Nursing Malpractice

Volume I: Foundations of Nursing Malpractice Claims
Fourth Edition

Compiled and edited by

Patricia W. Iyer, MSN, RN, LNCC
Barbara J. Levin, BSN, RN, ONC, LNCC
Kathleen C. Ashton, PhD, APRN, BC
Victoria Powell, RN, CCM, LNCC, CNLCP, CLCP, MSCC, CEAS

Contributors

Tonia D. Aiken, JD, BSN, RN
Stephen Appelbaum, CEP, EPIC
Peter I. Bergé, JD, RPA
Robert B. Buckalew, Esq.
Stephanie B. Camarda, Esq.
Helen Griff Chalier (formerly Weisgal), Esq.
Barbara Cohen, RN, M.S., M.Ed., JD
David Cohen, Esq.
Deborah D. D'Andrea, BSN, BA, RN
Samuel L. Davis, Esq.
Alisa Mintzer Dayanim, RN, BSN, MSN, CRRN
Sean J. Doolan, Esq.
Susan Egger, MSN, RN
Raymond Fleming, Esq.
Kenneth F. Fulginiti, Esq.
G. Ann Geyer, Esq.
Peter A. Greene, Esq.
Douglas S. Grossbart, MD, JD
Louise H. Hayes, Esq.

Nursine S. Jackson, MSN, RN
Monica M. Kenny, Esq.
Sharon L. Koob, RN, BSBA, CPHRM, ARM
Mark F. Kowal, Esq.
Thomas D. Lewis, Esq.
Bryan A. Liang, MD, PhD, JD
Mark Lukas, Ed.D., CRC
Timothy Mackey, MAS
Irmo Marini, PhD, CRC, CLCP
Susan Mellott, RN, CPHQ, FNAHQ, PhD
Wendy Neggers, Esq.
John M. Parisi, Esq.
Judith D. Rottkamp, MA, RN, CNA
Mindy M. Steichen, FCAS, MAAA
Frank D. Tinari, PhD
Diane Warlick, JD, BSN, RN
Peter G. Wick, FCAS, MAAA
Diane Wiley
Mona Goldman Yudkoff, RN, BSN, MPH, CRRN, CCM, CLCP

**Lawyers & Judges
Publishing Company, Inc.**
Tucson, Arizona

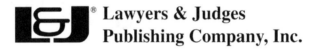 **Lawyers & Judges Publishing Company, Inc.**

P.O. Box 30040 • Tucson, AZ 85751-0040
(800) 209-7109 • FAX (800) 330-8795
e-mail: sales@lawyersandjudges.com
www.lawyersandjudges.com

Library of Congress Cataloging-in-Publication Data

Nursing malpractice / compiled and edited by Patricia W. Iyer ; contributors Tonia D. Aiken ...[et al.]. -- 4th ed.
   p. cm.
Includes index.
ISBN-13: 978-1-933264-94-3 (hardcover : alk. paper)
ISBN-10: 1-933264-94-2 (hardcover : alk. paper)
1. Nurses--Malpractice--United States. 2. Nursing--Law and legislation--United States. 3. Nursing errors. I.
Iyer, Patricia W. II. Aiken, Tonia D.
KF2915.N83N874 2011
344.7304'14--dc22

          2010053436

Printed in the United States of America
10 9 8 7 6 5 4 3 2 1

Dedications

Thank you to Kathleen Ashton and Victoria Powell for stepping up to assist with this revision. This revision would not have happened without their eager help. This book is dedicated to those affected by nursing malpractice—the nurses who are caught up in the legal system, sometimes without reason, and the patients and their families who are irreparably harmed. It is my great hope that application of the information provided in this work will provide a higher level of patient safety and avoid some of the tragedies that occur.

—Pat Iyer

Many thanks to my family and friends for affording me the luxury and opportunity to write and create. "The best and most beautiful things in the world cannot be seen or even touched. They must be felt with the heart." (Helen Keller) I give great appreciation to my friends Sue, Lesley, Michelle and Eileen for their continued friendship and support. Thank you, Pat Iyer, for inviting me on this journey and being an inspiration! A warm thank you to Kathleen and Victoria for their assistance with this book.

—With love, Barbara Levin

With gratitude to God, through whom all things are possible. With love and thanks to my husband, John, my best friend and the love of my life. With appreciation to Pat Iyer whose wonderful wit and wisdom have guided me since I first became a legal nurse consultant. And with warmest regards to my co-editors who lightened the load in so many ways and made the journey enjoyable.

—Kathleen Ashton

To my strongest supporter: my husband, Robert, who pushed me out of my comfort zone and thoroughly expected me to spread my wings so I could finally learn to soar. Thanks to my children, Lacy and John-Michael, for sitting patiently while I completed an e-mail or phone call before I could visit or tend to a concern. And a big hug goes to Remington Grace for helping me to find the smiles even when the pressure was on. Thank you to Pat Iyer for having faith in me and supporting us through this lengthy process. I appreciate your not laughing at my less-than-intelligent questions and not firing me for the incessant e-mails. I have learned so much, and I am grateful to have had the opportunity.

—Victoria Powell

Contents

Preface

Since its original publication in 1996, this book has become THE most comprehensive book on nursing malpractice. Written by experienced attorneys and nursing experts, this is the book needed to litigate nursing malpractice cases, assist in the screening and preparation of cases, and reduce risks of patient injury.

The efforts to reduce risks and improve patient safety have become more visible since the publication of the third edition of this book. The nursing shortage has worsened since the book was first published, raising concerns about patient safety. Faculty shortages and waiting lists for seats in nursing schools exacerbate the problem.

The chapters in this text have been updated to reflect the changes in nursing. A comprehensive review of the content of the third edition resulted in the identification of the need to add new material to broaden the range of the text. The publication of this edition includes nine new chapters to expand on the 45 in the third edition, 30 in the second edition, and 18 in the first edition.

The book is organized into two volumes. Volume I, *Foundations of Nursing Malpractice Claims*, contains four sections. Part One, *Patient Safety*, presents a comprehensive look at the factors that influence medical errors. All of the chapters in this section have been revised to detail the factors that contribute to patient injury and drive plaintiffs to seek attorneys.

Part Two, *Nursing Practice*, presents information on how nursing is practiced and documented. This section will enable attorneys to use the correct language when requesting documents or questioning nurses during depositions or trial.

Part Three, *Damages*, addresses the impact of injuries on a patient's future medical needs, vocational losses, economic claims, and pain and suffering. These chapters, like all of the chapters in the previous edition, were extensively updated.

Part Four, *Litigation of Nursing Malpractice Cases*, has the highest concentration of attorney authors. Experienced plaintiff and defense attorneys present their perspectives on nursing malpractice. This section includes two new chap-

ters: Chapter 17, *View of the Actuary* and Chapter 18, *E-Discovery*. Chapter 17 covers the types of malpractice policies, premiums, and rating variables. Chapter 18 covers rules, cases, and challenges associated with electronic discovery.

Volume II, *Roots of Nursing Malpractice*, begins with Part One, *Common Areas of Nursing Liability*. This consists of clinical topics written by nurses and attorneys to explain the clinical and liability issues specific to a wide range of nursing practice. New chapters have been added. Chapter 8, *Respiratory Malpractice*, discusses the role of healthcare providers in their care and treatment of a patient who has respiratory issues. Clinical issues, diagnostic tests and malpractice areas are discussed in this chapter. Chapter 14, *Dialysis Therapy Malpractice*, is another new chapter which educates the reader on types of dialysis therapy and the common complications and causes of action in this clinical area. Chapter 18, *Telephone Triage*, another new chapter, discusses the liability risks associated with telephone triage.

Part Two, *Advanced Roles*, focuses on the role of the nurse anesthetist, the nurse midwife and the newest chapter on the role of the nurse practitioner. All of these nurses work on the cusp of advanced practice nursing.

Part Three, *Causes of Action*, examines nursing liability from the perspective of sources of liability. Chapter 22, *Preventing Healthcare Acquired Complications Means You Never Have to Say You're Sorry*, a new chapter, focuses on the "never events" or hospital-acquired injury. Falls are one such type of injury. Another new chapter, Chapter 26, *Falls and Their Consequences*, addresses a widespread safety concern affecting all age groups, across both public and private locations as well as community and healthcare settings. Patient safety in hospitals has the attention of accreditation agencies, public health organizations, private insurance companies, and the government. This chapter provides the reader with important information to assist with the review of a medical record.

Key concepts are highlighted in figures throughout the book. An extensive appendix consisting of medical terms, abbreviations, and definitions, as well as websites, has been added to Volume II. This book is geared to attorneys who represent either plaintiffs or defendants and to legal nurse consultants. Insurance personnel such as claims investigators and risk management personnel who work in acute care settings will benefit from the information in this text. Legal nurse consultants and risk managers have come to rely on the comprehensive perspective of nursing malpractice presented in prior editions. Healthcare facility leaders are encouraged to use this valuable resource to educate and make a positive impact on the delivery of health care to patients. A unique blend of attorneys, nurse attorneys, nurse expert witnesses, legal nurse consultants, physicians, pharmacists, toxicologists, jury consultants, actuaries and legal photographers contributed chapters for this book. To our knowledge, this text remains the only one on the market written for attorneys on nursing malpractice using such a broad base of expert authors.

We would like to thank all of the authors for contributing their time and talents to this project. They poured enormous amounts of effort into the creation of this book. We appreciate having Kathleen Ashton and Victoria Powell join us as editors for this fourth edition of *Nursing Malpractice*. We hope you will find this book to be of great value.

Patricia W. Iyer, MSN, RN, LNCC
Barbara J. Levin, BSN, RN, ONC, LNCC

Part I:
Patient Safety

Chapter 1

The Roots of Patient Injury

Patricia W. Iyer, MSN, RN, LNCC

1.1 Introduction

The complexity of the hospital system becomes evident as soon as one walks through the doors of the building. The healthcare environment is made up of intertwined systems of people, equipment, procedures, and communication. Something as simple as finding a hospital department may become difficult due to lack of directions or absence of signs. Hospitals, nursing homes, and other healthcare facilities house a multileveled organizational structure consisting of separate departments. People of varying levels of education, experience, and communication abilities work within healthcare settings. There are multiple opportunities within this complex system for errors to occur that may result in patient harm.

Healthcare systems have been analyzed in comparison to high reliability organizations (HROs), such as aircraft carriers, nuclear power plants, firefighting teams, and others. High reliability organizations are institutions in which individuals work together in high acuity situations. They face great potential for error and disastrous consequences. They consistently perform and deliver their services with positive results and minimal errors. "Health care today in the United States can hardly qualify as an HRO."[1]

TIP: Patients enter hospitals and nursing homes to receive nursing care. The nurse is the only member of the healthcare team found at the bedside 24 hours a day and has the most contact with the patient. Errors or omissions in nursing care can have a profound impact on the patient. Nursing care delivered in a manner that conforms to the standards of care can have an equally profound impact.

This chapter explores the roots of patient injury: the factors in the healthcare environment and within nursing that contribute to untoward outcomes. Errors and harm can result from the complexity of the system, as well as from nursing performance. It is beyond the scope of this text to discuss errors committed by physicians and other non-nursing healthcare providers.

A compilation of all categories of root causes of sentinel events (1995-2004) by The Joint Commission yielded this listing (from most frequently implicated in a sentinel event to least frequently involved).[2] Sentinel events are so-named because they indicate the need for immediate investigation and response. The Joint Commission defines a sentinel event as "an unexpected occurrence involving the death or serious physical or psychological injury, or the risk thereof. Serious injury specifically includes loss of limb or function. The phrase, 'or risk thereof' includes any process variation for which a recurrence would carry a significant chance of a serious adverse outcome."[3]

This chapter addresses each of the factors listed below except staffing, which is discussed in Chapter 2, *Where Have All the Nurses Gone?*, and Chapter 8, *Inside the Healthcare Environment.*

1.   Communication
2.   Orientation/Training
3.   Patient Assessment
4.   Staffing
5.   Availability of Information
6.   Competency/Credentialing
7.   Procedural Compliance
8.   Environmental Safety/Security
9.   Leadership and Teamwork
10. Continuum of Care
11. Care Planning
12. Organizational Culture

1.2 Communication

TIP: "The problem with communication...is the illusion that it has been accomplished." —George Bernard Shaw

---

According to The Joint Commission, which accredits thousands of healthcare organizations, communication has been found to be the number one contributor to patient injury. In today's multicultural society, sources of misunderstanding and miscommunication can result in multiple opportunities for errors resulting in harm to patients. Communication barriers between patients and nurses, and nurses and other healthcare workers can result in inappropriate orders, incorrect interventions, or failure to take action.

Communication is a complex process affected by attention levels, needs, distractions, fatigue, cultural framework, accents, values, and many other factors. Seven percent of communication is verbal. Thirty-eight percent is tone and inflection. Fifty percent is nonverbal and symbolic.[4]

TIP: Language and cultural barriers can create hidden sources of misunderstanding. The nurse may have little insight into the way language and cultural differences influence communication. During nursing shortages, recruitment of nurses from foreign countries serves to increase the staff in United States hospitals. An influx of foreign-trained nurses to address the current shortage of nurses may exacerbate these communication difficulties.

Absence of communication also sets up a climate for errors to occur. Lack of communication may convey lack of interest, concern, leadership, or knowledge. Communication is the glue that holds a team together. Examples of communication gaps that may influence patient safety are shown in Figure 1.1.

- The nursing department has difficulty communicating to the pharmacists that in the middle of a cardiac arrest, the nurses on the unit are too busy to run to the pharmacy to retrieve a drug needed to resuscitate a patient.
- A female nurse who comes from a culture of subservient women may be reluctant to question a male doctor who writes an incorrect order.
- The housekeepers do not speak English, and the nurses are unable to communicate the need for a bed to be washed quickly in order to receive a critically ill patient.
- The nurses do not report that one of their beds has been vacated, because if the Admitting Department learns this, a new patient will be put in the bed. This will cause more work for the nurses.
- The nursing department's model of giving change of shift report through tape recordings does not permit the following shift to ask questions of the nurse completing the shift.
- The nursing department has no standardized data elements that should be conveyed in change of shift report.
- The emergency department nurse forgets to tell the critical care unit nurse at the time of transfer that the patient has already received heparin. A second dose is inadvertently given as soon as the patient arrives in the ICU.
- A patient's explanation of symptoms may be misinterpreted by a nurse with limited knowledge of English.
- Policy and procedure manuals are stored on an inaccessible shelf and are often out of date, not reflecting current practice.
- A stoic nurse who minimizes the patient's pain can delay reporting an ominous development of chest pain.
- There is no mechanism for an employee to make a suggestion to correct a safety problem, and no recognition for such ideas.
- An abusive physician is permitted to publicly chastise nurses because he brings a large volume of patients into the hospital.

Figure 1.1 *Examples of Communication Contributors to Patient Injury*

A. Nurse to Physician Communication

The nurses are the eyes and ears of the attending physician. Present 24 hours a day, the nurses and nursing assistants are responsible for communicating with each other and with the physician. The American Nurses Association's Scope and Standards of Practice emphasizes this critical role. Standard 11, Collaboration, states that "The registered nurse collaborates with patients, family, and others in the conduct of nursing practice."[5]

The willingness of nurses to timely report important information to a physician, physician assistant, or nurse practitioner may be influenced by several factors, including the:

- time of the day,
- recognition by the nurse that communication is needed,
- personality of the nurse, and
- personality and behavior of the physician.

1. Bullying

Definitions of terms related to bullying are found in Figure 1.2.

TIP: Increasingly, healthcare facilities and staff are identifying the impact of disruptive or abusive behavior on communication. Incidents of verbal abuse of nurses, typically by physicians, are unfortunately well-known. Employee morale and retention are negatively affected by such behavior.

a. The behavior

According to a VHA (Volunteer Hospitals of America) survey, an estimated 2-3 percent of physicians behaved badly toward their nurse colleagues. Specific triggers often precipitated events, such as:

- nurses calling the physician during evenings or weekends to question or clarify orders,
- orders carried out incorrectly or in an untimely manner,
- unexpected delays in care,
- difficulties with procedures or process flow, and
- changes in patient condition.[6]

Bullying—an offensive, intimidating, malicious or insulting behavior or abuse of power conducted by an individual or group against others, which makes the recipient feel upset, threatened, humiliated, or vulnerable, which undermines their self-confidence and which may cause them to suffer stress. Bullying is behavior that is generally persistent, systematic, and ongoing. Bullying is associated with a perpetrator at a higher level of authority or power.
"Lateral violence and Bullying in the Workplace," Center for American Nurses, February 2008

Workplace bullying—repeated inappropriate behavior, direct or indirect, whether verbal, physical, or otherwise, conducted by one or more persons against another or others, at the place of work and/or in the course of employment, which could reasonably be regarded as undermining the individual's right to dignity at work.
"Report of the Task Force on the Prevention of Workplace Bullying: Dignity at work—the challenge of workplace bullying." Dublin: Health and Safety Authority, Task Force on the Prevention of Workplace Bullying, 2001

Conflict—processes occurring within a group in any of several forms, such as hostility, decreased communication, distrust, sabotage, verbal abuse, and coercive tactics

Lateral violence, horizontal violence or horizontal hostility, nurse to nurse aggression—the physical, verbal, or emotional abuse of an employee. The violence is manifested in verbal and nonverbal behaviors. The ten most common forms of lateral violence are non-verbal innuendo, verbal affront, undermining activities, withholding information, sabotage, infighting, scapegoating, backstabbing, failure to respect privacy, and broken confidences.
Griffin, D., "Teaching cognitive rehearsal as a shield for lateral violence: an intervention for newly licensed nurses." The Journal of Continuing Education in Nursing, 35(6), 257-263, 2004

Culture of safety—characterized by open and respectful communication among all members of the healthcare team in order to provide safe patient care. It is a culture that supports organizational commitment to continually seeking to improve patient safety.
"Preventing Medication Errors," Institute of Medicine, The National Academies Press, 2007

Disruptive behavior—behavior that interferes with effective communication among healthcare providers and negatively impacts performance and outcomes. This type of behavior is not supportive of a culture of safety.
"Lateral violence and Bullying in the Workplace," Center for American Nurses, February 2008

Incivility—rude or disrespectful behavior that demonstrates a lack of regard for others.
Rau-Foster, M. "Workplace civility and staff retention," Nephrology Nursing Journal 2004: 47 (6): 664-671

Verbal abuse—a disruptive form of behavior involving verbal communication that is associated with horizontal violence and bullying. It is any communication a nurse perceives to be harsh condemnatory attack upon herself or himself professionally or personally. Such abuse may include gossiping, backbiting, silence, and passive aggressive behavior.
Cox, H., "Verbal abuse nationwide oppressed group behavior. Part 1. Nursing Management, 22 (2), 32-35
Rowe, M. and Sherlock, H. "Stress and verbal abuse in nursing: do burned out nurses eat their young? Journal of Nursing Management, 13(3), 242-248

Figure 1.2 *Definitions*

A study of 50 VHA hospitals culminating in data from more than 1,500 participants, primarily registered nurses or physicians, yielded these conclusions:

- There were 965 respondents to the question, "Have you ever witnessed disruptive behavior from a physician at your hospital?" Nearly three-quarters said "Yes."
- There were 960 respondents who answered the question, "Have you ever witnessed disruptive behavior from a nurse at your hospital?" Sixty-eight percent said "Yes."
- More than half of the respondents thought that 1-3 percent of doctors and nurses were disruptive.
- The majority believed that male physicians were more disruptive than females.
- Overall, between 73–95 percent of the respondents stated that disruptive behavior sometimes, frequently, or constantly resulted in:

  ◊ stress
  ◊ frustration
  ◊ loss of concentration
  ◊ reduced team collaboration
  ◊ reduced information transfer
  ◊ reduced communication
  ◊ impaired nurse-physician relationship

Effects of disruptive behavior on the patient included

- adverse events
- errors
- (impaired) patient safety
- (reduced) quality of care
- patient mortality
- (decreased) patient satisfaction

Some quotes from the respondents included:

- "Cardiologist upset by phone calls and refused to come in. Rx (treatment) delayed. MI extended."
- "Communication between obstetrician and delivery RN was hampered because of MD behavior. Resulted in poor outcome in newborn."
- "RN did not call MD about change in patient condition because he had a history of being abusive when called. Patient suffered because of this."
- "Disruptive behavior is not unique to physicians. Some nurses exhibit an air of superiority which makes communication difficult."

- "Physicians who are disruptive are usually chronic disrupters and have run-ins with several nurses. There are also nurses who are chronic disrupters. These people are often avoided by other staff which leads to lowered communication. I am sure that a serious incident is just around the corner."[7]

The American College of Physician Executives reported on a 2009 Doctor-Nurse Behavior Survey. More than 2,100 physicians and nurses completed the survey. These physician and nursing executives were asked how often behavior problems arose in their organizations. Thirty percent said they occurred monthly; 25 percent said they occurred weekly and 9.5 percent said they occurred daily. The most frequent behavior problem was yelling (58 percent) followed by degrading comments and insults (46.8 percent) and refusing to work together (24 percent). While there were complaints about nurse behaviors, both doctors and nurses who filled out the survey said physicians were to blame for a large part of disruptive behaviors. Many of the participants accused physicians of patronizing and belittling nurses. Some of the examples that were shared were:

- "Some ED physicians do not respect the nurses' opinions or suggestions. They will then appear to delay patient care 'just to show' the nurse."
- "A surgeon who was frustrated by a staffing issue in the OR stated loudly and publicly that monkeys could be trained to do what scrub nurses do."
- "A physician demanded a nurse be drug tested because she questioned an order. The order would have placed the patient at risk. He then demanded she be fired because she 'evidently wasn't competent to care for a slug.' He also called her names and cursed at her in front of staff and family members."
- "One surgeon threw himself on the OR floor while a patient was still open and under anesthesia because an instrument was not working properly."
- "Throwing objects to express frustration is apparently quite common. Nurses have ducked bloody chest tubes, scalpels, power tools, telephones, surgical instruments, clipboards, floor mats and more."[8]

b. The consequences

As the above results confirm, when nurses are too intimidated to contact a physician, patient safety is compromised. The responsibility of the nurse to act as a patient advocate to secure needed medical care may be deflected by fear of being chastised for contacting the physician.

In *Anonymous Parents and Deceased Five-year-Old Girl v. Anonymous Obstetrician and Anonymous Hospital*, the plaintiffs alleged their infant developed cerebral palsy after a difficult labor and delivery. Deposition testimony of the labor and delivery nurses indicated they were concerned about the lack of progress of the mother's labor, but they were reluctant to voice those concerns to the obstetrician because of the doctor's well-known tendency to respond negatively to such nursing input. This North Carolina case settled for $1.2 million.[9]

What are the consequences of such behavior? The Joint Commission issued a 2008 standard for hospitals to maintain a "zero tolerance" for such disruptive behaviors as uncooperative or abusive exchanges between doctors and nurses. Yet the PEJ study cited above found that outbursts, overreactions and refusals to work together continue to blanket healthcare environments.[10] In response to the question if nurses had been terminated in the previous year due to behavior problems, 61 percent said, "yes." Only 22 percent responded that physicians had been terminated due to behavior problems. Only 55 percent of the respondents had any training programs to reduce behavior problems.[11]

There are several factors changing the dysfunctional communication climate in health care. As the negative effects of disruptive behavior are recognized, firmer steps are being taken to impose a zero tolerance policy for abusive behavior. For example, nurses have begun calling a "Code Pink" when a physician is acting in an abusive manner towards a nurse. The nurses on the nursing unit converge on the scene of the confrontation and stand surrounding the nurse, staring at the physician. This has proven to be quite unnerving to the physician. In some VHA hospitals, the physicians sign a conduct contract. The first instance of abusive behavior is treated with counseling. The second incident results in termination. Physicians are being fired.[12]

The importance of a multidisciplinary approach to patient care is gaining greater recognition. Fostering a systematic and coordinated approach to patient care encourages collaboration and mutual respect for the contributions of each discipline. Costly teamwork failures are avoided, such as:

- failure to identify an established protocol for patient care or even to develop a treatment plan,
- failure to advocate and assert an alternative plan or corrective course of action when a question arises about the patient's care,
- failure to prioritize caregiver tasks for the patient, and

- failure to cross-monitor actions of other team members.[13]

The influx of masters-prepared nurse practitioners and clinical specialists also disturbs the traditional hierarchy of the authoritarian physician. Generally confident and assertive, these nurses are less likely to accept abuse. In one setting, a cardiothoracic surgeon was well-known for his pattern of screaming at nurses as soon as he came on the nursing unit. The staff learned to scatter and hide when they saw him coming. Shortly after a masters-prepared clinical specialist began work, she encountered the screaming surgeon for the first time. She stopped his screaming by saying, "Excuse me, you must have me confused with someone who will take this abuse." The surgeon quickly learned to change his communication pattern.[14]

Some of the suggested approaches for dealing with bullying behavior include:

- Medical and nursing school education on teamwork
- Clear policies and expectations for behavior with codes of conduct
- Early intervention by confronting the behavior
- Teamwork training
- Communicate consequences of disruption—negative behavior impacts patient care and silence kills
- Zero tolerance for the behavior—"It will only take one or two terminations of privileges to stop these offensive physician behaviors. Same thing applies to nurses who behave offensively."[15]

TIP: Nursing staff should be empowered to stop the behavior by simply saying, "I am sorry, but you may not speak to me in that tone of voice." It works.[16]

As collegial working relationships become more of the norm, such abusive behavior will subside, with a concomitant increase in communication and patient safety. The administration of a facility has to face and make tough decisions regarding disruptive physician behavior. Each of the physicians involved in the incidents described below lost their privileges:

- A cardiothoracic surgeon stormed into an operating room in his street clothes to berate a fellow who was in the midst of an operation.
- A chauvinistic male physician berated nurses on several occasions.
- An angry orthopaedic surgeon known to have temper tantrums threw open the door of the operating

room. A nurse standing behind the door was hit in the knee by the door and required surgery.

2. Hierarchical issues

Although it is comforting to think of nurses and physicians working together in a cohesive team, the reality still exists that communication is compounded by hierarchical issues. A power distance between team members deters "inferiors" from making themselves heard.[17]

A study of 20 medical and surgical residents reported in 2009 investigated these physicians' perceptions of nurses. Problems with nurse-physician collaboration or communication have been associated with medication errors, patient safety issues and patient deaths. In this study, residents repeatedly characterized the interdependence between nurses and physicians as a pattern in which residents gave orders that nurses carried out. "We make the decisions; they follow the orders, essentially." Most residents emphasized the one-way flow of information, in which they communicated treatment plans and orders to nurses. Some residents recognized that nurses did more than carry out orders, but their descriptions of nurses' roles did not place nurses at the center of the care process or consider them full partners in care. Overall, the residents' comments suggest a pervasive tendency to treat nurses as if they do not need to understand what is happening with patients because they merely follow orders. Only two residents said that frequent communication was important because of what the nurse had to say. One said, "Nurses' feedback is essential and important. Very, very important. Many times we may miss out on things and patients' conditions that the nurse may pick up and bring to our attention....Without a smooth communication and good rapport it wouldn't be possible for us to pick it up or treat that."[18]

In a different study, when nurses were asked about their perceptions of their relationships with physicians, some of the findings confirm the resident study. Of 511 nurses who responded to a survey, 66 percent did not think physicians understood what they did as nurses. When asked how frequently physicians consulted with them about the care and treatment of their patients, 40 percent said "usually" and 37 percent said "infrequently."[19]

3. Strategies

Communication within the team is improved by adopting techniques that have been found useful in other industries. These include:

- Requiring teamwork communication training for hospital credentialing

- Holding briefings and debriefings after specific events and procedures
- Creating standards for procedures
- Recognizing fatigue and age as factors in performance
- Scheduling meetings that focus on system deficiencies and minimize individual blame
- Testing all staff randomly for drugs[20]
- Use of the two challenge rule—the concept that a clinician must verbally express concern about patient safety at least twice if the problem is not corrected
- Check back—the practice of a person receiving an order or instruction repeating back those orders or instructions to the person giving them to ensure the receiver has understood the message correctly
- Call out—the practice of calling out important events, especially during rapidly changing situations, to facilitate anticipation of next steps
- SBAR—structured technique for presentation of relevant patient information (described below)
- DESC—structured technique for conflict resolution (described below)[21]

4. SBAR

Pronounced *S-Bar*, this term refers to a methodology designed to ensure effective, accurate, mistake-free communication among medical staff as well as between physicians and other healthcare professionals. It also promotes upfront dialog with the patients under their care. Proper medical care relies on precise communication. In order to coordinate any patient treatment, the professionals involved must interrelate with clarity. What does SBAR mean? It is an acronym for a formalized communication technique that is quickly becoming the standardized method in major hospitals and clinics throughout the United States. It stands for:

- Situation
- Background
- Assessment
- Request or recommendation

Originally established as a standard operating procedure of communication between the captain and the crew on U.S. Naval submarines, this methodology was adopted by Kaiser Permanente of Colorado several years ago to be used within the medical field in an effort to slash the rising statistics of human error. Based in Oakland, California, this organization operates 30 medical centers. It was instrumental in pioneering SBAR as a model to assist both the nurses and doctors to systematize their thoughts so they could convey the most critical information in under one minute. Each recorded medical update starts out with describing the *situation* surrounding the need for care, gives the *background* pertinent to that care, *assesses* what needs to be done and provides a *recommendation* as to a proper plan of action.

For example, Mr. Sanchez receives a medication prescribed by the physician on rounds. Within ten minutes of its administration, he develops a rash on his chest and abdomen and starts exhibiting diaphoresis. The nurse calls the physician to report the incident, giving her name, the patient's name, and a brief description of the *situation*.

> Dr. Smith, this is Delores Schwartz on 4 South at Mercy Hospital. This is the situation. Mr. Jorge Sanchez in 420B at 10:05 this morning received the dose of 0.5 mg Xanax you prescribed for anxiety on your morning rounds. At 10:15 this morning, he buzzed the floor nurse complaining of sweating and itching on his chest.

Then a brief *background* is given. This is two-fold. It clarifies the patient's history, so there is certainty the right patient is being discussed, and it reminds all personnel involved of the patient's history and condition leading up to the incident.

> Here is his background. As you know, Mr. Sanchez was admitted over the weekend for shortness of breath and chest pains. His EKG was unremarkable, but he had just lost his job, has a wife on disability, and has a son in Iraq. He has a reported history of medication sensitivity and is allergic to Codeine, penicillin and peanuts. He reports not sleeping well for the past month, and having bouts of severe indigestion. His vital signs are 185/96 with a respiration of 28 and a pulse of 82. Medication was verified as correct in quantity and dosage prior to administration via bracelet ID.

The *assessment* of the situation is given next. The nurse provides an analysis of the situation based on her observation and expertise.

> My assessment is that the patient seems anxious, having had bad reactions to medications in the past. His wife is here with him. He does have small reddish blotches on his abdomen and they are spread-

ing upwards into his chest. He is scratching vigorously. He is diaphoretic and his palms are clammy. His speech is clear and his tongue does not appear to be swelling. He can swallow without trouble and breathing is shallow but not labored.

Finally, the nurse offers her *request* related to the problem or *recommendation* of what she believes would be the best course of action. The nurse is not telling the doctor what to do, but clarifying options. This is often offered in a form of a question. Additionally, the nurse offers the listener a chance to ask questions. "I would recommend he be prescribed Benadryl and a cortisone cream, or do you want us to run lab work, or do you wish to return and reevaluate him? Do you have any questions?" For more on SBAR, see Iyer.[22]

Refer to Chapter 3, *Moving from Traditional Law and Medicine,* for additional information in strategies to promote patient safety.

B. Nurse to Nurse (and Other Staff) Communication

Nurses communicate with each other on an ongoing basis throughout their work. They communicate in every conceivable manner—in person, over the phone, in writing, in faxes and e-mails. A smoothly working team effectively exchanges information and is critical to patient safety. Numerous challenges contribute to poor communication, including hierarchical power differences, fatigue, distraction, stress, and conflict.

1. Bullying

Some speculate that verbal abuse by physicians contributes significantly to horizontal violence because nurses pass their anger and frustration with physicians onto other co-workers. Another set of behaviors is exhibited when nurses form a clique to exclude others, or make disparaging remarks or gossip about each other. Some of the examples that Bartolomew[23] shared were statements from nurses:

- "The smallest thing would trigger retaliation. [The charge nurse's] refusal to speak was the worst. Once she went 27 days without speaking."
- "It was the looks [the preceptor] gave me, like I was stupid. In my whole three months of orientation, I can't think of a single time anyone ever complimented me."
- This is what the group of nurses would do to me: I never sat down for 12 hours. It was horrendous. All I know is that if a group works together for long enough, they keep the others outside."

- "A root cause analysis performed after an episode of over-sedation revealed that the nurse was upset about an interaction with a co-worker. Tearfully she stammered to the charge nurse, 'I know I shouldn't have let [my co-worker] get to me, but he did, and I just wasn't thinking clearly. I felt so humiliated, so belittled.' The nurse had inadvertently programmed the PCA to deliver ten times the ordered dose of morphine. The patient was found unresponsive, with an oxygen saturation of 50%, and was transferred to the ICU. Two days later, a brain scan still showed areas of hypoxia, and the patient still could not put thoughts together clearly."

In addition to the risk of patient injury, bullying leads to turnover, burnout, depression, anxiety, absenteeism, physical ailments, strained relationships with one's family, anger, demotivation, decreased self-esteem, maladaptive responses such as overeating or substance abuse, reduced productivity at work, job dissatisfaction, and poor morale.[24]

2. Confronting risky behavior

Nurses are expected to function as patient advocates and to use communication skills to obtain the best possible care for their patients. At times, they need to confront each other to fix risky behavior or a risky situation. The work of Patterson, Grenny and McMillan uncovered the issue of people's unwillingness to confront risky topics, allowing risks to go unaddressed. Through firsthand observations in health care, they recognized seven crucial conversations people in health care frequently failed to hold, that likely added to unacceptable error rates. The nationwide study was conducted by VitalSmarts in partnership with the American Association of Critical Care Nurses. The seven most crucial issues were:

1. Broken rules: Dangerous shortcuts were taken.
2. Mistakes: Difficulty following directions and poor clinical judgment were displayed.
3. Lack of support: Reluctance to help, being impatient, and refusing to answer questions were observed.
4. Incompetence: Concerns about the competency of fellow workers (nurses and physicians) were voiced.
5. Poor teamwork: One or more workers who gossiped or formed a clique divided the team and affected morale.
6. Disrespect: Condescending, insulting, or rude behavior was displayed.

7. Micromanagement: Workers abuse their authority, pull rank, bully, threaten, or force their point of view on others.

The study showed that these issues were rarely addressed, creating common and dangerous problems. The authors recommended improving crucial conversations as a priority.[25]

Miscommunication affects patient safety in multiple ways. This pervasive problem is difficult to tackle, yet is of profound importance in health care.

3. Strategies
a. Handoffs

Patient safety efforts have focused on improving handoffs. This occurs whenever any information about a patient is transferred from one person to another, such as during change of shift or when a patient leaves one part of a facility to move to another. It is during these times of transition—admission, hospitalization, transfer, and discharge—that patients' vulnerability is revealed and patient safety may be compromised.[26] The potential for an ineffective handoff is present in any busy environment, such as the post anesthesia care unit, intensive care unit, or nursing units prone to noise and chaos. Each transfer of care carries a risk of information loss or distortion.[27]

For example, consider this situation: A nurse calls a physician because he is concerned about critical laboratory results. He fails to tell the nurse coming onto the shift why he placed the call to the physician and he goes off work before the physician returns the call. The physician calls back, and the nurse now assigned to the patient is unable to explain why the call was made. Both become frustrated; the critical laboratory results go unreported. Add in another compounding factor if the physician who returns the call is covering for the attending physician and is ill-equipped to deal with an unknown patient. In this situation, a nurse who communicates clearly will often be able to direct the covering physician to provide the requested medical orders.

Handoff communication may be improved by the opportunity to have face to face discussions about a patient's status, and the use of structured forms and tools to present important information. For example, nurses at one hospital developed a "round trip ticket," a one page, patient information sheet that provides basic, pertinent information when a patient is transported to another department. Simple questions are answered by checking off boxes, such as

- Can the patient ambulate and transfer independently?
- Does the patient speak English?

- Are there any special alerts or precautions?
- Is the patient NPO (not allowed to eat or drink)?

The nurse completes the top section of the ticket before the patient leaves the nursing unit and someone in the receiving department completes the bottom part of the form to relay pertinent information back to the patient's nurse.[28]

TIP: These documents might be retained as part of the medical record, and if so, are discoverable. This might be important in a case involving patient injury during transport.

---

b. DESC

The components of DESC are *describe, explain, state* and *consequences*. For example, consider the situation of Charlotte, a hospitalized woman who had a cardiac arrest. One of the factors that led to the arrest was an inability of the laboratory staff to obtain enough blood to test hemoglobin and hematocrit, and a failure to redraw the blood soon enough.[29] Charlotte's nurse could have used DESC to organize her thoughts and keep her emotions under control during discussions with the healthcare providers.

Describe: The nurse would describe the behavior, focusing on what she saw or heard that bothered her, without launching into a personal attack. "I am concerned about the inability to get Charlotte's blood drawn right now."

Explain: Explain the impact of the behavior. When someone learns the impact of her behavior, she may want to change or rethink the issue. Glossing over or minimizing the impact of the behavior lessens the possibility of any behavior changes. "Our inability to get a current hemoglobin means Charlotte has to wait an unacceptable period."

State the desired outcome: This prevents the listener from having to guess and gives the nurse a chance to ask for what she needs. "I need a current hemoglobin on this patient."

Consensus or consequences will help to get the listener's attention. The process of obtaining consensus means the achievement of agreement. DESC is also described with C being the consequences. This step may be the hardest because it is easier to avoid confrontation and work around a problem person while complaining about her to colleagues. But without consequences, the person who needs to provide help may not change her behavior. "What else do I need to do to get your attention? If I cannot get your help, I will need to talk to your supervisor."

C. Nurse to Patient Communication

The multicultural aspects of populations invariably lead to communication barriers. Many patients and their families have limited proficiency in English. Hospitals have a duty to provide professional medical interpreters. Research shows that patients with problems are at an increased risk of experiencing preventable adverse events and that patients with limited English proficiency are more likely to experience adverse events than English speaking patients.[30-32] The Joint Commission standards now address patient-centered communication. Standard PC.02.01.21 states, "The hospital effectively communicates with patients when providing care, treatment, and services." Elements of performance include:

1. The hospital identifies the patient's oral and written communication needs, including the patient's preferred language for discussing health care.
2. The hospital communicates with the patient during the provision of care, treatment, and services in a manner that meets the patient's oral and written communication needs.

Standard RI.01.01.03 states, "The hospital respects the patient's right to receive information in a manner he or she understands. Elements of performance include:

1. The hospital provides information in a manner tailored to the patient's age, language, and ability to understand.
2. The hospital provides language interpreting and translation services, which may include in person, or via telephone or video. The hospital determines which translated documents and languages are needed based on its patient population.
3. The hospital provides information to the patient who has vision, speech, hearing, or cognitive impairments in a manner that meets the patient's needs."[33]

Additional information is found in The Joint Commission's publication, *One Size Does Not Fit All: Meeting the Healthcare Needs of a Diverse Patient Population.*[34]

D. The Aftermath of an Error

Disclosure of the medical error to the patient is discussed in Chapter 5, *Medical Errors: Roots of Litigation*. Internal discussion of the error is limited in many settings. Sharing lessons learned within the organization and between organizations is difficult to achieve and an often-omitted step following an error. One study found that more than 50 percent of physicians and nurses found it difficult to discuss errors secondary to one of three major factors: personal reputation, threat of a malpractice suit and the egos of other team members.[35] After being involved in a medical error, these "second victims" describe a variety of physical as well as psychosocial symptoms. Nurses may fear termination, feel personal anguish, have symptoms of posttraumatic stress disorder, feel a loss of professional respect, anger, guilt and inadequacy. Many second guess themselves and wonder if they are right for healthcare.

One interviewed nurse said, "I will never forget this experience. This patient will always be with me. I think of her often. Because of this, I am a better nurse."[36]

1.3 Orientation/Training

One of the components of patient safety and prevention of medical errors is to define the roles and responsibilities of staff. Attorneys recognize that these documents can be obtained through discovery in the form of:

- policies,
- procedures,
- orientation manuals,
- continuing and inservice education records, and
- job descriptions.

Lack of knowledge of the standards of care can lead to errors. Inadequate knowledge has many causes, including failure to learn the applicable material during nursing school, failure to learn the institution's policies and procedures, and failure to learn how to correctly use new medical equipment, among others. Inadequate knowledge can lead to faulty nursing diagnoses and interventions. Knowledge deficits "may preclude nurses from considering other possibilities, interpretations and perceptions, because we only hear what we know."[37] In other words, we don't know what we don't know.

TIP: Inexperience can overwhelm a nurse at many points during a nursing career, but nowhere is it more acute than in the first job after graduation.

A. New Graduates

Marlene Kramer[38] was the first nurse to publish a work on the initial work experience of a graduate nurse, coining this "reality shock." She defined this as the "shock-like reaction that occurs when an individual who has been reared and educated in that subculture of nursing that is promulgated by schools of nursing suddenly discovers that nursing as practiced in the world of work is not the same—it does not

operate on the same principles."[39] This same issue continues to color the initial experiences of new graduates. More current literature confirms that new graduates continue to report feeling overwhelmed and unprepared for the demands of their new role. They stated that they did not fit in, lacked acceptance from their colleagues, and doubted their ability to acquire the required skills.[40] Inexperienced new graduates placed into the busy environment of health care are at risk for making errors. Many facilities will not hire new graduates until they have passed their licensing examination. New graduates require a high level of support, education, and supervision. Attorneys recognize that their inexperience may be a factor in making errors that harm patients.

B. Orientation

Healthcare institutions typically set up orientation plans to ease new employees into their jobs. The Joint Commission recognizes the importance of orientation by devoting standards to this topic. HR.01.02.07 states, "The hospital provides orientation to staff." The elements of performance include:

1. "The hospital determines the key safety content of orientation provided to staff.
2. The hospital orients its staff to the key safety content before staff provides care, treatment, and services. Completion of this orientation is documented. The hospital oriented staff on the following:

- Relevant hospital-wide and unit-specific policies and procedures. Completion of this orientation is documented.
- Their specific job duties, including those related to infection prevention and control and assessing and managing pain. Completion of this orientation is documented.
- Sensitivity to cultural diversity based on their job duties and responsibilities. Completion of this orientation is documented.
- Patient rights, including ethical aspects of care, treatment, and services and the process used to address ethical issues based on their job duties and responsibilities. Completion of this orientation is documented."[41]

TIP: Orientation programs and records are discoverable.

C. Floating

Inexperience and lack of knowledge leading to patient injury can occur when a nurse moves from one clinical setting to another. Some hospitals have responded to this risk by providing cross-training when it is anticipated a nurse will be routinely pulled to another unit. Nurses retain an individual responsibility to ask for help from more experienced staff and to appropriately use resources to obtain information needed for safe practice.

Borgatti[42] offered techniques needed to overcome the often negative reaction nurses feel when asked to float to another unit. She noted that floating forces nurses to leave their comfort zone and quite possibly their area of expertise. She suggests the following:

1. Know your limits. Do not accept an assignment beyond your level of competency and that could place a patient in jeopardy.
2. Face the unknown. Speak with the charge nurse and share any concerns you have about the unit and patient population.
3. Think FLOAT:
   F: Find a resource person, an experienced nurse who might be willing to act as a resource for you during the shift.
   L: Lower your stress level. Use stress reduction techniques such as deep breathing and orienting yourself to the unit's resources.
   O: Orient yourself to the unit. Take a few minutes to find the policy and procedure manuals, the crash cart (used for cardiopulmonary resuscitation) and other supplies.
   A: Ask questions and ask for help. Do not go it alone and try to struggle through the shift. Ask for help if you have never performed a particular task or procedure or are unsure how to do it safely and competently.
   T: Take five minutes to review your assignment. Anticipate where you might need help.
4. Check your attitude at the door. Some nurses can be mean-spirited to nurses who float onto their unit. Many have been at the receiving end of this behavior at one time or another.

Floaters are also expected to recognize that if they are asked to perform duties for which their competency has not been verified, they should report this to their supervisor immediately and document the concerns according to the institution's policy.[43] Cita provided the top ten tips for floating, including:

1. Be positive about floating.
2. Request an orientation.
3. Look for similarities between the care you deliver in your home unit and the care you give in the host unit.
4. Know normal physical assessment findings.
5. Know common practice norms in your facility.
6. Familiarize yourself with the host unit's documentation tools.
7. Always look up unfamiliar drugs or familiar drugs in unfamiliar places because doses may differ.
8. Ask questions.
9. Research the host unit's practice area if you have any free time.
10. Take care of yourself. Take your breaks and use stress-relieving techniques.

TIP: Determine if the nurse defendant was floated to the unit.

D. Ongoing Education

Health care is provided within an environment marked by a continuous flow of new products, procedures, regulations, and information from evidence-based studies. The Joint Commission recognizes the importance of ongoing education and training by devoting standards to this topic. HR.01.05.03 states, "Staff participates in ongoing education and training. The elements of performance include:

- Staff participates in ongoing education and training to maintain or increase their competency. Staff participation is documented.
- Staff participates in ongoing education and training whenever staff responsibilities change. Staff participation is documented.
- Staff participates in education and training that is specific to the needs of the patient population served by the hospital. Staff participation is documented.
- Staff participates in education and training that incorporates the skills of team communication, collaboration, and coordination of care. Staff participation is documented.
- Staff participates in education that includes information about the need to report unanticipated adverse events and how to report these events. Staff participation is documented.
- Staff participates in education and training on fall reduction activities. Staff participation is documented.
- The hospital provides education and training that addresses how to identify early warning signs of a

change in patient's condition and how to respond to a deteriorating patient, including how and when to contract responsible clinicians. Education is provided to staff and licensed independent practitioners who may request assistance and those who may respond to those requests. Participation in this education is documented."[44]

In a Massachusetts case, a confused and unsupervised resident wandered off the grounds of a nursing home and froze to death in a snowstorm. Training deficits were revealed in this case.

In *Anonymous 85-Year-Old Alzheimer's Patient, Deceased v. Anonymous Nursing Home*, the wandering resident was discovered missing at 4:15 A.M. Authorities were not notified until 5:38 A.M. The resident was found dead at 5:50 A.M. 100 feet from the building lying with her face against a rock where she had fallen. The plaintiff alleged the nursing home was chronically understaffed, had inadequate alarm systems, did not use alarms, and failed to train staff about alarms. The nurse in charge of the unit on the night in question stated that she assumed the orange warning light meant ready and armed, rather than that the perimeter had been breached.[45]

One of the consequences of the budget constraints and restructuring that occurred in hospitals in the 1990s and the recession that began in 2008 was a reduction in hospital education budgets to support orientation of newly hired nurses, and ongoing inservice and continuing education for nurses. The Joint Commission points out that hospitals (or other healthcare facilities) can ill afford—on a patient safety basis alone—to underfund these critical education and training needs.[46] Increasingly, facilities are rethinking methods of delivering education, and relying on computer-based training, simulations, distance learning, newsletters, and other means to make education available.

Gaps in knowledge about a patient's condition or the institution's policies can have devastating consequences. The complexities of the healthcare setting require that staff unfamiliar with a patient's care receive the appropriate education. Refer to Figure 1.3 for examples of education or orientation factors that contribute to patient injury.

In *Augustine Penalver, Individually and as independent executor of the Estate of Maria Belia Penalver, deceased, et al. v. Living Centers of Texas, Cyndi Brown, LNFA, and Kimberly Bordovsky,*

DON, a nursing home resident fell when a single person attempted to transfer her from wheelchair to bed. The resident fell, hit her head, and sustained a subdural hematoma. She died the following day. Her nursing care plan had required two people to assist in transfers, but the facility had been doing single-person assists safely for most of the time Penalver had lived there. On September 22, she had returned from the hospital where she had been diagnosed with a broken hip. On September 25, an inservice was provided to demonstrate a two-person assist due to her changed condition. The aide involved in the incident missed the inservice, however, and did a one-person transfer as she had done in the past. The fall resulted. The plaintiff alleged the facility, its nursing director, and its administrator were negligent in failing to, among other things, appropriately establish and follow a nursing care plan to safely transfer Penalver, appropriately supervise and train their employees, ensure compliance with state and federal regulations, and otherwise provide healthcare services reasonably prudent under the same or similar circumstances. The plaintiff was awarded $356,000.[47]

TIP: Providing ongoing education and training is challenging. Education should be geared for the different learning styles and generations of workers. It can also be difficult to teach part-time, per diem, and off shift (evening and night) nurses. The facility must find ways to reach these nurses through self-directed learning, computerized modules, off shift educators, and so on.

1.4 Assessment and Care Planning

Assessment is the first step in the nursing process—the universal thread that ties nurses together, whether they graduated from a diploma, associate's degree, or baccalaureate program. The nursing process forms the foundation for nursing education, practice, and documentation. The nursing process consists of a problem-solving approach directed toward meeting the needs and solving the problems of people.

TIP: The nursing process has five steps:
1. assessment,
2. diagnosis,
3. planning,
4. implementation, and
5. evaluation.

These steps are used daily by nurses to provide care.

A. Steps of the Nursing Process

Each of the steps of the nursing process is described below.

1. Assessment
a. Assessment process

During assessment the nurse collects information about the patient. This includes data about the patient's physical and psychosocial (emotional and mental) status. Data are obtained through interviews, observation, physical examination, the medical record, and discussion with the family. The initial collection of data occurs when the patient enters the healthcare system. A registered nurse assesses the patient and records this information on a document called the admission assessment or database. Whereas the physician completes a history and physical examination to diagnose the patient's condition, the nurse conducts a nursing history and assessment to obtain information on the patient's nursing needs. (Other healthcare professionals, such as physical therapists and occupational therapists, also collect information for their own database, or on a multidisciplinary document.) The database provides information that helps the healthcare professional determine the patient's priority needs and plan care accordingly. The time frame for completing the admission assessment is defined by agency policy.

TIP: The admission assessment contains valuable information about the patient's status on admission to the facility, which is often of great relevance in personal injury and malpractice cases.

Once the initial admission assessment database is completed, the nurse assesses the patient each time the patient is encountered. The assessment is an almost automatic process by which the nurse makes many observations such as the patient's grooming, skin color, facial expression, or body size.

Assessment plays a role in many of the high frequency sentinel events reported to The Joint Commission. Assessment may be involved in some of these outcomes in the following ways:

- **Operative or postoperative complication:** Failure to collect assessment data regarding the condition of the patient's skin (operative chemical burns or pressure ulcers); failure to assess for signs of bleeding, infection, or other complications
- **Wrong site surgery:** Failure to properly identify the patient

- **Delay in treatment:** Failure to collect assessment data needed to detect a change in condition
- **Medication error:** Failure to properly identify reasons for administering a medication
- **Suicide:** Failure to assess for signs of suicidal behavior; failure to monitor or observe the patient
- **Inpatient drug overdose:** Failure to assess for signs of respiratory depression from pain medication
- **Restraint-related event:** Failure to monitor patient/resident while restrained; failure to detect signs of circulation impairment from a tight restraint
- **Falls:** Failure to determine risk factors for falls; failure to assess for changes that warrant an intensified level of monitoring
- **Elopement:** Failure to assess wandering behavior of resident; failure to note signs of increased agitation and exit-seeking behavior

b. Failure to rescue

Failure to rescue is a term that describes the outcome when a patient's condition deteriorates before the changes are recognized and acted upon.

Imagine this scene: You are visiting your elderly father in the hospital when you notice his speech is becoming slurred and he is less awake than usual. Concerned, you call his nurse into the room. She assesses your father, then picks up the phone and requests an emergency response team. A team of professionals enter the room, assess and stabilize your father, and arrange for him to be transported to the ICU with a tentative diagnosis of rule out stroke. Your father's attending physician is called as the team is completing its assessment. The critical care nurse on the team pulls the floor nurse aside to congratulate her on her astute assessment. The process from start to finish has taken 20 minutes.

The use of rapid response teams (RRTs) to provide timely rescue efforts in hospitals has gained momentum and popularity, although not all hospitals have them. The concept originated with a critical care nurse from New Zealand who recognized the need to bring resources to the bedside of a patient whose condition deteriorated before more serious events occurred. Without rapid response teams, nurses who recognize ominous changes in the status of their patients are forced to contact the attending physician and wait for a return call. Should an attending physician refuse to deal with or minimize the concerns of the nurse, the nurse has to

- Education about a critical change in an intravenous pump is offered once. Those who were not on duty at the time of the educational program are unaware of how to use the pump.
- Nurses working for a staffing agency receive a few minutes of orientation and are unaware of facility policies on monitoring of vital signs.
- The pressure to hire, orient, and place new nursing employees on the nursing unit results in a new graduate being inappropriately assigned to a complex postoperative patient.
- The facility does not use posters or memos to provide information for those who need education on new changes.
- Once an important change in the process of healthcare delivery has been made, there is no follow-up review or monitoring to ensure the new system is being followed.

Figure 1.3 *Examples of Orientation/Training Contributors to Patient Injury*

use the chain of command within a facility—in effect, to go over the head of the attending physician with the assistance of nursing administration—to find a physician who will respond. This is a slow and difficult process. RRTs have the capability of bypassing the attending physician to turn what can be a 2-3 hour long process into a 5-10 minute arrival to the patient's bedside. The use of a team within a facility empowers the staff nurse, and provides a safety net for both the nurses and the patients. Implementation of RRTs has reduced cardiac arrests, deaths, the number of unexpected emergency admissions to ICU, and the length of a hospital admission for cardiac arrest survivors. RRTs build teamwork and spread knowledge and skills throughout the hospital. The goals of the team are to provide immediate detection and diagnosis, to treat patients early, and to mitigate harm by turning adverse events into "near misses." The system is designed to protect the patient from further harm and to allow for recovery from possible medical errors and system deficiencies.

Is the RRT system working? A survey of 56 staff nurses identified three categories of reasons for why the RRT was activated:

- The patient exhibited signs and symptoms that were either unexpected or significantly different from baseline.
- Despite the absence of objective data, the nurse had a "gut feeling" that "something was wrong."

- The nurse was convinced that the patient needed immediate evaluation and was unable to get the treating physician to respond as the nurse thought necessary. This is what one nurse said:

"It's during shift change so everybody's calling and running and doing this and that, and we called the doctor and he said, 'Well, she's got a pulmonologist on the case, call them.' He gave us nothing. No orders. No meds. No, no nothing....At that point we decided we're not going to wait for anybody else, we'll just call rapid response and get them down here."

Consider this comment in comparison to the often slow process of obtaining medical attention when a facility does not have a RRT. In addition to the direct patient safety benefits of such teams, RRTs empowered nurses and gave them a sense of control over the patient situation, identified other processes negatively affecting patient safety, and improved communication and respect between disciplines, thereby raising job satisfaction.[48]

TIP: Failure to rescue is a nursing-sensitive performance measure on the list of 15 identified by the National Quality Forum in 2004 to be collected by CMS (Centers for Medicare and Medicaid Services). A 2009 study performed by HealthGrades showed that patient safety incidents with the highest incidence rates were failure to rescue. There were 92.7 incidents (per 1,000 population).[49] Starting June 1, 2010, CMS began collecting data about a facility's failure to rescue rates.

---

2. Diagnosis

The nurse uses the assessment data to diagnose the patient's condition. A nursing diagnosis is a clinical judgment about individual, family, or community responses to actual or potential health problems/life processes. A nursing diagnosis provides the basis for selection of nursing interventions to achieve desired outcomes for which the nurse is accountable.[50] Nursing diagnoses are formulated by sorting, organizing, and analyzing the assessment data. Diagnoses are usually recorded in a variety of places, including the nursing care plan and the progress notes.

The nursing diagnosis usually consists of three components:

- The human response or problem
- The related factor
- The signs and symptoms

a. The human response

The human response describes a problem which the nurse has identified through assessment. After gathering and analyzing assessment data, the nurse formulates the nursing diagnosis by selecting the human response from a list of accepted nursing diagnoses, including North American Nursing Diagnosis Association and the Omaha (home care) diagnoses. A number of different nursing diagnosis systems are in use.

b. The related factor

The related factor is identified next. Related factors are physiologic, psychosocial, environmental, and spiritual elements. The words "related to" link the human response and the related factor. This relationship implies that if one part of the diagnosis changes, the other part may also change. "Related to" does not express a direct cause and effect relationship.

c. Signs and symptoms

Also referred to as "defining characteristics," signs and symptoms make up an optional third part of the nursing diagnosis. When they are included in the nursing diagnosis, they are linked to the related factor with the words "as evidenced by" or the abbreviation "AEB." Just as there are many possible related factors, the list of signs and symptoms associated with a human response can be extensive. Sometimes the signs and symptoms are omitted from the nursing diagnosis since they are described elsewhere in the nursing documentation.

d. Examples of nursing diagnoses

Putting this all together, here are some examples of nursing diagnoses:

- Risk for skin breakdown related to immobility as evidenced by open, red skin
- Altered coping related to separation from mother AEB crying and rocking in crib
- Risk for infection related to multiple open wounds

3. Planning

Once the patient's nursing diagnoses are identified, the nurse begins planning the care to be provided, which may be documented in the form of a nursing care plan. The traditional nursing care plan consists of three elements:

- Nursing diagnoses
- Outcomes
- Interventions

Outcomes are statements that describe the behavior the person will display if the nursing diagnosis is resolved. For example, if a patient is highly anxious, the outcome may be stated as "expresses less anxiety within two days."

The interventions are the specific actions the nurse performs to help the patient achieve the outcome. In the example mentioned above, the nurse may provide the patient with opportunities to discuss his anxiety and suggest strategies to deal with the anxiety more effectively.

Care planning was the eleventh most common factor identified as a root cause of sentinel events. It can be implicated in an injury through the failure to formulate or carry out a plan of care. In the following Washington case, the plaintiff alleged the care plan was not followed:

> The plaintiff's decedent, age 86, was transferred to the defendant nursing home in late June 2003 for rehabilitation of hip and back pain. He was at high risk for skin breakdown due to diabetes, incontinence of bladder and bowel, decreased hematocrit and hemoglobin, limited mobility and the need for frequent bed rest due to his hip and back pain. At admission, he had no pressure ulcers on his body. A care plan was established which was intended to address the high risk for skin breakdown, but the decedent claimed that this plan was not followed. Parts of the plan included physician orders. The decedent developed two stage I pressure ulcers eight days after admission. The plaintiff claimed that these were not properly treated and by late September the decedent had one stage I pressure ulcer, one stage II pressure ulcer and two stage IV pressure ulcers. He also developed anemia, several infections and weight loss. One day in early October the man was found unresponsive and he was transferred to a hospital, where he was noted to have multiple pressure ulcers, including necrotic and foul smelling stage IV ulcers on his sacral area and left heel and was lethargic, dehydrated, malnourished and anemic. The decedent required a below-knee amputation a week later. The defendant claimed the staff provided proper care and that the skin breakdown was unavoidable. A $101,500 settlement was reached.[51]

4. Implementation

The implementation phase involves administering direct care such as bathing, dressing changes and other treatments, and supervising the care provided by others, such as unlicensed assistive personnel or nursing assistants. It includes teaching and counseling patients and their families, identifying the need for referrals (such as to a home health agency), and carrying out orders of healthcare providers such as doctors, nurse practitioners, dentists, and others.

Considering the most frequent untoward outcomes reported to The Joint Commission, note how implementation of nursing care contributes to the result.

- **Operative or postoperative complication**: Failure to note the patient's allergy to iodine (a component of Betadine, a skin cleanser); failure to notify the physician of ominous changes in the postoperative patient's condition
- **Wrong site surgery:** Failure to properly identify the patient or location of the surgery
- **Delay in treatment:** Failure to contact the appropriate healthcare provider of the patient's need for attention or transfer to a higher level of care
- **Medication error:** Failure to administer the right dose of the right drug at the right time to the right patient by the right route for the right reason
- **Suicide:** Failure to carry out the plan of care
- **Restraint-related event:** Failure to implement least restrictive measures before applying restraints; failure to remove restraints periodically to assess skin
- **Inpatient drug overdose:** Failure to correctly set a pain medication pump
- **Falls:** Failure to implement safety measures
- **Elopement:** Failure to institute a plan of care to address wandering behavior of nursing home resident

5. Evaluation

The evaluation phase of the nursing process involves making a judgment about the effectiveness of the nursing care. One of the most significant professional functions of the registered nurse is evaluation of the patient's responses to nursing care. For example, when the nurse provides pain medication, the process is not complete without evaluating the medication's effectiveness. Using observation and questioning, the nurse makes a judgment about whether the person has obtained relief from the pain. Nurses make complex, sophisticated decisions concerning patient care, yet nursing documentation does not always reflect that decision making ability.

Evaluation is an ongoing process that occurs whenever the nurse sees the patient. It consists of reviewing the appropriateness of the nursing diagnoses, outcomes, and interventions. Based on the decisions made during the evaluation phase, the nurse may change the plan of care or continue

as originally planned. The patient may be injured when the nurse fails to evaluate the patient's condition and take the appropriate steps based on that evaluation. The patient could be injured if the nurse fails to

- collect the appropriate data about the patient's status (assessment)
- correctly identify the patient's problem or treat the patient for a problem that was nonexistent (diagnosis)
- develop a plan of care to address the patient's problems (planning)
- carry out a treatment in the proper way (implementation)
- evaluate the patient's response to treatment and make modifications in the plan of care accordingly (evaluation)

TIP: Failure to correctly carry out all of the steps of the nursing process may result in injury to a patient, thus sowing the seeds of a malpractice case. In fact, the majority of performance-related patient injuries occur because the nurse failed to properly follow the steps of the nursing process.

B. The Use of the Nursing Process in Litigation

The attorney should understand the nursing process for the following reasons:

1. Comprehension of the nursing process helps determine the nurse's responsibilities in order to identify any deviations from the standard of care.
2. The medical record is easier to interpret using a nursing process framework. Nursing documentation (discussed in greater depth in Chapter 7, *Nursing Documentation*) should contain evidence that the nurse followed the steps of the nursing process. For example, the medical record contains assessment data in the form of vital sign records, intake and output, neurological assessment checks, skin integrity assessments, and so on. The diagnosis is written on the nursing care plan which documents the planning phases. The nurse's notes and flow sheets show evidence of how the plan of care was implemented. The nurse's notes and flow sheets also contain information about the nurse's evaluation of the patient's response to care.
3. The nursing process language is readily understood by nurses. Use of the nursing process framework will

enable the attorney, claims adjuster, or risk manager to speak the same language as the nurses. Figure 1.4 offers examples of nursing process questions that could be used to depose a nurse defendant.

4. Expert witness reports usually reflect the nurse's responsibilities for following the nursing process. Expert witnesses may explain how the nurse did or did not carry out the steps of the nursing process.

5. The nursing process is useful when explaining to the jury the nurse's obligations. It can be used during the opening statement and closing argument and during direct and cross-examinations of witnesses.

C. Impaired Critical Thinking

The absence of critical thinking may lead to incorrect conclusions or a failure to take action when needed. Critical thinking is an elusive concept. The nursing literature defines critical thinking as both an outcome and a process. One definition that incorporates several perspectives of critical thinking identifies it as "a process influenced by knowledge and experience using strategies such as reflective thinking as a part of learning to identify the issues and opportunities and holistically synthesize the information in nursing practice. Clinical decisions are reached through multiple steps that include the opportunity for ongoing evaluation."[52] As noted above, the unlicensed assistive personnel employed in health care lack critical thinking. While it is their duty to report a dangerously low blood sugar of 30 (normal 80-120) to a nurse, it is the job of the nurse to synthesize and act on that information.

1. Importance of critical thinking

Fowler[53] recognizes that critical thinking is needed to form appropriate nursing judgments and points out that nursing judgment is the driving force and the expected outcome of the nursing process, regardless of the environment in which health care is provided. Without sound judgments, nurses are merely performing task-oriented care. Most patients are in the hospital because they need continual assessments and interventions based on nurses' judgments and plans.

TIP: The importance of critical thinking cannot be underestimated. It is an essential attribute of a professional nurse.

A large number of errors in nursing practice occur because the nurse fails to use critical thinking. The ability to think critically is a required part of daily nursing practice. Patients' lives depend on the nurse's ability to analyze, question, communicate, and relate theory to clinical realities. Critical thinking encompasses problem-solving behavior

and involves obtaining, analyzing, and evaluating information about patients. The benefits of critical thinking are clear: "Critical thinking offers the nurse the ability to make inferences, set priorities and construct an effective plan to assist patients in their recovery from illness and in promotion of their wellness."[54]

2. Evolution of critical thinking

The nurse with basic critical thinking skills is rule-guided and responds to authority figures. The competent critical thinker is able to perceive the situation more holistically. The most skilled critical thinker has vast experience and is keenly aware of alternative solutions. This nurse is able to reflect on past experiences and has a deep understanding of the situation.

When the technical aspects of nursing are mastered, the nurse is able to devote more attention to critical thinking. This is why it is so difficult for novices to think critically. Their attention is consumed by the tasks to be accomplished. When the technology of the practice becomes automatic, the more proficient person uses less energy to accomplish those tasks. Critical thinking employs cognitive knowledge, intuition, and experience to make clinical decisions.[55]

There is a fine line between failure to use critical thinking to identify and resolve a problem, and the use of nursing judgment in the same situation. The terminology in the previous sentence reflects the perspectives of the disciplines of nursing and law. The nursing literature offers much information on critical thinking, but little information on "nursing judgment." In a statement that linked the two overlapping concepts, the American Association of Colleges of Nursing stated, "the development of skills in critical thinking and clinical judgment should be the top curricular priority in baccalaureate and graduate nursing programs."[56] The use of critical thinking leads to a nursing judgment. When a bad outcome occurs, resulting in a lawsuit, the defense of nursing actions based on the use of nursing judgment may be an acceptable and successful strategy.

3. Errors and critical thinking

Several factors increase pressure on the registered nurse's ability to think critically. The rapid turnover of patients in hospitals prevents a nurse from getting to know a patient well enough to detect subtle changes. Lack of continuity of care (changing patient assignments frequently, use of part-time or per diem nurses) compounds the problem. Increasingly complex technology and knowledge must be managed by stressed nurses. Nurses with barely enough time to complete assignments have little opportunity to reflect on the data and define the appropriate interventions.

Assessment:
1. Could you please explain to me how patients were assigned to nurses at the time of the incident?
2. Was an acuity system used to make assignments?
3. Can you explain to me the rationale of assigning a nursing assistant to get Mr. R out of bed on his first day after surgery?
4. Did you have a physical assessment course as part of your nursing program?
5. Were you taught how to do a neurological assessment?
6. What are the signs of a compromised neurovascular system?
7. Describe for me how you performed a neurovascular assessment on Mr. Ginsberg.
8. What did your assessment of the plaintiff consist of at 12:00 P.M.?
9. Please show me the section of the chart that indicates that you assessed the patient's circulation every two hours.

Diagnosis:
1. Based on your assessment findings, what nursing diagnosis did you formulate?
2. Did you do anything to validate that diagnosis?
3. Did you reach any conclusions when you saw that the blood pressure was slowly dropping over the preceding eight hours?
4. Did your diagnosis of the plaintiff ever change over the course of your shift?

Planning:
1. What plan of care did you develop as a result of your diagnosis of risk for impaired skin integrity?
2. Please show me where you documented this plan of care.
3. During the change-of-shift report what did you hear about the plan of care for Mrs. Quick?

Implementation:
1. Was it customary for nurses to receive a computerized Kardex on each patient for whom they were to provide care?
2. Was it customary for the registered nurse to give the nursing assistant some type of report about the patients on the unit or in the rooms assigned to the nursing assistant?
3. Assuming the intermittent needle port was inserted into Mr. D on the 3-11 shift of December 2, and you cared for him on second shift on December 7, would you agree that you should have checked to see if the device had been changed in the interim?
4. Please show me the portion of the medication record that shows you administered the medication that was ordered "stat."
5. What did you tell Dr. Benjamin about the condition of the plaintiff at 5:30 A.M.?
6. Please show me the section of the nurse's notes which states that the side rails were up at the end of the evening shift.

Evaluation:
1. What do you understand to be your duty if the patient complains of pain at the site, or you observe warmth, redness, or swelling at the site of the intravenous needle?
2. Did you form an opinion about the amount of pain you would have expected the plaintiff to be displaying given her medical diagnosis?
3. Did you evaluate the patient's response to the pain medication?
4. When the plaintiff did not obtain relief from the pain medication, what did you do next?
5. Did you ever update the plan of care to reflect the new problems the plaintiff was experiencing?
6. Did you review the medical record to determine what the patient's blood pressure was before your shift began?

Figure 1.4 *Examples of Deposition Questions for Defendant Nurses Based on the Nursing Process*

The accumulation of stress has an impact on clinical performance. Job stress is defined as "the harmful physical and emotional responses that occur when the requirements of the job do not match the capabilities, resources or needs of the worker."[57] Job stress may impair critical thinking in addition to leading to health issues, conflicts with patients or staff, substance abuse, and depression.

Fatigue contributes to impaired critical thinking. 12-hour shifts, which can extend even longer, contribute to errors and near errors. A survey of 393 hospital staff nurses revealed that participants usually worked longer than scheduled and that approximately 40 percent of the 5,317 work shifts they logged exceeded 12 hours. The risks of making an error were significantly increased when work shifts were longer than 12 hours, when nurses worked overtime, or when they worked more than 40 hours per week.[58] Working shift work (which is defined as working outside normal daylight hours) is a requirement in healthcare settings that offer care 24 hours a day. The night shift and rotating shifts are of particular concern in terms of performance. Fatigue, irritability, reduced performance, and decreased mental agility may be present in some nurses working these hours.[59] The Institute of Medicine (IOM) concluded, "There is no evidence to suggest that any amount of training, motivation, or professionalism is able to overcome the performance deficits associated with fatigue, sleep loss, and sleepiness associated with circadian variations in alertness." The IOM concluded that the evidence related to prolonged work hours and fatigue was strong and recommended that state regulatory bodies prohibit nurses from working more than 12 hours in a 24-hour period and more than 60 hours per seven day period.[60] Some states have prohibited mandatory overtime and others have defined minimum staffing requirements.

TIP: Nurses who are otherwise competent may suffer a reduction in performance when they are fatigued. To combat fatigue, the Federal Highway Administration regulations limit truckers to working ten consecutive hours, followed by a minimum eight-hour break. Similar rules have been implemented by the Federal Aviation Administration, which requires airline pilots to have at least eight continuous hours of rest in the 24 hours before finishing their flight duty. Yet, there are no such regulations in the healthcare industry. A number of facilities follow the guidelines of the Accreditation Council for Graduate Medical Education for fatigue prevention, which suggest a broad limit of 60-hour work weeks for nurses.[61]

There is no consistent mechanism to detect or limit nurses who work two full-time jobs or a full-time and a part-time job, particularly if this occurs at different facilities. Sleep deprivation is a common problem among those who are employed to do shift work. Thirty-three percent of them average less than six hours of sleep per night on workdays even though the American Academy of Sleep Medicine says most adults need an average of seven to eight hours to feel alert and well rested. Inadequate sleep may be an annoyance to workers, but it has health and safety implications for healthcare practitioners and the patients in their care. Working longer hours, as many shift workers do, including the related fatigue and sleepiness they experience, is associated with accidents in the workplace. Shift workers are more likely than day-shift workers to make mistakes on the job and to be involved in accidents, increasing their risk of job-related injury and illness.[62]

4. Types of errors

Types of errors in critical thinking are described below, with true case examples.

a. Drawing incorrect parallels between two cases

The nurse's thinking about a situation may be influenced by a recent experience.

Example: A nurse is assigned to care for two patients with back pain. The first patient has fallen down some steps and has compression fractures in her back, causing pain. The second patient with back pain has no history of trauma. This patient's symptoms may be unfortunately minimized by the nurse. Back pain in this patient may signify spinal cord compression or a dissecting aortic aneurysm.

b. Making a premature diagnosis

Failure to consider all of the available information can result in mistaken diagnoses. Both nurses and physicians are prone to this trap.

Example: The restless patient treated with a sedative instead of an assessment for decreased oxygen is a victim of a premature diagnosis.

c. Overreliance on the findings of others

Not taking the time to investigate abnormal findings as reported by ancillary staff or other nurses may result in injury.

Example: A woman entered the hospital for laparoscopic surgery. Her vena cava was nicked during the surgery, and the bleeding was dismissed by the experienced surgeon. The patient was transferred to the recovery room, where her blood pressure steadily declined while her heart rate increased. Her last blood pressure was not taken by the recovery room before she was transferred to the next stage of the same-day surgery recovery area. The nurse who received her did not take a new set of vital signs, but rather copied down the values obtained by the recovery room nurse. This was standard practice for this facility. There were no vital signs taken on this patient before she arrested on the same-day surgery unit nearly two hours after arrival. An autopsy found a massive amount of blood pooled in her abdomen. The case settled.

d. Failing to recognize the significance of abnormal findings

A busy, inexperienced, distracted, or fatigued nurse may not correctly process information.

Example: A patient who was receiving morphine by PCA pump had a steady decline in vital signs. The nurse assigned to the patient failed to consider the significance of this trend or to report it to the physician. The patient had a respiratory arrest from oversedation. The case was tried for damages only.

e. Overreliance on protocols

Protocols are useful for giving guidance in situations, but cannot predict the unusual circumstance that demands critical thinking. The expression "rules are meant to be broken" may have applicability in those situations when the nurse must act as a patient advocate to gain attention for the patient.

Example: The patient was a young man who developed an acute clot in his leg. The surgeon took him to the operating room. After being unsuccessful in restoring circulation, the doctor completed the surgery without correcting the problem. While the alarmed mother and nurses continued to observe deterioration of the patient's circulation, the surgeon chose to take another patient into the operating room for an elective gall bladder operation. The nurses were unable to transfer the patient to another hospital without the surgeon having a discussion of the case with a doctor at a receiving hospital. The nursing supervisor waited outside the

operating room for the surgeon to finish the gall bladder surgery. The surgeon then made arrangements for the transport. The patient was rushed into surgery at the second hospital; his leg was saved, but he suffered a series of postoperative complications that resulted in severe scarring. The plaintiff charged that the nurses should have facilitated the transfer in a timelier manner. The defense's position was that the nurses did not have the authority to transfer the patient. However, what was overlooked was the possibility of having the surgeon use a speakerphone to speak to the doctor at the receiving hospital while the surgeon was in the operating room with the gall bladder surgery. This would have saved three hours of time. The defendants settled the case.

f. Overconfidence

Just as too little experience can result in errors, too much confidence in one's own abilities and experience can increase the likelihood of error. Overconfidence can result in incorrect use of the nursing process. For example, the overconfident nurse may perform an inadequate assessment by failing to gather enough information on the patient's status.

Example: A patient who had knee surgery was restless and agitated. The nurse concluded that since he required significant amounts of pain medication to treat his knee injury before surgery, that he was drug seeking. She advised him that if this was the most amount of pain he would experience, he would be lucky. The patient's pain persisted at intense levels all night. The next morning, a markedly swollen and pulseless leg was noted. Later that day in the operating room, the surgeon found a severed popliteal artery. The case was settled.

Factors that contribute to overconfidence include:

1. Large amounts of positive feedback from peers, other professionals, or the public
2. The reliance on unaided memory
3. The lack of awareness of environmental or treatment effects on outcomes (i.e., focusing on outcome feedback as opposed to process feedback)
4. The failure to search for disconfirming evidence[63]

Components of overconfidence include:

1. The failure to consider alternative perspectives

2. The failure to distinguish inferences from assertions
3. Favoring positive over negative information
4. Unwarranted certainty in the individual's accuracy of prediction
5. Enjoying a feeling of control and self-confidence.[64]

g. Caring for patients with similar names

Nurses are encouraged to avoid having an assignment of patients who have similar names. There is a great deal of room for error in treatment and medication administration. Many facilities ensure patients with identical names are not assigned to the same nursing unit.

As can be seen from these causes of critical thinking errors and case examples, the consequences can be serious—patient injury or death may result.

1.5 Availability of Information

Clinical and administrative information drives decision making. From a nursing perspective, information affects every aspect of care. Some of the components that have a positive effect on patient safety are listed below.

- Stat test results are available in a timely manner and are appropriately conveyed to the physician.
- Nurses are aware of the rate of falls on their unit and suggest changes to improve safety.
- Critical laboratory results are recognized and shared with the physician.
- Nurses have been trained and are comfortable with retrieving information from the medical record, whether in paper or electronic form.
- Nursing care plans define the patient's significant problems.
- Unlicensed assistive personnel have a method of retrieving information pertinent to the care of the patient.
- Medical records from a prior admission are available for consultation.
- Monitoring of oxygen levels through equipment such as pulse oximeters is performed to assess the patient's status.
- Change of shift reports convey crucial information about the patient.
- Available resources such as empty beds, empty operating rooms, and necessary equipment are identified and used appropriately.

In this Cook County, Illinois case, *Aaron Garcia, Minor v. Edward Hospital*, Dr. John Rigali, a labor-

ing woman had signs of fetal distress. Despite these signs, the nurses allowed the defendant obstetrician to use the only operating room in the labor and delivery suite for an elective tubal ligation. The fetal monitor strip deteriorated further shortly thereafter, until the nurses discovered a prolapsed umbilical cord. An additional 20-minute delay ensued before an operating room and personnel could be secured for an emergency cesarean section. The child was born with brain damage secondary to decreased oxygen and blood flow to the brain. The obstetrician settled for $1.5 million and a jury returned a $12.5 million verdict against the hospital.[65]

1.6 Competency/Credentialing

Experts agree that there are incompetent and irresponsible healthcare providers who should be held accountable, but incompetent professionals do not comprise the majority of those who make mistakes that hurt patients.[66] Outright incompetent nurses are rare. Several safeguards filter out the inept person. Student nurses must perform well enough in both academic and clinical courses to meet standards. Various standardized examinations are used to test the student's ability during the curriculum. Schools of nursing are accredited by the National League for Nursing or the Commission on Collegiate Nursing Education, which have standards regulating such areas as content of the curriculum, the degree of clinical supervision required (no more than eight students per instructor in the clinical courses), and passing scores on the standardized exams. As described in Chapter 6, *The Foundations of Nursing Practice*, graduates must pass the NCLEX-RN exam to earn a license to practice. Security measures in these examination areas are designed to detect cheating. The system is designed to screen out the incompetent nurse.

Further, the employer plays a role in identifying competent employees. Joint Commission standards address this in the hospital accreditation manual through the HR standard HR.01.02.01: "The hospital defines staff qualifications" and HR.01.02.05, "The hospital verifies staff qualifications." The hospital is expected to verify current licensure, certification or registration, to obtain a criminal background check on the applicant, and to credential physician assistant and advanced nurse practice registered nurses who practice within the hospital.[67]

A. Continuum of Competency

Patricia Benner[68] conceived of the concept of competency on a continuum:

1. The novice has no experience in the situations in which he is expected to perform and requires detailed analysis for problem solving. This individual is not necessarily incompetent, but rather is inexperienced.
2. The advanced beginner can demonstrate marginally acceptable performance, and has some experience, but requires support in clinical decisions.
3. The competent nurse can master, cope with, and manage the many contingencies of clinical nursing, but may not have speed and flexibility.
4. The proficient nurse perceives a clinical situation as a whole, including its implications for long-term planning and modification.
5. The expert nurse has sufficient experience to intuitively grasp clinical situations, rather than rely on analysis for routine problem solving.

According to this analysis, the novice is closer to the level of incompetence than the expert. However, factors such as working in an unfamiliar area or substance abuse may alter the skills of an otherwise competent nurse and result in patient injury. This is discussed in greater detail below. In the previously cited article about residents' perceptions about nurses, most residents associated experience with competence, as in the following observation: "You have more older nurses that know how the system runs; they know what to do with a patient." But experience was not synonymous with competence. Many residents pointed to the importance of education, either on its own or combined with experience.[69]

In *Estate of Oscar Gonzales, Deceased, O. Lopez De Gonzalez et al. v. Unidentified Nursing Home, Unidentified Parent Company of Nursing Home et al.*, a charge nurse in a Texas nursing home forced Oscar Gonzales, a nursing home resident, into his room. Subsequently, he fell over in his walker, struck his head, and then was put to bed. With the help of other nurses, the charge nurse concealed all evidence of the fall. The resident's roommate observed the fall, and testified that the charge nurse and the other nurses cleaned blood from the floor after the fall. One of Gonzales' daughters discovered him the next morning and arranged for him to be hospitalized. The hospital staff found that he had a "panic level" of the blood-thinning medication Coumadin in his system, and he died five days later of intracerebral bleeding. During discovery, it was found that the resident had fallen earlier that day. The care plan prepared by the facility failed to address the life-threatening risks such as his propensity to fall, wander, and the risk of bleeding from Coumadin. The charge nurse did not know what a care plan was and could not identify one. The facility records indicated that the nursing home employed the charge nurse as a supervisory nurse even though he had no prior nursing experience. This was in violation of the facility's requirement that the position required a minimum of one year of nursing experience. The charge nurse testified that he had no idea what any of the facility's policies or procedures were on any medical or nursing topics, much less topics pertinent to the care of Gonzalez. He had a second full-time job at a prison and the facility was aware of this. The nursing home settled for $1,275,000. A physician settled for $190,000 and a clinical laboratory added in $125,000.[70]

TIP: In the current system, the truly incompetent nurse practicing in a dangerous manner may be able to take advantage of holes in the legal system to move undetected into another state. After an incident has occurred or a complaint is filed, the nurse may disappear. Most attorneys have experienced the frustration of trying to locate a nurse defendant who has vanished.

Incompetent nurses may easily disappear from view. States vary in how they define a complaint, providing an important loophole of inconsistency. In one state, a call to the licensing board may be considered a complaint. In another, a complaint may be defined as filing a formal charge. It is not clear what information can be shared from one state to another when a nurse applies for a license to practice. These inconsistencies permit unsafe nurses to move to different jurisdictions before a complaint can be investigated and handled.[71] The Internet has made location of these individuals easier. Phone and property records are useful for finding nurses, as well as using the Board of Nursing if the individual's state can be identified.

The National Council of State Boards of Nursing has endorsed a mutual recognition model for interstate nursing practice to encourage reciprocal arrangements between states for licensing and disciplinary action. The goal would be to make licensure more like the rules used for a driver's license. That is, licensure would be recognized across state lines, but the nurse would still be subject to the rules of a state while in that state.[72]

B. Delegation

Nurses are expected to work as part of a team and to delegate tasks to others. Registered nurses must work with others to accomplish the goals of care. This requires the nurse to delegate safely. Nurses must know what the Board of Nursing allows to be assigned to others. For example, a state Board of Nursing may not allow licensed practical nurses to administer intravenous medications. Huston[73] defines the tips for safe delegation.

1. Delegate for the right reason. The nurse should not delegate an unpleasant task simply because he or she does not want to do it or is too disorganized.
2. Delegate to the right person. The nurse should know the capabilities of the person's skills, responsibilities and abilities. This is particularly important when the individual is an unlicensed assistive personnel (nurse's aide or technician) who lacks the education to recognize the significance of abnormal signs and symptoms.
3. Delegate at the right time. The nurse should avoid getting overwhelmed before asking for assistance to complete tasks.
4. Others should have the right to refuse a delegated task. The nurse should secure the agreement of the person and respect an inability or refusal to help.
5. Choose words carefully. Requests for help should be accompanied by "please" and thank you."
6. Do not create situations that require the nurse to redo delegated tasks. Others find this demoralizing. Consider why the task was not completed successfully and provide assistance in finding strategies to bring about the desired outcome.
7. Define the desired outcome of delegation, but allow latitude in how the delegated task is completed.
8. Never delegate responsibility for a task without providing the authority and resources needed to accomplish the task. The helper should have the time, equipment and resources to complete the assignment.
9. Oversee completion of the delegated task. The nurse should use the appropriate degree of supervision and periodically seek feedback to evaluate if things are going smoothly.
10. Celebrate successful completion of the delegated task. The nurse should recognize the good work and contribution to shared goals.

C. Discipline

In addition to licensing nurses, the second major responsibility of the Board of Nursing is to discipline nurses. The Board of Nursing may take action against a nurse's license. It may refuse to issue or renew; limit or restrict; suspend; revoke; place on probation; or place conditions on a license. A nurse may be reprimanded or disciplined, and civil penalties or fines may be imposed.

Grounds for discipline include:[74]

- failing to meet requirements for licensure
- licensing examination violations
- criminal convictions
- fraud and deceit
- unethical conduct
- action taken against the nurse in another jurisdiction
- unsafe or unprofessional practice
- misconduct
- drug diversion
- failure to comply with alternative program agreement
- other drug-related behavior
- unlawful practice

TIP: Actual injury to a patient does not have to be established for a nurse to be found guilty of unethical conduct. It must be proven the nurse performed actions that created an unnecessary danger to a patient's life, health, or safety. Failure to practice within the scope of the profession may also subject the individual's license to suspension or revocation.

An investigation may be initiated upon receipt of a complaint about a nurse. The accused nurse is entitled to due process, with the right to question witnesses, be represented by an attorney, have a record of the hearing, and have recourse to review by a judge. States vary as to when and how information regarding the allegations is communicated. Many states are barred from sharing information until the Board takes final action. In others, laws may require the Board to share information earlier in the process.[75] The nurse's name and a summary of the case may be published by the agency in a newsletter or on the Internet. The nurse must, by law, reveal the discipline when applying for a job, licensure in another state, or registration renewal.[76] Discovery that a nurse has been reprimanded by the Board of Nursing may have an impact on a nursing malpractice suit, as the following case demonstrates:

In *Alice Fay, Individually and on Behalf of Kayo Fay, Velvet Parker and Tasha Johnson v. Shannon Medical Center and Charles Phillips, RN*, a 41-year-old woman suffering from chronic degenerative cervical spine disease underwent a cervical laminectomy. Postoperatively, she developed numbness and tingling, which over the course of the next 14 hours progressed into an inability to move her upper and lower extremities. Emergency surgery was performed, during which a hematoma was allegedly discovered and removed, but the spinal cord had sustained permanent injury. The patient and her children sued the medical center and the nurse in charge, alleging they were negligent for failing to conduct a proper neurological assessment and failing to timely contact the surgeon about the patient's deteriorating condition. The plaintiffs accepted a confidential settlement from the defendants. Plaintiff counsel reported that while the case was pending, he learned that the defendant nurse was reprimanded by the Board of Nurse Examiners in connection with his care of the patient.[77]

TIP: Ask the nurse if her license to practice has ever been suspended or revoked.

One of the most common charges against nurses is substance abuse. A study of 249 Louisiana nurses disciplined by the Board of Nursing found that substance abuse was the most common reason for discipline, followed by violating the terms of the recovering nurse program. The other high-frequency violation was practicing without a valid license. In a Texas study, the most common violation was failure to administer medications or treatments responsibly.[78] In a New York study of 177 nurses disciplined in 1998, the five most common types of misconduct were criminal convictions, medication errors, falsification of information, documentation errors, and narcotics issues.[79]

D. Chemical Dependency

Cognitive and performance skills clouded by the effects of narcotics may contribute to patient injury. Substance abuse problems are prevalent in nursing, with the exact numbers difficult to establish. The National Institute on Drug Abuse estimates that 10 percent of U.S. adults abuse drugs during their lifetime. Accurate statistics are difficult to obtain because drug abuse and addiction are often cloaked in silence. The American Nurses Association says that 10 percent of nurses are dependent on drugs. With nearly 3 million RNs employed in the U.S., that means almost 300,000 nurses

may be substance abusers. Just in one state, of the hundreds of cases that come before the Ohio Board of Nursing each month, well over half of them deal with addiction. Nurses are considered to be vulnerable to addiction because of occupational triggers: easy access to medications, long shifts, mandatory overtime, and physically and emotionally taxing work. Nurses with untreated addiction can jeopardize patient safety because of impaired judgment, slower reaction time, diverting drugs from patients, neglecting patients, and making mistakes.[80]

The typical ways nurses obtain drugs in a healthcare setting include:

- Asking a prescriber to write a prescription for them
- Administering a partial dose of a medication to a patient and saving the rest for themselves
- Asking a co-worker to sign that a drug was wasted without witnessing the drug's disposal
- Signing out medications for patients who have left the unit
- Obtaining as needed medications for patients who have refused or not requested them[81]

It is a nurse's responsibility to identify colleagues with substance abuse problems, yet this is difficult for many. It is especially difficult for nurses to report a peer, given that nurses often empathize with the problems of their colleagues. Substance abuse is one of the most frequent reasons nurses are disciplined by the Board of Nursing.

TIP: Nurses often practice for several years with undiagnosed or unrecognized chemical dependency problems. It may take as long as five years before the nurse's addiction problem is discovered by others. Patients may have been endangered for this extended period of time.[82]

The "Alternative to Discipline Monitoring Program" described by the National Council of State Boards of Nursing creates a non-punitive and non-public approach for monitoring nurses' recovery from substance abuse as well as their ability to provide safe nursing care. This program is designed to promote early identification and close monitoring of nurses who are impaired due to substance abuse, and to decrease the time between the nurse acknowledging a substance abuse problem and the entrance into a treatment program. It is designed to ensure that recovering nurses are compliant with treatment, recovery, and work plans, and to monitor when the nurse returns to nursing practice to ensure safety of the public. It provides education to nurses, nursing schools, and employers regarding the disease of chemical dependency, and the implications for nursing practice. Finally, it promotes nurse self-reporting as well as earlier identification and treatment.[83]

E. Profile of the Nurse Practice Act Violator

According to three studies, men were disciplined disproportionately more than women. In Arizona, men made up 4.5 percent of all nurses statewide, but represented 19 percent of the disciplined nurses. In Great Britain, men made up 9 percent of the workforce, but 47.5 percent of nurses appearing for disciplinary hearings. In Louisiana, 10 percent of the nurses were male, but represented 18 percent of those disciplined.[84] Studies have shown that males are found in higher concentrations in critical care and emergency departments, where they may have greater access to narcotics.[85]

Nurses with no more than an associate's degree in nursing are more likely to be disciplined than nurses with baccalaureate degrees. These conclusions were reached in Arizona,[86] Texas,[87] Colorado, and Louisiana.[88]

Contrary to common belief, disciplined nurses are not young and inexperienced. Nurses between the ages of 40 and 49 are more likely to be disciplined. This finding was consistent in the Texas, Colorado, and Louisiana studies cited above. More studies of this nature are needed to determine if this profile can be generalized across the country.

Common reactions to being disciplined included shame and adverse effects on physical or mental health or on personal relationships. Lost income, lost job opportunities, financial hardship, and inability to work in the profession may follow the actions of the Board of Nursing.[89]

1.7 Procedural Compliance
A. Impact

Failure to follow a physician's order or an agency's policy can contribute to patient injury or death. Here are some examples:

1. Failure to correctly administer tube-feeding solution into the stomach, but instead instilling it into the lung or bladder can harm the patient.
2. Failure to administer the correct dose of a medication can cause death.
3. Failure to keep door alarms may permit confused elderly patients to wander out of a facility and onto a highway.
4. Failure to keep ventilator alarms may allow an undetected blockage of the airway to cause brain damage.
5. Failure to report the late decelerations seen on fetal monitoring strips may delay an emergency delivery.
6. Failure to keep crib rails up may allow a child to fall out of bed, causing a fractured skull.
7. Failure to intervene to prevent skin breakdown may result in pressure ulcers that literally deepen to the bone.
8. Failure to change an intravenous site according to policy may cause an infection.
9. Failure to monitor a suicidal patient with the necessary frequency may result in the patient's death.
10. Failure to correctly identify a surgical site may lead to an incision on the wrong leg.
11. Failure to inform the physician of seriously abnormal lab results may result in untreated conditions.
12. Failure to question an inappropriate physician order or to go up the chain of command may result in patient harm.
13. Failure to follow a valid physician's order or agency policy may lead to harm.

Performing correct sponge counts is the responsibility of the operating room nurses.

The plaintiff mother, age 29, underwent a cesarean section delivery performed by defendant Dr. Shaw in March 2004. A laparotomy sponge was left inside the plaintiff, but was undiagnosed until October 2004, when she was examined by a surgeon for what was believed to be a stitch abscess. The surgeon pulled out the 12-inch sponge through the plaintiff's abdomen while she was awake because he thought it was just a retained stitch. This caused the plaintiff severe pain. The plaintiff underwent laparotomy surgery with placement of drains the next day and was hospitalized for several days, followed by six days of postoperative drainage. No permanent injuries were claimed as the laparotomy incision was made at the same site as the cesarean section incision and the plaintiff subsequently gave birth to another child without complication. The defendant claimed that the nurses assisting in the surgery were responsible for the retained sponge. The plaintiff had settled with the hospital prior to trial. According to Cook County Jury Verdict Reporter a $110,410 verdict was returned.[90]

At times, a series of errors culminates in the untoward outcome. The story of Joe Wilson (Figure 1.5) illustrates how the actions of several people resulted in the patient's death. Patient safety experts refer to the Swiss Cheese model as a concept of how several holes in the system line up to permit the patient to be injured.

B. Causes

Nursing school teaches nurses the principles and procedures for providing care. The employer provides a policy and procedure. Yet, a nurse does not follow the procedure. There are several reasons that may contribute to this.

1. Safety standards are not monitored or enforced

Nursing managers must be clear about the need to follow policies and procedures and the consequences of not doing so. Continual monitoring and education about the importance of patient safety sends an obvious message about the value of patient safety policies.[91]

2. Lack of knowledge about the causes of error

Staff nurses may be unaware of how errors occur. Integration of patient safety information into the curriculum of schools of nursing helps to increase knowledge and skills.

3. Dysfunctional systems

Convoluted systems are sometimes created by providers or administrators who lack essential training in human factors and systems engineering, which may make it too hard to adhere to the practice.[92] This invites workarounds because it becomes too difficult to follow the procedures.

4. Normalization of deviance

This occurs when a nurse knowingly disregards a safety practice, such as using two patient identifiers to verify patient identity. Repeated deviation from the safe practices tends to "normalize" the risky behavior in the nurse's mind.[93] In another example, The Joint Commission Medication Management Standard requires labeling of all medications. Yet a survey by the American Nurses Association indicated that only 37 percent of nurses surveyed reported they always label syringes and 28 percent never label syringes when administering medications.[94] Despite awareness and education, some providers choose to willfully disregard safety practices. Patient safety experts define a "no blame" culture as one that argues that most errors are committed by hardworking people; the traditional focus on identifying who is at fault is a distraction. A "just culture" differentiates between blameworthy and blameless acts. Wachter and Pronovost[95] acknowledge that there are areas of performance that pose a clear risk to patients, such as failure to practice hand hygiene, use a checklist to reduce blood stream infec-

tions, mark the surgical site to prevent wrong-site surgery, or perform a preoperative time out.

Nurses are implicated in some of these issues. They work for the organization, which typically has relatively clear lines of authority and procedures for dealing with failure to follow accepted practices. On the other hand, physicians have traditionally been independent entrepreneurs, not employees. They are subject to weak peer enforcement. Peers often recoil from disciplining each other and hospitals have been reluctant to punish physicians for fear of alienating them and losing the business they bring in. The tradition of lax enforcement of safety rules has led too many physicians to ignore them. Wachter and Pronovost[96] argued for a clear definition of unacceptable behaviors, with the initial warnings and counseling. Continued failure to adhere to safety practices after the initial penalty would lead to suspension or loss of clinical privileges (for physicians and others subject to credentialing, such as advanced practice nurses) or firing.

1.8 Environmental Safety/Security

Maintaining a safe environment encompasses many aspects of nursing activities. This includes using equipment properly; supervising patients within the environment; and protecting patients from hazards, each other, or from visitors or intruders. A study by the American Nurses Association[97] showed that 75 percent of nurses surveyed stated that unsafe working conditions interfered with their ability to provide quality care.[98]

A. Equipment

Healthcare facilities contain patients with a variety of medical equipment such as Foley catheters, feeding tubes, ventilators, assistive devices for walking, physical therapy splints and whirlpool tubs, side rails, wheelchairs, lap buddies, intravenous and dialysis catheters, cribs, and others. Nurses have a duty to exercise reasonable care in the use of medical equipment. They are expected to understand how to safely use equipment, follow procedures, and never guess about how to operate the equipment. Misuse of equipment can cause patient injury in several ways, as shown in Figure 1.6.

Eskreis,[99] a nurse attorney, provides these suggestions to nurses:

1. Trust your instincts. Refuse to use a device if you have misgivings, assuming no extraordinary situation exists.
2. Remove and examine questionable equipment.
3. Report adverse events related to equipment to your supervisor or risk manager.

Two elderly men from the same city were admitted to ABC Hospital. Both had the same name, Joe Wilson (ficti-tious name). The first Joe Wilson (1) had gastrointestinal bleeding, became anemic, and needed blood. After he was tested for blood type, he was given two units of blood without incident.

A few days later, the second Joe Wilson (2) was transferred from one nursing unit to another. The nursing unit sent a piece of paper down to the admitting office requesting a new name plate to be created with Joe Wilson's (2) new room number.

The admitting office clerk, who was new on the job, did not know there were two Joe Wilsons in the hospital since there were no alerts in the hospital's system to advise her of this fact. She opened a drawer where the two Joe Wilson files were stored. The first one she came to was for Joe Wilson (1). She looked no further. She pulled Joe Wilson's (1) file, created a new hospital identification name plate, and sent it to the nursing unit of Joe Wilson (2). The name plate listed Joe Wilson's (1) hospital number, address, age, and doctor, which did not match Joe Wilson's (2) information. The incorrect information on the name plate was not recognized when the nursing unit received it from the admitting clerk. The faulty plate was put into use.

The family of Joe Wilson (2) saw a sign in Mr. Wilson's room that was stamped with the new plate. When the family recognized that the address, age and doctor were incorrect, they told a licensed practical nurse at the nurses' station, but no action was taken.

As luck would have it, Joe Wilson (2), who had cancer, also needed blood. The laboratory technician re-ceived a request to have Joe Wilson's (2) blood drawn for blood type. The blood request slip was stamped with the faulty name plate. The technician drew the blood, and recorded the specimen in her log book. Her log book showed that she had already typed and cross matched blood for Joe Wilson, as indeed she had for Joe Wilson (1). Therefore, she discarded the blood specimen without testing it. Two units of blood were prepared for Joe Wilson (2).

On Mr. Wilson's (2) final day of life, two units of blood were administered to him. Unfortunately, he had a different blood type than did Mr. Wilson (1). The hospital policy (and national standard of care) required that the blood be checked at the bedside by two nurses. The blood bag should have been checked with the patient's identification band (which listed his correct, original hospital number). Instead, the two nurses involved in checking each of the two units of blood performed the check at the nurses' station. The blood bag was checked with the blood request slip, which had been stamped with the faulty plate. These two pieces of data matched.

While the second unit of blood was being administered to Mr. Wilson, he began showing signs of a blood transfusion reaction. The symptoms were not recognized by either his oncologist or the nurse who was assigned to care for him. He died in front of his family, a few minutes after the completion of the second unit of blood.

When his body was being prepared for the morgue, body tags were stamped with the hospital identifica-tion plate. His son recognized that the address, age and doctor on the tags were not correct. An investigation ensued and within three hours, the dimensions of the errors began to take shape. A few days later an article appeared in the local newspaper about the tragedy. In the ensuing lawsuit, the discovery process revealed the multiple systems and performance errors and knowledge deficits that contributed to the outcome.

The nurses who checked the blood with the nurses who actually hung the blood settled before trial. The jury found all individuals negligent (clerk, laboratory technician, nurses) except the oncologist. The verdict was $125,000 in this 1993 case. The verdict was believed to be low in part because the patient was quite ill with a poor prognosis at the time of the blood transfusions.

The system errors that can be identified in this case include:
Orientation/Training: Inadequate training of the clerk to teach her how to ensure she had the correct patient.
Communication: Failure of the nurse at the desk to respond to family's report of wrong name plate.
Procedural compliance: The laboratory tech failed to type and cross match the blood. The two sets of nurses failed to follow the procedure to verify the patient's identity at the bedside.
Assessment: Neither the physician nor the nurse recognized the declining blood pressure as a sign of a transfu-sion reaction.

Figure 1.5 *A Fatal Mixup*

- Improper use of a Hoyer lift (used to move a patient from one surface to another) resulted in a patient being dropped on his head.
- Use of patient gown with metal snaps resulted in burns on the back of patient's neck when electrocautery was used in the operating room.
- Placing a surgical grounding pad over the patient's antiembolism stocking resulted in the fabric being burned into the patient's skin.
- The call bell is taken away from a patient who constantly uses it, thus preventing the patient from asking for help.
- Failing to dampen a sponge on a patient's face resulted in the sponge igniting when electrocautery was used.
- Applying a hot diaper to the heel of an infant caused severe burns.
- Failing to monitor the tightness of wrist restraints resulted in massive swelling and nerve damage to the hands of an agitated patient.
- Instructing a family member that it was alright to push the PCA pump button and that it is not possible to overdose a patient with a morphine patient-controlled analgesia pump resulted in reduction in blood pressure and a cardiac arrest from an overdose.
- Removing the external fetal monitor from a laboring patient resulted in a delay in detection of late decelerations and fetal distress.
- Failing to apply proper wrist restraints enabled a patient to slip her hands from homemade restraints and climb out of the second-story window of her hospital room, resulting in her death.
- Improperly inserting a nasogastric tube allowed delivery of tube-feeding solution into the lungs of an elderly woman, causing her death.
- When a newly inserted percutaneous gastrostomy tube came out of the patient's abdomen, the nurse re-inserted it instead of notifying the physician of the problem. Unfortunately, it was not properly inserted, resulting in tube feeding solution draining into the patient's abdomen.
- Intubating the esophagus rather than the trachea resulted in filling the stomach rather than the lungs with air, causing brain damage.
- Failing to provide an elevated toilet seat to a patient who had a total hip replacement resulted in displacement of the prosthesis.
- Striking a patient in the back of the knees with a wheelchair seat resulted in displacement of two newly inserted total knee replacements.
- A nurse who dropped the weights attached to the patient's cervical traction caused a herniated disc to worsen.
- Failing to apply brakes to a wheelchair resulted in a nursing home resident falling onto the floor and fracturing a hip.
- A restrained patient managed to wedge her body between an opening in two side rails, resulting in her strangulation.
- Improperly applying chest restraints causing patients to become strangulated.
- Not having an adapter for a metal tracheostomy tube prevented resuscitation of a patient with an Ambu bag.
- Incorrect programming of a patient-controlled analgesia machine resulted in the patient receiving five times the prescribed dose of morphine, causing respiratory arrest.

Figure 1.6 *Examples of Injuries Caused by Nursing Use of Equipment*

4. Ensure that equipment is being used as indicated.
5. Monitor patients who are using equipment.
6. Take extra care when the patient is unable to discern or communicate discomfort—especially if the patient is young, sedated, or anesthetized.
7. Document equipment-related injuries.

In *Madeline Weinberg as Executrix of the Estate of Joel Weinberg etc. v. Westchester County Healthcare Corp., Westchester Medical Center, Rafik El-Sabrout MD and Eric Presser MD*, the 62-year-old patient was admitted to the hospital for a kidney transplant. Doctors placed a feeding tube in the left side of the patient's abdomen and a drainage tube in the right side. The rubber tubes were red and the feeding tube was marked with tape. Five days later, the patient was fed by a nurse, who administered the feeding through the drainage tube. One of the defendant doctors realized the error four hours later. He performed an immediate operation to clean the feeding material out of the abdomen. Cultures from this procedure revealed the presence of streptococcus, enterobacter, and acinetobacter, a hospital-acquired infection. The decedent developed sepsis and his wound failed to heal properly. Several months later the kidney was rejected and subsequently removed. The patient developed adult respiratory distress syndrome and died shortly thereafter. The defendants argued that the infection existed before the feeding error occurred and that there was not enough time for the feeding to colonize the bacteria. A $1.45 million settlement was reached.[100]

The potential for this type of disaster exists whenever there are several tubes in place, one of which is used for feeding. Diagrams on the patient's Kardex or over the bed, and clear labels and instructions are needed to prevent mix-ups of this nature.

Patient safety experts have made inroads in helping healthcare providers recognize the hazards associated with wrist bands. This effort began when a Patient Safety Advisory was issued by the Pennsylvania Patient Safety Authority in 2005. A patient experiencing a cardiac arrest almost was not rescued because the patient had mistakenly been given a yellow wristband, which signified a do not resuscitate order. The nurse who had placed the yellow wristband on the patient also worked at another hospital in the area where yellow meant "restricted extremity." Fortunately, the mistake was recognized in time and the patient was resusci-

tated. Study of this issue revealed that Pennsylvania healthcare facilities were using nine different colors of wristbands communicating 22 different messages. Colors and messages differed among all of the facilities, indicating there was no standardization. About 35 states now have some form of standardized color-coded wristbands.[101]

B. Protection and Supervision of Patients

Nurses are expected to provide a reasonable level of supervision of patients. Those who are particularly vulnerable include the elderly, infants, anesthetized, and patients with psychiatric disorders. A variety of devices help protect the patient from injury, including alarms used to alert staff when a patient is attempting to leave a secure facility, alarms on equipment warning of changes in vital signs, straps on stretchers, intravenous pumps that control the flow of IV fluids, and other equipment.

A Massachusetts settlement flowed from a series of injuries sustained by a woman in a nursing home who developed blisters on her hand, a fracture of her hand, and a culture result of Trichomonas vaginalis. The fracture, blisters, and sexually transmitted disease led physicians to conclude that the plaintiff was the victim of elder abuse. An investigation revealed that the defendant had housed a known sexual predator as a temporary resident. A $300,000 settlement was reached.[102]

In this situation, the plaintiff alleged the nursing staff failed to protect the patient from the attention of the predator. In the next case, the charge was that the staff failed to protect the patient from herself.

In a Wisconsin case, *Peggy O'Hern v. Earlene Ronk; Brown County; Brown County Department of Human Services, Brown County Mental Health Care Center; Chandra Boomakanti; Mary Johnson; Stephanie Hueseman; Debra Miller; Barbara Radant; Dennis Hayes*, a 21-year-old woman had been a resident of the defendant county mental health center for three months when she ran away. The patient returned later in the day; an hour later she was left unattended and attempted to escape through a laundry chute in an unlocked utility room. She fell two stories to the basement and died. The plaintiff claimed that the defendants failed to provide adequate treatment and a safe environment and should not have left the decedent unattended for an extended period of time in light of her history and impulsive, dangerous behavior. The case settled for $1.5 million.[103]

1.9 Leadership and Teamwork
A. Leadership

The leaders of any healthcare organization are responsible for setting the tone for the environment of care delivery. Expectations for behavior, performance, and following procedures and policies are all defined and reinforced by leaders. Here are some important actions the leader must take to guarantee effective communication and patient safety:

- Speak the same language—literally and figuratively—as the staff.
- Educate others about their responsibilities.
- Respect the staff.
- Set goals and expectations.
- Encourage questions.

In addition, the leaders are responsible for:

- Appropriately allocating resources or workload to ensure no patient is at risk due to overworked staff
- Ensuring that the team meetings, briefings, debriefings, and other teamwork activities occur
- Helping to resolve interpersonal or medical conflicts using structured language and a chain of command[104]

Barriers created by the leadership include:

- Loss of control
- Time constraints
- Distractions
- Cultural differences
- Unclear goals
- Intimidation

Refer to Figure 1.7 for additional examples.

Ella Louise Wall, Individually and as PR of the Estate of Joseph Roy Hall v. Senior Living Properties and Complete Care Services, Inc. is a case in which the actions of a leader had a direct bearing on the patient. An 89-year-old man was a resident of the defendant nursing home for several years. He was transferred to the hospital to have his leg amputated because of diabetic complications. The physician declined to amputate because of his poor

The administrator of the hospital does not make rounds on the nursing units and is unaware of the rationale in the budget for more intravenous pumps. He has never seen the constantly empty storage room where the pumps are supposed to be housed.

Hospital executives are not part of key committees addressing patient safety issues.

Changes are forced on staff, who have had no input into them.

Figure 1.7 *Examples of Leadership Barriers*

condition. The patient was returned to the same nursing home at the request of its administrator to regain his strength. Upon his arrival, two registered nurses immediately advised the administrator of the need to transfer him back to the hospital because of his condition, and that caring for him at the nursing home would put his life in jeopardy. The administrator refused to allow the transfer, and instructed the nurse that she could not call the doctor to ask his advice. The patient died the same evening. The decedent's daughter claimed the administrator refused to transfer him back to the hospital because her corporate employer had told her that improving patient census, and therefore Medicare per diem payments, was its first priority. She also claimed the administrator had attempted to cover up her culpability by pressuring the nurse to rewrite her notes on the decedent's chart, to remove documentation that the administrator had refused to allow the transfer several times on the day of the patient's death. The administrator had threatened to fire the nurse if she did not comply. The nurse did what she was asked, but retained a copy of her original notes, and furnished them to the plaintiff's attorney. The case settled for $975,000.[105]

The overwhelmingly poor condition of this resident may have resulted in his death at the hospital before being sent back to the nursing home. Placing reimbursement over the needs of the patient intensified the difficulties of the administrator and the patient, and the subsequent actions of coercion worsened the situation.

TIP: Nursing employees desire recognition for their efforts. Lack of feedback from managers can increase frustration and turnover. Moreover, leaders reluctant to confront errors or patient safety issues increase the risk in the work environment.

B. Teamwork

Lessons learned from the aviation industry are part of crew resource management (CRM) and are increasingly being adopted by our highly complex healthcare systems. Many facilities are becoming more attentive to the nuances of team functioning and are providing education on teamwork. Some of the concepts include:

- Situation monitoring—active scanning of the nursing unit to assess patients and their plans of care, team member performance, and the environment and to look for potential errors
- Situation awareness—the state of knowing one's surroundings and what factors affect the environment. In times of high stress, situation awareness may decrease.
- Shared mental model—situation where caregivers are aware of the same information, and thus are able to plan and solve problems together.[106]

In addition to the hierarchical issues described in Section 1.2, teamwork is affected by differences in generations. There are four generations of workers in the workforce today.

1. Veterans or Traditionalists

This generation was born between 1927 and 1946. They have specific values such as "remember the lessons of history." They have loyalty to the organization. The Veterans worked to get their retirement. They have a nose to the grindstone work ethic. They are the keepers of the institutional memory. They tend to be patriotic, polite, and fiscally conservative. They have a high work ethic and are the senior employees and physicians, eyeing retirement and considering slowing down trial practice. Many of them are influenced by a military model as they grew up in World War II. They understand and follow a chain of command.

2. Baby boomers

Born between 1946 and 1964, Baby Boomers are the largest group. They were influenced by several events in the tumultuous world of the 60s including the civil rights movement. The Baby Boomers have a strong work ethic. They are workaholics and loyal to the organization. They will stay until the work is done. They are highly competitive, question authority, and invented the Type A personality. They have an overwhelming need to succeed. The Baby Boomer believes in teamwork and consensus building. They are optimistic. Baby Boomers are often found in management positions. It is hard for them to ask for help; they have difficulty admitting something is wrong. This may influence their behavior when caught up in a situation that could lead to patient injury. The Baby Boomer is uncomfortable with conflict and reluctant to go against peers. They are part of the "me" generation.

3. Gen X

Gen Xers were born between 1965 and 1978. The Watergate debacle, which revealed the extent of dirty politics, was an influence on this generation. Women's liberation affected traditional household roles and saw the rise of strong feminists. The gas crisis in 1973 resulted in a sudden feeling of vulnerability. The Gen Xers were the first generation of children affected by both parents working. They were exposed to massive corporate layoff, leading them to value self-reliance. Quality of life and balancing work and home life affects this generation. They saw an increase in divorce rates. This is the impatient generation. They are in a hurry, and want quick promotions and for work to be fun and informal. The Gen Xer tends to be more productive, producing more work in less time. They often prefer to work alone and may distrust and challenge authorities. This may influence their ability to work as part of a team and affect the need to communicate with others. They may be less likely to accept working long hours and schedule changes as they are driven by a need for life and work balances.

4. Gen Y or Millennials

The Gen Y population was born between 1981 and 2000. This is the generation that is drawn towards the family for safety and security. They are a global generation who accept multiculturalism and multitasking as a way of life. The Gen Ys are savvy about technology and instant communication. They are highly creative and well-educated, confident, hopeful and goal-oriented. They enjoy teamwork. They are a digital generation that is globally concerned. They expect 24-hour a day information. They have difficulty dealing with complex problems and are inexperienced within the medical world. They benefit from mentoring and structure. This is a group who has a high need for feedback and structure. Data show that 30 percent of Gen Y nurses turnover in the first year of practice and 57 percent by the second year. They have been taught to question each situation, to find meaning in every task.[107]

5. Conflict

The Veterans do not challenge authority. The Baby Boomers, Gen Xers and Gen Yers have been taught to speak up.

Gen X and Gen Y healthcare providers get frustrated with older people who resist technology. "All generations want to be respected, valued, and rewarded for their efforts."[108] Healthcare workers do best when they recognize there may be generational differences, and welcome the diversity. Communication can break down if the information is presented in a way that is not comprehensible to the listener.

1.10 Continuum of Care

The continuum of care encompasses several aspects that affect communication regarding the needs of the patient:

- Delegating care to unlicensed assistive personnel
- Assigning the patient to the same caregivers
- Transmitting information about the patient from one setting to another, such as the hospital to the nursing home or home care agency
- Providing discharge instructions
- Transferring the patient from one unit within a facility to another

In any of these situations, important details may be lost. This potential is addressed by The Joint Commission Patient Safety Goal relating to handoff of information, and is covered in more detail in Chapter 4, *Patient Safety Initiatives*.

1.11 Organizational Culture
A. Underreporting of Errors

The traditional shame and blame culture of organizations causes individuals to hide their mistakes. Only a small percentage of errors are captured in this type of system, with numbers estimated to be as small as 5 to 25 percent.[109-110] The major reason for underreporting is the culture of blame that exists in health care. As one expert notes, "The healthcare system is locked into a paradigm of preventing errors by training people very highly, holding them to high standards, and expecting them to make no mistakes: when they do, we punish them. We train and blame. What we need to think about is not who is at fault or who is to blame, but why and how errors occur and more importantly, what can be done to prevent them."[111] In reporting his hospital's attempt to change the culture to a non-punitive one, Thomas Alvey noted that an amnesty program is one that protects individuals from disciplinary action for errors they may report. The policy does not protect individuals who consistently fail to participate in detecting, reporting, and preventing errors. Nor does it protect individuals in which there is reason to believe criminal activity or criminal intent may be involved.[112]

The following is a list of reasons why the organizational culture may support non-reporting or underreporting of errors and incidents:

- inability to capture all types of incidents
- incident did not meet the definition of the criteria list
- patient was not harmed
- departure from the expected method of practice seemed reasonable[113]

TIP: Some studies have found that only 5 to 10 percent of all medical errors are reported to hospital administrators.[114]

Incident reports that are filed represent the tip of the iceberg of all reportable incidents. While most incidents do not qualify as sentinel events, the underreporting of incidents provides a bird's-eye view of the scope of this problem. Concerns about the current climate in healthcare facilities are increasing doubts about the accuracy of incident reporting. Feeling overworked and stressed, the employees' morale may sink, leading to an increase in errors. Although system errors may contribute to incidents involving patients, many healthcare professionals believe finger-pointing will be the result of incident reporting. Witness these concerns, which were shared with Joint Commission surveyors, as to why incidents were not being reported:

- "I knew I gave him the wrong dose, but I was afraid I'd lose my job."
- "There were so many incidents we decided we couldn't do them all, so we did nothing."
- "I observed the wrong treatment being administered but was too scared to do anything about it."
- "Incident reports used to be routine, now they are performance continuances."
- "We turned our unit into a place that was so different—we were used to helping each other out and knowing that mistakes or errors happened and it was dealt with. Now we know if we fudge, lie, ignore—then we might stay here."
- "A group of nurses on the critical care unit said that each time the surgeon is written up, the vice president of medical affairs comes to the unit in a tirade to 'get to the bottom of this.' The nurses are reluctant to document errors—they don't go anywhere and we get yelled at."[115]

TIP: Administrative actions that may result in reluctance to report incidents include withholding promotions or raises, disciplinary action, or firing an employee who reports an incident. While some situations may warrant these actions, routine use of these actions following an incident hinders forthright reporting of incidents.

As patient advocates, nurses are charged with the ethical responsibility to promote, advocate for, and strive to protect the health, safety, and rights of the patient. Part of the advocate role involves reporting mistakes and seeking care for the patient when it becomes clear the primary care provider is being ineffective. Juries are holding nurses accountable to be patient advocates. Rather than take that risk, the defense settled in the case described below.

In a Massachusetts case, the defendant obstetrician ordered Pitocin be administered to the plaintiff's mother to stimulate uterine contractions, and this order was carried out by one of the defendant labor nurses. The plaintiff alleged the contraction pattern indicated Pitocin was not needed, and that the mother's uterus was hyper-stimulated. The nurses failed to discontinue the Pitocin in the face of an abnormal fetal heart rate pattern, and actually increased it, according to the plaintiff. The nurses reported the abnormalities to the defendant doctor. The plaintiff alleged that the obstetrician failed to perform an emergency cesarean section. Prolonged oxygen deprivation was alleged to cause cerebral palsy and spastic quadriparesis. However, if the case had not settled, the expert testimony was expected to show that the nurses had an obligation to initiate the chain of command at the hospital because the doctor's decisions so clearly disregarded the health and safety of the fetus. There was a total of $2 million awarded to the plaintiff from the obstetrician's personal and corporate policy, and $1,750,000 from the nurses' individual policies.[116]

As described in Chapter 4, *Patient Safety Initiatives*, The Joint Commission asks its accredited facilities to report sentinel events. The implementation of this policy resulted in a dramatic increase in the reporting of sentinel events. Before the implementation of the policy described above, a small number of sentinel events were reported to The Joint Commission. In 1995, there were 23 such events with only one being self-reported. As of March 31, 2010, a total of 6,782 had been reported, with 4,381 being self-reported (64.4 percent). The sentinel events that came to the attention of The Joint Commission that were not self-reported were

- reported as a result of a complaint (15 percent),
- identified during The Joint Commission survey (8.5 percent),
- reported by the media (6.1 percent), or
- found through other sources such as a state or CMS report (5.9 percent).[117]

Current statistics regarding sentinel events can be found at www.jointcommission.org. As of March 31, 2010, the top ten types of sentinel events were:

- Wrong site surgery
- Patient suicides
- Operative or postoperative complication
- Delay in treatment
- Medication error
- Patient fall
- Unintended retention of a foreign object
- Assault/rape/homicide
- Perinatal death or loss of function
- Transfusion error

Death of the patients occurred in 67 percent of the incidents. Nine percent of the patients experienced loss of function, with other effects occurring in 24 percent of the incidents. The majority (67.7 percent) of the events occurred in general hospitals. Psychiatric hospitals were the settings for 10.8 percent of the incidents. Behavioral health facilities accounted for 4.4 percent of the sentinel events, whereas psychiatric units in general hospitals furnished another 4.4 percent of the incidents. The rest occurred in other settings.[118]

The number of incidents reported to The Joint Commission still represents only the tip of the iceberg. It is clear that United States hospitals are far from complying with full disclosure of mistakes. Compliance with self-reporting of sentinel events has dropped off in recent years. When data was first collected in 1995, only 4 percent of sentinel events were self-reported. The highest level of self-reporting was achieved in 2001 with 77 percent of events voluntarily reported. Self-reporting of sentinel events has dropped steadily since that time.

In December 2002, Joint Commission President Dennis O'Leary wrote a "Dear Colleague" letter to healthcare agencies accredited by The Joint Commission, stating that several types of reportable sentinel events had a disproportionately low frequency in the Sentinel Event Database. Specifically, he was referring to unanticipated deaths or permanent loss of function in patients which appeared to be related to nosocomial infections. Also included were long-term care incidents reportable to federal and state agencies as part of the Minimum Data Set, and home care incidents reportable to federal and state agencies as part of the OASIS requirements.

Dr. O'Leary acknowledged that reporting to the Sentinel Event Database was voluntary, and that The Joint Commission had thus far been able to maintain the confidentiality of all sentinel event data, but admitted that confidentiality concerns limited the number of cases actually brought to its attention.[119]

Near misses or close calls provide tremendous opportunity for identifying risks. Near misses occur three to 300 times more often than adverse events. There are fewer barriers to collecting the data.[120] However, to learn from near misses or errors, there needs to be some agreement about what constitutes an error. A study of personnel in 29 hospitals revealed that many physicians used terms like practice variances, suboptimal outcomes, or differences in clinical judgment to describe problems associated with:

- delays in treatment
- errors in administration of treatment
- the failure to use current treatment modalities
- the failure to act on the results of testing
- the failure to communicate with staff and patients

In this study, physicians, nurses, and administrators tended to perceive patient safety as primarily a nursing responsibility. Only 22 percent of respondents said physicians, nurses, pharmacists, and administrators should share responsibility equally for patient safety.[121] There is much education needed to increase awareness of the multifaceted nature of patient safety.

This chapter has addressed The Joint Commission's identification of roots of sentinel events. Another perspective is provided by the National Survey on Consumers' Experiences with Patient Safety and Quality Information, published by the Kaiser Family Foundation, Agency for Healthcare Research and Quality, and the Harvard School of Public Health. This November 2004 survey found that the public had perceptions about what caused medical errors. The comparison with The Joint Commission-identified factors is shown in Figure 1.8. It is intriguing to see the areas of agreement and differences in perceptions. Here are some areas of agreement:

- The Joint Commission factor of staffing, which corresponds with the Kaiser factor of overwork, stress, or fatigue and insufficient numbers of nurses in hospitals
- The Joint Commission factor of communication, which relates to the Kaiser factor of healthcare professionals not working together or communicating as a team
- The Joint Commission factor of education and training, which the Kaiser survey identified as poor training
- The Joint Commission factor of availability of medical information, which can correlate with the Kaiser factor of poor handwriting and lack of computerized medical records

TJC
1. Communication
2. Orientation/Training
3. Patient Assessment
4. Staffing
5. Availability of Information
6. Competency/Credentialing
7. Procedural Compliance
8. Environmental Safety/Security
9. Leadership
10. Continuum of Care
11. Care Planning
12. Organizational Culture

Public
1. Overwork, stress, or fatigue of health professionals
2. Not enough nurses in hospitals
3. Healthcare professionals not working together or not communicating as a team
4. Poor training of healthcare professionals
5. The influence of HMOs and other managed care plans on treatment decisions
6. Poor handwriting by healthcare professionals
7. Medical care being very complicated
8. Lack of computerized medical records

Figure 1.8 The Joint Commission's Identification of Contributing Causes of Medical Errors Versus the Public's. Public data from National Survey of Consumers' Experiences with Patient Safety and Quality Information, November 2004, the Henry J. Kaiser Family Foundation, Agency for Healthcare Research and Quality and Harvard School of Public Health

The public survey identified areas not specifically defined by The Joint Commission, yet may be incorporated in the complex analysis of sentinel events.

B. Strategies

This chapter has included descriptions of some of the strategies aimed at altering the environment and culture of care to minimize the roots of patient injury. Some additional ones include:

1. Use electronic boards on each nursing unit to show the number of days since the last patient fall and that day's patient satisfaction scores.
2. Plan team huddles to communicate plans for the day.
3. Use color-coded uniforms to help patients identify the role of anyone who enters their room.
4. Have top hospital executives make patient rounds.
5. Reduce hunting for and gathering equipment. The VHA has an initiative to RetuRN to care (return the RN to the bedside) by putting equipment such as IVs and blood pressure pumps and supplies in or outside every room, and using preprinted order sets and patient care pathways.
6. Provide nurses and patients with cell phones so that nurses spend less time running to answer call buttons or looking for a free phone to call a physician for an order.
7. Offer nurses a room where they can de-stress.
8. Provide consistency of assignment so nurses stay with the same patients for as many days in a row as possible.[122]

C. Cultures of Patient Safety

Organizations that adopt, integrate and promote a culture of patient safety will ultimately save lives. Making these changes requires tough decisions, behavior changes, and adherence to what is best for the patient. Organization culture is affected by the four subcultures needed to create a culture of safety: a reporting culture, a just culture, a flexible culture and a learning culture.

- A reporting culture consists of people who willingly report accidents and near misses because they are encouraged to disclose this information.
- People work in a just culture when they trust that the information will be handled in a just manner.
- A flexible culture requires that control of certain situations shifts from conventional hierarchical structures to a flat, professional structure in which

experts are used for their expertise. Those individuals most able to respond to an unsafe situation take control irrespective of rank.
- The organization must be willing to look carefully at the safety Information systems in place and come to the proper conclusions regarding changes to the system when indicated.[123]

1.12 Summary

Multiple complex systems and individual factors contribute to the roots of patient injury. This chapter is intended as an overview, as entire books could be written to address such a multifaceted subject. The medical and legal personnel involved in nursing malpractice cases should be mindful of the complicated interplay of factors that culminate in patient injury. With the release of more information to the public concerning medical mistakes, new attention is being given to tackling the many factors that contribute to patient injury.

Endnotes

1. Sundar, E., Sundar, S., Pawlowski, J. et al., "Crew resource management and team training," *Anesthesiology Clinics*, 25 (2007), 283-300.

2. http://www.jcaho.org/accredited+organizations/ambula-tory+care/sentinel+events/root+causes+of+sentinel+event.htm, last accessed December 10, 2005.

3. Sorbello, B. "Responding to a sentinel event," *American Nurse Today*, 39 (10) October 2008, 30-32.

4. Presentation by Spencer Byrum, Society for Healthcare Risk Management-NJ, Princeton, New Jersey. September 9, 2005.

5. American Nurses Association, *Scope and Standards of Nursing Practice*, Washington, D.C., pg. 38, 2004.

6. Joint Commission on Accreditation of Healthcare Organizations, *Health Care at the Crossroads*, http://www.jointcommission.org, last accessed July 8, 2010.

7. Rosenstein, A. and M. O'Daniel, "Disruptive behavior and clinical outcomes: perceptions of nurses and physicians," *AJN* 105, no. 1 (January 2005): 54–63.

8. Johnson, C, "Bad blood: Doctor-nurse behavior problems impact patient care," *PEJ*, November-December 2009, 6-11.

9. Laska, L. (ed.), "Hypoxic brain damage to infant," *Medical Malpractice Verdicts, Settlements, and Experts* (March 2003): 34.

10. Newitt, V. "Crossing the divide*," Advance for Nurses: Pennsylvania, New Jersey, Delaware*, April 26, 2010, 10-12.

11. See note 8.

12. Mason, D., "Safe Practices and Quality Health Care," presentation at 3rd Annual Patient Safety Conference: University of Pennsylvania, December 1, 2005.

13. Barrett, J., C. Gifford, J. Morey, D. Risser, and M. Salisbury, "Enhancing Patient Safety Through Teamwork Training," *Journal of Healthcare Risk Management* (Fall 2001): 57–65.

14. Crow, G., "Gerontological Nursing: Looking Toward the Horizon," presentation at National Gerontological Nursing Association, October 21, 2005.

15. "In their own words," *PEJ,* November-December 2009, 16-22.

16. *Id.*

17. O'Byrne, W., Weavind, L. and Selby, J. "The Science and Economics of Improving Clinical Communication," *Anesthesiology Clinics* 26 (2008), 729-744.

18. Weinberg, D, Miner, D. and Rivlin, L., "'It depends': medical residents' perspectives on working with nurses," *AJN,* July 2009, 109 (7), 34-43.

19. Sirota, T. "Nursing 2008, Nurse/physician relationships survey report," *Nursing 2008,* July 2008, 28-31.

20. McGreevy, J., Otten, T., Poggi, M. et al., "The challenge of changing roles and improving surgical care now: Crew resource management approach," *American Surgeon,* 2006, 72: 1082-7.

21. Nielsen, P. and Mann, S. "Team function in obstetrics to reduce errors and improve outcomes," *Obstetric Gynecology Clinics of North America,* 35 (2008), 81-95.

22. Iyer. P. "SBAR: Creating Clear Communication," http://www.medleague.com/webstore/med_league/sbar_communication.htm.

23. Bartolomew, K. *Ending Nurse to Nurse Hostility: Why Nurses Eat Their Young and Each Other*, Marblehead, MA: HCPro, 2006.

24. *Id.*

25. Patterson, K., Grenny, J. and McMillan, R. *Crucial Confrontations*, New York: McGraw Hill, 2005.

26. Arora, V. and Farnan, J., "Care transitions for hospitalized patients," *Medical Clinics of North America* 92 (2008), 315-324.

27. Parker, J. and Colera, E. "Improving clinical communication: a view from psychology," *Journal of the American Medical Information Association*, 2000: 7 (965): 453-61.

28. Mascioli, S., Laskowski-Jones, L., Urban, S and Moran, S., "Improving handoff communication," *Nursing 2009*, February 2009, 52-55.

29. http://www.patientsafetynow.com/products/untangling_charlottedvd.htm.

30. Bartlett, G, Blais, R, Tamblyn, R et al., "Impact of patient communication problems on the risk of preventable adverse events in acute care settings," *CMAJ* 178 (912): 1555-1562, June 3, 2008.

31. Divi, C., Koss, R, Schmaltz, S. et al., "Language proficiency and adverse events in U.S. hospitals: A pilot study. *Int. J. Qual Health Care* 19 (2): 60-67, April 2007.

32. Cohen, A., Rivera, F., Marcuse, E. et al., "Are language barriers associated with serious medical events in hospitalized pediatric patients?" *Pediatrics* 116(3): 575-9, September 2005.

33. The Joint Commission, *New and Revised Standards and EPs for Patient-Centered Communication,* Accreditation Program: Hospital, Pre-publication Version, 2010.

34. Wilson-Stronks, A., Cordero, C., Kopp, A. and Galvez, E., *One Size Does Not Fit All: Meeting the Healthcare Needs of a Diverse Patient Population*, Joint Commission, The California Endowment, 2008.

35. Sexton, J., Thomas, E. and Helmreich, R., "Error, stress and teamwork in medicine and aviation: cross sectional surveys," *British Journal of Medicine*, 2000, 106: E 45.

36. Scott, S., Hirschinger, L. and Cox, K. "Sharing the load: rescuing the healer after trauma," *RN,* December 2008, 38-43.

37. Wong, S., "Outcomes of nursing care: how do we know?" *Clinical Nurse Specialist*, 12, no. 4 (1998): 147.

38. Kramer, M., *Reality Shock: Why Nurses Leave Nursing*, St. Louis, Missouri: CV Mosby, 1974.

39. Kramer, M., "Why does reality shock continue?" In *Current Issues in Nursing*, edited by J. McCloskey and H. Grace, 891. Boston: Blackwell Scientific Publication, 1985.

40. Beeman, K., A. Jernigan, and P. Hensley, "Employing new grads: a plan for success," *Nursing Economic$*, 17, no. 2 (March-April 1999): 91.

41. "Human Resources" *CAMH Refreshed Core*, Joint Commission, January 2010.

42. Borgatti, J. "Tips for floaters," *American Nurse Today*, March 2010, 15-16.

43. Cita, B. "Top ten tips for fearless floating," *Nursing 2010*, February 2010, 57-58.

44. See note 41.

45. Laska, L. (ed.), "Unsupervised and confused Alzheimer's patient walks off facility grounds and freezes to death during snowstorm," *Medical Malpractice Verdicts, Settlements, and Experts* (March 2004): 45.

46. See note 6.

47. Laska, L. (ed.), "Ninety-year-old woman falls during single-person transfer, resulting in death," *Medical Malpractice Verdicts, Settlements, and Experts* (March 2003): 29–30.

48. Shapiro, S., Donaldson, N., and Scott, M. "Rapid response teams: seen through the eyes of the nurse," *AJN*, June 2010, 110 (6), 28-34.

49. www.healthgrades.com/media/dms/pdf/patientsafety-inamericanhospitalsstudy2009.pdf.

50. North American Nursing Diagnosis Association (NANDA), *Nursing Diagnoses: Definitions and Classifications 2001–2002*, Philadelphia, 2001.

51. Laska, L. (ed), "Man develops pressure ulcers while in nursing home, necessitating below-knee leg amputation four months after admission," *Medical Malpractice Verdicts, Settlements and Experts*, February 2010, 23.

52. Bittner, N. and Tobin, E. "Critical thinking: strategies for clinical practice," *Journal for Nurses in Staff Development* (November-December 1998): 267.

53. Fowler, L., "Improving critical thinking in nursing practice," *Journal for Nurses in Staff Development*, (July-August 1998): 183.

54. Cook, P., "Using critical thinking skills to improve medication administration," *MEDSURG Nursing*, 4, no. 4 (August 1995): 309.

55. See note 52.

56. American Association of Colleges of Nursing, *The Essentials of Baccalaureate Education for Professional Nursing Practice*. Washington, D.C., March 1998.

57. National Institute for Occupational Safety and Health: Stress at Work. Cincinnati, Ohio: NIOSH. Publication No. 99-101, 1999.

58. Rogers, A., W. Hwang, L. Scott, L. Aiken, and D. Dinges, "The working hours of hospital staff nurses and patient safety," *Health Affairs*, 23, no. 4 (July/August 2004).

59. Hughes, R. and P. Stone, "The perils of shift work," *American Journal of Nursing*, 104, no. 9 (September 2004): 60–63.

60. Labyak, S. et al., "Effects of shift work on sleep and menstrual function in nurses," *Health Care Women Int*, 23, No. 6–7 (2002): 703–714.

61. Harrison, B. "Healthcare travelers need restorative sleep," *RN Career Search*, 2009, 24-26.

62. Fuller, T. and Bain, E. "Shift workers give sleep short shrift," *AJN*, 110 (2), February 2010, 28-30.

63. Kissinger, J., "Overconfidence: a concept analysis," *Nursing Forum*, 33, no. 2 (April-June 1998): 18.

64. *Id.*

65. Laska, L. (ed.), "Failure to timely perform cesarean section," *Medical Malpractice Verdicts, Settlements, and Experts* (December 2004): 29.

66. Gerlin, A., *Curing a Culture of its Denial*. Philadelphia Online, September 15, 1999.

67. See note 41.

68. Benner, P., *From Novice to Expert: Excellence and Power in Clinical Practice,* Menlo Park, California: Addison Wesley, 1984.

69. See note 18.

70. Laska, L. (ed.), "Nursing home staff accused of concealing fall, but man had excessive Coumadin in system and died," *Medical Malpractice Verdicts, Settlements, Experts* (March 2003): 28.

71. Kohn, L., J. Corrigan, and M. Donaldson (eds.), *To Err Is Human: Building a Safer Health System. Institute of Medicine,* Washington, D.C.: National Academy Press, 1999.

72. *Id.*

73. Huston, C., "10 tips for successful delegation," *Nursing 2009*, March 2009, 54-56.

74. www.ncsbn.org/pdfs/chapter10.pdf, last accessed October 30, 2005.

75. Sheets, V., "Licensure discipline: a challenge for boards of nursing-and nurses," *AJN* (July 2005): 83–84.

76. LaDuke, S., "The effects of professional discipline on nurses," *AJN* (June 2000): 26.

77. Laska, L. (ed.), "Nursing negligence causes permanent quadriparesis," *Medical Malpractice Verdicts, Settlements, and Experts* (February 2003): 24–25.

78. Green, A., O. Fitzpatrick, R. Crismon, and L. Waddill et al., "Are you at risk for disciplinary action?" *AJN* (July 1995): 36.

79. See note 76.

80. Copp, M. Drug addiction, *RN*, April 2009, 40-44.

81. *Id.*

82. Carruth, A. and D. Booth, "Disciplinary actions against nurses: Who is at risk?" *Journal of Nursing Law* 6, no. 3 (November 1999): 55.

83. See note 74.

84. See note 78.

85. *Id.*

86. Murphy, J. and C. Connell. "Violations of the States' Nurse Practice Act. How Big is the Problem?" *Nursing Management,* 18 (1987): 44.

87. See note 78.

88. See note 82.

89. See note 78.

90. Laska, L. (Ed), "Laparotomy sponge left after cesarean section," *Medical Malpractice Verdicts, Settlements, and Experts*, February 2010, 26.

91. Beaulieu, L. and Freeman, M, "Nursing shortcuts can shortcut safety," *Nursing 2009*, December 2009, 16-20.

92. Wachter, R. and Pronovost, P., "Balancing 'no blame' with accountability in patient safety," *New England Journal of Medicine*, October 1, 2009, 1401-1406.

93. See note 91.

94. Cohen, M. "Risky imposter," *Nursing 2008*, May 2008, 20.

95. See note 92.

96. *Id.*

97. American Nurses Association, Health and Safety Survey, September 2001.

98. See note 6.

99. Eskreis, T., "Seven common legal pitfalls in nursing," *American Journal of Nursing* 98, no. 4 (April 1998): 34.

100. Laska, L. (ed.), "Kidney transplant given feeding through drainage tube instead of feeding tube," *Medical Malpractice Verdicts, Settlements, and Experts* (April 2005): 20.

101. Cizek, K, Estrada, N., Allen, J. and Elsholz, T., "A crystal clear call to standardize color-coded wristbands," *Nursing 2010*, May 2010, 57-59.

102. Laska, L. (ed.), "Nursing home resident attacked by known sexual predator housed as a temporary resident," *Medical Malpractice Verdicts, Settlements, and Experts* (March 2005): 30.

103. Laska, L. (ed.), "Patient's escape attempt ends in death," *Medical Malpractice Verdicts, Settlements, and Experts* (November 2005): 43–44.

104. See note 21.

105. Laska, L. (ed.), "Elderly man dies in Texas nursing home after its administrator refuses, against advice of nurses, to transfer him to hospital," *Medical Malpractice Verdicts, Settlements, and Experts* (May 2003): 34.

106. See note 21.

107. Chambers, P., "Tap the unique strengths of the millennial generation," *Nursing 2010*, February 2010, 49-51.

108. McKnight, L. "Generational diversity in today's legal market," *For the Defense*, May 2010, 46-48.

109. Cullen, D. and D. Bates et al., "The incident reporting system does not detect adverse drug events: a problem in quality assurance," *Joint Commission Journal on Quality Improvement* 21 (1995): 541–548.

110. Bennett, B. S. and A. G. Lippman, "Comparative study of prospective surveillance and voluntary reporting in determining the incidence of adverse drug reactions," *American Journal of Hospital Pharmacy* 34 (1977): 931–936, as quoted in Alvey, T., "Our experience in developing a non-punitive culture and an effective amnesty policy," *Journal of Healthcare Risk Management* (Fall 2001): 37–39.

111. Buerhaus, P., (No title supplied) *Journal of Nursing Scholarship* 31, no. 3 (1999): 281–286, as quoted in Alvey, T. "Our experience in developing a non-punitive culture and an effective amnesty policy," *Journal of Healthcare Risk Management* (Fall 2001): 37–39.

112. Alvey, T. (see note 110).

113. Cohoon, B., "Learning from near misses through reflection: a new risk management strategy," *Journal of Healthcare Risk Management* (Spring 2003): 19–25.

114. Gerlin, A., "Health care's deadly secret: Accidents routinely happen," *Philadelphia Online*. http://health.philly.com/specials/mistakes/hosp13.asp., last accessed September 12, 1999.

115. Jones, L. and G. Arana. "Is Downsizing Affecting Incident Reports?" *Journal of Healthcare Quality, The Joint Commission Journal* (August 1996): 592.

116. Kessler, B., *New Jersey Jury Verdict* 24, no. 10 (March 2004): 24.

117. http://www.jointcommission.org/SentinelEvents/Statistics/, last accessed July 8, 2010.

118. *Id.*

119. Dear Colleague Letter, www.jcaho.org/accredited+organizations/sentinel+event/dear+colleague+letter.htm, last accessed 2005

120. See note 113.

121. Cook, A., H. Hoas, K. Guttmannova, and J. Joyner, "An error by any other name," *American Journal of Nursing*, 104, no. 6 (June 2004): *32–45*.

122. Shaw, G. "Time to put patients first," *HealthLeaders*, May 2010, 17-27.

123. See note 21.

Additional Reading

Atkinson, L., "Who's really in charge?," *TRIAL*, May 2007, 30-39.

Bartolomew, K. Speak your Truth: Proven Strategies for Effective Nurse-Physician Communication, Marblehead, MA: HCPro, 2005.

Dellasega, C., "Bullying among nurses," *AJN*, January 2009, 109 (1), 52-58.

DiCecco, K., Cohen, M. and Levin, B., "Failure to communicate," *TRIAL*, May 2010, 38-44.

Kiekkas, P., Sakellaropoulos, G. Brokalaki, H. et al., "Association between nursing workload and mortality of Intensive Care Unit Patients," *Journal of Nursing Scholarship*, Fourth Quarter 2008, 385-390.

Nadzam, D. "Nurses' role in communication and patient safety," *Journal of Nursing Care Quality*, 24, (4), 184-188, 2009.

Northam, S. "Conflict in the workplace: part 1," *AJN*, 109 (6), June 2009, 70-73.

Northam, S. "Conflict in the workplace: part 2," *AJN*, July 2009, 65-67.

Pope, B., Rodzen, L. and Spross, G. "Raising the SBAR: How better communication improves patient outcomes," *Nursing 2007*, March 2007, 41-43.

Weick, K. and Sutcliffe, K., Managing the Unexpected: Assuring High Performance in an Age of Complexity, University of Michigan Business School Management Series, San Francisco, Jossey Bass, 2001.

Yu, K and Green, R. "Critical aspects of emergency department documentation and communication," *Emergency Medical Clinics of North America* 27 (2009), 641-654.

Chapter 2

Where Have All the Nurses Gone?

Patricia W. Iyer, MSN, RN, LNCC

2.1 Introduction

This text focuses on the impact of nursing care. The multiple cases cited throughout this text define the ways in which nursing negligence, systems errors, miscommunication, and other factors result in untoward outcomes. Every action a nurse takes contributes to the outcome of a patient who receives appropriate, thoughtful care. Nurses make up a large portion of the healthcare workforce. When their numbers dwindle, as is happening now, the care of patients is affected. Staffing is one of the top causes of sentinel events.[1] This chapter explores the reasons for the nursing shortage and offers some suggestions for addressing it.

2.2 Deliberate Understaffing
A. Reasons

Understaffing in the context of this chapter refers to the deliberate control of staff nurse positions at a point below the level of safe care. The incentive to the organization that engages in this practice is financial. Nursing salaries comprise a large portion of any healthcare organization's budget. A reduction in nursing salaries may translate into large salaries for administrators and profits for the corporation.

Reengineering was used to reduce the number of nursing positions in the 1990s. "Reengineering" refers to redesigning work to modify the processes of care and who performs them. For example, reengineering may result in a decision to put a small pharmacy department on each nursing unit for the dispensing of drugs, rather than having all medications come from a centralized department. With appropriate planning and feedback mechanisms, reengineering can maintain a safe balance between production and protection. However, the potential for injury increases when registered nurses are replaced with unlicensed assistive personnel who are then performing tasks without adequate understanding, skill, or experience.

In the mid to late 1990s, many hospitals changed the composition of the nursing staff by reducing the number of registered nurses and increasing the number of unlicensed assistive personnel. As a result of this change, the demands on registered nurses to be more proficient and skilled have intensified. New employees are expected to get "up to speed" as quickly as possible.

The potential for errors rose as downsizing and reengineering placed more unlicensed staff members at the patient's bedside. At the center of the controversy was the mistaken belief among some hospital administrators that nursing tasks are simply tasks—feeding patients, moving or washing them, and so on.[2] Administrators often did not recognize that the nurse performing these tasks was also simultaneously assessing the situation, teaching the patient, and critically evaluating the condition of the patient. The effort to reduce the nursing payroll by replacing nurses with unlicensed assistive personnel resulted in the loss of knowledgeable professional nurses and specialists, with fewer resources available to the less-experienced nurse.[3] Deliberate understaffing still exists although reengineering to eliminate nursing positions is no longer a dominant focus of health care.

B. Detection

Defense attorneys involved in handling nursing malpractice claims may suspect, as a result of interviews with defendants and fact witnesses, that deliberate understaffing was a factor in the events that led up to a claim. Discussions with employees or physicians may result in the defense attorney becoming aware of this concern. Plaintiff's attorneys may seek out former employees to probe into the usual staffing patterns. For example, they might discover that nursing homes may list employees as being on an active status, even though the people have been on disability for six months. Depositions of defendants and fact witnesses may reveal concerns about consistent understaffing, or beefed up staffing at the time of regulatory surveys. Some understaffing is driven by a financial motive. The dwindling supply of nurses may be responsible for some of the understaffing, but it is the deliberate understaffing for financial reasons that surfaces as an allegation in some litigation.

> In *Elijah Rockwell, as Executor of the Estate of Gertrude Hollins, Deceased v. Cleaver Memorial Convalescent Center, in its assumed or Common Name et al.*, an 89-year-old nursing home resident died after staying in the facility for 32 months. When she was admitted to the facility, the resident was alert, could walk independently, appeared stable, and had no history of pressure ulcers, dehydration, malnutrition, or end-stage disease processes. During her stay at the facility, the resident developed an infected 10-inch diameter stage IV pressure ulcer, lost 90 pounds, and was admitted to the hospital four times for dehydration. The plaintiff alleged the nursing home engaged in a pattern and common practice of dangerous understaffing; they destroyed personnel files and time cards to cover up the understaffing; they sought heavy care patients despite intentional understaffing; and they falsified staffing level records. The home denied these allegations and argued that their staffing was sufficient. The charge nurses and the dietician testified in deposition that the home had grossly neglected the resident. The resident's treating physi-

cian testified that this was one of the worst cases of nursing neglect she had ever seen. The home had been cited by the Texas Department of Health and Human Services for neglect of this resident. The case settled for $5.3 million.[4]

2.3 Impact of the Shortage
A. Impact of Registered Nurses on Safety in Hospitals

Patient care suffers whether understaffing is deliberate or the result of the growing nursing shortage. Several studies have suggested that higher nurse-to-patient ratios are associated with improved patient outcomes, affecting both morbidity (illness) and mortality (death). An American Nurses Association study[5] found that higher nurse-to-patient ratios were associated with shorter lengths of stay in hospitals and a reduction in complications such as pressure ulcers, pneumonia, urinary tract, and postoperative infections.[6] These results were consistent with a study published in 1993[7] that suggested that a higher ratio of RNs to other nursing personnel (licensed practical nurses, nursing assistants) was associated with lower patient mortality. A large-scale study of 589 randomly selected community hospitals[8] found an inverse relationship between the number of registered nurses and adverse events following surgery. In other words, the fewer the registered nurses, the more frequent the complications.[9]

TIP: Linda Aiken's University of Pennsylvania study published in 2002 showed that patients who have common surgeries in hospitals with the worst nurse staffing levels have an up to 31 percent increased chance of dying.[10]

More nurses at the bedside could save thousands of patient lives each year. Every additional patient in an average hospital nurse's workload increased the risk of death in surgical patients by 7 percent. Patients with life-threatening complications were also less likely to be rescued in hospitals where nurses' patient loads were heavier. Costs may increase when there are too few nurses due to the high costs of replacing burnt-out nurses and higher costs of caring for patients with poor outcomes. The Aiken study examined data collected from 168 hospitals, 232,342 surgical patients, and 10,184 nurses in Pennsylvania from 1998 to 1999. The researchers examined data from relatively common general surgeries (such as gall bladder removal), orthopaedic surgery (knee or hip replacement), and vascular surgeries excluding cardiac surgery such as coronary bypass.[11]

The findings of Aiken et al.'s study were confirmed by examination of 26 studies, most of which examined nurse staffing levels and adverse occurrences in the hospital setting, including in-hospital deaths and nonfatal adverse outcomes such as nosocomial (hospital-acquired) infections, pressure ulcers, or falls. Lower nurse-to-patient ratios were associated with higher rates of nonfatal adverse outcomes. The evidence did not consistently show that lower nurse staffing levels (more patients assigned to each nurse) were associated with higher mortality.[12] A survey of more than 75 nurse executives revealed that the nursing shortage was of prime concern. When asked to name the top barriers to improving safety, 71 percent of the nurses listed the nursing shortage first, followed by lack of a team approach, lack of management commitment to safety, and lack of access to clinical information.[13]

Reduced numbers of staff increase the potential for patient injury in a number of ways. One aspect relates to cutting corners and omitting steps which previously had been provided for safety. A simple example is the requirement of some hospitals that two nurses check insulin dosages drawn up in a syringe before the insulin is given to the patient. Staffing shortages may eliminate this step. The process of having two people perform checks is successfully used in several key aspects of nursing. The counting of narcotics at change of shift by two people or the counting of needles and sponges in the operating room are a few examples. This deliberate redundancy provides a safety net.

B. Impact of Registered Nurses on Safety in Nursing Homes

The benefits of nursing care are evident in nursing homes as well. More time spent by registered nurses in direct care of nursing home residents translates into improved outcomes:

- fewer pressure ulcers,
- fewer hospitalizations,
- fewer urinary tract infections,
- less weight loss,
- less catheterization,
- less deterioration in the ability to perform activities of daily living, and
- greater use of oral standard medical nutritional supplements.[14]

A New York nursing home resident had been a resident of the defendant facility for ten days when she went to the restroom alone after failing to receive a response to her call button request for assistance. She fell from the toilet and sustained injuries to her head which ultimately led to her death. The plaintiff alleged the facility's staff had determined there was insufficient staff to assist the decedent at every

trip to the bathroom and one employee installed a device which raised the seat's height, but it did not properly fit the toilet. A $300,000 verdict was returned against the facility.[15]

C. Impact of Excellence

Extensive studies have shown that nurse practitioners and clinical specialists decrease the number of hospital admissions, lower the lengths of patient stays, and result in cost savings for the hospitals where they were employed.[16] The contributions of the healthcare system to improve patient outcomes have also been studied.

Researchers evaluated whether or not patients admitted to top-ranked hospitals had lower short-term mortality than those admitted to other hospitals. In a study focused on cardiac patients, the researchers found that patients in the best hospitals in cardiology had a lower mortality rate and were more likely to use aspirin and beta-blocker medication in treatment. Other factors considered important in explaining the lower mortality rates were the development of clinical algorithms (decision trees) and improved training of the medical staff.[17]

HealthGrades analyzed all-payer data of approximately 14 million hospital delivery and neonate records from 2006 through 2008 at more than 1,600 hospitals in the 19 states which make their data available. To identify maternity care program performance, HealthGrades studied overall maternal complication rates for vaginal deliveries, C-sections, and patient-choice C-sections (non-clinically indicated C-sections), as well as neonatal mortality. In the 19 states studied, 1,546 hospitals (of the 1,616 hospitals) were eligible to be considered for the maternity care rating. Of these eligible hospitals, 232 best performers ranked in the top 15 percent and were recognized with a 5-star rating in maternity care. Of these 5-star hospitals, 154 are recipients of the Health-Grades 2010/2011 Maternity Care Excellence Award™ representing the top 10 percent of hospitals in the 19 states studied. The HealthGrades study found that best-performing (5-star rated) hospitals had fewer maternal complications and fewer neonatal mortalities. If all hospitals, among the 19 states studied, performed at the level of best-performing hospitals, 176,654 women may have avoided developing one or more in-hospital major obstetric complications (2006–2008).

The study also found:

- The best-performing hospitals had a 51.30 percent lower maternal complication rate among women who had vaginal births compared to poor-performing hospitals, and a 74.34 percent lower complication rate among women who had C-sections. Patient-choice C-sections had the largest difference at 84.14 percent between best- and poor-performing hospitals.

- C-section rates average approximately 32.59 percent among the 19 states studied with a range between 22.04 and 37.80 percent.
- Of hospitals in the 19 states studied, nearly 80 percent of Maternity Care Excellence Award hospitals are in five states: California (42), Texas (26), New York (24), Florida (18) and New Jersey (13).[18]

Facilities that go through the arduous and expensive process of seeking Magnet Recognition find that this results in valuable improvements in their facilities. The Magnet Recognition Program is designed to recognize healthcare organizations that provide nursing excellence. The management changes tied to Magnet status can have a positive impact on recruitment and retention. Features of magnet status include shared governance, focus on supervisory effectiveness, scheduling innovation, performance measurement and feedback, quality improvement, and interdisciplinary working relationships. The creation of a Magnet culture has also shown to improve patient quality outcomes.[19] Refer to Chapter 8, *Inside the Healthcare Environment*, for more on Magnet status.

D. Production versus Protection

There is a constant need to identify the appropriate levels of staff that are compatible with providing safe nursing care. Reason[20] calls this the constant tension and fundamental incompatibility between production and protection. He points out that administrators are trained in, develop, and possess production rather than safety skills. This is understandable because production, not safety, creates and sustains an organization in the first place.[21] For example, hospitals market themselves as having the best cardiovascular surgery department, not as having the lowest medication error rate. Data related to production are direct, continuous, and readily understood. Hospitals can measure length of stay, occupancy rate, utilization of the operating room, and so on. In contrast, measures of safety are indirect and difficult to interpret.[22] Near misses are not often documented. It is difficult to arrive at an accurate "accident" rate because of the underreporting of incidents.

In a major study[23] nurse researchers found that state-mandated minimum nurse-to-patient staffing ratios were associated with significantly lower patient mortality. At present, only California has required minimum nurse-to-patient

ratios in acute care hospitals. When compared to nurses in Pennsylvania and New Jersey, California nurses cared for one less patient on average and two fewer patients on medical surgical units per shift. Besides lower patient mortality, improved nurse staffing was associated with less nurse burnout and more job satisfaction, predictive of better nurse retention.

Concerns about legislated ratios revolve around treating nurses as numbers rather than recognizing them as professionals. Other concerns are that mandated ratios. Some people fear that the minimum ratios of nurses to patients will become an average of maximum level of care. There is a fear that it will be difficult to adjust ratios to meet staffing needs and that facilities will reduce the number of ancillary staff to finance increased RN staff.[24]

TIP: Production pressures are often unrecognized sources of patient injury. These may begin when a nursing school is pressured to accept less than qualified applicants, and to be lenient about passing students.

Students who have been held back or failed out of the program may initiate legal action against the school, claiming bias or unfair practices. Such litigation exacts a toll on instructors, who may become less willing to take on this challenge with other marginal students. Once a new graduate emerges into the healthcare system, other production choices are raised, as shown in Figure 2.1.

---

1. Does the nurse spend time with the patient who needs it the most, at the expense of falling behind in the care of the rest of the patients?
2. Should the nurse manager call in extra staff to work when the needs of the patients are complex, yet knowing the extra staff has not been budgeted?
3. Should the nurses begin using a new intravenous pump when not all staff have been taught how to use it?
4. Should a nurse with a year of experience be put in charge of the nursing unit on the night shift because an opening exists?
5. Should the new graduate be placed in the emergency department because there is insufficient staff there?

Figure 2.1 *Examples of production pressures that may lead to errors.*

TIP: Choices about production pressures determine whether the organization delivers safe care. Downsizing creates a clear organizational message that these crucial choices are, particularly at this point in time, to be decided on the side of production.

The shift in values towards production and away from safety is foreign to the core values of nurses and doctors ("first do no harm"). The turmoil that the values conflict creates is thought to be as important as the declining number of professional staff in creating increased complications and decreased patient safety.[25]

E. Turnover

Job dissatisfaction is a significant cause of turnover. One study showed that 40 percent of U.S. hospital nurses reported job dissatisfaction, and more than 43 percent demonstrated high levels of burnout. Nearly 23 percent of U.S. nurses said they planned to leave their current job within the next year. For nurses under 30 years of age, that figure was 33 percent.[26] Many new graduates do not pursue nursing as a career. Of those who do, half leave their first employer after two years.[27] Hospital turnover has been correlated with a higher adjusted mortality index and severity adjusted average length of stay, as well as a higher cost per discharge.[28] What does this mean? More patients die in hospitals with high turnover. They stay longer, and it costs more to care for them.

TIP: Loss of experienced nurses can produce depression, survivor guilt, lowered morale, and increased stress. All of these can lead to distraction and a resultant increase in errors and injury.

The loss of nurses is costly. A cost estimate would include these factors:

- Recruiting, advertising, and placement
- Orientation
- Human resources costs (new hires, recruiting agency)
- Ongoing training
- Additional overtime and pressures on remaining staff
- Staffing agency costs during the vacancy
- Opportunity costs (delays in expansion, diversion of patients to other facilities)
- Lost team cohesion and productivity
- Quality[29]

The total cost of the loss of a nurse can equate to as much as two times the annual salary of that nurse.[30]

The loss of experienced nurses directly affects safety. These nurses may contribute to the safety of patients in varied ways. They have an understanding of how the system works, which a new employee lacks. They are more likely to understand how to implement the standards of care for a particular patient population and how to deal with the unexpected. The "institutional memory" consists of unwritten rules which are needed to mount an effective response to the unexpected event.[31] Experienced nurses are often much more effective in communicating with other healthcare professionals. For example, the older nurse who has developed a rapport with the physicians is able to effectively question inappropriate orders with greater success than the new nurse can. This is particularly important because most physicians have difficulty acknowledging mistakes. Gerlin notes that beginning in medical school, the culture of medicine discourages acknowledgment of mistakes, asking for assistance, exhibiting any weakness, or challenging a supervisor.[32]

The American Nurses Association noted nursing is a knowledge-based profession.[33] Experienced nurses possess a wealth of information. Although registered nurses perform tasks, their knowledge guides decision making, critical thinking, and the use of the nursing process to provide appropriate patient care. Sufficient staffing allows the registered nurse the freedom to apply that knowledge in an effective and efficient way. The advent of the Centers for Medicare and Medicaid Services and many private payors' refusal to pay for preventable complications (described in Chapter 22, *Preventing Healthcare Acquired Conditions,* in Volume II) gives hospitals an incentive to retain nursing staff, including seasoned, clinically astute nurses. These nurses form the safety net in the hospital.

Changes in the quality of care may become evident as healthcare agencies supplement their staff with agency nurses. A lack of knowledge of the patients, physicians, and policies of the facility may hamper effective decision making.

TIP: It is critical for attorneys to determine if a nurse involved in an incident was employed by the hospital or an agency. There is no obvious way to identify an agency nurse from the documentation in the medical record. This information can be investigated during the discovery process.

F. Errors Caused by Stress and Burnout

As staffing shortages deepen, nurses work longer hours, and with inadequate amounts of staff, stress and burnout accumulate. Several types of errors (failure to follow orders and policies, improper use of equipment, medication errors, communication issues, as well as others) may result from high levels of stress and burnout.

Researchers have investigated the relationship between levels of stress and burnout with nurse injuries (needle sticks, back injuries), patient incidents (medication or IV errors, falls), personal incidents (sick leave, absenteeism) and staff turnover. Six hundred and one registered and licensed practical nurses working on hospital units were surveyed. Two self-assessment instruments were used to measure stress levels over a three-month period. Incidents were tracked through records kept in nursing administration, personnel, and risk management departments. A stress scale ranging from 0 (no stress) to 10 (maximum stress) was correlated with incidents. The average stress score was 5.8 for the three months. More than half of the nurses (56 percent) reported a stress level of 6.0 or higher. Twenty-seven percent rated their stress as 7.5 or higher. There was a statistically significant correlation between the stress scores and patient incidents (medication errors and falls). When the stress scores were categorized by hospital units, the units with the higher stress scores experienced more patient incidents. For example, units with mean stress scores of 0 to 4 had 0.6 percent patient incidents per nurse shift. Units with mean stress scores of 7.1 to 10 had an average of 2.2 percent patient incidents per nurse shift. The researchers concluded that hospital efforts to reduce stress or encourage staff to participate in stress-reduction activities might reduce the number of patient incidents and the related costs.[34]

2.4 Extent of the Shortage
A. Need for Nurses

The need for nurses continues to escalate. As the population ages, and people live longer, they develop more chronic illnesses that require medical and nursing attention. There is an estimated pool of 75 million baby boomers who will be increasingly in need of medical care as they age. Ironically, the baby boomer generation is filled with nurses who are approaching or are in retirement. The job market is affected by the health needs of the aging population and the increased complexity of health care. The Health Care Reform Bill passed in 2010 added 32 million U.S. citizens to the health care system. Employment of registered nurses is expected to grow by 22 percent from 2008 to 2018, much faster than the average for all occupations. Growth will be driven by technological advances in patient care, which permit a greater number of health problems to be treated, and by an increasing emphasis on preventive care. In addition, the number of older people, who are much more likely than

Table 2.2
Growth Rate for New Nursing Jobs

Industry	Percent
Offices of physicians	48
Home health care services	33
Nursing care facilities	25
Employment services	24
Hospitals, public and private	17

younger people to need nursing care, is projected to grow rapidly. The growth rate for new nursing jobs is highest in physician offices.[35] Refer to Table 2.2.

Although hospitals employ the most nurses, the growth rate for new jobs in hospitals is projected to be the smallest. Patients are discharged more quickly and more surgery has been moved to the outpatient setting.

Since 1999, hospitals have been on a constriction binge, heightening the competition for nurses. Eighty-three percent of hospitals report they plan to add capacity.[36]

Healthcare consumers are increasingly becoming more educated about the management of their health conditions. Now more than ever they search for healthcare-related information on the Internet. A 1999 survey performed by Cybercitizen Health showed that of those healthcare consumers using health websites, 73 percent were looking for information about specific conditions. More than four out of ten consumers looked for sites on diet, nutrition, medications, and women's health.[37] In addition to all of the healthcare information readily available to consumers, the web contains a number of sites which allow consumers to get a report card on the hospitals in their areas, such as www. healthgrades.com or www.leapfroggroup.com. These sites permit comparisons of outcomes and complication rates. Buerhaus notes that "hospitals are now feeling the pressure to compete on the basis of quality. As they decide what kind of staff they will hire to help them increase efficiency, reduce costs, move acute patients out, and still raise quality, they will bring in registered nurses."[38]

However, can those nurses be found? The United States is in the midst of a nursing shortage that is expected to intensify as baby boomers age and the need for health care grows. In 2010, the average age of the RN was 45.4. The employment of RNs older than age 50 is growing faster than among any other age group.[39] With the average nurse in his forties, and a fairly substantial number of nurses in their fifties and sixties, a large segment of the current workforce will be retiring in the upcoming years. These individuals cannot be replaced, either in experience or in sheer numbers. Nurses will start to retire at the time baby boomers begin turning 65 years of age and start using more care. Forecasts for a registered nurse shortage in 2020 range from 400,000 to more than 1 million.[40]

TIP: If the number of registered nurses under 30 entering the labor market is compared with the number of nurses who need to be replaced, the shortfall will be tremendous. A huge amount of knowledge and experience will be lost at the same time that the demand for these skills will be increasing.[41]

In addition to the number of RNs who leave nursing, there are almost one-half million licensed nurses who are not employed in nursing. About 69 percent of the 490,000 RNs not employed in nursing in 2000 were 50 years or older.[42] The problem is compounded by the fact that nursing colleges and universities are struggling to expand enrollment levels to meet the rising demand for nursing care. More than one million new and replacement nurses will be needed by 2012. There are nearly 100,000 vacant nursing positions in long-term care facilities on any given day, and the nurse turnover rate exceeds 50 percent. The shortage is costing long-term care facilities an estimated $4 billion a year in recruitment and training expenses. This turnover statistic is in comparison to a survey that found that the average registered nurse turnover rate was 13.9 percent, the vacancy rate was 16.1 percent, and the average RN cost-per-hire was $2,821.[43]

The supply of nurses in hospitals can be compared to a pipeline. Fewer people are entering nursing school (the opening of the pipe). As nurses age, they reduce their working hours and eventually retire. The pipe has developed leaks as nurses leave hospitals to work in other healthcare settings. The resultant stream of nurses through the pipe is not sufficient to meet the ever-increasing demands for skilled healthcare providers.

According to a 2002 report by the American Hospital Association, the nursing shortage reflects fundamental and basic changes in population demographics, career expectations, work attitudes, and worker dissatisfaction.[44] A federal government study predicts that hospital nursing vacancies will reach 800,000, or 29 percent, by 2020.[45] The number of nurses is expected to grow by only 6 percent by 2020, while demand for nursing care is expected to grow by 40 percent. Healthcare reform has created an even greater demand for nurses with advanced degrees in nursing who have been educated to provide primary care to patients in nurse-run clinics and physician's offices.

TIP: The nursing shortage that exists at the turn of the new century differs from prior shortages; the numbers of nurses as well as the amount of experience are reduced.

B. Career Expectations

Young women have many more choices for careers than existed in the past. A drop in the enrollment in nursing programs was evident beginning in 1995, according to annual surveys by the American Association of Colleges of Nursing. After a decline in applications to entry-level nursing programs during the 1990s, interest in nursing has soared[46] but enrollment in educational programs has risen only 2 percent per year, for eight straight years, indicating students are being turned away because of lack of capacity.[47] The shifting job market has had a ripple effect on nursing educational programs. Faculty in many nursing programs are expanding students' exposure to community health and geriatric care programs, including adult-care and daycare programs and boarding homes.

C. Faculty Shortage

A shortage of faculty directly affects nursing program enrollments. The National League for Nursing released a preliminary report that showed that an estimated 99,000 qualified applicants were turned away from nursing schools in 2006-2007.[48] The percentage of qualified applicants who were turned away by associate's degree programs was significantly higher than the rate of BSN programs.[49] The American Association of Colleges of Nursing reported that 550 entry-level baccalaureate programs had to turn away about 39,400 qualified candidates in 2009, primarily because of a shortage of nursing educators.[50] This figure does not include associate's degree and diploma program rejections. An insufficient number of faculty, clinical sites, space in classrooms, clinical preceptors, and budget constraints are factors.[51]

The nursing faculty shortage is influenced by several factors, including the need to be clinically active, be involved in one's professional association, publish, and teach. The two most common reasons for difficulty recruiting faculty, according to a National League for Nursing survey, were not enough qualified candidates and an inability to offer competitive salaries.[52]

The Council on Physician and Nurse Supply urged a national effort to substantially expand nursing education. The profession needs more graduates with baccalaureate degrees to help solve the faculty shortage. This will require substantial investments in subsidizing nursing education programs.[53] Public colleges have tuition set by the state, and cannot pass on the higher costs of salaries to students. As a result, those who are qualified to teach often do not. Another problem for colleges is the scarcity of clinical training sites. Overburdened hospital staff are reluctant to take on the additional work of teaching and supervising students. Some are asking for payment, thereby adding to the college's costs.[54]

TIP: Despite all of these responsibilities and a high level of academic preparation, many salaries paid to faculty remain consistently low.

Nurses who in the past would have entered doctoral programs in order to become educators, were drawn to the nurse practitioner role beginning in the 1980s, resulting in a reduction in graduate programs to prepare nurse educators. The average salary of master's-prepared nurse practitioners remains higher than that of nursing professors, exacerbating the nursing faculty shortage. Efforts to expand the nurse educator population are also frustrated by a shortage of openings in graduate programs.

The requirement for doctoral degrees in order to provide nursing instruction automatically places many faculty on the older end of the age spectrum with retirement plans. The average age of nurse faculty at retirement is 62.5. A wave of retirements is expected within the next ten years with the average age of doctorally prepared faculty currently 53.5 years.[55] Seventy-five percent of current nursing faculty members are expected to retire by 2019, creating tremendous opportunities for those who want to become full-time or part-time nurse educators.[56]

Some of the suggestions proffered to address faculty shortages include:

- Hire nurses enrolled in masters in nursing programs to teach
- Redesign the curriculum to more effectively use scarce resources[57]
- Use advanced practice nurses to teach, precept and mentor nursing students
- Provide online courses for subjects that do not require supervision of care
- Use non-nurses to teach subjects like biology, languages, sociology and psychology[58]
- Offer loan forgiveness for nursing students who pursue graduate education and teach nursing undergraduates in state schools[59]

D. Alternatives to Working in the Hospital

Not only are sheer numbers of nurses reduced according to the need, but experienced, competent nurses are in short supply. The shortage primarily involves specialty areas of critical care, emergency department, operating room, and pediatric intensive care units. Although the census of patients in American hospitals has been reduced by the swing to outpatient care, the patients who are in the hospital are more acutely ill. Their care requires highly skilled nurses who are no longer available in the numbers needed.[60]

Many experienced critical care nurses are choosing options such as case management, nursing education, clinical information management systems (computers), and outpatient surgicenters.[61] Critical care nurses are caring for patients at home on ventilators and continuous intravenous infusions, and many are enjoying the change from hospital nursing. Outpatient surgical centers have drawn operating room nurses out of the hospital.[62]

Some nurses, burned out with the stress of the hospital environment, have discovered that work opportunities for nurses have expanded beyond the traditional hospital walls. Rotating shifts, weekend work, and working on major holidays have added to the stress of employment in a hospital. Jobs are available which permit a work life that fits in better with family responsibilities. Attractive career options for nurses are increasingly being found outside of hospitals. Nurses can work in utilization review or computer information, as administrators, nurse practitioners, and nurse midwives managing a case load of patients. Nurses are employed by insurance companies to review files for medical issues, for physicians in office settings, or in ambulatory care settings, to name a few non-hospital jobs.

2.5 Strategies to Alleviate the Shortage
A. Use of Unlicensed Assistive Personnel

In an effort to react to the nursing shortage, many facilities have increased their use of unlicensed nursing assistants. Improper delegation, whether to a licensed or an unlicensed person, creates the risk of error and harm to patients. Delegation, according to the American Nurses Association, is the transfer of responsibility for the performance of an activity from one individual to another, with the former retaining accountability for the outcome. Assigning patient care or tasks to unlicensed assistive personnel creates the opportunity for risk to patient safety.[63]

Unlicensed assistive personnel proliferated in hospitals in the 1990s and continue to maintain a place in hospitals, nursing homes, and other sites. Unlicensed assistive personnel (UAP) are defined by the American Nurses Association as individuals who are trained to function in an assistive role to the licensed professional nurse in the provision of patient or client care activities as delegated by the nurse. The activities generally can be categorized as either direct or indirect care. Direct patient care activities include feeding, assisting with drinking, positioning, ambulating, grooming, toileting, dressing, and socializing, and may involve collecting, reporting, and documenting data related to these activities. Indirect care includes housekeeping, patient transport, clerical, equipment stocking, and maintaining supplies. In many hospitals, UAPs retrieve supplies, fill water pitchers, distribute snacks, and so on.[64]

TIP: In many hospitals, UAPs collect routine vital signs and answer call lights, particularly when nurses are in change of shift report.

UAPs may fulfill the roles of the certified nursing aide, clinical assistant, orderly, home health aide, nursing assistant, certified nursing assistant, personal care assistant, patient care technician, attendant, or certified phlebotomist. UAPs are required to perform increasingly complex tasks, necessitating the registered nurse to provide increased supervision. Delegating tasks to unlicensed assistive personnel (UAP) creates a situation ripe with opportunities for liability. The unlicensed assistive personnel may be performing tasks that were formerly carried out only by the registered nurse, such as drawing blood from arteries, veins, and catheters, checking blood glucose levels with blood pricked from fingers or earlobes, as well as monitoring vital signs. The UAP is taught how to perform the task, but not how to critically evaluate information. For example, the UAP may carefully record that the blood pressure of a postoperative patient is going down, but not understand the significance of this information in relation to hemorrhage.

Additionally, literacy issues arise. Many illiterate individuals have developed methods to conceal their problems with reading. It may never occur to a nurse that the nursing assistant is unable to read. However, it is the responsibility of the hospital to address basic literacy skills before placing unlicensed assistive personnel in contact with patients. It is the duty of the nurse to evaluate the skills of those to whom care is delegated.

TIP: Some unlicensed assistive personnel are poorly educated and lack reading skills. Ten to 33 percent of Americans are functionally illiterate, meaning that their reading ability does not exceed the fourth grade level. Some experts estimate that as much as 70 percent of workplace materials are written at the ninth to twelfth grade level.[65]

In response to concerns about maximizing patient safety and quality care, The American Association of Nurse Attorneys (TAANA) recommended the following:

- Nurses should be educated about team nursing and supervision of UAPs.
- Since many nurses work in states where there is no guidance regarding delegation to and supervision of UAPs by registered nurses, the state Board of Nursing should provide guidance and direction. This would include defining the tasks that can be delegated, as well as those that are non-delegable.
- Standardized curriculum and testing procedures should be instituted for all UAPs, similar to those for nursing assistants in long-term care. Demonstration of competency and resulting certification, and continuing education requirements should be defined.
- A multidisciplinary patient care team should be convened to evaluate, formulate, and implement the use of UAPs before UAPs are used in the facility. The team would draft job descriptions for the UAPs and the nurses who are supervising them.
- The use of UAPs should be periodically monitored and reevaluated to identify the need to revise job descriptions and identify educational needs.
- Facilities using UAPs should include in their inservice and education classes for both UAPs and RNs information and training concerning the areas of delegation and supervision.

TAANA recognizes that the use of UAPs presents opportunities and concerns, and that nurses are ultimately responsible for the provision of nursing care to their patients. That responsibility holds them accountable for the care given by UAPs.[66]

TIP: In today's hospital, the former housekeeper or dietary aide may be providing patient care. The nurse retains responsibility for the care provided and for acting on the information obtained by the UAP.

The nurse doing the delegating is responsible for the five rights of delegation:

1. The right tasks should be delegated. In general, the appropriate activities to delegate to a UAP include those which frequently recur on a daily basis, do not require the UAP to exercise nursing judgment, are not complex or multi-dimensional, for which the results are predictable and the potential risk is minimal, and use a standard and unchanging procedure.
2. The delegation should occur in the right circumstances. The patient's needs should be assessed

and the complexity of needs and activities matched with the competency of the UAP.

3. The delegation should be made to the right person. The staff nurse, or person making the assignment, should verify the competency of the UAP.

4. The delegation should include the right direction or instructions. The staff nurse should communicate the delegation decision and provide details of the assignment. The UAP may be told which specific data to collect, the method and timeliness for reporting, and the expected results or potential complications and how timely to report such information.

5. The right level of supervision must be employed over the person who will be carrying out the task. The staff nurse should provide clear directions and expectations for how an activity is to be performed, and how to monitor performance, obtain and provide feedback, intervene if necessary, and ensure proper documentation. As the professional, the RN should evaluate the client and evaluate the performance of the activity.[67]

Ultimately, it is the responsibility of the registered nurse to supervise the unlicensed assistive personnel. The American Nurses Association is quite clear on these points:

- It is the nursing profession that determines the scope of nursing practice.

- It is the nursing profession that defines and supervises the education, training, and utilization of any unlicensed assistant who is involved in providing direct patient care.

- It is the registered nurse who is responsible and accountable for the provision of nursing practice.

- It is the registered nurse who supervises and determines the appropriate utilization of any unlicensed assistant involved in providing direct patient care.

- It is the purpose of unlicensed assistive personnel to enable the professional nurse to provide nursing care of the patient.[68]

B. Use of Supplemental Staffing

In the face of shortages, healthcare facilities sustain operations by contracting with supplemental staffing agencies as needed. As the workforce shortages grow, the number of supplemental RNs and LPNs is projected to grow 57 percent by 2012. Hospitals are using temps to supplement about 5 percent of nursing work hours on average. A study by Aiken and several others addressed quality concerns that have been raised regarding the use of supplemental staff. It concluded that temporary nurses are as qualified as staff nurses (employed by the facility). Deficits in the hospital environment play a greater role in poor quality of care.[69]

Temporary nurses are compensated at higher levels, with basic per diem rates ranging from 25 to 40 percent of the average employee's wage.[70] This can lead to resentment and dumping on the temporary nurse. Use of internal registries or PRN pools may eliminate supplemental staffing agencies. Some facilities permit their employees to bid on open positions. The bid amount is more than they would receive in normal wages, but less than it would cost the facility to use an outside staffing agency. This has an added benefit of exposing nurses to different areas of the hospital, so that internal transfers may be requested. Increased productivity and morale may result.

C. Import Foreign Born Nurses

By 2005, 13 percent of all newly licensed nurses were international nursing graduates.[71] Foreign born nurses are typically younger than the U.S. born nurse. The growth of this segment of the workforce is far larger than the usual yearly immigration of 3,000-4,000 RNs during previous shortages. As the demand for nurses accelerates, hospitals and other healthcare providers will increasingly rely on foreign-educated nurses. Social, political, and regulatory issues arise as shortages develop within the countries sending their nurses to the U.S. Other questions are raised about the technical and cultural competence of foreign nurses.[72] The United States, Australia, New Zealand, Ireland, and Canada's top 12 source countries are India, the Philippines, Pakistan, South Korea, the United Kingdom, Egypt, South Africa, China, Germany, Mexico, Ireland, and Nigeria. However, some of these countries do not have enough clinicians to treat their own populations.[73] Approximately 42 percent of foreign born nurses who take the NCLEX exam to qualify to work in the U.S. pass the exam the first time. Complex cultural issues drive the market for these nurses. Many desire to emigrate to improve their salaries and to be able to send money back home to improve the standard of living for their family. They may be drawn to modern medical environments, better pay, career-advancement opportunities, physical safety, and political freedom.[74] Ninety percent of Filipino nurses are produced for export to other countries.[75] Some of the nurses were originally trained as doctors. For example, Filipino physicians frustrated with their job prospects in the Philippines have retrained as nurses. Since 2000, 3,500 Filipino doctors have graduated from nursing school, and another 4,000 Filipino doctors are in nursing school.[76] However, these nurses face food, language, and other adjustment issues in living in the United States. American patients may react negatively to hearing non-English speaking workers. At least two hospitals in New Jersey have lost market share because their nurses spoke foreign languages in front of the patients.[77] The United States' need for nurses is creating shortages in the countries that supply the nurses.

D. Change the Nature of Nursing Education

Recruitment and retention issues may be alleviated by shifting the focus of nursing education. The National League for Nursing issued a position statement in August 2003 calling for reform in nursing education. According to this view, students must be helped to learn to practice in rapidly changing environments where short stays in acute care faculties are common, and complex care is being provided in a variety of settings. The new methods of instruction must be research based and responsive to the unpredictable nature of the contemporary healthcare system. Nurses must be able to function effectively in ambiguous, unpredictable, and complex environments; demonstrate critical thinking and flexibility; teach health promotion and disease prevention; and execute a variety of roles throughout a lifetime career.[78] To prepare for the complex and challenging work of nursing, the American Organization of Nurse Executives (AONE) released a position statement in April 2005 that the educational preparation of the nurse for the future should be at the baccalaureate level. This preparation will prepare the nurse of the future to function as an equal partner, collaborator, and manager of the complex patient care journey that is envisioned by AONE. The baccalaureate curriculum will need to be re-framed.[79] The authors of *Educating Nurses: A Call for Radical Transformation* (2009) recommend essential changes in policy, curriculum and in the way nursing programs approach student learning. One of their recommendations is that the baccalaureate degree in nursing should be the minimal educational level into practice, and that within ten years after graduation all nurses should complete a master's degree in nursing.[80]

Transformation of the classroom is occurring now. Some schools have effectively integrated technology:

- Patient simulators can provide clinical training scenarios that mimic a particular patient pathology by using computer simulation monitoring systems that track clinician performance and grades against institutionally established best practices. Remote distance learning can be used to expand educational programs to underserved areas.[81]
- Educators can use slideshow presentations, to integrate web-based video clips, computer-generated graphics and research findings.

- Many programs use e-learning management systems, such as Blackboard to let faculty give online exams and quizzes, use software to identify plagiarized papers, and post resources for reinforcement and enrichment.
- Students can also use clickers (handheld remotes) to let the instructor know immediately how well they understand information in a lecture.
- Many instructors record lectures so students can listen to them on their iPods.
- A school may provide an e-learning discussion board to allow students to post assignments and information for classmates and faculty.
- Students and faculty may use blogs and wikis. Blogs may promote peer support. Wikis are collaboratively constructed websites where content is added and edited.
- Students may use PDAs (personal digital assistants) to quickly access information about disease processes, evidence-based nursing interventions and drug and treatment information.[82]

The need to make it easier for nurses to earn advanced degrees continues to motivate many schools to be flexible in their programs.[83] More programs now provide online education.

E. Recruit More Men into Nursing

Men represent 9 percent of registered nurses in the United States workforce, and this percentage has been increasing. As many as 20 percent of nursing students may be men.[84] According to a survey of male nurses, the top three reasons why men chose nursing as a career were:

- a desire to help people
- nursing is a growth profession with many career paths
- the desire to have a stable career

The difficulties in recruiting men to the field of nursing were identified in this survey as related to the negative stereotyping about men in the profession being gay, the reality that nursing is traditionally a female profession, poor pay, and lack of role models. Recommendations included presenting male nurses as models, providing non-gender-specific messages, stressing stable employment opportunities, and stressing the need for nurses to be skilled and autonomous.[85]

Male nurses may have a harder time expressing emotion and may not establish therapeutic relations with patients in the same way that most female nurses do. Men may be more likely to use humor and less likely to use touch.[86]

F. Improve Working Conditions in Nursing

Job satisfaction contributes to retention. Data suggests that there is much to do to improve retention.

TIP: Requiring nurses to work additional hours contributes to the vicious cycle of fatigue, job changes, and leaving the profession.[87]

Current national information on why nurses are dissatisfied and leave their jobs reveals these factors, in this order:

- Excessive administrative paperwork
- Workload too heavy due to acuity levels
- Workload too heavy due to inadequate staff
- Inadequate compensation
- Disruptive physician behavior
- Inadequate preparation/training
- Lack of information technology support
- Not enough direct patient care activity
- Unpleasant or inefficient physical environment
- Reliance upon agency nurses
- Scheduling mandatory overtime
- Excessive employment cost sharing for benefits[88]

Registered nurses who perceived that nursing was satisfying had opportunities to influence decision making, were recognized for their accomplishments, and were physically healthy. On the downside, nurses still reported that respect was not up to par in the workplace. Feeling stressed to the point of burnout or feeling overburdened with non-nursing tasks had a negative impact on their career perceptions. Ideal candidates for a career in nursing were men, people who want job security, and those who do well in the sciences or rank in the top 20 percent of their high school class.[89] Additional suggestions for increasing retention and alleviating the shortage include:

1. Make improvements in the work environment. Limit mandatory overtime to avoid the fatigue that contributes to medical errors. Discipline or remove from the medical staff those physicians who are abusive towards others. Foster respect for nurses.
2. Improve efforts to recruit minorities and those who make nursing a second career. Provide scholarship funds to permit low income potential students to complete a nursing education program.
3. Increase the supply of nursing educators by providing salaries that are competitive with career options for highly educated nurses. A nurse practitioner who could earn over $100,000 per year is not likely going to consider a job offer to work at $50,000 as an educator.
4. Provide new graduates with a year-long internship under the guidance of an experienced mentor. Turnover rates of first year nurses from those programs drop to 5.7 percent compared with the national average of nearly 30 percent.[90]

The Robert Wood Johnson Foundation and the Institute for Healthcare Improvement (IHI) teamed up to produce a program called Transforming Care at the Bedside, which was implemented in ten hospitals from 2003 to 2008. The work from this initiative continues as the IHI Collaborative on Transforming Care at the Bedside. It explores four aspects of the healthcare environment:

1. Safe and Reliable Care (Reliability)

Care for hospitalized patients is safe, reliable, effective and equitable.

Safe and reliable care hinges on a culture of safety where people are not just encouraged to work toward change, but to take action whenever necessary. A hospital is able to improve safety only when the leadership is visibly committed to change and when staff is empowered to openly share safety information. Organizations that do not have such an open culture often find staff members unwilling to report adverse events or unsafe conditions because of concerns of reprisal.

Because of their proximity to patients and the direct care they provide, nurses and other frontline staff are uniquely capable of identifying and implementing process improvements that could result in safer, more reliable care.

TIP: Examples of safe and reliable care include: reducing medication errors and adverse drug events, establishing rapid response teams and preventing inpatient falls.

---

2. Vitality and Teamwork (Vitality)

Effective care teams continually strive for excellence when they work in a joyful and supportive environment that nurtures professional training and career development.

Vitality can be facilitated by formal and informal leadership. Team vitality starts when teams are allowed to work on issues relevant to their success. Effective teams work together and get great results. The mindset of effective teams is that they must act in ways that make excellent work possible, sustainable and satisfying. They are always looking for ways to improve their work. Teams with strong vitality strive to reduce or eliminate blame, name-calling, cynicism, conflict and apathy. Developing a process for improving care and teamwork greatly increases team vitality by improving how the team acts and interacts.

TIP: Examples of vitality and teamwork include: optimizing communication among team members, engaging frontline staff, fostering personal and team recognition, and incorporating management and professional development programs for staff.

---

3. Patient-Centered Care (Patient Centeredness)

Truly patient-centered care on medical and surgical units honors the whole person and family, respects individual values and choices and ensures continuity of care. Patients will say, "They give me exactly the help I want and need exactly when I want and need it."

Patient- and family-centered care is essential to cultivating a partnership at the bedside in making decisions, healing relationships and facilitating interactions between the individual patient and the professional. A key aspect of patient- and family-centered care includes health care practitioners listening to and honoring patient and family perspectives and choices, including beliefs and cultural backgrounds. Sharing complete, unbiased information between health care providers and patients and families should be affirming and useful. Encouraging patients and families to participate in care and decision-making is important.

Because patients and their families spend most of their time with nurses and other frontline staff—and often express their preferences, expectations and frustration with them—nurses are in a great position to help ensure that the care a hospital provides is as patient-centered as possible.

TIP: Examples of patient-centered care include: involvement in the discharge process, adjusting medications to the patient's schedule, sitting for a few minutes with each patient at each shift, being pain free and having daily information regarding plan of care, schedule of tests and prognosis.

---

4. Value-Added Processes (Lean)

All care processes are free of waste and promote continuous flow.

Developing lean operations requires distinguishing value-added and nonvalue-added steps in every process. Commitment to a lean organization must begin with leadership and become a part of a culture that is receptive to and rewarding of lean ideas. Staff should be involved in helping to redesign processes to improve flow and reduce waste.

Because nurses and other frontline staff spend so much time in activities that take away from the amount of time they have to spend in direct patient care, they are well-suited to identify processes that increase leanness in a unit.

TIP: Examples of value-added processes include: application of lean strategies such as space redesign and having all needed equipment at the bedside at all times. Also, use of cell phones to reach staff where they are.[91]

Much can be done at low or no cost: creating a positive organizational climate, improving working relationships among personnel, respecting nurses' clinical judgment, and recognizing the professional autonomy of nurses in their daily work life decisions.[92] Facilities should use advanced practice nurses such as nurse midwives, clinical specialists, nurse anesthetist and nurse practitioners to supplement staff. Additionally, facilities are providing more flexible schedules to better meet the needs of the staff. For example, one group of nurses said they wanted four to six hour shifts so their children would not be impacted. Recently retired or baby boomer nurses may prefer short shifts.

Healthcare facilities should use information technology to best effect, including:

- Documentation, such as bedside wireless transmission to monitors and electronic medical records
- Medication administration, such as computerized physician order entry, bar coding, and robotic delivery
- Location and retrieval of patients, supplies and equipment, such as bar coding, radio frequency identification, and electronic patient progression tracking
- Communications, such as "one and done" calls: immediate responses from attending physician versus making multiple calls[93]

2.6 Summary

Nurses play a vital role in the healthcare delivery system. Their numbers and capabilities have a direct impact on patient outcomes. The nursing shortage is affected by retirements in the baby boomer population, a diminished supply of faculty prepared to educate students, and retention issues that drive nurses out of the field. Although solutions of increasing recruitment and retention are provided, the growing numbers of nurses leaving the profession continue to be of concern, and will affect the healthcare system for decades.

Endnotes

1. http://www.jointcommission.org/NR/rdonlyres/ FA46564-5F5F-4543-AC8F-E8AF6571E372/0/root_ cause_se.jpg last accessed April 17, 2006.

2. Canavan, K., "Combating dangerous delegation," *American Journal of Nursing* 97, no. 5 (May 1997): 57.

3. Boucher, M., "Delegation alert!" *American Journal of Nursing*, 98, no. 2 (February 1998): 26.

4. Laska, L. (ed.), "Neglect, malnourishment, and dehydration blamed for bed sores, decubitus ulcer and death," *Medical Malpractice Verdicts, Settlements, and Experts* (August 2003): 33–34.

5. American Nurses Association, *Implementing Nursing's Report Card: A Study of RN Staffing, Length of Stay and Patient Outcomes*. Washington D.C., 1997.

6. Knox, G., M. Kelley, K. Simpson et al. "Downsizing, reengineering and patient safety: numbers, newness and resultant risk," *Journal of Healthcare Risk Management*, 19, no. 4 (Fall 1999): 18.

7. Prescott, P., "Nursing: an important component of hospital survival under a reformed health care system," *Nursing Economic$* 11 (1993): 192.

8. Kovner, C. and P. Gergen, "Nurse staffing levels and adverse events following surgery in U.S. hospitals," *Image—The Journal of Nursing Scholarship*. 30, no. 4 (1998): 315.

9. See note 6.

10. Aiken, L., D. Sloane, and E. Lake et al., "Hospital nurse staffing and patient mortality," *JAMA*, 288, no. 16 (October 23 and 30, 2002): pgs. 1987–1993.

11. *Id.*

12. "The Effect of Health Care Working Conditions on Patient Safety, produced by an AHRQ-funded Evidence-based Practice Center" as quoted in *Hospital Nurse Staffing and Quality of Care*, March 2004, www.ahrq. gov.

13. "Frontline nurses speak out about medication safety," *NurseAdvise-ERR* 3, no. 7 (July 2005): 2.

14. Horn, S., P. Buerhaus, N. Bergstrom, and R. Smout. "RN staffing time and outcomes of long-stay nursing home residents," *American Journal of Nursing*, 105, no. 11 (November 2005): 58–69.

15. Laska. L. (ed.), Woman falls from toilet which had improperly fitted toilet seat height adjustment device. *Medical Malpractice Verdicts, Settlements and Experts*, January 2009, 31.

16. Brooten, D. and M. Naylor. "Nurses' effect on changing patient outcomes," *Journal of Nursing Scholarship* 27 (1995): 95.

17. Pinkerton, S., "Best nursing practices and best hospitals," *Journal of Professional Nursing*, 15, no. 4 (July-August 1999): 207.

18. www.healthgrades.com/cms/ratings-and-awards/2010-Maternity-Care-Excellence-Award-Announcement. aspx, last accessed 02/25/11.

19. What Works: Healing the Healthcare Staffing Shortage, http://www.pwc.com/us/en/healthcare/publications/ what-works-healing-the-healthcare-staffing-shortage. jhtml.

20. Reason, J., *Managing the Risks of Organizational Accidents*, Brookfield, Vermont: Ashgate Publishing Company, 1997.

21. See note 6.

22. *Id.*

23. Aiken, L., D. Shane, and J. Cimiotti et al., "Implications of the California nurse staffing mandate for other states," *Health Serv Res*, 4/9/2010.

24. Rajecki, R. "Mandatory staffing ratios: boon or bane?" *RN*, January 2009, 22-25.

25. See note 6.

26. Cited in Gelinas, K, Bohlen, C "Tomorrow's Work Force: A Strategic Approach," VHA Research Series, 2002; 1.

27. See note 19.

28. VHA Research Series; 7. The Business Case for Work Force Stability.

29. See note 19.

30. Atencio, B., Cohen, J, Gorenberg, B. "Nurse retention: is it worth it?" *Nursing Economics* 21 (6), via http://medscape.com/viewarticle/465918.

31. See note 6.

32. Gerlin, A., "For a systemic problem, no easy fix," Philadelphia Online, September 13, 1999. http://health.philly.com/specials/mistakes/hosp13.asp.

33. *Utilization Guide for the ANA Principles for Nurse Staffing*, American Nurses Association, September 2005.

34. DePalma, J., "How stress on nurses affects patient outcomes," *American Journal of Nursing* 98, no. 4 (April 1998): 37.

35. http://stats.bls.gov/oco/ocos083.htm#outlook, last accessed 02/25/11.

36. Medicare Payment Advisory Commission Report to the Congress: Medicare Payment Policy, March 2007, 57-58.

37. Haugh, R., "The new consumer," *Hospitals and Health Networks* (December 1999): 30.

38. Buerhaus, P., "Is a nursing shortage on the way?" *Nursing Management* (February 1999): 55.

39. Buerhaus, P., D. Staiger, and D. Auerbach, "New signs of a strengthening U.S. nurse labor market?" *Health Affairs* (November 2004): 17.

40. See note 19.

41. See note 38.

42. *Projected supply, demand, and shortages of Registered Nurses.* HRSA website: http://bhpr.hrsa.gov/healthworkforce/reports.rnproject/default.htm.

43. www.aacn.nche.edu/Media/FactSheets/NursingShortage.htm, last accessed July 18, 2005.

44. *Hospital nurse staffing and quality of care*, www.ahrq.gov, March 2004.

45. See note 42.

46. Cleary, B., Hassmiller, S., Reinhard, S. et al., "Forging partnerships to expand nursing education capacity," *AJN*, January 2010, 43-50.

47. www.aacn.nche.edu/media/newsreleases/2008/enrlgrowth.html, last accessed 02/25/11.

48. National League for Nursing, NLN annual nursing data review documents application, admission, enrollment, and graduation rates for all types of prelicensure nursing programs, March 16, 2009, http://www.nln.org/newsreleases/annual survey 031609.htm.

49. www.nln.org/newsreleases/datarelease05.pdf, last accessed July 18, 2005.

50. Hebel, M and Kim, A, Teaching tomorrow's nurse: what's happening in the classroom?" NY. nurse.com, May 2, 2010.

51. www.aacn.cnhe.edu/Media/FactSheets/NursingShortage.htm.

52. See note 46.

53. Roman, L. "Nursing shortage: Thought leaders discuss the future of the profession," *RN*, March 2008, 34-41.

54. See note 19.

55. See note 51.

56. See note 50.

57. See note 46.

58. See note 53.

59. See note 19.

60. Hawke, M., "Nursing Workforce 1999: a year of challenges and opportunities," *Nursing Spectrum* (November 29, 1999): 7.

61. *Id.*

62. Gray-Siracusa, K., "The roller coaster is running: shortages in specialty nurses are happening again," *Advance for Nurses, Greater Philadelphia* (September 27, 1999): 18.

63. See note 33.

64. *Id.*

65. Hess, V., "Literacy and learning for hospital employees," *Journal for Nurses in Staff Development* (May-June 1998): 143.

66. For the full text of the TAANA position, see www.ta-ana.org/shownews.asp?newsid=50.

67. Davidson, S. and R. Scott, "Thinking critically about delegation," *American Journal of Nursing* 99, no. 6 (June 1999): 61, and The Five Rights of Delegation, www.ncsbn.org/pdfs/fiverights.pdf, accessed July 18, 2005.

68. See note 33.

69. Aiken, L. Xue, Y et al., "Supplemental nurse staffing in hospitals and quality of care" *Journal of Nursing Administration* 37(7/8) 2007, 335.

70. See note 19.

71. *Id.*

72. See note 39.

73. See note 19.

74. *Id.*

75. Joel, L. personal communication, November 2005.

76. Academy Health 2006 Health in Foreign Policy Forum, 2/8/06. Migration and Global Shortage of Healthcare Professionals (transcripts) at http://kaisernetowrk.org/health cast/hcast index. cfm?display=detailandhc=1622.

77. See note 75.

78. www.nln.org/aboutnln/PositionStatements/innovation.htm, last accessed July 18, 2005.

79. *AONE Statement, AONE Practice and Education Partnership for the Future*, Marilyn Bowcutt, MSN, RN, AONE President, April 18, 2005.

80. www.carnegiefoundation.org/print/7186, last accessed 02/25/11.

81. See note 19.

82. See note 50.

83. Bensing, K., "Nursing education today," *Advance for Nurses*, Greater Philadelphia, 14, November 22, 1999.

84. www.nursingjobshelp.com/male_nurses.htm, last accessed 02/25/11.

85. "What do men in nursing really think?" *Nursing 2005* (November 2005): 47–48.

86. See note 50.

87. Trinkoff, A., J. Geiger-Brown, J. Brady, J. Lipscomb, and C. Muntainer, "How long and how much are nurses now working?" *American Journal of Nursing* 106, no. 4 (April 2006): 60–71.

88. See note 19.

89. Buerhaus, P., K. Donelan, and B. Ulrich, "2004 National Survey of Registered Nurses," *Nursing Economic$* (May/June 2005), as quoted in Steefel, L., "Survey shows first real positive workforce change," *Nursing Spectrum*, Pennsylvania, June 20, 2005.

90. Ericksen, A. "Recruiting nurses," *RN*, April 2009, 36-39.

91. www.rwjf.org/qualityequality/product.jsp?id=30051, last accessed 02/25/11.

92. See note 53.

93. See note 19.

Additional Reading

Douglas, K, Pledger, R. and Schulman, C., "Self-directed floating," *RN*, May 2009, 32-35.

Unruh, L. "Nurse staffing and patient, nurse and financial outcomes," *AJN*, January 2008, 108 (1), 62-69.

Chapter 3

Moving from Traditional Law and Medicine to Promote Safety and Effective Risk Management

Bryan A. Liang, PhD, MD, JD and Timothy Mackey, MAS

3.1 Introduction

Patient safety requires a fundamental reassessment of traditional legal and medical principles to promote effective and safe health care. By understanding the theory of complex systems, the processes that relate to these principles, and the legal issues associated with performing systemic patient safety work, the reader can better understand the interventions that can promote patient safety. This chapter presents an overview of systems theory, legal issues associated with patient safety, including the enacted Patient Safety and Quality Improvement Act of 2005, and several safety principles that may reduce error, mitigate its effects, and improve communications within the health care delivery team.

An increased awareness of patient safety resulted after the Institute of Medicine (IOM) Report was released in late 1999.[1] Recognition of medical error as the predominant mechanism by which patients are injured—and the inability for poor systems to mitigate its inevitable occurrence—provided an extremely important insight into the operation of the medical delivery system.[2-5] This recognition was and is the basis of reform within the systems of delivery, with the goal of minimization of the tremendous toll that iatrogenic injury causes to patients who access medical services.

Critical to any progress in patient safety is the participation by key providers. Because patient injury results in thousands of deaths annually in the inpatient setting alone, nurses and other providers are in positions to promote patient safety. Yet although professional ethics and performance improvement are perhaps the most important reasons for participating in patient safety activities, practically speaking, however, there are legal risks to those performing this work.

This chapter seeks to provide a foundation of information on medical error and systems theory to assist readers in their efforts to understand patient safety. It reviews some of the legal issues associated with patient safety work that may create issues of liability and risk for the practitioner and their legal advocates. The Patient Safety Quality Improvement Act of 2005 is also reviewed. Finally, some practical tools gleaned from the aviation industry are provided that may assist the nurse and provider community, the healthcare team, and risk managers in improving safety in the health delivery system by reducing the risk of patient injury and the concomitant potential for liability. The complex interplay of safety principles is defined to help the attorney reader understand why errors occur.

3.2 Systems Thinking

TIP: Medical error can be defined as a mistake, inadvertent occurrence, or unintended event in the delivery of care that may, or may not, result in patient injury.[6]

A. An Overview of Medical Error and Patient Injury

Medical error is *not* purposeful or reckless action that is intended to directly or indirectly harm. These latter kinds of actions represent only a small fraction of patient injuries and, furthermore, are malicious and volitional rather than error. Instead of focusing on bad actors, we are interested in the common, indeed prototypic, problem of error by individuals who are acting in the best of faith, but are working in systems where mistakes can occur that may reach the patient and cause harm.[7]

Deaths attributable to medical error are virtually epidemic, although estimates vary as to its specific magnitude.[8-12] Of course, the human toll associated with medical error is significant. High financial costs also attend: estimates indicate that between $17-29 billion annually is due to medical errors, which does not include the roughly $8-9 billion spent on the medical injury litigation and insurance.[13,14] In addition, studies indicate that a high percentage of these medical errors are preventable and that between 50 to 96 percent of adverse events go unreported annually.[15,16] Thus, the public and private costs of medical error represent a major social concern for providers, patients, and the public alike.

It must be reemphasized that errors are inevitable. Systems must try to eliminate preventable errors, but as humans, we will always err. The commercial and military aviation communities recognized this decades ago.[17] They moved away from the "top gun" paradigm, where the mission is perceived to be accomplished, or not, based on one person's performance. In the medical world, there is a similar ethic: the "gentlemanly honor" paradigm, where the provider believes he is personally responsible for any and all patient benefit—and hence harm—that occurs.

Instead of the top gun paradigm, the aviation industry accepted error occurrence and developed a systems-focused, team outcome approach, grounded in non-punitive reporting of system weaknesses and errors. The principles include:

1. Share information—make the system transparent through open non-punitive reporting so that problems can be fixed, the system made resilient, and harm more effectively averted.

2. Do not blame the messenger—listen for the information so that others (including you) won't be put in the same position to make the same error.

3. Individually oriented humiliation and blame is ineffective—it does not promote optimal individual or system performance and only encourages hiding important system information.

Through adopting these principles and culture change, aviation went from being less safe than driving on the nation's highways—truly a dismal statistic—to becoming the safest means of travel. And the industry accomplished this feat in less than 40 years.

B. Theory

Systems theory that accurately describes healthcare delivery focuses on two models: the systems pyramid and the Swiss cheese model, developed by James Reason, a noted human factors researcher.[18] The pyramid's "sharp end" represents the interface of the provider and patient, built on a foundation of blunt end administration, policy and procedures, human resources, conflicts, resource constraints, turf battles, rules, regulations, and formal and informal interactions and processes.

Layers of healthcare activity have Swiss cheese holes and barriers at that sharp end. The holes are weaknesses that let error through to the next layer of activity. The barriers are defenses that stop errors from reaching the next layer. Holes are generally "latent failures," manifestations of systemic processes and design—including the gaps and created by the ill-fitting parts of the pyramid.

Some important implications of this model affect patient care. First, the sharp end interface between provider and patient depends on how well the messy blunt end is put together. If the structure is constructed with well-fitting pieces, the foundation is firm and stable. Hence, the provider-patient interaction is stable and the provider may dedicate all her attention to the clinical task. If, however, the pyramid is more akin to a random, scattered, ill-fitting pile of firewood forming a rickety, unstable structure, the provider will be trying to treat the patient while trying to keep her balance—not a situation that allows full or even most attention to the clinical matter at hand.

Second, when considering the holes in the various Swiss cheese layers that comprise all healthcare activities, another lesson attends. If all the holes in the layers line up, the error reaches the patient and we have an accident. What is essential to realize is that it is generally not a dramatic and/or single error or failure that results in patient injury. Instead, it is the combination of multiple small failures in multiple layers of activity, each alone not enough to cause harm, that can result in a medical accident. Only in the relatively rare situation when all the holes line up do we risk a medical accident. Importantly, the holes and barriers are dynamic, making any single static action insufficient to ensure permanent safety in the delivery system.

Assume we have a drug dispensing error as a triggering event. The physician, the first possible defense barrier and activity level, is distracted due to latent system weaknesses: too many patients secondary to coverage requirements in his group, a misplaced paper chart due to outdated storage methods, and other elements beyond his control. These holes allow the error to penetrate this level of activity to the next. The physician writes an order that constitutes an overdose.

A possible second defense barrier/activity level is a drug tracking program using a computer physician order entry system with pharmacist cross checks. The program is not in place due to resource constraints, the staff's unfamiliarity with the technology, reduction in pharmacy coverage by the hospital, and other factors. So the error slips by this second possible barrier to harm.

Finally, the third defense barrier/activity level is the nurse, who is covering 30 patients, doing a double shift, exhausted due to mandatory overtime, and unfamiliar with the medication since she was pulled to this unit to fulfill staffing requirements and has had little time for effective orientation. The overdose error gets past this barrier as well—and onto the patient.

Of course, one other aspect of this situation bears noting. If the patient (or a patient advocate) were considered part of the team, informed as to relevant treatment, side effects, and provided an explanation of care, he could participate in the system and act in concert with providers. Indeed, the patient is the last barrier to harm. But without inclusion, the error reaches the patient, leading to harm.

Open and transparent communication of system weaknesses at all activity levels could make obvious where we need to change our delivery systems. Physician, pharmacist, nursing, and/or patient reports of system weakness and analysis would have allowed blunt end, administrative changes that could have firmed up the foundation and closed holes at the sharp end, providing useful intelligence to make sharp end activity more safe, effective, and efficient. As well, errors that were caught, reported, and communicated could have served the same purpose without any medical accident required. This also indicates another important lesson: just because an injury does *not* occur does not mean the system is safe.

C. A Few Consequences

Some important conclusions about complex system function bear noting. First, the last person to touch the patient cannot take all credit, nor all blame, for any medical accident, since she does not represent the entire pyramid or all the Swiss cheese. Second, the occurrence of an error does not mean that person is uncaring, lacks compassion, or is unethical. Instead, she is placed in a position where error can occur, which has as its basis a much deeper set of relationships and causes. Finally, if a last layer of defense does block the error from reaching the patient, it is a success. These "last layer success stories" should be celebrated, disseminated, and used for internal learning to improve the processes of care.

Well-functioning systems need front line, sharp end providers to report to blunt end designers and decision makers where the weaknesses and holes are, and how they can be addressed. Those on the blunt end do not work on the sharp end, so they require feedback on the results blunt end actions create at the sharp end, and, more practically, what approaches will be effective there. In addition, sharp end reports will also provide intelligence as to where the institutional latent weaknesses reside, and how best to fill them by those in the position to do so. A system that values and encourages the staff nurse to report safety hazards will reap the rewards.

3.3 Lawsuits and Legal Discovery

A primary issue of concern to providers, and one of the most formidable barriers to patient safety work, is use of patient safety information to support lawsuits. Providers may not report information that may assist in avoiding patient injury if they believe such reports will be used against them in a patient injury lawsuit. This information is generally obtained through legal discovery.

The Federal Rules of Civil Procedure, which have been adopted by most state court systems where patient injury suits are usually tried, allow for discovery of almost all information not protected by some legal privilege. Even inadmissible trial information is discoverable as long as it is "reasonably calculated" to lead to discovery of some information that would be admissible at trial.[19-22] The U.S. Supreme Court has created rules that also mandate automatic production of "all documents, data compilations, and tangible things in the possession, custody, or control of the party that are relevant to the disputed facts," and holding that excluding evidence by legal privilege is discouraged.[23-25] This general situation indicates the importance of possible protections represented by legal privilege.

3.4 Legal Privilege

TIP: The major legal privileges considered "protective" include the state peer review/quality assurance (PR/QA) privilege and the attorney-client privilege.[26]

A. PR/QA Privilege

PR/QA privilege purportedly protects PR/QA committee quality reviews of provider activities from legal discovery. The theory rests upon the ideal that full and candid assessments of clinical activities is made best in open, nonthreatening, cooperative environments where discussions are kept confidential.[27] However, state-based PR statutes are quite variable in their coverage, with some having extensive coverage while others are much more limited. PR/QA privilege coverage is also subject to differing interpretation by multiple courts across states, which makes predictability of coverage uncertain. It also bears noting that there has been a significant trend of narrowing privilege "in favor of full disclosure of relevant facts."[28]

TIP: As applied to patient safety, medical error and safety materials may not be protected by PR/QA privilege.[29]

First, although PR/QA statutes may protect some information generated by a PR/QA committee, they generally do not extend to information from an original source. In other words, one cannot simply present the information to a PR/QA committee to protect it from discovery. Second, broad PR/QA laws often do not protect "administrative information":

- incident/occurrence reports;
- investigation reports;
- documents in the possession of and information known to the hospital's board and CEO;
- information originating outside the PR process;
- personnel, administrative, and other hospital records;
- PR/QA proceeding effects;
- PR/QA information from other sources; documents created for legal opinions and/or weighing liability risks;
- documents instituting corrective action; and,
- most broadly, any information created in the normal course of business.[30-32]

PR/QA privilege also generally does not extend to non-healthcare entity information; for example, a third party consulting firm brought in to collect data on error and assist in systems analysis and corrective action.

Importantly, on the basis of the vagaries of state-federal jurisprudence, PR/QA privilege does not apply if a federal claim is attached to the medical liability claim and the federal court exercises supplemental jurisdiction over it. Because of its state law basis, PR/QA privilege is only applicable in

federal court if the federal court chooses to adopt it. However, due to the U.S. Supreme Court's perspective on limiting exclusionary privileges, federal courts have rejected privilege claims based on state law.[33,34] This conflict of PR/QA privilege at the state and federal level makes it exceedingly difficult for health care organizations to exchange relevant patient safety information for purposes of quality and safety improvement.[35] Exacerbating this situation, PR/QA privilege does not apply to institutional review board (IRB) information provided under federal law, criminal cases, nor to information disclosed to an investigating state provider board.[36]

In addition, it appears that sensitive error and safety information may still be obtained through the general subpoena and testimony process. Although some, but not all, state peer review laws protect various participants from being called to testify, that protection is not extended to non-members of the PR/QA committee.[37] This is particularly important for safety activities due to the large number of persons whose input is needed to perform an adequate systems analysis of error through a root cause analysis or other similar activity. Therefore, anyone can be called to testify in a lawsuit, including nurses as well as technicians, laboratory personnel, physicians, board members, and administrative staff, if they were present at the time of an error, or have relevant information about an error, and/or participated in its analysis outside the PR/QA committee forum. In fact, some courts reject plaintiff requests to break the PR/QA privilege because the same information may be elicited by the standard subpoena and testimony mechanisms.[38]

B. Attorney-Client Privilege

The rationale for attorney-client privilege is similar to PR/QA privilege. Attorney-client privilege exists to provide clients written confidential venue so they may communicate all relevant information to their attorney to permit the attorney to most effectively protect that client's rights.[39] However, like PR/QA privilege, there are significant weaknesses in relying on this privilege to protect patient safety information.

TIP: Error and safety information must often be disclosed to third parties, such as the state department of health under adverse event reporting statutes or The Joint Commission (TJC) under its sentinel event policy (discussed in Section 3.5.B in this chapter).

However, because this information has gone beyond the attorney and client, the privilege may be waived and the information deemed discoverable because it has been disclosed to parties not contemplated by the privilege.[40]

Error and safety information may be used by a wide array of personnel if a patient injury has occurred. For example, when a wrong-sided surgery occurs, members of the system—the nurses, hospital, physicians, administration, and others—participate in reporting and analyzing the event from their diverse perspectives to understand its root causes and approaches for corrective action. When there is a patient injury conflict, any of these parties may wish to introduce information gleaned from this error reporting and analysis to support their defense or perspective, perhaps indicating the systems involved and the identified factors leading to corrective action. This might occur in a patient injury lawsuit or in a professional board hearing. Hence, the error and safety information has gone beyond any client and attorney for the purpose of communication to protect the client's legal rights. In fact, if information regarding an error and safety analysis is discussed for any reason *other than* in preparation for litigation—e.g., to improve safety—the privilege is lost because it has gone beyond what is traditionally within the rationale of the privilege.[41,42]

3.5 Laws and Risks
A. State Adverse Event Reporting Statutes

Approximately half the states require adverse patient care events to be reported to a state agency, usually the department of health or a facility therein under quality of care regulations.[43,44] Three major legal risks are associated with reporting under state adverse event reporting statutes that may allow its use for sanction and/or to support lawsuits rather than being limited to intended safety purposes.

First, information submitted under state adverse event reporting laws may be used by the state agency or department to sanction the provider, usually for poor quality of care.[45] Indeed, such information may be disclosed to the public, depending on the specific provisions of the state statute.[46] Second, this information may be subject to legal discovery in a patient injury lawsuit. Because any documents relating to an error and adverse event that occurred can be "reasonably calculated" to lead to admissible information, the information provided under state adverse event reporting statutes may be at high risk for inappropriate disclosure and use for non-safety promotion purposes. Third, beyond issues of legal discovery, it is important to note that information and documents submitted under the state's adverse event reporting statutes may be accessible under the state's Freedom of Information Act. Unless protected by some legal privilege, reports of adverse event information to a state agency are akin to provision of this information to the public. As such, it may be accessible by members of the public through a Freedom of Information Act request to the state agency or department.

Standard legal privileges do not appear to be helpful in protecting safety information.

- Adverse event information submitted under state adverse event reporting statutes is reasonably considered administrative information, and is not therefore covered as peer review committee deliberations.
- Safety information may not be considered within peer review privilege if others external to the facility, such as a department of health, are involved in reporting, analyzing, and creating and implementing corrective action.
- Adverse event information for safety analysis may be submitted to or shared with—not created by—the PR/QA committee, and thus be considered outside any privilege for peer review committee deliberations.
- Safety reports under state mandating reporting are created in the normal course of business due to the state's reporting mandate; information collected and created in the normal course of business is not traditionally protected by peer review laws.
- Safety information and analysis may be used by codefendants in court or in front of professional boards for their defense; and in particular, may be discussed in any manner other than in preparation for litigation—for patient safety and error reduction purposes. Thus, attorney-client privilege is limited in protecting this information from use in non-safety sanction and suit circumstances.

B. The Joint Commission Reporting Requirements

Federal law requires that providers, such as hospitals, fulfill legal requirements known as Medicare Conditions of Participation if they wish to serve Medicare beneficiaries. Although other mechanisms are available, The Joint Commission (TJC) accreditation is "deemed" by state and federal governments to fulfill these requirements.[47] Thus, a vast majority of hospitals in the U.S. seek TJC accreditation and must fulfill TJC requirements in order to serve patients in the U.S. In fact, the TJC estimates that approximately 81 percent of U.S. hospitals are currently accredited.[48] One key policy relating to patient safety is the Sentinel Event Policy (SEP).

TJC implemented the SEP in 1996[49]; there have been more than 6,000 Sentinel Events reviewed by TJC since then.[50] The SEP requires[51] that certain adverse or "sentinel" events be reported to TJC, that the hospital perform a self-critical, systems and process-based root cause analysis (RCA) of these adverse events, and the facility develop a corrective action plan in response to this analysis designed to implement improvements to reduce risk, and monitor the effectiveness of such improvements. The hospital must submit this information to TJC for its review and approval. As might be imagined, the self-critical nature of the analysis makes this document and supporting materials very sensitive and damaging to the provider if inappropriately disclosed.

The SEP defines a sentinel event as "an unexpected occurrence involving death or serious physical or psychological injury, or the risk thereof," including, but not limited to:

- unanticipated death or major permanent loss of function unrelated to the patient's condition;
- patient suicide;
- unanticipated death of a full-term infant;
- wrong-sided or wrong body part surgery;
- patient abduction/discharge of infant to the wrong family;
- unintended retention of a foreign object after surgery or other procedure;
- severe neonatal hyperbilirubinemia;
- prolonged fluoroscopy with cumulative dose;
- rape; and
- hemolytic transfusion reactions involving major blood histocompatibility groups.[52]

However, in contrast to established error reporting systems such as the Aviation Safety Reporting System (ASRS),[53,54] the SEP excludes "near miss" reporting—reporting events that would have progressed to patient injury had there not been a last layer of protection that fortuitously stopped the accident chain from reaching the patient. This may result in significant loss of system learning opportunities.[55] Near misses have a higher frequency than actual adverse events, and they are available for use for both systems analysis that identifies failure holes as well as success strategies, since the circumstance did not proceed to a medical accident. There is much greater willingness of system members to participate in reporting, analysis, and corrective action, due to lack of any patient injury.[56] Evidence of organizational responses to sentinel events is evaluated by TJC as part of the accreditation requirements.[57,58] Hence, SEP activities, though labeled as "self-reporting," are compelled if a provider desires to maintain TJC accreditation.[59] Though TJC can become aware of a sentinel event through means other than a provider's self reporting, such as reporting by a third party or through a TJC surveyor, there are distinct disadvantages to failing to self-report.[60]

TIP: Under the SEP, the RCA is a detailed qualitative systems assessment by members of the health delivery system that reviews the entity's performance pathway that led to the sentinel event; an "action plan" addressing identified problems is the ultimate goal. The resulting action plan identifies strategies the provider will implement risk-reducing measures for similar adverse events including timelines to implementation, oversight, and measuring of effectiveness.

The RCA and action plan must be submitted to TJC within 45 days of event occurrence or organization or TJC learning of the event. If the adverse event report is not made to TJC, or the root cause analysis is not considered acceptable to TJC, its accreditation decision will automatically be changed to either Provisional Accreditation, Conditional Accreditation, or be recommended for a Denial of Accreditation depending on the time frame and status of the response. In the event that a provider fails to submit an RCA within 90 days of its due date, TJC's decision to recommend for a Denial of Accreditation is unappealable.

If the provider does not report the event and TJC discovers it (e.g., via the media, provider employees, patient, patient family, or through survey), the entity will be contacted and must submit an RCA under the same 45 day schedule. If a determination that the event is reviewable under the SEP is made more than 45 days after the event has occurred, the organization will have only 15 days to provide its response. Ultimately, if the provider does not fulfill this timeline, TJC may revoke the provider's accreditation.[61] Importantly, if TJC deems the reported or discovered event a continuous threat to patient safety that represents significant noncompliance with a TJC standard, it can immediately instigate an on-site sentinel event review and assessment.

Legal risks for inappropriate disclosure of SEP information are significant under the SEP, both due to the TJC's information policies itself as well as legal rules that may not protect this safety information. Indeed, the American Society for Healthcare Risk Management characterized SEP-mandated materials a "lawsuit kit for attorneys."[62] Further, significant negative effects on the provider's reputation can accrue under the SEP. TJC may unilaterally disclose to third parties upon request, including the lay press, that the reporting entity is under sentinel event review.[63] Though TJC's Public Information Policy classifies a provider's RCA and action plan as confidential, these SEP reports may be subject to compelled disclosure or other means of discovery as discussed below.[64]

The critical risk for the provider is legal discovery of sensitive SEP materials, beyond the rather unrealistic timetable for sentinel event reporting and analysis. TJC expects providers to send the RCA and action plan to TJC electronically using an online RCA collection tool which includes certain waivers of confidentiality protections.[65] However, because of provider resistance to this default due to legal concerns for inappropriate use and disclosure of the materials, TJC promulgated four alternatives:[66]

- Alternative 1 allows an entity employee to hand deliver the RCA to TJC, where it will be reviewed and returned on the same day.
- Alternative 2 allows a TJC surveyor to come to the facility and conduct an on-site RCA review.
- Alternative 3 allows the entity to have a TJC surveyor conduct an on-site RCA review without viewing the RCA documents; the surveyor conducts interviews and reviews "relevant documentation," which include selected policies and publications relevant to the organization's process for responding to sentinel events, and the action plan resulting from the analysis of the subject sentinel event.
- Alternative 4, which attempts to address legal discovery directly, allows a TJC surveyor to conduct an on-site review through interviews and review of relevant documentation. No surveyor reference to the RCA or action plan is made, and the focus is on review of the entity's analysis process. Alternative 4 is only available if the entity's CEO affirms that she has considered relevant statutes and case law, considered alternatives 1-3 above, and that the provider has completed a thorough RCA for the subject sentinel event.[67]

TIP: All alternatives require at least five business days prior notice to TJC, and all associated TJC costs are the entity's responsibility.[68]

To make matters clear about the SEP, TJC provides for stages of response and review of SEP documents for a reportable event. If after a fourth submission the SEP documents continue to not meet the established criteria, the Accreditation Committee will be requested to issue a decision of Preliminary Denial of Accreditation, which will result in eventual loss of accreditation.[69] This policy may include provider refusals to furnish what they consider to be inapplicable materials to TJC. Maintaining accreditation after SEP documents have been accepted is contingent upon a provider meeting certain follow-up activity measurements of success (MOS) conducted by TJC to ensure that an action plan was effective and sustained.[70]

TIP: In terms of discovery and PR/QA privilege, it is important to recognize that SEP materials, like state reported adverse event materials, may be considered administrative information, nonhospital information, information merely submitted to or shared with PR/QA committees rather than being generated by them, and certainly information collected in the normal course of business. Therefore the PR/QA privilege against discovery may be ineffective in protecting SEP information, TJC claims notwithstanding.[71,72]

With respect to attorney-client privilege, SEP materials may be shared with third parties—TJC and possibly the state under state adverse event reporting statutes. Additionally, the materials may be used by defendants at trial or at professional board hearings in support of their defense in a patient injury suit or disciplinary hearing, and certainly they are discussed in a manner other than in preparation for litigation—for safety and error reduction. Hence, attorney-client privilege will likely have limited application for information created under the SEP.

Finally, SEP alternatives address neither the standard subpoena and testimony access to the SEP information nor how these alternatives protect against discovery in federal court. Indeed, discussion of SEP data, analysis, and information with TJC—a third party not contemplated by any privilege—could waive any privilege extant before the information is supplied to TJC.[73]

C. TJC Standard RI.2.90

Beginning with the 2001 standards, TJC created another medical error mandate that may subject providers to legal risk under hospital accreditation standard RI.2.90: "Patients and, when appropriate, their families are informed about the outcomes of care, including unanticipated outcomes."[74]

The standard has been interpreted to require providers to "tell patients when they received substandard care."[75] Providers have understandably been concerned about provider liability under this standard and its unworkability. For example, substantively, every admission has unanticipated outcomes, and the standard has the potential for creating awkwardness between hospitals and medical providers. Because the disclosure of all "unanticipated outcomes" by any provider may be required, medical activities may be viewed under tremendous scrutiny by hospitals attempting to fulfill this TJC rule. Similarly, hospital-based workers such as nurses may be directed by administrators and be obligated to point to errors there to avoid sanction and suit. Unfortunately, this TJC standard may foster "shame and blame" oriented approaches that are antithetical to open, honest, nonthreatening and cooperative environments between providers, essential for effective communication, error reduction, and safety promotion. It thus may create conflicts between providers that may chill cooperation and analysis within these delivery systems. Refer to Chapter 4, *Patient Safety Initiatives*, for more information on TJC, and to Chapter 5, *Medical Errors: Roots of Litigation*, for a perspective on disclosure of errors.

3.6 Other Considerations
A. Liability Insurance

One practical concern relating to discovery and privilege may also substantially chill error reporting and assessment: the vagaries of medical liability insurance. Generally, within these policies, there is a standard clause requiring the covered entity to immediately report the event to it and make no statements or take no actions that would impede the insurer from defending the claim.[76]

However, in any thorough systems analysis, healthcare analysis teams will obtain a report, act to interview relevant parties, perform rigorous analysis to assess the root and system causes of the error, design corrective action strategies to ensure an error's incidence is minimized and/or system resilience improved, and assess if new interventions have created any additional sources of error.[77-80] These appropriate actions may delay reporting to an insurer, and, perhaps more critically with respect to potential breach of a liability insurance contract, create a discoverable, highly sensitive self-analysis. If this information is in fact deemed discoverable, the entity can certainly be seen to have made statements and taken actions that would hinder the insurer from defending the claim. Hence, although a medical error may result in a lawsuit, professional board hearings, and accreditation difficulties, participation in error reduction and system improvement efforts may subject entities to lawsuits without liability insurance coverage.[81,82]

In fact, both medical liability insurers and states have moved in the opposite direction to establish full disclosure and early offers of compensation programs in the event of medical error.[83] These programs aim to provide disclosure and explanation of medical errors to patients and what constitutes an "apology" in order to reduce litigation costs. In conjunction with these efforts, approximately 30 states have enacted apology laws protecting voluntary disclosures.[84]

B. Federal Freedom of Information Act

In addition to potential disclosure of safety information under state Freedom of Information Acts, information may also be disclosed via the federal Freedom of Information Act (FOIA).[85] Federal regulation related to hospitals that are TJC accredited require that hospitals permit TJC to release, to both the state and to the Centers for Medicare and Medicaid Services (CMS), a copy of the most current accreditation survey. This release could include anything related to the survey, including, potentially, SEP or safety information. Hence, through this process, patient safety and medical error information in CMS's hands may be amenable to a FOIA request similar to the state level adverse event reporting mechanisms. Even if a particular state's PR/QA privilege governs and a court rules in favor of protection, it is feasible that a plaintiff could still obtain the RCA and related information through the FOIA-CMS mechanism.[86,87] It should be noted that although there are government exemptions to FOIA requests,[88] exemptions are generally construed quite narrowly,[89] and have been largely unsuccessful when based on peer review status.[90]

3.7 The Patient Safety and Quality Improvement Act
A. An Overview of the Act

As noted above, patient safety activities have been limited by risks associated with the legal system. Assessment and discussion of medical errors, system weaknesses, as well as proactive efforts to promote safety can and are subject to legal discovery by attorneys to support lawsuits, and potentially used against providers in professional board hearings. This situation chills work in this area.

However, in an effort to address this issue, the Patient Safety and Quality Improvement Act of 2005 was signed into law on July 29, 2005 and became effective in January 2009.[91,92] Under this law, both individual and organizational providers can voluntarily report, share, discuss, and formulate information on medical errors and patient safety across facilities and locales of practice. The information provides federal confidentiality and privilege protections, and cannot be used to support non-intended uses of the information, including lawsuits and professional disciplinary hearings. The Act amends Title IX of the Public Health Service Act[93] to protect a provider's "patient safety work product."[94] Patient safety work product is data, reports, records, and other materials (e.g., root cause analyses), and analyses in any form assembled in a provider's "patient safety evaluation system"—a provider's system created to promote quality and safety in health care delivery.

To obtain the statute's legal protections, a provider must use information from its patient safety evaluation system and work with a "Patient Safety Organization" (PSO). A PSO is an entity that can provide analysis and feedback as to best practices, improvements in care, and other activities that promote quality and safety in health care and that meets the requirements and certifications necessary in accordance with the Act.[95] The Agency for Healthcare Research and Quality (AHRQ) of the Department of Health and Human Services (DHHS) will oversee the certification and listing of PSOs. As of the beginning of 2010, 79 PSOs were listed with the AHRQ.[96]

The statute prohibits any patient safety work product from being disclosed or used in any administrative, civil, or criminal proceedings.[97] The law also exempts the work product from all state or federal Freedom of Information Act requests.[98] Hence, the law's reach is very broad and provides extensive protection for safety and quality data, yielding significant opportunities to participate in patient safety improvement and promotion removing many of the legal barriers extant before its enactment.

In addition, the AHRQ will administer a Network of Patient Safety Databases (NPSD) that will provide a interactive, evidence-based resources by analyzing and reporting on aggregated and de-identified patient safety data provided by providers, PSOs and other entities. The NPSD will collect this de-identified patient safety work product for the purposes of providing meaningful analysis and safety event information with the goal of reducing adverse events and improving quality of healthcare.[99] This data will be made available to the public in hard copy and on the AHRQ's website on an annual basis.[100]

A recent report by the Government Accountability Office of the DHHS found that AHRQ is still in the preliminary stages of implementing the Patient Safety Act and that few of the listed PSOs have begun to collect patient safety data from providers.[101] It is anticipated that the NPSD may be operational and available to receive patient safety data from hospitals in early 2011.[102]

B. Exceptions

There are some limitations to the Act's scope of material protection. First, standard discoverable materials such as the patient's chart, billing records and discharge information, any other original patient or provider record, or any information existing separately from the patient safety evaluation system are not considered patient safety work product.[103] In addition, separately collected or maintained information cannot be made into patient safety work product merely by submitting it to a PSO.[104]

There are also some exceptions to the privilege and confidentiality provision of the law. However, they are circumscribed. For example, disclosure of patient safety work product for use in criminal proceedings is permitted. But to do so, a court must make an *in camera* (i.e., judge made) determination that: the work product contains evidence of a

criminal act; that it is material; *and* it is not reasonably available from any other source.[105]

Disclosure of previously privileged and confidential patient safety work product can occur if authorized for disclosure by all providers identified in the work product materials.[106] De-identified patient safety work product disclosure is allowed, as is work product disclosed for FDA-governed products and activities.[107]

In an important recognition of the risks associated with accreditation bodies, the statute allows voluntary disclosure to a provider's accrediting body.[108] However, due to the punitive nature of some accreditors that may use patient safety work product to sanction providers, the Act specifically states that providers cannot be forced by an accreditor to reveal its communications with any PSOs; further, accreditors cannot take accreditation action against a provider on the basis of provider collection, development, reporting, or maintenance of patient safety work product.[109]

Importantly, in contrast to state peer review privilege, which usually bases material protection upon discussion or presence of materials within a specific committee, the federal law's protections of the safety materials travels with the materials themselves.[110] Hence, protections still apply when patient safety work product is transferred to another party, discussed with others, or disseminated for broader learning and benefit. This is a critical provision of the Act because, as noted above, disclosure of privileged information, such as peer review information, to third parties often vitiated any privilege that protected materials might have had before disclosure. This prevented information from being disseminated or discussed by a broad array of providers within and outside an institution.

Finally, the Act does not affect state laws requiring provider reports on non-patient safety work product.[111] This would include, for example, state-mandated nosocomial infection reports, or mandated FDA reports.

C. Penalties

There are penalties for violating the privilege and confidentiality provisions. For reckless or knowing disclosure of patient safety work product, penalties include civil monetary penalties of up to $11,000 per violation.[112] The statute also protects good faith reporters of safety information against wrongful adverse employment actions. If an employer retaliates against persons who report safety information either to the provider or a PSO, these affected persons can bring an equitable civil suit against the provider. This includes orders to stop providers from acting wrongfully against reporters, employment reinstatement, back pay, and benefit restoration.[113]

D. HIPAA and PSOs

The Health Insurance Portability and Accountability Act (HIPAA) medical privacy provisions are specifically addressed by the Act. PSOs are to be treated as provider business associates, and PSO patient safety activities are to be considered "healthcare operations" of the provider.[114] Hence, under the regulations of the HIPAA privacy rule, authorization from individual patients is not required for provider patient safety activities. Compliance with the confidentiality and privilege provisions of the Act will be enforced by the Office for Civil Rights (OCR) of the DHHS.

3.8 Some Tools to Promote Patient Safety

A. Checklists

One of the most difficult aspects of dealing with a high stress environment is staying focused. Aviation recognized long ago that human memories fail under stress, often without the individual realizing it.[115] Consequently, aviation largely eliminated reliance upon human memory. When one boards an aircraft, note what the pilot, co-pilot, maintenance crew, and stewards are all doing: they are using checklists for pre-flight safety assessments. Further, note also that passengers also participate in the checklists on flights: virtually every passenger knows about seatbelt operation, oxygen, and life vest operation as well as what to do in an emergency, and where all of this information is located (on the information card in the seat pocket in front of us). Unfortunately, in health care, memorization has been relied upon improperly for the delivery of care, and results in error and potential patient injury.

Instead, to reduce the chance of error and injury, a piece of paper is a simple and effective tool method for having information always available, consistent, and accurate. Because human beings skip steps under stress, well-formed checklists not only serve as reminders of appropriate and necessary actions, they are extremely helpful in ensuring that the provider stays focused and provides high quality, efficient, and effective care for each and every encounter/procedure.

Further, another benefit is that the creation and consistent improvement of checklists also provides an opportunity for reflection about organizing and streamlining a provider's routine. This ensures that appropriate actions, procedures, notice, and follow-up are performed effectively for patient care as well as non-patient care activities. Hence, checklists promote not only consistent clinical performance but also can encompass broader systems issues (e.g., notation into chart and computer flagging for patient notification of results).

The preoperative checklist is a universally used checklist that ensures that all necessary steps have been followed before surgery. The preoperative checklist is successfully used by nurses to work through a series of specific items. Items on the checklist cover completion of history and physical and required diagnostic testing preparation of the patient; preoperative medicine, removal of jewelry, voiding, nothing to eat or drink after midnight, and so on. Studies have shown that checklists are extremely effective at increasing favorable outcomes for patients as well as reducing surgical mortality and morbidity, especially in high-pressure situations such as intensive care units and trauma patient care as well as increasing safety during hospital discharge or transfer of patients.[116-118] Many facilities are now using a checklist to ensure that the correct surgery site has been identified.

However, it should be noted that while checklists are an important tool in improving patient safety, they need to be complemented with evidenced-based data supporting the checklist items, may not be effective in situations which require non-standardized behavior or decision-making, and must be implemented in a safety culture environment.[119]

B. Standardization

Similar to checklists, standardization is an important tool in improving safety and preventing injury. Again, using aviation, passengers are fully aware of the aircraft emergency procedures due to the standardized briefings provided each time we board an aircraft.

Standardization in organization also assists us in processes of care. Consider the time that could be saved searching for "lost" supplies, if each examination room, crash cart, or supply closet were organized in the same way, with clear labels and a checklist for contents.

Moreover, procedure standardization provides us with a "cultural baseline," that is, an environmental gestalt that gives us warning or notice when something is done differently—we recognize or feel unease when the routine is interrupted. For example, nurses are taught to initial that a medication has been given after it is administered, not before. An interruption during the medication administration process disrupts the flow of the procedure. Use of standardized methods of giving medications permits the nurse to accurately resume. Hence, performing activities in a standardized way helps identify when something is performed in a *non*-standard way. Thus, standardization provides transparency and gives providers an opportunity to reevaluate and intercept errors that may lead to patient injury.

Finally, standardization helps ensure that we perform correctly in high stress situations, providing a means to address the faulty human memory. If providers have done the same action in the same way a thousand times, we will be less likely to skip a vital step. Flagging the chart the same way every time helps us ensure that nothing is left out, even if we are interrupted or distracted.

C. Redundancy

Redundancy encompasses several related considerations. First, personnel or human redundancy that double check vital procedures and processes is an important barrier to error and its untoward effects. By having two or more persons reviewing key/important actions, there is a reduced likelihood that such a key or important action is missed or performed incorrectly. An aviation example of safety redundancy is when two pilots check that the landing gear is down and locked on runway approach; similarly, in medicine, when two nurses check that blood to be infused is appropriate for a particular patient is also an example of safety redundancy.

Redundancy also is represented by the use of backup systems. When one system fails, another that is functionally redundant can provide a barrier to harm. A typical example here would be equipment driven by separate power sources in case one fails—virtually every aviation flight data instrument has power redundancy. In medicine, an electrically driven infusion pump with battery backup is a common example of power redundancy, or emergency hospital generators that exist to power equipment in the event of large scale power loss or natural disaster is another.

D. Designing Out the Problem

Since humans inevitably err, designing a system to literally eliminate the possibility of error is extremely useful in ensuring safety. For example, in more mundane situations, newer automobiles automatically turn the lights on and off for us, prevent us from removing the key if the car is in gear, and will not allow us to lock the car with the key in the ignition.

In medicine, this approach is also available. For example, concentrated potassium chloride (KCl) can kill patients if mistakenly infused. This was (and, unfortunately, still is in some places) a common problem in hospitals. The solution that designed out the problem is to eliminate it in the supply closet or on the crash cart and from the hospital generally; then no one can ever make the error.

Another example relates to the hook up for anesthetic gases. The nurse anesthetist cannot physically hookup a line to the wrong type of gas. The couplings are designed to work with only one type of gas.

Of course, sometimes complete design-out is impossible. However, close approximations can be almost as effective. For example, there are instances where a note is erroneously written in the wrong patient's chart. Sometimes, in the outpatient setting, this is due to a policy of having all charts for patients that will be seen that day (or morning, or afternoon) placed in the examination room. A simple solution is to have only one patient chart in the room at a time, a redundancy check by the nurse, nurse practitioner, and/or physician, and an "exit" check by the person who replaces the chart into the files. A similar system can easily be adopted when practices use an electronic medical record.

E. Self-Checks

Because the human is the weak point in any complex system, and the breadth of performance is influenced by many human factors, humans should take into account their condition each day and before each activity to identify potential sources of error. A standard self-checklist that aviation pilots use is the I'M SAFE checklist.

This checklist can be adapted to health care. One should ask oneself:

I   Illness: am I/will I be less effective due to illness?

M   Medications: am I impaired or less effective due to medications?

S   Stress: is there undue stress that will affect my performance and capabilities?

A   Alcohol/other drugs: am I impaired due to alcohol and/or other drugs (the aviation regulatory standard is a minimum of eight hours "bottle to throttle," with many pilots adopting a 12 hour standard)?

F   Fatigue/food: have I had appropriate rest to perform competently? Have I had appropriate meals and food to perform competently?

E   Emotion: am I emotionally stable to perform well? Does this patient/situation/day create any emotional concerns that may distract me in my care delivery efforts?

Each person working in the health delivery environment should ask himself these questions at least once before the day starts. Preferably, providers should reassess themselves periodically throughout the day. Posting this checklist at each workstation and giving workers copies on an easily accessible card or notepad can reinforce the need to consistently evaluate one's own human factors. This will lead to a regular assessment and situational awareness that could influence performance, error occurrence, and error mitigation of and by the worker.

F. Last Layer Success Stories

Last layer success stories (LLSSs) are often known as near misses. LLSSs should be an important component for system learning and improving safety. LLSSs illustrate how a system worked successfully to avoid an accident and harm to the patient. They also provide an opportunity to improve system function by identifying activity level holes that can be filled so that the system can perform even better. Industrial research has shown that using success stories is a much better means to improve operational safety and efficiency than stories of failure. Hence, LLSS discussions should be an important and consistent tool used to enhance safety systems. For example, a nursing student observes that a patient named Smythe in the same room as a patient named Smith is getting what may be the wrong drug due to confusion of the correct patient. The nursing student then questions the order and checks the chart to find that indeed, due to name confusion, the drug was almost administered to the wrong patient. This LLSS shows the importance of the nursing student team member as a redundancy for safety, and allows reflection and review of the system to put changes into place to minimize the potential for such an error and potential medication accident to happen again.

G. Patient Briefing

Although providers often focus upon themselves as safety guardians in health care delivery, the patient himself is the last layer of defense against potential harm when error penetrates all previous safety barriers and delivery activity layers. Hence, like aircraft passengers, patients should be briefed on their role as a member of the health care team, and what to expect in their care. Individuals are better participants in virtually any complex endeavor when given an overview of what is expected, their well-defined role in that activity, and when they are encouraged to participate. Of course, any patient participation must be sensitive to reality; some patients are debilitated, and others prefer a passive role. However, engaging the patient by communicating that their help and input is desired can instill trust and improve the therapeutic relationship, whatever the participation level.

During the patient briefing, patients should be informed that if an error does occur, they will be informed of it. Disclosure to patients of medical errors and adverse events is becoming more accepted as a practice by physicians and providers beyond accreditation and legal mandates. It calls for disclosure, explanation of why an error occurred, how the provider will minimize the effects of an error, and the steps a provider will take to prevent reoccurrence.[120] Though the effectiveness of disclosure on provider liability is unclear,[121] it is evident that health care practitioners need more training on how to discuss and brief patients about errors and adverse events as they arise. Such disclosure is an important adjunct to a patient briefing, because it is also an opportunity to solicit information on system safety that otherwise would not arise, and respects the patient as a member of the health care team.

H. Communication

Effective communication amongst members of the health care delivery team—including patients—is the foundation of any successful safety system and its improvement. To be effective, communication must be honest, open, and mutually respectful.[122] In fact, communication breakdowns have been cited as the root cause for almost all sentinel events reviewed by TJC and have also been reported as the leading cause of preventable error in certain medical malpractice claims.[123,124]

Specific to the relationship between nurses and physicians, communication barriers such as lack of communication structure and policies, differing rules for verbal transmission of information, differing opinions of what information should be reported, and disruptions caused by interruptions and distractions, can lead to breakdown of team collaboration.[125] Improving communication goes hand in hand with promoting teamwork with efforts towards implementing team training, eliminating hierarchy, delineating roles and responsibilities, and enforcing a zero-tolerance approach towards disruptive behavior as key to fostering an environment focused on safety and quality of care.[126] Using these techniques, providers can create a lower stress workplace while flattening hierarchy and encouraging more effective collaboration between team members.[127]

Effective communication is also essential in ensuring effective transitions of care with improvement of communication between caregivers and implementing standardized approaches to handoff communications required by TJC as part of its National Patient Safety Goals.[128,129] The importance of establishing safe care transitions is growing more important as health systems shift to more outpatient and ambulatory settings and as handoff in the inpatient setting gets more complicated.[130] Patients in periods of transition such as admission, hospitalization and discharge, are especially susceptible to medical errors. Through standardizing approaches to handoff communication, ensuring communication of up-to-date information, and using the situation briefing model (Situation, Background, Assessment, Recommendation [SBAR]) to structure and increase efficiency of communication, staff can improve patient outcomes, reduce medical errors and satisfy TJC accreditation requirements.[131-133]

In addition, two critical concepts require attention when considering effective communication. The first concept is "no ego." What this means is that communications have to be openly accepted from anyone and everyone in the practice environment, *no matter who they might be*. Everyone must feel empowered to point out an actual or potential weakness, and everyone's input must be valued and welcomed. No one should be derided or shamed for discussing the delivery system, and no one should take offense.

The second concept is "staying on your side of the net." In other words, discussing system weakness when it involves human action must be phrased objectively. As we all know, often it is not *what* is said, but *how* it is said that determines interpretation (or someone taking offense). Hence, when discussing humans in a system, one should not use names or finger point, and instead simply describe effects. For example, "Dr. Smith is always bothering me when I'm trying to give meds" is not objective nor does it describe effects. This is the "why you make things bad for me" approach, which immediately results in conflict. Instead, objective description would be preferable, for example, "While I am giving medications, interruptions can cause me to lose my place and make a mistake." This method provides an objective description of the issue, makes it more amenable to analysis, does not offend or immediately create conflict and personality issues, and is more accurate.

Finally, each person has to include *internal, self-communications* when applying no ego and staying on your side of the net concepts. One has to be honest with oneself (for example, when engaging in the I'M SAFE checklist), and have self-respect when thinking about safety issues.

I. Teamwork Training

Healthcare settings provide for complex, high pressure and high risk environments comprised of technically skilled professionals where safety is paramount. Hence, the complexity of the health care system requires strategies designed to improve effective teamwork and communication between health care professionals with multi-disciplinary backgrounds and varying roles.

Again, the aviation industry provides some important parallels in measuring and improving teamwork based on concepts such as Crew Resource Management (CRM) and establishment of a Safety Culture.[134] CRM in the context of aviation recognizes the limitations of both humans and machines and establishes a management system utilizing all team members to reduce the likelihood of human error.[135] Such approaches have been successfully implemented in aviation and have led to a transformation of the climate and culture of the cockpit by which interpersonal skills have been enhanced along with situational awareness leading to a safer industry. CRM is now mandated by aviation regulatory bodies such as the Federal Aviation Administration.[136]

Teamwork training as adopted in the healthcare setting is defined as a range of approaches to train medical profession-als to function as a team instead of as individuals and focuses on the role of "human factors" such as fatigue, predictable perceptual errors, and the impact of different management styles and organizational cultures.[137] Though there is no one standardized form of CRM for the clinical setting, all teamwork training focuses on minimizing the occurrence of error and training team members to respond appropriately through increasing communication skills, cross-checking of actions of others, and encouraging team members to raise questions without fear of judgment.[138] Four core competencies of CRM include concepts of team leadership, situational monitoring, mutual support and communication.[139] Team leadership focuses on directing and coordinating activities by task assignment; situational monitoring emphasizes common understanding and monitoring of team member performance; mutual support assesses team member performance and makes changes accordingly; and communication encourages open questioning of information that is suspected to be incorrect or unsafe.[140] Implementation of these CRM techniques can lead to a transformation of the teamwork culture and improved patient safety if followed consistently and used in conjunction with staff meetings as described in the next section.

J. Staff Meetings

Integrating safety into the culture of a delivery system can create a safe(r) environment and reduce risk of patient injury. That means that providers in an effective safety culture are always thinking about safety as well as how safety can be improved.

A corollary to this principle is that people in the organization must consistently talk about safety at regular intervals. This allows them to evaluate and improve safety efforts using the tools above, and ones they create.

Staff meetings are a virtually made-to-order opportunity to discuss safety and safety improvement. As part of the delivery culture, when safety becomes part of the staff meeting, it too becomes part of the culture of the delivery system.

Staff meetings are the place where LLSSs should be routinely raised, discussed, and congratulated, with lessons learned and disseminated while making adjustments to further improve system function. Staff meetings are also outstanding opportunities to brainstorm about new methods to close system holes on the sharp end activity layers, such as improving checklists, standardization efforts, and redundancy. The staff meeting can be a positive, creative session for improving safety that recognizes success and uses a team approach to make performance even better. Creating time for staff meetings in a busy nursing unit is a challenge faced by many organizations, yet the results are rewarding.

3.9 Summary

To promote patient safety, one must understand concepts of medical error, systems theory, and the legal issues in performing this important work. However, through understanding these concepts and the legal issues, including the opportunities presented by the Patient Safety and Quality Improvement Act, patient safety and quality improvement is possible. In fact, a recent study reports that hospital staff trained on aviation cockpit safety techniques as one part of their training on safety initiatives, and similar to those described in this chapter, resulted in improvements in staff attitudes towards improving patient safety, "personal empowerment" regarding safety initiatives, increased use of pre-surgery checklists, and an increase in self-reporting of errors.[141] By using some basic tools garnered from the aviation industry, and drawing upon an understanding of human factors, prevention and mitigation of error occurrence can inure to this generation and future generations of patients and providers.

Endnotes

1. Institute of Medicine. *To Err is Human: Building a Safer Health System.* Washington, D.C.: National Academy of Sciences, 1999.

2. Id.

3. UK Department of Health. *An Organization with a Memory: Report of an Expert Group on Learning from Adverse Events in the NHS.* London: NHS, 2000.

4. Tito, F. *Compensation and Professional Indemnity in Health Care: Review of Professional Indemnity Arrangements for Health Care Professionals.* Canberra: Commonwealth Department of Human Service and Health, 1994.

5. Wilson, L.L. "Quality management: Prevention is better than cure." *Australian Clinical Review,* 13, 75-82, 1993.

6. Liang, B.A. "The Adverse Event of Unaddressed Medical Error: Filling the Holes in the Legal and Health-Care Systems." *Journal of Law, Medicine, and Ethics,* 29, 346-368, 2001.

7. Leape, L.L. "Error in Medicine." *Journal of the American Medical Association,* 272, 1851-1857, 1994.

8. Wilson, R.M., W.B. Runciman, R.W. Gibberd, et al. "The quality in Australian health care study." *Medical Journal of Australia,* 163, 458-471, 1995.

9. McDonald, C.F., M. Weiner, S.L. Hui. "Deaths Due to Medical Errors Are Exaggerated in Institute of Medicine Report." *Journal of the American Medical Association,* 284, 93-95, 2000.

10. Leape, L.L. "Institute of Medicine Medical Error Figures Are Not Exaggerated." *Journal of the American Medical Association,* 284, 95-97, 2000.

11. Sox, H.C., S. Woloshin. "How Many Deaths Are Due to Medical Error? Getting the Number Right." *Effective Clinical Practice,* November/December, 2000. Available at http://www.acponline.org/clinical_information/journals_publications/ecp/novdec00/sox.htm (Retrieved February 8, 2010).

12. HealthGrades. *Medical Errors Cost U.S. $8.8 Billion, results in 238,337 potentially preventable deaths, according to HealthGrades Study.* (8 April 2008). Available at http://www.healthgrades.com/media/DMS/pdf/HealthGradesPatientSafetyRelease2008.pdf (Retrieved February 8, 2010).

13. See note 1.

14. Weiler, P.C. *Medical Malpractice on Trial.* Cambridge: Harvard Univ. Press, 1991.

15. Agency for Healthcare Research and Quality. *Medical Errors: The Scope of the Problem.* (February 2000). Available at http://www.ahrq.gov/qual/errback.htm (Retrieved February 8, 2010).

16. Barach, P., and S.D. Small, "Reporting and preventing medical mishaps: lessons from non-medical near miss reporting systems." *British Medical Journal,* 320, 759-763, 2000.

17. Reason, J. *Human Error.* New York: Cambridge Univ. Press, 1995.

18. *Id.*

19. See note 6.

20. Federal Rules of Civil Procedure. "Rule 26(b)." Minneapolis, MN: West Pub., 2001.

21. Liang, B.A. "Risk of reporting sentinel events." *Health Affairs,* 19(5),112-120, 2000.

22. Liang, B.A., K. Storti. "Creating problems as part of the 'solution': The JCAHO Sentinel Event Policy, Legal Issues, and Patient Safety." *Journal of Health Law,* 33, 263-285,2000.

23. *Univ. of Penn. v. EEOC*, 493 U.S. 192 (1990).

24. *Trammel v. U.S.*, 445 U.S. 40 (1980).

25. *U.S. v. Nixon*, 418 U.S. 683 (1974).

26. Bressler, H.J. "Sentinel events and the JCAHO: The genesis of patient safety." *Proceedings of Addressing the Medical, Legal, and Ethical Dilemmas in Modern Health Care, 39th Annual Conference of the American College of Legal Medicine*, New Orleans, LA, March 11-13, 1999 (Milwaukee: ACLM, 1999).

27. Scheutzow, S.O. "State Medical Peer Review: High Cost But No Benefit—Is It Time for a Change?" *American Journal of Law & Medicine*, 25, 7-60,1999.

28. Cepelewicz, B.B., L.J. Dunn, D.M. Feltch, et al. Recent Developments in Medicine and Law, *Tort and Insurance Law Journal*, 33, 580-603,1998.

29. See note 21.

30. See note 6.

31. See note 21.

32. See note 22.

33. See note 21.

34. *Adkins v. Christie*, 488 F.3d 1324 (11th Cir. 2007).

35. Suydam, S., B.A. Liang, S. Anderson, and M.B. Weinger, "Patient Safety Data Sharing and Protection from Legal Discovery." *Advances in Patient Safety*, 3, 361-370, 2005.

36. See note 21.

37. *Id.*

38. See note 22.

39. See note 6.

40. *Id.*

41. *Id.*

42. See note 21.

43. Office of Inspector General. *Adverse Events in Hospitals: State Reporting Systems*. Department of Human and Health Services, December 2008.

44. Adams, D. "Bills have been proposed in several states aimed at reducing medical errors and improving patient safety." *American Medical News*, Mar. 12, 2001.

45. Howley, C.J. "Error analysis and reduction: Part I." *Proceedings of Medical Errors and Quality Assurance: A Local, Regional and National Perspective*, Grants Pass, Oregon, November 9-10, 2000. Medford, OR: Asante/Providence Health Care Systems, 8-26, 2000.

46. *Id.*

47. Liang, B.A. *Health Law & Policy*. Boston: Butterworth-Heinemann, 93-114, 2000.

48. The Joint Commission. *Joint Commission Fact Sheets.* (January 15, 2010). Available at http://www.jointcommission.org/AboutUs/Fact_Sheets/hospital_facts.htm (Retrieved February 8, 2010).

49. The Joint Commission. *Patient Safety.* (December 17, 2009). Available at http://www.jointcommission.org/GeneralPublic/PatientSafety/#2 (Retrieved February 8, 2010).

50. The Joint Commission. *Sentinel Event Statistics.* (September 30, 2009). Available at http://www.jointcommission.org/NR/rdonlyres/377FF7E7-F565-4D61-9FD2-593CA688135B/0/SE_Stats_9_09.pdf (Retrieved February 8, 2010).

51. Liang, B.A. "Comment: Other People's Money: A Reply to The Joint Commission." *Journal of Health Law*, 33, 657-659, 2000.

52. The Joint Commission. *Sentinel Events Policy and Procedures*. Available at http://www.jointcommission.org/NR/rdonlyres/F84F9DC6-A5DA-490F-A91F-A9FCE26347C4/0/SE_chapter_july07.pdf (retrieved February 5, 2010).

53. See note 21.

54. Dorheim, M.A. "ASRS fights to curb dangerous trends." *Aviation Week & Space Technology*, 145(19), 72, 1996.

55. See note 21.

56. See note 51.

57. *Id.*

58. See note 52.

59. *Id.*

60. *Id.*

61. *Id.*

62. See note 21.

63. The Joint Commission. *Facts about the Public Informa-tion Policy.* (June 17, 2009). Available at http://www. jointcommission.org/AboutUs/Fact_Sheets/08_pip. htm (Retrieved February 8, 2010).

64. *Id.*

65. The Joint Commission. *Alternatives for Sharing Sen-tinel Event-Related Information with The Joint Com-mission.* (April 1, 2009). Available at http://www.joint-commission.org/SentinelEvents/ReportingAlternatives (Retrieved February 8, 2010).

66. *Id.*

67. *Id.*

68. See note 52.

69. *Id.*

70. *Id.*

71. Becker, C. "Root-cause trouble: Court ruling in N.J. could set precedent for making JCAHO reports public." *Modern Healthcare*, 11, June 18, 2001.

72. Crane, M. "Peer Review: Breaking the Code of Si-lence." *Medical Economics,* 76, 158-60, 1999.

73. See note 21.

74. TJC. *Revisions to Joint Commission Standards in Sup-port of Patient Safety and Medical/Health Care Error Reduction.* Available at http://www.dcha.org/JCAHOR-evision.htm (retrieved February 5, 2010).

75. Lovern, B. "JCAHO's new tell-all; Standards require that patients know about below-par care." *Modern Healthcare,* 2, Jan. 1, 2001.

76. Rozovsky, F. "The JCAHO Sentinel Event Policy." *Health L Digest,* 3-11, May 1998.

77. See note 13.

78. Liang, B.A. Error in medicine: Legal impediments to U.S. reform. *Journal of Health Politics, Policy and Law,* 24, 27-58,1999.

79. Cooper, J., D. Gaba, B.A. Liang, et al. *Agenda for Re-search and Development in Patient Safety.* Chicago: National Patient Safety Foundation, 2000.

80. Moray, N. "Error Reduction as a Systems Problem." In Bogner, M.S. (Editor). *Human Error in Medicine.* Hill-sdale: Lawrence Erlbaum Assoc., 1994.

81. See note 6.

82. See note 21.

83. Agency for Healthcare Research and Quality. *Review of Reforms to Our Medical Liability System.* (January 4, 2010). Available at http://ahrq.hhs.gov/qual/liability/re-forms.htm (Retrieved February 8, 2010).

84. McDonnell, W.M., E. Guenther. Narrative Review: Do State Laws Make It Easier to Say 'I'm Sorry?' *Annals of Internal Medicine*, 149, 811-815,2008.

85. 5 U.S.C. §552 (2004).

86. See note 76.

87. See note 21.

88. 5 U.S.C. §§ 552 (b)(4),(6) (2004).

89. *Department of Interior v. Klamath Water Users Protec-tive Association*, 121 S.Ct. 1060 (2001).

90. *Washington Post Co., v. United States Dep't of Health & Human Servs.*, 865 F.2d 320, 324 (D.C. Cir. 1989).

91. Public Law 109-41 (2005).

92. Department of Health & Human Services. *Understand-ing Patient Safety Confidentiality.* Available at http:// www.hhs.gov/ocr/privacy/psa/understanding/index. html (Retrieved February 8, 2010).

93. 42 U.S.C. 299 *et seq.* and 42 C.F.R. Part 3 (73 FR 70732).

94. 42 C.F.R. Part 3, §3.20.

95. Agency for Healthcare Research and Quality. *Patient Safety Organization Information.* Available at http:// www.pso.ahrq.gov/psos/overview.htm (Retrieved Feb-ruary 8, 2010).

96. Agency for Healthcare Research and Quality. *Al-phabetical Directory of Listed Patient Safety Orga-nizations.* Available at http://www.pso.ahrq.gov/list-ing/alphalist.htm (Retrieved February 8, 2010).

97. 42 C.F.R. Part 3, §3.204, §3.206.

98. *Id.*

99. Agency for Healthcare Research and Quality. *Network of Patient Safety Databases.* Available at http://www. pso.ahrq.gov/npsd/npsd.htm (Retrieved February 8, 2010).

100. Agency for Healthcare Research and Quality. *PSO Fast Facts.* Available at http://www.pso.ahrq.gov/psos/fast-facts.htm#ff25 (Retrieved February 8, 2010).

101. Government Accountability Office. *Patient Safety Act: HHS Is in the Process of Implementing the Act, So Its Effectiveness Cannot Yet Be Evaluated.* January 2010.

102. *Id.*

103. See note 94.

104. *Id.*

105. 42 C.F.R. Part 3 §3.206 (b)(1).

106. *Id.* §3.206 (3).

107. *Id.* §3.206 (5), (7).

108. *Id.* §3.206 (8).

109. *Id.* §3.206 (8)(B)(iii).

110. 42 C.F.R. Part 3 §3.208.

111. Public Law 109-41. §922(d)(1).

112. 42 C.F.R. Part 3 §3.402, §3.404.

113. Public Law 109-41. §922, (f)(4)(a).

114. See note 105 §3.206 (ii).

115. See note 17.

116. Pronovost, P., D. Needham, S. Sinopoli, et al. An Intervention to Decrease Cather-related Bloodstream Infections in the ICU. *New England Journal of Medicine*, 355(26), 2725-2732, 2006.

117. Haynes, A.B., T.G. Weiser, W.R. Berry, et al. A Surgical Safety Checklist to Reduce Morbidity and Mortality in a Global Population. *New England Journal of Medicine*, 360(5), 491-499, 2009.

118. Agency for Healthcare Research and Quality. *Patient Safety Primer: Checklists.* Available at http://www. psnet.ahrq.gov/primer.aspx?primerID=14 (Retrieved February 8, 2010).

119. *Id.*

120. Agency for Healthcare Research and Quality. *Patient Safety Primer: Error Disclosure.* Available at http:// www.psnet.ahrq.gov/primer.aspx?primerID=2 (Retrieved February 8, 2010).

121. *Id.*

122. Liang, B.A. *Report Cards Key to Health Reform,* San Diego Union Tribune, November 19, 2009, at B7. Available at http://www.signonsandiego.com/news/2009/nov/19/report-cards-key-to-health-reform/ (Retrieved February 8, 2010).

123. Kachalia, A., K.G. Shojania, T.P. Hofer, et al. "Does Full Disclosure of Medical Errors Affect Malpractice Liability? The Jury Is Still Out." *Joint Commission Journal on Quality and Patient Safety*, 29(10), 503-511,2003.

124. Nadzam, D.M. "Nurses' Role in Communication and Patient Safety." *Journal of Nursing Care Quality*, 24(3), 184-188,2009.

125. *Id.*

126. *Id.*

127. *Id.*

128. *Id.*

129. Agency for Healthcare Research and Quality. *Patient Safety Primer: Handoffs and Signouts.* Available at http://www.psnet.ahrq.gov/primer.aspx?primerID=9 (Retrieved February 8, 2010).

130. Arora, V.M., J.M. Farnan. Care Transitions for Hospitalized Patients. *Medical Clinics of North America,* 92, 315-324, 2008.

131. *Id.*

132. Yu, K.T., R.A. Green. Critical Aspects of Emergency Department Documentation and Communication. *Emergency Medical Clinics of North America,* 27, 641-654, 2009.

133. O'Byrne, W.T., L. Weavind, J. Selby. The Science and Economics of Improving Clinical Communication. *Anesthesiology Clinics,* 26, 729-744, 2008.

134. Thomas, E.J. *Aviation Safety Methods: Quickly Adopted but Questions Remain.* AHRQ Perspectives on Safety. Available at http://webmm.ahrq.gov/perspective.aspx?perspectiveID=16#ref8 (Retrieved February 8, 2010).

135. Nielsen, P., S. Mann. Team Function in Obstetrics to Reduce Errors and Improve Outcomes. *Obstetrics Gynecology Clinics North America,* 35, 81-95, 2008.

136. Federal Aviation Administration. *CFR NPRM.* (May 1, 2009) Available at http://rgl.faa.gov/Regulatory_and_Guidance_Library%5CrgNPRM.nsf/0/934D6204C4AF66E7862575A9006DC19D?Open Document (Retrieved February 8, 2010).

137. Agency for Healthcare Research and Quality. *Patient Safety Primer: Teamwork Training.* Available at http://www.psnet.ahrq.gov/primer.aspx?primerID=8 (Retrieved February 8, 2010).

138. *Id.*

139. See note 135.

140. *Id.*

141. Sax, H.C., P. Browne, R.J. Mayewski, et al. Can Aviation-Based Team Training Elicit Sustainable Behavioral Change? *Archives of Surgery,* 144(12), 1133-1137, 2009.

Chapter 4

Patient Safety Initiatives

Patricia W. Iyer, MSN, RN, LNCC and Susan Mellott, PhD, RN, CPHQ, FNAHQ*

---

*The authors appreciate the contributions of Thomas Haas RN, LNHA to the first edition of this chapter.

*This chapter is reprinted, with modifications, from *Medical Legal Aspects of Medical Records* (2010), published by Lawyers & Judges Publishing.

4.1 Introduction

Despite remarkable advances in almost every field of medicine, an age-old problem continues to haunt healthcare professionals—the occurrence of errors or failures. These events cast a shadow on the public's trust of healthcare. People justifiably ask, "What's going on?" When such failures harm individuals receiving healthcare services, the problem is extremely disturbing. Many, if not most errors or failures are the result of problems with processes within the healthcare system. These problems inherently cause failures to occur and individuals to be harmed. Although the rate of such failures in healthcare is unknown (and may be unknowable), any failure is a cause for concern. These events can result in tragedy for individuals served and their families, add cost to an already overburdened healthcare system, adversely affect the public's perception of an organization, and lead to prolonged litigation. They can also deeply affect healthcare professionals who are dedicated to helping individuals receiving care, treatment, or service.

4.2 The Current Healthcare Environment

Health care continues to experience dramatic change. As healthcare organizations become more complex, their systems and processes are increasingly interdependent and often interlocked or coupled. This makes the opportunity for failure more frequent and the recovery from failure by those involved more difficult. The rapid explosion of the medical knowledge base has made it increasingly challenging for practitioners to stay up-to-date. Yet, despite technological advances and great gains in knowledge, healthcare systems are, and will continue to be, appropriately dependent on human intervention. The rigorous financial constraints imposed by managed care and the need to reduce healthcare expenditures have affected every type of healthcare organization and the records it keeps. No organization is immune. Organization leaders are reassessing their workforces. Workloads are heavier, creating increased stress and fatigue for healthcare professionals, and affecting the quality of care and quantity of documentation in the medical record. Caregivers are working in new settings and performing new functions, sometimes with minimal training. Skill mixes are shifting. In short, the healthcare environment is ripe for serious problems caused by systems failures.

Instances of errors and failures within healthcare organizations have been reported in the media with increasing regularity. A galvanized industry is responding. Failure detection, reduction, and prevention strategies are receiving necessary new impetus as the healthcare industry recognizes the need for a proactive approach to reduce the risk of failure.

A. New Spotlight on Safety

In recent years, as a result of academic studies and highly publicized incidents of hospital error, patient safety has moved to the forefront. Starting in 1991, multiple articles in prominent medical journals reported on the Harvard Medical Practice Study of about 30,000 randomly selected records of patients hospitalized in New York State. The research determined that adverse events occurred in 3 percent of hospitalizations and that 14 percent of these events were fatal. In a dramatic illustration of the problem's scale, the authors extrapolated that as many people were dying from preventable deaths in American hospitals as would die if three jumbo jets crashed every two days.

Then, at the end of November 1999, *To Err Is Human,*[1] a report from the prestigious Institute of Medicine (IOM), received wide public attention. Extrapolating from the 1991 Harvard study and several more recent ones, the report estimated that anywhere from 44,000 to 98,000 Americans die each year because of medical errors in hospitals. If even the lower estimate was correct, more people die from medical errors than from motor vehicle accidents, breast cancer, or AIDS. While errors may be more easily detected in hospitals, they affect every healthcare setting: day-surgery and outpatient clinics, retail pharmacies, nursing homes, as well as home care. Medication errors alone were estimated to cause more than 7,000 deaths annually. William C. Richardson, the panel's chairman, said "these stunningly high rates of medical errors…are simply unacceptable in a medical system that promises first to 'do no harm.'"[2]

A variety of factors were identified in this report as contributing to medical errors. One of the most important findings is that no one person or group of individuals is to blame for these errors. Instead it is the healthcare system itself that produces the conditions that lead personnel to make a medical error. Processes within the healthcare system need to be improved in order to prevent errors and make it easier to do the correct thing, thus avoiding the errors.[3]

In response to the 1999 report, *To Err Is Human,* there was a major shift in regulatory and accreditation organizations' attention to patient safety issues. The National Quality Forum, HCFA (now Centers for Medicare and Medicaid Services) and The Joint Commission developed initiatives to improve and standardize various measures and increase accountability to the healthcare community.

In March 2001, the IOM issued a second report called *Crossing the Quality Chasm: A New Health System for the 21st Century.* This report examined the U.S. healthcare system and resulted in a recommendation that the entire healthcare system should be re-designed and that healthcare policy needed to be revised. The report established a strategy and an action plan for this re-design of the systems of care delivery. This report also established ten general rules or principles for healthcare systems and professionals to utilize when caring for patients. The report stressed the importance of interdisciplinary teams, especially with the chronically ill patient populations.[4]

In 2002, the IOM issued a third report called *Fostering Rapid Advances in Health Care: Learning from System Demonstrations.* This report focuses on primary care models for the chronically ill, as well as on communication, malpractice reform, and affordable insurance coverage at the state level.[5]

In 2003, the IOM issued a report, *Priority Areas for National Action: Transforming Health Care Quality,* which focuses on 20 priority areas that covers all areas of healthcare from prevention to palliative care. The report also focused on the importance of patient self-management and care coordination.[6] Also in 2003, the IOM released *Leadership by Example: Coordinating Government Roles in Improving Health Care Quality.* This report focused on the federal government, and the use of multiple approaches to improve the quality of care.[7] It is from this report that CMS has developed the "Pay for Performance" program.

In November 2005, the IOM released *Improving the Quality of Health Care for Mental Health and Substance-Use Conditions: Quality Chasm Series.* This report applies the knowledge learned from the "Crossing the Quality Chasm: A New Health System for the 21st Century" report to the mental illness and substance-use clinical environments.[8]

In July 2006, the IOM released *Preventing Medication Errors: Quality Chasm Series.* The Centers for Medicaid and Medicare Services commissioned the IOM to study medication errors and develop a national guideline for reducing these errors. This report found that medical errors were common and costly and outlined a comprehensive approach to decreasing the prevalence of these errors.[9] The IOM continues to study ways to identify and prevent medication errors, understanding drug safety, cost of medication errors, and several other factors regarding medication errors.[10]

In July 2005, the Patient Safety and Quality Improvement Act of 2005 was signed into law. This act "will promote cultures of safety across healthcare settings by establishing federal protections that encourage thorough, candid examinations of the causes of healthcare errors and the development of effective solutions to prevent their recurrence. Previously, evaluative information about the underlying causes of adverse events was not always considered confidential or protected from lawsuits, a fact that the Institute of Medicine blamed for driving errors underground and slowing the progress in improving patient safety."[11]

The Patient Safety and Quality Improvement Act of 2005 charged the Department of Health and Human Services to establish criteria and a process for designating *Patient Safety Organizations* (PSO). The final Patient Safety Rule was published in the Federal Register on November 21, 2008, and outlined the process for organizations to become a Patient Safety Organization. This act also describes the privilege and confidentiality protections of the information submitted and the penalties for impermissible disclosure of this information. The Agency for Healthcare Research and Quality administers the provisions of this rule and has approved numerous organizations as PSOs.[12] Any data submitted to these organizations will be provided full federal privilege to patient safety information.

B. Understanding Effective Patient Safety

Effective patient safety entails proactively identifying the potential and actual risks to safety, identifying the underlying cause(s) of the potential risks, and making the necessary improvements so that the risk is reduced. It also requires establishing processes to respond to sentinel events, identifying causes through root cause analysis, and making necessary improvements. This involves a systems-based approach that examines all activities within an organization that contribute to the maintenance and improvement of patient safety, such as performance improvement and risk management to ensure the activities work together, not independently, to improve care and safety. The systems-based approach is:

- driven by organization leadership;
- anchored in the organization's mission, vision, and strategic plan;
- endorsed and actively supported by the medical staff and nursing leadership;
- implemented by directors;
- integrated and coordinated throughout the organization's staff; and
- continuously re-engineered using proven, proactive performance improvement modalities.

In addition, effective reduction of errors and other factors that contribute to unintended adverse outcomes in an organization requires an environment in which patients, their families, and organization staff and leaders can identify and manage actual and potential risks to safety.

Elements of patient safety include:

- planning and designing services,
- directing services,
- integrating and coordinating services,
- reducing and correcting errors,
- using sentinel event alerts,
- adhering to National Patient Safety Goals,
- using clinical practice guidelines, and
- actively involving patients in care.

This chapter discusses the efforts of four organizations to promote patient safety through the use of standards or best practices. The safety programs of The Joint Commission, the Leapfrog Group, the National Quality Forum, and the Institute for Healthcare Improvement are described. There are other organizations involved in promoting safer health care. The reader is encouraged to explore the websites included in the end of the chapter. This chapter presents an overview of the framework for promoting a reduction in medical errors.

4.3 The Joint Commission

The Joint Commission sets standards for, evaluates, and accredits more than 16,000 healthcare organizations and programs in the United States. These include hospitals and home health agencies as well as ambulatory care services, behavioral health programs, clinical laboratories, and long term care organizations. In addition, The Joint Commission provides certification of disease-specific care programs, primary stroke centers, and health care staffing services.[13] The Joint Commission's comprehensive accreditation process evaluates an organization's compliance with these standards and other accreditation requirements.

The Joint Commission moved on multiple fronts to address the issues of continuous improvement in the safety and quality of healthcare services to the world's healthcare organizations. The Joint Commission received praise in a Washington congressional hearing for three patient safety initiatives:[14]

- collaboration with the centers for Medicaid and Medicare on their *Speak Up Campaign*, a national program that urges patients to take an active role in preventing healthcare errors by becoming active, involved, and informed participants in the healthcare team,
- implementation of their new survey process *Shared Visions—New Pathways* which resulted in strongly positive industry feedback, and
- development of National Patient Safety Goals.

If you want to find out anything from the theoretical physicists about the methods they use, I advise you to stick closely to one principle: Don't listen to their words, fix your attention on their deeds.
— Albert Einstein, *The World As I See It*

The Joint Commission began this journey by implementing the *Shared Visions—New Pathways* initiative, designed to progressively sharpen the focus of the accreditation process on care systems critical to the safety and quality of patient care, in effect in 2004. *Shared Visions—New Pathways* was designed to help organizations achieve 100 percent compliance 100 percent of the time and thereby consistently improve the safety and quality of the care they provide.

The changes brought about by *Shared Visions—New Pathways* were comprehensive, affecting every aspect of the accreditation process and representing a paradigm shift away from survey preparation and towards continuous operational improvement. Changes included the following:

- tracer methodology, that focuses on how services were delivered to actual patients as a way to explore healthcare system effectiveness at the facility,
- reformatting, clarifying, and streamlining standards to focus more directly on safety and quality, which, in turn, will increase their relevance and value,
- a Priority Focus Process (PFP) that incorporates presurvey organization-specific data and informs the on-site visit,
- a Periodic Performance Review (PPR) to drive organizations' continuous standards compliance efforts,
- a more continuous accreditation process that will facilitate an organization's incorporation of the standards into daily operations,
- revised Accreditation Reports and Quality Reports that emphasize performance, improvement in important safety and quality areas and de-emphasize compliance scores,
- more rigorous accreditation decisions,
- more follow-up after the survey, and
- clearer reporting on survey findings.

Each of these improvements helped to increase the value of accreditation to all healthcare organizations while improving the quality and safety of health care provided to the public—the heart of The Joint Commission's mission. The objectives of streamlining the standards included:

- ensure the relevance of The Joint Commission standards to safety and quality,
- reduce redundancy,
- improve the clarity of the standards, and
- reduce the associated burdens of paperwork and documentation.

The new accreditation process shifted the emphasis away from survey preparation and the consequent ramp-up activities completed by some organizations to prepare for it, to the continuous improvement of operational systems. Not only was the ramping-up process expensive, but it could put patient safety and quality of care in jeopardy. Organizations that focused on the standards only around the time of survey might miss issues that arise at other times. By encouraging organizations to maintain continuous compliance, The Joint Commission hoped to help reduce unnecessary costs associated with accreditation while improving safety and quality of care. The new process was highly focused on direct clinical care, information-driven, and systems-centered.

In October 2006, The Joint Commission began another revision of its standards as part of the Standards Improvement Initiative (SII).[15] The goals of this initiative were to:

- Clarify standards language
- Ensure that standards are program-specific
- Delete redundant or non-essential standards
- Consolidate similar standards

In addition, the manuals were reorganized and the scoring and decision processes were refined. Five new chapters were added, but they contained existing standards that were simply reorganized into the new chapters. The new chapters include the following:

- Emergency Management (EM)
- Life Safety (LS)
- Record of Care, Treatment, and Services (RC)
- Transplant Safety (TS)
- Waived Testing (WT)

In January 2009, the new standards manuals were rolled out for hospitals, ambulatory services, critical access hospitals, home care and office-based surgery programs. The standards manuals for the remaining types of organizations were implemented in January 2010.

A. The Mission of The Joint Commission

The stated mission of The Joint Commission is to *continuously* improve the *safety* and quality of care provided to the public through the provision of healthcare accreditation and related services that support performance improvement in healthcare organizations.[16]

B. Eligible Facilities

The Joint Commission's evaluation and accreditation services are provided for the following types of organizations:[17]

- general, psychiatric, children's, and rehabilitation hospitals,
- critical access hospitals,
- medical equipment services, hospice services, and other home care organizations
- nursing homes and other long term care facilities,
- behavioral healthcare organizations, addiction services
- rehabilitation centers, group practices, office-based surgeries and other ambulatory care providers
- independent or freestanding laboratories

C. Certifications

The Joint Commission also awards Disease-Specific Care (DSC) Certification to health plans, disease management service companies, hospitals, and other care delivery settings that provide disease management and chronic care services. The Joint Commission's Certification Program for DSC provides a comprehensive evaluation of disease or condition-specific services, including, but not limited to asthma, diabetes, congestive heart failure, coronary artery disease, chronic obstructive pulmonary disease, skin and wound management, and primary stroke care. The Joint Commission also provides a Health Care Staffing Services Certification Program.[18]

D. Benefits of Accreditation and Certification

The Joint Commission accreditation is recognized internationally as a symbol of quality that reflects an organization's commitment to meeting certain performance standards. To earn and maintain The Joint Commission's Gold Seal of Approval™, an organization must undergo an on-site survey by a Joint Commission survey team at least every three years. Laboratories must be surveyed every two years.

Joint Commission accreditation and certification promote the following benefits and advantages:[19]

- provides a framework for organizational structure and management
- strengthens community confidence in quality and safety of care, treatment, and services
- provides a competitive edge in the marketplace
- improves risk management and risk reduction
- provides education on good practices
- enhances staff recruitment and development
- provides deeming authority for Medicare certification
- recognized by insurers and third party payers
- validates compliance with recognized national standards

E. Standards and Performance Measurement

The standards focus not simply on an organization's ability to provide safe, high quality care, but on its actual performance as well. Standards set forth performance expectations for activities that affect the safety and quality of patient care. If an organization does the right things and does them well, there is a strong likelihood that its patients will experience good outcomes. The Joint Commission develops its standards in consultation with healthcare experts, providers, measurement experts, purchasers and consumers.

While a Joint Commission Surveyor will evaluate compliance with these standards using various methods (i.e., interviews, observations, and policy reviews) a major element of compliance will be based on review of patients' medical records. The survey agenda provides the surveyor significant time for tracing a patient's care at the organization through review of the patient medical record. As the standards are modified and strengthened each year, it is important to obtain the information management standards that were in place during the year(s) involved in the litigation process.

F. Periodic Performance Review

Beginning in November 2003, The Joint Commission-accredited organizations were required to complete a Periodic Performance Review (PPR) 18 months after their last Joint Commission survey. This included all freestanding ambulatory health care, behavioral health care, home health care, hospital, and long term care accreditation programs. The first group of organizations were those due for survey on July 1, 2005. At that time, the PPR was available on the "Jayco" extranet site for those hospitals whose time had come for the completion of the PPR. The PPR is a self analysis of how well the facility is meeting each of The Joint Commission standards and their Elements of Performance. When an organization is evaluated as being out of compliance with a standard, the organization must develop an action plan addressing each Element of Performance that was scored as either partial compliance or not compliant. If the organization did not complete the PPR within 30 days of the due date, the organization's accreditation status could change.[20]

In July 2005, The Joint Commission announced that the PPR must be submitted annually beginning in January 2006. The annual submission is based on the date of the organization's last full survey. For example, if an organization had its last full survey in October 2007, then its PPR was due in October 2008, and in October every year after that until its next full survey occurs. Since The Joint Commission is now conducting unannounced surveys, the date that the PPR is due will fluctuate with the date of the last full survey. For example, if the next full survey for the organization were to occur in December 2009, then the PPR will become due every December until the organization's next full survey.[21]

Beginning in 2006, laboratories that are accredited by The Joint Commission also had to complete the PPR for the laboratory accreditation program. The timing of the PPR completion coincides with the organization's primary program PPR, if the lab is part of an organization that provides more than one level and type of care. For free standing laboratories, the PPR due date is based on its laboratory's last full survey.[22]

There are four options to the completion of the PPR.[23] The first option is the full PPR utilizing The Joint Commis-

sion automated tool on the extranet. The transmission of the completed PPR and action plans are sent to The Joint Commission through a secure password-protected extranet site. Before 2006, following submission of the completed PPR, Joint Commission Standards Interpretation Group (SIG) would arrange a conference call with the organization to review the action plans and make suggestions for other improvements. In 2006, this SIG conference call became optional.

The second option for completion of the PPR is called Option 1. This option requires an organization to complete the full PPR and develop action plans as in the full PPR; however they are not required to submit the documentation to The Joint Commission. If this option is chosen, the organization must affirm in the PPR electronic notification that it has performed the complete review and that legal counsel has advised the organization not to participate in the full PPR. This group may still submit standard-related issues to the SIG for discussion, without indicating its own level of compliance.

Option 2 is the third way to complete the PPR. This option is completed by a Joint Commission surveyor who comes to the organization for an on-site survey. The on-site survey will last about one-third of the length of the triennial survey, and consists of only one surveyor. These organizations must also affirm that they have been advised by legal counsel not to participate in the full PPR. If this option is chosen, the organization must submit action plans to The Joint Commission within 30 days of the completion of the survey addressing any non-compliant standards. Before 2006, the SIG would then schedule a conference call to review the action plans with the organization. In 2006, these calls also became optional.

Option 3 is the last method that an organization may choose to complete its PPR. This option is similar to Option 2 in that a surveyor will conduct an on-site survey; however, no written report will be left by the surveyor. The surveyor will inform the organization orally of the findings in lieu of a written report. No findings are transmitted to The Joint Commission.

With either Option 2 or Option 3, if a surveyor finds anything that is having or may potentially have a serious, adverse effect on patient health or safety, the surveyor will take immediate action that could lead to an unfavorable change in the accreditation of the organization.

Legal concerns were voiced during the pilot of the full PPR revolving around the potential discovery of the self-assessment information. Option 1 was created in 2003 to address whether sharing the information with The Joint Commission could waive state law protection from discovery. Other organizations felt that the completion of the PPR would put them at risk for disclosure of the information, so The Joint Commission developed Option 2. Following further discussion with healthcare entities, The Joint Commission formed a Legal Issues Task Force to address these concerns. The Task Force consisted of members from the legal field, state hospital associations, and the American Society for Healthcare Risk Management (ASHRM). Option 3 was developed in late 2003 to address other concerns.[24]

G. Deemed Status

In 1965, Congress passed legislation that gave The Joint Commission "deemed" status, meaning that The Joint Commission surveys can be used in lieu of state agency certification. As a result, 92 percent of all hospital beds are TJC-accredited. The Joint Commission also has "deemed" status in regard to facilities with other patient populations. In 2002, the Centers for Medicare and Medicaid Services granted deemed status to The Joint Commission so that it could also survey eligible health maintenance organizations (HMOs) and preferred provider organizations.

In 2008, CMS enacted the Medicare Improvements for Patients and Providers Act of 2008. This act superseded the previous 1965 legislation and required The Joint Commission to apply for deemed status rather than automatically awarding such status. The act also allowed for a transition period in order to minimize and disruption to The Joint Commission accredited hospitals. CMS awarded deemed status to The Joint Commission for hospital surveys in July 2010 through July 15, 2014.[25]

The Joint Commission accreditation is voluntary and represents an organization's willingness to demonstrate a higher standard of care than simply meeting the minimum requirements put forth by the Centers for Medicare and Medicaid Services. The Joint Commission's Gold Seal of Approval™ is a clear sign that the accredited facility has demonstrated compliance to the most stringent standards of performance.

TIP: A recent study by LTCQ, Inc. demonstrated that The Joint Commission-accredited long term care facilities had significantly fewer health and immediate jeopardy deficiencies, better occupancy and payer mix and lower predicted litigation risk.[26]

H. The Joint Commission's Public Information Policy

The Joint Commission is committed to making relevant and accurate information about surveyed healthcare organizations available to interested parties. In February 2009, The Joint Commission's Board of Commissioners approved a revision to the Public Information Policy. This revision allows The Joint Commission to report to appropriate governmental and licensing authorities serious safety issues even if those issues are not determined to be an "Immediate Threat to Health and Safety." Prior to this date, The Joint Commission could only report information to appropriate authorities if they were taking action to deny accreditation under their "Immediate Threat to Health and Safety" process.[27]

1. The Joint Commission website (www.jointcommission.org)

The Joint Commission's website provides a comprehensive guide to help individuals learn more about the safety and quality of Joint Commission accredited healthcare organizations and programs throughout the United States. The main headers on the website include:

- Accreditation Programs
- Certification Programs
- Standards
- Patient Safety
- Sentinel Event
- Public Policy Reports
- Performance Measurement
- Library
- About Us

Each of these headers has a dropdown menu that lists the topics discussed in that section of the website. There is also a search field where the user can search for specific information that she is looking for. The right-hand column has the most recent news and updates from The Joint Commission. At the bottom of the page are links to various other items including the Quality Reports discussed in the next section. The website is continuously updated with information that is useful to healthcare professionals, consumers, and others.

2. Quality Reports

The Quality Reports provide summary information about the provision of quality and safety at an accredited organization. Quality Reports are created at the organization level and are designed to provide national and state information that can be compared against other accredited organizations and non-accredited organizations. Quality Check®, located at http://www.qualitycheck.org/consumer/searchQCR.aspx, includes Quality Reports for both Joint Commission-accredited, and/or certified organizations and health care organizations not accredited or certified by The Joint Commission. This report provides detailed information about an organization's performance. If the organization is not Joint Commission-accredited, the Quality Report will include the organization's name, address, type of facility (hospital, nursing home, etc.), a minimum of one service that they provide and a link for directions is included in their listing.

The Joint Commission Quality Reports for each accredited organization includes the following information:[28]

- Most recent accreditation decision
- Locations and services offered at each accredited organization
- Special Quality Awards the organization has achieved
- National Patient Safety Goals compliance
- Data for hospitals that submit National Quality Improvement Goals performance measures results (hospitals only).

TIP: The areas of patient care that are reported by accredited hospitals will change as new measures are included and older measures are deleted. Current measures are for Children's Asthma, Heart Attack, Heart Failure, Pneumonia, Pregnancy and related conditions, and the Surgical Care Improvement Project.

The Joint Commission Quality Reports regarding the Disease Specific and Health Care Staffing Services certification programs includes the following information:[29]

- Advanced Certification Programs
- Certified Programs
- Certification Decision
- Effective Dates
- Last Full Review Date
- Last On-Site Review Date
- National Patient Safety Goals Compliance

Each Joint Commission-accredited organization is afforded the opportunity to prepare a commentary of up to two pages regarding its Quality Report. The commentary accompanies any Organization Quality Reports distributed by The Joint Commission, whether via hard copy or The Joint Commission's website. In 2009, The Joint Commission added for hospitals the patient satisfaction data from the CMS Hospital Consumer Assessment of Health Providers and Systems (HCAHPS) program, the CMS 30-Day Mortality Measures for hospitals. The HCAHPS data and the Mortality measures are continuously updated, but have a lag time due to reporting processes.[30]

Each Quality Report released by The Joint Commission also includes appropriate background information. The Joint Commission may also make information contained in Quality Reports available to other third-party providers of information.

I. Sentinel Event Reporting

The Joint Commission began in early 1996 to formulate specific policies on sentinel events. When The Joint Commission became aware of a possible sentinel event, it conducted an unannounced survey. If during the unannounced survey it was determined that the organization had substantial control over the circumstances that led to the event, the organization would be given conditional accreditation pending the completion of an acceptable analysis of the event focused on reducing the risk of similar events occurring in the future.[31] Since that time, The Joint Commission has revised their definition and policies regarding sentinel events. According to The Joint Commission:[32]

"A sentinel event is an unexpected occurrence involving death or serious physical or psychological injury, or the risk thereof. Serious injury specifically includes loss of limb or function. The phrase 'or the risk thereof' includes any process variation for which a recurrence would carry a significant chance of a serious adverse outcome." The medical record is a vital component of all reviews of the sentinel events, sometimes called "never events" by some organizations. The medical record can be utilized to determine the need for implementation of improvements in processes that have been identified in Sentinel Event Alerts and is essential in completing a root cause analysis (RCA) once a sentinel event has occurred.

1. Sentinel Event Alerts

One of the outcomes from The Joint Commission Sentinel Event policy was the development of a newsletter, *Sentinel Event Alert*. Sentinel Event Alerts are designed to inform organizations concerning sentinel events and how they can be avoided. These alerts are not issued on any time schedule, but rather are released when the Sentinel Event Advisory Group determines that one should be published. The first Sentinel Event Alert was issued on February 27, 1996 regarding "Medication Error Prevention—Potassium Chloride."

Organizations should review all sentinel event alert recommendations and determine their applicability to their organization. Each Alert discusses the sentinel event, the root causes and risk reduction strategies, and finally Joint Commission recommendations to prevent the occurrence. All issues of *Sentinel Event Alert* are available for reference on The Joint Commission website at www.jointcommission. org. Click on the Sentinel Event tab at the top of the page and select the alerts from the drop down menu.

Reporting of sentinel events has had worthwhile results. For example, the data showed that potassium chloride came in vials that closely resembled sterile saline and other commonly used injectable medications and was, upon occasion, mistakenly injected intravenously in concentrated form—a process error that resulted in a significant number of accidental deaths. After The Joint Commission issued a sentinel event alert to the field explaining how such accidents could be prevented, the frequency with which they were reported or otherwise brought to the attention of The Joint Commission fell dramatically. For example, potassium chloride has been removed from nursing units and kept under tighter control. Following dissemination of sentinel event alerts, there have also been reductions in the frequency of reports to The Joint Commission of accidental deaths from restraints, inpatient suicides, and infant abductions.

TIP: From the reports and "root cause" analyses, The Joint Commission looks for common patterns of errors in order to inform and educate the field. As many experts have argued, errors are usually the result of poor processes, not of incompetent or inattentive people, or more rarely, of malicious professionals or impostors.

---

2. Root cause analysis (RCA)

When a sentinel event occurs, the accredited organization is expected to complete a thorough and credible root cause analysis (RCA), implement improvements to reduce risk, and monitor the effectiveness of those improvements. A root cause analysis is a method used to identify the special cause versus common cause variation in organizational processes and systems that are the "root" of why such an event occurred. The RCA focuses on the processes rather than the individuals involved in the sentinel event or near miss. The RCA identifies the potential improvements in processes or systems that would decrease the likelihood of the sentinel event occurring again in the future. Root cause analysis techniques use investigative methods to unravel complex situations (often found in health care). The process involves identifying causal factors, checking for generic implications of an event, determining if an event is recurrent, and recommending corrective action.[33]

All root causes that are identified should be the basis for an appropriate action plan to revise the process. In developing the action plans, there should be a literature search done to identify best practices and thus how they can be used to improve the current processes. There should also be selected

measures developed that will identify the effectiveness of the actions taken.

J. Failure Mode Effectiveness Analysis (FMEA)

The Joint Commission requires each healthcare facility that it accredits to identify at least one high-risk process for proactive risk assessment at least every 18 months. The medical record is crucial in indicating when and where events have occurred that could lead the organization to identify the process for their proactive risk assessment.

The Joint Commission describes one method of completing a proactive risk assessment through the following steps:[34]

1. Describe the chosen process (flowchart is an excellent tool for this step).
2. Identify ways in which the process could break down or fail to perform its desired function, which are often referred to as "failure modes."
3. Identify the possible effects that a breakdown or failure of the process could have on patients and the seriousness of the possible effects.
4. Prioritize the potential process breakdowns or failures.
5. Determine why the prioritized breakdowns or failures could occur, which may involve performing a hypothetical root cause analysis.
6. Redesign the process and/or underlying systems to minimize the risk of the effects on patients.
7. Test and implement the redesigned process.
8. Monitor the effectiveness of the redesigned process.

This proactive risk assessment can also be accomplished through a Failure Mode Effectiveness Analysis (FMEA). The purpose of the FMEA is to proactively examine a process and prevent errors from occurring. The FMEA process was developed first in industry and has now been adapted for health care. One of the best examples of the process for health care use can be found at http://www.patientsafety. gov/SafetyTopics.html#HFMEA. The Healthcare Failure Mode Effects Analysis (HFMEA) was designed by the VA National Center for Patient Safety (NCPS). The HFMEA tool simplifies the FMEA process by the utilization of a decision tree. The Risk Priority Score used in the FMEA is replaced by the Hazard Matrix Table, which was developed for this model.[35] A second example was developed by the Institute for Healthcare Improvement. Its FMEA process for health care can be found at their FMEA Info Center located at http://www.fmeainfocentre.com. A third example is from the American Society for Quality; its process can be found at http://www.asq.org/learn-about-quality/process-analysis-tools/overview/fmea.html.

4.4 The Joint Commission Survey Process

The Joint Commission accreditation is based largely on formal surveys of the subject organization conducted by The Joint Commission surveyors. The glossary of this book provides terminology and definitions that are important to the survey process. Each year The Joint Commission publishes a Survey Activity Guide describing how the survey process is conducted that year. There are not usually big changes to the process, but changes are always possible. The guide describes the survey process for each type of organization being surveyed.

A. The Unannounced Survey

Historically, The Joint Commission's regular, triennial surveys have been conducted in an announced fashion. Beginning in 2004 and through 2005, The Joint Commission began conducting unannounced triennial surveys on an optional and limited basis for organizations that volunteered. Since the beginning in 2006, all accreditation resurveys have been unannounced. All surveys conducted for CMS recognition through deemed status are unannounced. Initial (first-time) surveys remain announced.

B. The On-Site Survey

An organization that has applied for an accreditation survey will receive an on-site survey. The Priority Focus Process guides the survey process. These surveys are conducted at least every three years, but can also be conducted more frequently for cause, or for validation of a previous Joint Commission survey.

1. Priority Focus Process

The Priority Focus Process guides the overall survey process, including planning and the on-site survey, by providing enhanced insight into and information about each organization before its survey. This directs survey activities to organization-specific issues that are most relevant to safety and quality of care, referred to as priority focus areas (PFAs). The Priority Focus Process can be considered as a process for standardizing the PFAs for review during survey.

As part of the Priority Focus Process, an automated tool called the Priority Focus Tool (PFT) takes data about an organization gathered before the survey and, through the use of algorithms or sets of rules, transforms the data into information that guides the survey process. Examples of sources

for the data may include but are not limited to the following:

- data from an organization's application,
- complaint and sentinel event information,
- performance measurement data, when applicable,
- an organization's previous survey results, and
- data collected from external sources, such as the Nursing Home Compare section of the Medicare website (for a long term care survey).

2. The survey process

During an accreditation survey, The Joint Commission evaluates an organization's performance of functions and processes aimed at continuously improving patient/resident outcomes. The survey process focuses on assessing performance of important patient or resident-centered organization functions that support the safety and quality of care.

This assessment is accomplished through evaluating an organization's compliance with the applicable standards in the Standards manual published by The Joint Commission based on the following:

- tracing the care delivered to patients based on patient and staff interviews and medical record reviews,
- verbal and written information provided to The Joint Commission,
- on-site observations and interviews by The Joint Commission surveyors, and
- documents provided by the organization.

In addition, throughout the survey, any measure of success (MOS) identified by an organization as part of its periodic performance review (PPR) process will be validated. The Joint Commission's accreditation process seeks to help organizations identify and correct problems and improve the safety and quality of care and services provided. In addition to evaluating continuous compliance with standards and their Elements of Performance (EPs), significant time is spent on education.

Surveys are designed to be individualized to each organization, to be consistent, and to support the organization's efforts to improve performance. The length of the survey is determined by The Joint Commission based on information supplied in the application describing organization size and scope of services. The Joint Commission is no longer conducting portions of its survey after business hours. However, if during the regular patient tracers the surveyor feels that care on the other shifts needs to be evaluated, the surveyor is free to continue the survey at those other times.

3. The survey agenda

The survey agenda will contain the following elements:[36]

- *Surveyor Preliminary Planning Session.* During this session, the surveyors will review organization documents and plan for tracer activities.

- *Opening Conference.* The opening session of the survey process is an opportunity for organization leaders and key staff to meet with the surveyor(s) and make any last-minute adjustments to the survey schedule or elements. During this time the surveyors become further acquainted with the organization through a discussion with the leaders of the organization who are present.

- *Individual Tracer Activity.* These two elements of The Joint Commission's survey process, priority focus process and tracer, allow surveyors to analyze the functioning of organization systems.

- *Tracer Methodology.* One element driving this revised accreditation process is analysis of the organization's systems of providing care and services using actual patients as the framework for evaluating compliance with selected standards. This process, called tracer methodology, works with the priority focus process to trace patients, using priority focus areas as a starting point, within the healthcare organization's systems. Each type of organization has program-specific tracers that will be conducted during the individual Tracer Activity. For example, during the individual tracers for a home health agency, the surveyors will be specifically looking at fall reduction and hospital readmission.

- *Team Meeting/Surveyor Planning—End of Each Day.* The surveyors utilize this time to debrief themselves regarding the findings of that day and to plan for the next day's activities.

- *Daily Briefings.* During this session, organization staff will be briefed on the previous day's survey findings and any significant patterns or trends that are becoming evident in the survey.

- *Systems Tracer Sessions.* During these sessions, high-priority safety and quality-of-care issues on a system-wide basis are evaluated throughout the organization. Typically, for hospitals, these System Tracers consist of a Data System Tracer, a Medication Management Tracer, and an Infection Control System Tracer.

- *Environment of Care Session.* During this session the surveyor will assess the organization's compliance with the Environment of Care standards and identify vulnerabilities and strengths of the organization's processes in this area. For all hospitals this session will also include an Emergency Management tracer.

- *Life Safety Code Building Assessment.* This session will be conducted by a Life Safety Code Surveyor in all hospitals and by the other surveyors in other settings. The surveyor will evaluate the effectiveness designing, and maintaining the buildings, identifying and resolving Life Safety Code® problems, and the degree of compliance with the Life Safety Code® requirements.

- *Competence Assessment Process.* The surveyor(s) will determine how well the organization is meeting the competence assessment process for staff, licensed independent practitioners, and other credentialed practitioners. Included in this session is also a review of the organization's orientation, education, and training processes as they related to these types of individuals.

- *Medical Staff Credentialing and Privileging.* This session is for all hospitals. During this session the surveyors will evaluate the credentialing and privileging processes for the medical staff and other licensed independent practitioners who are privileged through the medical staff. The surveyors will also learn about the process used to collect data relevant to appointment decisions, the process for granting and delineating privileges, and the policies and procedures that assure consistency of the implementation of these activities.

- *Special Issue Resolution.* During this time period the surveyors explore issues that surfaced during the survey process that could not be resolved previously.

- *Leadership Conference.* During the conference, surveyors discuss with leaders (including medical staff leaders, governing body members, nursing, performance improvement, and safety leadership) their roles in performance improvement and other key issues of organization operations, such as patient safety, review of National Patient Safety Goals, and Priority Focus Process output related to clinical/service groups and clinical focus areas. Some organizations might experience two Leadership Conferences, as necessary.

- *Exit Briefing/Conference.* The surveyors will first meet with the CEO/administrator or designee to summarize their findings. At that time the CEO determines if the report should be copied and distributed to those attending the exit conference. The exit conference is devoted to a summary of the surveyor's findings and compliance issues.

- *Other Specialized Sessions.* Depending on the type of organization being surveyed, there may be other sessions specific to that type of facility.

Several chapters of the TJC accreditation manual and policies designed by the healthcare organization specifically define the composition of the patient's medical record. Through the review and evaluation of the medical record entries and other documents, and through the interaction with staff and patients, surveyors will determine compliance with The Joint Commission standards for that organization. They will also determine if appropriate patient care is being delivered to the patients/residents.

Three processes are viewed as necessary in identifying and delivering appropriate care, treatment, and services:

- *collecting data* about each patient's health history; physical, functional and psychosocial status; and needs as appropriate to the setting and circumstances,
- *analyzing data* to produce information about patient's needs for care, treatment, and services and to identify the need for additional data, and
- *making care, treatment, and services decisions* based on information developed about each patient's needs and his response to care, treatment, and services.

Qualified staff assesses each patient's care needs throughout the patient's contact with the organization through assessments or screenings. These activities may also identify the need for additional assessments or planning. These assessments are:

- defined by the organization,
- individualized to meet each patient's needs, and
- expected to address the needs of special populations.

The surveyor can use the accreditation manual, general clinical practice, and the organization's own procedures to identify medical records that should contain the appropriate documentation for a particular patient. These records are reviewed by the surveyor to help ascertain compliance with standards.

As part of the medical record, information gathered at the first contact can indicate the need for more data or a more intensive assessment of the patient's physical, psychological, cognitive, and communication skills, or development or social functioning. At a minimum, the need for further assessment is determined by the care, treatment, and services sought; the patient presenting condition(s), and whether the patient agrees to care, treatment, and services.

4. Survey team composition

The composition of an organization's survey team is based on the information provided in its application for accreditation. In most instances, an organization survey team is composed of one to five surveyors, including physicians, nurses, administrators, or other specialties as needed. A Life Safety Specialist is part of the survey team for all hospitals and critical access hospitals for one day. If the hospital has more than 750,000 square feet, the Life Safety Code Specialist will be there for two days. All surveyors perform evaluations and provide consultation regarding all functions addressed by the standards.

If more than one surveyor is required, one of the surveyors on the survey team is designated as the team leader. The team leader is responsible for integration, coordination, and communication of on-site survey activities. In addition to direct participation as an active member of the survey team, the team leader serves as the primary point of on-site contact between the organization and The Joint Commission. Among other responsibilities, the team leader leads the opening conference and the daily and exit briefings.

In addition, depending on the organization's service configuration, other surveyors may be assigned to survey specialized areas, such as long term care, home care, and behavioral healthcare. The findings of additional surveyors are integrated into the organization's accreditation decision and survey report.

5. Scoring compliance

In January 2009, a new scoring process was implemented for all Joint Commission surveys. The scoring is based on the "criticality" of the Elements of Performance within four levels of criticality:[37]

- Immediate Threat to Health and Safety
- Situational Decision Rules
- Direct Impact Requirements
- Indirect Impact Requirements.

The Joint Commission defines "criticality" as "The immediacy of risk to patient safety or quality of care as a result of noncompliance with a Joint Commission requirement."[38] The Immediate Threat to Health and Safety category is the most critical of the four. If the surveyors identify an Immediate Threat to Health and Safety in an organization, the facility will receive an expedited decision of Preliminary Denial of Accreditation (PDA). This decision remains in place until corrective action is taken and the action is validated by an on-site follow-up survey. At that point the organization moves into the Conditional Accreditation decision pending another on-site survey within 4-6 months.[39]

Situational Decision Rules are represented in The Joint Commission manuals by the symbol **A**. Based on the situations encountered by the surveyors during the survey process, a recommendation of PDA or Conditional Accreditation is made. If the organization is placed in Conditional Accreditation, there must be resolution of the issues within 45 days. There will be an onsite validation survey to assure the issues have been corrected.[40]

Direct Impact Requirements are represented in The Joint Commission manuals by the symbol △. These Elements of Performance (EP) have a direct impact on the implementation of care processes. If the lack of compliance with these EPs is likely to result in an immediate risk to patient safety or the quality of care being provided, the element is considered in non-compliance. If the organization receives a recommendation for improvement (RFI) regarding a Direct Impact EP, there must be resolution of the issues within 45 days. There will not be an onsite validation survey to assure the issues have been corrected.[41]

Indirect Impact Requirements are not represented in The Joint Commission manuals by any symbols. These Elements of Performance are based on planning and evaluation of care processes. Failure to be compliant with these EPs can still result in increased risk to patient safety or quality of care, but they are not as immediate of an impact as the Direct Impact Requirements. If the organization receives a recommendation for improvement (RFI) regarding an Indirect Impact EP, there must be resolution of the issues within 60 days. There will not be an onsite validation survey to assure the issues have been corrected.[42]

The scoring of the specific elements of performance remains dependent on a three point scale as follows:

0   Insufficient compliance
1   Partial compliance
2   Satisfactory compliance
NA Not applicable

In addition to the criticality levels of the elements of performance, each standard is designated as an "A" standard, or a "C" standard for scoring purposes. "A" standards

are typically related to structural requirements that are either in place or they are not. These standards will only receive a score of 2 or 0. "C" standards are scored based on the number of times an organization does not meet any given EP. These standards can receive scores of 2, 1, or 0.[43]

Two other symbols are currently being utilized with the standards. If an EP must be documented, the symbol Ⓓ will be indicated at the beginning of the EP. If an EP requires a "Measure of Success" (MOS) then the symbol Ⓜ will appear at the beginning of the EP. A Measure of Success is defined as a quantifiable measure which is utilized to determine if the EP has been met.[44]

C. Joint Commission Accreditation Decisions
The Joint Commission has six accreditation decision categories. Each decision and the conditions that lead to it are described in Table 4.1.

TIP: Accredited organizations are expected to remain in continuous compliance with the standards and their elements of performance throughout their accreditation cycle.

4.5 National Patient Safety Goals
A. Purpose of National Patient Safety Goals
The Joint Commission established the National Patient Safety Goals (NPSGs) to help accredited organizations address specific issues of patient safety and to promote specific improvements in patient safety. The goals highlight problematic areas in health care and describe evidence- and expert-based solutions to these problems. Recognizing that sound system design is intrinsic to the delivery of safe, high-quality health care, the Goals focus on system-wide solutions, wherever possible.

B. Establishment of the National Patient Safety Goals
In February 2002, the Sentinel Event Advisory Group was formed to advise The Joint Commission in the development of the Sentinel Event Alerts and NPSGs. The Advisory Group is charged with conducting a thorough review of all *Sentinel Event Alert* recommendations and other sources of patient safety recommendations. The Sentinel Event database, which contains de-identified aggregate information on sentinel events reported to The Joint Commission, is an important source of information from which the recommended changes to the NPSGs are derived. The latest Sentinel Event database report can be found at http://www.jointcommission.org/SentinelEvents/Statistics/.

Table 4.1 Accreditation Decisions

Decision Category	Explanation
Accredited	In compliance with all standards at the time of the survey or successfully addressed all requirements for improvements cited during the survey within 45 or 60 days following posting of the final report.
Provisional Accreditation	Organization fails to successfully address all requirements for improvements cited during the survey within 45 or 60 days following posting of the final report.
Conditional Accreditation	Organization fails to successfully address all the requirements for improvement by: • Previously being in Preliminary Denial of accreditation due to an Immediate Threat to Health or Safety situation; • Failure to resolve the requirements of a Provisional Accreditation; • Not in compliance with applicable standards due to a single or multiple issues that pose a risk to patient care or safety; • Failure to meet accreditation participation requirements. Must undergo an unannounced on-site-survey after submitting report of compliance in 45 or 60 days.
Preliminary Denial of Accreditation	Organization fails to successfully address all the requirements for improvement by: • An Immediate Threat to Health or Safety situation; • Failure to resolve the requirements of a Conditional Accreditation; • Not in compliance with a significant number of Joint Commission standards; • Failure to meet accreditation participation requirements. Decision is subject to review and appeal prior to determination to deny accreditation;
Denial of Accreditation	The organization has been denied accreditation. All appeals and reviews have been completed.
Preliminary Accreditation	For Early Survey options, the organization demonstrates compliance in standards surveyed under this type of survey. An unannounced survey will occur within six months of the first survey and all applicable standards will be surveyed.

Adapted from The Joint Commission. 2009 Hospital Accreditation Standards. The Joint Commission, Illinois. 2009, pages 409-410.[45]

The Advisory Group identifies recommendations as candidates for inclusion in the annual NPSGs if they are evidence- or consensus-based, cost effective and practical. Each year, new recommendations are added to the pool of candidates and the Advisory Group reevaluates the NPSG goals and requirements and suggests modifications, additions or deletions for the next year. A period of public comment on the proposed NPSGs is provided. The Advisory Group's suggestions are then forwarded to The Joint Commission Board of Commissioners for approval before the year in which they are to be implemented. Typically, the new NPSGs for the next year are finalized and published around July in order to give organizations the time to implement them prior to January 1 the next year.

C. Collaboration with Other Organizations

While some of the NPSGs are straightforward, others require collaboration with key professional associations and organizations to help strategize effective ways to meet the goal. One example is the Universal Protocol for Preventing Wrong Site, Wrong Procedure, Wrong Person Surgery. This protocol and its related implementation guidelines have now been endorsed by nearly 50 organizations including the American Hospital Association, the American Medical Association and the American Society of General Surgeons.

D. New Patient Safety Goals Annually

Every year around July, The Joint Commission announces the Patient Safety Goals for the upcoming year. The Joint Commission accredited facilities then have the remainder of the year to implement the upcoming goals. All of the goals must be fully implemented by January 1 of the next year. The Joint Commission expects The Joint Commission-accredited organizations to be in continual compliance with the pertinent Patient Safety Goals in addition to its continual compliance with The Joint Commission standards for that type of facility.

The Joint Commission posts on its website "Implementation Expectations" for the goals that are to be used by healthcare facilities in the implementation of the goals. Also found on The Joint Commission website are Frequently Asked Questions (FAQs) regarding the NPSGs. These FAQs are designed to answer questions from healthcare organizations that became apparent after the goals are announced for implementation.

TIP: Additional Patient Safety Goals will be added each year. Refer to The Joint Commission website (www.jointcommission.org) for current information about the National Patient Safety Goals.

TIP: The Joint Commission eventually retires the Patient Safety Goals, but when it does so, the goals are incorporated into The Joint Commission standards; they do not just go away.

E. Alternative Approaches

The Joint Commission NPSGs are more prescriptive than The Joint Commission standards. Accredited healthcare organizations may request approval of alternative approaches to The Joint Commission's requirements. Alternatives must be at least as effective as the published requirements in achieving the goals and be approved by the Sentinel Event Advisory Group. Organizations that wish to submit alternative approaches to the requirements associated with NPSGs can do so by filling out a "Request for Review of an Alternative Approach to a NPSG Requirement" form, found on The Joint Commission website. Members of the Advisory Group will review each form and advise The Joint Commission on the acceptability of the alternative. If not accepted, the organization will be provided with the rationale and will need either to revise the alternative until it is approved or to implement the requirement as issued by The Joint Commission.

F. National Patient Safety Goals for 2003

The Joint Commission established its first annual National Patient Safety Goals and associated recommendations for improving the safety of patient care in healthcare organizations. Only six goals were selected for the first year to allow for the healthcare organizations to adjust to the implementation and management of these goals.

G. National Patient Safety Goals for 2004

Since the advent of the NPSGs in 2003, additions and modifications in the Goals have been made each year. In July 2003, The Joint Commission Board of Directors approved the 2004 National Patient Safety Goals. These goals include the six 2003 NPSGs and their accompanying requirements and one new goal focusing on reducing the risk of healthcare acquired infections.

H. National Patient Safety Goals for 2005

In July 2004, the 2005 NPSGs were approved. For 2005, The Joint Commission developed program-specific goals for all accreditation programs that include continuation of the 2004 goals.

"The National Patient Safety Goals were intended from the outset to apply to all settings of care and all patient populations," notes Richard Croteau, M.D., The Joint Commission's director of strategic initiatives. "However, the language of the current requirements is decidedly 'acute care.' These program-specific adaptations will emphasize the Goal's applicability and enhance their effectiveness across healthcare settings."[46]

I. National Patient Safety Goals for 2006

In late May 2005, the 2006 NPSGs were announced. For 2006, The Joint Commission Board of Directors determined that there would be no more than two new requirements per program without any increase in the total number of requirements. Several goals and requirements were retired for 2006, while others were added and clarified.

J. National Patient Safety Goals for 2007

In June 2006, the 2007 NPSGs were announced along with a new process for scoring the goals. Implementation expectations have been added to make the goals more in line with the structure of the standards. The goals are scored as either compliant or non-compliant, unless the goal does not pertain to that type of organization. When a goal is scored as non-compliant, the organization will receive a requirement for improvement for that goal. All requirements for improvement must be addressed in the same manner as any non-compliant The Joint Commission standard.[47]

There are a few other changes in the 2007 NPSGs. A new goal regarding suicide risk assessment applies to most organizations. The existing patient-centered care goal (Goal 13) was expanded to more types of organizations. Medication reconciliation goal was expanded to require that the patient receive a copy of the list of medications upon discharge. A goal regarding risk assessments of patient homes and the risk for suicide was also added this year. No standards were removed from the list this year and the Laboratory is the only type of organization that had no changes at all.

K. National Patient Safety Goals for 2008

In May 2007, the 2008 NPSGs were announced. Some standards were consolidated, or expanded, and some were retired to the standards.

L. National Patient Safety Goals for 2009

In June 2008, the 2009 NPSGs were announced. For the 2009 NPSGs, there were many changes made, beginning with the renumbering of the NPSGs to match the renumbering of the standards. The scoring was changed also to match that of the standards. The NPSGs were modified in content and several were retired to the appropriate standards.

During 2009, The Joint Commission reviewed all of the current NPSGs and how they were developed. The Joint Commission stated that there would be no new goals for 2010, but this does not mean that the current 2009 goals will not be revised. Also, starting January 1, 2009, The Joint Commission was no longer accrediting networks and assisted living facilities so these two areas were dropped from the NPSG listings.

M. National Patient Safety Goals for 2010

In late 2009, the 2010 NPSGs were announced. While no new goals were added, several goals were revised and/or retired to the standards section of the manuals. The following goals were retired to the standards and are now being scored there: Abbreviations, Look-Alike Sound Alike Medications, Falls; Early Response to Patient Changing Needs; Read Back of Orders and Test Results; Handoff Communication; and Patient Involvement in Care. The goal of reporting hospital acquired infections associated with a death as a sentinel event has been deleted as it is covered with the sentinel event standards already.

N. Changes and Enhancements of NPSGs and Requirements

Comparison of goal requirement language for each year reveals specific changes and enhancements. The Sentinel Event Advisory Group is responsible for annually recommending retirement of selected requirements and goals. As these goals and/or requirements are retired, the numbering will be maintained for future reference. For example, NPSGs 5 and 6 have been retired and moved into the standards. The remaining goals will not be renumbered, so there will not be another NPSG with those numbers. In 2009, all of this was changed with the renumbering of the NPSGs to match that of the standards.

O. Application of National Patient Safety Goals and Joint Commission Standards to Legal Cases

The NPSGs and Joint Commission Standards define the quality of care that patients and nursing home residents and other such clients should be able to expect from The Joint Commission accredited organization. The accreditation process identifies the degree to which an organization's systems comply with NPSGs and Standards. Sentinel Event Alerts publicize issues that have been identified as potential problems usually across multiple organizations. Each patient contact has a high probability of being governed by a NPSG and/or a Joint Commission Standard (if the organization is accredited by The Joint Commission). In the following sections, specific cases are presented in which a patient's experience highlights a potential breakdown in how NPSGs and Standards were or were not employed in the delivery of medical care.

Appendix 4.1 at the end of this chapter discusses The Joint Commission National Patient Safety Goals and provides ideas for the titles of the documents relating to the goals that may be helpful in the course of discovery. Relevant policies and procedures may be stored in manuals or in electronic form. The manuals have different names in different facilities such as: Patient Care Standards, Nursing Department Manual, and Administrative Manual. Electronic storage of scanned policies and procedures may safely store outdated material. Some facilities store their policies and procedures on an intranet (accessible only within the facility) or on the Internet where anyone can access them.

The next section presents each of The Joint Commission National Patient Safety Goals current as of this writing in 2010. Each goal is explained and illustrated with a legal case, if available.

4.6 NPSG.01: Improve the Accuracy of Patient Identification

There is significant liability when treatments meant for one patient are delivered to the wrong person. An obvious source of error occurs when patients with the same or similar names are on the same nursing unit. Hospitals and other healthcare facilities typically try to keep patients with the same name separated. Misidentification can occur to any patient, however. Fatigued, distracted, or stressed healthcare providers may experience a slip and not verify the identity of the patient before beginning to render care. The first NPSG addresses this issue.

A. NPSG.01.01.01: Patient Identifiers (Implemented January 1, 2003) (All Organizations)

The Joint Commission NPSG advises that healthcare providers should use at least two patient identifiers (neither to be the patient's room number) whenever administering medications or blood products, taking blood samples *and other specimens for clinical testing, or providing any other treatments or procedures. The containers must be labeled in the presence of the patient.*[48]

The patient's identity can be confirmed by:

- asking the patient to state his name,
- asking the patient to state his date of birth,
- looking at the patient's identification band,
- looking at a patient identification number,
- asking the patient to state his phone number, or
- using photographs of the patient's face.

TIP: The medical record may not state how the patient was properly identified when an error resulted from misidentification. Post-incident statements or deposition testimony may reveal more details about how the patient was identified (or misidentified).

This section also addresses the use of patient identifiers for labeling specimens. Placing an incorrect label on a specimen can result in unwarranted treatment or failure to provide needed treatment. The consequences of these errors can be devastating.

B. NPSG.01.02.01: Time Out (Implemented January 1, 2003) (Long-Term Care, Home Health Care, Laboratory)

This NPSG advises that prior to the start of any surgical or invasive procedure, the healthcare providers should conduct a final verification process, such as a "time out," to confirm the correct patient, procedure, and site, using active—not passive—communication techniques. This applies to anywhere that a surgical or invasive procedure takes place, whether in the operating room or at any other location in the organization. This goal applies to Home Care, Laboratories, and Long-Term Care. For Ambulatory Health Care, Office Based Surgery, Critical Access Hospitals, and Hospitals, this goal is replaced with the Universal Protocol discussed later in this chapter.

C. NPSG.01.03.01: Eliminating Transfusion Errors (Implemented January 1, 2009) (Ambulatory Care, Behavioral Health, Critical Access Hospitals, Hospitals, Office-Based Surgery)

This NPSG was initiated to further prevent transfusion errors related to patient misidentification. Before the blood or blood product transfusion is initiated, the patient and the blood are matched utilizing two patient identifiers. One of these individuals must be a qualified transfusionist, such as a registered nurse, who will be administering the blood to the patient. The second person who is involved in the matching of the blood to the patient must also be a qualified transfusionist. An automated identification technology, such as barcoding, may be used if two qualified individuals are not available.[49]

4.7 NPSG.02: Improve the Effectiveness of Communication Among Caregivers

In today's multicultural society, sources of misunderstanding and miscommunication can result in errors which harm patients. Language and cultural barriers between patients and nurses, and nurses and other healthcare workers can result in inappropriate orders, incorrect interventions or not taking action when it is needed. Failure to communicate can contribute to patient injury in multiple ways. These are just a few:

- A female nurse who comes from a culture of subservient women may be reluctant to question a male doctor who writes an incorrect order.
- A patient's explanation of symptoms may be misinterpreted and documented by a nurse with limited English.
- A stoic nurse who minimizes the patient's pain can delay reporting and recording of an ominous development of chest pain.

As can be seen from the few examples above, miscommunication is a global issue. The Joint Commission standards address a narrow aspect of this issue: the reading back of telephone and verbal orders, as well as test results.

A. NPSG.02.01.01: Read Back Process (Implemented January 1, 2000 and Updated January 1, 2004) (All Organizations) (Retired to Standards in 2010)

The Joint Commission NPSG advises that healthcare providers should implement a process for taking verbal or telephone orders and critical values that require a verification "read-back" of the complete order or value by the person receiving the order or report. The Joint Commission recommends that a qualified healthcare professional taking a telephone or verbal order should write down the complete order or enter it into a computer, then read it back and receive confirmation from the individual who gave the order. This requirement also applies to physicians who give orders to each other, such as when an attending physician gives an order to a resident. This same requirement pertains to critical value results received from laboratory tests, radiologic examinations, and other such locations defined by the organization.[50]

Some healthcare organizations have implemented a policy of requiring the qualified healthcare professional who takes a verbal or telephone order or critical value report to document that it was read back to the prescriber/reporter. The Joint Commission does not require this to be done. The Joint Commission has not established any documentation requirements for this goal, but asks organizations during an accreditation survey to describe how they track performance against this Patient Safety Goal.

TIP: Critical tests and values were added to this requirement effective January 1, 2004.

The organization is expected to define what constitutes critical tests and critical test results. These may typically include:

- stat (immediate) orders,
- panic level test *results*, such as high or low blood sugar, high or low white blood cell counts, elevated or decreased electrolytes, dropping hemoglobin and hematocrit, prolonged clotting times, and so on, or
- diagnostic *tests* that require an urgent response, such as studies showing spinal cord injuries, intracerebral bleeding, free air in the abdomen which may indicate a perforation, vascular studies that show acute clotting, and so on.

Abnormal laboratory results are sorted into normal, abnormal, critical, and panic levels. The Laboratory staff typically calls the nursing staff to alert them of critical and panic values. The name of the healthcare professional that answered the phone and took the information is often requested and documented by the laboratory, and shows up in the medical record along with the test result. The nurse is typically the person receiving this report from the labo-

ratory, although depending on state laws, other healthcare professionals may also receive this report. Nursing notes are usually good sources to check to verify that a physician was notified of a critical test results. The nurse has the advantage of having the ability to readily document this conversation. The physician, who may be answering a cell phone or off premises, has no immediate way to acknowledge receipt of the results. The physician must have in place a system for addressing abnormal laboratory results. The nursing staff is required to notify the doctor about abnormal or critical test results, and may do so in a variety of ways. As long as the healthcare professional documents that the physician was notified, the onus is then on the physician to document what action was taken or not taken and why. Clearly, the physician will bear most of the responsibility if no action was taken and the patient suffers an adverse outcome. However, the nurse is also expected to follow the chain of command if an unsatisfactory response is obtained from the physician.[51]

Example: At 2:10 A.M., the nurse wakes the house physician up to report that a patient has a hemoglobin of 5 (normal 12-16). The physician responds "OK," and returns to sleep without issuing any orders or coming to evaluate the patient. The nurse is expected to contact the nursing supervisor and act as a patient advocate to obtain appropriate treatment for the patient

---

The results of abnormal radiological studies are typically conveyed from one physician to another, without involving the nursing staff. This is a physician to physician responsibility. However, if the results are conveyed to a health care professional other than the physician, that person must notify the physician utilizing the process described above.

B. NPSG.02.02.01: 'Do Not Use' Abbreviations (Implemented January 1, 2003) (All Organizations) (Retired to Standards in 2010)

The appendix of this text contains but a sampling of medical abbreviations that can be found in medical records. New staff members bring abbreviations used in other facilities. Abbreviations can create the potential for misunderstanding and errors. Some medical abbreviations have many different meanings, thus increasing the risk of error.

The Joint Commission asks healthcare organizations to address this issue by standardizing the abbreviations, acronyms, and symbols used throughout the organization, including a list of abbreviations, acronyms and symbols not to use. Healthcare providers are expected to not use:[52]

- U, u for units,
- IU for international units,
- QD, Q.D, qd, q.d. (every day),
- QOD, Q.O.D, qod, q.o.d (every other day),
- trailing zeros (X.0 mg) [permitted when reporting laboratory results in order to make the values precise],
- lack of a leading zero (0.Xmg), and
- MS, MS04 for morphine, or MgS04 for magnesium sulfate.

The implementation of this goal requires healthcare organizations to revise existing medical record forms. For example, specialized order sheets might include these unacceptable abbreviations. Some organizations have moved to allow only forms approved by the healthcare organization to be placed on the medical record. The healthcare organizations must work with physician offices and contracted services to assure that they also remove these abbreviations from the forms that they contribute to the healthcare organization's medical records. The forms that are approved by a facility for use in their medical records may have the organization's name or logo, as well as the form number and the date created and/or revised.

TIP: Commonly the date of the revision is listed on the bottom of the medical record form. Review medical record forms to see when the form was created. (This is useful information when tampering with the medical record is suspected.)

C. NPSG.02.03.01: Timeliness of Reporting and Receipt of Critical Values (Implemented January 1, 2005) (All Organizations— Expanded to Include Long-Term Care in 2008)

The Joint Commission addresses the area of critical tests and critical results by advising healthcare organizations to measure, assess and, if appropriate, take action to improve the timeliness of reporting, and the timeliness of receipt by the responsible licensed caregiver, of critical test results and values. For critical tests, the organization must determine what an acceptable length of time is for ordering the tests through receiving the results. The organization must also determine the appropriate length of time for reporting the results of critical values or findings. They must also define an acceptable length of time between the availability of the critical tests and critical results/values and the receipt by the responsible licensed caregiver.[53]

This NPSG was deleted for the ambulatory health care, home care, long-term care, and office-based surgery programs in 2010.

TIP: The attorney should request the facility to supply a policy that defines the acceptable length of time from ordering a critical test to reporting the results. Review this policy to determine if it defines the acceptable mechanism for reporting the critical value when the patient's responsible licensed professional is not available within those time frames.

D. NPSG.02.04.01: Critical Test Results and Values (for Laboratories Only) (Implemented January 1, 2005) (Retired January 2007)

This NPSG addresses the responsibility of the laboratory to assure that the critical values are communicated to the patient's responsible licensed caregiver in a timely manner. If the patient's responsible licensed professional is not available within the established time frames, there must be a mechanism to report the critical value to an alternative caregiver.[54]

E. NPSG.02.05.01: Managing Handoffs Communication (Implemented January 1, 2006) (All Organizations)

This NPSG was new for 2006 and applies to all accredited programs. This goal addresses these handoffs and the passing of patient-specific information from one caregiver to another for continuity of care and patient safety. This goal requires a standardized approach to *handoff* communications, including an opportunity to ask and respond to questions. There are many times and places where handoffs occur.[55] Just a few are:

- from one nursing shift to another,
- from the operating room to the recovery room,
- from the recovery room to the medical surgical unit or critical care unit,
- from the emergency department to be admitted to a medical surgical unit,
- from the intensive care unit to the step-down unit or medical surgical unit,
- from a hospital bed to a long term care facility,
- from the hospital bed to home, and
- from one physician to another who is taking call.

Communication gaps can result in loss of continuity. Lapses on the part of the healthcare practitioners can result in important information being overlooked.

Each organization should identify a standardized hand-off policy/procedure that includes the following information:

- the handoff situations,
- who is, or should be, involved in the communication,
- what information should be communicated,
- opportunities to ask and respond to questions,
- method to verify received information such as repeat-back, or read-back techniques, and
- the print or electronic information that should be available.

There can be more than one process of handoffs as appropriate. For example, the handoff between nursing shifts may be different from the handoff between nursing and radiology when the patient goes for a radiologic exam. However, each of these processes must have a standardized process developed that includes the following up-to-date information as appropriate:[56]

- patient's condition
- care and treatment
- medications
- services
- any anticipated changes

In addition, interruptions should be kept at a minimum. Interruptions have shown to lead to information that fails to be communicated or is forgotten.

TIP: Determine where handoffs have occurred in the case. Ask for the policies regarding these handoffs to determine if there is an indication that the handoffs were conducted correctly as per the policy.

4.8 NPSG.03: Improve the Safety of Using Medications
A. NPSG.03.01.01: Concentrated Electrolytes (Implemented January 1, 2003) (Retired to Standards January 2006)

Potassium chloride has been responsible for many medication errors and deaths. This concentrated electrolyte has been confused with similar size ampules of Lasix or saline. In response to multiple reports of medication errors, The Joint Commission recommended that potassium chloride be removed from nursing units. The NPSG recommended that all concentrated electrolyte solutions be carefully controlled and removed from nursing units. (These substances include, but are not limited to, potassium chloride, potassium phosphate, and sodium chloride greater than 0.9 percent.) The facility's medication administration policy and procedure should specify that these medications are not available on the units and the standardized dosing and admixtures are done by pharmacy.[57]

B. NPSG.03.02.01: Drug Concentrations (Implemented January 1, 2003) (Retired to Standards January 1, 2008)

The Joint Commission's objective was to have organizations standardize and limit the number of drug concentrations available in the organization.[58] This requirement primarily applies to drugs that are compounded in the hospital. The principle of standardization is to increase safety. When there are several strengths of a medication or intravenous fluid available, the chances are increased that the wrong one will be selected.

C. NPSG.03.03.01: Look-Alike, Sound-Alike Medications (Implemented January 1, 2005) (All Organizations Except Laboratory) (Retired to Standards in 2010)

The Joint Commission addressed the hazards of medications in a NPSG about the need to identify and, at a minimum, annually review a list of look-alike/sound-alike drugs used in the organization, and take action to prevent errors involving the interchange of these drugs. At a minimum, the list must contain ten look-alike/sound-alike medication combinations selected from the tables located on The Joint Commission website.[59]

The pharmaceutical industry contributes to this problem by assigning names of medications that are similar to others already on the market. Increased awareness of this risk has led to the use of "TALL man" lettering to capitalize portions of the name to make them stand out. The agencies responsible for approving trademarks and established names (i.e., nonproprietary generic names) for new drug products, primarily the U.S. Food and Drug Administration (FDA) and the United States Adopted Names Council (USANC), lack valid and reliable methods for assessing the likelihood of errors from look- and sound-alike medication names. Computerized methods could perhaps be used to reduce the number of confusing drug names that reach the marketplace and to identify confusing pairs within existing databases of medication names.

Once these pairs were identified, safeguards could be built into drug information systems to reduce the probability of confusion in clinical practice. Increasingly, companies are taking additional measures to determine if there are unacceptable similarities between the proposed trademark and products on the market. Therefore, a growing number of companies are now turning to ISMP (Institute of Safe Medication Practices) as an unbiased resource for error evaluation. The guiding principle for ISMP trademark evaluation is built upon Failure Mode and Effects Analysis (FMEA), a technique that places proposed trademarks in a clinical or pharmacy context and simulates actual work conditions. Thus, practicing nurses, pharmacists, and physicians are a major source of information during ISMP's error evaluation process. There are several other error evaluation services available to companies. ISMP anticipates that even more will become available as the FDA and other regulatory groups around the world encourage error potential evaluations. Toward that end, the FDA has established a Labeling and Nomenclature Committee to review every trademark as part of the new drug application (NDA) process. Among the criteria for the FDA trademark review are look- and sound-alike issues.[60]

D. NPSG.03.04.01: Labeling of Medications and Solutions On or Off the Sterile Field (Implemented January 1, 2006) (Ambulatory Care, Critical Access Hospital, Hospital, Office-Based Surgery)

This NPSG addresses the labeling of all fluids in and around the sterile field. This standard requires the labeling of all medications, medication containers (i.e., syringes, cups, basins), or other solutions on and off the sterile field in perioperative and other procedural settings, even if the procedure is not an "invasive" procedure. This labeling must occur when any medication or solution is transferred from the original packaging to another container. All original containers from medications or solutions must remain available for reference until the conclusion of the procedure. If there is a break or shift change, all medications and solutions both on and off the sterile field and their labels must be reviewed by the entering and exiting personnel.

All medications and containers are to be labeled at a minimum, with the following:

- Drug name, strength, and amount.
- Expiration date when not used in 24 hours.
- Expiration time when expiration occurs in less then 24 hours.
- The date prepared and the diluent for all compounded IV admixtures and parenteral nutrition solutions.
- The patient's name and location as well as directions for use should be added if the person prepar-

ing the medication is not the one who will administer it. These medications must be verified both verbally and visually by two qualified individuals.

All medications and solutions must be labeled even if there is only one medication to be used, and regardless of how obvious the medication/solution is. This includes anesthesia medications that are drawn up and placed on the anesthesia cart for use during the case. Any medications or solutions that are drawn up and used immediately are not required to be labeled. Any medications and solutions that are unlabeled must be discarded immediately. Any medications or solutions remaining after the completion of the procedure are also to be discarded.[61]

E. NPSG.03.05.01: Reducing Harm from Anticoagulation Therapy (Implemented January 2008) (Ambulatory Care, Critical Access Hospitals, Home Health, Hospitals, Long-Term Care)

The goal of this NPSG is to utilize standardized practices for anticoagulant therapy that includes patient involvement. This should result in a reduced risk of adverse drug events associated with the use of heparin (unfractionated) low molecular heparin, and warfarin (Coumadin). This goal was phased in during 2008 with full implementation by January 1, 2009. There must be an implemented defined anticoagulant management program which is utilized to individualize care. The facility must use only oral unit dose products, pre-filled syringes, or pre-mixed infusion bags when these are available. The facility must have approved protocols that address the anticoagulant therapy to be utilized, the patient to be treated, and the potential medication interactions. If the patient is on warfarin, there must be a baseline INR prior to initiating the therapy, and then the INR must be utilized to monitor and adjust the warfarin therapy. The Food Drug Interaction education should be supplied to the patient and utilized by the dietary department for patients on warfarin. If IV heparin is administered continuously, it must be administered via a programmable infusion pump. There must be written policies that address baselines and ongoing lab tests that are required for the heparin administration. The goal also requires that the patient, family, staff, and prescribers all receive education information about the anticoagulation therapy. The facility must also evaluate the safety and effectiveness of the anticoagulation therapy practices, take appropriate actions to make improvements in the processes and then measure the effectiveness of those actions on a regular basis.[62]

4.9 NPSG.04: Eliminate Wrong-Site, Wrong-Patient, Wrong-Procedure Surgery (Implemented January 1, 2003) (Changed to Universal Protocol July 1, 2004)

This goal consisted of preoperative verification, and site marking. This goal will be discussed as the Universal Protocol later in this section.

4.10 NPSG.05: Improve the Safety of Using Infusion Pumps: Ensure Free Flow Protection (Implemented January 1, 2003) (Retired to the Standards January 2006)

Focusing on prevention of free flow of intravenous fluids, this NPSG directs organizations to ensure free-flow protection on all general-use and PCA (patient controlled analgesia) intravenous infusion pumps used in the organization.[63] Free flow of fluid refers to the unimpeded flow of fluid when the tubing is removed from the pump and the roller clamp is opened.

Accidental, uncontrolled flow of intravenous fluids or medications can cause overdoses. In these incidents, free-flow occurs either because a nurse has not used an intravenous pump to control flow of fluid, or the caregiver has temporarily removed the tubing from the pump, but not closed off the clamp that controls flow of fluid. In one incident, a neonatal nurse removed the tubing from the IV pump, but failed to close off the flow of solution to the neonate. The infant received 180 ccs of lipids in three hours, which had previously been running at 0.5 cc per hour. The precise amount of lipids that was infused was not recorded in the medical record. The error was discovered when the laboratory technician inserted a needle into the infant's vein and got milky white fluid, which is the color of lipids, in the vial instead of blood. Massive brain damage resulted, leading to a large seven figure settlement (unpublished settlement). It is because of incidents like this one that The Joint Commission called for the elimination of IV pumps that permit a free flow of IV fluids.

4.11 NPSG.06: Improve the Effectiveness of Clinical Alarm Systems (Implemented January 1, 2003) (Retired to Standards January 2005)

A. NPSG.06.01.01: Check Alarm Systems

This NPSG stated that the facility should implement regular preventive maintenance and testing of alarm systems.[64] The facility should have criteria for periodically inspecting and testing the alarms.

TIP: Maintenance logs should be obtainable through discovery.

B. NPSG.06.02.01: Activate Alarms

The concern that promoted this NPSG was the need to assure that alarms are activated with appropriate settings. Alarms should be sufficiently audible with respect to distances and competing noise within the unit. The Goal dealing with alarms applied to a broad range of equipment, including ventilators, cardiac monitors, apnea machines, elopement/abduction alarms, infusion pumps, and panic buttons in bathrooms.[65] The medical record may have a checklist that the nurse uses to signify that alarms are activated, although there are no specific criteria for documenting that alarms are activated, set properly, and sufficiently audible.

1. Critical care alarms

A physician may write an order that specifies the upper and lower limits for alarms. For example, a heart rate under 50 or over 130 may trigger an alarm.

2. Elopement/departure alert systems

There are several vendors of elopement alarms, but the systems work primarily in two ways. The first kind involves a nursing home resident wearing an electronic device as a bracelet, anklet, or necklace which when it comes near a signalling device, sounds a loud audible alarm. The second electronic approach is the resident's alarming device sounds audibly and locks the exit door so that the resident may not use the door for egress. Audibly alarmed doors are also frequently used. These doors are alarmed to ring centrally at a nurse's station, locally at only the door, or at both sites. The preferred system is that the door alarms centrally and the local alarming device is an adjunct and second layer of protection. It is important that the alarms not be disarmed or turned off at the nurse's station which effectively destroys the central system. The staff should have to reset the alarm after each alarming episode to make sure that the door is checked and the staff is assured that a resident did not use the door as an exit.[66]

The medical record should make references to the ongoing use of alarm systems. The care plan should specify the device used for the resident.

4.12 NPSG.07: Reduce the Risk of Healthcare-Acquired Infections

A. NPSG.07.01.01: Meeting Hand Hygiene Guidelines (Implemented January 1, 2004) (All Organizations)

Healthcare personnel are directed to comply with current World Health Organization (WHO) or CDC (Centers for Disease Control and Prevention) hand hygiene guidelines (category I recommendations) in this NPSG.[67] The WHO guidelines are very similar to those of the CDC. The CDC report is available at http://www.cdc.gov/mmwr/PDF/rr/rr5116.pdf, pages 30-34. The WHO report may be downloaded at http://whqlibdoc.who.int/publications/2009/9789241597906_eng.pdf, Part 2 Sections 1-9.

The CDC has extensive research-based recommendations to reduce nosocomial (healthcare-acquired) infections. The guidelines address:

- when to wash hands with anti-microbial soap,
- when to decontaminate hands with alcohol-based products,
- when to use antimicrobial-impregnated wipes (i.e., towelettes),
- how to wash hands,
- the steps involved to prepare healthcare workers' hands prior to operations,
- how to select hand hygiene products,
- how to reduce irritation of skin from hand hygiene,
- use of gloves,
- avoidance of artificial nails, and
- the importance of education and monitoring compliance with hand hygiene guidelines.

The CDC guidelines specify documentation (which may be discoverable) that healthcare facilities are expected to keep related to hand hygiene. This includes measuring improvements in hand-hygiene adherence:

- Periodically monitor and record adherence as the number of hand-hygiene episodes performed by personnel/number of hand-hygiene opportunities, by ward or by service. Provide feedback to personnel regarding their performance.
- Monitor the volume of alcohol-based hand rub (or detergent used for handwashing or hand antisepsis) used per 1,000 patient-days. Monitor adherence to policies dealing with wearing of artificial nails.
- When outbreaks of infection occur, assess the adequacy of healthcare worker hand hygiene.[68]

B. NPSG.07.02.01: Healthcare Associated Infections Resulting in Death or Major Permanent Loss of Function (Implemented January 1, 2004) (All Organizations) (Deleted from All Programs in 2010)

The Joint Commission specifies that all identified cases of unanticipated death or major permanent loss of function

associated with a healthcare-acquired infection should be managed as sentinel events. This goal refers to an unanticipated death or major permanent loss of function related to a health care associated infection. The root cause analysis needs to address the management of the patient before and after the identification of the infection.[69]

Medical records may refer to the signs of infection, such as redness, swelling, warmth, drainage, fever, increased white blood cell count, or positive cultures of blood, urine, stool, wound drainage, respiratory secretions, cerebral spinal fluid, and so on. A nosocomial infection is one that is acquired within the facility. An iatrogenic infection is one caused by a healthcare provider. Failure to wash hands is one of the primary causes of infection. Refer to Vance[70] for additional information on infections within healthcare facilities.

C. NPSG.07.03.01: Preventing Multi-Drug Resistant Organism Infections (Implemented on January 1, 2009 with Full Implementation by January 1, 2010) (Critical Access Hospitals, Hospitals)

This goal requires that the applicable organizations implement evidence-based practices to prevent health-care associated infections due to multidrug-resistant organizations. This applies to, but is not limited to, Methicillin Resistant Staph Aureus Vancomycin Resistant Enterococcus, C-difficile, and multiple drug-resistant gram negative bacteria. This goal is to be phased in during 2009 with implementation targets at three, six, and nine months in 2009.

The basic elements that must be in place by January 1, 2010 are:[71]

- Conduct periodic risk assessments for multi-drug resistant organisms acquisition and transmission.
- Educate staff, licensed independent practitioners about such infections, multi-drug resistant organisms, and prevention strategies at time of hire and annually.
- Educate patients and families of those who are infected or colonized with multi-drug resistant organisms.
- Implement a surveillance program.
- Measure and monitor multi-drug resistant organisms prevention processes and outcomes.
- Provide surveillance data to key stakeholders.
- Implement policies and procedures for reducing the risk of transmission of multi-drug resistant organisms.

- Implement a laboratory-based alert system that identifies new patients with multi-drug resistant organisms.
- Implement an alert system that identifies readmitted or transferred multi-drug resistant organism-positive patients.

D. NPSG.07.04.01: Preventing Central-Line Associated Blood Stream Infections (Implemented on January 1, 2009 with Full Implementation by January 1, 2010) (Critical Access Hospitals, Hospital, Long-Term Care)

This goal requires that the applicable organizations implement evidence-based practices to prevent central-line associated bloodstream infections. This covers short term and long term central venous catheters and peripherally inserted central catheter (PICC) lines. This goal was phased in during 2009 with implementation targets at three, six, and nine months in 2009.

The basic elements that must be in place by January 1, 2010 are:[72]

- Educate staff, licensed independent practitioners, and others who are involved in these procedures about such infections and prevention strategies at time of hire and annually.
- Educate patients and families about the possibility of central line infections and prevention prior to inserting the line.
- Conduct periodic risk assessments for central-line-associated bloodstream infection rates, monitors compliance with best practices, and evaluate the effectiveness of prevention efforts.
- Implement policies and procedures for reducing the risk of transmission of central-line associated bloodstream infections.
- Measure and monitor central-line infection prevention processes and outcomes and provide surveillance data to key stakeholders.
- Utilize a catheter checklist and a standardized protocol for central venous catheter insertion.
- Perform hand hygiene prior to catheter insertion or manipulation.
- Utilize a standardized supply cart or kit for insertion of central lines.
- Utilize standardized protocol for how to care for the central line catheter.
- Remove all nonessential catheters.

E. NPSG.07.05.01: Preventing Surgical Site Infections (Implemented on January 1, 2009 with Full Implementation by January 1, 2010) (Ambulatory Health Care, Critical Access Hospital, Hospital, Office-Based Surgery)

This goal requires that the applicable organizations implement evidence-based practices to prevent surgical site infections. This goal was phased in during 2009 with implementation targets at three, six, and nine months in 2009. The basic elements that must be in place by January 1, 2010 are:[73]

- Educate staff, licensed independent practitioners, and others who are involved in surgical procedures about healthcare associated infections, surgical site infections, and the importance of prevention.
- Educate patients and families prior to their surgical procedure about surgical site infection prevention
- Implement policies and procedures for reducing the risk of surgical site infections.
- Conduct periodic risk assessments for surgical site infections, monitor compliance with best practices, and evaluate the effectiveness of prevention efforts.
- Utilize evidence-based guidelines, monitor surgical site infections for the first 30 days following procedures that do not involve inserting implantable devices and for one year following procedures involving implantable devices.
- Measure and monitor surgical site infections and provide surveillance data to key stakeholders.
- Administer antimicrobial agents for prophylaxis for particular procedures according to evidence-based standards and guidelines for best standards.
- Utilize clippers or depilatories for hair removal.

4.13 NPSG.08: Accurately and Completely Reconcile Medications Across the Continuum of Care (All Organizations Except the Laboratory)

Medication errors are the most frequent cause of patient harm in health care. A Sentinel Event Alert issued in January 2006 clarifies the importance of medication reconciliation in preventing medication errors. The opportune time to do this is during a transition in care, such as a change in setting, service, practitioner, or level of care. The reconciliation process helps to avoid medications that are inadvertently discontinued, continued when they are not indicated for the patient's current condition, and incorrectly ordered in terms of dose or frequency. Additionally, reconciliation helps to reduce the amount of time nurses and pharmacists spend tracking down medications and prescribers and verifying accuracy. A one-time verification of medications helps to reduce the redundancy and inconsistencies inherent in recording medication usage in multiple places in the medical record.

This NPSG has been revised several times. After the goal was revised for January 1, 2009, The Joint Commission Advisory board determined that it needed to reevaluate this goal again. During 2009, The Joint Commission interviewed healthcare practitioners, healthcare organizations, surveyors and others to determine what is absolutely necessary for patient safety. Patients and families are expected to be able to supply complete lists of medications the patient is taking. The inability of the patient to provide accurate information about medications intensifies the risks associated with medication administration. During the first half of 2011, the survey findings regarding this goal will not be considered in terms of the requirements for improvement that from a survey. In July 2011, this revised goal will be counted in the requirements for improvement.[74]

A. NPSG.08.01.01: Comparing Current and Newly Ordered Medications (Fully Implemented January 1, 2006) (Modified January 1, 2009)

This Joint Commission Goal states that facilities, with the involvement of the patient and/or significant other, should use a process for obtaining and documenting a complete list of the patient's current medications upon the patient's admission to the organization, referred to as "home medication" list. This process includes a comparison of the medications the organization provides to those on the home medication list.[75] The reconciliation process involves five steps:

1. Develop a list of current medications the patient is taking.
2. Develop a list of medications to be prescribed.
3. Compare the medications on the two lists.
4. Resolve any discrepancies.
5. Communicate the new list to appropriate caregivers and to the patient.
6. This information should be referred to by the prescriber who writes the initial medication orders, and whenever ordering medications during the patient's stay.

B. NPSG.08.02.01: Communicating Medications to the Next Provider (Implemented January 1, 2005 and Updated July 1, 2006) (Modified January 1, 2009)

According to this NPSG, a complete list of the patient's medications is to be communicated to the next provider of service when an organization refers or transfers a patient to another setting, service, practitioner, or level of care within or outside the organization. This communication between providers must be documented. When a patient leaves the hospital, or other such organization, to go home, the complete reconciled medication list is to be provided to the patient's known primary care provider, the original referring provider, or a known next provider of service.[76]

TIP: Physicians commonly list the patient's medications at the time of discharge or transfer to the care of a nursing home, rehabilitation facility, assisted living home, or home care agency.

Analysis of the medical record may reveal discrepancies, such as omissions of medications that the physician intended to continue. For example, insulin or anticonvulsant medications may inadvertently not be reordered after surgery. It is against The Joint Commission standards for a physician to enter an order to "resume preoperative medications" without specifying exactly what needs to be given. Nurses and pharmacists are expected to question these orders. Following directions for maintaining medication protocols may be critical. Medications that are ineffective if under-prescribed or toxic if given in too high doses need to be monitored.

C. NPSG.08.03.01: Providing a Reconciled Medication List to the Patient (Previously Part of NPSG.08.02.01) (Modified January 1, 2009)

This NPSG now singles out the fact that a patient is to be given a copy of the patient's reconciled medication list and that the medication list is explained to the patient or family as needed. Patients and families must be reminded to discard any old lists and to update their records with any new medications that they are on at the time of discharge. This interaction and education must be documented in the medical record.[77]

D. NPSG.08.04.01: Settings in Which Medications are Minimally Used (Implemented January 1, 2009)

There are settings in hospitals and other types of healthcare organizations where medications are minimally utilized, if at all. Many of these settings may utilize medications one time or for a very short duration. In these settings, it is very difficult to complete the entire NPSG process as described in the first three parts of this National Patient Safety Goal. In these settings, the requirements are that the organization collect the names of the medications the patient is using, but need not obtain the dose, route, or frequency of use. Where this portion of the medication reconciliation goal applies, medications may be utilized for only short periods of time, and no changes are made to the patient's current medication list when they are discharged from the organization.[78] However, even in these settings a complete, documented medication reconciliation process is required when:

- Any new long-term (chronic) medications are prescribed,
- There is a prescription change for any of the patient's current, known long-term medications, and
- The patient is required to be subsequently admitted to an organization from these settings for ongoing care.

In these settings, when a full medication reconciliation process is required as described above, the organization must also comply with NPSG.08.02.01 and NPSG.08.03.01 above.

4.14 NPSG.09: Reduce the Risk of Patient Harm Resulting From Falls
A. NPSG.09.01.01: Identification of Patients at Risk for Falls (Implemented January 1, 2005) (Retired January 2006)

This NPSG addressed the need to assess and periodically reassess each patient's risk for falling, including the potential risk associated with the patient's medication regimen, and take action to address any identified risks.[79]

Many hospital nursing departments have incorporated an analysis of risk factors for falls as part of the admission assessment. Refer to Miceli et al.[80] for a perspective on the use of side rails and restraints in nursing homes.

B. NPSG.09.02.01: Implementing a Fall Reduction Program (Implemented January 1, 2006) (Critical Access Hospitals, Home Health, Hospitals, Long-Term Care) (Retired to Standards in 2010)

The previous "Fall" Patient Safety Goal requirement was discontinued and replaced with this requirement in January 2006. This requirement is less proscriptive than the previous requirement. With this goal, the organization must imple-

ment a fall reduction program and evaluate the effectiveness of this program. The items to be included in the program will vary based on the type of organization. For example, the program in a long term care facility should address transfer protocols, while this might not be necessary in the hospital program. The program should include assessment and reassessment of the patient for risk of falls, and the assessment of the patient's environment for factors that may lead to falls. For example, in the home care environment, the patient's throw rugs throughout the house could contribute to the patient falling. The program should include risk reduction strategies, staff education, and education to patients and families. Repetitive falls must be addressed to change the plan of care to reduce the risk of falling.[81]

4.15 NPSG.10: Reduce the Risk of Influenza and Pneumococcal Disease in Older Adults (Implemented January 1, 2005) (Long-Term Care)

Long term care facilities, by their very nature, are facilities where infections can be spread easily among the residents. This NPSG was established as a preventative nature for those facilities. Regardless, many other types of organizations are implementing this goal even though it is not required of them to do so.

A. NPSG.10.01.01: Protocol for Influenza Vaccine (Retired to Standards for Long-Term Care in 2010)

With the need to immunize against the flu every year, the elderly are at risk if they do not receive the vaccine. This NPSG was established to help assure that those older adults who are in residential facilities and those who are at high risk are immunized. This goal calls for the development of protocols that will determine whether or not to vaccinate these older adults.[82]

B. NPSG.10.02.01: Protocol for Pneumonia Vaccine

Pneumococcal disease kills more people in the United States each year than all other vaccine-preventable diseases combined. The pneumococcal vaccine is effective in preventing severe disease, hospitalization, and death. The Centers for Disease Control (CDC) recommends the vaccine if the person is over 65 years of age, has a serious long-term health problem, has a low resistance to infection, or is an Alaskan native or a Native American. Revaccination should be strongly considered greater than or equal to six years after the first dose for those at highest risk of a) fatal pneumococcal disease (such as asplenic patients) or b) rapid decline in antibody levels (e.g., transplant recipients or those with chronic renal failure or nephrotic syndrome).[83] This goal calls for the development of a protocol that establishes when patients should be vaccinated and how often a booster shot is required.[84]

C. NPSG.10.03.01: Protocol for New Cases

This goal requires organizations to continuously monitor infections to identify any new cases of influenza and to manage an outbreak. These facilities are required to develop a protocol regarding how they do this. Reports should be given to the organization's leadership and to the performance improvement committee on a regular basis.[85]

4.16 NPSG.11: Reduce the Risk of Surgical Fires (Implemented January 1, 2005) (Ambulatory Health Care, Office Based Surgery)

According to The Joint Commission, this NPSG pertains only to Ambulatory and Office-Based Surgery. However, it is applicable to all organizations that utilize oxygen and sources of heat during surgery.

According to the Centers for Disease Control and Prevention (CDC), in the period from 1996 to 2007, there was a threefold increase in freestanding outpatient surgery center visits. There were an estimated 57.1 million surgical and nonsurgical procedures performed during 34.7 million ambulatory surgery center visits.[86]

Fires are of grave concern in the healthcare setting. With this number of outpatient surgical procedures occurring, it is highly likely that surgical fires are occurring. When these fires occur, they frequently result in serious injury and sometimes death. The surgical environment is an oxygen-rich atmosphere with flammable materials and ignition sources.

For this goal, The Joint Commission requires organizations to establish guidelines and training for staff who work in surgical or procedural areas where oxygen is utilized. The guidelines must address ways to minimize oxygen concentration over drapes, avoid the use of flammable solutions and materials, and safely control potential ignition sources. The guidelines must also include the procedures to be followed if a surgical fire should occur.[87]

4.17 NPSG.12: Implementation of Applicable National Patient Safety Goals and Associated Requirements by Components and Practitioner Sites (Implemented January 1, 2005) (Deleted

2008 when The Joint Commission No Longer Accredited Networks)
A. NPSG.12.01.01

This NPSG is applicable to Integrated Delivery Systems, Managed Care Organizations, and Preferred Provider Organizations. The NPSG specifically advises these organizations to examine the other National Patient Safety Goals, and then encourage those that are associated with these organizations to implement the pertinent goals for their facilities. The goal states that consideration should be given to incentives for those that demonstrate compliance with applicable goals.[88]

4.18 NPSG.13: Encourage the Active Involvement of Patients and Their Families in the Patient's Care as a Patient Safety Strategy (Implemented January 1, 2006) (Updated January 1, 2007) (All Organizations)
A. NPSG.13.01.01 (Retired to Standards in 2010)

This NPSG is designed to have facilities define and communicate how patients and their families report concerns about safety, and encourage them to do so. It is recognized that patient involvement in care decisions improves compliance and informed decision making. Patients and their families must be aware of safety issues and how they can contribute to patient safety. The Joint Commission's Speak Up Campaign is one effort to educate patients about speaking up regarding any concerns or questions they have regarding their care. This can be invaluable in their care and assist in the prevention of medical errors. This NPSG requires that patients be educated about how to report their concerns, and to be given information regarding infection control, such as hand hygiene, contact precautions and so on. Surgical patients are to be educated regarding measures that will be taken during surgery to prevent any adverse events. The patient's understanding of the education must be evaluated and documented in the medical record.[89]

4.19 NPSG.14: Prevent Healthcare-Associated Pressure Ulcers (Decubitus Ulcers) (Implemented January 1, 2006) (Long-Term Care)
A. NPSG.14.01.01: Assessment and Periodic Reassessment

Long term care facilities are required to assess and periodically reassess each resident's risk for developing a pressure ulcer (decubitus ulcer) and then to take action if risks are identified. According to the National Center for Health Statistics (2009), in 2004, according to the National Nursing Home Survey, about 159,000 nursing home residents (11 percent) had pressure ulcers. Stage II ulcers were the most common stage found. Others have estimated that from 2 to 28 percent of nursing home residents have pressure ulcers at any given time.[90]

For this NPSG, each long term care facility that The Joint Commission accredits must develop a plan for assessment of the skin, prevention of pressure ulcers and early treatment for any pressure ulcers that develop. This includes identifying residents who are at risk for pressure ulcers and incorporating prevention methods into their plan of care. All residents must be assessed for risk of a pressure ulcer upon admission and reassessed at periodic intervals. The assessment must be completed utilizing a validated risk assessment tool such as the Braden Scale or Norton Scale.[91]

4.20 NPSG.15: The Organization Identifies the Safety Risks Inherent in its Patient Population (Implemented January 1, 2007)
A. NPSG.15.01.01: Identification of Patients at Risk for Suicide (Hospitals, Behavioral Health)

This goal applies to psychiatric hospitals and patients being treated for emotional or behavioral disorders in a general hospital. The phrase "emotional or behavioral disorders" refers to any Diagnostic and Statistical Manual diagnosis or condition, including those related to substance abuse. While in a general hospital, the types of patients that must have this assessment are usually seen in the Emergency Department. There are several cases in The Joint Commission's sentinel event database of suicides in emergency departments while the patients were awaiting transfer. These facilities are required to utilize a risk assessment to identify risks that may increase or decrease the risk for suicide, and then to address the patient's immediate safety needs and most appropriate setting for treatment. Organizations must provide information about the availability of a crisis hotline (not necessarily its own) or other resources, and how to access them if needed.[92]

B. NPSG.15.02.01: Identification of Risks of Long-Term Oxygen Therapy such as Home Fires (Home Health)

Home care agencies are to utilize a home safety risk assessment regarding potential causes of a fire in the home. The assessment must include the presence or absence and working order of smoke detectors, fire extinguishers, and fire safety plans, and a review of all medical equipment. The agency then must provide education to the patient and fam-

ily regarding fire prevention in the home, based on the risk assessment findings. The agency must assess the patient's understanding and compliance with fire prevention activities and report any concerns to the patient's physician.[93]

4.21 NPSG.16: Improve Recognition and Response to Changes in a Patient's Condition (Implemented January 2007) (Critical Access Hospitals, Hospitals)
A. NPSG.16.01.01: Requesting Additional Assistance When a Patient's Condition is Worsening (Retired to Standards in 2010)

Hospitals must select a method that enables the healthcare staff members to directly request additional assistance from a specially trained individual(s) when the patient's condition appears to be worsening. This NPSG does not require organizations to have a rapid response team; however, this is the route most hospitals have taken. The patient and family should also be encouraged to seek assistance, but they do not have to be allowed to call the rapid response team themselves. Some facilities do allow families to activate the rapid response team. Most frequently, they are instructed how to call for a nurse or other caregiver in an emergency. The hospital staff must be educated regarding the method chosen by the facility to provide this additional assistance. The hospital must also monitor the effectiveness of the methodology utilized and act to make improvements as they are identified.[94]

4.22 Universal Protocol (Implemented July 1, 2004) (Revised January 1, 2009) (Ambulatory Health Care, Critical Access Hospital, Hospital, Office-Based Surgery)

Portions of the Universal Protocol were initially included in the National Patient Safety Goal 01.02.01 and remain there for Long-Term Care, Home Health Care, and Laboratory Organizations. However, for all other types of organizations, the Universal Protocol contains this information. The types of organizations that utilize NPSG.01.02.01 have less of a need for utilization of the complete protocol due to the type of services provided in those settings. The Joint Commission reviewed the Universal Protocol during 2009 to determine if there are additional modifications needed. The Universal Protocol applies to operating rooms and to nonoperating room settings. It applies to all procedures that expose patients to more than minimal risk, including procedures done in settings other than the operating room. Preprocedure verification, site marking, and the time out procedures described below should be as consistent as possible throughout the organization.[95]

A. UP.01.01.01: Conducting a Pre-Procedure Verification Process

This portion of the Universal Protocol addresses the importance of creating and using a preoperative verification process, such as a checklist, throughout the preprocedure time period. This should begin at the time of the decision to perform the procedure and end immediately prior to the initiation of the procedure. The purpose of this verification process is to assure that the relevant documentation (including the informed consent, lab work, etc.), information and equipment are:[96]

- Available prior to the start of the procedure.
- Correctly identified, labeled, and matched to the patient's identifiers.
- Reviewed and are consistent with the patient's expectations and with the team's understanding of the intended patient, procedure, and site.

Any disagreements must be resolved prior to the initiation of the procedure. The Universal Protocol describes multiple time frames when this verification must occur, the exact items that are to be verified at what times, and what documentation is required.

B. UP.01.02.01: Mark the Procedure Site (Implemented January 1, 2003) (Changed to Universal Protocol July 1, 2004)

All procedures that involve incision, percutaneous puncture or insertion must have the intended procedure site marked prior to the initiation of the procedure. It is necessary to mark the site when there is a laterality, multiple structures, such as fingers or toes, and multiple levels, such as vertebral bodies. The site is to be marked by a licensed independent practitioner or other provider who is privileged or permitted by the hospital to perform the intended surgical or nonsurgical invasive procedure. For example, the operating room nurse can not mark the site for a patient having surgery in the OR. The site should be marked prior to the patient being taken to the procedure room, and the patient should be awake and able to participate in this process. How the site is marked and the type of mark utilized should be standardized throughout the facility. In cases when such organization-wide standardized site marking is not possible, another standardized method should be developed for those areas. For example, in Radiology, the use of a "BB" is commonly how the potential site is marked. Regardless, the site marking should:[97]

- Be made at or near the procedure site or the incision site.

- Include, preferably, the surgeon's initials, with or without a line representing the proposed incision.
- Be made using a marker that is permanent to remain visible after the completion of the surgical prep and sterile draping, and is visible when the patient is in the final draped position.

The organization must also have an alternative method identified in case a patient determines that she does not want her skin marked with the permanent marker. Surgery on the incorrect site may occur due to confusion associated with surgical consents.

C. UP.01.03.01: A Time Out is Performed Immediately Prior to Starting the Procedure

The "time out" term refers to everyone stopping what they are doing and taking time out one more time before the procedure begins to assure that everything is in order for the procedure to be conducted. There should be a single person, such as the circulating nurse, who is responsible for calling the time out. Active communication among all of the members of the procedure team is required. Ideally the time out is completed prior to the start of the anesthesia, but frequently the surgeon is not ready and available at that time. If during the time out any member of the team has a question or concern regarding the procedure, everything stops until that concern or question is resolved. The components of the Universal Protocol and the time out must be clearly documented within the medical record. The time out addresses the following:[98]

- the name of the patient,
- the correct side and site of the procedure are marked,
- the procedure consent is completed correctly,
- the agreement on the procedure to be done,
- the correct patient position,
- relevant images and results are properly labeled and appropriately displayed,
- the antibiotics have been administered and/or fluids for irrigation purposes are available, and
- safety precautions based on the patient's history or medication use.

The surgeon, anesthesiologist, and the rest of the surgical team must participate in the positive identification of the patient, the intended procedure, and the site of the procedure.

4.23 The Leapfrog Group

Other organizations besides The Joint Commission are working towards increased patient safety. The Leapfrog

Group is made up of more than 160 companies and organizations that buy health care. Leapfrog and its members work together to:

- reduce preventable medical mistakes and improve the quality and affordability of health care,
- reward doctors and hospitals for improving the quality, safety and affordability of health care,
- encourage public reporting of healthcare quality and outcomes so that consumers and purchasing organizations can make more informed healthcare choices, and
- help consumers reap the benefits of making smart healthcare decisions.[99]

The Leapfrog Group has focused on several patient safety issues, which they call "Leaps." These include:[100]

- Evidence-Based Hospital Referral (EHR)
- Computer Physician Order Entry (CPOE)
- ICU physician staffing (IPS) and
- Leapfrog Safe Practices Score.

Each of these leaps has an overwhelming amount of scientific evidence showing that the leaps will improve quality and safety, and reduce preventable medical errors. Leapfrog believes that each is implementable in the near future. It also asserts consumers can appreciate the value that each of these leaps can bring, and the health plans, purchasers, and consumers can determine the presence or absence of these leaps when selecting healthcare providers. The Leapfrog Group surveys hospitals annually to determine how the organizations are doing in terms of meeting these leaps. This survey is called the Leapfrog Hospital Quality and Safety Survey. The Leapfrog Group also has hospital recognition and reward programs based on the scores received annually during its survey. Approximately 1,300 hospitals participated in the 2008 survey; the ratings based on the survey are available at http://www.leapfroggroup.org/cp.[101]

A. Evidence-Based Hospital Referral

Liability issues surround errors made in the care of patients with complex surgical needs. A surgeon may be found to be liable for botching an operation that should have been referred to a facility skilled in performing that surgery. A surgeon or surgical team at a facility that performs high risk surgery may be held liable if established protocols are not followed and an untoward outcome occurs.

The premise behind evidence-based hospital referral is that patients can achieve the best outcomes if they receive care at hospitals that are very familiar with their specific health needs. Familiarity is measured by adherence to clinical practices that improve outcomes, and through high volume exposure to patients with particular needs. Leapfrog Group has focused on surgical outcomes and the proficiency exhibited by these hospitals. Leapfrog Group maintains a searchable database on its website that permits consumers to locate hospitals that have reported their performance measures. Several of the high-risk procedures that are part of their survey include heart bypass surgery, heart angioplasty, aortic valve replacements, abdominal aortic aneurysm repair, pancreatic resection, esophogectomy, bariatric surgery, and high risk deliveries. In the 2008 survey 43 percent of those performing heart bypass surgery met the standards. Unfortunately, all of the other procedures had even less compliance with the lowest being abdominal aortic aneurysm repair with only 5 percent.[102]

B. Computer Prescriber Order Entry (CPOE)

When Computer Prescriber Order Entry (CPOE) systems with intercept capability (intercept errors) based on protocols specified by the Institute for Safe Medication Practices are used in hospitals, they have been shown to reduce serious prescribing errors by more than 50 percent. Yet fewer than 7 percent of hospitals surveyed reported meeting the Leapfrog standards.[103]

CPOE systems can eliminate errors caused by misreading or misinterpreting handwritten instructions. Leapfrog Group identifies the benefits of computer prescriber order entry as:

- prompts that warn against the possibility of drug interaction, allergy, or overdose,
- accurate, current information that helps physicians keep up with new drugs as they are introduced into the market,
- improved communication between physicians and pharmacists, and
- reduced healthcare costs due to improved efficiencies.[104]

The use of computers for direct order entry and drug dispensing machines is costly and are not yet error-free systems, and often lack important screening features to detect unsafe orders. In fact, in December 2008 The Joint Commission issued its 42nd Sentinel Event Alert entitled "Safely implementing health information and converging technologies." The alert states that unintended medication and other errors stem typically from human-machine interactions or organizational/system design. The technology purchased may not be compatible with all of the other technology with which it must communicate. The users of the technology may not fully understand how to use the technology or may not stay updated by changes to the technology that may have occurred.[105] This Sentinel Event Alert also states that a 2007 study conducted by The American Society of Health-System Pharmacists indicated that only 18 percent of hospitals had CPOE at that time. President Obama's initiatives are expected to increase that number.

C. ICU Physician Staffing

According to the Leapfrog Group, scientific evidence exists showing that the ICU quality of care is influenced by the ICUs being staffed with intensivists. Leapfrog further states that in ICUs managed or co-managed by intensivists, there is a 40 percent reduction in ICU mortality and a 30 percent reduction in hospital mortality. The Leapfrog standard requires that intensivists be utilized for care management for all general medical, surgical, and neuro ICUs for seven days a week, and at least eight hours a day. The intensivists must also be available on call by pager within five minutes. According to the results of their 2008 survey, this standard is being met by 31 percent of the hospitals responding and another 7 percent planned to have the intensivists in place by the end of 2009. In 2002, only 10 percent of the hospitals met this standard.[106]

D. Leapfrog Safe Practices Score

The Leapfrog Safety Practices Score consists of 13 safety practices endorsed by the National Quality Forum. The 2008 survey found that only 32 percent of the hospitals fully met at least 90 percent of the expert-weighted recommended policies and procedures. Some of these safety practices include maintaining a safety culture, hand hygiene, nursing workforce, and prevention of infections. The National Quality Forum-endorsed Safe Practices are discussed in the next section.[107] Other findings from this 2008 survey found that among the participating hospitals:[108]

- Sixty-five percent did not have all recommended policies and procedures in place to prevent hospital-acquired infections (HAIs)
- Seventy-five percent do not fully meet the standards for 13 evidence-based safety practices, ranging from handwashing to competency of the nursing staff
- Only 26 percent are fully meeting standards for heart attacks
- Only 34 percent are fully meeting standards for pneumonia

- Only 30 percent are fully meeting standards to prevent hospital acquired pressure ulcers
- Only 25 percent are fully meeting standards to prevent hospital acquired injuries

4.24 National Quality Forum

The National Quality Forum (NQF) is a private, not-for-profit membership organization created to develop and implement a national strategy for healthcare quality measurement and reporting. The mission of the NQF is to improve American health care through endorsement of consensus-based national standards for measurement and public reporting of healthcare performance data that provide meaningful information about whether care is safe, timely, beneficial, patient-centered, equitable and efficient.[109]

Established in 1999, NQF has partnered with many organizations, including The Joint Commission. Together these organizations are developing a common approach to measuring and reporting quality initiatives and system-wide improvements in patient safety, and healthcare quality. The strategic goals of NQF support this collaboration:[110]

- The NQF will be the convener of key public and private sector leaders to establish national priorities and goals to achieve the Institute of Medicine Aims—health care that is safe, effective, patient-centered, timely, efficient and equitable.
- NQF-endorsed standards will be the primary standards used to measure and report on the quality and efficiency of health care in the United States.
- The NQF will be recognized as a major driving force for and facilitator of continuous quality improvement of American healthcare quality.

In 2003, the National Quality Forum released a set of Safe Practices for Better Health Care which were defined to be applicable to all clinical care settings. It is from these safe practices that the Leapfrog Group selected its indicators for its Leapfrog Safe Practices Score. These NQF safe practices were updated in 2006, and again in 2009. The current set of safety practices have been updated with current evidence and expanded implementation approaches. The 2009 update also provides additional measures for assessing the implementation of the practices. The updates to the practices incorporated several elements of a practice being separated out, practices that were combined under one practice, and the addition of seven new practices. The total number of Safe Practices is now 34, increased from the original 31 practices.[111] Table 4.2 displays the current Safety Practices for Better Healthcare.[112] More detail on each of these practices can be found at www.qualityforum.org.

The NQF has also published the "Compendium 2000-2005," which presents in one document the history of all the original NQF-endorsed™ consensus standards in a sourcebook. This compendium can be obtained at http://www.qualityforum.org/publications/reports/compendium.asp.

4.25 Institute for Healthcare Improvement Initiatives

A. 100,000 Lives Campaign

In 2005, the Institute for Healthcare Improvement (IHI) instituted the 100,000 Lives Campaign aimed at saving 100,000 lives in 18 months. The campaign was based on six changes to the way healthcare was provided. The six changes were:[113]

- Deploy Rapid Response Teams
- Deliver Reliable, Evidence-Based Care for Acute Myocardial Infarction
- Prevent Adverse Drug Events (ADEs)
- Prevent Central Line Infections
- Prevent Surgical Site Infections
- Prevent Ventilator-Associated Pneumonia

Over 3,100 hospitals participated in this campaign from January 2005 through June 2006. IHI estimates that during that time period, 122,000 lives were saved due to this initiative. The IHI website provides the interventions for these six changes which appear to enhance the initiatives.[114]

B. 5 Million Lives Campaign

Following the success of the 100,000 Lives campaign, IHI decided to expand its focus to include medically-induced injuries, and thus the 5 Million Lives campaign was initiated in December 2006. Over 3,700 hospitals participated in this initiative over a two year period. The 5 Million Lives campaign continued the six initiatives from the 100,000 Lives campaign and added six more initiatives:[115]

- Prevent Harm from High-Alert Medications
- Reduce Surgical Complications
- Prevent Pressure Ulcers
- Reduce Methicillin-Resistant Staphylococcus aureus (MRSA) Infection
- Deliver Reliable, Evidence-Based Care for Congestive Heart Failure
- Get Boards on Board

C. Improvement Map

In January 2009, IHI introduced the "Improvement Map" which will assist hospitals in focusing on what IHI feels is an essential set of process improvements. The Improvement Map is designed to help leaders in establishing their process improvement priorities, organize work, and optimize resources. The 12 changes/initiatives from the 100,000 Lives and 5 Million Lives campaigns will continue. IHI has added three additional interventions to the improvement map:[116]

- WHO Surgical Safety Checklist
- Prevent Catheter-Associated Urinary Tract Infections
- Link Quality and Financial Management: Strategies to Engage the Chief Financial Officer and Provide Value for Patients

For each of these 15 interventions, IHI has many valuable resources on its website at http://www.ihi.org/IHI/Programs/ImprovementMap/ImprovementMap.htm?TabId=2. Each intervention has a Getting Started Kit with a How-To-Guide for implementing change, including changes and measures of success, a PowerPoint presentation with facilitator notes, and an annotated bibliography. The website also has a list of mentor hospitals that have been able to implement and sustain these changes, and improvement tools submitted by participating hospitals, and other resources. Refer to www.ihi.org for ongoing information about the status of the Improvement Map campaign.

4.26 Summary

The Joint Commission National Patient Safety Goals and the efforts of the Leap Frog Group, the National Quality Forum, and Institute for Healthcare Improvement, among others, have redefined views on patient safety and are now driving the practices of healthcare organizations and workers. Physicians, nurses, therapists and other clinicians are acutely aware in most organizations of the value and rationale of Patient Safety Goals. One only need to look at a medical record today and compare it to a patient record of just five years ago—the information included, from intake assessments to daily status has evolved over time.

In any discovery process, it is important to determine what standards were in place at the time of the incident and to evaluate the patient record from that perspective. Applicable standards may come from The Joint Commission, from government and from the organization itself. Many organizations have seen that the new emphasis on safety has made the accreditation process itself more relevant and visible. After all, accreditation is part of the overall effort to reduce the risk in health care.

Table 4.2
NQF's 2009 Safe Practices for Better Healthcare[117]

Safe Practice 1:	Leadership Structures and Systems
Safe Practice 2:	Culture Measurement, Feedback, and Intervention
Safe Practice 3:	Teamwork Training and Skill Building
Safe Practice 4:	Identification and Mitigation of Risks and Hazards
Safe Practice 5:	Informed Consent
Safe Practice 6:	Life-Sustaining Treatment
Safe Practice 7:	Disclosure
Safe Practice 8:	Care of the Caregiver
Safe Practice 9:	Nursing Workforce
Safe Practice 10:	Direct Caregivers
Safe Practice 11:	Intensive Care Unit Care
Safe Practice 12:	Patient Care Information
Safe Practice 13:	Order Read-Back and Abbreviations
Safe Practice 14:	Labeling of Diagnostic Studies
Safe Practice 15:	Discharge Systems
Safe Practice 16:	Safe Adoption of Computerized Prescriber Order Entry
Safe Practice 17:	Medication Reconciliation
Safe Practice 18:	Pharmacist Leadership Structures and Systems
Safe Practice 19:	Hand Hygiene
Safe Practice 20:	Influenza Prevention
Safe Practice 21:	Central Line-Associated Bloodstream Infection Prevention
Safe Practice 22:	Surgical-Site Infection Prevention
Safe Practice 23:	Care of the Ventilated Patient
Safe Practice 24:	Multidrug-Resistant Organism Prevention
Safe Practice 25:	Catheter-Associated Urinary Tract Infection Prevention
Safe Practice 26:	Wrong-Site, Wrong-Procedure, Wrong-Person Surgery Prevention
Safe Practice 27:	Pressure Ulcer Prevention
Safe Practice 28:	Venous Thromboembolism Prevention
Safe Practice 29:	Anticoagulation Therapy
Safe Practice 30:	Contrast Media-Induced Renal Failure Prevention
Safe Practice 31:	Organ Donation
Safe Practice 32:	Glycemic Control
Safe Practice 33:	Falls Prevention
Safe Practice 34:	Pediatric Imaging

1. Adapted from National Quality Forum (NQF). Safe Practices for Better Healthcare – 2009 Update: A Consensus Report. Washington, DC; NQF; 2009.

Endnotes

1. Kohn, L.T., J.M. Corrigan, M.S. Donaldson (Editors). *To err is human: Building a safer health system*. Committee on Quality of Healthcare in America, Institute of Medicine, The National Academies Press, 2000. Retrieved 2/24/05. Available at http://www.nap.edu/catalog/9728.html.

2. Richardson, W.C. Opening statement at public briefing announcing release of *To err is human: Building a safer health system*. Retrieved February 24, 2005. Available at http://www4.nationalacademies.org/news.nsf/isbn/s0309068371?OpenDocument.

3. Institute of Medicine of the National Academies, "Healthcare Improving Quality, Ensuring Safety," retrieved www.iom.edu November 14, 2005. Fall 2005 Newsletter.

4. *Id.*

5. *Id.*

6. *Id.*

7. *Id.*

8. *Id.*

9. Institute of Medicine of the National Academies, "Preventing Medication Errors: Quality Chasm Series" retrieved from www.iom.edu/CMS/3809/22526/35939.aspx May 19, 2009.

10. See note 3.

11. The Joint Commission news release "Joint Commission Hails Enactment of Patient Safety and Quality Improvement Act of 2005," Oakbrook Terrace, Ill, July 29, 2005.

12. Department of Health and Human Services, *Patient Safety and Quality Improvement*. Federal Register, Vol 73. No. 226. November 21, 2008.

13. The Joint Commission, "Facts about The Joint Commission" retrieved from www.jointcommission.org/AboutUs/Fact_Sheets/joint_commission_facts.htm May 19, 2009.

14. Statement at opening conference of The Joint Commission Accreditation Services, The Joint Commission 2005 Annual Invitational Training Conference, January 6-8, 2005, Chicago.

15. The Joint Commission. "Facts about the Standards Improvement Initiative" retrieved from www.jointcommission.org/Standards/SII/sii_facts.htm May 19, 2009.

16. The Joint Commission, "About The Joint Commission" retrieved from www.jointcommission.org/AboutUs/. May 19, 2009.

17. The Joint Commission, "Facts about The Joint Commission" retrieved from www.jointcommission.org/AboutUs/Fact_Sheets/joint_commission_facts.htm May 19, 2009.

18. *Id.*

19. *Id.*

20. Joint Commission Resources: "Periodic Performance Review Key to Continuous Provision of High-Quality Care," Joint Commission Perspectives, pgs. 7-9, Vol 24, number 1, January 2004.

21. Joint Commission Resources: "Due Dates for Annual Periodic Performance Review Beginning in 2006," Joint Commission Perspectives, pg. 15, Vol 25, number 7, July 2005.

22. Joint Commission Resources: "Laboratories Must Now Complete the Periodic Performance Review," Joint Commission Perspectives, pg. 1, Vol 25, number 8, August 2005.

23. The Joint Commission. "Facts about the periodic Performance Review" retrieved from www.jointcommission.org/AboutUs/Fact_Sheets/PPR_QA.htm May 19, 2009.

24. Joint Commission Resources: "Joint Commission Offers Two Alternative Ways to Fulfill the Periodic Performance Review," Joint Commission Perspectives, pgs. 1-5, Vol 23, number 10, October 2003.

25. The Joint Commission. "Joint Commission Online" August 2008. retrieved from www.jointcommission.org/Library/jconline/jconline_aug_2008.htm. on May 20, 2009.

26. Long Term Care Accreditation Services, The Joint Commission 2005 Annual Invitational Training Conference, Chicago, January 6-8, 2005. Long Term Care/LT2 Program Update, Chart 21.

27. The Joint Commission. *Revisions to the Public Information Policy*. Joint Commission Perspectives. Vol 29, issue 4, page 3.

28. The Joint Commission. *Quality Check®—What can this site do for me?* Retrieved from www.jointcommission.org/qualityxheck/qc_what.htm. May 20, 2009.

29. The Joint Commission. *2008 Certification Quality Report User Guide.* Retrieved from http://www.jointcommission.org/NR/rdonlyres/831063C5-C514-4BB2-81EF-7F32CECF672C/0/DSC_QR_UGuide.pdf May 20, 2009.

30. The Joint Commission. What's New on Quality Check. Retrieved from www.jointcommission.org/Quality-Check/06_qc_new.htm. on May 20, 2009.

31. Standards for Long Term Care, 2005-2006. Oakbrook Terrace: Joint Commission Resources. Public Information Policy, APP12-13.

32. The Joint Commission. Sentinel Event Policy and Procedures. retrieved from www.jointcommission.org/NR/rdonlyres/F84F9DC6-A5DA-490F-A9FCE26347C4/0/SE_chapter_july07.pdf on May 20, 2009.

33. *Id.*

34. The Joint Commission. 2009 Hospital Accreditation Standards. The Joint Commission, Illinois. 2009, page 124.

35. U.S. Department of Veteran Affairs. *Healthcare Failure Mode Effectiveness Analysis* retrieved from http://www.patientsafety.gov/SafetyTopics.html#HFMEA, on May 21, 2009.

36. The Joint Commission. Healthcare Organization Survey Activity Guide. Illinois, 2009.

37. The Joint Commission. 2009 Hospital Accreditation Standards. The Joint Commission, Illinois. 2009, page 6.

38. The Joint Commission. 2009 Hospital Accreditation Standards. The Joint Commission, Illinois. 2009, page 405.

39. See note 37.

40. The Joint Commission. 2009 Hospital Accreditation Standards. The Joint Commission, Illinois. 2009, page 6-7.

41. The Joint Commission. 2009 Hospital Accreditation Standards. The Joint Commission, Illinois. 2009, page 7-8.

42. The Joint Commission. 2009 Hospital Accreditation Standards. The Joint Commission, Illinois. 2009, page 8.

43. The Joint Commission. 2009 Hospital Accreditation Standards. The Joint Commission, Illinois. 2009, page 10.

44. The Joint Commission. 2009 Hospital Accreditation Standards. The Joint Commission, Illinois. 2009, page 9.

45. The Joint Commission. 2009 Hospital Accreditation Standards. The Joint Commission, Illinois. 2009, pages 409-410.

46. Croteau, R. National Patient Safety Goals Adapted for Programs. Joint Commission Perspectives 24, No. 3, pg. 1, 2004.

47. http://www.jointcommission.org/NewsRoom/NewsReleases/nr_npsg_07.htm, retrieved July 3, 2006.

48. The Joint Commission. *National Patient Safety Goal 1.* 2009 Hospital Accreditation Standards. The Joint Commission, Illinois. 2009, page 225.

49. The Joint Commission. *National Patient Safety Goal 1.* 2009 Hospital Accreditation Standards. The Joint Commission, Illinois. 2009, page 226.

50. The Joint Commission. *National Patient Safety Goal 2.* 2009 Hospital Accreditation Standards. The Joint Commission, Illinois. 2009, page 226.

51. Locatell, K. "Physician liability issues" in Iyer, P. (Editor), *Nursing Home Litigation: Investigation and Case Preparation,* Second Edition, Tucson: Lawyers and Judges Publishing Company, 2006.

52. The Joint Commission. *National Patient Safety Goal 2.* 2009 Hospital Accreditation Standards. The Joint Commission, Illinois. 2009, page 227.

53. The Joint Commission. *National Patient Safety Goal 2.* 2009 Hospital Accreditation Standards. The Joint Commission, Illinois. 2009, pages 227–228.

54. Joint Commission 2006 National Patient Safety Goals Implementation Expectations, http://www.jcaho.org/accredited+organizations/patient+safety/06_npsg_ie.pdf retrieved October 3, 2005.

55. The Joint Commission. *National Patient Safety Goal 2.* 2009 Hospital Accreditation Standards. The Joint Commission, Illinois. 2009, pages 228–229.

56. The Joint Commission. *2004 National Patient Safety Goals.* Retrieved from http://www.jointcommission. org/PatientSafety/NationalPatientSafetyGoals/04_ npsgs.htm on May 26, 2009.

57. The Joint Commission. *2004 National Patient Safety Goals.* Retrieved from http://www.jointcommission. org/PatientSafety/NationalPatientSafetyGoals/04_ npsgs.htm on May 26, 2009.

58. *Id.*

59. The Joint Commission. *National Patient Safety Goal 3.* 2009 Hospital Accreditation Standards. The Joint Commission, Illinois. 2009, page 229.

60. Cohen, L., P. Iyer, J. O'Donnell. "Preventing medication errors," in O'Donnell, J. (Editor). *Drug Injury, Liability, Analysis, and Prevention*, Tucson: Lawyers and Judges Publishing Company, 2005.

61. The Joint Commission. *National Patient Safety Goal 3.* 2009 Hospital Accreditation Standards. The Joint Commission, Illinois. 2009, page 230.

62. The Joint Commission. *National Patient Safety Goal 3.* 2009 Hospital Accreditation Standards. The Joint Commission, Illinois. 2009, page 231.

63. The Joint Commission. *2005 National Patient Safety Goals.* Retrieved from http://www.jointcommission. org/PatientSafety/NationalPatientSafetyGoals/05_hap_ npsgs.htm on May 27. 2009.

64. *Id.*

65. *Id.*

66. Chizek, M. "Wandering and elopement," in Iyer, P. (Editor). *Nursing Home Litigation: Investigation and Case Preparation* (Second Edition). Tucson: Lawyers and Judges Publishing Company, 2006.

67. The Joint Commission. *National Patient Safety Goal 7.* 2009 Hospital Accreditation Standards. The Joint Commission, Illinois. 2009, page 232.

68. Center for Disease Control. *Guideline for Hand Hygiene in Health-Care Settings.* Retrieved from http:// www.cdc.gov/mmwr/PDF/rr/rr5116.pdf, pages 30-34 on May 27, 2009.

69. The Joint Commission. *National Patient Safety Goal 7.* 2009 Hospital Accreditation Standards. The Joint Commission, Illinois. 2009, page 232–233.

70. Vance, J. "Infections in the Nursing Home," Iyer, P. (Editor). *Nursing Home Litigation: Investigation and Case Preparation* (Second Edition) Tucson: Lawyers and Judges Publishing Company, 2006.

71. The Joint Commission. *National Patient Safety Goal 7.* 2009 Hospital Accreditation Standards. The Joint Commission, Illinois. 2009, pages 233-235.

72. The Joint Commission. *National Patient Safety Goal 7.* 2009 Hospital Accreditation Standards. The Joint Commission, Illinois. 2009, pages 235-236.

73. The Joint Commission. *National Patient Safety Goal 7.* 2009 Hospital Accreditation Standards. The Joint Commission, Illinois. 2009, pages 237-238.

74. The Joint Commission, Joint Commission Online, retrieved from http://www.jointcommission. org/NR/rdonlyres/BD8048E0-24DC-4BD4-8913- F4415BBD20F5/0/02_09_jconline.pdf on May 27, 2009.

75. The Joint Commission. *National Patient Safety Goal 8.* 2009 Hospital Accreditation Standards. The Joint Commission, Illinois. 2009, pages 238-239.

76. The Joint Commission. *National Patient Safety Goal 8.* 2009 Hospital Accreditation Standards. The Joint Commission, Illinois. 2009, page 239.

77. The Joint Commission. *National Patient Safety Goal 8.* 2009 Hospital Accreditation Standards. The Joint Commission, Illinois. 2009, page 240.

78. The Joint Commission. *National Patient Safety Goal 8.* 2009 Hospital Accreditation Standards. The Joint Commission, Illinois. 2009, pages 240-241.

79. The Joint Commission. 2005 National Patient Safety Goals. Retrieved from *http://www.jointcommission. org/PatientSafety/NationalPatientSafetyGoals/05_ hap_npsgs.htm.* on May 27, 2009.

80. Miceli, D, et al., Falls Handbook, 2007, Med League Support Services, Inc, available at www.medleague. com.

81. The Joint Commission. *National Patient Safety Goal 9.* 2009 Hospital Accreditation Standards. The Joint Commission, Illinois. 2009, pages 241-242.

82. The Joint Commission. *2009 National patient Safety Goals Manual Chapter, Long Term Care*. Retrieved from http://www.jointcommission.org/NR/rdonlyres/ BD44F7AA-84D6-45ED-A0C5-33D3118CF973/0/ LTC_NPSG.pdf on May 27, 2009.

83. Centers for Disease Control and Prevention. General Recommendations on Immunization. Recommendations of the Advisory Committee on Immunization Practices (ACIP) and the American Academy of Family Physicians (AAFP). Retrieved from http://www.cdc.gov/mmwr/preview/mmwrhtml/00025228.htm on May 27, 2009.

84. The Joint Commission. *2009 National Patient Safety Goals Manual Chapter, Long Term Care*. Retrieved from http://www.jointcommission.org/NR/rdonlyres/ BD44F7AA-84D6-45ED-A0C5-33D3118CF973/0/ LTC_NPSG.pdf on May 27, 2009.

85. The Joint Commission. *2009 National patient Safety Goals Manual Chapter, Long Term Care*. Retrieved from http://www.jointcommission.org/NR/rdonlyres/ BD44F7AA-84D6-45ED-A0C5-33D3118CF973/0/ LTC_NPSG.pdf on May 27, 2009.

86. American Association of Operating Room Nurses. *CDC see rise in outpatient surgery*, AORN Management Connections February 2009 retrieved from http://www. aorn.org/News/Managers/February2009Issue/ASC-News/ on May 27, 2009.

87. The Joint Commission 2009 *National Patient Safety Goals Manual Chapter, Ambulatory Health Care*. Retrieved from http://www.jointcommission. org/NR/rdonlyres/979098FA-74FD-4F25-AF41-EDD48FBD300E/0/AHC_NPSG.pdf on May 27, 2009.

88. The Joint Commission. 2008 National Patient Safety Goals – Networks, retrieved from http://www.joint-commission.org/PatientSafety/NationalPatientSafety-Goals/08_net_npsgs.htm on may 27, 2009.

89. The Joint Commission. *National Patient Safety Goal 13*. 2009 Hospital Accreditation Standards. The Joint Commission, Illinois. 2009, pages 242-243.

90. National Center for Healthy Statistics. *NCHS Data Brief, No. 14*, February 2009.

91. The Joint Commission. *2009 National Patient Safety Goals Manual Chapter – Long Term Care*. Retrieved from http://www.jointcommission.org/NR/rdonlyres/ BD44F7AA-84D6-45ED-A0C5-33D3118CF973/0/ LTC_NPSG.pdf on May 28, 2009.

92. The Joint Commission. *NPSG 15.01.01 Frequently Asked Questions* retrieved from http://www.jointcommission.org/AccreditationPrograms/Hospitals/Standards/09_FAQs/NPSG/Focused_risk_assessment/ NPSG.15.01.01/Suicide+risk+reduction.htm on May 28, 2009.

93. The Joint Commission. *2009 National Patient Safety Goals Manual Chapter Home Health*. Retrieved from http://www.jointcommission.org/NR/rdonlyres/ ABD0D499-A95A-4E33-BA18-6064EBA6C0B3/0/ OME_NPSG.pdf on May 28,2009.

94. The Joint Commission. *National Patient Safety Goal 16*. 2009 Hospital Accreditation Standards. The Joint Commission, Illinois. 2009, pages 244-245.

95. The Joint Commission. *Universal Protocol* 2009 Hospital Accreditation Standards. The Joint Commission, Illinois. 2009, page 245.

96. The Joint Commission. *Universal Protocol* 2009 Hospital Accreditation Standards. The Joint Commission, Illinois. 2009, pages 245-246.

97. The Joint Commission. *Universal Protocol* 2009 Hospital Accreditation Standards. The Joint Commission, Illinois. 2009, page 247-248.

98. The Joint Commission. *Universal Protocol* 2009 Hospital Accreditation Standards. The Joint Commission, Illinois. 2009, page 248-249.

99. The Leapfrog Group. Home page. Retrieved from http://www.leapfroggroup.org/ on May 28. 2009.

100. The Leapfrog Group. *The Leapfrog Group Fact Sheet*. Retrieved from http://www.leapfroggroup.org/about_ us/leapfrog-factsheet on May 28, 2009.

101. *Id.*

102. The Leapfrog Group. Leapfrog Hospital Survey Results 2008. retrieved from http://www.leapfroggroup. org/media/file/leapfrogreportfinal.pdf on May 28, 2009.

103. *Id.*

104. The Leapfrog Group. *The Leapfrog Group Fact Sheet—CPOE*. Retrieved from http://www.leapfrog-group.org/media/file/FactSheet_CPOE.pdf, on May 29, 2009.

105. The Joint Commission. *Sentinel Event Alert Issue 42*, December 11, 2008.

106. The Leapfrog Group. Leapfrog Hospital Survey Results 2008. retrieved from http://www.leapfroggroup.org/media/file/leapfrogreportfinal.pdf on May 28, 2009.

107. *Id.*

108. The Leapfrog Group. Leapfrog Group Hospital Survey Finds Majority of Hospitals Fail to Meet Important Quality Standards. Retrieved from http://www.leapfroggroup.org/media/file/2008_Survey_results_final_042909.pdf on May 28, 2009.

109. The National Quality Forum. *Mission Statement and Vision.* retrieved from http://www.qualityforum.org/about/mission.asp on May 28, 2009.

110. *Id.*

111. National Quality Forum (NQF). Safe Practices for better Healthcare – 2009 Update: A Consensus Report. Washington, DC; NQF; 2009.

112. *Id.*

113. Institute for Healthcare Improvement. Overview of the 100,000 Lives Campaign. Retrieved from http://www.ihi.org/IHI/Programs/Campaign/100kCampaignOverviewArchive.htm on May 29, 2009.

114. Institute for Healthcare Improvement. Overview of the 5 Million Lives Campaign. Retrieved from http://www.ihi.org/IHI/Programs/IHIOpenSchool/?TabId=1 on May 29, 2009.

115. *Id.*

116. Institute for Healthcare Improvement. Improvement Map Overview. Retrieved from http://www.ihi.org/IHI/Programs/ImprovementMap/ImprovementMap.htm?TabId=1 on May 29, 2009.

117. National Quality Forum (NQF). Safe Practices for better Healthcare – 2009 Update: A Consensus Report. Washington, DC; NQF; 2009.

Appendix 4.1
Suggestions for Legal Discovery of Compliance with National Patient Safety Goals*

National Patient Safety Goal	Potential Source of Information	Title of Policy/ Procedure	Other Resources
NPSG 1—PATIENT IDENTIFICATION **Improve the accuracy of patient identification.**	Nursing policy and procedure Checklists within the medical record that may reference the step of identifying the patient	Medication administration Blood transfusions Patient Identification	Medication Management Committee Minutes Pharmacy Committee Minutes
NPSG.01.01.01. Two identifiers—Use at least two patient identifiers (neither to be the patient's room number) whenever providing care, treatment, or services. [Applicable to all types organizations]	Laboratory manual	Phlebotomy Handling of Specimens	
• Taking blood samples • Administering medications • Administering blood products • Collecting specimens for clinical testing	Organizational policies/ procedures	Universal Protocol Handling of Specimens	
NPSG.01.02.01. Time out— Prior to the start of any surgical or invasive procedure, conduct a final verification process, such as a "timeout," to confirm the correct patient, procedure and site, using active—not passive—communication techniques. [Applicable to Home Care, Lab, Long-Term Care]	Nursing policy and procedure Pre-Procedure Verification forms within medical record	Time out Universal Protocol Patient Identification	See Universal Protocol information at the end of this table for additional information and resources
[**NOTE**: Hospitals, Ambulatory Health Care, Office Based Surgery, and Critical Access Hospitals follow the Universal Protocol and are scored in the standards rather than here]	Operating room policies and procedures	Universal Protocol	Association of Operating Room Nurses—Correct Site Surgery Tool Kit www.aorn.org WHO Surgical Safety Checklist www.who.int.

*All of these goals have implementation expectations listed on The Joint Commission's website at www.jointcommission.org.

National Patient Safety Goal	Potential Source of Information	Title of Policy/ Procedure	Other Resources
NPSG.01.03.01 Eliminating Transfusion Errors Eliminate transfusion errors related to patient misidentification [Applicable to Ambulatory Healthcare, Behavioral Health, Critical Access Hospitals, Hospitals, Office-Based Surgery]	Laboratory and Blood Bank policy and procedures Nursing policy and procedures Preprinted transfusion forms or computer record which include the steps taken to verify accuracy of information.	Issuing Blood and Blood Products Blood and Blood Product Administration	Blood bank logs Competency records The Joint Commission Sentinel Event Alert #10 – Blood Transfusion Errors: Preventing Future Occurrences issued August 1999 Transfusion slips
NPSG 2 —COMMUNICATION **Improve the effectiveness of communication among caregivers.**			
NPSG.02.01.01. Read back Process – Verbal/phone orders— Implement a process for taking verbal or telephone orders, and critical values that require a verification "read-back" of the complete order or results by the person receiving the order/ call. [Applicable to all types organizations]	Hospital/nursing policy and procedure Nurses may use abbreviations and terms in the medical record such as TORB (telephone order read back), VORB (verbal order read back), confirmed. All indicate that the order was read back to the physician. Facility may also have order forms with check boxes to indicate that the order was read back to the physician. Medical Records policy and procedures Laboratory policies and procedures	Telephone/Verbal Orders Verbal Read Backs Critical Tests and Critical Values Critical Tests and Critical Values Panic Values	

National Patient Safety Goal	Potential Source of Information	Title of Policy/ Procedure	Other Resources
NPSG.02.02.01. Do Not Use Abbreviations—Standardize the abbreviations, acronyms, symbols and dose designations that are not to be used throughout the organization. [Applicable to all types organizations]	Hospital policy and procedure Order form which includes a list of unapproved abbreviations Integrated or physician progress notes which include a list of unapproved abbreviations Medical Records Policies and Procedures	Prohibited abbreviations Do Not Use Abbreviations Medication Administration Policy and Procedure Unapproved abbreviations Do Not Use Abbreviations	The Joint Commission requires a specific list of nine "Do Not Use" abbreviations, which can be found on their website at www. jointcommission.org The Joint Commission Sentinel Event Alert # 23—Medication Errors Related to Potentially Dangerous Abbreviations—issued September 2001 Institute of Safe Medication Practices— www.ismp.org Quality improvement audit reports for a regular review of orders the facility and compliance checked, trends noted, and reported through committees such as the Pharmacy and Therapeutics committee, Medication Safety Committee, Medical Records Committee, Patient Safety Committee Committee minutes
NPSG.02.03.01. Timeliness of Reporting—Measure, assess and, if appropriate, take action to improve the timeliness of reporting, and the timeliness of receipt by the responsible licensed caregiver, of critical test results and values. [Applicable to all types organizations except Long-Term Care and Networks]	Hospital policy and procedure Laboratory or radiological test results which state the name of the person informed of the critical results Laboratory policy and procedure	Critical Values Verbal Read Backs Critical Radiology Values, Reporting of Critical Laboratory Results, Reporting of	See NPSG.03.01.01 for additional information

4. Patient Safety Initiatives

National Patient Safety Goal	Potential Source of Information	Title of Policy/ Procedure	Other Resources
NPSG.02.04.01 Laboratory Test Results [Applicable to Laboratories only] (retired 2007)			See NPSG.02.01.01 and NPSG.02.03,01
NPSG.02.05.01 Handoff Communications: Implement a standardized approach to "handoff" communications, including an opportunity to ask and respond to questions. [Applicable to all types organizations]	Hospital Policy and Procedure Manual The facility may have forms that are to be completed by staff as the patient is transferred to and from different departments or units in the facility. These are usually a part of the permanent medical record. Daily or monthly progress notes, nursing notes, and physician orders	Change of Shift Report Transfer Reports Post Anesthesia Care Unit Discharge of Patient	
NPSG 3—SAFETY OF MEDICATIONS **Improve the safety of using high-alert medications**			The Joint Commission Sentinel Event Alert # 16—Mix-up Leads to a Medication Error— issued February 2001

National Patient Safety Goal	Potential Source of Information	Title of Policy/ Procedure	Other Resources
NPSG.03.01.01 Concentrated Electrolytes—Remove concentrated electrolytes (including, but not limited to, potassium chloride, potassium phosphate, sodium chloride >0.9%) from patient care units. ***(Retired to Standards 2006)***	Pharmacy policy and procedure	Medication Administration Policy and Procedure High Risk Medications Individual policies on high risk medications: Potassium chloride Potassium phosphate Sodium chloride Concentrated electrolytes	The Joint Commission Sentinel Event Alert #11—High-Alert Medications and Patient Safety—issued November 1999 Potassium is still usually found in the Emergency Department, Intensive Care Units, and in the Perfusion Therapist's medication boxes. It may also be found in powder form in Dialysis Units. Institute of Safe Medication Practices— www.ismp.org Admixture program description
NPSG.03.02.01 Drug Concentrations—Standardize and limit the number of drug concentrations available in the organization. [Applicable to all types organizations] (Retired to Standards 2008)	Pharmacy policy and procedure	IV Medication Policy and Procedure	Pharmacy formulary: Drug concentrations available in facility Institute of Safe Medication Practices— www.ismp.org

National Patient Safety Goal	Potential Source of Information	Title of Policy/ Procedure	Other Resources
NPSG.03.03.01. Look-Alike, Sound-Alike Medications – Identify and, at a minimum, annually review a list of look-alike/sound-alike drugs used in the organization, and take action to prevent errors involving the interchange of these drugs. [Applicable to all types of organizations except Laboratory]	Pharmacy policy and procedure	Look-Alike, Sound-Alike Medications	The Joint Commission Joint Commission Sentinel Event Alert # 19—Look-alike, Sound-alike drug names—issued May 2001 Institute of Safe Medication Practices—www.ismp.org Pharmacy formulary Pharmacy and Therapeutics (P&T) Committee minutes The Joint Commission website www. jointcommission.org has lists the categories and specific medications to be considered for this goal (Look-alike/sound-alike Drug List)
NPSG.03.04.01 Labeling Medications— Label all medications, medication containers (e.g., syringes, medicine cups, basins), or other solutions on and off the sterile field in perioperative and other procedural settings. [Applicable to Ambulatory Healthcare, Office Based Surgery, Critical Access Hospitals, and Hospitals]	Nursing Policies and Procedures Radiological Department Manual Surgical Suite Manual	Medication Administration Invasive Procedures, Assistance with Medication Labeling Medication/Solution Labeling	Institute of Safe Medication Practices—www.ismp.org Labels available in the organization Sterile labels for sterile procedures

National Patient Safety Goal	Potential Source of Information	Title of Policy/ Procedure	Other Resources
NPSG.03.05.01 Anticoagulation Therapy – Reduce the likelihood of patient harm associated with the use of anticoagulant therapy. [Applicable to Ambulatory Healthcare, Critical Access Hospitals, Hospitals, Home Health, Long-Term Care]	Pharmacy policy and procedures Nursing policy and procedures Preprinted order sets for managing the patient on anticoagulation Medication administration records	Anticoagulation Therapy Heparin Utilization Warfarin Utilization Food-Drug Interactions	Anticoagulation Therapy Protocols FMEA on anticoagulant therapy Anticoagulation Therapy Patient education materials Documentation of anticoagulation therapy education of staff, and licensed independent practitioners The Joint Commission Sentinel Event Alert # 41—Preventing Errors relating to Commonly Used Anticoagulants— issued September 2008
NPSG 4 —WRONG-SITE, WRONG-PATIENT, WRONG PROCEDURE **Eliminate wrong-site, wrong-patient, wrong-procedure surgery. [See Universal Protocol information] (moved to Universal Protocol in 2006)**	Hospital policy and procedure	Universal Protocol	Universal Protocol pertains to all areas that perform surgery or invasive procedures, not just in the Operating Rooms. See Universal Protocol at the end of this table for more information
NPSG 5—INFUSION PUMPS **Improve the safety of using infusion pumps. *(Retired to Standards 2006)***			

National Patient Safety Goal	Potential Source of Information	Title of Policy/ Procedure	Other Resources
NPSG.05.01.01. Free flow— Ensure free-flow protection on all general-use and PCA (patient controlled analgesia) intravenous infusion pumps used in the organization. *(Retired to Standards 2006)*	Nursing policy and procedures	Free Flow of IV fluids, Prevention of Medication policy and procedures states that no free-flow devices are in use in the institution	The Joint Commission Joint Commission Sentinel Event Alert # 15—Infusion Pumps: Preventing Future Adverse Events—issued November 2000
	Biomedical policy and procedure	IV Pumps PCA Pumps, Setting Up and Monitoring of	Purchasing department records Biomedical engineering report on defective equipment. Med Watch reports about an incident involving equipment Staff development records for training on how to check pumps for free flow protection The Joint Commission Sentinel Event Alert #33 on PCA by Proxy issued December 20, 2004 Institute for Safe Medication Practices, www.ismp.org Pump manuals
NPSG 6—CLINICAL ALARMS **Improve the effectiveness of clinical alarm systems.** *(Retired to Standards 2005)*			

National Patient Safety Goal	Potential Source of Information	Title of Policy/ Procedure	Other Resources
NPSG.06.01.01. Testing Alarms—Implement regular preventive maintenance and testing of alarm systems. ***(Retired to Standards 2005)***	Hospital policy and procedure	Wandering Patient Protocol Critical Care Clinical Alarms Newborn Abduction	Biomedical department maintenance records for alarms Purchasing department records Test of alarm systems – failure mode effectiveness analysis
NPSG.06.02.01 Activated Alarms—Assure that alarms are activated with appropriate settings and are sufficiently audible with respect to distances and competing noise within the unit. ***(Retired to Standards 2005)***	Hospital/Nursing policy and procedure Nursing flow sheets which state the settings for alarms Nursing policy and procedure	Wandering Patient Alarm Systems Critical Care Clinical Alarms Newborn Abduction Elopement Prevention Door Alarms Critical Care Monitor Alarms IV Pump Alarms	Alarm systems manuals Safety Committee minutes: Inventory and walk through by safety team subgroup to look for potential problems with audibility of alarms Emergency drills reports: Newborn abduction, etc. Double doors system in mental health inpatient unit Maintenance records Records that door alarms in mental health are checked regularly Safety committee meeting minutes Biomedical engineering records Monitor manual IV pump manual

National Patient Safety Goal	Potential Source of Information	Title of Policy/ Procedure	Other Resources
NPSG 7—INFECTIONS **Reduce the risk of healthcare-acquired infections.**			
NPSG.07.01.01. Hand Hygiene—Comply with current WHO or CDC hand hygiene guidelines. [Applicable to all types organizations]	Hospital policy and procedure	Handwashing Fingernail Lengths for Staff	Infection control manual Staff are not allowed to have artificial nails and must clip nails to ¼ inch
	Infection control policy and procedure	Nosocomial Infections	Infection Control committee minutes Infection Control Plan Purchasing records: Purchase of waterless handwashing materials and installation in each patient room and other areas
	Operating room policy and procedure	Surgical Scrubs	Centers for Disease Control guidelines
NPSG.07.02.01 Healthcare acquired-infection—Manage as sentinel events all identified cases of unanticipated death or major permanent loss of function associated with a healthcare care-acquired infection. [Applicable to all types organizations]	Hospital policy and procedures Integrated or physician progress notes Infectious disease consultations Culture results Medication administration records Physician orders Infection control policy and procedure	Sentinel Event Policy Adverse Occurrence Infection Related Mortality	Root cause analysis records Mortality Review Infection Control Committee minutes The Joint Commission Sentinel Event Alert # 28—Infection Control Related Sentinel Events—issued January 2003

National Patient Safety Goal	Potential Source of Information	Title of Policy/ Procedure	Other Resources
NPSG.07.03.01 Multidrug Resistant Organisms – Implement evidence-based practices to prevent healthcare-associated infections due to multi-drug-resistant organisms in acute care hospitals [Applicable to Critical Access Hospitals, Hospitals]	Infection Control Policies Nursing Policy and procedures Laboratory policy and procedure Culture results	Multi-Drug Resistant Organisms MRSA VRE C-Diff Pre-admission Screening Handwashing Nosocomial infections, Prevention of	Association for Professionals in Infection Control www.apic.org Infection Control Plan Infection Control committee minutes Preadmission screening Infection control monitoring and laboratory reporting of infections IHI Improvement map materials www.IHI.org
NPSG.07.04.01 Central Line-Associated Bloodstream Infections – Implement best practices or evidence-based guidelines to prevent central line-associated bloodstream infections [Applicable to Ambulatory Healthcare, Critical Access Hospitals, Home Health, Hospitals, Long-Term Care]	Infection Control Policies Nursing Policy and procedures Insertion flow sheets	Handwashing Nosocomial Infections, Prevention of PICC Central Lines, Inserting and Maintenance of	Association for Professionals in Infection Control www.apic.org Infection Control Plan Infection Control committee minutes Infection control monitoring and laboratory reporting of infections IHI Improvement map materials www.IHI.org

National Patient Safety Goal	Potential Source of Information	Title of Policy/Procedure	Other Resources
NPSG.07.05.01 Surgical Site Infections – Implement best practices for preventing surgical site infection [Applicable to Ambulatory Healthcare, Critical Access Hospitals, Hospitals, Office-Based Surgery]	Infection Control Policies Nursing Policy and procedures Surgical Suite Manual Integrated or physician progress notes for observations of surgical site Nursing notes for observations of surgical site	Handwashing Nosocomial Infections Maintaining a Sterile Environment	Association for Professionals in Infection Control www.apic.org Infection Control Plan Infection control committee minutes Infection control monitoring and laboratory reporting of infections IHI Improvement map materials www.IHI.org
NPSG 8—MEDICATION RECONCILIATION **Accurately and completely reconcile medications across the continuum of care.**			The Joint Commission Sentinel Event Alert # 35—Using Medication Reconciliation to Prevent Errors—issued January 2006

National Patient Safety Goal	Potential Source of Information	Title of Policy/Procedure	Other Resources
NPSG.08.01.01. Complete list of medications— A process exists for comparing the patient's current medications with those ordered for the patient while under the care of the healthcare organization. [Applicable to all types organizations except Laboratory]	Hospital policy and procedure Pharmacy policy and procedures Nursing policies and procedures Medical staff policies and procedures Medication lists from home, nursing home, or wherever the patient came from Flow sheet used to document medications at admission Multidisciplinary or nursing admission assessment History and physical Emergency department records	Medication Reconciliation Policy Admission Assessment History and Physical	Institute of Safe Medication Practices— www.ismp.org The Joint Commission Joint Commission Sentinel Event Alert # 35—Using Medication Reconciliation to Prevent Errors—issued January 2006 Pharmacy and nursing audits P&T Committee, Medication use Committee and other committee minutes

National Patient Safety Goal	Potential Source of Information	Title of Policy/Procedure	Other Resources
NPSG.08.02.01. Communication of the list of medications—When a patient is referred to or transferred from one healthcare organization to another, the complete and reconciled list of medications is communicated to the next provider of service, and the communication is documented. Alternatively, when a patient leaves the healthcare organization to go directly to his/her home, the complete and reconciled list of medications is provided to the patient's known primary care provider, the original referring provider, or a known next provider of service. [Applicable to all types organizations except Laboratory]	Hospital policy and procedure Pharmacy policy and procedures Nursing policies and procedures Many facilities have developed Medication Reconciliation forms that are completed on admission and throughout the patient's stay. These are utilized as the patient transfers to different levels of care. These forms may even serve as order sheets. Flow sheet used to document medications at discharge Medical staff policies and procedures Transfer form listing medications Discharge forms have Complete list of medications	Medication Reconciliation Policy Intratransfer and Intertransfer of Patients Transfer of Patient to Another Facility Discharge of the Patient Discharge Summary	Computerized documentation may keep patient medication lists from visit to visit and be updated each time Institute of Safe Medication Practices— www.ismp.org The Joint Commission Sentinel Event Alert # 35—Using Medication Reconciliation to Prevent Errors—issued January 2006 Medication lists from home, nursing home, or wherever the patient came from Pharmacy and nursing Audits P&T Committee, Medication Use Committee and other committee minutes

National Patient Safety Goal	Potential Source of Information	Title of Policy/Procedure	Other Resources
NPSG.08.03.01 List to patient—When a patient leaves the healthcare organization's care, a complete and reconciled list of the patient's medications is provided directly to the patient, and as needed, the family, and the list is explained to the patient and/or family. [Applicable to all organizations except Laboratory]	Hospital policy and procedure Nursing policy and procedures Medication lists from home, nursing home, or wherever the patient came from Discharge instruction form Discharge forms have complete list of medications Many facilities have developed medication reconciliation forms that are completed on admission and through out the patient's stay. These are utilized as the patient transfers to different levels of care. These forms may even serve as order sheets. Computerized documentation may keep patient medication lists from visit to visit and be updated each time.	Medication Reconciliation Policy Intratransfer and Intertransfer of Patient Transfer of Patient to Another Facility Discharge of the Patient	Institute of Safe Medication Practices—www.ismp.org The Joint Commission Sentinel Event Alert # 35—Using Medication Reconciliation to Prevent Errors—issued January 2006 Pharmacy and nursing audits Pharmacy and Therapeutics Committee, Medication use Committee and other committee minutes

National Patient Safety Goal	Potential Source of Information	Title of Policy/Procedure	Other Resources
NPSG.08.04.01 Minimal Use Settings – In settings where medications are used minimally or prescribed for a short duration, modified medication reconciliation processes are performed. [Applicable to all organizations except Laboratory]	Hospital policy and procedure Departmental policy and procedure Many facilities have developed medication reconciliation forms that are completed on admission and through out the patient's stay. These are utilized as the patient transfers to different levels of care. These forms may even serve as order sheets. Computerized documentation may keep patient medication lists from visit to visit and be updated each time Discharge forms have complete list of medications Medication lists from home, nursing home, or wherever the patient came from	Admission Assessment Medication Reconciliation Policy Discharge of the Patient	Institute of Safe Medication Practices— www.ismp.org Pharmacy and nursing audits P&T Committee, Medication Use Committee and other committee minutes

National Patient Safety Goal	Potential Source of Information	Title of Policy/Procedure	Other Resources
NPSG 9—FALLS **Reduce the risk of patient harm resulting from falls.**			
NPSG.09.01.01 Fall risk—Assess and periodically reassess each patient's risk for falling, including the potential risk associated with the patient's medication regimen, and take action to address any identified risks. **(Retired to Standards 2006)**	Nursing policy and procedure Fall risk assessment recorded on admission and whenever there is a significant change in the patient's status Physical therapy assessments of balance, strength, and gait Nursing flow sheets	Fall Risk Assessment Falls Prevention Policy	
NPSG.09.02.01 Fall Reduction Program Implement a fall reduction program and evaluate the effectiveness of the program. [Applicable to Critical Access Hospital, Home Care, Hospital, Long-Term Care]	Hospital Policy and procedures Nursing Policies and Procedures Nursing flow sheets for evidence of implementation of program Physician orders for one on one observation	Incident/Occurrence Reporting Risk for Falls Assessment Admission Assessment, Completion of Reassessment of the Patient Falls Prevention Protocol Falls Prevention Policy Restraint and Seclusion Policy Falling Star Program Chair/Bed Alarms Low Beds Floor Mats	The Joint Commission Sentinel Event Alert # 14—Fatal Falls: Lessons for the Future—issued July 2000 Bed alarm manual

National Patient Safety Goal	Potential Source of Information	Title of Policy/Procedure	Other Resources
NPSG 10—INFLUENZA AND PNEUMOCOCCAL VACCINE **Reduce the risk of influenza and pneumococcal disease in institutionalized older adults. [Applicable to Long-Term Care]**			
NPSG.10.01.01 Influenza Protocol—Develop and implement a protocol for administration and documentation of the flu vaccine.	Infection Control policy and procedures Nursing policies and procedures Consent forms for administration of the vaccine Physician orders Medication administration records	Infection Control Immunizations Admission Assessment Physician Order Forms	Infection Control Plan Centers for Disease Control May take the form of a Protocol
NPSG.10.02.01 Pneumococcus Protocol—Develop and implement a protocol for administration and documentation of the pneumococcus vaccine.	Infection Control policy and procedures Nursing policies and procedures Consent forms for administration of the vaccine Physician orders Medication administration records	Infection Control Immunizations Admission Assessment Physician Order Forms	Infection Control Plan Centers for Disease Control May take the form of a Protocol
NPSG.10.03.01 New Cases Protocol—Develop and implement a protocol to identify new cases of influenza and to manage an outbreak	Infection Control policy and procedures	Flu Outbreak, Management of	Infection Control plan Pandemic Plan Emergency Management Plan

National Patient Safety Goal	Potential Source of Information	Title of Policy/Procedure	Other Resources
NPSG 11—SURGICAL FIRES **Reduce the risk of surgical fires.**			
NPSG.11.01.01 Educate staff, including operating licensed independent practitioners and anesthesia providers, on how to control heat sources and manage fuels, and establish guidelines to minimize oxygen concentration under drapes. [Applicable to Ambulatory and Office Based Surgery.]	Safety Manual Operating Room Manual	Fires, Prevention of Electrocautery, Use of Skin Preparation and Draping	Operative/procedure record The Joint Commission Sentinel Event Alert # 29—Preventing Surgical Fires—issued June 2003 Association of Operating Room Nurses (AORN) Fire Safety Tool kit and other resources Many resources available on the Internet
NPSG 12—NETWORKS **Implementation of applicable National Patient Safety Goals and associated requirements by components and practitioner sites.** [Deleted in 2008 when The Joint Commission no longer accredited Networks]			
NPSG.12.01.01 Inform and encourage components and practitioner sites to implement the applicable National Patient Safety Goals and associated requirements. [Applicable to Networks.]	Administrative policies and procedures	Patient Safety National Patient Safety Goals, implementation of	

National Patient Safety Goal	Potential Source of Information	Title of Policy/Procedure	Other Resources
NPSG 13—ACTIVE INVOLVEMENT OF PATIENTS **Encourage the active involvement of patients and their families in the patient's care as a patient safety strategy.**			
NPSG.13.01.01 Patients Encouraged to Report Concerns—Define and communicate the means for patients to report concerns about safety and encourage them to do so. [Applicable to all types organizations]	Administrative Policy and Procedures Nursing Policies and Procedures Nursing notes Patient Education Manual Many facilities are also including forms that the patients must sign upon admission indicating that they have been given information regarding their role in their own safety while in the facility.	Patient Complaints, reporting of Patient Satisfaction Coordinator job description Patient Education Hazards, Reporting of	Admission forms Patient education records Signs in the patient's room 'Speak Up' – The Joint Commission's patient educational materials www.jointcommission.org Patient Satisfaction reports frequently include questions regarding how the patient feels regarding safety in the facility. Patient advocates The Joint Commission Sentinel Event Alerts— www.jointcommission.org

National Patient Safety Goal	Potential Source of Information	Title of Policy/Procedure	Other Resources
NPSG 14—PRESSURE ULCERS **Prevent health care-associated pressure ulcers (decubitus ulcers).**			
NPSG.14.01.01 Assess and periodically reassess each patient's risk for developing a pressure ulcer (decubitus ulcer) and take action to address any identified risks. [Applicable to Long-Term Care]	Nursing Policy and Procedure Manual Wound Care policy and procedures manual Risk for skin breakdown assessment tool Admission assessment, Physician orders Nursing flow sheets for evidence of implementation of preventative and treatment measures Completion of pressure ulcer risk assessment tools Wound care consults	Braden Scale, use of Skin breakdown, treatment of	AHRQ Clinical Practice Guidelines for prevention and treatment of skin breakdown Wound/Ostomy notes Wound/Ostomy nurse job description Wound, Ostomy and Continence Nurses Society—www.wocn.org National Pressure Ulcer Prevention Advisory panel www.npuap.org Braden Scale for Preventing Pressure Sore Risk www.bradenscale.com Norton Scale for Predicting Pressure Sore Risk www.woundcarehelpline.com/NortonScale

National Patient Safety Goal	Potential Source of Information	Title of Policy/Procedure	Other Resources
NPSG 15—PATIENT SAFETY RISKS **Identifies the safety risks inherent in its patient population**			
NPSG.15.01.01. Suicide Risk—The organization identifies patients at risk for suicide. [Applicable to psychiatric hospitals and patients being tracked for emotional or behavioral disorders in general hospitals]	Nursing policies and procedures Suicide risk assessment forms Patient safety policy and procedures Patient education policies and procedures Multidisciplinary or nursing admission assessment of suicide risk Patient education forms Flow sheets Psychiatric consultations	Admission Assessment Suicide Risk Assessment Patient Education	The Joint Commission Sentinel Event Alert # 7—Inpatient Suicides: Recommendations for Prevention—issued November 1998
NPSG.15.02.01. Long-Term Oxygen Therapy—The organization identifies risks associated with long-term oxygen therapy such as home fires [Applicable to Home Care]	Nursing policies and procedures Respiratory therapy policy and procedures DME policy and procedures Home safety assessment forms OASIS forms Patient education forms Nursing notes Patient Education policies and procedures	Admission Assessment Safety in the Home Equipment Use Within the Home Patient Education	The Joint Commission Joint Commission Sentinel Event Alert # 17—Lessons Learned: Fires in the Home Care Setting—issued March 2001

National Patient Safety Goal	Potential Source of Information	Title of Policy/Procedure	Other Resources
NPSG 16—RECOGNITION OF PATIENT CHANGES IN CONDITION **Improve recognition and response to changes in a patient's condition**			
NPSG.16.01.01 Requesting additional assistance with patients – The hospital selects a suitable method that enables healthcare staff members to directly request additional assistance from a specially trained individual(s) when the patient's condition appears to be worsening. [Applicable to Critical Access Hospitals, and Hospitals]	Hospital policy and procedure Nursing policy and procedures Nursing notes Integrated or physician progress note regarding findings of rapid response team	Rapid Response Team Code Blue Team Assessment, Reassessment of the patient	Rapid Response Team forms Monitoring of the effectiveness of the Rapid Response Team or other such mechanisms Rapid Response Team Committee minutes LeapFrog Group www.leapfrog.org
Universal Protocol			The Joint Commission Sentinel Event Alert # 12—Operative and Postoperative Complications: Lessons for the Future – issued February 2000
UP.01.01.01 Preprocedure Verification Process – Conduct a preprocedure verification process.	Hospital policy and procedure Flow sheets Preoperative checklist Procedure Verification forms	Operative and Invasive Procedure Verification	World Health Organization Surgical Checklist www.who.int The Joint Commission Sentinel Event Alert #6—Lessons Learned: Wrong Site Surgery—issued August 1998 The Joint Commission Sentinel Event Alert # 24—A Follow-up Review of Wrong Site Surgery—issued December 2001

National Patient Safety Goal	Potential Source of Information	Title of Policy/Procedure	Other Resources
UP.01.02.01 Mark the Procedure Site – Marking the procedure site to identify without ambiguity the intended site for the procedure.	Procedure Verification forms	Operative and Invasive Procedure Verification Surgical Site Identification	Association of Operating room Nurses-Correct Site Surgery Tool Kit World Health Organization Surgical Checklist www.who.int The Joint Commission Sentinel Event Alert #6—Lessons Learned: Wrong Site Surgery—issued August 1998 The Joint Commission Sentinel Event Alert # 24—A Follow-up Review of Wrong Site Surgery—issued December 2001
UP.01.03.01 Time Out – A time-out is performed immediately prior to starting procedures.	Hospital policy and procedure Flow sheets Procedure Verification forms Operative, procedure and other nursing notes	Operative and Invasive Procedure Verification Time Out	Association of Operating room Nurses-Correct Site Surgery Tool Kit World Health Organization Surgical Checklist www.who.int The Joint Commission Sentinel Event Alert # 6—Lessons Learned: Wrong Site Surgery—issued August 1998 The Joint Commission Sentinel Event Alert # 24—A Follow-up Review of Wrong Site Surgery—issued December 2001

Chapter 5

Medical Errors: Roots of Litigation

Patricia W. Iyer, MSN, RN, LNCC and Peter I. Bergé, JD, RPA

5.1 Introduction

The extent of medical and nursing errors used to be a well-concealed issue within health care. Incompetent practitioners were allowed to remain on a facility staff or were encouraged to move to another town or state. There was no mechanism in place for the unsuspecting new facility to check the track record of the healthcare practitioner who was applying for privileges. Incidents within hospitals were quietly handled. Risk managers and other healthcare professionals who became aware of incidents often had no incentive or external standards to cite as to why the patient or family should be informed of the nature of and reasons for the injury that had occurred.

The climate has changed as a result of several factors, including the:

- establishment of the National Practitioner Data Bank, which keeps data on healthcare practitioners,
- publication of To Err is Human[1] which exposed the conclusions of the Harvard Practice Study performed in the mid-1980s,
- imposition of The Joint Commission standard requiring disclosure of untoward outcomes, and
- increasingly informed public demanding a safer medical environment with reduction in medical errors.

This chapter addresses the frequency and perception of errors and the reasons why individuals seek the services of a plaintiff's attorney. It concludes with statistics regarding the frequency of litigation.

5.2 Frequency, Cost, and Perception of Errors
A. Frequency and Cost

It is difficult to determine the scope of the problem of nursing and medical malpractice. The Harvard Practice Study was based on medical records of New York patients. Of 30,000 records examined, the investigators found that 1 percent of the patients had experienced errors that caused injury. This study was based on 1980s records and published in 1991. Although healthcare providers were somewhat aware of the results, the press remained uninformed. When the study was described in an Institute of Medicine study published in 1999, *To Err is Human*[2] the public first learned that 44,000–98,000 people die each year as a result of medical errors. Although these numbers continue to be quoted 20 years later, many patient safety experts are aware the actual numbers are unknown, as the Harvard Practice Study relied on examination of hospital charts. The investigators did not review physician office records, nursing home records, or clinic records, and did not detect unrecorded errors. Health-Grades[3] announced in July 2004 that as many as 195,000

141

people could be dying annually in U.S. hospitals because of easily preventable errors. Their data were based on three years of Medicare data in all 50 states and Washington, D.C. In 2008, HealthGrades announced that patient safety incidents cost the federal Medicare program $8.8 billion and resulted in 238,337 potentially preventable deaths from 2004 through 2006. Medical errors with the highest incidence rates were pressure ulcers, failure to rescue, and postoperative respiratory failure. They accounted for 63.4 percent of incidents. Analysis of 41 million Medicare patient records showed that patients treated at top-performing hospitals had, on average, a 43 percent lower chance of experiencing one or more medical errors compared to the poorest-performing hospitals. Refer to www.healthgrades.com for current information.

Note these statistics:

- Three percent or more of hospital patients are hurt by medical error.
- One in 300 patients dies from such mistakes.
- 24 percent of people say they, or a family member, have been harmed by a medical error.
- One hundred eighty thousand elderly outpatients die or are seriously injured by drug toxicity. Half of these incidents may be preventable.
- Seven thousand patients die from drug errors each year.
- Five hundred and 54 errors in four months were found at one six-bed intensive care unit: 147 were potentially serious or life-threatening.
- Fifty-five percent of recommended care is actually administered.
- Two thousand dollars is the annual cost to employers per insured worker, due to poor-quality care.
- Ninety thousand people die of hospital-acquired infections annually.[4]
- There is increasing evidence that many or most of these deaths may be preventable.)[5-8]

Healthcare-acquired infection is a costly complication. The Center for Disease Control (CDC) estimates that direct annual medical costs of healthcare-associated infection to U.S. hospitals ranges from $28.4 to $33.8 billion (after adjusting to 2007 dollars using the Consumer Price Index (CPI) for all urban consumers). The totals are $35.7 billion to $45 billion (after adjusting to 2007 dollars using the CPI for inpatient hospital services). After adjusting for the range of effectiveness of possible infection control interventions,

the benefits of prevention range from a low of $5.7 to $6.8 billion (assuming 20 percent of infections are preventable, using CPI for all urban consumers) to a high of $25 to $31.5 billion (assuming 70 percent of infections are preventable and using the CPI for inpatient hospital services).[9]

B. Perceptions of Errors

Patients have been asked about their perceptions of medical errors in their own care. In a random sample of 621 patients who received care over a two-year period in 12 Veteran Affairs Healthcare Systems, 82 percent of the patients had at least one error reported over a 13 month period. The average number of errors reported per case was 4.7. The vast majority (95.7 percent) of errors were problems of under-use or getting too little medical care. Inadequate care for people with chronic illnesses was particularly common. Among the errors of omission, inadequate diagnostic testing, obtaining insufficient information from histories and physicals, and patients not receiving needed medications were common. Of the 2,917 errors identified, only 27 were rated as highly serious and 26 (96 percent) of those were errors of omission.[10]

What do physicians think about medical errors? A sample of 831 physicians who responded to mailed questionnaires and a random sample of 1,207 members of the public were questioned about their view on preventable medical errors.

Many of the physicians (35 percent) and members of the public (42 percent) reported errors in their own or a family member's care, but neither group viewed medical errors as one of the most important problems in health care today. A majority of both groups believed the number of in-hospital deaths due to preventable errors is lower than that reported by the Institute of Medicine. The public and many of the physicians supported the use of sanctions against healthcare professionals perceived as responsible for serious errors.[11]

An accrediting body for hospitals and some nursing homes, among other healthcare facilities, The Joint Commission launched a "Speak Up" campaign to improve awareness of the problem of medical errors. The program urges patients to get involved in their care. The "Speak Up: Help Prevent Errors in Your Care" hospital poster provides advice to patients (Figure 5.1). Brochures and posters are available for ambulatory care, behavioral health care, networks, laboratory services, home care, and long-term care. Expansion of the main points of each of the items on the poster are found on The Joint Commission website.[12]

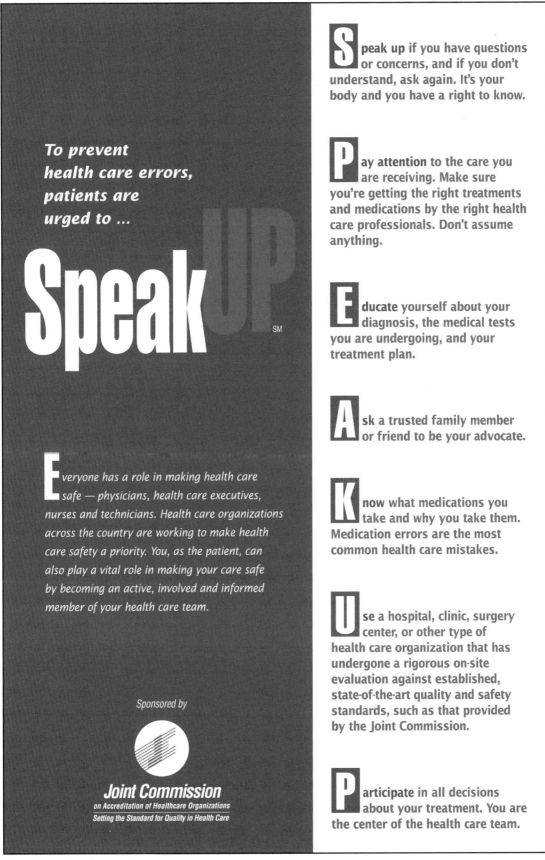

Figure 3.1 *Speak Up Poster, Joint Commission*

Another look at the public's perception of medical errors was defined in an evaluation of data about consumers' experiences with patient safety. The Henry Kaiser Family Foundation, the Harvard School of Public Health, and Agency for Healthcare Research and Quality conducted a survey of a nationally representative sample of 2,012 adults 18 years or older. The results published in November 2004 and updated in 2006 included some key findings:

- Over half (51 percent) of the public said that they were currently dissatisfied with the quality of health care in this country, compared to 44 percent who reported the same in 2000.

- Four in ten (40 percent) said the quality of health care had gotten worse in the past five years.

- Just over a third (36 percent) of the public said that in the past year they had seen information comparing the quality of different health plans, hospitals, or doctors.

- Sixty percent of the patients said that coordination among all of their different healthcare professions is a problem, including just over a quarter (26 percent) who said it is a major problem. Many people also reported specific problems with coordination of care, including having to wait longer for test results than they thought appropriate (48 percent), seeing a healthcare professional who did not have all of their medical information (42 percent), having to wait for a healthcare professional or make another appointment because they did not have the appropriate medical information (24 percent) and being sent for duplicate medical tests (19 percent).

- When comparing doctors, people were most likely to identify the top three factors that told them a lot about the quality of a doctor:
  ◊ How many times a doctor has done a specific medical procedure (66 percent)
  ◊ Whether a doctor is board certified (65 percent)
  ◊ How many malpractice suits a doctor has had filed against her (64 percent)

- When comparing hospitals, people were most likely to identify these factors as telling them a lot about the quality of a hospital:
  ◊ Reports of medical errors or mistakes that lead to harm of patients, such as a wrong dose or kind of medicine being given or the wrong operation being done (70 percent)
  ◊ How much experience the hospital has in performing a particular test or the surgery the respondent may need (65 percent)
  ◊ How many patients die after having surgery at the hospital (52 percent)

- In 2006, more than half the public reported knowing the meaning of the term "medical error," an increase from 2002 and 2004. More than four in ten said that when people sought help from a healthcare professional preventable medical errors occur "very" or "somewhat often."

- Americans continue to underestimate the number of people who die each year in hospitals from preventable medical errors: about half (49 percent) of the public said that 5,000 or fewer deaths occur in hospitals each year due to medical errors.

- After reading a definition of a medical error, about one in three said they, or a family member, experienced a medical error in their life.

- Those who experienced a medical error were most likely to place responsibility on the physician involved. Among those who said they or a family member experienced a medical error (34 percent of Americans), nearly three in four (72 percent) said the doctor involved had a lot of responsibility for the error. Fewer said that the institution (39 percent), nurses (28 percent), or other healthcare professionals (27 percent) involved had a lot of responsibility for the error.

- The public was more likely to blame individual healthcare professionals for causing medical errors, rather than the institutions where they worked. Nearly half (48 percent) of people said mistakes made by healthcare professionals were a more important cause of preventable medical errors than the mistakes made by the institutions. Just over one-third (36 percent) of Americans disagreed, saying mistakes made by institutions are a more important cause of medical errors.[13,14]

As insiders of the healthcare system, nurses have a unique perspective on patient safety. A 2005 Harris Interactive survey, commissioned by McKesson to determine how 216 registered nurses viewed the current state of medication safety, revealed that nurses had concerns about medication errors. The respondents were asked to discuss their perceptions of medication safety within their own hospital and at any hospital. When asked, "Concerning medication errors, how safe would you feel as a patient?"

- approximately 4 percent felt extremely safe in their own hospital,
- about 21 percent felt very safe,
- about 32 percent felt safe,
- about 33 percent felt somewhat safe, and
- about 9 percent said they were not safe at all in their own hospital.

The respondents were asked about their perception of medication safety in any hospital (as opposed to their own).

- none of the respondents felt extremely safe in any hospital,
- about 4 percent felt very safe,
- approximately 30 percent felt safe,
- about 51 percent felt somewhat safe, and
- about 15 percent did not feel safe at all in any hospital.[15]

In conclusion, perceptions of patient safety vary widely.

5.3 Motivation for Suits

This section provides an overview of the factors that affect a decision to seek a plaintiff's attorney. Both societal and personal factors influence how individuals react to an untoward outcome.

A. Societal Factors

1. Cost and complexity of health care

The costs associated with obtaining health care continue to rise in the United States. Those fortunate enough to obtain healthcare coverage through an employer are affected by the almost universal trend to pass on a portion of the premium payment to the employee. Individuals paying out-of-pocket for healthcare coverage or for services may have an expectation of a level of quality unmatched by the delivery of care. "This contributes to bad will towards the (healthcare) industry."[16]

Health care has become increasingly complex. Technological advances permitting interventions that were unthinkable five years ago also carry with them new risks. An expectation of quality of care is established by the opportunity to extend the ability to treat disease or perform intricate surgical techniques. Unrealistic consumer expectations may be created by the new advances.

2. Managed care

In the age of cost containment, nurses must perform increasingly complex tasks in less time, with fewer resources.

They are expected to document more extensively. Reliance on nursing assistants and technicians for greater amounts of bedside care, combined with the growing volume of time spent at the nursing station, decreases nursing time with the patient and degrades the quality of patient contact. The old adage that "the patient doesn't interrupt out work, the patient is our work" now seems archaic, particularly in the modern hospital context; yet adhering to the underlying philosophy can be key in decreasing the likelihood of legal claims.

TIP: The image of the nurse who sits at the bedside of the patient providing teaching and emotional support, or the kindly family doctor who had leisurely appointments with patients is long gone as managed care forces the healthcare door to revolve at a faster rate. The door of the hospital also revolves at a faster pace than ever before, with shorter lengths of stays, more outpatient surgery, and increased acuity of patients at all levels of care—hospital, subacute, home care and nursing home.

Nurses with no chance to get to know the patient who is briefly hospitalized do not have an opportunity to develop the individualized care that is a factor in patient safety. Resentment by patients may result.

The public is well aware of the decreased time available to spend with doctors. "Doctors not having enough time with patients" was the second most commonly cited cause of medical errors, according to the public surveyed for the National Survey on Consumers' Experiences with Patient Safety and Quality Information.[17] "Overwork, stress, or fatigue of healthcare professionals" was perceived as the number one reason for errors, and is a factor closely related to this concern of time or production pressure.

3. Depersonalized treatment

Health care has been slower than other industries to adopt the concepts of customer service and quality improvement. One of the roots of nursing malpractice suits is dissatisfaction with the quality of nursing care. Nurses have an advantage over other healthcare professionals in that public opinion polls consistently show that nurses are held in high regard. However, the protective halo over the nurse's head can be tarnished by unpleasant experiences. Johnson[18] identified the ten deadly sins of customer service, which can set the stage for an unhappy patient or family. Examples of how these sins contribute to the roots of a malpractice suit are included:

1. "I don't know." The nurse is unable to answer the patient's questions and does not make an effort to obtain the information.

2. "I don't care." Nurses are indifferent about their jobs and the patients.

3. "I can't be bothered." Ignoring the patient's requests for help or attention creates a negative impression that is hard to overcome.

4. "I do not like you." Nonverbal and verbal messages can clearly communicate this message to a patient or family. Avoidance of the patient worsens the situation.

5. "I know it all." Failing to listen to the patient increases frustration and impairs communication. Overconfidence, as previously mentioned, can lead to errors.

6. "You do not know anything." Negating the experiences of patients can lead to disasters. Patients are often finely attuned to their bodies and know when something is wrong. For example, one of the pearls of wisdom for obstetrical nurses is "When the patient says the baby is coming, believe her!"

7. "We do not want your kind here." Making negative assumptions based on appearance, color, age, class, educational level, sexual orientation or gender identity can lead to dissatisfaction and the development of hostility. Nurses may rush through their interactions with the patient and, therefore, miss important information or make errors.

8. "Do not come back." Every organization needs the return of satisfied customers. Consumers usually have a choice of providers, and spread the word of their unhappiness to other potential consumers of health care.

9. "I'm right and you are wrong." Arguing with a patient or family fuels the anger and sense of helplessness that many persons feel when their ability to control their situation is removed.

10. "Hurry up and wait." Many patients resent long waits for attention. Being left in the hallways of a hospital waiting for a transporter, or for someone to answer a call bell sends a message that their needs are not important.

An eleventh sin is emerging with the increasing usage of non-English speaking healthcare professionals. Healthcare workers speaking to each other in a language that excludes the patient may engender feelings of insecurity or anger. At least two major hospitals in one metropolitan state have lost market share because of this issue.[19]

4. Publicity about medical errors

Anyone with access to a newspaper, television, or the Internet has the capability of becoming informed of a medical error. An increasingly aware population may develop a level of cynicism regarding the promises of delivery of quality care. Many members of the public have heard about "never events" or the healthcare-acquired conditions which are supposed to never happen. The decision of CMS and many private payors to not pay for the care associated with these never events give support to an argument that the development of a never event is associated with substandard care. While there are many factors that result in never events, it is easier for plaintiff's attorneys to assert that the providers deviated from the standard of care. Refer to Armenti for more information.[20]

5. Independent research

Sophisticated patients and families may have access to information about current treatment that care providers are unaware of, and they can easily study the known risks and side effects of medications and other treatments. Less knowledgeable Internet surfers often misunderstand or misinterpret the information that is commonly available online, and may not easily differentiate between reliable sources of information, commercial claims, fringe movements and outright frauds. Whether the patients and their families are well-informed or misinformed, if their providers are not communicating with them, the next person to receive a summary of the research may be a plaintiff's attorney.

B. Personal Factors

1. Desire for answers

TIP: Studies show that the primary factor in a patient's decision to pursue a malpractice case is lack of communication from the provider after an unexpected outcome or undesirable result.[21]

Research demonstrates that a patient's decision to sue is influenced not only by the original injury, but also by insensitive handling, avoidance, silence, and poor communication afterwards. Patients want a clear, understandable explanation of what happened, the measures that will be taken to prevent a recurrence, if appropriate, and an understanding of the next steps in the treatment plan. Concealing an error in a shroud of mystery tends to intensify the agitation of patients leading them to become plaintiffs. Less than 15 percent of explanations patients received concerning their injury were considered satisfactory, and 37 percent stated they would not have sued if they had received an explanation and apology. Twenty-four percent recognized a cover-up, and 20 percent sued because they wanted information they could not get any other way.[22] The subject of disclosure of errors is addressed in more detail below.

2. Desire to improve patient safety

Some individuals file suit and endure through years of litigation because they do not want someone else to be injured by the same mistake. Patients do not want their experience to be repeated. Often the question asked of healthcare providers is, "What is the organization doing to find out how the event occurred and prevent it from happening again?[23] When patients or their families consult an attorney regarding a medical malpractice claim but the attorney does not wish to pursue the case, they are sometimes motivated to file complaints both with the hospital administration (when a hospital is involved) and with the state governmental agency or agencies responsible for oversight of the organization or practitioners who they believe provided substandard care. Their expressed interest is to prevent others from suffering the same experiences that they did.

The King family, parents of an 18-month-old who died in a major teaching hospital, is an example of those who have dedicated their attention to the issue of patient safety. In her book, *Josie's Story*, Sorrel King stated her attorney brought legal documents from Johns Hopkins University Hospital, where the error occurred. "There it was: the settlement offer. It was a concept that was difficult to comprehend—money for the death of our daughter. The concept of us accepting it was almost as appalling as them offering it. We didn't want their money and felt that by accepting it we would be letting them off the hook. We didn't want it to be so easy for them." When their attorney asked them what they did want, Sorrel said, "I wanted them to remember Josie, to learn something from her and to never let this happen again. 'I want every hospital in the country to know her name and why she died. I want them all to learn something,'" I said angrily. Her attorney replied, "'Then do that, do that with the settlement money. If you leave this money, it will just get sucked up in a black hole. Take the money and do something good. Do something for Josie. You can make this more than a sad story for the media to cover. You can create something much more.'"[24] The King family took their settlement check and funded patient safety efforts in the hospital in which their daughter died, and have been instrumental in improving safety in other hospitals throughout the world.[25]

In a case reported in 2010, a plaintiff's desire for changes in a system is fulfilled in the terms of a settlement. For example, actor James Woods brought suit on behalf of his brother's estate. His 49-year-old brother went to the emergency department complaining of a burning pain in his throat and vomiting. His respiratory and pulse rates were elevated. Although he had a history of a cardiac stent, he was triaged as less urgent. The nurse asked a physician to examine him. This doctor ordered an EKG, which was abnormal, and cardiac monitoring, which was not initiated. Mr. Woods was sent to the x-ray department, and when he was returned to the emergency department, he was left on a stretcher in the hallway. He suffered a fatal heart attack. A confidential settlement was reached after the hospital's president apologized to the family. In addition to the payment to the plaintiffs, the hospital agreed to spend $1.25 million over the next five years for the Michael J. Woods Institute, which will be charged with developing new procedures and training for the hospital's staff.[26]

In a second case reported in 2010, the plaintiff's decedent was a 32-year-old woman who underwent a cesarean section delivery of her second child. During delivery the woman's uterine artery was cut or torn, causing a severe obstetrical hemorrhage. She lost approximately 60 percent of her total blood volume. She developed hypotension, tachycardia, minimal urine output and metabolic acidosis, and deteriorated. A second surgery to explore her abdomen was performed. The surgeon found the retroperitoneal cavity was full of massive blood clots caused by continued internal bleeding. The family alleged after her death that the initial obstetrician damaged the uterine arteries in the retroperitoneum, which continued to bleed. The plaintiff also contended that due to a problem in the software of the OBIX Perinatal Data System monitoring machines, the decedent's vital signs were not accurately recorded while in the PACU.

The family reached a $5.2 million settlement. The hospital agreed to establish an annual quality lecture in the decedent's name which would focus on topics related to enhancing patient safety. They agreed to purchase a Noelle Maternal and Neonatal Simulator to use in training the labor and delivery staff. The hospital also agreed to change the default settings on its OBIX Perinatal Data System machines to prevent them from defaulting to record normal values for vital signs when the "add" button is pushed.[27]

While these stories are encouraging accounts of efforts to change the system through litigation, they are notable in that they are so rare.

3. Desire for Money

At one time, people were reluctant to make trouble for nurses or doctors, either out of respect for the services offered or because they had presumably so little money that it seemed unfair or pointless.[28] Today with all the publicity surrounding the rise in malpractice premium rates for doctors, the public is well aware that an insurance policy stands behind most healthcare professionals.

The families of patients who suffered a catastrophic adverse outcome and envision their loved ones requiring comprehensive and expensive care for the rest of their lives are highly motivated to seek compensation from those who they perceive to be responsible. A mother may wish to stay home and take care of her paralyzed child instead of having to work while the child is in the care of strangers. Relatives want their injured family members to have the best medical and nursing attention and equipment, and will look to the providers who contributed to the injury to make that possible.

Patients whose lives have been devastated by serious injuries that resulted from medical errors seek compensation for their pain, suffering, disability and other losses. The inadequacy of money to make an injured person whole reduces neither the desire nor the right to seek what recompense may be available.

Publicity regarding extraordinarily high verdicts or settlements may also affect perceptions. Some people think they will get rich quickly and are unaware that it typically takes three to five years for a claim to wind its way through the courts, and that there are difficult criteria that have to be satisfied to establish a valid claim. Plaintiff's attorneys who handle medical malpractice receive calls every week from people wanting to know if they have a valid claim. For example, Jonathan Schochor, a Maryland attorney, sees up to 3,000 potential cases per year and takes on about 80. He says, "You would have to be a fool to take a case that didn't have merit. Claims cost between $75,000 and $150,000 to pay for witnesses, life care planner, economists, and other basic business costs."[29]

TIP: Plaintiff's attorneys are wary of the potential client whose first concern is "how much is this worth?" There is rarely enough money available to satisfy this person. Plaintiff's attorney Eugene Horn commented that potential plaintiffs come to him wanting three things: to put the doctor or facility out of business, an apology, or money.[30]

---

4. Sense of entitlement

The injured patient may possess a "sue if possible, since I've been injured" attitude. There is strong evidence that some people are being socialized into thinking that if something goes wrong, they should sue. A factor may be the ubiquitous advertisements of attorneys on radio and television, on billboards, on the Internet, and in the Yellow Pages, promising legal help for a multitude of injuries and accidents.[31]

C. Predisposing and Precipitating Factors

Bunting, Benton, and Morgan[32] provide a framework of identifying predisposing and precipitating factors that can result in a lawsuit.

1. Predisposing factors: communication

The predisposing factors include events, which when viewed by themselves appear to be of little consequence to patient satisfaction. When viewed collectively, they may significantly influence the patient's perception about the quality of care provided. These predisposing factors may include a dirty room, a delay in having a request fulfilled, apathy, inattentiveness, rudeness, delays in obtaining pain or other medications, and minor errors not resulting in harm.

Para added to the list of predisposing factors as follows:

a. Failure to provide an explanation. The healthcare provider does not provide sufficient explanations for policies, procedures, or care decisions.

b. Failure to keep the patient or the family up to date. The healthcare providers do not recognize and address the patient's and family's need and right to have information about the patient's status. The patient has a fundamental right to be informed about and participate in decisions regarding his care. A common and unfortunate error is failing to inform the patient of what is being done on his behalf. The patient, or family member, who is not told that the doctor has been called or a special meal requested, is left feeling dissatisfied and resentful rather than appreciative.

c. Blaming a patient or the family for a bad outcome. Although contributory or comparative negligence is an appropriate legal defense in some circumstances, raising this defense at the bedside may not display the best timing.

d. Insensitivity in informing a patient or the family. Although in most settings breaking bad news or informing the patient or family about poor surgical outcomes or mistakes is in the realm of the doctor rather than the nurse, the nurse may be involved in revealing mistakes. Nurses generally handle these situations with compassion. Many physicians have difficulty breaking bad news because they feel an element of personal failure.[33]

e. Failure to effectively share the lessons learned. Although risk managers know a lot about the risks and opportunities for improvement in their organization, they may lack a framework to mine their data, link their findings to organizational efforts to improve safety, and deploy their knowledge on behalf of the organization. They need to make their knowledge actionable. The reluctance to share patient safety data has significantly impeded the opportunity to share improvement stories and establish best patient safety practices. Chances are high that valuable root cause analysis lessons are not routinely shared across managers and front line staff within the relevant specialty area, let alone across the institution or to a broader group.[34]

TIP: The nurse who forgets that caring for the family is an integral part of caring for the patient contributes to an atmosphere that makes legal claims more likely in the event of an adverse outcome.

These predisposing factors set the stage for an unhappy patient or family. Some of these individuals may have been involved in other types of lawsuits, and thus have familiarity with the legal system. On occasion, they may even inform the nurses and doctors that they have sued other people in the past.

Risk managers and others are increasingly educating healthcare providers to recognize the importance of the patient's perception of the quality of care. The tendency exists to minimize the patient's complaints about predisposing factors, resulting in a lost opportunity to intervene to de-escalate the situation.

2. Precipitating factors

Precipitating factors are those with significant influence on the patient's desire to file a claim against the healthcare providers. Unlike predisposing factors, which initially appear to be minor, the precipitating factors tend to be more serious. They may include a significant adverse patient outcome. Iatrogenic injuries (those caused by healthcare providers or the environment) are particularly likely to precipitate a lawsuit. Examples include burns caused by surgical grounding pads, instruments left in the body, medica-

tion errors, patients being dropped on the floor by the staff, and so on. The predisposing factors in the patient as well as the responses of the healthcare professionals to an adverse outcome determine whether the plaintiff's attorney is consulted.

As Adam Rothenberg of Levinson Axelrod said, "Certainly in cases in which there is a clear error, I am amazed how often the patient eventually turns to me (an attorney) because of the attitude of the doctor following a clear mistake. The comment I hear all too often is that it was bad enough that there was a mistake but the doctor's attitude, or lack of CARING (not care) that seemed to motivate them to seek counsel. One could say it is a rationalization, but often these people just want to know if they can get their medical deductible paid for the additional treatment; they do not even contemplate the pain and suffering awards. The best advice to doctors is that people who will sue, will sue—so do not turn your back on your patients. Many patients will never contemplate an attorney if you just own up to the act, take responsibility and show you care about the patient. And if he or she does sue, that is why you have insurance."[35]

5.4 Disclosure of Errors

As consumers have become increasingly aware of the problem of medical and nursing errors, a movement to persuade healthcare providers to be open about errors emerged. The movement to increase disclosure of errors is discussed below.

A. Compliance with Requirement for Disclosure

In most acute care facilities, the physician assumes the role of disclosing a medical error. This is true even if the error was made by a nurse and not the physician. Discussion of adverse events typically generates anxiety in the physician, as she anticipates the negative reactions, angry responses, and other reactions the patient or family may display. Ideally, physicians should receive education from their insurance carrier or facility on how to skillfully handle these discussions.

There continues to be a gap between the responsibility for advising the patient of an error and the actual practice of doing so. Much of the evaluation of this issue focuses on physician behavior, which may be applicable to how healthcare facilities handle disclosure. Key findings are summarized below.

Attitudes towards the risks and benefits of disclosure and apologies have varied over the years. A study published in the 1991 *Journal of the American Medical Association* reported that only 54 percent of 254 medical residents discussed their mistakes with their attending doctors, who are administratively responsible for them. Only 24 percent told the patients or families of the mistakes.[36]

The Joint Commission published a standard in 2001 effective in 2002 requiring healthcare providers to inform patients and their families about unanticipated outcomes. An immediate outcry was heard from risk managers, doctors, and others fearful of the implications of telling patients the truth about errors. Almost a decade later, compliance with this standard is not universal. There is still considerable resistance and fear, rooted in the perception that admitting mistakes is not safe in a culture that still subscribes to blame and punishment as methods for ensuring accountability and leading to litigation.[37] According to a 2002 survey of risk managers at 245 U.S. hospitals, 98 percent of the respondents reported that at their hospitals, there was an established practice of disclosing some or all harmful mistakes and other adverse events to patients. However, when the researchers asked risk managers to review actual cases of harm to patients and state whether they would disclose these specific incidents, 65 percent of respondents indicated an unwillingness to disclose preventable harms—a category that would include mistakes. The researchers also found that risk managers who expressed the most concern about malpractice litigation were the ones least likely to disclose mistakes.[38] Only 5.5 percent of the medication errors committed in 2003 and reported in the MEDMARX study were followed by the patient or caregiver being informed of the medication error.[39]

Many healthcare providers believe a number of myths, including that there is no ethical or legal duty to disclose medical errors to patients, or that patients do not really want to know about errors. On the contrary, Witman found that 98 percent of patients expected acknowledgment of even minor errors.[40] In one study, only 60 percent of doctors believed that a patient should always be told when a complication occurred.[41] The vast majority of consumers surveyed about patient safety by the Henry J. Kaiser Foundation believed that physicians should be required to tell their patients if a preventable medical error is made in their care. The vast majority also said that reporting of medical errors should be required and most said that this information should be released to the public.[42]

Doctors are less likely to disclose mistakes that result in serious injury or death. In some studies, physicians said they do not disclose errors for fear of further harming patients or of losing the patient's trust.[43,44]

The motivation to conceal the circumstances of a retained sponge is not clear in this case, but the results were concrete for the surgeon:

In a Washington case, the plaintiff's decedent was a 77-year-old woman who underwent surgery for early colon cancer. The defendant surgeon left a surgical sponge in the abdomen, requiring a second surgery to remove the sponge. According to the plaintiff, the defendant failed to inform the decedent or her family of the error until at least one month after the second surgery. By that time the decedent's condition had seriously deteriorated. She developed an abdominal wall abscess with a retained foreign body, resulting in sepsis secondary to a fistulous tract running from her small bowel to the exterior wall of her stomach, leading to her death. A $1.2 million settlement was reached.[45]

In one study, 33 percent of physicians said they would offer incomplete or misleading information to a patient's family if a mistake led to a patient's death.[46] The reasons for dishonesty to patients were associated with the emotional devastation felt by a physician involved in an error, pressure to be perfect, anxiety about losing professional reputation, and fear of litigation.[47]

TIP: The stress of being named in a malpractice lawsuit increases the risk of being named in other suits.

A study of 1,747 open and closed Michigan claims reported an analysis of the interval between the report date (when the doctor learned of the first lawsuit) for a first claim and the loss date (the date of the alleged negligent incident occurrence) of a second claim. During any given quarter, an insured physician's average risk of being named in a lawsuit was 5 percent. But during the three months following the report date for the first claim, a physician's risk for having a patient encounter that led to a second legal action almost tripled to 14.4 percent. The risk of a second lawsuit remained elevated for a two-year period after the initial notice. The study suggested a circular relationship: being named in a lawsuit increases stress, which in turn impairs clinical performance and increases exposure to subsequent liability.[48] The authors are unaware of any such study of nursing claims.

Although data from a similar study of nursing errors was not found, the authors are aware of nurses who have been so devastated by serious errors that they left nursing.

Some doctors do not disclose errors because of the belief that if they tell the truth, they increase their chances of being sued. Only 1 to 2 percent of negligent adverse events led to actual claims, but physicians estimated their risk of being sued is about three times the actual rate.[49] Few in the Kaiser

Family Foundation survey reported pursuing malpractice lawsuits after a medical error. Among those who said they or a family member experienced a medical error, 11 percent (or 4 percent of the total public) reported that they or their family member sued a healthcare professional for malpractice after experiencing the medical error. Of those who said that the medical error they or their family member experienced had serious health consequences, 14 percent (or 3 percent of the total public) reported that they or their family member sued a healthcare professional for malpractice after experiencing the medical error. Only 21 percent of the respondents thought that "more lawsuits for malpractice" was one of the potential ways to reduce medical errors.[50]

An American Medical Association ethical opinion states that when a doctor errs, "The physician is ethically required to inform the patient of all the facts necessary to ensure understanding of what has occurred" and that liability concerns should not impede disclosure.[51]

Some individuals do not seek out a plaintiff's attorney after a medical error, but instead:

- do not understand that an error has occurred,
- view the error as a mistake and are forgiving,
- view the outcome within a religious framework, such as seeing it as "God's will," or
- change providers rather than confront the individual.

B. Impact of Disclosure

Some experts in the patient safety field are urging more complete disclosure and alternatives to litigation. Healthcare facilities that practice a full disclosure model have seen a reduction in claims being filed and legal bills. The Lexington (Kentucky) Model, pioneered at a Veterans Administration Center, promotes assisting patients in filing compensation claims without first initiating litigation. The model emphasizes acting with extreme honesty, persuading the occasional reluctant victim to accept financial compensation, and advising injured patients and their families to hire their own lawyer to explain the compensation process and to represent them in settlement negotiations. As of 2007, Lexington was averaging $16,000 per settlement.[52] "Controlling anger is the reason that the Lexington VA was in the lowest quartile for total payments despite being in the highest quartile for claims. They removed anger from the process and in so doing removed customers' desire to financially punish the institution. Anger, not greed, is what drives severity."[53] The specifics of this model, which are not universally adaptable, are that the VHA:

- is a closed system,
- services a specific patient population,
- employs its own physicians,
- is protected by a federal statute limiting the liability of governmental institutions under the tort system, and
- is able to access a federal program to pay compensation settlements.[54]

However, there are non-VHA healthcare systems achieving results with disclosure models. Catholic Healthcare West supports "The Mistakes Project," which recognizes that patients are far more likely to seek legal representation if they believe information has been concealed. Timely disclosure of mistakes is cost effective from the standpoint of the institution. Fair compensation is discussed with the family as part of the disclosure of the mistake. In one situation, a family affected by a harmful mistake reflected on the question: "What do you need, based on what happened?" This family determined what they really needed was a trailer. The hospital agreed this was fair compensation and the family received the trailer.[55]

At University of Michigan Health Systems, encouraging doctors to apologize for mistakes is part of a broader effort to help doctors feel comfortable in being honest with their patients. They have seen their litigation costs drop in half and now claims drop by 40 percent.[56]

COPIC, a Denver-based malpractice insurer which provides malpractice insurance to 6,000 physicians and also insures hospitals and health plans, developed the 3Rs Program: "Recognize, Respond to, and Resolve Patient Injury." The program assists a physician by:

- Responding in a timely fashion to an unanticipated medical outcome,
- Communicating with the patient in an empathetic manner, and
- Arranging for additional care or services the patient might need as a result of the outcome.[57]

The objective of the program is to respond to patient injuries before they escalate into disputes, claims, or lawsuits by better preparing physicians to disclose unanticipated outcomes to patients. COPIC's own risk managers swiftly evaluate incidents and make settlement offers in cases in which a patient's need for fair compensation can be satisfied without a formal malpractice claim. Savings have been considerable. As of December 31, 2003, payments to patients under the 3Rs Program averaged $1,820, as opposed to an average cost of more than $250,000 for traditional paid claims handled by the same insurer, and an average cost of more than $78,000 for handling claims in which there was no payment to patients.[58]

TIP: Organizations that have practiced open disclosure with patients have found that it actually decreases their litigation by removing incentives to sue.

The West Virginia Mutual Insurance Company created a C.A.R.E program to assist their insured physicians in appropriately communicating unanticipated outcomes. Information about this program is included in this chapter because of the frequency with which physicians and nurses become defendants in the same suit. The specifics of the program are:

1. The physician must contact C.A.R.E. when there is an unanticipated outcome or error and discuss it with a C.A.R.E. representative. The Mutual will decide if the event meets the qualifications for the C.A.R.E. program.
2. If the situation meets the C.A.R.E. criteria, the physician must speak with the patient and/or family again and explain what happened, in terms they can understand, why it happened (if they know), what they are going to do about it to prevent this from happening again, and, if there is a medical error, accept responsibility and apologize for the error.
3. If it is an unanticipated outcome with no medical error, the physician should express sincere sympathy or regret for the outcome.
4. If the event qualifies for C.A.R.E., the patient or family member will be given contact information at this time. If they chose, they may call C.A.R.E.
5. Once the patient and/or family contacts C.A.R.E., the event is discussed with them to make sure they have no additional questions.
6. Discussions with the patient and/or family include out-of-pocket medical and non-medical expenses they may have incurred due to this unanticipated outcome and/or error.
7. Research is conducted on the medical and non-medical expenses and any other issues that are affecting the patient and/or family as a result of the error.
8. An offer of disbursement is made based upon the findings.

C.A.R.E. reinforces the apology in an attempt to meet the immediate needs of the patient. There are no disburse-ments for pain and suffering. The exclusions to the program include death, attorney involvement, Board of Medicine complaint, written demand, summons and complaint, and a Notice of Claim with Screening Certificate of Merit.[59]

The advice to disclose errors challenges the traditional legal view to remain silent when a mistake has affected a patient. That advice serves to block the ability of fellow doctors and nurses, even in the same facility, to get the clinical details of what went wrong in time to change their system to prevent a repeat tragedy.[60]

The process of apologizing and taking responsibility for errors is spreading. Much of the awareness is reflected in the mission of Sorry Works! Founded in 2005, The Sorry Works! Coalition has quickly become the nation's leading advocacy organization for disclosure, apology (when appropriate), and upfront compensation (when necessary) after adverse medical events. According to their website, the coalition believes and advocates that the medical malpractice crisis is a customer service crisis—not a legal problem—that can be solved anytime by medical, insurance, and legal professionals. Sorry Works! provides the customer service framework in a programmatic approach that encourages communication and problem solving with patients and families after adverse events. A simple three-step disclosure process is at the heart of the Sorry Works! program. Several states have enacted legislation prohibiting apologies from being used against a doctor in court. Refer to www.sorryworks.net for more information about efforts to foster disclosure and provide apologies to patients.

The value of offering apologies and the risks of these statements being seen as admission and used against the healthcare provider in court will be resolved as more healthcare providers begin to understand the benefits of being open and truthful with patients about medical errors.

For some plaintiffs, disclosure does not go far enough. Patients and patient advocates are asking for increased transparency and a greater role in the process of change. Some facilities have opened the doors to allow patients and families to participate in the failure mode and effects analysis (FMEA) and root cause analysis (RCA). The psychological benefits of including patients, when appropriate, can be profound. After an adverse event, many patients are able to understand the vulnerability of healthcare processes and although upset by their experience, wish to help improve the system. In group situations where caregivers are willing and able to listen, reveal vulnerability and concern, and patients can express feelings openly, a bond of experience can develop. This permits individuals to heal through shared understanding and empathy. Patients, who have long stated the desire to ensure that the system is changed as a result of their experience, are given the chance to participate in the process of improving the system. The process of bringing patients into the problem-solving environment requires careful screening, structuring of the process, adequate preparation and follow up.[61] For example, Sorrel and Tony King, the parents of a child killed by a medical error at Johns Hopkins, attended a root cause analysis meeting with a surgeon, an ICU doctor, an intensive care doctor, two pediatric nurses, and another risk manager. After the meeting, Sorrell handed each person a picture of Josie. "This is for you, to remind you that this is more than just a case study." On that day, she was unaware that this was the first time, not only in the history of Hopkins but possibly in the history of health care, that a family had been invited to attend a root cause analysis meeting. Years later, this approach to including the family would be slowly adopted in other healthcare institutions around the country.[62]

5.5 Frequency and Severity of Claims

The final section of this chapter summarizes allegations against nurses and offers data regarding claims. The Healthcare Protection and Integrity Databank 2002 report reveals that the Databank accumulated a total of 134,806 reports of 80,026 individuals and 2,213 organizations since 1999. Most of the reports involve physicians and nurses, but reports involving pharmacists, social workers, psychologists, optical practitioners, nurses' aides, and dentists also exist. Key findings of this report are listed below. The most common reasons why actions were taken against nurses' licenses were:

- unsafe practice or substandard care (24 percent),
- misconduct or abuse (22.7 percent),
- noncompliance with federal, state, or contractual requirements (9.6 percent), or
- other (36 percent).[63]

The most common actions taken against nurses were:

- probation of license or certificate (23.7 percent of those reported),
- suspension of license (13.6 percent),
- reprimand or censure (10.7 percent),
- reprimand, censure, and voluntary (license) surrender (10.8 percent),
- administrative fine, monetary penalty (6.2 percent), or
- revocation of license (6.1 percent).

Information about payments made on behalf of nurses may be found in the National Practitioner Databank (NPDB). Registered nurses are classified into five licensure categories: nurse anesthetist, nurse midwife, nurse practitioner, clinical nurse specialist/advanced practice nurse, and non-specialized registered nurse not otherwise classified. Key findings of the 2006 NPDB report are listed below.[64]

- One out of 50 malpractice payment reports were for nurses and most were for other classified registered nurses.
- All types of registered nurses have been responsible for 6,208 malpractice payments. or 2.1 percent of all payments, over the history of the NPDB.
- "Other-classified RNs" were responsible for 61.6 percent of the payments made for nurses. These claims fell under the category of monitoring, treatment, medication, obstetrics, and surgery-related problems.
- Nurse anesthetists were responsible for 19 percent of nurse payments, with anesthesia-related problems responsible for 84.1 percent of the payments.
- Nurse midwives were responsible for 9.6 percent of nurse payments. Obstetrics-related problems were responsible for 81 percent of these payments.
- Nurse practitioners were responsible for 9.6 percent of the payments. Diagnosis-related problems were involved in 44.9 percent of their payments. Treatment-related problems were involved in another 24.9 percent of the payments.
- The median nurse payment was $112,500. The median physician payment was $175,000.
- The mean nurse payment was $327,431. The mean physician payment was less at $311,965. The mean payment amount for nurses was likely larger because there were relatively fewer nurse payments, which means one significantly large payment can impact the mean more than if there were more nurse payments.[65]
- There was a wide variation in states' Nurse Malpractice Payment Reports compared to physicians. Vermont had only seven Malpractice Payment Reports while New Jersey had the most (752). (New Jersey statute requires the identification of a specific nurse defendant to surmount the institutional cap on liability.)

After several years of decreases in hospital professional liability claims, the number of claims was expected to rise at an annual rate of 1 percent in 2009 and 2010, according to a study by Aon Corp. and the American Association of Healthcare Risk Management. The 10th annual Hospital Professional Liability and Physician Liability Benchmark Analysis looks at trends in the number and cost of claims. "Worsening economic conditions in 2008 may have influenced individuals to assert claims," said Erik Johnson, healthcare practice leader for Aon's Actuarial and Analytics Practice. "In 2003 through 2007 public attention was directed on tort reform activity and prohibitive medical malpractice costs for physicians. This coincided with significant reductions in professional liability claims."[66]

5.6 Summary

Much of the impetus to file a suit after an injurious medical error lies in the way the incident is handled. Although patient factors may dampen the desire to seek a plaintiff's attorney, many do so because of a desire to obtain answers or an apology for a medical error. The movement to promote disclosure of errors seeks to fulfill professional obligations to tell the truth. A byproduct of this movement seems to be the reduction in litigation and the resolution of claims in what the consumer sees as a fair manner.

Endnotes

1. Institute of Medicine, To Err is Human: Building a Safer Health System, Washington, D.C.: National Academies Press, 1999.

2. *Id.*

3. http://www.healthgrades.com/media/dms/pdf/Health-GradesPatientSafetyRelease2008.pdf (last accessed 6/11/2010).

4. Langreth, R., "Fixing hospitals," Forbes (June 20, 2005): 68-82.

5. Cunningham R. et al. Effect on MRSA transmission of rapid PCR testing of patients admitted to critical care. J Hosp Infection Control, 65:1, 24-28. 2007.

6. Günter, K. and Kramer, A. "Epidemiologic Background of Hand Hygiene and Evaluation of the Most Important Agents for Scrubs and Rubs," Clinical Microbiology Reviews, Oct. 2004, p. 863-893 Vol. 17, No. 4.

7. Hany, A., Herson, V., Duncan, A. et al., Bloodstream Infection Preventable Among Premature Infants? A Tale of Two Cities—Pediatrics 2005; 115; 1513-1518.

8. Pronovost, P., Needham, D., Berenholtz, S. et al., An Intervention to Decrease Catheter-Related Bloodstream Infections in the ICU—JAMA December 28, 2006 vol. 355 no. 26.

9. Scott, R. The Direct Medical Costs of Healthcare-Associated Infections in U.S. Hospitals and the Benefits of Prevention, 2009, http://www.cdc.gov/ncidod/dhqp/pdf/Scott_CostPaper.pdf.

10. Hayward, R., S. Asch, M. Hogan, T. Hofer, and E. Kerr, "Sins of omission," Journal of General Internal Medicine 64 (June 2005).

11. Blendon, R., C. DesRoches, M. Brodie, J. Benson, A. Rosen, E. Schneider, D. Altman, K. Zapert, M. Herrmann, and A. Steffenson, "Views of practicing physicians and the public on medical errors," The New England Journal of Medicine 347 (December 12, 2002): pgs. 1933-1940.

12. http://www.jcaho.org/accredited+organizations/speak+up/hospital+brochure-eng.htm, last accessed December 31, 2005.

13. The Henry J. Kaiser Family Foundation, AHRQ, Harvard School of Public Health, National Survey on Consumers' Experiences with Patient Safety and Quality Information, November 2004.

14. 2006 Update on Consumers' Views of Patient Safety and Quality Information, The Henry J. Kaiser Foundation and AHRQ, http://www.kff.org/kaiserpolls/upload/7560.pdf.

15. "Frontline nurses' perceptions of the state of patient safety," Nurse Advise-ERR, 3, no. 7 (July 2005). www.ismp.org.

16. Greve Jr., P., "Malpractice insurance: riding out the storm," ASHRM Journal (Fall 2002): 7-11.

17. See note 13.

18. Johnson, C., "Knock your socks off service," Nursing Management (July 1999): 16.

19. Personal communication, Lucille Joel, November 2005.

20. Armenti, C. Preventing Healthcare-Acquired Conditions Means Never Having to Say You're Sorry, in Iyer, P. and Levin, B., Medical Legal Aspects of Medical Records, Second Edition, Tucson, Lawyers and Judges Publishing Company, 2010.

21 Hickson, G. and E. Clayton et al., "Factors that prompted families to file medical malpractice claims following perinatal injuries," JAMA 267 (1992): 1359-63.

22. Hicks, R., J. Santell, D. Cousins, and R. Williams, MEDMARX 5th Anniversary Data Report: A Chartbook of 2003 Findings and Trends 1999-2003, Rockville, MD: USP Center for the Advancement of Patient Safety, 2004.

23. Vincent, C., M. Young, and A. Phillips, "Why do people sue doctors? A study of patients and relatives taking legal action," Lancet 343, no. 1 (1994): 609-10.

24. Sorrel King, Josie's Story, New York, Atlantic Monthly Press, 2009.

25. Sorrel King's presentation, ASHRM conference, October 24, 2005.

26. Laska, L. (Ed), "Failure to properly evaluate man suffering from throat pain with abnormal EKG," Medical Malpractice Verdicts, Settlements, and Experts, March 2010, p. 11.

27. Laska, L. (Ed), "Failure to return woman for further surgery after repairing damaged uterine artery from cesarean section," Medical Malpractice Verdicts, Settlements, and Experts, May 2010, 24-25.

28. Joel, L., Nursing Experience, Fifth Edition, McGraw-Hill, 2006.

29. Anderson, T., "Taking medicine to court," Baltimore Business Journal, www.bizjournals.com/baltimore/stories/2004/12/20/focus1.html, accessed December 21, 2004.

30. Personal communication, Eugene Horn, April 2010.

31. See note 28.

32. Bunting, R., J. Benton, and W. Morgan, "Practical risk management principles for physicians," Journal of Healthcare Risk Management (Fall 1998): 29.

33. Para, P., "Patient relations for modern times," Journal of Healthcare Risk Management 17, no. 4 (Fall 1997): 23.

34. Data for Safety: Turning Lessons Learned into actionable Knowledge Monograph, American Society of Healthcare Risk Management, Vol. 28, No. 2, 7-15, 2008.

35. Personal communication, Adam Rothenberg, December 2004.

36. Gerlin, A., "Mum is often the word when caregivers stumble," September 14, 1999, Philadelphia Online. http://health.philly. com/specials/mistakes/hosp14.asp.

37. Porto, G., "Disclosure of medical error: Facts and fallacies," Journal of Healthcare Risk Management (Fall 2001): 67–76.

38. Berlinger, N., "Fair compensation without litigation: Addressing patients' financial needs in disclosure," ASHRM Journal 24, no. 1 (2004): 7-11.

39. See note 22.

40. Witman, A., and D. Park et al., "How do patients want physicians to handle mistakes?" Archives of Internal Medicine 156 (1996): 2565-69.

41. Hingorani, M. and T. Wong et al., "Attitudes after unintended injury during treatment: A survey of doctors and patients," Western Journal of Medicine 171 (1999): 81-83.

42. See note 14.

43. Sweet, M., and J. Bernat, "A study of the ethical duty of physician to disclose errors," The Journal of Clinical Ethics 8, no. 4 (1997): 341-48.

44. See note 41.

45. Laska, L. (ed.), "Sponge left in abdomen after surgery for colon cancer causes abscess and sepsis, leading to death," Medical Malpractice Verdicts, Settlements, and Experts (November 2005): 47.

46. Novack, D. and B. Detering et al., "Physicians' attitudes toward using deception to resolve difficult ethical problems," JAMA 26, no. 20 (1989): 2980-85.

47. See note 37.

48. Bartlett, E., "Physician stress management: a new approach to reducing medical errors and liability risk," ASHRM Journal (Spring 2002): 3-7.

49. See note 37.

50. See note 13.

51. www.ama-assn.org/amednews/2010/02/01/prsa0201. htm, last accessed 02/25/11.

52. Bridgeman, E. and Malinowski, A., The disclosure of unanticipated medical outcomes: better communication, better care, better patient satisfaction," *Journal of Legal Nurse Consulting*, 20, no. 1, Winter 2009, 13-18.

53. Wojceiszak, D., Saxton, J. and Finkelstein, M. Sorry Works! Disclosure, Apology, and Relationships Prevent Medical Malpractice Claims, AuthorHouse, 2007.

54. See note 38.

55. *Id.*

56. See note 51.

57. See note 52.

58. See note 38.

59. See note 52.

60. Nance, J., "A tragic error, and a laudable response," http://seattlepi.nwsource.com/opinion/202730_sorry12.html, accessed December 14, 2004.

61. Zimmerman, T. and Amori, G., "Including patients in root cause and system failure analysis: legal and psychological implications," *Journal of Healthcare Risk Management*, Vol. 27, No. 2, 27-34, 2007.

62. See note 24.

63. Healthcare Protection and Integrity Databank 2002 Annual Report, U.S. Department of Health and Human Services.

64. National Practitioner Data Bank 2006 Annual Report. www.npdb-hipdb.hrsa.gov/annualrpt.html, last accessed 02/25/11.

65. National Practitioner Database Annual Report 2003, U.S. Department of Health and Human Services.

66. www.ashrm.org/ashrm/news/forum_newsletter/forum_newsletter_archives/2009/Forum09NovDec.pdf, last accessed 02/25/11.

Additional Reading

Bewley, E. *Killer Cure,* Indianapolis, Dog Ear Publishing, 2010.

Kumar, S., *Fatal Care: Survive in the U.S. Health System,* Minneapolis, MN: IGI Press, 2008.

Part II:

Nursing Practice

Chapter 6

The Foundations of Nursing Practice

Patricia W. Iyer, MSN, RN, LNCC and Susan Egger, MSN, RN

6.1 Introduction

Nurses make up the largest healthcare profession, with 26 million jobs within the United States.[1] All of us interact with nurses throughout our lives, both within the healthcare setting and our social lives. Nurses are found in hospitals, homes, public health agencies, retirement communities, work settings, schools, outpatient surgical centers, camps, nursing homes, assisted living facilities, physicians' offices, insurance companies, military, governmental, and regulatory agencies—in short, wherever people live and work. The nursing profession continues to be highly regarded. This chapter provides an overview of the educational preparation of nurses, licensing and certification system, and definitions of standards of care. The information is useful when investigating potential claims or litigating nursing malpractice cases. The more the attorney knows about nursing practice, the easier it is to identify or refute nursing liability.

6.2 Nursing Education

Those involved in litigating or defending nursing malpractice claims must understand the different types of nursing programs and varieties of nurses who graduate from these programs.

There are several paths to enter practice as a registered nurse, but all lead to a role that contains some of the elements defined below.

A. Registered Nurses

The Department of Labor describes registered nurses as those who:

- work to promote health and prevent disease,
- help patients cope with illness,
- act as advocates and health educators for patients, families, and communities,
- observe, assess, and record symptoms, reactions, and progress of patients,
- assist physicians during surgeries, treatments, and examinations,
- administer medications,
- assist in convalescence and rehabilitation,
- develop and manage nursing care plans,
- instruct patients and their families in proper care, and
- help individuals and groups take steps to improve or maintain their health.[2]

159

The National Council of State Boards of Nursing defines the practice of nursing:

> Nursing is a scientific process founded on a professional body of knowledge; it is a learned process founded on a professional body of knowledge. It is a learned profession based on an understanding of the human condition across the lifespan and the relationship of a client with others and within the environment; and it is an art dedicated to caring for others. The practice of nursing means assisting clients to attain or maintain optimal health, implementing a strategy of care to accomplish defined goals within the context of a client-centered health care plan and evaluating responses to nursing care and treatment. Nursing is a dynamic discipline that increasingly involves more sophisticated knowledge, technologies and client care activities.[3]

The American Nurses Association defined nursing in *Nursing's Social Policy Statement:*

> Nursing is the protection, promotion, and optimization of health and abilities, prevention of illness and injury, alleviation of suffering through the diagnosis and treatment of human response, and advocacy in the care of individuals, families, communities, and populations.[4]

Nursing is viewed as both an art and a science. It is a learned profession based on an understanding of the human condition across the lifespan and the relationships of an individual with others and within the environment. Nursing practice is founded on a professional body of knowledge that integrates concepts from the biological, behavioral, and social sciences.[5] Three types of programs prepare students to sit for the licensing examination to become registered nurses: diploma, associate's degree, and baccalaureate degree programs. Traditionally all nursing education has been delivered in person in a classroom setting, but there are increasing numbers of courses completed, at least in part, online.

1. Diploma programs

The diploma school is the oldest type of nursing educational program. Approximately 17.5 percent of registered nurses are diploma graduates.[6] Typically a three-year program associated with a hospital, this was the most common setting for nursing education from the late 1800s through the mid-1900s. In the early 1960s, hospitals relied on student nurses to staff nursing units. Nursing leaders began

recognizing the exploitative nature of this arrangement and eliminated this practice. Diploma programs used to have a heavy emphasis on clinical experience for the students. In response to the increased complexity of nursing and the need to add theory classes, the amount of clinical experience was reduced. The number of diploma programs has declined as a result of a push to establish a college education as the entry route for nursing practice. Many surviving diploma programs have teamed up with community colleges to provide a diploma and an associate's degree in nursing.

2. Associate's degree programs

Associate's degree graduates make up 33.7 percent of the nurses in the workforce.[7] Community colleges are commonly the settings for associate's degree programs. Designed in the 1950s to promote more rapid education of student nurses, associate's degree programs are usually two-year programs. This type of program is often an affordable, convenient option for aspiring nurses. It provides college credits applicable toward a bachelor's degree in nursing. The degree granted at the end of the program is an associate's degree in applied sciences (AAS), associate of arts (AA) or is simply referred to as an associate's degree (AD).

3. Baccalaureate degree programs

The typical baccalaureate degree program is a four-year college program including basic nursing and liberal arts courses. The first baccalaureate degree in nursing was granted in 1916. Baccalaureate nursing education continues to be on the rise. Between 2008 and 2009 there was a 3.5 percent increase in enrollment into baccalaureate nursing programs.[8] Bachelor's degree graduates make up 47.2 percent of nurses in the U.S. workforce.[9] Most graduate schools offering master's degrees in nursing require a bachelor's degree in nursing (BSN) in order to be admitted.

There are programs that accelerate the education of a person who entered a nursing program having already earned a baccalaureate degree in another program of study. Accelerated BSN programs last 12 to 18 months and provide the fastest route to a BSN for individuals who already hold a bachelor's degree.

The existence of three different entry level programs for registered nurses creates confusion and difficulties in distinguishing capabilities of graduates. Some states have designated the graduates of an associate's degree or diploma program as "technical nurses" and those of a baccalaureate degree program as "professional nurses." The "technical nurses" have strenuously resisted this trend because they are unwilling to accept that their skills are anything less than professional.

Some healthcare employers differentiate among the graduates of educational programs when hiring and assigning responsibilities. They usually assign the associate's degree and diploma nurses to bedside care. New baccalaureate graduates begin in bedside care but may have the opportunity to advance to case management or unit management positions. (More information on case management will be presented at the end of the chapter.) Many employers make little or no distinction in salary or scope of practice when hiring nursing graduates.[10]

TIP: A baccalaureate degree in nursing, also called a bachelor of science in nursing, or BSN, is often a prerequisite for management positions in today's healthcare environment.

In 1999, the American Association of Colleges of Nursing (AACN) published a position paper stating in part that a baccalaureate degree is the minimum qualification to function in professional practice roles. The healthcare system requires decision making and services that respond to the complex, unpredictable situations of living: social, physical, economic, technological, and political. Nurses need specialized knowledge and skills to practice in this environment. Knowledge of the sciences, humanities, nursing, and other healthcare research, and leadership principles applicable to acute and community-based care settings is necessary to function in the healthcare setting. The American Association of Colleges of Nursing took the position that preparation of nurses at the baccalaureate degree level is essential for the acquisition of these skills.[11]

In May 2005, the American Organization of Nurse Executives (AONE) issued a statement recommending the education level of registered nurses be moved to the baccalaureate level in the future. In applauding this statement, AACN asserted that nurses with baccalaureate degrees are well-prepared to meet the demands placed on today's nurse. Baccalaureate-educated nurses are prized for their critical thinking, leadership, case management, and health promotion skills and receive an additional layer of entry-level education which enhances their professional development. This preparation assists the nurse in assuming a broader scope of practice including public and community health roles, and provides the nurse with a better understanding of the political, cultural, economic and social issues affecting patient and healthcare delivery systems.[12]

As the number of BSN graduates continues to increase, the trend to move the baccalaureate degree to the required level of entry into the nursing profession continues to be debated in many states. There are internal and external factors that contribute to the need to place the entry level into nursing practice at the BSN degree. The changing role of the registered nurse in an ever-changing and increasingly complex healthcare system serves as an internal force that demands the employment of more BSN-prepared RNs. In many healthcare facilities RNs are increasingly involved in the interdisciplinary care team in an attempt to provide holistic, high quality nursing care. As a member of this care team, RNs communicate and interact with varied healthcare professional who themselves are educated at advanced levels.[13] As a contributing member of this integrative team, the RN must possess the knowledge and skill to contribute to the management of the patient and integrative team goals, communicate with advanced professionals of other disciplines and interpret research findings to further support the integration of nursing research into nursing care.

Recent nursing research has reflected the benefits of having BSN nurses working at the bedside. In a landmark study at the University of Pennsylvania School of Nursing in Philadelphia, research data reflected a decreased mortality rate in a surgical patient population when this population was cared for by a majority of BSN-prepared nurses.[14] The U.S. Bureau of Labor Statistics has reported that RNs with at least a bachelor's degree will have much better job prospects than those candidates without a bachelor's degree.[15] There are persuasive external forces that also contribute to the BSN trend. One current and strongly influential factor is Magnet status. (Magnet status is discussed in detail in Chapter 8, *Inside the Healthcare Environment*). As more nursing departments in hospitals and medical centers compete for and acquire Magnet certification, the requirement to have a majority of BSN-degree-prepared nurses employed at those facilities is essential. In response to this, many associate's degree nursing programs have made articulation agreements with four-year colleges providing a continuous and relatively seamless pathway for the AD graduate to immediately continue on to baccalaureate education. Other ASN programs are closing.

4. Graduate degree programs

The nurse wishing to earn an advanced degree in nursing may enroll in a master's degree program. As of 2004, 13 percent of American nurses had earned a master's degree in nursing.[16] While most graduate schools grant a master of science degree in nursing (MSN), some confer a master of arts degree in nursing (MA). These programs, if completed full-time, are one and one-half to two years in length and diverse in nature. Some are designed with a heavy clinical component, while others focus on management theory, education or research. A number of programs have combined a master's degree in nursing with a master's degree in business administration, permitting nurses to earn two degrees simultaneously.

Nurses with advanced degrees may assume responsibilities for advanced roles including certified nurse midwives, certified registered nurse anesthetists, clinical nurse specialists, and nurse practitioners. With the exception of clinical nurse specialists and nurse practitioners, these programs may or may not require a master's degree in nursing.

5. Doctoral programs

A number of programs exist to prepare nurses at the doctoral level. The degree granted at the completion of the dissertation process is the Doctor of Philosophy, PhD, which is research-focused. The Doctor of Nursing Practice (DNP) degree is a practice-focused doctoral degree.[17] A doctoral degree in nursing is often a prerequisite for nurses wishing to teach in a school of nursing. The American Association of Colleges of Nursing[18] has taken the position that nursing faculty (who usually have doctorates) must be clinically competent and sound in the art and science of teaching. This is often accomplished by faculty working in clinical settings during or outside of the school year.

TIP: When looking for a nurse expert witness, consider retaining a nurse with a master's degree or doctoral degree in nursing. The advanced degree enhances credibility and expertise in the case.

B. Licensed Practical Nurses

The National Federation of Licensed Practical Nurses views the practical/vocational nurse as using specialized knowledge and skills which meet the health needs of people in a variety of settings. The licensed practical nurse works under the direction of qualified health professionals.[19] The role of licensed practical nurses is that of an assistant to physicians and registered nurses and they ordinarily work under the supervision of a registered nurse, who assigns patients and responsibilities to the licensed practical nurse.

The performance of treatments is a major focus for most licensed practical nurses. The responsibilities of the licensed practical nurse are directed toward health teaching, providing supportive care which alleviates the patient's problems, and restorative care, which is designed to improve function and regain strength. The curriculum of the student practical nursing program has a heavy emphasis on how to perform basic bedside care and technical procedures, such as dressing changes and irrigations. Basic bedside care includes:

- taking vital signs,

- preparing and giving medications, often with the exception of administering medication directly into the veins,
- administering enemas,
- applying dressings,
- monitoring catheters,
- turning patients,
- collecting specimens,
- reporting adverse changes in the patient,
- feeding and recording food and fluid intake and output, and
- assisting with bathing, toileting, and grooming.[20]

The National Association for Practical Nurse Educators and Services (NAPNES) defines the role of the licensed practical/vocational nurse as using a clinical problem-solving process—the nursing process (defined in Chapter 1, *The Roots of Patient Injury*)—to collect and organize relevant healthcare data. This process is designed to assist in the identification of health needs and problems throughout the client's lifespan and to contribute to the interdisciplinary team in a variety of settings. The entry level practical/vocational nurse should demonstrate the essential competencies needed to care for clients with commonly occurring health problems with predictable outcomes. NAPNES defines competency as applying knowledge, understanding and skills that transcend specific tasks and is guided by a commitment to ethical and legal principles.[21]

In a nursing home, the licensed practical nurse is usually given more autonomy, with responsibilities for taking and transcribing physician orders, adding to plans of care and supervising the care given by nursing assistants.

Licensed practical nurses (also called licensed vocational nurses in some parts of the United States) are usually educated in a vocational school setting. These programs are usually not part of a college setting. During the educational program, which is typically a year long, the nursing students are referred to as student practical nurses (SPNs).

After completion of the educational program, the graduate practical nurse is eligible to sit for a licensing examination, described as NCLEX-PN, below. Rarely, if ever, would a licensed practical nurse be in a leadership position, such as a charge nurse position.

C. Accreditation of Nursing Programs

There are two entities that accredit schools of nursing. The National League for Nursing (NLN), which was started as the American Society of Superintendents of Training Schools for Nurses in 1893, began as a society formed to establish and maintain a universal standard of training for nursing. In 1952, the NLN assumed responsibilities for accrediting nursing education programs.[22] The NLN Accrediting Commission is the only nationally recognized agency able to accredit all five types of post-secondary and higher degree education nursing programs including:

- Master's Degree
- Baccalaureate Degree
- Associate's Degree
- Diploma
- Practical Nursing[23]

Most state boards of nursing (described below) approve or accredit basic registered nurse and practical nursing programs.[24] Officially recognized by the U.S. Secretary of Education as a national accreditation agency, the Commission on Collegiate Nursing Education (CCNE) is an autonomous accrediting agency contributing to the improvement of the public's health. CCNE ensures the quality and integrity of baccalaureate and graduate education programs preparing effective nurses. CCNE serves the public interest by assessing and identifying programs that engage in effective educational practices. As a voluntary, self-regulatory process, CCNE accreditation supports and encourages continuing self-assessment by nursing education programs and the continuing growth and improvement of collegiate professional education.[25]

D. Nursing Assistants and Technicians

Collectively, nursing assistants, aides, and technicians make up a category of unlicensed assistive personnel. These individuals may be called:

- nursing aides,
- nursing assistants,
- psychiatric aides,
- home health aides,
- medication administration aides,
- personal aides,
- home care aides,
- certified nursing assistants,
- technicians,
- orderlies,
- personal care assistants, and
- patient care assistants.

In a hospital or nursing home setting, the nursing aide performs tasks under the supervision of a registered or licensed practical nurse. Their responsibilities include:

- answering the patient's call bell,
- changing bed linens,
- bathing and cleaning incontinent patients,
- assisting with feeding, grooming, and toileting,
- walking patients,
- taking vital signs,
- transporting patients within a facility, and
- obtaining specimens.

Home health aides help individuals living at home or in an assisted living facility. They provide primarily health-related services, whereas personal and home care aides are homemakers, companions, or personal attendants. Routine housekeeping and personal care services are provided by these individuals.[26] Nursing homes require nursing aides to complete a minimum of 75 hours of training and pass a competency evaluation program within four months of their start date. The aides who pass are designated as certified nursing assistants and are registered with the state. Home health aides are required to pass a competency test after receiving at least 75 hours of classroom and practical training.

Specialized training may prepare an individual to assume the responsibilities of a technician involved in the care of patients receiving dialysis, surgery, anesthesia, orthopaedic traction, psychiatric care, cardiac monitoring, and other areas.

6.3 Employment and Compensation

Registered nurses constitute the largest healthcare occupation, with 2.6 million jobs. More new jobs are expected to be created for registered nurses than for any other occupation. Employment of registered nurses is expected to grow by 22 percent from 2008 to 2018.[27] Employment in hospitals, the largest sector of nursing jobs, is expected to grow more slowly than in other sectors because of earlier discharges and the move to outpatient settings for procedures. Rapid growth is expected in outpatient settings, physician's offices, nursing homes, and home healthcare. In 2008, the median annual earnings of registered nurses was $62,450.[28]

Licensed practical nurses held about 753,600 jobs in 2008. Approximately 25 percent of LPNs worked in hospitals, 28 percent in nursing care facilities, and another 12 percent in physicians' offices. Employment of LPNs is expected to grow by 21 percent[29] in response to the needs of an increasingly elderly population and the general growth of health care. Although the need for LPNs in hospitals is declining, employment is expected to grow in nursing homes and home healthcare services. In 2008, the median annual earnings of LPNs was $39,030.[30]

Nursing, psychiatric, and home health aides held about 1.5 million jobs in 2008. Forty-one percent of nurses aides work in a nursing care facility and 295% work in hospitals. Fifty percent of psychiatric aides work in hospitals. Median hourly earnings was $12.77 for psychiatric aides and $11.46 for nursing aides, orderlies, and attendants in 2008.[31]

6.4 Regulation of Nursing Practice

In the early days of nursing, there was no regulation of nurses or nursing practice, no recognized curriculum of study and no licensure for nurses. There were no laws or regulations delineating what a nurse could or should do. There was no true definition of a "nurse" or "nursing." There was no consistency in the early registration acts. All nursing care was directed by a physician.[32] Nursing practice is regulated because it is one of the healthcare professions that pose risk of harm to the public if practiced by someone who is unprepared or incompetent.[33]

A number of groups now regulate nursing practice. These include:

- State legislatures
- Boards of nursing
- Departments of Health
- Centers for Medicare and Medicaid Services
- The Joint Commission, as well as other regulatory agencies.

It is beyond the scope of this book to provide a detailed description of each of these agencies, but a brief description of each follows. Standards can be obtained from the agencies for use with specific nursing malpractice cases.

A. The State Legislatures

Beginning in the late 1930s and early 1940s, states began enacting laws to define nursing practice and create the basic requirements for entering the practice of nursing. The Board of Nursing is the state entity with the legal authority to regulate nursing practice through laws. These laws, most commonly called Nurse Practice Acts, set forth the specific requirements to practice nursing in each state. The Nurse Practice Act is a statute that defines in general terms the practice of registered nurses and licensed practical nurses. (There are separate acts for registered nurses as opposed to licensed practical nurses.) The Nurse Practice Act typically

- defines the authority of the Board of Nursing, its composition and powers,
- defines nursing and the boundaries of the scope of nursing practice,

- identifies types of licenses and titles,
- states the requirements for licensure,
- protects titles, and
- identifies the grounds for disciplinary action.[34]

Nurses may be disciplined for:

- patient abuse
- practicing without a license
- practicing outside the scope of the nursing license
- sexual misconduct, particularly with patients
- illegally obtaining medications, including writing illegal prescriptions or diverting a patient's medications
- practicing while impaired from alcohol or drugs
- abandoning patients
- making practice errors, such as serious medication errors
- making documentation errors, such as using another person's password to access electronic medical records
- refusing care to a patient based on prejudice or discrimination
- violating privacy or revealing confidential information
- hiding prior criminal convictions
- gross incompetence
- failure to monitor

Allegations of misconduct are investigated by review of records and interviews. There may be a hearing, to which the licensee is well advised to bring an attorney. When there are sufficient grounds to take action, the licensee may receive a warning, a restriction on practice, suspension of a license, or revocation of the license. Most states make it possible for the public to find out who has been found guilty of misconduct. Some boards post this on their website.

Most states have now amended Nurse Practice Act laws to provide standards and requirements for advanced practice nursing. All states have some form of licensure law. Most states adopted the recommended language of the American Nurses Association. Nurse practice acts are amended and updated periodically. Many state Nurse Practice Acts now include language indicating that it is the nurse's responsibility to make diagnoses within the context of nursing practice.

B. Board of Nursing and Entry into Practice

Basic requirements to practice nursing include completion of an accredited educational program (associate's degree, diploma, or baccalaureate program) and passing a national licensing examination. In April 2010, the NCSBN (National Council of State Boards of Nursing) raised the passing standard for the NCLEX exam in response to the increasingly complex and diverse patient population.[35] In 1994, the National Council of State Boards of Nursing implemented computerized testing (called the NCLEX and pronounced N-Clecks) for administering the licensing examination to new graduates. In the former system, nurses sat in large rooms filling out answer sheets as they took a licensing exam offered only twice a year. The computerized exam is available 15 hours a day, six days a week, throughout the country. The same system is used to test graduate nurses who aspire to become registered nurses or practical nurses. Different tests are used for each level of graduate (registered versus practical).

The test is designed to test the knowledge, skills, and abilities essential to the safe and effective practice of nursing at the entry level. The test is administered in the United States, American Samoa, Guam, the Northern Mariana Islands, and the U.S. Virgin Islands. Beginning in January 2005, the NCLEX was administered in Hong Kong, Special Administrative Region of the Republic of China, London, and Seoul.[36] The test uses standard, multiple-choice questions with the addition of some alternate question formats. Each test is unique, ranging in length from 75 to 265 items.[37] As the graduate nurse answers a question, the computer calculates a competence estimate based on earlier answers. It then scans the test bank for the questions that most precisely measure the knowledge of the graduate nurse. This results in a test individualized for each candidate, while fulfilling the requirements to measure general nursing knowledge. The length of the test is determined by the applicant's answers. Once the minimum number has been answered, testing will stop when the candidate's ability is determined to be either above or below the passing standard with 95 percent certainty.

Because the NCLEX-RN examination is administered using computerized adaptive testing, the passing standard does not translate directly into a specific number of items that need to be answered correctly to pass the test. Results are available to the graduate within a month of completing the examination. Nursing graduates who fail the exam are allowed to retake the examination as directed by the individual state boards of nursing.

TIP: When deposing a nurse defendant, the lawyer should ask the nurse how many times he had to take the licensing examination before passing it.

As a result of changes in the licensing process, new graduates are becoming licensed as registered nurses much sooner. They receive the results quickly and do not have to wait. Under the old system, this delay afforded the new graduate an opportunity to gain experience under the guidance of the more experienced staff.

Nurses may be licensed in more than one state, either by examination or by endorsement of the license granted by another state. The Nurse Licensure Compact is a model that allows a nurse to have one license (in her state of residency) and to practice in other states (both physical practice and electronic practice), subject to each state's practice laws and regulation. To achieve mutual recognition, each state must enact legislation authorizing the Nurse Licensure Compact. Current information about the identity of states that accept the Nurse Licensure Compact may be found at www.ncsbn.org/158.htm.

Upon passing the national licensing examination, an individual is granted a license by the Board of Nursing to practice nursing and use the title "nurse." Nursing boards are made up of registered nurses, licensed practical nurses, and consumers. Members of the board in some states are appointees and consist of nurses and non-nurses. An attorney from the state's attorney general's office may also sit on the board to offer guidance in legal matters. The state Board of Nursing is given the authority to regulate nursing practice and may only exercise the power conferred upon it by the legislature. This may vary from state to state but usually includes matters of licensure, disciplinary actions, and determination of scope of practice. In many states, the same legislation that provides for the licensing of nurses also establishes the state Board of Nursing.

Since the Nurse Practice Act defines in broad terms the scope of practice of the registered and licensed nurse, the Board of Nursing is charged with the responsibility to govern specific actions of nurses. The Board of Nursing is authorized to develop administrative rules and regulations that further define nursing practice in response to new technology or trends. As health care changes and new responsibilities emerge, the Board of Nursing is queried as to whether the activity falls within the practice of nursing. For example, in the mid-1980s, licensed practical nurses were allowed to assume the new responsibility of administering intravenous antibiotics if they were mixed by a registered nurse or pharmacist. In some states, registered nurses are allowed to place and remove sutures, while in others they are not. A third party, such as a hospital, may authorize a nurse to engage in a nursing activity, as long as that activity is not prohibited by law or would not constitute the illegal practice of medicine. For example, the hospital may train the nurse to insert peripheral intravenous lines, but the same nurse would not be permitted to perform an invasive procedure such as a cardiac catheterization.

Nurses are expected to continue their education after graduation by reading professional journals, attending conferences, and participating in employer-provided inservice education. Nursing is a fast-paced profession in a constant state of change. Some states require a certain number of continuing education credits to be earned within a specific time in order to renew a nurse's license. The acceptable methods of earning continuing education credits vary from state to state. Commonly, continuing education credits may be awarded for attending conferences, enrolling in a degree program, completing self-study packages, writing an article or book, or presenting a paper. Nurses in these states are expected to maintain records to demonstrate compliance with the state's requirements.

C. Department of Health

The Department of Health establishes standards that govern hospitals, boarding homes, nursing homes, and other settings. Nursing practice issues may be regulated as well. For example, the state's Department of Health regulations may require that a nurse certified in Advanced Life Support be assigned to each shift in the emergency department. These standards are readily obtainable at a nominal cost.

TIP: The Department of Health will often send a surveyor to a hospital or long-term care facility if it receives a complaint about the care provided to a patient. The department will begin the investigation upon the request of a family or an attorney.

D. Centers of Medicare and Medicaid Services (CMS)

CMS (formerly HCFA or Healthcare Financing Administration) is a federal agency that administers the Medicare program and works in partnership with the states to administer the Medicaid, State Children's Health Insurance Program, and health insurance portability standards. It is heavily involved in the regulation of the nursing home industry. Under the Quality Improvement Organization program, CMS contracts with independent medical organizations to ensure medical care paid for under the Medicare program meets professional standards and is provided in the most economical setting. CMS is working to improve the quality of care by measuring and improving outcomes of care. Education is provided to healthcare professionals about quality improvement opportunities. Comparative data is provided about nursing homes and home care agencies on the CMS web-

site. As of this writing, comparative data about hospitals was under development.[38]

E. The Joint Commission (TJC)

Approximately 82 percent of U.S. hospitals are accredited by TJC.[39] Although TJC certification is not mandatory, participation in Medicare/Medicaid is dependent upon having TJC accreditation. The nursing departments of hospitals are heavily involved in the survey and accreditation process. TJC has developed standards for the various agencies it surveys. The format for the hospital standards has undergone marked changes in the last several years. The standards are broad and address topics such as leadership, assessment of patients, surveillance, and control of infection. TJC standards are less proscriptive than they have been in the past. They do not regulate the minutiae of running a nursing department, but do provide a broad framework of principles. Some TJC data about an agency is available for public review. This can be accessed on its website at www.jointcommission.org. See Chapter 4, *Patient Safety Initiatives*, for more information about The Joint Commission.

TIP: Since the standards of TJC have undergone marked revisions in the last decade, be sure to obtain the standards in effect at the time care was provided to the plaintiff.

F. Professional Organizations

As one of the largest nursing organizations, the American Nurses Association (ANA) represents the interests of nurses in many nursing specialties and has an active lobbying group in Washington, D.C. Members of the ANA receive a monthly newspaper called *The American Nurse*. The ANA has developed a number of standards of care that define professional practice. The ANA has also defined standards for specialty groups within nursing, such as medical surgical nurses, community health nurses, and school nurses. There are many other nursing organizations for nurses addressing such diverse nursing groups as intravenous therapy, post anesthesia care unit, and critical care. Several of these organizations publish standards in booklets or on their websites. Few will share membership information, although their boards of directors may be listed on their websites. The organizations may be located through Internet searches or a reference listing professional organizations found in the reference section of a comprehensive medical library.

G. American Hospital Association Patient Care Partnership

The American Hospital Association (AHA), as well as other groups, has defined the rights of patients (Appendix

6.1) in a document called *The Patient Care Partnership: Understanding Expectations, Rights, and Responsibilities.* Although the document contains several references to the patient's role with the physician, these standards can be used to judge nursing conduct. For example, the AHA states that the patient has the right to refuse a recommended treatment or plan of care to the extent permitted by law and hospital policy and be informed of the medical consequences of this action.

6.5 Certification

Certification is a voluntary way for a nurse to demonstrate expertise in a given subject area, increase credibility, and, in some instances, obtain salary increases and promotions.

A. Professional Associations

There are two broad types of certifications: clinical and non-clinical. Clinical certifications are available for a wide variety of areas, such as neonatal, obstetrical, emergency, post anesthesia care (recovery room), psychiatric, medical surgical, geriatrics, pediatric, and rehabilitation nursing, to name a few. Non-clinical certification exams are available for nurses in nursing administration, legal nurse consulting, quality improvement, risk management, and staff development (inservice education), among others.

A variety of nursing organizations provide certification exams for the registered nurse. ABSNC is the American Board for Specialty Nursing Certification; it used to be called the American Board of Nursing Specialties. It is the nursing equivalent of the American Board of Medical Specialties, the entity involved in board certification for physicians. ABSNC is the only accrediting body specifically dedicated to nursing certification. It has 19 rigorous standards that must be met for a certification program to be recognized by ABSNC. Nurses who successfully complete professional certifications offered by these ABSNC-recognized organizations are considered to be board certified. The nurse must meet certain criteria in order to take the exam. These criteria may specify the minimum number of hours per year or number of years the nurse must have worked in that specialty area. The nurse may also be asked to provide letters of reference and evidence of continuing education credits.

NCCA is the National Commission for Certifying Agencies. The website of NCCA is www.credentialingexcellence. org. There are several nursing organizations that have met the accreditation standards of NCCA.

Some types of certification are available only if the nurse has a specific educational background. In order to be certified in nursing administration, the applicant must have held a position in management for at least five years and

have a master's degree in nursing. A fee is required to take the comprehensive written exam. If the nurse passes the test, the nurse is entitled to add the initials for the certification after the nurse's name. The reader may see any of the following initials:

RNC	Registered Nurse, Certified
CPAN	Certified in Post Anesthesia Nursing
CEN	Certified in Emergency Nursing
CCRN	Certified Critical Care Registered Nurse
CNA	Certified in Nursing Administration
CNAA	Certified in Nursing Administration, Advanced
CRON	Certified Registered Operating Room Nurse
CRRN	Certified Rehabilitation Registered Nurse
CRNA	Certified Registered Nurse Anesthetist

These are only a few of the certifications available. Refer to Appendix 6.2 for a listing of titles found within medical records. The attorney should inquire about certifications when retaining nurse expert witnesses or determining the background of a defendant nurse.

TIP: During the discovery process determine whether the nurse has any certifications. When deposing a nurse, inquire about the meaning of any initials after the nurse's name and their significance. Certification enhances the credentials of the nurse expert witness. This should be stressed when qualifying the expert witness at trial.

Each organization that provides certification exams publishes a catalog explaining the prerequisites and process of certification and the topics included on the examination. There is a growing trend within nursing to expand the number of certification exams. As is true of board certification of physicians, the organizations that offer certification have criteria for recertification.

The Nursing Credentialing Research Coalition reported that "the majority of nurses it surveyed said that they experienced fewer adverse events and errors in patient care following certification. These nurses also reported that they felt more confident in their ability to detect early signs or symptoms of complications in their patients and to initiate early and prompt interventions."[40]

B. Cardiac Resuscitation Certification

Nurses frequently become certified in CPR (cardiopulmonary resuscitation). Most settings require current cardiac resuscitation certification as a condition of employment.

Certification in CPR may be essential in settings without immediate access to skilled emergency care, such as an outpatient surgical center or an urgent care center (freestanding emergency clinic).

The awareness that CPR can restore life fuels the drive to teach this essential skill to healthcare providers and lay people. In the 1980s, the American Heart Association (AHA) began encouraging hospitals and other agencies to meet criteria in order to become certifying centers. The goal was to increase the availability of training as well as to maintain a high quality of education and consistency of skills.

There are several Heartsaver courses. The Heartsaver CPR course is taught to non-medical personnel including day-care workers, airline personnel, babysitters, and others who need or want to learn CPR. There is an adult and pediatric module. The Heartsaver AED (Automated External Defibrillator) course combines hands-on AED instruction with adult CPR training. The course is designed for individuals who need to learn CPR and how to operate an AED.

Basic Cardiac Life Support (BCLS), which was renamed as Basic Life Support (BLS) in the early 1990s, is offered to healthcare providers and lay people. A variety of courses is available. Advanced Life Support (ALS) certification is available only to healthcare professionals and "first responders" such as paramedics. It provides the knowledge and skills needed to evaluate and manage the first ten minutes of an adult cardiac or respiratory arrest. Providers are expected to learn to manage ten core ALS cases:

- respiratory emergency
- four types of cardiac arrest: simple VF/VT, complex VF/VT, PEA (pulseless electrical activity) and asytole (absence of heartbeat)
- four types of prearrest emergencies (bradycardia, stable tachycardia, unstable tachycardia and acute coronary syndromes)
- stroke[41]

The American Heart Association also offers an ALS-EP (Experienced Provider) Course for seasoned ALS providers who want to renew their provider status. The Pediatric Advanced Life Support Course (PALS) focuses on arrests in infants and children. This course is designed for healthcare personnel responsible for the care of children. More information on basic and advanced life support, pediatric advanced life support, and advanced trauma life support courses is provided in Chapter 17, *Emergency Nursing Malpractice*, in Volume II.

6.6 National Standard of Care

At one time, nurses were judged by the standard of care of nurses working in the same geographical area or the locality rule. This rule was based on the premise that there were wide differences in the quality of health care available in urban versus rural settings. *Leonard v. Watsonville Community Hospital*, 47 Cal.2d 509, 305 P.2d 36 (1956), showed that the locality rule could not be used to justify substandard care.

In *Leonard*, a Kelly clamp, which is a steel scissor-shaped instrument, was left inside a patient's abdomen. The hospital had no provisions for counting instruments either before or after surgery. The defendant argued there was no duty to count instruments since other hospitals in the community did not require instrument counts and they were held to "exercise only that degree of skill employed by other hospitals and nurses in the community." The court held that the negligence of the nurses could not be excused "on the ground that others in the same locality practice the same kind of negligence." 305 P.2d at 42.[42]

Changes in technology, communication, and transportation have caused the locality rule to become obsolete. One of the cases which was instrumental in sending this message was *Wickliffe v. Sunrise Hospital*. In this case, a healthy 13-year-old girl underwent surgery to correct scoliosis of her spine. After the patient was transferred to the postoperative medical surgical unit, the nurse's aide checked her at 11:30 A.M. because the girl's nurse was at lunch. At 12:15 P.M., when the nurse filled her water pitcher, she noticed the patient was snoring. At 12:30 P.M., when a nursing assistant took her a food tray, the patient was still snoring. The assistant left to determine if the patient was to have lunch. On her return ten minutes later she found the patient in a state of cardiac arrest. Although the girl was resuscitated, she died 12 days later.

In the suit, the parents pointed out that the patient's vital signs were not checked between her return to the floor at 11:30 A.M. and the discovery of her respiratory arrest at 12:40 P.M. They argued that the hospital's procedures and nursing standards require a post surgical patient's vital signs to be monitored every 15 minutes during the first hour after the return to the surgical unit. A nurse expert witness testified that this lack of monitoring violated a national standard of care and thus the nurses were negligent. The district court ruled that this nurse's testimony as an expert witness should be excluded because she was not familiar with practices in the locality in which the case occurred. The jury returned a verdict in favor of the hospital. When the case was appealed the judgment was reversed. The court found that national nursing standards exist and cited TJC standards. The court also noted that nursing education and licensing had become standardized. A nurse who passes a licensing exam in one state does not need to take another state's licensing examination. The court concluded that an expert witness familiar with the standard of care expected of a reasonably prudent nurse, regardless of where that nurse is located, may testify in a negligence action against a hospital. *Wickliffe v. Sunrise Hospital, Inc.*, 706 P.2d 1383 (Nev. 1985).[43] In 1991, a South Carolina court held that the evolution of the law appears to support the adoption of a national standard of care throughout the healthcare system. Most nurses are judged by a national standard. *McMillan v. Durant*, 439 S.E.2d 829 (S.C. 1991).[44]

The prevalence of national professional organizations and associations, as well as the ease with which we share information today, has caused the majority of American courts to abandon the locality rule. The locality rule or community standards referred to the standard of care exercised by the healthcare providers in the defendant's own community or locality. One of the inherent weaknesses of this approach is evident in specialty areas where the defendant may be the only specialist of that kind on the facility's staff, or the impossibility of finding an expert willing to testify on behalf of a plaintiff located in his own backyard. Additionally, if the medical care is substandard at a particular facility, the standard practices may be below the accepted standard of care found elsewhere.

In addition to all of the national regulatory bodies whose standards govern nursing practice, nursing has its own body of knowledge. A quick walk through a medical library will show that there are many nursing journals. Most publish a mixture of clinical and management content. The clinical articles usually define the applicable standard of care at the time of the malpractice suit. Online searches of nursing literature save much time in retrieving information. It has become easier to obtain full-text articles online.

Many libraries have agreements with larger libraries to obtain articles from journals not carried by the local library. Nursing textbooks are updated periodically and provide a wealth of information about the standard of care associated with nursing techniques and care. The creation of a huge body of knowledge regarding nursing practice has influenced the development of a national standard of care.

6.7 Standards of Care versus Practice Guidelines

Standards of care are well-defined actions that lead to positive patient outcomes. The early 1990s saw the emergence of a new set of terms for guidelines designed to lead to positive patient outcomes. The terms include "clinical practice guidelines," "practice parameters," "protocols," "clinical pathways," "critical paths," and "Caremaps."

There is much overlap and confusion about the difference between practice guidelines and standards of care. For example, the National Academy of Sciences' Institute of Medicine adopted the term "clinical practice guideline" to refer to systematically developed statements used to assist practitioner and patient decisions about appropriate health care for specific, clinical circumstances.[45]

The purposes of the clinical practice guidelines are to:

- assist clinical decision making by practitioners and patients,
- educate individuals and groups,
- assess and assure quality care,
- guide the allocation of resources for health care, and
- reduce the risk of legal liability for patient care.[46]

A. Critical Paths

One method of documenting the implementation of a clinical practice guideline is the use of critical paths, a version of the nursing care plan. This is a multidisciplinary plan also known as the clinical pathway or Caremap which defines the plan of care for a specific type of patient or procedure. For example, a critical path may identify the plan of care for a patient who has a total hip replacement. The interventions of the physical therapist, physician and nurse will be specified on a daily basis from preadmission to discharge.

These plans fit within a healthcare delivery system called "case management." Increasingly, hospitals are adopting this method of organizing and overseeing care. Experience has shown that case management benefits nurses, patients, physicians, and other healthcare workers by increasing satisfaction and coordination of care; promotes earlier communication of discharge planning and patient education; and reduces costs and length of stay.

The critical path is one of the principal tools of case management. It is usually a one-page timeline that outlines the expected care for the patient day by day throughout the hospitalization. It is a set of proactive daily prescriptions for the care of a specific patient population whose length of stay and clinical needs can be defined. Some critical paths even include the period before and after hospitalization. A patient coming in for elective surgery may receive some of the patient education during the preadmission testing. The critical path would identify what the patient should be taught preoperatively. Postdischarge interventions may relate to coordinating the patient's care with community resources.

Often the critical path is structured with the care elements down the left column, and the days of the hospitalization across the top. The care elements might fall into broad categories of activity, diet, medications, diagnostic tests, and so on. In the column under each day of the hospitalization, specific entries are made that define the care for that day. For example, the activity for Day One may specify that the patient can sit on the edge of the bed. The Day Two column may read that the patient can sit in the chair twice a day for 30 minutes at a time, and the patient may be allowed out of bed as desired by Day Three. In addition to the activities and treatments, some critical paths include a nursing diagnosis and outcome for each day.

The critical path is a roadmap that defines the predictable, important events that must occur to move the patient along. The difficulties that arise in using critical paths often occur at the development stage. It is usually not easy to obtain agreement on the daily elements of care, particularly when individuals vary in their practices. However, in the act of laying out the critical path, important differences of opinion are uncovered, as well as system issues that affect the delivery of care. For example, closing the physical therapy department for the weekend slows the recovery of patients who have had total hip replacements.

Critical paths are usually placed on the chart or at the bedside during the patient's stay in the hospital. Some paths are structured to permit the documentation of variances on the reverse side of the form. Variances are deviations from the path. They fit into three categories: patient, system, and practitioner. A patient variance occurs when changes in the patient's condition prevent the expected outcomes. Systems variances are barriers in the process of providing care that disrupt the critical path. Practitioner variances occur when the expected elements of care are not provided. As part of the quality improvement program, variances are usually tracked and analyzed to see if changes need to be made in the provision of care.

Critical paths are usually not retained as a permanent part of the record unless they are written on by the healthcare team. They are meant to be guidelines that can be modified if required by the circumstances of the patient's care. No matter how precise the plan of care, there are often factors that change the critical path.

B. Drawbacks of Critical Paths

Deets[47] comments that the quality of critical pathways is inconsistent, depending on the research base available for pathway development. Sometimes a critical pathway reflects the beliefs of those who developed it (and are not validated by research) or the idiosyncratic issues of the practitioners or of the institution in which the pathway was developed. For example, Dr. Jones wants his total hip replacement patient to stay in bed for three days, whereas the literature advocates early ambulation to prevent pulmonary embolism.

Deets charges that critical paths are often based on current practice rather than on research. If the interventions in the critical path conflict with the standard of care as defined in the literature, the nurse is put in an awkward position, for which there is no easy answer. As the patient's advocate, the nurse who recognizes the conflict must strive to change the critical path. This may require negotiating with powerful forces within the organization.

C. Agency for Health Care Research and Quality

Many healthcare institutions churned out critical paths, clinical practice guidelines, and practice parameters that include information on the nursing interventions associated with the care of the patient. A federal agency, the Agency for Health Care Policy and Research (AHCPR), was funded in 1989 to foster the development of clinical guidelines. This agency is now called Agency for Health Care Research and Quality (AHRQ). Between 1989 and 1992, it funded 14 large projects known as Patient Outcomes Research Teams (PORT). These large multidisciplinary teams analyzed medical literature on specific topics and developed models for clinical decision-making and treatment. One of the tangible products of its mission is the clinical practice guideline. The guidelines are based on the knowledge of clinical reviewers, literature review, and clinical evaluations. Some of the original clinical practice guidelines have been withdrawn as a result of being outdated. Refer to the National Guideline Clearinghouse at www.ahcpr. gov/clinic/ngcfact.htm for a public database of evidence-based clinical practice guidelines and related documents.

D. Legal Implications of Practice Guidelines

Guidelines are voluntary, which means they can be modified or abandoned as the patient's circumstances warrant. Treating critical paths as *guidelines* (which implies they are desirable options) rather than as *standards* (which must be followed) has obvious legal implications. Feutz-Harter[48] notes that failing to follow a clinical practice guideline does not inherently represent a breach of the standard of care. Rather, it is understood that alterations in treatment will occur because of patient variances, the environment, the providers involved with the patient's care or the result of clinical creativity. The ultimate applicability of a clinical practice guideline depends on the clinical circumstances.

Nevertheless, questions about the legal admissibility of practice guidelines continue to be raised. Documents such as those produced by the Agency for Healthcare Research and Quality, which are founded on sound research and the experience of clinicians, should define a baseline quality of care. They act as a model for the development or refinement of agency-specific policies and procedures. The practice guidelines on the prevention of skin breakdown have formed the basis for innumerable hospitals' and nursing homes' policies and procedures. Careful adherence to these research-based practice guidelines should promote a higher quality of care and reduce liability.

6.8 Evidence-Based Nursing
A. Definition
The incorporation of research into nursing practice is growing as a result of many factors. The increased use of informatics, the widespread availability of computer-based data and the increase of baccalaureate prepared nurses are factors that promote evidence-based practice in nursing practice. Evidence-based practice (EBP) guides the development of policies and procedures and drives nursing practice. It is the process by which nurses make clinical decisions using the best available research evidence, their clinical expertise, and patient preferences. Evidence-based nursing practice solves problems encountered by nurses when they carry out four steps:

- clearly identify the issue or problem based on accurate analysis of current knowledge and practice
- search the nursing literature for relevant research
- evaluate the research evidence using established criteria regarding scientific merit
- choose interventions and justify the selection with the most valid evidence[49]

B. Barriers
Some barriers to evidence-based practice still exist.

1. The revision of nursing textbooks used in the preparation of new nurses is a lengthy process, spanning several years.
2. Some nurses claim that insufficient time or lack of staff prevents involvement in evidence-based practice[50]
3. There is not usually a system in place to track, review, teach, implement, and evaluate "best" practices. Such a system would include reengineering, process improvement, patient care redesign, clinical resource management, and productivity benchmarking.[51]
4. Establishing, implementing, and updating evidence-based clinical practice guidelines to fit insti-

tutional requirements is labor-intensive and time-consuming.[52]
5. Nurses who have not had a research course in their education may have insufficient skills to evaluate research. This applies to most graduates of associate's and diploma nursing programs. The majority of nurses in practice were educated before 1990 and the widespread use of electronic information resources and personal computers.[53]
6. The inability to ask a focused and precise clinical question can be a major impediment to evidence-based practice.[54]
7. Many nurses see their co-workers as more accessible than journal articles, research reports, or libraries. In a study of 760 nurses, 67 percent said they always or frequently sought information from a colleague rather than from a reference text or journal article.[55]

C. Incentives
Awareness of evidence-based practice is growing. The nursing profession continues to incorporate evidence into practice. These factors promote use of research in nursing practice:

1. Nurses' attitudes towards research findings.
2. Level of education—nurses with baccalaureate or higher degrees are more likely to incorporate EBP into their respective nursing practice.[56]
3. Knowledge gained in research courses—the majority of BSN programs contain a research component in the nursing curriculum.
4. Increased clinical nursing knowledge base as a result of research data.
5. Increased use of technology on clinical units allowing instant access to nursing databases and literature.
6. Established nursing research committees, journal clubs and grand rounds in healthcare facilities.
7. Organizational support to use research.[57]
8. Magnet designation of hospitals.
9. An expansive amount of clinical literature is available in several databases. For example, CINAHL is a database that contains 2 million records dating back to 1981. This translates into thousands of professional journals from the nursing and allied health fields.

Over the last two decades, there have been numerous advances in the dissemination of evidence-based medicine.

Many of these improvements apply to nursing as well. These improvements include:

- production of streamlined guides to aid in critical appraisal of the literature,
- evidence-based abstraction services,
- online and other forms of electronic literature searching,
- growing numbers of high quality systematic reviews,
- frequently updated textbooks in paper and electronic formats, and
- "point of care" service in the clinical settings.[58]

Some of the resources available for disseminating information about evidence-based practice include:

1. Evidence-based practice centers have been created with help from the AHRQ which currently funds 14 EBP centers.[59] One such center is the Gerontological Nursing Interventions Research Center at the University of Iowa, which was established with funding from the National Institutes of Health. The center's purpose is to increase gerontologic interventions, conduct outcomes research in nursing and related disciplines, and disseminate research-based guidelines for care of the elderly.[60]
2. Throughout the United States there are many Nursing Research Centers. One such center is the Center for Excellence for Cardiovascular Health in Vulnerable Populations at John Hopkins University School of Nursing. The goals of this center are to improve cardiovascular health in vulnerable populations, promote nursing scholarships and increase the dissemination of this cardiovascular research.[61]
3. The Cochrane Library is a global network that provides systematic reviews by the Cochrane Collaboration and is committed to improving global health care by preparing, maintaining, and disseminating systematic up-to-date reviews of the effects of health care.[62]
4. Twenty-five nursing organizations have organized a website in which they disseminate best practices: www.best4health.org.[63]
5. The Agency for Healthcare Research and Quality has a list of evidence-based practice reports. Refer to www.ahcpr.gov/clinic/epcix.htm

Many other initiatives exist and will certainly increase with time. Refer to HealthLinks of the University of Washington for more information and resources.[64]

6.9 Summary

Nursing practice is continuing to change and evolve. Many regulatory agencies have standards which dictate nursing care. The ever-evolving nursing literature is slowly moving in the direction of using research to identify best nursing practices. The modification of the standards of care using evidence-based practice offers the promise of improving patient care through sound interventions.

Endnotes

1. *Occupational Outlook Handbook* http://www.US.gov/oco/ocos083.htm accessed December 17, 2009.

2. *Id.*

3. NCSBN, Model Nursing Practice and Model Nursing Administrator Rules Article II-Scope of Nursing Practice, Section 1 http://www.ncsbn.org/Model_Practice_Act_December09_final.pdf., 2009 accessed December 27, 2009.

4. American Nurses Association, *Nursing's Social Policy Statement*, Second edition. Washington, D.C., 2003.

5. 2005 NCLEX-PN Test Plan, NCSBN. http://www.ncsbn.org/pdfs/NclexPN2002.pdf, accessed August 13, 2005.

6. Rosseter, R. AACN Fact Sheet: Creating a More Highly Qualified Nursing Workforce http://www.aacn.nche.edu/Media/pdf/NursingWorkforce.pdf,2009, accessed January 8, 2010.

7. *Id.*

8. (AACN) Press Release: Student enrollment expands at U.S. nursing colleges and universities for the 9th year despite financial challenges and capacity restraints http://www.aacn.nche.edu/Media/NewsReleases2009/StudentEnrollment.html, accessed January 8, 2010.

9. See note 6.

10. Acord, L., "Where have all the future nurses gone?" *Journal of Professional Nursing* 15, No. 3 (May-June 1999): 135.

11. American Association of Colleges of Nursing, "A vision of baccalaureate and graduate nursing education: the next decade," *Journal of Professional Nursing* 15, no. 1 (January-February1999): 59.

12. AACN Applauds Decision of the AONE Board to Move Registered Nursing Education to the Baccalaureate. http://www.aacn.nche.edu/Media/NewsReleases/2005/AONE505.htm, accessed July 18, 2005.

13. See note 6.

14. Aiken, L. et al., "Educational Levels of Hospital Nurses and Surgical Patient Mortality," *JAMA*, 290 (12), 2003,1617–1623.

15. See note 1.

16. http://www.worldwidelearn.com/healthcare/nursing/nursing-facts.html.

17. AACN Position Statement (2004) AACN Position Statement on the Practice Doctorate in Nursing Accessed January 24, 2010 http://www.aacn.nche.edu/DNP/DNPPositionStatement.htm.

18. *Id.*

19. National Federation of Licensed Practical Nurses, Inc. *Nursing Practice Standards for the Licensed Practical/Vocational Nurse*, Raleigh, North Carolina, 2003.

20. Licensed Practical and Licensed Vocational Nurses, http://bls.gov/oco/ocos102.htm, accessed January 25, 2010.

21. See note 19.

22. History of the National League for Nursing (NLN), Supporting Nursing Education for over a Century, http://www.nln.org/aboutnln/info-history.htm, accessed July 19, 2005.

23. NLNAC, National League for Nursing Accrediting Commission, Inc. http://www.allnursingschools.com/local/nlnac.htm, accessed August 13, 2005.

24. White Paper on the State of the Art of Approval/Accreditation Processes in Boards of Nursing, May 30, 2004, www.ncsbn.org/pdfs/Approval_White_ Paper_Final.pdf, accessed July 17, 2005.

25. CCNE Accreditation, http://www.aacn.nche.edu/Accreditation/, accessed August 14, 2005.

26. Personal and Home Care Aides, http://bls.gov/oco/ocos173.htm, accessed July 17, 2005.

27. See note 1.

28. *Id.*

29. See note 20.

30. *Id.*

31. Occupational Outlook Handbook, 2010-11 Nursing and Psychiatric Aides, http://www. bls.gov/oco/ocos327.htm accessed January 30, 2010.

32. Weiss, J. P., "Nursing practice: a legal and historical perspective," *Journal of Nursing Law* 2, no. 1 (1994): 17–36.

33. Nursing Regulation, www.ncsbn.org/regulation/index.asp, accessed July 18, 2005.

34. *Id.*

35. The NCLEX® Examination 2010, http://www.pearsonvue.com/nclex/ accessed December 20, 2009 and NSCBN 2010 NCLEX® Candidate Bulletin http://www.vue.com/nclex/bulletin_2010.pdf accessed January 30, 2010.

36. *Id.*

37. *Id.*

38. Facts about the Centers of Medicare and Medicaid Services, http://www.cms.hhs.gov/researchers/projects/APR/2004/facts.pdf, accessed July 19, 2005.

39. JC, 2010, http://www.jointcommission.org/AboutUs/Fact_Sheets_/hospital_facts.htm accessed January 25, 2010.

40. "Certified nurses report fewer adverse effects," *RN* (May 2000): 14.

41. ALS,www.americanheart.org/presenter.jhtml?identifier=3011972, accessed July 17, 2005.

42. Ramson, J., "Nursing liability: confusion in the courts," *For the Defense* (March 1999): 13.

43. Fiesta, J., "Look beyond your state for your standards of care," *Nursing* 86 (August 1986): 41.

44. Tammelleo, A. (ed.), "Doctor testifies as to national standards of nursing care," *Regan Report on Nursing Law* (April 1994): 1.

45. Feutz-Harter, S., "Clinical practice guidelines," *Journal of Nursing Law* 4, no. 2 (1997): 51.

46. *Id.*

47. Deets, C., "Evidence-based practice: been there, doing that!" *Journal of Professional Nursing* 14, No. 6 (November-December 1998): 322.

48. See note 45.

49. Evidence-based Nursing, http://evidence.ahc.umn.edu/ebn.htm, accessed July 21, 2005.

50. Van-Patter, G. and Schaffer, M. "Organizational Readiness for Evidence-Based Practice," *Journal of Nursing Administration* 19, no. 2 (February 2009) 91-97.

51. Pinkerton, S. "Best nursing practices and best hospitals," *Journal of Professional Nursing* 15 No. 4 (July-August 1999): 207.

52. Bailey, D., D. Litaker, and C. Mion, "Developing better critical paths in healthcare: combining 'best practice' and the quantitative approach," *Journal of Nursing Administration* 28 (1998): 21.

53. Pravikoff, D., A. Tanner, and S. Pierce, "Readiness of U.S. Nurses for evidenced-based practice," *AJN* 105, No. 9 (September 2005): 40–51.

54. Introduction, www.med.ualberta.ca/ebm/ebmintro.htm, accessed July 21, 2005.

55. See note 53.

56. Koehn, M. and Lehman, K. "Nurses' perceptions of evidence-based nursing practice," Journal of Advanced Nursing 62, No. 2 (April, 2008) 209-215.

57. Tittler, M., J. Mentes, and B. Rakel et al., "From book to bedside: putting evidence to use in the care of the elderly," *Journal on Quality Improvement, The Joint Commission Journal* (October 1999): 545.

58. See note 54.

59. Participating AHRQ Evidence-Based Practice Centers. January 2010. Agency for Healthcare Research and Quality. Rockville, MD http://www.ahrq.gov/Clinic/epc/epcents.htm.

60. See note 57.

61. John Hopkins University School of Nursing Center for Excellence for Cardiovascular Health in Vulnerable Populations http://www.nursing.jhu.edu/research/p30, 2010.

62. The Cochrane Collaboration http://www.cochrane.org, 2009, accessed January 30, 2010.

63. Lang, N., "Discipline-based approaches to evidence-based practice: a view from nursing," *Journal on Quality Improvement, The Joint Commission Journal* (October 1999): 539.

64. http://healthlinks.washington.edu/hsl/classes/evidence/, accessed July 21, 2005.

Additional Reading

Van Achterberg, T., Shoonhoven, L. and Grol, R. (Fourth Quarter, 2008), "Nursing implementation science: How evidence-based nursing requires evidence-based implementation," *Journal of Nursing Scholarship*, 302-310.

Appendix 6.1
The Patient Care Partnership: Understanding Expectations, Rights and Responsibilities

(Reprinted with permission of the American Hospital Association, ©2003.)

When you need hospital care, your doctor and the nurses and other professionals at our hospital are committed to working with you and your family to meet your health care needs. Our dedicated doctors and staff serve the community in all its ethnic, religious and economic diversity. Our goal is for you and your family to have the same care and attention we would want for our families and ourselves.

The sections explain some of the basics about how you can expect to be treated during your hospital stay. They also cover what we will need from you to care for you better. If you have questions at any time, please ask them. Unasked or unanswered questions can add to the stress of being in the hospital. Your comfort and confidence in your care are very important to us.

What to Expect During Your Hospital Stay

- **High quality hospital care.** Our first priority is to provide you the care you need, when you need it, with skill, compassion, and respect. Tell your caregivers if you have concerns about your care or if you have pain. You have the right to know the identity of doctors, nurses and others involved in your care, and you have the right to know when they are students, residents or other trainees.

- **A clean and safe environment.** Our hospital works hard to keep you safe. We use special policies and procedures to avoid mistakes in your care and keep you free from abuse or neglect. If anything unexpected and significant happens during your hospital stay, you will be told what happened, and any resulting changes in your care will be discussed with you

- **Involvement in your care.** You and your doctor often make decisions about your care before you go to the hospital. Other times, especially in emergencies, those decisions are made during your hospital stay. When decision-making takes place, it should include:

- *Discussing your medical condition and information about medically appropriate treatment choices.* To make informed decisions with your doctor, you need to understand:
  ◊   The benefits and risks of each treatment.
  ◊   Whether your treatment is experimental or part of a research study.
  ◊   What you can reasonably expect from your treatment and any long-term effects it might have on your quality of life.
  ◊   What you and your family will need to do after you leave the hospital.
  ◊   The financial consequences of using uncovered services or out-of-network providers.

  Please tell your caregivers if you need more information about treatment choices.

- *Discussing your treatment plan.* When you enter the hospital, you sign a general consent to treatment. In some cases, such as surgery or experimental treatment, you may be asked to confirm in writing that you understand what is planned and agree to it. This process protects your right to consent to or refuse a treatment. Your doctor will explain the medical consequences of refusing recommended treatment. It also protects your right to decide if you want to participate in a research study.

- *Getting information from you.* Your caregivers need complete and correct information about your health and coverage so that they can make good decisions about your care. That includes:

◊   Past illnesses, surgeries or hospital stays.
◊   Past allergic reactions.
◊   Any medicines or dietary supplements (such as vitamins and herbs) that you are taking.
◊   Any network or admission requirements under your health plan.

•   *Understanding your health care goals and values.* You may have health care goals and values or spiritual beliefs that are important to your well-being. They will be taken into account as much as possible throughout your hospital stay. Make sure your doctor, your family and your care team know your wishes.

•   *Understanding who should make decisions when you cannot.* If you have signed a health care power of attorney stating who should speak for you if you become unable to make health care decisions for yourself, or a "living will" or "advance directive" that states your wishes about end-of-life care; give copies to your doctor, your family and your care team. If you or your family need help making difficult decisions, counselors, chaplains and others are available to help.

•   **Protection of your privacy.** We respect the confidentiality of your relationship with your doctor and other care-givers, and the sensitive information about your health and health care that are part of that relationship. State and federal laws and hospital operating policies protect the privacy of your medical information. You will receive a Notice of Privacy Practices that describes the ways that we use, disclose and safeguard patient information and that explains how you can obtain a copy of information from our records about your care.

•   **Preparing you and your family for when you leave the hospital.** Your doctor works with hospital staff and pro-fessionals in your community. You and your family also play an important role in your care. The success of your treatment often depends on your efforts to follow medication, diet and therapy plans. Your family may need to help care for you at home.

You can expect us to help you identify sources of follow-up care and to let you know if our hospital has a financial interest in any referrals. As long as you agree that we can share information about your care with them, we will coordinate our activities with your caregivers outside the hospital. You can also expect to receive information and, where possible, training about the self-care you will need when you go home.

•   **Help with your bill and filing insurance claims.** Our staff will file claims for you with health care insurers or other programs such as Medicare and Medicaid. They also will help your doctor with needed documentation. Hospital bills and insurance coverage are often confusing. If you have questions about your bill, contact our business office. If you need help understanding your insurance coverage or health plan, start with your insurance company or health benefits manager. If you do not have health coverage, we will try to help you and your family find financial help or make other arrangements. We need your help with collecting needed information and other requirements to obtain coverage or assistance.

While you are here, you will receive more detailed notices about some of the rights you have as a hospital patient and how to exercise them. We are always interested in improving. If you have questions, comments, or concerns, please contact

_____.

Appendix 6.2
Professional Acronyms

ABPS—American Board of Podiatric Surgery Certification.

ACNP—Acute Care Nurse Practitioner.

ACSM—American College of Sports Medicine Certification.

AIYS; Dip Aroma—Association of International Yoga School, Diploma in Aromatherapy.

AIYS; Dip Mass—Association of International Yoga School, Diploma in Massage.

AIYS; Dip Yoga—Association of International Yoga School, Diploma in Yoga Teaching.

AP—Acupuncture Physician.

AOBTA Certified Practitioner—Certified Practitioner Member of the American Oriental Bodywork Therapy Association.

AOCN—Advanced Oncology Certified Nurse.

ANP—Advanced Nurse Practitioner.

ARP—Accredited Rehabilitation Professional (Canada).

ATC—Certified Athletic Trainer.

ATR—Registered Art Therapist.

ATR-BC—Registered Art Therapist; Board Certified.

AuD—Audiology Doctorate.

BA—Bachelor of Arts Degree.

BAMS—Bachelor of Ayurvedic Medicine and Surgery.

BC—Board Certified.

BCEN—Board Certified in Emergency Nursing.

BCNP—Board Certified in Nuclear Pharmacy.

BCNSP—Board Certified in Nutrition Support Pharmacy.

BCPP—Board Certified in Psychiatric Pharmacy.

BCPS—Board Certified in Pharmacotherapy.

BS—Bachelor of Science Degree.

BSN—Bachelor of Science, Nursing.

CA—Certified Acupuncturist.

CAc—Certified Acupuncturist.

CAMT—Certified Acupressure Massage Therapist.

CAPA—Certified Ambulatory Perianesthesia Nurse.

CCH—Certified in Classical Homeopathy.

CCNS—Certified Critical Care Nurse Specialist.

CCRC—Canadian Certified Rehabilitation Counselor.

CCRN—Certified Critical Care Nurse.

CCRF—Certified Flight Registered Nurse.

CCRP—Certified Clinical Research Professional.

CD—Certified Doula.

CDE—Certified Diabetes Educator.

CFC—Certified Fitness Consultant (Canada).

CGN—Certified Gastroenterology Nurse.

CGP—Certified Geriatric Pharmacist.

CGRN—Certified Gastroenterology Registered Nurse.

CH—Certified Herbalist.

CHHP—Certified Holistic Health Practitioner.

CHom—Certified in Homeopathy.

CHPN—Certified Hospice and Palliative Nurse.

CHt—Certified Hypnotherapist.

CMT—Certified Massage Therapist.

CNM—Certified Nurse Midwife.

CNN—Certified Nephrology Nurse.

CNS—Certified Nurse Specialist

COHN—Certified Occupational Health Nurse.

COHN/CM—Certified Occupational Health Nurse Case Manager.

COHN-S—Certified Occupational Health Nurse Specialist.

CPAN—Certified Post-Anesthesia Nurse.

CPed—Certified Pedorthist.

CPHQ—Certified Professional in Health Quality.

CPhT—Certified Pharmacy Technician.

CPHT—Certified Practitioner of Homeopathic Therapeutics.

CPN—Certified Pediatric Nurse.

CPNP—Certified Pediatric Nurse Practitioner.

CPON—Certified Pediatric Oncology Nurse.

CRNA—Certified Registered Nurse Anesthetist.

CRNH—Certified Registered Nurse Hospice.

CRNP—Certified Registered Nurse Practitioner.

CRRN—Certified Rehabilitation Registered Nurse.

CRRN-A—Certified Rehabilitation Registered Nurse, Advanced.

CRC—Certified Rehabilitation Counselor.

CRT—Certified Respiratory Therapist.

CSN—Certified School Nurse.

C-SSWS—Certified School Social Work Specialist.

CST—Certified Surgical Technologist.

CWOCN—Certified Wound Ostomy Continence Nurse.

CWS—Certified Wound Specialist.

DAAPM—Diplomate of the American Academy of Pain Management.

DAc—Diplomate in Acupuncture; Doctor of Acupuncture.

DABIM—Diplomate of the American Board of Internal Medicine.

DABMA—Diplomate of the American Board of Medical Acupuncture.

DACBN—Diplomate of the American Chiropractic Board of Nutrition.

DC—Doctor of Chiropractic.

DCSW—Diplomate in Clinical Social Work.

DDS—Doctor of Dentistry.

DHANP—Diplomate of the Homeopathic Academy of Naturopathic Physicians.

DHM or DHm—Doctor of Homeopathic Medicine.

DHom—Homeopathic Diplomate (UK).

DHt—Diplomate in Homeotherapeutics.

DiplAc (NCCAOM)—Board Certified Diplomate in Acupuncture of the National Commission for the Certification of Acupuncture and Oriental Medicine.

DiplCH (NCCAOM)—Board Certified Diplomate in Chinese Herbology of the National Commission for the Certification of Acupuncture and Oriental Medicine.

DiplOBT (NCCAOM)—Board Certified Diplomate in Oriental Bodywork Therapy of the National Commission for the Certification of Acupuncture and Oriental Medicine.

DNP—Doctor of Nursing Practice.

DMD—Doctor of Medical Denistry.

DNBHE—Diplomate of the National Board of Homeopathic Examiners.

DO—Doctor of Osteopathy.

DOM—Doctor of Oriental Medicine.

DPM—Doctor of Podiatric Medicine.

DtP—Registered Dietitian (French-Canadian).

DTR—Dietetic Technician, Registered.

DVM—Doctor of Veterinary Medicine.

EMT—Emergency Medical Technician.

EPC—Certified Exercise Physiologist.

FAAD—Fellow of the American Academy of Dermatology.

FAAFP—Fellow of the American Academy of Family Physicians.

FAAO—Fellow of the American Academy of Optometry.

FAAP—Fellow of the American Academy of Pediatrics.

FACE—Fellow of the American College of Endocrinology.

FACP—Fellow of the American College of Physicians.

FACS—Fellow of the American College of Surgeons.

FADA—Fellow of the American Dietetic Association.

FAGD—Fellow of the Academy of General Dentistry.

FAPhA—Fellow of the American Pharmaceutical Association.

FASHP—Fellow of the American Society of Health-System Pharmacists.

FCCM—Fellow Critical Care Medicine.

FCCP—Fellow of the College of Chest Physicians.

FIACA—Fellow of the International Academy of Clinical Acupuncture.

FNP—Family Nurse Practitioner.

FNP-C—Family Nurse Practitioner, Certified.

HMD—Homeopathic Medical Doctor.

HNC—Holistic Nurse Certified.

ICCE—ICEA Certified Childbirth Educator (ICEA—International Childbirth Education Association).

ICPE—ICEA Certified Postnatal Educator.

ICPFE—ICEA Certified Perinatal Fitness Educator.

LAc—Licensed Acupuncturist.

LCSW—Licensed Social Worker.

LHom—Licensed Homeopath (UK).

LicAc—Licensed Acupuncturist.

LM—Licensed Midwife.

LMP—Licensed Massage Practitioner.

LMT—Licensed Massage Therapist.

LN—Licensed Nutritionist.

LNC—Licensed Nutritionist Counselor.

LNCC—Legal Nurse Consultant Certified.

LNHA—Licensed Nursing Home Administrator.

LNCC—Legal Nurse Consultant Certified.

LPC—Licensed Professional Counselor.

LPN—Licensed Practical Nurse.

LSHom—Licensed Member of the Society of Homeopaths (UK).

LSW—Licensed Social Worker.

LVN—Licensed Vocational Nurse.

MA—Master of Arts Degree.

MAc—Masters in Acupuncture.

MD—Medical Doctor.

MFCC—Marriage, Family, and Child Counselor.

MFT—Marriage and Family Therapist.

MH—Master Herbalist.

MHSc—Master of Health Science.

MNIMH—Member National Institute of Medical Herbalists.

MNNP—Master of Nursing, Nurse Practitioner.

MPH—Master of Public Health.

MS—Master of Science Degree.

MSN—Master of Science in Nursing.

MSW—Master of Social Work.

NBCCH—National Board Certified Clinical Hypnotherapist.

NBCDCH—National Board Certified Diplomate in Clinical Hypnotherapy.

NCC—National Certified Counselor.

NCSN—Certified by the National Board for Certification of School Nurses.

NCTMB Certified—Board Certified by the National Certification Board for Therapeutic Massage and Bodywork.

ND—Naturopathic Doctor.

NMD—Naturopathic Medical Doctor.

NP—Nurse Practitioner.

NP-C—Nurse Practitioner, Certified.

NREMT—National Registry of Emergency Medical Technicians.

NREMT-P—National Registry of Emergency Medical Technicians—Paramedic.

OCN—Oncology Certified Nurse.

OD—Doctor of Optometry; Optometrist.

OMD—Oriental Medicine Doctor.

ONC—Orthopaedic Nurse Certified.

OPA-C—Orthopaedic Physician's Assistant-Certified.

PA—Physician's Assistant.

PA-C— Physician's Assistant, Certified.

PDHom—Practitioner Diploma in Homeopathy (UK).

PDt—Professional Dietitian (Canada).

PFLC—Professional Fitness and Lifestyle Consultant (Canada).

PharmD—Pharmacy Doctorate.

PhD—Doctor of Philosophy (Doctoral Degree).

PsyD—Doctor of Psychology.

PT—Physical Therapist.

PTA—Physical Therapist Assistant.

QCSW—Qualified Clinical Social Worker.

RAc—Registered Acupuncturist.

RD—Registered Dietitian.

RD, CSP—Board Certified Specialist in Pediatric Nutrition.

RD, CSR—Board Certified Specialist in Renal Nutrition.

RDN—Registered Dietitian and Nutritionist.

RDt—Registered Dietitian (Canada).

RKT—Registered Kinesiotherapist.

RN—Registered Nurse.

RN-C—Registered Nurse, Certified.

RNCS—Registered Nurse Clinical Specialist.

RN/NP—Registered Nurse, Nurse Practitioner.

RPh—Registered Pharmacist.

RRT—Registered Respiratory Therapist.

RSHom—Registered with the Society of Homeopaths (UK).

RYT—Registered Yoga Teacher; Yoga Alliance.

SLP.D—Doctorate in Speech-Language Pathology.

Chapter 7

Nursing Documentation

Patricia W. Iyer, MSN, RN, LNCC and Sharon L. Koob, RN, BSBA, CPHRM, ARM

7.1 Introduction

The information in nursing documentation is often one of the deciding factors in both medical and nursing liability claims. Nursing records may be used to support the nurses' version of events, and used to refute the claims of a physician. Documentation, or charting, is a vital part of professional nursing practice. The nursing process is the framework for practice, with documentation being an essential link between providing and evaluating care. All aspects of nursing documentation are a permanent part of the medical record, with the exception of nursing assignment worksheets.

7.2 Importance of Documentation

Nursing documentation is often the key to understanding the events that spawn a nursing or medical malpractice claim. The medical record can refute or support the plaintiff's or defendant's version of events. Careful scrutiny of the medical record can eliminate many potential suits and lead to early settlements of claims that have merit. Nursing documentation often paints a vivid picture for both the plaintiff and defense attorneys, with each side using the record to draw conclusions about the events of the case. Expert witnesses will rely on the charting to form opinions about adherence to or deviations from the standard of care. It is therefore essential that the attorney have an intimate understanding of the medical record and how nurses document.

Nursing documentation provides essential information that describes a patient's injuries or health status, major problems, effectiveness of treatment, and cooperation or lack of compliance with treatment. When correlated with other parts of the medical record, nursing documentation usually provides a complete picture of the patient's condition. Discrepancies, if any, between the nursing documentation and that of other healthcare providers, can be crucial in a particular case.

Nursing documentation is often the most legible part of the chart and contains information that must be considered when evaluating a personal injury, malpractice, or product liability case. Comments that patients make about their injuries or the details of a personal injury case are often recorded verbatim by nurses. For this reason the attorney should request a complete medical record in order to gather facts that bear on the patient's injuries. It is imperative to know how nursing records are organized in order to decipher medical records to find the facts that will hurt or help the case.

7.3 Why Nurses Document
A. Professional Responsibility

The primary reason for nursing documentation is to accurately and completely describe the patient's status and the care rendered. The medical record is a communication tool that acts as the central repository for information about the patient. Nurses document care as part of their professional responsibilities to the patient. The medical record facilitates care, enhances continuity of care, and helps coordinate the treatment and evaluation of the patient. "The patient care record is used to evaluate patient status. All health professionals need to evaluate the patient's health status, interventions, effectiveness of care and needed changes in the patient's plan of care."[1] Nursing notes should be reviewed by other healthcare professionals for a picture of the patient. Nurses are the only professionals who are in contact with the patient 24 hours a day in the hospital. The medical record should verify that the nurse adhered to the standard of care. Conversely, it is used to prove that the nurses did not follow standards, policies or procedures. Likely documentation of turning and repositioning would have been key in this case.

The plaintiff, age 26, sustained a traumatic injury in November 2005 which caused permanent quadriplegia. The plaintiff's treatment was overseen by general surgeon, Dr. Francis Baccay. The plaintiff was hospitalized for six weeks, followed by a lengthy rehabilitation. During the hospitalization the plaintiff developed three pressure ulcers which progressed to stage IV status. The plaintiff ultimately underwent surgery to close the wounds in 2007 and 2008. The plaintiff claimed that the decubitus ulcers negatively impacted his rehabilitation. The plaintiff claimed that he was not provided a proper diet and that he was not repositioned regularly. The defendants claimed the plaintiff received proper care and maintained that the plaintiff had reached the expected degree of functionality. According to a published account the plaintiff and Sodexho, the company which employed the hospital's dieticians, reached a confidential settlement prior to trial. A $2.25 million verdict was then returned. The plaintiff's recovery was reduced to the stipulated limit of $800,000.[2]

TIP: Many clinicians do not realize that the chart will be compared to the healthcare facility's written regulations, policies, procedures and guidelines. For example, if the facility policy requires turning a patient with a pressure ulcer once every two hours, failure to do that constitutes a breach of the standard of care.[3]

B. Regulatory Standards

Nursing documentation is used to demonstrate compliance with the standards of regulatory agencies. As discussed in Chapter 6, *The Foundations of Nursing Practice*, The Joint Commission is the most prominent regulatory agency for hospitals. Nursing homes are regulated by a number of agencies including the federal Department of Health and Human Services through the Centers for Medicare and Medicaid Services (CMS). This governmental agency has strict standards that affect nursing practice and documentation in long-term-care facilities. See Chapter 10, *Subacute and Long-Term Care Nursing Malpractice Issues*, in Volume II, for more information. Rehabilitation centers and home care agencies have their own accrediting bodies and regulatory standards which also dictate documentation practices. See Chapter 15, *Home Healthcare Nursing Malpractice Issues*, in Volume II. In fact, every organization that provides health care is affected by a host of standards that influence the way care is delivered and nurses chart in medical records.

C. A Word About "If You Didn't Chart It, You Didn't Do It"

This expression engenders more fear in nurses than almost any other phrase as it is used to reiterate the importance of documentation. The phrase is also used to accuse nurses whose documentation is not complete. Incomplete documentation can dramatically affect a malpractice case. In the ideal world all pertinent observations and interventions are recorded. However, for a variety of reasons, medical records may be incomplete. Emergency situations, such as cardiac arrests, often result in gaps in documentation as patient needs take priority. Ideally the nurse tries to record detailed notes after the emergency is over, but this does not always happen because the nurse must direct attention to the other patients who took a back seat to the crisis. Sketchy documentation complicates the defense of a case and provides the plaintiff's attorney with an opportunity to advance theories of liability.

Plaintiff's attorneys may use the phrase "if you didn't chart it, you didn't do it" to convince the jury that essential care was not given. Defense attorneys sometimes attempt to preempt the anticipated attack on the nurse's credibility or documentation. This can be brought up on direct examination of the nurse during trial by having the nurse testify about the impossibility of recording every detail or observation of the patient. Another useful technique is to have the nurse testify about the nurse's usual practice which may or may not be recorded in the medical record.

Missing documentation coupled with a poor outcome complicates the defense of cases no matter what strategy is employed, and it provides the plaintiff with an opportunity to successfully argue that care was not rendered. In the case below, the nurses could not prove they contacted the physician, if they did.

The plaintiff, age 63, suffered a back injury and could not return to work as a nurse. She decided to have an anterior approach lumbar fusion of the spine. This was to include surgery to the spine from the front of the body and then a day or two later, surgery from the back. For the anterior approach the plaintiff's abdomen was opened and her internal organs were moved in order to get to the spine. After surgery the plaintiff had fluctuating blood pressure and no pulse in the left leg. The nurses noted the lack of pulse in the leg but did nothing about it. The next morning, when Dr. Brown arrived to perform the second part of the surgery, he discovered her problems and had her rushed for a CT scan which showed internal bleeding in her abdomen and a blockage of the artery which supplies blood to the left leg. The plaintiff was transferred to another hospital by helicopter, but the surgeons there were unsuccessful in salvaging the leg and an above-knee amputation was performed. The plaintiff was unaware of the problem with the leg overnight due to being heavily medicated. The plaintiff's abdomen took four years to heal because the surgical incision wouldn't fully close due to the swelling of her organs and the internal bleeding. The plaintiff also had infections and required repeated surgeries to repair the damage to her abdomen. The matter settled for $5.25 million.[4]

TIP: Good documentation is consistent, concise, chronological, continuing, and reasonably complete.[5]

7.4 Obtaining Medical Records
A. Necessary Records

The practice of health care requires maintaining medical records. The entity that generates the physical record itself has been deemed to be the "owner" of the record. For practical purposes, this remains true in most cases when referring to the actual pieces of paper or other recording material that may contain patient data. The patient data itself, however, is generally thought to belong to both the provider and the patient. Both parties have rights and responsibilities that attach. The healthcare provider's "ownership" or "property" rights are not absolute. Possession confers, among others, the responsibilities of safeguarding the record from physical harm.[6]

Failure to create a medical record results in loss of a source of information to establish the condition of the patient and an inability to communicate important health information.

> In *Grady Cleveland, PR of the Estate of Francis Cleveland v. St. Michael Nursing Center*, a 67-year-old woman who had suffered a stroke was admitted to the defendant rehabilitation center for further therapy. The decedent suffered a cardiopulmonary arrest within four hours of arrival. She died six months later after remaining in a coma in the hospital to which she was transferred. The plaintiff claimed that the decedent developed respiratory compromise due to the inability to clear oral secretions. The plaintiff claimed the defendant's suctioning machine was missing a part which rendered it inoperative. The plaintiff claimed the defendant had inadequate staffing, failed to reassess the decedent after her arrival, and did not create a chart or any documentation regarding the decedent's presence. The defense argued that there was no evidence that the suctioning machine was not working as required. The jury found in favor of the plaintiff for $1,050,000.[7]

To decide what medical records to request, the plaintiff's attorney must first identify all the healthcare providers the client has seen. It is best to have a detailed form for each client to fill out, listing all physicians seen, the dates, the complaint, the treatment, tests, medications and the outcome of the treatment. The form should be detailed enough to include all contact information for each provider listed: names, addresses and phone numbers. It is essential the client fill out the form thoroughly and completely. This will help identify which records need to be obtained, and which ones might be unnecessary.[8]

If the plaintiff is unable to cooperate with completing a form, a legal nurse consultant will interview the plaintiff to obtain as complete a medical history as possible. Pharmacy records provide a thumbnail sketch of the patient's medical care prior to the incident in question and reveal prescribing physicians. Obtain all of the records—nursing home, clinic, hospital, urgent care, ambulance, visiting nurse, therapy, physician office and emergency department. See Figure 7.1 for a list of the different types of medical records. Even if all of the available medical records are not part of the alleged incident, they should still be obtained as reference material. The records just before and after the alleged incident are especially important in providing the documentation as to the person's medical condition, the extent of the injuries, as well as an indication of any probable long-lasting complications that may exist.[9] Surprising information may sometimes be found in medical records.

In the event that it is suspected that the client/claimant has been treated for an injury but withheld information about healthcare providers, the attorney may query clinics and emergency departments in the vicinity.[10] Sometimes the timely provision of medical records can make a difference in a person's care.

> The plaintiff, age 59, was taken to an emergency room with acute chest pain, diaphoresis and pain radiating to the left arm with numbness. While on the way to the hospital, an emergency medical technician called to alert the hospital to prepare the catheterization lab. An EKG was performed on arrival, which revealed a left bundle branch block. The plaintiff had undergone a heart catheterization in 2003. Medical records were ordered and received by fax at 10:00 A.M., but were not charted until after 3:00 P.M. These records indicated an ejection fraction of 42 percent, compared to a normal level of 55 to 70 percent, and evidence of infarcts. These records were inconsistent with the plaintiff's understanding and his report in the emergency room that he had a clean history after a prior cardiac work-up. Initial cardiac enzymes were not

A host of records may be relevant in a specific case. Depending on the circumstances, of the claim, the attorney should examine:

- hospital, emergency room, or emergency center records where the injury was initially treated;
- emergency medical services records (ambulance or medical intensive care unit/MICU);
- hospital records that relate to treatment and surgery;
- records of physicians and specialists who examined or treated the plaintiff before and after the incident;
- outpatient imaging (x-rays, MRI scans, CT scans and so forth);
- any outpatient labs where blood work or other tests (EMG, EKG, and so forth) were done;
- inpatient and outpatient rehabilitation records including physical therapy, occupational therapy, and so forth;
- records of outpatient pain treatment centers;
- the actual radiographs and reports that relate to the injury;
- the actual pathology specimens and reports that relate to the injury;
- billing records;
- visiting nurse home care records;
- mental health, substance abuse records and HIV records;
- autopsy reports; and
- nursing home records.

A liability expert will have limited need to review voluminous medical records for care rendered after the care alleged to be negligent.

Figure 7.1 *Types of Medical Records*

elevated. Only after the enzymes became elevated, about nine hours after admission, was a cardiac consult ordered. Catheterization was performed, but not before a myocardial infarction occurred. The plaintiff was discharged nine days after admission. The plaintiff's ejection fraction after this incident was between 22 percent and 35 percent. The plaintiff claimed that catheterization should have occurred within 90 minutes of admission to the emergency room. According to a published account a $690,000 settlement was reached.[11]

B. Right to Access Records

To avoid alerting the medical records department or risk manager to a potential suit, many plaintiff's attorneys request the client to obtain a copy of the medical record to screen a potential nursing malpractice case. The Health Insurance Portability and Accountability Act (HIPAA) which has been phased into effect in stages between 1996 and 2009, regulates the patient's right to access protected and individually identifiable health information. HIPAA sets a national standard on how medical information may be accessed. The regulations apply to both paper and electronic medical records. HIPAA security rules guard against unau-

thorized transmission of PHI (Personal Health Information) only in electronic form—over the Internet, extranet, private networks and leased and dial-up lines. Other technologies used to transmit PHI—voice over the telephone, paper-to-paper fax machines, and videoconferencing and voicemail systems—are considered analog transactions and therefore outside the scope of HIPAA's security rules.[12] Those handling medical records need to be well aware of the consequences of violating confidentiality. Although outside the scope of HIPAA, disclosure of information by fax may result in a lawsuit.

The plaintiff's mother found a note written by her 14-year-old daughter in November 2003 which reflected suicidal thoughts. The parents spoke with a school counselor and the next day the teenager was evaluated at a hospital. A decision was made to admit her for psychiatric treatment. At admission her parents, who worked in the school system in the small-town area, were adamant that the school not be notified of the hospitalization. The parents feared that their daughter would be further traumatized if her mental illness became public and known to her peers. The daughter only agreed to enter the hospital after being told that her information would be private and no one at school would know. The next afternoon a hospital therapist faxed a letter to the high school office revealing the hospitalization. It was sent to an open fax which was available to anyone in the office—student, teacher, or administrator. There was evidence that a number of teachers and administrators learned of the hospitalization from the fax. When the girl returned to school, she believed that her hospitalization had been a secret. Upon returning to basketball practice, it was clear that her coaches and fellow players all knew.

The teen was distraught and believed that her confidence had been betrayed. She was readmitted to the hospital and placed on a suicide watch. She refused to treat with mental health providers after her release. She and her family later moved to another area so she could have a fresh start. The plaintiffs alleged failure to maintain confidentiality by sending the fax. The plaintiffs specifically maintained that the fax was not for communication with school administrators about the teenager's condition, but was an effort to generate more business, as the fax stated "thanks for the referral," and finished with "thanks again." The trial court initially granted summary judgment to the hospital, finding that the matter was a malpractice case which required a medical review panel. The Court of Appeals reversed, holding that the negligent or reckless dissemination of confidential patient information was not covered by the applicable law. The hospital, at trial, claimed that their conduct was appropriate and that the teenager had not suffered injury. The defendant also alleged that there had been a failure to mitigate damages in the refusal to continue treatment with mental health professionals. The jury returned a verdict in favor of the daughter only, on the claim of invasion of privacy. The jury awarded $200,000, but found 45 percent fault by the plaintiff, reducing the verdict to $110,000.[13]

Access to medical records, prior to HIPAA, was not guaranteed by federal law. Only about half the states had laws requiring patients to be able to see and copy their own medical records. Now HIPAA gives everyone the right to see, copy, and request to amend their own medical records.[14] The required language must be found in "HIPAA-compliant" authorization forms. Refer to Stromberg et al.[15] for additional information and samples of HIPAA-compliant medical records requests forms.

TIP: Some hospital and healthcare entities place information on how to obtain medical records on their websites. The healthcare entity is expected to comply with the request for the records within 30 days from the date the request is received. If the covered entity provides a reason for a delay, the time frame may be extended for an additional 30 days. Many firms use software to keep track of deadlines for the provision of medical records. Fees for medical records are supposed to be reasonable and cost-based.[16]

HIPAA regulations state that fees for copying and postage costs provided under state law are presumed to be "reasonable"; however, per-page costs that include costs excluded under the Privacy Rule (e.g., processing, retrieving and handling) are not acceptable. As a result, state-mandated fees for copying charges may be preempted by HIPAA and the Privacy Rule. Many state-mandated copying fees are higher than the costs involved in copying the information and therefore these fees may be preempted by the lower "reasonable" cost standard. In connection with providing copies to individuals or their personal representatives, covered entities will need to carefully review the state-mandated fees and determine whether they meet the Privacy Rule reasonableness standard.[17]

A new provision under the Health Information Technology for Economic and Clinical Health (HITECH) Act places an administrative burden on physician practices that could discourage them from adopting electronic health record (EHR) systems, according to the Medical Group Management Association (MGMA). A 2003 Health Insurance Portability and Accountability Act privacy rule allowed patients to request from practices an accounting of disclosures of their protected health information. The new provision expands the type of information that practices are required to provide in this accounting, necessitating medical groups with EHR systems to track all disclosures of patient information, including those made for treatment, payment, and healthcare operation. According to new MGMA online research, of more than 360 practice administrators, 69 percent stated that they had received no accounting-for-disclosure requests from patients in the previous year, and an additional 22 percent had received ten or fewer requests during that time. Administrators participating in the survey expressed concerns regarding the cost, staff training, and computer upgrades necessary to comply with the new provision.[18]

C. HIPAA Impact on Law Firms

Details of HIPAA may be accessed in the Code of Federal Regulations (CFR Title 45 Part 164).

HIPAA restrictions on use of protected health information do not apply to a plaintiff's attorney because the medical records are obtained through a signed valid authorization form prepared by the patient or legal representative.

The defense attorney is identified as a business associate of the healthcare provider. (See section 160.103 for the definition of business associate.) Before the disclosure can be made, the provider and the law firm must enter into a written business associate agreement or arrangement. (See section 164.502(e)(1) and (2) for general standards for disclosure to a business associate and requirements for written agreements or arrangements.) The business associate agreement defines how the law firm may use the medical record it receives from the provider. (See section 164.504(e)(2) for implementation specifications related to business associate contracts.) Under the rule, the business associate agreement must establish the required and permitted uses and disclosures of any protected health information (PHI) received by the business associate. The agreement cannot authorize the business associate to use or further disclose information in any way that would violate the requirements of the privacy rule if done by the provider.[19]

D. Complete Records

The attorney should request a full certified copy of the medical record when reviewing nursing malpractice cases. Although a received record's cover letter states that it is a certified copy, this does not mean that both sides of every page have been properly copied. Sometimes a medical records clerk or an employee of a copying service may fail to turn over a page, or may omit some of the pages of a multi-page flow sheet. Be particularly alert to narrative notes that stop in mid-sentence or state "continued" or "cont" when the first part of the note is missing. This may signify that a double sided page was copied only on one side.

TIP: The attorney may request the facility staff to staple multi-page flow sheets in order.

The attorney should expect an expert witness, or a legal nurse consultant reviewing the medical records, to draw omissions to the attorney's attention. If appropriate, original records may be reviewed on site by the attorney. If the records are to be viewed on site, this should be promptly done. Records are eventually put on microfilm which is more difficult to read than a hard copy. Original records may also be produced at the time of deposition. Medical bills are helpful in identifying tests and treatments which were done, even when the record does not mention them. The bills can be compared with the medical record to determine if the records are complete.[20] This is particularly effective when reviewing physician office records and may reveal bills for office visits that are not matched with office notes.

As noted, incomplete records can be the result of simple human error; however, there are occasions when healthcare workers tamper with the record. It is important, therefore, that the attorney be aware of this possibility and be ready to respond to it. Record tampering is reviewed in greater detail in Section 7.12 of this chapter.

E. Subsequent Medical Record Requests

Many attorneys request a second copy of the medical record just before trial. This enables the attorney to detect changes that may have been made in the medical record after the initiation of a lawsuit. Record tampering can profoundly affect a malpractice case. That information will also be found in Section 7.12 of this chapter.

TIP: The attorney may use software to keep track of deadlines and to follow up on records requests.

7.5 Components of the Medical Record

This section provides details about hospital records. The unique forms found in nursing home records are discussed in Chapter 10, *Subacute and Long-Term Care Nursing Malpractice Issues*, in Volume II. The typical paper hospital chart is kept either in a binder, with the pages opening like a book, or in a clamp-type chart holder, with the pages opening at the bottom of the chart holder. Sections of the record are separated by plastic dividers and labeled for ease of locating specific types of documentation when the medical record is in use in a hospital or clinic. Though these plastic dividers are not maintained with a stored medical record, section integrity is preserved. The sections found in a typical hospital chart are described below.

A. Face Sheet

The face sheet contains basic data about the patient, including name, address, sex, marital status, religion, employer, insurance information, dates of admission and discharge, admitting physician, and initial medical diagnosis. This sheet often also contains the diagnoses at the time of discharge, operations and complications. Complications are often coded with a number that is in the 900 series. The attending physician signs the bottom of the face sheet at the time of discharge, and the medical records department assigns diagnostic-related group (DRG) codes to the diagnoses. Nurses refer to the information on this page when contacting family members about the patient and for other basic demographic information such as age and address. Websites providing an interpretation of DRG codes may be found with search engines. Texts provide this same information.

B. Discharge Summary

The discharge summary is usually found under the face sheet. It is a dictated summary that should be prepared, according to hospital bylaws and Joint Commission standards, within 30 days of the patient's discharge. The attorney can determine the date it was dictated by looking for the notation "D:" (followed by a date) in the lower left corner of the last page of the discharge summary. The date the discharge summary was typed is noted with the letter "T:" (followed by a date). Be alert for a long period of time between the time the patient was discharged and when the discharge summary was dictated, or dictation of a discharge summary after the patient was readmitted with complications from the first admission. There may be significant altering of the facts or attempts at cover-up when the discharge summary is not dictated within the usual time. Also, be alert to a code that would indicate that the discharge summary was revised. This may be indicated by the abbreviation "DR" (date revised). The discharge summary typically describes the:

- patient's condition on admission;
- results of key diagnostic studies;
- medical diagnoses;
- treatment that was rendered;
- patient's status at the time of discharge; and
- details of discharge instructions, which may include directions regarding medications, physical activity, self-care instructions, and a time frame for returning to the physician's office.[21]

C. Discharge Instruction Sheet

A one or two page document including discharge instructions is typically given to the patient by the nurse assigned to care for the patient on the last day he or she is in the hospital. This form contains self care instructions, time of next physician office appointment following discharge, names of medications to be taken at home, and reportable signs, such as fever, signs of infection or other concerns specific to the patient's nursing and medical diagnoses. In many settings the patient or a family member signs the form to verify understanding of instructions.

D. Transfer Forms

When a patient is sent to or from a nursing home or to a home care agency, a form is filled out by nurses that documents key aspects of the patient's assessment. Treatment orders are often documented on the form as well. The form may include the date and time of transfer, where the patient was sent or received from, and the patient's diagnoses, vi-

tal signs, and condition. An accurate listing of medications should also be included in this document. The Joint Commission has emphasized that all of a patient's medications be reconciled when care level is changed. Refer to Chapter 4, *Patient Safety Initiatives*, for additional information.

E. Emergency Department Records

Emergency department records are often at the front of the chart following the discharge summary. They usually include:

- a face sheet,
- a note by the triage nurse documenting condition on arrival and chief complaints,
- notes by the nurses who provided care,
- the examination by the physician, either handwritten or dictated,
- diagnostic test results ordered during the stay,
- a consent for treatment,
- recommendations for admission, referral, transfer to another facility, or discharge,
- discharge instructions signed by the patient if the patient was not admitted to the facility, and
- a transfer form if the patient was sent to another agency.

Records of the rescue squad may be contained in this section of the chart, but often must be requested separately.

F. Treatment Orders

Medical orders may be initiated by physicians as well as physician assistants and nurse practitioners. Orders cover treatment, diagnostic tests, transfers to another service, requests for consultations, medications, and so on. The orders are to be signed by the person who provided the order. A supervising attending physician cosigns orders provided by interns and residents, as well as any telephone and verbal orders which may have been issued. A variety of doctors use this section of the chart, including consultants, residents, interns, and attending physicians. These orders are documented on handwritten forms, computer-printed order forms or preprinted order forms. Preprinted order forms may include specially prepared order forms for hyperalimentation (high calorie intravenous fluids), heparin administration, PCA pumps (patient-controlled analgesia or narcotic infusions), telemetry and critical care standing orders, postpartum obstetrical orders, and so on. Orders are transcribed by a nurse and possibly cosigned by a second person or by a unit secretary and always cosigned by a nurse. The co-signature verifies that the order was accurately transcribed.

- Nursing admission assessment (this may be a multidisciplinary assessment in some settings)
- Nursing care plan which defines problems or diagnoses, outcomes, and interventions individualized for the patient
- Critical pathway and variances for care to be provided each day of the admission
- Nursing flow sheets that document routine aspects of care (baths, treatments)
- Specialized flow sheets for patient-controlled analgesia pumps, restraints, neurological and neurovascular assessments, pressure ulcer, fall risk, frequent vital signs, altered behavior, suicide checks
- Patient education records
- Critical care flow sheets
- Narrative nurse's notes
- Intravenous therapy records
- Medication administration records for routine medications given every day, PRN (as needed medications) and one-time-only medications
- Discharge instructions
- Interagency transfer forms

Figure 7.2 *Components of Hospital Nursing Documentation*

TIP: Increasingly, reviewers see TORB or VORB to indicate a telephone or verbal order was taken by a nurse and read back to the prescriber.

G. Graphic Records

Graphic records include charts consisting of displays of temperature, pulse and respirations, and blood pressures. Some hospitals have intake and output totals on the bottom of the graphic record and provide per shift and per day totals, and also use this sheet to record weights. These records are kept by nurses and nursing assistants. It is often difficult to determine the identity of a person who recorded vital signs on one of these documents, as there are typically no signatures or initials.

H. Nurse's Notes

Nursing documentation makes up one of the largest parts of the medical record. Components of nursing documentation are shown in Figure 7.2. These forms record the patient's condition, complaints, treatment, and responses to care. Various flow sheets are used depending on the patient population. For example, neurological assessments, Glasgow Coma Scores, dialysis treatment records, and so on, are used. Nursing records incorporate changes in the standard of care. For example, the recommendations for prevention of ventilator-associated pneumonia are frequently incorporated into critical care flow sheets. Also, documentation of a risk assessment of falls and/or pressure ulcers may be part of the nursing records.

I. Laboratory Test Results

The laboratory section contains results of testing on blood, urine, spinal fluid, sputum, wound drainage, and so on. Abnormal results are typically flagged in some way (bold, H for "high," or L for "low," or C for "critical"). Critically abnormal results are usually called to the nursing unit with notation of the time and name of the person so informed. This section often includes forms filled out by nurses when they hang blood transfusions.

J. X-Rays and Other Diagnostic Test Results

Other test results are found in this section, such as x-rays, ultrasound, CT scans, EEGs, MRIs, bone scans, arterial studies, and echocardiograms. The reports include the name of the physician who interpreted the x-ray, nuclear medicine test, CT scan, ultrasound, or MRI, and the name of the physician who ordered the test.

K. Surgical Records

Surgical records consist of the following:

1. Preoperative checklist, completed in the nursing unit before the patient is sent to the operating room suite and verified in the surgical holding room (where patients are kept waiting for the operating room).
2. Informed consent form, which may be witnessed by a nurse, for the surgical procedure.
3. Anesthesia clearance form, consisting of a brief listing of medical problems and an assignment of an anesthesia risk score. (See Chapter 20, *Nurse*

Anesthesia Malpractice Issues, in Volume II, for more information about the ASA score.) The anesthesia form also contains a note after the anesthesiologist sees the patient 24 hours after discharge from the recovery room.

4. Anesthesia record, documenting the medications and vital signs of the patient during the surgery, which is completed by an anesthesiologist or nurse anesthetist.

5. Correct site verification, which may be signed by a nurse and others in the surgical area.

6. Dictated operative report (most hospitals require the operative report to be dictated within 24 hours after surgery). In some medical malpractice cases, the operative report may not be dictated for months. This always arouses suspicion about the validity of the report.

7. Operating room nurses' notes regarding the evaluation of the patient before and during surgery, the names of the circulating and scrub nurses and the times they were involved in the patient's care (particularly when relieved for a break).

8. Cell saver flow sheets.

9. Operating room nurses' care plan.

10. Count sheets for needles and sponges completed by the circulating nurse and scrub nurse or technician.

11. Equipment sheets, recording numbers of implants and other types of equipment put into the patient. These sheets may also contain identifying information on the implants themselves, such as serial numbers. Or this area may contain actual paperwork which came with the implant, containing these identifiers.

12. Postanesthesia care unit (PACU) notes, consisting of vital signs, medications administered, intravenous fluids given, Aldrete score (standardized method of assessing patient on admission, throughout stay and at discharge) and observations of the patient recorded by the PACU nurse.

13. Pathology report on tissue removed from the patient's body.

L. History and Physical

The admission history and physical may be prepared in advance of the admission. This can be handwritten or dictated by the physician, resident, nurse practitioner or physician's assistant. It contains details of the patient's medical, surgical, and social history, current medications, findings of physical examination, initial impressions or diagnoses, and treatment plan. Refer to Levine[22] for more information.

M. Progress Notes

Depending on the hospital policy, physicians, physician assistants, and nurse practitioners may document on their own section of the medical record or all progress notes may be combined. Interdisciplinary notes contain the entries of physicians, nurses, therapists and others. Medical progress notes may include:

*   diagnoses and findings of assessments
*   plans of care
*   patient's response to care
*   prognosis statements
*   courtesy statements such as "appreciate the consultation of Dr. King...."
*   reminders to physicians by other professionals, such as nurses and therapists who request reordering medications and treatment
*   comments that a diagnostic test has been done, such as "CT scan complete."[23]

N. Consultations

Consultation reports are written by doctors or specialized nurses, such as psychiatric or wound care experts, who are brought into the case at the request of the attending physician. An abbreviated version of the consultation report may be handwritten on a consultation form or briefly summarized in the progress notes, followed by a more detailed dictated version. Consultants may suggest care to be ordered by the attending physician or in some circumstances may take the initiative to write orders.

O. Notes of Ancillary Departments

Notes from dietary, respiratory, physical, speech and occupational therapy, and social services are included as applicable. These records will consist of initial assessment and ongoing treatment or interventions.

P. Miscellaneous Forms

These include the patient's consent to be treated at the hospital and other consents (which may be witnessed by a nurse) for invasive procedures. A clothing list, which contains information about what clothing the patient was wearing upon entrance to the hospital and the disposition of any valuables such as money or jewelry should be present. Chart forms may also include advance directives which specify the patient's wishes for care in the event of a terminal illness. Legal papers such as involuntary or voluntary commitment documents may also be incorporated.

7.6 Other Sources of Information about the Patient

Not all information about the patient makes its way into the medical record. Some of the following documents may be available and obtainable through discovery:

1. OR log, which gives data about each operation performed in the operating room
2. Labor and delivery log, which gives details about every delivery
3. Emergency department log, which provides information about all patients who are registered to be seen in the ER
4. Infection control surveillance reports prepared by the infection control nurse
5. Pharmacy drug profiles, which list every medication ordered by the doctor
6. Utilization review reports, which address the necessity for the admission
7. The shift supervisor's report, which usually lists new admissions, discharges, deaths and seriously ill patients
8. The Kardex, which is a document that lists the care ordered by the physician, and may be discarded at the time the patient leaves

9. Risk management reports or incident reports if there is an unusual occurrence
10. Fetal monitoring strips
11. Patient advocacy records
12. Billing records
13. Autopsy records

7.7 Organizing Medical Records

Locating information in medical records is a source of great frustration for attorneys and risk managers. A little time spent organizing the record saves much time and effort, and avoids agony. Figure 7.3 lists suggestions for a workable system for organizing medical records. Table 7.1 helps to ascertain that all applicable records have been provided. Refer to Figure 7.4 for medical record management tips.

Organizing electronic medical records can be more challenging. The way the information is printed out may result in a mixture of different types of records back to back. An operative report may follow a physician progress note, which may follow a diagnostic test result. Additionally, nursing information may be aggregated by topic, rather than printed out sequentially. For example all notes about skin integrity may be gathered together. It is usually possible to organize printed electronic records into categories by the type of provider or documentation.

---

1. Obtain hospital chart dividers from a hospital supplier or a legal supplier. The most economical dividers are made of heavy paper with plastic coated tabs that mark the various sections of the chart. Dividers are available for hospital charts as well as for nursing home charts.
2. Have your legal nurse consultant or paralegal start at the top of the stack and place the pages into piles that correspond with each divider. Once each paper is sorted into the right category, organize each section chronologically, starting with the first day of the admission and so on. (When charts come from duplicating services they are often in reverse order, with the end of the hospitalization at the top of the stack.)
3. Once the medical record is organized, ask that the pages be numbered in the lower left or right corner. This can be accomplished with a Bates stamp (machine that prints numbers) or with clear labels imprinted with numbers. If the documents are scanned, they can be printed and numbered at the same time.
4. Have the medical record taken to a copying service and request that the record be duplicated on predrilled paper (paper with three holes in it). Photocopying the records at 95 percent will prevent loss of information if the pages are three-hole punched. Some attorneys have records copied on legal paper to provide a margin at the bottom for notes. Avoid having the record copied on two-sided paper. If the records are not properly organized, it will become very difficult for the medical expert to reshuffle the documents.
5. Have at least two copies made. Set aside the record supplied by the hospital and keep it in a safe place.
6. Place the copies of the record in three-ring binders organized with the hospital chart dividers.
7. Identify one of the two copies that have been made as the "working copy." This copy can be flagged, underlined, highlighted, and written on. The second copy will be used for expert witness review if the case proceeds further. Since your set of records and the expert's will be identical, it will be easy to discuss the case and refer to specific page numbers.

Figure 7.3 How to Organize Medical Records

1. Be very specific about whether you need a certified medical record or an abstract. A nursing malpractice case involving a specific admission would be difficult to evaluate without a full certified copy of the medical records.

2. Be aware that the production of the nursing home chart is regulated by the Federal Government. Under 42 CFR 483.10, the nursing home is required to produce a medical record within two working days of a request. "The resident or his or her legal representative has the right (1) upon an oral or written request, to access all records pertaining to himself or herself, including the clinical records, within 24 hours (excluding weekends and holidays); and (2) after receipt of his or her records for inspection, to purchase at a cost not to exceed the community standard, photocopies of the records or any portion of them upon request and two working days advance notice to the facility."

3. Use a logical system for staying on top of medical records requests so your office will know when to send a second request.

4. Do not accept a poor quality copy of a medical record. A poor copy may be light, misfed into the copier so that only part of the page is visible, or missing pages. A copy that is double sided, with the pages jumbled and placed front to back in random order, will be almost impossible to follow.

5. Do not put yellow or pink highlighting on the medical records you forward to the expert. The expert may have to explain that highlighting in a deposition one day. The other side may assert that the highlighting assumes the expert cannot find the relevant material without hints from the attorney.

6. Do have someone with medical knowledge organize records before they are sent to an expert or consultant. Organizing means using hospital or nursing home tabs to divide medical records into sections. You will save money on expert witness bills by sending organized records.

7. Do not jumble medical records. Hospital and nursing home records should be organized chronologically within each section of the records. For example, the physician orders should start with the initial set written when the patient was admitted to the hospital, and end with the discharge order.

8. Do not send your expert your only copy of the medical records. You may need to refer to them while the expert has them.

9. Do not send medical records by a method by which they cannot be tracked if lost.

10. Do not send physician's office records without identifying the name of the physician on a cover sheet or without the records request letter. It may be difficult for the expert or consultant to determine the author of the records without this identification.

Figure 7.4 *Top Ten Hints for Medical Records Management: Attorneys Will Save Time and Money by Avoiding These Pitfalls*

Table 7.1
Hospital Admission Record Organization

	Present	N/A	Missing	Need
(Before first section):				
Attorney's letter requesting record				
Certification letter				
Face Sheet/Front Index Sheet				
Dictated Discharge Summary				
Discharge Instructions by MD/RN				
Death Certificate/Autopsy Records				
Transfer Form to Hospital				
Rescue Squad/Helicopter Transport Sheet				
ER Records:				
Triage/Trauma Records, Nurses Notes, MD Exam, MD Typed H&P				
Physician's Orders				
Handwritten, computer generated or standing (preprinted) orders in date order				
TPN orders (nutritional IV supplement)				
Graphic Chart				
Temperature, Blood Pressure, Respirations				
Frequent Vital Signs				
Intake/Output				
Nurses Notes				
Nursing Admission Assessment/Database				
Nursing Care Plan				
Nursing Kardex (handwritten or computerized)				
Nurses Progress Notes/Narrative Notes				
Patient Care Flow Sheets				
Critical Care/ICU Notes				
Code Sheets (if any)				
Pressure Ulcer Assessment/Flow Sheet				
Neurological Assessment/Flow Sheet				
Neurovascular Assessment/Flow Sheet				
Dialysis Flow Sheet				
Restraint Sheets/Flow Sheet				
Medications (Regular and PRN)				
IV Care, IV Fluids				
Patient Education/Teaching Documentation				

continued on next page…

Table 7.1 (continued)

Discharge Instructions by Nurse				
Death Checklist done by nurse				
Laboratory Reports				
Blood Test, Cultures (Pathology Reports—Except Operative), Urine Tests, Other Body Fluids Tests				
Blood Transfusion Slips				
ABG (Arterial Blood Gases)				
X-ray Reports				
Radiology				
MRI				
CT Scan				
EEG – Brain Wave Test				
EKG – Cardiac Tests				
EKG Monitor Strips				
Ultrasound				
GI Studies/Barium Enema				
Report of Operation				
OR Consent				
Pre-op Checklist done by Nurse				
Pre-anesthesia Assessment				
Report of Operation (Typed)				
OR Nurses Notes (care plan, instrument and sponge counts, assessment)				
Anesthesia Record (Graphic Sheet)				
PACU Notes/Recovery Room Notes				
Pathology Report (surgical specimen report)				
(place a divider page between operations)				
History and Physical				
Handwritten or Dictated Admission Exam Notes				
History and Physical Exam Notes (Form)				
Progress Notes				
Physician (or integrated) Progress Notes				
Consultations in Date Order				
Misc. Records				
Permission (Admission Consent)				

continued on next page…

Table 7.1 (continued)

Special Consents (Photograph, Experimental Drugs, Release of Restraints, Invasive (non-surgical) Procedures)				
Organ Donor Forms				
Blood Transfusion Consent				
Advanced Directives/DNR Forms				
Dietary/Nutrition Notes				
Occupational Therapy				
Physical Therapy				
Respiratory Therapy (including Ventilator Sheets)				
Social Services				
Social Services – Discharge Plan/Home Care				
Speech Therapy				
Clothing List, Valuables				
Billing Information				

7.8 Physician Practice Records

Physician practice and clinic records also are pivotal in nursing liability cases. These records can be obtained in the same way as hospital records; and nursing documentation in physician practices and clinics follow the same rules as those noted in this chapter, with a few notable exceptions and/or specifics.

- Nurses are not employed in all physician practices; however, the rules of documentation which apply to them still apply to other practice staff (technicians, therapists, advanced practice nurses, and others) who are required to chart in those practices.
- The components of a practice chart are usually more limited than hospital or nursing home records. They may include:
  1. A face sheet which contains patient demographics such as name, age, gender, insurance coverage, and possibly working diagnoses.
  2. A cover sheet which tracks medications the patient is on (this page may also be found in other areas of the chart).

TIP: If no centralized tracking of the patient's medications is found on a practice or clinic record, the chart should be carefully reviewed for possible medication error.

3. Progress notes, which may include notations by physicians, nurses, and other clinical professionals who work in the practice.

TIP: These notes need to be dated and signed just like those in hospital charts, unless there is only one person who documents in this area. If there is only one person using the progress notes, then this person's notes must be dated.

4. Laboratory and other test results.

TIP: Test results should be initialed by the physician or nurse practitioner to note that they have been reviewed. If no notation indicating review is found, the result may have been filed in the chart without the physician seeing it.

5.   Reports from consultants; these reports should be handled in the same way as test results

- Documenting in a practice record is almost always done using one of two documentation styles, narrative charting and electronic recordkeeping. These two methods of charting are discussed in detail in Section 7.9 of this chapter.

- In an effort to save space, some practices layer lab test results in a tiered effect, either by taping them on a progress note, or by using pages especially designed to stick the results on the page in this way. If this is done, a copy of the record may show only the top result. The attorney must request that multiple copies of the page be made, each copy showing a different test result.

Other issues specific to this type of office record are noted throughout this chapter where appropriate.

7.9 Nursing Charting Systems

The heart of analysis of a nursing malpractice case is the review of nursing documentation. Various methods of documenting the nursing process have developed over the years. These include narrative charting, problem-oriented charting, PIE charting, Focus Charting®, and Charting By Exception. These systems are used to document on the nursing progress notes and on associated nursing forms in the medical record. The attorney may encounter any of these charting systems when reviewing medical records. A brief description of each system with its key elements and advantages and disadvantages follows.

A. Narrative Charting

1. Key elements

Most attorneys are familiar with narrative charting. It is the most commonly used method for documenting the nursing process. Narrative charting uses a simple chronological format to document patient care over the course of the shift. Nursing notes usually consist of a series of timed entries that describe the patient's status, nursing interventions and treatments, and the patient's response to the interventions. For example:

Date	Time	Progress notes (Narrative charting)
3/17	0830	OOB to chair for the first time this A.M. Unsteady on her feet, weak and complaining of nausea. Returned to bed with assist of two. Medicated with Compazine for c/o of nausea.
	0930	States relief of nausea.

2. Flow sheets

Nurses develop flow sheets to reduce the volume of information that needs to be charted and to standardize the elements which are documented. Because most habits die hard, however, many nurses continue to duplicate information in the narrative note which is already on the flow sheet. This practice creates double documentation. This is one of the reasons why some physicians state that they do not read nurses' notes as they often perceive that the nurses' notes contain a lot of repetitive information. Many doctors assume they will be told about significant findings or changes. In an ideal world this occurs, but with today's fast-paced healthcare environment, nurses tend to assume that the doctor will read the chart as well. Juries tend to believe that nurses have important information to convey and that doctors should read nurses' notes. Depending on the attorney's theories of the case, it may be very useful to question the physician about whether the doctor read the nurses' notes. If the doctor admits to not having read the notes, the witness may be asked the reasons why nurses document, the legal importance, the need to communicate important findings, and so on.

Flow sheets are found in virtually every area of nursing and vary a great deal in appearance. There are a few elements common to most flow sheets. Most use columns for documenting information, usually according to the time or shift. Another common element is the use of brief words, symbols or abbreviations to enter information onto the form. With the development of flow sheets which capture the routine, repetitive aspects of care, the narrative note has the potential to become shorter and more meaningful. However, the attorney may encounter charts consisting of several days' worth of flow sheets that are not accompanied by narrative entries. This type of documentation can present an incomplete picture of the patient's status and may complicate the case because of omissions in charting.

3. Advantages and disadvantages of narrative charting

Narrative charting is the system that most nurses learned in nursing school and is one that nurses use with comfort. If used correctly, the narrative note contains information on the patient's problems, nursing interventions, and the response or lack of response to interventions. Narrative charting is quick and easy in emergency situations. Nurses can quickly document the chronological events of the situation using this system.

The primary disadvantage of narrative charting is the disorganization of the typical narrative note. The attorney or paralegal often spends much time scanning notes trying to find key information. Narrative notes often contain observations of the patient and treatments that were rendered, but may omit evaluation of the patient's response to treatment. The unstructured narrative note does not provide a cue to remind the nurse to evaluate the patient's reactions to treatment.

The attorney often experiences frustration when trying to track a particular aspect of the patient's condition only to discover that some nurses charted information about the problem and others have omitted any mention of the issue.

B. Problem-Oriented Charting (SOAP)

Problem-oriented charting, introduced in the late 1960s by Dr. Lawrence Weed, was originally a system designed to be used by doctors to systematically record information about the patient's medical problems. The format used in problem-oriented charting is called SOAP:

S— subjective data: what the patient tells the healthcare provider

O— objective data: what is observed

A— assessment: the nursing diagnosis or conclusion based on the data

P— plan: what the healthcare provider is going to do about the problem

This is an easily recognizable format. Although the system was initially designed for physicians' documentation, nurses began using SOAP charting because its structured format is an improvement over the free-form narrative note.

1. Key elements

Problem-oriented charting has two unique components: the problem list and structured SOAP progress notes.

a. Problem list

Once a database of information is compiled during the patient's assessment, a problem list is created that identifies the patient's important problems. Nurses use numbered nursing diagnoses as the problems. Physicians and nurses may use the same problem list. If the problem list is not shared the nurse may document the problems directly on the nursing care plan, eliminating the need for a separate list. The list is updated as new problems arise and others are resolved.

b. Progress notes

In traditional SOAP format, progress notes document information about patient problems or nursing diagnoses

which are on the problem list or the care plan. The SOAP format is missing the elements of implementation and evaluation, since the SOAP format ends with the "P" for the plan of care. Over the years, the SOAP format has been modified to reflect the entire nursing process more adequately. The SOAPIE format is a modification of the SOAP format:

S: subjective data—what the patient or family tells the healthcare provider

O: objective data—factual, measurable data gathered during the assessment, such as observed signs and symptoms, vital signs and lab test values

A: assessment—conclusions based on collected data and formulated as patient problems or nursing diagnosis

P: plan—what the healthcare provider is going to do about the problem, including the immediate and long term measures

I: interventions—the specific interventions that are implemented to achieve the outcomes

E: evaluation—the analysis of the effectiveness of the interventions[24]

The SOAPIE modification incorporates all the steps of the nursing process. An example of a SOAPIE note follows:

Date	Time	Progress notes (SOAPIE Note)
1/6	0800	S: "I am in pain" Rates pain as a 9.
		O: Holding abdomen and moaning.
		A: Pain related to surgery
		P: Medicate for pain
		I: Morphine 1 mg IV given
	0900	E: Patient expresses relief of pain to level 2.

2. Advantages and disadvantages of SOAP(IE) charting

SOAP(IE) charting provides a structured format that makes it easy to locate a specific piece of information. Its format reminds the nurse to use the nursing process to organize information. The problem-oriented medical record was the first system that advocated having all healthcare professionals document progress notes on the same page using the SOAP format. The integrated progress note can foster collaboration and enhance communication among health care professionals. Many nurses believe that physicians are more likely to read nursing entries when they appear on the same page as the physicians' progress note. This makes it more probable that the patient's needs will be addressed in a coordinated fashion. Settings in which the integrated progress note is commonly used include hospitals, rehabilitation, clinics, and psychiatric care units.

The biggest disadvantage to SOAP(IE) charting is its inefficiency; it is a cumbersome system to use. For example, each problem or nursing diagnosis requires a separate SOAP(IE) entry even though there may be overlap between problems. Creating a separate entry for each problem may involve repeating assessment data and interventions that apply to more than one problem.

Another disadvantage of SOAP charting is the considerable redundancy in the system. As a general rule, the more places a nurse has to enter the same piece of information, the less likely the information will be recorded everywhere it is needed. The SOAP system has built-in redundancy between the care plan and problem list, and between the flow sheets, care plan, and SOAP(IE) note.

C. PIE Charting

Although many attorneys are familiar with narrative charting and SOAP(IE) charting, PIE charting is less commonly encountered. The initials in PIE represent the documentation of problems, interventions, and evaluation of nursing care. The goal of PIE charting, as originally designed in 1984, was to streamline documentation. This was accomplished by eliminating the traditional care plan and incorporating an ongoing plan of care into the daily documentation.

1. Key elements

The PIE system of charting consists of flow sheets and the progress notes. Progress notes use nursing diagnoses as the problem. The problem statement is labeled with a "P" and numbered for easy reference. For example:

Date	Time	Progress notes (PIE charting)
1/7	1300	P#1 Risk for impaired skin integrity related to decreased mobility

Nursing interventions, in response to a specific nursing diagnosis, are recorded next to an "I" and are numbered to correspond to the problem. The evaluation of the effectiveness of the interventions is recorded next to an "E" and numbered. For example:

Date	Time	Progress notes (PIE charting)
1/7	1300	P#1 Risk for impaired skin integrity related to decreased mobility
		I#1 Turn and repositioned every 2 hours. Kept clean and dry.
	1400	E#1 Skin intact without evidence of pressure

An evaluation of each problem is to be made at least once a shift in this system of documentation. Current problems are addressed each day until the problem is resolved.

2. Modifications of PIE charting

The PIE method is often modified in one or both of the following ways:

- A problem list is developed to record the patient's identified problems.
- An additional entry is made in the PIE note. Assessment findings are added to make the actual entry "APIE." For example:

Date	Time	Progress notes (APIE note)
6/11	1200	A#1 Area of redness 2 cm x 2 cm noted on left hip.
		P#1 Impaired skin integrity related to immobility
		I#1 Turned and repositioned. Duoderm applied to left hip and Dr. Wilkes notified.
	2300	E#1 Duoderm intact

3. Advantages and disadvantages of PIE charting

The major advantage of PIE charting is that its format encourages the use of the nursing process by structuring the progress note to include nursing diagnoses, interventions and evaluation. The system also promotes the systematic evaluation of each identified problem once every shift.

The primary disadvantage of PIE charting is that the planning step of the nursing process is not documented. PIE charting skips from the problem to the interventions that were carried out. Although experienced nurses can make the leap from nursing diagnosis to interventions without documenting planning, novice nurses often have difficulty performing without a plan of care. Staff nurses usually do not have time to review pages of progress notes to determine which approaches have been used to resolve nursing diagnoses. They often rely on change-of-shift reports to determine the important needs of the patient, as knowledgeable attorneys discover when they question nurses in depositions.

D. Focus Charting®

1. Key elements

Focus Charting® is a method of organizing the narrative documentation to include data, action, and response for each identified concern or focus. The use of the term "focus" broadens the scope of identified concerns and eliminates the negative connotations of the word "problem." The medical record chart reviewer will recognize Focus Charting® by a column in the nursing progress notes labeled "focus." The focus may be any of the following:

Focus	Example
Current behavior or concern	Anxious
	Loss of income
Signs and/or symptoms	Increased blood pressure
	Vomiting
Acute change in status	Acute dyspnea
	Onset of delirium tremens
Significant patient care event	Return from PACU
	Discharge
Nursing diagnosis	Risk for falls
	Risk for aspiration

Information entered into the medical record next to the "focus" is organized into data, action and response entries. The data are the subjective and objective information which describes the focus. The actions are the nursing interventions which were carried out. The nurse's evaluation of the effectiveness of the intervention is documented in the response section of the note.

Date	Time	Focus	Progress notes (Focus Charting®)
5/6	1530	Constipation	D: Requested laxative, said he had not moved bowel since admission
			A: Order for MOM 30 cc obtained from Dr. Wilkes, administered
	2330		R: No response to MOM yet

2. Advantages and disadvantages of Focus Charting®

The use of the focus column and the DAR format permits the reader to quickly scan to find information on specific concerns without having to search through an unstructured narrative. Focus Charting® encourages the nurse to use the nursing process and to evaluate the patient's response. Focus Charting® stimulates nurses to identify a broader scope of patient concerns, not just problems. The format of Focus Charting® prompts the nurse to identify and document the patient's needs.

As is true of SOAP or PIE charting, if Focus Charting® is not used correctly, nurses can switch to narrative charting without charting evidence of patient response to interventions. In addition, Focus Charting® requires a reorganization of how nurses chart information. To use this system correctly the nurse must be able to identify the focus accurately, and sort the data into the appropriate categories of data, action, and response. In addition, the nurse must evaluate the patient's progress toward outcomes to document the response. These problems are also found when nurses adjust to SOAP charting or PIE charting.

E. Charting By Exception

1. Key elements

Charting By Exception (CBE) is a charting system that has been in use since the mid-1980s. The principle behind Charting By Exception is to document only significant findings or exceptions to defined norms or standards. CBE consists of several components, including flow sheets, standards of practice, a nursing database, nursing care plans and progress notes. The two pieces which are unique to this system (a nursing assessment/order flow sheet and documentation according to standards of practice) are described below.

2. Nursing assessment/order flow sheets

The bedside nursing assessment/order flow sheet is used for two purposes:

- It standardizes the documentation of physical assessment findings.
- It is used to chart the implementation of physicians' and nursing orders.

The nurse decides which elements of physical assessment to carry out based on the condition of the patient. The standards of practice for the institution and the clinical area may also specify what needs to be assessed. The flow sheet is accompanied by a description of the specific elements which constitute a standard normal assessment for a particular body system. For example, the form may specify that a patient with a normal neurological system would be alert, know who she was, where she was and what day it was (oriented X3), be free of pain, be able to swallow without coughing or choking, and be free of numbness or tingling.

The attorney may encounter a set of specific symbols used in CBE to document the assessment of the patient. CBE uses these abbreviations on the nursing assessment/order flow sheet:

√ = The assessment was completed and no abnormal findings were noted.

* = Significant abnormal findings are present and are described in the nurses' notes or elsewhere on the flow sheet.

→ = The patient's status remains unchanged from the previous entry with an asterisk (*).

The nursing assessment/order flow sheet is also used to document the completion of nursing and physicians' orders. A nursing order that might be included on this flow sheet would be pressure ulcer care. The completion of the order is documented using the same symbols as described above:

√ = The order was carried out.

* = The nurse's note contains a description of the ulcer.

→ = The ulcer has not changed appearance from the previous description.

3. Standards of practice

The institution establishes standards of practice that govern the provision of nursing care to the major patient populations served by the facility. In CBE, standards of practice are incorporated into the documentation system to eliminate the need to record routine nursing interventions such as hygiene care, irrigation of tubes, and monitoring of the IV site. Check marks are used to indicate that the standard of practice was carried out. An asterisk indicates that not all the standards were followed. The parts of the standard that were not followed or modified should be described in the nurse's notes.

4. Advantages of Charting By Exception

Although CBE is not the only documentation system that uses bedside forms, one of the primary advantages of the bedside nursing assessment/order sheet is that the most complete data are available at the bedside and thus accessible to the healthcare team. One of the major pluses of this system is the establishment of agreement on the elements of normal findings. For example, using narrative charting, a nurse may document "normal cardiac assessment" without defining the elements of that assessment. This ambiguity can cause confusion and leave everyone wondering about the completeness of the assessment.

CBE also streamlines charting since much of the repetitive charting of routine care is eliminated. Charting consistency is improved because the system reduces individual variations in documentation quality and quantity.[25] The use of standards of practice reduces charting time, improves productivity, reduces the need to obtain routine orders from physicians, and reduces costs by decreasing overtime. Other advantages, defined by one hospital after using Charting By Exception for four years, are as follows:

- Eliminated redundancy in documentation
- Reduced documentation by approximately 75 percent
- Reduced paper use and associated costs by 50 percent
- Ensured concise documentation of routine care
- Emphasized abnormal findings, thus facilitating the implementation of appropriate treatment plans
- Helped to identify trends in clinical care across the three nursing shifts
- Made medical records more comprehensive[26]

5. Disadvantages of Charting By Exception

CBE's major disadvantage from a liability perspective relates to concerns about the defensibly of this charting system. Refer to Figure 7.5 for comments expressing reservations about this system. Charting By Exception, through its use of well-defined assessments, completion of orders and standards of practice, is a clearly structured system. The developers of the documentation system had it evaluated from legal, quality and cost perspectives.

Each nurse using this system must carefully adhere to the standards of practice and conscientiously complete each element of the physical assessments. There are potential problems of undercharting or differences in performing assessments. Clarifying notes have to be written if the flow sheet does not provide enough information about the patient's condition. The integrity of the charting system and accuracy of documentation can be attacked if a nurse charts as if all elements had been completed but fails to record the omissions. There are many insignificant reasons why a nurse would not follow all of these standards. Once a pattern of mechanical or rote charting is established, the nurse may become careless about documenting exceptions to the standards. This may become an issue in a malpractice case in which the attorney is trying to establish whether the standards were followed.

TIP: If the plaintiff's attorney can obtain an admission from the nurse during a deposition or trial that the nurse failed to document omissions, the attorney can question the accuracy of the information documented about the patient.

Cummins and Hill[27] provide recommendations to organizations to avoid legal problems. These elements should be reviewed by both defense and plaintiff's attorneys when a nursing malpractice case involves care documented under a Charting By Exception model:

"All of the risk and claims managers I spoke with told me it is extremely difficult to successfully defend claims when clinics use the Charting By Exception documentation method because of inconsistencies that inadvertently happen. In fact, I was told that with this style of reporting, you typically lose more cases than you win. Why? Because most applications of Charting By Exception assume that all routine or non-critical processes are done but are not documented—and it is on this assumption that your defense will rest. Unfortunately, if a plaintiff's attorney can prove that even once something routine that is not typically documented was not really done, your ability to defend the fact that you really did do any other specific test or intervention and did not document it is markedly decreased."[1]

"If your facility uses a Charting By Exception (CBE) format, you'll need to take extra precautions. In a CBE system, only exceptions to expected observations are charted. Because minimizing documentation is risky, you'll need to use well-designed flow sheets in a CBE system. If the CBE documentation doesn't give a clear, accurate description of the patient's condition, write it out in a narrative note. If you're asked to testify several years later, you'll be able to reconstruct an accurate picture of your patient's condition."[2]

"At our facility we do not chart by exception. After going through a few state surveys I am very leery of doing this. They expect and have asked me for nurse's documentation to show assessment of the resident condition, such as a Foley catheter that has been in for years. We usually have to prove we are monitoring to prevent a condition from developing."[3]

"My experience has always been that if you did it, you charted it" Rowell (senior policy fellow of the American Nurses Association) said. "With checklists, people just whip down them. It becomes so rote that you don't think about it anymore."[4]

1. Abeln, M. Llability awareness: reporting risk check-up, www.apta.org/pt_magazine/Oct 97/liab.htm, accessed 2/15/04
2. Habel, S., Document it Right, January 13, 2003, Nurse Week, www.nurseweek.com/ce/ce670a_print. htm, accessed 2/15/04
3. Mabel (no last name), NADONA's Director of Nursing Forum, http://pub34.bravenet.com/forum, accessed 2/15/04
4. Federwisch, A. Charting your way to valid outcomes, www.nurseweek.com/features/98-3/chart/html, accessed 2/15/04

Figure 7.5 Comments by Nurses about Disadvantages of Charting By Exception

1. The nursing department must have a written copy of CBE policies, procedures and guidelines.
2. Policies must be clear and understood by all staff members (and agency nurses) who write in the medical charts.
3. Policies must specify by license and title who may document data, observations, and interventions.
4. Policies must address how the CBE format links to each required element of charting.
5. Definitions of "normal" findings of physical assessment must be specified, along with what qualifies as an "exception" to normal findings.
6. Documentation should be legible and up-to-date, with all pertinent information concerning medical and nursing problems clearly specified.
7. Observations, emerging complications, significant conversations, interventions, treatment plans (and the rationale behind them) must all be included.
8. Charting should be time-sensitive, not merely a summary of events. Caregivers must note the date and time of each entry.

Healthcare organizations should ensure that the charting policies and procedures associated with Charting By Exception do not conflict with state, federal, or Joint Commission standards. Risk managers, facility attorneys, multidisciplinary committees, and state human services representatives should review and approve of Charting By Exception protocols and structures. Reviews of this system should be documented. Staff will need extensive training and reinforcement on the correct use of the system.[28] Additionally, staff should recognize when care and documentation is not routine or unanticipated outcomes occur. Charting By Exception may be problematic if the policy, protocols, and guidelines are not in place to guide the nurse and clarify the use of this form of documentation.[29]

6. Charting By Exception versus charting by exception

There is some confusion between the charting system called "Charting By Exception" and the practice of charting by exception, or omitting documentation of routine aspects of care. The practice of charting by exception is related to the familiar saying "If it wasn't charted, it wasn't done." The difficulty with this old saying is that it sets a standard that is impossible to achieve. Nurses will readily testify that they do not chart everything they do. It would be physically impossible to document all of the nursing actions and thought processes involved in providing care. In reality, the nurse sorts through all of the data and establishes priorities regarding which negative charting to chart. Some nurse defendants justify omission of documentation by saying they use "negative charting." This implies that they do not document normal findings. While current documentation standards do not require extensive documentation of normal findings, they do require noting the pertinent information about a patient. "No symptoms of chest pain" may be an important entry for a 51-year-old man in the coronary care unit with a diagnosis of "rule out myocardial infarction." The same entry in the chart of an 82-year-old woman with cellulitis of the legs may be meaningless. After an incident, it is difficult for nurses to justify scant documentation by saying they practice negative charting. Sketchy documentation provides opportunities for the plaintiff's attorney to assert care was not properly rendered and complicates the nurse's defense. The omission of documentation of important information then raises the question of whether the nurse actually carried out the action but forgot to document it, or more significantly, did not perform the action at all.

F. FACT Charting

FACT documentation facilitates transition to computerized documentation. The FACT ("Flow sheets, Assessment, Concise progress notes, Treatment") documentation system incorporates many CBE principles in that the nurse documents only exceptions to what is normally expected or significant information about the patient. The FACT documentation system contains flow sheets, assessments with baseline parameters, concise progress notes flow sheets documenting the patient's condition, and response to treatment when care is given.[30]

1. Key elements

The FACT system uses three components:

- An assessment and action flow sheet is used to document ongoing assessments and interventions or actions. Normal assessment findings for each body system are printed on the form along with the planned actions. This flow sheet is designed to be individualized.
- A frequent assessment flow sheet is used to document vital signs and frequent physical assessments.
- Progress notes are documented on integrated notes (all disciplines document on the same progress notes). The patient's progress and any significant events are recorded on these notes. The notes are formatted into data, action, and response.[31]

2. Advantages

The advantages of this charting system are similar to those identified for Charting By Exception and Focus notes. The use of integrated progress notes helps to facilitate communication among healthcare professionals, as there is a greater likelihood that the various healthcare providers will read each other's notes when they are located within the same section of the medical record.

3. Disadvantages

The disadvantages of FACT charting are similar to Charting By Exception.[32]

7.10 Computerization of Nursing Information

In April 2004, President Bush called for the majority of Americans to have interoperable (the ability to securely exchange clinical, demographic, and financial data by using a method of capturing, storing, and securely transmitting and receiving data) health records within ten years. President Obama continued the focus on electronic heath records when he slated more than $19 billion for health information technology under the American Reinvestment and Recovery Act of 2009. The Act provides incentives for physicians who purchase and make "meaningful use" of electronic medical records. Medicare will pay incentives for computerized documentation starting in 2011 to a variety of healthcare providers, such as physicians, dentists, certified nurse-midwives, nurse practitioners, and physician assistants who are practicing in federally qualified health centers or rural health clinics led by a physician assistant.[33] See Figure 7.6 for information on the privacy, confidentiality and security of medical records.

Privacy: the right of individuals to determine when, who and to what extent information is transmitted about themselves

Confidentiality: the trust placed that the information that is shared will be respected and used only for the purpose disclosed

Security: the protection of information from accidental or intentional access by unauthorized people, including modification or destruction of the information

Styffe, E., "Privacy, confidentiality, and security in clinical information systems: Dilemmas and opportunities for the nurse executive," *Nursing Administration Quarterly*, 21 (3), 1997: 21.

Figure 7.6 *Privacy, Confidentiality, and Security of Computer Records*

A. Advantages

Regardless of the type of record, computerization of medical records has many advantages.

1. Efficiency

- The enormous amount of data that are collected about a person's health can be stored and organized in a more efficient method than our current paper system permits. It is time consuming to find data in a patient's chart. The larger the chart becomes, the less easy it is to use it to locate key information. An electronic medical record can be searched to find key pieces of information. One facility found 61 percent of respondents (28 out of 46 nursing home employees) reported that their computerized patient record system had increased efficiency by being able to find necessary patient information. Time studies verified the employees' perceptions of time savings.[34] The ability of electronic health records to compress large amounts of data into minimal space relieves providers of the pressure to cull files.[35]
- Placement of bar codes on medical record forms permits a handwritten form to be scanned and saved in the correct section of an electronic chart.
- Being able to use standardized order sets saves the prescriber time. For example, certain patients with specific diagnoses may need the same laboratory work ordered every time a treatment regimen begins. The ability of prescribers to access the order sets, without having to remember what they are, facilitates care.
- The electronic medical record could lead to a more efficient transfer of information from one health-

care provider to another. When using manual methods of documentation, duplication of testing and data collection can occur during care transfer from one provider to another. Cost containment and healthcare reform mandate improving efficiency in the management of healthcare data.

- An electronic record may be simultaneously viewed by more than one person.
- The electronic medical record can be accessed by authorized people located at a remote site. For example, the physician managing the care of a nursing home resident or hospital patient can access laboratory results, orders, and medical and nursing documentation in order to make clinical decisions.
- Computerized documentation supports economical use of the data entry process by reducing or eliminating redundant charting. A one-time entry of a piece of information into the program can be sent to all of the appropriate places. For example, the patient's allergy to Morphine should show up wherever this information is needed, such as in the pharmacy, on the medication administration record, and as an alert in the clinical information system.
- Copying of medical records prior to transferring a patient to a different facility can be eliminated under the electronic health record model. This system would permit the receiving facility's providers to be able to access the information gathered at the sending facility.
- Hospital bedside monitors, laboratory equipment, and other devices provide data which may be electronically incorporated into the patient's medical record.
- The ability to review records of prior hospitalizations permits the healthcare team to obtain data

about prior medical problems. For example, a nurse could scan a number of hospitalizations to see if the patient experienced pressure ulcers in the past or if the patient had a pattern of becoming acutely delirious after receiving anesthesia. The admission assessment of a prior admission could be referenced so that the nurse does not have to repeat all of the same questions, but simply confirm or add new information.

2. Quality of information

- Electronic medical records manipulate and display information in a way that no paper and pen system could duplicate. All notes related to a specific aspect of care can be collated and printed out. The paper chart cannot be reorganized in this manner, nor can it be merged with records from another facility or healthcare provider.
- Medical records can be used to more effectively track outcomes of care. Instead of using ineffective methods of treating medical problems, data collected about outcomes can be used to define the most appropriate approaches to care. This would facilitate clinical research and outcomes analysis.
- Electronic charts standardize terminology to conform documentation to common terms and permit aggregation of data. For example, one handheld PC program designed to document risk assessment and pressure ulcer documentation resulted in all wounds being documented in an identical manner with very little room for misinterpretation. An aggregate of all wound data allowed for real-time review by clinical managers and administrators.[36]
- Electronic medical records (EMR) promote standardized documentation, providing consistent information about patients.
- EMRs help support evidence-based criteria. Standards of care are supported when the system prompts the nurse to enter information that conforms to appropriate protocols.
- Continuity of care (CCR) records would permit ready access to an individual's healthcare information. For example, a CCR system would permit the emergency department staff to determine the medical history of an unconscious patient brought into the emergency department of a hospital.
- Electronic medical records may improve a facility's ability to recruit and retain healthcare providers. Anecdotal information has shown that computers

tend to increase job satisfaction and morale. This is a significant advantage, given the high cost of turnover.
- In some systems, the patient can access parts of his medical record over the Internet. Links to sites that provide information about medical conditions could be made available.

3. Medical errors

- Pen and paper medical records are plagued by illegible handwriting along with non-standardized and dangerous abbreviations, which can lead to medical errors. Electronic records are legible and are programmed to use only approved terminology and abbreviations.
- Electronic medical records may be supplemented with resources, such as information about medications, which is useful when prescribing drugs. Systems that include data from laboratory systems can incorporate clinical prompts, for example, which may warn against prescribing a specific medication in the presence of declining kidney or liver function. A prescriber can be warned when an order is entered for a medication to which the patient is allergic. These decision-making supports may improve the quality of care and reduce medical errors.
- Use of bar coding technology reduces medication errors. The patient, medication, and nurse's badge are all bar coded. Matches must occur before the medication is administered to the patient. Institutions observing nurses attempting to work around the system may make revisions to block these efforts to negate the safety features.
- Programs can be designed to include unit-specific and agency-wide standards of care and practice. The effect of these programs is to remind the provider of the essential elements that must be documented, through the use of clinical flags. For example, if the standard states that a fall prevention program must be initiated for high-risk patients, the program can remind the nurse of the standard. The nurse will not be allowed to delete required interventions and will be prompted to enter specific interventions and observations.
- Programs which incorporate the facility's standards of care prompt the nurse to enter the essential information. For example, an admission assessment would include information that would identify the patient's risk for skin breakdown or for a fall. This

type of prompting focuses the nurse's attention on key clinical issues and reminds the nurse to collect and enter data that would fulfill the standard of care.

4. Forensic issues

- Access to a medical record may be electronically limited. For example, a nursing assistant may be permitted to only enter vital signs but not review orders or laboratory results, or write nursing notes. A paper medical record may be viewed by anyone.
- It is possible to determine who has accessed an electronic chart. For example, Registered Nurse Charles Cullen, who confessed to killing many patients, was finally caught in 2003 through the use of computers. His excessive use of digoxin, a medication used to kill his victims, was preceded by accessing medical records of patients to whom he was not assigned. The digoxin was stored in a computerized drug dispensing cart, which recorded his removal of the drug.

TIP: Each entry in the electronic medical record carries a time and date stamp, as well as the identity of the user.

- Tampering with the medical record is much more difficult to do with an electronic system. Software typically permits the healthcare professional to correct errors in typing and phrasing immediately after the error is made. Software programs contain a feature that makes the entry unalterable after a certain time or event. Typically, the entry is made unchangeable once it is authenticated. There is also a regularly scheduled backup time to store data, making it impossible for someone to delete previous entries once they are saved. If a correction (such as revision of an incorrect entry, misspelled word, or typographical error) is to be made after an entry is saved or authenticated, the software program should contain a way to accomplish this task. This is often achieved in the same way it is done in paper systems, by bracketing the mistaken entry, adding the correct information, and giving a reason for the change, such as "wrong chart." A clock embedded in the software program indicates the precise time and date of an entry; and in this way it becomes impossible to backdate information to make it look as if it was entered earlier.

- With sufficient safeguards in place, an electronic record is more reliable and less likely to be lost.

5. Operational issues

- Many facilities are also putting their policy and procedure manual online. The unit's policies and procedures are thus readily available instead of being contained in huge three-ring binders. Thus it becomes easier to use the policies and procedures to follow the standard of care and to document accordingly. A work list of activities that need to be completed for a patient can be created in some electronic medical records systems. For example, the treatments and medications that are due to be administered over the course of a shift may be printed out for a nurse.

TIP: When asking a facility for a policy/procedure saved in an electronic form, the attorney may need to identify the key words of the document. For example, the facility's employee might be able to insert the word "falls" into a search box to retrieve all relevant electronic policies.

6. Benefits to the attorney of computerized documentation

Computerization of documentation provides some benefits for those involved in litigation.

- One of the most obvious benefits is the creation of legible records. Computer printed records are completely legible, therefore eliminating the confusion caused by guessing at the meaning of handwritten words.
- The identities of the healthcare providers are easy to determine, as each entry is followed by either initials or a full name and status (MD, RN, LPN and so on). If the entry is followed by initials, somewhere else in the document the person's full name will appear.

The benefits of computerized medical records are clear cut. Vital information about patients is available to those who need it immediately. Costly duplication of testing is avoided. Errors in care should be reduced, particularly as clinical aids flag information that needs to be considered in care.

B. Disadvantages

There are troublesome issues surrounding implementation of electronic medical or health records.

1. Privacy, security, confidentiality

- There are problems with security and confidentiality of patient information inherent in computerized medical records. Refer to Figure 7.6 for definitions. The consequences of inappropriate release of private health information can be severe, including ruined careers, public ridicule, social rejection, and economic devastation of individuals and their families.[37] A New Jersey hospital employee, Enzima Obie, undergoing testing in anticipation of surgery received a false positive HIV test result. A second test returned a negative result, leading her physicians to conclude that the false positive was related to her recent case of malaria. A suit ensued after a lab employee reported the first test result to the employee's supervisor. HIV test results were kept in a binder that could be viewed by any hospital employee. When Obie applied to return to work after surgery, her supervisor advised her that she would be placed on a preferred hiring list, but she was never rehired even though there were several vacancies she was qualified to fill. After a 10-day trial, the jury found the hospital violated the AIDS Assistance Act and awarded $200,000 in compensatory damages.[38]

- Computerized medical records pose new challenges to the healthcare provider's ethical and legal obligation to safeguard confidential information and comply with the provisions of the HIPAA. The ability of individuals to access the patient's computerized medical record from distant sites requires rigorous adherence to security measures. The placement of computer screens in a healthcare setting needs to be considered in relation to the presence of patients and visitors. Specifically, screens, and the information displayed on them, should not be visible to anyone without appropriate access to that information.

TIP: Dedicated hackers may breach the security of electronic health records, gaining access to potentially embarrassing details about an individual.

- Documentation about sexual preferences, histories of abuse, incest, mental illness, pregnancies, substance abuse, suicide attempts, HIV status and other personal medical history details may provide fodder for blackmail and other schemes. This is not a far fetched concern. A January 2003 theft of computers from an Arizona-based medical records contractor resulted in loss of the confidential and personal files of more than 500,000 members of the military, retirees, or their families.[39] Resistance to plans to computerize medical records is pervasive. Critics reacted to the plans of the Department of Health and Human Resources to implement a medical database system known as the National Health Information Network. The plan will include the creation of electronic health records that could be shared by doctors, insurance companies, and governmental healthcare providers. Opponents of this plan took the position that electronic health records were a major violation of a patient's privacy. Critics and others expressing concern posited that records would not only be accessible to healthcare providers without patient consent but any number of other people and organizations. These could include universities conducting research, medical students, and bureaucrats at every level, from entry-level data processors to registration clerks at medical clinics.[40]

- Critics point out misinformation would be difficult to correct as electronic health records are shared around the medical community.[41]

- A November 2004 Gallup poll found that a large majority of Americans did not want their medical information shared with anyone other than the doctor with whom they shared the information without their consent: this included other doctors. Ninety-two percent opposed giving government agencies access, and 84 percent opposed giving insurance companies access without prior consent.[42]

2. Forensic issues

- Failure to authenticate a medical record may permit alterations of data after the entry should have become permanent. Authentication finishes a record entry, making it permanent. For example, a nurse who fails to authenticate nursing notes until the end of an eight-hour shift may make changes after an event has occurred. A software solution that deals with this issue may include automatically making an entry unalterable after a certain period of time, such as within a few minutes or a couple hours. Some software systems lack the capability of locking if the author of the entry does not sign an entry. If a record is never locked, clinicians may make changes until the day the record is sent to auditors or litigators.

If information needs to be added or comments made after an entry has been locked, a new entry should be written and clearly identified as an addendum, following the guidelines for late entries.[43]

- Some electronic medical records have the capability of assembling and printing out all of the data related to specific aspects of the patient's care. For example, all of the nursing entries referring to elimination, skin integrity, or patient education are collected and printed out in chronological form. When reading a record which is assembled in this manner, it becomes difficult for the reviewer to identify a picture of the patient's overall condition at any one point in time.

- Most EMR software systems have the ability to "auto-populate" data fields, as described earlier. In this situation a key data element, such as an allergy to penicillin, need only be entered into the record once and it will be automatically entered into every other area of the record which requires allergy information. When the wrong information is entered into one of these key fields, that error will be auto-populated throughout the record and may cause medical error. The reviewing attorney should be aware of this weakness in electronic records and its connection with adverse events.

- Obtaining a copy of an electronic medical record has proved to be a significant challenge. Unlike paper records, which are usually organized in a specific fashion, electronic records often make little sense when simply printed out. Frequently, a printed out record uses excessive amounts of paper to record a limited amount of information; and that information is not presented in a logical format. The requesting attorney may wish to assure the receipt of an understandable record by confirming the facility uses a forensic record retrieval firm.

- All facilities which have converted to EMR need to have tested protocols which allow all practitioners to continue documenting smoothly during those times when the EMR system is "down." When reviewing a copy of an electronic record, the attorney should note any unusual gaps in the record since those gaps may indicate a systems issue and the existence of (or lack of) manual records produced during those gaps.

- Some practitioners have discovered that they can "copy and paste" sections of electronic documentation. Because people who engage in this behavior are trying to save time, they may be less likely to take care to make sure the copied section is completely accurate in its new position. What seems like a time-saver to the caregiver can diminish the validity of the record, create miscommunication, and lead to medical error when the pasted note contains inaccurate information. The reviewing attorney should watch for verbatim sections of notes appearing in more than one place in the chart; if it is apparent that the practitioner copied and pasted this material the attorney can use this information to discredit the caregiver at deposition or testimony.[44] Even if one provider copies and pastes his own text, entries may not be suitably updated with changes in the patient's condition.

3. Operational issues

- Start-up costs for transition to electronic medical records represent a large financial burden for facilities. Hardware, software, and training costs can range from $3 to $10 million per hospital. Fewer errors and higher productivity may more than offset the expense, but those savings are initially obtained by health insurance carriers, not hospitals since fewer complications and improved efficiency add up to shorter hospital stays.[45]

- Physician and nursing resistance to the use of computers is a factor that complicates the introduction of computers to a healthcare setting. Resistance to change is a potent force that can affect the acceptance of terminals. The attorney may be able to see some evidence of this resistance by examining the record of a patient who was hospitalized during the organization's transition to computerized documentation. The attorney may observe that some of the documentation is done in a manual manner while other providers have used the computer to document. While this may reflect that the healthcare providers have not all gone through training on the computers or with the software, it may also be due to resistance to change. Partial use of the computer and partial use of handwritten entries can create a confusing record. Buppert[46] shared the story of a cancer center that decided to adopt electronic order entry and documetnaiton. When some of the physicians resisted, the facility had to maintain two systems for ordering and recording data. This required the nurses to know which physicians used the EMRs and which did not, increasing the time and risk associated with checking for chemotherapy and other orders. In these situations the requesting attorney should take extra care to make sure that all records have been received.

- It may be more time consuming for the healthcare provider to navigate through a series of screens in order to select the appropriate data elements than it would to handwrite a brief note.

- Computer systems may become unavailable due to unexpected crashes or routine downtime. Medical information becomes inaccessible during these times, creating potential for medical errors.

- The adage "garbage in, garbage out" applies to the computer medical record just as it does to other aspects of computer programming. Incidents may increasingly occur in which clearly inaccurate information has worked its way into the medical record (as in auto-population errors, described above), but has not been questioned by healthcare professionals because computerized information is perceived to be infallible. No machine can replace a healthcare professional who can critically evaluate patient data and question information that does not make sense. Attorneys and healthcare personnel must guard against the temptation to deify the computer. Meaningless documentation can also be generated when templates are used without modification or individualization.

- It may be possible for one clinician's entries to appear as another clinician's entries if the first person does not sign off the record or log off.

- Healthcare personnel who work at several hospitals may be asked to remember a series of passwords to log into different computers. Unable to keep all of the codes memorized, some personnel keep a list of passwords. The act of writing down passwords in order to use them to access systems compromises security.

- Computer equipment is subject to breakdown and software problems. A facility or entity that uses electronic records must make sure that functional equipment is available for those who document to prevent interruptions in the charting process.[47]

TIP: Some nurses who have learned to electronically chart, and have never worked in a system that requires manual charting, may have difficulty adjusting when computer downtime occurs.

- Devastation of medical records through computer viruses which are introduced via disks or by files downloaded from the Internet may cause massive losses of data. Adequate backup solutions must be in place.

- The transition from paper to electronic records has to incorporate a way to capture paper documents. Forms brought to the hospital or physician office will have to be scanned to add them to an electronic record. This is time-consuming and labor intensive.[48]

- Customer service issues are created when healthcare professionals lose eye contact with the patient in favor of documenting on the computer.

- Rigidity is a problem with many electronic health records. Many records become electronic versions of checklists, which may not permit individualization for a patient. For example, the system may limit free text entries needed to clarify information.[49]

4. Potential problems for the attorney associated with computerization of nursing documentation

- Electronic health records can spread information about controversies concerning a patient. Patients may have difficulty finding physicians willing to treat them after a conflict has occurred with a healthcare provider. A threat of, or an actual, malpractice suit, a patient who is labeled as difficult or non-compliant, or a conflict with a nurse or physician that is memorialized in medical records may dissuade other providers from assuming care of the patient. While these deterrents have always existed, the ability to find this information about a prospective patient is made much easier when electronic health records can be accessed by other providers.

- A common complaint about computerized documentation is that some of the individuality of charting is lost. Since the same stock phrases are used over and over, charting on patients can end up sounding alike. While this is also a potential pattern in manual documentation, it is more clearly evident with computerized documentation. Although software programs usually allow free text entry (narrative notes), many nurses either do not know how to type or do not take the time to create free text entries. This can create frustration for the attorney trying to obtain a clear picture of the patient's status.

- Free text entries are often brief and may not adequately describe an incident or series of events leading up to an emergency. This greatly increases the difficulty in analyzing liability in medical malpractice cases.

Computers may confuse the ability to determine what actually happened before an incident.

In *Jason Peterson and Alicia Peterson, Individually and as Next of Friends of Alyssa Peters, a Minor vs Mckenna Memorial Hospital, Inc. and Dr. Zachary Window,* confusion surrounded the dosage of Pitocin given to a laboring mother. This 2003 Texas case involved Alicia Peterson, who was in labor. Her physician ordered Pitocin to augment labor. The records indicate the Pitocin was doubled and tripled by the nurse in violation of the doctor's orders and that the nurse exceeded the maximum dosage ordered by the physician. The nurse denied violating the doctor's orders and testified she made a computer entry error. She testified she was trying to record an increase of the epidural, not an increase of the Pitocin. The child was born with a broken clavicle, a broken ulna, and Erb's palsy. The verdict was $35,000. The hospital and physi-

cian settled before trial. The award was reduced to $15,000 by credit.[50]

Refer to Figure 7.7 for some questions that may be appropriate when pursuing a case involving electronic medical records. Iyer contains more information on the topic of computerized medical records.[51]

7.11 Guidelines for Charting

Nurses are taught to follow certain key guidelines when documenting on a patient's medical record. The following information provides an overview of these rules. Adherence to these guidelines can make the difference between a defensible and an indefensible case. Readers interested in more information on this subject are referred to Iyer.[52]

A. Labeling Pages

The attorney should look at each page to be sure that the page matches the patient's name when reviewing medical records. Occasionally pages are misfiled and an attorney, legal nurse consultant, or expert witness may find that a page of one patient's medical record has been inserted into another patient's chart. Addressographs or name plates are

---

- How were you taught to use the electronic medical record?
- How much time was devoted to training?
- Who could you go to if you had questions about how to use the software?
- Did you double check the information you entered before you completed your entry?
- What are the safeguards in the system designed to prevent charting or user errors?
- Did you override any safeguards in the system?
- Did you share your password with another individual?
- How often did you change your password?
- Did you leave the information about the patient visible on the computer screen after you left the terminal?
- Did you log off the terminal when you were not using it?
- How often did the electronic health record "go down" or become inaccessible to you?
- How did you handle disposing of printouts of patient information?
- Did you take any patient-specific information home?
- How did you correct an error in data entry?
- What safeguards were in place to protect the electronic information from tampering?
- What did you do to protect the data?
- At what point in time are you required to authenticate an entry?
- Up to what point in time are you able to make changes in a medical record?
- Did you alter the medical record in this case?
- What are your facility's policies regarding maintaining confidentiality of patient data?
- What did you do to follow this policy?
- What are your facility's policies regarding disclosure of patient data?
- In what format is the electronic medical record kept: paper copies, computer CDs, or some other form?

Figure 7.7 Questions of Nurses about Computer Documentation

used to stamp each page of the record. In emergencies, the healthcare professional often will grab a page, handwrite the patient's name on the sheet, and stamp the page later, if at all. Potential for error exists when the nurse documents on a sheet and then stamps it with another patient's name. Take careful note of the flow of information from page to page and from page front to page back. If the medical record page seems to be referring to a totally different person, this might be true. This discrepancy can be effectively called into question in depositions and at trial.

B. Dating, Timing and Signing Entries

Medical records must contain the date on which the entries were made. It can be very difficult to piece together a multi-page flow sheet if the date is not documented on every page. The request for hospital records may specify that critical care flow sheets be provided stapled together as a unit.

Timing can be an important factor in many nursing malpractice suits, as the following case shows.

> The plaintiff's decedent, age 43, went to a hospital in July 2006 for the delivery of her third child. She was at high risk for a ruptured placenta due to placenta accrete. She had been scheduled for a cesarean section delivery. The woman went into labor and underwent a cesarean section delivery followed by a hysterectomy. Complications arose and she died three days later. The plaintiff claimed that the defendant's staff failed to timely perform the hysterectomy. The plaintiff maintained that the plaintiff's risk factors required a hysterectomy tray, blood transfusions and other medical devices be prepared prior to the cesarean section in case a hysterectomy was needed. The plaintiff argued that the hemorrhage occurred almost immediately after delivery, but the hysterectomy was performed about 30 minutes later. The defendant denied any negligence and maintained that the hysterectomy was performed immediately after the cesarean section. The plaintiff and defendant argued over the timing of the hysterectomy based on a nurse's note (there were no times for the procedures in the anesthesiology charts) which had 3:49 P.M. written as the time the hysterectomy ended, which had been crossed out and 3:15 P.M. written above it. According to a published account a $950,000 settlement was reached.[53]

The nurse's name should appear at the end of each chart entry. It will be evident if one chart note covers all or most of a shift because there will be only one signature to document all that happened during that extensive period of time. If the nurse charted at various times during the shift, each entry should have a date, a time, and a signature. This gives any reader of the chart a better understanding of what happened during the shift. Though it was meant to help concurrent and subsequent caregivers, this charting is also invaluable to the attorney who can use it to evaluate the chart, construct a case, and develop a timeline of events.

Entries are signed with the first initial of the nurse's first name, followed by the last name and the nurse's status such as RN, SN, LPN, SPN (student practical nurse), and so on. Nurses are expected to draw a line through any empty space on the line between the end of their charting and the beginning of their signatures to prevent someone else from inserting words into their entry.

When the nurse's charting continues from one page to the next, the nurse signs her name at the bottom of the first page. The top of the next page should be dated, timed and include the words "continued from previous page." If the nurse does not do this, or follows a different method of contiguous charting, the difference should be supported by the facility's documentation policies.

C. Cosigning Notes

Student nurses' notes are frequently cosigned by the instructor. Cosigning implies that the instructor approved the care given, and assumes responsibility for it. See below for an example of the correct identification of a student nurse's entry and the use of lines to fill in blank spaces:

> 11:30 A.M. Back from physical therapy. Complains of weakness and fatigue. P. Watson SN MCC/R. Hill RN-----------

TIP: Cosigning an entry on a medication record means the instructor is accepting the responsibility that the patient received the correct medication.

If an instructor signs an entry without reading it or overlooks a problem the entry raises, he could share liability for any injury that results. Lawsuits in which student nurses are named are rare. However, if a plaintiff initiates a suit against a student, the instructor, school, agency, physician, and other nurses may be included as well.

The recommended procedure for cosigning is as follows: the student writes the note and signs it with the first initial, last name, S.N. for student nurse, and the name of the school. Students should write the initials or abbreviated name of their nursing program, i.e., "MCC" for Mercer County College.

After reading the note and drawing a slash, the instructor signs the note with the first initial, last name, and R.N.

Although student nurses provide nursing care, the healthcare organization's nursing personnel are ultimately responsible for the patient. The fact that a student nurse was assigned to the patient does not absolve the nursing staff from their obligation to document important observations or nursing interventions.

Cosigning also occurs in situations where a nurse is being precepted or mentored by another nurse. This is usually done in situations where the nurse is new to a unit or to a procedure. Mentoring or proctoring co-signatories accept the same responsibility for the nurse's actions as nursing instructors.

D. Using Neat and Legible Handwriting

Illegible and sloppy handwriting can cause confusion, miscommunication, and medical error during the care of a patient. It can be the reason a record finds its way into an attorney's hands. Sloppy, illegible handwriting complicates both plaintiff and defense work. It makes screening of the nursing malpractice case for merit more difficult; and it complicates the defense of the nurse. The challenge of deciphering illegible handwriting is one of the biggest complaints of attorneys who are trying to interpret what could be an essential entry in the medical record. The plaintiff's attorney can request that the nurse transcribe the handwriting once a case is in suit. Some plaintiff's attorneys save this for the deposition of the defendant nurse.

TIP: The plaintiff's attorney should consider enlarging a page containing illegible nurses' notes and using it to cross-examine a nurse defendant on the stand. The attorney can lead the defendant through a cross-examination on the importance of the medical record for communication, and draw out a concession on why handwriting should be clear and legible. Nurses who cannot read their own handwriting are particularly vulnerable to this line of questioning.

E. Using Correct Spelling and Grammar

Progress notes that are filled with misspelled words and incorrect grammar create negative impressions about the nurse's abilities. They imply that the nurse has a limited education or intellect, or is careless and distracted when charting. Spelling and grammatical errors can be enlarged into poster size if they are related to the alleged acts of negligence, and the errors pointed out to the jury. Knowing the educational level of the jurors is important when using this tactic, though.

F. Using Authorized Abbreviations

Abbreviations, acronyms, and symbols have often been the source of confusion and misinterpretation in medical records. At times they lead to medical errors. Some problems have occurred because incorrect interpretation of abbreviations or symbols was fostered by illegible handwriting; other difficulties have arisen when practitioners use abbreviations which are not approved by the facility.

Institutions which are accredited by The Joint Commission (TJC), and many who are not, have been engaged in a process to reduce the number of abbreviations allowed in their organizations. This movement has had strong backing by NAHQ (the National Association of Healthcare Quality), AHRQ (the Agency for Healthcare Research and Quality, U.S. Department of Health and Human Services), as well as many other national organizations devoted to quality improvement and patient safety. One of The Joint Commission's National Patient Safety Goals is to standardize a list of abbreviations, acronyms and symbols which are not to be used in their organization; they have also published an official "Do Not Use" list.[54]

All healthcare and malpractice attorneys should update themselves on this continuing process since the nation's largest healthcare-accrediting organization, multiple national organizations, and the federal government have taken such a strong stand on the issue. (Refer to Chapter 4, *Patient Safety Initiatives*, for additional information.) When case issues involve an abbreviation, acronym, or symbol, the attorney should have no difficulty obtaining the facility's policies on this type of documentation. The healthcare facility's list of approved and unacceptable abbreviations can be obtained through discovery.

This national and institutional focus on abbreviations has not eliminated all incorrect abbreviations, however. Unapproved abbreviations enter the organization when new healthcare personnel come on staff, and during moments of levity or black humor (used to cope with traumatic events). An attorney who has a case involving a misused abbreviation can cite the facility's approved abbreviation list as well as current literature from The Joint Commission and other national organizations whose goal is to improve healthcare quality. There will be a great deal of supportive information to be found at these organizations' websites and in professional journals. All of this information can make a nurse who uses an incorrect or dangerous abbreviation look like she does not keep up with the profession. Employers have a responsibility to update their staff, to ensure that the policies of the facility are revised to conform to TJC National Patient Safety Goals, and to provide education to nursing staff on their important role in ensuring compliance with the Goals.

G. Performing Prompt Charting

Large gaps in documentation times raise the suspicion that information was not promptly charted or that information was left out. Attorneys are often fond of asking nurses if the documentation was done at the time of the events or at the end of the shift. Asking this question can fluster a nursing witness who may have difficulty explaining to a jury how charting gets done on a timely or untimely basis. Nurses know that, although it is sometimes possible to document on the medical record as events occur, more frequently they chart during the middle of the shift, at the end of the shift, or on worksheets as events conclude. Information on the worksheet is later entered into the medical record.

Each healthcare facility should have specific rules for recording information which the nurse has captured over a period of time. An attorney who is reviewing documentation for a case may find that the timeline of events portrayed by the chart does not make sense or does not match the recollections of the initial people interviewed. In these situations, the attorney may wish to obtain the facility's documentation policies for use in deposition of the nurses who did the charting.

TIP: When there is a question about the accuracy of the medical record, the attorney should ask the nurse whether the entry was made at the time given in the time column, or at the end of the shift.

Ask the defendant nurse if a worksheet was used during the course of the shift, and if the nurse saved the worksheet. The worksheet may contain important data that never made its way to the medical record. Nurses also refer to the worksheet as the "cheat sheet" because it is a shorthand notation of the patient's needs and the critical data.

H. Leaving Blanks on Forms

Flow sheets at the patient's bedside make it easier for the nurse to record important information promptly before it is forgotten or overlooked. While providing easy ability to document a large amount of information in one place, flow sheets also have inherent weaknesses. Facilities and nursing departments tend to design flow sheets to accommodate many pieces of data in a small space; unfortunately, the data is often redundant. Thus, a nurse caring for a patient has many small boxes in which to record vital signs, medications, neurological signs, the status of the bed rails (up or down), the status of various alarms (on or off), and so on. Flow sheets of this nature vary from department to department and facility to facility. The almost mindless repetitiveness of completing them does not vary.

Nurses will often look for ways to shortcut the seemingly endless number of empty boxes on a flow sheet. A favorite time saver is filling in one box and then drawing a line through all the other boxes on that line or column for that shift, indicating that all values were the same for each time checked. Attorneys can attack this method of charting by asking directly, at deposition or trial, "Did you check this value each hour (or 15 minute period, as indicated on the flow sheet)?"

Another problem encountered with flow sheets is gaps in charting. Just like nursing progress sheets, where lines must be drawn between the end of charting and the nurse's signature, no empty spaces may be left on a flow sheet. An attorney can question this lack of documentation at deposition and at trial.

Forms are also a popular chart format. Though not as large or as complex as a flow sheet, a form also allows routine documentation to be condensed onto one sheet. Even though they are simpler, forms have all the weaknesses of flow sheets. Nurses are tempted to leave blanks in forms or they may fail to document something that is significant. If there is a blank to be filled in on a chart form, nurses are taught to fill it in, or draw a line through it if it is not applicable. A blank space raises questions that complicate the patient's immediate, and any future, care; however the pace of daily practice may make cutting corners seem attractive. Therefore, the plaintiff's attorney may argue that there was an important observation or element of care that was omitted. The defense attorney may discover in talking with the nurse defendant that the nurse cannot remember why the medical record is incomplete. Blank spaces can have a critical effect on the case. Absence of documentation was an issue in the following Florida case:

In *Susan Meek. v. Southern Baptist Hospital of Florida, Inc. d/b/a Baptist Medical Center,* the 42-year-old plaintiff was admitted to the hospital for a hysterectomy. After surgery she developed bleeding and was taken to the radiology department for uterine artery emoblization to stop the bleeding. The physicians ordered the nurses at the hospital to perform frequent leg examinations to detect possible diminished blood flow and nerve injury, a known complication of the procedure caused by clotting of the external iliac artery due to arterial wall injury. The plaintiff claimed the leg examinations were not performed based on the lack of documentation of the exams. Permanent nerve injury developed after a massive clot in the external iliac artery was removed. A $1.55 million verdict was returned.[55]

I. Adding Late Entries

Few parts of the medical record are scrutinized by attorneys more closely than late entries. Key information is often contained in a late entry. Nurses make late entries when they remember important information that needs to be added to the medical record after documentation has been completed. For example, after completing charting, the nurse may review the entry and realize that something crucial was left out. A late entry also may be written if the patient was out of the nursing unit at the end of the shift, and the documentation cannot be completed until the next day. On rare occasions, the nurse completely overlooks a particular chart and does not realize until the next day that documentation had been omitted.

Late entries are also written when there has been a poor patient outcome and the healthcare professionals are worried about being sued. (This is commonly called "buffing the chart.") It is this type of late entry that is the greatest concern to risk managers and attorneys. These entries are usually recognized with ease because of the length of time between the event and the entry, and because of the tone of the entry itself. Invariably these chart entries are made by a physician or nurse to "explain" what really happened. No matter how sincere the writer is in this effort, the documentation often sounds like an effort at a cover-up.

The practice of leaving blank lines is discouraged. If the need arises to add information to the medical record out of sequence or at a later date than the shift on which the nurse provided care, the nurse is supposed to do the following:

1. Add the entry to the first available line.
2. Identify the time the nurse is making the late entry. Start the entry with the words "Late entry for (date and time)."

Attorneys often ask, "When is a late entry suspect?" The rule of thumb is the sooner the nurse adds a late entry, the better. Figure 7.8 shows a portion of nurses' notes which contains two late entries. It is clear from the sequence of entries that these late entries were written the day of the incident. In this lawsuit the plaintiff was claiming that she asked the nurse for toilet paper. According to the plaintiff the nurse stood in the doorway of the bathroom, said "Here, catch" and tossed her a roll of paper. The plaintiff claims she fell into the tub while trying to catch the paper. The nurses' notes provide a very different description of the fall that led to the fractured arm. The author acted as a defense expert witness in this case. The plaintiff eventually dropped the suit.

Late entries should not be squeezed into an existing note or placed in the margins. Attorneys on both sides of the bar should scrutinize late entries. The plaintiff's attorney may attempt to prove that the nurse tried to alter a record to cover up an error instead of making an addition. Tampering with the medical record is covered in detail later in the chapter.

TIP: Late entries can look self-serving; they often look like they are written in response to fear of liability, particularly when the patient has had a bad outcome. The agency's policies and procedures usually describe the proper way to add information to the record. These policies can be obtained through discovery.

J. Using Ink Colors

In the past many hospitals color-coded charting by using blue (or black), red, and green to denote documentation on the three different nursing shifts. Most institutions have moved to the exclusive use of blue or black ink for documenting on medical records. This switch away from the use of green or red ink has made it easier to decipher a photocopy of the medical record supplied by the hospital. A few institutions still may use a different color, usually red, to chart a specific item; in many cases they use this method to chart a pain medication variation or some other event to which they wish to draw attention. Color variations in the ink still show up poorly in photocopies, even with improved photocopying technology. Color photocopies may be made when the expense is warranted by the details of the case.

TIP: When legibility of the medical record is an issue, ask to see the original. Additions to the record in a different color ink will become obvious when the original is examined. Color photocopies are also effective in revealing these additions.

K. Recording in Military Time

Attorneys will encounter the use of military time in medical records; most healthcare facilities have chosen this style of documentation. Medical records documented in military time eliminate much confusion about the time of day of the events in question and make the development of an event timeline much easier.

L. Documenting Omitted Care or Medications

Facility policies and procedures specify the protocol for documenting omitted medications or treatments. In most cases omitted medications are documented on the medication administration record. This is usually done by drawing a circle around the nurse's initials in the block that corresponds to the omitted dose. The reason for the omission is meant to be written in the nurses' notes. Omitted treatments are supposed to be recorded in the nurses' notes as well.

11/30 7:30 Awake and resting easily in bed. Suture line to left hip dry and intact. No drainage noted.
8:30 Afebrile. V/S stable. breakfast taken fully. Intercath left arm intact. No swelling noted. Voiding qs clear yellow urine.
10:45 Dr. L. vs. Dressing applied (dry) to left hip by Dr. L.
11:00 OOB with walker to bathroom for voiding.
11:05 Pt states she was reaching for toilet paper and slipped and fell. Found pt. on floor in BR lying on left side against tub. Left upper arm appears swollen. Dr. L. present. NPO status now in effect.
12:30 X-ray done. Volpe cast applied to left arm by Dr. L.
1:30 Re-x-ray done. Med for pain with Levo 2 mg SQ with relief.
3 P.M. Brother vs. Hep lock was in right hand. Antibiotics infusing easily. Cast damp and open to air. Fingers cool and mobile. Color good.
Late charting
3:45 Pt advised when OOB to BR to put call light on when wanting assistance. Assisted earlier to BR by G. D. RN, also advised that she use call bell when needing assist. When found on floor lying on left side, floor dry and uncluttered except for walker also lying on left side on floor. Pt seen in BR by Dr. L and then assisted to bed by G.D. and J. S. LPN and Dr. L.————————J.S. LPN
9:30 Late note. Assisted OOB to BR. Ambulated well. Asked if she should put called light on. — told her that she should put the light on for assistance.
9:45 Bathroom call light on. Stated "I was going to get up by myself but I know if I fell you girls would get in trouble." Reminded she was asked to put light on for assistance and should do so to avoid injury. G.D. RN
9:45 Assisted back to bed without difficulty. G.D. RN

Figure 7.8 *Late Entries*

When medications or treatments were omitted because of a busy shift or short staffing, it is likely that there was little time to document the reasons for omissions in the progress notes. Therefore, this information will often be missing. The defense of the nurse is complicated when the reasons for the omissions are not provided; and conversely, plaintiff's counsel can often use the absence of information to their benefit. More information on the documentation issues surrounding medications is presented in Chapter 28, *Medication Errors*, in Volume II.

M. Charting in Blocks

Block charting occurs when the nurse enters a broad time frame in the "time of" column in the nurses' notes, such as "4-6 A.M." or "3 P.M.-11 P.M." This type of charting is disappearing because nurses are instructed to enter accurate times next to their entries, but occasionally a reviewer will find block charting in medical records.

Although it initially seems innocuous, block charting makes it difficult to establish when certain events occurred and permits the plaintiff's attorney to question the nurse about

the exact times that the events occurred. When the nurse has no recollection of the events, a block charting entry provides no help. Defense counsel has little opportunity to prepare the nurse for this questioning in either deposition or at trial.

If the chart does indicate that an event occurred during the block of time, this type of charting usually gives no details as to the sequence of actions. During questioning the plaintiff's counsel is again free to ask the nurse anything about the event and the nurse has little hope of being able to respond with clarity.

N. Identifying Mistaken Entries

Most entries that are marked as an error or mistaken entry are purely innocent mistakes. Nurses may pick up the wrong patient's chart, only to discover they are documenting on the wrong record part of the way through charting. Spelling mistakes or the use of the wrong word are also common errors. In the past, before a lot of attention was paid to this issue, nurses corrected these errors with correction fluid or black markers. As a result of education, most nurses understand the proper way to correct mistaken entries.

It is common practice to remove correction fluid from any areas containing medical records. A director of medical records told one of the authors that a physician asked a medical records clerk for a bottle of correction fluid. The clerk came to her boss to ask where it was kept, and the medical records director was able to thwart the doctor's plan to alter the records. All staff, including unit secretaries, should understand why correction fluid cannot be used on medical records.

TIP: When the attorney is confronted with a medical record containing correction fluid and the obliteration appears in a crucial part of the record, consider having the original page x-rayed. Words covered by correction fluid have been deciphered with x-ray equipment.

Following is the recommended approach taught to nurses for correcting mistaken entries:

1. Draw a single line through the entry so that it is still readable. It should never be crossed off with a heavy marker, heavily scratched out, or covered with correction fluid.
2. Write the word "mistaken entry" above or beside the original words. The use of the word "error" is no longer advised because juries tend to associate the word "error" with a clinical error that affected the patient.
3. Place the date and your initials next to the words "mistaken entry."
4. This process is made easier when the abbreviation "M.E." for "mistaken entry" is added to the list of approved abbreviations in use in the facility.

An alteration should be made only to truthfully document the care provided to the patient or to protect the patient's interests. Changes should not be made purely to justify decisions after the fact or for other "cosmetic" reasons. Generally an appropriate late entry may be made if it is clearly documented that it is a late entry, is dated correctly, can be justified, does not attempt to falsify the record, and is signed by the recorder.[56]

O. Making Inappropriate Comments

When a patient's care is handled by more than one physician, and those physicians are not in agreement on the best way to manage the case, disagreements can surface in the chart's documentation. Similar conflicts between nurses, between hospital units or departments, or between staff and physicians can also be found. Statements are written in different ways in the chart, but they most often take the form of finger pointing and accusations. Some of the notes are written boldly, while others are done in a more subtle fashion. Documentation of this nature is often made in disgust, anger, or exasperation. Three common situations in nursing malpractice cases can give rise to finger pointing by another person:

1. The patient has been injured.
2. The patient could have been injured.
3. The plan of care of the physician's orders has not been carried out and the individual is trying to cover himself.

The mere presence of an inappropriate comment does not mean that the patient has suffered from an injury. Clinical outcomes should be carefully examined to determine if any harm has occurred. Risk managers have spent a great deal of time educating healthcare professionals about the consequences of inappropriate comments and accusations. Aside from memorializing what could be an inaccurate description of the events, finger pointing draws attention to what could be a minor omission with no untoward effects on the patient.

TIP: Evidence of fighting among healthcare professionals facilitates the job of developing a case for the plaintiff's attorney and can create nightmares for the defense. These comments are most likely to appear in the progress notes of the nurses and doctors. Look for accusations of blame after an incident.

P. Describing an Incident

Although the attorney reviewing a chart may know or suspect that an untoward event has happened to the patient, the chart may not give a clear picture of what happened. In fact, it may seem impossible to find evidence that anything out of the ordinary happened at all.

> In *Estate of Gladys Forbis v. Pavilion Health Care Center*, the nursing home resident was suffering from Alzheimer's disease. The cause of her death was asphyxiation from blood which traveled into her lungs from a cut on her lip. There was no direct evidence about precisely how the cut was sustained. Her estate claimed it was the result of trauma, and the plaintiff pathology expert opined that the lip injury was either inflicted or related to the failure to use softer restraints. He doubted the cut was in any way self-inflicted. The plaintiff alleged the nursing home provided substandard care and had treated the decedent with reckless disregard. The defense

pathologist denied the death had been the result of aspiration, whereas another defense expert testified that the resident could have bitten herself. The jury imposed $320,000 for the resident's suffering and punitive damages of $2.2 million.[57]

Absent documentation is one of the biggest sources of frustration for attorneys involved in nursing malpractice cases. The medical record may also contain more than one version of the events in question. To complicate matters, these versions may be incomplete, and the plaintiff may have an entirely different version. A description of the event may be recorded in the following places:

- Nursing progress notes
- Physicians' progress notes written by the house physician or doctor who examined the patient right after the injury
- Attending physician's version in the progress notes
- Operative report if the injury occurred in the operating room (OR) or resulted in a trip to the OR
- The discharge summary
- Logs (OR, labor and delivery)
- Progress notes of ancillary staff (respiratory, physical or occupational therapists)

In an initial review of the medical record, the reviewer should look in all of these places to determine what was written about the incident. Prescriber order sheets and all progress notes should also be read for references made to an event report, situation report, or incident report. Facilities have changed the name of the report which details an unexpected event over the years and, as patient safety and computerized documentation systems are put in place, further name changes have occurred. The chart reviewer must be aware of references which sound like they are referring to an incident report, though the reference may use another name. As discovery progresses, consider interviewing or deposing people with knowledge of the event, which may include the patient, visitors, roommates, physicians, nursing staff and others.

Nurses are instructed to document an incident immediately when details are fresh. The details should include:

- the time of the incident,
- what happened,
- the name of the physician who was notified of the event,
- the physician's response (physician orders given or whether she came to examine the patient),

- follow-up care, and
- the patient's response to the treatment which was ordered.

Nurses are instructed to be very cautious in documenting an incident and not to offer opinions, place blame or make accusations regarding the events associated with the occurrence. In some situations, nurses fail to record the facts of an occurrence in the chart. This is often due to their concern about appropriate documentation of an event and their conclusion that no documentation is better than incorrect documentation, or the conclusion that documenting an event will get them into trouble. Unfortunately, lack of documentation of an event more often than not will look like an attempt to cover up the occurrence to an attorney and, subsequently, to a jury. A random sample of 26 medical residents who were involved in medical errors showed that of 73 cases, only 30 (41.1 percent) formally acknowledged and documented the error in the medical record.[58] Lack of clear cut documentation about an incident also complicates the ability of all parties to figure out what happened; this includes not only the after-the-fact reviewer, but concurrent and subsequent caregivers.

Part of careful screening and review of a nursing malpractice case includes making decisions based on the credibility of the plaintiff as well as the perceived accuracy of the medical record. Always recognize what is at stake when considering the statements of the defendants and the plaintiff. Documentation that is prepared as events are unfolding before the outcome is known is presumed to be more accurate than memories of the event. Sometimes the attorney's intuition or common sense will result in a suspicion that the truth lies somewhere between the defense's and the plaintiff's version of the events.

1. "Incident report filled out"

Details of the incident are to be documented in the medical record with an objective description of the events free of accusations or self blame. Self-blaming statements include words like "I was tired and distracted and therefore...." "The incident report should contain the same details as the medical record does, including a physician's examination of the patient if warranted by the circumstances. Nurses and physicians are instructed not to document that an incident report has been completed. Discoverability of the incident report varies from state to state, though it has become increasingly difficult to protect as a result of changes in state laws and court decisions in a majority of states.

The premises behind not referring to the incident report in the medical record are:

- The opportunity to maintain the confidentiality of the incident report may be lost if the report is mentioned in the medical record or incorporated into the record by reference to it.
- If a plaintiff's attorney sees a reference to an incident report, it will draw attention to an incident that might otherwise be overlooked. For example, the attorney may be investigating a case involving a fractured hip that occurred after a fall from a stretcher. In a separate incident, the patient may have received the wrong medication. The attorney may not be aware that the second incident occurred in the absence of a reference to the incident report that was prepared.

Increasingly, healthcare professionals are recognizing their responsibility to inform the patient and family when an untoward outcome occurs, as is required by Joint Commission standards. As described in Chapter 5, *Medical Errors: Roots of Litigation*, controversy and anxiety surrounds the nature of the disclosure of a potential medical error and the impact on a possible lawsuit. Documentation surrounding the incident becomes part of the evidence of the event. It is recommended that healthcare professionals do the following:

- Describe the event in factual terms.
- Avoid using the medical record as an emotional catharsis.
- Record only known facts, avoiding speculation.
- Avoid recording opinions that a particular event caused a specific result.
- Describe any discussions held with the patient or family.
- Record the facts of the discussion—who was there, when it was held, the facts that were presented.
- Avoid documenting opinions and suppositions.
- Note the next steps to be taken.[59]

One of the best approaches for analyzing incidents involves careful reading of the nurses' notes and physician's progress notes. Descriptions of incidents involving wrong treatments, injuries, omissions of medication or care, and so on, need to be detected early in the litigation process. The plaintiff's attorney may want to build these incidents into a theory that there is a pattern of substandard care. The defense attorney will need to consult with experts to evaluate the potential clinical effect of additional incident(s) on the patient. With this information, the attorney will be prepared to refute the plaintiff's claims that the incident affected the patient.

2. Obtaining the incident report

It is often far easier to obtain a medical record than it is to get a copy of an incident report, unless the defense attorney is the person requesting the document. In an attempt to keep an incident report confidential, the hospital may identify it as a work-product document prepared in anticipation of litigation, or as a privileged quality improvement document. The hospital's policy and procedure manual may contain a document that describes the types of situations which warrant the completion of an incident report. Many policies simply describe a need for an incident or event report whenever something happens which is not consistent with the routine or usual operation of the hospital. Some hospitals require that a report be created when an incident results in harm to another person or when a "near miss" occurs. A near miss is an incident having the potential for creating harm to another person. A near miss can also be used to recognize the need to change an aspect of patient care or a system to avoid repetition of the circumstances that almost harmed a person.

The plaintiff's attorney may wish to inquire about how the incident report is handled within the hospital. As one nurse attorney said, "I always ask about the incident report, review the policy and procedure and review how the report itself was treated:

1. Was it left at the nurses' station for all to read?
2. Was it discussed with or shown to independent contractor physicians?
3. Was it left in an in-box that is nailed to a door in a hallway?
4. Was it discussed with others not involved in the incident?
5. Was it not labeled as a confidential document?
6. Are there triplicates, but no one knows where the other copies are, or are they not locked up?"[60]

If, indeed, the incident report has been treated in this fashion, then the attorney can make a strong case for its easy release through discovery. A truly confidential document must be treated as such by the institution well before a plaintiff's attorney requests it.

Q. Charting Care Given by Others

Nurses are obligated to describe the care that they have given or supervised. This makes the licensed nurse responsible for documenting the care provided by unlicensed assistive personnel (UAP). In some settings the UAP are allowed to document on flow sheets. For example, in a long-term-care facility the UAP may document the type of bath that was given and the activity of the patient (out of bed, bed rest, etc.).

The medical record may not include the names of the UAP who gave the patient care, and documentation rules may not require that they do so. However, when a specific occurrence happens and a UAP has reported facts to the nurse, it is appropriate that the nurse record the UAP's name in the patient's record as the source of the information. When this information is not present in the chart it may be difficult to obtain after the fact.

Staffing sheets maintained by the hospital or nursing home will list the names of the personnel assigned to work in a specific unit for the day in question. Assignment sheets indicating which personnel were assigned to a particular patient are usually not retained. In fact, in some units the assignments are written on blackboards or are posted using magnetic name tags. In these settings, there is no retrievable record of the patient care assignment.

TIP: When interviewing or deposing a nurse defendant, ask if a nursing assistant was involved in providing care to the patient. The nurse's documentation may include any unlicensed person's observations that the nurse may not have witnessed.

R. Revealing Bias in Documentation

Sooner or later every plaintiff's attorney who screens nursing malpractice cases will hear complaints about the way the nurses interacted with the patient or family. Sometimes these complaints are based on unrealistic expectations about the level of nursing care that can be provided. However, antagonism can and does develop between nurses and patients and their families. Look for evidence of this antagonism revealed in nursing documentation.

TIP: Words that reveal negative attitudes toward the patient include: complainer, abusive, drunk, lazy, spoiled, problem patient, demanding, obnoxious, nasty, and disagreeable. If a jury reads progress notes with these types of words, they may infer the patient received substandard care because the nurses disliked the patient.

Nurses are supposed to describe the patient's behavior objectively. For example, instead of charting that the patient was obnoxious, the nurse would describe the specific behavior of the patient, such as swearing, verbally abusive, or demanding constant attention. The attorney reviewer should carefully evaluate the effect of documentation which reveals antagonism between the patient and the nurses. This could be a significant factor in the resolution of the case.

S. Communicating with the Physician

The care of a patient depends on clear communication, both verbal and written. Errors can happen when that communication fails in any way. As discussed in Chapter 1, *The Roots of Patient Injury*, miscommunication is the most frequent cause of sentinel events. Many of the cases included in the clinical chapters of this text refer to liability situations in which the communication between the nurse and the physician is the center of the problem. The nurse is expected to monitor the patient's condition and notify the patient's physician of pertinent information, using judgment about when and what to communicate. Depending on the situation, communication may be in person, by phone, or through documentation. Urgent situations require notification in person or by phone.[61] Frequently, nursing malpractice cases deal with what the physician was told about the patient's condition, particularly when deterioration results in a poor outcome for the patient. The nursing malpractice case may hinge on this point. Issues include:

- Should the nurse have called the doctor and was the call made?
- What did the nurse say?
- What time was the call made?
- What should the nurse have done next?

1. Should the nurse have called the physician and was the call made?

The role of the professional nurse includes communication of important findings to the physician. A multiplicity of factors complicates this simple statement. The factors that influence this phone call include:

- Does the nurse have the critical thinking skills to recognize that a call should be made?
- Does the nurse personally make the call or does the nurse ask a nurse manager to call?
- Does the physician receive the message that the nurse called?
- Is accurate information conveyed to the physician?

The plaintiff was diagnosed in 1990 at the age of four months with hydrocephalus. A shunt was installed for drainage of excess cerebrospinal fluid. The plaintiff experienced recurrent infections, obstructions and other malfunctions which required 30 surgeries for shunt replacement or revision. The plaintiff was admitted to Primary Children's Medical Center in March 2005 at the age of 15 for another such procedure. The plaintiff claimed that nurses ignored excessively high pressure readings during this stay and failed to contact physicians when the pressure exceeded 20 mm Hg for more than five minutes. The plaintiffs claimed that the plaintiff's pressures spiked for three days, then remained high for the next two days, finally rising to 140 and spiking as high as 165. The plaintiff ultimately became unresponsive and curled into a fetal position before going into respiratory arrest. Doctors responded at this time and immediately opened valves to allow pressures to return to normal levels. The plaintiff very quickly became responsive. The plaintiff suffered brain damage causing memory loss, with a marked decline in short term memory, depression, emotional distress, decreased physical abilities and cognitive and social disabilities. The plaintiff will need lifetime assistance and medical care. The defendants admitted that an acute injury occurred at the time of this hospitalization, but claimed that later incidents caused most of the plaintiff's problems.[62]

This case illustrates the importance of not only documenting abnormal findings, but in communicating these findings to the physician, and documenting that communication. The nurse's role as a patient advocate provides support for the responsibility to contact the physician with this information.

2. What did the nurse say?

Nurses are taught to document, with as much detail as possible, what they told the physician about the patient. The nurse also needs to make sure that the documentation is clearly written because detail alone does not always explain what happened. It is important that nurses read their own charting to make sure it makes sense and is inclusive. Failure to document the phone call or notification to the physician opens the nurse to the accusation that the physician was not informed.

TIP: Carefully note an entry written after a nurse calls a physician about the patient. The words "physician called" are used in two confusing contexts. This could mean that the nurse called the doctor, or the doctor called the nurse. It could be a critical distinction in a specific case. Note the symptoms that the nurse conveyed to the doctor. Nurses often tell the doctor more than they document, while all the chart reflects is a vague phrase "physician updated on patient's condition."

---

3. What time was the call or notification made?

Nurses are instructed to document on the clinical record the time of a phone call or that they informed a physician of a change in the patient's condition or a critical abnormal laboratory value. This documentation must be very specific and very clear.

In a Michigan case, a 48-year-old man was admitted to the defendant hospital with a diagnosis of acute diverticulitis. His condition deteriorated after admission, with the development of high temperature, respiratory rate, and pulse rate, combined with low blood pressure. The plaintiff claimed that a nurse at the defendant hospital had called the defendant physician at 2:30 A.M. on the day after the decedent's admission. The original nursing notes—which the plaintiff alleged would have documented this call—were missing from the chart. The defendant physician testified that no phone call was ever placed to him and that if the information regarding the decedent's condition had been provided to him (as the nurse clearly testified it was), the defendant doctor would have been able to prevent the patient's death. The nurse testified that she did telephone the physician to provide pertinent information concerning the patient's condition. She testified that the doctor's reply was that he would be in during the morning hours to see the patient. The decedent's condition continued to deteriorate. Surgery was not performed until 11 A.M., revealing an obstruction of the sigmoid colon, with infarction during surgery. The patient died the next day. The case settled for policy limits for the defendant hospital and defendant physician for $2.2 million.[63]

4. What should the nurse have done next?

If the situation warrants further action, the nurse uses the chain of command to resolve the concern. In the Michigan case described above, it must be asked what the nurse should have done when the patient's condition continued to deteriorate and it was obvious that the physician was not going to come to the hospital. The nursing supervisor and chairman of the surgery department were appropriate people to address this problem. The role of the nurse as a patient advocate is clearly defined in the ethical responsibilities of the nursing profession. This was concretely demonstrated in the *Darling v. Charleston Community Memorial Hospital*, 33 Ill.2d 326, 211 N.E.2d 253, 14 A.3d 860 (1965), in which a young man developed a foul smell under the cast on his leg. The physician did not respond to the nurse's concerns about the patient's condition. The young man ultimately lost his leg, and the nurses were held liable for not pursuing the issue beyond the patient's physician.

Each facility should have a chain of command policy; this can usually be found in the nursing department's policy and procedure manual. This policy should describe alternative approaches to be taken when normal processes used to report patient problems do not result in appropriate response to patient care concerns. These alternative approaches should take into account times when the physician is unresponsive and times when the nursing manager is unresponsive. Unresponsiveness to patient issues challenges a nurse's ability to think critically and document it well. When the chain of command is used, the nurse should document the names of the individuals that were notified of the concerns.

TIP: If the nurse documents "nurse manager informed" or "supervisor notified" without identifying the name of the individual, request the staffing sheets for that day. The names of the managers can usually be determined through the staffing sheets. These individuals may carry some liability depending on the circumstances of the case.

---

5. Communication with the physician and proximate cause

Though a patient suffers an untoward outcome, and the nurse may have failed to communicate important information to the physician, the nurse may not necessarily be found liable for the patient's outcome. The plaintiff must prove that this breach of duty by the nurse was the proximate cause of the patient's injuries. The intervening negligence of the physician may have been responsible for the injuries. In these types of cases plaintiff's attorneys frequently name the nurse and the physician and let the defendants point fingers at each other. Failure to name all of the potential defendants allows the defense to point to the empty chair that should have been occupied by one of the parties involved in the incident. A defense that is often effectively used is to assert that even if the nurse had informed the physician of the findings, the doctor would not have done anything differently.

T. Documenting Exact Quotes

Carefully review medical records containing quotations from the patient or physician. Nurses are taught to document exact quotes, particularly when those quotes contain highly significant information. When patients are verbally abusive, however, the nurse is taught not to use specific quotes using that language. Exact quotes contain a high degree of cred-

ibility and are usually of great help to both plaintiff and defense reviewers.

On occasion, physicians respond inappropriately to nurses' concerns and make flippant or exasperated responses. Although nurses are supposed to document that they informed the doctor of the patient's condition (including the specific symptoms) and did not receive any new orders, occasionally nurses document the verbatim response of the doctor. Particularly damning comments such as "Do not call me again" or "Do not bother me with this again" can be potent weapons in a malpractice case. These quotes are forms of inappropriate comments in the chart.

U. Taking Telephone and Verbal Orders

Misunderstandings or documentation of wrong orders are prevalent when orders are received verbally or by phone. Background noise, accents, and distractions may result in misunderstanding the order. Another risk with phone orders is that the physician may misdiagnose the problem and provide inappropriate orders. This is an even greater problem when the physician has signed out to a covering physician who does not know the patient. Writing a verbal or telephone order on a piece of paper other than a chart form may result in the need for others to decipher the document. There is a risk of a transcription error occurring as a result.

In hospitals, physicians are expected to verify the accuracy of a telephone or verbal order, sometimes within 24 hours. In nursing homes, a telephone order may be recorded on a chart form, photocopied, and mailed to the physician for cosignature. Unfortunately, because of misunderstandings, the order may differ from the order that was given; and, by the time the physician receives it, the order has already been transcribed and implemented. Also, the clinician may not recall the order several days later. A study of seven 99-bed skilled nursing facilities in Southern California concluded that there was an error rate of 6.1 per 1000 telephone orders. In all cases, the order error was not identified in routine physician phone order review when the clinician had an opportunity to compare the transmitted order with his memory of the actual order.[64]

Most agencies attempt to discourage verbal orders in circumstances other than emergencies. Every facility should have well-known and enforced policies that specify the criteria for dictating and accepting verbal and phone orders. The Joint Commission brought this issue to the forefront when it was included as one of the 2004 Patient Safety Goals. The Joint Commission's second Patient Safety Goal emphasizes their commitment to improve the effectiveness of communication among caregivers. Accredited facilities must implement a process for taking verbal or telephone orders that require a verification "read-back" of the complete order by the person receiving the order. Simply repeating back the order is not sufficient. Whenever possible, the receiver of the order should write down the complete order on an order sheet or enter it into a computer, then read it back, and receive confirmation from the individual who gave the order. This goal applies to all verbal and telephone orders. It also applies to reading back critical test values that are reported verbally or by telephone to a nurse, unit secretary, or physician in an institutional setting. Critical test results are defined by the healthcare organization and typically include "stat" tests, "panic value" reports, and other diagnostic test results that require urgent response.[65]

Voicemail orders at home care agencies are not acceptable within the context of this Patient Safety Goal. Most state laws require nurses and pharmacists to obtain the order directly from the prescriber or her agent. When not received directly, the nurse or pharmacist must call the prescriber back to get the order directly, including a "read-back." Patients or their family members are not considered physicians' agents, nor are they qualified by law and regulation in most (if not all) states to receive orders for care. If this is legally permissible in a particular venue, then a "read-back" of any verbal or telephone order should be carried out, and the family member would have to be trained to do this.[66]

V. Transcribing Orders

Accurate transcription of orders is essential. Although unit secretaries may transcribe orders, the registered nurse has ultimate responsibility for the accuracy of transcription. It is a common practice to check off each order as it is processed or to document a number next to the order as assigned by the computer. In a manual medical record system, the nurse draws a bracket alongside the orders, and beneath the last order writes the date and time, and signs the nurse's name. This indicates that all orders within that bracket have been transcribed. In some facilities, one shift (usually the night shift) is responsible for checking all charts to be sure that there are no overlooked orders written in the last 24 hours. This may be noted as "24 hour check" on the order sheet.[67] Medical errors may occur when an order is transcribed inaccurately or overlooked.

W. Providing Telephone Triage and Advice

Nurses and physicians are often put in the position of answering questions from family and patients over the phone. Calls come into medical offices, clinics, emergency departments, and other settings. The chief components that need to be documented in these circumstances include:

- date and time of the call;
- caller's name;
- caller's request or chief complaint;
- advice the healthcare professional gave;
- protocol that was followed (if any);
- other caregivers that were notified; and
- the name of the person who took the call.[68]

X. Documenting Allergies

Facility policy usually defines how allergy information is documented. Commonly used facility records for documenting allergies are the emergency department triage record, physician's history, nursing admission assessment, medication administration record, front of the patient's chart and sometimes the top or bottom of every physician order sheet. Facilities with computerized medical records may have a warning system to flag an order which is contrary to a known allergy.[69]

7.12 Tampering with Medical Records

Whenever attorneys review medical records they should be alert to signs of tampering with the record. The true incidence of tampering with the record will never be known. Healthcare professionals have tampered with medical records in a number of ways. Tampering with the record involves any of the following:

1. Adding to the existing record at a later date without indicating the addition is a late entry
2. Placing inaccurate information into the record
3. Omitting significant facts
4. Dating a record to make it appear as if it were written at an earlier time
5. Rewriting or altering the record
6. Destroying records
7. Adding to someone else's notes

Medical records departments often alert their risk managers when a record request comes from a plaintiff's attorney's office. The risk manager may then make the decision to have the record sequestered in anticipation of possible future legal action. Sequestering the record is not designed to impede the facility's response to a record request. It is done to protect the integrity of the record and to assure that no part of the record is lost or destroyed. Without sequestration, healthcare professionals involved in the care of the patient may be informed of a request and take an opportunity to review the medical record without supervision. Some professionals have yielded to the temptation to embellish or otherwise alter the medical record. Changes that are made in a medical record before it is supplied to the client or attorney may require the services of a forensic documentation specialist. These specialists are able to test inks and writing styles to determine if an alteration has been made; in many cases they are able to determine some or all of the original charting.

In suspected tampering situations where the patient is still in the hospital, the medical records department and the risk manager may copy the chart every 24 hours and keep those copies under lock and key. In this way, a running record is kept; this record is hopefully as comprehensive and tamper-free as possible.

TIP: If the patient has obtained a portion or all of the medical record for the plaintiff's attorney, it is also wise for the plaintiff's attorney to request a copy from the hospital. Compare the patient's copy of the record with that supplied by the hospital to see if there are any changes or omissions in the record

---

A. Effect on the Case

Showing that records were tampered with will increase the case value, help prove the attorney's due diligence, and prevent witnesses from committing perjury.[70] Proof that a healthcare professional has altered or falsified medical records is the holy grail of discovery. Such evidence will normally be decisive and nullify an otherwise strong defense. The changing of a record may require defense counsel to settle the case out of court even if no negligence has occurred. Once the accuracy of the record is challenged, the integrity of the entire record becomes suspect. Rubin[71] notes that in virtually all cases, the imagination of the jury will be significantly worse than whatever was contained in the destroyed record.

Plaintiff's attorneys who have successfully proven that tampering has occurred have had some success in getting the statute of limitations extended based on the premise that fraud has been committed. When records are destroyed, the plaintiff's attorney can request sanctions against the defendants for failure to comply with the orders to produce documents. The plaintiff's attorney can argue in court that the records were intentionally altered or lost because of conspiracy or fraud.

TIP: Successful arguing of "aggravated or outrageous conduct" can result in the granting of punitive damages.

If the plaintiff can show that a defendant is guilty of spoliation of evidence, the burden of proof may shift to the defendant. When medical records are missing for unexplained reasons, a plaintiff is at a disadvantage in the legal process and should not be prejudiced because of the missing records.[72]

A Texas case resulting in an extraordinary verdict included the failure of the defendant to produce documents.

> In *Cecil Fuqua, as Executor of the Estate of Wyvonne Fuqua, Deceased, v. Horizon/CMS Healthcare Corporation f/k/a/ Horizon Healthcare Corporation*, a Texas nursing home was sued for the care provided to a woman who developed multiple adverse changes in her physical status, which the plaintiffs alleged were the direct result of negligence. The resident developed malnutrition, dehydration, contractures and 16 pressure ulcers (five of which deteriorated to stage IV). The defendant failed to produce subpoenaed documents. The jury returned a unanimous plaintiff verdict, and awarded $2,710,000 for pain and suffering, impairment, disfigurement, and mental anguish of the decedent in the two and one half years of care before her death. They additionally awarded $310,000,000 in punitive damages.[73]

B. Jury Charge

Many states recognize that juries may infer that a defendant was trying to avoid liability by altering or destroying evidence. That a jury may infer either criminal guilt or civil liability from the destruction or suppression of evidence is well-established. *Omnia praesumuntur contra spoliatorem: All things are presumed against the despoiler or wrongdoer.*[74]

In most states, if there is evidence of alteration or falsification of medical records, the judge will instruct the jury they can infer from the altered record that the healthcare provider knew he was at fault. For example, in New Jersey, jurors receive the following instruction:

> Physicians have a duty to ensure that all treatment records accurately reflect the treatment or services rendered. Corrections or changes to entries may be made only where the change is clearly identified as such, dated and initialed by the person making the change. In fact, it is against the law in this State to alter medical records with the intent to deceive or mislead anyone. In this case you have heard evidence that Dr. [insert the doctor's name] altered his records in the following manner: [here describe the actions]. The alteration of medical records is ad-

missible as evidence of a defendant's own belief that the actual records do not support his defense. If you find that Dr. [insert the doctor's name] altered the medical records with the intent to deceive or mislead anyone, you may infer that the alteration of the records in this case occurred because Dr. [insert the doctor's name] believed that the original record would have been unfavorable in the trial of this matter.[75]

Juries tend to believe what they see in black and white. Written or typed words about a patient's medical history, chief complaints, examinations, and treatment often make or break a case.[76] Preserving evidence provides each party with an opportunity for a fair trial. Juries respond unfavorably to people who lie or cheat in connection with a criminal or civil matter. This is exactly the type of misconduct the spoliation inference brings into a case. An appropriate jury charge tells the jurors that they are fully able to consider the spoliator's misconduct when deciding liability.[77]

C. Effect on the Healthcare Provider

1. Insurance coverage

A medical malpractice claim that includes an allegation of alteration of records may not be covered by a commercial professional or individual's liability policy. The insurer may reserve its rights to not pay any judgment that might be entered against the provider. Institutional providers participating in self-insured trusts may have similar coverage limitations. Some states recognize a separate cause of action for alteration of medical records, whereas other states deal with it as a jury charge. If the provider admits that he made the alteration, the policy may be completely voided, including coverage for medical negligence, depending on that state's law. The provider may find the carrier refusing to renew the policy the following year after the insured was found to have altered records, or on whose behalf a settlement was paid in a case involving alleged alterations.[78]

2. Regulatory agencies and privileges

Some state regulatory or licensing boards may investigate the healthcare provider; and, in the wake of record alterations, disciplinary action may follow. The healthcare system that has provided privileges to the healthcare provider may be reluctant to allow that individual to continue on the staff.[79] Those who falsify medical records risk more than just the loss of a malpractice case. Medical boards have been known to suspend or revoke the licenses of healthcare professionals caught tampering with records, for example,

In re Jascalevich License Revocation, 182 *N.J. Super.* 455 (App.Div. 1982).

3. Criminal/civil offenses

In many states, falsification of medical records is also a criminal offense punishable by fines and incarceration, for example, *California Penal Code* section 471.5. The Health Insurance Portability and Accountability Act was used to put a nurse in prison.

A former nurse was the first in her profession nationwide to go to prison for falsifying medical records, an act which contributed to the death of an 84-year-old nursing home resident. The LPN was sentenced to 10 to 16 months in federal prison, and surrendered her nursing license. The LPN received a verbal order to reduce the resident's anticoagulant (increases clotting time) medication. A short time thereafter, the resident's condition worsened, and the LPN realized that she failed to transcribe accurately the order to reduce the anticoagulant medication. The LPN then falsified the resident's medical record to indicate that the physician's order had been implemented correctly. It was this falsification of the medical record, not the initial error itself, which formed the basis for the criminal charges. The law used by the federal prosecutor to prosecute the LPN had never been utilized in this way before. The federal law was incorporated into the 1996 Health Insurance Portability and Accountability Act (HIPAA) and precludes the making of "false statements" in a matter involving a federal healthcare benefit program. The healthcare benefit programs that are usually involved are the federal Medicare and Medicaid programs. Attorney Prosecutor David Hoffman admitted that he had chosen this case to make a statement regarding what he perceived to be a significant problem. He maintained that medical records are "routinely falsified" and that if such falsifications are prosecuted as federal offenses, it will deter such behavior. Attorney Hoffman said that the nurse took advantage of a defenseless victim and the government needed to send a message that such behavior will not be tolerated. "It is a betrayal of trust that thousands of elderly people in nursing homes throughout the country rely on. It is not OK to document care that was not provided." The LPN cared for two adopted teenage sons and a two-year-old daughter. She had just divorced her husband around the time she falsified the records. Job-related stress was difficult due to understaffing at the nursing home, said her sister. Although her family begged the judge not to send the LPN to jail, some violations of HIPAA result in a mandatory prison term, leaving the judge no choice. The case was decided in November 2001.[80]

In a second Pennsylvania case, the head of a now-defunct nursing home was indicted on federal fraud charges. The indictment followed the death of a woman who wandered outside in the cold and was locked out in 40-degree temperatures. Fraud charges were added to involuntary manslaughter charges. According to the indictment, the administrator and nursing home altered nurses' notes to hide bruises and sores, forged doctor's signatures on medical records, altered doctors' orders and did not hire enough employees. The federal prosecutors also claim the facility defrauded Medicare and Medicaid from 1999 to 2003 by forging records and inflating care. The administrator was also accused of skimming money by having the nursing home make payments to three nonprofit organizations she ran. The supervisor is awaiting trial on perjury, conspiracy, and tampering with evidence charges. Investigators believed that the resident walked out a door that was propped open or one where the alarm was deactivated so workers could go outside to smoke. The prosecutors claim that the administrator ordered the supervisor to have the resident's body carried back inside the home and to alter records to make it appear as if the resident died in her sleep. The attorney for the nursing home and administrator argued that they should not be held responsible for the resident's death because there was no way to know she would wander outside.[81]

D. Detection of Tampering

Fraudulent addition to a record for the purposes of covering up an incident can be detected by current technology. Expert document examiners have many sophisticated techniques to detect altered records. Some of these methods include chemical analysis, ultraviolet and infrared examination, spectrophotometry, and chromatography. They can date ink samples the size of a pinprick. Many manufacturers change the composition of the ink in pens and typewriter ribbons at the beginning of each year, permitting the dating of entries.[82]

Ideally, the forensic documents examiner will use the original of the disputed, or questioned, document. Even a very good quality photocopy will not reveal as much detail about the ink (or pencil) lines in the writing as will the original. Having the original will allow microscopic examination of the ink line morphology. This allows the examiner to observe any striations in the ink line. Striations are caused by uneven deposition of ink by a ball point pen, resulting in either un-inked or very lightly inked lines that run through the ink line. These are useful in determining the direction of rotation of the ball in the pen, which, in turn, allows the examiner to determine exactly how a letter was formed. There is other important information in an original document that will not be reproduced in a photocopy. For instance, variations in pen pressure will sometimes not be evident in a copy. The nature of line endings, whether tapered or blunt, may also be concealed by the photocopying process. These characteristics can be clear indications of tracings or simulations, so the inability to observe them will limit the strength of any opinion which can be reached. If the original is not available or does not exist, the best quality photocopy available should be submitted. A facsimile copy displays even lower resolution than most photocopies. Facsimile copies should be used only as a last resort if no originals or quality photocopies are available. Finally, lack of original documents totally prevents some examinations, such as ink comparisons and the visualization of indentations in the paper.[83]

The following are clues used to detect altered records:

1. Chart entries crowded around existing documentation
2. Changes in slant, pressure, uniformity or other variations in handwriting
3. Erasure or obliteration; smeared spots on document
4. Use of different pens or typewriters to write one entry
5. Misaligned typed notation
6. Impressions or lack of impressions from writing instruments on the following pages
7. Ink offsets or lack of offsets on the back side of the preceding page
8. Additions on different dates written in the same ink, while original entries were written in different ink[84]

A legal nurse consultant is an invaluable resource to the attorney who suspects tampering with medical records. Nurses are familiar with the information that should be recorded in the medical record and can quickly spot missing pieces, information out of order and inconsistencies in the medical record. For example, one hospital was asked to produce the medical record for a six-month admission. The patient was in an intensive care unit for several months. The hospital's medical records department failed to copy a few pages of the multipage critical care flow sheet that covered the first 24 hours after the patient was brought into the ICU. This time frame was critical to the case. The legal nurse consultant spotted the omission because she was familiar with the information that should have been on the flow sheet and recognized that two shifts' worth of documentation was not copied.

E. Types of Tampering

1. Adding to an existing record at a later date

In reviewing medical records the attorney may find incomplete records. One of the roles of the medical records department (now often called the Healthcare Information Department) is to review the chart at the time the patient is discharged and to ask the physician to complete the chart. The doctor may be asked to sign telephone orders, dictate operative reports and discharge summaries, and so on. This job is supposed to be completed within a specified time, usually 30 days after the patient has been discharged. Nurses are not usually asked to go through a medical record after the patient is discharged to "finish off" the chart.

As noted earlier, many hospital risk managers attempt to prevent tampering by securing the medical record after a patient has sustained an adverse outcome. The record may be locked in the risk manager's office. If this first line of defense fails (because there is no risk manager or the risk manager is unaware of the patient's circumstances) and the defendant physician is allowed to review the record, the temptation is high to alter the medical record.

TIP: The attorney should be alert to the possibility that the defendant may have attempted to add or actually added information to the medical record upon becoming aware of a potential malpractice suit. Some healthcare providers become panic stricken when notified of an impending lawsuit and are tempted to review the medical record for completeness. They may be unaware that by the time they realize a suit has been filed the plaintiff's attorney has a copy of the record. Defense attorneys should consider this possibility when questioning their clients since the plaintiff's attorney is likely to explore this possibility during the defendant's deposition, particularly if there is anything suspect about the medical record.

Healthcare professionals are taught that the correct way to add to an existing record is to document the time and date that the addition is being made. The addition should not be squeezed into an earlier entry but should appear on the next available line in the medical entry. This is known as a late entry as discussed above.

The plaintiff, age 22, had sickle cell trait and became pregnant. After delivery of her child she suffered a precipitous drop in blood pressure. She was initially given phenylephrine. The blood pressure rose, but then dropped quickly again with the blood pressure being as low as 94/17. When the second drop occurred no action was taken for nearly 30 minutes. After her discharge from recovery it was discovered that she was unable to move her legs. She continues to be paraplegic. During discovery the plaintiff learned that a note had been added by a nurse at a later time indicating that she had received approval to transfer the patient from another nurse who received approval from the anesthesiologist. This was vigorously disputed by the second nurse and the anesthesiologist. A third party claim was filed by the hospital against the nurse and her employer. The plaintiff claimed that the most likely cause of the paralysis was a drop in blood flow and proper perfusion in the area of the artery of Adamkiewicz, causing a sludging and subsequent paralysis. According to a published account a confidential settlement was reached.[85]

2. Placing inaccurate information into the record

False information in a medical record can sometimes be hard to detect after the fact. At times common sense or the clinical knowledge of a legal nurse consultant or expert witness will lead to the suspicion that the documentation is not entirely truthful. At other times, the plaintiff will convincingly assert that the information is inaccurate.

The plaintiff's decedent, age 65, was admitted to the defendant facility after knee surgery in October 2007. The decedent had a history of blood clots in her lungs and was taking the anticoagulant Coumadin. Blood work done a week after her admission showed her clotting factor to be dangerously high and a nurse who received the test results did not forward them to the physician. The medical records indicate that the results had been given to the physician, but the plaintiff claimed that the nurse altered the records. The decedent died two days later. According to a published account a $900,000 settlement was reached.[86]

3. Omitting significant information

The deliberate omission of significant information may be more difficult to detect. Omission of information was at one time very difficult to identify, but currently has become easier due to changes in documentation styles and changes in regulations by The Joint Commission and CMS (Centers for Medicare and Medicaid Services). As an example, charts now use forms and flow sheets more frequently. The omission of information from a flow sheet or a nursing form may be easy to spot. For example, some neonatal and pediatric flow sheets are set up with blanks to be filled in every hour to indicate that an intravenous site was examined for signs of infiltration. A flow sheet of this nature would be an important piece of evidence in a case involving a child with an intravenous-associated injury.

The Joint Commission and CMS have set goals and regulations for hospitals and long-term care facilities to clearly and accurately record patient complaints of pain, the medications given for that pain, and the relief (if any) the patients experienced. Omission of any of that information is usually simply an error in documentation, but could also be deliberate.

Common sense is often applied to identify the information that is missing. In the following case, common sense was used to identify missing information:

A New Jersey nursing home resident had a significant risk for falls. During a visit by his son, his son noticed that he was in severe pain. The son reported his father's pain to a nurse and a nursing home supervisor subsequently told the son that the decedent had fallen the day before. The incident went unreported. The decedent was diagnosed with a left hip fracture which required surgery. The plaintiff alleged negligence in monitoring the decedent and failure to adequately restrain him in bed. The plaintiff also alleged negligence in failing to chart the fall. The defendant argued that the decedent was in good condition after the fall and that no charting was necessary under the facility's protocol, which called for charting only when a patient's condition changed. An $80,000 settlement was reached.[87]

4. Dating a record to make it appear as if it had been written at an earlier time

Many people involved in malpractice litigation recognize that more tampering occurs in doctor's office records than in the hospital, where it is easier to spot an alteration. The following describes clues used by attorneys and expert document examiners to detect fraudulent dating of records:

1. Unnatural order of writing and uniformity of handwriting, ink margins, and spacing
2. Intersecting fountain pen entries of different dates that bleed together
3. Differences between pages as to folds, stains, offsets, impressions, holes, tears, and type of paper used
4. Use of forms not approved or adopted at the purported time of entry
5. Use of later year (1995 for 1994), especially if it has been corrected several times[88]

5. Rewriting the record

One of the most damaging admissions occurs when a healthcare professional testifies that a medical record was rewritten. There can be completely innocent reasons why a medical record was rewritten. Occasionally a page from a chart will be recopied if it is torn or liquid is spilled on it. The appropriate procedure to follow when this occurs is to identify the page as rewritten. The original page should be retained in the medical record. The deliberate rewriting of a record with attendant changes in the content, timing, and sequence of events is tampering with the record.

In a Utah case involving an infant diagnosed with an anoxic brain injury, the plaintiff claimed the hospital failed to properly activate the hospital's emergency call system and failed to have proper resuscitation equipment available. One of the nurses had allegedly prepared a signed flow sheet showing the arrival time of the physicians. Another unsigned flow sheet showed the arrival time of these doctors to be several minutes sooner. The nurse who prepared the flow sheets was medically unable to be deposed. The jury returned an $892,214 verdict.[89]

Defendants should be carefully questioned when rewriting of the medical record is suspected. This issue can have a major effect on a case.

6. Destroying medical records

The destruction of pages, sections or an entire medical record creates a strong suspicion that the information in the record was so damaging that it had to be concealed. Medical records are usually carefully safeguarded by the medical records department of a healthcare institution as well as by the risk manager when an untoward event has occurred.

When a record, or pages of it, disappear(s), part of the discovery process involves determining who had access to the record. Missing records are always difficult to explain and in most cases the mystery is never completely solved. As discussed earlier, the missing records negatively affect both plaintiff and defense attorneys.

In a New York case, a laboring mother was monitored in labor and delivery by nurses and a resident. Shortly after birth, the infant was diagnosed with cerebral infarctions which caused mild, partial paralysis. The child also suffers some reduction in cognitive ability. The plaintiff claimed that the infarctions were due to hypoxia and that an earlier cesarean section would have prevented the hypoxia. The defendant claimed that the fetal heart monitor had shown normal readings during the hour and one-half to two hours just prior to the delivery, although the hospital could not produce the fetal heart monitor tracings. A $3 million settlement was reached.[90]

7. Adding to someone else's notes

Even though it is unacceptable for a healthcare professional to alter someone else's documentation, it happens, and more commonly than attorneys would believe. Physicians have altered nursing records, and nurses have altered each other's notes. This alteration may be as simple as a rather bold addition to a note, with the addition done in an obviously different handwriting. In a case like this the alteration may have been done by a physician who is adding comments to another's note. Physicians may be very casual about editing someone else's notes because of the practice of overseeing the documentation of residents.

Risk managers are often involved when the alteration of medical records is discovered. The risk manager becomes involved in re-educating the person who has been discovered editing or changing another person's documentation.

Tampering with records can have profound implications for the attorney. It will make the defense of a malpractice case difficult and the pursuit of a settlement easier for the plaintiff. The attorney who suspects that tampering has occurred needs to validate these concerns in order to make the appropriate strategic moves. Refer to Konray and Iyer[91] and Iyer[92] for additional information on this topic.

7.13 Summary

The ability to decipher and interpret nursing documentation is often the key to analyzing a nursing malpractice case. A malpractice case can be won or lost on a few words in a medical record. It is essential that the attorney be able to

review and understand medical records in order to make appropriate legal decisions. As more medical documentation becomes computerized, the task of understanding nursing documentation will become easier.

Endnotes

1. Chelewski, P. "Designing a patient-care 24-hour flow sheet" *Nursing Management*, pg. 37, April 1998.

2. Laska, L. (Ed), "Failure to prevent decubitus ulcers during man's recovery from injury which caused quadriplegia," *Medical Malpractice Verdicts, Settlements, and Experts*, May 2010, page 14.

3. Legal issues in the care of pressure ulcer patients: Key concepts for healthcare providers, *International Expert Wound Care Advisory Panel*, 6/22/2009.

4. Laska, L. (Ed), "Woman suffers lack of pulse in leg after spinal surgery," *Medical Malpractice Verdicts, Settlements, and Experts*, January 2010, page 37.

5. See note 3.

6. Northcutt, C. and Shea, M.A. , "Generation and retention of medical records," Iyer, P., and Levin, B. *Medical Legal Aspects of Medical Records, Second Edition*, Tucson, Lawyers and Judges Publishing Company, 2010.

7. Laska, L. (Editor) "Woman suffers arrest hours after arrival at nursing home" *Medical Malpractice Verdicts, Settlements, and Experts*, pg. 31, September 2004.

8. Clark, K. P. Iyer, B. Levin and M.S. Shea, "Unlocking medical records," *Legal Assistant Today*, July/August 2004, http://www.legalassistanttoday.com/issue_archive/feature2_ja04.htm, accessed 2/11/06.

9. Taylor, J. "Tips for requesting and reviewing medical records," *Journal of Legal Nurse Consulting*, Fall 2009, Vol. 20, No. 3, 13-15.

10. Cauler, G. "Obtaining necessary medical records" http://www.tthlaw.com/Articles/Articles/106/?vobid=467&pm=151, accessed 2/11/06.

11. Laska, L. (Ed), "Failure to immediately perform heart catheterization on man with chest pain," *Medical Malpractice Verdicts, Settlements, and Experts*, February 2010, page 11.

12. HIPAA Compliance, http://www.networkcomputing. com/showArticle.jhtml?articleID=21401318, accessed 2/10/06.

13. Laska. L. (Ed), "Fax sent to teenager's school regarding hospitalization for psychiatric treatment alleged to violate confidentiality," *Medical Malpractice Verdicts, Settlements, and Experts*, January 2010, page 34.

14. HIPAA Basics: Medical Privacy in the Electronic Age, www.privacy.org, accessed 2/11/06.

15. Stromberg, M. et al., "HIPAA," in Iyer, P., Levin, B. *Medical Legal Aspects of Medical Records, Second Edition*, Lawyers and Judges Publishing Company, 2010.

16. Schwartz, S. Rights to access medical records under the HIPAA Privacy Regulation, http://www.healthassistancepartnership.org/assets/pdfs/HIPAA_Privacy_Q_A_MA2003-017298.pdf, accessed 2/11/06.

17. Fox, S. and R. Monson, HIPAA and Medical Records Copy Charges, http://www.hipaadvisory.com/action/LegalQA/law/Legal47.htm, accessed 2/11/06.

18. Rajecki, R. MGMA: HITECH provision puts unnecessary burden on practices http://medicaleconomics.modernmedicine.com/memag/article/articleDetail.jsp?id=673588&sk=107019ef288e121ae9e4aa2580761740.

19. Hatton, M. HIPAA Protection of Medical Records Involved in a Malpractice Case, http://www.medscape.com/viewarticle/462439, accessed 2/11/06.

20. Iyer, P. and J. Barone, "Obtaining and organizing medical records," in Iyer, P., and B. Levin, *Medical Legal Aspects of Medical Records, Second Edition*, Tucson, Lawyers and Judges Publishing Company, 2010.

21. *Id.*

22. Levine, J. "Physician documentation in hospitals and nursing homes" in Iyer, P. and Levin, B., *Medical Legal Aspects of Medical Records, Second Edition*, Tucson, Lawyers and Judges Publishing Company, 2010.

23. See note 20.

24. *Mastering Documentation*, Springhouse, PA: Springhouse Corporation, 1999.

25. Smith, L. "How to chart by exception" *Nursing 2002*, Vol. 32, No. 9, pg. 30 September 2002.

26. Cummins, K. and M. Hill, M. Charting By Exception. *American Journal of Nursing*, 99(3), 24G. March 1999.

27. *Id.*

28. Smith, L. "How to chart by exception," *Nursing 2002*, Vol. 32, No. 9, pg. 30, September 2002.

29. Brent, N. "Nurse attorney answers common legal questions," nurse.com, March 22, 2010.

30. Methods for documenting nurses' notes, www.corexcel. com/html/body.documentation.page8.ceus.html, accessed 2/11/04.

31. Document It Right: A Nurse's Guide to Charting. http://69.3.158.146/nurse/courses/nurseweek/nw0400/c2/p01.htm, accessed 8/27/04.

32. Iyer, P. "Charting systems," in Iyer, P., and Levin, B. *Medical Legal Aspects of Medical Records, Second Edition*, Tucson, Lawyers and Judges Publishing Company, 2010.

33. Buppert, C. "Electronic medical records: 18 ways to reduce legal risks," *Topics in Advanced Practice Nursing*, 1/13/10, accessed 1/20/10.

34. Id.

35. Tan, R., S. Isaacks. "Computerized records and quality of care," *Annals of Long Term Care* 7 (9), September, 1999.

36. Jergesen, A., "The challenge of computerized medical records," www.physicianlawalert.com/publications/articles/PLA_Conf_eHealth_02.html, accessed 2/13/05.

37. Milholland D., "Privacy and confidentiality of patient information: Challenges for nursing," *Journal of Nursing Administration* 24, February, 1994: 19.

38. "$200K for HIV Test Disclosure," *New Jersey Law Journal*, pg. 9, October 17, 2005.

39. French, M., "DOD examining health records security," www.fcw.com/fcw/articles.2003/0106/web-med-01-10-03.asp, accessed 2/13/05.

40. Dougherty, J., "Critics blast electronic medical records plan," www.news.max.com, accessed 2/15/05.

41. *Id.*

42. Dougherty, J., "Critics blast electronic medical records plan," www.news.max.com, accessed 2/15/05.

43. See note 33.

44. Gaffey, A. "Communication and documentation considerations for electronic health records," *Journal of Healthcare Risk Management*, Volume 29, Number 2, 16-20, 2009.

45. See note 33.

46. Turner, R., "A high dose of tech," www.USNews.com, 8/2/04, accessed 2/13/05.

47. See note 44.

48. See note 33.

49. See note 3.

50. Laska, L. (Editor), "Mishandled delivery leaves baby with broken clavicle, broken ulna, and Erb's Palsy." *Medical Malpractice Verdicts, Settlements, and Experts,* May, 2003: 39.

51. Iyer, P. "Computerization of medical records: in Iyer, P, and Levin, D. *Medical Legal Aspects of Medical Records, Second Edition,* Tucson, Lawyers and Judges Publishing Company, 2010.

52. Iyer, P. and N. Camp, *Nursing Documentation, Fourth Edition,* Med League Support Services, Inc. Flemington, NJ, 2005.

53. Laska, L. (ed), "Failure to timely perform hysterectomy on woman with bleeding due to placenta accrete following cesarean section delivery," *Medical Malpractice Verdicts, Settlements and Experts*, March 2010, 26.

54. www.jointcommission.org.

55. Laska, L. (Editor) "Failure to perform exams on legs following uterine artery remobilization," *Medical Malpractice Verdicts, Settlements, and Ex*perts, p. 15, July 2005.

56. "Punitive damages allowable for record alteration." *Journal of Healthcare Risk Management*, pp. 43-45, Winter 1995.

57. Laska, L. (Editor) "Alzheimer's patient asphyxiates on her own blood drained into her lungs from trauma-induced blow to her lip," *Medical Malpractice Verdicts, Settlements, and Experts,* pgs. 41-42, April 2004.

58. Rosenthal, M., P. Cornett, K. Sutcliff, and E. Lewton, "Beyond the medical record: other modes of error acknowledgement," *J. Gen Intern Med*, 20 (5) pgs 404-9, May 2005.

59. "Disclosure: what works now and what can work even better," *ASHRM Journal* Vol. 24, No. 1, pgs 19-26, 2004.

60. Klepatsky, A. Personal communication, March 2, 2000.

61. Austin, S. "Ladies and gentlemen of the jury, I present the nursing documentation," *Nursing* 2006, Vol. 36, No. 1, pgs 56-62, January 2006.

62. Laska, L. (ed), "Failure to report teenager's rising intracranial pressure during hospitalization for shunt malfunction," *Medical Malpractice Verdicts, Settlements and Experts*, April 2010, page 14.

63. Laska, L. (Editor) "Delay in assessment and surgical intervention in intestinal obstruction results in death," *Medical Malpractice Verdicts, Settlements, and Experts*, pg. 23, December 2003.

64. Randolph, J., J. Magro, D. Stalmach, B. Cermak, and B. Wilson, "A study of the accuracy of telephone orders in nursing homes in Southern California," *Annals of Long-Term Care*, 7 (9): 334 338, (1999).

65. http://www.jcaho.org/accredited+organizations/patient+safety/04+npsg/04_faqs.htm#goal%202   accessed 4/19/04.

66. *Id.*

67. Iyer, P. "Legal aspects of charting," in Iyer, P., Levin, B. *Medical Legal Aspects of Medical Records, Second Edition,* Tucson, Lawyers and Judges Publishing Company, 2010.

68. Why is there so much hoopla about documentation anyway?   www.corexcel.com/html/body.documentation.page4.ceus.html accessed 4/19/04.

69. See note 66.

70. Palmer, R. "Altered and 'lost' medical records." *TRIAL*, May, 1999.

71. Rubin J. "An overview of the legal implications of medical documentation." www.woundcare.org/newsvol.4n3/ed1.htm, accessed 11/16/04.

72. Tammelleo, A. (Editor). "Spoilation of evidence shifts burden of proof." *Regan Report on Nursing Law* 1, July, 1995.

73. Laska, L. (Editor). "Death of nursing home resident following development of pressure ulcers, contractures, and malnutrition," *Medical Malpractice Verdicts, Settlements, and Experts,* pg. 37, August, 2001.

74. See note 69.

75. New Jersey Model Civil Jury Charge 5.36H.

76. Palmer, R. "Altered and 'lost' medical records." *TRIAL,* May, 1999.

77. Wirtes, D., A Citrin. "Spoliation of evidence as proof of guilt or liability." www.cunninghambounds.com/htm/lawyers/resources/wirtes/spoliation.

78. Baxter, M. "Managing medical malpractice: the documents, the providers, and the lawyers." www.bbsclaw.com/med_mal_baxter.htm, accessed 11/16/04.

79. "Ballard doctor fined for lying." http://seattlepi.nwsource.com/local/159084_doctor03.html, retrieved 1/5/05.

80. Grossman, E. "Bethlehem nurse pleads guilty to covering up error." *The Morning Call,* Allentown PA, May 24, 2001.

81. Crissey, M. "PA nursing home administrator indicted." http:news.yahoo.com/news, 8/25/04, accessed 8/28/04.

82. Nygaard, D. and S. Deubner, S. "Altered or 'lost' medical records." *TRIAL,* 46, June 1988.

83. Hicks, A. R. "The forensic examination of records," in Iyer, P., Levin, B., *Medical Legal Aspects of Medical Records, Second Edition,* Tucson, Lawyers and Judges Publishing Company, 2010.

84. See note 81.

85. Laska, L. (ed), "Woman's drop in blood pressure after delivery of child not properly treated, resulting in paraplegia," *Medical Malpractice Verdicts, Settlements and Experts,* March 2010, p. 15.

86. Laska, L. (ed), "Failure to relay information to doctor regarding dangerously high clotting factor in woman on Coumadin," *Medical Malpractice Verdicts, Settlements and Experts,* January 2010, p. 24.

87. Laska, L. (Editor) "Failure to properly monitor man at risk of falling and failure to chart fall." *Medical Malpractice Verdicts, Settlements, and Experts,* June 2008, p. 32.

88. See note 80.

89. Laska, L. "Failure to properly resuscitate newborn following placental abruption." *Medical Malpractice Verdicts, Settlements, and Experts,* February 2009, p. 32.

90. Laska, L. "Failure to timely perform cesarean section blamed on hypoxia and cerebral infarctions." *Medical Malpractice Verdicts, Settlements, and Experts,* March 2008, p. 36.

91. Konray, R. and P. Iyer, "Tampering with medical records," in Iyer, P., Levin, B,. *Medical Legal Aspects of Medical Records, Second Edition,* Tucson, Lawyers and Judges Publishing Company, 2010.

92. Iyer, P. "Tampering with medical records," in Iyer, P. (Editor) *Nursing Home Litigation: Investigation and Case Preparation, Second Edition,* Tucson, Lawyers and Judges Publishing Company, 2006.

Additional Reading

Brous, E. Documentation and litigation, *RN,* February 2009, 40-43.

Ericksen, A. "Informatics: the future of nursing," *RN,* July 2009, 34-37.

Frampton, S. Horowitz, S and Stumpo, B., "Open medical records," *American Journal of Nursing,* August 2009, 59-63.

Krasner, D. "Safeguard your wound and skin care practice from litigation," *ECPN,* April 2007, 28-32.

Yu, K and Green, R. "Critical aspects of emergency department documentation and communication," *Emergency Medical Clinics of North America,* 27 (2009), 641-654.

Chapter 8

Inside the Healthcare Environment

Judith D. Rottkamp, MA, RN, CNA

8.1 Introduction

The healthcare environment is in a constant state of change, impacted equally by regulators; third-party payers, especially Medicare and Medicaid; educators; researchers; and stakeholders. Each entity has appropriate reasons for imposing the recommendations for change based on experience, research, and expert opinion, all of which should be validated in practice by utilizing performance improvement, quality indicators, and desired outcomes.

Statutes and regulations to enhance practice and adjust the environment for the good of the patient and community guide the healthcare team. The recent addition of never events and the impact on outcomes of care as well as reimbursement will continue to evolve. The nurses and the healthcare team who continuously incorporate evolving changes into daily practice provide a safe environment. Members of the team use education, knowledge, and experience to provide a culture of safety for the patients. They adjust performance and professional practice to adhere to the standards of care and standards of practice that are reviewed and revised as needed, so change and professional practice can evolve. Nursing administration will need to validate the competency of the staff and the outcomes of care on a continuous basis. Ongoing education and support for the staff to meet the standards of excellence are key to the success of the department.

Nurses utilize a combination of critical thinking, assessment skills, and scientific evidence-based knowledge to perform as professionals with total accountability and responsibility for their actions. Change is ongoing, occurring at a rapid rate, and challenging to the professional nurse.

8.2 Hospital-Wide Delivery Systems

Hospital personnel investigate and invest in delivery systems that work best in their organizational environment. In discussion with nursing executives and senior leadership, a delivery system is chosen that provides safe quality patient care for the clients and community served. The acuity system (method of categorizing level of illness of a patient) in healthcare organizations provides the data from which the staffing model is designed. Once a staffing model is selected a staffing pattern or matrix is developed as a guide to provide nursing with appropriate staff and team support. As acuity increases, adjustments accommodate and reinforce the staffing model. Examples of staffing models follow.

A. Functional

The functional model is simply the assigning of specific tasks on a nursing unit. Each staff member is responsible for completing an aspect of the total care required by the patients on the unit. The tasks can be anything such as an assignment for the medication nurse to distribute all medications for the unit, or to a specific number of patients on the unit for a large unit. Another nurse coordinates all preoperative and diagnostic treatments. The nurse assigned to the desk is responsible for the administrative or indirect care such as completing physician orders and communicating required care or changes in care to the appropriate individual. The desk nurse also coordinates ancillary scheduling of physical

therapy, radiation therapy, speech and hearing, social services, and so on. Finally, this nurse completes the assignments for the nursing assistants or support staff on the unit.

TIP: Functional nursing can stretch staffing and is not favored in the acute care setting. Nurses find that repetitive tasks decrease individual skills and decrease the flexibility needed to provide safe quality care to the patients. Communication is also difficult with this method. The patient care frequently becomes fragmented leading to decreased patient and staff satisfaction and increased potential for error.

B. Team Nursing

In this method of nursing delivery, a group of patients is provided care by a team of personnel assigned to the unit. This team, depending on the size, is led by a RN and may include additional RN or LPN staff with nursing assistants. The leader of each team coordinates the plan of care for all of the patients on the team. It is the leader's responsibility to communicate well with the physician and professional staff. The leader must be proficient in the delivery of care and also possess managerial skills such as delegating, communicating, monitoring patient outcomes, and planning care.

A well-organized team is evident by patient, physician, and staff satisfaction as well as positive patient outcomes. Nursing leadership must facilitate a team that complements the whole unit and the specific needs of the patients; it must also facilitate the assignment of the appropriate skill mix of staff to provide safe quality care. The communication, collaboration, cooperation, and coordination of care encompass true team nursing. Each team member fulfills an assignment based on education, competencies, abilities, and professional regulations. The members can seek guidance within the team when a unique situation arises which is beyond their knowledge and skill.

Individual accountability and responsibility is a given at each professional level. The leader of the team has increased responsibility and accountability as dictated by the structure. The team leader, working within the scope and standards of the nursing profession licensure, has the responsibility to delegate to the individual with appropriate skills to complete tasks necessary to meet the patient plan of care.

C. Primary Nursing

In this system, the primary care nurse has complete responsibility from the admission assessment to the final discharge process of the assigned patients. The nurse deals directly with the physician and other professional members of the staff responsible for the patient. This nurse meets all of the requirements of licensure and standards of care as an independent provider of care. The patient plan of care is initiated, implemented, evaluated, and revised by the primary nurse.

This model creates a close relationship between the patient and nurse, as well as the physician and nurse. Leadership is responsible for assuring the appropriate case load based on the competencies of the primary care nurse by evaluating these competencies and any additional competencies as needed. Constant evaluation is needed as the healthcare environment is on a course of change, growth, and medical advancement. The RN is responsible for directing total patient care, even as shifts change.

TIP: In this model, communication by the original caregiver is imperative. The decision-making skills and empowerment of the nurse are most evident in this model of nursing. A LPN is not appropriate for this role based on educational preparation and licensure standards.

D. Modular

This system focuses on a small team of nurses and patients with a primary nurse responsible for a patient from admission to discharge. The RN guides the care and the plan of care for each patient in this module. It may be established with a few patients who have a similar diagnosis or DRG in close proximity to each other on the nursing unit. "Pods," mini-units within a unit, and a sense of specialization can be found in this method of delivery of care. Patients become familiar with the caregivers and the process, and recognize achievement of goals within the plan of care. Satisfaction is gained and trust is established with this familiarity and consistency of caregiver and processes. Leadership maintains responsibility for the individual nursing competencies and monitors patient outcomes. Leadership also monitors patient, physician, and staff satisfaction.

E. Case Management

The case management delivery system focuses on the patient length of stay and efficient achievement of specific patient outcomes. Health care focused on cost containment and efficiencies of care in the 1970s and 1980s. The evolving critical pathways or plans were the basis for planning individual patient care. Patients with similar diagnoses were assigned a specific plan or pathway, which could be adjusted for changes in condition, comorbid conditions, physician preference, and individual response to treatment. Specific patients are placed on a plan and the case manager coordinates and monitors care throughout the hospital stay.

Case managers can be direct patient caregivers with responsibility for compliance with the plan or pathway. Alternatively, the case manager can monitor the plan, evaluate the patient outcome and deviations from the plan, as well as work with the care providers to accomplish the plan. Case managers can follow the patient from admission to a change in the level of care to transfer within the organization and finally to discharge.

Today, most case managers are unit based and communicate the patient status, plan of care, goals, and outcomes when a patient is transferred from one unit to another. Case managers may have advanced education, such as a BSN, certification, or both. Many case managers are certified by individual organizations or governing medical staff bylaws. In addition, some case managers have achieved the title of Clinical Nurse Specialist (CNS). The CNS is master's-degree prepared and will follow the patient with a specific protocol from admission to discharge. These nurses develop the protocol based on education and clinical expertise. They are completely involved with each patient and the achievement of the goals with appropriate outcomes.

Timelines are important with case management, and when variances occur, explanations are required and the plan or protocol is altered. Case management is a collaborative model in which positive interaction with ancillary departments is established in order to expedite care. The knowledge and experience of the case manager is recognized and facilitates the achievement of the plan. A positive patient outcome in a timely efficient way is a strong result of this model. Team cooperation and an esprit de corps make this model work.

TIP: In the early stages of case management, data collected regarding the patient length of stay and delivery of ancillary services revolutionized the delivery of patient care. Departments originally operating five days per week on the day shift found it difficult to justify the delay inservices due to a weekend, holiday, or an off-shift. It is not uncommon to find departments open 24 hours per day, seven days per week to meet the needs of the community.

F. Patient-Focused Care

The 1990s brought the patient-focused care model to improve patient care. Cost, competition and the beginning of a worsening nursing shortage were present. The focus of this initiative was to make the patient the center of all activities. The patient is no longer seen by a multitude of staff, nor moved through many departments and asked the same or similar questions repeatedly. The process of tests, questions, and traveling are changed. The patient is moved as little as possible; all entities come to the patient. A team of cross-trained caregivers provides patient care in a patient-focused environment. The patient receives care from one, or at most two, individuals.

The organization must decentralize all of the departments in this model. The services a patient requires are all available on the nursing unit. A patient does not need to travel to the lab, radiology, or physical therapy. In this system, supplies, equipment, and medications are in the patient room. The patient receives care from fewer personnel, which adds a positive comfort measure because of a familiarity with all of the caregivers. The staff communicates more efficiently and thus the care is more comprehensive. The follow-up communication is decreased since the caregiver knows what has occurred.

Training, retraining, and redesign of nursing units are a major undertaking. Competency monitoring is a priority with the increased cross training. It can be difficult to maintain all competencies and have the staff fill the roles in this model of care. The model may preclude the use of nurses who wish to work on a part-time basis. The infrequent requirement to perform skills such as taking blood, performing EKGs, starting IVs, or providing respiratory therapy can result in a nurse who has difficulty maintaining a competent performance level.

TIP: Role responsibility must be clear and concise. This can be challenging with the nurse responsible for all aspects of patient care. Some facilities have abandoned the model because of this problem.

G. Theorist Based

Nursing theorists have evolved throughout the history of nursing. These theorists have guided the beliefs and practice of nursing in various settings and delivery models as they set standards. They have allowed the nursing profession to grow and formulate professional decision making based on valid theories. Nursing theorists have influenced nursing values and beliefs, and have guided the profession. Nursing leadership must be knowledgeable about many theorists in order to produce a model of care that is best for the patients, families, and staff they guide.

Professional nurses are exposed to nursing theorists in their basic nursing education. The experience and knowledge of theoretical frameworks strengthen a nursing career and can be the basis for structuring the model of care or practice. With the autonomy and empowerment of nurses today, we can recognize the continued influence of the nursing theorists.

8.3 Magnet Culture
A. Overview

The Magnet culture has enhanced the professional environment and professionalism of every nursing staff that meets the Magnet standards and criteria. This culture is realized when an organization has been awarded the magnet recognition designation. The Magnet Hospital Recognition Program for Excellence in Nursing Service was established in 1990. This designation was approved by the American Nurses Association (ANA) under the American Nurses Credentialing Center (ANCC). This proposal was built upon the 1983 Magnet Hospital Study conducted by the American Academy of Nursing. At that time it was decided the baseline for Magnet development was the *Standards for Organized Nursing Services and Responsibilities of Nurse Administrators Across All Settings*. The goals of this program are consistent with those of the ANCC, where Magnet is based. The number of applicants and organizations has grown since 1994 when the first Magnet award was given.

In 1997, the program changed to the Magnet Nursing Services Recognition Program. The program criteria was revised, utilizing the *Scope and Standards for Nursing Administrators*. The number of recipients earning the award has increased. In 1998, the program was expanded to long-term care facilities. Also in 1998, ANCC established the Institute for Research, Education, and Consultation (IREC). The goal of this institute is to ensure that there are broad and balanced products and services offered. As growth continued in all of the ANCC certification programs, ANCC established an international division to expand to all settings in 1999.[1]

B. Goals

The Magnet Recognition Program has the following goals:

- Identify excellence in the delivery of nursing services to patients, clients, or residents.
- Promote quality in a milieu that supports professional practices.
- Provide a mechanism for the dissemination of "best practice" in nursing services.[2]

The Magnet standards have been updated to reference ISO 9000 standards. Plexus ISO 9000 and Healthcare Training System was created by the Plexus Corporation. This is a federation comprised of national standard bodies from approximately 120 countries around the world.

TIP: The ISO standards promote worldwide standardization and facilitate international exchange of goods and services. They lead to enhanced quality and reliability at a reasonable cost, improved health, safety and environmental protection, cost reduction, greater comparability, improved usability, and distribution efficiency.

Quality of Nursing Leadership Our leadership brings a wide range of experience and education to the organization, patients, and staff. We value, appreciate, and recognize our nurses' efforts to advance their knowledge and provide quality care to our patients.	**Organizational Structure** Our structure uses a decentralized unit based decision making with strong nursing representation evident in the organizational committee structure.
Management Style Shared governance has been in place since 1990. This style provides the nurse with control over his/her practice, enhances communications, and impacts patient care.	**Personnel Policies and Programs** Salaries and benefits are competitive. Rotating shifts are minimized and flexible staffing model are used. Personnel policies are created with staff involvement, and significant administrative and clinical promotional opportunities exist.
Professional Models of Care Models of care give nurses the responsibility and authority for the provision of care. Nurses are accountable for their own practice and are coordinators of care.	**Quality of Care** All of our nurses provide high quality care to their patients.
Quality Improvement Quality Improvement activities are viewed as educational. Staff nurses participate in the quality improvement process to ensure the highest quality of care is given to their patients.	**Consultation and Resources** We have many consultants available to our nurses. We have experts in education, research, DVT, dialysis, psychiatric, smoking cessation, pain management, etc.
Autonomy Nurses practice autonomously consistent with professional standards. Independent judgment is expected within the context of a multidisciplinary approach to patient care.	**Community and the Hospital** We maintain a strong community presence with a variety of ongoing, long term outreach programs.
Nurses as Teachers Our nurses are permitted and expected to incorporate teaching in all aspects of their practice.	**Image of Nursing** Our nurses are seen as essential by other members of the healthcare team.
Collegial Relationships Our nurses work closely with all interdisciplinary disciplines to provide the highest level of patient care.	**Professional Development** Our nurses are provided with many opportunities for professional growth and development. We provide orientation, inservice education, continuing education, formal education, and career development opportunities. We also provide competency based clinical advancement along with the resources to maintain competency.

Figure 8.1 Forces of Magnetism

C. Requirements

To receive Magnet status, an organization and the nursing services department must have

- a nursing management philosophy and practices of nursing services,
- an adherence to quality standards,
- a chief nursing officer (CNO) supporting professional practice and competence, and
- an awareness of cultural, ethical diversity of patients, families, and their providers.

A benefit of this designation is recognition in the community. In addition, the organization can have increased utilization, enhanced marketing strategies, and improved nursing recruitment. Stability in nursing care is provided with positive patient outcomes. Nursing autonomy, in which nurses problem solve and actively participate in decision making with positive outcomes for patients and peers, is evident throughout the organization in collaboration with the CNO.

D. Characteristics

Research projects by Linda Aiken, PhD, RN, FAAN indicate that Magnet awardees have similar characteristics:

- reduced Medicare mortality and morbidity rates,
- reduced mortality rates associated with the care of patients with AIDS in the acute care setting,
- increased patient satisfaction,
- decreased likelihood of nurses being dissatisfied and burned out,
- reduced needle stick injury rate among nurses,
- improved patient care ratios, and
- powerful and influential CNOs.[3]

Upon initiating the Magnet Journey, required eligibility criteria has to be met. There are fees to be paid and deadlines to be met. Compliance in meeting the *Magnet Standards of Care and Standards of Professional Performance* must be documented. It is then decided if the organizational overview and measurement criteria are met. If these are met a site visit is planned, after which the final report goes to the Magnet Commission on Recognition. The decision is determined regarding recipients of Magnet status. The healthcare organization is then notified of its Magnet status and this award is good for four years. Thereafter, an annual report must be submitted to assure the Magnet status is being maintained regarding quality outcomes and nurse-sensitive quality outcomes.

In 2004, the Forces of Magnetism (Figure 8.1) replaced previous standards of care and professional practice. These forces must be visible and verified in the nursing environment and practice.

In 2008, Model Components with the Forces of Magnetism were published. These Models replaced the previous forces of magnetism. The five Model Components are:

- Transformational Leadership
- Structural Empowerment
- Exemplary Professional Practice
- New Knowledge, Innovations, and Improvements
- Empirical Quality Results

The Models are evidence of continued efforts to demonstrate quality and excellence in nursing practice in Magnet Nursing Organizations. See www.nursecredentialing. org/Magnet/ResourceCenters/Magnet-Overview-Brochure. aspx pages 6–8 for more information.

E. Forces of Magnetism

The Forces of Magnetism are summarized on the St. Francis Medical Center website (www.stfrancismedicalcenter. com):

> The standards of care and professional performance can be utilized when an organization demonstrates the "force." The forces focus on descriptive qualities of the professional RN and showcase the true Magnet culture. The presentation of the information in a clear, concise narrative will impress the Magnet appraisers. The final preparation for the Magnet visit must prepare all staff, including ancillary staff, to speak knowledgably about the Forces of Magnetism. The healthcare organization receives the award, and the nursing department leads the journey.

The site visit demonstrates, through interviews and presentations, behaviors validating compliance with the material submitted. The facility must showcase examples and present proof of specific requests for information. The facility only has one chance as there is no appeal or resubmission permitted. It behooves the organization to seek education or consultation to assist with the initial application.

The survey team consists of two appraisers and the visit is usually three days in duration. The visit has a planned agenda, which can be revised by the surveyors without notice. The organization must be fully prepared from the physical appearance and cleanliness to the information posted on bulletin boards. The staff must be prepared and comfortable discussing the material submitted and addressing questions or concerns from the surveyors. The appraisers also request the assistance of a staff nurse during the tours and scheduled meetings. The material submitted will be challenged throughout the visit to validate the information provided and to verify the staff's knowledge and comfort with the Magnet standards. All nursing shifts are invited to participate with the interviews, validating compliance with the standards around the clock.

Maintaining the Magnet culture after a survey is a colossal job. The forces must be updated, data collection continued, benchmarking completed, and statistics collected regarding recruitment and retention, education, and advancement. The information is submitted in an annual report (in a set format) to the Magnet organization. The data is reviewed by accrediting staff, and comments or concerns must be addressed by the organization. The Magnet designation can be jeopardized if there is a serious occurrence or significant change in the management of the organization, or in the outcomes collected regarding the nurse-sensitive outcomes. Not all organizations are redesignated or provide sufficient evidence to support Magnet designation.

8.4 Standards of Care
A. Definition
Professional practitioners of nursing have the primary responsibility and accountability for their patients and clients. Nursing practice is a goal-oriented service and is adapted to the individual patient or client in all areas of care, for example, acute, long-term, and community. Standards are guides to provide the nurse with a reference useful for the completion of duties. These guides focus on nursing practice in any setting where care is provided by a professional nurse with or without nonprofessional assistants. Standards of care usually begin with complete ongoing collection of data and a nursing assessment in order to develop nursing diagnoses. Once the nursing diagnosis is determined, the standards establish a plan of care and prioritize the implementation of care. At all times, the professional nurse encourages patient, client, and family participation in health promotion, maintenance, and restoration. Finally, progress (or lack of progress) towards goals must be determined by the individual and the nurse, then reassessed and revised with priorities and goals redefined in a plan of care.

The ANA began developing basic standards for nursing in the late 1960s. These standards are generic and focus on the basic nursing process. This is a critical thinking model for all RNs, beginning with assessment, diagnosis, planning, implementation, and evaluation. This demonstrates the strong connection between the ANA and state statutes guiding nursing practice. Refer to Chapter 1, *The Roots of Patient Injury*, for more information on the nursing process.

Over the years, specialty nursing practice groups have developed scope of practice standards and statements (i.e., pediatrics, gerontology, rehabilitation, psychiatric and mental health, and others). In 1991, the collaboration with ANA and specialty nursing organizations published *Standards of Clinical Nursing Practice*.[4] A common language was utilized with a predetermined format to clarify and strengthen nursing's ability to define the actual conduct of nursing practice in all practice areas. Thus, a framework was established in which specialty organizations and the ANA collaborate to decide standards for the practice of nursing. These standards have shaped nursing practice, provided a model for regulatory language, and provided a model for other specialty groups to define specific scope and standards of practice.

RNs throughout the U.S. confirmed the usefulness and necessity to have the standards. The Congress on Nursing Practice and Economics (CNPE) established a group to review the *Standards of Clinical Practice*[5] and incorporated all RN specialties and their standards of practice. These standards are the authoritative statement describing nursing responsibility and accountability and also reflect the values and priorities of the profession. By providing direction and a framework for the evaluation of nursing practice, it provides accountability to the public and provides positive outcomes for the population served.

B. Policy and Procedure
Specific standards are provided by healthcare organizations' nursing departments.

These standards are developed to provide guidelines for a nurse in performing specific duties. They provide a step-by-step procedure to assure each RN is performing the procedure the same way. In each organization, policies and procedures are developed.

TIP: The policy is that which cannot change; the procedure is how to do a task. An example would be a patient who is to receive a bath each day. Patient status determines how the bath is given (such as a shower or a bed bath) and whether it is a partial or complete bath. This decision will vary depending on the patient.

Policies and procedures may be found in a manual in the department. However, they are increasingly found on the hospital intranet, providing increased accessibility for the staff. In addition to providing the staff with a reference tool, the policy and procedure manual is developed to meet a state regulation, or a requirement from another external agency such as The Joint Commission. For the professional nurse who participates in policy formation, it is a positive experience to develop and implement a policy or a procedure. New staff members are introduced to the policy and procedure manual during the orientation process. If evaluators, surveyors, the state department of health, or corporate representatives inquire about nursing practices, the policy and procedure manual will provide evidence of compliance and a tool to evaluate the care rendered.

Most organizations have professional committees that provide oversight by the professionals involved in the care. These professionals expertly provide knowledge for a specific policy or procedure. The procedure is researched and prepared, reviewed by professionals involved, approved by a committee, and signed and approved by the CNO or designee. Policies should be utilized when:

- the nurse needs to review a procedure that is not used on a frequent basis;
- there is a new requirement or piece of equipment; or
- a complicated procedure needs specific direction, step by step.

Policies and procedures need to be based on current literature, research, knowledge, and manufacturer recommendations, when appropriate. They need to be clear and concise. All policies and procedures need to be reviewed and revised as needed or based on state requirements. Policies and procedures need to be available for the caregiver via the intranet or in a specific manual on the unit or department. It is common practice to utilize policies and procedures provided from another resource deemed appropriate by the organization. Professional writers and publishing companies have produced books on basic professional practice. If a book is deemed to be in alignment with the organization practice it can be utilized as a reference tool for the staff. This practice has been in use since the 1990s.

TIP: Policies and procedures are often used in litigation; therefore, they must be maintained by the organization as a legal document. When policies or procedures are revised, the original version must be maintained on file to meet statutory requirements. Statutes of limitations for suing an organization or a staff member may vary and the policy and procedure in place at the time of the occurrence is beneficial to both parties. The attorney should always carefully check the date of a policy or procedure supplied during discovery to ensure the one in use at the time of the patient's care was provided. Careful maintenance of policies and procedures is highly recommended.

C. Universal

Universal standards of care arise from basic professional practice in many occupations. These standards define the basic foundation for a professional unit. They can be changed to meet state or local initiatives, but remain a standard by which practitioners abide. Universal standards are promulgated by a demonstration that a standard can effectively be utilized with a positive outcome for all (e.g., handwashing). It is documented in all literature, research, and regulations that if all practitioners would wash their hands, it would decrease infection and cross contamination for the patients. (Refer to Chapter 23, *Infections in Hospitals and Nursing Homes*, in Volume II, for additional information.) Mortality rates would be decreased.

Universal standards of care assist in expanding this knowledge to the public; thus more lives are saved with appropriate practices. The public can use this knowledge when selecting a healthcare organization or discussing concerns with community leaders, physicians, and healthcare personnel. This knowledge can only assist in prevention, maintenance, and positive self-care outcomes when followed. It is a positive collaboration of leaders and healthcare teams to assist the community in knowing and accepting these standards.

D. Unit Specific

Specialty units have specific policies and procedures in addition to the hospital's basic policies and procedures. These are necessary due to specialization and the care variation of the patient or client. These policies and procedures define the philosophy and provide guidelines to be followed in a special unit by the staff assigned. The approval process is contained on the unit, but developed in coordination with the CNO or designee. These policy and procedure manuals are available on the unit and in nursing administration in a paper copy or online. The state regulations apply to the policy and procedure manual as well as review and revision of materials. This information must be provided to regulators when requested. The index demonstrates the original date of the policy or procedure completion, last review or revision date, and any deletion of procedures.

When a particular policy or procedure is no longer in practice, a deletion should be noted in committee minutes. If the procedure is from a specialty unit the deletion should be documented in staff minutes. The format of a policy and procedure should be consistent throughout the organization. Staff responds to the standardization as it simplifies the maintenance process. Most policies and procedures have a set format, beginning with a policy statement that defines the policy's purpose. Finally, the procedure is detailed. Research or literature references should be noted at the conclusion of the procedure. In addition, the professional experts assisting with the procedure development or review should be listed, documenting the approval and appropriateness of the procedure. This format is simple and when presented to staff, new orientees, and even regulators, is accepted and found to make policies and procedures more useful.

TIP: Long, complicated policies and procedures do not capture the interest of the reader nor are they followed to the degree or detail they require. The attorney may find the policies and procedures combined, depending on the institution. Some organizations have stand-alone policies and stand-alone procedures. Again when requesting information in discovery it is important to obtain all available information.

E. Department Specific

Policies and procedures may be relevant to several units, with similar patient populations, care, and standards. These are developed for staff to understand the particulars of department-specific procedures with the appropriate providers. Department-specific policies and procedures are few in number. They are developed in collaboration with the CNO and the RNs working in the department with the assistance of other practitioners that coordinate care in the department. The same review and revision practice for policy and procedure development is followed with the departmental policies and procedures.

F. Administrative

Administrative policies and procedures impacting the professional nurse are frequently related to aspects of performance instead of direct patient care. An example would be staff schedules, sick calls, holiday pay, and so on. The policies and procedures impact the caregiver but do not directly define the care provided. The procedures are reviewed in committee and included in the unit staff meeting minutes. The development and review process is the same as listed in the other sections regarding standards.

G. Local, State, National

Standards of care provided by any level of authority complements the nursing practice by providing specific guidelines of care and practice. These guidelines become standards and every nurse must have knowledge of them, follow them, and participate in changes that become necessary. Local, state, and national standards of care all focus on the practice of nursing, have similar goals, and complement each other. When a difference of opinion occurs, the highest standard

has priority. For example, a nursing home might write a policy that the family be informed of all incidents involving the resident. The state may require notification only for injurious incidents. The nursing home's policy sets a higher standard and would thus be used to evaluate the actions of the staff.

The impact of ANA and the ANA Standards of Nursing Practice is held nationwide. The standards are inclusive of the Standards of Practice; the Standards of Professional Performance can be viewed at www.ana.org.[6] The addition of the 14 Forces of Magnetism gives credibility to the empowered, autonomous RN of today.

Today, as we continue our mission and goals to provide quality care with positive outcomes of care, we are faced with the development of the never event. A never event is a negative outcome of care that should be avoided within every patient care environment. For example, these events include care resulting in a patient acquiring a urinary tract infection as an outcome of the foley catheter and resulting care. In any never event, it is important for the nurse executive and staff to identify the potential event, identify best practice to avoid a negative outcome, and design concurrent monitoring tools to identify potential contributing events. When a patient has a foley catheter, data regarding the reason for insertion, the professional completing the insertion, compliance with daily care, and the evaluation of the patient daily for the continued need of the catheter need to be considered as the care is monitored. If the staff monitors the events maintaining quality and limiting the use of the catheter it will have a positive impact on the outcomes.

As a result of the monitoring, corrective/professional development action tools should be developed and utilized. In the event the concurrent monitoring tools regulating a patient with a foley catheter identify that a professional inserting the catheters has one or more patients with an identified infection, an action plan needs to be initiated. The professional should be notified of the infection rate. Education needs to be in place to review best practice. Monitoring the professional is completed with the documented competency for performing the procedure.

In order to continue the efforts and results of the concurrent monitoring the staff needs to know the environment is not an environment for punishment, but one for enhancing growth and increasing quality of care. However, once the professional is notified, re-educated, and documented as competent, resulting action for a continued infection rate will involve the use of the human resources policies and procedures in place for the discipline of staff failing to follow policies and procedures.

H. Benchmarking

Benchmarking is utilized in most organizations to determine effectiveness of policies, procedures, and delivery of care. The organization may review specific outcomes of care with other healthcare organizations. In addition, the organization can compare results on a unit-by-unit basis. An example includes the comparison of patient satisfaction scores, patient falls, medication errors, or antibiotic usage in the preoperative patient. Benchmarking with other organizations (by system, statewide, or nationwide) enhances professionalism and productivity by comparing similar nurse-sensitive quality outcome indicators. This practice can produce best practice information and instill a competitive sense to do better and collaborate with peers. Outcomes are clearly noted with benchmarking, and investigation into individual practice can be performed. This practice benefits all participants and improves outcomes for patients and clients.

Benchmarking is a positive way to perform checks and balances on the individual organization and nursing staff. It provides leaders with a point of reflection and pins discussion on ways to improve goals. Regulators look upon benchmarking as a significant source of data and outcomes. It is imperative that an organization's staff participates in the benchmarking of common indicators. How else would they have the knowledge of where or how they are providing quality care? Magnet organizations are required to participate in national benchmarking. Many of the organizations participate in NDNQI (National Data for Nursing Quality Indicators). NDNQI offers benchmarking statistics related to nurse-sensitive outcomes. It linked with the ANCC and Magnet to encourage active sharing and evaluation of data for Magnet organizations. Currently, organizations are participating in NDNQI to meet the Magnet requirement of one year of benchmark data. NDNQI was a quality initiative that has become a serious provider of data needed for professional collaboration.

8.5 Management Style

Management style is a standard that is either followed or determined by a professional leader. There are several management styles documented in the literature including participative, dictatorial, hierarchical, and so on. There are also variations within the styles. Different styles produce different cultures within an organization. A professional nurse prefers to have a voice (as demonstrated in the Force of Magnetism) of empowerment within the organization. The RN usually has a formal chain of command structure within the work environment, with the expectation that other resources can be utilized if needed. This knowledge, autonomy, and empowerment acknowledged by nursing leadership encourages

the professional nurse to speak up, no matter what management style is in place. There are a variety of leadership styles and thus one should seek assistance from mentors and utilize the chain of command if any questions arise. The ability to be comfortable in seeking to protect the safety of patients or to secure needed medical attention can make the difference between life and death of a patient. This subject is expanded upon in Chapter 1, *The Roots of Patient Injury*.

A. Shared Governance

TIP: Shared governance is a format for empowered decision making. It is a relevant and vital issue in the structuring of professional practice and fits well in nursing.

In making decisions about professional practice in shared governance, there must be a working relationship between the leader's ability to facilitate this model, the professional nurse, the standards, and staff competence. The process and structure can be different in each organization. The staff nurse may have control over practice and influence decisions in higher administrative areas. Our present nursing shortage has revitalized this concept.

Three general models of shared governance have emerged:

- The Councilor Model is the most popular model where a coordinating council integrates decisions made by managers and staff in subcommittee.
- The Administrative Model resembles a more traditional bureaucratic structure that divides the organization chart into two tracks with either a management or clinical focus.
- The Congressional Model relies on a democratic component to empower nurses to vote on issues as a group. The people make up the membership; that makes a difference in any model or variation thereof.

Predictors of success or failures are based upon the expertise of nurses and their commitment to the process. In Magnet hospitals, a structure for empowering nurses exists. Nurses must have influence over themselves as a professional group. A special characteristic of the model is that nurses feel they have access to information necessary to make effective decisions. It is not easy to establish shared governance. Staff can distort it if they are not vested in the process or it could meet with resistance from a previous structure that is not flexible. The following are insights regarding shared governance:

- Shared governance is a journey, not a destination.
- The journey can be long and steep.
- Not every environment is conducive to shared governance.
- Although not everyone will make the journey, it should be open to all.
- Some question if the journey is worth the price.

B. Structure (Organizational Chart)

The structure of the nursing department can be presented in chart format, showing areas of responsibilities and the reporting mechanism of both higher and lower management. The chart can be utilized by caregivers, patients, families, physicians, and the community to locate a unit or manager and to seek assistance, clarification, or information. Often if there is a concern by either staff or patients it is helpful to visualize the next level of management. Structures may vary from organization to organization. There is the normal pyramid chart, with increased levels of responsibility evident at a glance. There is a fair delegation of authority.

In the flat chart, the entire nursing leadership has equal responsibility and all report to a single entity. This chart usually is cumbersome when only one person handles the multitude of responsibility and accountability issues. A new trend is to have the organization chart with the patient or client in the middle and the reporting structure around the patient. This chart provides a visual image of the patient-centered philosophy of care. The largest organization chart showcases the entire organizational leadership, with nursing being predominant.

8.6 Job Responsibilities
A. Chief Nursing Officer (CNO)

The CNO is responsible for defining, approving, and upholding the standards of quality nursing care, and holds all nurses in the organization accountable for following the standards. The nursing leaders and staff must have verified education and competencies. Policies and procedures are designed and validated by the CNO. The state regulatory organization has specific requirements for the CNO, that is, master's degree and five years experience in nursing administration recommended. Certification can be varied in different specialties, but the CNA (Certified Nursing Administrator) or CNAA (Certified Nursing Administrator Advanced) is highly recommended. Other additional education, certification, accomplishments, or publications are desirable.

The areas of responsibility, besides overseeing nurses housewide and in the nursing department, can vary. It is not uncommon for a CNO to also have responsibility for physi-

cal therapy, laboratory, or pharmacy. The CEO decides on the total scope of responsibility. The CNO is usually a vice president and reports to a senior vice president or the CEO. The CNO's job description is structured to include compliance to the philosophy of the organization and the nursing department with adherence to the mission and values of the organization. The job description includes routine and specific job criteria and defines direct reporting lines and evaluation responsibility. The annual competency requirements are also included in the structure of the job description. As part of the evaluation process, the CNO with the appraiser (CEO or senior vice president) will develop annual goals. The compliance with the goals for the previous year is rated as part of the annual performance review. The evaluation also includes a report of educational achievements for the rating period by the CNO. This places a high level of importance on the necessity to maintain education and skills. The CNO should prepare a report of all educational programs attended or presented to the appraiser as part of the evaluation, since the CNO must meet the requirements of the job and demonstrate skills as a role model. Excellence begins at the top and the others will follow.

B. Assistant Vice President (AVP)

AVP responsibilities are assigned by the CNO, and can include:

- overseeing specific nursing units,
- serving as chair of committees, such as quality assurance,
- being a liaison for regulators (Joint Commission, Department of Health, and so on),
- leading special projects (i.e., Magnet),
- being an advisor for shared governance, and
- credentialing responsibility for allied health.

Although it can vary per organization, the reporting structure is usually to the CNO (VP of Nursing). The job description is individualized and complements the scope of services covered under the responsibilities assigned. The organization philosophy, mission, and values are included, along with annual competencies and personal goal setting.

The qualifications for an AVP of nursing are similar to the CNO; usually a BSN (master's degree preferably in nursing) and at least five years experience in a management administrative role are required. Certification in nursing administration at the CNA or CNAA level is recommended. All other specialty certifications are highly regarded and add to the individual credentials.

C. Director of Nursing

A director's area of responsibility is usually unit, or similar service, specific. Directors oversee more than one unit or specialty. For example, there may be a director of perioperative services who oversees the same day surgery unit, operating room, recovery room, and sterile supply department. The job description would address the organization's philosophy, mission, values, compliance with general management responsibilities, and specific job requirements. Annual competencies and personal goals are required. The director reports to the AVP or CNO. Qualifications for a nursing director include an experienced RN preferably BSN or master's prepared (or both) with at least five years management experience. Certification in a specialty is recommended for a CNA or CNAA.

D. Nurse Manager

The nurse manager has responsibility for a single nursing unit or a few similar units. The unit or units may vary in size; the staffing required is equated to the patient caseload. The manager oversees the organization of the unit and placement of equipment, supplies, and medications. Responsibility for hiring, counseling, assigning, or terminating staff on the unit lies with the nurse manager. Awareness of individual competency is key to assigning appropriate patients to the appropriate team member. For example, a nursing malpractice case may revolve around a failure to detect critical changes in a patient. Upon discovery, it may be learned the patient was assigned to an individual fatigued from working a double shift or assigned to a new employee, when a LPN or RN was needed.

Keeping the patient, client, and family aware of the plan of care is strategic in the process of assessment, diagnosis, implementation, outcome monitoring, and evaluation. The unit manager keeps communication lines open, conducts staff meetings, and encourages unit practice councils in order to assist the staff in decision-making skills. Leadership meetings are required in order to help the management staff remain well informed. The nurse manager is then responsible for disseminating the information to the staff in a timely fashion. Being alert to specific behaviors can avoid team disgruntlement or disruption of patient care. A nurse manager's knowledge of patient issues or concerns is enhanced with frequent rounding. This enables the manager to problem solve in a timely fashion and therefore increase patient, staff, and customer satisfaction. It is highly recommended the manager round on the unit with the staff. Unit-specific policies and procedures are also developed, monitored, and reviewed annually, following most state regulations.

The nurse manager can motivate staff members to continue their education by adjusting the work schedule to maximize attendance for classes. Encouraging staff growth (via mentoring or precepting) is rewarding and results in improved skills, communications, and competencies for increased clinical support. Preparation of budgets and staff schedules tends to be time consuming. These activities can be shared with staff as an initiative that may be used to achieve a level of the nursing clinical ladder program. Unit-based managers have the ability to provide the most organized productive team with the highest positive patient care outcomes.

The job description usually mirrors the generic standard for the other leadership staff with a narrower scope of responsibility. A nurse manager can be an experienced RN, usually with five years experience in nursing and some experience or expertise in the unit or chosen specialty. A minimum of a BSN is required, with a MSN recommended; certification in medical surgical nursing or other specialty is often required.

E. Supervisor

The supervisor represents administration on the evening, night, weekend, and holiday shifts when other nursing leaders are off site. The responsibilities are many, starting with oversight of all clinical areas, staffing concerns, and needs. The role requires a high level of critical and creative thinking when facilitating movement of staff. The goal is to have the appropriate competent staff in the right place and on the right team wherever necessary. The staff who call in sick make the decision making and adjustment of staffing levels a constant challenge.

The supervisor wears multiple hats, covering nonclinical areas such as medical records, warehouse, dietary, and other areas necessary to meet the special needs for any patient or physician. Problems or concerns must be dealt with quickly. The supervisor is an important person in the chain of command. Nursing negligence claims often include an allegation that the staff nurse failed to inform the charge nurse or supervisor of a concern regarding a patient. The supervisor has the authority to intervene, deal with physicians, or go over the physicians' heads to a department chair in order to gain care for the patient. The supervisor must be knowledgeable in emergency management and access the right mix of staff and equipment at the right time.

Counseling and disciplinary action may also be required during the course of a shift. For example, a nurse may come to work in an impaired state. Immediate action may be needed to protect the patients from the nurse who is unable to make correct judgments. The supervisor is also responsible for knowing the current policies and procedures or at least the resources needed to address the policy or procedure.

The administrative supervisor must have exemplary critical thinking skills, at least five years nursing experience, clinical competency, and exceptional public relations and communication skills in dealing with personnel, medical staff, patients, the media, and the community. The supervisor must possess diplomacy and the ability to handle confrontations without backing down. Leadership skills are essential.

F. Charge Nurse

The charge nurse is responsible for oversight and coordination of a unit's activity. This nurse can be assigned on an individual shift or all shifts. This individual can be a specific person in a permanent position or a position rotated amongst existing qualified, competent staff. Organizational preference usually determines the practice of a charge nurse. A charge nurse's responsibilities may be defined or changed as needed. An example of the flexibility in the role is the need for the charge nurse to take a patient care assignment in addition to the duties of the charge nurse. The priorities include an awareness of the unit activities, patient condition or change in condition, and the coordination of the overall plan of care. Some charge nurses give and receive the entire unit report at the change of shift; others expect the team members to do so.

The job description of the charge nurse has generic standards for the professional nurse and specific responsibilities related to the charge responsibilities. High levels of competency and goal setting are the norm. A charge nurse is a RN with reasonable experience and competencies for the assigned unit. The role is not assigned based upon seniority. Certification in nursing or the nursing specialty is recommended but not required.

G. Staff Nurse

A staff nurse is responsible and accountable for the patients assigned. The coordination of the plan of care and patient assessment dictate next steps in the quality care provided and outcomes monitored. The staff nurse coordinates individual patient care with the interdisciplinary team by initiating referrals and following up with members of the team. Competencies are maintained and monitored. Attendance at staff meetings and educational programs is recommended. Completing the clinical ladder program of the organization is also recommended.

Just as with the charge nurse, a staff nurse's job description has both generic standards and specific responsibilities related to the position of staff nurse. High levels of competency and goal setting are the norm.

Qualifications include graduation from nursing school and licensure in the state of employment. The initial inter-

view tends to be a positive experience and is conducted with the nurse manager, selected peers, and in certain areas a member of the medical staff. The human resources department is responsible for referrals and initial screening. The orientation process is completed with the assistance of an experienced preceptor on the nursing unit and the competencies of the staff nurse are closely monitored. The staff nurse must complete one year of employment prior to applying for the clinical ladder program.

H. Licensed Practical or Vocational Nurse (LPN/LVN)

A LPN or LVN is responsible for patient care assigned or delegated by the RN. Assignments are based on individual competencies, education, organization policies and procedures, and the Nurse Practice Act. The role of the LPN or LVN may easily be confused with the role of the RN. However, the Nurse Practice Act limits the role of the LPN or LVN. For example, the RN is responsible for assessing the patient. The LPN or LVN may collect data used for the assessment, but the RN completes the process. The job description of the LPN or LVN has generic standards for the licensed practical nurse and then specific responsibilities related to nursing. A qualification includes current licensure in the state of employment. Previous experience is recommended and additional education or certification is encouraged.

I. Unlicensed Assistive Personnel (UAP)

A UAP is responsible for specific tasks assigned by the RN or LPN. The UAP renders patient care by bathing patients, taking vital signs, and performing other tasks based on education and validated competency. The job description for the UAP has generic standards and specific responsibilities based on education, experience, validated competency, and organizational policies and procedures. Qualifications of the UAP include graduating high school, completing a standardized test related to the role, and possessing any additional education or certification necessary to enhance skills. A UAP in long-term or home care is required to complete the requirements for a certified nursing assistant (CNA).

More information on the education of RNs, LPNs or LVNs, and UAPs is found in Chapter 6, *The Foundations of Nursing Practice*.

J. Unit Secretary

The unit secretary is responsible for maintaining the patient chart, transcribing physician orders, and communicating with other disciplines for purposes of assisting with the coordination or scheduling of patient care. The orders transcribed by the unit secretary are validated by the RN on the unit. The unit secretary answers phones and manages communications on the unit. The secretary will enter orders and information into the computer, will fax information, and will communicate with patients and families as a liaison for patient advocacy. The job description has generic standards for the unit secretary in addition to specific responsibilities based on education, experience, validated competency, and organization policy and procedure. Qualifications for the unit secretary include the ability to read and write, use of the computer, communication and public relation skills, organizational skills, and telephone etiquette. A high school diploma is required.

8.7 Staffing Issues
A. Staffing and Scheduling

The challenge of having the right staff, the right mix, and the right number is paramount in a healthcare organization. Creativity and flexibility are required. The primary goal of the nursing department is to provide quality care to the patients, families, and community served.

To validate nurse-sensitive quality, patient outcomes are monitored closely. Staffing can be adjusted based on the outcomes and the right team members can be assigned to a patient unit. Acuity measurement is often completed prospectively and is constantly used as a measure in the department.

Position control is developed as a tool to hire a predetermined (budgeted) number of staff to meet the anticipated needs of the patients on a particular unit. Nurse managers use this tool to document the hiring process to maintain the right mix of staff—RN, LPN, UAP, and secretaries for the unit. The position control process is completed in conjunction with the development of a staffing matrix to schedule the hired staff to meet the anticipated needs of the patient population.

The nurse manager completes the schedule. The staff in the nursing office or staffing office assists the management staff by inputting the information in the scheduling system, completing schedule changes, printing daily rosters, and so on. In addition, the staff in this office manages a group of personnel assigned to float. The staffing office will schedule the personnel to fill in for call outs, or to alter the staffing based on census and acuity of illness of the patient population. The use of agency staff is also coordinated and managed in this office. This department also documents the names of staff that call in sick. Staff competencies of float or agency staff are monitored and maintained by the staff in this office. An additional concern is the impact of staffing levels on the healthcare worker's well-being. In case a state

of emergency is declared, a disaster tree for all nursing staff is maintained and activated by the organization leadership staff. This ensures quality of care is maintained in difficult times.

TIP: Reaching the right staffing levels is inclusive of the number of staff, but also the education, experience, and competency of the staff.

There exists a severe nationwide undersupply of nurses. There will be an even shorter supply of staff in the future. Recruitment and retention of nurses is a daily priority in health care. Competition is rampant, and nurses follow the market and choose accordingly, which tests the financial constraints. The organization must stay competitive and bolster pay with other positive incentives to retain the staff, especially the experienced staff.

Maintaining position control charts assists with managing open positions and increasing awareness of staffing needs. Once the basic FTE (full-time equivalent) per unit is determined or budgeted, nursing management can post and recruit for open positions in the department. It has been the trend to increase the number of part-time staff to provide the flexibility needed to increase and decrease staff based on patient census and patient acuity.

As roles in health care evolve and change and nurse executives manage more departments, staffing concerns grow. A staffing model should be developed that is capable of maintaining positive patient outcomes in order to survive financially.

Staffing ratios are already mandated in some states. It has become law in California. This mandate places pressure on nursing to either meet the ratios or close nursing units. In some states, healthcare organizations are mandated to post staffing for all units on all shifts. This will potentially be a concern of the public and advocates of union activity, regulators, and patients.

Monitoring patient outcomes is important, and it behooves the nursing department and organization to creatively design a way to do this daily. Scheduling is often a difficult activity; accommodating requests, special shifts, and unforeseeable events can be an awesome responsibility. Nursing has empowered many units to do self scheduling, with management oversight as needed. Special bonuses or programs are offered to fill difficult shifts, such as weekend, evening, and night shifts. Meeting scheduling needs is key to maintaining staff satisfaction and to retaining staff.

State and federal legislators are responding to public outcries, data, and regulatory organization concerns. The information in newspapers, journals, magazines, and billboards has awakened these individuals. The statistics were determined in order to place blame for increasing medical errors. Professional healthcare providers should be aware and get involved in proposed regulations that will eventually affect the work care environment. Staffing levels are usually presented by the state department of health codes or regulations. The Centers for Medicare and Medicaid (CMS) provides criteria to be met in order to participate. In 1999, California's governor signed legislation requiring the State Department of Health to establish a regulation for staffing levels in acute care hospitals by 2002.[7] This is the first state to accomplish this, and despite the initial problems it is working in most areas.

B. Productivity

Productivity is a monitoring tool designed to control utilization of resources and the amount of money budgeted. Fixed budgets usually remain constant and a flexible budget is a target to work toward. Acuity, quality, census, and standards of care influence the budget system. A nurse manager can impact the productivity monitoring by position control and staff performance. With money variables and other unpredictable occurrences in health care, managers must be aware of all external and internal factors and how they impact productivity. A nurse can be very productive when the environment is organized, and supplies and medications are available. Information system capabilities make communicating an efficient and timely process, allowing peers and team members to work cohesively.

C. FTE (Full-Time Equivalent)

A full-time equivalent is a budget term. It is equal to 2,080 hours per year or 40 hours per week. In an organization, a number of FTEs are budgeted to staff a unit. The variable in the staffing or use of FTE is the number of days and shifts the department is open. If a department is open seven days a week, 1.4 FTEs will need to be budgeted to have one person on seven days a week for a two-week pay period. By using the FTE process, the manager is not hiring a person; instead the manager is hiring a FTE or portion of a FTE. A creative manager can have a multitude of variations in the number of staff used to fill the budgeted FTEs. Determining the direct care man-hours leads to an outcome of FTEs for the fiscal year. Standards of care and preselected levels of quality are a part of the decision-making process and lead to positive quality outcomes.

D. Direct versus Indirect

Direct caregivers provide direct hands-on patient care. These include the nurse manager, RNs, LPNs, UAPs, technicians,

and so on. Indirect caregivers include those who do not provide direct care; rather they provide support (e.g., unit secretary, environmental personnel, and educators).

E. Alternative Scheduling Patterns

Alternative scheduling patterns are unique approaches to scheduling staff. A nursing unit might rotate an on-call nurse to provide coverage for a call out or unscheduled event. Care units or organizations can post a needs list for unfilled shifts on the schedule, for per diem or other interested staff. Bidding programs are designed and marketed to provide a computerized notification of available shifts for staff to bid on over the Internet. There may or may not be a financial incentive for the early participants. This program is monitored frequently and positions are added, updated, confirmed, or removed.

F. Staffing Systems

Staffing systems are selected by the organization. The organization may choose a computerized or paper version of staffing and scheduling. Some organizations use a combination of the two. In a true computerized system, the computer generates the schedule. In a combined system, the manager may do the schedule with paper and pencil. However, the staffing office will enter the information into a computerized system.

TIP: Whatever system is used, the facility should be able to provide the staffing schedule upon request of an attorney.

An organization may prepare a staffing matrix to guide the development of the schedule. A work allocation system is a unit designed by type of patient, number of patients, a specific clinical ladder, and predetermined staffing. For example, 6 East has 24 beds, and is an orthopaedic unit staffed by eight full-time RNs, four LPNs, six UAPs, and two unit secretaries. There are four positions of Clinical III orthopaedic RNs, and four new RN staff. All of the LPN and UAP staff are experienced in orthopaedics. If a nursing unit has a less acute population then the staffing mix could vary with less professional staff and more support staff.

G. Acuity Systems

A variety of acuity systems are available to determine the level of care required for a patient for a specific period of time. The system must be designed to equate the care provided or anticipated into staffing requirements. The objectivity of the system is difficult to maintain based on nursing perceptions. Therefore, it is advisable to complete interrater reliability studies (a way nurse managers check the acuity of the patients; it is known as a checks and balances system) on completed acuities to validate the measures selected. In most cases, acuity systems are used to project long-term budget needs. It is difficult to use this system to manage daily staffing needs, especially if, based on acuity, the unit needs three float staff and there are only two.

Frequently the usefulness for daily staffing is to assist the staffer in the critical-thinking process. If acuity is considerably higher on unit A, the individual can therefore send extra nurses there. Per diem and float pool nurses provide the scheduling office with a list of availability and can fill unit positions as needed. These nurses may be used to fill vacancies, depending on staffing needs and individual competencies. They usually receive a higher hourly rate because they do not receive benefits. However, they may also receive additional incentives to work evenings, nights, and weekends depending on the particular needs of the organization. The program provides both the nurse and the organization with additional flexibility to meet the needs of increasing or decreasing acuity, census, and staffing.

Fluctuating census and acuity can affect staffing in both directions. Overstaffing and understaffing occur, and nursing leaders are required to make decisions or utilize predetermined strategies to cope. Management reacts to the constant communication of changing situations. When the facility is overstaffed, staff may be asked to take time off, leave early, be reassigned to another unit, or serve on call. When understaffed, nursing leadership may elect to utilize float or per diem staff, call unscheduled staff to work extra, pull a nurse from another unit, or call a staffing agency.

H. Staffing Effectiveness

A staffing effectiveness requirement was designed by The Joint Commission in 2002 in the Human Resources standards. The Joint Commission presented a format with approximately 20 indicators: ten human relations and ten clinical indicators. Organizations were required to select two from each group and collect data.[8] The data was converted into the rate per 1,000 patient days. A continual comparison was developed and monitoring tools and action plans were designed. Several years after organizations developed these tools, no meaningful correlation was noted regarding the relationship of the indicators. In 2004-05, the regulators recognized this phenomenon and presented another way to compare the indicators. By being more specific and drilling down into the data, it is expected that relationships will be documented. For example, the data will be more specific in the definition of the indicator, that is, not just amount of overtime, but more specifically shifts longer than 12.5

hours, greater than two to three shifts in a row, and so on. This information is beginning to be presented and healthcare providers are awaiting conclusions regarding the results.

I. Reengineering and Patient Safety

TIP: Healthcare organizations use reengineering to redesign the delivery model, improve productivity, and restructure. This process produces changes (by saving financial costs) that healthcare organizations measure to check or increase competitiveness and to improve outcomes.

Reengineering focuses on change to improve patient safety. Organizations use the cause and effect model to make things better and shake up a stable environment. To succeed, leadership must support this process. If the process, structure, and outcomes of an organization are currently not perceived as meeting standards, reengineering can provide a new vision, uplift spirits, and encourage change in a positive way. A "new beginning" is a frequently used term in the reengineering arena.

J. Nursing Shortage and the Impact on Staff

Statistics show a nursing shortage is occurring and predict a persistent shortage in the future. Nursing shortages developed from a decreased interest in the profession, and multiple career options available. Regulators who decrease reimbursement to the healthcare organizations force cutbacks; thus safety issues can intimidate possible candidates. Creative staffing and staffing models are developed when a shortage impacts the number of nurses available.

The awareness of regulators and businesses has corrected shortages over time. Regulators influence the educators to produce more professional RNs, and businesses advertise the positive aspects of the frontline providers and encourage enrollment into this profession. The company Johnson & Johnson has devoted major resources to improving the image of nursing by increasing the number of individuals enrolling in nursing education programs. This company offers a number of scholarships to nursing students.

State nursing organizations provide statistics and oversight to the number of nurses currently active in the profession. These statistics, which include nurses' ages and employment information, provide guidelines concerning how to deal with the shortage.

The U.S. Bureau of Statistics divides healthcare workers into "health diagnosing" (physicians), "health assessing" (RNs), "health technicians" (lab, x-ray), "health services" (nurse aide), "home health" (home health aide), and "other."[9] This is not necessarily the way educators and managers would categorize the healthcare workers, but it is the way it is done nationally.

The nursing profession has a wide variation in educational routes, experiences, and roles. "A nurse is a nurse" is not always an accurate description of nursing: there are LPNs, RNs, RNs who become NPs (nurse practitioners), and so on. When a shortage is in progress, attention focuses on the employment and deployment of the right mix of nurses to best deliver quality patient care. Shortages will persist and nursing leadership must keep this as a priority in promoting the role of the professional nurse, setting reasonable educational goals, and mentoring the new inexperienced nurse.

For organizations to retain the RN staff and avoid a shortage, they must provide the right environment together with a competitive salary structure with additional benefits to encourage additional education, certification, and professional growth. Refer to Chapter 2, *Where Have All the Nurses Gone?*, for more information on this subject.

K. Hospital-Wide Standards to Facilitate Staffing

Hospital-wide standards facilitate staffing and can provide the way to efficient practice. Incorporating written standards into daily documentation can meet the quality care requirements of the hospital and regulators (state, Joint Commission, Magnet) that monitor quality care and outcomes.

TIP: If the standards are used house-wide then nursing staff can easily move unit to unit; agency personnel can be oriented to one standard documentation tool; and the stability and knowledge of the standards become a practice due to continually assessing and reassessing the patient's care and documenting findings.

Meeting clinical standards is a challenge and the creative design of the medical record can incorporate mandatory standards. For example, pain management relates to the standard of assessing every patient's pain; noting an intervention and an outcome is required by all regulators. Some states (e.g., New Jersey) have mandated that pain assessment, usually using a pain scale with a 1-10 rating, be the fifth vital sign when following the organization's vital sign policy and procedure. If triggers are placed in a specific format, compliance with the standard cannot be avoided. Double documenting is undesirable when nurses design a nursing documentation tool. It takes a creative team to come to consensus, be concise, avoid duplication, and streamline the tool.

Plans of care are developed by diagnosis to provide a standard of care for patients with a specific DRG. Generic plans of care are developed for the patient when a specific diagnosis is not confirmed. Policies and procedures define the what, why, and how to initiate the assessment on admission, which is a more comprehensive and inclusive intake and includes the basic assessment of:

- vital signs
- pain
- intake and output
- neurological signs
- skin and wound
- psychosocial
- education
- high-risk events (falls)
- discharge planning
- respiratory indicators
- activities of daily living

Narrative nursing notes communicate unique, unusual changes in any aspect of the patient condition or treatment modalities that occurred on a particular shift and their impact on the outcome of care. To evaluate the standards, performance improvement indicators are in place to validate compliance and determine if certain elements should be revised or eliminated; they should be continually updated to stay current with new regulations or new standards of care. The failure to evaluate the plan of care, recognize when care needs to be altered, and define a new set of interventions can result in a poor outcome. For example, a pressure ulcer flow sheet documents a deepening of a pressure ulcer, despite use of a skin barrier dressing. The nurse would be expected to recognize the need to change the plan of care. A tool that streamlines evaluation by staff is an important source of staff satisfaction. If a product is concise in a contained format (one tool, not multiple separate papers), easy to follow, and organized, then RNs have more time to be with the patient and therefore documentation improves.

L. Incentive for Staffing

A variety of initiatives in staffing have a positive impact on maintaining safe staffing levels. Flexible shifts, bonuses for special or periodic commitments, a guaranteed team of cohesive staff, and offering a per diem or float pool within the organization are all positive incentives for nursing staff. Recruitment and retention committees focus on unique ways to retain staff:

- educational offerings

- tuition reimbursement
- holiday celebrations
- staff recognition luncheons or dinners
- flexible benefit packages

Having a thorough orientation and offering specialty courses can provide nurses opportunities for personal growth and additional competencies, which is a positive incentive. An environment of professionalism, autonomy, and empowerment is welcomed by nurses and allows decision making related to patient care and control over practice, which stimulates knowledge and critical thinking resulting in improved outcomes in the nurse-sensitive quality indicators.

M. Staffing and Assignments

Assignments are developed to facilitate efficient patient care and meet the needs of the patient. The assignment provides structure for communications within the patient care team. Assignments usually are communicated at the change of shift. The assignment is developed by the nurse manager, charge nurse, or designee. Specific attention is paid to the acuity of the patient, the patient care needs for the shift, the competencies of the individuals available to be assigned to the patient, and the location of the patient. The acuity of a patient can be defined by a set of indicators predefined to address the severity of the patient needs. The nursing assessment partially determines the acuity of care needed by the patient. The medical orders for the period also impact the acuity of the patient illness. The need for several diagnostic tests or immediate postoperative care can definitely impact the amount of care required.

The report is then focused to provide information to the caregiver. If a patient condition changes after the assignment is completed, the staff needs to be flexible enough to revise the assignment. The nursing leader or RN in charge should be able to rely on the staff to apprise the leader of the patient's status. The nurse learns this type of decision making in school; however, the main education occurs after graduation with direct clinical experience on the unit. Some units attempt to assign the same caregiver to a patient for several days or shifts in a row. This improves the continuity of the delivery of care and also has a positive impact on patient satisfaction.

Changes in assignment can occur:

- when a patient's condition changes,
- when an individual assignment is extremely heavy,
- when activities increase for more than one patient or a particular patient and family require special care, or
- when the nurse schedule changes.

It is pertinent to rotate a difficult patient among the team, and collectively determine the best method of dealing with the particular difficulties encountered.

Many times a patient requires consultation beyond the team on the unit. The extended team for individual care could include a pain management expert, social worker, physical therapist, nutrition expert, respiratory therapist, case manager, and so on. Whatever care needed by the patient or family must be addressed with the appropriate resources available to the team. A patient assignment can be a one-to-one (1:1) nurse-patient ratio (or 1:2, 1:3, and so on, per patient need); ratios are determined by regulatory agencies or individual staff competencies. Astute and creative leadership is necessary to complete the correct assignment of care. The transfer of care usually occurs at the change of shift with appropriate documentation and a change of shift report.

TIP: There must be sufficient staffing on the nursing unit during change of shift report to meet a patient's needs. Patient incidents may occur when the professional nursing staff is busy with shift report or completing documentation. This leaves the UAP to answer call bells and respond to patient requests.

Many organizations do rounding at the change of shift to more accurately transfer the care. In addition, the rounding provides an opportunity to introduce the patient and family to the nursing staff taking over the care for the shift. Transfer of care can also occur during a given shift due to patient or staff leaving the unit for lunch, education programs, and so on. One team member will be given a report and have responsibility for the patient while the assigned nurse is off the unit. Thus there is no interruption in the delivery of care. Another transfer of care occurs when the patient is moved to another unit or another level of care such as intensive care, telemetry, oncology, and so on. In addition, the patient can be sent to a more appropriate facility.

N. Alternatives to Pulling and Floating

This concept needs to be introduced during orientation. Staff needs to be aware of the possibility of being pulled to another nursing unit. Standardization can facilitate this practice and nurses will have less fear of different practices and policies on a different unit. Competencies must be considered and levels of care decided so staff is aware of individual limitations. Shared governance models can decide unit-specific rules regarding pulling. Rotational on-call lists can be developed to provide staff in the case of acuity, call outs, increased census, or other emergent situations. Maintaining a per diem float team or calling contracted agencies are alternatives. Offering monetary incentives to staff who work on unscheduled days and rewarding staff who work extra shifts by offering the next day off are additional alternatives.

TIP: Nursing staff reacts negatively to the practice of pulling or being floated to another unit.

O. Agency Use

The use of agency nurses is costly to an organization. (The agency hourly fee is higher than the organization would pay an employee.) Their usage can vary from a contracted amount of time to daily requests. Agencies provide educational, licensure and credentialing, and competency information to the organization's staffing office or human resources department. Agency use can provide support when nursing has open positions or shifts. The staff relies on this support in unique or emergent situations. Agency nurses can work well within an organization if they are familiar with the standards of care and practice. Cohesive personalities develop over time; trust is evident and they become a partner in quality care delivery. Travel nurses learn about an organization's culture while working on a timed assignment, such as 12 weeks on a telemetry unit. This nurse may opt to take a permanent assignment on that unit once the contract has been fulfilled.

8.8 Patient Safety—Culture of Safety

One of the byproducts of media coverage of nursing and other medical negligence claims is that an informed public is aware of occurrences, problems, and poor outcomes. The public has become more knowledgeable about how to prevent personal injuries, oversights, and medical errors to itself, its families, or significant others. Public fact finding is reported in newspapers, in magazines, online, on television, and through regulatory statistics at local, state, and national levels. An organization receives more attention due to the significance of the occurrence. The administration may be called upon to reveal the actions it has taken to assure itself this occurrence will not be repeated.

The regulators (Joint Commission) have recommended a "culture of safety" be encouraged and publicized. This culture is one that guides the public to inquire about a healthcare organization and statistics regarding safety. Healthcare providers owe the public the requested information, and this questioning can prevent future occurrences. Today's informed public can sense a culture of safety in the healthcare environment by asking or observing specific behaviors. If handwashing is reported to decrease infections and the spreading of disease, it is imperative caregivers wash their hands or be asked "why not?" by an informed consumer. This process can only lead to a safer, more aware health-

care team and a healthy public. Brochures are available that provide key points on the "how to" of a culture of safety environment. These pamphlets are key in encouraging the public to ask questions, and self advocate for a safer healthcare environment.

8.9 Satisfaction
A. Patient Satisfaction

In today's competitive healthcare environment organizations must maintain a high level of patient satisfaction. The satisfaction is measured utilizing a monitoring instrument designed by the organization or an outside provider of a tool. In addition to consumers, regulators and third-party payers also review patient satisfaction results. Patient satisfaction in some institutions is based on the patient's perception of quality. The healthcare organization would be remiss not to rely on and utilize the data collected to validate positive patient satisfaction outcomes. The organization must respond to the issues as quickly as possible if there are concerns. This practice assists an organization in providing best practices and responding to patient concerns. Responding to individual patients also can avoid legal implications or negative publicity based on dissatisfaction. Organizational benchmarking can occur with like organizations, units, and quality indicators. This communication is needed for organizations to remain stable within the community. In addition, CMS can refer to patient satisfaction results in the decision making involving payment and benefits for the organization.

B. Staff Satisfaction

Staff satisfaction surveys allow leadership to evaluate the environment, resolve perceptions of dissatisfaction, and develop work plans to address the concerns of the staff. Knowledge of staff satisfaction assists in the development of recruitment and retention strategies for the organization. The survey assists management in opening dialogues when issues are identified. The dialogue leads to development of plans with the assistance of the staff to resolve the identified issues. Accrediting organizations, e.g., Magnet, require staff satisfaction data in the initial application and the annual report. Magnet facilities can develop or work with the individual organization staff satisfaction or utilize the survey provided by NDNQI. Staff dissatisfaction can negatively impact patient satisfaction. In addition to recruitment and retention of staff, the survey assists with the overall patient satisfaction initiatives.

8.10 Competencies

The competency requirement begins during employee orientation and continues throughout employment in response to a change in position or unit, new job responsibilities, changes in equipment or medications, changes in procedures related to the delivery of care, and so on. Organizations meet the competency requirement by developing a competency program. This program is developed with the assistance of the educators and the leadership of the department. The program varies for individuals. The competency is selected for several reasons: new practices, new equipment, new treatment modality, low volume high-risk procedures, or tracking of patterns based on medication or safety issues. Certain units require competencies based on the population served. Unit-specific competencies must be completed in order to work in the particular unit.

TIP: The goal of The Joint Commission is safe quality care for the population. One of the main focuses of The Joint Commission visit is verifying the organization is validating the competencies of the staff.

A. Pre-Employment Testing

Pre-employment testing is completed in the human resources department. It assures the organization that the new employee meets standard criteria necessary for employment. The tests are usually a complete history and physical, urine screening for drug or alcohol use, and criminal background checks. In some states, fingerprinting of nurses is a new requirement. After the basic criteria are successfully completed, the employee is processed through the education department. Two basic standardized tests are usually administered to check or validate basic knowledge and competencies related to medication administration and nursing. If a potential employee cannot successfully complete the testing with a score of 80 or above, counseling can be provided and a second test can be scheduled. Other factors, such as the interview process and personal references, can be considered and have an impact on the hiring process.

B. Interview Process

The human resources department screens all applications. Nursing management is contacted to interview and concur on a prospective new hire. The manager conducts the next interview and reviews the job description and role expectations for the unit. Peer interviews are conducted in some settings. This initiative allows the RN autonomy and empowerment related to the staff joining the team. This is important in the Magnet culture and allows the staff to introduce the prospective employee to the shared governance and decision-making process at the institution. The same process occurs for nurses wishing to transfer to another unit or level of the organization. The interview process is different if the

applicant is seeking a management role. Several staff will be asked to interview the candidate peers; interdisciplinary staff members that would potentially work with the candidate are requested to participate in the interview process. The level of staff participating in the process increases as the management role and responsibilities increase. Senior management staff participate in the interviews for the higher levels of management.

C. Orientation

Orientation is an essential part of the employment process. All organizations have standards related to the orientation of new staff. This is the time to welcome the new staff member and to introduce the employee to the mission, values, and philosophy of the organization. The orientation also includes information on safety, such as fire Hazmat, infection control, emergency preparedness, and disaster procedures. Introduction to key leadership staff is also part of the process. The organization chart is reviewed as part of the program. A basic tour of the organization is included in the orientation. At this time the new employee receives an identification badge with name, department, and special credentials. In some settings photos are placed on the badge. This badge must be worn at all times while in the facility.

All of the mandatory education for staff and patient safety are covered during orientation. A formal checklist documents completion of the orientation requirements. This is completed as soon as possible and maintained in the employee file. The second portion of the checklist relates to specific duties and responsibilities for the assigned unit or department. Most organizations have a 90-day probationary period during which the organization can validate the competencies of the employee. If the employee is found incompetent during this time period, employment can be terminated for valid, documented reasons.

D. Preceptors

Preceptors are assigned to orient new staff to a particular unit or department. Preceptors are experienced, knowledgeable peers that emulate best practices, critical thinking, and good interpersonal skills. A preceptor works closely with the new staff, orienting and observing him and providing guidance to the organization standards of care and practices. Preceptors can enhance their skills through education and some organizations provide additional pay or recognition for continuing education. Performance outcomes can be measured on an ongoing basis to check for problems, monitor retention, and recruit new employees. The orientation period is extremely important for the individual and the organization. It determines if the employee and the unit are a good fit for the patients and other customers. A poor orientation frequently precipitates early resignations and therefore impacts staff retention.

E. Mentors

Mentors are staff members usually chosen by another staff member to provide guidance, information, and special insight into a particular job, or more likely professional development for the individual. A mentor can provide special sessions or education to facilitate a plan to increase the knowledge of the employee. A mentor provides encouragement and suggests possible ways to attain goals and accomplish tasks necessary to meet the goals. Mentoring is usually agreed upon by both parties. A mentor can work with a group with mutual needs and goals. Mentors can and do make a lasting impression and are frequently instrumental in the professional development of the person seeking assistance. It is a mentor's most cherished achievement to see an individual grow professionally and achieve new professional heights. Mentors have meaningful roles, as it takes willingness to go the extra mile and be a true leader and role model.

F. Annual Mandatory Education

Only by consistently monitoring staff skills and knowledge can management be assured that patients are receiving quality care. A process must be in place to have staff at all levels of the organization receive annual mandatory education. The mandatory education is a review of key aspects of the organization's beliefs, concerns, and expected outcomes. It is essential all staff participate in this education.

Compliance with the expected education is monitored by regulators at the state and national level. The education process challenges the creativity of the presenters and planners to provide the information in a unique way so it is memorable to the attendees. Retention of the facts and information presented is insignificant if the specific needs of the adult learner are not addressed. The presentation must be interesting. Individual state regulators can set standards that must be met by all employees on an annual basis. The organization may add educational standards to address the current needs of the staff and the community served. A hot topic in current literature or a Joint Commission, Department of Health, or Institute of Medicine issue can also be included to assure staff knowledge and compliance with current trends, safety goals, or mandates.

G. Continuing Education and Continuing Education Units (CEUs)

Nurses continue education to stay current, master new skills, advance to a higher educational level, or obtain national cer-

tification in a particular specialty. Continuing education is available within and outside of all organizations; however, the degree to which the organization or the individual education department functions is determined by the leadership, department or unit-specific education requests, and the needs assessment completed by the education department. This information is collated and evaluated to develop an education calendar of meaningful programs. The nurse's responsibility is to become aware of these educational offerings and select the ones to meet her needs. The attendance is either during work or personal time.

Professionalism may be demonstrated by the individual nurse's attendance at education and application of the material to the work setting. The unit of measure for the time spent in education is a Continuing Education Unit (CEU), which is given when the education provided meets the criteria and standards of the provider organization. The ANCC grants providership to sponsoring agencies.

TIP: One hour of education is equal to one contact hour.

In some states, nurses are required to earn contact hours for renewal of their professional license. Certified nurses value contact hours because they are needed in the recertification process. The certification exam can be taken if an insufficient numbers of contact hours have been earned. The professional nurse should prepare an education summary for the manager to include in the annual evaluation process. The certificates from outside programs should be submitted to demonstrate professional accomplishments and development. In addition, the certificates are needed for completion of the application for professional certification. Nursing leadership should encourage participation by preparing an education budget and facilitating schedule adjustments to allow for education time. Magnet organizations demonstrate a high level of participation in the education process.

H. Unit-Specific Requirements

As the nursing department is composed of a variety of units offering specific services to specific patient populations, staff providing the care may need unit-specific education to meet the needs of the population served. Upon hire or transfer to a specialty unit, orientation occurs and an assessment of the nurse's credentials and education needs is completed. The job requirements include years of experience, educational preparation, and certifications. There are times, due to changes in equipment or advances in technology, that new services are offered requiring development of further unit-specific competencies. The requirements are determined by the organization, nursing leadership, nursing education, or regulatory agencies. If a nursing unit or department delivers a specific treatment modality and it is high risk or low volume, that service is usually included in the unit-specific competencies.

I. Clinical Advancement Programs (CAP)

Clinical advancement programs (CAP) are available to staff to encourage professional growth and participation in the organization. Many times the opportunities for advancement in management are limited. In addition some staff prefer to advance clinically in the organization. Therefore the CAP program provides additional incentives for the nurse at the bedside. Some institutions provide a monetary award based on the level achieved. Clinical ladders or advancement programs can vary among organizations. However, in all cases, specific requirements must be met and maintained to enter or remain in the program. The accomplishments of the individual must be confirmed and validated by the management of the department and also by the committee of peers reviewing the information.

A basic requirement for participation is the overall evaluation score for the individual from the annual performance review. A low score prevents participation in the program. The time frame for the material submitted is one year. The data submitted includes but is not limited to hours worked, educational programs attended, certifications achieved, and hours utilized for participation in special projects.

The nurse completes an application to be reviewed by a committee of peers. The committee decides whether to accept or reject the application based on the material presented and on compliance with the requirements. The peers represent a variety of clinical areas and devote several hours monthly to reviewing of packets and applications, mentoring applicants as needed, and finally accepting or rejecting the application. The initial application is the most difficult and overwhelming, but with encouragement and mentoring, peer-to-peer review can make the goal achievable. The second application or renewal is easier to complete.

In some institutions the clinical ladder program has extended to the LPN staff. This reflects professionalism on the part of the RN staff mentoring and encouraging LPN staff to achieve higher levels of nursing. The program impacts nursing recruitment and retention and more importantly quality outcomes for the community served.

8.11 Continuum of Care
A. Sites of Care

Nursing across the continuum is important to patients in that it provides care in the appropriate setting from birth to death.

The patient becomes nursing's responsibility upon entering an environment of care and accepting care. No matter how the patient enters the system (direct admission, via the emergency medicine department, or an outpatient service) that patient gives consent to the organization and healthcare team to provide care. The initial nursing assessment is a collection of data regarding the patient and includes:

- the history of the current medical problem,
- current state of health and physical data such as height and weight,
- the medical history, and
- the physical, which provides the basis for the plan of care.

The patient is assessed for potential discharge needs (including medications) on this first encounter. As care is delivered and outcomes evaluated, the patient progresses through the healthcare system. The nursing shift-to-shift, day-to-day care is essential in achieving patient outcomes while preparing for discharge to the next stage in the continuum of care. The patient is discharged to the level of care necessary to return the patient to the optimum level of health achievable for the current problem. The patient may be discharged to home, home health care, long-term care, or rehabilitation, among others.

The movement of the patient through the continuum is facilitated by the provision of quality care in a timely fashion, in the correct setting, and with a detailed transfer-of-care plan. Nursing care across the continuum is the constant that enables the patient to achieve a positive outcome in each encounter. The continuum of care is enhanced when relationships among caregivers are established, focusing every member on the patient's plan of care. Nursing's role throughout the continuum is to coordinate services and care delivered. The responsibility of the nurse is constant and transferred among nurses in each setting.

B. Discharge Planning

1. Definition

Discharge planning is the coordination of care a patient requires in preparation for leaving the hospital setting. This planning includes, but is not limited to, scheduling transportation, arranging delivery of care, coordinating services with the agency responsible for the care, and educating patient and family. The team decides the level of care needed in the home. The planning and coordinating care is initiated in the acute care setting. The external agency involved in the process works with the acute care team and prepares to implement the plan of care postdischarge. The patient is assessed and evaluated at all times. A thorough discharge process leads to positive outcomes for the patient and decreases readmission rates and complications. Safe quality care is enhanced when this process is done well. Refer to Chapter 15, *Home Healthcare Nursing Malpractice Issues*, in Volume II, for more information on the post-discharge setting.

2. Timing

TIP: The discharge planning process is initiated at the time of admission to the acute care setting.

In the initial admission assessment, the answers to specific questions trigger further evaluation of potential needs at the time of discharge. A plan is initiated based on the results of the admission assessment, including support systems in the home in conjunction with the current diagnosis and health status of the patient. The case manager, if used in the hospital, continues the evaluation and meets with the healthcare team to facilitate care both in the hospital and in the appropriate setting after discharge. The case management staff works with the insurance companies to verify or validate coverage for the patient. The case management staff also advocates for the patient when necessary. A major role of the case manager is to coordinate the interdisciplinary team conference. During this conference the members of the healthcare team, including dieticians, physicians, nurses, physical therapists, social services, pain management, smoking cessation counselors, and so on evaluate the response of the patient to the care provided. The team facilitates the discharge of the patient to the appropriate care setting.

3. Admission and discharge nurse

Many organizations have identified the need for a skilled admission and discharge nurse. This nurse provides an added benefit for the planning and delivery of care. The admission and discharge process can be extremely stressful for the patient and family. The nurse, based on the assessment, initiates the plan of care, collects appropriate specimens for the diagnostic testing, and communicates with the patient, family, and healthcare team. The admission nurse initiates medication reconciliation, evaluates the patient's readiness to learn, assesses learning techniques best suited for the patient, and when appropriate, initiates patient and family education. The admission nurse is responsible for transferring the care report to the nurse receiving the patient. This is documented on the medical record. The discharge nurse provides the checks and balances needed in the care of the patient. This nurse reviews and reinforces the patient

and family education, plan of care, medication reconciliation, prescriptions needed, follow-up care, and final smoking cessation counseling if appropriate.

At the time of discharge the nurse also provides the patient with a phone number to call with questions. The opportunity for the nurse to allay fears and anxieties is crucial for the patient and family. The nurse secures information as needed and answers questions or refers the individual to the appropriate person for resolution of the question. In today's healthcare environment there is a decreased length of stay; thus the admission and discharge nurse can provide a needed service for the patient and family.

4. Education

Smoking cessation is a national initiative to decrease smoking and educate the public regarding the dangers to the secondhand smoker. Smoking is a known causative agent in lung cancer, heart failure, and pneumonia. This knowledge is well-known, and healthcare organizations have brought the significance of this habit to the forefront. It is a primary education initiative today and a regulatory requirement. To fulfill the nurse's role of "preventative health care maintenance," patients need to be told and retold the dangers of this habit to themselves and others.

The healthcare care team must evaluate the comprehensive abilities of each patient. This information facilitates the recovery process for the patient. It is important to have the patient repeat the education provided and demonstrate skills such as medication administration, dressing changes, and so on. This is a necessary step to make the patient feel safe leaving the organization. Some nursing units will call the patient after discharge. These calls provide evaluation of the education provided. In addition, they have been reported as high satisfiers for patients and families.

5. Medication reconciliation

Medication reconciliation is a Joint Commission National Patient Safety Goal for 2005.[10] This process, done on admission, can safely monitor medications (including herbal and over-the-counter medications) taken outside of the acute care setting. Allergies and sensitivities are also included in order to complete the initial intake information. This data is communicated to the hospital pharmacy and the admitting physician and resident staff. As nursing compiles the information, the admitting physician reviews and orders medications to be administered while in the hospital. Frequently the medications are new to the patient, based on diagnosis and condition of the patient. The medication may also be ordered via a different route or strength as determined by the patient condition. It is imperative preadmission medications be reviewed and evaluated to determine their continuance. Mediation reconciliation literature encourages the patient to ask questions when receiving unfamiliar medications. This initiative has decreased medication errors and prevented serious complications. The 100,000 Lives (now 5 Million Lives) campaign complements this process. Refer to Chapter 4, *Patient Safety Initiatives*, for more information on this campaign.

Medication reconciliation is repeated at the time of discharge. A member of the healthcare team, such as the discharge nurse, reviews the discharge medication orders, and compares the discharge medication with medication taken prior to admission and those medications added or changed during the inpatient stay. This reconciliation must be thorough and comprehensive. Missed medications are missed opportunities to provide a safe discharge process and transition to the next level of care.

6. Alternatives

Alternatives to discharge planning can occur when members of the healthcare team disagree. The appropriateness of the discharge plan can be questioned if the patient is not included in the plan or process, or if the patient does not have the resources but desires to return home anyway. Alternatives could include a change in destination such as a choice of rehabilitation or long-term care, or even the selection of a hospice unit. Shorter hospital stays can affect discharge needs and may affect the ability of the patient to return home with minimal change to the daily routine, capabilities, and resources.

7. Follow-up care

The positive acknowledgments and increased patient satisfaction ratings have proved that follow-up care enhances patient comfort and safety after discharge. Follow-up care provides information sharing and provides opportunities to address questions and review protocols. The caregiver monitors the outcomes, reiterates the educational parameters initiated in the acute care setting, and continues with positive relationships. Continual follow-up care can identify infections that can occur up to 30 days after a surgical procedure and can address comorbid conditions impacting recovery. Prior to discharge, the nurse confirms access to follow-up care by providing the patient or family with a phone number to call in order to alleviate fear and continue safe quality outcomes.

8. Emergent needs

Another area of concern in discharging a patient is the "what if" occurrences. Providing the process to follow when a problem occurs can decrease stress by assisting the patient in handling situations appropriately. Getting treatment immediately when the reportable signs and symptoms identified in the discharge planning process occur is imperative in avoiding serious complications.

8.12 The Future

The future of nursing in various settings will continue to grow with the increase in skills and knowledge and the increase in community needs. Nurses continue to be a critical component of the health care delivery system. In addition, if the predicted shortages occur, further redesign of the nurse's role in the health care delivery system will occur.

8.13 Summary

The healthcare environment is complex. The delivery of patient care is determined by the needs of the patient and the setting in which the needs occur. The care can occur in the home, the community, a surgicenter, a parish, a hospital, a nursing home, and so on. The delivery of care is no longer primarily found in the acute care setting. The patient is the center of the activity; however, the nurse is the coordinator of the care. The nurse has a direct impact on the outcomes of care and works in concert with the physician and other members of the healthcare team to assist the patient in achieving the optimum outcome.

Endnotes

1. Current American Nurses MAGNET Recognition Program Manual, (2008).

2. *Id.*

3. MAGNET Hospitals Revisited: *Attraction and Retention of Professional Nurses*, eds M. L. McLure and A. S. Hinshaw.

4. American Nurses Association, *Nursing scope and standards of practice*. Washington, DC: American Nurses Publishing, 2009 3rd Edition.

5. *Id.*

6. American Nurses Association, *Standards of clinical nursing practice*, Second edition. Washington D.C.: American Nurses Publishing, 2004.

7. American Nurses Association, *Nurse staffing plans and ratios*. Second edition. www.nursingworld.org/gova/state/2004/staffing.htm, re: Safe Staffing 2008.

8. The Joint Commission releases interim staffing effectiveness standards, December 28, 2009.

9. The Joint Commission *"Special Report! 2010 National Patient Safety Goals: The Official, Approved Goals and Helpful Solutions for Meeting Them."*

10. Dohm, A Shniper, L., Occupational Employment Projections to 2016.

Additional Reading

American Nurses Association Code of Ethics, Updated 2008 Publication.

"Approved: 2010 National Patient Safety Goals," Official Newsletter of T.J.C. October 2009.

Bogue, F. J., Joseph, M. L., Sieloff, C. L., *"Shared Governance as Vertical Alignment of Nursing Group Power and Nurse Practice Council Effectiveness" Journal of Nursing Management*, 2009.

Comah, H., "The Joint Commission 2010 Patient Safety Goals Reduce Requirements ", *for Health Leaders Media*, October 2009.

Manojlovich, M., *"Power and Empowerment in Nursing: Looking Backward to Inform the Future." The Online Journal of Issues in Nursing* from ANA January 2007.

Patient Safety and Quality, An Evidence Based Handbook for Nurses, Agency for Healthcare Research and Quality April 2008.

Smitt, T., *"To Err Is Human"*: Nursing's effect on patient safety, December 2009 by INQRI (Interdisciplinary Nursing Quarter Research Initiative).

The Joint Commission, National Patient Safety Goals Chapter Outline and Overview Hospital 2010.

The Joint Commission 1*"Facts About Patient Safety"* December 2009.

The Joint Commision (TJC), Performance Improvement Staffing Effectiveness 1-24-08.

Valentine, N. M., "Achieving Effective Staffing through a Shared Decision Making Approach to Open-shift Management," *JONA* Nov., 2008.

Welton, J. M., *"Mandatory Hospital Nurse to Patient Staffing Ratios: Time to Take a Different Approach." The Online Journal of Issues in Nursing*, ANA, September 2007.

Chapter 9

The Intersection of Nursing and Employment Law

Thomas B. Lewis, Esq., Stephanie B. Camarda, Esq., and Mark F. Kowal, Esq.[1]

9.1 Introduction

As reported by the American Nurses Association, there are approximately 2.9 million registered nurses in the United States; and as the highly publicized nursing shortage indicates, this is far too small a number especially as baby boomers age and the need for health care grows. A nursing shortage may cause a reduction in the quality of patient care as nurses become overwhelmed with patients. Thus, a nurse's continued employment can be influenced by a variety of factors, including competence and malpractice concerns. Some nurses may engage in conduct they believe is improper or otherwise not in the best interests of their patients because they fear they will be terminated from their job if they do not follow their employer's orders or the physician's orders. Others may be compelled to cover up what they know to have been improper conduct to protect their employer or the physician. Not only does the nurse risk opening himself to a malpractice claim, but legal protection may be available to guard against termination. It is a good practice for attorneys and nurses to have a working understanding of the basic tenants of employment law and how the duties as a nurse intersect with the rights of an employee.

9.2 The At-Will versus Contract Employee

There are two general types of employees: at-will employees and contractual employees. While many laypersons may not understand the distinction, it is nonetheless an important one, at least from a legal prospective, as it helps identify the rights and benefits due to the employee. The distinction determines the expectations of the employee and the employer, the terms and conditions of employment, under what circumstances an employer or the employee can terminate the employment relationship, and how the employee can challenge the termination.

A. Contract Employees

Contract employees are the distinct minority. These are generally highly paid, high-ranking employees with specialized knowledge and skill sets. Unlike their at-will counterparts, their employment is governed by a written agreement which sets forth the terms and conditions of their employment, such as their rate of pay, bonus structure, and a definitive end date for their employment. More importantly, these agreements will also set forth limitations on the employer's ability to terminate the employee. Also, these agreements may obligate an employee to remain employed for a period of time.

In those instances where a contract employee is terminated prior to the agreed upon end date, the remedies available to the employee are established by contract law. Once the validity of the contract is established, the employee must then demonstrate that the termination was made for a purpose outside those delineated by the contract. If the termination is not made according to the terms of the contract, the employee can seek to recover damages including wages and other benefits lost by the employer's breach of the contract.

B. At-Will Employees

Although nurses comprise a large segment of healthcare employees, they traditionally fall into the category of an at-will employee. While a small number of nurses, about 5 percent, are employed under some employment contract, most are rarely given the opportunity to negotiate a contract for employment. Generally nurses with an employment contract are those in executive positions, are advanced nurse practitioners, or are members of a nursing faculty. Staff nurses, nurse managers, and nurses in other healthcare organizations — such as private physician offices or nursing homes — are at-will employees. This is not to say that the work performed by these different groups are any less important than the other, it is just that the American workplace has long favored at-will employment over contractual employment.

This doctrine is premised on the understanding that both the employer and employee should have the right to terminate the employment relationship at any time for any reason that does not violate the law. While it has its origins in English law, it has been the preferred type of employment since the early 1900s. Because the relationship is for no definite duration, the employee can be terminated for any reason — either for good cause, bad cause, or no cause — as long as the reason does not violate the law. At the same time, this type of employment relationship also benefits the employee, who is free to resign the employment.

TIP: The at-will employment presumption was recognized by the United States Supreme Court as early as 1905.

9.3 Exceptions to the At-Will Employment Doctrine

Generally, if an at-will employee is terminated, she will have a limited basis for challenging the termination. While many employees question how their employer could terminate them without warning, or after numerous years of quality service, the law usually turns a blind eye to these concerns. However, the doctrine is not absolute and several exceptions have been carved out by legislatures and courts. Such exceptions include violations of law, statute, or regulation; "public policy exemptions"; the existence of an implied contract of employment; and a lack of good faith and fair dealing by the employer.

This chapter is designed to familiarize the reader with the hallmarks of each of these at-will exceptions. However, as laws vary from one jurisdiction to another, a nurse facing what is believed to be an improper termination should consult an attorney for specific analysis of the circumstances surrounding the termination and advice specific to that state.

A. Violations of Law, Statute, or Regulation

TIP: Perhaps the most widely known category of exceptions to the at-will doctrine is the anti-discrimination statutes that have been enacted on both the federal and state level.

Generally, these laws prohibit an employer from taking an adverse action against an employee, such as demoting or firing the employee, based on the employee's membership in a protected class, such as race, creed, color, sex, national origin, disability, age, and sexual orientation. State laws, which vary among jurisdictions, are often more favorable to the employee than their federal counterparts in the types of protections offered to employees.

In addition to banning discrimination, there is also a myriad of anti-retaliation laws which seek to protect employees who report, to a governmental agency or other regulatory body, what they believe is illegal or improper conduct by their employer or co-workers. These laws are often colloquially referred to as "whistleblower" statutes. Because the triggering events for such protections will vary among states, employees should consult with an attorney as to whether their conduct would fall under the protections of these types of statutes.

B. The "Public Policy" Exception

One of the earliest exceptions to the at-will doctrine was based on the idea that an employer does not have a right to terminate an employee who objects or refuses to participate in an illegal activity at the request of the employer. This exception, which has become recognized as the "public policy exception" is recognized in every state except Alabama, Florida, Georgia, Louisiana, Maine, Nebraska, New York, and Rhode Island. In its current form, the public policy exception also protects employees who exercise a protected right, such as filing a worker's compensation claim.

A nurse successfully challenging a termination on the basis of this doctrine must demonstrate that:

- the protected conduct is rooted in law and not the result of the nurse's definition of the "public good";
- a "clear mandate" of public policy exists and is relevant to the protected conduct; and
- the concern motivating the nurse's particular conduct must be within the "public interest," not just a "private concern."

In determining what constitutes "protected conduct," perhaps the best starting point is previous decisions applying the doctrine. Doing so uncovers a pattern of four broad categories of conduct that courts have routinely recognized as protected:

- refusing to perform unlawful acts;
- exercising legal rights;
- reporting illegal activity; and
- performing public duties.

In the context of nursing, refusal to perform unlawful acts and reporting illegal activity are most likely to occur. For example, a nurse may refuse to rewrite a medical record as ordered by a supervisor.

Several court decisions have demonstrated that the "public policy" exception is applicable to cases involving allegations of malpractice. For example, in *Sides v. Duke University Medical Center*, the North Carolina Appellate Court found a nurse's termination improper where she was fired for refusing to give false testimony in the context of a wrongful death action brought against the hospital-employer.[2] Similarly, in *Witt v. Forest Hospital,* the Illinois Appellate Court relied on the "public policy" exception to find the termination of a nurse working at a psychiatric hospital improper when the termination followed reports made by the nurse to a regulatory state agency complaining of improper treatment of patients.[3] Recently, in *Hughes v. Freeman Health System*, the Missouri Court of Appeals reversed and remanded the trial court's grant of summary judgment for the hospital where a nurse had previously been employed.[4] The Court noted that summary judgment was not appropriate because issues existed as to the actual reason for the nurse's termination. Instrumental in the court's decision was the fact that the nurse's refusal to delete portions of the patient's progress notes invoked the public policy protections exception to the employment-at-will doctrine.[5] In these cases, the court found the employees-nurses were acting in the best interests of the public, and as such the law offered protections from employment discharge.

Once a court determines the nurse's conduct is "protected," it will then look to determine whether there was some public good underlying the nurse's conduct. This analysis requires showing that the nurse was acting for the benefit of society at large rather than a purely personal or proprietary reason. To do so, employees will often tie their "protected conduct" to some well-established source of law, such as the federal or state Constitution, federal or state statutes and regulations, or common law.

Interestingly, some courts, such as those of New Jersey, may not recognize internal nursing codes of ethics as a valid source of public policy. For example, in *Warthen v. Toms River Community Memorial Hospital,* the New Jersey Appellate Court upheld the firing of a nurse who disobeyed a physician's order to give dialysis to a patient on the belief that the treatment would kill the patient.[6] The nurse argued that the American Nurses Association Code of Ethics supported her refusal to perform the treatment because of its requirement to provide care with respect to human life.[7] The court held that although the Code could possibly rise to the level of a public policy, it was generally designed to protect the interests of the nursing profession rather than the public.[8] As such, the Code could not be invoked as a basis to sustain a wrongful termination claim based on the public policy exception.[9]

C. Implied Contracts for Employment

TIP: A growing trend in the employment law arena is for at-will employees to challenge their termination on the basis of an implied contract theory.

Under this doctrine, an employer's conduct, communications, and even documents, are used to establish that the employee was hired for a specific and definite period of time. More importantly, this doctrine can be used to argue that an employer has agreed to terminate an employee only when there exists "good cause" or a good reason to do so.

As a threshold matter, a nurse employee must first demonstrate to the court that there was a reasonable basis for believing that the employment was for a finite period. To do this, many employees turn to the employer's policy and procedures manual, oftentimes known as an employee handbook. This avenue has been successfully used by nurses in several jurisdictions—including Arizona, Illinois, and Nebraska—to challenge their terminations.

Additionally, an implied contract can be formed orally, through written documents to the employee, or through the regular practices of the employer. For example, a promise of permanent employment—such as if a nurse is told during the job interview that the position would be for life if he does a good job—may be viewed as employment until retirement, death, or disability. Similarly, the employer's statements regarding the payment of bonuses, raises, or other benefits can be argued to have created something more than employment at-will. However, these types of implied contracts are more difficult to prove, and a reviewing court will closely scrutinize the purported promise to determine what degree of job security should be afforded the employee.

D. Breach of Good Faith and Fair Dealing

Depending on the state in which they are employed, some nurse-employees may be able to challenge a termination on the basis of an implied-in-law covenant of good faith and fair dealing. This exception may be of particular use in an instance where a nurse is terminated after being named in a malpractice claim, but before there is an investigation into the veracity of the allegations.

At the heart of this doctrine is the idea that "every contract imposes upon each party a duty of good faith and fair dealing in its performance and its enforcement."[10] If the employment relationship is viewed as an implied but terminable contract, it would be a breach of this covenant to discharge an employee except for reasons that are honest, consistent with the employer's normal policies and procedures, and relevant to the expectations of the parties.

Applying this theory to the nursing setting, a terminated nurse may have a claim against a former employer if the termination was done in such a fashion that it denied the nurse an accrued benefit, such as a pension or coverage under the employer's professional liability insurance. Additionally, if the discharge was done in a particularly abusive fashion or if it was done in a manner inconsistent with the employer's written policy or common practice, the nurse-employee may have a cause of action based on a breach of this implied covenant.

9.4 Tort Law Exceptions to the At-Will Doctrine

In addition to the exceptions described above, a terminated employee may have a cause of action against the former employer based on traditional tort claims, such as invasion of privacy, defamation, slander, libel, and intentional infliction of emotional distress. Such claims would arise from the employer's treatment of the nurse while still an employee or from the method used to terminate the nurse.

Improper treatment by an employer may include:

- making menacing threats which constitute assault or battery;
- holding and interrogating employees against their will, which may be false imprisonment;
- violating an employee's right to privacy by undue inquiries or physical invasion of work areas;
- accusing the nurse, if unfounded, of improper behavior—such as that which would constitute malpractice—may constitute defamation;
- behaving in an overzealous manner when dealing with the employee, such as using loud, obscene, or derogatory language, or attempting to humiliate an employee.

A. Intentional Infliction of Emotional Distress

Under the theory of respondeat superior, all employers are potentially liable for the negligent actions of their employees. Stated differently, employers have a legal duty to ensure their employees are carrying out their tasks in a safe and reasonable fashion. Where the employer is directly responsible for the welfare of members of the general public—such as in the medical setting—the employer's potential for liability is much greater. As such, employees in these types of industries may be subjected to more stringent supervision than their counterparts in other industries.

The most common, but perhaps not the most effective, tool used by employers in the clinical setting to monitor employees and gauge their abilities is a yearly or bi-annual performance evaluation. Performance evaluations not only ensure quality patient care, but are often used in making decisions concerning employee retention, promotion, and salary. Generally, such types of investigations—even if the employee disagrees with the employer's review of her work—will not give rise to a cause of action against the employer.

More serious investigations—where an employer may be specifically looking to uncover a nurse's mistake—often follow a claim for malpractice. In these instances, the employer may be looking for someone to shift liability to or for a reason to terminate the nurse. Regardless of motive, an exceptionally overzealous investigation by the employer, or one of its agents or employees, may give the targeted nurse a cause of action against the employer for intentional infliction of emotional distress.

To establish a claim for intentional infliction of emotional distress, a plaintiff-employee must show:

- that the employer's conduct was extreme and outrageous;
- emotional distress that is "so severe that no reasonable person could be expected to endure it";
- an intent on the part of the employer to commit the challenged act or acts; and
- a connection between the employer's conduct and the emotional distress suffered by the employee.

Interestingly, the touchstone for this type of claim is not the injury suffered by the employee, but rather the nature of the employer. Liability will only be found where the conduct is "so outrageous in character, and so extreme in degree, as to go beyond all possible bounds of decency, and to be regarded as atrocious, and utterly intolerable in a civilized community."[11] While this can be a high threshold for a plaintiff-employee to leap, courts have allowed a plaintiff-employee to recover against the employer.

The case of *Caesar v. Hartford Hospital* provides an interesting example of how this type of claim can be used by an employee challenging a termination.[12] Here, the plaintiff-employee was a Certified Nurse's Aide who was terminated following allegations of patient abuse.[13] The plaintiff-employee challenged her termination, inter alia, by arguing that the employer-hospital had purposely provided false information to the state Department of Public Health during the ensuing investigation with the malicious intent of retaliating against her. She maintained that such statements placed her professional career in jeopardy and had caused emotional distress to her. Although dismissing several of the plaintiff-employee's claims against the hospital, the claim for intentional infliction was allowed to proceed.[14]

Just as an employer may be liable for an overzealous investigation, it can also be liable for an overall pattern of dealing with an employee in an extreme and outrageous fashion. For example, had the hospital in *Caesar v. Hartford Hospital* retained the plaintiff-employee rather than terminating her, and in this capacity, assigned her demeaning tasks; assigned her unfavorable shifts; subjected her to verbally or physically abusive language; or expected her to perform at levels it did not expect of other employees, she may have also had a claim for intentional infliction of emotional distress.

Finally, employees who quit rather than endure this treatment may also have a claim for wrongful discharge on the theory that their resignation was in fact a "constructive discharge." The issue in a "constructive discharge" case is whether the employer's conduct is so extreme and intolerable that a reasonable person subjected to such acts would resign. As such, the test is an objective rather than a subjective one—the employee's own subjective beliefs are not enough.

B. Defamation

A common basis for liability against an employer is through defamatory communications to third parties. However, as shown in *Caesar v. Hartford Hospital*, nurses may also be damaged by an employer's statements to a state agency, regulatory body, or professional organization.[15] In these instances, the employer's comments can be particularly damaging as the comments may provoke an investigation by a regulatory agency and may affect the employee's ability to remain employed in the nursing profession.[16]

Legally, defamation is defined as an oral or written communication to a third party that is false and which tends to injure another's reputation (that is, diminish the esteem, respect, goodwill, or confidence in which that person is held)

or that causes adverse, derogatory, or unpleasant feelings or opinions against that person. In the context of employment, for a plaintiff-employee to establish a claim of defamation, she must be able to demonstrate the following:

1. The defendant-employer has made a false and defamatory statement concerning the employee;
2. An unprivileged publication (i.e., communication) by the employer to a third person who actually heard and understood the communication to relate to the employee;
3. Fault amounting at least to negligence on the part of the employer; and
4. Proof of special harm caused by the publication of the statements, such as pecuniary loss or loss of employment.

1. Defamatory meaning

An initial question in any defamation case is whether the challenged statement is reasonably susceptible to a defamatory meaning. This is ordinarily a question of law, which means it can be designed without submission to the jury. To answer this question, the court will consider the statements in context and consider the publication as a whole, and must give them the fair and natural meaning that would be given them by a reasonable person of ordinary intelligence.

To be defamatory, a statement must be false and either:

*   injure the reputation of another,
*   expose him to hatred, contempt, or ridicule,
*   cause him to be shunned or avoided, or
*   subject him to a loss of the good will, esteem, respect, and confidence shown by others.

The statement need not refer to immoral or illegal conduct to be defamatory; rather, statements concerning a person's trade, profession, or business can be actionable if made with respect to the manner in which the person carries out these activities.

If the statement is only susceptible to one meaning, and that meaning is defamatory, the statement is said to be defamatory per se, or as a matter of law. Conversely, if the statement is susceptible to only a non-defamatory meaning, it cannot be considered libelous, justifying dismissal of the action. Where the statement is capable of being assigned more than one meaning, one of which is defamatory and the other not, the question of whether its content is defamatory must be resolved by a jury. Further, if the statement or comment is truthful, it is unlikely it will be defamatory.

2. Publication

To be actionable, the allegedly defamatory statement or statements must have been communicated to someone other than the person defamed, and that third-party must have understood the communication to relate to the plaintiff. Publication can be made to any third person, including an employer's own officers, employees, or agents. Such communication may be made orally or in writing.

TIP: Traditionally, defamatory statements made in written or printed form were classified as "libel"; however, the term has more recently been expanded to include any fixed medium, such as a picture, a sign, an electronic broadcast, or e-mail.

Interestingly, libel is classified as both a crime and a tort, although it is no longer prosecuted as a crime. An employer's letter to a regulatory body, such as a nursing board or state agency, could qualify as libelous material, but may also be a privileged communication.

Oral statements may likewise be considered defamatory and can subject the maker of the statement to liability. Legally, defamatory statements made through some transient medium, such as speech, are referred to as "slander" as opposed to libel, although a claim for slander will generally require much the same proof as that of a claim for libel. However, an important caveat distinguishing the two is that in certain contexts a false oral statement will be considered slanderous per se and not require a showing of damages on the part of the plaintiff-employee.

Two of the slanderous per se categories are particularly relevant to the employment setting: those that charge the commission of a crime or those affecting a person in business, trade, employment, or office.

As to slanderous statements regarding criminal conduct, the general rule is that imputation of a crime is actionable per se if it involves a major social disgrace or moral turpitude. Typical examples of statements that would fall in this category include accusations of theft or larceny. False allegations that a nurse stole narcotics from a hospital pharmacy, or that she negligently caused injury to a patient, could constitute grounds for a claim for slander. Similarly, words concerning an employee in business, profession, or employment that impute a want of integrity, credit, or common honesty, or charge personal incapacity may be slanderous per se. Although negative job evaluations are not normally found to give rise to a claim for slander, similar negative comments regarding an employee's performance made to other co-workers or patients could give rise to a claim against the employer.

9.5 Conclusion

Although at-will employment remains the most prevalent form of employment for nurses in the United States, the doctrine is slowly being eroded by federal and state laws. As numerous exceptions exist to the at-will doctrine, a nurse should analyze all legal avenues if he believes termination of employment was improper.

Endnotes

1. The authors appreciate the contributions of David Krulewicz to the previous edition of this chapter.

2. *Sides v. Duke University Medical Center*, 74 N.C. App. 331 (N.C. App. 1985).

3. *Witt v. Forest Hospital*, Ill. App.3d 48 (Ill. App. Dist. 1983).

4. *Hughes v. Freeman Health System*, 283 S.W.3d 797 (Mo. Ct. App. 2009).

5. *Id.*

6. *Warthen v. Toms River Community Memorial Hospital*, 199 N.J. Super. 18 (N.J. App. Div. 1985).

7. *Id.*

8. *Id.*

9. *Id.*

10. Restatement (Second) Contracts, §205.

11. Restatement (Second) of Torts, §46 comment d.

12. *Caesar v. Hartford Hospital*, 46 F.Supp. 2d 174 (1999).

13. *Id.*

14. *Id.*

15. Hartford, 46 F.Supp.2d (1999).

16. *Id.*

Part III:

Damages

Chapter 10

Pain and Suffering

Patricia W. Iyer, MSN, RN, LNCC

10.1 Introduction

Nursing malpractice can have far-reaching consequences. An injury may set off a chain of medical events that causes a patient to spiral downwards into disability and death. For example, a fractured hip can result in:

- immobility,

- pneumonia,

- pressure ulcers,

- a reduction in limb length,

- nonunion of the bones,

- loosening of the prosthetic pieces with resultant need for re-operation,

- injury to the sciatic nerve with resultant foot drop, or

- overgrowth of bone (heterotopic ossification) with chronic pain.

An infant born with profound neurological impairment as a result of a failure to detect fetal distress during labor can require a lifetime of expensive and emotionally and financially draining medical care. A patient who becomes paralyzed from the nipple line down as a result of a failure of a nurse to detect signs of an epidural hematoma pressing on the spine will need a host of supportive services, including respiratory, physical and occupational therapy, restorative care, durable medical equipment, and so on. The damages resulting from nursing malpractice may range from temporary to permanent, mild to severe, and physical to emotional and psychological.

This chapter addresses the injuries causally related to nursing malpractice sustained by the plaintiff. The calculation of economic losses (medical bills, lost income, future wage loss and medical care) is relatively concrete and is discussed elsewhere. Refer to Chapter 13, *The Role of the Forensic Economist in Nursing Malpractice Actions*, Chapter 11, *Vocational Evaluations in Nursing Malpractice Cases*, and Chapter 12, *Life Care Planning*, which cover these subjects in-depth.

This chapter takes a narrower focus to explore the clinical aspects of pain and suffering. The strategies the attorney uses to explain pain and suffering, or to refute unwarranted claims of pain and suffering are illuminated through the use of an expert witness. This individual summarizes medical records and teaches the jury about pain and suffering or is used to refute claims of excessive pain and suffering. Additional aspects of the attorney's presentation of pain and suffering are covered in a variety of articles and texts.[1-7]

10.2 Pain as an Element of Damages

The assessment of pain and suffering sustained as a result of nursing malpractice is important in initially evaluating a potential case as few plaintiff's attorneys are interested in taking cases involving temporary and minor injuries. Although liability may be clear-cut, the damages may be negligible in some cases of nursing malpractice. For example, some attorneys would not file suit in the following limited damages cases:

- The elderly patient falls out of a hospital bed, breaking her nose.
- The premature infant's toe drops off after a pulse oximeter clip was allegedly left in one place too long.
- The young adult's tooth breaks during insertion of an endotracheal tube by a nurse anesthetist.
- There was a three-month delay in diagnosis of breast cancer by a nurse practitioner.

Plaintiff's attorneys must understand their clients' claims of injuries in order to evaluate the value of the case. Any state caps on recovery for pain and suffering should be taken into consideration when determining the value of a case.

Exploration of the extent of pain and suffering is accomplished by analysis of medical records generated both before and after the injury to determine if the results of the alleged malpractice produced a demonstrable change in the patient's life. The plaintiff's attorney may spend additional time investigating the damages. This may entail interviewing family, friends, and neighbors to determine how an individual has been affected by a trauma. If the liability, causation, and damages criteria meet the attorney's threshold for taking the case, the attorney proceeds to work up the case. Refer to Chapter 14, *Screening the Nursing Malpractice Case*, and Chapter 15, *Plaintiff's Attorney's Perspective*, for additional information on this topic.

Both defense and plaintiff counsel must understand the true impact of the injury on the patient's life. Defense counsel is likely to vigorously dispute a plaintiff's claim of injuries if none can be detected through observation or examination. Surveillance videotaping, although expensive, may be useful in some situations in which malingering or faking injury is suspected. Refer to Broderick and West for more information on the defense attorney's perspective of pain and suffering.[8]

10.3 Definitions of Pain

The International Association for the Study of Pain defines pain as, "An unpleasant sensory and emotional experience associated with actual or potential tissue damage, or described in terms of such damage."[9] Acute or chronic pain may result from the negligent care provided by a nurse. Acute pain has a sudden onset and has the potential to increase vital signs such as pulse and blood pressure. The patient expects that the pain will not be long-term. Very often the patient is anxious, and if the pain is severe, a "fight or flight" response may be evoked.

Chronic pain lasts longer than six months or beyond the normal period of recovery. The chronic pain patient experiences pain on a daily basis and expects the problem to be long-term and possibly without resolution. Vital sign changes are not a good indicator of chronic pain since the patient's body may physiologically adjust to the continued painful assault. Since chronic pain is an ongoing condition, depression is a common feature of this type of pain.[10]

Chronic pain is surprisingly widespread. Forty-two percent of United States households report one or more persons have chronic pain. Low back pain, fibromyalgia, arthritis, and neuropathies are common chronic conditions. Chronic pain may be well concealed by the patient who has learned how to use coping methods to avoid displaying the degree of pain being experienced. These coping skills may sometimes lead the healthcare professionals (and the attorneys) to conclude that the patient is not in pain. Thoughtful consideration must be given to the association of chronic pain with specific medical conditions. For example, chronic pain may result from arthritis or complex regional pain syndrome induced by a severe fracture. Relying on the patient's self report (if able to communicate pain) is also of prime importance.

Neuropathic pain is chronic pain caused by nerve damage. The pain is described in terms of burning, tingling, numbness, or shooting pain. Neuropathic pain syndromes may be caused by diabetic neuropathy, low back pain with radicular components of pain going down one or both legs, post-mastectomy pain, postherpetic neuralgia, and trigeminal neuralgia.[11]

TIP: Questions that have been asked of juries in an effort to put a dollar figure on the value of chronic pain are:

- Would you accept a job that made you work 24 hours a day, seven days a week with no respite?
- How much would you pay to avoid being a chronic pain patient?

10.4 Pain Assessment

This section addresses the components of pain assessment. The next section discusses the populations at risk for increased pain and inadequate pain assessment and management. The identification of pain as the fifth vital sign (after temperature, pulse, respirations, and blood pressure) was first proposed by the American Pain Society in 1995. Vital signs are monitored to detect changes or trends that signal a need for further assessment, diagnosis, and interventions. Making pain a vital sign ensures that pain is monitored on a regular basis.[12] The Joint Commission (TJC) developed pain management standards first implemented in 2000. These standards state that all patients should have their pain assessed and managed. With the implementation of these national guidelines, an increased emphasis is placed on the role of pain assessment and the resultant pain management. Since the inception of TJC standards, the assessment of pain has been prioritized, while healthcare consumers have become better advocates for their own pain management needs.[13] As a result of the attention of both The Joint Commission and professional nursing associations, nurses are becoming better attuned to the need to assess and document the patient's level of pain.

Medical records should document the patient's level of pain. Location, duration, radiation, quality, and aggravating/alleviating factors add important information about the pain. Healthcare professionals are trained to follow a model when questioning the patient about pain: LPPQRSTE. Refer to Figure 10.1. The patient's words are used to describe the pain, such as throbbing, aching, burning, sharp, dull, and so on.

- Location: Look at the medical records for drawings of various body figures (e.g., full torso, head).

- Provocation: What causes the initial pain or increases pain (activity, stress, touch)? What is the duration?

- Palliation: What reduces or relieves the pain (activity change, medications, heat, cold, massage, sleep)?

- Quality: What words does the patient use to describe the pain?

- Region: Is the pain localized or generalized? Does it radiate to other parts of the body, and if so, where?

- Severity: What is the pain intensity? (Use 0-10 scale, FACES, and/or category scale.)

- Temporal: Is the pain constant or intermittent? Is there a pattern or rhythm and, if so, describe it. (Does it occur during sleep, are there seasonal variations and overall trends?)

- Effects: How does the pain affect function and quality of life? Has the pain changed the daily routine or altered lifestyle? (Does pain affect sleep, appetite, physical activity, relationship with others [irritability, roles], emotions [anger, crying, suicidal], concentration?)

Figure 10.1 *The LPPQRSTE Model for Assessing Pain*

A number of pain assessment scales exist to identify pain in specific populations:

- The CRIES scale is used with neonates and is based on a group of observations and physiologic indicators. The behaviors are rated and scored with the higher score indicating the greater distress and pain.
- The FACES scale was developed to evaluate the pain of children. The six faces are aligned with a happy or no pain face at the left and the tearful or most pain face at the right. The patient is asked to point to the face that best represents the patient's pain.
- Behavioral pain rating scales are used to assess pain when the patient is unable to rate pain using a standard pain rating scale. Behaviors used by the healthcare professional to identify pain as being present are facial expressions, vocalization, or movement.
- The visual analog scale is a 100 millimeter horizontal line with zero as the anchor at one end of the scale and 100 at the opposite end of the scale. It is a very simple form of pain assessment which is suitable for most people.[14]

With acute pain, the medical chart often records the use of a simple 0 to 10 pain intensity scale, where 0 is "no pain" and 10 is "worst possible pain." This is usually adequate to assess and reassess pain intensity, and response to pain management modalities. The most common scale in use is this numeric pain intensity scale. Using this scale, nurse's notes and physician's progress notes often state the patient's pain score in terms of a point between 0 and 10. The record may have an entry such as "patient reports pain is a 6 out of 10" or "6/10." A number of studies have shown that a pain rating at 4 or more on a 0 to 10 pain rating scale interferes significantly with daily function. A pain rating this high indicates the need to revise pain treatment with higher doses of analgesics, different medications, or other comfort measures.[15] Some individuals are not able to provide a description of pain. These include infants and those who are cognitively impaired, have a language barrier, or are otherwise unable to communicate. The healthcare professional must use other signs to assess pain level. Interpretation of the patient's facial expressions, behavior, and body movements is less accurate than the individual's report of the level of pain. There are no objective measures of pain such as laboratory values, blood pressure or pulse. The most reliable measure of pain is the patient's self-report.[16]

TIP: The standard of care requires the healthcare professional to use knowledge of the sensations normally produced by procedures, injuries, and medical interventions to come to a conclusion about the presence of pain in an individual who is not able to report pain.

A resident of a nursing home suffered a fractured leg when she was dropped by two nursing aides. The leg was so badly shattered it had to be amputated. This confused patient could not ask for pain medication in the days following surgery. Review of the medical record showed that the nurses did not provide pain medication to this patient, although an order for medication had been written by the physician. The failure to administer pain medication was below the standard of care.

10.5 Populations at Risk

Some patients are at risk for increased pain due to the nature of their injuries or clinical condition, while others are at risk because of communication barriers or other factors that lead to inadequate pain management.

A. Patients at Risk Due to Injury or Disease

While there are many conditions that cause pain, this section discusses people with pain due to fractures, amputations, skin changes, or cancer.

1. Fractures

Nursing malpractice claims may center around fractures that allegedly occurred as a result of negligence. Injuries consisting of fractures of the hip, leg, arm, spine, and skull are the orthopaedic locations most often implicated in lawsuits. Although fractures may occur in any age group, elderly patients are at increased risk for fractures from falls due to weakening of the bones from osteoporosis.

Simple fractures are closed fractures with no broken bones protruding through the skin. Compound (open) fractures occur when broken bones protrude through the skin. Impacted fractures occur when broken bone edges are wedged together. Comminuted fractures occur when great force is applied to the bone, as the bone is literally shattered into many pieces. Spiral fractures are usually a result of a twisting injury. Linear fractures are parallel to the long axis on the bone, whereas transverse fractures occur when the bone is snapped across. A compression fracture results when one bone is forced against another, such as when a patient's vertebrae are crushed. This may happen with falls or direct blows. A burst fracture occurs in the spine when pieces of vertebrae are forced backwards into the spinal canal. A displaced fracture occurs when the two parts of the bone are not aligned.

The pain associated with fractures is caused by tearing of blood vessels, nerves, and tissues. The release of blood into the area and tissue trauma combine to cause swelling, which further increases pain as tissue is compressed. Immobilization and early surgical correction reduce pain. As a rule, fractures that can be splinted or put in a cast are less painful than fractures that cannot be stabilized. Fractures of the clavicles, ribs, pelvis, or vertebral bodies in the back cannot be casted. Fractured ribs and pelvic fractures tend to be very painful because these areas cannot be effectively immobilized. Hand fractures tend to be more painful due to the multiple nerve endings in the hands, as well as the associated swelling.

Severe fractures of the long bones in the arms or legs may require internal or external fixation. Internal fixation consists of drilling holes in the bone and screwing on plates. Sometimes crushed bone from cadavers or from another bone in the patient's body is needed to fill in the area of severely crushed bones. External fixation may be needed to align bone pieces. In this situation, screws are placed in the bone and connected to a long rod that stays outside of the body. Limbs may also be encircled by a frame that is attached to the bone with pins. These devices may be in place for weeks if not months, creating difficulties with mobility, function, dressing, and pain control.

Fractures inherently cause a degree of immobility which may lead to other problems without diligent medical and nursing care. Blood clots in the leg are a risk of immobility and are prevented with sequential compression devices which inflate and deflate to stimulate circulation in the legs. Injections of heparin or low molecular weight heparin (Lovenox) may be given to prevent clots. Pieces of fat can be released from the bone marrow and travel to the lungs causing fat emboli that can be fatal.

Pneumonia is a risk of bed rest and inactivity following a fracture. Patients are instructed to cough and deep breathe and blow into plastic devices (incentive spirometers) to prevent collection of secretions in the lungs. Skin breakdown can also result from immobility if proper attention is not paid to preventive measures.

When long-term traction is needed after a fracture, the sites where pins enter the skin are foci for infection or itching. Casts can create severe itching under the skin. Sometimes patients stick long objects into the cast to scratch skin, which may result in the object being retained in the cast or shredding the inner lining of the cast.

Fractures can result in long-term disability. For example, elderly patients may not regain their ability to walk after a fractured hip, or traumatic arthritis may develop at the site of the fracture. Complex regional pain syndrome (formerly RDS or reflex sympathetic dystrophy) may occur after a limb is fractured. Other complications of fractures include nonunion, traumatic arthritis, heterotopic ossification (excessive bony growth), and osteomyelitis (infection of the bone). All can be associated with chronic pain. Refer to Chapter 9, *Orthopaedic Nursing Malpractice Issues*, and Chapter 26, *Falls and Their Consequences*, both in Volume II, for more information.

2. Amputations

Significant swelling often occurs after an amputation of a limb. The recovery from amputation surgery is frequently prolonged. A period of time must transpire to allow swelling to reduce before the individual may be fitted with a prosthetic limb. Learning to walk on an artificial leg may require intensive stretching and physical therapy. The process of learning to put on and take off the limb, to adjust to a different body image, and to the limitations associated with prosthesis may take months.

Phantom limb pain may occur after a limb has been amputated. The person may feel sensation as if the amputated extremity was still present. This phenomenon is believed to be due to the slowness with which the brain learns the limb is no longer there. The patient's symptoms include pain, pins and needles, tingling, pressure sensation, burning, or itching in the absent limb. Phantom pain can also be experienced as cramped, twisted, and abnormal posturing of the phantom limb. The patient with a missing hand may have the sensation of the fist being clenched so tightly that the nails are tearing into the palm. Patients with amputated feet may experience their missing toes as tightly curled and cramped. The sensations are likely to be most painful immediately after the amputation.[17] These sensations are likely to last for months and are often very distressing to patients. A common request is to ask a nurse to scratch an absent foot.

3. Skin changes

The high concentration of nerve endings makes injuries to the skin painful. Pressure ulcers or burns are among the most frequent type of skin injuries cited in nursing malpractice suits.

a. Pressure ulcers

The most significant factor causing pressure ulcers is immobility. Debilitated patients frequently are in one position for a prolonged time period. They may not have the strength to shift positions. The blood supply, which carries oxygen and nutrients to the skin, is hampered by the immobility.

A patient laying on her back compresses the bony sacrum against the bed surface and squeezes the tissues in between, which creates pressures that exceed the capillary pressure. The tissue therefore does not receive adequate blood supply and begins to die. Any incontinence may macerate (moisten and irritate) the skin and lead to further breakdown. Additionally, the skin is exposed to bacteria and any disruption of the skin surface can easily become infected.[18] Pressure ulcers may develop in acute and long-term care settings. Liability issues center around recognizing that the patient was at risk for skin breakdown, initiating an appropriate plan of care to prevent skin breakdown, and implementing appropriate evidence-based interventions to effect healing without progression of the wound. The pain associated with pressure ulcers is related to swelling and exposure of nerves and tissues. Treatment of pressure ulcers is often prolonged, painful, and intensive.

Possible complications of pressure ulcers include fistulas, abscesses, osteomyelitis, cellulitis, and bacteremia. A fistula refers to an abnormal passage that can occur internally or externally. An internal fistula is a passage from organ to organ. An external fistula refers to a passage from organ to body surface. An abscess refers to a localized collection of pus. It is usually related to an infection and the area is surrounded by inflamed tissue. Osteomyelitis and cellulitis also are related to an infection. Osteomyelitis refers to the inflammation of bone due to an infection. Cellulitis refers to an inflammation of tissue and is characterized by redness, swelling, and tenderness. Bacteria in the blood is called bacteremia. Interventions should be implemented to treat the complication as soon as it is feasible. Complications should be closely monitored and reassessed for improvement or lack of improvement.[19]

Refer to Chapter 25, *Wounds*, in Volume II, for more detailed information about pressure ulcers.

b. Burns

Burns may be caused by scalding in a tub or shower, by flames, prolonged exposure to sun, steam, hot fumes, extremely acidic or alkaline chemicals or nongrounded electrical equipment. Nursing liability may be associated with any of these types of burns. Scalding may occur when the patient is left unattended in a shower with inadequate safeguards over the water temperature. Water exceeding a safe temperature of 105-110 degrees has been used to fill tubs into which patients are lowered for a bath. Unsupervised smoking is a common cause of clothing catching on fire. Residents of long-term care and assisted living facilities have developed severe burns from being left out in the sun too long. Use of the wrong strength acetic acid (97 percent versus 3 percent) for surgical procedures involving dermatological and gynecological lesions has caused severe burns in several operating rooms. Patients have been electrocuted by faulty use of electrical equipment.

TIP: Burn involvement is estimated based on the Rule of Nines.

The Adult Rule of Nines is used to calculate the percentage of the body that has been burned.

> Head = 9 percent
> Front = 18 percent
> Back = 18 percent
> Left arm = 9 percent
> Right arm = 9 percent
> Groin = 1 percent
> Left leg = 18 percent
> Right leg = 18 percent

The Baby Rule of Nines allows for the proportionate difference in head size related to lower extremity size in children less than three years of age compared with adults.

> Head and Neck = 18 percent
> Arm = 9 percent
> Posterior Trunk = 18 percent
> Anterior Trunk = 18 percent
> Leg = 14 percent
> Perineum = 1 percent

While one might assume that large burns cause the most severe pain, even a small burn can be extremely painful. Pain is common in all burn patients, regardless of the cause, size or depth of the burn. The pain they experience can be among the worst known.[20] Burn pain is related to the extent of tissue damage, the tissue surface involved, and the treatment modalities. Pain is further exacerbated by uncontrolled anxiety and fear. Burn pain can also be affected by an individual's psychological perception of life with a burn.

Tissue damage refers to the extent of tissue loss or the depth of the burn. Superficial burns (unblistered or first degree burns) or those burns resulting in partial thickness tissue loss (second degree burns) are painful. In a partial thickness burn, the outermost skin layer (epidermis) and the uppermost third of the underlying skin layers (dermis) are damaged, and peripheral nerve endings become exposed in the damaged dermal layer.[21] Edema and pressure resulting from the injury to the tissue, as previously described, results in pain.[22] In addition to the pain caused by direct tissue destruction, burn injury induces pain by stimulating both inflammation and hyperalgesia (extreme sensitivity to painful stimuli) which worsens when the burned area is handled during wound care. It was once believed that patients with full-thickness burns did not feel pain at the site because nerve endings were destroyed. Yet pain can occur in what appears to be a full thickness (third-degree) burn. A burn wound may have areas of both partial and full thickness burns, and there may be areas where nerves are still functioning. Full-thickness burns are often surrounded by painful partial-thickness burns. Patients with full thickness burns can also experience pain at the margins of the wound. An increase in pain in a full-thickness burn around the circumference of a limb may indicate a compartment syndrome-like process, necessitating escharotomy or fasciotomy (slicing the limb open to relieve pressure). Full thickness burns require repeated painful procedures to prevent infection and promote closure with minimal disfigurement.[23]

Acute burn pain has two distinct components: continuous background pain and intermittent severe pain induced by treatment.[24] Procedural burn pain is caused by:

- wound cleansing,
- debridement,
- skin grafting,
- insertion and inflation of tissue expanders,
- passive range of motion,
- splint application, and
- removal of adherent dressings and exposure of the wound to air without adequate premedication.[25]

Debridement of tissue is another source of pain. Debridement (pronounced *debreedment*) involves snipping away dead tissue until the wound consists of a bleeding healthy tissue. This is a painful process commonly preceded by the administration of intravenous narcotics to reduce awareness of pain. Manual debridement is done by nurses or burn care technicians who scrape or pull off loose dead tissue using a washcloth, tweezers or scissors. Enzymatic debridement with Travase or collagenase (Santyl) ointment has been used to remove small areas of eschar in an attempt to avoid surgical debridement; but some patients have reported the use of enzymatic therapy to be just as painful as traditional debridement. After wound cleansing and manual debridement are performed, as necessary, a topical antimicrobial agent is applied. Some of those most commonly used today can add to the patient's pain.[26] Extensive debridement is performed in the operating room under general anesthesia within three to five days after injury.

Surgery may be necessary to remove dead tissue or apply a healthy tissue graft from elsewhere on the patient's body (often the thighs or buttocks are used) or from a cadaver or pig. Skin grafting consists of use of a temporary graft (either synthetic or from a cadaver) or a permanent graft (donated unburned skin from another part of the person's body). The fragility of the new graft site mandates it be protected from trauma. This necessitates immobilization of the grafted part from 5 to 14 days or more. The patient's burned limb may be attached to a sling hung from an overhead sling to minimize swelling. The patient returns from the surgery with a painful burn wound that has been subjected to both debridement and grafting, as well as a painful donor site.[27]

TIP: The removal of the top layer of the patient's skin at the skin grafting site causes an additional source of postoperative pain. Many patients describe the pain at the skin donor site as burning and itching.

Post-burn physical therapy is designed to prevent scar tissue from causing contractures (bending of the joints). Contractures result in loss of range of motion, may require surgery to release, and if not corrected, limit functional ability. Once the skin grafts are stable, the physical therapist provides range of motion and strengthening exercises, which are in themselves painful. Any manipulation of the body is likely to be painful; therefore the burned patient requires immense and frequent doses of narcotics before dressing changes, debridement, and physical therapy.

Some individuals are prone to the development of keloids, which are raised, excessive scars. This type of scarring is pronounced and may make the burned individual feel even more conspicuous. Itching may result from the burns, which puts the tissue or newly grafted skin at risk for trauma from scratching. Oral and topical medications may reduce some itching. Other complications associated with burns include the risk of infections and pressure ulcers, additional damage to the tender new skin, an increased risk of getting skin cancer, the need to protect the sensitive skin from sun, and heat and cold. Refer to Webster for a firsthand account written by an attorney about his burns and recovery.[28]

Sources of suffering for the burned patient include:

- undertreatment of pain
- disfigurement, which can profoundly affect self-image
- functional losses
- boredom caused by long periods of immobility and lack of variation in routine
- anxiety and irritability from stress
- concerns about the future (employment, family relationships, appearance, limitations, additional surgery)
- isolation from others to prevent infection

- feelings of powerlessness to prevent or stop pain
- depression
- side effects of heavy doses of narcotics and antibiotics
- itching of graft donor sites and partial thickness wounds
- requirement to eat a large amount of food to increase healing
- exposure to unpleasant odors associated with the wound and treatment medications
- social isolation with loss of educational, employment and marital opportunities
- being stared at in public
- posttraumatic stress disorder (PTSD) manifested by nightmares and reliving the burn trauma

---

TIP: Recovery from the effects of burns can take months. Custom-made pressure garments that ensure scar tissue grows flat must be worn 23 hours a day for approximately a year. The risk of dislodging skin grafts may last for several months.

Refer to Chapter 25, *Wounds*, in Volume II, for additional information on this topic.

4. Cancer

Nurses in a variety of roles may be associated with litigation initiated by people with cancer. Nursing practitioners may be involved in nursing malpractice suits alleging a delay in diagnosis of cancer. Delays in the diagnosis of cancer may result in suffering associated with anger, frustration, and disillusionment. Waiting for the results of diagnostic testing done to stage the cancer can cause unbearable anxiety.

Staff nurses involved in inserting intravenous needles or using existing lines to inject chemotherapy may be named in a suit involving release of chemotherapeutic agents into the tissues instead of the vein or other medication errors associated with chemotherapy or pain relievers.

Buehle notes that approximately 50-80 percent of patients with advanced cancer experience pain during the course of their disease. The majority of these patients will not obtain satisfactory relief.[29] Unrelieved pain remains a major problem for patients with cancer. Along with lack of knowledge of healthcare prescribers and those who administer pain medication, patients continue to hold misconceptions about the use and effects of drugs commonly used to manage cancer pain. Control of cancer pain may be improved through patient education by helping patients have more control over the pain and by improving the patients' adherence to the scheduling of pain medications.[30]

Overall, bone cancer and pancreatic cancer are associated with pain that is the most difficult to treat. Cancers that have advanced to the stage that they are invading major nerve pathways cause intractable (unrelieved) pain that needs to be treated with surgical nerve blocks. Brain cancer can cause intolerable pain that can only be treated by heavy sedation and medically induced coma.

Attorneys can evaluate pain experiences by using the matrix of questions provided in Table 10.1, or they can use pain assessment questionnaires readily available on the Internet or in the literature. Information about clinical dimensions of pain may not be as useful as information about the impact of pain on the lives of the patients and their family. Refer to Bales for additional information on cancer pain and suffering.[31]

5. Surgery

Despite the increased focus on pain management, postoperative pain relief remains a concern for patients. Patients continue to suffer unacceptable levels of pain after surgery, with as many as 75 percent experiencing severe pain. Healthcare providers are barriers to achieving adequate pain relief. Their deficits may involve knowledge needed to prescribe and administer medications, assess and reassess postoperative pain, and understand cultural and ethnic responses to pain and pain control. Lack of understanding surrounds administration of opioids, and in particular concerns about respiratory depression, hypotension, and risk of addiction.[32]

B. Patients at Risk Due to Individualized Factors

Specific factors may influence a patient's level of pain and ability to communicate the need for pain relief. While it is difficult to define absolutes, there are some trends and studies which define populations at greater risk for undertreatment of pain.

1. Sex-related

The American Pain Society conducted a study completed in 2001 that included data collected from 967 females and 680 males who had chronic pain. They found differences in that the women reported more fear and frustration related to pain than men. Men reported more anxiety and frustration with intense pain, whereas women reported only frustration to intense pain. On the other hand, men reported only frustration to the highest pain intensities, whereas women reported depression with frustration. The researchers noted that, surprisingly, pain-related emotions were reported by men to be more strongly related to pain than those reported by women. They concluded that emotions were most closely related to the unpleasantness of pain rather than to the intensity of pain.[33]

Table 10.1
Pain and Suffering Matrix—Part B: Questions used to explore dimensions of pain and suffering.

QUESTIONS RE: PAIN/ SUFFERING EXPERIENCE	Physiological	Psychological	Spiritual	Cultural
Temporal	Where is your cancer? Where did it start growing? When did it begin?	Do you associate the pain with any event or experience?	Has the pain affected spiritual or religious aspects of your life?	Is your cancer experience the same as others in your community or culture?
Geographical	Where in your body is the cancer located? Where has it spread?	Do you associate the part of your body where the cancer is with a certain emotion?	Does your pain and suffering change when you are involved in spiritual activities?	Do your family and friends think they know why you developed this kind of cancer?
Historical	Have any of your family members had cancer?	How have your emotions been associated with physical symptoms in the past?	How are pain and suffering described historically by your church or religion?	How do people from your community or culture cope with pain and suffering?
Etiological	What is the physical cause for your pain and/or suffering?	Do you associate any emotional distress with your pain or cancer?	What does your pain or cancer mean to you in spiritual terms?	What is thought to cause pain and suffering in your community or culture?
Qualitative	What does your pain feel like? Can you describe it in terms that others would understand?	How do you feel emotionally and psychologically when you have pain and/or suffering?	How do you use spirituality to help you cope with your pain/suffering/cancer?	In what ways do people from your community or culture usually cope with or treat pain?
Quantitative	How severe do you feel your pain/suffering is at this time?	How much does your pain/cancer affect you psychologically?	To what degree does this pain/cancer affect your spiritual life?	How much does your pain/suffering restrict you socially?

Reprinted from Bales, C. "Cancer Pain and Suffering," in Iyer, P. (Editor) *Medical Legal Aspects of Pain and Suffering,* Tucson, Lawyers & Judges Publishing Company, 2003.

2. Critically ill

Often, in the face of life-threatening illness or injury, pain and its treatment are forgotten, or at least under-appreciated by the healthcare team. While a plethora of research exists regarding cancer pain and chronic pain, little attention has been paid to the evaluation and management of pain in critically ill patients. Assessment of pain may be hampered by age-related limitations of communication and cognition, level of consciousness, presence of endotracheal tubes, and the confusion of the ICU environment. It has been shown that caretakers commonly underestimate pain severity and thus may undertreat it.[34] The presence of ventilators prevents the critically ill patient from being able to speak to communicate pain. Although boards with commonly used words such as pain, bed pain, and water are available for the patient to point to, the use of wrist restraints to prevent removal of tubes also limits communication. Critically ill patients may be given sedation to diminish their awareness of the environment, but without concurrent administration of opioids, such as morphine, they will not experience pain relief. Approximately 50 to 64 percent of ICU patients have moderate to severe pain. In addition to the suffering associated with pain, pain can interfere with breathing, mobility, and even testing procedures. Anxiety associated with pain can worsen pain.[35]

Critical care nurses must carefully observe the responses of patients under their care to detect signs of pain, such as vital sign changes. D'Arcy and Puntillo found that critical care patients experienced a high level of pain and that these patients had recall of their critical care pain experiences.[36-37] Refer to the seminal work prepared by the Task Force of the American College of Critical Care Medicine for clinical practice guidelines for the use of sedatives and analgesics in the critically ill adult for additional information.[38] Refer to Cohen[39] for additional information on pain and suffering in the critical care unit.

3. Infants and children

The misconception that infants do not feel pain is long-standing. An analysis of 40 publications revealed that 77 percent of newborns undergoing surgical ligation of patent ductus arteriosus (heart surgery) received no anesthesia, only muscle relaxants or intermittent nitrous oxide.[40] Several studies have shown that children receive inadequate amounts of pain medication.[41]

Maintaining pain control in infants is particularly challenging. There is a small margin of error in dosages of medication. Infants are not able to rate their pain. Infants under six months of age are at the highest risk for clinically significant narcotic-induced depression of breathing. Some physicians place these babies on ventilators to ensure breathing functions continue during the administration of continuous narcotics. Children are at risk for scratching themselves due to the itching associated with opioids. Their nails must be kept short and smooth to prevent scratching.[42] Refer to the authoritative article prepared jointly by the American Academy of Pediatrics and the American Pain Society for standards regarding the assessment and management of acute pain in infants, children, and adolescents.[43]

4. Culturally diverse

Culture influences how each person experiences and responds to pain, including when and how to ask for pain management. Culture affects the pain experience in terms of the degree of expressivity (stoic versus demonstrative), how people describe and conceptualize pain, what they believe should be done to manage pain, and which treatments are appropriate. Cultural problems that complicate pain management include:

- Language and interpretation problems caused by not having competent interpreters
- Nonverbal communication problems resulting in an inability of nurses and others to recognize cues of pain
- Culturally or linguistically inappropriate pain assessment tools not translated appropriately, if at all

- Underreporting by stoic patients taught not to complain
- Reluctance to use pain medications because of cultural fears or taboos about their use
- Genetic differences that make pain medications more likely to cause adverse or ineffective effects
- Limited access to pain medications due to having inadequate health insurance
- Providers' fears of drug abuse caused by stereotyping certain minority groups and associating them with drug-seeking or abusing behaviors
- Prejudice and discrimination associated with negative judgments based on race or ethnicity[44]

The impact of ethnicity and minority status on pain control has been studied by a number of researchers. In a study of 1,308 outpatients with cancer pain, Cleeland found that 65 percent of minority patients did not receive appropriate analgesic prescriptions for their pain, compared to 50 percent of non-minority patients. The researchers discovered that Hispanic patients in particular were less likely to receive adequate analgesia.[45] A study found that African-American and Caucasian patients were prescribed more analgesics than Hispanics and Asians, with Hispanics receiving less medication than Asian patients.[46] Non-Hispanic Caucasians were twice as likely to receive pain relievers after a long bone fracture than were Hispanics visiting emergency departments.[47] Al-Atiyyat's review article cites several other studies of cultural expressions of pain and concluded that nurses need to understand cultural similarities and differences to prevent problems related to stereotyping, miscommunication, and interpersonal stress that lead to inadequate control of pain.[48]

5. Elderly

TIP: There is a mistaken belief that pain sensation decreases with age but there is no research evidence to support this. As a consequence of this misunderstanding, elderly patients receive significantly less analgesic medication than younger adults experiencing similar pain, leading to inadequate pain relief in older patients.[49]

Sometimes pain in elders is untreated or undertreated due to inadequate assessment, concern about effects of medications, or misconceptions based on ageism. While pain medications may contribute to cognitive dysfunction, untreated pain may have the same consequence.[50]

Many older people expect pain to be a part of aging and therefore fail to report it and fail to request pain management because they do not want to be a nuisance or they get tired of asking staff to treat their pain. The elderly may also fear that pain represents a deeper problem. Studies suggest that 25 to 50 percent of community-dwelling elderly suffer from pain, and up to 83 percent of the institutionalized elderly report at least one pain problem. Unrelieved pain can inhibit the ability to take deep breaths, cough, and be mobile, factors that could make an elderly person more susceptible to pneumonia, constipation, or deep vein thrombosis.[51] Another myth that affects pain management is that elderly patients experience less pain than do younger people. There is no research that shows that older people have a lesser ability to perceive pain, or do not experience the same pain as would a younger person suffering from the same trauma. There are additional factors that affect pain management. A nursing home resident who is alert and oriented may not always report pain. He may have an unrealistic fear of addiction or dependence on opioids or narcotics, believe it is a sign of weakness to need pain medication, or avoid taking medications because of unpleasant side effects. Many opioids cause nausea, constipation, itching, or drowsiness.

Healthcare providers contribute to undertreatment of pain through:

- inadequate staffing
- fears that providing adequate pain relief may lead to respiratory depression or addiction
- insufficient education on pain assessment[52]

6. Confused elderly

TIP: The confused elderly patient in acute pain is at even greater risk for inadequate pain relief since the patient may be unable to communicate the presence of pain.

Dementia affects pain assessment and management and the evaluation of damages. Although the demented resident cannot express pain, it is still experienced. One of the myths that affect pain management in the elderly is the nurse's belief that pain is a normal consequence of aging. In fact, pain is a signal of something wrong. Common causes of pain in the elderly are arthritis, cancer, spinal pathology, and postherpes neuralgia.[53-54] There is growing recognition of the problem of pain management in older adults, the effects of pain on everyday function and quality of life and the difficulties of assessing and managing pain in patients with dementia. Among older adults with dementia in long-term care, the prevalence of pain or potentially painful conditions is high, with estimates ranging from 43 percent to 71 percent.[55] A myth that affects pain management is that dement-

ed patients who report pain cannot be believed. Clinical staff members often discount complaints of pain in persons with cognitive impairment because their pain reports are inconsistent. Several studies, however, have indicated that verbal complaints of pain among the cognitively impaired are reliable and valid.[56-58]

The assessment of pain in the demented resident, or any resident for that matter, involves asking the patient if she is in pain. Many patients with mild or moderate degrees of dementia can still accurately describe the site of their pain and its severity. One study showed that 83 percent of elderly patients—demented or not—could describe their pain using a pain scale from one to ten, with ten being the highest. A demented resident may have an easier time using a pain scale with faces that indicate the level of pain.[59]

Another pain management myth that affects the analysis of medical records is that if the resident is in pain, the medical record will state this. Routine pain assessment is inconsistently performed in nursing homes. Even worse, several hours or days may go by after a resident is injured before the presence of pain is recognized by the staff. This results in delay of diagnosis of injuries such as fractures. The medical record may contain observations consistent with pain, such as the resident was grimacing or trying to push away healthcare workers. The resident may be restless, agitated, strike at others, display fidgeting, be withdrawn or have difficulty sleeping. Other signs of pain include holding an incision, refusing to move, assuming a distorted posture, having anxiety or depression, calling out for help, yelling and moaning. Blood pressure, heart rate, and breathing rate may be increased in acute (but not chronic) pain. Horgas and Miller note pain may be exacerbated by activities of daily living, such as bathing, dressing and transferring. During such activities, the pain may be exhibited by resisting care, clenching fists, grabbing the caregiver, guarding, and becoming rigid. In addition to causing needless suffering, unrelieved pain in people with dementia can have serious consequences, including declines in physical function, diminished appetite, irritability, reduced participation in social activities and depression. Untreated pain can delay healing, disturb sleep and activity patterns, reduce function, reduce quality of life, and prolong hospitalization.[60] Research indicates that failure to assess and treat pain in these individuals is often because of an unfounded belief by healthcare providers that pain sensations are diminished in individuals with cognitive impairments.[61] Refer to Assessing Pain in Older Adults and Assessing Pain in Persons with Dementia for more information.[62-63]

Pain medications can be a source of confusion in the elderly. Those which can increase confusion in elderly patients include nonsteroidal anti-inflammatory drugs, Demerol, Darvon, and Talwin.

10.6 Undertreatment of Pain
Pain management may be inadequate because of both underreporting and undertreatment of pain.

A. Causes

1. Behavior of the patient
Patients contribute to the undertreatment of pain for a number of reasons. Some patients refrain from admitting they are in pain for fear of being labeled as a complainer or whiner. Many have been raised in households where stoic behavior was valued and accepted. A "grin and bear it" philosophy prevails. Others view pain as punishment for doing something wrong. Some patients are fearful of taking medications in general, and pain relievers specifically, because of concerns of being overmedicated. They may have experienced side effects from pain relievers in the past. The pain associated with injections of pain relievers may lead to delays in reporting pain in an effort to avoid being stuck with a needle. Some medications (Demerol and Vistaril, among others) cause burning and pain as they are being injected. They may be fearful that the pain is an indication of a worsening health problem, and therefore believe if it is not reported, but ignored, it will go away. They may be concerned about distracting healthcare providers from other issues ("You're so busy, I hate to bother you…").

Pain may not be reported because it will signal the discomfort or expense of testing and treating the problem causing the pain. Reporting of pain may result in administration of narcotics or opioids, and cause a fear of addiction, side effects, or increased expense. The patient may not report pain because of a fear of being labeled as a complainer. Some patients are fatalistic and believe they are meant to endure pain. Others may infer that the healthcare provider should know that the condition is painful and would provide relief if it were available.[64]

Undertreatment occurs when the patient asks for pain medication before the allotted time span between doses (for example, asking for it at three and one-half hours after the previous dose, when the order is written for every four hours). Undertreatment may also result when the physician has provided an order for a dosage range of a medication, such as Morphine 1-2 mg or Percocet 1 to 2 tablets. The nurse is left with the choice as to how much pain medication to administer. Consistently selecting the smaller dose may result in undertreatment of pain when a larger dose is needed. In some states, orders that provide a range of medi-

cation dosages are not permitted by the regulatory agencies who oversee healthcare facilities.

TIP: Healthcare professionals continue to struggle with the need to accept the patient's report of pain regardless of the patient's behavior. Many nurses are still reluctant to relieve severe pain in a patient who is smiling. Most nurses expect patients who report severe pain to look as if they were hurt. Behavior is a poor indicator of pain intensity, because responses to pain vary among individuals.

---

2. Lack of knowledge of healthcare providers
Some healthcare providers need more education about pain assessment and management. Their lack of knowledge may contribute to the pain and suffering of patients under their care. A recent survey of nurses exposed some areas of misconceptions. The correct answers follow each statement.

1. Increases in vital signs are an indication that the patient is experiencing pain.
   False—correctly answered by 20 percent

2. Intramuscular injection is a good way to deliver pain medication.
   False—correctly answered by 75 percent

3. A patient may sleep despite being in pain.
   True—correctly answered by 94 percent

4. Depression is common in patients who have chronic pain.
   True—correctly answered by 98 percent

5. A nurse can tell how much pain a patient is experiencing by closely observing him.
   False—correctly answered by 82 percent

6. Behavioral pain scales using behaviors such as grimacing, moaning, or rubbing are effective for assessing pain in nonverbal patients.
   True—correctly answered by 91 percent

7. Patients who exhibit behaviors such as clock watching are showing signs of addiction.
   False—correctly answered by 80 percent

8. Continuous infusion via patient controlled analgesia pumps is a good way to provide analgesia for all patients.
   False—correctly answered by 83 percent

9. Differences in mu (opioid) binding sites account for differences in patient response to opioids.
    True—correctly answered by 93 percent

10. Management of neuropathic pain, such as diabetic neuropathy, often requires a combination of medications such as opioids and antidepressants for effective pain relief.
    True—correctly answered by 88 percent

11. There is no ceiling or upper limit on how far you can increase doses of opioid medication to improve pain relief.
    True—correctly answered by 42 percent

12. Nonsteroidal anti-inflammatory drugs used for relief of mild pain cause few adverse reactions.
    False—correctly answered by 52 percent

13. In patients with chronic pain, functionality may be a better measure of the efficacy of pain medication than decreased pain levels.
    True—correctly answered by 91 percent

14. Giving a patient a placebo is a good way to tell if he's really having pain.
    False—correctly answered by 92 percent

15. What percentage of patients who receive opioids for short-term treatment of acute pain (one to three days) will become addicted?
    Less than 1 percent. Correctly answered by 89 percent

16. What percentage of patients who have chronic pain and use opioids for one year become addicted?
    5 percent. Correctly answered by 40 percent

17. What percentage of addicted patients who abuse prescription opioids can be considered dependent on opioids?
    50 percent or more. Correctly answered by 54 percent

18. How comfortable are you giving opioids regularly to a patient who's been taking opioids for 12 months to control chronic low back pain?
    35 percent: Very comfortable
    45 percent: Comfortable
    15 percent: Uncomfortable
    4 percent: Very uncomfortable

19. Please check all of the following that apply to use of PCA in your practice.
    83 percent: Two nurses must sign when therapy is initiated and with all dosing changes.
    69 percent: Standardized education on PCA use is provided to patients.
    68 percent: Standard order sets are used for PCA.
    67 percent: PCA solutions and concentrations are standardized.
    63 percent: Annual competency on PCA use is required to assess your ability to correctly enter dose setting and parameters.
    19 percent: Nurse-activated PCA or PCA by proxy is permitted.[65]

Although the length of time on narcotics increases the likelihood that tolerance and physical dependence will occur, it does not increase the likelihood of addiction.[66] Blame is also laid at the door of the doctors doing the prescribing. Some physicians fear that if they deliver humane pain care, they will face prosecution by the Drug Enforcement Agency.[67]

B. Consequences

Studies of unrelieved pain in older adults have shown that the harmful effects of unrelieved pain include interference with sleep, difficulty walking, impaired cognition, altered nutrition, and decline in socialization. The number of falls increases, rehabilitation is slowed, and the level of independence declines.[68] Patients with unrelieved pain may lie quietly to avoid increased pain with movement. They may be reluctant to walk or perform range of motion exercises. This can lead to deconditioning, weight loss, or loss of muscle tone and strength. Decreased appetite associated with unrelieved pain can lead to weight loss, increased healing difficulties, and increased risk of skin breakdown. As can be seen from the information presented thus far, pain management is a significant problem for many patients. Inadequate pain management compounds the problems created by the original injury which precipitated the lawsuit.

Margaret Henry's postoperative pain was ineffectively treated by the nurses. She refused to be turned and repositioned because her pain level was so high. Her nurses labeled her as uncooperative instead of seeking a better solution to her pain management needs. Soon pressure ulcers began appearing on her heels and sacrum. The plaintiff nursing expert identified deviations from the standard of care in pain management and prevention of skin breakdown. Her nurses became defendants in a nursing malpractice suit.

C. Liability

As professional organizations and TJC standards reiterate the need to provide appropriate pain assessment and management, the failure to do so becomes a source of liability for healthcare professionals. Braun,[69] Furrow,[70] and Vaglienti and Grinberg[71] address this concern from the legal perspective. Theories of liability include:

- Failure to refer to a pain specialist
- Infliction of emotional distress
- Failure to provide informed consent regarding pain management[72]

Sources of standards of care for pain management are found in:

- Medical texts and journals
- Position statements of professional organizations
- Position statements of licensing boards
- State statutes
- Clinical practice guidelines
- Joint Commission standards[73]

10.7 Pain as a Part of Medical and Nursing Care

The medical treatment that becomes necessary to diagnose and treat negligence-inflicted injury becomes an additional source of discomfort. There are multiple ways that healthcare providers add to the pain and suffering of patients being treated for injuries. For example, insertion and removal of medical devices can cause pain. A research study at State University of New York at Stony Brook identified the following four emergency medical procedures that caused the most pain:

- Nasogastric intubation (insertion of a tube into the stomach by way of the nose)
- Incision and drainage of an abscess
- Reduction (setting) of a fracture
- Insertion of a urinary catheter[74]

The sensations associated with removal of tubes were studied in a group of hospitalized patients. Thirty-one had Jackson Pratt drains (small football-shaped drains attached to a long hollow tube with its end in the surgical wound) and 31 had chest tubes (tube the size of a person's thumb that is in the chest cavity). Both groups reported similar sensations when the tubes were removed: pain, pulling, pressure, and burning.[75] Pain is associated with dressing changes, wound care, administration of intramuscular and subcutaneous injections, insertion of intravenous needles, and so on.

Neurological injuries are often associated with a change in the patient's level of awareness or consciousness, requiring infliction of pain to stimulate a response. Examples of plaintiffs who may have experienced nursing malpractice-associated injuries that could cause altered level of awareness include:

1. The patient who showed beginning signs of a stroke that were not detected by the nurse practitioner, who should have referred him to the local emergency room for treatment to arrest the progression of the event.
2. The infant who is born with brain damage due to failure of the nurse to recognize the ominous patterns on the fetal heart monitoring strip.
3. The elderly patient who suffers a fractured skull and intracranial bleeding when she falls off the unsupervised loading dock of the hospital.
4. The postoperative patient who received an overdose of Morphine due to incorrect programming of the pump.
5. The critical care patient whose tracheostomy tube became dislodged, undetected by the nurse assigned to care for him.

In order to identify a change or improvement in level of consciousness when the patient is unable to effectively communicate, healthcare professionals are taught how to inflict pain. This specific type of pain is referred to in medical records as noxious stimuli. Light levels of pain may be inflicted by rolling or pressing a pencil over the fingernails or toenails. Pinching the skin may be used also, although if done repetitively can result in bruising. When the patient reacts to this type of pain, the medical record may state that the patient "localized" the pain, meaning she withdrew from painful stimulation. Deeper levels of pain are used when light pain does not elicit a reaction. This more vigorous infliction of pain is performed by pinching the shoulder muscle, pressing the fingers on the bony ridge above the eyes, or using the knuckles to press on the sternum. Older and less common methods include pinching the nipples, scrotum, or inner area of the thigh. Patients unable to localize or withdraw from the pain may grimace. No response to painful stimuli is synonymous with a deep level of sedation or coma.

10.8 Pain Treatment

There are varied ways to treat pain, with the use of analgesics as the main treatment method. However, the types of analgesics and the way in which they are administered are multiple; each has certain benefits and risks. It is important to remember that many of these strategies reduce the level of pain but not all can eliminate pain. Pain control options include those shown in Figure 10.2. The selection of the best combination of these options should be based on an assessment of a variety of factors including the patient's ability to cooperate, the level of pain, and the cause of the pain.

The principles of pain management are built on the World Health Organization analgesic ladder. The rule of thumb is to "start slow, go slow" by using the weakest drugs that are effective, and then moving up the ladder to find the drugs which make the patient comfortable. Refer to Table 10.2.

- Step 1 medications include aspirin, acetaminophen and nonsteroidal anti-inflammatories, although this third category of medications is used with caution given the many side effects associated with their use. Adjuvant medications enhance the effectiveness of the pain reliever.
- Step 2 medications for mild to moderate pain include aspirin or acetaminophen, dihydrocodeine, codeine, hydrocodone, oxycodone, and tramadol.
- Step 3 medications for severe pain include morphine, Fentanyl, hydromorphone, methadone, oxycodone, and levorphenol.

A. Analgesic Pain Medications

1. Types of analgesics
The next section of this chapter will provide an overview of some of the more commonly used analgesics.

TIP: Morphine sulfate is the pain medication against which all other pain relievers are judged.

a. Morphine
Most of the dosage information about pain medications is based on doses given at three to four hour intervals using Morphine 10 mgs intramuscular as a standard for comparison.[76] Morphine decreases pain impulse transmission and produces central nervous system (brain) depression and reduced awareness of pain. It is given for severe pain. Morphine is available in oral form (liquid or pills), or can be injected into the muscle or veins. Side effects of Morphine include constipation, low blood pressure, confusion, respiratory depression (slowing the breathing rate), itching, nausea, and sedation. This potent medication must be carefully prescribed, administered, and monitored. An overdose has the potential to cause respiratory arrest.

Table 10.2
WHO 3-Step Ladder for Cancer Pain Treatment

Step 1	Non-opioid +/- adjuvant drug therapy
Step 2	Opiate for mild to moderate pain + non-opioid +/- adjuvant as needed
Step 3	Opioid for moderate to severe pain +/- non-opioid +/- adjuvant as needed

- Massage, heat or cold, TENS (transcutaneous electrical nerve stimulation)
- Nonsteroidal anti-inflammatory drugs to supplement narcotics
- Around the clock administration of medication rather than only in the waking hours
- Patient-controlled analgesia machines to permit the patient to self-medicate with intravenous doses of a narcotic
- Permitting the patient to self-medicate for pain with oral or other forms of pain relievers
- Spinal analgesia using an epidural narcotic
- Intermittent or continuous local nerve blocks

Figure 10.2 *Methods of pain control behavioral interventions such as relaxation, distraction and imagery to reduce pain, anxiety and the amount of medications that are needed for pain control. Agency for Healthcare Policy and Research, (1992). Acute Pain Management: Operative or Medical Procedures and Trauma, U.S. Department of Health and Human Services, Rockville, Maryland.*

b. Demerol

Demerol (Meperidine) was once commonly used for pain control, particularly after surgery to relieve moderate to severe pain. Demerol can be given orally, subcutaneously, intramuscularly, or intravenously. It was often used in combination with Vistaril or Phenergan to enhance its effects. A common order is 75 mgs every four hours. This order is inadequate because Demerol provides pain reduction for only two and one-half to three and one-half hours. A dose of 75 mgs every four hours is equivalent to only 5–7.5 mgs of Morphine. To obtain the same amount of pain relief as that provided by 10 mgs of Morphine, physicians would need to prescribe 100-150 mgs of Demerol every three hours.[77] Demerol should not be used when kidney function is impaired, as it is excreted by the kidneys. Seizures, increased intracranial pressure, respiratory depression, confusion, and irritability may result from its use. The frequency with which prescribers have requested that Demerol be given to patients has substantially declined in recent years. It is no longer the pain reliever of choice, although it may be used to reduce shivering in a postoperative patient.

c. Fentanyl

As one of the fastest acting narcotics, Fentanyl (Sublimaze) is used in the operating room as well as on the hospital units. It inhibits the pain pathways and alters pain perception. A synthetic opiate, Fentanyl can be given in intramuscular and intravenous forms. Duragesic, which is Fentanyl in a patch form, is effectively used for pain control. It may be given orally in the form of a pop. It is given in small doses of 0.05 mg to 0.1 mg to adults. The risk of overdose is great if medication orders are not carefully written and transcribed. Serious side effects of Fentanyl can include slow heart rate, cardiac arrest, respiratory depression, and spasm of the larynx.

d. Dilaudid

Dilaudid (Hydromorphone) can be used to suppress coughing, but is most commonly used for moderate to severe pain. It is often reserved for the end stages of terminal cancer due to its potency. Dilaudid can be given in oral, intramuscular, or intravenous forms. It can cause sedation, confusion, low blood pressure or breathing rate, nausea, vomiting, constipation, or loss of appetite.

e. Percodan and Percocet

Percodan (also known as Roxicodone, Oxycodan) or Percocet (also known as Tylox, Roxicet) are often the first oral pain relievers used after intramuscular or intravenous analgesics are stopped. These oral opiates are used for moderate to severe pain. They are available in a liquid or pill form as well as a suppository. Percocet contains acetaminophen (Tylenol) whereas Percodan does not. A standard adult dose is either one or two tablets repeated every three to four hours as needed. Side effects include dizziness, drowsiness, confusion, headache, sedation, and euphoria. Nausea, vomiting, constipation, and respiratory depression may occur. The total dose of Tylenol must be limited due to liver toxicity risks. Older adults should not take more than 2 grams per day and younger, healthy adults may take up to 4 grams.[78]

f. Codeine

Codeine may be used alone or in combination with Tylenol for moderate to severe pain. Tylenol #3 contains 30 mgs of Codeine whereas Tylenol #4 contains 60 mgs of Codeine. It is also used in cough medicine. Codeine can be given orally or by injection. Side effects can include drowsiness, sedation, nausea, vomiting, constipation, and loss of appetite.

g. Nonsteroidal anti-inflammatories

Nonsteroidal anti-inflammatory drugs are frequently given to patients who sustain trauma. Commonly used drugs are shown in Table 10.3. Vioxx's withdrawal from the market raised questions about the safety of the category of COX-2 inhibitors. This category of NSAID is associated with a lower risk of gastrointestinal side effects. Heigh[79] commented that many patients stop taking NSAIDs because of gastrointestinal side effects after a period of time. In a sample of elderly patients, users of these drugs were four times more likely than nonusers to be hospitalized for ulcer disease or upper gastrointestinal hemorrhage. People who had taken the drugs for a total of 30 or more days had the highest risk. There was a relationship between the amount of the medication taken and the complications. In a study of patients treated with a variety of NSAIDs, only 32 percent did not have changes in their stomach and duodenum. Hemorrhage was present in 44.6 percent, erosions were seen in 53.8 percent and ulcers were found in 15.4 percent of the patients. Patients who take both steroids and NSAIDs are at higher risk for gastrointestinal symptoms.

NSAIDs that are the least harmful to the stomach and duodenum are Disalcid, Relafen, and Lodine. The patient may be given Zantac to protect the duodenum from injury. Zantac does not protect the stomach. Carafate is helpful for only one to two weeks. Cytotec is helpful to protect against damage during the early as well as late phases of treatment.

Table 10.3
Pain Relievers

Type of drug	Examples
Nonsteroidal anti-inflammatories (risk of gastric bleeding)	Aspirin, Voltaren, Dolobid, Ansaid, Lodine, Motrin, Advil, Nalfon, Indocin, Orudis, Toradol, Relafen, Mobic, Daypro, Anaprox, Naprosyn, Feldene, Clinoril, Tolectin
COX-2 selective NSAIDS (reduced risk of gastric bleeding)	Celebrex, Bextra
Opioid analgesics	Stadol, Morphine (MS Contin, Roxanol), Demerol, Codeine, Methadone, Sublimaze, Dilaudid, Nubain, Roxicodone, Percocet, Percodan, Codeine, Levo-dromoran, Darvon
Neuropathic pain relievers	Pamelor, Klonopin, Tegretol, Neurontin, Depakote

B. Timing and Methods of Pain Medications

1. PRN "as needed"

The traditional method of pain control in an institutional setting is based on the pattern of the patient asking for pain medication when needed. This method often results in undermedication and delays in receiving pain medication, since the patient must wait for the nurse to fill the request. Pain medication levels dip down when the patient is sleeping, resulting in increased pain upon awakening. Unrelieved pain after surgery or trauma is often unhealthy and is preventable or controllable in an overwhelming majority of cases.[80] The management of pain is still not well understood. Much education is needed to change the prescribing patterns of healthcare professionals.

2. Longer-lasting oral medications

In addition to Methadone, which has an extended effect with a half-life of 24 to 48 hours, other new medications are effective for once a day dosing. New extended release products on the market include Hydromorph Contin, a 12-hour extended release form of Dilaudid/hydromorphone. Kadian and Avinza are two forms of extended release morphine, and may be used for 24-hour dosing.[81] Both Fentanyl and Lidocaine can be delivered by patch. The Fentanyl patches take up to 48 hours to reach full effect and are changed every 72 hours. Lidocaine patches are applied over the painful area for 12 hours a day.

3. Patient controlled analgesia

Patient controlled analgesia (PCA) pumps were developed to address the problem of undermedication. They are used to permit the patient to self-administer small doses of narcotics (usually Morphine, Demerol, or Fentanyl) into the blood or spinal fluid at frequent intervals. PCA pumps are commonly used after surgery to provide a more effective method of pain control than periodic injections of narcotics. This method of pain control has been found to result in less pain and earlier discharge from the hospital. PCA pumps can be effectively used by children as young as six years old.[82] A continuous infusion (called a basal rate) of 1-2 mg/hour permits the patient to receive a continuous infusion of pain medication. This mode of delivery is now used only for patients who have had prior opioid use or are not "opioid naïve." The risk of respiratory depression is too great in patients who have not built up a tolerance to opioids. Typically the patient receives an intravenous "loading" dose to quickly raise the blood level of the pain medication.

Depending on how the physician orders the medication, doses of narcotics may be given in addition to or instead of a continuously running infusion of narcotics. These additional doses given on demand are usually limited to 1 mg of the narcotic in the pump. The pump is programmed to limit the number of additional doses that the patient can receive, so as to not exceed safe hourly limits of the narcotic. New pumps have touch screens and bar coding, which can be used to track pain medications as they leave the pharmacy, but also to identify the patient who receives the medication and the nurse who puts it in the pump. A handheld computer can be used to collect information from the patient's identification band and the pump. Infrared technology allows the data to be wirelessly downloaded to a central station where pain assessment and medication can be monitored.[83]

Morphine is the most common medication used with PCA pumps although Demerol is occasionally used. Its onset and duration are similar to Morphine. Fentanyl has a rapid onset but a shorter duration than Demerol or Morphine. Administration of narcotics through an epidural catheter usually involves a combination of narcotic (Fentanyl, Morphine, or Dilaudid) mixed with low doses of a local anesthetic (Lidocaine, Bupivacaine, or Ropivacaine) without epinephrine. Side effects of the anesthetics include sensory and motor deficits, low blood pressure, and urinary retention.[84]

Concerns have been identified in the last few years about the hazards of PCA by proxy, that is allowing nurses and family members to activate the PCA pump on behalf of the patient. Overdoses of medication have occurred due to this practice, which is now being discouraged. Careful PCA pump programming and patient selection, as well as vigilant monitoring for the patient's responses to medication are essential to provide a safe delivery of pain relief. There have been tragic instances of overdoses delivered through PCA pumps, resulting in respiratory arrest and brain damage.

A PCEA (patient controlled epidural analgesia) pump delivers pain medication into the patient's epidural space. Dilaudid, Morphine, or Fentanyl is used along with a local anesthetic such as bupivacaine or ropivacaine. The epidural method of pain medication administration should be done only by clinicians skilled in its use and when careful monitoring of the patient can be provided.

4. Other methods

A Fentanyl patient-controlled transdermal system consists of a credit-card sized system with an adhesive backing applied to the patient's upper arm. The patient pushes a button attached to the device. The medication is delivered into the tissues. The device can deliver 80 doses or last 24 hours, whichever comes first. This method of pain relief has proven to be as effective as Morphine PCA pumps for postoperative pain control. Spinal cord stimulators are used in patients with chronic neuropathic pain that do not respond to medication. Leads are implanted in the epidural space next to the nerves that affect the body area in pain. The leads emit a mild current that makes the patient feel less pain. The morphine pump is another device that is implanted. This device can deliver Morphine into the intrathecal space to reduce pain. The pump is placed in the abdomen and can be programmed from the outside. Additional medication may be needed to supplement the Morphine within the pump.[85]

10.9 Suffering

Although the phrase "pain and suffering" places suffering in a secondary position, suffering is a broader concept than pain, encompassing many aspects of life after injury. Certainly pain can cause suffering, but suffering may exist independent of pain. Patients may suffer from nausea, vomiting, diarrhea, shortness of breath, fatigue, anxiety, panic, and a host of other symptoms. Since medical records will rarely comment that the patient is "suffering," a basic understanding of causes and symptoms of suffering as well as

the ability to interpret medical documentation helps identify suffering.

The suffering associated with pain may be influenced by many factors, including:

- Stage of growth and development
- Personality
- Culture and societal influences
- Sexual identity and stereotypes
- Level of fatigue
- Communication skills
- Meaning of pain
- How long pain has been present
- Spiritual beliefs
- Family and occupational roles
- Level of excitement or distraction
- Attitude toward pain
- Pain threshold
- General state of health
- Intensity and frequency of the pain
- Pain location
- Underlying cause of pain
- Age
- Integrity of nervous system
- Pain quality[86]

A. Causes of Suffering

Nursing malpractice that results in injury can profoundly disrupt the life of an individual and his family. Suffering may result from any of these sources:

- Sensory overload: loud noises, strong smells, bright lights, interrupted sleep
- Strange tests filled with unfamiliar sensations
- Feeling depersonalized
- Lack of privacy
- Loss of control
- Inability to understand medical language
- Feeling lonely
- Exposure to multiple strangers performing intimate activities

Specific sources of pain and suffering include:

- Hurried staff, not allowing time to recover after the various steps in a procedure
- Rough handling of tubes, catheters, and surgical drains
- Rapid removal of tape, dressings adherent to the wounds

- Rapid and rough turning and positioning of the patient
- Repeated venipunctures and arterial blood gases, heel sticks in neonates
- Requirement to cough and deep breathe after surgery
- Suctioning
- Injections
- Being on a ventilator

In addition to pain, the patient may experience stress from many factors associated with the illness:

- Suddenness of illness without adequate time to prepare or plan
- Feelings of helplessness
- Anger about the injury or disease, and the circumstances surrounding it
- Loss of power
- Inadequate information about the injury and its treatment
- Waiting for medical attention (doctor's offices and clinics, in the hospital bed, or for diagnostic tests)
- Uncertainty about the chances of full recovery
- Side effects of medications
- Management of symptoms
- Learning how to care for oneself (perform dressing changes, use crutches, pack wounds, give medications, etc.)
- Emotional turmoil resulting from multiple losses, such as loss of normal role, functional abilities, energy, or body image
- Fear of dependence, pain, loss of love, and of stigma associated with some illnesses (cancer, epilepsy, HIV)
- Preparation for medical crises
- Loss of hopes and dreams[87]
- Boredom: Lack of variety in one's daily routine
- Fear of surgery, procedures, mutilation or death: Stress caused by worrying
- Disfigurement/change in body image: Alteration in appearance caused by trauma, surgery, burns and other causes
- Loss of recreation: Inability to participate in hobbies or other relaxing activities and for children, disruption in play activities
- Lost opportunities: The inability to participate in chances to improve one's life

- Loss of control over bodily functions: Incontinence of bladder and bowel, inability to eat or breathe on one's own, and being unable to get out of bed or wash oneself contribute to a feeling of helplessness
- Disruption in communication: The presence of a ventilator, tracheostomy, stroke or head injury impairs communication
- Restraints: Restricted movement prevents adjusting position or touching one's body, for example to scratch the face
- Being in unfamiliar surroundings: Exposure to new sights, sounds, smells, and people contributes to stress
- Loss of independence: The inability to care for one's own needs, on either a temporary or permanent basis
- Role disruptions: The alteration in one's usual roles and responsibilities
- Separation from loved ones or peers: The disruption in normal relationships imposed by isolation in the hospital, in the nursing home, or at home
- Disruption in routines: Alteration in lifestyle due to the need for medical treatment or by injuries
- Accumulation of tension: Inability to release tension by one's usual coping methods

Individual factors that prolong suffering and hinder coping include:

- Passive, helpless, pessimistic personality
- Lack of sense of humor
- Depression, guilt
- Sense of helplessness
- Lack of spirituality
- Denial of seriousness of illness
- Postponing decision making
- Unrealistic goal setting
- Low self-esteem
- Inability to ask for help
- Reluctance to discuss feelings or needs
- Small or inaccessible social network
- Lack of help from support system
- Inadequate support from healthcare providers
- No contact with others who have had similar experiences
- Inflexible concepts of one's role (either the patient or the caregivers)[88]

- Nausea
- Vomiting
- Anorexia causing loss of appetite
- Dyspnea (shortness of breath)
- Coughing
- Urgency (an inability to wait after the urge to urinate develops)
- Frequency of urination
- Burning on urination
- Itching
- Abdominal distention
- Constipation
- Diarrhea
- Fever
- Swelling of body parts
- Dizziness
- Weakness
- Fatigue
- Loss of memory and other cognitive deficits

Figure 10.3 *Symptoms that contribute to suffering*

Table 10.4
Medications Used to Treat Symptoms

Type of drug	Purpose	Examples
Anti-anxiety	To reduce anxiety	Ativan, Xanax, Librium, Klonopin, Tranxene, Valium, Serax
Antidepressants	To reduce depression	Zoloft, Elavil, Anafranil, Norpramin, Sinequan, Tofranil, Pamelor, Vivactil, Nardil, Parnate, Celexa, Prozac, Luvox, Wellbutrin, Serzone, Remeron, Desyrel, Effexor, Paxil
Antidiarrheals	To reduce diarrhea	Lomotil, Immodium
Antiemetic	To prevent emesis or vomiting	Pepto Bismol, Kaopectate Compazine, Tigan, Reglan
Anti-itching	To reduce itching	Benadryl
Hypnotic	To promote sleep	Ambien, Benadryl, ProSom, Dalmane, Doral, Restoril, Halcion, Sonata
Laxatives	To treat constipation	Milk of Magnesia, Metamucil, Citrucel, Fibercon, Surfak, Colace, Dialose, Mineral Oil, Citronesia, Magnesium Hydroxide, Fleets Phosphosoda, Glycerine, Lactulose, Golytely, Dulcolax, Cascara, Castor Oil, Senokot
Neuromuscular blockers	Paralyze the diaphragm	Tracrium, Nimbex, Nuromax, Mivacron, Pavulon, Zemuron, Anectine, Norcuron

B. Physical Stress

Physical symptoms resulting from injury contribute to suffering. Examples of symptoms that contribute to suffering are shown in Figure 10.3. Exposure to these symptoms can generate suffering in the patient and anxiety in the family, who often feel helpless to intervene to reduce the symptoms. Medications used to treat these symptoms are displayed in Table 10.4.

C. The Medical Environment and Treatment

Exposure to the medical environment can cause suffering by virtue of the assault on the senses. Unpleasant sights, sounds, and sensations multiply discomfort. Descriptions of some common sources of suffering from the medical environment and treatment follow.

1. Suctioning

Suctioning involves inserting a flexible clear tube down the nose or mouth. Once the tube has passed beyond the back of the throat where the gag reflex is located, suction is applied to remove accumulated secretions from the lungs. Deep suctioning involves advancing the catheter far into the airways of the lungs. The presence of thick yellow secretions necessitates frequent suctioning, as often as every 30 to 60 minutes. The risk of developing thick mucus plugs, which block off the airway is reduced with frequent suctioning. Suctioning is unpleasant for two major reasons. The gag reflex is stimulated when the catheter passes down the throat and the act of suctioning causes the patient to have a sensation of air being cut off while the tube is in the throat. The medical record may state that the patient has blood-tinged sputum after being suctioned. This usually indicates trauma to the airway and tissues from repeated suctioning.

2. Ventilators

TIP: Many patients experience great suffering when on a ventilator. Although the medical record does not graphically describe the discomfort associated with being attached to a ventilator, patients often report discomfort.

The complaints of patients who have been on a ventilator are shown below:

- finding the ventilator frightening, uncomfortable, and painful
- dreading suctioning
- being scolded for trying to shift the endotracheal tube to a more comfortable position, which nurses often mistake for attempts to pull it out

- having unexplained blurred vision
- becoming disoriented because they could not turn their heads, talk, or see clearly
- feeling helpless
- hearing nurses talking about them as if they did not exist
- being concerned if nurses wore worried expressions
- suffering from hunger and thirst[89]

Patients on ventilators often require frequent suctioning. Although the patient may be described as mouthing words in an attempt to talk, rarely can the healthcare providers understand them. The process of weaning off of the ventilator can create anxiety if the patient becomes short of breath and needs to be placed back on the ventilator or reintubated.

Having to depend on a machine to breathe and being unable to speak can bring about anxiety, sleep disturbances, and rapid heart and breathing rates. Prolonged use of an endotracheal tube can cause ulcerations of the vocal cords, narrowing of the larynx and trachea, and vocal cord paralysis. Hoarseness, redness of the larynx and scar tissue may remain as long as six months. A tracheostomy may become necessary if it is anticipated the patient will remain on the ventilator for longer than three weeks. Immediate complications following a tracheostomy include bleeding, collapse of the lung, and development of air under the tissues.[90]

3. ICU (Intensive Care Unit) psychosis

Exposure to intensive treatment can lead to profound disruptions in normal sleep wake cycles. Patients who require frequent interruptions for assessments, treatment, vital sign checks, blood work, and medications are at high risk for ICU psychosis. Sleep deprivation, sensory deprivation or overload, excessive fatigue, side effects of medications, and a prolonged stay in ICU all contribute to this condition. This syndrome is defined as a delirium manifested by the symptoms shown below:

- Agitation
- Restlessness
- Irritability
- Depression
- Withdrawal
- Anxiety
- Disorientation
- Memory loss
- Confusion
- Wakefulness
- Fatigue with decreased attention and concentration

- Delirium and inability to distinguish day and night
- Hallucinations
- Delusions
- Paranoia
- Distorted perceptual abilities[91-92]

4. Medical equipment

The liability issues associated with the use of restraints have been addressed in Chapter 10, *Subacute and Long-Term Care Nursing Malpractice Issues*, in Volume II. The use of restraints can engender feelings of helplessness, anxiety, loss of control, and anger at having one's will thwarted. Invasive equipment attached to one's body can contribute to suffering. The patient's movements may be hampered by devices such as:

- Tubes in the bladder, kidneys, heart, head, or chest
- Traction attached to the arms, legs, head, or spine
- Intravenous lines in the arms, groin, leg, upper chest, or neck
- Splints on arms or legs

The medical record may contain documentation that the patient's level of agitation was addressed through the use of restraints. It is common to see documentation of the use of wrist restraints to prevent removal of the endotracheal tube, intravenous lines, Foley catheter, and other equipment when the patient is in the Intensive Care Unit.

10.10 Symptoms of Suffering

Suffering is mostly manifested through emotional and psychological reactions. The patient may express anxiety or fear, or become agitated. Barsky[93] notes that "patients often become angry in response to the suffering and disability caused by disease, adverse life events or the psychological threats inherent in being a patient." He notes that illness often causes anger because it presents the threats of disfigurement, pain, lost opportunity, abandonment, and even death. Some patients are particularly enraged by the helplessness, lack of control, and enforced passivity that disease (or injury) confers. The patient may feel helpless, hopeless, powerless, lonely, and isolated. Depression and withdrawal from others may occur. Posttraumatic stress disorder may result after a traumatic event, such as the development of quadriplegia or being burned as result of nursing negligence. The diagnostic criteria for this disorder are shown below:

1. Exposure to a traumatic event in which the person has responded with intense fear, helplessness, or horror

2. Re-experiencing of the traumatic event in recurrent, intrusive, and distressing images, thoughts, or perceptions

3. Persistent avoidance of stimuli associated with the trauma, accompanied by a numbing of general responsiveness not present before the trauma

4. Persistent symptoms of increased arousal, such as hypervigilance or exaggerated startle response, which were not present before the trauma

5. Duration of disturbance symptoms for more than one month

6. Clinically significant distress or impairment in social, occupational, or other important areas of functioning[94]

Two qualities are common to patients affected by posttraumatic stress disorder: depersonalization (the stripping away of one's individuality) and entrapment (the sense that escape routes are non-existent or dangerous).[95] According to research published in the *Journal of Bone and Joint Surgery* people who suffer a traumatic injury, such as a fracture, may also develop posttraumatic stress disorder (PTSD). In one study, orthopedic surgeons found that 51 percent of patients who had sustained some type of fracture went on to develop PTSD. Symptoms of PTSD include recurrent flashbacks of traumatic events, anxiety, depression, insomnia, jumpiness, and irritability. For the study, researchers gave a standard PTSD questionnaire to 580 patients seen in an acute care facility after a trauma. The researchers plan to follow up this study with another that compares the rate of posttraumatic stress, depression, and anxiety between trauma patients who get cognitive behavioral therapy and those who get the current standard of care, which is no psychological treatment.[96] Refer to Pangia for more information on litigation strategies for handling a claim involving posttraumatic stress disorder.[97]

10.11 Treatment of Suffering

Treatments and medications to minimize distressing physical symptoms are useful. Other suggestions for healthcare professionals to lessen specific sources of distress include:

1. Control environmental stimuli such as noise, odors, and traffic.

2. Provide rest intervals between care to allow recovery from procedures and treatments.

3. Handle tubes, catheters, and drains gently.

4. Remove tape and dressings slowly and gently.

5. Allow patients to perform their own dressing changes and apply ointments to the skin.

6. Use moisture-retentive dressings that will not adhere to a wound.

7. Ask patients how best to turn and position themselves. Turn slowly and gently.

8. Permit the patient to sleep uninterrupted by clustering care activities.

9. Encourage the physician to insert arterial lines for blood gases to prevent repeated punctures.

10. Let a parent or guardian stay with infants and children during painful procedures.

11. Swaddle infants (wrap in bedding) and provide distraction by rubbing the opposite leg during heel punctures. Provide them with objects to hold or suck on.[98]

Refer to Lambert and Hudson-Barr[99] and Pollock, D'Lugo and Ford[100] for additional insights regarding pain and suffering in children.

Psychological stress is treated by reassurance, education, and compassion. Guided imagery, meditation, distraction, and relaxation exercises can be used. Counseling, group therapy, support groups, and other psychological interventions may be helpful in adjusting to changes and reducing suffering. Healthcare professionals are taught to acknowledge the patient's suffering using empathy and sensitivity.

TIP: Patients who use anger to express their suffering are particularly challenging for healthcare providers. The anger often interferes with therapy, recovery, and communication. Avoidance of the angry patients may increase their sense of isolation and despair. Setting limits on the angry behavior is often needed.

The nature of the patient's injuries, if associated with nursing malpractice, may complicate the treatment of suffering. Nursing staff may be uncomfortable caring for a patient whose condition was caused by negligent care. Suspicions of a future lawsuit may lead staff to avoid the patient, for fear of being swept up into the litigation. Interactions with the patient may be brief or the call light left unanswered for long periods of time. The patient's sense of isolation and anger may intensify. (See Chapter 5, *Medical Errors: Roots of Litigation*, for more information.)

10.12 Pain and Suffering Testimony

A nurse may testify in three specific roles—as a liability expert, as an expert in explaining the medical record, and as a life care planner to identify the cost of future medical needs. The role described in this chapter is an expert witness who focuses on summarizing medical records, and not on liability. The expert explains the facts of a case with regard to illness or injury, course of treatment, and impact on the client. Drawing on a healthcare background, preparation, and experience in educating clients and families, the expert explains the often technical and voluminous healthcare records to attorneys, judges, and juries. This expert witness serves as a reviewer and interpreter of the healthcare records rather than offering opinions on the care rendered.[101] A nurse is useful for preparing a summary of the plaintiff's pain and suffering. Instead of bringing in a parade of treating physicians or other experts: the attorney can retain a nursing expert who can review and summarize the medical records and present them in their entirety. The plaintiff's attorney's purpose may be to provide the jury with a clear, concise, and understandable accounting of the events in the medical records in order to persuade the jury to accept the attorney's depiction of the damages. Defense attorneys may wish to retain an expert witness to refute the findings of the plaintiff's expert.

TIP: Nurses' holistic perspective of patient care makes them uniquely qualified to testify as experts about the patient's experiences.

Physicians tend to concentrate on explanations of specific medical treatments and procedures and minimize pain and suffering. Unlike a nurse, a physician makes brief periodic visits to a patient's bedside. Physicians are rarely at the bedside for an extended amount of time, do not perform all of the painful procedures that nurses do, and do not share the same holistic perspective of nurses. A nurse is more likely to visualize and present a broader, more comprehensive, and more empathetic view of the events described in the medical records. Nursing expert witnesses have expertise in both the legal and nursing fields. This dual expertise makes them excellent choices to fulfill this testifying role. The person selected to perform this function should have excellent oral and written communication skills, and the ability to teach, be analytical and well-organized, and convey complex material in a clear manner.

A. Legal Basis

Rule 1006 of the Federal Rules of Evidence permits the use of summaries. The rule provides that when there are voluminous writings, recordings, or photographs that cannot be conveniently examined in court, a chart, summary, or calculation may be presented. The originals must be made available for examination or copying by the opposing party, and the judge may order their production in court. In many instances the use of summaries is the only practical means of presenting the contents of voluminous evidence to the judge and jury. There must be a reasonable guarantee that the summary is accurate and that the person who prepared the summary is available to testify at trial as to the method of preparation of the report or to give an explanation of the summary.

B. Use of Pain and Suffering Summaries

The pain and suffering report is usually prepared on behalf of the patient and is particularly helpful in malpractice and personal injury cases. They are particularly effective in the situations shown below:

Pain and suffering reports are effective if:

1. There are extensive medical records covering a long admission to the hospital or several admissions over a number of months or years.
2. The plaintiff is unable to describe his or her own pain and suffering due to death, disability, or lack of communication skill or memory.
3. The plaintiff experienced marked pain, has required extensive narcotic or analgesic medication, multiple medical and nursing interventions, surgical procedures, complications, noxious sensations, or emotional suffering.
4. The attorney wants the nurse to educate the jury about the plaintiff's unpleasant experiences.
5. The attorney wants to build maximum impact by having a nurse testify to the patient's pain and suffering rather than putting the patient on the stand and risk having the plaintiff being perceived as whining.
6. The nurse can explain medical procedures to educate the jury.

The report provides the attorney with a comprehensive overview of the contents of the medical record, with a specific focus on the problems the patient experienced. The summary is useful for the liability witnesses in the case, who may use it to refresh their recollection about the medical events when preparing for deposition or trial. The summary may reduce the need and cost of the liability experts to perform a complete review of all of the medical records.

When prepared for the defense attorney, the summary of the medical record reviews the plaintiff's claims in the complaint, deposition, expert witness reports, or pain and suffering summary. The expert witness reviews the medical documentation and refutes the plaintiff's exaggerations.

C. Case Examples

The following case histories demonstrate the range of nursing malpractice cases which can benefit from this type of report:

1. At age 17, Nancy was diagnosed with a bony tumor in her shoulder. She underwent a treatment regimen consisting of Methotrexate and leukovorin. She received the same regimen for 11 cycles. Her mother stayed at her bedside whenever she was admitted to the hospital. The physician incorrectly ordered the regimen for the last of the 12 cycles, permitting too much time to transpire from the end of the Methotrexate infusion before the administration of leukovorin. The nurse made a medication error by allowing the Methotrexate to run in over too long a period. When the patient's mother questioned the nurse about the errors, she was brushed off. Nancy developed a toxic epidermal necrolysis, which consisted of losing all of her skin. She died as a result of massive infection. An autopsy showed there was no evidence of cancer in her body at the time of her death. The case settled.
2. Mrs. G. was admitted to a psychiatric unit for detoxification from alcohol. Prior to admission she was being given Methotrexate twice a week by her internal medicine physician to treat her arthritis. Not understanding the dosing of Methotrexate, the psychiatrist ordered that it be given daily instead of twice weekly. The patient developed toxic levels of Methotrexate, and died within a few weeks. The pain and suffering report prepared in this case is contained in the appendix of Chapter 28, *Medication Errors*, in Volume II.
3. An 84-year-old woman spent several months in the hospital. Within a week of her admission her skin began to break down. Over the course of the next several months she developed stage IV ulcers on both hips and her sacrum. The heads of her femur became visible through the hip wounds. The family took photographs of these wounds in the hospital. The patient had contractures of her legs which kept her heels in contact with her rectal area. One particularly vivid photograph showed a feces-soiled dressing covering her heel ulcer. The jury awarded $1.1 million.
4. A quadriplegic patient was scalded in a nursing home bathtub filled with water that was 180

degrees. His legs were amputated. He was transferred to a different nursing home, where his skin did not heal and continued to be open. He died seven months after the scalding. The jury awarded $200,000. Under the terms of the high low agreement the award was increased to $900,000.

5. A woman's nightgown caught on fire while she was smoking at home in the presence of a home care nurse. The nurse put out the flames and called the physician's office for orders. She described the burn as a "sunburn." The physician's receptionist provided an order for Silvadene. For the next six days the nurse and home healthcare aide treated the burns with Silvadene and showers without the patient being seen by the physician. At the end of the six days the patient fell at home, striking her forehead and sustaining a laceration. When the patient was taken to the emergency room she was diagnosed with first, second, and third degree burns of her right neck, chest, abdomen, arm, hand, shoulder, breast, and axilla. She was admitted to a burn unit, where she was sedated with Morphine for the remaining 29 days of her life. The case was settled for an undisclosed amount.

10.13 Format for the Pain and Suffering Report
A. Analysis of the Medical Record

The expert witness typically reviews all medical documentation related to the plaintiff's medical condition before and after the care alleged to be negligent. While reviewing the care, the expert looks for the impact on the patient such as symptoms of pain and evidence of suffering. The expert may take notes, develop charts, and flag pages with poignant quotes. The expert also looks for information indicating relief of pain and suffering.

B. Pain Diaries

A pain diary is a document or computer file kept by a person in pain (or responsible adult). It typically lists the date and time, a pre-intervention pain score, the intervention, the post-intervention pain score, and comments. Templates for diaries are found on the Internet. The diary permits the patient to share data with healthcare providers, see correlations between interventions and pain relief, and improve the effectiveness of pain control. A pain diary provided to the expert witness is another source of data about the patient's experience.

C. Report Formats

The summary of the medical record can follow several formats. The report typically begins by listing the documents reviewed in preparation of the report. This includes the medical records from hospitalizations, outpatient visits to doctors, physical therapy, and so on. The body of the text describes the experiences the patient went through based on the nurse's review of the medical records and knowledge of the sensations typically experienced by a patient undergoing certain types of procedures.

The report can be organized to provide a chronological description of the patient's pain and suffering, or it can be organized to describe the major symptoms or complications the patient experienced. A chronological listing would typically describe each week, month and/or provide a summary of each hospitalization. A report organized according to symptoms would take each major problem and describe its progression or resolution over time. For example, a prolonged illness that occurred as a result of malpractice may be associated with skin breakdown; nutritional disruption; infections; respiratory problems; immobility; pain; use of multiple invasive devices such as chest tubes, catheters, and intravenous tubes; and surgical procedures. The report should contain quotations from the medical record to convey the suffering. Statements made by the patient for the purposes of medical treatment are considered admissible as evidence. This is an exception to the hearsay rule exclusion, and the medical record is also admissible as evidence as a business record. Table 10.5 contains medical record quotations from the case of an elderly woman who fell in the hospital, fracturing ribs and a vertebral body. This case was settled.

Tables can be used to supplement the information in the report. The tables that are natural additions to the pain and suffering summary include the following:

1. The amount of morphine a patient required during a hospitalization (Figure 10.4).
2. Injuries—Figure 10.5 shows those of a plaintiff who wandered off the roof of a hospital.
3. Invasive devices—Figure 10.6 depicts those that were used after a man stopped breathing due to overdose of narcotics.
4. Chronologies/timelines of admissions and key events (Table 10.6).

Ideally, the charts are designed so they can be enlarged and used as exhibits at the time of trial, as discussed elsewhere in Chapter 22, *Demonstrative Evidence.*

Table 10.5
Quotations from Medical Record of Woman Who Fell at Hospital

DATE	SOURCE	COMMENT
10/27/04	Nursing progress notes	Experiencing back pain and spasms upon any movement in bed
10/27/04	MD progress notes	Complains of back pain status post fall yesterday. Diagnosis: lumbar sacral sprain/contusion
10/29/04	MD progress notes	Severe pain in back. X-ray compression fracture T11
10/29/04	Physical therapy	Stabbing pain right mid and low back. Pain at times across low back bilaterally. Indicates she is fearful of falling.
10/30/04	Nursing progress notes	"I got some bad news this morning. My spine is fractured and I may have to go to a nursing home." Emotional support given. Still hesitates to cough related to back pain.
10/30/04	MD progress notes	Complained of back pain and right chest wall. Bone scan shows increased uptake in ribs. Right rib fractures.
10/31/04	Physical therapy	Complains of right low back pain and right rib pain both worse with coughing, yawning, hiccups.
11/5/04	Nursing progress notes	Patient complains of back pain when coughs and deep breathes. K-pad in place on back.
11/7/04	MD progress notes	Still complains of pain at night.
11/7/04	Physical therapy	Complains of back pain at night especially. Unsure of how long relief from pain lasts after PT.
11/8/04	Physical therapy	Complains of low back pain. She is afraid of falling.
11/9/04	Nursing progress notes	Patient still with lower back pain especially with movement.

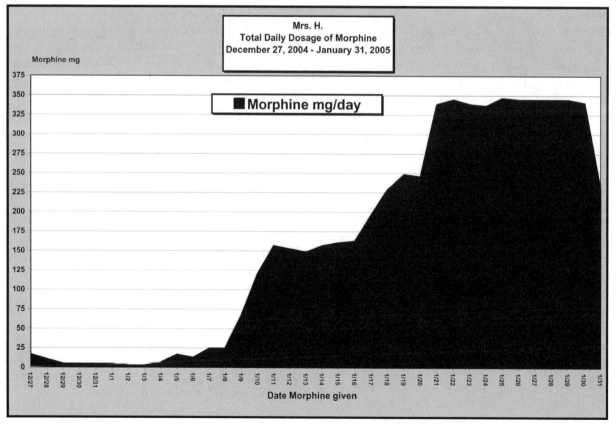

Figure 10.4 Morphine Chart

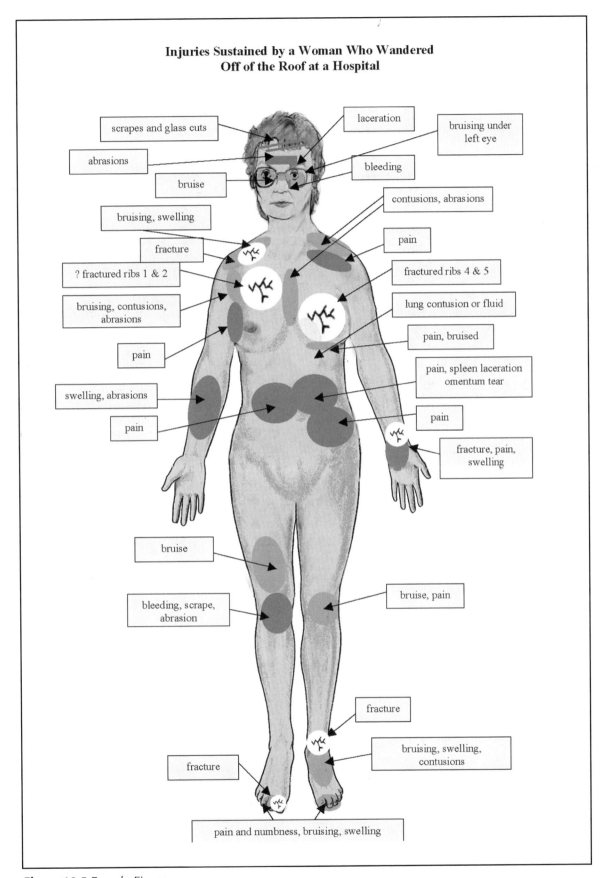

Figure 10.5 *Female Figure*

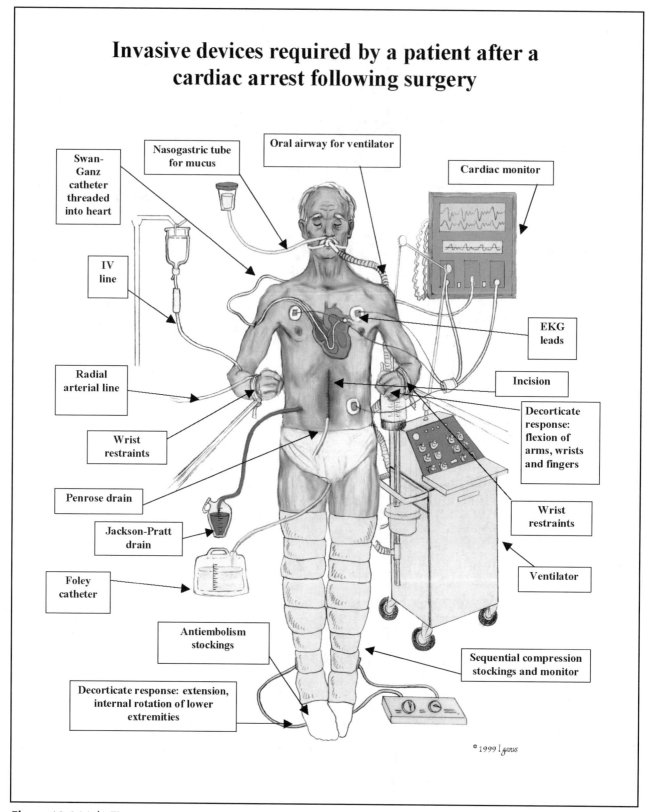

Invasive devices required by a patient after a cardiac arrest following surgery

Figure 10.6 Male Figure

Table 10.6
Description of Burns
December 26, 1994

Time	Staff	Description of Burns
Emergency Medical Services		
11:43 A.M.	EMT (not signed)	Second degree burns of 26% of body
The P Hospital		
	L. B., RN, Triage Nurse	First and second degree burns
9:00 P.M.	Dr. K., Emergency Room Physician	Second and third degree burns to right neck, chest, abdomen, arm, hand. 20% BSA (body surface area)
7:00 P.M.	Plastic Surgeon (name unknown)	Extensive second and third degree burns with increased e (erythema?) on neck, left shoulder, chest, abdomen, left arm and dorsum of hand. 20% BSA (drawing done).
4:45 P.M.	Dr. M., Surgeon	Second and third degree burns to neck, forearm, shoulder. No intact blisters. Macerated skin of left shoulder (drawing done).
	Dr. D. (coverage for Dr. O.)	Second degree burns to chest wall and left arm. Burns to entire chest wall and left arm per Dr. M's note. Infected skin throughout area.
5:15 P.M.	Dr. F., Medical Resident	Left anterior chest, left arm second degree burns (drawing done).
9:20 P.M.	EMT (unsigned)	Second and third degree burns to 20% BSA
C. Hospital		
10:20 P.M.	M. L., Triage Nurse	Second and third degree burns to neck, chest, abdomen, left shoulder, left hand.
	Burns Service	Deep second degree burns to bilateral neck. Bilateral extensive second and third degree burns to chest and breast, near circumferential burn to left upper arm. Left and dorsum with deep second and third degree burn. Burn to left axilla. Approximately 13% BSA
10:20 P.M.	I.W., Emergency Department Nurse	Second and third degree flame burns to neck, chest, abdomen, left shoulder, left hand.

10.14 Testimony at Trial

The use of a nursing expert in the role of expert witness or pain and suffering expert is a relatively new concept to some. (The author has testified in this role since 1982.) The plaintiff's attorney should be prepared for objections to this role and have researched the relevant state statutes and the Federal Rule of Evidence 1006, which permits testimony summarizing medical records. A brief or oral argument should be presented to provide the legal support for this testimony. The attorney may wish to provide the judge with a copy of the nurse's report for the judge's review. The defense attorney can be expected to object to the introduction of the report and the expert's testimony. The defense counsel usually does not want the jury to focus on the pain and suffering experienced by the victim of alleged malpractice, for fear that sympathy will be evoked and prejudice the jury's determination of liability and damages. Objections that may be raised by defense counsel are listed below.

A. Objection: Use of Treating Healthcare Workers

Argument: The plaintiff's attorney should present the treating doctors and nurses to provide the testimony on the patient's experiences.

This argument can be countered by pointing out the impracticality of having dozens of healthcare professionals come to court. In addition, the professionals would most likely not remember this patient and would end up relying on the records. The expert witness is uniquely qualified to rely on the records to summarize the patient's experiences.

The possibility of calling treating physicians to the witness stand to discuss medical care does not require the exclusion of the testimony of the expert witness. Keeping in mind practicality, a singular presentation from an expert witness offers an efficient and less costly alternative to presenting each doctor in turn to explain his portions of the medical records. A singular presentation is also apt to be more cogent than piecemeal accounts from each of the treating and examining physicians. Even if the plaintiffs or defendants choose to call those physicians at trial and admit the underlying records in toto, the expert witness' testimony may still be admitted as a secondary evidence summary.[102]

B. Objection: Repetitive with the Plaintiff's Testimony

Argument: The patient can describe her own pain and suffering.

This objection may be countered by arguing that the use of a nurse as an expert witness does not prevent the patient from also testifying about pain and suffering. However, the nursing expert's focus is not only on the information in the medical records but also on interpreting the information for the jury. The patient lacks the medical knowledge to explain the medical records to the jury. In some cases, the patient may be dead. If alive, the patient may have forgotten the details of what happened, spent part of the time in a coma, and/or sustained injuries or have communication barriers that prevent the patient from communicating with the jury.

The expert witness may use models, drawings, and other exhibits to explain the medical and nursing care the plaintiff experienced. The use of this demonstrative evidence will help the jury understand the experiences of the plaintiff. The plaintiff is not likely to be able to provide this type of testimony.

C. Objection: There are Only Two Types of Witnesses: Fact Witnesses and Expert Witnesses

Argument: A fact witness has personal knowledge of the issues of the case. An expert witness expresses an opinion about the conduct of the healthcare professionals. The testimony of an expert witness does not fit into either category. The expert witness did not render nursing or medical care or participate in the treatment of the patient. There are no opinions set forth in the summary of medical records. If the subject matter of expert testimony falls distinctly within a particular field or profession, the individual offered as an expert generally must be a licensed member of that profession. A nurse is not qualified to make comments about the entries of a physician or upon the significance of a physician's entry in a medical chart.[103]

Note that the American Nurses Association has endorsed the use of legal nurse consultants as expert witnesses and published a definition of this role in the 2006 standards.[104] Additionally, this objection may be responded to by pointing out that there are at least three kinds of evidentiary summaries that may be presented in a courtroom. First, there are "primary evidence summaries" that are typically used to condense voluminous materials that cannot be conveniently examined in court.[105] Second, "pedagogical-device summaries," more commonly described as "demonstrative aids," are presented to summarize, clarify, or simplify proofs admitted in the case. These devices include chalkboard drawings, graphs, charts, calculations, or models, and are not themselves admitted into evidence, but instead used as aids in presenting and understanding the evidence.[106] Third, a trial advocate may present "secondary evidence summaries." These are hybrids of the first two categories, admitted "not in lieu of the evidence they summarize but in addition thereto."[107] Secondary evidence summaries are permitted where, "in the judgment of the trial court such summaries so accurately and reliably summarize complex or difficult evidence…as to materially assist the jurors in better understanding the evidence."[108] Such devices are "not prepared entirely in compliance with Rule 1006 and yet are more than mere pedagogical devices." The summary of an expert witness should be analyzed under the first and last of these evidential categories, that is, either as a primary evidence summary under Evid. R. 1006 admitted in lieu of the medical records or as a secondary evidence summary designed to accompany the admission of these records.[109]

A nurse has the technical or specialized knowledge that will assist the trier of fact to understand the evidence.[110] The nurse need not be a physician to describe the medications or treatments the patient received, or to translate the common medical symbols appearing on the patient's charts. Also, the nurse need not offer any expert opinions in his limited trial role as a summary provider. As Rule 703 explicitly recognizes, an expert may testify in the form of an opinion "or otherwise."[111]

D. Objection: Jury Can Read Records

Argument: The jury can review the medical records the plaintiffs enter into evidence and consider those records during their deliberations.

A response to this objection includes noting that the role of the expert witness is to assist the jury in the damages phase of the trial. The expert witness extracts information from medical records and explains data to the jury in more understandable terms. Medical records are extensive and highly technical. Records are replete with technical medical jargon which would not be readily understood by lay jurors without substantial definition and explanation. If the records were admitted as exhibits at trial without explanatory testimony, they would be apt to cause serious confusion in the jury room.[112]

An evidential summary may be presented in the form of a written document or by live testimony. Live testimony can often be more readily understood and accessed by a lay jury than dry written materials. Moreover, such testimony may be more effectively impeached by an adversary than a stack of paper exhibits.[113]

The medical records must be voluminous and not conveniently examined in court. Definitions of voluminous vary. The author of this chapter testified at a deposition about pain and suffering that involved care of a woman whose medical records filled eight 3-inch binders. She brought the records to the deposition using a luggage cart and two boxes stacked on top of each other. The attorney taking her deposition tried to make the point that the records were not voluminous because she was able to move them herself without help of others. She responded by pointing out that about 48 pounds of records would be considered voluminous by any standard. There is no requirement in Rule 1006 that it is literally impossible to examine the underlying records before a summary or chart may be used. Rather than imposing such a harsh standard of impossibility, "all that is required for the rule to apply is that the underlying writings be 'voluminous' and that in-court examination not be convenient."[114-115]

E. Objection: Use Expert Witnesses to Present Information

Argument: The plaintiff's liability expert witnesses can discuss the medical records and any entries that the plaintiffs find relevant or significant in support of their case.

This argument may be countered with the perspective that the liability expert witness' report focuses on a detailed summary of the medical record. The liability expert witness's report typically provides a brief summary of the medical issues and then defines the standard of care and the deviations from the standards of care. The expert witness is concentrating on liability issues when reviewing the records. Moreover, when a physician expert witness reviews records, she is evaluating care provided by physicians. Nursing care, which makes up the bulk of the care provided in hospitals, rehabilitation facilities, and nursing homes, is best summarized by nurses.

F. Objection: Rule 403—Prejudicial Nature of the Testimony Will Outweigh the Probative Value

Argument: The jury should not be exposed to the graphic nature of the plaintiff's injuries.

This objection may be countered by stressing that the subject matter of a personal injury/medical malpractice claim is not pleasant, but is very relevant to the plaintiff's damages case. The plaintiff is to present the expert witness' testimony in a balanced, fair, and dispassionate manner. The summary of the medical record, and the exhibits created as a part of that process, should avoid incorporating particularly graphic photographs and other material that may be deemed prejudicial.

10.15 Summary

Pain and suffering may result from the injuries alleged to have occurred as a result of nursing malpractice. The consequences of these injuries can include pain from a variety of sources arising from the injuries and from treatments. The medical treatment designed to treat the injuries often creates even more discomfort. Pain medications, while effective in reducing discomfort, are accompanied by risks and side effects. In addition, pain medication is often underprescribed and underutilized, resulting in unrelieved pain. Suffering also results from the effects that the injuries have on the patient's quality of life. The expert fact witness can be an effective addition to the expert testimony used in malpractice and personal injury cases.

Endnotes

1. Ball, D. *David Ball on Damages*, Second Edition, NITA, 2005.

2. Duffy, T., "The Plaintiff Attorney's Perspective," in Patricia W. Iyer (Ed), *Medical Legal Aspects of Pain and Suffering*, Tucson, Arizona: Lawyers and Judges Publishing Co., 2003.

3. Perdue, Sr., J. M. and J. M. Perdue, Jr., "Putting the pieces together," *Trial* (May 2003): 39–47.

4. Turley, W., "Getting to 'yes' with the video settlement documentary," *Trial* (June 2003): 50–55.

5. Vesper, T. and R. Orr, "Make time palpable by using per diem arguments," *Trial* (October 2002): 59-65.

6. Becton, C., "Help the jury understand pain and suffering," *Trial* (March 2005): 60-65.

7. Spiva, H., "Unseen, but not unreal," *Trial* (June 2005): 18-24.

8. Broderick, T. and J. M. West, "The Defense Attorney's Perspective," In *Medical Legal Aspects of Pain and Suffering*, ed. P. Iyer. Tucson, Arizona: Lawyers and Judges Publishing Co., 2003.

9. Merskey, H. and N. Bogduk, *Classification of Chronic Pain*, Second edition, International Association for the Study of Pain, IASP Task Force on Taxonomy, IASP Press, Seattle, 1994.

10. D'Arcy, Y., "Pain assessment," in Patricia W. Iyer, (ed) *Medical Legal Aspects of Pain and Suffering*, Tucson, Arizona: Lawyers and Judges Publishing Co., 2003.

11. D'Arcy, Y., "Conquering pain," *Nursing* (March 2005): 37-41.

12. Mayer, D., L. Torma, I. Byock, and K. Norris, "Speaking the language of pain," *American Journal of Nursing* 101, no. 2 (February 2001): 44.

13. See note 10.

14. *Id.*

15. McCaffery, M., "Pain control," *American Journal of Nursing* 99, no. 8 (August 1999): 18.

16. Flaherty, E. "Using pain-rating scales with older adults," *AJN*, June 2008, 108 (6), 40-47.

17. Luckmann, J. and K. Sorensen, *Medical Surgical Nursing*, Third Edition, Philadelphia: W.B. Saunders, 1987.

18. Fried, G. and K. Fried, "Spinal Cord Injury," in Patricia W. Iyer (ed) *Medical Legal Aspects of Pain and Suffering*, Tucson, Arizona: Lawyers and Judges Publishing Co., 2003.

19. Jaszarowski, K., "Skin Trauma," In Patricia W. Iyer and Barbara Levin (eds), *Medical Legal Aspects of Medical Records*, Second Edition, Tucson, Arizona: Lawyers and Judges Publishing Co., 2010.

20. Connor-Ballard, P., "Understanding and managing burn pain: Part 1," *AJN*, April 2009, 48-56.

21. *Id.*

22. Jaszarowski, "Wounds and Burns," in Patricia W. Iyer (ed) *Medical Legal Aspects of Pain and Suffering*, Tucson, Arizona: Lawyers and Judges Publishing Co., 2003.

23. See note 20.

24. Connor-Ballard, P."Understanding and managing burn pain: Part 2," *AJN*, May 2009, 54-59.

25. See note 20.

26. *Id.*

27. *Id.*

28. Webster, H., "To make an injured person whole," *Trial* (November 2003): 72.

29. Buhle, E., "Introduction to pain," *OncoLink*, University of Pennsylvania Cancer Center, http://msc8a.upenn. edu/specialty/pain/intro.html.

30. Al-Atiyyat, N., "Patient-related barriers to effective cancer pain management," Journal of Hospice and Palliative Nursing, July/August 2008, 10 94), 198-204.

31. Bales, C., "Cancer pain and suffering," n Patricia W. Iyer, (Ed) *Medical Legal Aspects of Pain and Suffering*, Tucson, Arizona: Lawyers and Judges Publishing Co., 2003.

32. Grinstein-Cohen, O., Sarid, O, Attar, D et al., "Improvements and difficulties in postoperative pain management," *Orthopaedic Nursing*, September/October 2009, 28 (5), 232-239.

33. Riley, J., M. Robinson, J. Wade, C. Myers, and D. Price, "Sex differences in negative emotional responses to chronic pain," *The Journal of Pain* 2, no. 6 (December 2001).

34. Hamill-Ruth, R. and M. Marohn, "Evaluation of pain in the critically ill patient," *Critical Care Clinics* 15, no. 1 (January 1999): 35.

35. Greifzu, S., "Caring for the chronically critically ill," *RN* 65, no. 7 (July 2002): 42-48.

36. D'Arcy, Y. M., "Patient controlled analgesia (PCA) with fast track coronary artery bypass (CABG) patients," *Proceedings at the 9th World Congress on Pain*, Vienna, Austria, 76. August 22-27, 1999.

37. Puntillo K.A., and S. J. Weiss, "Pain: Its mediators and associated morbidity in critically ill cardiovascular patients," *Nursing Research* 43, no. 1 (1994): 31-36.

38. Task Force of the American College of Critical Care Medicine, "Clinical practice guidelines for the sustained use of sedatives and analgesics in the critically ill adult," *Critical Care Medicine* 30, no. 1 (January 2002).

39. Cohen, I. L., "Pain and Suffering in the Intensive Care Unit," in Patricia W. Iyer (ed) *Medical Legal Aspects of Pain and Suffering,* Tucson, Arizona: Lawyers and Judges Publishing Co., 2003.

40. McCaffery, M. and C. Pasero, *Pain Clinical Manual*, Second Edition, Mosby, St. Louis, 1999.

41. Martin, J. and G. Moore, "Pearls, pitfalls, and updates for pain management," *Emergency Medicine Clinics of North America* 15, no. 2 (May 1997): 399.

42. Pasero, C., "Epidural analgesia in children," *American Journal of Nursing* 99, no. 5 (May 1999): 20.

43. American Academy of Pediatrics and the American Pain Society, "The assessment and management of acute pain in infants, children, and adolescents," *Pediatrics* 108, no. 3 (September 2001).

44. Narayan, M. "Culture's effects on pain assessment and management," *AJN*, April 2010, 110 (4), 38-49.

45. McCaffery, M., "Pain control," *American Journal of Nursing* 99, no. 8 (August 1999): 18.

46. Ng, B., et al. "The effect of ethnicity on prescriptions for patient-controlled analgesia for postoperative pain," *Pain* 66, no. 1 (1998): 9.

47. Todd, K., T. Lee, and J. Hoffman, et al., "Ethnicity as a risk factor for inadequate emergency department analgesia," *Journal of the American Medical Association* 269 (1993): 1537-1539.

48. Al-Atiyyat, N. "Cultural diversity and cancer pain," *Journal of Hospice and Palliative Nursing,* May/June 2009, 11 (3) 154-164.

49. Young, D., "Acute pain management protocol," *Journal of Gerontological Nursing* 10 (June 1999).

50. "Changes in cognition and function: implications for caregivers of older adults," *Gerontological Nursing Counseling Points* (December 2005): 4-14.

51. Victor, K., "Properly assessing pain in the elderly," *RN* 64, no. 5 (May 2001): 45-49.

52. See note 16.

53. Stein, W., "Pain management in the elderly: pain in the nursing home," *Clinics in Geriatric Medicine* 17, no. 3 (August 2001).

54. Freedman, G. and R. Peruvemba, "Geriatric anesthesia: geriatric pain management," *Anesthesiology Clinics of North America* 18, no. 1 (March 2000).

55. AGS Panel on Persistent Pain in Older Persons. "The management of persistent pain in older persons." *J Am Geriatr Soc* 2002, 50 (6 Suppl): S205-S224.

56. Ferrell, B., B. Ferrell, and L. Rivera, "Pain in the cognitively impaired nursing home patients," *Journal of Pain Symptom Management* 10 (1995): 504.

57. Parmalee, P., B. Smith, and I. Katz, "Pain complaints and cognitive status among elderly institution residents," *Journal of the American Geriatric Society* 41, part 5 (1993): 517.

58. Parmalee, P. A., "Pain in cognitively impaired older persons," *Clinical Geriatric Medicine* 12, part 3 (1996): 473.

59. Ferrell, B., "Pain evaluation and management in the nursing home," *Annals of Internal Medicine* 30, no. 4 (November 1, 1995): 681-87.

60. Horgas, A. and Miller, L. "Pain assessment win people with dementia," *AJN*, July 2008, 108 (7), 62-72.

61. See note 49.

62. http://www.hartfordign.org/publications/trythis/issue07.pdf. last accessed 5/30/06.

63. http://www.hartfordign.org/publications/trythis/assessingPain.pdf, last accessed 5/30/06.

64. Lynch, M., "Pain as the fifth vital sign," *Journal of Intravenous Nursing* 24, no. 2 (March-April 2001): 85.

65. D'Arcy, Y. "Pain management survey report," *Nursing 2008*, June 2008, 43-49.

66. McCaffery, M. and B. Ferrell, "Opioids and pain management: what do nurses know?" *Nursing* 99 (1999): 48.

67. Yeoman, B., "Prisoners of Pain," *AARP Magazine* (October 2005): 49.

68. Loeb, J., "Pain management in long-term care," *American Journal of Nursing* 99, no. 2 (February 1999): 48.

69. Braun, J., "Pain mis(management)," in Patricia W. Iyer (Ed) *Nursing Home Litigation: Investigation and Case Preparation*, Second edition, Tucson, Arizona: Lawyers and Judges Publishing Co., 2006.

70. Furrow, B., "Failure to treat pain: no more excuses," *Trial* (October 2002): 32-40.

71. Vaglienti, C. and M. Grinberg, "Emerging liability for the undertreatment of pain," *Journal of Nursing Law* 9, no. 3 (2004): 7-17.

72. See note 70.

73. See note 71.

74. "Rating procedural pain," *American Journal of Nursing* 99, no. 9 (September 1999): 10.

75. "Patients' experience of tube removal," *American Journal of Nursing* 99, no. 8 (August 1999): 24AA.

76. Pasero, C., "Using continuous infusion with PCA," *American Journal of Nursing* 99, no. 2 (February 1999): 22.

77. Agency for Healthcare Policy and Research, *Acute Pain Management: Operative or Medical Procedures and Trauma*, Rockville, Maryland: U.S. Department of Health and Human Services, 1992.

78. D'Arcy, Y., "Conquering pain: Have you tried these new techniques?" *Nursing 2005* (March 2005): 36-41.

79. Heigh, R., "Use of NSAIDS," *Postgraduate Medicine* 96, no. 6 (November 1, 1994): 63.

80. See note 77.

81. See note 78.

82. Etches, R., "Pain control in the perioperative period," *Surgical Clinics of North America* 79, no. 2 (April 1999): 297.

83. See note 77.

84. See note 42.

85. See note 77.

86. See note 17.

87. Based on data in A. Maher, S. Salmond, and T. Pellino, *Orthopaedic Nursing*. Philadelphia: W.B. Saunders Co., 1994.

88. *Id.*

89. Jablonski, R., "If ventilator patients could talk," *RN* 32 (February 1995).

90. Lindgren, V. and N. Ames, "Caring for patients on mechanical ventilator," *American Journal of Nursing* 105, no. 5 (May 2005): 50-61.

91. Barker, E., *Neuroscience Nursing*. St. Louis: Mosby, 1994.

92. Wilson, H. and C. Kneisl, *Psychiatric Nursing*, Third Edition. Menlo Park: California, Addison Wesley, 1988.

93. Barsky, A., "Approach to the angry patient," In *Primary Care Medicine*, Third edition, ed. Goroll, 1061. Philadelphia: Lippincott-Raven Publishers, 1995.

94. *American Psychiatric Association, Diagnostic and Statistical Manual of Mental Disorders*, DSM-IV, Fourth edition, Washington, D.C.: The Association, 1994.

95. Clark, C., "Post traumatic stress disorder: how to support healing," *American Journal of Nursing* 97, no. 8 (August 1997): 27.

96. Starr, et al., "Symptoms of Posttraumatic Stress Disorder After Orthopaedic Trauma," *J Bone Joint Surg Am* 86 (2004): 1115–1121.

97. Pangia, M. "Post-traumatic stress disorder: Litigation strategies," *Trial* (September 2000): 18-30.

98. Smith, N., "Nondrug measures for painful procedures," *American Journal of Nursing* 97, no. 8 (August 1997): 18.

99. Lambert, S. and D. Hudson-Barr, "Pain and suffering of children," in *Patricia W. Iyer (Ed) Medical Legal Aspects of Pain and Suffering* Tucson, Arizona: Lawyers and Judges Publishing Co., 2003.

100. Pollock, M., M. D'Lugo, and R. Ford, "Pain and suffering in pediatric neurology," In Patricia W. Iyer (ed) *Medical Legal Aspects of Pain and Suffering*, Tucson, Arizona: Lawyers and Judges Publishing Co., 2003.

101. *Legal nurse consulting: scope and standards of practice*, ANA, 2006.

102. Judge Sabatino, Superior Court of New Jersey Law Division, Mercer County, May 9, 2002.

103. Letter by Joseph Lang, Esq. of Lenox, Socey, Wilgus, Formidoni, Brown, Giordano and Casey, to Clerk of Mercer County, October 15, 2001.

104. See note 99.

105. *United States v. Bray*, 139 F.3d 1104, 1112 (6th Cir. 1998); see also 1 Devitt, Federal Jury Practice and Instructions 14.02 (4th ed. 1992). See also Fed. R. Evid. 1006.

106. *United States v. Bray*, supra 139 F.3d at 1112; 1 Devitt, supra at §14.02. See also *White Industries v. Cessna Aircraft Co.*, 611 F. Supp 1049, 1069 (W.D. Mo. 1985) distinguishing between "pedagogical" demonstrative aids that undertake to "summarize or organize other evidence" and Rule 1006 summaries offered in lieu of the supporting materials.

107. *United States v. Bray*, supra, 139 F.3d at 1112; see also *United States v. Citron*, 783 F.2d 307, 317 n. 10 (2d Cir. 1986).

108. *United States v. Bray*, supra, 139 F.3d at 1112.

109. *Id.*

110. See note 102.

111. Evid R. 703.

112. See note 102.

113. *Id.*

114. *United States v. Scales*, 594 F.2d 558, 561-65 6th Cir. 1979).

115. *Id.*

Additional Reading

Abrahamson, K. "Dealing with cancer-related distress," *AJN*, April 2010, 110 (4), 67-69.

Aguirre, L, Nevidjon, B and Clemonds, A. "Pain diaries," *AJN*, June 2008, 108 (6), 36-39.

D'Arcy, Y. "Overturning barriers to pain relief in older adults," *Nursing 2009*, October 2009, 32-38.

Long, C, Morgan, B, Alonzo, T, et al., "Improving pain management in long-term care: The campaign against pain," *Journal of Hospice and Palliative Nursing*, May/June 2010, 12 (3), 148-155.

Chapter 11

Vocational Evaluations in Nursing Malpractice Cases

Irmo Marini, PhD, CRC, CLCP and Mark Lukas, Ed.D., CRC

11.1 Introduction

The purpose of this chapter is to provide the reader with information concerning the use of vocational evaluations within nursing malpractice cases. The chapter provides a brief history of the field of vocational rehabilitation and specifically the place for forensic services within the larger rehabilitation field. The chapter addresses the various elements of a vocational evaluation in determining vocational damages, including the individual's age, education, past work experience, transferable skills, labor market access loss, and potential wage or earning capacity loss. Vocational evaluators rely upon worker traits and skills necessary to perform jobs, and must consider how an individual's disability functionally limits that person from performing certain types of jobs. The vocational expert must determine whether an individual has sustained not only a disabling condition that has limited performance of a job in the economy, but also whether the individual has sustained a diminished future stream of financial gainful activity due to the limitations. Furthermore, the chapter discusses the effects of federal court cases reflecting the use of experts within the context of litigation and specific effects upon the methodologies employed in vocational evaluations. Concluding information encompasses a guide to critically evaluating vocational reports within a forensic context.

11.2 A Brief History of the Vocational Evaluation Process

TIP: The field of the forensic vocational evaluator exists within the context of the vocational rehabilitation field at large. Rehabilitation counseling has the unique distinction of being the only profession to be established by an act of Congress.

Following World War II and in response to returning veterans and societal needs, Congress enacted legislation to provide funding for university level rehabilitation programs in order to fulfill the need for rehabilitation counselors primarily in governmental settings. From the mid- to late-twentieth century, funding for graduate level rehabilitation programs extended to more than 100 universities.

Rehabilitation counseling is generally identified as a field allied with psychology, particularly as rehabilitation counseling issues fall generally within the science and art of the study of human behavior. Initially, rehabilitation counselors were employed within governmental settings, primarily state agencies mandated to assist individuals with disabilities with respect to coordinating necessary services, counseling, and ultimately helping with a return to work. The basis of the provision of rehabilitation services had been, and continues to be, through the implementation of an IPE (Individualized Plan for Employment). The IPE is, in a sense, both a planning tool and a contract between the rehabilitation agency provider and the disabled person, outlining agreed-upon services and the responsibilities of both the agency and rehabilitant in meeting the objectives of the written rehabilitation program.

The methodology initially employed in the implementation of the IPE has remained substantially unchanged for the past five decades. Counselors generally conduct a meeting with the individual for the purpose of performing a vocational rehabilitation evaluation. The counselor gathers information about the individual's age, education, work history, nature of the injury, limitations, occupational interests, and aspirations; he may either conduct or out-contract for intelligence, achievement, aptitude, and vocational interest testing. Thereafter, the IPE is fashioned to the needs of the individual, the results of the evaluation, and the scope and availability of rehabilitation services, which may include employability counseling, vocational rehabilitation, or job placement services.

TIP: The methodology employed in the compilation and implementation of an IPE is essentially the same method utilized and employed in forensic vocational evaluations with the objective of identifying an individual's capabilities with respect to the job market and vocational earning power.

The use of expert vocational services within the legal context began within the disability benefits portion of the Social Security Administration. In the early 1960s, court decisions concerning the adjudication of Social Security Disability cases began to mandate the use of vocational expert witnesses in cases in which the capacity to work was at issue. Court decisions indicated that disability benefits could not be denied based upon the theoretical ability to engage in substantial, gainful employment activities but rather the burden of proof fell to the Social Security Administration to identify the types of work the claimant could perform with respect to vocational characteristics including age, educational background, work history, and medically established limitations. Thereafter, through the late 1960s and 1970s, the use of vocational experts in Social Security Disability cases began to increase. Vocational experts were needed to assist the trier of fact and administrative law judge, and to deter-

mine the vocational capability and access to the job market of the individual claimant in response to medical limitations and the vocational characteristics. Vocational experts have continued a long association extending to the present, offering services to the Social Security Administration on a case-by-case basis. The vocational expert appears at the request of the administrative law judge, though at times claimants have secured independent vocational evaluations to assist the trier of fact in the adjudication of the specific disability cases.

Vocational experts have been employed in workers' compensation cases generally beginning in the 1970s, as many states had mandated more aggressive rehabilitation services in an effort to assist workers with job market re-integration. Through the 1970s and 1980s, and again extending to the present with various changes in legislation, vocational rehabilitation counselors continued to provide expert services within the context of workers' compensation cases adjudicated within various state systems. Vocational experts have also been employed in divorce cases to address the issues of vocational earning capacity and with respect to children; the Individuals with Disabilities Education Act (IDEA); and issues related to the Americans with Disabilities Act (ADA) concerning reasonable work accommodations and job market access. Finally, through the ascendance of rehabilitation services within the legal context, vocational rehabilitation experts have been employed within personal injury cases to assist the trier of fact with respect to the degree, and presence or absence, of vocational damages. Vocational rehabilitation experts help define the extent to which an individual's economic or vocational horizons have been adversely affected by the injuries sustained within the accident or incident in question.

Within the larger context of personal injury cases, nursing malpractice cases revolve about the issues related to professional nursing care, injuries sustained by the patient with regard to the care, and the specific vocational impact of the injuries. Within nursing malpractice cases, as with other forms of injury, essentially the same methodology is employed by the vocational rehabilitation consultant in order to assess the degree of vocational damages or the impact of an individual's health condition upon the ability to participate in the job market. Age, education, work history, and related issues form elements of the vocational evaluation. Section 11.3 addresses the objectives of the vocational evaluation and the general evaluation methodology employed.

11.3 Objectives of a Vocational Evaluation

Nursing malpractice may encompass a number of specific tasks and behaviors within the purview of the nurse including medication error, obstetrical error, failure to monitor the development of quadriplegia or paraplegia, a fall by a post-surgical patient resulting in greater injury, or neurological complications related to drawing of blood or peripherally inserted central catheter (PICC) line placement, among others.

From a methodologic standpoint, the services of a vocational expert are placed generally between the establishment of a medical impairment by a physician and a subsequent economic assessment of the vocational damages. The chronology of establishing vocational damages is first to determine the presence of a permanent medical impairment medically or causally attributable to the nursing incident. The medical statement should include some indication of the permanency of the medical condition and also a statement concerning specific limitations and restrictions imposed by the limitation. The treating, evaluating, or examining physician indicates the medical dimensions of the injury and impact upon function. At this point, following the determination of limitations and restrictions, a consultant conducts a vocational evaluation taking into consideration the presence of a health condition, limitations, permanency, and vocational factors including: age, educational background, work history, test results, and so on. Following definitive identification of medical restrictions and impairments, the vocational evaluation articulates the effect of the indicated limitations upon that specific individual's ability to participate in the job market and any limitations or impairments of earning capacity associated with the presence of the health condition. For example, orthopaedic limitations in regard to lifting, turning, bending, squatting, carrying, or reaching may adversely impact or preclude an individual's ability to engage in past work if that work had been exertional. The limitations may allow for a more restricted range of employment activities involving lighter functions with an associated diminution in vocational earning capacity. The U.S. Department of Labor categorizes all work by exertional demand level: sedentary, light, medium, heavy, and very heavy.[1]

The vocational evaluation establishes the degree of vocational impairment and may express that impairment by a comparison between pre- and post-injury earning capacity. The medical restrictions and limitations established by the physician are specifically addressed and delineated with regard to diminished labor market access and, in turn, vocational earning capacity. Thereafter, depending upon the skill, experience, and training of the vocational expert, the results of the vocational evaluation are expressed in wage or earnings terms over the course of an individual's work life which may include considerations regarding productivity, inflation, rises in wages, work life expectancy, or a range of additional issues affecting future workforce participation.

The latter information may be articulated by the vocational expert or, perhaps more appropriately, by an economist to project future effects of the damages established in the vocational evaluation. In short, the expert witness sequence of physician, vocational expert, and economist most adequately articulates the presence of the medical impairment and its permanency, the effects of labor market participation, and a projection into the future concerning diminished occupational access and earning capacity.

A further related area of damages refers to projections concerning future life care needs, which may include, among others: costs for further surgeries, physical therapies, counseling, and transportation or home modifications. These costs are best articulated by a life care planner (LCP). Analyses generally include an individualized and detailed projection of needs and quantification of costs over a lifespan. A life care planner is usually engaged in cases in which the injuries are significant and the patient requires long-term medical care. Please refer to Chapter 12, *Life Care Planning*, for a thorough discussion on life care planning.

11.4 Vocational Evaluation Parameters

TIP: The vocational evaluation is essentially an assessment to determine an individual's wage earning capacity in consideration of a number of pertinent factors.

The vocational evaluation considers a number of variables pertinent to an individual's vocational functioning, in the same manner a physician may conduct a physical examination of a patient, take a history, perform physical tests including range of motion and resistance testing, and review results of formal diagnostic testing. The vocational expert employs a holistic approach consistent with the methodology established within the rehabilitation field and, as importantly, exercises clinical judgment in regard to the dynamic interplay of a number of vocational factors and variables with respect to an individual's job market participation. This is essentially an underlying principle upon which the evaluation proceeds. The factors under consideration include:

- Age
- Educational background
- Work experience
- Skills and abilities
- Health-related limitations
- Ancillary or pre-existing health conditions
- Personal characteristics
- Labor market access
- Wages versus earning capacity loss

A. Age

Age is an important vocational variable. A younger individual may be, depending upon the nature of impairment, appropriate for participation in vocational retraining to enhance vocational profile. Older individuals with shortened future work lives may experience greater difficulty in returning to the job market, particularly those with single occupational histories. These patients may be less appropriate or inappropriate for participation in lengthy vocational rehabilitation programs which would impact vocational earning capacity.

Case example:

Two patients experience similar physical limitations following L4-L5 back injuries related to falls from nursing malpractice incidents, rendering each incapable of lifting beyond the light level. One is a 21-year-old telemarketer with a high school diploma. The other is a 48-year-old construction worker with a tenth grade education. From a rehabilitation standpoint, the younger telemarketer can either return to his same sedentary job or is more amenable to retraining than the older, lesser educated construction worker.

B. Educational Background

An individual's educational background forms a substantial basis with regard to the ability to engage in the job market. Higher levels of academic participation encompassing post secondary completion generally allow greater access to the job market depending upon the individual, as there may be greater acquisition of intellect as opposed to skills transmitted through physical prowess. Conversely, lower levels of education encompassing less than high school completion or diminished academic capabilities generally result in an adverse effect upon job market participation and tend to inhibit both pre-injury and post-injury vocational earning capacity.

Case example:

A 40-year-old technical writer and software engineer with a bachelor's degree in computer science supplemented by graduate training suffers from paraplegia after a nurse failed to detect signs of spinal cord compression. From a vocational rehabilitation standpoint, the software engineer, based on pre-morbid educational characteristics, has a reasonable likelihood of employment accommodation and ongoing attachment to the labor market.

C. Work Experience

Work history indicates an individual's acquired skills and abilities. A vocational assessment of transferability of skill analysis may conclude that an individual may possess transferable skills into lighter forms of work or alternate work more compatible with the medically identified restrictions and limitations. Work history further establishes an individual's position in the job market and may be assessed through a qualitative conceptual framework including exertional requirements, skill acquisition, industry affiliation, and job tenure. An individual may have a long, continuous, and single-industry occupational history and others may have work histories involving frequent job changing. Job changing may indicate advancement issues and, depending upon the nature of the qualitative assessment, this may identify an individual not adjusting well to the job market, which results in frequent job mobility.

Case example:

A 45-year-old registered nurse with 21 years of nursing experience sustains a L1 spinal cord injury and is unable to continue her nursing home duties classified at the medium level of lift/carry (up to a maximum of 50 pounds occasionally). Her physiatrist indicates she is otherwise relegated to sedentary work and therefore has transferable skills to the position of medical intake clerk or hospital admitting clerk.

D. Skills and Abilities

Occupation or work skills and abilities arise from a combination of educational and vocational factors. Some work skills may have been learned in a classroom context while others may have been acquired through on-the-job experience. An individual may have demonstrated transferability through significant alternate abilities beyond the specific parameters of an occupation, including supervisory skills, management or coordination capabilities, or specific knowledge.

Case example:

A 45-year-old male high school graduate has been employed as a pipefitter and lead-man for a large construction and contracting company. He now experiences a torn rotator cuff and shoulder fracture after being dropped from a stretcher by a nurse. The results of a vocational evaluation revealed the presence of supervisory skills transferable to less physically demanding supervisory jobs within his company.

E. Health-Related Limitations

Injuries from nursing malpractice confirmed through physician assessments form the basis for the vocational assessment. The physician's assessment establishes the medical parameters within which an individual may resume occupational participation. The presence of health-related limitations associated with allegations of nursing malpractice would most likely, but need not, result in adverse vocational impact. In essence, the vocational evaluation would address the specific impact upon the subject individual. Depending upon age, education, work experience, skills, and abilities, individuals are vocationally affected in different ways by health conditions, and hence, the need for a vocational assessment to identify and articulate the specific impact upon the subject of the evaluation.

Case example:

A 30-year-old female mechanical assembler with a high school education comes under surgical treatment for gall bladder removal. She sustains an anoxic insult and subsequent mild brain injury from respiratory arrest due to anesthesia. Her neuropsychological assessment indicates severe difficulty with speed and pace as well as problems with fine finger dexterity. With ten years tenure and earning $21 per hour, the claimant has no transferable skills within the company and commensurate with her education and past work experience, will either have to consider returning to school if feasible or reemployment in a job market where she will in all vocational probability see a wage loss of approximately 50 percent or more.

F. Ancillary or Pre-Existing Health Conditions

In a nursing malpractice case, the subject of the evaluation may have a pre-existing medical condition that imposes restrictions and limitations independent of any nursing-related incident. Prior to and independent of the nursing incident in question, an individual may experience a health condition that limits or impairs vocational earning capacity or access, which may comprise an additional factor for vocational scrutiny.

Case example:

A 45-year-old former carpenter with a high school education is seen in a clinical setting for a long-standing bilateral knee condition that has rendered him disabled from his past work but capable of sedentary assembly work. Improper venipuncture results in dominant arm pain and hand dysfunction.

He experiences a loss in earning capacity as he is vocationally unable to engage in bench assembly functions.

G. Personal Characteristics

Personal traits may include alternate skills and abilities an individual may have acquired outside or independent of the vocational realm including participation in avocational activities. Personal characteristics may also include job market or career interests specific to the individual which may be included in the vocational assessment in regard to return to work issues.

Case example:

A 36-year-old master electrician sustains a right lower extremity hemi-paresis from an improperly administered nursing injection, and is no longer able to wire homes for electricity. The gentleman has a side hobby of assembling and repairing computers using electronic computer parts, and since he has now been relegated by his physician to sedentary work, is able to transition into repairing computers.

H. Labor Market Access

A vocational analysis should include consideration of an individual's specific labor market area and access. Concerning alternate work, if appropriate, what would an individual's reasonable vocational alternatives be within the general labor market area accessible to the individual? This typically involves taking into consideration the Functional Capacity Evaluation (FCE) or some form of physician or physical therapist evaluation of an individual's residual physical and/or mental capabilities as well as her functional limitations (See Appendix 11.1 for sample FCE format). The Worker Trait Profile found in the government resource *Classification of Jobs*,[2] sets forth the worker trait frequencies for over 12,700 jobs in the U.S. economy. For example, 91 percent of all jobs require frequent reaching and handling with the hands; therefore, an individual who has an arm or hand amputation would be significantly limited in bilateral hand or arm use for jobs requiring frequent or constant reaching and handling. Additionally, only approximately 11 percent of all jobs in the U.S. economy are classified as sedentary in nature, requiring sitting for six or more hours in an eight hour workday, and lifting/carrying no more than 10 pounds occasionally. As such, when a physician renders a patient totally or partially disabled and limited to sedentary work, the vocational evaluator is dealing with a very small segment of an individual's remaining labor market. Other factors that must then be considered include the individual's educational and specific vocational preparation skill level, past work experience as well as any other notably specific limitations such as a visual impairment or upper extremity paralysis. The end result for the vocational expert is often to cite the local and/or national available job title base that represents the individual's available labor market access with a representative sample and rationale for such jobs. In many instances, depending on the type of case, vocational evaluators will be asked to call area employers or research and find available job openings in the local area.

Case example:

A 40-year-old male unskilled agricultural laborer with a less than high school education who had performed heavy work was appropriately treated for an arm laceration. While under the care of nursing staff in a clinical setting, he suffers a fall. This results in right knee internal derangement necessitating surgery and bracing resulting in the ability to return to sedentary work only.

I. Wages versus Earning Capacity Loss

Assessing pre- or post-injury vocational earning capacity necessarily requires some consideration of industries, labor market characteristics, and occupational areas that would otherwise be reasonably accessible to the individual once determining the available labor market after accounting for functional or mental limitations noted above. Furthermore, wages associated with specific occupations vary by geographic locality. Wages are influenced by a variety of factors beyond the scope of this discussion, but may include labor market supply and demand, urban versus rural areas, and other demographic and economic factors. National and local geographic area median wages by occupation can also be obtained by accessing information from the Bureau of Labor Statistics and is available online (www.acinet.org).

The vocational evaluator, if asked to determine future wage or earning capacity loss, must understand the difference between the two concepts. *Wage loss* should be utilized to estimate potential future vocational monetary damages when an individual has an established work history. For example, assume an individual has been a truck driver for over five years earning an average of $50,000 per year. He would, if determined to be totally and permanently disabled, sustain a future wage loss approximating this amount, not including fringe benefits. An economist is typically used to determine fringe benefits as well as inflation and discounting of the dollar, with the ability to determine present value. The vocational evaluator or expert becomes particularly useful in this process when the injured individual is deemed able to work, but unable to return to past relevant work. In this instance, the vocational evaluator will typically consider the available local labor market and representative jobs matching the residual functional capacity, averaging what those jobs pay, and subtract these totals from the truck driver wage. The result renders a vocationally probable future wage loss if retraining or returning to school is not an option. *Earning capacity,* as discussed later regarding vocational evaluation of children and adolescents, is considered when an individual does not have an established work history, or alternatively in the case of children, has not begun to work. In this instance, it is standard vocational protocol to consider the parents' educational and employment attainment. A rudimentary example would be two parents who both completed a bachelors' degree in all statistical probability having a child complete a bachelors' degree as well and then be expected to earn wages commensurate with this level of education. The U.S. Census Bureau compiles this information with its American Community Survey each year, noting differences in education level, race/ethnicity, and gender.

11.5 Methodology

The vocational evaluation involves a holistic approach considering a number of variables and factors. The analysis process relies generally upon deductive reasoning, that is, reasoning from an established conceptual framework to a specific case. The assessment is essentially an analysis of the patient's variables and factors with the objective of obtaining an appropriate assessment of vocational earning capacity in regard to the health issues affecting work and capacity.

TIP: The vocational evaluation employs established methodology in concert with clinical judgment.

The assessment encompasses factors including physical, intellectual, and emotional characteristics. Field and Choppa offer a more complete discussion of the clinical judgment model concerning vocational evaluations.[3] Furthermore, the evaluation methodology identified is essentially identical to the model employed in state and federal vocational rehabilitation agencies. The model is further articulated and found within the Social Security Administration Regulations.[4] Within sociology, rehabilitation, behavioral psychology, and educational literature, the effects of age, education, skill acquisition, and transference are addressed in specific study areas.

The objective of gathering information can be bifurcated in two areas:

1. the forensic vocational consultant is generally asked to assess an individual's earning capacity given the limitations imposed by the injury or health condition, and

2. the vocational expert identifies the individual's earning capacity absent the limitations imposed by an injury or health condition. The limitations are articulated by a physician in the form of medical information or a functional capacity evaluation.

That information partially forms the basis for health-related information associated with the vocational evaluation. The evaluation of earning capacity absent the limitations may require clinical judgment or may be reflected by an individual's earnings history. Theoretically, if an individual had maintained continuous employment in a single industry and occupation until alleged nursing malpractice, that may form a reasonable basis for earning capacity absent the limitations or health condition. In some instances, a patient has engaged in vocational skill-enhancing behaviors including completion of a specific training program prior to the onset of a health condition. When the injury prevents utilization of training, the person's previous earning capacity may not specifically represent the upgraded earning capacity.

When injured as a result of nursing malpractice, an individual may have been separated from the job market due to factors unrelated to vocational characteristics, including industry downsizing, layoffs, or other demographic or economic factors. An individual's earning capacity at the time of the nursing malpractice incident and perhaps in the months prior may have equaled zero. However, absence from the job market does not necessarily conclude that the individual had no earning capacity prior to the onset of health problems stemming from nursing malpractice. The vocational evaluation would articulate the individual's skills, abilities, and reasonable access to the job market prior to the onset of the health incident, recognizing fluctuations in labor markets.

A body of literature has been developed, primarily based upon governmental data sources, reflecting the effect of disability upon worklife expectancy. At the broadest level the presence of a disability has been known to affect both worklife expectancy and vocational earning capacity depending upon the characteristics of the individual. This model relies upon worklife expectancy tables indexed by age, gender, educational level, and disability status. Disability status is further specified by severely disabled, not severely disabled, and all disabled levels. A thorough discussion of the use of worklife expectancy tables can be found in *The New Worklife Expectancy Tables*.[5]

11.6 Vocational Report Content

The means by which data are secured relevant to the evaluation generally encompasses three areas: the vocational interview, vocational testing if appropriate, and a review of pertinent documentation. The format by which the evaluation is presented may vary considerably among individuals offering forensic vocational services. The evaluation may include multiple headings and subheadings with phrases or brief sentences attached to each. Other evaluations take the form of an expanded outline. A more traditional approach is the narrative form. General headings are offered pertinent to the assessment followed by a narrative discussion. Regardless of the form of presentation, the evaluation encompasses the vocational information and domain areas.

A. Vocational Interview

Customarily, forensic vocational consultants conduct an interview to obtain information pertinent to the evaluation directly from the subject of the evaluation or plaintiff. Regardless of the referral source, plaintiff or defendant, a personal interview is usually preferable, though not always possible or permissible depending upon jurisdiction and circumstances. However, evaluations may be completed based upon a comprehensive review of the records in the absence of a personal interview. The interviews may be conducted in a structured or semi-structured format. Structured interview formats may rely upon the use of a checklist or interview guide. Semi-structured interviews are generally completed absent a guide but follow a format sufficient to obtain information related to the pertinent areas. The vocational interview encompasses work history, educational background, health history, military service, and leisure or avocational activities. The interview may certainly not be limited to these areas and the focus of the interview varies depending upon the individual. A thorough discussion of the individual's work history includes the following:

- Job title
- Description of employment
- Duration
- Type of industry
- Specific occupational work tasks
- Acquired skills and abilities
- Exertional demands

The purpose of the work history information is to establish an individual's presence in the job market, types of skills and abilities acquired, and exertional demands of past work.

TIP: The work history essentially defines the subject of the evaluation in vocational terms.

B. Educational Background

The interview will include content information associated with educational background, whether the individual completed high school, post secondary or college level training, academic emphases, night school, trade school, community college, or formal training environments which would further enhance an individual's skill background and provide further knowledge concerning vocational and educational characteristics.

C. Health History

The health history portion of the vocational interview may include a comprehensive review of an individual's health condition, not only related to the effects of the nursing malpractice but also other health conditions, traumas, hospitalizations, and medical treatment which form an individual's health background. The health history generally includes a description by the subject of the evaluation with respect to perceived health limitations. These may include personal observations concerning ability to perform activities of daily living, perceptions of physical limitations and pain, as well as physical capacities and restrictions. The health history descriptions generally focus upon an individual's perception of capacities and limitations and may thereafter be supplemented by review of medical records forming a foundation for the types of limitations identified by the individual during the course of the vocational interview.

D. Military

Type of service and duration of military service, training received, and conditions of discharge form portions of an individual's background. Military training may offer some transferability into civilian employment; however, other aspects depend upon the duration of the training, time since last performed, and the demands of the job market.

E. Leisure or Avocational Activities

Individuals may engage in leisure activities that further illustrate the pre-injury level of capability and activity compared to post-injury levels of participation. At other times, the leisure activities may offer a potential area of career direction post-injury, depending upon the nature of the limitations and the level of development.

F. Testing

TIP: Some form of vocational testing is generally, but not always, employed during the course of the vocational evaluation. The purpose for test administration is manifold. The objective of the evaluation is to provide an accurate assessment of an individual's health condition and ability to participate in job market or vocational activities. Reliance on psychological and neuropsychological test findings is appropriate when relevant, and the vocational evaluator is not otherwise qualified to administer such tests.

Intellectual capabilities, skills, abilities, aptitudes, and personality characteristics influence an individual's vocational characteristics and ultimate ability to participate in job market activity. For example, during the course of a vocational interview, the subject of the evaluation may indicate that he possesses a high school diploma. Absent testing, a default conclusion would consider that the person has academic capabilities consistent with that of an individual possessing a high school diploma. Without further information, vocational planning and recommendations may be based upon this conclusion. Formal academic testing may reveal that an individual's reading or mathematical capabilities may fall below that of a high school graduate or similar age-group peers. Conversely, testing may reveal that the individual possesses academic capabilities superior to that of a high school graduate which may have been garnered through avocational interests or pursuits.

Intellectual testing, in the form of I.Q. measures, reveals an individual's level of intellectual development. Testing may indicate intellectual capabilities that offer further insight and enlightenment with respect to vocational access alternatives or intellectual fitness for engagement in a retraining program or to learn new skills in an alternate environment.

Case example:

A 25-year-old female sewing machine operator experiences a neurologic dominant hand impairment following an unrecognized massive infiltration of intravenous fluid causing nerve damage. Testing reveals intellect within the superior range with commensurate academic capabilities. The patient is a favorable candidate for rehabilitation including retraining.

Standardized aptitude testing identifies the presence or absence of vocational abilities which forms an additional foundation or basis for the evaluation. Aptitude testing may focus on clerical ability, mechanical skills, or supervisory or interpersonal capability for occupations involving contact with people as opposed to data or objects. Aptitude testing, as with other measures, is generally conducted in a standardized distraction-free environment and may encompass both timed and untimed measures. Testing undertaken under these circumstances is scored in a standardized fashion employing score sheets and norms tables appropriate to the aptitude measured and the individual assessed.

Case example:

A 30-year-old female package handler employed by a national delivery service sustains an orthopaedic lower back impairment limiting lifting after she fell in the bathroom of her hospital room, due to an unheeded request that the nursing assistant stay with her. She is unable to return to her past work and experiences a loss in vocational earning capacity. Aptitude testing reveals vocational interests and strengths in mechanical pursuits and she is retrained, acquiring technical computer skills.

Personality or emotional testing may also offer further enlightenment concerning an individual's emotional state. Depending upon the qualifications of the evaluator and the characteristics of the subject, testing may determine the presence or absence of depression or anxiety as emotional states along with a range of alternative personality characteristics. The presence of a significant emotional disorder, which may be brought to light during the course of the vocational interview or reflected in the treatment records, would present an additional factor for consideration with respect to vocational planning, recommendations, and the outcomes of the assessment.

Case example:

A 55-year-old construction worker with a less than high school education suffers disfiguring facial burns in the operating room as a result of improper equipment use by the operating room nurse. His extremely poor self image affects his attempts to return to the job market. His inability to return to work has resulted in marital tension, economic hardship, and mounting debt. He experiences the onset of reactive depressive symptomatology manifest by anhedonia, flat affect, ruminations, and fatigue. The symptoms are recognized by his treating physician. Testing reveals that his depression, if untreated, is of psychopathological intensity sufficient to impair occupational functioning.

Other tested facets may include dexterity or manipulative abilities, particularly for individuals who have experienced hand, arm, shoulder, or upper extremity impairments. Each level of impairment of this nature may affect an individual's ability to grip, grasp, feel, or use the fingers for fine or dexterous movements. Standardized measures are available within a cadre of test materials in order to assess these characteristics from a functional standpoint. Normative information generally compares the individual's test results with average test results for individuals engaged in specific occupational areas or age/gender appropriate norm groups. While medical determination may have indicated the presence of an upper extremity impairment or neurologic condition, vocational testing performance tends to express that level of impairment in vocational or occupational access terms.

Figure 11.1 contains commonly employed testing measures within a vocational assessment environment. This list is certainly not exhaustive of the testing tools available to the vocational examiner, nor should all individuals be subject to each assessment tool available. Clinical judgment is used to select testing materials based upon the specific characteristics of the individual: occupational history, health considerations, skills and abilities, and, ultimately, the objectives of the evaluation with respect to identifying appropriate labor market access issues.

Finally, it should be noted that vocational evaluators are not qualified to administer certain types of tests. In such instances, if test results do not exist, the vocational evaluator will instruct the attorney that specific tests from other experts such as clinical psychologists or neuropsychologists are needed. The vocational evaluator must be careful to remain in her area of expertise to avoid excluded testimony. Typically, vocational evaluators are not qualified to administer tests such as the Weschler Adult Intelligence Scale or younger age versions, neuropsychological tests such as the Reitan-Indiana Neuropsychological Test battery, and projective tests, to name a few.

G. Pertinent Documents

As previously described, the evaluation generally encompasses three information domains: information obtained during the vocational interview; test results and observations; and a review of medical and related pertinent documents. Legal counsel generally provides the documents and information to the forensic vocational consultant. The provided information forms the necessary medical foundation with respect to the presence or absence of a health condition, diagnoses, treatment, medical capacities, and restrictions. Furthermore, the provided records offer documentation con-

- Wide Range Achievement Test—test of academic ability: reading, spelling, mathematics
- Wexler Adult Intelligence Test—measure of global intellect
- Slosson Intelligence Test—measure of global intellect appropriate for children
- BETA III Test—non-reading test of general intelligence appropriate for evaluees of marginal literacy
- Career Ability Placement Survey—multiple test battery measuring vocational aptitudes
- Minnesota Clerical Test—a visual measure of clerical ability
- Purdue Pegboard Dexterity Test—a measure of fine finger dexterity
- Hamilton Depression Inventory—a test of current emotional state
- Personal Assessment Inventory—a measure of current emotional state
- 16 PF—multi-dimensional personality test
- Bennett Mechanical Comprehension Test—measure of mechanical ability
- Wiesen Mechanical Aptitude Test—test of mechanical aptitude
- Slosson Oral Reading Test—test of oral reading ability
- Grey Silent Reading Test—test of non-verbal reading
- Nelson Denny Reading Test—test of reading comprehension
- Self-Directed Search—vocational interest inventory

Figure 11.1 Commonly Used Standardized Tests

cerning vocational information secured during the course of the interview and form the record upon which the vocational evaluation is, in part, based. Pertinent materials include the following, among others:

- Narrative medical reports
- Treatment records
- Reports of surgery
- Physical therapy progress reports
- Independent medical evaluations
- Employment-related information
- Work performance appraisals
- Earnings documentation
- Physical Functional Capacity Evaluations and/or Mental Functional Capacity Evaluations (see Appendix 11.2)

11.7 Integration of Information and Vocational Analysis

The preceding discussion has focused primarily upon the types of information required for the evaluation, the general methodology employed, and the data necessary for the assessment. The analysis is based upon this information.

TIP: The vocational analysis essentially encompasses integration of the information provided including that from the interview, documentation, health capacities and restrictions, and test findings.

The assessment includes consideration of the individual's cognitive, intellectual, and aptitude capabilities, exertional requirements of work, and emotional reactions, if applicable. In all respects, the vocational evaluation considers the individual with respect to the customary demands associated with competitive employment, which include factors such as consistency and regularity in attendance and punctuality, an ability to meet reasonable employer-established productivity standards, and the capability to interact effectively with co-workers, supervisors, the general public, and so on. The subject of the evaluation must possess the capability to meet these very basic criteria with respect to the parameters of competitive employment. The evaluator may conduct a transferable skill assessment to identify any skills and abilities the subject of the evaluation may possess that are transferable to alternate occupations in compliance with the medical restrictions and limitations indicated.

The transferable skill analysis may be accomplished through the use of information provided by the U.S. Department of Labor including the *Dictionary of Occupational Titles*,[6] *O Net*,[7] *Classification of Jobs*,[8] *Handbook of Analyzing Jobs*,[9] or a range of resource materials available within the public domain concerning the characteristics, and exertional and intellectual demands of various occupations. A number of computer and Internet resources such as SkillTRAN may assist in the transferable skill analysis.[10]

The assessment concludes with a statement concerning the vocational effects of the health condition—which may have arisen from nursing malpractice—upon the subject's ability to participate in job market activity. These include the customary demands of employment, as previously described, and considerations offered to health, safety, and productivity. The assessment reflects an indication of pre- and post-injury vocational earning capacity. Any differential between the two parameters may further include an assessment of future work life.

11.8 Vocational Evaluations of Children and Adolescents

Evaluations associated with minor plaintiffs or individuals who have not yet entered the labor market confront the evaluator with additional issues for analysis. The data-gathering methodology remains unchanged. Such persons have no record of work from which to identify pre-injury work participation and skill development. The absence of a work record need not preclude a vocational analysis. A high correlation between educational attainment level and vocational earning capacity exists. From the broadest perspective, as individuals ascend the educational ladder (high school, college, graduate study and so on), there is a corresponding increase in vocational earnings. Independent of specific occupation or career path, each educational level has an associated average level of vocational earnings. It is standard protocol among vocational experts to extrapolate the probable career path of a disabled child by relying on the educational and occupational progress of the parents and involved family members. Based on research by Toppino, Reed and Agrusa[11] for example, statistics indicate that when both parents have less than a high school education, only 18 percent of their children will complete college; however, when both parents have post-graduate education, 70 percent of their children complete college.

TIP: Within our society there is a correlation between the educational attainment level of parents and children. The factors influencing this are manifold and include, but are not limited to, the following: the environment in the home, genetics, and economic resources available within the home for post secondary educational participation.

Upon the establishment of an appropriate pre-injury educational attainment level for the child, a corresponding level of earnings may be determined and serve as a reference level from which to assess the impact of the child's health condition.

11.9 Daubert, Kumho, and Forensic Vocational Opinions

Within the federal court system, the Federal Rule of Evidence 702[12] has been applied to vocational experts and in-

dividuals offering forensic vocational opinions within that forum. The Federal Rule 702 initially set forth in the *Frye* decision (1923)[13] has been known as the *Frye* Rule and established that: if scientific, technical or other specialized knowledge will assist the trier of fact to understand the evidence or determine affected issue, witnesses qualified as experts by knowledge, skill, experience, training or education may testify thereto, in the form of an opinion. Their qualifications and the testimony must be based upon sufficient facts, reliable principles and methods, and the witness must apply those principle methods to the facts of the case.

An appropriately qualified vocational rehabilitation expert witness under the *Frye* Rule would offer testimony concerning vocational earnings or lost earning capacity in accordance with the practices within the field of vocational rehabilitation.

In 1993, *Daubert v. Merrill Dow Pharmaceutical,*[14] heard by the Supreme Court, offered an additional test by which forensic scientific evidence could be introduced within the federal system. This present chapter is not intended as a legal discussion of the applicability or issues within *Daubert*. Subsequent rulings, including *Kumho Tire Company v. Carmichael,*[15] have influenced the introduction of scientific expert and vocational rehabilitation testimony within the federal court system, including testimony applied within nursing malpractice cases. *Daubert* offered a four-part test to evaluate expert testimony:

1. Can the theory of technique be tested?
2. Has the theory or technique been subjected to peer review and publications?
3. What is the known error rate of the particular scientific method?
4. Is there an explicit identification and acceptance of the theory and technique within a relevant scientific community?

While Federal Rule 702 (the *Frye* Rule) offers the trier of fact broader parameters with respect to the introduction of expert or scientific testimony, the *Daubert* ruling, as it applies to scientific testimony, specifically requires adherence to the four-part test. The applicability of *Daubert* to forensic vocational expert opinions has varied on a case-by-case basis.

From an epistemological standpoint, clearly *Daubert* assumes the positivist view of knowledge; that is, physical and social reality exist independently of those who observe it and, if unbiased, constitutes scientific knowledge. Positivist data tend to be more quantitative as opposed to qualitative and are gathered under rigorous experimental control

conditions. However, the practice of rehabilitation counseling has more in common with the post-positivist view,
which believes that social reality is constructed differently
by different individuals. It is more holistic. Data tend to be
more qualitative as opposed to quantitative. The qualitative
or post-positivist methodologies encompass case studies,
verbal data, interpretative analysis, and analytic induction.

While quantitative analysis can find close adherence and
expression within a number of fields including engineering,
medicine, and chemistry, the qualitative approach utilized in
the social sciences encompassing psychology, rehabilitation,
counseling, and sociology tend to capitalize upon methods
of inquiry and, in turn, scientific knowledge independent of
the strict adherence to the scientific method. Vocational testimony, which has strictly adhered to the methodology and
procedures found within the field of vocational rehabilitation counseling, may be admitted under the *Frye* Rule. This
testimony offers information to the disposition of the case
concerning the impact of a health condition upon vocational
earning capacity. The same analysis may be excluded under
the more confining *Daubert* standard which, in turn, would
tend to deny the trier of fact information useful to the case.
Discussions of error rates may be appropriately applied to
standardized testing, which forms a portion or component
of the evaluation. The holistic approach necessary in the vocational evaluation process encompasses review of data and
medical records, interviewing, testing, and a cogent analysis
encompassing the various factors important to the evaluation. The clinical judgment model articulated by Field and
Choppa[16] is likely the most succinct discussion and presentation of the vocational analysis process. While adherence to
the scientific method with respect to error rates may apply to
portions or elements of the evaluation, the global nature of
a vocational evaluation necessarily requires weighing, balancing, and analyzing multiple variables.

11.10 Critical Analysis of Vocational Reports in Nursing Malpractice Cases

The following questions may serve the reader of a vocational evaluation report direction to analyze the evaluation
process, assumptions underlying the opinion, and the value
or quality of the assessment.

- Does the opinion include all relevant medical information?
- Were specific medical reports ignored in the vocational opinion?
- What specific medical limitations arise from the
  nursing malpractice and what are the vocational
  consequences?

- Does relevant medical information post-date the
  vocational report?
- Was appropriate testing utilized as a foundation for
  the opinion? If not, why not?
- Was the testing valid?
- Has the vocational opinion considered all health
  conditions confronting the evaluee?
- What is the evaluee's labor market area?
- What is the quality of the wage or labor market in-
  formation contained in the vocational evaluation?
- What is the rehabilitation potential of the evaluee?

11.11 Summary

A vocational evaluation can form an important element with
respect to articulating vocational damages associated with a
particular case related to nursing malpractice. The forensic
vocational witness completes an interview and analysis, and
identifies the presence of a health condition and its functional impact upon job market participation. The expert articulates the impact of the health condition upon vocational
earning capacity, which is entirely within the purview of the
vocational consultant. From a practical standpoint, the vocational opinion testimony is, to a large extent, founded upon
the health-related information and is a functional extension
of the restrictions and limitations expressed in specific vocational terms. The opinions of the vocational expert offer
an indication, within reasonable vocational certainty, of the
specific access denied to the individual in the job market
owing to the health-related condition.

Endnotes

1. *Dictionary of Occupational Titles*. Washington, D.C.:
   U.S. Department of Labor, 1991.

2. Field, J. E., and Field, T. F. (1992). *Classification of
   Jobs*. Washington, DC: U.S. Department of Labor. Elliott & Fitzpatrick Inc. Publishing.

3. Field, T. F. and A. J. Choppa, *Admissible Testimony:
   A Content Analysis of Selected Cases Involving Vocational Experts with a Revised Clinical model for Developing Opinion*. Athens, Georgia: Elliott & Fitzpatrick
   Inc, 2005.

4. Federal Register. Washington, D.C. (20 CFR
   404.1560).

5. Gamboa, A. *The New Worklife Expectancy Tables*, revised. Louisville, Kentucky: Vocational Econometrics,
   Inc, 2002.

6. See note 1.

7. *O-Net,* Washington. D.C.: U.S. Department of Labor, 2000.

8. See note 2.

9. *The Revised Handbook of Analyzing Jobs*, Washington, DC: U.S. Department of Labor, 1991.

10. SkillTRAN™ (www.skilltran.com).

11. Toppino, D., Reed, W., and Agrusa, J. (1998). *The ABC's Of Rehabilitation Economics*. Athens, Georgia: Elliott & Fitzpatrick, Inc. Publishing.

12. Federal Rules of Evidence (as amended 2002). Washington, D.C.: U.S. Department of Justice, 2002.

13. *Frye v. United States.* 293 F. 1013 (D.C. Cir. 1923).

14. *Daubert v. Merrill Dow Pharmaceuticals.* 92-102, Sp Ct 1993.

15. *Kumho Tire Company v. Carmichael.* 97-1709, Sp Ct 1999.

16. See note 3.

Appendix 11.1
Physical Functional Capacity Evaluation

PATIENT: _____   FACILITY: _____

U.S. Department of Labor Definitions:

SEDENTARY WORK: lift 10 # maximum and occasionally carry small objects
LIGHT WORK: lift 20 # maximum; frequently lift/carry up to 10 #
MEDIUM WORK: lift 50 # maximum; frequently lift/carry up to 25 #
HEAVY WORK: lift 100 # maximum; frequently lift/carry up to 50 #

_____ It is my opinion that patient can now return to work without restrictions.

_____ Based on patient's demonstrated performance in our evaluation, the following limitations exist relevant to work activity:

1. LIFT:

	No Restriction	Occasionally (1%–11%)	Frequently (34%–66%)	Constantly (67%–100%)
a. up to 10 #	_____	_____	_____	_____
b. 11–20	_____	_____	_____	_____
c. 21–30	_____	_____	_____	_____
d. 31–50	_____	_____	_____	_____
e. 51–100	_____	_____	_____	_____

2. CARRY:

	No Restriction	Occasionally (1%–11%)	Frequently (34%–66%)	Constantly (67%–100%)
a. up to 10 #	_____	_____	_____	_____
b. 11–20	_____	_____	_____	_____
c. 21–30	_____	_____	_____	_____
d. 31–50	_____	_____	_____	_____
e. 51–100	_____	_____	_____	_____

3. CAN THE PERSON PERFORM THE FOLLOWING TASKS:

	No Restriction	Occasionally (1%–11%)	Frequently (34%–66%)	Constantly (67%-100%)
Pull–Seated	_____	_____	_____	_____
Pull–Standing	_____	_____	_____	_____
Bend	_____	_____	_____	_____
Squat	_____	_____	_____	_____
Crawl	_____	_____	_____	_____
Climb	_____	_____	_____	_____

4. ASSUMING AN 8-HOUR WORKDAY WITH TWO FIFTEEN (15) MINUTE BREAKS AND HALF-HOUR MEAL BREAK, I WOULD EXPECT THIS PERSON TO BE ABLE TO:

- Sit for _____ hours at a time, up to _____ hours over an 8-hour workday
- Stand for _____ hours at a time, up to _____ hours over an 8-hour workday
- Alternately stand/sit for_____ hours over an 8-hour workday
- Walking for _____hours over an 8-hour workday

5. CAN THE PERSON USE HANDS FOR REPETITIVE ACTIONS SUCH AS:

	Simple Grasping	Firm Grasp	Fine Manipulating
Right	Yes___ No___	Yes___ No___	Yes___ No___
Left	Yes___ No___	Yes___ No___	Yes___ No___

Estimated grip strength: Right_____   Left_____

6. CAN THE PERSON USE FEET FOR REPETITIVE MOVEMENTS AS IN OPERATING FOOT CONTROLS?

	Right	Left	Both
	Yes____ No____	Yes___ No____	Yes___ No____

7. ANY RESTRICTIONS OF ACTIVITIES INVOLVED?

	None	Mild	Moderate	Total
Unprotected heights	____	____	____	____
Being around moving machinery	____	____	____	____
Exposed to marked changes in temperature and humidity	____	____	____	____
Drive automotive equipment	____	____	____	____
Exposure to dust, fumes, gas	____	____	____	____

8. CAN THE PERSON NOW RETURN TO PREVIOUS JOB?

9. COMMENTS: _____

_____

_____

SIGNATURE:_____   **DATE:**_____

Appendix 11.2
Mental Functional Capacity Evaluation

_____   _____

Name of Individual   Social Security Number

Please assist us in determining this individual's ability to do work-related activities on a sustained basis. "Sustained basis" means the ability to perform work-related activities eight hours a day for five days a week, or an equivalent work schedule. Please give us your professional opinion of *what the individual can still do despite his/her impairment(s)*. The opinion should be based on your findings with respect to medical history, clinical and laboratory findings, diagnosis, prescribed treatment and response, and prognosis.

For each activity shown below:

(1) Respond to the questions about the individual's ability to perform the activity. When doing so, use the following definitions for the rating terms:

- *None*—Absent or minimal limitations. If limitations are present, they are transient and/or expectable reactions to psychological stresses.
- *Slight*—There is some mild limitation in this area, but the individual can generally function well.
- *Moderate*—There is moderate limitation in this area, but the individual is still able to function satisfactorily.
- *Marked*—There is serious limitation in this area. The ability to function is severely limited but not precluded.
- *Extreme*—There is major limitation in this area. There is no useful ability to function in this area.

(2) Identify the factors (e.g., the particular medical signs, laboratory findings, or other factors described above) that support your assessment.

	No Evidence	Slightly Limited	Moderately Limited	Markedly Limited	No Limitation
A. UNDERSTANDING AND MEMORY					
1. The ability to remember locations and worklike procedures	1.___	2.___	3.___	4.___	5.___
2. The ability to understand and remember very short and simple instructions	1.___	2.___	3.___	4.___	5.___
3. The ability to understand and remember detailed instructions	1.___	2.___	3.___	4.___	5.___
B. SUSTAINED CONCENTRATION AND PERSISTENCE					
4. The ability to carry out very short and simple instructions	1.___	2.___	3.___	4.___	5.___
5. The ability to carry out detailed instructions	1.___	2.___	3.___	4.___	5.___
6. The ability to maintain attention and concentration for extended periods	1.___	2.___	3.___	4.___	5.___
7. The ability to perform activities within a schedule, maintain regular attendance, and be punctual within customary tolerances	1.___	2.___	3.___	4.___	5.___

	No Evidence	Slightly Limited	Moderately Limited	Markedly Limited	No Limitation
8. The ability to sustain an ordinary routine without special supervision	1.___	2.___	3.___	4.___	5.___
9. The ability to work in coordination with or proximity to others without being distracted by them	1.___	2.___	3.___	4.___	5.___
10. The ability to make simple work-related decisions	1.___	2.___	3.___	4.___	5.___
11. The ability to complete a normal workday and workweek without interruptions from psychologically based symptoms and perform at a consistent pace without an unreasonable number and length of rest periods	1.___	2.___	3.___	4.___	5.___
C. SOCIAL INTERACTION					
12. The ability to interact appropriately with the general public.	1.___	2.___	3.___	4.___	5.___
13. The ability to ask simple questions or request assistance	1.___	2.___	3.___	4.___	5.___
14. The ability to accept instructions and respond appropriately to criticism from supervisors	1.___	2.___	3.___	4.___	5.___
15. The ability to get along with co-workers or peers without distracting them or exhibiting behavioral extremes	1.___	2.___	3.___	4.___	5.___
16. The ability to maintain socially appropriate behavior and to adhere to basic standards of neatness and cleanliness.	1.___	2.___	3.___	4.___	5.___
D. ADAPTATION					
17. The ability to respond appropriately to changes in the work setting	1.___	2.___	3.___	4.___	5.___
18. The ability to be aware of normal hazards and take appropriate precautions	1.___	2.___	3.___	4.___	5.___
19. The ability to travel in unfamiliar places or use public transportation	1.___	2.___	3.___	4.___	5.___
20. The ability to set realistic goals or make plans independently of others	1.___	2.___	3.___	4.___	5.___

Chapter 12

Life Care Planning

Mona Goldman Yudkoff, RN, BSN, MPH, CRRN, CCM, CLCP, Alisa Mintzer Dayanim, RN, BSN, MSN, CRRN, and Victoria Powell, RN, CCM, LNCC, CNLCP, CLCP, MSCC, CEAS

12.1 What is a Life Care Plan and Why Do You Need One?

Clients with physical or cognitive deficits secondary to catastrophic injuries or chronic illness will almost always have ongoing and complex needs. The cost of medical and supportive care often becomes a major portion of the damages that are awarded to these plaintiffs. This is true of cases involving medical malpractice, accidents, product liability and other areas of personal injury.

The life care plan, a comprehensive and organized analysis of current and future medical expenses, is an essential element in personal injury cases. This projection must be specific to the needs of each client, taking into account the nature of the illness, injury or disability. Each plan is annotated with the medical rationale for needed services. Consideration must be given to geographical differences in medical expenses. The finished plan is a holistic document, individualized to reflect the medical and non-medical needs, family composition, values, cultural variants and pre-morbid lifestyle of the client.

A well-prepared LCP should project damages in a defensible and organized report. The need for each item must be clearly stated and justified in relation to the injury. Recommendations of treating healthcare providers are clearly documented, and specific costs are referenced to local vendors. The anticipated dates of initiation and completion of required services are included in order to facilitate the economist's projection of the present value of the total needs.

When the LCP is submitted into evidence, the jury should have a clear picture of the total impact of the injury on the client and the family. In addition to knowing the cost of the future medical needs, the jurors can also appreciate the emotional and physical resources required to implement the plan of care.

This chapter provides a guide to understanding the application of life care planning in the forensic setting, from the selection of the life care planning expert witness through the evaluation and presentation of the LCP.

12.2 History of Life Care Planning

Insurance companies and medical case managers have traditionally used LCPs to set reserves for high-cost cases. The use of the LCP in the forensic setting was first described in the literature by Deutsch and his associates in the early 1980s. In *A Guide to Rehabilitation*, published in 1985, Drs. Paul M. Deutsch and Horace Sawyer outlined a methodology that considered the patient, disability, clinical team, service providers, family, and life cycle changes in needs. Today, the use of life care planners is standard procedure in presenting future medical damages for cases involving catastrophic injuries or illnesses.

The field has experienced significant growth and activity over the past two decades. The International Academy of Life Care Planners (IALCP) was originally formed in 1996 and merged with the International Academy of Rehabilitation Professionals (IARP, www.rehabpro.org) in 2005. The IALCP, a special interest section of IARP (www.rehabpro.org/ialcp), provides a professional organization for rehabilitation professionals from many disciplines engaged in the specialty practice of life care planning. The organization strives to advance the practice of life care planning by educational programs and the development of standards of practice and ethics relevant to life care planning. The American Association of Nurse Life Care Planners (AANLCP, www.aanlcp.org), founded in 1998, promotes the specialized contribution the registered nurse brings to the life care planning process and supports education, research, and standards related to the practice of nurse life care planning.

Growth of the professional aspect of life care planning is further evidenced by the development of specific credentialing processes. The International Commission on Health Care Certification (ICHCC, www.ichcc.org) certifies rehabilitation professionals from multiple disciplines, with the title of Certified Life Care Planner (CLCP). The American Association of Nurse Life Care Planners (AANLCP) certifies registered nurses with the title of Certified Nurse Life Care Planner (CNLCP). As with other specialty association certifications, these credentials recognize the skills of the experienced life care planner who has met the requirements to sit for the exam and successfully completed the testing process. Refer to Chapter 20, *Working with Legal Nurse Consultants*, for additional information on certification.

The Foundation for Life Care Planning Research (http://flcpr.org/index.html), a non-profit research group established in 2002, focuses on life care planning validation studies and rehabilitation research. Working with the Department of Rehabilitation Counseling at the Medical College of Virginia, Virginia Commonwealth University, the Department of Rehabilitation at Georgia State University and other state universities, private practitioners, university academics, and doctoral students, the Foundation has successfully initiated several research projects and supervises several doctoral students in the completion of their dissertation work.

12.3 Choosing a Life Care Planning Expert Witness

Successful life care planners typically come from a rehabilitation background. A strong background in the provision of care to persons with chronic and catastrophic deficits is essential. Case management experience, i.e., familiarity with the coordination of services to the catastrophically ill or injured, is a basic requirement. A working knowledge of health care providers and vendors is necessary. Experience with billing and coding procedures is also helpful. Although life care planners may come from a variety of professional disciplines, the basic

rules for choosing any expert witness apply. Education, relevant expertise, credentials, communication skills, and professional appearance are crucial to the credibility of any expert.

Nurses are often uniquely qualified to prepare LCPs. Nursing is a scientific discipline as well as a profession.[1] The science of nursing is based on the critical thinking framework known as the nursing process. This process is composed of assessment, diagnosis, outcomes identification, planning, implementation and evaluation. Registered nurses have the medical training and experience to understand the needs of the client and to anticipate those needs or services that have not yet been addressed by health care providers. Florence Nightingale taught nurses to employ critical thinking to integrate objective data with knowledge gained from the assessment of the patient. This critical thinking process, now known as the nursing process, is used to apply the best available evidence and research to the process of diagnosis.[2] Nursing employs practices that are supportive, restorative, and promotive in nature. One objective of nursing as outlined in our scope and standards of practice is to achieve positive patient outcomes that maximize one's quality of life across the entire lifespan.[3] Therefore in this role, nurses have traditionally played a pivotal role in rehabilitation medicine as facilitators of the management of disabled patients. Registered nurses facilitate the comprehensive and interdisciplinary care provided by collaborating with other colleagues to meet patient care needs. Nurses are well experienced in organizing plans of care, coordinating the recommendations of team members and regularly evaluating the cost, safety and effectiveness of care.

Nurses are diagnosticians. With the formal classification of nursing diagnoses published by NANDA International (North American Nursing Diagnosis Association), it is broadly accepted that nurses are diagnosticians who use diagnostic reasoning to identify the best diagnoses to guide interventions and achieve positive patient outcomes.[4] The focus of nursing care is the person's achievement of well-being and self-actualization. Nursing diagnosis requires competencies in intellectual, interpersonal, and technical domains as well as the development of the personal strengths of tolerance for ambiguity and use of reflective practice (NANDA).[5] Nursing diagnoses can be used to provide foundation for recommendations made by nurses. NANDA defines nursing diagnoses as, "A clinical judgement about individual family or community responses to actual or potential health problems / life processes. A nursing diagnosis provides the basis for selection of nursing intervention to achieve outcomes for which the nurse is accountable."

Certification as a life care planner (CLCP or CNLCP) and academic preparation at the master's or doctoral level enhances credibility and shows a commitment to professionalism and the acquisition of skills and knowledge in one's own field. Continuing education courses and attendance at professional meetings and conferences ensure that the nurse life care planner knows what is current in the field.

Certification by professional organizations shows peer recognition of experience and expertise. It is important to identify the life care planner whose background best suits the individual case. The CRRN (certified rehabilitation nurse) credential reflects experience in rehabilitation nursing and the strong knowledge base required to understand, address, and explain complex medical needs resulting from severe injuries or illnesses. This medical background may be especially important when the damages represent only a part of the total impairment, for example, a case with a pre-existing medical condition. Nurses may also obtain certain multi-disciplinary certifications that reflect expanded rehabilitation expertise. A certified case manager (CCM) has experience and expertise in coordinating and obtaining rehabilitation services. A Certified Rehabilitation Counselor (CRC) may be the appropriate expert in a case where significant damages are related to retooling the client's vocational life. Other credentials are listed in Figure 12.1. It is the responsibility of the attorney to evaluate the credibility of the certifying body.

In addition to professional education and certifications, the attorney should evaluate the potential expert's work experience, forensic experience and direct experience in preparing and testifying about LCPs. Professional work experience related to the injuries in question will enhance the creditability of the expert. For example, clinical pediatric experience is an important credential for the expert testifying about the needs of a child.

12.4 Methodology

Preparing the LCP using standard and accepted methodology is essential in providing a strong foundation for testimony. Nurse life care planners use the nursing process as the basis for developing a LCP. This methodology, standard to nurses across practice areas, includes assessment of the injured party's needs, nursing diagnoses of the human response to health issues and a plan of action for patient care. Once the clinical assessment is completed, the life care planning standard methodology is used to add the monetary cost of the individual needs to the process.

A. Assessment

At the outset, the life care planner requires medical records including physician and therapy notes, consultations, diagnostics, home health care records, hospital or facility records, and mental health care records. In pediatric cases, the life care planner will want to view early intervention records, Individualized Education Plans (IEPs), developmental testing and other school-related items.

Throughout this process, the life care planner can draw valuable insights from supporting information such as videotapes, log books, diaries, and calendars compiled by the attorney, treatment team, and family. Review of deposition transcripts from the treating physician or family can give the life care planner further insight into the day-to-day demands of caring for the individual.

The certified rehabilitation nurse (**CRRN**) credential reflects experience in rehabilitation nursing and the strong knowledge base required to understand, address, and explain complex medical needs resulting from severe injuries or illnesses. This medical background may be especially important when the damages represent only a part of the total impairment, for example, a case with a pre-existing medical condition. Nurses may also obtain certain multi-disciplinary certifications that reflect expanded rehabilitation expertise.

A certified case manager (**CCM**) has experience and expertise in coordinating and obtaining rehabilitation services.

A Certified Rehabilitation Counselor (**CRC**) or Certified Insurance Rehabilitation Specialist (**CIRS**) may be the appropriate expert in a case where significant damages are related to retooling the client's vocational life.

Certification specific to life care planners is currently offered by two agencies, one exclusively for nurses and one that is multi-disciplinary. The Certified Nurse Life Care Planner (**CNLCP**) is a registered nurse with experience and continuing education in rehabilitation and life care planning. The Certified Life Care Planner (**CLCP**) is a rehabilitation professional with experience and continuing education in rehabilitation and life care planning.

Figure 12.1 Life Care Planner Credentials

Interviewing the injured party, family members and direct caregivers is preferred to provide a strong basis for many of the recommendations in the LCP. It is often helpful to conduct the interview in individual's residence. Valuable information may be obtained when viewing the home for accessibility issues and safety. Observation of family dynamics can offer insight into issues such as caregiver burnout.

Treating physicians, therapists, other providers and expert witnesses may be asked for input regarding future medical surveillance and care, equipment, environment, additional services, and so on.

B. Establish a Plan of Treatment

The treatment plan is a projection based on the data collection and the rehabilitation specialist's experience. In addition to the recommendations set forth by treating or expert physician and care providers, the nurse makes appropriate nursing diagnoses regarding the individual's responses to the injuries, medical diagnoses and functional deficits. Nursing recommendations are derived from the nursing diagnoses. Specific areas to be considered in the LCP are described in the next section of this chapter.

The life care planner should be able to clearly explain the foundation for each recommendation. Frequency and duration of services are an essential part of the plan.

C. Costing the Life Care Plan

Although report formats vary among life care planners, each style should clearly document the need for and cost of each given item, the expected duration of that need, and the projected frequency and cost of the item's replacement.

The cost for services already in place, such as physician or therapy, should be a direct reflection of the current charges for that provider. The charges may come from billing records or direct contact with the billing office of the provider.

When new services are included in the LCP, the cost in the plan should reflect the average charge or range of charges of two or more appropriate providers, geographically proximate to the injured party. However, in some remote locations, it may be difficult to find even one appropriate provider, so that a range or average may not be possible and the plan may need to include the cost for travel to access specialty care. Resources such as national fee sources, various software programs or online databases are sometimes used for documentation of the costs associated with care. Medical services can sometimes be annotated with a CPT code (Current Procedural Terminology) to clarify pricing.

Researching costs for equipment, supplies, medications and other items that are not dependent on the location of the provider, allows the life care planner to use the lowest cost available from a reputable provider. The LCP should indicate the source of the cost projection, and when appropriate, the specific brand and model number of the item.

D. Periodic Review and Update

In some cases, the LCP will be completed many months, or even years, before deposition or trial testimony is scheduled. The LCP should be reviewed and updated as needed. The LCP is a dynamic document, which is subject to changes based on the patient's condition and response to treatment. Depending on the nature of the injury under discussion, an updated assessment of the patient may be helpful. The life care planner should be supplied with updated medical records, depositions and expert opinion reports that are relevant to the LCP.

12.5 The Components of the Life Care Plan

The foundation, rationale and relevant factors contributing to each specific recommendation are clearly delineated in the LCP. The recommendations are usually assumed "more likely than not" to be required. Potential complications and new developments in technology may be discussed, but the cost for these services is generally not included in the total LCP projection.

A. Medical Surveillance

The LCP includes routine medical surveillance required, as a result of the injury, to maintain health status. This section addresses the maintenance care required by the injured party to maintain the status quo by the institution of measures to prevent decline or complications and by early diagnosis of potential complications. Medical surveillance recommendations usually fall into the following categories: physicians (or other providers), diagnostics, procedures and hospitalizations.

The recommendations for medical providers include the frequency and duration of services. Projections should consider changes in care due to growth (pediatric), aging, changes in medical condition and expected outcomes based on condition or treatment. See Figure 12.2.

B. Therapy

Recommendations for therapeutic modalities in the LCP will include evaluations, acute therapy sessions and services for maintenance and crisis intervention over the lifespan. Modalities may include basics such as physical, occupational and speech therapy and more specific services including respiratory, vestibular, vision, aquatic, equestrian and recreational therapy and other specialties. See Figure 12.3.

Category	Areas to Consider	Other Factors	Sample Items
Providers	• Primary Care • Physiatrist • Neurologist • Psychiatrist • Urologist • Nutritionist • Other Specialty	• Visit frequency • Changes due to growth • Changes in condition • Expected outcomes	• Neurologist: 2/year to age 16, then 1/year throughout lifespan • Physiatrist, 1/year throughout lifespan • Primary care, 4/year to age 18; 2/year age 19+
Diagnostic Studies	• Specific blood tests • Imaging • Ultrasound • EEG • EKG	• Frequency changes due to growth or changes in medical condition • Expected outcomes for relevant diagnoses	• Dilantin level 4/year to age 16, then 1/year throughout life • EEG every three years • Renal ultrasound 1/year
Future Procedures or Hospital Stays	• Muscle/tendon transfers • Plastic surgery • Shunt revisions • Other procedures	• Length of hospital stays • Physician fees • Post-surgical therapy/nursing • Orthotics/equipment	• Muscle release, hospital fee for 3 inpatient days, surgeon / anesthesiologist fees, 24 sessions PT, twice in lifespan • Shunt revision, every 3-5 years, 3 inpatient days, plus professional fees • Inpatient stay for complications, average 6–10 days every 1–3 years.

Figure 12.2 Examples of Life Care Plan Items for Medical Surveillance

C. Psychological Support and Case Management

Rehabilitation nurses evaluate coping responses to injury or illness. Supportive counseling is often beneficial to develop or enhance coping mechanisms when there are functional deficits, body-image (cosmetic) changes or chronic pain. Coping mechanisms usually require reinforcement over time. Therefore, after an initial episode of intensive counseling, the LCP will often include intermittent episodes of counseling for maintenance, crisis intervention and support during new life cycle stages. Family members and caregivers may participate in some of the sessions.

The recommended professional(s) may be a psychologist, social worker or psychiatrist. The level of academic preparation of the professional recommended will depend on the type of service needed and geographic availability.

When the injured party is a minor or cognitively impaired, caregivers and family members may require counseling that focuses on providing appropriate care to and support of the injured party, while maintaining an intact, functional family. Specialized counseling may be required for behavior management of cognitively impaired adults or children.

A case manager with a specialty in catastrophic injury and chronic illness is included in the LCP to assist the injured party or the family to navigate the health care system, find cost effective, creative and functional solutions to obstacles to activities of daily living and ensure the implementation of the recommendations of healthcare providers.

An independent case manager is a rehabilitation professional responsible to the injured party and not to providers or payer sources. Case managers provided by government agencies, insurance companies or facilities do not replace the need for an independent case manager. Facility residents often benefit from an independent case manager to ensure appropriate care within the facility. Refer to Figure 12.4.

D. Equipment, Supplies and Medications

The LCP clearly itemizes necessary equipment, supplies and medications. Only those items specific to the injury under discussion are included in the LCP.

Durable equipment cost projection should include reasonable replacement schedules and maintenance costs. When items are covered under warranty for a limited period of time, the annual maintenance within the replacement schedule can be averaged to simplify the calculation. For example, if the maintenance on a chair that will need replacement every five years is $100 per year except the first year (warranty coverage), the average annual maintenance cost for the five-year period is $80 ($100 per year for four years divided by five years).

Category	Areas to Consider	Other Factors	Sample Items
Therapeutic Modalities	• Physical therapy • Occupational therapy • Speech therapy • Feeding therapy • Cognitive retraining • Audiology • Respiratory therapy • Other	• Frequency of service • Duration of service • Maintenance therapy	• PT, 3/week in summer to age 21, then annual evaluation throughout lifespan • ST, 3/week for two years, then maintenance therapy, average 6 sessions / year throughout life • Occupational therapy, 12 sessions, 4 times over adult lifespan
Adapted Recreation	• Summer programming • Extracurricular activities	• Availability in the community • Specific needs of the client/family	• Summer camp to age 21 • Special Olympics • Equestrian therapy 30 sessions / year

Figure 12.3 *Examples of Life Care Plan Items for Therapy and Adapted Recreation*

Category	Areas to Consider	Other Factors	Sample Items
Counseling	• Individual therapy • Family therapy • Behavior modification • Support groups	• Maintenance therapy as a follow-up to initial intensive therapy • Physician provider for medication needs	• Weekly counseling for one year at age 10 and again at age 16 • Maintenance therapy average six sessions/year to age 30
Case Management	• Private case management	• Current coordination of services and capability of caregivers	• Case management, four to six hours per quarter

Figure 12.4 *Examples of Life Care Plan Items for Support Services*

The LCP should show quantities and duration of use for supplies used in activities of daily living (ADL), respiratory care, enteral feedings, and so on.

The dosage should be included for each medication in the LCP. See Figure 12.5.

E. Accessible Housing and Transportation

Accessible housing is required when the injured party has mobility deficits. Consideration should be given to both function and safety. The injured party should have at least two readily available exits from the home. Protected parking is usually needed for access in and out of the home in inclement weather. Modifications to bathrooms, kitchens and electrical outlets and switches will depend on the level of function of the injured party, both at the current time and into the future, as the person ages with a disability. Caregiver function is also critical in designing an appropriate living space. The cost projection for purchasing a new home should be offset by the normally expected cost of housing.

The types of modifications to a vehicle in the cost projection will depend on whether or not the injured party is driving or is driven by a caregiver. It may be appropriate to include a driving evaluation or driving lessons for an adapted vehicle. The cost of the adaptions and vehicle should be offset by the expected cost of transportation for the individual absent the injury. Consult Figure 12.6.

F. Attendant Care, Nursing, Long Term Care and Replacement Services

The most expensive section of the life care plan is often the part that addresses home or facility care. The need for this service should be carefully documented, relative to both the level of care recommended and the intensity of service. Some injured parties will require an attendant (aide), licensed practical nurse (LPN), or registered nurse (RN) at home. These individuals may be hired privately or through a licensed agency. The use of more expensive agency-hired personnel has many advantages, including supervision, training, and bonding. Usually a replacement is available if the attendant cannot work and a registered nurse supervisor visits monthly. Privately hiring personnel may save some dollars, but the client is responsible for paying taxes and keeping financial records.

Category	Areas to Consider	Other Factors	Sample Items
Equipment	• ADL • Positioning • Mobility • Nutrition/hydration • Respiratory function • Hygiene, bowel and bladder function • Recreation • Other care needs	• Cost of purchase • Brand, model • Maintenance • Replacement • Growth and development • Aging	• Wheelchair, $2,500 every three years until age 16, then, $3,200 every five years, age 17+ • Wheelchair maintenance, $250/year • Adapted Tricycle, once • MAFOs, $1,100 every year to age 16, then $1,100 every two years
Supplies	• ADL • Nutrition/hydration • Respiratory function • Hygiene, bowel and bladder function • Other care needs	• Frequency • Quantity	• Suction catheters, 3 per day • Gloves, 10 per day • Foley catheter, 2 per month
Medication	• Prescription • Over-the counter	• Frequency • Strength • Duration	• Tegretol, 250 mg., 4 per day • MS Contin, PRN, average 10 per week

Figure 12.5 Examples of Life Care Plan items for equipment, supplies, and medications

Category	Areas to Consider	Other Factors	Sample Items
Housing	• Safety • Entry and egress • Storage • Bathroom • Bedroom exit • All-weather entry	• Assess current housing • Make recommendations based on disability and design of living space	• Ramps for doors • Wheel-in shower • Widen doorways • Lower storage • Create bedroom exit
Vehicle	• Driver vs. passenger • Wheelchair lift • Hand controls • Tie downs • Driver's education	• Assess ability to drive • Sitting height of patient	• Semi-automatic lift with tie-downs • Hand controls • Driver re-training

Figure 12.6 Examples of Life Care Plan items for accessible housing and transportation

Category	Areas to Consider	Other Factors	Sample Items
Home Attendant / Respite	• Level of care • Frequency • Duration • Respite for caregiver	• Nurse practice act if using agency • Needs of caregiver • Level of independence	• HHA, 12 hour/day, 50 weeks • HHA, 24 hour/day, 2 weeks • LPN, feeding visit 2/day • Live-in HHA • LPN, 24 hours/day
Residential Placement	• Prior to age 21 • After age 21	• Client's needs • Family's ability /desire to meet needs • Socialization needs • Medical and vocational needs	• Facility placement • Group home • Assisted living • Skilled nursing home
Replacement Services	• Maintenance • Child care • Care of spouse, parent • Car maintenance	• Pre-injury level of function • Family support • Housing	• Homemaker, 12 hours/week • Yard care, snow removal, 36 weeks/year • Home maintenance, 10 hours/month

Figure 12.7 *Examples of Life Care Plan items for attendant care / facility placement / replacement services*

Category	Areas to Consider	Other Factors	Sample Items
Vocational Planning	• Assessments • Training programs • Job coaching	• Planning for needs after school age	• Sheltered workshop • Life skills training program • Day activity program
Education	• Public school • Private school	• Special needs • Family resources	• Public / private day school • Residential programs • Tutors

Figure 12.8 *Examples of Life Care Plan items for vocational and educational services*

The need for skilled nursing (LPN or RN) care greatly increases the cost of the life care plan. The specific reasons for using skilled care should be carefully documented and may often be supported by the Nurse Practice Act for each state.

The need for awake nighttime care must be justified when providing around-the-clock hourly services. Often the use of a live-in aide, with or without some supplemental nighttime hours, can provide around-the-clock emergency attendance at a lower cost.

In addition to direct care services, persons remaining at home may require replacement of the home maintenance services or care provided to other family members that they would have provided absent the injury. Replacement services are sometimes addressed by an economist. The LCP should not duplicate services recommended by other experts.

The decision to place a loved one in a residential facility is very difficult for a family. The ability or inability to provide for physical care and supervision is often the primary factor in this decision. However, the need for structured activity and socialization for adults with disabilities is sometimes better met in a residential placement even when the family is capable of providing home care. The cost of residential placement as an alternative for individuals with cognitive injuries or severe physical injuries is usually presented as an alternative option.

The type of facility will have a significant effect on the cost of the LCP. The LCP should clearly show the basis for choosing between a group home, community-based residence, nursing home, assisted living facility or other level of residential care. Refer to Figure 12.7.

G. Vocational and Educational Services

The LCP may include the cost of specialized educational services or vocational support. Recommendations for vocational and educational services will be based on appropriate foundation from qualified experts in these fields. Some life care planners are also qualified to provide opinions on vocational issues. Life care planners qualified to render independent vocational opinions may request additional materials such as the school and employment records, tax returns, and information regarding academic levels of achievement and work history.

Vocational issues include retraining for a new skill set or learning a new trade to provide opportunities for employment. In catastrophic cases, the injured person is often unable to work at all, or will require significant support to maintain employment. Options include episodic job coaching, supervised employment or sheltered workshop environments. Some injured persons, who cannot work even with support, will attend a day activity program or medical day care center in lieu of a work program.

Educational support for children whose needs are not met in the public school setting may include placement in a specialized school program or supplementation to the current school placement. Transitional programs may be recommended for young adults with the potential to gain some level of independence. See Figure 12.8.

12.6 Reviewing a Life Care Plan

How does an attorney or insurance company know when the submitted life care plan is appropriate to the client's needs? Using a qualified life care planner to provide a review of the life care plan can often reveal inconsistencies in methodology, inadequate research into resources and costs, and flawed assumptions. In some cases, it may be helpful to have the life care planner perform an independent assessment of the injured party or attend an Independent Medical Examination by another expert. However, the reviewer retained by an attorney representing a defendant may not be allowed direct access to the injured party or his home. Therefore the life care planner providing the review may have to rely on consultations with other experts who have evaluated the current status of the injured party. Review of Day in the Life Videos of the individual in the home environment can also be extremely helpful.

The following questions should be addressed when reviewing a LCP:

- Are the recommendations in the LCP appropriate for the diagnosis(es) under discussion?
- Is there foundation from treating providers or qualified experts?
- Are recommendations made independently by the life care planner within that expert's scope of practice or area of expertise?
- Have services required for routine health maintenance or the care of unrelated comorbidities been identified and removed from the total cost projections?
- Do the services recommended in the LCP duplicate other services in the LCP or other expert reports?

- Is attendant care provided for more than 365 days when inpatient care is considered?
- Are replacement services included in both the LCP and the economist's report?
- Does the plan include multiple physician visits that may provide overlapping care?
- Are appropriate offsets considered for normal costs of child care, housing, transportation, extracurricular activities, etc.?
- Are the costs for each service appropriate? Are the mathematical calculations accurate?
- Are the recommendations consistent with the description of the injured party in depositions, videos and medical records?

12.7 Standards of Practice and Ethical Issues

Life care planners who serve as experts are expected to apply the basic methodology to the development of their plans. That methodology, as earlier reviewed in this chapter, involves collaboration with the treatment providers and the use of clinical guidelines to develop a medical foundation for various items in the life care plan.

Published standards of practice for life care planning outline the philosophy, goals, role, and functions of life care planning, and delineate standards of performance as defined by life care planning professionals. A major part of the life care planning methodology involves the use of a reliable system for the accumulation and documentation of information.

Ethics refers to a set of principles of "right" conduct, a theory or a system of moral values, or the rules or standards governing the conduct of a person or members of a profession. The primary goal of practice ethics is to protect clients, provide guidelines for practicing professionals, and enhance the profession as a whole. Within the life care planning industry all practitioners are licensed or certified members of one or more professional disciplines. It is expected that life care planners follow appropriate relevant ethical guidelines within their areas of professional practice and expertise.

Life care planners are expected to maintain appropriate confidentiality, avoid dual relationships, adequately advise clients of the role of the life care planner, and maintain competency in the profession.

Appropriate confidentiality is a sensitive and important concept. Some professionals will have communications protected by "privilege" which is statutorily based in each state. For example, although no life care planners are currently covered by privilege, many may be professional counselors, licensed psychologists or others who have the additional statutory protection. In addition, litigation has the additional component of attorney work product that may have an effect on what information may be disclosed. The life care planner must be thoroughly informed on this topic.

A personal relationship with a client is not appropriate during the course of service. Developing LCPs for friends, co-workers, professional colleagues, or anyone where the objectivity and professionalism of the care plan is questioned should be avoided.

Each client should be fully informed about the role of the life care planner. For example, the client should be fully informed about who is requesting the LCP as well as the confidentiality of communications. Also, life care planners who have dual role responsibilities should clarify that they are not acting as a case manager, psychologist, and so on, and what the limits of their participation might be.

The life care planner is expected to accurately represent any information received for a particular case. Medical recommendations are to have an appropriate medical foundation. Research information that the life care planner has obtained for all aspects of care should be readily available for examination by appropriate reviewers.

12.8 Conclusion

Nurse life care planners are a valuable addition to the forensic team when litigating cases involving significant personal injury. Choosing the life care planning expert wisely will ensure an accurate and appropriate presentation of the damages in a personal injury case.

Endnotes

1. American Nurses Association. *Nursing Scope & Standards of Practice.* "Scope of Nursing Practice." 2004 edition. Nursesbooks.org The Publishing Program of ANA. April, 2007.

2. *Id.*

3. *Id.*

4. Herdman, H. ed., *NANDA International Nursing Diagnoses: Definitions & Classification 2009-2011.* Blackwell Publishing, 2009. p. 4-5.

5. *Id.*

Additional Resources

Organizations

The International Academy of Rehabilitation Professionals (IARP) and The International Academy of Life Care Planners Section (IALCP)
1926 Waukegan Road Suite 1
Glenview, IL 60025-1770
888-472-7722
www.rehabpro.org
The IARP/IALCP promotes high standards of professional performance and ethics, inservice training, networking, and cooperative efforts to advance life care planning.

The American Association of Nurse Life Care Planners
3267 East 3300 South #309
Salt Lake City, UT 84109
888-575-4047
www. aanlcp.org
AANLCP recognizes the nurse life care planner as the Registered Nurse (RN) who assesses, identifies issues, and plans for appropriate interventions, implementation, and evaluation in the nurse life care planning process. AANLCP promotes the professional practice that the Registered Nurse delivers to the life care planning process.

The Care Planner Network
3126 West Cary Street #137
Richmond, VA 23221
800-252-1094
www.careplanners.net
The mission of The Care Planner Network is to support, enhance and promote the specialized practice of life care planning. The organization is dedicated to improving the reliability and validity of the life care planning process by narrowing the variance in practice patterns, and by providing resources and networking opportunities to all practicing life care planners.

Books/Journals

ANA Scope and Standards of Practice. (2004). Silver Spring, MD: American Nurses Association

Deutsch, P. and H. Sawyer (2003). *Guide To Rehabilitation.* Purchase, NY: Ahab Press.

NANDA International. *Nursing Diagnoses: Definitions and Classification 2009-2011.* Wiley-Blackwell Publishing, 2008.

Riddick-Grisham, Susan and Laura Deming (2004). *Pediatric Life Care Planning and Case Management.* Boca Raton, FL: CRC Press.

Weed, R. and T. Field (2001). *The Rehabilitation Consultant's Handbook.* Athens, GA: Elliot and Fitzpatrick, Inc.

Weed, R. (2009). Life Care Planning and Case Management Handbook. Boca Raton, FL: CRC Press.

Yudkoff, M. (2002). "The Life Care Plan Expert," In *Legal Nurse Consulting: Principals And Practice, Second Edition,* Boca Raton, FL: CRC Press, 867-894.

Journal of Life Care Planning
Elliott & Fitzpatrick
Managing Editor: Ms. Debbie Berens
1156 Master Lane
Snellville, GA 30078
770.978.9212
770.972.6112 (fax)
http://www.elliottfitzpatrick.com/jlcp.html

Journal of Nurse Life Care Planning
Published by American Association of Nurse Life Care Planners
3267 East 3300 South #309
Salt Lake City, UT 84109
888-575-4047
http://aanlcp.org/Journal.html

Chapter 13

The Role of the Forensic Economist in Nursing Malpractice Actions

Frank D. Tinari, PhD

13.1 Introduction

Forensic economists are often called upon to express their opinions regarding the pecuniary harm or damage incurred by an individual who is bringing suit as a result of a nursing malpractice claim. This chapter explores the many ways in which attorneys use a forensic economist during various stages of a case. For example, forensic economists are commonly contacted only in the last phases of a case, but such a strategy may be shortsighted. It may appear to be a reasonable and rational use of an attorney's time and a client's resources, but it may not make optimum use of the economist's services on behalf of the client. This chapter also addresses the selection of a forensic economist, what information the economist should be given, ethical concerns in using an economist and how to maximize the economist's contribution to a case.

13.2 What Can the Forensic Economist Contribute to Your Case?

A. In Initial Stages of Litigation

One of the first questions a plaintiff's attorney ponders in deciding on a proposed case is, "Does the case have sufficient economic value to justify the time and resources?" After hearing the facts of a case from a potential client, experienced plaintiff's attorneys are able to make a decision about the valuation of the case. Their experience with comparable cases and outcomes regarding proof of liability and the value of ultimate damages often allows them to estimate the value of a proposed case. This is also true of defense attorneys and insurance agents who see numerous complaints and know the history of their disposition. However, because each case is unique, there may be aspects of damages that require careful consideration and reflection before valuating a case. For those cases, a forensic economist should be consulted in the early stages of the litigation to assist either party in determining the magnitude of the economic damages.

B. In Settlement Negotiations

In some cases, settlement negotiations occur relatively early. It would be valuable to know the economist's valuation of damages before proceeding with settlement talks. From the plaintiff's perspective, this ensures any settlement would not appreciably underestimate the damages. Conversely, the defendant wants to know that its offer does not exceed the value of damages. Intangible damages must be accounted for in final negotiations in addition to economic damages. Knowing the economic damages component is a critical part of the picture and should not be treated lightly.

C. In Later Stages of Litigation

1. Preparation of full report

The parties must detail the damages, assuming a case proceeds normally. At this point, a forensic economist is engaged to prepare a full damages report. The preparation of this report requires that both the client and counsel work closely with the economist to ensure all relevant facts are communicated and considered, and that the theory of the case is properly reflected.

2. Role of the forensic economist for defendants

Forensic economists working for defendants often respond to the plaintiff expert's damages valuation. This provides a good check on the reasonableness of the opposing expert's methodology and assumptions. Such work by economists hired by defendants is frequently performed behind the scenes on a consultative basis and without the defendant naming, or revealing the usage of, the expert. Rebuttal reports focus on weaknesses in the plaintiff's report and suggest areas of questioning the plaintiff's expert at deposition or trial. Sometimes, defendants will engage the services of a forensic economist before any expert report is rendered by the plaintiff's economist, because the defendant wants to know the approximate magnitude of the potential pecuniary exposure. This engagement may occur for purposes of settlement negotiations or to determine if the full value of an insurance policy should be granted to a plaintiff.

13.3 How to Select a Forensic Economist

Before discussing the particulars of a forensic economist's report, it is worthwhile to explore the process of identifying and retaining a credible forensic economist.

A. Sources of Information

Attorneys have various means to locate economic experts. Some attorneys contact reputable universities, use expert directories and organizational membership lists as filtering devices and refer to advertisements placed in bar association publications. The Internet is of increasing importance. Many damage experts now maintain websites that reveal information about their experience and capabilities. Good sources of experts include trial lawyers groups, continuing legal education seminars, and bar seminars featuring forensic economists. At these sessions, attorneys determine the experts' knowledge, views, and speaking abilities. However, the majority of attorneys seek out colleagues with experience with particular experts. Attorneys rely on the firsthand knowledge of their compatriots because an economic expert could be deposed or required to testify at trial. Such testimony is critical to explain economic damages, so a reliable and credible expert is needed.

B. Importance of Competence and Credibility

1. The ideal economic expert

"In addition to being a skilled economist, the economics expert must exude confidence, be empathetic, sincere, and convincing. He must be able to explain difficult economic concepts in simple, concise, ordinary English and, most importantly, present a credible report by reasonable economic assumptions."[1] A few suggestions on how to locate such a person follow.

2. Competence and credibility of potential experts

Regardless of the method of obtaining the names of potential economic experts, attorneys should ensure the expert will be both competent and credible. Thus, an initial request should be made of the expert to obtain:

- a curriculum vitae or résumé
- a list of his or her publications
- a list of cases in which the expert has been deposed or has testified at trial
- a list of law firms and attorneys who have used the expert's services
- a sample (redacted) report.

Determine if the expert works solely or predominantly for one side in litigated matters. A "hired gun" who works only one side can be discredited. Attorneys are sometimes tempted to hire such experts with the belief that a loss value closer to their stated position will be generated, a shortsighted perspective that might help in some cases but could be detrimental in others. Federal rules require testifying experts to provide a list of all their deposition and trial testimony appearances during the preceding four years, thus offering an opportunity to find conflicting testimony.

TIP: Once materials are obtained from a forensic economist, the attorney should examine the expert's background, credentials, and experience. Does the expert possess a terminal degree in his or her field? Does the expert have experience in litigated matters? Has the expert published in the fields of forensic economics or labor economics? What do other attorneys say about the expert's testimony, work, and responsiveness to requests and deadlines? Attorneys should also carefully read the economist's sample report. Is it clearly written? Are there typographical errors? Does the expert have good command of the English language?

---

3. Competency and credibility guidelines set by federal case law

Federal case law has generated some classic findings regarding the acceptability of experts at trial, cited in many subsequent opinions. One of the important cases is *Daubert*.[2] Judicial opinion in that case identified several tests of the worthiness and acceptability of an expert's opinion. These were elaborated upon and solidified in the *Kumho Tire* case.[3] The expert's work must be found acceptable to professional peers, use a tested methodology that lies within the mainstream of the profession, adopt reasonable assumptions and provide evidence of the range of error in the expert's findings. The standard of credible testimony requires that the expert abide by high professional standards and be objective, careful and current in the work provided.

4. Caveats about competency and credibility: guidelines for forensic economists

Economic expertise straddles the worlds of pure science and applied practice. Applied economics is a science and an art, meaning that economic damages calculations are not purely scientific because the work cannot be replicated statistically or in the laboratory. It is unclear to what extent economic damages opinions will be subjected to *Daubert* or *Kumho Tire* challenges. These case guidelines apply in federal litigation, but may or may not be invoked in state jurisdictions. Nevertheless, the ideal expert economist must be knowledgeable in his field, experienced in litigation and seen as independent and objective. For more information about the selection of a qualified forensic economist, see Martin[4] and Gilbreath and Gilbreath.[5]

C. Cost Considerations

1. Different viewpoints on cost considerations

Costs should be explored once the attorney decides upon an expert. Attorneys have varying opinions on how expert fees affect the selection of an expert. One view is that the best expert should be retained notwithstanding costs. Another view is that costs should remain low because they can easily escalate and subtract from the total case value. Keeping costs low should be considered if the plaintiff is fully responsible for such costs and is already suffering economic deprivation.

TIP: Even if the attorney assumes costs in the hope of repayment from a settlement or award, the possibility of loss means cost consciousness should be considered.

---

2. Further consideration of cost issues

The two aforementioned views are closer than one would think since competitive pressures price services and rates comparably. While markets are imperfect and negotiation exists, the market rule applies in only broad terms. Obtaining cost estimates and hourly fees from several experts would help the final decision. However, asking the expert to wait for recompense until a settlement or award, even if agreeable to the expert, is inadvisable and may be unethical. (Ethical issues in connection with the use of a forensic economist are discussed in Section 13.5.)

D. Formalization of Agreement to Retain Services

Once the attorney is satisfied with the economist's background, education, experience and fees, retention of a forensic economist comes as a letter or formal contract with a written retainer agreement. The majority of matters in which the author has been retained involved a simple letter stating the work to be done, date of completion, and expected fees.

TIP: Before retaining the expert, the attorney should ask the expert about conflicts of interest, and ascertain if the expert has been approached by opposing counsel.

13.4 What to Provide to the Economist
A. Information to be Provided to the Economist

Experienced forensic economists often provide attorneys with a questionnaire completed by the plaintiff or plaintiff's counsel. The questionnaire elicits factual information necessary for the calculation of damages, such as the plaintiff's or patient's name, date of birth, date of incident, educational attainment, pre-incident health status, employment and earnings history and other relevant information. Provide support for all facts by corroborating documents such as school transcripts or diplomas, employment personnel files, income tax returns, and fringe benefit and pension plan booklets. Attorneys should also give the expert a copy of the complaint to offer background information concerning the sequence of events and the litigation parties.

Any available answers to interrogatories and deposition transcripts should also be given to the forensic economist. If an employability or vocational expert has been engaged and has issued a report about an individual impaired because of alleged nursing malpractice, the economist need not be provided with medical reports. The vocational expert should have reviewed these documents and incorporated data into the vocational evaluation report. (See Chapter 11, *Vocational Evaluations in Nursing Malpractice Cases.*) Many documents focus upon proof of causation, but the causation documents would be unhelpful because the economist is concerned only with calculation of damages.

B. Coordination with Other Experts

Economic experts' work must be coordinated with that of other experts used in a case. In addition to the vocational expert, a life care planner may be involved in nursing malpractice cases with significant injuries. (See Chapter 12, *Life Care Planning.*) If so, the life care plan should be provided to the forensic economist, who determines the present dollar value of its components. Moreover, the economist may question aspects of the life care plan, which sometimes results in modified or clarified details in a plan prepared by the life care planner.

C. Allowing Sufficient Time for Analysis

All of this assumes adequate time has been allotted the economist to review documents and communicate with the vocational and life care plan experts. As settlement negotiations proceed, some attorneys delay hiring the economist in order to minimize costs. Unfortunately, this pressures the expert to quickly complete the damages report, thereby leading to poor research and preparation. This is especially true in cases in which the economist desires an interview with the client. The author has conducted personal interviews in a relatively small number of cases. Personal interviews occur in cases in which few other experts have been involved or in which the economist's fact-finding questionnaire has not been adequately completed by the plaintiff.

TIP: Allow adequate time for the forensic economist's report preparation. Unexpected aspects of the calculation of damages could require longer than anticipated fact-finding, research, or analysis.

13.5 Ethical Dimensions of Using an Expert Economist
A. Need for Neutrality in Forensic Economic Testimony

1. Adversarial nature of civil lawsuits

Ethical issues arise in the use of any expert in litigation, but the discussion here focuses upon use of the expert economist. By their nature, civil lawsuits are adversarial. Our society trusts that the truth will ultimately prevail because both sides have opportunities to examine each other's facts and positions (motions, depositions, interrogatory questions, etc.) and opposing views will be presented both in writing and at trial.

2. The intended role of the forensic economist in litigation

Difficulties arise when the plaintiff's attorney presses the economist for the largest possible economic damages valuation or defense counsel pressures the expert for the lowest possible loss figure. By "managing" the expert's opinion, the attorney uses the adversarial process to its fullest extent; but the expert's approach is different. The forensic economist, as an expert, is responsible for developing the most accurate value of damages able to be generated, using the latest acceptable methods and data sources, as applied to the facts of a particular case. Whether hired by the plaintiff or defense, the expert should adhere to the principles of economics, not adversarial principles.

3. Effects of unethical behavior

This conflict of perspectives can lead to partial corruption of the economist's role. In the extreme, an expert selects certain values, rates and other aspects of the calculations to generate an extremely low (for the defense) or high (for the plaintiff) value of damages. Such experts become known to bar members and work almost exclusively for one side or the other. Attorneys using these experts know that the majority of cases depend on the damages figure to arrive at a settlement more favorable to their client. The problem is that attorneys do not know particular cases will settle and are exposed to the full litigation process, including an adversary's detailed examination of their expert's opinion.

4. The importance of the forensic economist's reputation

Many forensic economists, when asked to generate a particular value of losses, are put in an uncomfortable situation. With training and experience in the application of forensic economic methodology, it becomes difficult to change or even bend the rules to achieve a targeted outcome. Forensic economists are concerned not only about the case, but also their reputation and credibility should their opinions be scrutinized by forensic economists hired by the opposing party. The most valuable asset a forensic economist possesses, and which should be protected, is her reputation. If such an expert were disqualified by a court, or even bested by the logic and methodological standards of an opposing expert, it could be circulated among the bar and reduce the use of that expert. It is in the long-term interests of forensic economists to resist the pressures some attorneys might place on them regarding the valuation of damages.

5. Room for differences in opinion

There is room for differences of interpretation, application, and ultimate conclusions. As mentioned earlier, forensic economics is an art and a science. Differences of opinion among economic experts are inevitable. Consider the case of a permanently impaired plaintiff for whom further employment is not expected. The economic damages reports involve a calculation of the plaintiff's future losses, such as what incremental wage growth should be adopted in such a projection. Alternative bases in the rate's selection exist. The damages calculation may differ, depending on the rate used by the forensic economist. Similarly, in calculating the value of lost household services, the economist adopts some measure of the value of a decedent's or plaintiff's pre-impairment services. Depending on what has been told to the economist, the value of such services could also differ.

6. Focus of defense work

Experts retained by the defense are often asked to review the plaintiff expert's report and to render an opinion on the acceptability of the methods and calculations. In such cases, the defense expert is not rendering an independent valuation of damages but is providing a rebuttal commentary to the plaintiff's report and its findings. Therefore, the economist working for a defendant may not need to comment upon every element of damages or specify which methods used are acceptable. Rather, the focus is criticism of weaknesses in the plaintiff expert's report.

7. Court-appointed expert

Under Federal Rule of Evidence 706, the judge appoints an expert when data or methodologies employed by opposing experts significantly differ. Although this rarely occurs, the availability of this option has a sobering effect on the work and economic testimony of the prudent expert.

B. Information is Discoverable

Virtually all notes during telephone conversations and documents given to the expert are discoverable in court jurisdictions. Other than certain forms of privileged communication (on case or trial strategy) between the attorney and expert, all evidence and information evaluated by the expert can be examined by opposing counsel, either upon request for production or at deposition of the expert. The economist should have nothing to hide since such information exists. Nevertheless, attorneys sometimes fear information in the expert's possession may harm their side's position. These attorneys might be tempted to remove documents from the expert's file, a very dangerous act because it could lead to impeachment of the expert's opinion. It is a case of short-term expediency being traded against potential harm to the expert's reputation. The attorney should be careful about what is said and given to the expert. In this way, there is no basis for fearing the production of discovery.

C. Ethical Concerns Regarding Payment of Fees

Another area of concern is payment of fees, which should occur promptly by the retaining attorney. A retainer deposit is typically sent with the initial retention agreement and documents. Upon completion of a report, the expert submits an invoice for remaining monies owed. A payment dispute can escalate into an ethical problem at the point of deposition or trial. The expert should never be put in a position in which payment is dependent on her testimony. Economic experts quickly learn to say they are being paid for time and not content of opinions. It is in the interests of both the attorney and client to ensure the economist will speak truthfully about methods and opinions. Opposing counsel typically inquires about fees, payments and outstanding balances due, which is why this author, like many colleagues, insists on full payment of expected fees before taking the stand at trial.

TIP: The economist is under oath to tell the truth and should not be swayed by financial considerations.

D. Professional Codes of Conduct

The economics profession does not issue certifications. Organizations such as the National Association of Forensic Economics have developed and published statements of ethical principles for members. (The Association's statement and that of the American Academy of Economic and Financial Experts are shown in Figure 13.1 and Figure 13.2, respectively.)

13.6 Dimensions of Economic Damages
A. Damages Vary from Case to Case

Nursing malpractice cases vary in the medical and physical impairments (or death) that are the subjects of litigation. Persons who become impaired differ by age, sex, race, educational attainment, geographic region, work history, earnings, fringe benefits, pensions and medical care costs among others. Hence, economic damages vary with the particulars in each case. Nevertheless, it is possible to identify the general components of economic damages calculated by the forensic economist.

B. The Attorney is the Guide to the Components of Loss

Before exploring these components, one caveat is in order. The hiring attorney is responsible for guiding the economist with respect to the elements of loss. This author has experienced an attorney advising the expert, for strategic or legal reasons, to exclude certain components of damages that otherwise appear reasonable for the case at hand. It is perfectly legitimate for the economic expert to carry out his analysis on that basis. Conversely, what seems to be a reasonable adjustment in the analysis might not be legal. Thus, experts are required to follow the law and make appropriate accommodations in their loss appraisals.

C. Net Earnings Losses

1. What earnings losses involve

Most damages reports incorporate measures of earnings losses for working adults, or projected earnings losses of an impaired youngster. In some states, loss of earnings can even be calculated for a full-time homemaker with no recent employment history. The economist develops estimates of lifetime earnings based on reasonable assumptions about the expected educational attainment for infants and children. This is typically a function of the educational attainment of the child's parents as well as the child's pre-impairment school performance or abilities.

2. How net earnings loss is determined
a. Worklife and unemployment adjustments

"Net" in the phrase "net earnings loss" refers to various adjustments, both positive and negative, made by the forensic economist before arriving at an accurate measure of earnings losses. Apply worklife expectancy data to determine a reasonable number of years over which the plaintiff or decedent would have been employed had malpractice not occurred. Worklife expectancy statistics reflect that people leave the labor force, temporarily or permanently, for voluntary and involuntary reasons. Such data reveals that a 35-year-old who becomes impaired is unlikely to have been in the labor force for a continuous period of an additional 30 years until retirement. Another adjustment takes into account the future probability of unemployment due to work stoppages, temporary shutdowns, or other reasons causing unemployment of workers.

b. Income tax and fringe benefits adjustments

Another adjustment consists of subtraction of income tax liabilities in federal court cases and those state court jurisdictions that specify subtraction of taxes. "With reference to Social Security and federal employee retirement taxes, these should not be deducted as they may be viewed as a type of deferred wage, giving rise to a later purchased benefit, similar to any other type of private insurance."[6] Yet another adjustment takes into account the pecuniary value of various non-wage forms of compensation, referred to as fringe benefits. These benefits vary, but typically include one or more of the following employer-funded elements: pension benefit, 401(k) retirement plan, stock-savings plan, life insurance coverage, disability insurance, medical care insurance, dental insurance, prescription plan coverage, tuition payment, and company automobile. The forensic economist requests details about fringe benefits previously received by plaintiff or decedent and inquires about any such benefits continuing after the incident, thereby estimating a replacement value for lost benefits.

When providing expert opinion for use as evidence by the trier of fact, a NAFE member pledges, as a condition of membership, adherence to the following:

1. Engagement

Practitioners of forensic economics should decline involvement in any litigation when they are asked to assume invalid representations of fact or alter their methodologies without foundation or compelling analytical reason.

2. Compensation

Practitioners of forensic economics should not accept contingency fee arrangements, or fee amounts associated with the size of a court award or out-of-court settlement.

3. Diligence, Objectivity and Accuracy

Practitioners of forensic economics should employ generally accepted and/or theoretically sound economic methodologies based on reliable economic data. Practitioners of forensic economics should attempt to provide accurate, fair and reasonable expert opinions, recognizing that it is not the responsibility of the practitioner to verify the accuracy or completeness of the case-specific information that has been provided.

4. Disclosure

Practitioners of forensic economics should stand ready to provide sufficient detail to allow replication of all numerical calculations, with reasonable effort, by other competent forensic economics experts, and be prepared to provide sufficient disclosure of sources of information and assumptions underpinning their opinions to make them understandable to others.

5. Consistency

While it is recognized that practitioners of forensic economics may be given a different assignment when engaged on behalf of the plaintiff than when engaged on behalf of the defense, for any given assignment, the basic assumptions, sources, and methods should not change regardless of the party who engages the expert to perform the assignment. There should be no change in methodology for purposes of favoring any party's claim. This requirement of consistency is not meant to preclude methodological changes as new knowledge evolves, nor is it meant to preclude performing requested calculations based upon a hypothetical—as long as its hypothetical nature is clearly disclosed in the expert's report and testimony.

6. Knowledge

Practitioners of forensic economics should strive to maintain a current knowledge base of their discipline.

7. Discourse

Open, uninhibited discussion is a desired educational feature of academic and professional forensic economic conferences. Therefore, to preserve and protect the educational environment, practitioners of forensic economics will refrain from the citation of oral remarks made in an educational environment, without permission from the speaker.

8. Responsibility

Practitioners of forensic economics are encouraged to make known the existence of, and their adherence to, these principles to those retaining them to perform economic analyses and to other participants in litigation. In addition, it is appropriate for practitioners of forensic economics to offer criticisms of breaches of these principles.

Note: The NAFE board established this statement as a condition of membership in NAFE effective October 1, 2004.

Figure 13.1 *Statement of Ethical Principles and Principles of Professional Practice. National Association of Forensic Economics (NAFE). Reprinted with permission.*

The AAEFE Statement of Disclosure

The board of directors and the members of the American Academy of Economic and Financial Experts have adopted the following statement of disclosure:

The Statement of Disclosure
The American Academy of Economics and Financial Experts encourages its members to clearly state sources of information and material assumptions leading to their options. Such disclosure should be in sufficient detail to allow identification of specific sources relied upon and replication of the analytical conclusions by a competent economist with reasonable effort.

Figure 13.2 *AAEFE Statement of Disclosure. First published in the* Journal of Legal Economics, *Vol. 5, No. 3, Winter 1995. Reprinted with permission.*

c. Job maintenance expenses and personal consumption adjustments

Individuals permanently disabled from employment are entitled to another adjustment for job-related expenses. Before arriving at a net loss to surviving family members, the economist identifies a deduction for personal consumption or, in some states, maintenance expenses of a decedent had she lived.[7] While a detailed explanation of adjustments to earnings is beyond the scope of this chapter, forensic economists are expected to be aware of the ongoing research on their measurement and the data sources relied upon in making these adjustments. Any economist's report ignoring one or more of these is subject to critical and effective scrutiny and cross-examination by opposing counsel.

d. Legal requirements

Forensic economists must be familiar with the legal parameters permitting or prohibiting damages calculations within the jurisdiction of the venued case. For instance, New York court rules require subtraction of income tax liabilities from projected earnings losses in medical malpractice, but not accidental injury, cases.

D. Loss of Ability to Perform Household Services

1. General statements about loss of services

Courts have long recognized that an impaired individual and his family may suffer a loss of ability to perform services at home. Numerous studies have measured the quantity of such services, subdivided by family and demographic characteristics. These studies aid economists in measuring the value of lost services with a fair degree of accuracy. Household services should be included in the economic appraisal report of losses in most malpractice cases unless there are overriding reasons for ignoring them.

2. Evaluating the loss of services

Figuring the value of this loss component entails several steps. The expert should be given information about the plaintiff's household activities before impairment along with a list of activities no longer performed after impairment. In some instances, the inability to perform household services will change over the post-impairment period, and needs to be identified and estimated carefully.

3. Use of household data research

The estimates of hours of services performed pre- and post-impairment should be checked against statistical studies describing the experience of thousands of households in various profiles (e.g., with both spouses working, only one income-earner, households with and without dependent children). The analyst assures that the plaintiff's reported numbers are within national norms, or that there are good reasons for a discrepancy. An hourly rate is applied to the reduced hours of services to determine pecuniary value. Economists differ in their selection of the appropriate rate. Some select the rate of a paid homemaker, others use the minimum wage and still others use the average hourly rate in the services sector industry. The attorney should check that a reasonable basis and explanation are given in the report, without which the report is subject to criticism by the opposition.

4. Controversies surrounding valuation of household services

Attorneys should be aware of the controversies surrounding valuation of household services. One issue concerns the scope of the term. Should child care, guidance and counsel to family members or time spent together in various activities be included? Courts answer these questions differently, so the forensic economist must be made aware of the legal parameters in which the analysis is undertaken.[8] Judges sometimes disallow a lost services claim for years leading up to the trial if the person or family has not expended funds on replacing lost services. Economists see this as untenable since individuals, more often than not, have had income reductions subsequent to impairment and fewer resources to pay extra household assistance. Economists recognize that the person or family has suffered a real loss (i.e., either in money or actual services lost) and compensation is required proportionately.[9,10] Another issue concerns the time period over which this loss is calculated. Economists generally use the plaintiff's life expectancy notwithstanding impairment, but many make downward adjustments to account for reduced vitality in later years.

E. Valuation of Life Care Plan Costs

1. General statement about the valuation of life care plan costs

By far the largest component of damages in serious medical malpractice cases is the cost of lifetime care of the victim, sometimes running into the millions of dollars. Good medical care entails costly treatments, medications and specialized personnel. As noted in Chapter 12, *Life Care Planning*, these are typically specified in a life care plan detailing each form of therapy, procedure or treatment, and frequency and duration. The job of the forensic economist is to translate these specifications into annual costs and total cost for all care components combined.

2. Critical tasks facing the economist

Two critical tasks facing the economist in this process are the identification of an application of appropriate growth rates anticipated for the future and an appropriate interest or discount rate to reduce future values to present dollar value. This varies from state to state. Pennsylvania requires total offset, applying identical growth and discount rates; New York requires no discounting to present value in the damages portion of the case. (Reduction to present value is done in a separate post-trial hearing, in accordance with New York State Court Rules.) All federal courts and the majority of state jurisdictions require growth and discount procedures. The challenge to the analyst is to ascertain appropriate growth rates for each type of expenditure within a life care plan. For example, transportation costs have exhibited a different pattern of annual increase than that of medical costs.

To apply the same anticipated growth rates to both may be difficult to justify.

3. Presentation of life care plan costs

The forensic economist provides a monetary tabulation of the elements of the life care plan, presented in both annual value and lifetime totals, explaining all methodological assumptions adopted in converting the life care plan information to dollar value. If this component of damages is combined with others, such as a claim for lost earnings and household services, the forensic economist reviews the total picture of damages to ensure double counting has not occurred. If 24-hour care in an institutional setting is needed for a severely impaired individual, it is inappropriate to incorporate an additional claim for lost household services because all food, cleaning, and other services are included in the care setting. See Tinari[11] for a detailed description of this potential problem.

13.7 If the Case Does Not Settle
A. What Happens if the Case Does Not Settle?

Opposing counsel may depose and question the expert on the basis for opinions contained in the report. If the case is not settled after completing all discovery of documents and taking depositions, the expert may be called upon to testify at trial. Further collaboration is needed between the attorney and testifying expert at this stage.

B. Distinction Between Plaintiff and Defense Strategies

Distinguish between plaintiff and defense strategies with respect to use of the damages expert. Defense attorneys will infrequently call their damages expert to testify because they fear (1) it is an implicit admission that damages have been suffered by the plaintiff, and (2) presenting a value of losses, even if lower than the plaintiff's expert, gives the jury an easy way of calculating damages by averaging the two loss estimates. Not all defense strategies concur with this approach, so the economist may be called upon to testify, whether working for plaintiff or defense counsel.

C. Preparing for Trial

1. Providing trial developments to the economist

The attorney should provide the expert with relevant information on trial developments because the economist will be among the last experts to testify. If insufficient testimony is presented about the plaintiff's inability to perform household services, plaintiff's counsel may advise deleting any reference to such services in the presentation of damages to the trier of fact. Similarly, other salient facts may be unknown by the economic expert while preparing her report. Such information must be provided to the expert, who then modifies her opinion regarding damages and readily explains them at trial. At the very least, the economist needs to update all calculations at the time of trial. In the majority of cases, pre-trial losses must be expanded to include the time up to the trial date. This procedure typically creates a modest change in the ultimate opinion of losses, except when several years have passed.

2. Making the economist's testimony understandable to a jury

Another concern counsel may have is making the economist's testimony understandable to a jury. There is a great fear juries are incapable of understanding techniques and calculations used by economists. A long-winded explanation with a litany of charts and numbers may put the jury to sleep, defeating the purpose of the testimony. The attorney should consult the plentiful resources on how to make the best use of experts.

3. Brevity

Brevity means the questions and responses should be focused and to the point, particularly responses with numerical values. If allowed by the court, the expert's testimony should be a continuous narrative explanation to the jury rather than a question-answer format.

4. Clarity

Creative presentation skills are required to communicate detailed numbers effectively. The use of computer presentations, overhead transparencies and preprinted blown-up charts are effective techniques. Instead of spending time writing out the years and corresponding values, the economist can more effectively explain to the jury what the numbers represent and how they were calculated. Advance preparation is required if the economic expert plans to use supporting graphics. When using transparencies, for example, tables, graphs, and charts must be extracted from the expert's report and formatted and copied onto transparency material. With enlarged charts, the text and charts must be prepared on clean copy and sent out for enlargement.

TIP: Attorneys should give experts enough lead-time to prepare supporting materials needed for testimony. These need revision if done too far in advance, so timing is critical. In addition, the attorney should ensure the courtroom has appropriate technology and equipment to facilitate the presentation of demonstrative evidence.

5. Effective expert witnessing

The attorney should invest time to prepare questions and review the expert's testimony before trial, especially if the attorney is not experienced in directing the testimony of financial and economic experts. These extra investments of time and resources create more effective expert witnessing and, hopefully, a favorable outcome.

13.8 Summary

The forensic economist plays a significant and vital role in the effective demonstration of damages in civil nursing malpractice litigation. The integrity of the forensic economist's work is maintained through adherence to the principles of the discipline. Taking on an adversarial role risks the forensic economist's reliability, credibility, and effectiveness. Because expert reputation is so important, the forensic economist should be motivated to recognize ethical standards and procedures to prevent impeachment and discredit.

Attorneys provide forensic economists with full information about the case and allow sufficient time for the completion of the research, analysis, and report preparation required. Coordination with other experts is often necessary in order to build the proper foundation for the calculation of damages by the forensic economist.

Economic losses suffered by a particular plaintiff must be tailored to the circumstances of that individual. Lost earnings or earnings capacity claims must incorporate various adjustments, some of which are worklife expectancy, probability of unemployment, income tax liabilities, fringe benefits, job maintenance expenses, and, in death cases, personal consumption expenditures or personal maintenance expenses. Loss of services is often included in nursing malpractice actions and calculation must use personal circumstances and published data. The cost of life care plans in many nursing malpractice cases must be tallied and valued by the forensic economist. Be sure not to double-count losses in serious impairment cases since life care plans incorporate the patient's day-to-day household care, nutrition and utilities among others.

The services provided by forensic economists vary depending on the strategies pursued by the plaintiff's attorney or defense counsel. For trial testimony, the economic expert should be provided with updated information, particularly when reports were rendered an appreciable time prior to trial. The forensic economist should make his presentation with clarity and brevity, working closely with counsel in the preparation of testimony.

Endnotes

1. Gilbreath, K. and R. Gilbreath, "Working together: some practical advice for lawyers and forensic economists," *Litigation Economics Digest* 4, no. 1 (Spring 1999): 40.

2. *Daubert v. Merrell Dow Pharmaceuticals, Inc.*, 509 U.S. 579 (1993).

3. *Kumho Tire Co., Ltd. v. Carmichael*, 526 U.S. 137 (1999).

4. Martin, G., *Determining Economic Damages*. Costa Mesa, California: James Publishing, Inc., 2009, Ch. 1.

5. See note 1.

6. Slesinger, R., "How economists can help in litigation involving personal injury, death, or discrimination," *Journal of Legal Economics* 1, no. 1 (March 1991): 68–74.

7. Ireland, T. and T. Depperschmidt, *Assessing Family Loss in Wrongful Death Litigation: The Special Roles of Lost Services and Personal Consumption*. Tucson, Arizona: Lawyers & Judges Publishing Co., 1999.

8. Tinari, F., "Household Services: Toward a More Comprehensive Measure," (article reprint) In R. T. Kaufman, J. D. Rodgers and G. D. Martin, *Economic Foundations of Injury and Death Damages*. Edward Elgar Publishing Ltd., 2005.

9. See note 4.

10. See note 7.

11. Tinari, F., "Do we double-count damages in severe personal injury cases?" *Journal of Legal Economics* 5, no. 2 (Fall 1995): 23–32.

Part IV:

Litigation of Nursing Malpractice Claims

Chapter 14

Screening the Nursing Malpractice Case

David Cohen, Esq.

14.1 Introduction

For well over a decade, personal injury litigation involving nurses has consistently been increasing. Although the largest component of this trend involves nursing home litigation, other areas likewise contribute. With the advent of managed health care, there came a precipitous decrease in physician care and a concomitant increase in nursing involvement in multiple areas of discipline.

Both plaintiffs and plaintiff's attorneys have become much more sensitized and proficient in outlining very specific allegations against multiple healthcare providers, including nurses. There are additional realities of litigation lending a hand toward this increase. Many institutions, including nursing homes and hospitals, have either significant self-insured retentions or operate without outside insurance coverage. For cases that do involve or might involve such issues, plaintiff's attorneys typically individually name nurse defendants where historically they might have simply named the institution as the sole direct defendant. This places nurses in a precarious situation with regard to continued insurance coverage beyond the litigation at hand. It also places the nurses potentially at odds with the institutions that are their employers, or contracted places of employment when serving as agency nurses or independent contractors.

When addressing nursing malpractice cases, both the plaintiff and defense attorney should engage in serious, honest introspection to determine whether they are the right people to do this kind of work. The personal injury attorney who has never handled a medical malpractice case may ultimately be better served by referring the case to an experienced medical malpractice attorney. Many attorneys rush in where angels fear to tread and live to regret the day. This area of litigation grows increasingly complex with regard to the medical issues. It involves the interplay of local statutory schemes and their relationship to regulations, policies, and procedures, and the interactions with accreditation-related guidelines, such as The Joint Commission. Gone are the days when nursing experts could base their opinions solely on the general standard of care in the community. Rather, experts in the modern arena of nursing negligence litigation must develop an intimate familiarity with the interplay of standards, regulations, and the like.

One must also keep in mind that much of health care has shifted to the outpatient arena or home care, so that injuries in a same-day surgery unit, falls at home, and falls at adult daycare-type facilities will occur. In each of these venues, the nursing milieu predominates.

14.2 Who Suffered Harm?

As simple as it may initially seem, the process of determining who the plaintiffs are can be quite vexing. Just as difficult is the issue of which individuals might have standing to assert claims on behalf of injured parties.

When the injured party is a minor, parents generally serve as guardian ad litem. There are occasions, though, when the court wants or needs to appoint an independent guardian, typically an attorney. This can occur when a conflict of interest arises or when the judgment of the parents appears to be antithetical to the interests of the child.

When the injured party is a mentally competent adult, the assessment is much simpler. However, keep in mind that per quod claims recorded during the intake phase of a case are anything but simple when divorce or separation occurs during its pendency.

Significant challenges arise in situations involving declining physical or cognitive health and cases that involve an injured party who died intestate (i.e., without a will).

TIP: Preparing and maintaining an enforceable set of healthcare power of attorney and durable power of attorney documents speeds the process of opening and investigating claims. Similarly, developing a streamlined system to establish an estate representative, by way of direct estate work or contacts with a qualified estate attorney, helps to accomplish this same end.

A. Current and Pre-Existing Physical and Mental Conditions

For injured parties living at the time the case is either investigated or prosecuted, significant physical or mental disabilities may ultimately prevent an attorney's ability to prepare and enforce a power of attorney, as a consequence of the injured party's inability to appoint a trusted individual for this position. Equally difficult and ethically challenging is the situation where the injured party's mental acuity is limited, but without a judicial determination as to its extent. In such circumstances, the practitioner must be keenly aware of these issues and of potential infirmities in a power of attorney, if and when it is prepared.

In most jurisdictions, the process involved in achieving a court determination that a cognitively incapacitated individual is mentally incompetent and, accordingly, having a guardian appointed, can take as long as the underlying tort litigation that occasioned the need for such a guardian to be appointed. All of this is likewise problematic in light of the time it takes to investigate a claim prior to the expiration of the appropriate statute of limitations. It is important to carefully review with all family members whether or not there might exist a valid power of attorney prepared before the time of cognitive impairment.

B. Relationship to Patient

1. Family member/next of kin

In many jurisdictions litigation can be initiated by an individual with documentation confirming next of kin status. However, this is not a sufficient position to allow that individual to administer the estate or otherwise distribute assets.

2. Spouse

If the injured party is alive, the gathering of medical records and potentially filing of suit is much simpler if the spouse is also alive. In the event the injured party is deceased either at the time the case is established or at any point prior to disbursements, Medicaid estate liens may not be enforceable if there is a surviving spouse of the victim. This information is very important as oftentimes such liens can exceed the full value of a claim. Additionally, if the injured party is deceased and dies intestate, the surviving spouse should not have a difficult time obtaining the proper papers relative to the estate.

3. Legal guardian

As noted, the process of obtaining a legal guardian can be problematic in the event there is a living plaintiff who does not possess the cognitive ability to make decisions or otherwise appoint an attorney in fact. Many judges are willing to appoint either a family member or a member of the bar in good standing to serve as an administrator ad prosequendum solely for litigation purposes. By the same token, many judges are not so inclined. Practitioners should be cautious about filing suit without having resolved this issue or otherwise having established a focused plan.

TIP: Develop a clear understanding of your jurisdiction's view concerning the interplay between legal insanity and the tolling of a statute of limitations. Often, family members will approach counsel many years after the care occurred. Do not dismiss the potential of pursuing these out of hand. Rather, examine in great detail the level of mental cognition of the injured party going back to the period of time the incidents occurred up through the present. Quite frequently, injuries may be prosecuted in excess of five years old—even in a two-year statute of limitations jurisdiction.

When it is necessary to pursue a full mental incompetency/legal guardianship case, case manage this with the judge involved in the civil claim that comprises the tort action. Most judges permit these cases to run through the court system concurrently, rather than putting the injured party at risk of sitting on her rights while the other matter proceeds. It is very important to be judicious in the means by which the complaint is captioned when guardianship issues remain unresolved at the time of the filing by way of necessity. Remember that if the relief sought in the guardianship complaint concerning mental competence is denied, the plaintiff faces a res judicata decision that such individual is not mentally incompetent and thus otherwise is subject to a ruling that arguably suggests that individual was at all times capable of pursuing a claim for the injurious conduct of the defendant. Thus, if one waits until the conclusion of the guardianship complaint to file suit and loses the guardianship complaint, that party might be collaterally stopped from even pursuing the underlying claim subsequent to the denial of the guardianship matter.

4. Friend of family

Quite often, a case is brought on behalf of an injured party who has no living or interested relatives. Basically, the same formula follows. If the individual is alive and competent, that person may consider appointing a friend as the power of attorney. If there is a lack of competence, it is certainly more difficult to get a friend appointed as guardian, unless the proven facts of the relationship compel this.

However, with regard to a deceased plaintiff, remember that the appointment of an estate executor or executrix does not necessarily speak to the same issues as to who takes under the laws of in intestacy. Thus, to at least get a case moving, a friend can potentially get appointed as an administrator ad prosequendum prior to the determination as to who

might take under the estate. When such a delicate situation arises, it is important for the attorney prosecuting the injury-related claim not to confuse his ethical duties. Namely, that attorney's ethical obligation is toward the estate, not toward the individual with whom that attorney is working. If under this circumstance any other potential issues arise as to who might take from the proceeds of a personal injury settlement, it is quite prudent to refer disputing family members to other counsel, and at the same time allow the malpractice attorney to focus on the issues within that person's field of specialty.

C. How Often Did the Person or Family Visit the Resident or Patient?

At the screening stage of a case it is very important to determine what type of face will be put on the plaintiff's case. Namely, where there are situations when the plaintiff is either not alive or otherwise incompetent to testify, one must keep a close eye on what type of interest the jury would have in the people who ostensibly speak on behalf of the injured party. In this regard, and most notably when it comes to nursing home cases, it is important to carefully review how frequently the injured party was witnessed by the family members ultimately prosecuting the claim. Although most assisted living facilities and nursing homes maintain visitor logs, it is essential to determine whether or not those logs were truly signed on a regular basis when family members or friends visited. In most of these facilities, the visitors' log is not signed once there is a familiarity between the visiting party and the facility's representatives or front desk staff. If the log is a document that had to be faithfully signed in order to visit the injured party, a family who rarely visited can be painted as mercenary by the defense. On the other hand, families who can clearly be demonstrated as having visited nearly every day often may be seen as wearing the white hat in the litigation when the defendant is an institution such as an assisted living facility or nursing home chain. Additionally, medical records (nurses' notes and social services entries) may comment on the frequency of family visits.

14.3 Injuries and Damages

A careful review of the type of injury being alleged is crucial to the evaluation of a claim. Just as pivotal is critical analysis of all potential breaks in the causation chain between the alleged negligent conduct and the injuries suffered. Very often, plaintiff's attorneys are well into litigation before faced with the sad reality that a causal connection between the negligent conduct and the injury simply cannot be established. Thus, it is essential to address this during the screening stage of the case and not to focus solely on whether or not there was a deviation in the standard of care.

Ultimately, damages can often be much more or less significant than they appear at the time of the original client interview. As is discussed below, by way of just one example, injuries typically seen in assault cases can appear quite horrific, but can resolve completely by the time litigation ensues. On the other hand, what initially presents as a minor concussion can develop into a catastrophic injury with enormous damages. Similarly, the temporal relationship between negligent conduct and an injury does not necessarily confirm there is indeed a medical relationship between the two. Failure to administer medication does not confirm that its administration would have ensured a perfect result. Further, negligent conduct toward a patient with significant comorbidities might ultimately not have anything to do with a bad result, at least in terms of what can be proven by way of medical testimony.

Just as important is the analytical juxtaposition of the potential value of the claim against both liability issues and potential causation defenses. In the end, few cases are clear or perfect from the inception and accordingly require a balanced appraisal of risks versus benefits before investing significant time and money into them.

A. Pressure Ulcers

Pressure ulcer cases have swiftly begun to dominate the legal landscape with regard to nursing negligence claims. Litigation surrounding these injuries crosses the entire spectrum of settings where nurses practice. Namely, pressure ulcers are found in hospital claims, nursing home litigation, assisted living claims, and often are being found for claims which involve visiting nurses at the injured party's own residence. Although the medicine involving pressure ulcer claims is addressed in Chapter 25, *Wounds*, in Volume II, it should be noted that all participants in this area of litigation must develop an intimate familiarity with the ever-changing medical theories surrounding pressure ulcer prevention and treatment. In addition to a potential change in the definitions used by nurses that stage pressure ulcers, new medical concepts are emerging concerning the concept of "deep tissue" injury (pressure creates damage within the tissue, which works its way to the surface).

Pressure ulcers are characterized by four levels of severity: Stage I, II, III and IV. (Refer to Chapter 25, *Wounds*, in Volume II, for definitions.) As a general rule, it is not economically advisable to pursue claims for Stage I or II ulcers. Although they often arise solely as a result of negligence and can lead to pain and suffering, the cost of prosecution might exceed the compensation obtained for the plaintiff. On the other hand, Stage III and IV pressure ulcers are quite dramatic in appearance, have a profound negative impact on the health of patient (including osteomyelitis), and often cause extraordinary pain. Thus, they are worth pursuing and help with the laudable goal of providing an extra layer of incentive for healthcare providers to prevent avoidable pressure ulcers.

This source of damages is extraordinarily important for practitioners who face cases with long timelines of treatment. Often, medically debilitated individuals are on a revolving door from home to hospital, nursing home to hospital, and the like. Under the old paradigm, facilities or providers who discharge an individual without skin interruption would never be named as defendants in a pressure ulcer claim if treatment was demonstrated to have occurred prior to any notable skin interruption. Under the new paradigm, providers or institutions who cared for a patient just prior to the development of even a Stage I pressure ulcer typically are brought into the litigation as a consequence of the unknown status of that individual's skin under the top few layers.

Many cases involve a nursing home receiving an individual directly from a hospital where some minor redness might be noted at that individual's sacrum or heels. Typically, the hospital would not have made any note of these very minor skin integrity issues upon discharge. However, because nursing homes have become much more sensitized to both skin integrity care and litigation issues, even the most minor skin breakdown is typically noted upon admission. What remains a significant question at that precise point in time is what was going on with the deeper layers of tissue for that patient on that day of admission to the nursing home. Quite often, a mere three or four days after admission, that Stage I skin discoloration or irritation eventually opens up to a gaping Stage IV pressure ulcer with slough and osteomyelitis. Many medical and nursing experts will argue that significant damage had already been done before that individual even left the hospital. An unwary plaintiff's attorney might leave the hospital out of the litigation until it is literally too late, by way of the statute of limitations. Thus, for any case involving skin breakdown, it is essential not only to pinpoint the very first day that any form of skin interruption becomes evident in the medical records, but also to examine the medical treatment and the location of that individual just prior to the minor skin breakdown where it first appeared in the medical record.

It is also important to differentiate between pressure ulcers and peripheral vascular lesions, and arterial/venous stasis ulcers. Non-pressure related ulcers more typically arise in the absence of neglect, while liability more commonly attaches to pressure ulcer cases. Be wary of relying solely on the terminology used by nurses to characterize these lesions. A typical practice is to unscientifically refer to stasis ulcers as pressure ulcers. When photographs are available, they must be provided to experts to determine the appropriate classification.

Plaintiff's attorneys should endeavor to obtain photographs and videos of pressure ulcers for all living clients who suffer from them. Defense attorneys often benefit from photographic evidence that demonstrates pressure ulcers were inherited from another facility or treated prior to the time treatment began by that particular defendant. Many nursing homes and hospitals now make it a practice to photograph patients who suffer from pressure ulcers on the first day of their admission to such a facility. This allows defense counsel to clearly demonstrate that the skin integrity difficulties were inherited rather than caused by their clients. Increasingly, healthcare facilities are discouraged from taking photographs of wounds becoming progressively worse within their walls. Defense attorneys are well aware of the impact of these photographs on jurors. Refer to Chapter 25, *Wounds*, in Volume II, and Myers[1] for more on liability and damages.

Liability issues related to the screening of a case include the failure to identify the patient as being at risk for a pressure ulcer, failure to implement preventative measures, failure to use appropriate treatments based upon the stage of the ulcer, failure to seek orders from physicians for changes in treatment plan if the ulcer progresses, failure to implement a multidisciplinary plan of care, failure to report signs of deterioration of an ulcer, and, at times, failure to question or challenge the propriety of a physician's orders. Sources of the standard of care include the Agency for Health Care Research and Quality (AHRQ) or publications on pressure ulcers.[2,3] For TJC-certified facilities, The Joint Commission guidelines are also quite helpful.

TIP: Both plaintiff and defense attorneys should work diligently to obtain all photographic evidence of skin breakdown for pressure ulcer cases.

B. Malnutrition or Dehydration

As the medical portions of this text reveal, many issues in nursing negligence claims are highly interrelated. This probably is most evident when interpreting the interrelationship between skin integrity claims and that of malnutrition or dehydration. Although the latter certainly exist as independent claims, when there is smoke there is, generally, fire. Namely, poor care that permits pressure ulcers to erupt typically involves improper nutrition and hydration practices of facilities caring for otherwise debilitated patients or residents.

A detailed review of charting is essential in claims involving malnutrition or dehydration. Very difficult in this regard are the notoriously inaccurate weight charts taken at hospitals and long-term care facilities. It is not uncommon to see divergence in recorded weight as much as 40 pounds over a one or two day period. This occurs when there is a non-compliant patient; when one cannot properly stand in order to be weighed conventionally; or when the scale is not properly maintained and recalibrated. Additionally, weight is often inaccurately transcribed from one record to another, without any independent verification. What this means is that the attorney or expert reviewing the case involving malnutrition must carefully scrutinize many lines of parallel records to attempt to determine whether or not it is even possible to accurately transcribe an individual's weight throughout a carefully prepared timeline. In a rare case of acute renal failure, after massive fluid resuscitation, a patient may gain a great deal of weight overnight.

It is very difficult to defend cases of tube-fed patients who suffer malnutrition or dehydration. The exception is a properly documented end-of-life related decline or otherwise definable exacerbation of comorbid medical conditions. This results in an unavoidable inability to properly hydrate or nourish someone where the control of that is exclusively with the nurses and other care providers. Typically there is a significant interrelationship between oral feeding related malnutrition or dehydration and that of tube-fed patients. The end-stage Alzheimer's patient often experiences an inability to swallow, resulting in nutritional decline. The most common scenario is that of the individual whose onset of dysphagia (documented difficulty in swallowing) commences a decline in either an ability or willingness to consume sufficient caloric and liquid intake to maintain proper nutritional and hydration status.

Interrelated with this issue is the expected friction between the care providers who might be encouraging implantation of a feeding tube and resistance on the part of family members to accepting this. As the argument ensues, the family will allege the care providers are not taking the (now) increased time it takes to properly feed the resident, while the care providers will allege the family lacks a realistic appreciation for the declining physical health of the patient. Once the malnutrition and dehydration occur after the feeding tube is not initially implanted, the soon-to-be defendant will claim the family allowed this to occur by refusing the feeding tube. The family or plaintiff will allege the defendant simply was looking for an easy way out and did not appropriately ensure proper nutrition and hydration. For cases involving nursing homes, there are very clear regulations contained within the OBRA guidelines noting that a feeding tube should not under any circumstance be implanted unless its use is unavoidable and that the nursing home is otherwise compelled to ensure that an individual receives adequate hydration and nutrition. There is evidence that percutaneous endoscopic gastric (PEG) feeding tubes do not improve nutritional status, reduce aspiration risk, or improve pressure ulcer healing and functional status in patients with advanced dementia.[4]

A proper assessment must occur at the onset of any clinical indicators of malnutrition or dehydration. In the nursing home context, if there is a five percent or more weight loss within 30 days or a ten percent or more weight loss within six months, a full assessment must be completed. Failure to do so would constitute a violation of a nursing home resident's federal rights. However, the same type of standard exists in any institution. Namely, when such clinical signs occur, a proper assessment and change in course of treatment must occur. Dehydration may be manifested by rising sodium levels. The creatinine value and the blood urea nitrogen value may increase with dehydration-associated renal failure. The patient's mouth might be dry. Nursing notes may refer to poor skin turgor, or a tenting effect created when the skin is lifted from the arm. Other signs of dehydration and malnutrition involve dark colored urine, low albumin levels, documented loss of weight, and a host of other issues that an expert can help the attorney understand.

Fluid overload may occur if a nurse administers intravenous fluid too rapidly. A patient with congestive heart failure is at particular risk for this complication. A patient with fluid overload may "drown" in fluids. Screening of these cases is directed to reviewing the ordered rate of intravenous fluid versus what was actually administered. Intake and output records become important documents in an investigation of this type of claim. Autopsy reports may include details of lung tissue examination, noting congestion in the lungs.

C. Physical Abuse or Assault

These are among the most difficult cases to either prosecute or defend, based upon the usual lack of clear evidence as to what might have occurred. In most cases involving physical abuse or assault, there are either very few or no witnesses. These cases can involve patient-on-patient or resident-on-resident abuse, or that committed by a staff member. They can involve physical assault without sexual contact. Those involving sexual assault are the most potentially explosive, especially when they involve a member of an institution's staff.

From the nursing perspective, the chart should be carefully explored to see what the nursing progress notes might have said about the prior interrelationship with either the staff or fellow residents which might have resulted in notice to an institution of a potential for violence. Additionally,

nurses may be held liable as a consequence of a failure to quell an emerging violent situation.

The practitioner must keep in mind that intentional assault by a staff member is usually not directly covered by insurance. However, other related issues, such as a negligent hiring, training, and supervision are generally covered. Even more than with most other claims, counsel should carefully weigh damages and liability issues during the screening process of these claims. In the evaluation, consider:

- Who is the assailant?
- Who is the victim?
- Is the assailant a fellow patient or a staff member?
- What is known or what can be learned about the assailant (e.g., is the psychiatric history of the assailant inaccessible as a consequence of HIPAA)?
- Is the injury one that at first is quite dramatic, but ultimately leaves no significant residuals…such as a nasal fracture?
- What is the likelihood of ever learning what truly happened?
- Were roommates at a healthcare facility an obvious mismatch?

In the end, these are challenging claims on all fronts. Unlike more familiar negligence issues, determining the true facts of the case may not be possible. As inflammatory as the initial facts may sound, many injuries in this context resolve with little or no treatment. This should be kept in mind during the highly emotional initial interviews with prospective clients.

TIP: In all cases involving physical abuse and assault, it is important to commence investigation very early. To the extent possible, it is always advisable to involve the police and the Division of Health and Human Services/ Division of Health and Senior Services. Additionally, for nursing home cases, one should contact the Ombudsman's office. Typically, these agencies can obtain valuable discovery that is not otherwise immediately available to counsel. It also serves to preserve evidence and statements of individuals who might not be available for testimony after litigation is instituted.

D. Falls

Falls in both hospitals and nursing homes represent the second most common claim involving assertions of nursing negligence, second only to pressure ulcer claims. However, liability in these cases is almost always far from clear.

Fall prevention can be categorized into two types of claims: those involving competent and those incompetent patients or residents. Both involve dramatically distinct theories of liability and standards of care involving fall prevention. For individuals who are cognitively intact, liability is typically quite difficult. All regulations involving both hospitals and nursing homes place a focus on the responsibility of an institution and its nursing staff to ensure the maximum level of independence possible for an individual, and in a practical sense place fall-related safety issues second on the list. Thus, these cases are appropriately defended on the basis that institutions, through their nursing staffs, are compelled to ensure that otherwise frail individuals with significant comorbidities are nonetheless left free to engage in as many activities of daily living as their condition permits. This means that many types of fall prevention strategies are not authorized. The significant exception in this regard involves cognitively intact individuals not capable of independent movement and/or transfers. A common presentation in this regard is the drop case when a patient or resident is being transferred from bed to wheelchair, bath or toilet to wheelchair, or wheelchair to bed. When it can be demonstrated that this individual was fully dependent upon staff for all modes of transfer, the nursing staff will have a difficult time or an impossible time defending the matter.

TIP: For cases involving drops during transfer, one should carefully scrutinize issues related to short staffing. Many of these cases involve a very clear order requiring a two-person transfer, with the actual incident only involving one person. Nearly as common are transfers being attempted by people who simply are not physically strong enough to assist a large patient.

In the continuum from cognitively impaired to mentally competent lies the middle area, where a patient has diminished cognitive acuity, but is not fully appreciative of those limitations. This represents a very difficult situation for the care providers in balancing safety and independence. For such cases, all the medical records must be carefully scrutinized to determine whether the facility properly addressed that balance—or if the facility even addressed it with sufficient care to defend against a fall down accident.

The strongest claims for plaintiffs involve cognitively-impaired injured parties. All facilities, be they assisted living, hospital, or long-term care, are compelled to engage in a very detailed fall risk assessment and an appropriately tailored care plan which diminishes the risk for falls as much as possible. Cognitively impaired individuals represent the highest risk for falls and are least likely to respond to corrective instructions from nursing staff. Many cases in this regard are replete with nursing notes reminding individuals to use the call button instead of attempting to exit the bed independently. When this instruction has failed for a protracted period of time without a change in the care plan, negligence becomes apparent. That is, when a specific mode of fall prevention strategy repeatedly fails, nurses are obligated to take proper steps to ensure a new care plan is devised.

Before committing to prosecuting a fall case, carefully examine damage issues. While cases may present one or even many inexcusable falls, families often wish to pursue those that do not involve significant injuries. This is generally not advisable, as a consequence both of the expense of litigation and the lack of certainty with regard to liability—even with the seeming best of fact patterns. One should also think twice before pursuing even a fracture case, where there is either excellent healing or where there is no meaningful permanent impact on the patient's activities of daily living. On the other hand, a seemingly modest injury, such as a bump on the head, can ultimately prove catastrophic when the patient is already on blood thinning medications like Coumadin or heparin. In those circumstances, it is important to track the recovery of the patient before making a final decision. It is likewise essential to learn from treating and/or expert physicians as to what injury can specifically be linked to the fall.

All experts agree that numerous tools exist for nurses to work toward preventing falls—even though they are not always preventable. When a facility fails to explore all potential options and, importantly, fails to implement those they have chosen, liability is strong.

In summary, liability issues to consider in screening a fall case include:

- How did the fall occur?
- Was the patient appropriately identified as being at risk for falls?
- Was a plan of care implemented to reduce the risk of falls?
- Was the fall and injury promptly reported (versus being concealed)?
- What changes in the plan of care were made to reduce the risk of subsequent falls?
- Were these successful?

E. Improperly Administered Medication

These cases seem to appear much more often in hospital claims than at long-term care facilities or assisted living centers. However, they are extraordinarily common as an adjunct to other claims related to either skin integrity or other medically related disputes. Namely, even without the existence of a specific injury related to improperly administered medication, it often can serve as evidence of poor care. In the nursing home context, family members typically testify they find medication within the bed sheets of their loved one. Other cases might reveal improper dosages or improper transcriptions of a physician's order.

All of this requires careful scrutiny of the medical chart. This involves a careful day by day comparison of the medical administration record (MAR), nursing progress notes, physician orders and their transcriptions, and the controlled drug administration record. Very often, an error or inconsistency is made when comparing these records.

It is also important to consider ordering repeat copies of certain important records in the chart throughout the history of the claim. This sometimes results in a revelation concerning an intentionally altered record. A mistake commonly found with physician orders is the incorrect placement of decimal points on critical numbers. Refer to Chapter 28, *Medication Errors*, in Volume II, for additional information.

TIP: For cases involving nursing home care, it is a clear violation of the federal regulations (OBRA) for a nurse to fail in complying with a physician's admission order. These same regulations also strongly suggest that the failure to follow any physician's order, such as the administration of medication, constitutes a violation of a resident's nursing home resident rights. Should any documents have been intentionally altered, this may also give rise to a federal criminal prosecution.

As with assault claims, medication error cases often present with shocking and disturbing fact patterns, but just as often result in no permanent injury. Indeed, very few medication errors cause permanent or serious harm. The types of medications most often implicated in serious and permanent harm are narcotics, chemotherapeutic agents, and anticoagulants. Even when liability is quite strong, one should remember that patients with significant comorbidities are generally subject to strong causation defenses. That is, it is not always clear as to what type of harm was caused to an otherwise debilitated individual as a consequence of improper administration of medication.

F. Infections (Including Sepsis)

Infection cases rarely stand alone, but sometimes do. It is important to recognize at the outset that the vast majority of infections suffered by patients at institutions are not and should not be actionable. Namely, certain infections as a

general rule do not arise as a consequence of negligent conduct. Most predominant among these is Methicillin Resistant Staphyloccus Aureas (MRSA). This and a number of other infections are simply known risks for individuals residing at institutions. When faced with an infection claim either as a stand-alone matter or in conjunction with other claims, it is important to promptly speak with both a nursing expert witness and potentially an infectious disease physician to ferret through what issue might be the result of negligence and what might simply constitute a known and accepted risk for institutionalized patients. The most common reason why nosocomial (acquired in an institution) infections are transmitted is the failure of staff to simply wash their hands. However, proving first the lack of existence of this practice at the defendant healthcare facility and second that it is causally related to the infection suffered by the plaintiff, is extraordinarily difficult.

For individuals with compromised health and significant comorbidities, certain infections might be recognized by all experts as tremendously stubborn and difficult to resolve. However, this does not absolve the nursing staff from complying with the standard of care. Importantly, nurses are universally recognized to have an absolute duty to promptly notify their supervisors or the attending physician directly whenever the clinical signs of infection appear. Additionally, nursing experts and all applicable regulatory schemes recognize the nurse's affirmative duty to address all of these issues with the physician—and to potentially question the physician. This often arises as a consequence of a physician's repeated reliance on a given antibiotic—even when sensitivity lab work reveals that the infection is resistant to the currently used antibiotic—or the physician's use of a drug to which the patient is allergic. This particular scenario presents itself quite often in this area of litigation.

Nurses should be keenly aware of the fact that plaintiffs are much more apt to file a claim against a nurse than a physician. Physicians commonly complain they are not receiving enough or prompt information from the nurse to allow them to issue appropriate orders. Thus, the failure of a nurse to chart and act upon clinical signs of infection can result in a direct action against that nurse.

Infections also are quite common with skin integrity claims. The most common of these is sepsis in the presence of a pressure ulcer. However, sepsis does not arise solely from pressure ulcers. A patient can suffer from sepsis that did not develop in a wound site.

TIP: In all cases involving infection, the practitioner should consult with a physician to address causation issues involving the relationship between that infection and the injuries more directly involved in whatever items of negligence are in the case. Do not assume that all infections result from negligence.

One of the most insidious infections commonly seen in nursing home litigation is that of osteomyelitis. This is an infection of the bone typically arising after a Stage IV pressure ulcer develops. Osteomyelitis commonly results in amputation or death.

TIP: With infection and indeed all other medical claims, nearly all courts do not permit a nurse to address causation issues. It is essential to have a physician, on behalf of either plaintiff or defendant, relate an injury to the asserted act of negligence. A burgeoning and narrow exception to this relates to skin care. Some experts agree that wound care nurses might ultimately be qualified to relate skin interruption to negligence. However, it remains prudent for either side of a litigated matter to have a physician address these issues.

In summary, the attorney should address both damages and liability issues when screening infection cases. When considering damages, determine:

- What type of infection developed?
- What were the effects?
- How long did it take to treat it?
- Was long-term antibiotic therapy required?
- Was the patient affected by a blood infection?
- Did the patient die?
- Could earlier treatment of the infection have changed the outcome?

From a liability perspective, consider:

- Was the infection hospital-acquired?
- Should the claim be accepted, would knowing the hospital's infection rates be of benefit?
- Is the claim related to treatment with the wrong medication?
- If the cultures showed that the organism was resistant to the antibiotic, was there evidence that the nurse notified the physician?
- Were antibiotics given by the nurses as ordered?
- Does the medical record verify that an antibiotic was promptly begun after the infection was diagnosed?

Refer to Chapter 23, *Infections in Hospitals and Nursing Homes*, in Volume II, for more on this subject.

G. Aspiration Pneumonia or Improper Administration of Feeding Tube Solution

Aspiration pneumonia cases are quite common in nursing litigation. Much more challenging, as with many of the above categories, is the issue of causation. That is, many different aspirants can lead to aspiration pneumonia. These can include secretions or food, among others. The most common scenario involves a patient or resident with a feeding tube. For reasons most likely related to improper training and staffing, many tube-fed patients at nursing homes or hospitals are fed purely horizontally. This practice clearly is contrary to the appropriate nursing standard of care and generally contrary to the physician's orders that accompany tube feeding. Namely, tube-fed individuals should be fed at either the Fowler's (45 degree) or semi-Fowler's (30 degree) positions. This allows gravity to work in favor of the patient and reduces, to some extent, the risk of aspiration.

Unfortunately, when patients are changed or cleaned, nurses or nurses' aides permit these individuals to be placed in a horizontal position without turning off the tube feeding. Sometimes at the conclusion of such a changing, the bed is not once again raised. This dramatically increases the risk of aspiration. These types of cases present very challenging factual and medical obstacles for the plaintiff.

In the first instance, it is very rare that a chart would disclose the fact that a tube-fed patient was left in a purely horizontal position. The only scenario where this seems to arise is when fingers are pointed in multiple directions by staff members who recognize a mistake has been made. More generally, there is an absence of nursing notes related to bed position or notations that might be correct or incorrect reflecting that the head of the bed (HOB) is in the up position ("HOB up"). This might fly in the face of what family members have to say about the bed position. However, this would be known only if the family member was aware of the required bed position.

Once that hurdle is overcome by the plaintiff, the defense is in a position to place serious focus on the nature of the aspiration, its relationship to bed position or other aspiration issues, and its potential relationship to the causes of death of the patient.

TIP: In all aspiration cases, it is important to have a physician carefully scrutinize all x-ray reports. These often provide a significant set of clues as to the nature of the aspiration and whether or not it is causally related to the asserted negligence.

Many other aspiration cases involve allegations that nurses failed to timely notify physicians or nurse supervisors of what were later characterized as clinical signs of an individual suffering from an aspiration-related event. These cases involve relatively significant hurdles with regard to causation, but often are much simpler with regard to negligence. Namely, certain clinical signs that highlight the fact a person is suffering an aspiration-related event are clear enough to warrant a simple call to a physician—who might literally be in another part of the building. It is very difficult for nurses to defend claims when the only thing the plaintiff alleges should have been done is a phone call to a physician on duty. Many of these cases involve precious wasted time where nurses are alleged to have been much too lax in light of clinical signs of a serious aspiration.

As noted, aspiration typically involves feeding tube claims. However, these are certainly not limited to tube-fed patients, but also patients at high risk for aspiration pneumonia by way of a pneumonia-related history and individuals at any stage of the development of dysphagia. Many dysphagia patients have very restricted diet regimens. Oftentimes, nurses are alleged to have failed to adhere to dietician orders—such as the need for pureed food. The introduction of a hard food can create an aspiration risk for individuals with compromised swallowing capacity.

Finally, many cases arise out of an allegation that extraordinary pressure was placed on a family to introduce tube feeding for an individual who otherwise did not need tube feeding. If it is later demonstrated that this particular individual was able to live and meet caloric, liquid, and protein needs without a feeding tube, there might be a claim under federal regulations related to tube feeding.

Feeding tubes are associated with risks. Equipment-related problems include:

- Accidental removal of PEG tubes, followed by incorrect reinsertion into the abdominal cavity instead of the stomach.
- Too rapid administration of tube feeding solution, resulting in vomiting and inhalation of vomitus (aspiration).
- Administration of tube feeding solution into a suprapubic tube instead of a PEG tube.

The Joint Commission issued a sentinel event alert in April 2006 regarding the risks associated with tube feeding. For more information, see www.jointcommission.org. Screening of an aspiration or tube feeding misadventure involves evaluating damages and liability. Aspiration may result in pneumonia, which may kill a fragile patient. Aspiration of food boluses resulting in an obstructed airway may cause catastrophic anoxic brain damage, requiring a lifetime of care. Misplacement of feeding tubes resulting in instil-lation of tube feeding solution into the lungs can be fatal. Instillation of feeding into the abdomen can result in massively painful peritonitis and death.

Liability issues surrounding aspiration revolve around correctly carrying out nursing procedures.

- Did the nurse recognize the risk of aspiration?
- Was the nurse permitted to replace a displaced nasogastric tube?
- Did the nurse verify correct placement of a feeding tube before instilling solution?
- Was the patient correctly positioned during tube feeding?
- Was the solution administered at the correct rate?
- Did the nurse promptly recognize signs of aspiration?

The attorney screening a tube-feeding related incident should review the medical record for comments about the prognosis of the patient (terminally ill versus expectations to recover) and the associated comorbidities. All too often, a concerned family has unrealistic expectations about the present and future states of these patients. To assess damages, causation, and liability, an interview with the family physician may shed some light on the true condition and prognosis of the tube-fed patient.

H. Theft

Theft cases are rare in the hospital context, but prolific in nursing home and assisted living claims. Indeed, most plaintiff's attorneys advise that with regard to nursing home claims, all involve theft. These rarely represent independent claims, but instead are institutional systemic problems alleged by plaintiff's attorneys to be related to the poor delivery of care. Many issues of theft actually have a significant relationship to deleterious health situations. Namely, care in such institutions typically involves the theft of hearing aids, eyeglasses, dentures, and assistive walking devices. All of these need to be closely monitored by nursing staff to ensure replacements are promptly obtained. The loss of dentures can quickly lead to a significant loss of weight and loss of enjoyment of life for a resident unable to process non-pureed food. Similarly, significant emotional, psychological, and safety consequences accompany the loss of either a hearing aid or eyeglasses. Significantly, individuals with such losses typically are unable to engage in nearly all of the activities of daily living, already limited due to their comorbidities. A physically disabled, but mentally intact individual might derive pleasure solely from watching television or reading. Because of theft of hearing aids or eyeglasses, such individual's activities might be limited to listening or watching without supplementary vision or hearing, respectively. Institutions typically lose assistive devices and rob residents of their ability to fully engage in these activities. In many persons, this leads to a snowball-effect decline in mental status and, in turn, physical health. Additionally, loss of hearing aids and eyeglasses may increase safety hazards, resulting in falls, burns, and other injuries. Nurses who fail to act upon these issues could be accused of negligent conduct toward the resident. Refer to Chapter 10, *Subacute and Long-Term Care Nursing Malpractice Issues*, in Volume II, for additional information on the effects of sensory deprivation or loss of senses.

I. Wrongful Death/Survivorship

It is essential that practitioners carefully research the statutes for their jurisdictions related to these particular claims. In the nursing home context, it is quite rare that a wrongful death claim has a specific pecuniary value, based on the general rule that nursing home residents are not income producers and are perceived as individuals for whom society and family members must provide, rather than vice versa. No specific value is assigned to cases in jurisdictions that limit wrongful death claims to pecuniary loss. However, the impact of being able to allege wrongful death might have a significant impact on a putative jury.

Outside of the nursing home context, many cases at assisted living facilities and a higher percentage of cases involving other venues of care certainly might have wrongful death claims.

TIP: It is common with nursing neglect claims to focus on nursing negligence and thus hinge on the review of a nursing expert. However, it is critical to determine early on whether it is possible to have a physician specifically relate wrongful death or other claims to the negligence at hand. Similarly, the defense should shore up its defenses that do not relate the ultimate outcome to the act of nursing neglect.

Survivorship claims deal with the loss of enjoyment of life and pain and suffering the patient or resident endures as a direct or indirect consequence of the asserted items of neglect. In this regard, the chart should be carefully scrutinized not only to find all indications of pain from the nursing progress notes, but also from the medical administration records. Even when an indication of pain does not find its way into the progress notes, the administration of PRN pain medication found in the medical administration record certainly reflects that the medication was given in response to a demonstration or utterance of pain.

Nursing standards and federal regulations strictly compel nurses to pay close attention to pain management. A failure to do so can place a defendant in a very precarious situation. Such conduct could theoretically allow the defendant to win on areas of negligence or causation, but expose that same defendant to a significant judgment as a consequence of the failure to properly manage pain and treat the patient humanely in light of whatever injury cause exists. This is particularly true in pressure ulcer claims in which nurses fail to pre-medicate before dressing changes or other forms of treatment for pressure ulcers. There is a movement among healthcare providers to ensure individuals subject to painful debridement or dressing changes be subject to pre-medication—to make the procedure as humane as possible. The most significant violations in this appear to arise when patients do not have the physical or mental capacity to outwardly complain of pain. There is an underlying assumption that if the patient is not verbally complaining, pain management is not necessary. This could not be further from the truth. Chapter 10, *Pain and Suffering*, discusses this topic in more detail.

As discussed in Chapter 10, *Pain and Suffering*, the pain and suffering or loss of enjoyment of life suffered by a decedent results in compensation that flows into the estate. The question of determining which family members receive money when the decedent dies intestate can be quite problematic. It is often difficult to get cooperation among living family members. This is especially true when there is a strong emotional overlay with the loss of a loved one.

J. Violation of State and Federal Laws, Codes, and Regulations

It is important that all practitioners become keenly aware of all statutes and regulations that apply to a given case. This review must start with the nature of the facility or site where the alleged negligence is claimed to have occurred. The regulatory scheme differs significantly from nursing home to assisted living facility to hospital. It is also quite different in a physician's office and differs again with the advent of home care. The Joint Commission standards in effect at the time of care rendered in a hospital are useful in evaluating a case.

Attorneys having a focus on nursing home cases should be familiar with the OBRA regulations (Omnibus Budget Reconciliation Act of 1987; 42 C.F.R. 483). These regulations are quite extensive, but do not contain language that includes a cause of action for their violation. Instead, some states contain statutory schemes that incorporate these federal regulations. For those states that do not, the OBRA standards might be argued to establish the standard of care or be used as guidelines for Medicare reimbursement. This latter issue is the fodder of dueling expert testimony across the nursing home litigation landscape. However, in cases with statutory schemes that specifically incorporate federal regulations and their own causes of action, OBRA violations have routinely been successfully litigated by plaintiff's attorneys in addition to the underlying malpractice cause of action. Most states contain their own regulatory scheme that might mirror OBRA or contain different standards. On a case-by-case basis, this might be demonstrated to constitute the standard of care, a separate cause of action, or neither. Still, in the nursing home context, a number of states have specific enabling statutes that include a direct cause of action. Other states have consumer fraud statutes that might apply to nursing home or assisted living care.

The assisted living claims are exposed to slightly different laws and regulations. However, many of those statutory schemes contain definitions of nursing homes that appear to address most or all of the functions that modern assisted living facilities attempt to fill. In other words, many assisted living claims can be pled as nursing home claims. Much of the litigation involving assisted living facilities includes the very real allegation that such facilities are attempting to step into the shoes of long-term care facilities without the proper personnel or expertise to do so. In those circumstances, plaintiff's attorneys have been successful in pursuing nursing home litigation against assisted living facilities. The position of plaintiffs in such cases is that the means by which the facility was licensed is irrelevant to the analysis. Rather, the role that the facility takes in the care of its residents is relevant. Thus, if the facility is caring for chronically ill, sick, significantly dependent long-term care residents, it is acting in the role of a long-term care facility and, thus, subject to the regulatory and statutory schemes involved therein.

Many of these statutes contain fee and cost shifting provisions. Similarly, punitive and treble damage provisions exist in them. For those states that do not have such statutes, many plaintiff's attorneys are attempting to utilize consumer fraud law to invoke these same types of punitive, treble damage, and fee/cost shifting laws into play. Related to both of these types of facilities are certain accreditation agencies, such as The Joint Commission, which, if adopted by that facility, may ultimately establish the appropriate standard of care and contractual obligation of that facility toward its patients or residents. This potentially applies to hospital claims where the hospital is a Joint Commission-accredited facility. Similarly, the American Medical Directors Association maintains standards for the care provided to nursing home residents. A failure to follow these might not necessarily result in a statutory violation, but might be proven to establish a breach in either the standard of care or the contractual obligations of that facility toward its residents or patients. In all of these circumstances, most such violations involve allegations of negligent nursing care rather than physician care.

It is also important to recognize that many statutory or regulatory claims can potentially stand independently from the underlying malpractice claim, meaning a plaintiff can potentially lose under the theories of deviation of causation, but still receive a recovery that invokes fee shifting on a statutory violation. Many of these claims are more akin to laws against discrimination claims or civil rights claims. Jury verdict research reveals a significant appreciation of jurors for the plight of the geriatric population when faced with either nursing home or assisted living care. Chapter 11, *Assisted Living Liability*, in Volume II, discusses this topic in more detail.

14.4 Potential Defendants
A. Healthcare Facility (Is There More Than One?)

As noted above, it is essential to establish a very detailed timeline to determine which items of nursing negligence are being alleged and where the injury ultimately manifested itself. What seems apparent to either the plaintiff or family members when first presenting a claim might not be borne out in the records. Thus, many cases involve significant dispute between different facilities in the successive line of treatment. Typically, nursing home and hospital charts involve widely divergent views of the status of an individual's skin, weight, or hydration between discharge and admission records. The only means by which a plaintiff's attorney can ferret through these issues is to ultimately name all facilities. This is because those issues simply cannot be determined with ironclad assuredness prior to the institution of suit. When any such facility is left out of the litigation, it provides an excellent opportunity for defense attorneys to focus on the empty chair.

TIP: In any nursing negligence claim, it is advisable to retain a legal nurse consultant—who is not necessarily the ultimate expert in the case—to provide a detailed timeline, to examine all claims and all sites of alleged negligence or manifestation of injury, and to determine the proper players in the case. This is frequently inexpensive and provides an excellent foundation for all of the future litigation from either the plaintiff or defendant's point of view.

---

1. Publicly or privately owned

Many care institutions are publicly owned or operated without any indication of that status being contained within the name of the institution. This is very dangerous territory for plaintiff's attorneys—due to the fact that most states have very specific public entity statutes, requiring detailed tort claims notices or other requirements to proceed with litigation. Most of the interpretive laws contain an inherent assumption that any plaintiff prosecuting a claim will engage in a due diligence effort to learn about the potential defendants in the case. Thus, many a plaintiff's attorney prosecuting a claim against a state, county, or city facility might face applications for dismissal for failure to provide proper tort claims notices. It is not enough to claim ignorance of the status of the facility. It is incumbent upon any prosecuting attorney to determine the ownership of that facility.

Just as important with private institutions is to determine the corporate structure of the ownership. In today's climate, many nursing home chains do not carry insurance for the individual nursing home and have erected significant barriers between the local facility and the national parent corporation that arguably manages, runs, or otherwise supervises that facility. Without a proper understanding of that relationship and a complaint that names all appropriate entities, a plaintiff might ultimately obtain no money on an otherwise meritorious claim. Many states do not require nursing homes to carry liability insurance or otherwise maintain any type of minimal coverage. Thus, a significant number of nursing homes carry $50,000 or less in coverage, while many others have no coverage and operate under the constant threat of bankruptcy. For these reasons, it is essential to develop a keen understanding of the corporate structure.

2. Charitable immunity

Another minefield for plaintiff's attorneys is claims involving charitable institutions. Most states have some type of statute either rendering such facilities totally immune from suit or involving caps on damages for them. Inherent in the process of interpreting one's case is the relationship between the plaintiff and the charitable institution. In most jurisdictions, a beneficiary of the charitable activities of that institution is subject to that jurisdiction's charitable immunity statute. Some jurisdictions contain statutes that allow a plaintiff to pursue claims directly against various individuals at those facilities without the cloak of charitable immunity. Thus, nurses are a frequent target of such claims. When a charitable institution, such as a hospital or nursing home, is named in a case, but is otherwise considered to be charitable and subject to that state's statute, plaintiff's attorneys frequently individually name nurses who provided care. As noted above, this can often result in some amount of legal friction between the nurse and the employing institution or place of contractual engagement. More hospitals are being

named directly for nursing negligence matters. Many more hospitals than nursing homes are subject to the local jurisdiction's charitable immunity statute simply by virtue of the means by which many hospitals are established and taxed.

B. Assisted Living Facility

Please see discussion above for assisted living facilities. Lawsuits against such facilities can and should under the right circumstances be pled to specifically allege nursing home rights violations and OBRA violations. It is also essential for attorneys handling such claims to obtain as much advertising and promotional data as possible. This is especially true of the assisted living facilities that heavily market their services. This can ultimately be argued by the plaintiff to fall within the consumer fraud statute and also serve to bolster an argument that the facility had a contractual obligation to the plaintiff.

14.5 Statute of Limitations Concerns
A. Is There a Specific Date of Incident? (i.e., Date of Fall, Assault, or Formation of Pressure Ulcer)

Most nursing negligence cases significantly diverge from traditional medical malpractice claims in that they are not focused on one act or omission. This may be true in nursing home claims but is not usually true in hospital claims. Hospital claims are usually focused on a single issue case—a fall from bed, a treatment error, a failure to report abnormalities of a patient, or a medication error, to name a few. For claims such as these, the seminal event creates a concise date-based source for the litigation. Although there may still exist discovery-rule-related issues or issues related to the mental incompetence of the plaintiff, the determination of the statute of limitations for nearly all hospital claims is a relatively straightforward matter.

On the other hand, nursing home claims generally involve a long line of conduct that involves detailed analysis. It is essential to understand the appropriate jurisdiction's law concerning continuing torts. Whenever possible, commence an action within the appropriate statute of limitations period from the first asserted act of negligence. With pressure ulcer claims, it is quite challenging to determine not only when the first evidence of skin breakdown appeared, but also when the first negligent conduct related to that breakdown occurred. The same analysis applies to malnutrition or dehydration cases—though a typical added issue often involves whether the nurses acted appropriately and promptly enough when the malnutrition or dehydration reached a level requiring hospitalization. Further complicating matters is that negligent conduct not only occurs over a prolonged period of time, but is also related to the conduct of multiple individuals, crossing varying fields of specialties.

B. Dates of Admission and Discharge to Each Facility

In determining what statute of limitations to apply in a multi-defendant case, it is important to develop a timeline that establishes the admission and discharge dates for each institution involved. When time permits, it is likewise advisable to file within the appropriate statute of limitations period from the very first admission of the very first facility involved in the case. This is important to do even when the asserted acts of negligence did not occur until some time later. This is because it is extraordinarily difficult to develop a full understanding of each of the asserted negligent acts that led to the injury.

TIP: Never take a statute of limitations determination for granted prior to a full evaluation of a claim. Very often, issues that appear to be beyond the statute of limitations are not. Conversely, many claims falsely seem to enjoy significant additional time before the statue of limitations expires. An exhaustive analysis at the outset of a case to determine this seemingly simple issue can prove invaluable.

C. Is the Statute of Limitations Tolled Due to Resident's or Patient's Mental Incapacity or Incompetence?

In many cases, the statute of limitations is tolled as a consequence of the injured party's legal insanity or mental incompetence for certain periods of time. The computations involving this issue can become quite complex when there is a documented degradation of one's mental acuity throughout a particular institutionalization. This involves circumstances in which a seminal event decreases an individual's mental acuity or in which there is a general aggravation over time of either dementia or Alzheimer's disease. While it is certainly preferable to avoid all of these issues from the plaintiff's point of view and simply file suit within the appropriate statute of limitations, families frequently do not approach counsel in sufficient time to meet all of these statutes of limitations. Many apparently expired claims are, in fact, not expired if the injured party was mentally incompetent for all or part of the time the incidents occurred.

This issue can potentially involve a battle of the experts, attempting to specify the level of competence of a plaintiff for particularly targeted dates. Obviously, this science is tremendously imprecise since it rarely involves the findings of a specific, independent medical examination. In

other words, these experts might attempt to utilize nursing progress notes, psychiatric consults, and social worker interviews to address the level of mental acuity for a five-month window of time. This is clearly a minefield for the plaintiff's attorney and can cast a dark cloud over the entirety of the litigation. Whenever possible, it remains advisable to avoid this issue and simply file within the appropriate statute of limitations from the first act of negligence.

The discovery rule can vary entirely or subtly among states. Under the discovery rule, a statute of limitations theoretically does not begin to run until the party not only learns of the potential negligent conduct, but also can reasonably be expected to have understood a direct relationship between negligent conduct and injuries suffered. This represents a two-tiered defense to statute of limitations assertions when the plaintiff is or was mentally incompetent. In the first instance, the statute is directly tolled by virtue of the incompetence; in the second, there remains an argument that this individual could not have appreciated the negligent conduct or its relationship to the injury at any relevant period of time—perhaps even before that individual's death. The issue also surfaces when charts are altered or when negligent conduct is not apparent until perhaps a subsequent care provider suggests it to the plaintiff or a family member. Because this rule varies so much among states, it is important at the outset of such litigation to develop a keen understanding of the discovery rule for the appropriate jurisdiction. This discovery rule potentially allows plaintiff to move much farther back than the statute of limitations alone would otherwise suggest.

Challenging issues abound in pediatric cases. In investigating any malpractice case for a minor, it is wise not to put off a full medical review because of false security arising from an extended statute of limitations. Many hospitals or medical providers either purge documents after a number of years, or simply lose them. More importantly, key witnesses become impossible to locate or might die. Important policies and procedures documents are updated such that the version that existed at the time of the seminal event no longer exists. Similarly, The Joint Commission standards in effect during the time of the treatment at least partially no longer apply and might be quite difficult to access. In the end, however, these cases often reach counsel's desk within the statute of limitations, but many years after the conduct occurred. At the very least, be mindful of these issues and challenges for the screening process.

D. Review if Wrongful Death Alleged

As a general rule, the statute of limitations for most jurisdictions related to wrongful death is much simpler. Basically, look to one's own jurisdiction to determine the specific amount of time to file suit based on a wrongful death claim. However, this can vary from state to state and also from one type of claim to another. It also might vary depending upon the specific cause of action being alleged. Namely, in certain jurisdictions a consumer-fraud-based claim or a breach of contract claim might extend the statute of limitations. However, the personal injury or malpractice statute of limitations is generally the most applicable. There may exist rare circumstances where a discovery rule extension may be applied. However, the death of an individual is much more obvious than some of the more subtle injuries to which the discovery rule more commonly applies. Nonetheless, there may be situations in which a death initially seemed innocuous, but additional information made family members suspect more was at play.

14.6 Obtaining Records
A. Color or Black and White Copy

While it is always preferable to have a color copy of a chart, the realities of practice do not always permit this. Most facilities (hospitals, nursing homes, or assisted living facilities) are appropriately reluctant to allow a chart to exit their physical site. This makes getting color copies quite difficult when most facilities only have a black and white copier. It is sometimes necessary to get early court intervention. Alternatively, the depositions of the medical records custodian may be taken on the premises of a company that provides color duplication. The medical records custodian brings the chart to the copy center, attests to its creation as part of the business practices of the facility, and the record is copied and handed back to the custodian.

TIP: Although expensive, it is often advantageous to obtain three copies of a chart. The first should be obtained by the plaintiff or plaintiff's family without attorney intervention; the second by the attorney pre-suit; and the third by the attorney during litigation. The advantage is that charts are obtained during periods of widely varying levels of concern from the putative defendants. Comparing each copy frequently reveals alterations to the chart.

There are a number of inherent advantages to a color chart. It is physically easier to read. As any nurse expert or practitioner would attest, poring through hundreds of pages of handwritten records is very fatiguing. Critical information might be buried in a nursing progress note that is quite difficult to read. There is often a tendency to move quickly through entries with bad handwriting and focus on those

typewritten or with better handwriting. While this obviously is not the appropriate way to review a chart, it is a reflection of simple human nature. When charts are copied in color, it is easier to pick up details.

Additionally, the color of ink in a chart is often very relevant and signifies which shift has made an entry. When reviewing a file for potential falsification, a black and white copy cannot reveal different shades of the same color pen or different colors when records have been altered. A number of copying services will go to a nursing facility with its own equipment to obtain a color copy of the chart. Oftentimes, defense counsel is entrusted to personally bring the chart to a copy center with color copying capabilities. However, it is all too frequently necessary to obtain court intervention to obtain this. With the busy day-to-day realities of malpractice litigation, it is easy to overlook the extra effort required to get color records. However, in cases that warrant the additional expense, they prove invaluable in permitting a more in-depth review and understanding of those records.

B. Obtain All Other Medical Records

After a review of the primary records believed to be at the core of the case, the need for other records typically becomes apparent. Family members of patients with significant co-morbidities frequently forget various outpatient stays, tests, and even protracted hospitalizations sandwiched between long-term care center admissions.

TIP: After receipt of all known medical records, conduct a review of those to determine what records are not yet available. Put all of this together to complete the timeline of all medical treatment.

When developing a full chronological set of records, comparing discharge to admissions from various facilities will sometimes reveal diverging assessments of the patient. This is especially true in cases surrounding skin integrity issues. Many times the facility in which the skin breakdown was acquired will understate the severity of a pressure ulcer, while the admission papers from the very same day at the facility where the problem did not arise will accurately assess it. Thus, subsequent admission records can serve as a check on the accuracy of previous discharge records.

C. Obtain Department of Health Licensure, Survey, and Complaint Files

For any case involving an institution, a state or federal survey file should be available through Freedom of Information Act or Public Records Act-related requests. These can be used to identify potential systemic problems that pre-date the injury that marks the core of the case. The judicial view of the admissibility of such records varies among judges, not just jurisdictions. However, these records at times reveal the very incident that marks the core of the litigation. Sometimes when a family makes a complaint with the state, they are not apprised as to what the state did with that complaint. A careful review of complaint files reveals remarkably similar incidents. When these are dated, it is possible to specifically relate them to the case at hand. These complaint files also often reflect statements made by facility administrators and employees. Such statements might turn out to be admissible in discovery.

TIP: In addition to state records, check to see if the facility involved is a Joint Commission-accredited facility. If so, The Joint Commission will have surveys available to identify potential systemic problems at such a facility. Many of these are available online from The Joint Commission website at www.jointcommission.org.

Request the survey, complaint, and licensure file when requesting state records for a facility. Each contain different information that may prove relevant to a case.

14.7 Organize the Chart
A. Separate the Chart into Subfolders or Tabbed Binders

It is nearly impossible to review an unorganized chart. Even the largest of charts become digestible when broken down into basic components. Organizing the records also reveals what is missing. It is important to prepare a list of all the types of records that should be within the chart. Refer to Chapter 7, *Nursing Documentation*, in this volume and Chapter 10, *Subacute and Long-Term Care Nursing Malpractice Issues*, in Volume II, for additional medical information on medical record components. By way of just one example, a nursing home chart should contain at a bare minimum, the following records:

- Nursing Progress Notes
- Physician Orders
- Medical Administration Record (MAR)
- Treatment Administration Records (TAR)
- Minimum Data Set (MDS)
- Resident Assessment Protocols (RAPS)

B. Scan Each Page of the Record

For cases that warrant additional labor and expense, it is often advantageous to electronically scan these records. This provides for the easier dissemination of discovery and its transmittal. It also can serve as the basis for preparing mediation, arbitration, and trial presentations. Before such scanning occurs, however, it is essential to develop a game plan, so that access of these records does not become problematic. One way to do so is to utilize UPC codes on each record so that the equivalent of Bates stamping has been accomplished. It is also important to have the proper software to access these records once they are scanned.

14.8 Liability Evaluation
A. In-House Review

As noted, it is always advantageous to employ a legal nurse consultant (either an in-house or outside consultant) to review files and to sit in on original interviews. While most cases are aggressively defended on the issues of causation and damages, liability is rarely as simple as it seems.

TIP: Be alert to the possibility that critical documentation concerning the liability issue may not be found in nursing notes. Very often treatment may be in other ancillary records such as flow sheets, treatment administration records, the notes of physical or occupational therapy, or the Minimum Data Set (for nursing home cases). Experts need to review all parallel sections of a chart before a criticism arises related to lack of treatment.

From the outset, it is imperative that all parallel lines of care and treatment be analyzed and segregated within a file. Once chronology is established, the liability evaluation will flow much more smoothly.

B. Outside Nurse and Medical Doctor Expert Review

Before the completion of the liability evaluation, it is essential to employ both an outside nurse and a physician.

TIP: A common problem in the prosecution of nursing negligence claims is an overemphasis on liability (i.e., the conduct of nursing staff) with an underemphasis on the issues of causation. Many cases fail in their prosecution as a consequence of this oversight. Before pursuing any claim, it is essential to ensure there is a strong and legitimate causation relationship between the conduct complained of and the injury itself.

As a general rule, an independent legal nurse consultant can perform the most extensive of the four reviews involved in a liability evaluation: the in-house review of the attorney and a legal nurse consultant; the nursing expert witness review; and a physician expert witness review. The physician may be asked to focus attention on whether the medical care met the standard of care or if nursing deviations caused harm to the patient. Physician experts should not be used to opine on the nursing standard of care. Refer to Chapter 21, *Working with Nursing Expert Witnesses*, for more information on the current thinking regarding experts for nursing liability reviews. A physician may also be asked to determine if the deviations from the standard of care caused the patient to be injured or die. It is generally advantageous to employ a nurse first because of the relatively lighter expense and the comprehensiveness of that review. However, the review remains incomplete until it is determined whether or not a physician can and will relate the events which mark the core of the claim to the actual injury. Most medical malpractice claims are more successfully defended on causation issues than on the actual negligence issues. Indeed, this accounts for the vast majority of defense verdicts in nursing and medical malpractice claims.

It is imperative to check the rules of one's jurisdiction to determine whether communications between counsel and counsel's experts are discoverable. Some jurisdictions authorize oral and written communications between counsel and experts to be protected as work product privilege; other jurisdictions do not. The initial liability evaluation portion of the investigation is critical in terms of how the experts communicate with counsel and each other. It is also important to ensure the expert clearly delineates what documents were relied upon in the review of the file—especially when preparing a report that will eventually be released to opposing counsel. Again, in some jurisdictions, draft reports are discoverable. It is important to recognize that while nurse and physician experts might cooperate and coordinate with each other, the communications involved between the experts may or may not be discoverable by one's adversary once the matter is in suit. Sensitivity to the local rules on this issue allows the investigation stage to proceed in a manner that might not in the future jeopardize the litigation of the claim.

C. Affidavit of Merit

Originally implemented in many jurisdictions as a component of tort reform legislation, the affidavit of merit and other similar statutes in other jurisdictions have become the fodder of extensive litigation and have consistently served as a trap for unwary plaintiff's attorneys. Superficially, the concept is simple enough. Prior to the institution of suit, the plaintiff's attorney must retain a qualified expert and receive confirmation that the claim about to be prosecuted does indeed have merit. The details of the form of that proof, and how to get to it, vary significantly among jurisdictions.

However, issues related to timing and completeness of an affidavit of merit have led to many legal malpractice claims against plaintiff's attorneys for failing to adequately satisfy their local statutes.

TIP: Before considering entering plaintiff's malpractice litigation, it is imperative to become intimately familiar with one's jurisdiction's malpractice law, including certificates of merit, affidavits of merit, and the like. In many jurisdictions, the failure to fully comply with these statutes serves as a complete bar to recovery and forms the basis for a dismissal of plaintiff's claim.

If one's case screening infrastructure is well organized, the affidavit of merit is an integral component of the case screening process. Namely, the procurement of an affidavit of merit can act as a tickler or reminder to prompt the initiation of suit and a clear indication that the review has proven the case worthy for prosecution.

As with many other traps facing practitioners, the devil is always in the details. When pursuing a nursing malpractice claim, it is extraordinarily important to ensure the expert furnishing the affidavit of merit has the proper qualifications to criticize the putative defendant. The jurisdiction's statute typically is instructive. It is also essential to review the case law that interprets the statutory scheme. For example, a triage nurse might not be qualified to provide an affidavit of merit critical of a nurse in a geriatric setting, while the converse could also serve true. Many malpractice claims involve complaints of negligence against different professionals and specialties. If a claim involves asserted negligence against the surgeon, neurologist, and nurse, it will likely be necessary to procure three separate affidavits of merit, applicable to each defendant.

Certain realities in litigation make conformity with affidavit of merit statutes either difficult or impossible. The typical scenario involves plaintiffs who approach counsel shortly before a statute of limitations is about to run out. In jurisdictions that require an affidavit of merit to be submitted to counsel and the court very shortly after a complaint is filed, this proves to be impossible. The appropriate strategy in this regard is either to reject the case in its entirety or to employ early intervention with the court to obtain court orders for prompt production of medical records in sufficient time to have them evaluated and to obtain the affidavit of merit within the parameters of whatever statute applies.

TIP: Some jurisdictions, New Jersey being one example, include provisions of the affidavit of merit statute that address situations in which a defendant fails to produce a medical record, despite a legitimate request via certified mail. Under certain circumstances, the statute allows an affidavit to be presented to the court indicating that despite an appropriate and timely presented request for records with a HIPAA-compliant authorization, such records were never presented and otherwise would have been necessary to have the matter evaluated by an expert.

In the context of nursing home litigation, the federal regulatory scheme, 42 C.F.R. 483.10, Resident Rights, includes a subsection that compels defendants to produce a nursing home chart within two days of the date of a request. Thus, even though nursing homes rarely, if ever, produce such records in conformity with this very tight time limitation, an order to show cause filed pre-suit for a delinquent defendant can often serve to solve the dilemma faced by plaintiff's attorneys without sufficient time to have records reviewed.

14.9 Potential Liens
A. Medicaid Recipient

The payor source for all forms of medical treatment received by the plaintiff must be determined before pursuing any claim for nursing negligence. As a general rule, all bills related to a cause of action paid by Medicaid are subject to recovery prior to payment to the plaintiff. Within the realm of Medicaid liens there are two significantly differing forms.

The primary and more familiar Medicaid lien simply involves medical bills paid by Medicaid for treatment of injuries that mark the subject matter of litigation. As a general rule, Medicaid will allow a reduction in the gross amount of the lien by the percentage of the attorney's fee applicable for that case. Thus, a claim involving a one-third attorney's fee with a $100,000 lien would represent a $66,666 net lien for the plaintiff. However, under scenarios where there exists both a significantly sized lien and problematic liability, local representatives of Medicaid are often willing to compromise these claims.

The U.S. Supreme Court decided the seminal matter of *Arkansas Department of Health and Human Services et al. v. Ahlborn, 547 U.S.* 268 (2006). In a unanimous opinion, the Court found that an Arkansas law requiring Medicaid recipients to give all funds received from an award or settlement of a case to Medicaid violated Medicaid law. Rather, the Court held that the state can only recover that portion of the award of settlement specifically related to the repayment of medical expenses. Practitioners should carefully track those decisions that follow and interpret *Ahlborn* with regard to both Medicaid liens and its potential impact on Medicare liens.

TIP: Because of the length of time it takes to determine the amount and applicability of both Medicaid and Medicare liens, inquiries to these entities should be made as soon as a case is opened. It is not uncommon for Medicare to take in excess of two years to determine the amount and applicability of liens.

B. Estate Lien

The second and more onerous form of Medicaid liens is known as the Estate Lien. Although the statutory scheme is governed by one's local jurisdiction, the form of the statute appears to be uniform across multiple jurisdictions. The Medicaid Estate Lien is limited to non-spousal survivorship claims. Wrongful death claims are not affected. In sum, an Estate Lien is a claim filed by the state against the estate of the deceased plaintiff for any and all claims ever made by Medicaid on behalf of the decedent—whether or not they have any relationship to the claim at hand. The seeming justification for the Estate Lien is premised in the fact that Medicaid is a needs-based form of public assistance and is only provided when one's assets are at a sufficiently low level to employ public assistance. When there is any type of financial windfall to the estate, Medicaid enjoys a lien with a higher priority than that of the beneficiaries. There are certain exceptions to the applicability of the Estate Lien and thus, the statute and its interpreting case law should be examined before paying such liens. These may include cases of a surviving spouse or claims that involve legitimate assertions of undue hardship for surviving family members.

Additionally, Estate Liens do not apply to wrongful death claims, which are generally considered direct claims and do not need to flow through the estate. However, the strategy of simply characterizing a survivorship claim as a wrongful death claim will be highly scrutinized by Medicaid. It is generally believed that the recent *Ahlborn* decision will have no impact on the Estate Lien.

C. Medicare Recipient

Medicare is considered to represent a higher priority lien than Medicaid and has developed a reputation for taking extraordinary lengths of time to provide liens to attorneys. Attempts are being made on a legislative level to address this, but have not yet proven fruitful. Thus, it is important to get Medicare letters out quite early and to follow up. It is also essential to have the itemization of such liens carefully scrutinized by one's expert. Remember that the subrogation agencies for Medicare do not have nearly as intimate an understanding of plaintiff's claim as plaintiff's counsel or, indeed, defense counsel does. Thus, they generally err on the side of caution and include as many bills as can be related to the claim. For this reason, an early review of that itemization allows counsel to narrow the list down to bills that indeed bear relation to the claim at hand. However, as a claim progresses through litigation, more often than not, some allegations that seemed meritorious at the outset will fall by the wayside. Thus, continued communication with Medicare allows at least the effort to have portions of the claim redacted.

Medicare's subrogation entities have historically employed some rather confusing tactics in computing these liens. One that seems at least superficially egregious is the notion that if one very small portion of an extraordinarily large hospital bill bears any relation to the claim, Medicare takes the overt position that the entirety of that hospital bill can potentially serve as a lien against a claim. The typical example involves pressure ulcer claims. Under this scenario, an individual suffering from pressure ulcers and receiving inexpensive treatment at a nursing home might be sent to a hospital for a cardiac event. That particular hospital bill could reach the tens of thousands of dollars and have been occasioned solely as a result of the cardiac event. However, should Medicare's subrogation analysts find that in the diagnostic codes, pressure ulcer (diagnostic code 7070) exists, they generally will attempt to enforce a lien for the entirety of that hospital bill, arguing that there is no way to determine the cost of treatment for the pressure ulcer versus the myriad of other treatments provided and which otherwise clearly represent the vast majority of the bill. Medicare's representatives have expressed the view that these are supported in Medicare's regulations, but historically have not provided any detail as to how they have reached this conclusion. This certainly represents an issue that both plaintiff and defense attorney should address before paying an entire lien without close scrutiny.

Finally, it is vitally important to review the current status of the law pertaining to enforceability of Medicare liens on a federal level and with regard to the local jurisdiction's collateral source rule. These issues have been extensively litigated and have generally fallen on the side of confirming enforceability of Medicare liens. However, there is such a significant volume of litigation in this regard, that the law should be closely followed before such liens are paid.

It is also important to note that Medicare does, under certain circumstances, permit compromise or waiver of liens. These include cases involving liens much larger than the value of a claim or demonstrated proof of hardship if the full lien is enforced. It is also vital to understand that there exists a bureaucratic distinction between the vendors on the front line enforcing Medicare's liens and what is known as the "regional office" of Medicare. The regional office generally bears responsibility for request of either waiver or com-

promise while the computation itself occurs at the offices of the vendors. When significant dispute occurs as to the applicability of certain bills, much letter writing needs to occur before the attorney's allegations of inappropriate lien amounts can be addressed.

At the time of this writing (January 2011), there exists a significant concern on behalf of defense attorneys, their insurers, and many of their clients that recent amendments to Medicare regulations require something known as "Medicare Set Asides" to be utilized in liability settlements. One might argue that this is born out of a fear of the unknown. However, through a series of town hall meetings, position papers, and the like, Medicare has made clear that with the exception of workers' compensation settlements, there is no indication in the statutes which references any requirement for Medicare set asides to be established for liability claims. Further, Medicare has published documents known as "User Guides" and interpretive "alerts" which indicate that they have never stated that they intend to require Medicare set asides for liability settlements.

All of this being said, the regulatory and legal landscape often changes with tremendous velocity. Thus, practitioners must be careful in relying upon texts and findings rendered months or even years before a settlement. The challenge, of course, is that very often defense carriers insist upon putting together an impossible-to-construct instrument (the Medicare set aside) as a condition precedent to settling. For practitioners settling cases under this backdrop, the first order of business is to determine whether or not the lack of requirement for Medicare set asides as existed in the middle of 2010 persists. Should that status remain the same, counsel should work toward agreeing upon language in a release which relieves the defense of concerns over being independently pursued by Medicare and similarly should explore language to protect plaintiffs, in order that they do not potentially lose their benefits. In reality, absent a change in the status of the law and Medicare's position on such matters, neither side faces significant, if any, risk. Should all of this lead to a stalemate, the parties can literally attempt to establish a Medicare set aside and then learn the hard way that it is impossible to establish one with the guidance of Medicare — in the absence of a rule or regulatory change.

One should understand that the Medicare set asides relate solely to future medical expenses and their interrelationship with that component of the settlement which is specifically designated for future medical treatment and its attendant expenses. This discussion has nothing to do with payment for past case-related Medicare expenditures — which present themselves in the form of a more traditional Medicare lien.

14.10 Conflict of Interest

At the beginning of any claim, attorneys should ensure that a complete list of all plaintiffs and all defendants is addressed and that complete communication occurs with all other attorneys at one's firm to ensure there exists no conflict of interest. The obvious conflicts occur when a potential defendant has been represented by the plaintiff's attorney. This is axiomatic. However, it more subtly exists when addressing issues involving family members of deceased plaintiffs.

One's fee agreement needs to be carefully tailored to clearly delineate whom the plaintiff's attorney represents. In circumstances where there are divergent family members with varying interests, outside counsel will typically need to be employed to ferret out differences among the beneficiaries. If an attorney solely represents the estate, one must question how issues involving wrongful death claims will be handled vis-à-vis those of the survivorship claim. All issues that could potentially have a bearing on conflict of interest should be carefully reviewed and documented to ensure the parties and counsel are well aware of the issues that exist.

14.11 Summary

Careful case screening will make the difference between an effective plaintiff practice and one that drains the firm's resources without a meaningful return. Meticulous evaluation of liability and damages issues at the outset of a claim help the attorney make the necessary judgments about whether a claim should be pursued. This extra effort on the front end of case development also generates significant benefits once litigation ensues.

Endnotes

1. Myers, S., "Defense attorney perspective," In *Nursing Home Litigation: Investigation and Case Preparation*, Second edition, ed. P. Iyer. Tucson, Arizona: Lawyers and Judges Publishing Co., 2006.

2. Agency for Health Care Research and Quality, *Publications Pressure Ulcers in Adults: Prediction and Prevention* (Clinical Practice Guideline Number 3), 1994.

3. Agency for Health Care Research and Quality, *Treatment of Pressure Ulcers* (Clinical Practice Guideline Number 15), 1992.

4. Plunk, Dr. William, "Use of Percutaneous Endoscopic Gastrostomy Tubes in the Nursing Home," American Medical Directors Association Conference, 2006.

Additional Reading

The Joint Commission, *Comprehensive Accreditation Manual for Hospitals: The Official Handbook,* http://www.jointcommission.org.

Medicare Secondary Payer (MSP) Manual, Chapter 7—Contractor MSP Recovery Rules, http://www.medicare.gov.

National Senior Citizens Law Center, *Nursing Home Law Letter* (periodical).

OBRA Regulations, http://www.access.gpo.gov/nara/cfr/waisidx_03/42cfr483_03.html.

Winter, S. M., "Terminal Nutrition: framing the debate for the withdrawal of support in terminally ill patients," *American Journal of Medicine 9 (2000): 723-26.*

Chapter 15

The Plaintiff's Attorney's Perspective: Working Up a Case

Robert B. Buckalew, Esq., Tonia D. Aiken, JD, BSN, RN, and Diane Warlick, JD, BSN, RN

15.1 Introduction

Properly screening a potential nursing malpractice case is the first step on a pathway that hopefully results in a satisfied client. For some plaintiffs, getting questions answered about the origin of the damages, whether or not related to nursing care, is the prime motivation to seek the services of an attorney. For others, a desire to improve care for other patients is the prime motivating factor for instituting litigation. Some are so angry about the outcome of care that they want to see the nurse lose her license to practice. This chapter takes the reader through the initial intake and discovery phase of the case. It provides practical pointers for handling a claim from the plaintiff's attorney's perspective. Contrasts to defense of a case are noted in some areas.

In representing a plaintiff in a nursing malpractice case, the plaintiff's attorney keeps in mind that the eventual outcome of the case starts with the client and with the gradual development of the overall case. From the time a client becomes a plaintiff in a nursing malpractice case, case development begins, and it evolves from the time of the initial interview up until the time all information, witnesses and documentation are acquired. While such a case may eventually result in a settlement, attorneys representing plaintiffs should prepare their case from the outset as if they were planning to go to trial.

15.2 Setting Up the File

The beginning steps of filing a nursing malpractice claim involve learning what the plaintiff perceives as the cause of the injuries sustained or in some cases the death of the plaintiff. A frank discussion about the realities of filing a nursing malpractice claim including the costs, length of time, and likelihood of recovery is part of the initial work with the plaintiff. During the interview process, it is important that the plaintiff's attorney determine the expectations of the client with regard to a nursing malpractice case. Not only should the attorney explain the current state of law to the plaintiff, but the attorney should explain the type of recovery to which the plaintiffs may be entitled if their nursing malpractice case is successfully litigated or even settled. It is also important that the attorney explain the amount of preparation that will be needed to pursue a nursing malpractice case. The plaintiff's attorney should develop a bond of trust from the outset so that information will be forthcoming and the plaintiff's attorney will not be caught off guard with surprises at a later date. This means taking time out with the client to answer questions and address concerns. An attorney's time should not be any more important than the client's. Otherwise the client may perceive the attorney as uncaring and will not want his services.

The attorney representing the plaintiff will focus on three factors in a nursing malpractice claim, namely (1) liability, (2) extent of the plaintiff's damages, and (3) credibility and character of the plaintiff. With regard to the third factor (i.e., credibility and character of the plaintiff), remember the old defense adage: *"juries try people and not the facts of the case."* Absent either liability or damages, the nursing malpractice case is worthless. However, even when liability is clear and substantial damages are shown, a jury can still render a defense verdict if the plaintiff lacks credibility and character, or the jury could substantially diminish the award because of this one factor. It is vital to remember that all three of these factors reinforce each other in a nursing malpractice claim; and it is even more important to remember that a nursing malpractice case is no better than the client an attorney represents. In other words, the attorney takes clients as she finds them. Besides questions of liability and damages, always size up a potential client's character and credibility before agreeing to undertake representation.

Assuming liability is clear, always determine if the potential damages are substantial enough to justify pursuing a nursing malpractice claim. These claims can be expensive and time consuming and the costs of such a case have to be justified by the potential recovery. If the latter is lacking, the attorney may well decline to pursue such a claim.

The initial interview with the client and the initial case evaluation are crucial, but frequently overlooked, areas of preparation. Seldom can a nursing malpractice case be properly tried to a jury if there has not been good foundation work from the very commencement of the case. The initial interview should be conducted with more than a "get the facts" perspective. Although obtaining information from the client is the primary goal of the initial interview, it cannot be relegated to merely obtaining information. The client's family situation, as well as the emotional ordeal of going through a potential trial, must also be considered. Nonetheless, the interview should be conducted with some form of interview sheet in mind.

After a frank discussion has taken place and all questions and concerns of the attorney and the client have been addressed, the attorney will have the client sign a retention agreement which will be discussed in greater detail under Section 15.3. Forms providing permission to release medical records will also be signed, and records will then be requested. Other attorneys may choose to wait until the records are received and a positive opinion is obtained from an expert witness before having the client sign a retainer form.

TIP: The timing of when to sign the client up may vary from attorney to attorney, case to case, and state to state.

In some states, if a retainer agreement is signed after the attorney-client relationship has been established, the client may be deemed to have signed under duress if an attorney-client disagreement arises later.

15.3 The Client Retainer Form

The majority of plaintiff medical malpractice cases are handled on a contingency fee basis. Expert witnesses are paid costs up front—usually before testifying. The attorney may advance these costs on behalf of the plaintiff but should be repaid from the plaintiff's recovery at the end of the case. The maximum percentage of the recovery a plaintiff's attorney can earn may be regulated by the state bar. The attorney and the client must negotiate the actual percentage and the agreement must be put in writing. Contingency fee agreements are required to be in writing under the ABA Model Rules of Professional Ethics,[1] which have been adopted by all state bars in some form.

While the type of nursing malpractice case will dictate the percentage of an attorney's contingency fee, in states where permitted, the representing attorney should make certain that the contingency fee allows for more in-depth preparation, complexity and resistance from the defense in preparing and getting the plaintiff's case to trial. It should also be noted that in nursing malpractice death cases, the plaintiff's attorney should make sure the contract is with the administrator or the executor of the estate. In representing an injured minor, the plaintiff's attorney should make sure the contract is with the guardian of the minor's estate. In either case, it is prudent to get the court's permission to enter into the contract at the time the estate of the decedent or the minor is established.

While it is rarely used, an alternative to a percentage or contingency fee contract is an hourly fee. Most plaintiff clients will not select this method of payment in personal injury litigation because they cannot afford hourly representation. Malpractice and personal injury cases normally last several years and require hundreds of hours of legal work. The expenses for pursuing the case may also be quite large. Expert witness costs range from hundreds to many thousands of dollars depending upon witnesses' particular expertise and credentials. The contingency fee system was devised to make litigation feasible for injured parties without financial means to "pay as you go" for representation.

By way of contrast, representation of defendants is generally handled on an hourly fee basis. This is necessary since there is no sum of money paid to the defendant at the end of the case from which the attorney can take the fees. In addition, malpractice insurance companies usually pay for the defense of personal injury and malpractice cases. The insurance company negotiates an hourly fee with a defense firm to handle all its cases. This fee may be lower than the attorney's usual hourly rate based on the volume of cases handled for the insurer.

15.4 Medical Records

If a plaintiff client does not already have medical records in hand when seeking legal representation, it may take several weeks or months to acquire a complete copy. In malpractice cases it is highly preferable for the prospective plaintiff to request the records directly from the provider or facility. A records request from a plaintiff law firm is an automatic red flag, which may generate alterations or additions to the records. In addition, a patient's legal entitlement to a copy of the record should shorten the time it takes to obtain the record and reduce the fee charged for the copy. Many states have legislatively mandated time limits within which the medical record copy must be delivered to the patient. The law may also set the maximum per page amount that may be legally charged for photocopies, which might be lower for the patient.

At the time of the initial interview, it is extremely important for the plaintiff's attorney to get a complete list of the plaintiff's treating doctors, as well as the names of any hospitals, treatment facilities or other providers where the plaintiff has received medical care for the nursing malpractice case. It is also necessary for the plaintiff's attorney to inquire if the plaintiff has had any prior or subsequent injuries, as these may influence the outcome of the plaintiff's nursing malpractice claim.

In a nursing malpractice claim, since the treating doctor is the only one qualified to make an assessment of the plaintiff's physical condition, the eventual outcome of the plaintiff's damages at trial will largely hinge on the doctor's opinion, assuming liability is shown. Therefore, at the time of the initial interview, not only will the plaintiff's attorney have the necessary HIPAA medical authorizations signed, allowing the release of medical information, but the plaintiff's attorney will want to get the medical records and bills from the providers in case these cannot be obtained directly by the plaintiff. This applies not only to the medical providers involved in the plaintiff's current nursing malpractice case but to those providers involved in any prior or subsequent injuries that may be relevant to the current claim.

A large percentage of nursing malpractice claims involve the development of medical issues. Therefore, after the plaintiff's attorney has reviewed the plaintiff's medical records and identified any medical issues, he will then ask for the doctor's opinion or a separate medical expert's opinion, with regard to these medical issues.

An attorney cannot make an informed decision on whether or not to accept a malpractice case in the absence of a complete medical record. When medical records are extensive, the plaintiff may not have the funds to pay for the complete record. It may not be necessary to review an entire record to conduct a preliminary analysis related to specific time or provider-limited allegations of negligent medical or nursing care. In these cases, only limited pertinent portions of the record may need to be reviewed before a decision to accept the case can be made.

Nursing homes are subject to specific federal regulations with respect to who may obtain copies of a patient record. Krisztal[2] notes that when requesting the records from a nursing home, the records manager should be advised that the law firm is requesting the records pursuant to 42 C.F.R. 483.10, which states in part:

> Only the resident or his or her legal representative has the right (i) upon an oral or written request, to access all records pertaining to himself or herself including current clinical records within 24 hours (excluding weekends and holidays); and (ii) After receipt of his or her records for inspection, to purchase at a cost not to exceed the community standard photocopies of the records or any portion of them upon request and two working days advance notice to the facility.

Medical record departments of healthcare institutions and providers require a medical authorization signed by the patient (or a legally authorized representative in the event the patient is mentally incompetent or deceased) before release of the records to an attorney. HIPAA[3] regulations include very specific requirements for maintaining confidentiality of records and patient privacy.

An institution is required to release records once appropriate medical authorization has been signed and presented to the hospital. A 2005 Mississippi appellate court decision was held that the failure of the hospital to provide a complete medical record "tolled" or interrupted the statute of limitations. This allowed the plaintiff to file suit even though the statutory amount of time during which suit must be filed or precluded had already expired.[4]

Medical records may also be obtained by using a subpoena duces tecum under certain circumstances. Certain documents which are not part of the patient's record or which are protected from disclosure by law do not have to be produced, including peer review reports and incident reports. The individual requested to produce the record must object to the production of confidential documents and assert the legal basis for non-disclosure.

The original copy of the medical record should be placed in a sealed, dated envelope after copying to verify later whether pages are missing.

TIP: There have been many cases in which pages have been added to the record or altered before they are sent to the attorney. Sealing the medical record in an envelope preserves the true condition of the original record in the event there are alterations, insertions, or questions about the content.

The working copy can be reorganized in any manner most conducive for pre-trial work-up. After all medical records have been obtained, they must be organized and reviewed. See Chapter 7, *Nursing Documentation,* for suggestions on how to organize the medical record.

Some attorneys prefer the records be maintained in the original sequence, as records get shuffled and pulled out of sequence. In this system the pages of the medical record are numbered consecutively when obtained, in the order they are in when received. Others prefer the file be organized first and then numbered according to the sections of the chart. Often the facility will already have numbered the pages. Pages may be numbered with a Bates stamp or with clear numbered labels.

A brief written summation of the pertinent facts must be done by the attorney or a legal nurse consultant (LNC). The review should hone in on the pertinent issues and provide the reader with guidance on whether the claim has potential merit and should be sent to an expert witness for formal evaluation. If an expert witness is retained, a complete copy of the medical record should be duplicated, placed in a binder, organized, labeled, and sent to the expert witness, along with the attorney's or LNC's summary. The transmittal must list exactly what documents are being sent, inclusive dates of care they represent, and the number of pages.

TIP: Never give the expert the only copy of the medical record. Although delivery services and express mail carriers cost money, a lost medical record costs more to replace or may be irreplaceable. Experts are generally reliable, but they do on occasion lose records, x-rays, slides, and so on. In one other instance, original x-ray films were inadvertently left in a taxicab. There were no copies.

In most circumstances anything sent to the expert is discoverable. Thus, the case summary and request for an expert opinion must contain only the bare facts without any interpretation, opinion of merit, or legal analysis. The analysis of liability issues should be kept in a separate document which can be protected from disclosure as an attorney work product.

It is better not to discuss with or provide to the expert the attorney's liability theories before he has reviewed the records.

15.5 Researching the Issues and Setting Up the File

Some unique fact patterns of nursing malpractice claims may require legal research. The attorney's task is to interpret the potential effect of the laws, regulations, and judicial opinions to specific factual circumstances and then advise the client on how the law may apply to that situation. To do this the attorney must be fully knowledgeable about the language of applicable laws, regulations, and court opinions. Some LNCs and paralegals do the research for the attorneys or the company by whom they are employed. The research must be updated regularly because the law evolves on a daily basis.

Legal research previously required hours and often days of sitting in law libraries going through cases and statute indexes, books, and updates to be sure they were aware of the latest laws and court rulings on an issue. Today most of the research can be done on the Internet, and the cases, statutes, and regulations downloaded for future reference. Congress, all state legislatures, and most courts that issue written opinions have websites updated daily, if not hourly. To find a specific court case on a court website, the researcher must know the name and type of the court, and the docket or case number or names of one or more of the parties. Courts began posting opinions on their websites in the late 1990s. Earlier cases may not be available directly from the court. Refer to Table 15.1 for information regarding Internet sources for legal research.

Once the attorney has decided to accept representation of the client in the medical malpractice case, as documents are obtained in the case, a record must be kept of the date when each document is received in the office, the number of pages, and who provided them. A reliable reminder system is critical for legal professionals who have numerous cases to keep track of at one time. Before computer technology, deadlines were managed by tickler systems—a process using index cards and file boxes with data organized sequentially and cross indexed. Various deadlines and other critical dates were put on individual cards and filed by date. Computer technology has superseded tickler systems and provides the ability to organize data and track deadlines electronically with increasing sophistication. Various software programs are on the market for case management and docketing specifically for the law office. In addition, most attorneys carry personal data assistants (PDAs) or smartphones to keep track of deadlines, create lists, and store client and contact information and appointments. The information on PDAs or smartphones can be shared or synced with the office computer database so the staff has access to the same up-to-date information.

Table 15.1
Websites for Legal Research

- http://www.firstgov.gov/Agencies/Federal/Judicial.shtml—List of federal courts by type of court.
- http://www.uscourts.gov/—Alphabetical list of courts by state.
- http://www.uscourts.gov/images/CircuitMap.pdf—A map showing location of federal trial and appeals courts.
- http://pacer.psc.uscourts.gov/psco/cgi-bin/links.pl—Federal court cases including all pleadings filed with the court are available on the "pacer" system. This requires an individual account, password and payment of $.08 per page to view and download.
- http://www.findlaw.com/casecode/—Links to state websites as well as federal courts.
- www.usa.gov/Citizen/Topics/PublicSafety/Courts.shtml—Click on either "Federal Judicial Branch" or "State Courts."

Legal Research Web-Sites

Federal Judiciary	www.uscourts.gov
Links to all Federal Courts	www.uscourts.gov/links.html
Links to Federal and State cases and codes	
(Findlaw has links to everything)	www.findlaw/casecode
U.S. Supreme Court	www.supremecourtus.gov
U.S. Supreme Court opinions at Findlaw	www.findlaw.com/10fedgov/judicial/supreme_court/
	opinions.htm
U.S. Supreme Court cases at Cornell	www.supct.law.cornell.edu/supct/index
Thomas—Federal Legislative info	
at Library of Congress	www.thomas.loc.gov
Links to hundreds of legal sites—some	
free and some forms for sale	www.lawyertool.com
Federal and state court forms—some free	http://findforms/uscourtforms.com
Findlaw State law and agency links	www.findlaw.com/11stategov/indexcode.htm
State statutes organized by topic	www.law.cornell.edu/topics/statestatutes.html#
Code of Federal Regulations	www.access.gpo.gov/nara/cfr/index.html
Federal Register	www.gpoaccess/fr/index.html
All Uniform or Model Codes	www.law.cornell.edu/statutes.html#state
Case Summaries since 2000 for	
all Federal Courts, NY and CA	www.caselaw.lp.findlaw.com/casesummary
Tarlton Law Library, Univ of Texas	www.law.utexas.edu/research
Georgia State Univ meta-index	
for legal research	http://gsulaw.gsu.edu/metaindex
Univ of Pa Law School Library	www.law.upenn.edu/bll/res/research.htm
American Law Institute	www.ali.org
U.S. Code—Cornell	www4.law.cornell.edu/uscode/#TITLES
U.S. Code—official site	www.access.gpo.gov/congress/cong013.html

continued on next page...

Table 15.1
Websites for Legal Research (continued)

Professional Association Websites

Academy of Medical-Surgical Nurses	www.medsurgnurse.org
Aerospace Medical Association	www.asma.org
Air and Surface Transport Nurses	www.astna.org
American Academy of Allergy and Immunology	www.aaaai.org
American Academy of Ambulatory Care Nursing	www.aaacn.org
American Academy of Child andAdolescent Psychiatry	www.aacap.org
American Academy of Cosmetic Surgery	www.cosmeticsurgery.org
American Academy of Dermatology	www.aad.org
American Academy of Facial Plastic & Reconstructive Surgery	www.facial-plastic-surgery.org
American Academy of Family Physicians	www.aafp.org
American Academy of Insurance Medicine	www.aaimedicine.org
American Academy of Neurology	www.aan.com/professionals
American Academy of Ophthalmology	www.aao.org
American Academy of Orthopedic Surgeons	www.aaos.org
American Academy of Otolaryngologic Allergy	www.allergy-ent.com
American Academy of Otololaryngology—Head and Neck	www.entnet.org
American Academy of Pain Medicine	www.painmed.org
American Academy of Pediatrics	www.aap.org
American Academy of Pharmaceutical Physicians	www.aapp.org
American Academy of Physical Medicine and Rehab	www.aapmr.org
American Academy of Physician Assistants	www.aapa.org
American Academy of Sleep Medicine	www.aasmnet.org
American Association for Continuity of Care	www.continuityofcare.com
American Association of Critical Care Nurses	www.aacn.org
American Association of Legal Nurse Consultants	www.aalnc.org
American Association of Neuroscience Nurses	www.aann.org
The American Association of Nurse Attorneys	www.taana.org
American Association of Occupational Health Nurses	www.aaohn.org
American Association of Spinal Cord Injury Nurses	www.aascin.org
American Association for Thoracic Surgery	www.aats.org
American Association for Vascular Surgery	www.aavs.vascularweb.org
American Association of Clinical Endocrinologists	www.aace.com
American Association of Clinical Urologists	www.aacuweb.org
American Association of Electrodiagnostic Medicine	www.aaem.net
American Association of Gynecological Laparoscopists	www.aagl.com
American Association of Hip and Knee Surgeons	www.aahks.org
American Association of Neurological Surgeons	www.neurosurgery.ord/aans
American Association of Nurse Anesthetists	www.aana.com
American Board of Bariatric Surgery	www.asbs.org
American Board of Medical Specialties	www.abms.org
American Board of Surgery	www.absurgery.org
American Chiropractic Association	www.amerchiro.org
American College of Healthcare Executives	www.ache.org

continued on next page…

Table 15.1
Websites for Legal Research (continued)

American College of Nurse Practitioners	www.nurse.org/acnp
American Dental Association	www.ada.org
American Health Information Management Association	www.ahima.org
American Holistic Nurses Association	www.ahna.org/home
American Society of Perianesthesia Nursing	www.aspan.org
American Medical Association	www.ama-assn.org
American Medical Informatics Association	www.amia.org
American Medical Women's Association	www.amwa-doc.org/index
American Nephrology Nurses Association	www.anna.inurse.com
American Osteopathic Association	www.aoa-net.org
American Psychiatric Association	www.psych.org
American Psychiatric Nurses Association	www.apna.org
American Society for Clinical Pathology	www.ascp.org
American Society for Dermatologic Surgery	www.asds-net.org
American Society for Gastrointestinal Endoscopy	www.asge.org
American Society for Parenteral and Enteral Nutrition	www.clinnutr.org
American Society for Reproductive Medicine	www.asrm.org
American Society for Surgery of the Hand	www.hand-surg.org
American Society for Therapeutic Radiology and Oncology	www.astro.org
American Society of Abdominal Surgeons	www.gis.net/~absurg
American Society of Addiction Medicine	www.asam.org
American Society of Cataract & Refractive Surgery	www.ascrs.org
American Society of Clinical Oncology	www.asco.org/asco
American Society of Colon & Rectal Surgeons	www.fascrs.org
American Society of Cytopathology	www.cytopathology.org
American Society of General Surgeons	www.theasgs.org
American Society of Hematology	www.hematology.org
American Society of Maxillofacial Surgeons	www.maxface.org
American Society of Neuroimaging	www.asnweb.org
American Society of Neuroradiology	www.asnr.org
American Society of Plastic Surgeons	www.plasticsurgery.org
Association of Perioperative Registered Nurses	www.aorn.org
Association of Rehabilitation Nurses	www.rehabnurse.org
Assn of Women's Health, Obstetric & Neonatal Nurses	www.awhonn.org
British Medical Association	www.bma.org.uk/ap.nsf
Canadian Medical Association	www.cma.ca/cma/common
Developmental Disabilities Nurses Association	www.ddna.org
Dermatology Nurses Association	www.dna/inurse.com
Emergency Nurses Association	www.ena.org
Federation of State Medical Boards	www.fsmb.org
Infusion Nurses Society	www.ins1.org
International College of Surgeons	www.icsglobal.org/aboutus
National Association of Clinical Nurse Specialists	www.nacns.org
National Association of Neonatal Nurse Specialists	www.nann.org
National Association of Orthopaedic Nurses	www.orthonurse.org
National Assn of Pediatric Nurse Practitioners	www.napnap.org

continued on next page...

Table 15.1
Websites for Legal Research (continued)

National Association of School Nurses	www.nasn.org
National Conference of Gerontological Nurse Practitioners	www.ncgnp.org
National League for Nursing	www.nln.org
National Organization of Nurse Practitioner Faculties	www.nonpf.com
North American Nursing Diagnosis Association	www.nanda.org
Nurses Organization of Veteran's Affairs	www.vanurse.org
Nurse Practitioners in Women's Health	www.npwh.org
Oncology Nursing Society	www.ons.org
Sigma Theta Tau International	www.nursingsociety.org
Society of Otorhinolaryngology, Head & Neck Nurses	www.sohnnnurse.com
Society of Urologic Nurses and Associates	www.suna.org
Wound, Ostomy and Continence Nurses Society	www.wocn.org

Government and Nonprofit Healthcare Organization Websites

Agency for Healthcare Research and Quality	www.ahcpr.gov
American Hospital Association	www.hospitalconnect.com/aha/index
American Public Health Association	www.apha.org
Center for Disease Control	www.cdc.gov
Joint Commission on Accreditation of Healthcare Organizations	www.jacho.org
Kaiser Family Foundation	www.kaisernetwork.org
Morbidity, Mortality Weekly Report	www.cdc.gov/mmwr
National Academies Press	www.nap.edu
National Assn of Public Hospitals and Health Systems	www.naph.org
National Cancer Institute	www.nci.nih.gov
National Center for Infectious Diseases	www.cdc.gov/publications
National Eye Institute	www.nei.nih.gov
National Guideline Clearinghouse	www.guideline.gov/index
National Heart, Lung and Blood Institute	www.nhlbi.nih.gov
National Institute on Aging	www.nia.nih.gov
National Institute of Allergy and Infectious Disease	www.niaid.nih.gov
National Institute of Child Health & Human Development	www.nichd.nih.gov
National Institute of Diabetes & Digestive & Kidney Diseases	www.niddik.nih.gov
National Institutes of Health	www.nih.gov/icd
Institute of Medicine	www.iom.edu/iom/iomhome.nsf
National Institute of Mental Health	www.nimh.nih.gov
National Institute of Neurological Disorders And Stroke	www.ninds.nih/gov
National Institute of Nursing Research	www.ninr.nih.gov
National Institute for Occupational Safety & Health	www.cdc.gov/niosh/homepage
National Library of Medicine	www.nlm.nih.gov
National Practitioner Data Bank	www.npdb-hipdh.com
U.S. Dept. of Health and Human Services	www.os.dhhs.gov
World Health Organization	www.who.int.en

---

1. Records management system software:

Legal Specific
- Legal Trax: www.interwoven.com/company
- Legal Key

Generic
- Infolinx
- Trim Captura
- QRMS Record Management Software

2. Personalized file management system database software such as:
- Microsoft Access
- Corel's Paradox
- InMagic's DB Textworks

3. Comprehensive case management programs such as:
- Abacus Law
- Time Matters
- Amicus Attorney

Figure 15.1 *Computer Applications for Law Firms*

Case management and docketing, or scheduling, software programs organize and handle information, which can be accessed and retrieved in pre-programmed formats. They range from offering calendar and scheduling functions to producing detailed data on individual cases. It is beyond the scope of this chapter to analyze or critique the various programs on the market. In addition, the usefulness of a particular system will be based upon personal preferences and needs. The American Bar Association has detailed office technology reviews with links to the commercial websites. Refer to Figure 15.1 for some well-known computer applications reviewed by the American Bar Association (ABA). More detailed information on the functions of the various programs can be found on the ABA website: www.abanet.org/tech.

The usefulness and accuracy of these care and record management systems always depends upon the accuracy and timeliness of the information keyed into the database. One of the most important dates to docket is the last date the case may be filed—that is, the statute of limitations deadline. Missing this deadline can rarely be remedied and is automatically a breach of the attorney's duty to clients. The case docket and daily schedules should be printed ev-

ery morning to check dates and so on, and distributed to all office personnel. These must be coordinated with the individual attorney's and legal nurse consultant's calendars on a daily basis. Rigid adherence to this process keeps the law office efficient and organized; the attorney should never miss another deadline.

15.6 Expert Witnesses

The term "expert" almost defies meaning, use and application. The determination of the validity of an expert witness in trial is most frequently made at the time the expert is initially selected. Unfortunately, a common mistake is made by retaining an expert without sufficient background investigation as to credentials, prior testimony, criminal problems and credibility issues. While expert witnesses may be either local or national experts, it is recommended that local experts be retained whenever possible. There are frequently experts available in most geographic locations if one takes the time to search. Generally, local experts are better received by local juries than experts of another region.

By the end of the 1980s, all state courts recognized that medical and nursing standards of care are national in scope. If it becomes difficult to find a local expert who will review a case and testify against a healthcare provider in the same community, then it may be necessary to find an expert outside the locality or state who can review and evaluate the nursing malpractice claim. When looking for a nursing expert, consider the following:

1. Is the expert currently practicing or teaching in the specialty at issue?
2. Has the expert published textbooks, journal articles, or research papers?
3. Has the expert testified for plaintiff or defendant in a deposition or at trial? How many for each?
4. Has the expert been qualified or disqualified as an expert in her field in any court?
5. Has the expert reviewed cases or testified in cases for primarily plaintiffs or defendants?
6. Does the expert have "presence" and present well before a jury?
7. Can and does the expert teach?
8. Can the expert be understood or is there a language barrier, for example, an accent?
9. Is the expert likable?
10. Does the expert have references so that you can call and speak to other attorneys about working with the expert?
11. Is the expert easy to work with?
12. What are the expert's fees?

13. Is the expert knowledgeable about proving liability, or (if appropriate) causation and damages?
14. What are the qualifications of the expert and board certifications?
15. Has the expert testified before in a factually similar case?[5]

The attorney should also check on the data banks such as IDEX for defense attorneys and Trialwatch for plaintiff's attorneys and court records for prior testimony by experts. Transcripts of prior testimony can be obtained from the attorneys in the case or court reporters after searching court records online for the names of testifying experts. The prior testimony may be used in preparing for an expert's deposition to see how he has previously performed under pressure and to identify prior testimony that may affect or contradict the expert's opinion in a current case.

Many state laws now restrict the qualification of an expert based upon the years and nature of their clinical practice. An expert may be required to have been practicing in the same specialty in which testimony will be given at the time of the incident at issue or within a specific number of years from the incident. To qualify as an expert in a nursing malpractice case, Texas, for instance, requires that the expert have been practicing nursing at the time such testimony was given or at the time the claim arose.[6]

Plaintiff's experts may be asked to do various tasks such as:

1. Determine which records are needed to properly review the case
2. Perform a detailed review of the records
3. Render an oral report
4. Render a written report
5. Determine what other experts are needed for the case
6. Define the breaches of the standard of care
7. Define the damages
8. Outline the elements of negligence: duty, breach of duty, proximate cause, and damages
9. Define the economic losses
10. Assist in preparing the case for trial or a medical review panel
11. Assist in preparing the case for mediation or arbitration
12. Assist the attorney in preparing for depositions
13. Assist the attorney in preparing discovery (e.g., interrogatories, requests for production of documents, and so on)
14. Work with other experts in preparing the case for trial
15. Assist in developing and selecting the appropriate visual aids and demonstrative evidence to be used at trial (e.g., medical illustrations)
16. Assist the attorney in developing the theme of the case to the jury
17. Determine if the claim is defensible
18. Determine if the plaintiff has a claim for damages and liability[7]

Experts can be found through various sources. A literature search on the specific topic at issue in the case (e.g., decubitus ulcers or assessment techniques) will identify the authors who are experts on the subject matter. Nurses who have authored textbooks, chapters, or articles are usually seen as authorities and many will review and evaluate cases for attorneys. Other attorneys who have successfully used a particular expert may be good sources of referrals. The local universities and medical and nursing schools are great sources for experts. Teachers are accustomed to explaining their area of expertise, which is exactly what the expert will do at trial for the jury. If an expert is not willing to review a case, she may be willing to refer a colleague.

Other possible ways to find expert witnesses include case reporters and legal publications. National and local attorney associations have expert data banks containing copies of deposition testimony by experts that are available to its members and can be purchased. The review of prior testimony is invaluable for assessing: the clarity with which an expert explains the facts, the expert's strengths and weaknesses, and any skeletons lurking in the expert's background. Attending seminars is an excellent means of identifying potential experts who enjoy public speaking on their area of expertise.

Experts can also be found through expert referral services or consultants; however, it is very important the expert not be viewed as a "hired gun" in the industry. "Hired gun" is a term used for an individual whose current professional practice consists almost exclusively of providing expert witness services for hire. Legislation restricting expert qualifications may ultimately eliminate these experts from the pool. Specifically ask what percentage of a potential expert's income is derived from testifying as an expert witness. Additional information about the location and screening of expert witnesses is found in Chapter 21, *Working with Nursing Expert Witnesses.*

It is important to use great care in communicating with experts from the outset. The assumption should be made that every conversation among counsel, client, attorney and anyone else concerning the expert's work on the case along with all material in the expert's file and documents generated by the expert, will be discovered. Therefore, the plaintiff's attorney has to be extremely careful in dealing with an expert. Otherwise, it is better to look for another expert than to try to block discovery that might be embarrassing.

Be aware of the court rules regarding the use of written reports. Some require them; others do not. The plaintiff's attorney should remember to give the client clear guidelines as to what can and cannot be discussed with the expert. In fact, plaintiff's counsel may want to consider proposing an agreement with opposing counsel which will allow experts to communicate in writing but only permit discovery on that which is relied upon.

15.7 What Do You Have to Prove?

In professional malpractice cases, including alleged nursing negligence, the plaintiff must prove two distinct components: liability (breach of duty and causation) and damages. It is necessary in most cases that one expert testify that there is a breach of the standard of care that caused the damages suffered by the plaintiff. In some cases two experts may be required. For example, a nurse may testify in nursing negligence cases on the deviation from the standard of care, but not to causation. Courts have held that since determining the cause of an injury involves the making of a diagnosis, only a physician may testify that the deviation from the applicable standards caused the alleged harm to the patient.[8]

TIP: A case must be looked at in great detail. Although a case may appear to have extensive damages, if the injuries cannot be related to any breach of the standard of care by a nurse, it is just a bad result.

There are various types of damages that can be part of a claim:

1. Special Damages—actual monetary losses, such as lost wages for the past, present, and future, caused by the defendant's acts.
2. General Damages—awarded for the plaintiff's non-economic losses such as pain and suffering caused by the defendant's acts.
3. Punitive Damages—intended to punish the defendant for the egregious nature of the tort. The defendant's actions must be willful and wanton, and the damages are not based on the plaintiff's actual monetary loss but in the wealth of the defendant to "punish" the defendant economically to prevent re-

currence of the reckless behavior. Many states limit punitive damages to an amount double or triple the actual damages. Punitive damages are not common in nursing malpractice suits except those involving nursing home patients.

In addition to damages for wrongful death, some states, such as Arkansas, allow the decedent's estate to recover for the decedent's loss of life as an independent element of damages.

15.8 Discovery Tools

Discovery is a critical aspect of every case. At this time an attorney can learn the intricate details surrounding the alleged acts of malpractice and circumstances of the plaintiff's alleged damages. There are several different discovery methods that are utilized by attorneys. They include informal and formal discovery.

A. Informal Discovery

Informal discovery includes those techniques for gaining information about the case that do not require specific authority from state civil procedure rules. Informal discovery techniques can often be more effective than formal discovery devices in gathering information. In part, informal discovery may be more effective because the techniques involved can generally be used without notice to the other side. The methods of informal discovery are limited only by the lawyer's creative imagination and ethical constraints. Some of the suggested methods of informal discovery include: (1) interviewing the client; (2) interviewing the witnesses; (3) visiting the scene where the malpractice allegedly occurred; (4) inspecting and/or photographing the scene, equipment and other evidence; (5) inspecting physical evidence; and (6) consulting with experts. Informal discovery also includes anything else the attorney can think of that is not illegal or prohibited by the rules of professional conduct.

One of the most successful informal discovery tools is a unique device called a telephone. It is amazing how much information one can obtain informally by establishing an honest and trusting relationship with the attorneys with whom you normally work. Other sources of informal discovery include the Internet generally, databases such as Lexis, Westlaw, MySpace, Facebook, and other social networking sites, as well as other research websites.

Another form of informal discovery involves independent physical examinations. These are usually performed by a healthcare provider that has been selected by either or both of the parties if there is a dispute as to the plaintiff's or patient's actual damages. While these examinations are usually called "independent examinations," "IME's," "insurance medical examinations," or "defense medical examinations," it is suggested that these terms not be used at all. When used, these terms imply that the examining doctor second guess a treating provider. Many doctors get caught up in semantics and do not like being put in a position of second guessing a treating doctor. Therefore, it is suggested that the term "medical evaluation" be used at all times.

Presumably an objective third party practitioner selected by both defense and plaintiff can render an unbiased opinion as to the actual cause of injuries. In recent years, many attorneys have lost faith in this practice as producing an independent result, and as such this practice has been somewhat discouraged.

B. Formal Discovery

Naturally there is some discovery on a formal basis that is needed for most all cases, including nursing malpractice cases. However, the client's rights and the attorney's responsibilities should not be minimized by excessive informality to the sacrifice of proper preparation and preservation of legal rights and remedies. Where needed, types of formal discovery include:

- interrogatories,
- requests for production of documents,
- admissions of fact, and
- depositions.

Some attorneys prefer to retain expert witnesses to review the medical record before filing claims and initiating discovery so that the expert can assist with or direct discovery. Attorneys knowledgeable in the subject matter of the case may prefer to simply present the expert with all of the information that has been gathered through the methods outlined below.

A paper system for tracking documents involves assembling a discovery notebook or binder for various subjects, witnesses, and so on; it is very useful for organizing the information collected through discovery. The notebook may include:

1. Complaints
2. Documents produced in response to a request for production
3. Interrogatory responses
4. Pertinent medical, hospital, and office records
5. Summaries of medical records
6. Chronology of events

7. Medical research and applicable case law
8. Deposition transcripts
9. Deposition summaries
10. Expert reports

Electronic methods of assembling material involve scanning documents or saving documents as PDF (portable document format) files. A PDF file may be read by a user regardless of software or computer operating system. PDF documents cannot be edited or changed, but with Adobe Acrobat the document may be saved in rich text format, and then opened in Microsoft Word for editing. PDF files may include bookmarks, password protection, and digital signatures. Files may be saved and loaded onto an intranet (computer system within a law firm that is accessible by the firm's attorneys and other employees) or extranet (an extension of an institution's intranet, especially over the World Wide Web, enabling communication between the institution and people it deals with, often by providing limited access to its intranet). Once pages of the medical record, policies and procedures, incident reports, and other documents are in an electronic format, it becomes easy to locate specific information and incorporate material into demonstrative evidence.

1. Interrogatories

Interrogatories are written questions sent by either party requesting specific information such as the background of the defendants, plaintiffs' job experience, information on disease entities, fact or expert witnesses, specific allegations of negligence, insurance policies, and so on. Some states have uniform interrogatories that are answered for any medical malpractice claim. Supplemental interrogatories may be served on the opposing counsel to clarify answers to the interrogatories or to explore other individualized issues.

There is usually a time limit within which the opposing side must answer the interrogatories, and there may be a limit on the number of questions asked. Interrogatories are posed to the party but generally answered or carefully reviewed by the attorneys. For this reason, interrogatories are designed to obtain factual background information, the response to which does not benefit from spontaneity. Questions an attorney wants an opposing party to answer without a great deal of reflection or attorney consultation are reserved for depositions. Objections to interrogatories must be provided in response to questions not answered along with the reason for the objection. Figure 15.2 lists sample interrogatory questions.

INTERROGATORY NO. 1:
Please state your full name; the date and place of your birth; and your residential address and telephone number.

INTERROGATORY NO. 2:
Have you ever been known by any other name? If so, for each other name, state:
- (a)   The name in full.
- (b)   The inclusive dates you were known by that name.

INTERROGATORY NO. 3:
Have you retained an expert to act on your behalf in any matter pertaining to this action? If so, for each expert, state:
- (a)   Name, office address, and telephone number
- (b)   Occupation and specialty
- (c)   A description of qualifications
- (d)   The number of years of experience he or she has in the specialty
- (e)   Whether he or she practices nursing, and, if so, the name of the locality in which he or she practices
- (f)   The name of each nursing organization of which the expert is a member
- (g)   A description of the services the expert has been employed to perform
- (h)   A description of the remuneration for which you employed the expert
- (i)   Whether you propose to call the expert as a witness
- (j)   Whether the expert has ever been a witness in any other lawsuit, and, if so, for each lawsuit, give the name of the suit, the kind of suit involved, the name of the court, the date of filing, and the name and address of the party for whom the expert gave evidence
- (k)   List of all materials including but not limited to textbooks, journal articles, and standards the expert has reviewed and used to render an expert opinion about the liability and damages in this case
- (l)   Scope of facts and opinions to which the expert is expected to testify

INTERROGATORY NO. 4:
Please list all fact witnesses you will call at the trial of this matter
- (a)   Fact witness's name, address, and telephone number
- (b)   Scope of facts to which the witness is expected to testify

INTERROGATORY NO. 5:
Is there any person who has knowledge or information concerning this case whose name and address is not listed in the preceding interrogatories? If so, for each such person, state:
- (a)   His or her name, address, and telephone number
- (b)   The address of the place where he or she is employed
- (c)   His or her occupation and job title
- (d)   What information or knowledge concerning this case the person possesses

Figure 15.2 *Sample Interrogatories*

The following tips are useful for writing effective interrogatories:

1. Write clear and simple interrogatories.
2. Outline the type of information you are trying to elicit from the opposing side.
3. Develop specific interrogatories that will produce information rather than being objected to by the opposing attorney—avoid a "fishing expedition."
4. Ask general interrogatories about the defendant's address, education, and background.
5. Ask information related to the allegations in the lawsuit.
6. Ask specific questions about the claim.
7. Do not ask compound or complex questions that may be objected to by opposing counsel.

Examples of Interrogatories:

1. Please list and describe common signs and symptoms of sepsis.
2. Please list and describe common signs and symptoms of fetal distress.
3. Please list all signs and symptoms of fetal distress exhibited by plaintiff _____ on November 18, 2006.
4. Please list all signs and symptoms of sepsis exhibited by plaintiff _____ on _____ between 10 A.M. and 7 P.M.

Procedural aspects of discovery practice:

1. Docket the time when answers to interrogatories are due by opposing counsel.
2. If answers are not received on the date, call opposing counsel and follow with a letter confirming the conversation.
3. If you do not receive the answers on the date agreed upon, file the necessary documents in court to compel answers.
4. It is important to keep track of dates so that the case can be moved quickly.

2. Requests for production of documents and things

Requests for production of documents and things are written requests for documents pertinent to the circumstances surrounding the alleged act of malpractice or negligence. Items of equipment that may have failed and harmed the patient may also be requested. The actual item involved in the incident in question must be preserved and is subject to examination under carefully controlled circumstances.

A request for production of documents and things includes requests for computer disks and other data in electronic format, personnel files, medical records, fetal monitoring strips, office records, physician records, OR or labor and delivery logs, ambulance run sheets, emergency room reports, autopsy reports, policy and procedures, standards of care or expert witness reports, telephone records, and anything else that is arguably pertinent to the case.

In nursing home cases, Krisztal[9] suggests asking for:

*   Programs, textbooks, manuals, or other materials in connection with training given to all employees of the facility and of the facilities responsible for nursing services, such employees including, but not limited to, Director of Nursing and assistants, Health Service Supervisor and assistants, staff nurses, charge nurses, certified medication technicians, certified medication aides, certified nurses' aides, nurses aides, social service workers, activity directors, and restorative aides.
*   Names of individuals contacted, and the dates of said contacts, to verify the background of nursing employees prior to commencement of employment with defendant's nursing home.
    [The above information may verify the claim of negligent hiring. In one instance, a case was litigated wherein a resident was injured as she was transferred from the wheelchair to the bed. The aide failed to follow the facility's policies which required the assistance of two people when transferring a resident. The aide listed two previous jobs with other nursing homes. He was fired from the other nursing homes for his failure to properly transfer residents, and failure to follow the facility's policies and procedures in transferring the resident.]
*   Complaints made to defendants regarding treatment, abuse, or injuries sustained by residents of the nursing home.

TIP: If the facility received a complaint previously, be it from an employee or another resident, it would go to the issue of notice.

---

*   Records of all safety-oriented inservice meetings held and evidence as to who attended such meetings.
*   Weekly census sheets from the time of plaintiff's admission until the time of final discharge. If your client was a resident of the facility for several years,

and the issues which you are litigating relate to the last six months, for example, you may want to start by asking only for that period of time. The above will be necessary to establish whether the facility had sufficient staff to meet the resident's needs.

- Copies of the nursing policy and procedure manual(s) in use during the time plaintiff was a resident at the institution, as well as a list of all policies and procedures manuals in use at the facility.
- Copy of the Wound Care Manual.
- Copy of the Dietary Manual.

[The defendants have developed a tendency to offer the index for review and have the plaintiff's attorney inform them what sections she or he wishes to receive. Refuse such an offer and demand the entire policy manual. Relevant policies can be more readily identified. Moreover, there is generally no privilege attached and no reason for the limitation. Additionally, it may infringe on the analysis of the case.]

[As it relates to the policies and procedures, defendants have requested counsel to agree to a Protective Order. The courts do not favor Protective Orders, and the defendant has the obligation to demonstrate the reasons for the Protective Order to be issued. The simple fact that it wants one does not mean it is entitled to it. It is strongly suggested the plaintiff's attorney oppose such requests.]

- Corporate policy regarding hiring, retention, and termination of employees.
- Copies of any and all policies of insurance in effect during the time alleged in the petition that would cover the incidents in question (if discoverable).
- A list of nursing homes owned, managed, and/or operated by defendant.
- Copies of any and all investigative reports conducted by defendants, other than those commenced at the instruction of counsel, or in anticipation of litigation, pertaining to the injuries sustained by plaintiff while residing at defendants' nursing home.
- There are numerous laws requiring certain injuries to be investigated. OBRA provides that the facility must ensure that all alleged violations involving mistreatment, neglect, or abuse, including injuries of unknown source, be reported immediately to the administrator of the facility and to other officials in accordance with state law. (See 31 U.S.C.S. 3730 et.seq.) The facility "must have evidence that all alleged violations are thoroughly investigated." (See 42 C.F.R. 483.13(c) (2).)

- Copies of defendants' policies and procedures regarding investigation of accidents pertaining to injuries suffered by residents of the nursing home. [This is helpful to determine if the facility followed its own policies, and for the administrator and management to explain why not, if that is the case.]
- Employee's personnel file. Most of the daily care is provided by certified nurse's aides. OBRA requires the facility to complete performance reviews at least once annually. (See 42 C.F. R. 403.75 (e) (8).)
- Quality assessment reports. [OBRA requires the facility to maintain a quality assessment and assurance committee consisting of the director of nursing, a physician, and at least three other members of the facility staff. (See 42 C.F.R. 403.75 (O)] [It has been opined that records created in response to state surveys and deficiencies issued by the state do not fall within the definition of "peer review." (See 42 C.F.R. 483 et seq. (requirements for states and long-term care facilities). Moreover, look at the Peer Review Statute in the jurisdiction. The defendants have argued that the same is a public record and they do not have to provide the same since it is equally available to an attorney through other sources. It has been successfully argued that the fact that the material is available through the state is not a valid objection to the production. Additionally, the attorney will want to know what material they have and what they have sent to the corporate office.]
- Request the photos of decubitus ulcers (if any).

TIP: If a decubitus ulcer is described as 7.8 cm by 8.3 cm in the medical record, the jury will not understand the measurements. Translate them into inches. Remember a picture is worth a thousand words.

- Produce the original schedule identifying the individuals assigned to work, along with the original "time cards" reflecting the individuals who actually worked.

TIP: The staffing schedule for the employees may be made as much as two to four weeks in advance. It is possible the scheduled employee no longer works for the facility or did not go to work on a particular day. If there was no replacement, the staffing was worsened. The care provided to the resident suffers accordingly.

- In the event of an abuse case, request the medical records of the resident suspected of the abuse. If it is a sexual abuse case, the perpetrator's records (if another resident) more likely than not will have the material to support the allegation that the facility knew about the perpetrator resident's propensities, and chose to keep the perpetrator in the nursing home anyway whether for financial or for other reasons.
- The original incident report pertaining to the accident-injuries suffered by your client.

TIP: The incident report may have more accurate information than the nurses' notes.

- Public relations and advertising campaign programs and materials directed to physicians and residents and/or the families of residents.
- Copies of the Residents' Council Committee Minutes.
- Records of all inservice meetings held at the facility (for the period of time at issue), including records of attendance at said meetings, and records of persons excused from said meetings.
- Contract(s) entered into at the time of admission, and any amendments between the plaintiff or plaintiff's representative and the defendant.
- If you are dealing with a fall case, you may also consider asking for a copy of all incident reports related to falls, be it observed or unobserved, as well as incident reports dealing with residents who were found on the floor, and/or were lowered to the floor.
- Copies of any and all management agreement(s) entered into by and between defendant(s) and any third parties.
- Copies of any and all written, recorded or transcribed statements by plaintiff, defendant, or any witnesses to the events which are the subject of this action and which were obtained by any representatives and/or agents of the defendant, or in the possession of the attorneys or agents of said defendants and obtained prior to the notification of the lawsuit.
- Any and all documents, correspondence, memoranda or other written materials of any kind identified in defendants' answers to interrogatories.
- Any and all documents, correspondence, reports, summaries, memoranda or written materials of any kind provided to, prepared by, and/or received

from any and all expert witnesses whom defendant reasonably expects to call as an expert witness at trial.

- Copies of the job descriptions and duties of the employees who charted the nursing care to plaintiff, including the responsibilities and duties of the administrator and director of nursing.
- Job application and any and all notices, memorandums, letters, correspondence, and suspensions issued to employees of defendant, during the time at issue.
- Copy of the Proposed Budget for the period of time at issue.
- Produce the actual budget used during the time at issue.
- Any and all records which would identify the amount which was spent for nursing services for the time at issue when plaintiff resided at the facility.
- Any and all records which would identify the amount which was spent for staffing agency services to provide nursing services, and any amendments thereto, for the time at issue when plaintiff resided at the facility.
- The acuity reports prepared at the facility during the time at issue. For purposes of this request, the facility is instructed to delete the name of every resident from the documents, other than the plaintiff.
- Any termination letters and/or resignation letters provided by any nursing, administrative, or social services employees at the facility during the time at issue.
- Copies of any and all correspondence, memoranda or written materials sent by the facility administrator or the medical director to corporate offices or representatives, and responses thereto, regarding the quality of care provided to its residents, staffing levels, budgets, finances and acuity of the resident census. For purposes of this request, the facility is instructed to delete the name or other identifiable information pertaining to each individual resident.
- Copies of the Cost Reports submitted to the state and to HCFA during the period of time at issue when the plaintiff resided at the facility.
- Copies of the agency employee's employment records, vouchers, and invoices submitted to agencies for work performed by the agency personnel for the nursing home during the time at issue.
- Copies of the labor distribution reports and the bi-weekly payroll distribution reports for the nursing

home during the time that plaintiff resided at the facility, during the time at issue.

- Copies of the document retention policy.
- The corporate chart as it relates to the individuals from corporate office, be it regional or national level, who visited the nursing home during the time at issue.
- An executed copy of the Medical Director's Agreement.

This discovery method allows many different items to be discovered. States vary with regard to the time limits for answering such requests. Figure 15.3 shows a sample request for production.

The following are tips for requesting appropriate documents in requests for production:

1. The attorney should confer with the expert or legal nurse consultant when requesting documents or things needed to fully identify what may be relevant and helpful. At times inexperienced attorneys fail to request crucial documents because:
   a. They do not know what to ask for;
   b. They do not know that such documents exist;
   c. They do not know what to name or call the document needed; or
   d. They do not understand the importance of such documents to the case.
2. Call friends or acquaintances in the healthcare industry who can be of help when requesting documents.
3. Call other attorneys who have worked on the same type of case.

PLEASE PRODUCE THE FOLLOWING:

1. All documents, letters, ledgers, notes, minutes or memoranda, either recorded, contained on a computer disk or hard drive, typed or handwritten, which, either in whole or in part, contain any information which relates to the allegations in the pleadings.
2. Any and all hospital records, physician office records, medical reports, laboratory results, medical consultations, or other medical records in your possession, including x-ray films and reports thereof, nurses notes, physician progress notes, doctors orders, and any other items which make up your complete record for the Plaintiff, _____.
3. Any and all statements concerning this action or in any way related to the Plaintiff or treatment you provided to Plaintiff, including those from witnesses, parties, their agents, servants, or employees.
4. Any and all documents, letters, memos, or other writing containing the names of any individuals contacted as potential witnesses in this matter.
5. Reports of any and all experts who will testify at trial including any and all transcriptions, tapes, documents, letters, memoranda, notes, or other information prepared by the expert.
6. Any and all reports, documents, letters, memoranda, notes, articles, or other information supplied by Defendant or their agents to any expert expected to testify at trial.
7. The curriculum vitae of any expert expected to testify at trial.
8. Any and all exhibits that are anticipated to be introduced at trial of this matter.
9. All articles, books, treatises, or other documents authored by the Defendant.
10. All articles written or co-authored or otherwise contributed to by any expert expected to testify at trial, which in any way relates to issues which may arise at trial of this matter.
11. Any report or writing of any kind in the possession of the Defendant or the Defendant's attorney which is claimed to have been completed or signed by any Plaintiff or their agents, servants, employees, or representatives in connection with this litigation.
12. Any and all photographs in any way related to the incident alleged in the complaint or the injuries alleged to have been suffered by plaintiff as a result.

Figure 15.3 *Sample Request for Production*

4. Contact national attorney associations that may have data banks or resources available.

5. Check legal publications. Many have developed a list of standard interrogatories and requests for production for certain types of cases, for example, brain-damaged baby cases, sepsis cases, retained surgical instruments cases, falls cases, and so on.

3. Admissions of fact

Admissions of fact (also called "submission to a finding or requests for admissions") are written requests to admit or deny facts regarding issues of the lawsuit. This technique attempts to limit the number of facts that actually are disputed and argued at trial. (See Figure 15.4 for the format.)

4. Physical examinations

As stated previously, physical examinations can be a form of informal discovery. Physical examinations are performed by a healthcare provider that has been selected by either or both parties in a case where there is a dispute over actual damages. Many times a legal nurse consultant may be retained to attend the IME to document the process and determine if an appropriate and complete examination is performed. Refer to Zimmerman[10] and Buchanan and Anderson[11] for additional information on this topic.

5. Depositions

There is one key word necessary to obtain all that you can out of a malpractice deposition. It is "preparation." In this regard, preparation begins with a thorough understanding of the case, which includes not only the facts at issue but also the legal theories of recovery that affect both liability and potential damages. Each side should also take a hard look at the overall case to determine not only its strengths but also weaknesses and areas of uncertainty. Legal research may be required as to any recent changes in the law.

Malpractice depositions may be very simple and timely or very detailed and lengthy. An attorney's technique and strategies depend on the nature of the witness and purpose of the deposition. If the attorney is trying to determine how the defendant or defendant's expert will comport himself under pressure, the technique may be very hard-hitting and include accusatory questions. On the other hand, if the attorney wants to try to "bleed" the expert and get as much information as possible, a more relaxed and "please educate me—you're the expert" attitude would be used. A word of caution—attorneys must prepare thoroughly and know the subject about which the witness is being deposed. Attorneys who walk into a deposition with little or no preparation and then ask irrelevant questions or who do not have sufficient knowledge of the subject to ask appropriate questions or follow-up on the answers given are wasting time and money. In addition, an attorney who walks into a deposition without adequate preparation is not only bound to be unsuccessful, but is sure to lose credibility in the eyes of the client as well as the other participants.

TIP: The questioner at a deposition can become educate through Internet resources such as WebMD, WebRN, Medscape, PubMed, and Nurselaw.com to name a few. An expert in the relevant field may be consulted in preparation for the deposition.

REQUEST FOR ADMISSIONS UNDER FEDERAL RULE 36

_____ hereby requests that _____, within 30 days after service of this request to make the following admissions for the purpose of this action only and subject to all pertinent objections to admissibility at trial:

1. Do you admit or deny that each of the following documents, exhibited with this request, is genuine?
   List and describe each document.
2. Do you admit or deny that each of the following statements is true?
   List and describe each statement.
3. Do you admit or deny that plaintiff was an inpatient at General Hospital on the following dates:
4. Do you admit or deny that you [defendant] scheduled [plaintiff] for [procedure] on [date] at [time]?
5. Do you admit or deny that you provided plaintiff with pre-operative instructions to _____?
6. Do you admit or deny that you informed [plaintiff] that a first year resident would be performing portions of the surgical procedure?

Figure 15.4 Sample Request for Admission

a. Reasons for depositions

Depositions can be used by the attorney:

1. To gather or discover all available information about the allegations and circumstances surrounding the lawsuit
2. To evaluate the demeanor and credibility of the witnesses and parties to the lawsuit
3. To discover facts and the circumstances of the alleged malpractice
4. To determine availability of insurance coverage
5. To assist attorneys in formulating strategies for litigation or negotiations
6. To assist attorneys in assessing the strengths or weaknesses of their cases and their opponent's cases
7. To determine the existence of pertinent documents
8. To preserve the testimony of a witness who may be unavailable at the time of trial (e.g., out of town)
9. To refresh the witness' memory during trial
10. To impeach the witness' credibility during trial[12]

b. Preparation of the witness for the deposition

Witness preparation must address the following:

1. What is the purpose of the deposition?
2. What are the common types of questions that will be asked?
3. What is the opposing counsel's style of deposing?
4. What are the potential "danger" zones in her testimony?
5. Where will the deposition be taken?[13]

c. How the witness should appear at the deposition

The witness should be instructed on appropriate behavior for depositions including the following manners and attitudes:

1. Professional
2. Confident
3. Organized
4. Knowledgeable
5. Honest and credible
6. Polite
7. Attentive
8. Not defensive[14]

d. Tips for deposing nurse defendants and expert witnesses

Most experienced experts will know how to conduct themselves in a deposition because they have done so in the past. However, not all experts or nurse defendants have been involved in litigation and therefore may not be totally experienced in conducting themselves at a given deposition. They should be instructed to focus on two things. First, they should concentrate on what is actually being asked; and secondly, they should be instructed to answer the question truthfully with the least amount of words necessary. If the opposing attorney wants them to elaborate he will ask them to do so. Otherwise, the witness should not volunteer information that is not elicited by the opposing attorney.

The following are tips for conducting a deposition:

1. Know the pertinent materials and documents better than the witness.
2. Let the defendant know that you have a nursing or medical background if that is the case.
3. Do the appropriate research prior to the deposition.
4. Do not go on a "fishing expedition."
5. Know the case and the relevant medical and nursing information to prove the points.
6. Talk to the expert before taking the deposition to be sure you are asking key points and eliciting the necessary information required to support the case.
7. Read all articles, books, and chapters that the nurse defendant or expert has written or co-authored.
8. Use the articles, books, and chapters to your advantage. Ask key questions about theories, points made in the documents, and so on to see if the defendant or expert agrees or disagrees with her own work. This can be used later at trial to damage the credibility of the witness.
9. Read articles, books, and chapters from other experts that may disagree with the expert's works and use those in the deposition to question the testimony of the defendant's or expert's viewpoint.
10. Always question the witness on what she reviewed to prepare for the deposition.
11. Ask to see the witness' file if she brought it to the deposition.[15]

Refer to Chapter 21, *Working with Nursing Expert Witnesses,* for more information on deposing experts.

15.9 Legal Doctrines, Liability, and Damages

A number of legal doctrines may apply to the specialty of nursing malpractice. *Res ipsa loquitur* is a legal doctrine used when it is more probable than not that the defendant has breached the standard of care, causing damages. This doctrine may also be used when the lack of medical or nursing care skills is obvious to the ordinary person. The use of this doctrine in nursing malpractice cases allows the plaintiff a shortcut to proving a claim; the plaintiff can usually make a prima facia case without an expert witness.

The following three facts must be present for the res ipsa doctrine to apply:

1. The type of injury does not normally occur in the absence of negligence.
2. Healthcare professionals had exclusive control of the instrumentality or treatment of the injury (e.g., patient under anesthesia).
3. The patient did not cause or contribute to the injuries.

This topic is discussed in more detail in Chapter 5, *Perioperative Nursing Malpractice Issues*, in Volume II. Another legal doctrine commonly used in malpractice cases is respondeat superior: "Let the master answer." This holds the employer responsible for the legal consequences of the acts of the employee while the employee is acting within the scope of employment. Common allegations of damages by plaintiffs include:

1. pain and suffering
2. mental anguish
3. emotional distress
4. loss of companionship
5. loss of guidance
6. loss of nurturance
7. decrease in life expectancy
8. loss of enjoyment of life
9. loss of wages
10. past, present, and future medical bills

Loss of chance is a damage allegation most commonly used in failure to diagnose or timely treat cancer cases. If a patient has a claim against a nurse practitioner based on a failure to timely diagnose breast cancer, the plaintiff can allege that the delayed diagnosis deprived him of the possibility of successful treatment. The complaint can define the allegation stating that because the defendants failed to timely treat and diagnose the patient, he or she has a decreased chance of survival because it is too late to initiate treatment that would have been available at an earlier time, and the cancer has now metastasized. In addition to a nurse practitioner being named as a defendant, an office nurse may be

brought into this type of suit if the nurse's actions contributed to a delay in diagnosis of cancer. For example, an office nurse or a nurse employed in a HMO may be responsible for notifying the physician or patient of abnormal lab results or diagnostic tests.

Many states have placed caps or limitations on damages the plaintiff can receive in a medical malpractice claim. The caps vary throughout the country. For example, Louisiana has a $500,000 cap for noneconomic damages in addition to any future medical expenses.

15.10 Settlement Strategies
A. Empty Chair Defense
Settling with one defendant can be dangerous at times. If one defendant is dismissed from a lawsuit after settling, it creates the possibility of using the empty chair defense. The remaining defendants can allege the dismissed defendant was solely responsible for the damages suffered by the plaintiff. If the remaining defendants all adopt this approach, it can be extremely difficult for a plaintiff to prevail, especially against individual practitioners. On the other hand, if all defendants except one settle, the remaining defendant will be the only target, and the jury will be left to wonder why the other potential defendants are not in the case.

B. Presuit Settlement
In some situations, it may be wise to attempt to settle the case before filing the lawsuit. The attorney must decide whether or not the client has a good chance of winning the case. Questions that should be considered include:

1. Is there clear-cut liability and considerable damages?
2. Who is the defendant—is it only a facility or are nurses involved? Many nurse practitioners, nurse midwives, and nurse anesthetists will not settle because this action will be reported to the National Practitioner Data Bank.
3. Is this a case the defendants may want to settle quickly because of potentially harmful negative publicity?
4. Is this a case the defendants may want to settle quickly to avoid disclosure of damaging information that has been uncovered? For example, did the nurse defendant have a substance abuse problem, criminal conviction, or a history of being fired from prior employment?
5. Is there enough time to negotiate and work out settlement details before the claim prescribes or the statute of limitations expires?

6. Can this case be settled through mediation thus avoiding a trial?

7. Can the plaintiff obtain a court-ordered mediation?

8. Is discovery necessary to gain a sufficient understanding of the potential liability and damages before settlement can be considered?

To be good negotiators, both plaintiff and defense counsel must know the traits and characteristics of each other and plan their settlement strategy accordingly. In conducting settlement negotiations, both attorneys must be courteous, friendly, and patient, but also firm and never in a hurry. They must never appear too anxious and must be willing to litigate the case should it become necessary.

Besides standard negotiation practices, trends in the judicial process include mandatory pre-trial mediation or arbitration. Mediation is the process in which both sides agree on a third party mediator who facilitates an analysis and step by step moves the parties toward a mutually beneficial and acceptable solution of the issues.[16] Resolution of issues through mediation is voluntary; all parties must be in agreement. The mediator may not force resolution of the parties. Arbitration is more of an out-of-court private trial process with a third party serving as the arbitrator. The arbitrator, like judge and jury, evaluates the evidence presented and makes a decision for the parties.

Facilitation is an alternative dispute resolution process used prior to or following litigation. A facilitator is an outside or impartial party, neutral with respect to the parties, the dispute, and the negotiation. The facilitator assists or facilitates the parties in clarifying issues, overcoming obstacles to agreement, breaking impasses, and identifying needs, interests, motives, and goals of the parties. The role of the facilitator is to provide structure and advance discussions among the participants.[17]

Whether the parties engage in standard negotiation practices, or the mediation or arbitration process, before doing so, one should determine the potential problems and weaknesses in the plaintiff's case prior to participating in any type of settlement. Factors to consider include:

1. Is the plaintiff believable?
2. Are the witnesses believable?
3. Are the damages purely subjective?
4. Does the plaintiff have a preexisting condition that makes it hard to determine damages caused by the defendant?
5. Are the treating physicians and expert witnesses able to substantiate liability or damage claims?

6. Did the plaintiff contribute to the injuries?

7. Was the plaintiff's condition difficult to diagnose?

8. Has the jury been exposed to unfavorable news media regarding the case?

9. Will the appearance or mannerisms of the plaintiff make a favorable or unfavorable impression on that particular jury in state or federal court?[18]

15.11 Summary

Malpractice cases rarely involve only nursing acts or omissions. The typical scenario is that the plaintiff will bring suit against the facility, physicians, and nurses for damages caused by a combination of breaches of standards of care by all nurses and physicians involved in the particular aspect of care at issue. The case can be very simple and straightforward or very complex and requiring detailed organization, a thorough work-up, and tenacity. Although years may pass before trial is scheduled and a settlement or judgment is awarded, the client can be vindicated for the harms suffered as a result of malpractice. If the case is tried, the verdict is necessarily in the form of monetary compensation. If the case is settled, a more flexible agreement can be reached that might include, for example, facility agreement to changes in procedures to prevent harm to future patients.

The attorney should develop skills of trial preparation and technique, seasoned with compassion and concern for the human impact on the injured party or the surviving family members. The case should never be prepared without due consideration for the fears and stresses that the client faces in dealing with an uncertain world dominated by a system they do not understand. Wrongful death cases that result as a result of nursing malpractice require aggressive preparation and a genuine effort to be compassionate without losing objectivity.

Endnotes

1. Cornell Legal Information Institute, www.law.cornell.edu/ethics/compare. See Rule 1.5: Fees for text of rules and state to state comparisons.

2. Krisztal, R., "Investigation and Pretrial Preparation of Nursing Home Cases," *Nursing Home Litigation, Investigation and Case Preparation*, Second edition, ed. P. Iyer. Tucson, Arizona: Lawyers and Judges Publishing Co., 2006.

3. Health Insurance Portability and Accountability Act of 1996, Pub.L. 104-191 and implementing regulations for privacy standards, 45 CFR Parts 160, 162, and 164 (as amended through February 16, 2006). For detailed

analysis and information, see Dept. of Health and Human Services website, http://www.hhs.gov/ocr/hipaa.

4. *Forrest County General Hospital v. Kelley*, 914 So.2d 242 2005 WL 1530515 (Miss. App.).

5. Aiken, T., *Legal, Ethical and Political Issues in Nursing*, Second Edition. F.A. Davis, 2004.

6. Tex. Civil Prac & Rem Code§74.401-§74.403.

7. See note 5.

8. See for example, *Costello v. Christus Santa Rosa Healthcare Corporation*, 141. S. W. 3d 245 (Tex. App. 2004).

9. See note 2.

10. Zimmerman, J., "The Plaintiff Attorney's Perspective," In *Medical Legal Aspects of Medical Records*, Second Edition, P. Iyer, and B. Levin, (eds.) Tucson, Arizona: Lawyers and Judges Publishing Co., 2010.

11. Buchanan, L. and Anderson, T, " Defense Medical Evaluations" in Peterson, A. Kopishke, L. (Eds) Legal Nurse Consulting Principles, Third edition, Taylor and Francis, 2010.

12. See note 5.

13. *Id.*

14. *Id.*

15. *Id.*

16. *Id.*

17. *Id.*

18. Trine, W. and P. Luvera *Winning Medical Negligence Cases*. Washington, D.C.: ATLA Press, 1993.

Chapter 16

Defense Attorney's Perspective: Working Up a Case

Peter A. Greene, Esq.

16.1 Introduction

While litigation is an adversarial process, the best defense attorney keeps an open mind and sees the case from the plaintiff's and defense's side. The attorney should take a neutral attitude while investigating the facts. The goal must be a thorough investigation, even if facts emerge that can hurt the client. It is better to know the worst early than to be blind-sided at trial. If damaging facts do emerge, the attorney must resist disclosure by invoking all possible permissible privileges; but failing in this, the facts must come out. This does not constitute "failure" by the attorney but a higher duty to assist in fair and equitable dispute resolution. While an attorney is a "zealous advocate," she must maintain professional separation from the client and occasional overzealous insurance adjuster. To slightly revise a cliché, "Winning may be the biggest thing, but it is not everything." The defense attorney's biggest prize and weapon in trial or settlement is a reputation for personal integrity, no matter what other attorneys might do.

One other preliminary caution: It is not enough to know the facts of a case. One must prove the facts in open court, meaning a case is only as strong as the admissible evidence placed before a jury. At every step, the attorney must ask, "How can I get this fact before a jury?" Witnesses must be physically located, convinced to testify, and kept track of to prevent disappearance before trial. Records must be located, inspected for legibility, transcribed if necessary and certified as complete. Most importantly, defense experts must review all discovery before trial, since the expert witness is the single most efficient and effective conduit to introduce medical facts into evidence at trial.

TIP: With a thorough investigation, well-prepared client and competent expert with a viable defense theory and complete familiarity with the records, the attorney has all the necessary tools to try, and probably win, a nursing malpractice verdict in favor of the defendant nurse.

16.2 Developments in the Litigation Climate

Foreign observers of our legal system often express surprise at the litigious nature of our society. Many nations will not even entertain a medical malpractice action, but litigation in the United States has reached what many see as crisis proportions. Nursing malpractice suits account for less than 2 percent of the malpractice payments reported to the National Practitioner Data Bank (NPDB), but the yearly number of payments for nursing malpractice claims has increased steadily, from 253 in 1998 to 488 in 2004, the latest year of available NPDB data. Median and mean payments for nurses in 2004 were $100,000 and $302,738, respectively. Little academic analysis has been done on nursing malpractice, but a study of 253 cases by Croke[1] broke down cases into six categories of negligence :

- failure to follow standards of care
- failure to use equipment in a responsible manner
- failure to communicate
- failure to document
- failure to assess and monitor
- failure to act as a patient advocate

This is good background reading for defense counsel.

Like it or not, litigation is here to stay, and if cases are to be tried, there is no fairer system in the world than the United States jury system. Many nursing clients feel they will be "persecuted" by a gang of ignorant, pro-plaintiff bleeding-hearts sitting in the jury box, and that the deck is stacked against them. It is easy for a defense attorney to reinforce this perception by blaming the "unfair jury system" in advance for any possibility the nurse will lose the case. But this unjustly denigrates what is truly a brilliant mechanism for dispute resolution. The defense attorney does favors for no one by bad-mouthing the jury system to the client or insurance carrier.

However, there are undeniably broad forces at work which have the capacity to distort the outcome of any case and which the defense attorney must understand and discuss with the client and carrier. These include those described below.

A. Tort Reform

Tort reform refers to the general concept and belief that plaintiffs' "jackpot" verdicts have gone too far and must be reined in by legislation, including caps on verdict amounts and requirements of affidavits of merit or similar preliminary proofs that a case has merit before it can proceed.

This movement can have a negative impact on nurses, since when collection against doctors is limited by law, pressure is created to seek additional deep pockets, which often results in nurses being sued where they would previously not be targeted by plaintiff's attorneys.

B. National and State Data Banks

As a companion to tort reform, a concurrent movement exists to identify the few "bad apples" in the healthcare professions who are unfairly hurting the majority of competent and caring doctors and nurses. Federal and state reporting mechanisms have been in effect for several years to identify repeat offenders and remove them from their professions.

However, this otherwise commendable movement has negative effects on nurses, as follows: while both doctors and nurses get reported to federal and state agencies based on their claims histories, doctors have more to lose and have more clout with insurance carriers who report them. This results in doctors more often blaming nurses in discovery and at trial, and in carriers more often settling cases on behalf of nurses to protect co-defendant doctors whom they also insure. The argument goes that a staff nurse is usually insured through a hospital and will not lose insurance coverage based on a poor litigation history, whereas a doctor is usually insured individually and could lose the entire practice for failure to qualify for insurance coverage. Note that nurses in advanced practice roles may be individually insured: nurse midwives, nurse practitioners and nurse anesthetists.

A related trend is the liquidation of a number of medical malpractice insurers across the country due to high payouts, bad payments and poor business decisions, resulting in state takeovers with statutory caps on payouts for doctors and concurrent pressure to name more nurses as co-defendants to increase the available pot of insurance money.

C. High Profile "Mega-Verdicts"

With the rise of tort reform as a national political issue, and with increasing high profile trials involving drugs like Vioxx, most jurors are aware that verdicts of $50 million and up are a possibility. Some jurors will react with disgust and want to find the defendant not negligent in any case they hear. Others may feel empowered or compelled to award a multi-million dollar verdict for any significant injury; most will obey the instructions of the judge to disregard all political concerns and decide each case on its merits.

TIP: The mega-verdict syndrome, whether real or perceived, has increased the fear of insurance carriers and proportion of cases settled rather than tried to verdict.

D. Alternate Dispute Resolution (ADR)

Across the country, the number of full trials is down and mediation, arbitration and mini-trials are on the increase. One of the reasons for this trend is fear of mega-verdicts. For the defense counsel, it means preparing the nurse client for the increased possibility that the case will be settled rather than tried. Most nurses are relieved at this, but some may complain, with some merit, that their cases will be settled despite their innocence. Nurses may feel they are being scapegoated to protect co-defendant doctors from losing their insurance or from suffering an astronomical increase in premiums. This may be a particular issue for nurse practitioners, whose supervising physicians may go without insurance coverage. Three particular problems arise for the defense counsel in ADR:

1. The usual result is that the settlement is smaller than the potential jury verdict but that "no plaintiff goes away empty-handed," so the attorney may have to accept and explain to the client nurse why the case settled even though he arguably did nothing wrong.
2. The attorney must not lose his edge by thinking all cases will be settled rather than tried. Preparation must proceed on the assumption of a full trial.
3. Before and after a case is settled, careful attention must be paid to allocation of liability among the defendants. A carrier insuring multiple defendants tends not to care how the settlement is divided; but the defendant nurse certainly does, and it is the attorney's duty to fight for the client on allocation issues. (Due to NPDB policies, if a nurse is to be dismissed and not contribute to a settlement, this must occur several weeks before the actual settlement, or the nurse will be presumed to have contributed, so advance plans must be made.)

E. Global Politics

In the post-9/11 world, one cannot ignore a heightened awareness of ethnic and social differences, and, sadly, the reality of increased prejudice toward some racial and ethnic groups. With nursing tending to be a highly international profession, and active recruiting from the Middle and Far East, the possibility of ethnic bias exists in a jury trial and must be discussed openly by counsel, client and carrier alike.

16.3 Initial Intake and Setup of the File

The defense attorney has it easy in a sense. No financial or moral dilemmas exist over whether to bring a case or not. No preliminary hurdles, such as "affidavits of merit," must be vaulted. Few problems exist in locating or serving parties.

The other side "started it." All the defense attorney needs to do is respond. But defense counsel has its own problems:

- a high volume of cases;
- intense competition with other law firms for large blocks of business from a small number of insurance carriers; and
- a high proportion of clients who are initially angry, uncooperative, scared, in denial or all of the above.

Fortunately, once the initial anxieties are overcome, there are few better or more satisfying clients to represent than nurses. They are smart, committed to their profession (and their defense), and cooperative, as long as the attorney makes the effort to engage them in their own case. Many years of experience have highlighted recurrent "start-up" issues, including the following:

(a) Location of the client can be challenging. Nurses tend to move a lot, so they must be impressed with the need to keep their attorneys advised of all current phone numbers, e-mail, work and home addresses.

(b) The client must be explicitly informed that a nursing malpractice suit is not a criminal complaint or an action against her nursing license, although in limited circumstances a state Board of Nursing can independently investigate the case. The client should be advised not to discuss the case with anyone other than the attorney, insurance representative and facility's risk manager.

(c) Many nurses purchase their own nursing insurance in addition (and almost always in excess) to the facility's policy. Nurses commonly pay a small amount for these policies and misplace or forget about them. The defense attorney must explicitly question the nurse on other insurance policies and help her locate and notify the other insurer. Keep all insurers advised of the case's progress. A significant delay in notification to a carrier can possibly result in denial of coverage.

(d) By the time the complaint filters through the nurse, employer and carrier, down to the defense attorney, the time to answer has usually expired and a default may already be entered by the plaintiff's attorney. This can cause the client anxiety but is hardly ever a problem, because plaintiff's attorneys are glad to see defense counsel and the insurance money they represent enter the case.

(e) The relationship between counsel and client may start with some suspicion and hostility, but early care, concern and time put forth pays off in making the client a valuable ally in many ways:

- discovering the fact pattern;
- interpreting the chart;
- identifying signatures;
- getting "the story behind the story"; and
- helping identify potential experts or professional organizations which can provide experts.

(f) Even before contact with the client, the defense counsel usually discusses the case with the insurance claims representative and risk manager, a four-sided relationship continuing throughout the case and sometimes leading to tension, as discussed below.

(g) Conflict checking must be done initially and throughout the case. Conflicts are such a difficult part of defense representation that they will be discussed in a separate section.

(h) Cross claims should always be filed against all co-defendants whom the defense attorney does not represent. If the attorney represents two nurses who have reason to file cross claims against each other, that is a sure sign of conflict and one client should be reassigned (see below).

TIP: The time when it was thought impolite to cross-claim against a fellow defendant is long gone. Indeed, failure to pursue a substantive cross claim could now be legal malpractice.

Beyond filing a cross claim, a defense attorney must prepare to prove it at trial, which may mean engaging an expert witness against a co-defendant. While normally a defendant can rely on a plaintiff to provide expert testimony against all parties, a plaintiff may sometimes settle with a co-defendant before trial and not call an expert against that co-defendant at trial. Unless a nurse has his own expert to attack the co-defendant, the cross claim cannot get to the jury, which could be a catastrophe. This is a prime example of the difference between knowing something and proving it to a jury. So, plan for cross claims early.

(i) The defense counsel must likewise be prepared to respond to an expert retained by a co-defendant who has filed a cross claim. For example, a physician's defense position may be based on blaming a nurse for the events. A nursing expert may be hired by the physician's attorney, requiring defense counsel for the nurse to respond to the expert through use of a defense nursing expert.

(j) Perform a checklist of possible affirmative defenses and immunities under statute and case law, including but not limited to:

- statute of limitations;
- statutory immunity or cap on damage;
- "Good Samaritan" immunity;
- immunity involving suicides; and
- particular statutory immunities peculiar to each state.

(k) Identify distorting factors in the case, such as a potential defendant who should be in the case but is not named by plaintiff (often because of a special relationship with the plaintiff) or co-defendants with strong liability but insufficient or lapsed insurance (like a doctor whose carrier is in liquidation). A defendant nurse will rarely have to bring an additional nurse or doctor as a third party defendant, but it should always be considered. A politically safer tactic is an off-the-record call to the plaintiff's attorney suggesting she add another party defendant.

16.4 Dealing with Conflicts

Conflicts are a common and aggravating part of defense work. Most malpractice complaints name multiple defendants, often represented by the same insurance carrier. Most hospital employees, including nurses, are insured under the same policy. Insurance claims representatives like to have all hospital co-workers in a case represented by the same law firm, and most law firms likewise prefer to represent all hospital co-workers.

While the insurer and the defense attorney may be content with multiple representation, the client and court may be dissatisfied and, most importantly, justice may not be served. The interests of justice and the interests of business may pull in different directions. Assigning multiple defendant nurses to one law firm saves legal fees for the carrier and assures a defense attorney with whom the adjuster is comfortable. Accepting multiple defendants increases a law firm's billing and protects valuable contacts at a hospital from raiding by other firms. After all, relationships are crucial. Additionally, representation of multiple clients assures the most coordinated defense possible and reduces finger pointing at trial.

Nonetheless, a significant conflict frequently develops between co-defendant nurses or between a nurse and the co-defendant hospital whom the defense attorneys also represent, requiring appointment of separate counsel by the carrier.

A far from exhaustive list of potential conflicts includes:

- A nurse questions the adequacy of staffing, equipment or training at the co-defendant hospital;
- Two nurses on the same shift or successive shifts assert the other was responsible for a decision or an action;
- Two nurses give different versions of the same event;
- A nurse is terminated on hostile terms from the hospital which is represented by the same firm; or
- A nurse is expected by the hospital, also represented by the attorney, to accept blame to protect a co-defendant doctor who generates large amounts of business for the hospital, which really happens and once cost this author a major client.

TIP: Insurance carriers are becoming more sensitive to conflicts and will take an attorney's word that a conflict exists, but it still creates an uncomfortable business situation to allow access to "your" healthcare facility client by a potential rival law firm.

Nonetheless, the attorneys' code of ethics forbids an attorney from representing two clients in conflict, and if a judge learns of it, the defense firm may be ordered to give up representation of both parties and leave the case altogether. It always pays to do the right thing: the sooner the better.

16.5 The Complex Four-Sided Relationship Between Attorney, Client, Risk Manager and Insurance Representative

Most attorney-client relationships are just attorney and client, but for nursing defense counsel there are four people in the relationship. The legal duty is unequivocally the same: the attorney represents only the defendant nurse, even though two others are involved. The insurance representative assigns work to the defense firm on an ongoing basis, pays the legal fees, dictates settlement or trial and consents to key legal strategies. The risk manager controls the attorney's access to records and other key hospital employees, and is the attorney's contact for discovery and trial. Furthermore, if the attorney does not maintain a warm, personal rapport with

the insurance representative and the risk manager, the firm may lose business.

It is obvious that, in many ways, the client nurse is the least important of the quartet. The nurse does not pay the bills, assign future business, decide on settlement or trial or have an ongoing relationship with the attorney before or after the case. Yet the attorney has taken an oath to protect the nurse without reservation. Any defense attorney in the profession long enough will encounter serious ethical issues due to the incompatibility of this four-way relationship. How well an attorney finesses this situation is as important to the long-term success of his law firm as any brilliant victory in court.

The best advice is to always fight as hard as one can for the nurse client and to work equally hard to maintain politically secure and personal ties with the insurance company and hospital so the nurse client is never compromised for the sake of business.

16.6 Investigating the Claim

Much of the early work in a case involves the hospital's risk manager, with whom the attorney must maintain good relations. A risk manager can be anyone from an executive secretary at the hospital to a senior vice president, but almost always has multiple jobs and works only part-time with the attorney.

TIP: Typically, and ideally, the risk manager is a nurse with staff nursing experience and some degree of influence in the hospital.

The keys to dealing with a risk manager, as with anyone else, is showing respect, courtesy and understanding. The risk manager is not a servant, secretary or "go-fer." A little concern for the risk manager's problems goes a long way. Conversely, if one offends a risk manager, a complaint may be carried to the highest level of the hospital and its insurance representative, which is no minor matter. Risk managers come with all levels of experience. Some will get everything needed with little prompting. Others will do very little unless requested.

TIP: The risk manager is an important bridge between law, medicine and nursing.

Nursing clients feel comfortable with a fellow nurse or hospital employee. Also, as a fact of geography, the risk manager is on the scene with immediate access to records, policies, and other documents. The risk manager may call the nurse in for an initial meeting to explain the legal process and help with answers to interrogatories. Since the risk manager is such an important person to the defense attorney, the following are some tips for maintaining good relations:

- If the risk manager is new, expectations should be clear about how much detail to put in interrogatory answers, what records to check, etc.

- The risk manager should be informed about the legal process as it unfolds, so she can report to the nursing or hospital administration.

- The attorney might suggest a "legal insurance" program for the nursing staff, such as a mock trial;

- Requests for information should be specific, with deadlines set far in advance. It is a good idea to visit the risk manager and have lunch with him or her periodically.

- The attorney should be available to advise the risk manager about other legal aspects of the job, even though the time is not billable. (Be careful about advising on personal legal matters)

- Do not abuse the risk manager by asking her to do the attorney's job. For example, the risk manager can identify, locate and even contact possible hospital employee witnesses, but cannot interview, evaluate or prepare them for deposition or trial, which is the attorney's job.

- A risk manager is not part of the attorney's office. One cannot be totally candid with all risk managers all the time. Understandably, risk managers are loyal to their hospital. Too negative an assessment of a case may be viewed as treason and bring the attorney's loyalty into question. Carefully balance expressions of optimism with the possibility of losing a case.

- Likewise, be very careful about pointing out areas for improvement in hospital nursing care. It may not be appreciated.

16.7 Getting the Records

It seems obvious that one needs the medical records to evaluate the case, but a number of considerations could be overlooked. Not all documents are kept in the medical records department. Enlist the risk manager to assemble documents from other hospital departments.

- Make sure the medical records department retains the original chart and does not send it for scanning or microfilming in the middle of the case pursuant to its normal schedule. This can be embarrassing and prevent examination of the medical record by

a document examiner if tampering with the record is suspected.

- In a major case, the attorneys should go to the hospital and read the original chart early in discovery to avoid hidden surprises like notes on the backs of pages.

- Assure all sections are in the chart before distributing certified copies.

- Develop a personal relationship with the records custodian, apart from the risk manager. He can track down missing documents, identify who has been reviewing the file and make it easier to get documents into court at trial time.

- The hospital must keep all charts in litigation in a secured cabinet. The original should not be kept in the attorney's office.

- One must never change a record or allow anyone to alter it. Tampering with the record will be discovered. Refer to Iyer[2] and Konray and Iyer[3] for more information on this subject.

- A plaintiff or plaintiff's attorney has full access to the original chart at the hospital without notice or consent, under the doctrines of freedom of information and patient's rights, before or after litigation begins.

- Once a plaintiff begins litigation against a hospital, she waives the physician-patient privilege for all her medical records at the hospital. If the plaintiff had other treatment at the defendant hospital, the hospital's attorney may obtain all treatment records of the patient at that hospital, even for admissions before and after the incident in question. For treatment records elsewhere, the attorneys need a signed authorization from the patient in the specific form required by the federal HIPAA statute. Since the passage of HIPAA, the use of a subpoena to obtain medical records, without a proper authorization signed by the patient, will not satisfy the requirements of the law.

A. Incident Reports

The principle of self-critical analysis states health care institutions must have free rein to candidly discuss accidents and errors in care to avoid recurrence. Public policy dictates that hospital personnel must be free to express their opinions without fear of being hauled into court to testify in some future civil litigation.

TIP: In most jurisdictions, the general rule is that incident reports are discoverable and admissible in evidence as business records, but privileged if they contain "self-critical analysis," as opposed to mere recitation of the incident's facts.

A related principle is *subsequent remedial action*. If a hospital corrects a procedure or re-trains or counsels a nurse, that is unusable against the hospital or nurse in a civil suit. If it were usable, mistakes would not often be corrected.

It is the defense counsel's job to evaluate reports and assert the claim of privilege. When in doubt, privilege should be claimed and the plaintiff forced to bring the issue to a judge for in camera (private by the judge) inspection and ruling.

B. Minutes of Hospital Committees

Occasionally a case will be the subject of review by a hospital committee, grand rounds or a nursing inservice meeting. The same considerations apply as for aforementioned incident reports. Various states also have statutory privileges for certain hospital committees with which the counsel should be familiar.

C. Personnel Files

A troublesome tactic for a plaintiff's attorney is attempting to review a defendant nurse's entire career and life because the plaintiff has sued the defendant, and is seeking personnel files, job applications, letters of reference, personal medical records and so forth. These requests must be strenuously resisted. Reports of incidents, admonishments, reprimands and so on in a personnel file are usually irrelevant to the current case. Likewise, requests for medical, housing, financial, and family data are an invasion of privacy. Typically, the only relevant items are training records and certifications involving the particular area of nursing at issue in the case.

TIP: It is a general rule of evidence that one cannot establish negligent conduct on a given occasion by evidence of prior negligence, such as might appear in personnel files.

D. Signatures and Names on Records

One early task in reviewing a case is identifying the people involved. The best source for this is the hospital's nursing department, either directly or through the risk manager. Other sources are the personnel and medical staff office. Unlike board certified and other physicians located through directories, no national directory exists for nurses. The state Board of Nursing can often supply information about a nurse's current address if the nurse has remained licensed in the state. Co-workers of the defendant can sometimes supply a current address. An investigator is occasionally required to locate a

nurse. The Internet has a number of sites helpful in finding a missing nurse, such as those that list phone numbers like Switchboard.com. A state registry keeps track of certified nursing assistants.

E. Logs, Nursing Supervisor Reports, Security Records, and so on

Beyond the hospital chart are a number of secondary documents useful in proving times, personnel present and so forth. Records are increasingly kept on computer, so check with the computer directors at the hospital for backup disks.

TIP: Since the name and medical record of any patient who is not a party to the lawsuit is protected by the physician-patient privilege, be sure to redact all non-party names in any records served on the adversary. One exception to this is the name and address of a roommate or other eyewitness to an incident, but it is safer to withhold all names and make the plaintiff obtain a court order to disclose anything.

Some sources of information about a case beyond the chart are shown in Figure 16.1.

16.8 Meeting with the Client and Answering Interrogatories

Meet the client face-to-face early in the proceedings. In a small case or when the nurse has only peripheral involvement, a telephone contact may suffice. At the initial meeting, explain the legal process and expected time frame. Most nurses have no idea how long it can take for a case to work its way through the various stages. The attorney should review the facts of the case and ask the nurse specific questions. Figure 16.2 displays some suggested questions for several types of cases.

16.9 Continuing Contact with the Client

Use judgment on how closely to stay in contact with the client. For many clients, a call or letter is unnerving, so contact should not be overdone, but keep the client involved in all significant developments.

The first major litigation hurdle may be answering interrogatories in a jurisdiction using them in malpractice cases. The general rule is to say as little as possible. For all their burdensomeness, interrogatories are rarely used at trial and usually play unsubstantial roles in the case.

If the case involves a narrow issue, such as a fall out of bed, medication error or retained sponge in surgery, set forth fully in the interrogatories the client's actions at the time in question. This includes both charted and unrecorded recollections.

- Ambulance report
- Emergency room log
- X-ray department log
- Intensive care unit, critical care unit, other unit logs
- "Code" log (when an emergency resuscitation is called, see the switchboard operator's log for exact timing)
- Nursing supervisor's shift reports
- Lab logs
- Lab computer tapes, discs and records
- Medication wastage records
- Fetal monitor strips (look for handwritten or typed nursing comments and printed times, although times may be inaccurate)
- EKG, Holter monitor and telemetry strips
- Autopsy reports
- Staffing schedules, planned and actual
- Patient census sheets
- Employees' time cards
- Narcotics sign out sheets
- Prescriptions
- Nursing worksheets
- Anecdotal records kept by nurse
- Incident reports
- Operating room logs
- Communication books used to exchange information among nurses

Figure 16.1 Sources of Information about an Event

Fall-out-of-bed cases:

Do you remember this patient?

Was the patient on "fall precautions"?

Were you told in report about this patient?

(If the fall was out of bed):

> Were the side rails up?
>
> How many side rails were up?
>
> What was the hospital's policy on side rails?
>
> Were bed alarms available and used on this unit?
>
> What was the patient's condition?
>
> Could the patient use the call bell?
>
> Did the patient have out-of-bed privileges?
>
> Did you observe the patient trying to get out of bed before the fall?

Had you read the chart earlier?

Did you update the plan of care?

Where was the last time you saw the patient before the fall?

Was there any history of confusion, restlessness or other risk factors?

Was the patient on medication which altered consciousness?

What was done on earlier and later shifts?

What was your patient load?

Where were you at the time of the fall?

Were there any emergencies on your shift?

How often did you make rounds?

Did you fill out an incident report?

Wrong-medication cases:

Was the order for medication written or verbal?

If it was a verbal order, is there proof that it was read back to the prescriber?

Who wrote the order?

Who read the order?

Was there any difficulty interpreting the prescriber's handwriting?

Were you familiar with the medication involved?

Was the order correctly copied onto a medication Kardex?

Who measured the medication dose?

Figure 16.2 Questions to Ask Nurse Defendant

Did you question anything about the medication? What was said?

Did you consult the pharmacy, a supervisor or a doctor?

Were there any changes in the order for the medication?

Who observed the patient take the medication?

Did you notify the physician of the error?

Did you see any changes in the patient as a result of the error?

Was an incident report prepared?

Was there anything about how this error occurred which is not in the chart?

Were you tired or distracted when the error occurred?

Operating room sponge cases:

What are the hospital's policies on sponge counts?

Who counted the sponges before the operation began?

Who counted the sponges as they went in?

Were strips or rings kept outside the operative field?

Were the sponges radio-opaque?

Did the surgeon change the normal procedure?

Was the patient's condition unstable at any time?

Was the count suspended or not done at all? If so, why?

Did you advise the doctor of an incorrect sponge count?

If so, what was said by the nurse and the doctor?

Was an x-ray done when the count was incorrect?

Was an incident report prepared?

Failure-to-communicate cases:

When did you recognize the need to call a physician?

Had you cared for this patient before?

What led to your decision to call a physician?

When did you call the doctor?

Which doctor did you call?

How many times did you call the doctor?

Did you call the house doctor? Did you call a supervisor?

What did the answering service or doctor's office staff say?

Did you call another doctor when you could not reach the first one?

Did you alert your supervisor? If not, why not?

What did the physician say to you?

Do you have any notes about the incident?

What is the hospital's policy on notifying the doctor?

What is your usual chain of command?

Did you document each call?

Do you have any notes about the incident?

Pressure ulcer cases:

What is the facility's policy on identifying patients at risk for skin breakdown?

Was the patient identified as high risk?

Was the identification accurately performed?

Once the patient was at high risk, what ordinarily occured?

Did that occur in this patient's case?

Was a form to document turning in use at this facility?

Is it contained in the chart?

Were these forms a permanent part of the record?

Please show me the initials on the form that you added.

Were specialty beds in use at the facility?

What was the procedure for getting one for a patient?

Fetal distress cases:

What was the policy in recording fetal heart tracings?

What was the policy on making marks on the strips and flow sheets?

Was Dr. X or Nurse Midwife Y on the labor and delivery unit during the patient's labor?

At what points?

What did you tell Dr. X or Nurse Y about the patient's tracing?

What did you do in response to changes in the strip?

Where is this documented?

At what time did you contact the doctor, nurse, midwife or supervisor?

Was there a delay in obtaining a delivery room?

Elopement from nursing home cases:

How long was this resident at the facility?

Was the resident identified as a wanderer?

Was the care plan altered to include this safety risk?

What measures were implemented to reduce the risk of the resident getting out of the facility?

Was a door alarm in use at the time of escape?

What measures were used to verify that the door alarm was functional?

What were you doing at the time the resident escaped?

When did you discover the resident was missing?

What happened next?

When were the police notified?

Figure 16.2 Questions to Ask Nurse Defendant (continued)

TIP: If the nurse recalls taking action or making observations that were uncharted, she may be open to a credibility attack at deposition or trial. Therefore, it is better to get these actions and observations on the record as soon as possible by putting them in answers to interrogatories.

Because interrogatories come so early in discovery, one can use the answer "unknown at this time, pending further discovery" as often as possible to avoid touchy questions. By the time of trial, however, counsel must be sure to amend interrogatory answers to list all potential witnesses or risk being barred from producing a witness at trial. Likewise, list the "learned treatises," which may be relied upon to examine any witness.

TIP: A good test for interrogatories is: "If this response were read to a jury, would it hurt me?" If the answer is yes, change the response if possible.

When typing answers in final form and sending them to the client for certification, the cover letter should urge the client to read them carefully and make all necessary corrections. This will fend off the occasional client who testifies not having read the answers written by the attorney. Also, retain the client's draft in the file.

16.10 Developing the Theory of Defense

The defense attorney should compile a checklist of potential defenses early in every case. These include those listed below.

A. Factual Denial

- Mistaken identity, including name read incorrectly off the chart; name read correctly from the chart but another nurse performed the work; nurse was probably on vacation or off work at the time of the incident; plaintiff identifies nurse from a written record but plaintiff was mistaken.
- Written notes contradict plaintiff's allegations. For example, plaintiff claims side rails were down, but notes state otherwise; or plaintiff claims injection was in center of buttock but nurse writes it was in right outer quadrant.
- Independent witness contradicts plaintiff's story.
- Plaintiff's case relies solely on plaintiff's own testimony and is an unreliable witness. For example, the incident involves an unwitnessed fall by a patient with dementia.

- Plaintiff's case relies on the event without corroborating testimony. For example, the plaintiff is found on the floor, but unable to testify due to severe dementia.

B. Patient Care was the Responsibility of Others

- Physician or senior nurse was present at the time of the incident and made the medical decisions involved.
- Client did not have responsibility for the patient, and nurses with responsibility were aware of patient's condition at the time.
- Nurse was acting as a Good Samaritan, volunteering to help a patient to whom she had no duty (only applies to incidents outside the workplace).

C. Recognized Complications

The plaintiff's injury could have occurred even in the absence of negligence by the nurse, since it was a known risk of the patient's condition or the procedure being administered. This defense usually requires expert testimony and support in the literature.

D. Nursing Judgment

The nurse has some latitude in her actions depending on the facts of the case. Many situations are "a judgment call" and a healthcare professional should be permitted to exercise that judgment.

E. Two Schools of Thought

Although an expert might testify the nurse could have handled the situation one way, there is valid medical support for the nurse handling the situation another way. This again requires expert testimony and, preferably, medical literature.

F. Lack of Proximate Cause

Volumes could be written about this defense as it is one of the most difficult concepts in law. The attorney is arguing that even if the nurse was negligent, the outcome would have been the same even without the nurse's negligence. Among many examples are these:

- The nurse was negligent in charting, but no one relied on the charting error so it had no effect on patient care.
- The nurse was negligent but the patient would have died of an unrelated condition anyway.

- The nurse was negligent but the negligence did not materially increase the patient's injury.
- The nurse was negligent but the patient suffered no harm as a result.

G. Contributory Negligence of Plaintiff

The defense of contributory negligence can be effective in limited circumstances, such as a patient:

- leaving the hospital against medical advice;
- failing to follow instructions for follow-up care;
- with diabetes continuing to smoke or eat an unhealthy diet despite instructions;
- failing to call a nurse when the patient was mentally competent and a call bell was easily within reach;
- bringing his own medications into the hospital and taking them without advising a nurse, or a patient secretly abusing medications provided at the hospital; and
- tampering with medical equipment (but not a delusional patient pulling out an IV, because that is an expected risk of the patient's condition and should have been anticipated).

Severe limits exist on this defense, as follows:

- If a patient is under medical care due to a certain condition and a nurse fails to prevent a known risk of that condition, the nurse cannot invoke contributory negligence of the patient. If a suicidal patient jumps out a window at the hospital, the nurse cannot blame the patient, as it was her duty to prevent this known risk. Likewise, if a feeble, elderly patient is allowed to walk unattended and falls and hurts himself, the nurse cannot blame the patient;
- If a nurse fails to perform a task or collect data as required, the nurse cannot claim that the patient is unable to prove he had the condition, which the data might have shown if the nurse had collected it; and
- Even without legal prohibition on the defense of contributory negligence, it is often a risky maneuver to blame an injured or ill patient for her own problems. Juries tend to disfavor this tactic.

H. Failure of Plaintiff's Expert to List a Deviation from Nursing Practice

The failure to provide a comprehensive list of deviations is one of the key points of any defense. With few exceptions, such as the common knowledge doctrine or *res ipsa loquitur*, the only way that a plaintiff can prove negligence by a nurse is through expert testimony. If plaintiff's expert, either in a written report, affirmation, deposition testimony or trial testimony, fails to articulate a particular deviation by the nurse, it cannot be considered by a jury.

If a deviation is not listed as one of the plaintiff's nursing expert's opinions, the defense attorney should not elicit it at deposition or trial. The expert should be pinned down at deposition with the open-ended question, "Have you now set forth all the deviations from nursing practice that you find in this case?" Once the expert agrees that she has, the scope of trial is set. It is difficult for the plaintiff to add a deviation at trial which was not set forth by the expert previously, which is why it is such an important job of the defense counsel to limit plaintiff's expert opinions before trial. Any attempt by plaintiff to expand on those theories at trial should be met with strenuous objection, which will probably be sustained by the trial judge.

The defense is also constrained to follow the opinions of its nursing expert. The attorney is not allowed to argue to a jury defenses which are not supported by expert testimony. Find a good expert and fully prepare that witness before trial.

16.11 Locating Experts

TIP: Obtaining a strong report from a well-qualified nurse expert is crucial to the defense of most cases; but good experts are hard to find, so start the search early.

Experts can come from several sources:

- A "stable of tried and true regulars" who can be counted on to prepare timely reports in proper legal format
- An agency specializing in finding nursing experts
- Recommendation by the client
- Recommendation by a nursing society or organization specializing in the appropriate nursing area

Each of these sources has its benefits and drawbacks. Most nursing malpractice defense attorneys have a group of nursing experts whom they know and trust. The advantage of using such experts is that they are familiar with the process and understand the importance of providing a timely report containing the requisite legal language, including the fact that the defendant nurse complied with reasonable standards of nursing practice to a reasonable degree of nursing probability. The disadvantage of using such a nurse is that the plaintiff's attorney may well have a "book" on the expert, including reports and depositions from previous cases, which, in the worst case scenario, could include statements contradictory to those made by the expert in the present case. Additionally, an experienced expert can be made out on cross-examination as a hack.

It is increasingly common for defense, as well as plaintiff's attorneys, to turn to expert-finding services, often run by nurses who find and cultivate well-qualified experts in various nursing fields. The advantages to this route are:

- the agency, not the attorney, spends time and money locating qualified, interested experts;
- the agency gives experts preliminary training in the expectations of attorneys; and
- the agency helps the attorney review and edit the report if necessary.

The disadvantages of working with an agency include:

- opposing counsel can expose in cross-examination that the expert was procured through an agency, making the witness look biased or mercenary unless opposing counsel also uses an agency;
- the agency takes a cut of the expert fee, pushing up the hourly rate unless the expert accepts a lower than market rate; and
- the expert could be a stranger to the attorney, from a distant area and have a history unknown to the attorney.

It is always a good idea to ask the nurse defendant to recommend potential experts in his own defense, the advantages of which include:

- the client feels happy and empowered that an expert whom he knows and respects will defend him;
- the expert is highly motivated to write a favorable report due to the personal connection with the defendant; and
- the expert may not be a professional witness, but instead a practicing nurse, whom a jury would find more convincing.

A drawback of using an expert recommended by the client is that anything more than a professional relationship between the client and the expert will create an obvious conflict of interest, which the plaintiff's attorney can exploit. Under no circumstances should the defense attorney engage an expert who is a relative, social friend, former employer

or former co-employee of the client. A former teacher of the client should be looked at with great caution. However, fellow members of nursing societies and lecturers at nursing conferences or continuing nursing education classes should not pose a problem.

Professional nursing organizations, such as specialty groups, are another fertile source for experts, especially in cases involving specialized areas such as ostomy and wound care. These organizations usually have websites, membership lists (which may or may not be shared with non-members) and even lists of nurses willing to be experts.

There is a group of nurses known as legal nurse consultants. The advantage is their motivation and enthusiasm for preparing legal expert reports and their training in style and format. However, the disadvantage is that a jury might assign less credibility to the testimony of such an expert, as opposed to a "real nurse." Refer to Chapter 20, *Working with Legal Nurse Consultants*, for more information on this role.

Under the Rules of Federal Evidence and the rules of most states, the communication between the defense attorney and the expert is confidential and not discoverable by the plaintiff. Each state's rules must be consulted on this issue. If back-and-forth communication with the expert is not discoverable, the attorney should carefully review an expert's report before serving it and ask the expert to revise and re-submit the report. If a state deems communication between the attorney and the expert discoverable, however, the defense attorney must rely on verbal communication with the expert before any draft report is submitted in writing, as drafts and requested changes by the attorney could be discovered by the plaintiff and used effectively against the expert on cross-examination.

Under no circumstances should the plaintiff or defense nursing expert and the defendant nurse be in direct communication with each other. This is discoverable and would seriously damage the credibility of both the experts and client.

By the time of trial, the expert must have reviewed all medical records, interrogatories, depositions (at least as to liability), and other expert reports served by any party in the case. A defense counsel should never expose an expert to criticism on the grounds that the expert has not seen all the relevant documents in the case. This would be a self-inflicted wound. To the contrary, the expert should have all relevant documents handy at deposition and trial. A well-prepared expert will render an opinion that the defendant nurse complied with all accepted nursing standards, summarize all medical facts favorable to the defendant nurse and refute the arguments of the plaintiff's expert. There is no more powerful witness in a nursing malpractice case than a well-prepared defense expert.

By analogy to chess, the defense expert is the Queen, who can testify as to both facts and opinions, summarize medical treatment, cite effective medical literature and, by virtue of the expert's typical position as the last witness called in the case, presage the defense attorney's summation of the case, all under the guise of an objective medical advisor to the court. It is said many cases come down to a battle of the experts and, in the author's experience, this is true. (Refer to Chapter 21, *Working with Nursing Expert Witnesses*, for more information.)

For all these reasons, selection of the expert and assistance with preparation of the expert report are two of the defense attorney's most crucial tasks in the defense of any case.

Refer to Figure 16.3 for a list of organizations which might assist in the location of experts.

16.12 The Deposition

Deposition of the client nurse and the plaintiff are the most important events in the discovery process. Depositions should always be taken and the attorney should personally supervise everything concerning the deposition, beginning with the mundane arrangements.

A. Scheduling

Consider the following points:

1. The nurse's convenience comes first, if possible.
2. The hospital is generally the best deposition site for a currently employed nurse.
3. Be mindful of the nurse's schedule when making contact or scheduling (try to learn the nurse's shift from the risk manager before contacting the nurse).
4. When dealing with a nurse no longer employed by the hospital:

    • learn from risk management if the termination was friendly or unfriendly;

    • attempt to contact the nurse by letter before providing any information to the adversary; enclose relevant sections of the patient chart to provide knowledge of the case;

    • treat the nurse just as if she were still employed (i.e., prepare the nurse defendant and represent her at the deposition) if the nurse responds to counsel's inquires;

    • offer to speak or write to her employer if the nurse is concerned about the effect on a current job; arrange to have the insurance carrier reimburse the nurse for lost wages if possible; and

    • give the last known address to the adversary with the suggestion for a subpoena only if the terminated nurse cannot be reached after several attempts (i.e., Board of Nursing, DMV, Internet, etc.); never give out a phone number.

A nurse who left on hostile terms can be a problem. If she is a direct defendant, there is an incentive to cooperate, but the attorney has a conflict if involved in representing the hospital. If the nurse is crucial to the case, not a direct defendant and proves hostile by either non-response or open expressions, consider settlement.

B. Sequestration

When more than one nurse will be deposed at one session, the plaintiff's attorney often asks that only one nurse be present at a time. If the nurses are parties, they have a right to be present at all depositions. However, as a strategy one might consider agreeing to sequestration if one is confident the nurses will testify consistently. This takes away an argument from the plaintiff.

C. Preparing the Witness

Allow sufficient time for preparation. Same-day preparation is acceptable if the deposition will not be complex or crucial to the case. It is safe to assume that the attorney or client

---

1. American Association of Legal Nurse Consultants (www.aalnc.org)
2. American Association of Nurse Attorneys (www.taana.org)
3. American Health Lawyers Association (www.healthlawyers.org)
4. Nurses Service Organization (www.nso.com)
5. Nursing Net (www.nursingnet.org)
6. Wound, Ostomy and Continence Nurses Society (www.wocn.org)
7. Association of Women's Health, Obstetric and Neonatal Nurses (AWOHN) (www.awhonn.org)

Figure 16.3 Potential Sources Useful for Locating Nursing Expert Witnesses

may be late, so time should be added to the schedule: plan on at least an hour of preparation for each nurse, unless there is considerable overlap of facts. For complex depositions, consider preparing on a separate day.

D. Subjects to Cover in Preparing the Nurse

The defense attorney should cover these issues when helping the nurse get prepared for the deposition.

- Mechanics of the deposition. Go over the standard instructions. These can be left until the end or integrated with the factual preparation. If discussed at the start, they may be forgotten by the end of the preparation.
- An overview of the case. Include other parties, theories of liability, theories of defense and where this nurse fits in. This lets the nurse become a partner in the defense.
- Nursing credentials. Make sure the nurse recites them, with specific years and names of institutions. Get the nurse talking, not just listening, during preparation.
- "Dirty laundry." Any problems with licensing, employment, drugs, alcohol and so on, must come out. Impress the confidentiality of the conversation, but advise the nurse that this information will probably be discoverable if directly asked about. "Dirty laundry" also includes questions on overworking or understaffing. Was the nurse working a double or triple shift without sleep? Was she working two jobs? Was the floor understaffed? Many nurses are eager to blame a situation on management, but must understand that the sins of management will not absolve the nurse and may bring an inquiry such as, "Well, what did you do to protect your patients?"
- Review of the chart. Have the nurse read aloud everything he wrote in the chart. Have the nurse review the entire chart for his entries, remembering narrative notes, flow sheets, medication records, order and code sheets and so forth. Discuss any cross-outs and revisions.
- Change-of-shift procedures (report). What the nurse knew about the patient, when and how he knew it and how the information was passed on are subjects at deposition. This involves the procedure for taking and giving report and reading portions of the chart from past shifts.
- The nurse's charting routine. Were entries made contemporaneously or at the end of the shift?

Did the nurse use a worksheet? How were notes timed or, if not, why? Were the notes rewritten and why? Was everything supposed to be recorded or just positive findings? Was the patient observed at times without a note being made? Was every doctor visit to the patient necessarily recorded by the nurse? Were different inks used for different shifts? (If the deposition is at the hospital, have the original chart at the deposition.) Did other nurses chart during the defendant nurse's break? Where are vital signs recorded and by whom? How are input and output charted?

- Investigations. Explore committee meetings, counseling sessions, formal or informal discussions, procedure changes and reprimands resulting from the incident. (Whether privileged or not, these must be known by the attorney.)
- Other witnesses' versions of the same events. Be familiar with all other versions of the incident given in prior depositions or interviews with other witnesses. Orally brief the nurse on these. This is protected by attorney-client privilege. If counsel shows the nurse a deposition transcript, he must testify honestly that the transcript was reviewed, if asked. Explain that all versions of an incident should be consistent, and work to achieve consistency, but emphasize that the nurse must tell the truth as it is recalled. Nurses must protect their own interests first, especially if named as defendants.
- Healthcare facility policies related to the case. Policies must be reviewed and discussed with the witness, especially those already, or soon to be, known to the plaintiff's attorney. This is a sensitive area but facility policies are not necessarily the standard of nursing practice. The nurse should not concede that facility policies set standards of practice. Often the proper care was given but it was not recorded in the specific format required by the hospital's policy. Sometimes the facility's policy was ignored or abandoned as unwieldy. Remind the nurse to explain that patient care comes before charting.
- Nursing standards of care. Plaintiff's attorneys are permitted to question standards of nursing care to determine the competence of a witness. For example, in a medication error case, a nurse could be asked about standard dosages of relevant drugs, routes of administration or how and where to administer an injection. Counsel should anticipate relevant "standard of care questions" and discuss them with the nurse.

- The nurse's memory of the patient or the incident beyond the written notes. Explain how important it is to tell everything the nurse remembers, if asked. Explain the difference between specific recollections of this incident and general recall of habit, custom and standard procedure.

E. The Perils of Non-Recollection

One may be surprised at some nurses' lack of memory of events which lay people might recall vividly. Memory loss can be attributed to the thousands of patients seen over the years. Other "amnesia" may be a defense mechanism to block out unpleasant events. But, a percentage of so-called memory loss is intentional misrepresentation. As noted earlier, an attorney may think the client views her as a friend and confidant, but the client nurse may distrust the attorney for a number of reasons:

- The attorney is a stranger assigned through the insurance company and hospital administration.
- A nurse may lose his job if a confidential statement to an attorney gets back to the employer.
- The nurse may not want to inform on a friend or colleague.
- A nurse may be afraid to criticize a doctor or administrator.
- If a nurse did make a mistake, he may feel ashamed to tell a stranger.

All this feeds into a culture of non-recollection. It is easy, safe and avoids problems. However, the inability to recall a significant event can hurt the defense.

In one case, a wife and husband vividly testified how a nurse jumped up on the bed and held the wife's knees together to inhibit a baby's delivery, a definite deviation. But the nurse testified she couldn't recall because she was present at thousands of deliveries. The defense attorney encountering this memory loss is tempted to say, "Either admit or deny, but in the face of dramatic events, please don't claim loss of memory," which goes for interrogatory answers and deposition testimony alike. Aside from loss of credibility, a nurse's failure to remember an event leaves the field open to the plaintiff, whose words are essentially uncontested.

TIP: A position of not remembering is the same as a plea of no contest in a criminal case.

A companion to non-recollection is the position that "I do not recall anything outside my notes." This may be quickly and easily said in interrogatories or depositions. The client can be hurt with this statement when the nurse does try to defend herself later in the suit with a fuller recollection.

Clients will often be closed-mouthed and reserved early, but by the trial they become more aggressive and eager to win. The counsel's job is to make sure they do not claim non-recollection in early discovery. Take the time to gain the client's confidence and, thereby, truth. Failure of memory is legitimate in many situations, but when common sense says an event is too dramatic to forget, the jury will feel the same and brand the client a liar. The defense attorney should get the straight truth from the client before the deposition using sweetness, anger, persuasion or whatever works.

F. Anticipating the Attack or Taking the Offensive

So far, the preparation has been defensive, but often the best defense is a good offense. If a nurse can be prepped to answer logically and confidently why a certain action was taken, a giant step has been made toward victory. This does not happen without preparation. Asked why he did or did not do a particular thing with a patient, an unprepared nurse is likely to say, "Gosh, I don't know," or "How do you expect me to remember that?" However, if counsel has a careful discussion, the client can organize and articulate the factors which entered into judgment at the time. Take the probably accurate view that nursing conduct can be justified by logical reasoning.

Unless chemically impaired, the nurse was probably sincerely trying to help the patient and not being grossly negligent. In hindsight, nursing conduct can be made to look bad by a plaintiff's attorney, especially if the plaintiff has been hurt.

TIP: Show that the conduct in question was well thought out and justified when preparing a witness for deposition. Ideally, the nurse's stance should be, "That was my judgment at the time and I would act the same way today." It is not as hard as it sounds, but does take preparation.

During the deposition, the attorney should minimize off-the-record conferences with the client, which look like both are hiding something. Advise the defendant that she is obligated to answer any question to which there is no objection. If things start to go seriously wrong, stop the deposition. If the client seems tired, confused, upset or angry, take a break or adjourn for the day with some scheduling excuse.

After the deposition, always discuss the event with the client and give words of encouragement. Counsel should stay available by phone for questions, and send the client a copy of the transcript. Counsel and client should part cordially. It may be the last face-to-face meeting until shortly before trial.

TIP: Inaccuracies can be corrected through questioning on the record, but only if the distortion was serious and central to the case. As a rule, defense counsel will virtually never question his own client on the record at a deposition.

16.13 The Impending Trial

Eventually, sometimes after years of waiting, the day of reckoning may arrive: the trial notice. Immediately notify the client in writing and ask that she acknowledge availability for trial. Impress upon the nurse the need to be present daily through all or most of the proceedings, making necessary arrangements with employers, childcare and so on. Also explain that trials are often adjourned or delayed and dates are unsure. Advise the risk manager as well as the client, since nursing departments can be run much like the army in that the nurse must obey an order to cooperate from above, and conversely, if there is no prior approval, it puts the client in an awkward position.

The trial notice usually causes anxiety, which can be reduced by a phone call with the client. Emphasize the need to study, but not memorize, the deposition transcript sent to the client earlier. Re-emphasize the plan of defense, such as "nursing judgment," "not my job," "it didn't happen," or "even if it happened, it didn't matter." Reassure the client that counsel will meet before the testimony and discuss specific questions.

Give an early warning of the day of testimony, but tell the client that there will likely be only a day or two of notice. Give clear directions to the courthouse or suggest the hospital provide transportation. Ask the client to arrive early

and do not schedule too many witnesses in one day. It is difficult on the witness to be brought to court only to have the testimony postponed.

Above all, before trial and at all stages of discovery, listen carefully to the client. Counsel may be an experienced lawyer, but the client is the experienced nurse. The client can often come up with a line of questioning or a theory that can win the case. Do not be blinded by pride or ego to a good suggestion. As a team, the attorney and the nurse client should be unbeatable.

16.14 Summary

Always keep in mind that the defense attorney's primary responsibility is to the nurse client. Careful preparation and strong support will help the client weather a highly stressful period. A client who understands the steps in the legal process is in the best position to aid in the defense effort. Most nurses are eager to help and easily motivated to learn the rules of the legal proceedings. By keeping a strong relationship with the risk manager and insurance personnel, counsel will enhance his effectiveness in defending nurses.

Endnotes

1. Croke, E., "Nurses, Negligence, and Malpractice," *American Journal of Nursing* 103, no. 9 (September 2003): 54-63.

2. Iyer, P., "Tampering with Medical Records," In *Nursing Home Litigation: Investigation and Case Preparation,* Second Edition, ed. P. Iyer. Tucson, Arizona: Lawyers and Judges Publishing Co., 2006.

3. Konray, R. and P. Iyer, "Tampering with Medical Records," In *Medical Legal Aspects of Medical Records, Second Edition*, eds. P. Iyer, B. Levin, Tucson, Arizona: Lawyers and Judges Publishing Co., 2010.

Chapter 17

View of the Actuary

Mindy M. Steichen, FCAS, MAAA and Peter G. Wick, FCAS, MAAA

17.1 Introduction

The medical malpractice insurance industry is a multi-billion dollar per year industry. This chapter provides an overview of some of the important aspects of and issues regarding medical malpractice insurance. It also discusses some current trends and how these trends are affecting the current claim environment of nursing and general malpractice claims.

17.2 Medical Malpractice Insurance
A. Types of Policies

There are three main types of medical malpractice policies. The first two, *occurrence* and *claims-made* policies, are mutually exclusive of one another. A medical professional or hospital will carry one type or the other of these two policies. A *tail* policy is a third type of policy that is issued to a professional who at one time carried a claims-made policy, but for various possible reasons no longer carries the coverage. In 2008, industry-wide gross earned premiums for medical malpractice occurrence policies were approximately $2.5 billion, while gross earned premiums for medical malpractice claims-made policies were approximately $9.5 billion.[1] These premiums only include the commercial insurance market; it is estimated that approximately another $10 billion of premium is self-insured. The differences between the types of policies are described below.

1. Occurrence policies

Occurrence medical malpractice policies cover all claims against the policyholder that occurred in the covered policy period. The incident that triggered the claim may not be reported or become a claim for several years. Therefore, occurrence policies are often considered long-tailed.

For example, assume a nurse is covered by a 2009 occurrence policy. An incident occurs in February 2009 and a suit is brought about in March 2009; this claim will be covered by the 2009 occurrence policy. A different incident occurs in June 2009, but a suit is not made for several years, until 2012. This claim will also be covered under the 2009 occurrence policy. Finally, a suit is made in October 2009 against the nurse regarding an incident that occurred in 2007. This claim will not be covered under the 2009 occurrence policy. Assuming the nurse had the same occurrence coverage in 2007, the claim will be covered under that policy instead. Occurrence policies were originally the only type of medical malpractice insurance coverage available. Due to the fact that medical professional liability claims can sometimes take upwards of 10 or 20 years to be reported, it became increasingly difficult to estimate the ultimate claim costs for occurrence policies. Therefore, claims-made policies were created.

2. Claims-made policies

Claims-made policies cover all claims reported against a policyholder in a given policy period, as long as the incident occurred after claims-made coverage was first initiated or back to some initial date established in the policy known as the retro date. As the length of time between the retro date and the policy start date increases, eventually (usually around five years) the policy will be known as a mature claims-made policy. In our example from above, now assuming the nurse has purchased claims-made policies instead, the incident that occurred in February 2009 and the suit that was made in March 2009 would be covered by the 2009 claims-made policy. For the incident that occurred in June 2009, but the suit was not made until 2012, this claim would not be covered under the 2009 claims-made policy, but would be covered under the 2012 policy if coverage is still in place at the time. Finally, the suit that is made in October 2009 for a 2007 incident would be covered under the 2009 claims-made policy assuming the nurse has a coverage retro date prior to 2007. Because claims-made policies cover only the claims against the provider in a specific policy year, they are much shorter tailed then occurrence policies. While the total dollar amount of specific claims might not be known for several years until claims are settled, the number of claims will be known shortly after the close of the policy year.

TIP: Occurrence policies are triggered by the date the incident occurred, while claims-made policies are triggered by the date the claim is brought against the insured.

---

3. Tail policies

The third type of medical malpractice insurance policy is usually purchased when the provider will no longer be carrying claims-made coverage. The reasons for the provider to end claims-made coverage are varied, and can be due to retirement, death, disability, leaving the profession, switching carriers or becoming self-insured. In our previous example, if the nurse with claims-made coverage decides to retire after the 2009 policy year she will no longer purchase claims-made coverage, and instead could purchase one final tail policy that will cover any future claims brought against her. The suit that is brought in 2012 for an incident that happened before the nurse retired in 2009 would then be covered

under this tail policy. Some claims-made insurers offer what is known as a DDR (death, disability, retirement) provision to its policyholders in conjunction with their claims-made policies. In these cases, if the insured experiences death, disability or retirement a tail policy will be provided. A provision for the DDR coverage is built into the claims-made premium.

B. Limits

Policy limits for medical malpractice insurance policies vary based on who is purchasing the policy and her individual insurance needs. Limits for policies are most commonly stated on both a per claim and per aggregate basis. For example, a policy with a $1 million per claim and $3 million aggregate limit would most usually be described as a $1M/$3M policy. In this case, the insured would be covered for up to $1 million per each claim and up to $3 million in the aggregate or for all claims during a given policy period. Similarly, a $200K/$600K limit policy would provide coverage of $200,000 per claim or $600,000 total for each policy period. The entities or individuals that require and purchase medical malpractice insurance vary, and therefore several different types of insurance policies are available. Some of the most common types of policies are as follows.

1. Hospital professional liability

Hospital and healthcare facilities may purchase commercial hospital professional liability (HPL) insurance to cover their medical malpractice liabilities. In some cases they may self-insure a portion of these liabilities through trusts, captives or other arrangements. If the hospital or healthcare facility directly employs physicians or other medical staff they will typically buy a policy that covers claims against the hospital and against the employed physicians or other medical staff. Due to the amount of exposure usually covered by the HPL policy, the limits on these policies are often large and usually greater than those purchased by healthcare providers.

2. Physicians professional liability

Most states require physicians and surgeons to have liability coverage. They will usually buy a physician's professional liability (PPL) policy from a commercial insurer or a physician-owned mutual group. Many physicians who are employed by a hospital will also be covered by the HPL policy purchased by that hospital. Physician policy limits tend to also be large, as settlements for suits brought against physicians can be high. Limits between $200K/$600K and $1M/$3M are common, with physician groups many times purchasing larger amounts. Many physicians are also covered by state-based patient compensation funds (PCF) that provide excess insurance coverage above the physician's primary limit. The PCFs are funded by mandatory surcharges on the primary limit policies.

3. Nurses professional liability

Nurses who are employed by a hospital are usually covered by that hospital's HPL policy. There are several reasons why the nurse may want to purchase an additional nursing professional liability (NPL) commercial policy, including coverage for off-duty incidents, coverage in the event of a job change and to provide additional limits or tail coverage. NPL policies are usually written at lower limits than PPL or HPL policies. A $100K/$300K or $200K/$600K limit policy are common limits for nurses.

4. Allied professionals

Allied professional can be defined as all other non-medical or nursing professionals. Some examples of allied professionals are speech and language therapists, lab technicians and pharmacy assistants. These professionals also require medical malpractice insurance and may be insured by the healthcare facility by whom they are employed or can also purchase commercial allied professional malpractice insurance.

TIP: Attorneys may want to consider policy details and their ramifications when evaluating cases involving nursing malpractice.

C. Components of Premium

The total claim amount covered by an insurance company or self-insurance can be divided into several components.

1. Indemnity payment

The indemnity payment is the actual settlement or loss amount paid to the claimant. This settlement amount is usually broken out into the economic and non-economic damages.

a. Economic damages

The economic damages are the actual damages suffered by the claimant such as medical expense and lost wages from time unable to work.

b. Non-economic damages

The non-economic damages include awards for pain and suffering and monetary payments for disability or disfigurement. These are more difficult to quantify than the economic damages and are subject to interpretation.

2. Allocated loss adjustment expenses

Allocated loss adjustment expenses (ALAE) are the expenses associated with a claim that can be attributed to that specific claim. Examples are medical tests, private investigators, attorney fees and expert witness fees.

3. Unallocated loss adjustment expenses

Unallocated loss adjustment expenses (ULAE) are costs associated with medical malpractice claims. These expenses, unlike the ALAE, usually cannot be assigned to a specific claim. They include administrative expenses, claims handling expenses, and overhead expenses.

D. Breakdown of Costs

Several industry studies have broken down the distribution of premium dollars in the medical professional liability industry. One study by Studdard[2] estimates that approximately 40 percent of premium dollars in the medical professional liability industry are used to pay claimants. A study of more than 30 years of industry insurance data by Karls[3] found similar results. The results of that study estimated the breakdown of medical professional liability costs as follows:

- 39 percent: final payments to claimant
- 27 percent: insurance industry's claims management costs (including court costs, attorney fees, individual claim costs, expert witness fees, and all other litigation costs)
- 19 percent: claimant's attorney fees
- 15 percent: insurance company expenses and overhead

TIP: Payouts to claimants are estimated to be approximately 40 percent of premium dollars while claimant attorney fees are typically about 20 percent of premium dollars.

E. Biggest Players

Medical malpractice insurance can be largely influenced by state-specific laws on statute of limitations, rate filing processes, and settlement awards. Therefore many medical malpractice insurance writers specialize in specific states, regions or territories. Looking at total direct written medical malpractice premiums on a nationwide basis for 2009, Table 17.1 lists the largest writers of medical malpractice insurance in the United States and their market share of the commercial insurance market.[4] As shown in Table 17.1, the six largest writers of medical malpractice insurance in the United States in 2009 made up approximately 35 percent of the total market.

Table 17.1
2009 Direct Written Premiums and Market Share

Company	Direct Written Premiums	Market Share
MLMIC Group	$757M	7.1%
Berkshire Hathaway Insurance Group	$726M	6.8%
Doctors Company Group	$601M	5.6%
ProAssurance Corporation Group	$541M	5.1%
American International Group	$524M	4.9%
CNA Insurance Group	$517M	4.9%

CNA Insurance Group, the sixth largest medical malpractice insurer in total, is also the largest insurer of nurses in the United States. They have provided professional liability coverage to nurses since 1984 and currently insure more than 650,000 nurses. Their coverage is typically sold directly to the nurse or nurse practitioner[5].

F. Rating Variables

The rates that insurance companies charge hospitals, doctors, nurses or other medical professionals for medical malpractice insurance are based on many different variables. Rates are usually calculated and filed on a state-specific basis.

1. Line of business factors

Some examples of variables that are used to determine the rate an insurer will charge for a specific coverage are: historical frequency (number) of claims, historical severity (dollar amount) per claim, ultimate (final) loss and ALAE for the historical business, ULAE load as a percentage of premium, and loss and ALAE trend rates.

2. State-specific factors

State-specific factors are also used to determine rates such as state premium tax rates and territory relativities. Another state-specific factor that may affect a company's rates is the presence or absence of tort reform legislation. Several states have initiated tort reform policies where the non-economic damages portion of the settlement amount of a medical malpractice claim may be capped at a certain dollar amount. States also have different time frames for the statute of limitations for when a claim can be filed. This legislation and in some cases the repeal of the legislation can influence the company's rates in that specific state.

3. Company-specific factors

Company-specific factors such as acquisition expenses, general expenses (both fixed and variable), risk management expenses, and commission and brokerage expenses are also used as rating variables. Additionally, company-specific expense, and surplus and investment ratios are often used, such as the company's premium or reserve to surplus ratio, rate of return on assets, and federal income tax rate.

4. Insured specific factors

Once the line of business, state- and company-specific factors are combined to determine the specific rate for that line of business, insured-specific factors are then used to derive the specific rate charged to each insured. Some examples of these factors are: claims-made step factors (factors to adjust the rate to the insured's number of years since the retro date), class plan or specialty relativities (for example, a nurse practitioner will be charged a higher rate than a staff nurse practice physician), and increased/decreased limit factors (used to calculate the rate at the specific policy limit).

17.3 Drivers of Medical Malpractice Costs
A. Examples

1. By state

The rates charged to hospitals, physicians, nurses, or other healthcare professionals can vary significantly by state, by insurance company and by specialty. The Medical Liability Monitor's Annual Rate Summary Issue published in October 2009[6] found a broad range of medical professional liability rates. For example, insuring a physician specializing in internal medicine and purchasing $1M/$3M limits of mature claims-made coverage produced the rate examples by territories seen in Table 17.2.

For nurse professional liability (NPL) coverage, the differences in rates charged by state or territory are not as extreme. One reason for this is the much smaller volume of NPL claims versus doctors or hospital claims. Due to a much smaller database of available claim history, NPL insurers often must rely on nationwide data when developing

Table 17.2
Internal Medicine $1M/$3M Rate Examples

Minnesota	$3,000
Los Angeles, California	$10,000
New Jersey	$20,000
New York City	$26,000
Miami, Florida	$32,000
Chicago, Illinois	$38,000

The sampling shows the large variability found in physicians' professional liability rates by state or territory and insurer.

Table 17.3
Nurse Rates by State

	Georgia	Iowa	Maine	Minnesota	Pennsylvania	N. Carolina	Washington
Registered Nurse	$98	$98	$98	$106	$98	$106	$98
Nurse Practitioner	$1,247	$1,133	$1,247	$1,247	$1,309	$1,247	$1,195

Table 17.4
Physician Rates by Specialty

Specialty	Relativity
Internal Medicine—No Surgery	1.13
Radiology Diagnostic	1.70
Family/General Practice – Surgery	1.88
General Surgery	2.74
OB / GYN	4.30
Neurology	6.26

Table 17.5
Nurse Rates by Specialty in North Carolina

Specialty	Employed Rate	Self-Employed Rate
Registered Nurse	$106	$345
Clinical Nurse Specialist (No Prescriptive Authority)	$106	$345
Nurse Practitioner		
A. Adult/Family Planning/Women's Health	$683	$842
B. Psychiatric	$964	$1,191
C. Pediatric/Family Practice/Acute Critical Care	$1,247	$1,539
D. Obstetrics/Gynecology	$1,530	$1,890
E. Nurse Practitioner Student	$275	N/A
F. Clinical Nurse Specialist—Educator, Consultant, Administrator	$512	$631

rates and give very little credibility to state-specific data due to the limited loss data. For example, rates for an employed registered nurse and a family practice nurse practitioner for American Casualty Company (part of CNA Group) are listed in Table 17.3 for several states.[7]

2. By specialty

For physician professional liability rates there is significant variability in the rates charged by specialty. For example, from a January 1, 2008 rate filing in the State of Ohio for the Medical Protective Company, with a family/general practice (no surgery) physician used as a base, rate relativities were assigned to some of the other specialties as seen in Table 17.4.[8] From Table 17.4, a general surgeon would be charged 2.74 times more than a family physician, while an OB/GYN physician would be charged 4.3 times more than a family physician.

While NPL rates many times do not vary significantly by state, there is variability when looking at the rates by specialty. Table 17.5 shows an example of rates for employed and self-employed nurse specialists in the state of North Carolina for the American Casualty Company.[9]

As Table 17.5 shows, rates range from $106 for an employed registered nurse to $1,890 for a self-employed nurse practitioner specializing in obstetrics/gynecology. Employed rates are usually lower than self-employed rates due to shared limits of coverage among the employees.

B. Frequency of Claims

1. PPL claims

The frequency, or number of claims, per physician, per hospital, or even per nurse are often examined on an industry-wide basis in order to analyze the trends in the medical professional liability industry. In an analysis using publicly available insurance data, we found the closed claim frequency per physician has decreased steadily for the years 2001 through 2008.[10] Some reasons for the declining number of claims per physician for these years include the influence of tort reform legislation in many states and increased risk management initiatives throughout the health care industry. The analysis also shows that the frequency of physician claims may have reached its lowest levels. Economic conditions, and in some states the repeal of tort reform initiatives, may cause claim frequencies to remain constant or even start to increase in the future.

2. HPL claims

A study of hospital professional liability claims by AON Corp. and the American Society for Healthcare Risk Management (ASHRM) published in 2009[11] indicates that the frequency of hospital professional liability claims is expected to rise for the first time, after showing decreasing frequencies in the previous ten years. The study expects HPL claims to start increasing at a rate of 1 percent per year. The study points to factors such as the economic downturn, less public sympathy towards healthcare providers and changes in Medicare reimbursement policies as driving the increasing claim frequencies.

3. Nursing claims

Though not much industry data are available focusing specifically on nurse malpractice claims, frequency trends for nursing-specific claims data may show different trends than the downward frequency trends for PPL and HPL claims. A study by CNA[12] of nursing claims showed that from 1997 to 2007 the ultimate frequency of nurse claims generally increased each year. This steadily increasing number of claims can partly be explained by changing trends in the nursing litigation environment. In the past, nurses were seen as playing a limited role in patient care and were not often named in lawsuits. This has shifted over time and nurses are now being specifically named in suits as being responsible for decisions regarding patient care and being held liable for patient injuries.

TIP: Nurses are increasingly the target of malpractice litigation.

C. Severity of Claims

1. PPL and HPL claims

The severity of a medical professional liability claim is equal to the settlement dollar amount of that claim. An analysis of severities of publicly available countrywide closed claims shows claim severities steadily increasing over the past 20 years. In 1991, the average claim severity was slightly higher than $150,000 per claim; by 2000 the average severity per claim was approaching $250,000; and by 2009 the average severity for this database of claims was about $325,000 per claim. The analysis shows the trend in average severities is rising higher than the general inflation rate as measured by the Consumer Price Index.[13]

The AON study[14] also shows HPL claim severities steadily increasing over time. This study estimates claims are increasing at a rate between 3.5 to 6.0 percent per year and estimates claims will continue to increase at about 4.0 percent per year.

Economic factors such as costs of lost wages and medical costs are the main drivers of increasing claim severities.

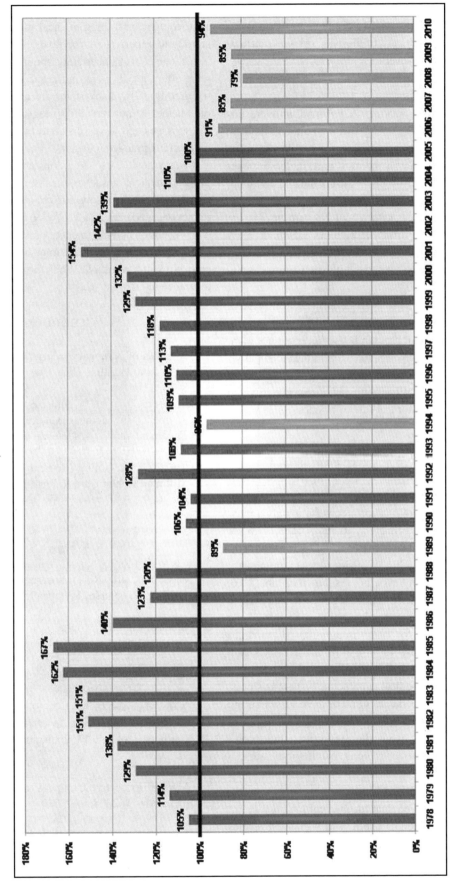

Table 17.6
Medical Professional Liability Combined Ratio after Dividends

Note: 2009 and 2010 figures are estimated.

The cost to defend claims is also increasing and juries are becoming more likely to award very high severity multi-million dollar settlements. All of these factors are contributing to increasing claim severities.

2. Nursing claims

The CNA study[15] on nursing claims found similar results in the severity trends for nursing-specific claims. Like PPL and HPL claims, the average severities for nursing claims on a closed-claim basis are, for the most part, increasing over time. In a different study by CNA,[16] using nurse practitioner claims, they found that accident year indemnity payment severities have been increasing at about 2.3 percent per year from $168,600 in 1999 to $189,300 in 2008. Similarly, average expense payments for nurse practitioner claims have been increasing at about 2.9 percent per year from $28,500 in 1998 to $42,900 in 2008.

D. Combined Ratios

One common measure of profitability for an insurance company is called the combined ratio. An insurance company's combined ratio for a line of business is equal to the expected liability on claims plus all administrative expenses divided by premiums collected for that line of business.

$$\text{Combined Ratio} = \frac{\text{Incurred Losses} + \text{Expenses}}{\text{Earned Premiums}}$$

An important item to note is that an insurer's combined ratio does not include investment income; it is only a measure of underwriting profitability. Refer to Table 17.6 for a depiction of the historical combined ratios for the medical professional liability line of business based on industry data on a nationwide market basis.[17] As shown in Table 17.6, medical professional liability insurance experienced periods of very poor underwriting results throughout most of the 1980's and then again for 1994 through 2004. Companies were paying out much more for claims and expenses than they were collecting in premium dollars. Due to the long-tailed nature of some medical malpractice lines of business, investment returns helped ease some of these losses during those time periods. Starting in the late 2000s and estimated to continue in the future, medical professional liability combined ratios have been much more favorable for insurers.

17.4 Summary

The current claim environment for medical malpractice insurance can be described as one in which claim severities are steadily increasing, while claim frequencies are showing

signs of increasing for the first time in many years. Insurance companies writing medical malpractice coverage are starting to experience more favorable underwriting results. Yet, there is also uncertainty about healthcare reform and what effect it will have on the medical malpractice industry. Additionally, many states are awaiting court decisions on whether or not tort reform legislation will be repealed. These issues add to the uncertainty about the future of the medical malpractice industry.

Many healthcare institutions are stepping up efforts to prevent medical misadventures and improve outcomes in the area of patient safety. Efforts are focusing on falls risk reduction, medication safety, wrong site surgery reduction, and prevention and treatment of pressure ulcers. The success of these efforts will not only improve the delivery of health care, but will have implications for the medical malpractice insurance industry as well.

Endnotes

1. Analysis of National Underwriter Insurance Data Services from Highline Data.

2. Studdert, D. et al. "Claims, Errors and Compensation Payments in Medical Malpractice Litigation." *New England Journal of Medicine.* May 11, 2006.

3. Karls, C. "Retooling Medical Professional Liability." Milliman Health Care Reform Briefing Paper. September 2009.

4. See Note 1.

5. CNA Healthpro Nurse Claims Study, "An Analysis of Claims with Risk Management Recommendations 1997-2007." Nurses Service Organization.

6. Medical Liability Monitor's Annual Rate Survey Issue. October 2009.

7. American Casualty Company's Rate Filings for the states of: Georgia as of February 1, 2007, Iowa as of July 15, 2009, Maine as of July 15, 2009, Minnesota as of July 15, 2009, Pennsylvania as of February 1, 2007, North Carolina as of July 15, 2009, and Washington as of July 15, 2009.

8. Medical Protective Company's Rate Filing in Ohio as of January 1, 2008.

9. See note 7 for the State of North Carolina.

10. Analysis of AM Best Aggregates and Averages – Property/Casualty. Analysis of National Underwriter Insurance Data Services from Highline Data. 2009 and 2010 estimated from A.M. Best Review & Preview, February 2010.

11. "Hospital Professional Liability and Physician Liability 2009 Benchmark Analysis," AON and American Society for Healthcare Risk Management, October 2009.

12. See Note 5.

13. Analysis of National Practitioner Data Bank Public Use Data File, December 31, 2009.

14. See Note 11.

15. See Note 5.

16. CNA Healthpro "Nurse Practitioner Claims Analysis 1998-2008." Nurses Service Organization.

17. See Note 10.

Chapter 18

E-Discovery

G. Ann Geyer, Esq.

18.1 Introduction

Thirty-five years after the introduction of computer technology, America has truly become a digital society. According to a University of California study, 93 percent of all information generated in 1999 was created digitally.[1] Well-known market research firm IDC estimates that by 2012 the amount of digital information will have reached 2500 exabytes[2] and will continue to increase about 5 percent annually.[3] In the last ten years, the media for digital information storage has shifted. No longer restricted purely to computers, digital information appears as cell phone images and text messages, instant messages, social networking postings, business and personal blogs, in addition to the more common e-mail and voice messages. Digital information can be stored on highly portable devices such as USB ports, smart cards, laptops, and cell phones in addition to more traditional computer tapes, disks, and hard drives.

In 2006, the Federal Rules of Civil Procedure (FRCP) were modified to officially recognize the existence of digital information and provide specific discovery procedures. These amendments are colloquially referred to as "e-discovery." Before the e-discovery rules were approved, the federal courts spent considerable time struggling to fit digital information into older discovery rules. Most of the difficulties were associated with the scope of discovery which was limited to "documents or tangible things." The e-discovery rules do not change the fundamental principles or practices of discovery in general; rather they defined a new class of discoverable information, namely "electronically stored information" or ESI.

TIP: Even though the FRCP apply only to federal cases, healthcare organizations and counsel need to become familiar with the rules since at least 26 states have adopted their own versions of e-discovery, many of which are similar or identical to the FRCP rules.[4]

ESI changes the discovery landscape in several ways. First, the volume of discoverable information is greatly expanded over paper documents. ESI includes not just the information from applications, file servers, and core computer systems, but also any information sources that duplicate, replicate, or consolidate information in other storage locations. Any type of ESI is discoverable including e-mail, voicemail, instant messaging, cell phone data, iPod and iPad data, cookies, browser favorite listings, USB stores, backup stores, audit logs, and even deleted files under some circumstances. Additionally ESI is not limited to an organization's own computer systems but extends to any ESI under its control which might include employees' home computers, business associate systems, and third-party service providers.

Consider this scenario: A nurse receives a text message from the hospital lab on her cell phone with the results of certain stat blood tests. The results indicate the patient is now in a distressed condition. The nurse does not view or respond to the message for 30 minutes. Not only is the text message subject to discovery under the e-discovery rules but so is the time it was received, opened, and acknowledged by the nurse.

TIP: The best practice is to consider any information which has ever been stored as ESI in some type of electronic device, not just the traditional notion of a computer, and apply the e-discovery rules to all such information.

The e-discovery rules include a class of ESI known as "metadata" which is information that provides authenticity, history, context, statistics, or other information to assist with data management. Metadata can be quite extensive, difficult to search, and presents some unique privilege issues not present with paper documents. One of the more troublesome aspects of managing metadata for discovery purposes is avoiding spoliation which can occur merely because the metadata information was copied or forwarded. Consequently, e-discovery places a greater emphasis on sound computer forensic methods to collect and preserve ESI subject to discovery requests. New policies and procedures specifically addressing preservation of metadata are necessary to avoid such issues and their associated sanctions.

E-discovery rules put a greater burden on effective communications between the legal process and information management policies. This is particularly true for "litigation hold" procedures. Under discovery rules, once a party has a reasonable anticipation of litigation, it has an obligation to preserve relevant information and to notify key employees that data relevant to the anticipated litigation must be preserved.

Consider this scenario: A former patient sues the hospital and names two nurses as defendants, claiming that the hospital was negligent in supervising and monitoring its nursing staff and that the named nurse defendants failed to follow proper standards in monitoring the patient's status and informing the physician of changes. The hospital provides all nurses with smartphones that allow phone, voice and text messaging, e-mail and instant messaging communications. The nursing staff has received no instructions on how to archive cell phone messages. Once the hospital or the nurses have any reasonable anticipation that a lawsuit may occur, they each have an obligation to preserve relevant information. The cell phone usage records and incoming or outgoing messages pertaining to this patient are relevant and should be preserved. This also means that the cell phone batteries must stay charged so as not to inadvertently delete any internally stored data.

To effectively and efficiently manage e-discovery, healthcare organizations need to implement or revise policies that address:

1. discovery and disclosure procedures;
2. information retention and destruction;
3. litigation hold and information preservation; and
4. spoliation.

This means that legal e-discovery obligations must now be closely aligned with information technology (IT), risk management, and compliance practices. Key clinical and support departments with data custodian responsibilities or with super-user status may need specialized training to implement some of these policies. Litigation hold training should become a standard part of employee compliance training.

To prepare and plan for e-discovery requires understanding five critical elements:

1. how ESI is treated differently than documents and things;
2. the scope of e-discovery and the accelerated time frames for the meet and confer conference;
3. the two-tier approach to ESI production;
4. the effect of inadvertent production of privileged ESI; and
5. the safe harbor protections from sanctions.

In addition to the legal rules of e-discovery, attorneys are expected to have the skills and knowledge to make good faith negotiations with opposing counsel about all aspects of e-discovery. While attorneys are not expected to become IT professionals, they must be familiar enough with clients' information systems to ask probing questions and be able to manage the preservation and discovery obligations. This means that attorneys should have a working understanding of:

1. their clients' information infrastructure;
2. what information sources exist and how they can be effectively searched;
3. information retention, deletion, and preservation policies to prevent spoliation; and
4. clients' capabilities to produce ESI in useable form.

New terms such as "native file format," "metadata," "Boolean searching," and "hashing" will become standard vocabulary for healthcare attorneys, nurse managers, and HIM personnel.

18.2 The New E-Discovery Rules

The first formal rules for discovery of digital information went into effect on December 1, 2006. Prior to this time, the FRCP addressed only documents and things, which meant many of the original rules had to be distorted to accommodate methods and disputes associated with the discovery of digital information. The 2006 amendments apply primarily to FRCP 16, 26, 33, 34 and 37. Together they act to:

1. encourage cooperation between parties about e-discovery parameters very early in the litigation process;
2. require the preservation of electronic information as soon as there is a reasonable likelihood of litigation;
3. determine in what form ESI should be produced;
4. identify when ESI is inaccessible and the procedures for compelling production and cost sharing of production expenses;
5. establish a safe harbor for privileged ESI; and
6. provide for sanctions if the e-discovery rules are not complied with appropriately.

A. ESI—Electronically Stored Information

ESI is now a defined term that is used to govern the proper scope of an e-discovery request.[5] According to the Judicial Conference Committee notes to Rule 34(a)(1), the proper scope for a request to produce ESI is "expansive."

TIP: An expansive ESI request, such as "all information which constitute, refer or relate to any exact copies of all relevant computer disks, CDs, DVDs, USBs, or other removable media related to this action during the relevant time period of this litigation,"[6] can be quite difficult to respond to if prior preparation has not been made to identify and track portable media or data stored in volatile memory.

The Rules require the parties to provide "a copy or a description by category and location of all documents, electronically stored information…that the disclosing party has in its possession, custody or control and may use to support its claims or defenses…."[7]

This means that any type of ESI is discoverable including not just the originally collected or created information, but any duplicates, replicates, or amalgamations kept for backup purposes, stored in multiple locations, used for con-

venience in supporting different business functions, or used as an interim device for managing the information. The consequence of this expansive scope is that ESI discovery overwhelms the paper environment in terms of both the volume of information produced and the costs associated with identification, production, and privilege review.[8] With a gigabit of data being the equivalent of 75,000 pages and even the smallest computers and data storage devices having multi-gigabit capacity, e-discovery is a mega-sized proposition.

TIP: Courts have frowned on the use of ESI discovery solely for purposes of burdening the opposing party. Attorneys should develop a working understanding of when to use ESI discovery rather than paper documents, keeping in mind the associated cost and time burdens.

B. New Meet and Confer Obligations

Under the e-discovery rules, the Rule 26 "meet and confer conference" must take place within 99 days of the complaint filing.[9] Recognizing the complexity of ESI production and the likelihood that several meet and confer conferences may be necessary, the rules specifically require the parties to address their ESI discovery issues as early as possible with the intent to avoid downstream disruptions in the case proceedings.

In addition to all regular discovery issues, three specific ESI topics must be covered in the meet and confer conference:

1. issues relating to disclosure of ESI including the form or formats for production;
2. issues related to preserving discoverable information; and
3. issues relating to claims of privilege including whether the parties may assert a privilege claim after production has occurred.

In order to have a productive conference, attorneys are expected to come prepared with the requisite knowledge of their client's information sources and preferences for complying with e-discovery requests. This means that attorneys must become familiar with a number of new parameters. A well designed e-discovery plan requires attorneys to understand what types of ESI exist, where and how the ESI is stored, how the ESI is routinely used, and what types of information maintenance policies apply to the ESI. Attorneys also need to understand how the ESI is structured and what types of searching keywords are possible for each ESI data set. Without such knowledge, it is likely the discovery plan will lack the specificity needed to produced the data efficiently and may lead to costly rework later in the litigation schedule or to sanctions for unnecessary delay or uncooperative behavior.

TIP: When time is of the essence, pre-planning is critical. If an organization waits until an e-discovery request is made, the likelihood of finding all responsive data is limited. E-discovery compliance depends upon developing a working inventory of information sources and methods for searching, preserving, and producing the necessary information.

C. Production Formats

As amended, Rule 34(b) gives the requesting party the right to specify its preferred data format. The responding party may object to any of the requested formats by including the objection and specifying the reasons in the customary objection response. If the responding party objects, or if the requesting party never stated a format preference, then the responding party must provide information about the formats it will produce.

TIP: The responding party is always obligated to produce ESI in the form in which it is routinely maintained in the course of its business or in a form that is reasonably useable.

It is important that production formats be negotiated by the parties during the meet and confer conference. A mutual agreement early in the discovery process streamlines the responding party's production process and avoids the risk of a usability challenge which tends to result in unnecessary duplicative efforts by the responding party to produce a usable alternative format.

Despite the obligation to discuss production form in the meet and confer conference, usability challenges still occur and can be contentious. The benefit of agreement during the meet and confer is that the court can issue an order consistent with the agreement thus effectively ending subsequent challenges. If no agreement was reached, then a dispute is resolved by court order—effectively putting the choice of production format in the hands of the court. The court has discretion to order any format and is not bound to choose an alternative proposed by either party.

The parties need to agree on format requirements to ensure that the disclosing party can provide the ESI in a form that is useable by the requesting party. Under e-discovery rules, the ESI must be produced "as it is ordinarily maintained or in a reasonably useable form."[10] Essentially, a disclosing party is prohibited from merely printing to paper and dumping boxes of paper copies of ESI, provided a request

for ESI has been made. This requirement is particularly relevant for information stored in proprietary systems for which export options might be limited. For example, in some EMR systems, the normal expectation is that stored information is presented according to a particular screen format. Without the associated application, information in a file format may be difficult or costly to display and the data in the file itself quite unintelligible without its display formatting.

The e-discovery rules provide for agreement regarding alternative formats. The first alternative is the "native" format which is defined as an electronic document that is produced with "the associated file structure defined by the creating application."[11] An example of a native format would be a document created in Microsoft Word, but not the same document converted to PDF. The second alternative is any non-native format that is "reasonably usable." Here the PDF format in the previous example would be reasonably useful as it makes ESI stored in a proprietary or uncommon format readable. A major caveat in producing alternative, non-native formats is that the ESI may not be converted from a searchable to a non-searchable form. This means that a native Word document which is searchable could not be produced as a TIFF file which is not searchable. Once the ESI is produced in an electronic format there is no requirement to provide it in other form.[12]

TIP: The disclosing party should include the form it intends to use in the Rule 24 written response to avoid the possibility of subsequent challenges about the reasonably useable character of the ESI produced.

D. Metadata

Metadata is a term used to describe information that is maintained about other information and used for various business and data management purposes such as to establish authenticity, communicate context or history, or provide statistics about the associated information.[13] For example, the properties fields of a Word document are metadata.

Prior to the e-discovery rules, parties often argued about whether metadata was discoverable because it was not actually part of a document. The amended FRCP 34(a) has ended this debate. Metadata is electronically stored information and thus is by definition ESI. Each layer of an information architecture tends to have its own collection of metadata which means that each application, file system, or database may have different metadata fields. Metadata is typically generated either by user input or automatically by system design. For example, a Word document author can open the properties field and input the document title, purpose, or keyword—while the Word application supplies the creation, modification, and access dates, number of words and other statistical information. Application metadata is normally stored as part of the application data. On the other hand, system servers—file servers, web servers, database servers—create and store metadata separately. Audit logs routinely include information that acts as metadata for the system producing the audit logs.

A party need not expressly request metadata for it to be discoverable. In some early cases, parties tried to remove the metadata prior to production of the native format, but courts have rejected this approach as insufficient and have ordered sanctions in some cases. In *Williams v. Sprint/United Mgmt. Co.*, the court held that "when a party is ordered to produce electronic documents as they are maintained in the ordinary course of business, the producing party should produce the electronic documents with their metadata intact, unless that party timely objects to production of metadata, the parties agree that the metadata should not be produced, or the producing party requests a protective order."[14]

More recently courts have started to inspect the parties' arguments for requesting or excluding metadata more seriously because of the volume of metadata and the likelihood of privilege issues. Metadata is often the source of inadvertent disclosure of privileged information. Even where parties attempt to redact privileged information, the associated metadata may be used to reveal the redaction. Metadata production can result in volumes of information that without a compelling rationale unduly burden the pre-production review, delay discovery progress, and add unproductive costs to the procedures.

TIP: Since metadata is a frequently disputed topic, attorneys should be prepared to discuss and reach an agreement during the meet and confer conference. Unilateral decisions to remove metadata are not likely to be accepted and can lead to additional discovery work and the possibility of sanctions.

E. Inaccessible Information

Rule 26(b)(2) as amended for e-discovery establishes a two-tiered discovery process. The first tier is the information which can be disclosed through the normal e-discovery process, that is "…a responding party should produce [ESI] that is relevant, not privileged, and reasonably accessible."[15] The second tier is information the responding party identifies as being "not reasonably accessible." The responding party must identify by category or type any ESI sources that might contain responsive information that it will not search or produce as part of the tier one discovery because of practical difficulties or costs.

The responding party must provide sufficient detail about inaccessible information to allow the requesting party to assess the burdens and determine the likelihood that the first tier information sources will provide sufficient responsive information. If a dispute between the parties arises over the second tier ESI sources, the court may order production if the requesting party can show good cause for the discovery.[16] The court will balance the burdens with the benefits by looking at various factors such as

1. the specificity of the request;
2. whether the information requested is available in other accessible information sources;
3. the likelihood of finding relevant information in the inaccessible information source;
4. the importance or utility of the requested information to the issues of the case; and
5. the parties' capabilities and resources.

TIP: The burden is initially on the objecting party to show the costs and burden of production and then shifts to the requesting party to demonstrate good cause for an order to compel.

There are legitimate reasons why organizations maintain inaccessible information. The information may be archived to backup media with no index and limited searching capabilities. The information may be from a legacy application or system that is currently readable only by obsolete hardware or software. The most problematical situation is for "deleted" information. Modern computer forensic techniques make it possible to recover information that has been deleted by the user or even under some normal system deletion procedures. The recovery process can be time-consuming and labor expensive, so attorneys should be careful to clarify whether deleted information is part of the discovery request.

TIP: An organization may choose to preserve discoverable information in formats that are "not reasonably accessible" but runs the risk of having to produce native or useable forms of the information if ordered to do so.

TIP: A request to sample inaccessible data, as opposed to a motion to compel production, is a viable strategy to minimize the likelihood the court finds the request unduly burdensome or triggers a cost shifting order.

F. Preservation

ESI preservation is important because ESI and its associated metadata can be altered, deleted, or destroyed through routine operations often without the awareness of the user or system administrator; the mere opening of a record or file can and often does change the ESI content.

Consider this scenario: A hospital has fully implemented an EMR system which captures all patient charting; there is no paper charting except for backup during system downtime. When a patient is discharged, the system automatically archives any records for that patient older than 90 days, but retains an entry in the index. The archive system overwrites the file creation date when it enters the file and data into the archive index. This is a clear example of failure to preserve the file creation date metadata.

In many cases, the event that triggers the duty to preserve information is clear, for example, receiving a letter from an attorney advising the organization of a potential claim. Other times the circumstances are much less certain. For example, nurses or clinical managers discussing an adverse patient event may trigger the duty. At least one court has held that a management discussion of an event that may lead to litigation will trigger the duty to preserve related records.[17]

Every organization has "a duty to disclose all potentially relevant sources of information" to the courts as soon as they 'reasonably anticipate' litigation.[18] For example, in *Blinzler v. Marriott International, Inc.*, the court held that an inference of spoliation is proper only when the destroying party knows "of circumstances that are likely to give rise to future litigation."[19] *Testa v. Walmart* is a case in which the court found the defendant should have anticipated litigation several years before the lawsuit was filed. The court held that because Walmart had conducted an accident investigation and included in its report the victim's threat to sue, Walmart had notice of the possibility of litigation.[20] Walmart failed to trigger a litigation hold and consequently destroyed ESI (e-mails and electronic forms) that were vital to its defense. The court gave the jury an adverse inference which Walmart appealed but the decision was upheld.

TIP: *Testa* emphasizes the need for companies to devise and implement early detection measures for potential lawsuits and to suspend where necessary routine destruction of information relevant to potential litigation.

G. Spoliation

Consider this scenario: A nurse is informed he has been named as a defendant in a patient lawsuit. The nurse fails to copy all information in his assigned file area and IT staff fail to suspend routine deletion of system copies and backup overwrites.

Spoliation of evidence is "the intentional destruction of evidence...."[21] However intent is not required for a court to make a spoliation determination and sanction a party for failing to produce ESI. Courts have held that poor document retention practices or failure to maintain such practices are sufficient to impose sanctions. For example, in *Mosaid v. Samsung*, the court determined that because the defendant failed to place a "litigation hold" on its ESI and the files were deleted pursuant to a standing retention policy, the defendant was subject to an adverse evidentiary inference instruction to the jury. The court reasoned "[i]f a party has notice that evidence is relevant to an action, and either proceeds to destroy the evidence or allows it to be destroyed by failing to take reasonable precautions, common sense dictates that the party is more likely to have been threatened by that evidence."[22] In *Broccoli v. Echostar*, the court held that "Echostar acted in bad faith in its failure to suspend its e-mail and destruction policy or preserve essential personnel documents in order to fulfill its duty to preserve the relevant documentation for purposes of potential litigation."[23] The sentiments expressed by the courts in *Mosaid* and *Broccoli* are supported by a number of additional findings[24] and make it clear that organizations have an affirmative obligation to ensure information subject to discovery is preserved and not deleted because of inattention to preservation duties.

Knowing when an organization should anticipate the likelihood of litigation is a critical factor in complying with preservation obligations and avoiding spoliation sanctions. There is no bright-line rule indicating when a party should be on notice that it has sufficient information to constitute reasonable anticipation; the determination is a fact-specific analysis that involves a number of factors. For example, courts have ruled in each of the following cases that the duty to preserve was triggered prior to notice of litigation:

1. terminated employee's threat to file a class action discrimination suit that was communicated to management;[25]

2. pre-litigation negotiations that failed to resolve the dispute;[26]

3. a complaint was made specifically and repeatedly without resolution;[27] and

4. a complaint was made that expressly threatened a lawsuit in a credible manner.[28]

Courts have held that a duty to preserve existed for a plaintiff who destroyed information prior to filing the complaint but after the plaintiff had decided to sue.[29]

H. Privilege

The e-discovery rules expressly recognize the risk that the volume of relevant ESI may lead to an unintended disclosure of privileged information; therefore the rules encourage the parties to discuss in the meet and confer conference methods for dealing with this issue—notably "clawbacks" and "quick peeks." Neither method is unique to e-discovery, but take on new importance because of the increased risks attendant with ESI.

A clawback agreement between parties stipulates that information will be produced without any intent to waive privilege and that if privileged information is inadvertently produced privilege is not lost and the receiving party, regardless of who first discovers the privileged information, must return the information and not use it in litigation. Clawback agreements had been losing popularity with courts prior to e-discovery but have come back in favor as a means of speeding up production and reducing costs.

A quick peek agreement is also designed to make discovery more efficient by delaying the privilege review until after the receiving party has looked at all information and decided what it actually wants. Quick peek agreements are less favored because the risk of privileged information being disclosed is quite high. Even where the parties agree that privileged materials will not be used, most parties will not want the other to see the information in the first place.

In *Hernandez v. Esso*[30] the defendant asserted a claim of privilege one year after production. The problem was only recognized by the defendant after the plaintiff counterclaimed using paper copies of the defendant's previously disclosed electronic information. The defendant asserted an unintentional error that resulted in the merger of two electronic files: one containing the privileged information and one without any privilege. The court was not impressed, reasoning that parties that choose to use technology to store privileged information should also use technology to avoid disclosure mistakes.

Inadvertent disclosure is a critical issue as many jurisdictions apply a general waiver not only to the disclosed information that is privileged but also to the entire subject matter. Because FRCP does not automatically have the effect of changing substantive law, jurisdictions that take a strict approach may disregard the federal rules even where the parties have reached an agreement during the meet and confer conference and a court order has instantiated that agreement. To eliminate any conflict between procedural and substantive law, the e-discovery rules clearly prevent a court from ordering clawback or quick peek or equivalent methods unless the parties agree.[31]

TIP: Most nursing malpractice claims fall under state court jurisdictions. Attorneys representing these nurse defendants should continue to incorporate pre-production privilege reviews even when a waiver agreement has been reached between the parties.

I. Interrogatories

As amended, Rule 33 provides that a response to an interrogatory that refers to business records, where such records are ESI, means that the respondent may provide the interrogating party access to the ESI if the requestor can readily find the answer. The Advisory Committee has noted that a party that chooses to allow access to its ESI may be required to provide technical support and other assistance with using the application to inspect the ESI at issue.

J. Sanctions and Safe Harbor

Rule 37(f) is a new e-discovery rule that limits the court's ability to issue sanctions for spoliation if the party has exercised good faith in its preservation efforts. Rule 37(f) states that "absent exceptional circumstances, a court may not impose sanctions for failing to provide [ESI] lost as a result of routine, good faith operation of an electronic information system."[32] For example, if an organization initiates a litigation hold and undertakes reasonable measures to preserve potentially responsive ESI after the organization knows of the possibility of litigation, then it could claim protection under the safe harbor if the targeted ESI were inadvertently deleted. The claim of good faith generally would require a party to modify certain routine operations such as suspending an automatic 45-day destruction rule, preventing changes to configuration rules that govern how or what data is displayed, or modifying a drop-down list of user-selectable input options.[33] Rule 37(f) expressly recognizes the differential difficulty in keeping ESI data intact and requires the court to factor in such difficulties as part of its analysis prior to determining whether sanctions are warranted.

TIP: The safe harbor applies only to FRCP sanctions and not sanctions that are under the court's jurisdictional authority.[34]

18.3 Key E-Discovery Cases

The *Zubulake* cases (I, III, IV, V) are generally considered landmark cases for e-discovery principles even though these cases were decided between 2003 to 2005 before adoption of the e-discovery rules in 2006.

Zubulake I[35] and *III*[36] address a discrimination suit against a former employer in which the plaintiff, Laura Zubulake, maintained that evidence critical to her case existed in e-mails sent between other employees. Ms. Zubulake was able to produce approximately 450 pages of e-mails and requested the defendant to locate all relevant e-mails from its backup tapes and e-mail archives. The defendant objected, citing undue burden and requested the court to shift the costs of production to the plaintiff. In its ruling the court articulated five categories of electronic storage—(1) online data, such as hard disks; (2) near-line data, such as optical disks; (3) offline storage, such as magnetic tapes; (4) backup tapes; and (5) fragmented, erased and damaged data. Categories four and five were declared inaccessible for e-discovery purposes. The court also created a new seven factor test for inaccessibility. The defendant was ordered to produce all responsive e-mails from its disks, servers and backup tapes at its costs but conducted a separate cost-shifting analysis after reviewing the restored backup tape contents. Applying the seven factor test, the court determined that the plaintiff should pay for 25 percent of the costs, excluding attorney review costs.

In *Zubulake IV*[37] discovery disclosed that the defendant had overwritten some of the relevant backup tapes and that some relevant e-mails originating after the initial proceedings began had been deleted. The court found that the defendant had a duty to preserve evidence since it should have known the e-mails would be relevant for future litigation and ordered the defendant to cover the production costs.

In *Zubulake V*[38] the court held that the defendant had failed to take the steps necessary to ensure that relevant data was preserved and produced. The court ordered both sanctions and an adverse inference instruction against the defendant. The court noted that defendant's counsel had failed in its duty to locate and preserve relevant information by not affirmatively monitoring its client's discovery procedures.

The *Zubulake* cases set the stage for how digitally stored data (ESI) would be treated during discovery. In the ensuing years after 2006, various state and federal courts have tackled a number of e-discovery issues including when the duty to preserve ESI is triggered, whether attorneys are competent to define ESI searching keywords, and what types of digital information qualify as ESI. A number of new tests have been created and an impressive degree of thoughtful and sound reasoning has been forthcoming. The following sections summarize some of the recent notable cases.

A. Duty to Preserve

Although a party reasonably knows of litigation when a complaint is filed, the duty to preserve evidence often begins much closer to the events that are claimed as the underlying cause. In *Beard Research v. Kates*[39] the court held that a former employee's duty to preserve attached when he gave a presentation to the employer's competitor using information he knew was confidential. The implication is that when a party has knowledge that acts have occurred that could lead to litigation, the duty to preserve is possibly triggered and remains in effect until the potential claim has been resolved or the statute of limitations has run.

The duty to preserve has also been linked to the existence of widespread litigation on the basis that the defendant's similar actions should have made it reasonable to anticipate litigation of its own. *Adams v. Dell*[40] is a patent infringement case in which the plaintiff claimed that one of the defendants destroyed critical pieces of evidence. The defendant claimed that its duty to preserve did not arise until it received a letter warning of potential litigation. However, the court held that "counsel's letter is not the inviolable benchmark" and in this case, the defendant's duty to preserve was triggered five years earlier because at that time similar litigation cases were rampant in the defendant's industry.

TIP: Waiting for a lawsuit complaint to be served is much too late to begin preparing for the preservation of data. Attorneys, risk managers, and nursing managers should begin to understand how information contained in risk reports, nursing communications, and informal discussions about untoward outcomes can be used to argue anticipation of litigation existed and the duty to preserve was triggered.

B. Litigation Hold

A 2010 decision in *Pension Committee of Montreal v. Banc of America Securities*[41] expands on the original *Zubulake* opinions by reinforcing the importance of preserving and collecting all potentially relevant data once litigation is reasonably anticipated. The new decision holds that failure to issue *written* litigation hold instructions, identify *all* custodians of potential evidence, ensure custodian's preservation of the data, and preserve sole source backup tapes constitutes gross negligence. Judge Scheindlin felt compelled to review the parties' discovery efforts and found no excuse for a failure to preserve stating that "by now, it should be abundantly clear that the duty to preserve means what it says and that a failure to preserve records—paper or electronic—and to search the right places for those records, will inevitably result in the spoliation of evidence."[42] Actual failure, not intent, is the measure of negligence and whether the negligence is simple, gross or willful misconduct will be determined by the totality of circumstances surrounding the failure to preserve.[43]

TIP: An effective litigation hold memo should be written and include information that identifies the parties, provides a brief description of the legal claims, explains the scope of the hold, suggests likely sources of potentially relevant ESI, and provides general technical advice about how to preserve the ESI.

C. ESI Data

A number of cases from different states and federal courts have weighed in on the scope of information that can be classified as ESI. The general trend is that any information that is digitally stored even if only in temporary memory is ESI and may be discoverable under the 2006 rules.

Flagg v. City of Detroit[44] is one of the first cases to clarify that text messages are ESI and thus discoverable. Flagg also points out that communications between parties is subject to discovery regardless of whether business or personal property is used to make the communications.

In *Columbia v. Bunnell*[45] the defendants were ordered to begin capturing and preserving Internet Protocol (IP) addresses which were stored only temporarily in volatile memory (RAM) and never written to any type of permanent storage media. The decision was very fact-specific and based on well-supported arguments that the IP addresses were critical evidence that could not be obtained by other means. The court's analysis did not approve boilerplate requests to preserve temporary digital information; rather it reinforced the principle that producing parties should have full opportunity to oppose such requests by showing the burden and perhaps the impossibility of complying with RAM data production.

TIP: Any digital device that is used to communicate or document information relevant to potential litigation should be part of the organization's ESI discovery planning process, including devices personally owned by employees.

D. IT Expertise

The e-discovery rules require attorneys to have a good understanding of their client's IT systems, communications methods, and data retention and destruction policies and practices. This understanding is necessary to competently represent clients and perform e-discovery duties to preserve, search, produce and protect privilege. Attorneys are not normally proficient in IT ways and means and courts have started to lose patience when ignorance is served up as a good faith excuse for errors. In response a number of recent cases have seemingly created a duty to solicit professional IT involvement in preserving and producing ESI data.

In *Victor Stanley v. Creative Pipe*[46] the court took issue with whether attorneys are competent to determine keywords for e-discovery searching. During discovery, the defendants turned over 165 ESI files that contained privileged information. The defendants argued that privilege should not be waived because the disclosure was an "honest error" and the search and review was made in "good faith." The court was not impressed, admonishing the defendants that no credible

evidence was presented to establish reasonable search and review efforts had been performed. Consequently the court held that the disclosure of the privileged ESI acted to waive privilege. The 43-page opinion has been called a roadmap for attorneys and judges in determining what constitutes appropriate search and review actions for privilege protection. The opinion cites The Sedona Conference, Best Practices Commentary on the Use of Search and Information Retrieval[47] and the National Institute of Standards and Technology (NIST) Text Retrieval studies[48] for guidance.

Other cases that also address the need for competent searching and technical expertise include *Gross Construction v. American Manufacturing* (ESI search must be based on competence, quality control, testing, and cooperation between counsel),[49] *Equity Analytics v. Lundin* (whether a particular search methodology is effective requires expert testimony),[50] *Diabetes Centers of America v. Healthpia* (inadequate keyword searches may be sanctionable),[51] In *re Seroquel* (refusal to allow contact with IT experts),[52] and *U.S. v. O'Keefe* (holding that ESI searching is too complicated for lawyers and judges to address without the aid of expert testimony).[53]

TIP: Counsel need to plan and conduct search and review procedures with serious consideration for consequences. Good planning means either being competent in IT search methods or engaging experts who are. Prudent counsel will prepare a formal search and review plan and documentation to support a potential "good faith" argument if needed. Evaluation of the search strategy success rate in a sample of files will be critical evidence.

The *Phoenix Four v. Strategic Resources*[54] case takes the IT knowledge requirement to a higher level. Not only does counsel have a duty to proactively supervise the client's e-discovery efforts, counsel has a duty to find the relevant information if it exists. In *Phoenix Four*, the defendant had ceased operations and had been evicted from its offices after the litigation had started, leaving behind ten computers that the landlord then disposed of. Former associates of the defendant also took several servers and computer workstations away with them. During discovery, defendant claimed there were no computers or computerized records available. The court found that, even though counsel had communicated the need to locate and gather paper and ESI records, counsel had nonetheless "failed in its obligation to locate and timely produce the evidence."[55] The court held the attorney responsible for not asking about hidden partitions in his client's servers, where the majority of evidence was subsequently located. The attorney erred in accepting the client's representation that because it had ceased operations there was nothing remaining to search. The court set a high standard for the attorneys by stating that counsel was expected to inquire into the whereabouts of the client's computers and business data. If no satisfactory answers were forthcoming, then counsel would be expected to obtain a technical review of the equipment in question. The court found counsel's failure to inquire into the existence of ESI to constitute gross negligence and sanctioned both the client and counsel.

E. Cooperation

Courts are consistently admonishing attorneys of the need to cooperate, not compete, when conducting e-discovery. In *Mancia v. Mayflower Textile*[56] the court took the opportunity to use a case full of boilerplate objections and delaying tactics to reinforce the cooperation principles articulated by the Sedona Conference Cooperation Proclamation.[57] The *Mancia* decision states that cooperation between counsel is not a mere courtesy but a requirement stemming from FRCP 26(g) where discovery requests and responses must be preceded by "reasonably inquiry." The court also took aim at plaintiffs making e-discovery requests that were not reasonably limited in scope stating that if an attorney certifies discovery documents "without substantial justification, the court (on motion or sua sponte) must impose an appropriate sanction."

Other cases citing the Sedona Conference Cooperation Proclamation include *Gross Construction v. American Manufacturing*,[58] *SEC v. Collins & Aikman Corp.*,[59] and *Technical Sales Associates v. Ohio Star Forge*.[60]

TIP: Counsel should be wary of using open-ended phrases such as "any and all" in e-discovery requests or overusing the "overbroad and burdensome" response objections without adequate justifications, or risk having this language be sanctioned as a violation of FRCP26(g)(3).

F. Sanctions

In 2009 more than half of the e-discovery opinions issued involved the consideration of sanctions, and actual sanctions were awarded in more than one-third of the cases in the first part of the year.[61,62]

Keithley v. Homestore.com, Inc.[63] is an example where the e-discovery sanctions were substantial even when the party prevailed on the merits of the case. In *Keithley*, the defendants prevailed on a motion for summary judgment. Nonetheless the court ordered them to pay $283,000 in fees for the "systematic failure to preserve and produce relevant electronic evidence."[64]

Perhaps the most attention-grabbing case of sanctions occurs in *Bray and Gillespie*[65] where new counsel was sanctioned for inadequate supervision of the production process. The *Bray and Gillespie* decision addressed some basic e-discovery errors surrounding a request for production of ESI in its native state including the associated metadata. The original mistakes were then exacerbated by material misrepresentations and omissions by counsel for the producing party. The court determined that it was not appropriate to sanction the client for decisions made by the outside counsel. The court went further to state that additional sanctions against counsel would be considered, including outright dismissal, if the information produced under the new order contained more metadata than that originally produced by the sanctioned attorneys. This decision reinforces the obligations of counsel who take over the case midstream to thoroughly review all e-discovery actions and be accountable for the earlier discovery decisions made by prior counsel.

G. Adverse Inference

Dismissals and adverse inferences are intended to address egregious violations where the "very integrity of the litigation process has been impugned."[66] Nonetheless the number of adverse inference orders for e-discovery disputes have increased over the last several years signaling courts' general dissatisfaction with less than serious attention to cooperative, compliant ESI production.

In *Nursing Home Pension Fund v. Oracle*,[67] the court held that adverse inference instructions against the defendant were warranted when it produced only 15 e-mails out of more than 1,500 original messages and failed to prevent destruction of ESI evidence it could have controlled. The court reasoned that because the defendant had notice of the impending litigation, the spoliation of the e-mails and other ESI data was willful. The court held that the plaintiff was entitled to adverse inference instructions.

18.4 E-Discovery Implications for Nursing Malpractice

Inadequate communication is at the heart of many nursing malpractice claims. As a consequence one should expect that discovery requests in nursing malpractice cases will focus heavily on nurse communications—what was said, when it was said, the patient's status at the time, time delays, follow up with the physician, and escalation in appropriate cases. Depending on the facts of the case, any type of communication made using a digital device is potentially discoverable. In particular voicemails, e-mails, and text messaging will have increasing importance in establishing proper communications occurred and that the appropriate nursing process was followed.

Taking due care to preserve patient records and nursing communications is important particularly in light of the fact that willful failure to do so may lead to an adverse instruction. Given the nature of nursing malpractice suits, an instruction that says the information deleted is presumed to be prejudicial to the nurse defendant may be insurmountable.

TIP: All nursing staff and support personnel should be warned that voicemail, e-mail, and other forms of electronic communications are discoverable. Staff should be trained in proper methods to search and preserve messages when a litigation hold instruction is issued.

ESI metadata changes the evidence landscape. Because metadata routinely conveys the context in which information is created, modified, used, disclosed, copied, or deleted, it has the ability to expose the inner workings of the nursing process and specific care protocols. Many malpractice cases will rest on what the nurse did or did not do relative to the applicable standard of care. Disputes often arise about the patient's symptoms and complaints, problem indications that may have existed, treatment recommendations that may have been ordered, and communications between the nurse and physicians that may have been made. Metadata places more emphasis on good documentation practices because it exposes the timing of entries not just by the nurse but other relevant caregivers, and it indicates what clinical information about the patient was available and should have been known by the nurse at the time any action was taken.

Metadata does more than expose the nursing context; it can also call into question the information's integrity and its reliability as evidence. Preserving nursing data now requires stronger attention on systems administration to ensure that metadata is not accidently or willfully overwritten or changed during the litigation hold period.

18.5 Preparing for E-Discovery

Knowledge, pre-planning, and attention to detail are the cornerstones of a well-managed e-discovery plan.

A. The E-Discovery Plan

A successful e-discovery plan follows the same principles as a traditional discovery plan. There should be an analysis of the discovery request, a data collection process, attorney review, and production to the requesting party. In addition, there must be careful consideration given to: identifying all possible locations of potentially relevant ESI, including copies, backups, archives, consolidations, and compilations; understanding how ESI searching terms should be created, coded, executed, and verified; determining how the privilege review will oc-

cur; developing a discovery negotiation strategy for use with opposing counsel; and documenting the plan and subsequent actions for any good faith arguments. Successful e-discovery cannot occur without considerable pre-planning.

B. Take a Team Approach

A good starting place is to review, or establish if necessary, clear cut policies that address discovery and disclosure; retention and destruction; litigation hold; ESI preservation; and disaster recovery. To obtain the necessary knowledge and competencies, a team approach is best that includes executive management, clinical management, finance, risk management, HIM and, of course, legal and IT. Depending on the case, specific clinical departments should be brought in as needed. The e-discovery team can oversee a number of preparatory activities including an assessment of current discovery practices; procedures to educate staff; methods to increase communications between legal and IT procedures, and determination of monitoring and auditing requirements.

C. Develop Policies and Procedures

Many existing IT policies should be reviewed and updated for e-discovery purposes. A key target is the data retention and destruction policy. These policies should cover what information must be retained, and methods and time periods for retention and destruction. Special attention for preservations should be inserted into system lifecycle management policies that ensure that ESI stored in systems undergoing upgrades or decommissioning remain accessible.

D. Use Available Resources

There is little advantage in developing a unique e-discovery plan. There are a number of excellent resources available to guide the e-discovery team including The Sedona Conference, an educational organization active in developing e-discovery standards;[68] the Federal Judicial Center that provides educational material;[69] the E-discovery Institute that is researching ESI search techniques;[70] and a number of websites and blogs.

18.6 Summary

E-discovery is a complex and evolving set of issues. Organizational processes for e-discovery are largely nascent as attorneys, executives, IT, and clinical managers struggle to develop cost-effective strategies both for using e-discovery wisely in litigation and for effectively responding to e-discovery requests. Case law is developing in a number of areas particularly the ethics of cooperation, litigation hold, ESI searching, production formats, not reasonably accessible information, and spoliation.

To prepare for e-discovery, healthcare organizations, nurses, and their counsel should immediately familiarize themselves with the e-discovery rules; prepare for e-discovery by forming and participating in their e-discovery team; develop e-discovery policies and procedures; provide litigation hold training; and ensuring that legal and IT are closely aligned to avoid costly communications and data preservation mistakes. Litigation is a costly activity, and e-discovery violations can only add to the total expense. Having a pre-planned, proactive e-discovery approach that clearly integrates IT technical knowledge with sound legal supervision will go a long way in reducing the overall risk.

Endnotes

1. *New Study Tracks Increasing Use Of Digital Information*, Telecom Policy Report, FindArticles.com. Jul 23, 2009, available at http://findarticles.com/p/articles/mi_m0PJR/is_29_1/ai_110308282/ (last visited 3-8-2010).

2. An exabyte is 1000 petabytes; a petabyte is 1000 terabytes; a terabyte is 1000 gigabytes; and a gigabyte is 1000 megabytes. One exabyte = 10^{18} bytes = 1000^6 bytes = 1,000,000,000,000,000,000 bytes.

3. *The Expanding Digital Universe*, IDC, May 2009, available at http://www.emc.com/collateral/demos/microsites/idc-digital-universe/iview.htm (last visited 3-8-2010).

4. http://www.ediscoverylaw.com/2008/10/articles/resources/current-listing-of-states-that-have-enacted-ediscovery-rules (last visited 3-8-2010).

5. Fed. R. Civ. P. 16(b).

6. *Columbia Pictures Industries v. Justin Bunnel*, (C.D.Cal May 29, 207), aff'd. (C.D.Cal Aug. 24, 2007)

7. Fed. R. Civ. P. 26(a)(1)(A)(ii).

8. Skamser, *The E-discovery Paradigm Shift* available at http://ediscoveryconsulting.blogspot.com/2008/09/cost-of-ediscovery.html (last visited 8-5-09).

9. Fed. R. Civ. P. 16(b).

10. Fed. R. Civ. P. 34(b)(2)(E)(ii).

11. *See, The Sedona Conference Glossary: E-discovery & Digital Information Management*, available at http://www.thesedonaconference.org (last visited 3-8-2010).

12. Fed. R. Civ. P. 34(b)(2)(E)(iii).

13. *See generally*, Ball, *Beyond Data about Data: The Litigator's Guide to Metadata*, available at http://www.craigball.com/metadata.pdf (last visited 8-4-09).

14. *Williams v. Sprint/United Mgmt. Co.*, 2005 WL 2401626 (D. Kan. Sept. 29, 2005) (providing a detailed review of metadata issues).

15. FRCP 26(b).

16. Fed. R. Civ. P. Rule 33(d).

17. *Doe v. Norwalk Community College*, 248 F.R.D. 372 (D.Conn. 2007).

18. Fed. R. Civ. P. Rule 26(b).

19. *Blinzler v. Marriott Intern., Inc.*, 81 F.3d 1148, 1159 (1st Cir. 1996).

20. *Testa v. Wal-Mart Stores, Inc.*, 144 F.3d 173 (1st Cir. 1998).

21. *Black's Law Dictionary* (Eighth Ed. 1999).

22. *Mosaid Tech., Inc. v. Samsung Elect. Co.*, 348 F.Supp. 2d 322 (D.N.J. 2004).

23. *Broccoli v. Echostar Comm. Corp.*, 229 F.R.D. 506 (D. Md. August 4, 2009).

24. *Coleman (Parent) Holdings, Inc. v. Morgan Stanley & Co., Inc.*, 2005 WL 679071 (Fla. Cir. Ct. Mar. 1, 2005); *In re Prudential Ins. Co. of America Sales Practices Litig.*, 169 F.R.D. 598 (D.N.J. 1997); *Wachtel v. Guardian Life Ins. Co.*, 2006 WL 1286189 (D.N.J. May 8, 2008); and *U.S. v. Arthur Andersen, LLP*, 374 F.3d 281 (5th Cir. 2004).

25. *Wm. T. Thompson v. General Nutrition Corp.*, 593 F. Supp. 1443 (C.D. Cal. 1984)

26. *Blinzler v. Marriott Int'l Inc.*, 81 F.3d 1148 (1st Cir. 1996).

27. *Computer Assoc. Int'l, Inc. v. Am. Fundware, Inc.*, 133 F.R.D. 166, 168 (D. Colo. 1990).

28. *Patent Corporation v. Nestle Co.*, 558 F. Supp. 747, 758-59, 765 (D.N.J. 1981).

29. *New York State National Organization for Women v. Pataki*, 261 F.2d 156 (2d Cir.2001).

30. *Marrero Hernandez v. Esso Standard Oil Co.*, 429. F. Supp. 2d 469 (D.P.R. May 2, 2006).

31. Fed. R. Civ. P. 26(f) and Committee Notes.

32. Fed. R. Civ. P. 37(f).

33. *Heng Chan v. Triple 8 Palace, Inc.*, 206 U.S., Dist. Lexis 15780 (D.N.Y. 2006); *Lewy v. Remington Arms Co.*, 836 F.2d 1104, 1112 (8 th Cir. 1988) and *Zubulake v. UBS Warburg LLC*, 220 FRD 212 (S.S. N.Y. October 22, 2003).

34. *Nucor Corp. v. Bell*, 251 F.R.D. 191, (D.S.C. 2008).

35. *Zubulake v. UBS Warburg*, LLC, CIV.02-1243, 2003 WL 21087884 (S.D.N.Y. May 13, 2003)(hereafter *Zubulake I*).

36. *Zubulake v. UBS Warburg LLC*, 216 F.R.D. 280 (S.D.N.Y. Jul 24, 2003) (hereafter *Zubulake III*).

37. *Zubulake v. UBS Warburg LLC*, 220 F.R.D. 212 (S.D.N.Y. 2003)(hereafter *Zubulake IV*).

38. *Zubulake v. UBS Warburg LLC et al.* (2004 WL 1620866 S.D.N.Y.) (hereafter *Zubulake V*).

39. *Beard Research v. Kates*, 2009 WL 1515625 (Del. CH. May 29, 2009).

40. *Phillip M. Adams & Assoc., LLC v. Dell, Inc.*, 2009 WL 910801 (D. Utah Mar 30, 2009).

41. *The Pension Committee of Montreal et al. v. Banc of America Securities et al.*, 05 Civ. 9016 (SDNY Jan. 15, 2010).

42. *Id.* at 2.

43. *Id.* at 8.

44. *Flagg v. City of Detroit*, 252 F.R.D. 346 (E.D. Mich. 2008).

45. *Columbia Pictures Indus. v. Bunnell et al.* (C.D. Cal. May 29, 2007).

46. *Victor Stanley, Inc. v. Creative Pipe*, Inc., 2008 WL 2221841 (D. Md. May 29, 2008).

47. 8 The Sedona Conf. J. 189 (2007).

48. NIST Text Retrieval Conference website available at *htpp*://trec.nist.gov (last visited 3-8-2010).

49. *William A. Gross Constr. Assn. v. Amer. Mfgr Mutual Ins. Co.*, 256 F.R.D. 134 (S.D.N.Y. 2009).

50. *Equity Analytics, LLC v. Lundin*, 248 F.R.D. 331 (D.D.C. March 7, 2008).

51. *Diabetes Centers of America, Inc. v. Healthpia America, Inc.*, 2008 U.S. Dist. LEXIS 8362, 2008 WL 336382 (S.D. Tex. Feb. 5, 2008).

52. *In re Seroquel Products Liability Litigation*, 244 F.R.D. 650 (M.D.Fla. Aug. 21, 2007).

53. *U.S. v. O'Keefe*, 537 F. Supp. 2d 14 (D.D.C. 2008).

54. *Phoenix Four, Inc. v. Strategic Resources Corporation et al.*, No. 05-CIV-4837 (HB), 2006 WL 1409413 (S.D.N.Y. May 23, 2006).

55. *Id.* at *5.

56. *Mancia v. Mayflower Textile Servs. Co.*, 253 F.R.D. 354, 359, 363 (D. Md. 2008).

57. The Sedona Conference Cooperation Proclamation, available at http://www.thesedonaconference.org/.../ tsc_cooperation_proclamation (last visited 3-8-2010).

58. *See* [49] at 136.

59. *SEC v. Collins & Aikman Corp.*, 256 F.R.D. 403, 415 (S.D.N.Y. 2009).

60. *Technical Sales Assn. v. Ohio Star Forge Co.*, 2009 WL 728520 at *4 (E.D. Mich. March 19, 2009).

61. Flanagan and Borden, *2009 Mid-Year Update on E-Discovery Cases* available at http://www.gibsondunn.com/ publications/pages/2009Mid-YearUpdateonE-DiscoveryCases.aspx (last visited 3-8-2010).

62. *Year in Review: Courts Unsympathetic to Electronic Discovery Ignorance or Misconduct*, Kroll Ontrack, Dec. 2, 2008 available at http://www.krollontrack.com (last visited 3-8-2010).

63. *Keithley v. The Home Store.com, Inc.*,. 2008 U.S. Dist. LEXIS 61741 (August 12, 2008).

64. *Id.* at *43.

65. *Bray & Gillespie Mgmt. LLC v. Lexington Ins. Co.*, 2009 WL 546429 (M.D. Fla. Mar. 4, 2009).

66. *Micron Technology, Inc. v. Rambus, Inc.*, 255 F.R.D. 135, 151 (D. Del. 2009).

67. *Nursing Home Pension Fund et al., v. Oracle Corporations et al.,* 254 F.R.D. 559 (N.D. Ca. 2008).

68. www.thesedonaconference.org (last visited 3-8-2010).

69. www.fjc.gov (last visited 3-8-2010).

70. www.ediscoveryinstitute.org (last visited 3-8-2010).

Additional Reading

Electronic Discovery Law, K&L Gates website, available at http://www.ediscoverylaw.com.

Losey, R. *An Introduction to Electronic Discovery*, American Bar Association (2009).

Paul, G. and. Baron, J. *Information Inflation: Can the Legal System Adapt?* 13 *Rich. J.L. & Tech.* 10 (2007).

Rothstein, Hedges and Wiggins, eds., Managing Discovery of Electronic Information: A Pocket Guide for Judges, Federal Judicial Center (2007).

Scheindlin, S. and Capra, D. The Sedona Conference, *Electronic Discovery and Digital Evidence*, Thomson/Reuters (2009).

The Sedona Conference Commentary on Legal Holds: The Trigger & The Process, available at www.thesedonaconference.com/dltForm?did=Legal_holds.pdf, last accessed 02/25/11.

Chapter 19

Working with Claims Adjusters

Barbara Cohen, RN, MS, M.Ed., JD and Louise H. Hayes, Esq.

19.1 Introduction

Claims adjusters are an essential part of the litigation process. State licensure rules for claims adjusters vary by individual state. Approximately half of the states in the nation require independent claims adjusters to be licensed.[1] Provision can be made for claims adjusters to work under the supervision of a licensed adjuster. Resources for further information concerning licensure of claims adjusters can be found in the additional reading section at the end of this chapter.

Insurance carriers rely upon claims adjusters to accurately evaluate the value of a case and to manage the case from inception to trial and a defense verdict or to settlement in a manner that protects the carriers' interests. Claims adjusters must evaluate and reevaluate their cases multiple times during the life of an action. They must set reserves and adjust those reserves as additional information is accumulated. A reserve set too high has significant financial implications in tying up funds unnecessarily. This can ultimately result in increased premiums being charged to the insureds without an accurate basis. If a reserve is set too low and not raised in response to negative information, the im-

pact on insurers and re-insurers can be disastrous. Nobody likes surprises! Even surprises that result in last minute favorable developments are not surprises at all. Rather, these "surprise" developments can call into question the judgment and evaluative skills of the claims adjuster, and the truthfulness and forthrightness of attorneys assigned to a case. Moreover, having an open, cordial and honest relationship with the claims adjuster handling a matter can potentially result in a fair and early settlement of a meritorious claim. Counsels' relationships with claims adjusters from both the defense and plaintiffs' sides can be built over time such that the parties have a trusting business relationship and the work of the day will proceed more smoothly and swiftly to conclusion

---

TIP: If there is a golden rule that governs the relationship between claims adjusters and the attorneys handling their cases, it is to communicate—early, often, succinctly, and in the most cost-efficient way possible throughout the lifetime of a lawsuit.

19.2 Receipt of Letter of Claim or Summons and Complaint

The insured may forward a letter of claim[2] or a summons and complaint to the claims adjuster. This forwarding can be via direct receipt and mailing or via forwarding to the insured's supervisor or risk management office. The letter of claim may be written by the claimant herself or by claimant's counsel in an effort to resolve the matter without proceeding to litigation.

19.3 Handling of a Letter of Claim

In general, a claims adjuster will evaluate and manage a letter of claim without involvement of defense counsel. The claims adjuster will contact the complainant or complainant's counsel, obtain all documentation relevant to the claim, interview the insured(s), and make a determination of liability. The claims adjuster will present the matter to the insured, the insured's employer and the carrier, and request authority to settle a meritorious claim. If monies are to be paid on account of a letter of claim, the claims adjuster will, in general, negotiate either with the claimant directly or with the claimant's counsel. On rare occasion, a letter of claim will be referred to defense counsel when the claim could potentially involve a very high exposure or other related legal issues for the insureds. If no payment is to be made on a claim, the claims adjuster will send a denial letter to the claimant, denying the claim and informing the insured that he is free to seek legal counsel. If a letter of claim is not settled, in some instances, claimant's counsel or the claimant may allow the matter to languish beyond the Statute of Limitations. Alternatively, if compensation is denied at this stage of a claim, the claimant may seek legal counsel or claimant's counsel may commence legal action.

19.4 Assignment of Case to Law Firm

Assuming a case is commenced by service of a summons and complaint, when the claims adjuster opens a case he will review the information available about the nature thereof and will make a preliminary determination with respect to issues concerning coverage for each of the insureds. It is at this time that any disclaimer letters as required would be sent to the insureds. The bases for disclaimers are many. Two more frequent bases are (1) a disclaimer may be based upon a lack of coverage for the time period(s) alleged in the complaint or (2) a disclaimer may be based upon the fact that the nature of the claim is beyond the scope of the coverage. The disclaimer letter may disclaim both defense and indemnity for the claim, in which case no counsel is assigned and the matter is referred back to the defendant for forwarding to current carriers. Alternatively, the disclaimer letter may disclaim coverage for damages, but may provide a defense, pending further development in the matter. The latter scenario may arise when the underlying claim is an intentional tort or a crime. In the latter scenario, the claims adjuster will forward the case to defense counsel and the matter will proceed until the developing facts dictate otherwise.

The claims adjuster will also frequently review the applicable statutes of limitations and make a preliminary assessment of the same. As the next step in the process, the claims adjuster will assign the matter to the law firm best able to handle the case. The basis for case assignment varies, depending upon the carriers' claims office policies and procedures. On occasion, the adjuster will designate a particular attorney who has been requested by the healthcare professional or medical facility involved based upon prior history or personal recommendation. A copy of the summons and complaint in the matter along with any records or other data available will be forwarded to defense counsel along with a retainer letter. Policy information as well as the addresses of the carriers to be copied on all correspondence is generally included.

As soon as the case is assigned to a law firm, an avenue of communication is opened by the claims adjuster. The law firm must convey its acceptance of the case assignment. It must also designate which lawyer(s) will be responsible for handling the case and submitting the necessary reports to the adjuster and the respective carriers for the primary and excess layers of insurance.

The acceptance of the assignment letter should contain the names and phone numbers of the attorneys who will be working on the case. This information should also be e-mailed to the claims adjuster as soon as possible. In general, law firms assign teams to represent a person or entity being sued. The team may include a partner who is in charge and who will ultimately take the case to trial, and several middle and junior associates who will be assigned to do much of the day-to-day work on the file and to handle routine court appearances. On occasion, a paralegal will be assigned to handle some details of the matter. These team members must be identified and approved by the claims adjuster. The team members selected must be on the approved counsel list for the carrier. If an insured requests representation by an attorney not on the approved counsel list, individual attorneys can be approved to handle a matter and the rates charged will be negotiated by the claims adjuster with that attorney or with the law firm's managing partner.

At the same time the adjuster will send a letter to the nurse or facility being sued informing that person or entity of the name and address of the law firm that has been assigned the case. The letter contains assurances that someone from that firm will be calling or writing directly to introduce herself and to provide appropriate phone numbers if questions arise. These steps create another avenue for the exchange of information—this one between an insured and the attorney handling the case. The adjuster will have already spoken by telephone with the insured upon receipt of the summons and complaint by the carrier and adjuster. If the jury facility is named, the adjuster will have spoken with the facility's risk manager by telephone to obtain an overview and background of the matter at hand.

The attorney who has accepted assignment of the case will write an introductory letter directly to the facility or individual being sued to suggest documents that should be retained and to advise defendants of certain "dos and don'ts." Original medical records should be copied by the insured facility or healthcare professional and the original sequestered. Such ancillary things as fetal monitoring tapes should also be copied and the originals sequestered with the chart. X-rays and medical or other hospital equipment such as beds involved in the incident should be secured as well. Instructions should be sent at this time to the facility also requesting a search for and sequestering of any policies and procedures in place at the time of the incident as well as any maintenance logs and/or manufacturer's instructions for matters involving claims of defective devices.

It is critical for counsel to note at this time the absence of any evidence critical to the defense of the matter. Missing evidence such as fetal monitoring strips, incident reports, maintenance logs, etc. can result in a missing evidence charge at the time of trial. Such a charge generally results in the jury making an adverse inference with respect to the weight of such evidence against the insured and in favor of the plaintiff. A missing hospital record could result in early settlement of a matter that would now be considered by the claims adjuster to be a poor risk for a defense verdict at the time of trial. Defense counsel must immediately inform the claims adjuster of any missing evidence by letter and it is recommended that an e-mail be sent and a telephone call be made to provide this information via multiple venues. In many circumstances, the insurance company will be able to provide investigators, often nurses themselves, to search for missing items. Exhaustive searches can be made of both the healthcare facility's record rooms and individual locations such as radiology, as well as offsite record storage facilities.

Date

Ann Jones, ANP
400 East 37th Street
New York, NY

     Re: *Adam Smith v. Add Jones and Lessex Nurse Practitioners, PC*
            File No.:

Dear Nurse Jones:

Enclosed is a copy of the answer to be served on your behalf in the above-entitled case. This law firm has been assigned by your carrier to handle your defense in this matter.

Please review the answer and, if it meets with your approval, please sign it in the prescribed place and return it to us in the enclosed, self-addressed, stamped envelope. If there is some alteration you feel is necessary, please contact us at _____ so that we can discuss your concerns.

As soon as possible please direct your secretary or office manager to make a complete copy of the medical record concerning this patient. Place the original chart and ancillary documents in a secure place for the duration of this action. We will call your office within the next few weeks to try to find a time convenient to your schedule when we might meet and go over the facts and claims in this case. In the meantime, please do not discuss this lawsuit with any of your colleagues.

If you have any questions at all concerning this matter, please do not hesitate to call us at the above number. We look forward to working with you in the successful defense of this action.

Very truly yours,

Xxx/xx
Enclosures

Figure 19.1 Letter to Insured

TIP: If the entity being sued is a hospital or nursing home the risk management department usually provides a secure location for original records to be kept. (See Figure 19.1.)

19.5 Assignment of Separate Counsel

On very rare occasion, the claims adjuster will be required to assign separate counsel to one or more insureds. This greatly increases the cost of litigation. In addition, in light of the increased opportunity for the plaintiff to "divide and conquer" every effort is made to avoid splitting the defense. In rare occasions, the interests of the insureds, albeit under the same

policies, are so vastly different that assignment of separate counsel cannot be avoided in order to comply with best practices for claims adjusters. If there comes a time when defense counsel is unable to continue to zealously represent the interests of all insureds, the same must be promptly reported to the claims adjuster who will either re-assign the defense of one of the parties or, if necessary, remove the entire case from defense counsel's caseload and re-assign the matter to two separate law firms. While this causes a rise in defense costs, the provision of ethical and zealous representation on the part of defense counsel along with claims handling best practices may well require this course of action.[3]

Practices to be avoided:

- Too many attorneys working on a case
- Rotation of attorneys on and off a case
- Significant assignments (e.g., depositions, court appearances) given to attorneys unfamiliar with the case
- Failure to develop individual case strategy
- Inefficient case handling, e.g., repeated file review and intra-office conferences
- Failure to seek approval before making motions

CASE TEAM
A litigation team will handle defense of a claim. Only previously approved attorneys will be allowed to bill on a case. Each team shall be headed by a trial attorney (partner) who will direct and oversee the litigation in all stages. One or two associates will be engaged to handle tasks as delegated and instructed by the partner. A paralegal may be assigned to a team to provide legal research.

MANAGEMENT OF LITIGATION
Prior approval from claims adjuster must be received before initiating work on any of the following:

- Motions
- Legal or medical research exceeding $_____
- Depositions of non-parties
- Third party impleaders
- All appeals

FORMAL REPORTING
The following reports should be made on a timely basis to claims adjuster:

- Preliminary report upon receipt of complaint and initial papers and service of answer
- Report on bill of particulars
- Reports after each deposition
- Report on opinion of outside expert
- Report after filing of note of issue
- Daily verbal progress reports during trial
- Trial report after verdict

Figure 19.2 *Excerpts from Guidelines to Attorney from Claims Adjuster*

19.6 Reporting Guidelines for Counsel

Before a firm is retained for a case, it will have been provided a copy of the "Guidelines for Defense Counsel" or "Rules for Defense Attorneys" specific to a carrier. This document will cover in detail the rules and regulations set forth by each carrier for any attorney handling a case for it. (See Figure 19.2, which contains excerpts of this type of document.) It is important that defense counsel follow these guidelines to the letter including length of reports, formatting of reports including font type, activities for which only one attorney may bill for time spent, etc. Failure to do so can result in the claims adjuster or the carrier decreasing defense counsel's billing on a matter or denying payment altogether for services inappropriately rendered or rendered without permission. It is important to note that some actions that may be more costly such as out of town depositions may require advance permission to be granted by the claims adjuster.

A. Preliminary Report from Assigned Counsel

The initial report from counsel to the claims adjuster follows the first of those reporting rules. In it the attorney acknowledges receipt of the case by the law firm, briefly reiterates the facts apparently giving rise to the lawsuit, and states specific claims, if any, cited in the summons and complaint. This preliminary or initial report should be written by the lawyer who drafted the answer, usually the senior partner in the law firm or the most senior attorney handling the case. The report outlines the points asserted in the complaint and the responses made in the answer. Any affirmative defenses included in the answer should be listed and have their significance explained. In addition any investigation needed should be outlined so that collection of documents in the possession of the insured can be secured, possible witnesses can be identified, and any data or documents likely to be needed to defend the case can be obtained. Those items listed for discovery should be tracked by the defense team to ensure that appropriate follow-up with the insureds and the claims adjuster took place such that all relevant and requested evidence is found and secured in a timely manner.

This first report from counsel should also contain, to the extent possible, some preliminary analysis of the possibility of liability being found and the probable exposure if that occurs. Of necessity, this analysis is very general, but should assure the claims adjuster that an attorney with experience has taken note of the action. It is helpful at this time for defense counsel to provide case citations and other hard evidence of potential exposure in the instant matter based

upon the facts as they are known at this preliminary stage. For example, if a married 40-year-old father of two, working as a construction worker, lost his leg due to medical malpractice, counsel should include jury verdict search reports of potential verdict and ultimate appellate division ranges in similar cases. This information assists the adjuster in refining the reserve in a matter. Any contact already made with the insured should be confirmed. (See Figure 19.3.)

TIP: In addition to formal reports in writing, frequent conversations between the claims adjuster and attorney on a particular case ensure that each knows how the other views the case and that each is advised of any potential problems in a timely fashion. All conversations should be documented in a follow-up letter to the claims adjuster, to any excess carriers and to the insured to prevent surprises. All parties at larger facilities should be copied particularly on high exposure or politically sensitive matters when considering settlement. Timely and complete reporting enhances the likelihood of receipt of future assignments to defense counsel.

Both the attorney and the claims adjuster should create notes for the file reflecting the substance and dates of any conversation between them. E-mail provides a quick and easy way to communicate, but each person is well advised to print out hard copies of any such conversations and place them in the file. This will avoid misconceptions and contribute to the smooth handling of a case.

B. Bill of Particulars

1. Recap of steps in litigation

What follows is a description of the steps in litigation in the State of New York. There may be variations of these steps, or terms may differ, in other venues. After a complaint is filed to start a lawsuit, an answer is served by the defendant or defendants. Demands for additional information such as authorizations to obtain other medical records, names of witnesses, statements, experts, and so on are served along with the answer. One of these is called a demand for a bill of particulars (or interrogatories in other states). The demand contains a series of questions requiring the plaintiff to add specificity to the allegations in the complaint as well as to provide additional information about the plaintiff such as date of birth, social security number, marital status, place of employment, and so on. (See Figure 19.4.)[4]

Date

Claims Adjuster

    Re: Claimant: Belinda Mattera
               Insured: Elise Wilson and Floria Ramirez
               Claim No:
               File No:

Dear Claims Adjuster:

    Thank you for referral of the above case. The following is our preliminary report.

STATEMENT OF FACTS

    Plaintiff, Belinda Mattera, apparently was scheduled on June 4, 2006 for a partial colectomy done by Dr. Jones for the purposes of removing a colon tumor. It was during this surgery that the sponges were allegedly left inside her. During the course of this procedure the sponge count was allegedly incorrect, resulting in retention of three sponges. Belinda Mattera had surgery six months (on December 14, 2006) later because of persistent abdominal pain. In between the two surgeries, she received chemotherapy and suffered from side effects of these drugs, including weight loss and dehydration. Her surgery of December 14, 2006, was performed following the detection of three radioopaque densities within her right upper quadrant. The pathology report revealed that they were sponges.

ANALYSIS OF SUMMONS AND COMPLAINT

    Plaintiff's complaint against the nurses contains two causes of action. She alleges that the surgical nurses deviated from the standard of care by failing to perform an accurate sponge count. Plaintiff also alleges spoliation of records, stating that the sponge count was altered after the fact, by changing the number 8 to a 5. On behalf of Elise Wilson and Floria Ramirez, we served an answer denying all plaintiff's allegations of negligence and asserting the affirmative defense that Dr. VonDyke, whom we do not insure, was negligent in leaving the three sponges within the patient's abdomen. A copy of the answer is enclosed for your file.

    Along with the answer we served a demand for bill of particulars, a notice to take the deposition of plaintiff and a notice of objection to service of legal papers by electronic means. We also served demands for additional discovery.

    Plaintiff is represented in this action by the law firm of _____, ____, and ____. Address_____. Joseph _____ is the attorney on the file.

ANALYSIS OF LIABILITY AND EXPOSURE

    We do not yet have in our possession a copy of the hospital records of Belinda Mattera or of Dr. VonDyke so we are unable at present to make any meaningful analysis of possible exposure in this case. If plaintiff's claim that a second surgery was required to remove the sponges, it sounds as if Ms. Mattera had some significant sequelae to the surgery performed by Dr. VonDyke and the allegedly inaccurate sponge count. We do need to stress that much of her debilitation was due to the weight loss (almost 40 pounds in seven months) associated with the chemotherapy.

    We have written to Nurse Wilson and Nurse Ramirez to advise them of the attorney who will be in charge of their defense and to remind them not to discuss the case with anyone. A copy of that correspondence is also enclosed for your file. Rest assured we will keep you advised as additional information comes to us. In the meantime if you have any questions at all, please do not hesitate to refer them to my partner, _____ , at ___ _____ or to me at ___ _____. Thank you again for referral of this case.

Very truly yours,

Figure 19.3 Preliminary Report on Liability and Damages

SUPREME COURT OF THE STATE OF NEW YORK
COUNTY OF

—————————————————————————————————x

                                    Plaintiff   DEMAND FOR BILL OF
                                                        PARTICULARS
        Against

                                    Defendant.

—————————————————————————————————x

        PLEASE TAKE NOTICE that defendant_____ hereby demands that plaintiff serve on the under-
signed within twenty (20) days from the date of service hereof, a Verified Bill of Particulars with respect to the
following matters concerning the allegations in the complaint against the above named defendant:

1. State the date and place of birth of plaintiff.
2. State the residence address of plaintiff at the time of negligence claimed.
3. State plaintiff's marital status.
4. Give name of spouse, if married.
5. Give names and dates of birth of any dependents.
6. Set forth a general statement of the acts or omissions of this defendant that are claimed to constitute
    departures from good and accepted medical practice.
7. Set forth date or dates of defendant's alleged negligence
8. Set forth:
    a. Dates of first and last services rendered by defendant
    b. Place or places where services were rendered.
9. If plaintiff charges defendant with a misdiagnosis, identify the alleged misdiagnosis and set forth the diag-
    nosis claimed to be the proper one.
10. If plaintiff charges failure to administer a diagnostic test, identify the test.
11. If plaintiff charges failure to administer a particular therapy, state the medicines, treatments and surgical
    procedures claimed to have been required and where and when each should have been done.
12. If plaintiff charges defendant with having administered contraindicated treatments or medications, iden-
    tify each.
13. If plaintiff claims special damages, please state the following:
    a. Charges for any and all hospitalizations
    b. Physician's charges
    c. Charges for medicines (itemized)
    d. Nursing charges
    e. Any other special damages
14. If any of the above charges were reimbursed by and insurance company, set forth the complete name
    and address of the company, person in whose name policy was issued and policy number and group
    number.

Figure 19.4 Demand for Bill of Particulars

15. If plaintiff claims injuries alleged here were caused in whole or in part by use of defective equipment, specify the piece of equipment and set forth facts that support those allegations.
16. Set forth full names and address of each and every person plaintiff, at time of trial, will claim observed defendant's acts of negligence.
17. If plaintiff charges defendant with lack of informed consent, set forth:
    a. Aspect of defendant's treatment claimed to have exposed plaintiff to material risks sufficient to require disclosure.
    b. Identify each risk plaintiff will claim was not disclosed by defendant
    c. State in what respect defendant's disclosure was unreasonably inadequate
    d. Set forth alternative choices of treatment that should have been disclosed and describe each
    e. Set forth date on which plaintiff claims defendant should have obtained consent
18. Set forth name and address of each and every nurse from whom plaintiff received treatment subsequent to the alleged negligent acts.
19. Set forth the nature of the condition for which plaintiff sought and received medical treatment rendered by defendant.
20. Give the nature, extent and duration of each injury plaintiff claims as a result of alleged negligence of defendant.
21. Set forth each and every condition, if any, that plaintiff claims this defendant exacerbated.
22. If plaintiff claims the aforesaid injuries necessitated any hospitalizations state name and address of hospital with dates of confinement or outpatient treatment.
23. If plaintiff claims aforesaid injuries required confinement to bed or home, set forth the following:
    a. Dates of confinement to home
    b. Dates of confinement to bed
24. If plaintiff claims aforesaid injuries resulted in loss of earnings set forth:
    a. Name and location of employer
    b. Dates of absence from job
    c. Lost wages claimed

PLEASE TAKE FURTHER NOTICE that in the event of plaintiff's failure to comply with the foregoing Demand for a Verified Bill of Particulars within the time allowed by statute, defendant will move to preclude offering of any evidence as to the matters of which particulars were herein demanded and not provided and will demand reimbursement for the costs of such motion.

Dated:

                                        Yours, etc.,

                                        _____

                                        By:
                                        _____,_____ and _____

To: _____,_____ and _____
         Attorneys for plaintiff

Figure 19.4 *Demand for Bill of Particulars (continued)*

2. Report on bill of particulars

When the bill of particulars is received from the plaintiff, the attorney will make the next formal report to the claims adjuster. This report is a detailed one that reviews and comments upon plaintiff's specific claims. The bill of particulars should be sufficient to apprise defendants of plaintiff's theory of the case and the medical errors alleged to have caused injury to the plaintiff. If there is insufficient specificity in plaintiff's papers then the attorney should also include a request for permission from the claims adjuster to make an appropriate motion to demand that plaintiff provide a more informative bill of particulars.

Plaintiff's theory of malpractice must be examined against the information contained in the insured's own medical records. An early determination should be made as to whether plaintiff's claims appear to be supported in whole or in part by the chart. Are there any indications in the insured's own records of departures from good and accepted medical practice, problems in the treatment given, of evidence of bad results sustained by the patient, who has now become a plaintiff? In preparing this report for the claims adjuster, the lawyer has a further opportunity to assess possible liability and exposure in light of the additional information received. The claims adjuster, upon receipt of the report, can discuss with his supervisors the need to evaluate litigation strategy and, perhaps, to adjust reserves. (See Figure 19.5.)

The report on the bill of particulars should contain references to prior reported cases' verdict, appellate and settlement values based upon a review of plaintiff's claims such that the claims adjuster can, at this time, adjust the reserve if necessary. It is important that defense counsel take present value into account when calculating future lost earnings. It is insufficient to simply multiply the plaintiff's annual lost earnings claim by the number of work years left as lost earnings awards will be reduced to present value and that is the value that is utilized by the claims adjuster to set the reserve.[5]

In wrongful death cases, it is important for defense counsel to properly calculate the value of loss of parental care and guidance based upon the ages and needs of the children, rather than giving a blanket figure without regard for such particulars.[6]

Along with the bill of particulars, plaintiff will provide authorizations to permit defendants to access records regarding any further medical treatment received. These additional medical records may demand further investigation and require yet another evaluation of liability and exposure to be communicated to the claims adjuster.

The defense attorney should at every stage in a lawsuit affirm or alter the preliminary litigation strategy. Initially the determination of strategy is made by use of a triage process not unlike medical triage done in an emergency room setting. If it is clear, for example, from the medical chart that nursing mistakes were made and that injuries were suffered, then counsel should relay this information to the claims adjuster in clear and certain terms and suggest that early settlement be pursued. Likewise, if it becomes clear that the nurse's actions were not related to the plaintiff's injuries, then defense counsel should suggest making a motion to dismiss the claim as against the nurse. That suggestion should be renewed post-deposition if depositions clarify liability in such as way as to exculpate the nurse. Affidavits from nursing experts should be obtained in order to properly support a motion to dismiss.[7]

If there is question whether there were any departures from good nursing practice or that those departures actually caused the injury the plaintiff is claiming, counsel will recommend the case be litigated at least through discovery. During depositions and other discovery the attorney will try to acquaint plaintiff with the problems proving the case or convincing a jury to make a monetary award. This may lead both parties to a place where reasonable settlement can be reached. Perhaps the plaintiff can be convinced to discontinue the case against one or more of the defendants or possibly to accept a "nuisance value" or moderate settlement so that both parties can save trial costs. If there is no indication that the nurse departed from good and accepted nursing practice, defense counsel should make every effort to obtain discontinuance prior to trial or settlement on behalf of the nurse. Should such discontinuance be affected, no verdict or settlement would be reported to the National Practitioner Data Bank as against the nurse.[8]

If the attorney litigating the case feels plaintiff's claims are ill-founded, she may advise holding firm against plaintiff's demands through trial and possibly through appeal if an adverse verdict is handed down by a jury.

C. Report on Preliminary Conference

The next report to a claims adjuster will typically come after a preliminary conference before the court.[9] (22 NYCRR 202.12) A party to the action, usually the plaintiff, will file a document called Request for Judicial Intervention with the court, and representatives of every party will be required to appear to set up a schedule for depositions and other discovery. At the preliminary conference, basic information is exchanged such as names, addresses, and phone numbers of counsel representing each party and insurance coverage information. Discovery demands are discussed and augmented, and a schedule is set for depositions of all parties and completion of all discovery. All of this information is contained

Date

Claims Adjuster

        Re: Claimant: Belinda Mattera
                   Insured: Elise Wilson and Floria Raimerez
                   Claim No.:

Dear_____,

        We have recently received plaintiff's bill of particulars. As you will recall, this case involves a 59-year-old woman who required a partial colectomy for colon cancer. At the completion of the surgical procedure done by codefendant, Dr. VonDyke, the two operating room nurses allegedly miscounted the sponges, resulting in retention of three surgical sponges. A copy of the bill of particulars is enclosed.

PLAINTIFF'S BILL OF PARTICULARS
        According to plaintiff's bill of particulars, Mrs. Mattera was born in 1947 and was married at the time of the surgery. She was a homemaker; there is no claim for lost earnings. The bill of particulars alleges that Elise Wilson and Floria Ramirez failed to properly count sponges, failed to alert Dr. VonDyke of the discrepancy in the count, and altered the medical record to make it look as if the count was correct.
        Plaintiff experienced several months of side effects of chemotherapy between the first surgery (performed to remove the colon tumor) and the second surgery to remove the sponges. During the last month before the second operation, she complained of intermittent abdominal pain and showed some signs of dehydration. These symptoms were attributed to her colon cancer and the chemotherapy, until an ultrasound of her abdomen revealed the presence of the sponges. Following the second surgery, the plaintiff made a strong recovery and has been well since. She is being followed by her oncologist with biannual colonoscopies because she had two positive lymph nodes at the time of her colon resection.

ANALYSIS OF LIABILITY AND EXPOSURE

        It seems likely that a finding of liability will be made against our insured nurses. It is the responsibility of operating room nurses to perform accurate counts. Any discrepancies in the count should be brought to the attention of the surgeon so that appropriate diagnostic studies (x-ray of the abdomen) may be performed. We are concerned that the plaintiff is alleging spoliation of evidence. Interviews with the nurses have revealed that the nurses have no explanation for why the numbers on the surgical count sheets were over written. They displayed marked evasion of discussion of this point, a factor that is of concern.
        Plaintiff is afflicted with colon cancer and has a poor prognosis given the presence of tumor in two of her lymph nodes at the time of the June 2006 surgery. However, the chemotherapy may have been effective is slowing the spread of cancer, thus making her long term prognosis unclear.
        We estimate this case to have a sustainable value of $450,000 to $700,000. If plaintiff's attorney is interested in reaching an early settlement in order to save time and litigation expenses, we should express a willingness to negotiate in good faith. The success of any negotiations will depend on plaintiff's willingness to settle for an amount significantly discounted from the lower of the figures mentioned above. This would appear to be the wisest early litigation strategy. If plaintiff is not currently interested in settlement negotiations, he may agree to mediation of this case before a judge at a later date.
        Rest assured we will keep you advised as additional information comes to us. In the meantime if you have any questions, please do not hesitate to call.

                              Very truly yours,

Figure 19.5 Report of Bill of Particulars

in a Preliminary Conference Order signed by the judge. It is important for defense counsel to notify the insured as soon as possible of any dates for upcoming depositions to maximize the likelihood of the availability of the insured and to avoid unnecessarily prolonged litigation. Prompt forwarding of the Preliminary Conference Order can allow the claims adjuster time within which to request appropriate motions to be made to object to production of certain documents.

TIP: In recent years some adjusters and carriers have asked simply to be supplied with a copy of the Preliminary Conference Order rather than a report commenting upon that order. This is part of an effort to contain litigation defense costs.

19.6 Expert Review

There is no hard and fast rule about when an expert review of the medical care at issue should be obtained. Often a medical facility will have an early, informal, internal review by a physician affiliated with the facility. This report will be sent to the claims adjuster who will share the opinion offered with the attorney in charge of the case. This process can lead to an early determination to settle.

At some point in litigation the services of an outside, impartial expert will be required both to evaluate the case and, possibly, to testify for the defense at trial. Sometimes the attorney is asked to recommend an expert, but more often the claims adjuster will select a name from the carrier's list of approved physicians or nurses. The claims adjuster will also frequently do independent medical research to find an appropriate expert in the event of an unusual situation or rare illness or new medical procedure. The claims adjuster will contact the expert's office to discuss fees, payment schedule and interest in reviewing the matter. It is at this time that the claims adjuster will also determine any additional fees to be paid at the time of deposition or trial, such as travel expenses, hotel, limousine service, etc. These items can significantly impact the cost of retaining a particular expert and so can result in the retention of an expert whose fees will be more reasonable. The claims adjuster will also explore any possible litigation conflicts as well as any availability issues on the part of the physician. All new experts will require approval by the claims adjuster's supervisor in accordance with company policy. The attorney will then contact the potential expert, and if she continues to agree to review the matter, the claims adjuster will send a letter outlining the fees to be paid and any special expenses that may have been agreed to beforehand. Additionally, the retention letter will confirm that the reviewing physician has no conflict of interest with respect to the pending matter. Thereafter the attorney han-

dling the file will provide the physician with all records to be reviewed, speak directly with the physician, outline the facts of the case, list the claims plaintiff is asserting, and suggest issues that should be kept in mind during the review. At some point, the attorney trying the case will meet face to face with the expert to go over the medical records in detail, and will then write a cogent report to the claims adjuster about the findings of the expert and the impact these should have on the earlier assessment of liability and exposure.

The report should be complete and candid, laying out both the pros and cons of taking the case to trial. Every effort should be made to eliminate the possibility of any unpleasant surprises. If a significant revamping of litigation strategy is indicated, the claims adjuster and attorney should make it together at that time. (See Figure 19.6.) If the care provided is felt to be negative the insured is granted a second independent review. Occasionally, additional reviews will be completed. Depending upon the claims in a matter, several experts may be retained in a case to address the variety of plaintiff's claims.

19.7 Depositions of Parties

TIP: Each deposition in a case should be reported within a few days of the event. Many carriers provide rules for timely reporting of depositions. Failure to adhere to those rules can result in decreased or denied payments to defense counsel and/or client dissatisfaction.

The report must not be just a line-by-line regurgitation of the testimony itself. A very brief one paragraph reminder of the facts of the case should start the report followed by names and titles of all persons present at the deposition and their roles in the case. Some succinct comments on the appearance and demeanor of the deponent should follow. These comments should give clues to the claims adjuster as to the probable effectiveness of deponent as a witness at trial. Comments should offer an educated opinion about the believability of a deponent's testimony and the response a jury may have to that person. This kind of assessment should be made of both plaintiffs and defendants.

Information obtained about the deponent's education, background, and family status should be elicited. Questions should be asked point-by-point and day-by-day of every contact between plaintiff and each defendant, conversations, treatments proposed, treatments given, and results of treatments. The testimony should be summarized in a logical order. In the final paragraph of each deposition report, the attorney should revisit issues of liability and exposure and any impact thereon from the deposition testimony. If additional investigation or documents are needed, their request should follow. (See Figures 19.7-19.9.)

Date

Claims Adjuster

     Re: Claimant: Plaintiff
                 Insured: Elise Wilson and Floria Ramirez
                 Claims No.:

Dear _____,

In accordance with your instructions, the nursing care provided in this case was reviewed and evaluated by a certified operating room nurse. We have had an opportunity to meet with the nurse and discuss the case with her in detail.

As you will recall, plaintiff in this case alleges that the operating room nurses were negligent for failing to perform an accurate operating room sponge count and for attempting to alter the records after the fact. The patient underwent a second surgery six months later for removal of the three retained sponges.

EXPERT OPINION

Nurse _____ reviewed records of the operating room nurses and records of subsequent surgery to remove the sponges. The expert nurse opined that the anesthesia record shows a dramatic drop in blood pressure midway through the operation. The dictated operating room report shows that the surgeon encountered uncontrolled bleeding during this time. It is likely that the state of emergency that existed within the operating room contributed to the undetected retention of sponges. Our nurse also pointed to the fact that the operating room nurses were relieved partway through the procedures, and that plaintiff did not name the second set of nurses, who were ultimately the ones who performed the final counts.

Nurse_____ pointed out that the first set of nurses (Elise Wilson and Floria Ramirez) likely did not have liability because they were not in the room at the time the counts were performed. However, our insured nurses, Betty Bentley and Marcelia Moira, who did perform the final counts, were likely negligent for failing to perform accurate counts and not detecting the three missing sponges in the counts. Although the state of crisis midway through the operating may have caused the sponges to be left in the abdomen, by the time the case ended, the patient was stable. An accurate sponge count should have been performed at that time. The overwritten sponge count record concerned our expert, who believes that a jury would agree with the plaintiff's theory that the nurse attempted to cover up the inaccurate count.

In light of the nurse's findings, we believe a jury is likely to make a finding of liability against our insured. There is exposure. The second surgery to remove the sponges would not have been necessary had the sponge count been done correctly. Plaintiff came across in her deposition as a likeable woman, a church goer, with many friends and ties within the local community.

We believe it is prudent to attempt to settle this case sooner rather than later for a sum that represents our estimation of trial costs ($75,000) or less. Please contact me if you have any questions.

Very truly yours,

Figure 19.6 *Report of Expert Review*

This case is currently pending in the Superior Court of New Jersey, County, with a trial date of 2006. The depositions of your insured Nurse M has now been taken and the following is a summary of her testimony.

Nurse M was the charge nurse on the 7 to 3 shift on June 9, 1998, the day that C jumped out of a van. Nurse M had also attended to C on several other dates during her admission to the acute care adolescent hospital, beginning on, 2006. She also had some familiarity with C from prior admissions.

Nurse M obtained a nursing diploma in 1964 from Hospital and has worked all but two years since then as a registered nurse. She worked at Hospital in Pediatrics for one year; as a nurse to two oral surgeons for two years; as an industrial nurse for a drug company for two years; at Medical Center at the Mental Health Unit for four years; at K for 24 years; and currently works at Medical Center in the Eating Disorder Unit. She still works an occasional shift at K. She started at K in 1975, in the acute care adult unit. She eventually worked on all the units at K. In 1997 and 1998, she was full-time at the adolescent unit. This unit had 32 to 34 beds and served acutely ill patients who were suicidal, homicidal, otherwise mentally ill or who had a combination of mental illness and substance abuse. The population ranged from ages 13 to 18. The staffing was two to three nurses, four nurses' aides, two doctors, four social workers, two secretaries and two members of the allied clinical therapies, who ran groups. It was a double locked unit, meaning that there were two sets of locked doors.

Ms. M's job duties included giving and taking verbal reports on tape, talking to the night nurse when she came on if she had any questions, preparing the point sheets for the residents to tell them what privileges they were entitled to based on their conduct of the day before, administering medications, assigning nurses' aides, doing morning rounds, and meeting with the doctors, nurses and social workers to discuss problems. She would also meet with patients individually and make contracts with them for privileges. She would also make sure that everyone attended their scheduled groups and handle any disruptions that may have occurred. The doctors on the unit were X and Y.

Ms. M remembered C as being very provocative, very attention seeking, always oppositional and defiant. She would often have an incident in the morning and later calm down and follow limits. By "provocative" Ms. M explained that she would dress provocatively, and act and talk sexually. She would also threaten other patients, start fights and complain of being unfairly treated. She needed firm limits and could be angry or cooperative. She would have mood swings and on a bad day would not comply with her limits. She would agree to contract for behavioral limits but often would not follow them.

Ms. M knew that the patient was admitted on, 2006 with a history of running away and attempting to harm herself and drinking White-Out. She had been a patient at the Facility. She was then transferred to the intensive care unit awaiting a bed in the acute care hospital. At that point she apparently had sex with a male patient.

Nurse M's first note is dated, 2006. C was in a quiet area in the acute care adolescent unit to prevent her from having sex with male peers. She was not on suicide watch, and Ms. M wrote that she was not suicidal. In fact, a review all the nursing notes through the entire hospitalization gives no indication that the patient was suicidal. She was on check every 15 minutes due to her behavior and to prevent her from having sex. This was not for suicide, however. Dr. T in his deposition said that the patient was on 15 minute check for suicide, but Ms. M disagreed with this.

On June 3, the patient met with a DYFS worker, and the nursing team decided to keep the patient visible at all times in the lounge area. On June 4, Nurse M noted that the patient was angry, defiant, profane and refusing to write an assignment about why she had acted badly the day before. Ms. M's notes indicate that the patient complained of a vaginal itch and had her period. A doctor was notified, who ordered Monistat cream by telephone. On , 2006 the primary social worker, J, wrote that he and Ms. M met with the patient.

On June 9, C had to go to court for a judge to review her hospital stay. The hearing was in another building on the Campus. A nurse's aide escorted over those patients who were scheduled to have hearings that day. However, C was brought back to the unit from the hearing by a crisis intervention person, who stated that she had tried to run out of the hearing lounge area to go outside for some "fresh air." The crisis worker considered this to be an escape attempt but caught her before she made it outside. At 2:00 P.M. Nurse M and Dr. T, the patient's treating psychiatrist, met with C in the quiet area to discuss C's scheduled appointment for that evening at Planned Parenthood. C was to go with staff from Facility for the appointment, because she had been a Facility resident before her acute hospitalization. Nurse M noted that the patient verbally contracted with Dr. T not to run away during the

Figure 19.7 Deposition Report

Planned Parenthood appointment. Ms. M called the Facility to discuss the transport. She does not recall to whom she spoke. Ms. M wanted Facility to be aware what happened with C in court that morning. Her nurses notes state:

> Writer called Facility staff to tell them of incident this A.M. and to tell them to discuss more than one staff member going, which they agreed to do.
>
> Nurse M knew that the person she spoke to was on the regular counseling staff at Facility but does not know her name. She did not know if Dr. T also called the Facility, as he testified at his deposition recently. She said it was the doctor's role to write an order about the transport and to specify how many escorts would go with the patient. Ms. M assessed the patient and suggested that two escorts go with her to the Planned Parenthood meeting. Nurse M's shift ended at 3:15 and she left at about 3:30. L, who is also a defendant in the case, relieved her. Ms. M did not speak directly to L but instead recorded a report on tape. That taped report no longer exists, but Ms. M thinks she would have stated that the patient had attempted to bolt in the morning and would have stated her feelings that two people should be considered to escort the patient to Planned Parenthood.

Ms. M said that Dr. T did not order two staffers to escort the patient, although he could have done so. She said that the nurses on the 3 to 11 shift also had a duty to assess the patient before she left for her Planned Parenthood visit. L, according to her own notes, actually did assess the patient. Ms. M did not know whether L spoke with G, the young counselor from Facility, before Ms. G transported the patient. Ms. H learned of the incident the next day and was surprised and upset. She has not spoken to H about the incident. Although she was not on duty at 6:00 P.M. when the patient left, Ms. M said that it was her practice to advise transporters to lock the doors on the van and make sure the patient was wearing a seatbelt. This was a written policy at C as well.

This concluded the deposition of Nurse M.

Impact of Deposition:

With the doctor and the two nurses who dealt with C on the afternoon of June 9 now having been deposed, the situation is more in focus. It appears that Dr. T bears a large portion of responsibility since he assessed the patient at 2:00 P.M. and did not order two escorts to accompany her to her Planned Parenthood appointment. Instead of an order to this effect, he merely "recommended" that the Facility staff "consider" bringing two escorts. Nurse M, on the 7 to 3 shift, was largely covered by Dr. T, since the doctor and Nurse M jointly assessed the patient, and the doctor decided one escort would be sufficient if Facility could not spare two people. However, Nurse M would theoretically have an independent duty to challenge this decision but did not. Nurse H, on the 3 to 11 shift, seems to have more of a problem, since she had a duty to independently assess the patient. From her note, it appears that she did assess the patient, but she arguably made the wrong decision in allowing the patient out with only one escort. In her deposition, Ms. H, stated that she viewed it as a decision of the prior shift to allow the patient out with only one escort. This position is not very defensible. G, the young counselor from Facility who escorted the patient, also bears a large portion of responsibility since she allowed the patient alone in the back seat without a seatbelt and with the doors unlocked. She was very new to the job and inexperienced. Plaintiff will argue that she did not get the help she required from the nurses on the floor, namely H.

In short, liability seems most focused on Dr. T and P. This is a case where someone will have to pay. We will keep you advised of all significant developments.

Very truly yours,
PETER A. GREENE

Figure 19.7 *Deposition Report (continued)*

This case is currently pending in the Superior Court of _____, _____ County, without trial date. The deposition of your insured Nurse E, has now been taken and the following is a summary of her testimony. Nurse E flew in for the deposition from her home in_____.

Nurse E graduated from_____Community College with an associate's degree in nursing. Before she became a nurse she was an emergency medical technician (EMT). Her date of birth is_____. Upon graduation from nursing school in_____, 2006, she began working on a medical surgical floor at_____Medical Center and floated in the emergency room for two or three shifts. She always wanted to become an emergency room nurse and in_____2006 she transferred to the emergency department at_____Medical Center. In fact, Mr. B was her very first patient as an emergency room nurse. She worked at_____Medical Center until she recently moved to_____, leaving the hospital on good terms. She now works as a trauma nurse care coordinator at_____Regional Medical Center in_____.

In _____ 2006, Nurse E was beginning a six-week orientation program in the emergency department at_____Medical Center. On the first day, she reviewed policies and procedures. On the second day she began working with her mentor, experienced ER Nurse H. Her duty was to be Nurse H's "shadow," following her and carefully observing her treatment of patients. Nurse H would perform most of the hands-on care and Nurse E would write the nursing notes. Nurse E has some limited recollection of the Patient B. She recalls a security guard calling out that the patient was seizing. She recalls moving the patient to a room close to the nursing station. She also recalls Dr. C, an intensivist, examining the patient. Her shift began at 8 A.M. and she participated in taking verbal report from the prior nurse, although she does not remember what was said in the report. She said the emergency department at_____ Medical Center contained 12 rooms, plus beds in the hallway. There were five nurses normally on the day shift. On the day in question,_____, 2006, there were four other nurses plus Nurse H and Nurse E.

Nurse E does not think that she and Ms. H checked the patient's prior chart when they first came on duty. Portions of the chart would have been on the wall at the nursing station. Once the patient started seizing at about 9:10 A.M., the nurses caring for him basically stayed with him and would not have had a chance to read the chart. Nurse E specifically recalls being asked by Dr. C to check for the patient's glucose level at about 1:00 P.M. and finding out for the first time that the EMTs had taken a glucose level in the field which was about 40. The glucose at 1:00 P.M. was 49. She said that she has since learned that, while low, a glucose of 49 would probably not cause seizures. She was not aware of that at the time, however. Nurse E said she did know how to check for glucose with a glucometer which pricks the patient's finger and that such a machine was available at the nursing station in_____, 2006. However, she said, a nurse could not take a blood glucose reading without being ordered by a doctor. Dr. C was the first to order a glucose reading, shortly after 1:00 P.M. on_____, 2006. Nurse E said that normal glucose would be between 60 and 120. Thus a reading of 40 or 49 was not drastically low.

Nurse E was asked by plaintiff's attorney to read her notes into the chart. At 8:25 A.M. Nurse E wrote in her first note that the patient was arousable and responsive and talking to the nurses. He had not eaten breakfast yet. He was on room air. She did not remember whether he had an IV line in place as of 8:25 A.M. She said Dr. H was the attending emergency room doctor on duty, but the first note explicitly stating that Dr. H examined the patient was at 10:45 A.M. However, Nurse E stated that Dr. H could well have come in earlier to see the patient, especially after seizures began at 9:10 A.M. There are several notes stating that Ativan was administered to the patient after 9:15 A.M. These would have required a doctor's order, although not necessarily the presence of the doctor. Nurse E said that currently she records whenever a doctor visits a patient. However, at the time of this incident, she may not have written that.

Figure 19.8 Deposition Report

Nurse E denied that her comment at 8:25 A.M. that the patient was feeling "lousy" indicated a change in status. She had not reviewed the prior notes on this patient but relied on verbal report recently received from the prior shift. She was not aware from report that the patient had received a bolus of dextrose from the EMTs for hypoglycemia. At 9:10 A.M. the patient began seizing with spastic movements of his arms and legs. He was unresponsive, with snoring respirations. He was placed on a non-rebreather mask at 100% oxygen. From that point on, his vital signs remained abnormal with increased pulse, respirations and blood pressure. He remained unresponsive until he was transferred to the ICU at 2:20 P.M. He was reported to be seizing periodically throughout this entire time. Nurse E also recorded decerebrate posturing, which she said was a description of the patient's arm position which could indicate brain injury. An oral airway was placed at 10:42 A.M. The patient was intubated at 10:48 A.M. by Dr. H. He had a CAT scan of the head and a chest x-ray between 11:10 and 11:20 A.M.

Nurse E does not know what caused this patient's seizures. He first received additional dextrose on Nurse E's shift at 1:20 P.M. in the form of one ampule of dextrose IVP and an IV of D5 normal saline.

Nurse E made a good witness. She did say that her mentor, Nurse H, did most of the treatment. Nurse H is not a defendant in this case. If plaintiff does not bring Nurse H in as a defendant, this would be a good defense for Nurse E. However, even without this defense, it is unclear that Nurse E did anything wrong in the treatment of this patient. There is, as you know, a dispute as to whether nurses can order blood glucose levels on their own. Plaintiff's expert says they can, whereas our expert and our nurses say that nurses need a doctor's order to take a blood glucose. There is also doubt as to whether low glucose was the cause of this patient's seizures. Alcohol withdrawal could be another cause, although the patient still had alcohol in his blood at the time of the seizures. Nurse E made no accusations against any co-defendant or any other medical treater.

We will continue to keep you advised of all significant developments.

Very truly yours,

PETER A. GREENE

Figure 19.8 *Deposition Report (continued)*

Date

Claims Adjuster

       Re: Claimant Linda Stern
       Insured:
       Claims No.:

Dear _____,

    We recently conducted the deposition of a co-defendant physician in the above-entitled case. As you will recall, this case involves the wrongful death of a 55-year-old woman who died of complications and an external wound infection following cardiac bypass surgery.

Those present at the deposition were as follows:

Defendant, Dr. C_____, primary care physician for deceased, plaintiff;

_____ _____, Esq., of the Law firm of _____, attorneys for
Dr. C_____;

_____, Esq. of the Law firm of _____, attorneys for co-defendant
physician, Dr. D_____;

_____, Esq. of the Law firm of _____, attorneys for plaintiff.

The report was Joanne P_____ of _____Reporting Service.

DEPOSITION OF DR. C.

    Dr. C testified he had been plaintiff's primary care physician for the eight years prior to her death. He obtained his medical degree from Georgetown University in 1964 and his residency in _____Hospital in New York City. He has been board certified in Internal Medicine since 1970.

    Although Dr. C is a distinguished looking, gray-haired man, his manner is arrogant, and he speaks in a derogatory way about his deceased patient. He is not likely to make a favorable impression on a jury. Dr. C. initially saw plaintiff in 1990. Mrs. Stern was overweight with a history of smoking a pack and a half of cigarettes. She had diminished pedal pulses indicating peripheral vascular disease, and her blood tests showed elevated levels of cholesterol and triglycerides. Dr. C. testified he recalled telling plaintiff that she was a candidate for COPD, lung cancer and heart disease. Howeve, nothing in the record confirmed such a conversation.

    At the plaintiff's second visit a week later, Dr. C. prescribed a low cholesterol diet and asked plaintiff to return in three months for further blood tests. Mrs. Stern did not, however, return until some ten months later when she came in without an appointment complaining of leg pain. She was referred to a vascular surgeon to rule out acute thrombosis of the left femoral artery. The vascular surgeon diagnosed neuralgia. When Mrs. Stern returned to Dr. C. he ordered a CT scan of the spine and x-rays of the pelvis and hip to rule out a disc problem. He also ordered further blood tests as her cholesterol levels remained elevated.

    Although Mrs. Stern made an appointment two months later, she cancelled it and did not return for four months. Dr. C. testified he continued to advise plaintiff to stop smoking, but this is not documented in the chart. He went on to state that he did not consider prescribing appetite control medications because of her PVD and did not prescribe medications to control cholesterol levels because the patient was not compliant enough to return for regular monitoring visits and sometimes refused medications because of allergies.

Figure 19.9 Deposition Report

Dr. C. went on to say that he wanted to see plaintiff every three months to monitor her blood pressure, but this, also, was not documented in the chart.

In March of 1992 Mrs. Stern's blood work showed a continuing high cholesterol level. Dr. C. felt the elevated cholesterol might come from hypothyroidism. An EKG was taken. This was abnormal and showed nonspecific T wave changes indicative of remote anteroseptal ischemia or infarction. There was no note in plaintiff's medical record to indicate that Dr. C. reviewed the EKG or discussed it with Mrs. Stern although Dr. C. testified he had a clear recollection of telling plaintiff she had atherosclerotic heart disease.

Two visits in 1993 were for shoulder injury and loose bowel movements diagnosed by a gastroenterologist as colitis. In early 1994, Mrs. Stern came in with complaints of upper respiratory infection. Dr. C. recalled examining lung and heart, but no results are documented in file.

Dr. C. testified that plaintiff did not return until March 1997 for her annual checkup. Mrs. Stern had cut back on smoking to three cigarettes per day, and her cholesterol was still elevated. Dr. C. documented that he found no change in her EKG. However, she had complaints of chest pain at rest when she returned in June of 1997. Dr. C. ordered an echocardiogram and a drawing of arterial blood gases. Dr. C. testified that he advised her to see a cardiologist. A chart entry shows recommendation to a cardiologist, but it is crossed out. He did refer her to a pulmonologist who prescribed prilosec for acid reflux. The patient reported that this medication relieved the chest pain symptoms.

Several walk-in visits with complaints such as ear infection and leg pain were made during 1998. When Mrs. Stern returned in February 1999 she reported she had been hospitalized with severe shortness of breath. Dr. C. believed this to be from bronchitis and acute exacerbation of chronic obstructive pulmonary disease. He did not refer her to a cardiologist at that time, but did a week later when she returned for her next visit.

Dr. C. went on to testify that he medically cleared plaintiff for cardiac catheterization some five weeks later. He recalls telling plaintiff she would probably have to have cardiac bypass surgery, but there is nothing in the chart that reflects such a disclosure. He did not follow plaintiff after that, but was advised by plaintiff's husband that she had come through the surgery all right and later learned she had died.

CONCLUSIONS

Dr. C's testimony about undocumented conversations with plaintiff are not believable. At the time he testified he had between 600 and 1100 patients on his active list, so to say he has crystal clear recollection of conversations that took place on specific visits 12 years earlier is ridiculous.

Dr. C. had reviewed the autopsy report of Mrs. Stern in preparation for his deposition. This was most unusual, but in addition to that, he proceeded to misstate the findings in the report saying she had only single-vessel bypass (there was in fact two-vessel bypass) and ignored the cardiac catheterization report that identified severe left triple vessel disease and severe left ventricular dysfunction as well as mitral regurgitation.

Dr. C. is obviously aware that he is a target in this case. Mrs. Stern's attorney has now indicated that he may be willing to forego a deposition of our insured physician and hospital. If this occurs we will seek a voluntary discontinuance as to each.

Rest assured we will keep you advised of any further developments as they occur. In the meantime if you have any questions, please do not hesitate to call.

Very truly yours,

Figure 19.9 Deposition Report *(continued)*

Again, defense counsel should include references to actual sustainable value for both settlement and trial results in the case such that the claims adjuster can review the reserve and re-set as necessary. The failure to provide this sort of legal analysis is seen by the claims adjuster as a significant weakness on the part of counsel.

19.8 Cost Considerations

TIP: In recent years some insurers have placed stringent limits on formal reporting in an effort to cut back on litigation defense costs. Consistent efforts on the part of defense counsel to circumvent these limits or to create additional billing is held in very poor regard by claims adjusters who are responsible for ensuring compliance with company guidelines and can result in a reluctance by the claims adjuster to assign further work to defense counsel whose billing is outside of the norm.

Certainly the claims adjuster and the attorneys working on a case must do whatever reporting is necessary to keep each other fully informed of the status of a case. A well-written report can be both succinct and thorough, and can even be done by e-mail. However, remember the caveat, "Make a hard copy of any e-mail you send and keep it in the file."

As a basic, cost-saving effort, a carrier will often refuse to reimburse a law firm if billing on a file is done by too many attorneys. Carriers do not like to be billed over a period of months or years by an ever-changing succession of attorneys who come in contact with a file for the first time. In fact, no billing for "review of file" by a new attorney is likely to be paid for by the carrier. Claims adjusters and carriers deplore redundant work and are not willing to pay for it. When claims adjusters and attorneys consistently work with a file from commencement of a case to its final disposition, the efficiencies are instantly apparent and will be reflected in the statistical litigation expense to indemnity ratio.

Prompt consideration of appropriate or early settlement of a matter where warranted will contain costs. The claims adjuster and his supervisors will compare the ratio of legal expenses paid out to the ultimate settlement paid. When the legal expenses paid on a claim far outweigh the ultimate settlement value, the judgment of both defense counsel and claims adjuster will be called into question.

19.9 Claims Conferences

Most claims departments and insurance companies have periodic meetings to review cases in litigation. The number of attendees will vary, but in almost every instance will include several claims adjusters, supervisors, risk managers, and administrators from the medical facility, as well as the attorney handling each case. As a cost saving measure and in light of developing technology, it is not unusual for a claims conference to take place by telephone or teleconference. When the nursing case to be discussed appears on the agenda, the case presentation varies from company to company. In many settings, the claims adjuster will set out a brief summary of the facts of the case and then outline the progress of the case to date, the status of discovery, the positive or negative judgment by the expert reviewer or reviewers of the medical care provided, the problems uncovered, the personalities involved, the experience and reputation of the opposing attorney who will be taking the case to trial, and again, the likelihood of liability being found and, if so, the probable exposure. The claims adjuster will present sustainable jury verdict value for the matter at hand. In other settings, the claims adjuster will present the facts of the case and defense counsel will present the remaining details.

These presentations are followed by a period of questions posed to the attorney and the claims adjuster and their respective answers. After further discussion the conferees will make a recommendation to counsel and to the claims adjuster to begin efforts to negotiate a reasonable settlement or to proceed with preparations for trial. At that time, if authorization is granted to settle a matter, the claims adjuster will then obtain any further authority to settle a case from any excess carriers that may be involved. The claims adjuster will also notify all excess carriers potentially affected by any settlement of a matter and, if necessary, obtain further authority to settle the matter. Failure on the part of the claims adjuster to obtain appropriate authority can result in the affected carrier's refusal to pay its fair share of any settlement.

National Practice Data Bank reporting issues will also be sorted out at the time of the claims conference. All practitioners who have committed medical/nursing malpractice such that an award is granted or settlement paid out on their behalves are reported to the National Practitioner Data Bank (NPDB).[10] Data Bank reporting and consent to settlement, and thus reporting thereto, should be obtained by either defense counsel or the claims adjuster. Carriers may have a procedure set up for insureds to object to settlements made on their behalves. Insureds may be entitled to an internal appeal before any settlement being effected that would include them, thus requiring an NPDB report. Some nurses are not aware that they will be reported to the NPDB as a result of settlement of a matter and must be informed prior to obtaining their consent to settle a case. In other carrier settings, the insureds are not granted the right to object to a settlement nor are they permitted to appeal any intention to settle a case on their behalves. It is very important for both the claims adjuster and defense counsel to be familiar with the NPDB reporting procedures and the objection to settlement rights of any insured. If an insured wins an internal appeal with respect to the effecting of any settlement on her behalf, then the case would proceed to trial, sometimes to the detriment of the carrier.

Reporting to the NPDB can pose an issue for individually named insureds such as CRNAs, CNMs, etc. Hospitals must query the NPDB to ascertain whether or not a practitioner, including a nurse or advanced practice nurse (APRN) such as a certified registered nurse anesthetist (CRNA), has been reported to the NPDB (45 CFR Part 60). This can potentially have an effect upon the insureds' job prospects. Most, if not all insureds, object to being reported to the NPDB. If it is determined that the outcome of the case was not caused by any neglect on their part, defense counsel can be instructed at the claims conference to obtain a discontinuance of a legal matter as against the nurse insured or other insureds named in a litigation, before the settlement of the case. No discontinuance can be a condition of settlement in order to be a validly non-reportable event.

Although NPDB reports are not accessible to the general public, various states currently have reporting requirements for medical malpractice settlements. New York, for example, has a physician profiling website, www.nydoctorprofile.com. When a physician has settled a matter for a sum beyond the usual limits, or has a grievous injury case or has three or more settlements, the physician's settlements are placed on the New York state physician profiling website.

TIP: The claims adjuster and defense counsel should confer by telephone prior to the claims conference which takes place in the presence of the client/insured. This conference will allow for discussion of any inconsistencies, unpleasant developments, "stones unturned" or "sleeping dogs" in a case. It is universally regarded as exceedingly poor form for defense counsel to unexpectedly contradict the claims adjuster's position in a public meeting without the courtesy of advance notice such that the case can be effectively, completely and clearly presented to the client/insured.

19.10 Trial

When discovery has been completed in a case, plaintiff will file a document with the court called a note of issue. This tells the court that the case is ready to be placed on the trial calendar. The attorney must inform the claims adjuster immediately, and, as further court conferences are scheduled, the claims adjuster must be kept fully informed. Frequently a judge will ask that the claims adjuster be present at a particular conference when the court will be trying to facilitate a settlement. In many jurisdictions a case may not actually come to trial for a period of months or even years after filing the note of issue.

At some point the court will assign a firm trial date. When that date has been designated, the claims adjuster should try to clear his calendar in order to be present in the courtroom during as much of the testimony as possible. Even on days when the adjuster is present, daily or twice-daily verbal or e-mail reports should be made to the adjuster by the trial attorney. There should be assessment and reassessment at every stage of the trial. Full two-way communication between counsel and adjuster is mandatory. The performance of each witness on the stand should be assessed, her credibility should be evaluated and any facial or body-language response by jurors should be noted. If, during the course of a trial, a plaintiff or co-defendant expresses an interest in talking settlement, the claims adjuster must be advised and included in any response either positive or negative to that initiative.

Last minute telephone calls from court requesting settlement monies far outside any amounts previously set forth and discussed between claims adjuster and defense counsel create a myriad of judgment and trust issues in the adjuster-counsel relationship, absent a totally unforeseen turn of events. Requesting settlement authority for heretofore unheard of sums of money from overseas or excess carriers is exceedingly poor form and is viewed as a very poor performance by the claims adjuster who is held responsible for failing to evaluate and manage defense counsel's handling of the matter. Further, sums of money beyond the reserves set in the matter can have an impact upon carrier stability, premiums charged to the insureds and willingness to continue to provide insurance to insureds.

If the case goes through trial and a verdict is reached, a full trial report must be provided by the trial attorney to the claims adjuster. (See Figures 19.10 and 19.11.) This document will summarize all testimony, comment on any unexpected twists in the trial, assess the outcome, and recommend any future steps to be taken. These include motions to set aside or reduce a verdict or the filing of a notice of appeal.

Dear_____,

        As you know, this case was tried before Judge _____ and a jury over seven days, between _____ and _____, 2006 in the Superior Court of _____, _____ County, resulting in a verdict of $500,000 against _____, which was reduced on our motion to $250,000 by the Charitable Immunity Statute. Co-defendant _P_____, M.D., a first year UMDNJ rotating surgical resident, was found not negligent. Other codefendants, _JT_____, M.D. and _SW_____ M.D., whom we represented, were dismissed on our motion before trial. Plaintiffs' recent attempt to amend the Complaint to name _J_____, R.N., was opposed by us and was denied by Judge _J_____ in April. This became crucial, since Nurse _J_____ emerged as the target of the case and would have been assessed the full $500,000 had she been a named defendant.

        The seven-member jury was satisfactory. It contained blue collar and white collar workers, men and women, three blacks and four whites. All decisions were unanimous.

        There were several key elements in this strange case which contributed to the outcome.

        1)   The overriding factor was extreme emotionality. A bright, accomplished 16-year-old African-American boy from a loving, clean-cut religious family suddenly suffered a cardiac arrest 20 minutes after receiving an intravenous dose of Compazine, an anti-nausea medicine with a known tendency to cause hypotension when given IV. The trial was attended daily by a number of family members and church members. The jury question, in reality, changed from whether to blame anyone to "who should we blame?"

        Other key elements included these:

        2)   Nurse _J_____ took upon herself virtually all responsibility for the ordering, administration and monitoring of the Compazine IV, leaving the impression that she may have overstepped her authority as a nurse and possibly tampered with or caused the falsification of records in the chart.

        Going into trial we did not believe that a registered nurse could be found negligent for properly carrying out a doctor's order which complied with the Physician's Desk Reference. However, Nurse _J_____ ___ appeared so strong and Dr. _P_____ so weak that the jury found her de facto in charge of the patient's care at the crucial time on _____. 2006.

        3)   Drs. _JT_____ and _SW_____, the treating hematologists-oncologists, in giving testimony to clear themselves during discovery, made several important statements which hurt the defense of Nurse _J_____ and the hospital. They inadvertently became the plaintiffs' star witnesses against us.

        These last points require further exploration.

        Nurse _J_____ was a favorite of the _____ family during _S's_____ _ hospitalization. She appears highly trained, well spoken and compassionate. However, her memory at trial may have seemed a little "too perfect"; she also was contradicted on two significant points by fellow Nurse _BP_____; and she had to concede a serious intentional charting inaccuracy, i.e., that she gave the Compazine IV whereas she asked Nurse _BP_____ to chart it. We knew about the discrepancies and charting problem before trial, but felt that we could overcome their impact. However, plaintiff's attorney used these facts as a springboard to argue that Nurse _J_____ actually may have modified Dr. _P's_____ _____ order without consulting him and may have lied in other ways.

        Dr. _SW_____ provided the plaintiffs with a key liability argument when he stated at deposition, and had to repeat at trial, that a nurse should monitor a patient's blood pressure, pulse and respirations while giving medication IV. Our excellent nursing expert, _AE_____, R.N., together with Nurse _J_____, tried to refute this statement as inaccurate. However, the credibility of Drs. JT_____ and _SW_____ as "the only truly objective witnesses in the case," was extremely high and the damage was done. (We were further hurt by the absence of a hospital nursing policy on administration of IV medication). Nurse _J's_____ failure to take vital signs during the administration of the Compazine IV became one of plaintiffs' main theories of negligence.

Figure 19.10 Trial Report

Whereas we went into trial with the family alleging that they saw Dr. _P_____ inject the Compazine quickly into S's_____ IV line, Nurse _J_____ testified (as she had at deposition) that she herself gave the Compazine. She effectively neutralized the family's charge against Dr. _P_____ by reminding Dr. _P_____ that he must have tested the placement of _S's_____ NG tube by injecting air into the line with a syringe. Dr. _P_____ then testified to this custom and practice, which explained the family's observations, thus eliminating Dr. _P_____ and confirming Nurse _J_____ as the giver of the medication. (For his part, Dr. _P_____ had no specific recollection whatsoever of the case).

Nurse _J_____ further testified that Dr. _P_____ changed his Compazine order from "IM" to "IV" at her request. She said that Dr. _P_____ wrote "IV" over "IM" in the chart. However, Dr. _P_____ could not confirm that the write-over letters on the order sheet were in his handwriting. Further suspicion may have been raised because Nurse _J_____ was not even assigned to care for _S_____ on the day of the incident but simply took over when Nurse _BP_____ became busy with another patient. Plaintiff argued on summation that Nurse _J_____ may have changed "I" to "IV" on the chart herself without ever asking Dr. _P_____.

We argued, through three experts, that IV was actually a superior route of administration for Compazine in this patient. We further argued that although IV administration had risks, it was safe if pushed slowly, which Nurse _J_____ testified she did. We argued that a pump on the IV line made it impossible to give the medication too fast, unless it was injected below the pump, which Nurse _J_____ denied. The jury may have rejected the nurse's testimony and found she injected it too fast. Or they may have accepted her testimony but also accepted the testimony of plaintiffs' expert, Dr. _M_____, that Compazine should virtually never be administered intravenously, no matter how slowly. All three defense experts testified that IV is a legitimate route of administration for Compazine, listed in the PDR and other literature. However, their endorsement of Compazine was somewhat tepid since by 1996 it had largely been replaced by Zofran as the drug of choice for nausea.

In sum, experienced Nurse _J_____ rather than first year resident _P_____, emerged as the driving force behind the administration of Compazine to _S_____, for better or for worse. The jury found "for worse."

We also had a proximate cause defense, which was effectively, if inadvertently, undermined by Drs. _JT_____ and _SW_____. Our causation experts, Drs. _D_____ and _R_____, testified that _S_____ was already in a terminal state prior to administration of Compazine due to sepsis caused by suppression of his immune system by powerful chemotherapy for his newly diagnosed leukemia. The experts kindly avoided blaming Drs. _JT_____ and _SW_____ for missing this diagnosis by saying that it was very elusive. However, Drs. _JT_____ _and _SW_____ testified that _S_____ was not especially sick beyond the normal reaction to chemotherapy; they were surprised by his sudden death, and that even after autopsy the cause of death remained inconclusive. They further testified that although the 5-year survival rate for teen-onset leukemia is only 65 percent, _S_____ was more likely to be a survivor since he had rapid initial response to chemotherapy. (Incidentally, we called Drs. _JT_____ and _SW_____, and Nurses _J_____ and _P_____ as our own witnesses because both other counsel had subpoenaed them, and we felt it would look better for the hospital if we put them on ourselves). Because of _JT's_____ and _SW's_____ testimony, the jury gave us no Scafidi percentage for preexisting risk of death.

As to damages, $500,000 was high but not outrageous. With the reduction to $250,000 there is no hope of a remittitur.

Figure 19.10 *Trial Report (continued)*

As to appellate prospects, the most dangerous issue is plaintiff's possible appeal of Judge _I's_____ _____ denial of the motion to amend the Complaint to add _J_____, R.N. as a direct defendant. If that were reversed, the verdict would immediately jump to $500,000, plus prejudgment interest. We feel that Judge _I's_____ decision was correct, but he made it without oral argument and we are aware of no opinion on the record. Plaintiffs could also appeal Judge _C's_____ barring of damages for pain, suffering and loss of enjoyment of life.

Our own issues on appeal seem weak. They include: remittitur, weight of the evidence (which would require making a new trial motion by June 28th), refusal to charge "judgment," allowing a bottom line economic number to go to the jury (although this is now permitted by law), and barring testimony about the results of an x-ray which was lost by the hospital. On balance we might do better trying to discourage plaintiff from appealing and trying to settle the case for about $250,000. We will argue to plaintiff's attorney that his clients were willing to take less than $250,000 anyway, and that an appeal on the amendment of the Complaint issue could expose them to a legal malpractice claim if denied, since Judge _I's_____ _____ basis for denying that amendment was lack of diligence in discovery by plaintiff's attorneys. If we take an appeal, it would force plaintiff to cross-appeal, and their issues appear stronger than ours.

Please call me if you need any further information.

Very truly yours,

Peter Greene Esq.

Figure 19.10 *Trial Report (continued)*

Claims Adjuster

      Re: Claimant
                 Insureds: Hospital, Dr. Blank and Nurse Nemo

Dear_____,

    On May 20th through June 9th we were on trial in _____ County before Justice John J. Judge in the above-entitled matter.

    As you will recall, this case involved a cancer patient who was being given a combination of drugs one of which was Adriamycin. During one of the infusions, the Adriamycin extravasated causing a serious burn to claimant's arm. The chemo was being administered by Nurse Nemo in a cancer treatment center in _____Hospital under the supervision of Dr. Blank, the oncologist.

    The burn on claimant's arm was treated over a significant period of weeks and resulted in a large keloid scar on the right arm. Claimant ultimately died of the underlying cancer. The lawsuit that had been started by her was continued by her estate.

PLAINTIFF'S CASE

    Plaintiff's attorney presented two witnesses on her behalf. The first was an adult son who testified that his mother had suffered significant pain from the burn on her arm, both for a number of months following the extravasation during which the burn was healing and thereafter as skin grafts were attempted. He also stated that his mother had lost almost all the use of her affected arm which was her dominant one.

    The second witness presented on plaintiff's case was a physician who testified that recognition of the extravasation was delayed, that the nurse had not followed the appropriate protocols, that she had put in the IV at too acute an angle so that it went through the vein and out into the surrounding tissue. This witness also faulted the defendant doctor for not supervising closely enough and not detecting that the nurse had used poor technique in placing the infusion.

    Little was attempted on cross-examination except to verify with the son that his mother who had a fatal form of cancer had lived for some seven years after the incident complained of and had seen three grandchildren born during those years.

    The physician on cross-examination admitted that he was familiar with the facility where chemotherapy was given at the insured hospital. He testified that the room is set up with no more than four reclining chairs and was probably no larger than 10 by 15 feet. He admitted that this meant that Dr. Blank, whose desk was there, would have had his patients in view and would have been close enough for supervision.

DEFENDANTS' CASE

    Defense called three witnesses. The first was defendant, Dr. Blank, who had diagnosed plaintiff's cancer and had prescribed the treatment she was to receive. He testified categorically that he was constantly present in the room when his patients were receiving chemotherapy. He also testified that Nurse Nemo had received special training and had extensive experience in starting chemotherapeutic infusion. It was his custom and practice to examine the infusion lines and the insertion points at the commencement of each chemo session. Dr. Blank testified that the chemo cocktail with Adriamicin was the most effective protocol for the plaintiff's form of cancer and was clearly the treatment of choice. Dr. Blank made a deliberate and effective witness.

Figure 19.11 Trial Report

The second witness was a nursing supervisor familiar with the techniques involved in chemotherapy infusion. She testified about the training involved required before a nurse could give chemotherapy and about the procedures to be followed.

The third and most important witness was Nurse Nemo, and she was by far the most persuasive witness. She described her training and the years of experience she had had giving chemotherapeutic infusions before the date when she first saw plaintiff. She then described in exacting detail each and every step she took in ensuring that the butterfly needle went into the vein at the correct angle, pulling it back slightly to make sure it had not gone completely through the vein to the other side and the number of times the infusion was checked during the time it was dripping into the patient's body. She then testified about her concern when the chemo medications were seen to have extravasated, her prompt reporting of that event to the physician in charge and the immediate application of ice to reduce swelling and to counteract the effects of the burn as much as possible, and the subsequent treatment given by the oncologist.

The cross-examination of Nurse Nemo was thorough and frequently unpleasant. However, she maintained throughout several hours a firm resolve, a quiet conviction that she had done her best, and the unswerving realization that extravasation of chemotherapeutic agents is one of those things that happens from time to time in spite of the best precautions and attention to detail. She was a totally convincing witness.

Summations reiterated the theories of both plaintiff and defendants concerning the medical care given. Plaintiff's thesis was simply that extravasation should not have happened and asked for sympathy for the patient who was dying of cancer and had to suffer an additional injury.

Our summation emphasized the care that Nurse Nemo had exhibited, the breadth of her training and the unchallenged presence of Dr. Blank during the infusion. We conceded that it was unfortunate that the plaintiff had to endure pain and suffering additional to that from her cancer, but pointed out that because of the chemo she had enjoyed another seven years of life beyond her life expectancy and had had the joy of seeing several grandchildren born.

The jury deliberated for just over an hour and returned a verdict in favor of the hospital, Dr. Blank and Nurse Nemo.

Thank you for the opportunity to work with you on this case. We very much enjoyed getting to know Dr. Blank and Nurse Nemo-both of whom are extraordinary medical professionals. We are delighted that this case could be brought to a successful conclusion.

Very truly yours,

Figure 19.11 *Trial Report (continued)*

19.11 Summary

Claims adjusters and attorneys must deal with each other candidly, respectfully, and in good faith throughout the course of litigation. Full, but not verbose, reports must chronicle every step. Queries must be answered, doubts must be disclosed, opinions must be exchanged, and records must be kept of all events important to the case. Communication is still the key to providing outstanding legal services in response to a claims adjuster's assignment of matters and to manage a case from start to a satisfactory conclusion.

Endnotes

1. Bureau of Labor Statistics Outlook Handbook (2010-2100) http://www.bls.gov/oco/ocos125.htm retrieved 2/23/10.

2. A letter of claim is an informal demand for compensation due as a result of the injuries alleged. Letters of claim are sent in an effort to resolve claims prior to commencement of a formal legal action by filing of a Summons and Complaint.

3. ABA Model Rules of Conduct.

4. N.Y.S. C.P.L.R. sec. 3402.

5. N.Y.S. C.P.L.R. sec. 4111 et seq.

6. N.Y.S. E.P.T.L. 5-4.3 et seq.

7. N.Y.S. C.P.L.R. Sec. 3211.

8. 45 C.F.R. Part 60.

9. 22 N.Y.C.R.R. 202.12.

10. See note 8.

Additional Reading

Adler, S. and J. Adler, "The Claims Adjuster's Perspective," In *Nursing Home Litigation: Investigation and Case Preparation*, Second edition, ed. P. Iyer. Tucson, Arizona: Lawyers and Judges Publishing Co., 2006.

Licensing and Training Resources for Claims Adjusters

American Institute for Chartered Property Casualty Underwriters and the Insurance Institute of America, 720 Providence Road, Suite 100, Malvern, PA 19355-3433. Internet: http://www.aicpcu.org.

Independent Automotive Damage Appraisers Association, P.O. Box 12291, Columbus, GA 31917-2291. Internet: http://www.iada.org.

Insurance Information Institute, 110 William Street, New York, NY 10038. Internet: http://www.iii.org.

International Claim Association, 1155 15th Street NW, Suite 500, Washington, DC 20005. Internet: http://www.claim.org.

National Association of Public Insurance Adjusters, 21165 Whitfield Place, Suite 105, Potomac Falls, VA 20165. Internet: http://www.napia.com.

Chapter 20

Working with Legal Nurse Consultants

Patricia W. Iyer, MSN, RN, LNCC and Deborah D. D'Andrea, BSN, BA, RN

20.1 Introduction

The focus of this chapter is the use of legal nurse consultants (LNCs) in nursing malpractice cases. Legal nurse consulting is the evaluation and analysis of facts and the rendering of informed opinions related to the delivery of nursing and healthcare services and outcomes. The legal nurse consultant is a licensed registered nurse who performs a critical analysis of clinical and administrative nursing practice, healthcare facts and issues, and their outcomes for the legal profession, healthcare professions, consumers of healthcare and legal services, and others as appropriate. With a strong educational and experiential foundation, the legal nurse consultant is qualified to assess adherence to standards and guidelines of nursing practice.[1] LNCs can be successfully used in litigation other than medical malpractice. Nurses providing legal nurse consulting can be found as employees in many settings, including in the plaintiff or defense firm, the risk manager's office, federal and state agencies, and the insurance companies. An equal number of legal nurse consultants are self-employed (called "independents") and provide services to clients on both sides of the bar. The knowledge and capabilities of a nurse can be used at any stage in a nursing malpractice case. This chapter first focuses on the LNC's contributions that are common to the role of the legal nurse consultant, whether self-employed or working as an employee. We then present information about the self-employed LNC. The chapter ends with an explanation of the functions of a nurse who works in a law firm.

20.2 American Association of Legal Nurse Consultants

While nurses have been providing attorneys with consulting advice for quite some time, the organized profession of legal nurse consulting is a new one. The founding of the American Association of Legal Nurse Consultants (AALNC) occurred in 1989. The organization has grown from a core of 40 members to a membership of several thousand. AALNC provides a professional framework for the practice of legal nurse consulting and has published a scope of practice, a code of ethics, a core curriculum,[2] and a text on business principles for legal nurse consultants.[3] (See www.aalnc.org for more information about the association.)

20.3 Paralegal versus Legal Nurse Consultant

Role confusion exists regarding the differences in preparation and functions of a paralegal versus a legal nurse consultant. By definition, paralegals and legal assistants are qualified by education, training, or work experience to perform specifically delegated substantive legal work for which a lawyer is responsible. Legal education is typically a requirement for paralegals. Although many legal nurse consultants have acquired knowledge of the legal system through such experiences as consulting with attorneys and attending seminars, legal education is not a prerequisite for the independent practice of legal nurse consulting. Professional nursing education and healthcare experience make LNCs unique and valuable partners in legal processes.[4] A simple explanation is that the paralegal has some education about law, and the legal nurse consultant is a nurse who has developed expertise in assisting attorneys with medical issues. Paralegals learn about general law, legal research, torts, legal writing, civil litigation, and technical litigation support.

Many attorneys, unfamiliar with the term legal nurse consultant or its abbreviation, LNC, may refer to the nurse as a nurse paralegal. Unless the nurse has taken a paralegal program, this term is a misnomer. A nurse paralegal is a paralegal who is also a nurse. A legal nurse consultant is a registered nurse who consults on healthcare issues within the legal arena.[5] Confusion about roles arises also because in some settings legal nurse consultants perform some of the same work that legal assistants and paralegals do, par-

ticularly in small law offices. The American Association of Legal Nurse Consultants has defined legal nurse consulting as a specialty practice of the nursing profession, a position endorsed by the American Nurses Association in 2006 (Figure 20.1). Refer to Figure 20.2 for the standards of practice and performance for the legal nurse consultant.

While legal nurse consultants may acquire knowledge about legal documents, such as complaints, interrogatories, requests for production, and the like, most LNCs have no legal training and are not frequently used to draft legal documents. Their focus does not include wills, real estate transactions, and other areas of non-healthcare-related law which is a typical part of paralegal education. Legal education programs offered for nurses by legal assistant or paralegal education programs also cause confusion about roles. To the extent that legal education is provided to nurses by legal assistant or paralegal education programs, it should be considered separate from the education of paralegals and legal assistants because of the differences in their practice in the legal arena. AALNC's position, therefore, is that legal nurse consulting education should be developed and presented as specialty nursing curricula by nurse educators in partnership with legal educators.[6]

Research performed by one of the authors (PI) provided some surprising information about the functions of legal nurse consultants and paralegals. Data was collected from paralegals, legal nurse consultants (LNCs), and attorneys in order to define the most common activities performed by paralegals and legal nurse consultants. The 76 paralegal respondents ranged from students to those with 19 years of experience. The legal nurse consultants (27 in number) had zero to nine years of experience as LNCs. The perceptions of 16 attorneys who had one to 29 years of experience were also elicited. Each person was asked to review a list of functions and indicate if each function was an activity that a paralegal or legal nurse consultant (or both) could perform.

Despite wide differences in experience and perspectives, a consensus emerged among all of the groups. The most commonly identified legal nurse consultant activities were:

1. Identify medical management issues
2. Identify medical issues not addressed or explained in the records
3. Identify malingerers
4. Point out potential medical complications of injuries
5. Identify medical malpractice

AALNC
American Association of Legal Nurse Consultants
The Specialty Practice of Legal Nurse Consulting 2005

Summary

The purpose of this position statement is to define the specialty of Legal Nurse Consulting as a Registered Nurse Practice and reinforce that Legal Nurse Consultants therefore must maintain an active registered nurse license.

Introduction

This position statement is the outcome of extensive discussions and public dialogue about the scope of practice and many roles of Legal Nurse Consultants when providing for direct and indirect patient care, as well as consultation and education.

Background

In 2003 the American Nurses Association's *Nursing's Social Policy Statement* introduced an updated, contemporary definition of nursing: "Nursing is the protection, promotion, and optimization of health and abilities, prevention of illness and injury, alleviation of suffering through the diagnosis and treatment of human response, and advocacy in the care of individuals, families, communities, and populations."

The *Nursing Scope and Standards of Practice* (2004) and *Code of Ethics for Nurses with Interpretive Statements* (2001) of the American Nurses Association provide additional details and further description of nursing and the associated standards of practice. These foundational references provide a framework for the definition of specialty nursing practice, including Legal Nurse Consulting.

Legal Nurse Consulting

The American Association of Legal Nurse Consultants (AALNC), the professional nursing specialty organization for Legal Nurse Consultants, defines legal nurse consulting as the evaluation and analysis of facts and the rendering of informed opinions related to the delivery of nursing and healthcare services and outcomes. The legal nurse consultant is a licensed registered nurse who performs a critical analysis of clinical and administrative nursing practice, healthcare facts and issues and their outcomes for the legal profession, healthcare professions, consumers of healthcare and legal services, and others as appropriate.

As knowledge-based professionals, Legal Nurse Consultants use information learned in the research and development of a case to improve future health care for patients, to advocate for remedies for patients who have received inadequat care, and to provide education to clients, patients, health care providers, and the public as appropriate. Legal Nurse Consultants seek adequate protection of patients and the public and promote accepted standards of care that will serve to prevent injury and alleviate suffering.

Figure 20.1 *The Specialty Practice of Legal Nurse Consulting, reprinted with permission of the American Association of Legal Nurse Consulting*

Similar to other registered nurses working in research settings, informatics, administrative positions, and other role settings, Legal Nurse Consultants engage in specialty nursing practice that covers many roles, some including direct patient care and others influencing patient care indirectly. For example, the nurse Case Manager or Life Care Planner directly influence patient outcome by assessing patient needs and making appropriate recommendations. The expert witness Legal Nurse Consultant educates the public when testifying before a jury. As knowledge-based professionals, Legal Nurse Consultants use information learned in the research and development of a case to improve future health care for patients. For example, researching and explaining medical issues in malpractice cases may lead to revised nursing policies and procedures; help identify those with legitimate injuries, evaluate the impact of injuries on level of function and advocate for remedies when these result from receiving inadequate care. Legal Nurse Consultants provide education to clients, patients, health care providers and the public, when attending and explaining an independent medical exam or injuries sustained in an accident. By virtue of nursing knowledge, training and experience (including Legal Nurse Consulting training and experience), all of these roles are implemented by nurses who are considered to be practicing nurses and whose contributions further the nursing profession itself as well as promote effective patient care.

In many jurisdictions, the state Nurse Practice Act and associated regulatory language have conveyed title protection for the term "nurse." When the word "nurse" is used in the professional title, that user must be actively licensed as a registered nurse. Nursing is a knowledge-based profession and when using that knowledge base, the legal nurse consultant is indeed practicing the profession of nursing.

The American Association of Legal Nurse Consultants AALNC is the organization that:

- Provides the foundation for best practices within the multitude of legal nurse consultant roles.
- Incorporates cutting edge clinical and consultative education to promote the practice of legal nurse consulting.
- Supports "Legal Nurse Consulting: Scope and Standards of Practice."

Conclusion

Legal Nurse Consulting is an expanding nursing specialty practice. Legal Nurse Consultants must maintain an active Registered Nurse license as an integral requirement of the practice discipline.

Resources

American Nurses Association. (2001). Code of Ethics for Nurses with Interpretive *Statements.* Washington, D.C.
American Nurses Association. (2003) *Nursing's Social Policy Statement,* 2nd edition. Washington, D.C.
American Nurses Association. (2004). *Nursing: Scope and Standards of Practice,* Washington, D.C.
American Association of Legal Nurse Consultants (AALNC). (Iyer, P., Ed.) (2003). *Legal Nurse Consulting: Principles and Practice.* (Second ediiton) Boca Raton, Florida: CRC Press.
Approved by the American Association of Legal Nurse Consultants Board of Directors, September 2005.

Figure 20.1 *The Specialty Practice of Legal Nurse Consulting, reprinted with permission of the American Association of Legal Nurse Consulting (continued)*

Legal Nurse Consulting Standards of Practice

Standard 1. Assessment
The legal nurse consultant collects comprehensive data pertinent to the health case or claim.

Standard 2. Issue or Problem Identification
The legal nurse consultant analyzes the assessment data to determine the issues in the health case or claim.

Standard 3. Outcomes Identification
The legal nurse consultant identifies expected outcomes for the individualized plan for a given health case or claim.

Standard 4. Planning
The legal nurse consultant develops a plan that prescribes strategies and alternatives to attain expected outcomes.

Standard 5. Implementation
The legal nurse consultant implements the identified plan.

Standard 5a: Coordination of Services
The legal nurse consultant coordinates services related to the health case or claim.

Standard 5b: Health Teaching and Health Promotion
The legal nurse consultant employs strategies to promote a better understanding of health and safety related to a health case or claim.

Standard 5c: Consultation
The legal nurse consultant provides consultation regarding a health case or claim to influence the identified plan, enhance and support the contribution of others, and effect change.

Standard 6. Evaluation
The legal nurse consultant evaluates progress towards attainment of outcomes.

Standards of Professional Performance

Standard 7. Quality of Practice
The legal nurse consultant systematically enhances the quality and effectiveness of nursing practice.

Standard 8. Education
The legal nurse consultant attains knowledge and competency that reflect current nursing practice.

Standard 9. Professional Practice Evaluation
The legal nurse consultant evaluates one's own nursing practice in relation to professional practice standards and guidelines, relevant statutes, rules, and regulations.

Standard 10. Collegiality
The legal nurse consultant interacts with and contributes to the professional development of peers and colleagues.

Figure 20.2 *Legal Nurse Consulting Standards of Practice and Performance. Reprinted with permission from the American Association of Legal Nurse Consultants.*

Standard 11. Collaboration
The legal nurse consultant collaborates with clients and others in the conduct of legal nurse consulting practice.

Standard 12. Ethics
The legal nurse consultant integrates ethical provisions in all areas of practice.

Standard 13. Research
The legal nurse consultant integrates research findings into practice.

Standard 14. Resource Utilization
The legal nurse consultant considers factors related to safety, effectiveness, cost, and impact on practice in the planning and evaluation of the health case or claim.

Standard 15. Leadership
The legal nurse consultant provides leadership in the professional practice setting and the profession.

Figure 20.2 Legal Nurse Consulting Standards of Practice and Performance (continued)

The most common activities attributed to the role of the paralegal were:

1. Obtain medical records
2. Identify costs causally related to the accident
3. Organize medical records
4. Summarize medical records
5. Identify missing records

Paralegals were more easily able to identify functions of their own profession than they were able to define the role of the legal nurse consultant, and vice versa. Experienced paralegals and the attorneys identified more functions of the legal nurse consultant than did less experienced paralegals. One of the conclusions of this data was that rather than being in competition with each other, legal nurse consultants and paralegals perform important functions that complement each other. For example, analysis of key medical issues by a legal nurse consultant cannot occur without the appropriate retrieval and organization of medical records by a paralegal. The identification of costs associated with an injury can be competently performed by a paralegal, allowing the legal nurse consultant to use medical expertise to focus on the clinical issues in the case.[7]

20.4 Qualifications

The qualifications and competence of the LNC must be appropriate to the attorney's needs. The significant qualifications are described below.

A. Education

Each LNC must have a current nursing license as a registered nurse. Licensed practical nurses are not considered to have the requisite educational background to provide consulting services in this role. A minimum of a bachelor's degree in nursing science (BSN) or in the arts (BA) is preferred.

B. Clinical Experience

At a minimum, the attorney should expect the LNC to have five years of clinical experience in any field of nursing. The longer a nurse has been clinically active, the more knowledge and experience the nurse will bring to the evaluation of the attorney's cases. Each year of clinical service results in a vast wealth of knowledge.

C. Preparation

There are many routes for a nurse to travel to achieve the goal of becoming an LNC. Some nurses are introduced to the LNC role through attendance at a seminar offered by one of several nurse entrepreneurs who teach the basic skills of legal nurse consulting. Others take an extensive certificate program, such as those offered by colleges. Self-learning through texts and other resources is another way to gain basic knowledge of the field. On-the-job training is how many LNCs acquire the skills to be effective in this role. AALNC's online legal nurse consulting course is another valuable option for entry into practice.

D. Business Structure

The independent legal nurse consultant may practice within the framework of a sole proprietorship, partnership, or become incorporated. As the LNC's business grows, a common growth pattern is to add secretarial support first, then become affiliated with a partner or nurses who will serve as subcontractors to the LNC. These subcontractor nurses will ordinarily perform legal nurse consulting services for the LNC on a per project basis. As the business expands, the LNC may add nurses as part-time or full-time employees and will then be responsible for paying salaries, benefits, and taxes for these assistants. A few LNCs will go on to open offices in other geographical areas to expand their business. The independent LNC may provide behind-the-scenes consulting assistance only or may also serve as an expert witness.

E. Certification

Certification in a specialty area of nursing is definitely a plus. Certification validates competency in a specialty area and is independent of the state licensure. Certification has emerged as the recognized and accepted method for identifying those who have attained advanced knowledge, experience, and expertise in a specialty area.[8] As acknowledgment of the mastery of a body of knowledge and skills related to a nursing specialty area, certification provides a level of recognition well beyond the minimal competency level required by the state licensure.

TIP: Only by identifying the standards and understanding the quality criteria utilized by each certifying organization and its respective certification program, can the true value of its certification be established.[9]

The American Association of Legal Nurse Consultants' certification program is the only one approved by the American Board for Specialty Nursing Certification (formerly the American Board of Nursing Specialties). Attorneys may be familiar with the American Board of Medical Specialties, the entity involved in board certification for physicians. ABSNC is the nursing equivalent of the American Board of Medical Specialties. ABSNC is the only accrediting body specifically dedicated to nursing certification. It has 19 rigorous standards that must be met for a certification program to be recognized by ABSNC. The LNCC certification program has met these rigorous criteria and is available only to LNCs with experience in the field, making it similar to other nursing specialty certifications. To be eligible to take the examination, candidates must have the following at the time of the application:

- a current, unrestricted registered nurse's license in the United States or its territories;
- a minimum of five years of experience practicing as a registered nurse; and
- evidence of 2,000 hours of legal nurse consulting experience in a staff, administrative, teaching, or private practice setting within the last three years.

The certification designation granted after passing a comprehensive exam is LNCC (Legal Nurse Consultant Certified). The LNC's achievement of certification by taking a competitive examination developed by the AALNC assures the attorney that the LNC has mastered a body of knowledge and developed consulting skills through extensive experience. LNCs who have achieved the distinction of earning the LNCC are board-certified. Recertification is required every five years. It is granted if the LNC has an active license, provided 2,000 hours of legal nurse consulting in the previous five years, and has evidence of 60 hours of continuing education that meets specific criteria. The LNCC also has the option of taking the examination again.

The LNCC certification serves to assure the client/patient population, attorneys, other health professionals and the general public of the LNCC's advanced knowledge, skills, and practice experience. Entry-level certifications offered by private companies lack the validation of experience and expertise.[10]

TIP: If an LNC presents herself as being certified as a legal nurse consultant, ask more details about the nature of the certification and the criteria that must be fulfilled to take the certification exam. Ask if the nurse needed a certain level of experience as an LNC before being able to sit for the examination. Inquire as to the organization that provided the certification. See Figure 20.3 for a comparison between certification and a certificate in legal nurse consulting.

F. Communication Skills

The LNC needs to possess good written and oral communication skills, and should be an active listener. Good communication skills are important when working with the attorney or the client, or talking with the various physicians, nurses, scientific or healthcare provider experts, and defendants. Nursing malpractice cases are complex. Consequently, the LNC must be able to teach the attorney this scientific and medical information so that the attorney can use it to review, litigate, settle, or defend a case. It is imperative the LNC be able to put complex, confusing information into words that are easily understood by the lay person. The LNC should

American Legal Nurse Consultant
Certification Board

Certification vs. Certificate

People often ask, "What is the difference between certification and a certificate?" To assist you in communicating with your colleagues and clients and to help avoid confusion in the marketplace, we have provided you the comparison below.

By setting and enforcing standards for certification, the American Board of Nursing Specialties (ABNS) seeks to protect the public and consumers through their mission to provide assurance to the public that the nurse holding the credential from an accredited certification program possesses the knowledge, skills and competency for quality practice in the specialty. In compliance with ABNS standards and requirements, the American Legal Nurse Consultant Certification Board (ALNCCB) certifies legal nurse consultant professionals through the Legal Nurse Consultant Certified (LNCC) program. Unlike many certificate programs being offered by colleges and private educational providers, the LNCC program is practice-based. It is not intended to teach individuals how to become legal nurse consultants. Rather, it is designed to measure an individual's "knowledge-in-use" – the application of knowledge and skills by those with real-life experience in this role.

Certification	Certificate
Results from an assessment process that recognizes an individual's knowledge, skills and competency in a particular specialty	Results from an educational process
Typically requires professional experience	For newcomers and experienced professionals
Awarded by a third-party, standard-setting organization, typically not for profit	Awarded by educational programs or institutions often for-profit
Indicates mastery/competency as measured against a defensible set of standards, usually by application or exam	Indicates completion of a course or series of courses with a specific focus (different than a degree granting program)
Standards set through a defensible, industry-wide process (job analysis/role delineation) that results in an outline of required knowledge and skills	Course content determined by the specific provider or institution, not standardized
Typically results in credentials to be listed after one's name (LNCC, ONC, CCRN)	Usually listed on a résumé detailing education
Has on-going requirements in order to maintain; holder must demonstrate he/she continues to meet requirements	Demonstrates knowledge of course content at the end of a set period in time

Certification generally refers to an earned credential that demonstrates the holder's specialized knowledge, skills, and experience.

Certification differs from a certificate program, which is usually an educational offering that confers a document at the program's conclusion.

Accreditation of a certification involves a voluntary, self-regulatory process. Accreditation is granted when stated quality criteria are met.

LNCC is the only legal nurse consulting credential recognized by AALNC and accredited by ABNS.

Figure 20.3 Certificate versus Certification, reprinted with permission of the American Legal Nurse Consultant Certification Board (ALNCCB)

possess the skills to accurately proofread various documents and be able to amend documents without modifying the specific content.

G. Organizational Skills

The ability to take complex information and organize it in a logical fashion is one of the most important skills the LNC brings to the legal arena. Nurses working in the clinical setting typically take an assignment consisting of a group of patients with diverse needs, and transform that group of patients into an organized workday. Rarely can a nurse complete a task without being interrupted. Organizational skills assist the LNC when sorting through and organizing medical records, developing case strategies, suggesting which expert witnesses to retain in what order, and managing the volume of paper generated by a lawsuit. In many nursing malpractice cases the records tend to be voluminous and repetitive. The LNC should possess the skills needed to organize this material into a format which makes it easier to review.

The same organizational skills are used to meet deadlines. Clinical nurses have been drilled in the importance of completing their assignment before the end of the shift. They tend to carry over the same emphasis on task completion when they provide legal nurse consulting. This way of thinking is of infinite value when the attorney is racing to meet deadlines imposed by the courts or statute of limitations.

H. Resourcefulness

The resourcefulness with which nurses approach patient care is easily converted into the skills required by the LNC, such as ferreting out medical information, developing exhibits, and suggesting case strategies. Nurses possess persistence when searching for specific circumstances or details, yet also are flexible.

I. Ability to Work with Difficult People

Rarely can nurses choose to not care for a difficult patient. They may develop a plan of care to deal with the angry, manipulative, or withdrawn patient. Attorneys experiencing the pressures of practicing law, taking depositions, preparing for trial, or settlement conferences can experience stress that manifests itself in a variety of ways. The LNC is often a helpful support person in these circumstances. LNCs have to be able to work with a range of personalities, some of whom are challenging, and some who flare under tight deadlines and stress. Not every nurse has the ability to be an LNC. The special communication skills, detective-like thinking, detail-oriented behavior, and ability to teach and research are not universally present in all nurses.

J. Research Skills

Strong Internet search skills are a must including those needed for medical literature searches, obtaining hard copies of journal articles and medical textbooks, locating current contact information for medical providers and doing background checks of defendant physicians and opposing counsel's experts.[11]

TIP: Conducting medical literature searches is somewhat of an art—the more time you spend doing it the more proficient you become.[12]

20.5 Roles of the LNC

There is a strong parallel between the roles that are filled by the nurse in the clinical role and the legal nurse consultant. The clinical nurse is an educator, a skilled communicator, and a person who juggles several simultaneous responsibilities. The clinical nurse is also analytical and makes decisions based on experience, intuition, and clinical judgment. Nurses frequently act as detectives, monitoring and assessing their patients, investigating, scrutinizing, and recognizing subtle changes in the patient's condition. The vast majority of the malpractice cases cited in this text which resulted in injury to the patient occurred because of the failure to carry out these critical skills.

The LNC is first and foremost a nurse. The LNC holds a primary allegiance to nursing, and a professional practice that emphasizes the contributions of a nurse to the legal arena. Most LNCs find that their nursing skills such as teaching, communicating, and analyzing are readily appreciated and valued by attorneys and others involved in the claims management process. The LNC looks for evidence of negligence and assesses each case for merit utilizing investigatory and detective skills. The following section discusses how each role of the LNC is important in litigation.

A. Educator

The skills of the LNC will assist the attorney in evaluating the strengths and weaknesses of each case. Many firms ask the LNC to provide medical education to the associates to assist them in better management of files. The LNC can provide instruction on how nurses and others in the healthcare facility function as well as case specific information. For example, the attorney should use the LNC to learn how to correctly pronounce medical terms, or to interpret The Joint Commission (TJC) standards or professional nursing organization's regulations. The LNC will educate the attorney and the attorney's associates regarding the medical facts and issues relevant to the case. In addition, the LNC can teach attorneys how to recognize the claims that have obvious merit and how to use the LNC to screen the more difficult nursing malpractice cases.

TIP: The basic role of the LNC is to be an educator and teacher to the attorney regarding the medical facts and issues relevant to a particular nursing malpractice case.

B. Analyst

While the paralegal and a law clerk can successfully compile a medical chronology, it takes an LNC to analyze the nuances and identify the inconsistencies and specifics of the health care provided in order to ascertain if the care was or was not appropriate. The LNC will not only be able to define when an untoward event occurred, but will be able to explain why it occurred. An LNC can identify the risk factors that contributed to an incident, such as a fall or the development of an adverse reaction to medication. See Appendix 20.1 for an example of this type of analysis. This knowledge is gained only through working within the healthcare system, and from past experiences and situations. What sets the LNC apart from non-health professionals used to review, summarize, and prepare a chronology of a medical record, is that a nurse can analyze and interpret what is documented in the record. The non-nurse can only regurgitate what has been written. The LNC can spot the inconsistencies and missing records because of the LNC's familiarity with medical records and facts. Often what is not contained within the medical record is extremely important in a nursing malpractice case. The LNC should assist the attorney in spotting concealment of information, rewriting of the record, and destruction of documents. Chapter 7, *Nursing Documentation,* provides additional information on this subject.

TIP: It is efficient to place all medical records in three-ring binders, separating each hospital visit and outpatient records with appropriate tabs. Various specific sections of a hospitalization can also be separated by the use of tabs. This system is a replication of the system employed by hospitals. These records will then be reviewed, summarized, analyzed, and interpreted.

When the medical records have been obtained, the LNC will assemble and organize the medical records in an efficient manner. Clifford[13] provides some suggestions for organizing voluminous medical records:

1. The LNC should begin by determining what records have been received. Create a list of records.
2. Determine if the records were certified.
3. Determine if the attorney has a preference for organization.
4. Avoid reading the records for content until they are organized.
5. Physically organize the records in chronological order by year, month and dates.

Refer to Iyer and Barone[14] for additional suggestions on obtaining and organizing medical records.

The LNC will readily spot the incomplete record that looks complete to someone without a medical background. Alterations or tampering with the medical records may be detected at this stage. Refer to Konray and Iyer[15] for more information. The LNC is usually skilled at identifying the sequence of events that may seem out of order.

LNCs are frequently used to help an attorney with a medical malpractice claim. The LNC's medical knowledge permits an analysis of liability, damages, and causation. This is a particularly important role for a plaintiff's attorney who has to make decisions about the viability of a claim. During the process of analyzing the medical records, the LNC searches for specific medical-legal concerns such as deviations from the standards of care by the nurse and other healthcare providers. All pertinent information will be abstracted from the medical records. The LNC will analyze the physician's, nurse's, or unlicensed assistive personnel's responsibilities in their care and treatment of the patient. The LNC will be able to reconstruct a series of events to determine what should have been done for the patient. The LNC will then render an opinion regarding the liability issues and negligence in reference to the claims and damages. The LNC will use some or all of the following resources to render this opinion:

- experience,
- education,
- research of previous cases,
- the Nurse Practice Act,
- written national standards,
- a current review of the medical literature,
- TJC regulations,
- nursing specialty or professional organization guidelines,
- state regulations, and
- facility policies and procedures.

The opinions of the consulting LNC may be discoverable if that individual is functioning in the role of expert witness, but are protected by the work product doctrine if the LNC is serving as a consultant.

Throughout the entire review process, the LNC will look for conflicts among the various caregivers such as areas where the nurse's documentation states one thing and the physician's states another. A simple example of this is a case in which a patient hospitalized for an elective prostatectomy experienced a heart attack. The LNC noted that on the day of the event, the nurse documented that the patient had been experiencing increasing episodes of chest pain, but the physician documented that the patient had no complaints and there was no change in clinical status. The LNC would analyze the record and provide information on the nurse's responsibilities for informing the physician of the complaints of chest pain.

The LNC working on the defense side (as either an employee of the insurance company, defense law firm, or independent legal nurse consultant) is usually not involved in a case until the complaint is filed. Sometimes the claims adjuster and defense counsel become aware of a case through the risk manager before receiving a complaint and bring the LNC into the case at that point.

Examples of the types of incidents (all real examples) that may result in an internal investigation with the participation of the LNC include:

• the hospitalized patient who was alert, oriented, and ambulatory until the nurse administered an inappropriate dose of Morphine, resulting in a serious overdose;

• the emergency department patient who developed quadriplegia after the nurse removed the cervical collar without an order and without the spine being cleared;

• the unsupervised nursing home resident on a pureed diet who choked on deli meat he grabbed off another resident's tray;

• the newborn infant delivered by vacuum extraction who experienced signs of respiratory distress that went unnoted by the nursery staff until the infant experienced a respiratory arrest and expired due to complications from a subgaleal hemorrhage;

• the critical care sitter who sexually assaulted a patient;

• the intubated patient who pulled out his endotracheal tube because the nurse did not restrain his hands:

• the paraplegic receiving supplemental nutrition via a nasogastric feeding tube who experienced an aspiration event and died because the RN programmed the feeding pump incorrectly, resulting in the infusion of an excessive amount of feeding over a short period of time;

• the unsupervised emergency department psychiatric patient who jumped off the roof of the hospital while waiting to be admitted to a psychiatric unit;

• the medical surgical patient who rolled off the bed while the sheets were being changed because the nurse did not put the side rail up;

• the trauma patient who developed compartment syndrome and nerve damage because the nurses did not perform neurovascular checks;

• the oncology patient who suffered from a large extravasation of a chemotherapeutic drug;

• the patient who fell off the operating room table because the nurse did not apply safety straps;

• the postoperative patient who developed a wound infection from poor dressing changing techniques of the nurses;

• the man who jumped through a window because the nurse did not recognize the need to start one to one supervision;

• the surgical patient diagnosed with a retained sponge despite the "correct" sponge count;

• the nursing home patient scalded in a bathtub;

• the psychiatric patient who had a history of suicidal ideation and attempts, who was unmonitored, left the hospital, and hung himself in the nearby woods;

• the pediatric patient who went into respiratory distress and whose home care nurse asked his father to come home instead of following directions to call 911;

• the surgical patient who fractured a hip after being dropped by a nursing assistant, who did not report the incident; and

• the postoperative patient who experienced intra-abdominal hemorrhage and subsequent shock that went undetected by the Post Anesthesia Care Unit nurse.

In any of the above situations, which healthcare personnel sometimes refer to as "train wrecks," the legal nurse consultant may be assisting the defense team in the initial claims investigation.

The LNC can help develop pleadings, requests for production, interrogatories tailored to the case, the complaint and jury demand for the plaintiff, and demand letters outlining specific claims and injuries. For the defense, the LNC can review these pleadings to delineate and evaluate the medical issues and the specific claims being presented or made. The LNC also prepares expert witness affidavits for the expert to review as required by state law.

August 2, 2010

Mr. Jones
100 Jefferson Street
Mid America, USA

Re: SC v. ABC Health Center et al.

Dear Mr. Jones:

A review and analysis of medical records related to the above named case revealed that Ms. SC was admitted on 10/8/09, and underwent a right total knee replacement on that same date. Documentation reflects that Ms. SC suffered a hypotensive event late on the night of the first post-op day, 10/9/09. She was evaluated by the house physician several hours later, and subsequently transferred to the Intensive Care Unit (ICU).

Multiple specialists were called into consult for evaluation and treatment of:
• Possible myocardial infarction (MI)
• Acute renal failure (ARF)
• Acute respiratory insufficiency (ARI)
• Shock liver and ensuing toxic encephalopathy (manifested by confusion and delirium).

This multi-system failure resolved with treatment over the next five days. Ms. SC transferred to telemetry on 10/15/09, from there to a regular orthopedic floor on 10/19/09, and was ultimately discharged to rehab on 10/28/09. By the date of discharge all specialists had documented resolution of the above named conditions, with no need for further specific medical diagnostic testing and/or care.

The discharge summary did not state any definitive etiology for the hypotensive event. Most significantly, the patient had a preoperative Persantine Stress Test (10/01/09) that demonstrated an ejection fraction of 69%. A postoperative cardiac catheterization (10/24/09) revealed an ejection fraction of 55%. Simply stated, ejection fraction is the percentage of blood ejected from the left ventricle with each heartbeat. According to Cecil Textbook of Medicine (22nd Edition, 2004), a normal ejection fraction ranges from 55-70%.

There is no evidence that the event itself was precipitated by any deviation from the standard of care. Rather, nursing documentation demonstrated a failure to assess and address an acute hypotensive episode in a timely fashion, resulting in delayed treatment. If the delayed treatment had resulted in measurable damages, one could consider this case meritorious. However, the fact that all complications were self-limiting, and the post-event ejection fraction – albeit lower than the preoperative measurement – remained within the normal range, suggests insufficient damages.

Thank you for retaining my services to assist in the evaluation of this most interesting case. Feel free to call with any additional questions you may have.

Sincerely,
Barbara A. Boschert RN, BSN
Legal Nurse Consultant

Figure 20.4 *Screening for merit (courtesy of Barbara Boschert, Myriad Medical Legal Consulting, Inc, St. Louis, MO)*

The LNC involved in personal injury or workers' compensation cases focuses on establishing a chronology of care, searches for evidence of pre-existing injuries, and determines if damages (medical and financial) are plausibly related to the accident.

C. Preparer of Reports

The most frequently used reports generated by the LNC include those listed below.

1. Merit determination report

A merit determination report is the initial review and report that assists the plaintiff's attorney in eliminating non-meritorious cases by highlighting pertinent issues, potential defendants, and the specific departures from the standards of care. It may also supply the research necessary to understand case issues, and identify the type of potential testifying experts needed. The insurance carrier may request the report to analyze liability if there is concern on the part of an insured that a claim may be filed after an incident involving high liability or large damages. Refer to Figure 20.4 and Appendix 20.2.

2. Case summary

A case summary defines the theories and case issues; provides a detailed review of the care rendered; defines medical terms; summarizes the medical literature; lists discrepancies in charting and deviations from the standards of care; addresses causation, pain and suffering and damages; and discusses prognosis. This is useful for identifying the key information and refreshing the attorney's memory about the facts of the case when work on the file progresses over a number of years. See Appendix 20.3.

3. Chronology

A chronology of the most important dates, times, and facts assists with interviewing defendants or fact witnesses, in preparation for depositions or trials, and as exhibits for trial. The chronology may be customized based on the case facts and the purpose of its preparation. For example, is the purpose of the chronology to:

- focus on precise timing of events?
- correlate several factors?
- define deviations from the standards of care related to events?
- compare the observations of different providers?
- contrast deposition testimony with the events recorded in the medical record?

- create a chronological description of symptoms and treatment?[16]

Suggestions for evaluating the quality of the chronology prepared by the LNC are shown in Figure 20.5.

4. Timelines and calendars

Timelines and calendars present key pieces of information. Timelines are useful for understanding relationships between events and providing a quick reference for locating dates and events. There are many possible ways to extract information from records to create a timeline. The LNC may use one, two, three or more columns to present key elements.[17] A variety of software programs may be used to create them, including Time Map (Figure 20.6), PowerPoint (Figure 20.7), Adobe Illustrator (Figure 20.8), as well as other programs.

5. Demand letters

The LNC assisting the plaintiff's attorney may facilitate the preparation of the demand letter by comprehending the medical issues of the case from the outset. The LNC may be involved in gathering the medical records, contacting the patient for monthly updates, and reviewing the records to confirm the patient is following instructions and that the treaters' records are consistent with the patient's story. The LNC will note if the primary care physician is seeing the patient in conjunction with physical therapists or chiropractors. The LNC may meet with the treating physician, along with the attorney, to discuss preparation of a written report that comments on damages, proximate cause, and prognosis. The LNC may be asked to assemble medical records for the treating physician to review to obtain a picture of the entire treatment history. The LNC may research various aspects of the injuries, using peer-reviewed medical literature, to explain uncommon injuries. Additionally, the LNC may interview the client to identify all activities that were impaired as a result of an incident.[18] See Figure 20.9. The liability aspects of this case are described in Appendix 20.2.

The LNC assisting the defense attorney would review the demand letter for accuracy, correlating the claims with the information found in the medical record.

6. Expert witness reports

Nursing expert witnesses constitute a subset of legal nurse consultants. Figure 20.10 presents a report written by a nursing expert. Additional examples of expert reports are located in Chapter 21, *Working with Nursing Expert Witnesses,* in this volume and Chapter 5, *Perioperative Nursing Malpractice Issues,* in Volume II.

The top 13 ways to evaluate the quality of a chronology

- Did the chronology address the important issues in the case? Is the information useful?
- Are Bates stamped pages referenced (if pages are numbered)?
- Is the font easy to read? Times New Roman or Arial are two fonts that are commonly used and easy to read.
- Is there a header at the top of the page?
- Are the providers identified?
- Are the dates consistently formatted? For example, the chronology should either use numbers, such as 1/25/10 or words, such as January 25, 2010 but not both formats within the same document.
- Is the time consistently formatted? Many people find military time confusing and prefer that military time be translated into A.M. and P.M. for ease of understanding.
- Are entries written in complete sentences?
- Are medical abbreviations spelled out the first time they are used? For example, the sentence may say, "The physician ordered MTX (Methotrexate) 2.5 mg six per day."
- When there is an extensive amount of abbreviations used in a chronology or medical summary, is there an appendix of all of the abbreviations in alphabetical order for use by the reader?
- If a word cannot be deciphered, does the chronology indicate this by using ___ or ??? (cannot decipher)?
- Has the document been thoroughly proofread? Look for errors in dates, in referring to the sex of the patient, and for words that the spell checker will gloss over because they are correctly spelled but wrong within the context of the sentence.
- Are extras included, such as photographs of providers, diagrams of anatomy, information on medications, and pertinent charts?

Modified from Iyer, P. *Medication Errors Toolkit,* www.medleague.com and Parker Jones, M. "Strategies for an effective medical chronology," *Journal of Legal Nurse Consulting,* Summer 2008, 7-20.

Figure 20.5

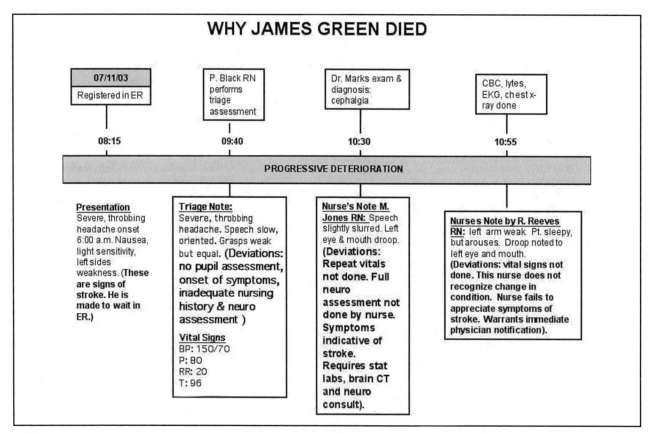

Figure 20.6 Timeline of Emergency Department Case Created in Time Map, courtesy of Jo Ann Kuc BSN, RN, LNCC

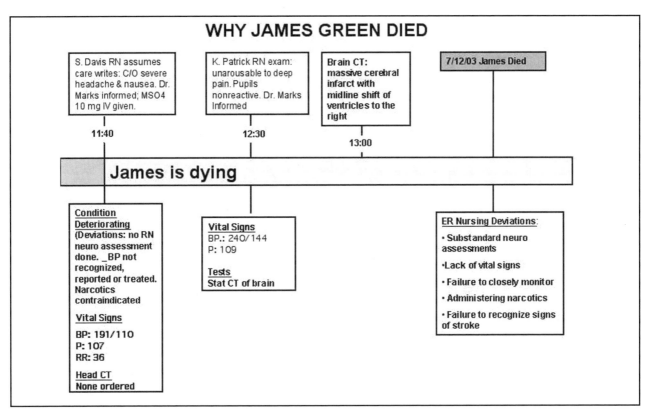

Figure 20.6 *Timeline of Emergency Department Case Created in Time Map, courtesy of Jo Ann Kuc BSN, RN, LNCC (continued)*

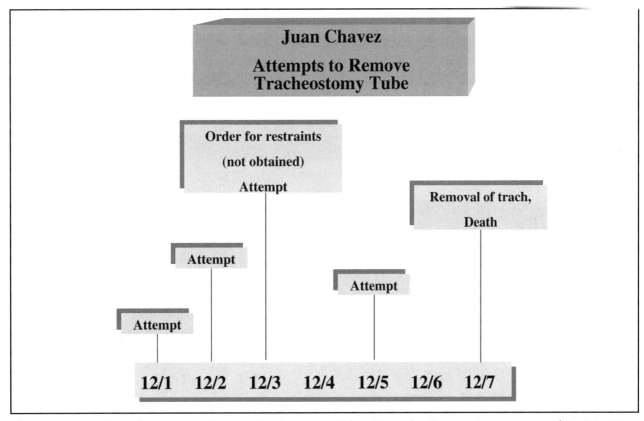

Figure 20.7 *Timeline of Attempts to Remove Tracheostomy Tube. Created in Powerpoint, courtesy of Patricia W. Iyer, MSN, RN, LNCC*

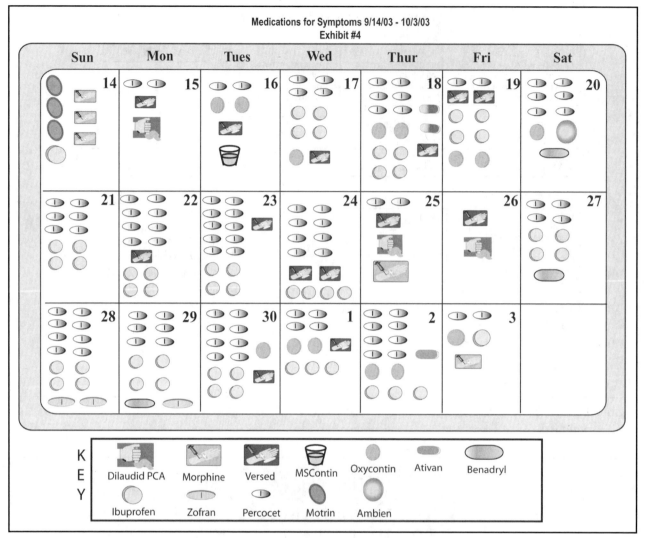

Figure 20.8 *Timeline of Medications Needed for Pain Created in Adobe Illustrator, courtesy of Patricia W. Iyer, MSN, RN, LNCC*

Pain and Suffering

David's family and close friends describe multiple conversations with David in the months before his death where he verbalized his fear that something was seriously wrong with him. In a phone conversation, David told his sister Jane "something is wrong, something just doesn't seem right." She recalls David describing numbness and tingling on one side of his face in between the two visits in question. He verbalized his fear and impending sense that something bad was going to happen.

Jane recalls talking with David after the 10/29/09 visit to Ms. Brown. She describes David saying that Ms. Brown told that he had some kind of anxiety simply because he had told her that sometimes he gets nervous in class. He was upset and frustrated with Dr. Schwartz's office and in pain. Jane told him not to take the Paxil and David said he wanted to take it if it would help his pain. He was willing to take anything that might somehow alleviate the pain he was in.

When Jane told David that Paxil takes weeks to have any effect at all and that it would not help his pain, David was very upset and frustrated. Jane feels David knew there was something wrong and no one would take him seriously. He was seeking help from his doctor for pain that was being minimized as a "symptom" of other problems like a neck strain that occurred eight years earlier and anxiety.

David was confused, doubting himself in terms of whether the symptoms he considered serious were of any consequence at all. Further, this intelligent young man who was trying so hard to succeed in his life after many setbacks, was wondering whether the pain and photophobia that was making it so difficult for him to attend classes, were "all in his head."

David told Jane in this conversation that at the end of his office visit with Ms. Brown, she came up behind him and rested her hand on his shoulder and said, "Ya know, Dave, it takes a really big person to admit when they have a problem." Even if David had an anxiety disorder—which is doubtful at best—he still had severe pain and serious symptomology that was plainly unrelated to "anxiety." From a pain and suffering standpoint, there was no reason at all that these extremely painful and debilitating symptoms could not have been further addressed, investigated and adequately treated at the same time as the Paxil was reaching its therapeutic level. Photophobia, intensely painful headaches, nausea and nuchal rigidity warrant more attention, merely from the pain and suffering standpoint, than a hand on the shoulder and a bottle of Paxil.

David's mother Carol James, spoke with David shortly before the 10/29/09 visit to Dr. Schwartz's office. David said, "Mom, I am in so much pain. I'm dying, Mom. I'm dying." David was in severe pain. He felt he was dying and he was right. Carol told David he had to go back to the doctor immediately and tell them how severe these headaches were. David did return as his mother urged him to. He was ignored.

David's close personal friend, Dr. Brian Regan DC, vividly recalls David describing the intensity of his headaches. Brian expressed to David the importance of seeking medical attention, as there was a chance that something was seriously wrong. He vividly recalls David talking to him after the 10/29/09 visit with Ms. Brown. David said that he was told his headaches were due to anxiety and essentially, "all in his head." David expressed to Brian that he feared he was dying and that he did not expect to live past his 30th birthday.

Figure 20.9 Portion of a demand letter that focuses on pain and suffering, courtesy of Ann Steinmetz, Rochester, NY

Re: *Est. of John R. Smith Jr. et al. v. Community Hospital et al.*

Dear Ms. Murphy,

I have reviewed the following materials in relation to the above captioned matter:
* Records from Community Hospital for the admissions of May 5, 2001, April 23, 2001, March 11, 2001 and February 22, 2001;
* Autopsy report dated May 7, 2001;
* Defendant's response to request for production of documents, dated April 5, 2004;
* Plaintiff's answers to interrogatories;
* Defendant's answers to interrogatories;
* Deposition transcript of Dr. R. dated May 2, 2005;
* Deposition transcript Dr. R., dated November 4, 2005;
* Notes of Nurse W.;

* Deposition transcript of PD, dated August 25, 2004;
* Deposition transcript of John Smith Sr., dated July 26, 2005;
* Deposition transcript of WS, dated July 26, 2005;
* Deposition transcript of JP, dated July 26, 2005;
* Deposition transcript of Dr. B., dated November 30, 2005;
* Deposition transcript of JM, dated November 16, 2005.

Brief Summary of Medical Record

John Smith was admitted to Community Hospital via the emergency room on 5/6/01 with complaints of back and chest pain and was admitted to the medical floor with the diagnosis of neutropenic fever. Past medical history was significant for acute myelocytic leukemia. Mr. Smith had recently (April 23–April 27) completed consolation chemotherapy with ARA-C, Idarubicin, and Altrans retinoic acid. He was treated in the emergency room with Vancomycin and Ceftazidime and narcotic analgesics for pain management. At approximately 3 P.M. he was transferred to a medical floor (3C). Mr. Smith became unresponsive and developed respiratory failure and cardiac arrhythmias. He was intubated, placed on mechanical ventilation and transferred to the intensive care unit. His condition continued to deteriorate and he suffered a cardiac arrest. He was pronounced dead at 12:20 A.M. Final cause of death as per autopsy report was septic shock.

Analysis and opinion

I have been asked to review the care rendered by the nursing staff at Community Hospital. My analysis is based on my knowledge of the scope of nursing practice, accepted professional standards regarding patient assessment and monitoring, and over 20 years of clinical experience in the care of the critically ill patient.

After careful analysis I am of the opinion that the nursing staff delivered care that deviated from the accepted standards of care, specifically while Mr. Smith was a patient on unit 3C.

* **The nursing staff failed to properly assess and monitor a patient who was hemodynamically compromised as evidenced by the limited nursing data in the medical record.**

The standard of nursing care as defined by the American Nurses Association requires the nurse to collect data about the health status of the patient. The collection should be systematic and continuous. The purpose is to determine the immediate health care problems and develop a nursing diagnosis. The initial nursing assessment was performed at 3 P.M. There was no continued assessment of pain, mental status, blood pressure, heart rate, or respiratory rate. There was no record of interventions or notification of physicians. The only nursing

Figure 20.10 Expert witness report (courtesy of Cheryl Gatti, Lark and Gatti, Watchung, NJ)

documentation of his continued decompensation is in the nursing transfer summary.

The initial (and only) assessment performed at 3 P.M. by PK contained the following data. Blood pressure was 140/78 (after receiving 2 liters of fluid in the emergency room), heart rate 108, and respiratory rate 24. Mr. Smith is described as pale and shocky (or shaky). The pain assessment was negative, however he continued to be medicated for pain. The Pain Assessment Sheet was not initiated as required. He presented with dizziness, chest pain, shortness of breath, palpitations and diaphoresis. All these are clear cut signs of ineffective tissue perfusion. Ineffective tissue perfusion is a decrease in oxygen resulting in the failure to nourish the tissues at the capillary level.[1] This is a recognized nursing diagnosis that was not identified, and consistent with shock.

Mr. Smith remained in this critical state from 3 P.M. until he went into acute respiratory failure and was intubated ay 6:57 P.M. Most importantly, Mr. Smith is described as unresponsive from approximately 5 P.M. on. There is no documentation as to when or if the physician was notified of the significant changes in Mr. Smith's mental status as outlined in the nursing transfer summary (confusion to unresponsiveness). There was no documentation of his vital signs during that time. It is common nursing knowledge that continued oxygen depletion leads to organ failure

and ultimately death, and urgent intervention is required to prevent organ failure. This lack of nursing assessment and failure to recognize acute changes in the patient's condition clearly deviated from the standard of care.

- **The nursing staff continued to medicate for pain without regard to the effectiveness and effect on the circulatory and respiratory status of Mr. Smith.**

The patient with ineffective tissue perfusion is already compromised. Narcotic analgesics have the potential to cause respiratory depression and hypotension. Ativan, a benzodiazepine, has the potential to cause sedation, respiratory depression, hypotension and tachycardia. The probability to develop these side effects increases in a patient with compromised circulatory and respiratory function. Mr. Smith was placed at an even higher risk without proper monitoring.

The following medications were administered to Mr. Smith from his presentation In the emergency room to 5:15 P.M. on 5/5/01:

- 1045 – Morphine 4 mg IVP (intravenous push) for pain 10/10 (ER record)
- 1110 – Morphine 4 mg IVP for pain 8/10 (ER record)
- 1200 – Demerol 50 mg IVP for tremors/pain (ER record)
- 1305 – Morphine 4 mg IVP (ER record)
- 1500 – Morphine 1 mg IVP (Medication administration record)
- 1530 – Morphine 2 mg IVP (Medication administration record)
- 1630 – Ativan 1 mg IVP (Medication administration record)
- 1715 – Demerol 50 mg IVP (Medication administration record)

This was a significant amount of narcotic administered. It is interesting to note that in the initial nursing assessment, the pain level was rated as 0 (no pain). From 1500-1715 there was no assessment of response to the medication or as stated previously ongoing assessment of hemodynamic status (blood pressure, pulse rate). There is a lone blood pressure written on the nursing transfer summary (109/56). I have no idea what time that blood pressure was taken. Patricia Smith states there was a point where one of the nurses took his blood pressure and couldn't read it, another nurse tried to get it. It was really low. (PS dep. p.120). This was not documented in the medical record. Again, there was failure to properly monitor, and Mrs. Smith's testimony indicates that there was a low blood pressure issue that was not addressed by the nursing staff.

The nursing transfer summary stated Mr. Smith became unresponsive anywhere from 5-5:30. The medication

---

1. Nursing Diagnoses: Definition and Classification, NANDA International.

Figure 20.10 Expert witness report *(courtesy of Cheryl Gatti, Lark and Gatti, Watchung, NJ) (continued)*

administration record states Narcan was administered at 5:15 P.M., however the physician order was written at 6:15 P.M. There was no documentation of the response to the Narcan. Dr. K did not know how long Mr. Smith was unresponsive before he was intubated. She replied "no" when she was asked if there was anything in the medical record that shows how long he was responsive before somebody got to him (K dep. p.99). The progress notes document that Mr. Smith was intubated at 6:57. The data from the medical record, physician testimony and the wife's testimony, defines a time frame of approximately 1.5–2 hours when there was evidence of critical changes in Mr. Smith's mental status related to ineffective cerebral tissue perfusion. I reiterate my opinion that the nursing care deviated from accepted standards as detailed above. My opinions are given within a reasonable degree of nursing probability.

Thank you for the opportunity to assist you with this case. I reserve the right to amend my opinion should additional information become available.

Respectfully submitted,

Cheryl Gatti RN BSN CCRN LNCC

Figure 20.10 *Expert witness report (courtesy of Cheryl Gatti, Lark and Gatti, Watchung, NJ) (continued)*

There are a variety of styles of reports that the LNC generates as well as many graphs and timelines, all designed specifically for an individual case. The LNC uses creativity to design the most effective demonstration of case-specific information.

TIP: The main skill of the LNC is the ability to analyze complex information and present this information in a simple, professional manner.

D. Medical Resource Person

Years as a clinical nurse help the LNC become familiar with various policies and procedures as well as the standards of TJC and other regulatory agencies. This knowledge will be invaluable as the attorney proceeds through discovery and is searching for the documents relevant to the particular case. The skilled LNC educates the attorney in the nuances of each particular case. The LNC's clinical knowledge should help the attorney recognize an outcome related to negligence.

During the discovery phase, the LNC advises the attorney concerning the types of documents—such as medical records, incident reports, citations by the Department of Health, bills, x-rays, and so on—that the attorney should be requesting from the defendant healthcare facilities and other healthcare providers.

TIP: The LNC's knowledge of how the healthcare system works, which is just as intricate as the legal system, will provide the attorney with an inside edge.

Once discovery documents are ordered and received, the LNC will review these documents for completeness. The defense LNC assists the firm in responding to the requests for production. The LNC advises the attorney concerning the procurement of various policies and procedures, available standards, clinical protocols, and guidelines applicable to each case, whether requested by the plaintiff or not.

As the case develops, the LNC explores the various nursing, medical, federal, hospital, or other healthcare standards. The LNC obtains copies of these standards, and reviews and analyzes all relevant policies and procedures, looking for discrepancies or practice deviations. This information will be summarized or abstracted, and organized in a logical fashion.

E. Investigator

Third-party administrators are finding it beneficial to ask LNCs to conduct on-site investigations. Usually these requests occur after serious accidents or injuries have occurred at the facility and when these events are under the potential threat of a negligence suit. As investigators, LNCs are adept at navigating the inner workings of facilities, are able to extract pertinent medical record data and identify red flags, and can assist in the identification of information that will help defend various allegations. The LNC assists in interpreting the multi-layered, mandated federal and state regulations, as well as other universally accepted standards of care.

The LNC has the advantage of being able to "speak the same language" as the nursing staff. The LNC can provide an early assessment and evaluation of the facility staff as witnesses. Frequently the investigating LNC will have training in forensics, which can be helpful when evaluating safety issues such as falls, progressive infections, elopements, chart tampering, and abuse claims.

In a new trend, LNCs are frequently being hired by insurance underwriting departments to conduct on-site reviews or facility risk assessment of the potential risk exposures in the clinical care area. A facility risk assessment usually requires one or two days, and a written report of the final findings is sent to the underwriter or risk management department of the insurance company. This standard of care report provides objective insight and assistance in determining exposure before a problem develops. Refer to Appendix 20.4 for an example of an on-site evaluation of liability at issue in an assisted living facility.

F. Medical Expert

The LNC has comprehensive knowledge of human anatomy and physiology that far exceeds the knowledge of any lay person. The LNC is able to combine this comprehensive knowledge of anatomy and physiology and integrate this information into the specifics of the client's case. The LNC possesses knowledge of the local medical community totally unknown to anyone who has never worked in the healthcare field.

The LNC, as the attorney's medical expert, has the education, training, and experience, and possesses knowledge of a specialized nature beyond that of the normal lay person. Part of this process is demonstrated during the review of the case to determine if the damages claimed by the plaintiff could be proximately related to the actions or inactions of the nurse or physician. The medical knowledge possessed by the LNC permits the LNC to readily correlate claims and damages in obvious cases, and to perform the required research when the proximate cause is not quite as apparent.

TIP: Many unnecessary and expensive lawsuits can be avoided by using the clinical knowledge of the LNC. The meritorious versus non-meritorious claim can be identified early on before filing the complaint, thus saving the plaintiff's attorney much time, money, and effort. On the defense side, the skills of the LNC help defense counsel differentiate between the claims that should be settled and those that should be taken into the courtroom for trial.

The LNC can assist in the development of the theories of liability which will eventually be pleaded or help develop countervailing defense strategies. One of the primary roles of the LNC is to perform medical research regarding specific case subject areas and standards of care. The LNC will identify pertinent medical literature that the attorney should be familiar with pertaining to each issue. In analyzing the various medical research, the LNC searches for articles that

- define the standard of care,
- refute the position of the opposing expert witness, and
- support or refute the attorney's theories of the case.

This medical research is then organized and summarized in an appropriate manner. The summary will include the incorporation of the published medical research into the case analysis. If desired, each article can be abstracted. The LNC can also assist in recommending and obtaining appropriate medical texts, standards, and guidelines for the attorney's medical library.

G. Team Player

Appropriate use of the unique skills of the nurse can mean that the attorney ultimately prevails and excels in the litigation of the nursing malpractice case. Nurses are, by nature and practice, quite comfortable with the team approach. They have been working within interdisciplinary teams their entire careers. The LNC is part of the team that does the initial intake work on the file. When the plaintiff's attorney decides not to accept a malpractice case that the LNC has screened for merit, the LNC may attend the appointment with the clients to explain the medical rationale for turning the case down. Support during settlement conferences, arbitration, depositions, and trials is discussed below.

The LNC frequently functions as a liaison between the physician, attorney, and the client (either the hospital's risk management staff, plaintiff, defendant or insurance company's claims representatives) for responsibilities related to propounding or responding to interrogatory responses, requests for admission, and requests for production.

H. Strategist

The LNC can demonstrate great insight into the allegations, which can then assist the attorney in the development of legal theories and strategies. Anticipating the position of the other side helps the attorney prepare rebuttal. During the medical record review, the LNC identifies all key personnel. The LNC drafts medically related questions appropriate for each care provider. These questions can be employed informally when asking an expert's opinion, or during deposition or trial. The LNC can also advise the attorney on appropriate strategy to be used with the medical witnesses.

TIP: Early in the development of each case, include the LNC in discussions concerning the various strategies and legal theories. As the LNC becomes familiar with this process, he will begin to make insightful contributions.

I. Location and Facilitation of Communication with Expert Witnesses

LNCs often have a wide network established in the medical community. Thus, the LNC can be exceptionally helpful in identifying and locating all healthcare experts (medical, nursing, pharmaceutical, or dental) or other experts such as engineering experts. First, medical personnel readily communicate using medical terminology that may be foreign to an attorney. Second, the nurse will be able to explain the events of the case more accurately than a lay person will. The potential expert will often have specific questions about the events that occurred in the case. The LNC will have the ability to accurately answer these questions posed by the expert. Frequently, a potential expert will become disinterested in a case when the case facts are presented in a jumbled, incoherent manner or if the questions about the case are not able to be explained or answered. This means the attorney possibly has lost an excellent expert even before she was hired.

Once the LNC has contacted a potential expert, the LNC determines if there is any conflict of interest and will ascertain the expert's availability to serve as an expert on a specific case. If the expert has no conflict of interest and is available, the LNC provides the expert with a brief overview of the case facts. This overview allows the expert to determine if this case falls within the parameters of the expert's expertise and if the expert has continued interest in the case.

Once this has been specified, the LNC will request a copy of the expert's curriculum vitae. The curriculum vitae is passed on to the attorney client. The LNC may be asked to assist the attorney in the screening process of the expert, including reviewing the expert's qualifications and drafting pertinent questions to ask the expert. Ultimately, though, the decision to hire the expert is the responsibility of the attorney. During the entire course of the case, the LNC may act as a liaison between the testifying expert and attorney.

In some instances, once the expert has been identified and retained, the LNC may then be responsible for forwarding all medical records and other pertinent documentation to the expert. Chronological organization and tabbing of the medical records in the format that is familiar to all medical personnel is extremely helpful for the expert. The organization of records speeds the expert's review of the case and saves the firm money in expensive expert witness time.

After the expert has had a chance to review the medical records and form an opinion, the LNC may then contact or interview the expert to ascertain the expert's opinions of the case facts and relevant medical issues. The LNC can then prepare a summary of the medical expert's review and opinions for the file and review by the attorney, particularly if the attorney's state does not require the production of written expert witness reports. The LNC will maintain ongoing contact with the expert and assist in preparing the expert for the deposition and trial. The LNC also can be used to review the

Area of Nursing	Nursing Standard of Care	Care Provided		
		Yes	No	Partially
PACU	PARS assessment during PACU stay	☐	☐	☐
	Vital signs per protocol	☐	☐	☐
	Accurate documentation (Vital signs, Narcotic administration, Complete discharge assessment, Discharge note)	☐	☐	☐
Admission to 6N	Complete transfer assessment (Vital signs, Oxygenation, Neurological status, Pain)	☐	☐	☐
	Recognize abnormal findings (Sedation and lethargy; Responds sometimes, only with encouragement)	☐	☐	☐
	Responds to abnormal findings	☐	☐	☐
Duties of an Incoming Nurse	Prioritize patients for initial assessment (New post-operative patient admitted by LPN, Patient status less than optimal)	☐	☐	☐
	Assess patients based on prioritization	☐	☐	☐
CPR	Initiate immediately/Assistive breathing (Deposition testimony contradicts 15 minute lag time noted in records)	☐	☐	☐

Figure 20.11 Trial exhibit (Courtesy of Mindy Cohen, MSN, RN, LNCC of Mindy Cohen & Associates, Inc. Villanova, PA)

publications of the attorney's expert as well as the opposing expert to check for contradictions in the opinions expressed in this particular case. Refer to Chapter 21, *Working with Nursing Expert Witnesses,* for more on this subject.

J. Preparer of Demonstrative Evidence

The LNC can be instrumental in locating and preparing demonstrative evidence for deposition or trial. Demonstrative evidence plays an increasingly large role in trial. During a trial the courtroom becomes a classroom; thus the presentation of the facts of a case becomes an exercise in teaching and learning for the participants. In today's litigation environment, it is necessary to teach the jurors the science and mechanics of a particular subject before they can be expected to judge if the standard of care was violated. See Figure 20.11 for an example of a trial exhibit prepared by an LNC.

Effective demonstrative evidence starts with the proper presentation of all important aspects of the case that can be visually documented. This documentation or demonstrative evidence may include photographs, videotaping, scene diagrams, radiographic displays, anatomical models, custom medical illustrations or computer animations, a "blow-up" of specific aspects of the medical records, and chronologies or timelines. Demonstrative evidence need not be complicated. Legal nurse consultant Karen Haviland shared this story:

> I was doing a nursing home case and in the opening statement the attorney was trying to explain to the jury the size of this lady's wound which happened to be 15 by 8 centimeters. I drew a round circle that was about 15 by 8, on a little piece of paper. He folded it up, put it in his pocket and when he was describing the wound in his opening statement he opened up the piece of paper which looked quite large and then turned around and slapped it on the middle of his back. And you could see the size. That was much more effective than just saying to the jury, "You know, Ms. Smith had a 15 by 8 centimeter wound in her lower back." When he put that on his back you could see the white piece of paper and the size. It was effective and anyone can do something like that.[19]

Refer to Chapter 22, *Demonstrative Evidence,* for additional information on this topic.

K. Deposition Support Person

The LNC can play an instrumental role during pre-deposition conferences by assisting in the preparation of the expert and the client for their depositions. The LNC can help in predicting the questions posed by the opposing counsel, thus facilitating in the witness-client preparation process. The LNC can assist the attorney in interviewing the physician, nurse or other healthcare personnel who are fact witnesses or defendants. The LNC will be instrumental in the development of deposition questions in conjunction with strategy development (see Appendices 20.5 and 20.6). Before the deposition, the LNC can prepare the attorney by advising or suggesting specific questions and appropriate strategy to be used with each individual medical witness or expert.

TIP: Although the LNC is not permitted to ask questions of the witness during the deposition, the LNC may write questions on a pad for the attorney to consider, and confer with the attorney during a break to suggest an additional line of questioning. Through remote videoconferencing technology, the LNC may be able to monitor the deposition while off-site.

After the deposition is completed, the LNC and the attorney can meet with the client or expert witness to provide feedback on the deposition. Frequently, the LNC is in a better position to provide feedback than the attorney who has taken the deposition. The attorney is caught up in the deposition process while the nurse can be an observer of nonverbal communication and the dynamics of the witness's answering of questions. Once the transcript is received, the nurse can prepare a summary of the deposition transcript. During this summarizing process, the LNC will analyze the deposition for the purpose of identifying any medical fallacies, inconsistencies, and incompatible theories or statements.

L. Observer at the Independent/Insurance Medical Examination (IME)

The LNC assumes a few different types of roles with respect to IMEs. First, the independent LNC or in-house LNC may be involved in assembling medical records for the person performing the IME. The LNC may be asked to locate a physician who is qualified to perform the exam.

After scheduling the examination, the in-house LNC can make sure the examining physician receives a summary of the alleged injuries, all medical records, x-rays, or other necessary diagnostic tools prior to the examination.

Second, the independent LNC may be asked to observe the exam. While some attorneys send their secretary or paralegal to attend an IME as an observer, the LNC can provide a more comprehensive service including the observation and summary report. The plaintiff may be more comfortable with being assisted by a nurse rather than a non-medical person. Additionally, the LNC understands the elements of the physical assessment in a way that eludes the non-medical person. In fact, the LNC may have clinical experience performing most of the same tests that the physician will be using on the patient.

Client: John Smith (hereinafter referred to as JS)

Appointment Date:

Appointment Time:

Healthcare Provider: Dr. James Brown (hereinafter referred to as MD)

Location:

Witness: Barbara A. Boschert RN, BSN

1200: MD entered the room

MD: Tell me about the accident.

JS: I was admitted to a rehab facility after I fractured my hip. The nurse did not lock the wheels of my wheelchair, and I broke the other hip when I fell while trying to get into it.

MD: Did you have problems with your hip prior to the accident?

JS: No

Transcript would go on to read like this for all questions/answers. If you have specific recall of a statement, verbatim, put it in quotation marks. Otherwise, it is understood that this is a reflection of the essence of the conversation.

1:00: Physical exam began.

Tested range of motion (ROM) of hip: (appeared to be stiff and have some difficulty with these maneuvers, based on facial grimacing, body language, and grunting noises)

Flexion
Extension
Lateral bending
Rotation

Tested reflexes bilaterally:

Triceps
Patellar
Achilles
Babinski

Transcript would go on to describe all activities of the physical exam. The LNC should remain objective and concise with descriptions, i.e., "appeared to be stiff and have some difficulty," as opposed to stating, "maneuvers caused pain"—if the patient did not actually state he was having pain. Most often, the LNC will not be able to document actual responses/measurements, i.e., degree of ROM, intensity of reflex response, etc.

1:30: Exam ended. MD exited the room.

The LNC will record all events and the time they occur, i.e., each time the MD leaves the room, if the patient goes to x-ray, etc.

The LNC may be called into deposition, if there are discrepancies between the transcript and the report of the examining physician. The LNC must understand all the details in the report, even months/years later, as he or she will likely not have an independent recollection of the event.

Microsoft Word is the easiest program for formatting this report. The LNC may build a "table," then "hide" the "gridlines" on the finished product. The report looks clean, professional, and easy to read. Pages should be numbered.

The disclaimer further reinforces the fact that this is a reflection of the essence of the exam/conversation.

To the best of my ability, this is a record of the interview and exam that transpired on DATE during the Independent Medical Examination of Mr. NAME by Dr. NAME.

_____

Barbara A. Boschert RN, BSN

___/___/___
Date

Figure 20.12 *IME template, courtesy of Barbara Boschert BSN, RN*

ORTHOPEDIC
Independent Medical Exam

Doctor's Name:_____   **Specialty**:_____
Location of Exam:_____   **Phone**:
Date of Exam:_____

Patient's Name_____
Birth Date:_____ Sex: Male / Female   Height:_____ Weight:_____
_____   R/L Handed:_____

ARRIVED AT OFFICE: _____A.M./P.M.   EXAMINATION STARTED: _____A.M./P.M.

I. History of present condition:

1. Date of Accident:_____

2. Type of Accident: Workers' Compensation/Motor Vehicle/Other

3. Seat belted? Yes / No
A. Driver / Passenger? B. Front seat / Back Seat?

4. Description of accident:

_____

_____

5. Injuries: _____

_____

6. Loss of consciousness?   Yes/No How Long? _____

7. Taken to the emergency room?   Yes/No Where and When?

8. Admitted to the hospital?   Yes/No How Long?_____

9. Re-hospitalized for these injuries?   Yes/No
If so, where, when, and why?_____

Figure 20.13 *IME Template, courtesy of Karen Cebulko RN*

II.   Subjective complaints:

_____

_____

_____

III.   Interaction/Exam Technique

Gentle   Moderate   Forceful   Thorough

IV.   Physical Examination: Time started: _____ Time ended: _____

_____

_____

_____

Checked for the following:

Cervical Thoracic Region	Yes/No
Lumbar Sacral Region	Yes/No
Paresthesias Upper Extremities	Yes/No
Paresthesias Lower Extremities	Yes/No
Range of motion	Yes/No
Reflexes	Yes/No
Flexion	Yes/No
Extension	Yes/No
Gait	Yes/No
Leg Raising	Yes/No

V.   Presence of Medical Records and/or X-rays in Exam Room?   Yes/No

   Does Examiner Indicate Whether they were Reviewed?   Yes/No

Figure 20.13 _IME Template, courtesy of Karen Cebulko RN (continued)_

VI.   X-rays Taken?   Yes/No

VII.   Use of Examination Tools? (ie. reflex hammer)   Yes/No

VIII.   Impression:

_____

_____

_____

IX.   Other Information:

_____

_____

_____

_____

EXAMINATION ENDED: _____A.M./P.M.

Figure 20.13 *IME Template, courtesy of Karen Cebulko RN (continued)*

It is frequently recommended the LNC meet the client before the examination. The LNC can educate the client concerning what to expect during the examination. The LNC may accompany the client to the physician's office and be present during the examination process, whether that is a physical examination or psychological testing. The presence of an LNC at the examination tends to increase the likelihood that the physician will provide a more thorough evaluation.

TIP: The examining physician should always be informed that the LNC will be accompanying the client, and that the LNC will be expected to remain during the examination.

Once the IME has been completed, the LNC is responsible for giving the attorney an oral report which is then followed up with a detailed written report. This report should include information concerning how the examination was conducted by the physician. The report would include such observations as the physician's manner towards the client, demeanor, the treatment of the client (i.e., courtesy extended to the client), the demeanor of the client, and the client's reaction to the physician and examination itself. While the report cannot capture verbatim what transpired, the attorney should expect the report to reflect the substance of what occurred, along with the length of time of each component (history and physical). (See Figures 20.12 and 20.13.)

When the examining physician's report has been obtained, the LNC reviews and analyzes this report and compares it with the LNC's observations made during the IME. The LNC can begin to formulate questions and strategies to be used during the deposition of this examining physician, if applicable. Using the report, the LNC can evaluate the effect of the harm the plaintiff allegedly received from the malpractice. The LNC is an invaluable person when there is a discrepancy between the information the doctor puts in the IME report and the observations made by the LNC. The LNC's detailed report and testimony can be used to refute the claims made by the physician.

M. Presenter of Damages at the Settlement Conference or Arbitration

Arbitration is becoming increasingly common in nursing negligence cases. This is because more facilities are placing an arbitration clause in the patient's admission contract. These arbitration clauses generally provide for arbitration under state or federal procedures. The LNC can be a valuable resource at settlement conferences when medical damages are being discussed. The LNC helping the plaintiff's attorney can explain the effect of the damages that are being claimed to have resulted from the malpractice. The LNC at the defense table can assist the attorney in attacking the proximate cause and the validity of the damages. With the LNC's assistance, the defense attorney can minimize the impact of the damages or question damages that could not have been causally related to the alleged malpractice.

N. Trial Support Person

Nurses are usually adept at handling emergencies. LNCs liken a trial to the excitement that surrounds a sudden cardiac arrest. A crucial statement by a witness or a ruling by a judge can change the nature of the trial in an instant. Many firms ask the LNC to sit in the second chair during the trial to provide assistance to the attorney, expert witness, client, or all three. One managing partner of a prestigious plaintiffs' law firm stated that using the LNC during trial as the second chair was a much better management decision than having one of the associates, a law clerk or paralegal, spend the entire day in the courtroom.

In general, during trial, the LNC performs the duties and tasks once previously reserved for the associate attorney. This may include maintaining the trial book in appropriate order or organizing and arranging demonstrative evidence for easy accessibility. Other tasks may include scheduling witnesses for their appearances, taking notes, and observing jurors during voir dire. Throughout the trial, the LNC will make observations that the attorney may miss because of concentration on courtroom strategy. The LNC can make suggestions concerning strategies and compile questions to be asked during cross-examination or redirect. Attorneys benefit from the LNC's skills as a counselor who helps reduce the anxiety levels of the clients, the expert witnesses, and attorney during trial proceedings. The LNC can assist

in developing trial strategies to be used with the opponent's experts and be responsible for bringing exhibits to the courtroom. Increasingly, LNCs are being used to present demonstrative evidence in electronic format. This allows the attorney to concentrate on the case instead of the equipment.

20.6 Advantages of Using a Nurse Rather than a Physician to Consult on Nursing Malpractice Cases

LNCs often hear, "I have doctors screen my malpractice cases. Why do I need a nurse?" The use of an LNC to screen malpractice cases is cost-effective and efficient for the following reasons.

LNCs are the most appropriate people to assist with nursing malpractice claims. The nurse possesses the background to understand and explain the nursing milieu: the aspects of nursing practice that are second nature to a nurse, and are not understood by others outside of the field. Nurses understand nursing practice in a way that eludes most physicians and attorneys. For example, LNCs understand how the policy and procedure manual is organized, and which policies are likely to exist and can be requested during discovery. Physicians rarely become involved in the development and review of nursing policies.

Working with nurses is cost-effective. The groundwork laid by the LNC enables the attorney to more effectively use the physician's time when the malpractice case involves both doctors and nurses. Nurses acting as consultants on a case rather than as nursing expert witnesses are able to provide opinions on the liability of nurses and other healthcare providers such as doctors, physical therapists, and so on.

Nurses are thorough, detail-oriented individuals. Doctors rarely read the entire medical record, even when caring for their own patients. LNCs are in a better position to review and interpret nursing documentation. The LNC's familiarity with nursing documentation enables the LNC to quickly spot incomplete medical records and tampering with the record.

LNCs do not have the sometimes endemic mistrust of attorneys that doctors may express. They tend to understand how the legal system works and find that the advocacy role (whether for the defense or the plaintiff) fits into the nursing code of ethics, which also places the nurse in an advocacy role. The advocacy role is appropriate for the behind-the-scenes LNC consulting on a case but is not appropriate when the nurse is serving as an expert witness. David Cohen Esq. states that "[u]tilizing a legal nurse consultant isn't just helpful with my nursing home practice—it is absolutely essential. Developing a core understanding of the chart and guidance from the LNC in interpreting it is the key to developing and prosecuting a claim. The LNC provides insights which are quite distinct from those of the physician expert and often serve to assist the physician in her own understanding of the case."[20]

LNCs are familiar with medical literature, governing agency and accreditation requirements, and the Nurse Practice Act; they recognize the authoritative texts and journals, and are familiar with the national specialty nursing organizations and medical organizations. For this reason alone they are a much better resource on nursing malpractice cases than physicians.

A plaintiff's attorney expressed the advantages of using a nurse this way:

> I have found that a nurse, especially one who has served as a director of nursing or in a risk management position, is able to complete an evaluation quicker and at a much reduced cost than a physician. In New York, I find that such a quick and timely review of the records allows me to advise the client of the intricacies faster and with less cost than with a physician. In addition, the nurse is usually more concerned with the hour by hour care of the patient than is the doctor, and sees accreditation guidelines and issues clearly. Finally, after a positive nurse review, I then seek out my physician opinion, with some confidence that I have a meritorious claim and am ready to engage the physician at a higher level of conversation.[21]

20.7 Limitations of the Legal Nurse Consultant's Role

While the LNC can perform many of the activities within the scope of the paralegal, the LNC is usually not a paralegal as well. Many LNCs are technically proficient with the use of the computer, but they are not secretaries and should not be used as such. Independent LNCs building a business often find that as their business grows, it makes sense to hire a secretary to take on more involved word processing and billing.

The LNC is capable of providing a screening opinion on the merits of a medical or nursing malpractice case. This service can be performed for either the plaintiff or the defense attorney once the plaintiff has obtained representation. The LNC who works directly with a person who wants to know if he has a viable medical malpractice claim can be accused of practicing law without a license. The LNC should avoid working with pro se plaintiffs for the same reason. After reviewing the details of the case (and often the medical or nursing literature), the LNC will come to one of three conclusions:

- the case has merit (or is indefensible, if the LNC is working for the defense),
- the case does not have merit (or is defensible), or
- the case is "gray" and warrants involvement of an expert witness for a definitive opinion.

Although the LNC has a broad range of knowledge about many aspects of medical care, the LNC's knowledge base is usually not identical to that of an expert witness. The expert witness has focused knowledge about a limited field, while the LNC has broad knowledge about many subjects.

While the expert witness is retained to review a nursing malpractice case and testify if need be, the consulting legal nurse consultant is working behind the scenes. The LNC can therefore provide an open and objective analysis of the case without fear that the work product will be discoverable.

20.8 The Independent Legal Nurse Consultant
A. Getting Started

Entrepreneurial nurses with a desire to enjoy the benefits of being self-employed enter this field of consulting from a variety of starting points. Some get their start by gaining knowledge working in a law firm for a period of time before cutting the ties and opening their own offices. Others attend a course to learn more about the field, while yet others are tutored by an overworked attorney who desperately needs help.

The independent LNC may choose to provide behind-the-scenes consulting assistance only. Some LNCs serve only as expert witnesses. (The role of the expert witness is discussed in Chapter 21, *Working with Nursing Expert Witnesses*.)

B. Advantages of Working with the Independent LNC

There are many advantages to retaining an independent LNC to work on cases for the attorney's firm, as opposed to hiring a nurse as an employee.

- Many firms do not have the volume of work to justify hiring a part-time or full-time LNC. By establishing a relationship with an independent LNC, they are able to use the skills of the LNC on a case-by-case basis.
- The independent LNC is responsible for paying all overhead costs associated with the LNC's business. The independent LNC pays for equipment, furniture, and other costs. Benefits such as vacation, taxes, insurance, and so on are borne by the

independent, not the law firm. The benefits can add 25-33 percent to the base cost of having an employee.

- Independent LNCs perform their services off-site and therefore do not require space allocated for their use in the law firm. With many firms bursting at the seams, this is a real advantage.

- A nurse employed at a law firm will, in most cases, need a secretary so that when the attorney considers hiring a nurse, it often means hiring a support person for the LNC as well. This adds another person to the payroll with a salary, benefits, and requirements for space and equipment. The independent LNC is responsible for paying for secretarial services.

- As a result of working with many clients, the independent LNC is more likely to have a broader perspective than the nurse employed by the law firm. The independent LNC comes in contact with many attorneys who have similar practices and can often offer suggestions (without violating confidentiality) on how other firms handle aspects of managing their files.

- The LNC who works with several firms can assist attorneys to network with each other by suggesting that the attorney contact another attorney who has handled a similar malpractice case.

- The location of expert witnesses is often easier for the independent LNC than for the nurse employed in the law firm. The independent LNC is more likely to have a broader fund of knowledge about experts used by a variety of firms.

- There are no geographical limitations on the location of the LNC. The attorney may work with an LNC in any part of the country. Both of the authors of this chapter have clients who are hundreds or thousands of miles away whom they have never met. Case materials are delivered by mail, e-mail, or express delivery services and returned the same way. Fax machines make it easy to transmit documents in seconds for analysis by an LNC at a different site.

- When the attorney retains an independent LNC with consulting experience, the attorney reaps the benefits of the time other attorneys have spent developing that nurse. The approaches the LNC uses may be different and far more effective than any the attorney would have suggested to an in-house nurse.

- The fees paid to the LNC are billable to the client's file. They are taken off the top of any settlement that is negotiated for a plaintiff.

C. Locating an Independent LNC

The following suggestions will help the attorney locate an independent legal nurse consultant.

- Watch the mail for letters, brochures, or newsletters sent to the attorney by legal nurse consultants. Many nurses have gotten their start by sending various types of printed advertisements out to attorneys. They obtain the attorney's name from mailing lists, word of mouth, by researching Martindale Hubbell, or through the Internet.

TIP: Although many nurses express an interest in legal nurse consulting, and may enroll in a seminar or course to learn more about it, only a small percentage go on to establish a business, and even fewer possess the necessary skills and knowledge to be successful in their business.

- When attending professional conferences, spend time with the exhibitors. The more successful legal nurse consultants may be exhibiting at programs that deal with personal injury or malpractice issues. Ask the LNC exhibitor for sample reports, a fee schedule, and a curriculum vitae.

- Talk with colleagues and ask if they are using a legal nurse consultant. Ask for their impressions of the individual who has provided services to them.

TIP: Do not be surprised if reluctance is expressed when asking a colleague for information on how to contact the consultant. Many attorneys become protective of their LNC, because of their concern that the LNC will become too busy to handle their files if the attorney refers the LNC to others. (Many LNCs address this concern by subcontracting their cases to other qualified LNCs.)

- Look in the local legal papers for a directory of expert witnesses and consultants. This is usually printed annually and contains advertisements by a variety of consultants, including legal nurse consultants.

- Place an advertisement in a nursing newspaper such as *The American Nurse*, published by the American Nurses Association, stating the desire to retain an LNC.

- Do an Internet search looking for websites of legal nurse consultants.

Experience

1. How much experience do you have in consulting? How long have you been in business as an independent consultant?
2. How did you get started consulting?
3. Are you in business full-time or part-time?
4. Do you have subcontractor nurses who also consult on cases?
5. Do you have a secretary?
6. What type of cases do you generally consult on?
7. Do you limit your practice or do you consult on medical malpractice, nursing malpractice, long-term care, personal injury, etc?
8. Are you also an expert witness and if so, in what areas?
9. Discuss the types of demonstrative evidence that you have been involved with preparing.
10. Discuss the type of work-product that you have produced as a legal nurse consultant.
11. Do you have samples of the materials you have prepared that I may review?
12. What techniques do you utilize when looking for an expert witness?

Background

1. What is your educational background?
2. What type of clinical background do you have and are you still practicing nursing?

Fees

1. What do you charge? Do you charge for travel time to come to my office, and what is the travel rate?
2. Do you charge an interest rate or a rebilling fee if invoices are not paid within a specified period of time?
3. Do you require a retainer and if so, how much?
4. Do you have a written fee agreement, and if so, may I see it?

References

1. For whom have you consulted? May we contact these references?
2. Do you work for both plaintiff and defense counsel?
3. In what geographical area are most of your customers?

Figure 20.14 Questions to Use to Interview an Independent LNC, originally published in Iyer, P. and D'Andrea, D., "The Role of the Legal Nurse Consultant" in Patricia W. Iyer (Ed.) Nursing Home Litigation: Investigation and Case Preparation, Lawyers and Judges Publishing Company, Second Edition, 2006

D. Interviewing the Independent LNC

Laying a proper foundation for the attorney's relationship with the independent LNC is essential for the development and maintenance of a productive experience. The questions in Figure 20.14 are useful when the attorney is inquiring about the services and background of the independent LNC. Since many independents are in home-based businesses, the attorney's firm is the most appropriate setting for an interview. There is usually no charge associated with this initial meeting. However, if the attorney is so impressed with the LNC that the attorney asks this individual to stay to work on files after the interview, the attorney should expect to compensate the LNC for this time.

TIP: If at all possible, set aside a half-hour to meet with the LNC to conduct an interview. Most independent LNCs, unless they are far away, are quite willing to come to the firm to speak in person.

E. Compensation

The behind-the-scenes LNC is paid on an hourly basis with the typical range for hourly fees ranging from $100–$175. The general rule of thumb is that independent LNCs usually charge three to four times the average staff nurse salary in the area. With staff nurse salaries running as high as $45–$70 per hour, expect to pay more for an LNC's services. Expert witness hourly rates may range from $150-$400 per hour.

Some services are charged on a per-project basis. For example, it is quite common for LNCs to charge a flat rate for locating an expert witness. On the other hand, some LNCs mark up the expert's hourly rate and split the hourly fee with the expert. Some consultants have a flat rate for accompanying an attorney to deposition or court. It is common practice for the LNC to charge for travel time and expenses such as binders, indexes, delivery charges, copying, parking, mileage, and so on.

Factors that influence the fees charged by the LNC include:

- Years of experience as a nurse. Experienced nurses often charge more than a nurse with less clinical experience.
- Years of experience as a legal nurse consultant. Experienced consultants may have higher fees, but balance that with greater efficiency and skill.
- LNCC—Certification from the American Association of Legal Nurse Consultants
- Educational preparation and advanced degrees. Nurses with advanced degrees can charge more.
- Cost of living associated with the area of the country. The LNCs on the east and west coasts generally have higher costs of living.
- Overhead expenses associated with running an office. The less costly and most common arrangement is the home-based business. LNCs who run a business in commercial office space will have increased overhead expenses including rent, payroll, computer equipment costs, and so on.
- Nature of the LNC's relationship with the law firm. The LNC may offer a decreased rate based on volume of work.
- The "aggravation factor." The LNC may charge some clients more if the LNC has had difficulty collecting money from the firm in the past. In this situation, the LNC may ask for a greater retainer, ask for the retainer to be replenished when exhausted or, in extreme cases, decline to work with the attorney again.
- The urgency of the job. The rush job may cost the attorney more. Some LNCs double their fees if there is a very short turnaround time that requires the LNC to work evenings and weekends to meet the deadline or put aside commitments to other clients.
- The LNC's awareness of what the market will bear. The inexperienced LNC may undercharge or overcharge.

Many LNCs use a fee agreement, which they may ask the attorney to sign at the beginning of their relationship or for each case given to the LNC. The use of this type of agreement provides protection to both the attorney and the LNC and prevents misunderstandings. Many attorneys recognize that paying their consultant and expert bills promptly helps to assure excellent service and that the consultant will go the extra mile for the attorney. Unfortunately, not all attorneys have this philosophy or the cash flow to promptly pay the bills of the LNC. One of the common difficulties that LNCs experience is collecting fees for services rendered. The authors have heard many frustrated LNCs discuss their problems getting payment for work that is rendered. The best policy is to be honest with the LNC when there are cash flow problems. Most LNCs are very reasonable people and will be willing to work with the attorney to arrive at a plan to receive payment for the invoice.

F. Tips for Establishing a Strong Relationship with an LNC

1. Send a retainer letter with the case materials defining what the attorney needs, saying that the attorney is retaining the LNC's services in anticipation of litigation or trial, and specifying that the LNC is not expected to testify. This helps to preserve the confidentiality of the work product. The retainer letter should specify a deadline, acknowledge the LNC's fees for providing this service, and mention that a retainer is enclosed.
2. Whenever possible, give the LNC as much lead time as possible. The attorney may avoid costly rush fees and will get a better product in return if the LNC is not rushed to complete the project.
3. Be as explicit as possible in defining the final product that is desired. A letter or phone call defining what would be most helpful to the attorney is preferable to a letter accompanying materials that states, "Would you please analyze this case?" The LNC will need direction to prepare an analysis that is most useful to the attorney. LNCs, as nurses, are quite skilled at pleasing people and are usually

willing to go the extra mile to meet the needs of the attorney.

4. Although the attorney may be pressured to work within a budget or obtain approval from a client before retaining the LNC, the attorney should not be surprised if the LNC cannot give a precise answer to the question, "What is it going to cost me?" Assignments which sound relatively simple when the attorney first contacts the LNC can turn into major projects. Factors which increase the difficulty of the LNC's job include:

- receiving totally unorganized medical records,
- trying to transcribe or decipher illegible copies or poor handwriting in medical records,
- locating obscure literature on arcane aspects of medicine or nursing, and
- locating an expert witness for a narrowly defined subject area or within strict time, and geographical constraints (e.g., "I want an obstetrical nurse who was working in a nursery in 2004" or "I want someone to review this case this weekend because the statute of limitations will run on Tuesday.").

The attorney has the right to expect the LNC to inform her when the costs are going to greatly exceed the projected ones to gain approval before proceeding, and to be able to explain why the project took longer to complete than expected.

5. Do not expect the LNC to work on a contingent fee basis. This violates both the ethical codes of the LNC and the attorney. This concept can be misunderstood by attorneys in a few ways. The examples that follow have been suggested to LNCs. The proposal that the LNC receive a percentage of the final settlement is easily recognized as a prohibited arrangement because it distorts the motivation of the LNC and would provide an incentive to do anything to win the case. Another prohibited proposal is to ask the LNC to agree to be paid if something is found in the medical records that helps the attorney win the case. If the LNC finds nothing of value, the LNC would not be paid. While this proposal would seem advantageous to the attorney who wants to minimize fees, it ignores the fact that the LNC's services are based on billable hours and not a 25-33 percent contingent fee that attorneys receive. The LNC has no control over what is in the records

and there is no justifiable business reason for the LNC to accept this suggestion. Another variation of a contingent fee occurs when the attorney settles a case for less than she or he expected, then asks the expert to reduce the final bill so that the client (and attorney) will keep more of the settlement. The expert's fees are, in effect, contingent on how well the plaintiff's attorney has been able to negotiate. This is unfair to the expert, who has provided services on a billable hour basis. Also, do not expect the LNC to wait until the case is settled before paying for those services. LNCs typically cannot defer payment for the years it takes to settle or take a case to trial. Replenish retainers as agreed upon to enable the LNC to keep working steadily on the case.

6. The LNC may not work directly with a plaintiff without a relationship being established with an attorney. The LNC screening a nursing malpractice case for merit on behalf of a family who has not retained an attorney may be construed as practicing law without a license. Only the attorney can make a decision about whether to accept or reject a potential claim against a nurse. Only the attorney can pay the LNC's bills. Checks should be written from the attorney's bank account, not the plaintiff's.

7. Thank the consultant and give feedback on the finished product. Tell the LNC what you like and what should be done differently next time. In general, LNCs value that type of information because it helps them continuously improve their service.

TIP: One of the most valuable tools the attorney possesses is the ability to give feedback to the LNC on how the LNC helped with a particular case. This type of feedback, coupled with experiences, provides the LNC with a foundation for improving skills.

G. Evaluation of the Independent LNC

Every attorney uses criteria to judge the quality of the work provided by a support person such as an LNC. Here are some questions to ask as the attorney progresses in the relationship with the independent LNC:

- Was the LNC able to provide the desired services?
- Were the services provided in a timely manner?
- Was the quality of the work product what I expected it would be or was it better?
- Did the LNC identify something in the case I would have completely missed?

LNC Evaluation Form

Date:

Client:

LNC:

Was the LNC able to follow directions?

Was the document/report proofread with correct grammar, spelling, and complete sentences used?

Was analytical thinking present in the work product?

Was the invoice reasonable?

Was the work delivered in a timely manner?

Other comments:

Figure 20.15 *LNC Evaluation Form, courtesy of Patricia W. Iyer, MSN, RN, LNCC*

- Did the LNC provide me with something extra I did not expect to receive?
- Was the LNC able to readily communicate opinions and provide material that made it easier for me to understand the case?
- Did the LNC adhere to the opinions expressed and explain the rationale behind them?
- Was the LNC able to anticipate the strategies raised by the other side of the case?
- Was the LNC knowledgeable about national, federal, and state nursing regulations?
- Did the LNC tell me the strengths as well as the weaknesses of the case?
- If the LNC was asked to provide literature, did it address the applicable standards of care at the time of the incident? Was the literature complete? If I asked the LNC to summarize the literature, was the summary easy to follow?

- Does the LNC have a good understanding of the legal system?
- Is the LNC easy to work with?
- Are the invoices prepared by the LNC well documented with explanations of the services provided?
- Have there been any surprises in the invoices?
- Have the invoices fairly represented the services provided and the hours spent on the file?
- Has the LNC asked me for comments on the work product and made changes to suit my needs?
- Would I use this LNC again?
- Would I recommend this LNC to others?

Refer to Figure 20.15 for some of the questions useful for evaluating an LNC.

H. The LNC Employed within Physician's Offices or Ambulatory Care Settings

There are a variety of ambulatory care settings in which an LNC can be employed as a risk manager. These settings may include physician offices or clinics, freestanding surgical centers, public health facilities, and urgent- or emergent-clinics.

The roles and functions of the risk manager within these settings remain similar to those roles within hospitals and other healthcare systems; however, the uniqueness of these outpatient settings lend a variety to the general flavor of risk management. Within the outpatient settings, the care rendered to individuals may be fragmented because of increased patient encounters and varying caregivers. Continuity is a large issue. However, the issues of liability exposure, including training and education of staff members and the review and analysis of incident reports, remain the same. The credentialing and granting-of-privileges process will be similar to that of larger institutions. The risk manager may be responsible for reviewing all individual, professional liability insurance coverage. The risk manager will be responsible for developing or reviewing policies and procedures to ensure the incorporation of all state, federal, and regulating agencies' guidelines. An integral part of the risk manager's job will be providing ongoing chart review, and analysis and interpretation to ascertain that all clients are receiving the highest level of care possible and that the quality of care has not diminished because of caregiver fragmentation.

The role of the risk manager may include the development of a systemic approach for investigating claims, assessing potential liability exposure, and establishing and maintaining a claims file. The risk manager will develop a system for reporting and investigating all potential claims.

The role of the risk manager in the future will continue to focus on some ongoing issues such as sentinel events, safety and security, and infection control, as well as telemedicine, fraud and abuse, electronic exchange of information, and alternative medicine.

20.9 The Legal Nurse Consultant Employed by a Law Firm

Some attorneys choose to employ nurses as part-time or full-time staff. Hiring an LNC for one's firm can be a monumental task. The same amount of care and consideration used to hire an associate attorney is required when hiring a nurse to augment the attorney's support staff. In the following section, we refer to the nurse employed in a law firm as an "in-house" nurse. Depending on the firm, the LNC may be called a legal nurse consultant, nurse consultant, nurse paralegal, nurse legal assistant, or medical legal consultant.[22] The material is also applicable to hiring a nurse to work in an insurance company.

A. Advantages of Having an In-House LNC

The advantages of having an in-house consultant are numerous. The most obvious advantage is having someone immediately available to discuss some phase or aspect of a particular case.

It is frequently more cost-effective, and reviews are completed in a more timely fashion, when the attorney has an in-house LNC perform an initial review of potential cases, instead of having these cases sent out to experts. The cases initially reviewed for merit by the in-house LNC are then sent to an expert for review.

Voluminous records do not need to be copied to send to the expert for the review, as the in-house nurse can simply review the original records. In cases with voluminous records, the LNC can assist in focusing the expert on the pertinent event or alleged deviations from the standard of care.

The time-saving element of having an in-house LNC can be of extraordinary value. If the attorney is in the middle of trial and needs immediate research conducted, the attorney already has someone with a working knowledge of the case, and this is consequently of great benefit to the attorney. The LNC will assist in uncovering relevant medical information, developing a case theme, supporting this theme with standards, clinical protocols, and policies, and anticipating opposing counsel's arguments, tactics, and strategy.

The LNC can contribute to the financial success of the firm by providing a high quality work product that will hone in on the medical issues, by enhancing client satisfaction by regular contact by updating clients on the progress of their cases, and by nurturing referring attorneys. The LNC can bring in new business through networking with colleagues. In many firms, the LNC does work formerly performed by attorneys at higher rates, such as reviewing records. The use of an LNC is cost-effective for the client and allows the attorney to perform the required legal work.[23]

The in-house LNC often acts as an interface or conduit to the testifying experts. Frequently, the nurse and the nursing expert will exchange theories of nursing practice, as well as standards of care pertinent to the attorney's specific case. The LNC can frequently save the expert a great deal of time by performing the specific research and procurement of nursing literature. Often the expert is quite busy maintaining a job, fulfilling teaching engagements and other academic obligations; thus it can be difficult for the expert to obtain the desired research.

The in-house LNC has a broader knowledge base than non-medical personnel and will be more adept at investigating the inconsistencies and nuances of medical records. As one attorney said, the in-house LNC will "turn over all the rocks" while exploring for problem areas and looking for inconsistencies. This advanced knowledge will enable the LNC to determine the effects of one negligent action on the entire body, not just on the initial area affected. Knowledge of anatomy and physiology will also enable the LNC to make a more thorough analysis of the medical literature.

Another advantage of having an in-house LNC is the opportunity for the attorney to mold and sculpt this nurse. This enables the attorney to direct the format of the report and provide feedback to hone the LNC's writing skills to perfection. As the LNC becomes familiar with the firm's style, he may be able to anticipate needs even before the attorney is aware of those specific needs.

A cost-effective and useful strategy used by some firms is to maintain a mixture of in-house LNCs and independent LNCs. These circumstances may include the times when there is an unusually high influx of cases requiring merit reviews.

TIP: The independent LNC is also used when the in-house nurse lacks a very specialized knowledge base, or when the in-house nurse is busy with trial preparation. This is a cost-effective use of the in-house LNC as well as the independent contractor.

B. Hiring the In-House LNC

1. Advertising

Hiring an in-house LNC can begin with placing an advertisement in a conspicuous journal or newspaper. Advertisements may be placed in the *Journal of Legal Nurse Consulting*, published quarterly by the American Association of

Legal Nurse Consultants. This journal is focused directly toward nurses who are either working in or have a strong desire to work in the area of legal nurse consulting. Other successful avenues for job advertisement placement include nursing newsletters such as *ADVANCE for Nurses*, which is published monthly, or in the local newspaper's medical job section.

The attorney may find an independent LNC who may post the opening on a listserv. Other Internet job bulletins are available. The attorney will be surprised at the number of applicants received from the initial advertisement. Once the applications start arriving the attorney will need to proceed with the review and selection process by narrowing the selection down to a manageable number of applicants to interview.

TIP: One of the basic questions that needs to be asked is whether the attorney is willing to train a nurse without previous legal nurse consulting experience, or is looking for someone with experience.

In addition to or instead of advertising, many firms look for an in-house LNC by using their networks. Speak to other attorneys who have LNC employees to let them know the firm is looking for an in-house LNC. The LNCs employed at other firms may know of someone searching for the type of job the attorney is offering. Talk with the independent LNCs to see if they are interested in accepting a position as an employee. The advantages of being self-employed are sometimes overshadowed by the need for the security that a paycheck and medical insurance benefits provide. Find out if there is a local chapter of the American Association of Legal Nurse Consultants in the area, and contact the president or a board member to provide information about the job opening. Talk with hospital-based risk managers. These individuals may know of someone looking for a job as an in-house LNC. Once the attorney has begun receiving responses to the networking and advertising efforts, it is time to set up interviews.

2. Screening

Some attorneys prefer to use an office manager to sort through résumés to identify those who look promising. Other attorneys want to see each one to select those to be interviewed. Carefully review each résumé and look for the qualities that match your needs. Some of the factors that employers may consider when hiring employees are:

1. Evidence of spell checking and proofreading—LNC work demands an eye for accuracy in written

materials. Individuals who cannot proofread are not suitable for this type of work.

2. Absence of gaps in employment—A long time out of the workforce may convey a lack of contact with the clinical world and may be a deficit when it comes to understanding medical issues.

3. Evidence of frequent job changes—A pattern of brief periods of employment may result from an inability to get along with others or to stay with one environment for any length of time.

4. Clinical experience related to the needs of the firm—A personal injury firm may prefer nurses with particular expertise, such as orthopedic or neurosurgical, for example. A company that handles a lot of birth injury cases may look for obstetrical nurses.

5. Educational preparation—Some attorneys prefer LNCs with bachelor's degrees. Refer to Chapter 6, *The Foundations of Nursing Practice*, for an explanation of the educational preparation levels. Few firms hire licensed practical nurses, who have only one year of educational preparation, and typically do not have the breadth of knowledge needed to work in a law firm.

6. LNCC certification—As described in Section 20.4.E of this chapter, LNCC certification designates the LNC with expertise in the field.

7. Competence in using a computer—At a minimum, the LNC should be comfortable using word processing software.

8. The ability to express opinions logically and coherently, both verbally and in writing.[24]

3. Interviewing

Attorneys are well-trained for the interviewing process. Approach each interview in a positive manner, realizing that this interview is likely to be a major event in the applicant's life and this is a great public relations opportunity for the attorney's firm.

The main purpose of this interview process is to obtain information and to explore how well each applicant meets the attorney's needs and how each interviewee fits into the attorney's "ideal employee profile." The field of legal nurse consulting requires an ability to proofread, use correct grammar and spelling, set up letters or reports in proper format, and be able to organize information. The screening tools in Appendix 20.7 (with answers in Appendix 20.8) can eliminate many weaker candidates. To assist with the interview process, we have included some typical interview questions in Figure 20.16. Evaluate the candidate's presentation style, critical thinking skills, and sample work product, if any.

The following are typical selection questions that tend to avoid pitfalls and gather important job-related information:

Important Questions
1.   What experience do you have with computer systems?
2.   Why do you want to work for a law firm?
3.   What type of clinical background do you have and when did you last work clinically?
4.   Are you a member of the American Association of Legal Nurse Consultants?
5.   Is there a chapter near here? If so, do you attend chapter meetings?
6.   Have you ever done this type of work before?
7.   Why are you interested in this field?

Interest in the Law Firm
1.   Why would you like to work for this law firm?
2.   How did you hear about this opening?
3.   What material have you read about our firm?
4.   What do you know about the history and focus of this firm?
5.   What interests you most about this position?
6.   Why should I hire you?

Work Related (General)
1.   What did you do that was innovative in your last position?
2.   What do you think your previous supervisors would cite as your strengths?
3.   What did you like best about your previous job?

Work Related (Specific)
1.   What strategies do you use to get your point across?
2.   What criteria do you use when assigning work to others?
3.   How do you follow up on work assigned to subordinates?
4.   Tell me about a situation in which you made a wrong decision and how you corrected it.

Education and Training
1.   What special skills do you have?
2.   What aspects of your education or work experience have prepared you best for this position?
3.   Are you certified by the American Association of Legal Nurse Consultants? If not, when will you become eligible to take the certification examination?
4.   Do you possess a certificate in legal nurse consulting? If so, who granted the certificate? What were the criteria you had to meet to earn the certificate?

Career Plans and Goals
1.   What are your long-range career goals?
2.   If you join this firm, what would you like to be doing in five years from now?
3.   How do you feel about the way your career has gone so far?
4.   What are you doing in order to prepare yourself for advancements?
5.   Who influenced you most in your career choice?

Figure 20.16 *Questions to Use to Interview an Applicant for an In-house LNC Position, originally published in Iyer, P. and D'Andrea, D., "The Role of the Legal Nurse Consultant," in Patricia W. Iyer (Editor), Nursing Home Litigation: Investigation and Case Preparation, Lawyers and Judges Publishing Company, Second Editioan, 2006*

Job Performance

1. What do you believe are the most important performance criteria in your area of expertise?
2. How do you ensure that you are receiving feedback pertaining to your performance?
3. What criteria do you use when making decisions?
4. All of us have pluses and minuses in our performance; what are some of your pluses?
5. How were you evaluated during your last two evaluations?

Salary and Benefits

1. What kind of salary would you need to join this firm?
2. What would you consider to be a good annual increase?
3. How does our salary range compare to your last position?
4. If you had to do without a fringe benefit, which would it be?
5. Are you currently covered by health and dental insurance?

Career Field (General)

1. What do you think is the greatest challenge facing the legal nurse consultant today?
2. What do you think will be the next major breakthrough in the field of legal nurse consulting?
3. What do you see as the major trend in the field of legal nurse consulting?
4. What do you see are the benefits for having an in-house legal nurse consultant?
5. What benefits can you provide to this firm?

Career Field (Specific)

1. Discuss one of the closed cases in which you acted as the expert witness (if applicable).
2. What techniques do you utilize when looking for an expert witness?
3. Discuss the types of demonstrative evidence that you have been involved with preparing.
4. Discuss the type of work-product that you have produced as a nurse consultant.

Figure 20.16 Questions to Use to Interview an Applicant for an In-house LNC Position, originally published in Iyer, P. and D'Andrea, D., "The Role of the Legal Nurse Consultant," in Patricia W. Iyer (Editor), Nursing Home Litigation: Investigation and Case Preparation, Lawyers and Judges Publishing Company, Second Editioan, 2006 (continued)

To ascertain if the prospective legal nurse consultant has a valid current nursing license, the attorney may contact the state's department responsible for professional education and license registration, known as the Board of Nursing. Also, follow the requirements of the Patriot Act and perform criminal background checks. A job description and profile for the LNC should be developed in order to separate the LNC from any other staff group in the firm. A performance evaluation can be developed using this job profile. This job description can be developed to incorporate the firm's overall objectives and philosophy. The attorney may wish to discuss the main points of the job description during the initial interview. Nurses readily understand the concept of a job description and are accustomed to thinking in terms of the structure that a written job description provides. Although the nurse quickly understands what a RN does in a healthcare facility, the same nurse may have little or no idea how a RN would function in a law firm.

TIP: When verifying the authenticity and currency of a nurse's license, do not accept a photocopied license as evidence of current licensure. Such copies have been used fraudulently. See that the original license is current and valid and that the name on the license is the legal name of the prospective employee.

A prominent Chicago plaintiff's attorney asks all interviewees to bring a sample of their writing to the interview. He also sets aside a portion of the interview for what he calls the "practical aspect." During this portion of the interview, the nurse is given an example of a case study to review. This interviewee is then asked how she would analyze the case. This attorney is looking for an innovative and thought-provoking discussion concerning this case. This approach may not be effective when interviewing a nurse without experience as a legal nurse consultant.

While the attorney is interviewing the LNC candidates, the LNCs may also be eliciting information either before or during the interview that affects their decision making. Some of these factors include:

- The size of the firm—this affects the firm's culture, decision making and ease of communication
- Who are the clients—some LNCs may have a strong preference for working for one type of client, such as defendants
- Number of attorneys who work on medical malpractice and other personal injury cases
- The reputation of the firm and its attorneys—are they involved with prestigious professional attorney organizations
- The culture of the firm—hierarchical or informal
- The ratio of LNCs to attorneys—this impacts workload and job security
- How the firm measures productivity
- The rating of the firm on Martindale Hubbell
- Involvement of the attorneys in making presentations to their peers
- Mission and vision statement or set of core values
- Appearance and content of the firm's website
- Number of certified trial attorneys
- Availability of secretarial support
- Job description
- Firm philosophy and expectations for the role of the LNC
- Prior experience with LNCs as employees[25]

4. Compensation

The salary range for the LNC depends on many factors that include the number of years spent in active clinical nursing, whether the firm has plaintiff or defense clients, diversity of nursing experience, educational background, as well as the number of years spent as an LNC. Nurses are hired for their medical background and knowledge and command higher salaries than paralegals. Nurses perform high level tasks on projects that are medically complex.[26]

Salaries have a tendency to vary regionally, commensurate with the region's cost of living and the salaries paid by the major employers in the area, such as the hospitals. Salaries on both the east and west coast are higher than those salaries offered in the south or midwestern states.

Frequently, the LNC is expected to work "overtime." This may include some late evenings as well as Saturdays and is usually related to trial preparation. The attorney should be aware of state and federal laws, which may govern reimbursement for overtime and define which employ-

ees are exempt or nonexempt. Generally nurses are in salaried positions.

Another form of compensation is a yearly bonus usually distributed at the end of each fiscal year. The bonus system is firm-specific and has many contributing factors, such as years of employment with the firm, number of new cases, number of cases settled, jury verdicts, number of cases dismissed, and the number of billable hours.

5. Orientation

In order to assure the nurse will appropriately represent the attorney's firm and be able to supply the attorney with the information the attorney needs, the training and orientation of an LNC should be performed by the attorney. The orientation should include relevant information concerning the day-to-day operation of the attorney's firm. Information that is quite basic to the attorney, such as "diarying" a date for a deposition, will be foreign to the nurse. But remember that nurses will be very familiar with "scheduling" events or tests. The concept is the same; it just needs further illumination. The LNC should not only be given time to learn the role of the people in the firm, but to meet the key people outside of the firm. The LNC working for a defense firm should meet the claims adjusters and other important employees of the insurance company and the local hospital risk managers. The LNC employed by a plaintiffs' firm should become familiar with the attorneys who refer cases to the law firm. The introduction of the LNC to the attorney's referral base can be a valuable marketing strategy, inspiring confidence in the firm's ability to handle a nursing malpractice case.

Frequently, previous work examples, if any are available, are given to the LNC as part of the orientation so the LNC can become familiar with the formatting preferred by the attorney's firm. The law firm's database should contain the names, addresses, and phone numbers of the most frequently used vendors and other litigation support personnel, such as the record copy service that obtains the attorney's medical records, the company that duplicates the attorney's x-rays, and the company that produces the attorney's poster-size, color reproductions.

Introduce the LNC to the system for storing information about the expert witnesses the firm has retained or has researched. If a database of experts does not exist, consider having the LNC establish one. Encourage the LNC to update, reinforce, and fortify the database with information about experts whom the LNC personally knows.

Keep in mind that unless the LNC has previous in-house experience, the LNC may be somewhat naive concerning the workings of an office, especially the intricate processes of a law firm. Most clinically active nurses have never worked in the business field or in an office and sometimes do not know how to operate various commonly used business machines. The nurse should spend some time with a clerk to become oriented to these procedures. Binding machines may be foreign to the attorney's LNC. On the other hand, the LNC can operate high-tech medical machinery with ease and grace. Once the nurse is shown how to appropriately and accurately operate office machinery, it will become second nature.

TIP: Even though the LNC will not normally be expected to perform these tasks in the firm, it is always beneficial to know how to operate the various machines, in the event of an emergency that is bound to occur.

Another important aspect to remember is that legal terms are frequently gibberish to the novice LNC. These terms, such as requests for production, interrogatories, summary judgment, and so on are second nature to the attorney, but the LNC can pronounce and define complex medical terms. Consider developing a list of the most common legal terms and their definitions and applications for the LNC. One law firm presents the LNC with a personal copy of *Black's Law Dictionary*. Alternately, introduce the LNC to the legal websites that the firm uses most often.

TIP: Before asking the LNC to provide support at a deposition or at trial, give the LNC an opportunity to observe these proceedings. Unless the LNC has been in court on some type of civil matter, the LNC's understanding of a deposition or a trial is likely to be governed by television and movies. It is quite possible the LNC has never seen the inside of a courtroom.

For the novice LNC, orientation and training is an ongoing activity. Use the same type of mentoring and guidance the attorney uses with the law clerks and new associates. This assures the attorney will mold the LNC to the attorney's specifications. Attorneys have told us it takes many months of support before the associate becomes comfortable enough to practice law without ongoing supervision. The LNC may need a similar time frame to learn the workings of the attorney's firm.

TIP: Nurses are natural team players and are accustomed to getting feedback on their performance. This type of feedback will help to avoid possible conflict that can arise from inadequate communication between the attorney and the LNC. The firm should devise, implement, and monitor an effective system for communication necessary to complete assignments appropriately.

C. The Role of the In-House LNC

The contributions of the LNC to the legal team have been described in detail earlier in this chapter. The specific roles that an in-house LNC can fill are described below. LNCs working in either plaintiff and defense firms perform similar services.

If the attorney's firm is plaintiff-oriented, engage the LNC in screening cases from the beginning. This means having the nurse present during the attorney's initial interview with the prospective client. By using well-developed assessment skills, many LNCs have created comprehensive intake forms, which are used during the initial client interview session. The development and use of this form has proven to be quite successful in elucidating the facts concerning events, obtaining a complete and accurate medical history, as well as illuminating the client's/plaintiff's interpretation and beliefs. The LNC possesses refined assessment skills that can be channeled into the evaluation of the client during the initial interview as well as review and analysis of the medical records.

TIP: The LNC can focus on the medical aspects of the nursing negligence case during the initial interview, thus freeing the attorney to concentrate on the liability issues.

As Zorn notes,[27] the LNC may conduct a preliminary medical literature search to identify issues related to liability and causation. The LNC may prepare a case screening memo recommending whether the firm should take the case to the next step of expert review. The memo would include the LNC's conclusions and excerpts from the medical literature. After locating the expert and preparing an organized package for the expert, the LNC may develop a list of questions for the expert witness to consider in his review as well as in a meeting or phone conference with the expert once the review is finished. The plaintiff LNC is responsible for keeping abreast of the client's current medical condition and periodically updating the client's medical records. The defense LNC may comb through the medical records to look for additional providers the plaintiff forgot to mention at the deposition. Both LNCs should note and report to the attorney any details that would affect the plaintiff's credibility, such as a history of drug or alcohol abuse or a criminal record or facts that would give rise to a defense that the plaintiff is partially responsible for her injuries.

Refer to Figure 20.17 for a chronology prepared to show the plaintiff's failure to follow medical instructions.

The LNC working for a defense firm performs many of the same roles and tasks as the independent LNC. The LNC

Date	Document	Description	Treatment
7/10/05	Smiley	Wrist pain. Able to move wrist. Mild sprain both wrists	Motrin
7/23/05	Smiley	R & L wrist pain with numb fingers 1-3 on L	
9/10/05	Smiley	Pain in L wrist on motion	Analgesics. MRI.
10/8/05	MRI	Fracture L wrist	
10/24/05	Smiley	Severe pain.	Oxycontin and IR-Oxycodone.
11/5/05	Welby	Surgical repair; splint provided.	Splint
11/12/05	Smiley	Dressings completely off. Redressed. Not wearing splint.	Dressing; encouraged splint use
11/21/05	Welby x-ray	Sutures removed. X-ray shows fixation at fracture site. Has not worn splint; Cast applied	Cast
12/1/05	Smiley	No show	Missed appt.
12/5/05	Welby	No show	Missed appt.
12/16/05	Welby x-ray	Cast cracked. Some tenderness. Refused new cast –splint made. Instructed to wear splint or risk non-union and other problems. X-ray (no reading)	New splint
1/15/06	Welby	No show	Missed appt.
2/13/06	Welby x-ray	Pain. X-ray shows minimal healing at fx site.	Bone stimulator
3/13/06	Welby x-ray	Not wearing splint. Instructed to wear at all times. X-ray – loosening of hardware. Loose hardware may be explained by noncompliance. Needs continued immobilization	
3/27/06	Smiley	Not wearing electrical stimulator.	
4/14/06	Welby x-ray	Not wearing splint. X-ray shows non-union left scaphoid. Using bone stimulator occasionally. Constant pain in wrist. Refuses surgery-wants to live with symptoms despite knowledge this will cause permanent partial disability.	
4/15/06	Welby	Reluctant for further treatment. Will be discharged.	
11/22/06	Smiley	Hopefully will convince him to get wrist scan and therapy	

Figure 20.17 Chronology of John Smith. Non-compliance related to wrist fracture post fall (Courtesy of Mindy Cohen, MSN, RN, LNCC of Mindy Cohen & Associates, Inc. Villanova, PA.)

usually becomes involved in the case as soon as the firm receives a negligence case. Defense LNCs may assist with drafting portions of the initial legal pleadings, or responses to summons and complaints, and answering interrogatories and other discovery demands. Job responsibilities may include identification of experts, organization and review of medical records, and preparation of other documents for the expert's review. The defense LNC may undertake a similar process as does the plaintiff LNC to summarize, analyze, and evaluate the merits of the claims. The defense LNC may help the attorney prepare for the plaintiff's deposition by developing a chronology of the past and present medical care. Additional important job duties include analysis of the fac-

tors that might impact the liability, causation, damages, or contributory negligence issues of a case. The defense attorney can expect the LNC to abstract the expert witness's depositions and to discuss with the attorney any new or significant information gleaned from these depositions. The LNC performs research pertaining to the standards of care and has conferences with the attorney to discuss the strengths and weaknesses of the case. In addition, the defense LNC drafts a detailed assessment of the proximate cause and damage issues. As in plaintiff cases, the defense LNC plays an important role in assisting in trial preparation. The LNC may be called on to act as in-house counselor, to assist the defendant by answering questions concerning the legal process, as well as to assist in alleviating the psychological stressors that may occur and plague the defendant. In other words, the nurse becomes the counselor and support person of a nervous client or defendant.

LNCs working with either the plaintiff or the defense attorney may perform more in-depth medical literature reviews as the issues in the case become more focused regarding liability or damages. They may review key policies and procedures and participate in focus groups as the attorneys present the case to participants recruited from the community.[28] Refer to Chapter 23, *Keeping the Jurors in Mind*, for additional Information.

D. Billing Practices of the In-House LNC

Most law firms, whether they primarily represent plaintiffs or defendants, request that the in-house LNCs provide an accurate accounting of time spent on each case. The goal behind this process is to:

- facilitate effective communication of the tasks and costs of litigation, and
- provide each client and law firm with a means to understand the cost of litigation.

The billing practices within a large law firm are frequently based upon the client's specifications. This billing practice usually incorporates two specific aspects: the number of hours billed per year and the increment in which that billing takes place.

Billing increments in one law firm may be based upon one-quarter hour increments while another law firm bases billing practices on increments of tenths of an hour or in ten-minute increments. In a very large national law firm, one group of clients requested that the LNCs bill in five-minute increments. Again, this billing practice is dependent upon the stipulations of the client and the law firm's relationship with that client. Many clients, when entering into a contract with a new law firm, are more structured in their demands than if this relationship has been ongoing for many years. In the case of a long-term relationship, the structuring and client demands may be more flexible.

Most defense firm clients scrutinize their bills carefully and may question the level of personnel who performed a task or the number of hours billed to the file. The LNC must comply with company policies regarding recording time.[29]

Every client and law firm understands that the workday contains non-billable hours. As one in-house LNC put it, "No matter what you do, each day has a few non-billable hours; however, the daily goal is to keep those non-billable hours to a minimum." Alternatively, in completing a project

or meeting a deadline, the LNC may end up working after-hours or on the weekend in order to maintain a quota of billable hours. The minimum yearly billable hours tend to be law-firm specific. An example would be: one law firm requires that the LNC be accountable for billing a minimum of seven hours a day, five days a week for 52 weeks per year, equaling a total number of billable hours to 1,820 per year. Another law firm requires that the LNC be responsible for billing a total of 2,080 hours a year with no specifications as to how many hours must be billed each day. It is up to each LNC to make sure that weekly or monthly hours eventually add up to the minimum required amount.

Other firms question the validity of expecting staff to bill 2,080 hours and derive a number less than this to take into account breaks and other unavoidable downtime. It is important to note that unrealistic requirements for a high number of billable hours are generating controversy within the legal community. Many associates identify these demands as the source of burnout and rapid turnover. Concerns have been raised that padding billable hours or double billing (billing on two cases simultaneously) raises ethical and integrity issues. The law firm's partners may find the same concerns raised when imposing high billable hour requirements on nurses. While accountability for the use of one's time (and the client's resources) is important, forcing employees to work 60 to 70 hours per week in order to get in 40 hours of billable time may be counterproductive in the long run. Turnover of burned out LNCs is expensive, given the learning curve associated with this type of work.

Not only is the LNC responsible for keeping track of all billable hours, these hours are frequently broken down into phases or aspects of litigation, or in task-specific categories. Many law firms have developed their own billing systems while others use a billing and coding system developed by individual corporate clients. Some law firms are beginning to adopt the recently designed Uniform Task-Based Management System, developed by the American Bar Association Section of Litigation.

While employed as an in-house LNC, one author (DD) utilized a task-oriented and very simplistic billing system. Under this system, not every task or project neatly fit into each category; however, it allowed one to record the time spent on each case in specific categories of activity. These categories included:

- medical records: organization, review, and analysis
- case issues and strategy: review and analysis
- conference with attorney, client, experts
- deposition: preparation, review, and abstraction

- research, or
- trial preparation

The Litigation Code set developed by the ABA is grouped into five basic phases or aspects of litigation, which include:

- case assessment, development, and administration
- pre-trial pleadings and motions
- discovery
- trial preparation and trial
- appeal

Each of these basic phases is further broken down into specific tasks or projects. An example of some of the subcategories contained within the L100 case assessment, development and administration section include:

L110 Fact Investigation/Development
L120 Analysis/Strategy
L130 Experts/Consultants
L140 Document/File Management

The ABA suggests that when using the Uniform Task-Based Management System, all work associated with a task should be included within that category. The ultimate goal of using this system is to provide a true picture of the labor cost of each task. For the LNC, an example of this would be: "Case assessment (L100), Analysis/Strategy (L120)." This would encompass all time spent on:

- reviewing the medical records,
- determining what medical records needed to be ordered,
- ordering the necessary records,
- organizing these records,
- summarizing the medical care rendered, and
- preparing chronologies of medical events, and comparing and correlating these events to the allegations.

One in-house LNC who utilizes a variety of billing systems, including the ABA's system as well as client-specific systems, relates that for the most part these systems were developed as broad general guidelines. While not all of the tasks or duties of an LNC neatly fit into the specific categories (because many of the tasks overlap or the categories are imprecise) the LNC is able to categorize his work and the primary purpose of each task.

Regardless of the size of the law firm, type of law practiced, or the client's specifications, the LNC is responsible for accurately recording the time spent on individual cases

and identifying the areas in which this time was spent. In most law firms, the individual billing practices will be factored into the LNC's bonus and raise at the time of the yearly evaluation.

E. Performance Evaluations

Performance evaluations should be conducted at specified intervals during the course of employment. The job description can be used to develop the LNC's performance evaluation. The frequency of evaluations should be based on the experience of the nurse as a consultant. For instance, a nurse who has many years in the clinical arena but no experience as an LNC may need extra guidance in the business or law-firm arena. Consequently, this first evaluation should be performed at the end of the first three months and then repeated at the end of six months and then at the end of the first year. After the first year, evaluations need only be performed on an annual basis. If the attorney has hired an experienced in-house LNC, the evaluation should be performed at the three-month time frame, corresponding with the probationary period, and again at the end of the first year. At the time of the evaluation and throughout the year, provide the nurse with specific feedback about the valuable contributions the LNC is making as well as the activities that need to be improved or changed.

20.10 Summary

The major benefit of using the legal nurse consultant's expertise in litigating malpractice cases is being able to draw on the nurse's expertise. The combination of the attorney's legal knowledge and skills and the nurse's medical knowledge and skills provides a dynamic team.

Endnotes

1. *Legal Nurse Consulting: Scope and Standards of Practice,* Washington, D.C.: American Nurses Association, 2006.

2. Peterson, A. and Kopishke, L. (ed.), *Legal Nurse Consulting Principles and Practices, Third Edition.* Boca Raton, Florida: CRC Press, 2010.

3. Iyer, P. (ed.), *Business Principles of Legal Nurse Consulting,* Boca Raton, Florida: CRC Press, 2005.

4. See note 1.

5. Conklin, M. and K. Jeffries, "Nurse paralegal/legal nurse consultant: similar work product. What is the controversy?" *Journal of Legal Nurse Consulting* 17, no. 1 (Winter 2006): 21-23.

6. AALNC Position Statement, 1999. http://www.aalnc. org/hire/roll.cfm.

7. Paralegals and legal nurse consultants: Perfect together? 2000   http://www.medleague.com/Articles/president/ Paralegals_LNC.htm).

8. Scherubel, J. "Nursing licensure and certification," *Contemporary Nursing: Issues, Trends and Management*, St. Louis, Elsevier Mosby, 2005.

9. Feliciano, M. "Q: There are several Legal Nurse Consultant (LNC) certifications currently available," *Journal of Legal Nurse Consulting*, Spring 2006, 18-21.

10. *Id.*

11. Zorn, B. and Iyer, P, *Secrets of Success of an Inhouse LNC Teleseminar*, www.medleague.com.

12. *Id.*

13. Clifford, R. "Approaching the initial review of voluminous medical records," *Journal of Legal Nurse Consulting*, Spring 2009, 23-24.

14. Iyer, P. and Barone, J. "Obtaining and organizing medical records," in Iyer, P. and Levin, B. (eds), *Medical Legal Aspects of Medical Records, Second Edition,* Lawyers and Judges Publishing Company, 2010.

15. Konray, R and Iyer, P, "Tampering with medical records," in Iyer, P. and Levin, B. (eds), *Medical Legal Aspects of Medical Records, Second Edition,* Lawyers and Judges Publishing Company, 2010.

16. Iyer, P. *LNC Writing Handbook*, www.medLeague.com, 2010.

17. *Id.*

18. Blank, A. and Kennedy, P. "Dynamic demand letters," *TRIAL*, December 2009, 28-31.

19. Haviland, K. and Iyer, P. *Visual Evidence Teleseminar*, Med League, 2009 www.medleague.com.

20. Personal communication, David Cohen Esq., 2004.

21. Personal communication, Robert Hyman Esq., 2004.

22. See note 11.

23. Zorn, B. and Manz, M. "Legal nurse consultant practice within a law firm," In A. Peterson and L. Kopishke (eds.) *Legal Nurse Consulting Principles and Practices, Third Edition*, Boca Raton, Florida: CRC Press, 2010.

24. See note 11.

25. *Id.*

26. *Id.*

27. *Id.*

28. *Id.*

29. See note 23.

Appendix 20.1: Medication Overdose (Courtesy of Jean Dworniczek RN)

Mrs. Horn's husband sought counsel from the leading medical negligence attorney in his area as he felt that his wife had not received proper care when she was first hospitalized. It was his belief that this inappropriate care directly resulted in her deficits and ultimate death. The attorney requested the medical records and had an independent LNC review these records to specifically determine the cause of the alleged neglect. Upon review of the records, the LNC was able to calculate the exact amount of narcotics that Mrs. Horn had received prior to the event to determine as the cause of her respiratory failure.

Summary of Clinical Events:

On 4/21/2006, Mrs. Horn, age 62, was admitted at 6:15 P.M. to Southlake Community Hospital with uncontrolled pain related to her metastatic disease. Her history included cancer of her right breast diagnosed in 2001 at which time she had a lumpectomy. Subsequently, she was treated with radiation therapy and six cycles of chemotherapy. In March of 2005, her cancer metastasized to her lungs and eventually to her bones by late December 2005. She was receiving chemotherapy with her last treatment three weeks prior to admission. Her history also included chronic obstructive pulmonary disease and hypothyroidism. Mrs. Horn was a two packs per day smoker for over 30 years but quit six months prior to admission. She was functioning independently at home and was working part-time two to three days a week in an office setting. During the three weeks prior to this admission, her medication regimen included oral opioids of Roxicodone and Lortab at home for the past three weeks. She reported poor relief in the past five to seven days. She was unable to sleep for longer than two hours at a time, was eating one small meal a day with one to two snacks and had been unable to work for one to two weeks. Her oncologist, Dr. Bobby Parsons, planned her direct admission to the oncology unit for acute pain management. His orders included oral, topical and intravenous administration of narcotics and NSAIDs to gain control of her pain. The ultimate outcome would be to gradually find the correct oral and topical dosage for pain control.

Her admitting pain medication orders were Roxicodone 5 mg orally every six hours, Fentanyl 50 mcg topical patch, change every 72 hours, Morphine 2 mg IV every one hour for breakthrough pain and Motrin 400 mg orally every six hours. In addition, Ambien (sleeping pill) 10 mg Q HS PRN was prescribed.

Mrs. Horn was initially assessed at 6:45 P.M. She had a blood pressure of 102/56, pulse 92, respirations 18 and oximetry of 99% on room air. Her nursing admission assessment was completed by 7:15 P.M. with significant findings of alert, oriented x4, and lungs clear but diminished in the bilateral bases. She had slight pedal edema. She had a steady gait but easily fatigued after walking 30 feet to use the washroom. She reported her pain, located in her left chest and mid back, as 8/10 and described it as constant, aching and nagging. It was aggravated by activity, eating and deep breaths. She did not eat prior to arrival so she was served a light meal. She only drank 6 ounces of juice and ate 4 ounces of Jell-O. IV fluids of normal saline were started at 50cc per hour via her existing venous access device [VAD]. Her last bowel movement was three days prior to arrival.

She received her first dose of Morphine 2mg at 7:20 P.M. with instructions on calling for assistance to get up. Her reassessment of pain at 8:10 P.M. noted her pain was 7/10 so she was administered a second dose of Morphine 2 mg. Her Fentanyl patch was applied at 9:25 P.M. and she received her first dose of Motrin at the same time. She continued to utilize the Morphine doses as needed until the Fentanyl patch achieved its effect. [See Table]

On 4/22/2006 at 6 A.M., Mrs. Horn stated she did not sleep well but the nursing notes reported sleep episodes after administration of pain medications. She ate 25% of her breakfast, sat in a chair for most of the morning and was walking to the bathroom independently. Her blood pressure was 90/62, pulse was 86 and respirations were 16. She had clear lungs with diminished bases and reported her pain as 6/10. The nurse continued to administer the Morphine 2 mg for pain to achieve a rating less than 4/10. Mrs. Horn again ate only 25% of her lunch and was sleeping after lunch for about two hours. She was easily arousable, alert and oriented x4. She walked with a steady gait but continued to complain of fatigue with activity. By dinner, her family visited and it was noted she was cheerful. She ate 50% of her dinner while her company was present. By 8 P.M. her pain rating was increasing from earlier in day. Her vital signs were checked every shift and remained stable.

On the morning of 4/23/2006, Mrs. Horn remained alert, oriented x4 and easily arousable. She reported her pain in the same location and with the same description but the rating fluctuated from 4-6 based on her activity. Her blood pressure was 98/52, pulse 92, respirations were 16 and oximetry was 96% on room air. Her vital signs were again checked every shift and remained stable. She sat in the chair for only one hour in the morning and then returned to bed. Her appetite remained decreased and a dietary assessment noted diet supplements were sent with each meal. In addition, the nurse encouraged oral fluid intake and her IV rate was increased to 75 cc per hour. At 2 P.M., the nurse noted instructions on deep breathing exercises, but following this activity, Mrs. Horn's pain increased significantly to 9/10. Additional Morphine was administered for pain control. Mrs. Horn remained in bed for the rest of the afternoon due to her pain and her fear of pain returning with activity. Her family visited again but the nurse charted she was resting with eyes closed during this time. She continued to report her pain from 6-9 and additional doses of Morphine were administered.

At 8 p.m., Mrs. Horn was moaning with pain and crying that she could not get comfortable. The nurse administered the prescribed pain medication. At 9:10 p.m. her pain status was reassessed as 7/10, she was drowsy but arousable. Her blood pressure was 90/74, pulse was 68, respirations were 12, shallow and her pulse oximetry was 92%. At 11:30 p.m., her blood pressure was 90/62, pulse was 62, respirations 12 and shallow, and pulse oximetry was 90%. She was groggy but arousable to voice and touch. She was not assessed for orientation at this notation.

On 4/24/2006 at 2:15 a.m., Mrs. Horn was found unresponsive by the nursing aide, Ms. Young. The nurse, Mary Hinkley, assessed her at 2:25 a.m. and noted her blood pressure was 86/50, pulse was 62, respirations were 8 and oximetry was 84%. With deep sternal rub, she moaned but was non-verbal. After this period, Dr. Parsons was paged at 2:35 a.m. through his service with a response time at 2:42 a.m. At 2:40, Mrs. Horn was unresponsive, no respirations or pulse. A Code Blue was called and CPR was initiated. Since Dr. Parsons' response was two minutes after the code was called he was updated per telephone by the nurses and the code team. Orders were noted to transfer to ICU. Mrs. Horn was intubated in the unit and remained on a ventilator for the next 16 hours. She was eventually weaned off but remained in the ICU for two additional days.

Mrs. Horn was progressing well in her functional level as she was walking with assistance due to weakness and loss of balance, she was able to feed herself but needed assistance to dress her lower extremities. Physical and occupational therapy were ordered to assist in these areas. She had significant delays of memory and speech. A CT scan and MRI of the brain reported insignificant findings. An EEG was performed with some reported conduction delays. A neurologist consultation by Dr. Bayer noted questionable ability for improvement. Speech therapy was then added by the team to address cognition and speech. The therapist evaluation noted moderate expressive aphasia that increased with fatigue. She had delay with responses and word selection. She lacked problem solving abilities and decision making. The discharge plan was transfer to the University Rehabilitation Center for continued PT, OT and ST services.

After four weeks of inpatient rehab services, Mrs. Horn was discharged to home with home care services consisting of short term therapy. Mr. Horn was unable to assume all their care so her daughter made daily visits to assist. They hired a CNA for four hours a day to assist with her bathing, dressing and some meal preparation. As her disease progressed, Mrs. Horn was moved to an inpatient hospice on 11-1-06 until her death on 12-22-06.

Review Findings:

According to the Medication Administration Record [MAR] dated 4/21/2004, Mrs. Horn received Roxicodone 5 mg every 6 hours beginning at 9:25 p.m. Fentanyl was applied at 9:25 p.m. with hand written notation to change Q 72 hours. Morphine 2mg was administered at 7:20 p.m. with several doses following on all shifts. The Table details all medications, doses and times administered from admission to the time she was found unresponsive.

The total amount of narcotics received in a 24-hour period, noted in the table, was significant based upon her medications taken at home prior to this admission.

Upon further investigation of the records, Mrs. Horn had been given 2 doses of Fentanyl patch within 48 hours. The MAR failed to have accurate transcription from 4/21/06 to 4/22/06 and again to 4/23/2006. The entry on 4/21/2006 had a date when the Fentanyl patch was placed but lacked location on the body. The record failed to have a date and time entered on the subsequent records for 4/22 and 4/23 when the Fentanyl patch was due to be replaced. This process error contributed to the nurse applying the second Fentanyl patch on 4/23/2006, in addition to the one that had been put on 24 hours earlier.

The nurse should have noted the admission date on the MAR and the order date to determine the patch most likely was placed the day of admission making it obvious it was less than 72 hours. In addition, the medication dispensing system had a process of verifying when the last Fentanyl patch was taken from the system. The nurse failed to check Mrs. Horn's skin for a previous patch to not only remove it but verify a date of placement on the patch. By not removing the Fentanyl patch, Mrs. Horn was receiving not only the 50 mcg of Fentanyl every hour of one patch but she was receiving a double dose of 100 mcg per hour since both patches remained in place.

The billing records and the pharmacy dispensing logs demonstrated additional doses of Morphine that were not noted on the MAR. These doses are asterisk-noted in the table. Failure to document these doses not only demonstrated ineffective communication among the nurses but allowed for the possibility of, or potential for administration of Morphine doses earlier than prescribed.

Mrs. Horn's vital signs were noted to have gradual decrease over time but the changes occurred most significantly the evening of 4/23/06. For the patient receiving this amount of narcotics, a more frequent assessment of vital signs, respiratory and neurological status was indicated to provide a more accurate reading of her response to the medications. One would also expect the nurse to notify the attending physician of this continued downward trend in vital signs and neurologic status.

Mrs. Horn received a significant amount of narcotics over a 24-hour period of time. The records did not indicate if the physician was informed of her total dosing as well her pain status. The double dosing of Fentanyl was the most pertinent action that led to her respiratory failure and eventual injury.

During the deposition of the nurses, issues of the amount of administered narcotics were addressed as well as the lack of notification of the physician of significant changes in Mrs. Horn's clinical status. Another issue that was explored extensively was the ten minute delay from the time that Mrs. Horn was found unresponsive by the aide and the time the nurse responded to the situation.

Shortly after the depositions of the nurses were taken, the case was settled for $2.5 million.

PAIN MEDICATION ADMINISTRATION

DATE	TIME	DRUG	DOSE	ROUTE
4/21/2006	7:20 P.M.	Morphine	2 mg	IV
4/21/2006	8:10 P.M.	Morphine	2 mg	IV
4/21/2006	9:25 P.M.	Fentanyl	50 mcg	TO
4/21/2006	9:25 P.M.	Roxicodone	5 mg	PO
4/21/2006	11:40 P.M.	Morphine	2 mg	IV
4/22/2006	3:30 A.M.	Roxicodone	5 mg	PO
4/22/2006	6:30 A.M.	Morphine	2 mg	IV
4/22/2006	8:00 A.M.	Morphine **	2 mg	IV
4/22/2006	9:30 A.M.	Morphine	2 mg	IV
4/22/2006	9:30 A.M.	Roxicodone	5 mg	PO
4/22/2006	12:00 P.M.	Morphine	2 mg	IV
4/22/2006	2:00 P.M.	Morphine	2 mg	IV
4/22/2006	3:10 P.M.	Morphine	2 mg	IV
4/22/2006	3:30 P.M.	Roxicodone	5 mg	PO
4/22/2006	5:00 P.M.	Morphine	2 mg	IV
4/22/2006	8:00 P.M.	Morphine	2 mg	IV
4/22/2006	9:30 P.M.	Roxicodone	5 mg	PO
4/22/2006	11:50 P.M.	Morphine	2 mg	IV
4/23/2006	3:30 A.M.	Morphine	2 mg	IV
4/23/2005	3:30 A.M.	Roxicodone	5 mg	PO
4/23/2006	6:00 A.M.	Morphine **	2 mg	IV
4/23/2006	8:10 A.M.	Morphine	2 mg	IV
4/23/2006	9:30 A.M.	Roxicodone	5 mg	PO
4/23/2006	12:15 P.M.	Morphine	2 mg	IV
4/23/2006	2:15 P.M.	Morphine	2 mg	IV
4/23/2006	3:15 P.M.	Morphine	2 mg	IV
4/23/2006	3:15 P.M.	Roxicodone	5 mg	PO
4/23/2006	4:30 P.M.	Morphine	2 mg	IV
4/23/2006	6:45 P.M.	Morphine	2 mg	IV
4/23/2006	8:15 P.M.	Morphine	2 mg	IV
4/23/2006	9:30 P.M.	Roxicodone	5 mg	PO
4/23/2006	9:30 P.M.	Morphine	2 mg	IV
4/23/2006	9:30 P.M.	Fentanyl	50 mcg	TO
4/23/2006	11:50 P.M.	Morphine	2 mg	IV

Total Dosing

Date	Morphine	Roxicodone
4/21/2006	6 mg	5 mg
4/22/2006	18 mg	20 mg
4/23/2006	20 mg	20 mg

Appendix 20.2
Liability

Common sense and critical thinking would guide the prudent nurse practitioner or primary care physician to rule out the more serious possible causes of the headaches, (especially given the classic features of the headaches), before settling for the least life-threatening and quite frankly, unlikely possibilities.

The American Academy of Nurse Practitioners' Standards of Practice states:

"The nurse practitioner utilizes the scientific process and national standards of care as a framework for managing patient care."

This process includes "utilizing critical thinking in the diagnostic process, synthesizing and analyzing the collected data and formulating a differential diagnosis based on the history, physical examination and diagnostic test results." Two nurse practitioners, Ms. White and Ms. Brown, deviated from the standard of care.

Ms. White's diagnosis of cervical strain in absence of any cause for cervical strain was devoid of critical thinking. The fact that she ignored hallmark signs of meningeal irritation or perhaps was unaware of what these signs are is malpractice.

Ms. Brown lost her focus on David's chief complaint of "severe headache" (severe enough to awaken him, accompanied by photophobia), when she elicited a history of his drinking and smoking habits. His chief complaint was demoted to a manifestation of "anxiety" with no formal diagnostic workup despite his symptoms. The fact that she also ignored David's changing symptoms and evolving pattern of headaches and all that it implies is malpractice.

David's blood pressure was 120/92. The record is unclear as to what size cuff this blood pressure was measured with. Ms. Brown notes that, at his last visit, the blood pressure was taken with a large cuff and was 130/82. Pulse is 80 bpm. Neurological exam is reported as negative.

Both Ms. White and Ms. Brown were negligent in failing to formulate a differential diagnosis. They both entertained their own single possible diagnosis despite symptoms that had more than one possible life-threatening etiology (aneurysmal bleed, AVM).

Because they failed to formulate differential diagnoses, Ms. White and Ms. Brown were negligent in failing to establish priorities to meet David's health and medical needs. In other words, it was a higher priority to assess for aneurysm than to treat for "anxiety." The failure to establish these priorities to meet David's health and medical needs falls below acceptable standards of care.

The American Academy of Family Physicians' Headache Consortium published evidence-based practice guidelines regarding the use of diagnostic neuro imaging in October of 2000:

1. Testing should be avoided if it will not lead to any change in management;
2. Testing is not recommended if the patient is not significantly more likely than the general population to have a significant abnormality; and
3. Testing that is not normally recommended may make sense in individual cases, such as in patients who are excessively worried about a serious problem as the cause of their headaches.

The AAFP goes on to explain the arguments for and against neuro imaging. NO recommendations are made regarding neuro imaging in the presence or absence of neurologic symptoms (David had no documented neurologic symptoms).

The data reviewed by the AAFP suggested that an increased likelihood of intracranial pathology exists in headaches worsened by valsalva maneuver, headache that awakens the patient, new onset headache in older patients or progressively worsening headaches. David's headaches were evolving in severity. They were awakening him. They were becoming progressively debilitating. They were rarely if ever mentioned in his medical record prior to these three consecutive visits. He was never asked if Valsalva made his headaches worse.

Despite the facts that David presented to Dr. Schwartz's office on two successive occasions with "his worse headache" and "a severe headache," with hypertension, tachycardia, signs of nuchal rigidity and nausea during the first visit, photophobia and disruptions in his ability to attend classes and disruptions in his ability to sleep, nothing was done to rule out serious intracranial processes. He was not referred to a neurologist or neurosurgeon. No neuro imaging was ordered to rule out aneurysm or AVM. He was not examined by any medical doctor nor is there any indication in the notes that Dr. Schwartz was consulted by his nurse practitioners for guidance.

The American Academy of Family Physicians' *Guidelines on the Supervision of Certified Nurse Midwives, Nurse Practitioners and Physician Assistants* states:

"The central principle underlying physician supervision of NPP's (non-physician providers) is that the physician retains ultimate responsibility for the patient care rendered."
"The physician must afford supervision adequate to ensure that the NPP provides care in accordance with accepted medical standards"

The guideline goes on to define "supervision" as:

"to coordinate, direct and inspect on an ongoing basis the accomplishments of another, or to oversee, with the power to direct, the implementation of one's own or another's intentions."

The guidelines clearly state "it is the responsibility of the supervising physician (Dr. Schwartz) to direct and review the work, records and practice of the NP on a continuous basis to ensure that appropriate directions are given and understood and that appropriate treatment is rendered." There is nothing in the medical chart indicating that Dr. Schwartz reviewed David's case with, or otherwise directed, the nurse practitioners in his office. This is substandard care. Furthermore, if he did review David's case and failed to develop a more comprehensive differential diagnosis, this would also constitute a deviation from acceptable medical standards.

According to the guidelines, it is the responsibility of the physician to ensure that appropriate direction is given, understood and executed. Direction may take the form of written protocols, in person, over the phone, etc. The degree of supervision should lessen only when the physician can ensure that the NP will provide care in accordance with directions and accepted medical standards. Both the physician and NP must ensure their currency in regard to the evolving standards of medical practice. The goal is to err on the side of the NP seeking physician involvement more often than proves to be necessary.

Dr. Schwartz did not adequately supervise or direct the nurse practitioners working in his office in David's care. The nurse practitioners did not appropriately seek physician involvement in David's care decisions. Failure to do so resulted in a missed diagnosis and David's avoidable death.

Wrongful Death

According to the medical literature, a warning leak, if interpreted correctly to diagnose aneurysmal subarachnoid hemorrhage, has significant potential to improve overall outcome. Our expert is strongly of the opinion that:

1. David's intracranial hemorrhage, to a reasonable degree of certainty based on his age, medical history and CT scan results, was due to a ruptured aneurysm.
2. David showed classic signs of a "sentinel bleed" (neck stiffness, nausea, vomiting, sensitivity to light; Aneurysm, Brain, Emedicine, last updated May 26, 2001), which should have been diagnosed by Dr. Schwartz, Ms. White and Ms. Brown.
3. Proper diagnostic workup and/or referral (neurology, LP, CT, MRI) by Dr. Schwartz's office most likely would have produced the correct diagnosis in time to avoid David's death.
4. David's aneurysm most likely would have been treatable either surgically or via interventional radiological procedures.
5. His death was the result of substandard medical care on the part of Dr. Schwartz's office staff.

(Courtesy of Ann Steinmetz, Rochester, NY)

Appendix 20.3
Medical Record Summary

Client: Dorothy Smith, Date: A while ago

Date of Accident: 1/1/09

Conditions Claimed: Nausea, vomiting, abdominal pain, irregular heartbeat, hypertension, bladder infection, decreased kidney function, medication overdose, gastroenteritis, failure to diagnose, failure to treat, failure to safely provide hypertension medications within the standard of care of dehydrated patient, volume depletion and dehydration.

Risk Factors Associated with Conditions Claimed: Spanish speaking

Conditions Treated/ Damages Bladder infection, hypertension, dehydration

Medical Providers:
A Large Hospital
Bob Jones, MD
Suzy Black, RN
Harry Hughes, RN
John Richards MD
Radiologist: Jimmy Peters, MD
Fred Red, MD/ED

Records are not available in the file for the following providers:
The following records are missing for the same date of 1/1/09 and 1/2/09
- Missing complete physical admission exam
- Missing physician transfer orders
- Missing abdominal CT scan and MRI of abdomen with complete reports (the reports are incomplete).
- Missing nursing notes denoting the change in patient status
- Missing physician contact sheet
- Missing respiratory therapy notes
- Missing authorization sheets for admission and tests performed
- Need medication MAR and IV intake and output sheets
- Need physician orders for these dates

The plaintiff is claiming the following injuries as a result of the accident (according to the medical records ONLY)
- Failure to provide lifesaving measures.
- Failure to obtain the health care power of attorney signed papers from patient.
- Failure to obtain an interpreter to secure no code status and prevent confusion in interpretation of medical information.
- Negligence and failure to treat resulted in ultimate death.
- Breach in the standard of care for prompt diagnosis.
- Breach in the standard of care for clear concise documentation when transferring patient to another floor.
- Breach in the standard of care for safe medication administration.
- Incongruent medical findings and physician interpretations of patient status.
- Failure to respond promptly to nurses call for change in patient status

SUMMARY OF CASE

Ms. Dorothy Smith was a 95-year-old patient who presented to the emergency department at A Large Hospital with nausea and vomiting for 24 hours. She was seen and evaluated in the emergency department where diagnostic testing proved she had a bladder infection, and also diarrhea, loss of fluids, and vomiting.

At some point (the medical records are unclear), Ms. Smith was given a dose of DrugXYZ. After the administration of the large amount of DrugXYZ, Ms. Smith's breathing changed drastically and she eventually died.

LNC Evaluation

The medical file is filled with incongruencies which make it difficult to read and interpret. The physicians document that Ms. Smith had a long history of medical issues when, in fact, the medical issues she did have were well controlled with her current conservative methods. When she presented to the ED, she was alert, oriented and her only complaints were nausea and vomiting (she did not speak English and a translator would have been appropriate rather than a family member—these standards of care for interpreters or translators are provided by The Joint Commission and can be read here:

The Joint Commission's Hospitals, Language, and Culture study: *http://www.jointcommission.org/NR/rdonlyres/ 3BEC48A2-5CAA-459F-9BD4-EFC8AC8F6F23/0/EffectiveCommunicationResourcesforHCOsrevised.pdf).*

There was never a diagnosis provided for the nausea and vomiting she presented with to the emergency department, aside from gastroenteritis, which is a physical condition.

When she was seen for radiological studies, the EKG was normal. Her heart was normal and without shadows, and even her abdominal studies appear to be normal. Yet, she was given a diagnosis of gastroenteritis. Complete physical exams by the physicians are missing pages. Also, there are pages missing from the radiological studies and I could not find the results of the MRI or the CT scan that was ordered.

The only positive testing was the advanced bladder infection. It makes sense that she would have nausea and vomiting with a bladder infection. There were no fever or chills which may lead us to believe that the kidneys were involved in the infection.

Therefore, the obvious cause in the change of Ms. Smith's condition would be the administration of the medication DrugXYZ and the medication error of double dosing the patient.

According to Drug Company XYZ, the pharmaceutical which produces DrugXYZ, the medication peaks in approximately one hour. It is used to control hypertension. (At the time of her admission to the hospital, it should be noted that Ms. Smith was hypotensive—this was related to her dehydration and volume depletion). Drug Company XYZ reveals the medication has a special warning when used with patients who are dehydrated. There are risks when the patient is dehydrated and there is loss of kidney function (radiological studies show that Ms. Smith's right kidney was atrophied).

Under all of these conditions, Ms. Smith had missed a dose of her DrugXYZ (typically provided twice a day) while she was at testing. When she returned to the medical floor, the nurse obtained her blood pressure (as prescribed by the treating physician). The medication was then given. However, shortly thereafter (I am unsure of the time), the DrugXYZ was again administered to the patient following the taking of her vital signs.

When DrugXYZ is given in an overdose, there is no remedy for the overdose. It cannot be removed from the blood with the use of hemodialysis.

Hannah, the patient's daughter, noticed a change in Ms. Smith's breathing and alerted the nurse. The complete nurse's notes are not available and it's difficult to tell what the nurse did—if she contacted the physician, if the physician came to the bedside, or if a no code status was indeed obtained. There are more questions than answers following this period of time.

By 7:05 A.M. (unsure of time of death—need death certificate), Ms. Smith was pronounced dead.

At best, the physician documentation is scanty. The nurse's documentation may have been more thorough and is not available to me for review.

There are several breaches in the standard of care. The most rudimentary, though, is the need for a translator to assist with the medical information and the interpretation of the patient's symptoms. Perhaps an interpreter would have been able to tell the nurse that the patient had just taken that medication. The physician documents the daughter told the nurse that she did not want the mother to be a full CODE. However, there is no documentation from the nurse that states this.

It appears the patient died and the family was unaware of how ill she was or that this would occur at this particular time.

The rapid onset of Ms. Smith's symptoms following the administration of the second dose DrugXYZ places the change in condition directly following her taking the drug.

You will need a testifying expert to speak to the standard of care concerning the following breaches:

- Failure to provide lifesaving measures
- Failure to obtain the health care power of attorney signed papers from patient
- Failure to obtain an interpreter to secure no code status and prevent confusion in interpretation of medical information
- Negligence and failure to treat resulted in ultimate death
- Breach in the standard of care for prompt diagnosis
- Breach in the standard of care for clear concise documentation when transferring patient to another floor
- Breach in the standard of care for safe medication administration
- Incongruent medical findings and physician interpretations of patient status
- Failure to respond promptly to nurse's call for change in patient status

The recommended physician testifying experts would possibly include an emergency room physician. Also, you need a pharmaceutical specialist who can speak to the consequences of double dosing DrugXYZ with dehydration and kidney insufficiency. You'll need a medical surgical nurse to address the standard of care for administration of medication and missed dose medications is recommended.

In addressing the communication needs of the patient, it would be best to have a clerk or physician from the emergency room who can discuss when translators are typically contacted for the patients who are admitted that do not speak English.

In closing, in this report are profiles for the treating physicians and nurses of Ms. Smith, who include:

- Bob Jones, MD
- Suzy Black, RN
- Harry Hughes, RN
- John Richards MD
- Radiologist: Jimmy Peters, MD
- Fred Red, MD/ED

Date Review Completed: Revised Sometime
Reviewed by: Clarann P. Hull, RN, CCM, MSCC, CLNC

(Courtesy of Clarann Hull, Raleigh-Durham North Carolina)

Appendix 20.4
On-Site Investigation of Assisted Living Facility

Period covered: April 2, 2006 through January 21, 2009
Review date: November 5, 2009
Insured: Southwest Assisted Living
Insured location: Valley Care Center
Claim: 123-465789
                         Marion Pepper

Background medical history:

Hypertension, myocardial infarction per history, cerebral vascular accident per history, anticoagulation therapy, pulmonary edema, coronary artery disease, cholangitis, type II diabetes, peripheral vascular disease, and transient ischemic attack.

Investigative focus

Change in condition acute hospital admission leading to death

Summary

Ms. Pepper was admitted to Southwest Assisted Living facility on April 2, 2006. Her overall stay was not significant except that she did have *"spells"* which were presumed to be small transient ischemic attacks. One of these spells occurred once while she was out with the group at the Wal-Mart and 911 was called. This resident had a history of laborious breathing and some gastrointestinal disturbances related to her gallbladder.

From admission in 2006 to her discharge in 2009, there had been a slow but steady decline in which she had begun to require more assistance from the staff as evidenced by being charged for Level 2 services.

This review focuses on Ms. Pepper's admission to Golden Regional Hospital on January 21, 2009.

According to the nursing note of January 20, 2009 at 0930, Ms. Pepper was noted to be limping when ambulating to the dining room with her walker and she was noted to have a dry non-productive cough.

At 1 P.M. that same day, a family member brought in some lunch from home according the nursing note. Ms. Pepper ate a small amount. The family members were concerned about her because she was *"not acting as she usually does"* and she had a *"hacking non-productive cough."* The family requested an appointment with the physician. The nurse, Crystal Steele, LPN noted that she would *"monitor."*

On January 30, 2009, the niece came to the facility to collect Ms. Pepper's items. According to Mr. Ramsey, *"Connie said that the doctor was not able to do anything to take the fluid off her abdomen because she is in congestive heart failure and won't make it out of the hospital. She blamed Crystal for not responding quickly enough to her concerns about the changes."*

On February 1, 2009, Connie came to turn in the keys and said that Ms. Pepper's death was near.

STAFF INTERVIEWS (deleted)

Investigator Summary/Opinions:

There is a significant gap in this resident's nursing notes. Prior to January 20, 2009 the last note was written on May 24, 2008. Ms. Pepper was requiring more assistance and her level of care had increased to a Level 2.

Upon review of Ms. Pepper's medication administration record [MAR], it appears that the resident did not receive her Lasix [diuretic] as ordered in the month of December. **It was to be administered daily and was only documented once**. The facility could not locate the January 2009 MAR which may impact this matter. [This medication is utilized to lower the circulating fluid volume in the system.]

The nursing note of January 21, 2009 indicates that Nurse Steele contacted the physician. The documentation of Mr. Ramsey indicates the resident's niece called the physician. This will be complicated by the fact that Nurse Steele was dismissed from the facility in April 2009 for among other things, **fraudulent documentation**.

Recommendations:
1. Reevaluate nursing documentation policies
2. Clear guidelines when the physicians are to be notified of changes in conditions
3. Refresher course for nursing staff on appropriate assessments
4. Clear guidelines for non-professional staff to contact licensed staff or physicians for guidance

Conclusion:
1. The community staff failed to appropriately assess Ms. Pepper's change in condition.
2. The community staff failed to document according to standard.
3. The community staff failed to follow orders regarding medication administration.
4. The community failed to keep an accurate and complete medical record.

Standard of practice-**Below**
Venue-**Good**
Defense witnesses-**Good to Very Good**
Medical record as evidence-**Poor**

For **eight months** nothing noteworthy occurred.

When Nurse Steele noted that Ms. Pepper was weak, needing to sit down on January 20, 2009 and that she was coughing, appropriate assessments should have occurred. There were no vital signs recorded, no assessment of the chest/lungs and no assessment evaluating why she was limping.

After the family visited and expressed concerns, there were still no documented assessments. The nurse indicated that she was going to follow up but it appears that nothing initially was even assessed. The family requested that the physician be called. Given Ms. Pepper's prior medical history, delicate health and that the facility was under the attack of a serious flu epidemic, a call should have been made to the physician prior to the family's request.

Once the family requested this, it should have been done that day. It was documented that this request occurred at 1 P.M. That would have been plenty of time to contact the physician's office before closing to relay the **change in condition and concern**.

There were no assessments documented for the remaining of that shift, the evening shift or night shift. Therefore the medical record does not reflect any **monitoring** at all.

It is not known by the investigator what Ms. Pepper's admission diagnoses were at Golden Regional Medical Center. However, the niece's conversation with Mr. Ramsey indicated an issue with fluid build up related to **congestive heart failure**.

The following morning at 9 A.M., the nursing note stated that *"Dr. Henry called and informed of Ms. Pepper's status."* The physician ordered a chest x-ray. Ms. Pepper's niece was called and informed and stated she would be at the facility at 10 A.M. to provide transport.

At 2 P.M. that day, the facility received a telephone message that Ms. Pepper had been admitted to the hospital.

The Executive Director, Matthew Ramsey had encountered the niece, Connie when she was getting ready to take Ms. Pepper to the physician's office that morning. She expressed that she was upset that it was she who obtained an appointment for Ms. Pepper and not the nurse. [See Quality Assurance Review for Marion Pepper.]

On January 28, 2009, staff members Lisa Allen and Michelle Aster visited Ms. Pepper in the hospital and encountered Connie. She relayed that Valley staff should have sent her to the physician sooner.

Appendix 20.5
Questions Written by a Legal Nurse Consultant to Assist an Attorney with the Deposition of a Defense Nursing Expert

1. What is the standard of care (SOC) in regard to post-op vital sign monitoring? (The standard is usually every 15 minutes for the first hour, every 30 minutes for the second hour, and then every four hours. It is up to a nurse to intervene if during that time the vital signs change. More frequent vitals should be done.)

2. What is the purpose of post-op vital signs? (To watch for a trend and if the vital signs are changing, to contact physician and alert him to a change in order to prevent any further untoward events from happening.)

3. When you look at the chart —how many times were post-op vital signs done on Mrs. Kestler? Do you feel this met the standard of care? (Especially with the changes that were occurring—BP was initially 152/77, pulse of 82, resp of 20. At 16:45: 147/70-92-36.)

4. Do you think that this change in respiratory rate was clinically significant? (Vitals at 20:30: 145/63-144-39.)

5. At 20:30 when both the pulse and respiratory rate elevated, what is the significance of these changes?

6. Did you see the order to monitor hourly urine output? Why is this important? As a nurse, what are you taught is the minimal amount per hour that is considered adequate? (30cc/hr)

7. Did you see anywhere on the night of the 8th that this was recorded? (It was recorded at 7 P.M. on the graphic record, but not mentioned or recorded until she arrived in ICU and the nurse made a comment that it was less than 30cc.)

8. As a nurse, you have been taught that 30cc urine output per hour is the minimal amount that you watch for. Is that correct?

9. From a nursing perspective, why is it important that a person puts out 30cc of urine per hour? (It indicates adequate urine production.)

10. Also, from a nursing perspective, if a person does not put out this amount, what is a general medical-surgical nurse supposed to do? (Notify the MD and tell her the current status of the patient, which includes vital signs, and any other assessment that is pertinent, in this case, abdominal assessment, skin color, respiratory pattern, pain level, and overall presentation.)

11. What is a normal pulse oximeter value? (95-100%)

12. First explain what a pulse ox is, and how it is different from arterial blood gases. How does it work?

13. From a nursing perspective, at what level does the standard of care indicate that the nurse should be concerned?

14. It was noted that at 20:30 her pulse ox was 84%. Is this normal? How much oxygen was she on at the time?

15. Would you expect someone with oxygen on to have this low of a pulse ox? From a nursing perspective what are some factors that could lead to a low pulse ox?

16. The nurse notified the doctor of the low oxygen saturation. Was this appropriate? (Yes.)

17. According to the nursing notes Mrs. Kestler was changed to a 50% Venti mask and her pulse ox came up to 89%. From a nursing perspective is this acceptable? (This is still too low.) Do you see any further monitoring of the pulse ox?

18. At 22:00, the respiratory therapist noted that the patient was desaturating (dropping oxygen level). What does this mean from a nursing perspective?

19. Would you think that the nurse should have noted that in her notes? Do you find any evidence of this issue being charted on?

20. As a nurse, would you expect that respiratory therapy and nursing would be in communication concerning the patient's condition? (Yes.)

21. Please turn to page 193 and look at the section titled "respiratory." Do you see continuous pulse ox written in? So this would mean that the nurses had this information available to them—correct? By this charting it means that she was continuously hooked to a machine, not just intermittently—correct?

22. Are nurses able to read the pulse ox machine? (Yes.) It is not exclusively just for respiratory therapists, is it?

23. The nurse charted that she was going to continue to monitor the patient closely as per her nursing notes at 20:30. Does the medical record indicate that this was done? If you look on pages 193 and 194, do you see if there are any assessments made after 20:00?

24. Does the SOC require the nurse to document why orders from an MD were received, or why the nurse is contacting the doctor? Does the medical record contain this information in Mrs. Kestler's case?

25. Does the SOC require the nurses to assess and chart an abdominal assessment on a patient who has had abdominal surgery? Do you see anything charted by nursing in regard to this after 20:00?

26. What is the SOC in regard to following orders to administer antibiotics?

27. Was the pre-op Claforan given? Who should have given this medication?

28. Was it a deviation from the standard of care to not give a preoperative medication that was ordered?

29. Zosyn was ordered at 00:50, but not given until 05:30—is this acceptable (especially when the drug is available on floor)?

30. As noted in the chart there are several Lasix orders given. There is a Lasix 40mg given at 22:00—correct? Then there is another Lasix ordered at 23:00—what amount was ordered at that time? (80mg.)

31. On the med sheet it is circled at 23:00 which means it is not given. Now turn to the nursing notes on page 288. The nurse noted that at 01:00 she held the Lasix due to a decrease in the blood pressure and she called Dr. Searley for orders. In the chart, the orders from Dr. Searley are timed for 00:50. What time do you actually think that this blood pressure was taken—23:00 when she circles the Lasix entry on the med sheet or the 01:00 entry on her progress notes?

32. If Mrs. Kestler's BP was really 99/44 at 23:00, is that not a breach in the SOC on the nurse's part to not phone the physician at that time instead of waiting almost two hours?

33. The order from Dr. Searley was to monitor blood pressure and notify him if the systolic blood pressure fell below 90 and diastolic below 50. Were any other vital signs taken between the value of 99/44 and the value of 40/22 obtained at 5:45 A.M.? (No.)

34. Also there was on order generated at 1:30 A.M. for a 300cc fluid bolus. Do you see any evidence that this order was completed? Did the nurse deviate from the standard of care by not administering the fluid challenge?

35. What does the SOC require for the nurse in regard to pain monitoring? (recording intensity of pain, site, quality of pain, whether pain was relieved.)

36. Did the nurse meet the SOC? Did you find any evidence that her pain was assessed? (The only place pain was noted was on page 194 under pain assessment: Level of 8 at 16:45, and 9 at 20:00.)

37. Explain the pain scale. Is it not a patient's right to be relieved of pain or made as comfortable as possible? Why is the pain scale used? What is the significance of it?

38. Do you know what TJC standards were in 2004 are in regard to pain? Do you see anywhere on the record that Mrs. Kestler received any type of pain medications?

39. On page 360, can you determine if at 17:30 the PCA was on or off? According to the signatures—Nurse Conrletter noted it was off, but Nurse Nuwool noted it was on. How can that be? Please explain, was it on or off?

40. In looking at the care received by Mrs. Kestler, do you believe it conformed to the standard of care?

Appendix 20.6
Questions Written by a Legal Nurse Consultant to Assist an Attorney with a Deposition of a Defendant Nurse

1. What is the primary aim of nursing management for an infant with DKA (diabetic ketoacidosis)?
    To achieve metabolic control, re-hydrate the patient and restore electrolyte balance without compromising patient safety. Meaning astute assessments, critical thinking and quick decision making.

2. What are some of the presenting signs and symptoms of DKA?
    Altered level of consciousness; tachypnea. In moderate to severe DKA deep rapid respirations (Kussmaul's respirations). Fruity odor to the breath. Other signs include: flushed skin (despite being hypotensive—when you would expect the patient to be pale). Tachycardia.

3. What does the fruity odor to the breath indicate?
    The presence of acetone.

4. Are you aware of nursing policies and procedures that address DKA (infants in DKA to be exact)?

5. What are general nursing functions when monitoring an infant in DKA?
    Monitoring the patient closely, documenting and taking appropriate actions such as notification of the MD. Assessments should include general appearance, temperature, pulse, respiratory rate, B/P and neurologic status.

6. What are other nursing observations that should be performed on an infant every hour?
    Observation of general condition, monitoring for signs of hypoglycemia and electrolyte imbalance. Frequent assessment of acid base status with venous pH measurements; monitoring of blood urea. While frequency is ordered by MD, it should be every two hours then every four hours based upon status and clinical condition of infant.

7. What is the major cause of fluid loss in DKA?
    Osmotic diuresis which is brought about by excess excretion of glucose in the urine. As a result of this osmotic diuresis, sodium, chloride and potassium are excreted in the urine in large amounts, accompanied by severe water loss. Thus, dehydration is seen and if severe enough, dehydration can cause cardiovascular instability leading to shock.

8. Discuss the nursing process pertaining to the rehydration of an infant who has had a DKA episode.
    This hydration should be gradual, using an isotonic fluid such as 0.9 NSS (normal saline). Because this fluid is restricted to the extracellular fluid space and more rapidly corrects plasma volume than hypotonic fluids. Rapid rehydration is thought to be a significant risk factor for cerebral edema.

9. What is the frequency of monitoring vital signs in an infant with suspected DKA?
    Frequent vital signs should be monitored every 15 minutes if unstable; hourly if stable; neuro status should be monitored as well. Urinary output should be monitored hourly to assess renal function. Glucose levels should be monitored via a finger prick method every hour.

10. Are you aware of the policy and procedure pertaining to the administration of intravenous insulin to an infant with DKA? Please indicate how you followed the policy.

11. What is the usual IV insulin dose?
    Even though dosage is ordered by the MD, the RN must know the normal parameters for correct administration.

Insulin is given by continuous infusion; initial dose is 0.05 unit per kg of weight per hour in children under eight years of age. The mixture is 50 ml of 0.9 NS and 50 units short-acting human insulin, giving a mixture of 1 unit of insulin per ml of fluid. A flow chart should be established (per policy) to document insulin administration.

12. Are you aware of the policy addressing the rate of reduction of the blood glucose levels? Are you aware that rapid reduction can be detrimental to the infant?
    Blood glucose levels should be restored to normal ranges as safely as possible, thus gradual reduction is necessary and usually no more than 5 mmol/l (millimoles per liter) per hour.

13. List the potential disadvantages of administering Sodium Bicarbonate.
    Worsening hypokalemia; production of paradoxical central nervous system acidosis; worsened intracellular acidosis due to increased carbon dioxide production; prolongation of ketoanion metabolism.

14. At what pH should Sodium Bicarbonate be given?
    Sodium Bicarbonate should not be given unless the pH is below 7.0.

15. What was the pH when you first started the administration of Sodium Bicarbonate?
    PH at 2200 on 1-29-09 was 7.03, critical level. Normal is 7.35–7.45.

16. What is the significance of the elevated potassium levels?
    Potassium leaves the cells and flows into the intravascular system when insulin levels are low.

17. Discuss potassium levels and insulin therapy.
    The potassium is driven back into the cells once insulin therapy is started (usually within one hour); thus the potassium levels will decrease. EKG monitoring should be performed as hypokalemia is seen on an EKG by prolonged QT intervals, flattened or depressed T waves, and depressed ST segments. Physical signs may include muscle weakness, hypotension and a weakening pulse. Lethal dysrhythmias may occur if the potassium level is allowed to drop too far.

18. What are the signs and symptoms of intracerebral crisis during the treatment of DKA?
    Decreasing sensorium; vomiting; agitation; change in vital signs (hypothermia, hypotension or hypertension, tachycardia or bradycardia or arrhythmias, gasping respirations or periods of apnea); pupillary changes (asymmetry, sluggish to fixed); posturing and seizures

QUESTIONS SPECIFIC FOR ADMITTING NURSE:
19. What is the significance of the statement (pg 10030) that you wrote during the admission assessment: "mother states diapers have been soaked more than usual the past 2 wks"?

20. Did you correlate the statement from mom with your assessment (pg 10028) that states the diapers were "very wet"?

21. Was there any significance to the fact that Hannah was lethargic? What are the signs of DKA? (see above)

22. Laboratory tests from 1900 on 1-28-09 reflect a glucose level of 672, marked as critical. Did the laboratory personnel advise you of this critical value?

23. Documentation reflects that Dr. Newley was called at 2000; documentation also reflects that the results of the laboratory tests were given to him at 2040. To the best of your recollection, is this when you informed him of the 672 glucose level?

24. At 2300, you have documented that there were 4+ ketones in the urine. Was this information relayed to Dr. Newley? Did you inform Dr. Newley that the glucose level from 2200 on 1-28-09 was 727, again in the critical range?

25. What is the significance of ketones in the urine?
    In diabetes the presence of large amounts of urine ketones is important confirmatory evidence of diabetic ketoacidosis or impending acidosis.

QUESTIONS SPECIFIC FOR 1st ICU RN:
26. What is the significance of Kussmaul respirations?

27. Did you notify a physician that Hannah was experiencing Kussmaul respirations?

Appendix 20.7
Screening Tools for Use with LNCs

A. Spelling Test 1

Circle the correctly spelled word.

accidently	accidentally
arguement	argument
competent	compitent
defendant	diffendant
irresistible	irresistable
referance	reference
seperate	separate
harrass	harass
indispensable	indispensible
liaison	liason
pursue	persue
privilege	priviledge
refferance	reference
subpoena	subpena
truely	truly
warrant	warrent
yeild	yield

B. Spelling Test 2

Some of the words below are incorrectly spelled. If the spelling is incorrect, write the correct spelling in the space after the word.

Accommodate	Maintenance
Administator	Mangement
A lot	Medial Malpractice
Appenddix	Murmur
Attendance	Nusing
Bussiness	Occurred

Calendar	Oxgen
Clincial	Paient
Correspondence	Pennyslvania
Definitely	Philadephia
Desperate	Postoperaive
Development	Priviledge
Disabilites	Pscyhology
Eligible	Questionnaire
Embarassment	Receipt
Equiptment	Recieve
Existence	Rhythm
Foreign	Sceinces
Forty	Seizere
Gauge	Strenuous
Hemorrhage	Succes
Hosptial	Tendency
Insitute	Theraputic
Irregardless	Trail attorneys
Leisure	Untied States

Your name_____   Date:_____
(Please print clearly)

HR use only   /50 Score for this page_____

C. Word Usage

For each of the following sentences, decide which of the words in parentheses represents correct usage. Write the letter or letters in the answer column.

1. She believed she had nothing to (a) loose (b) lose.   1._____

2. The (a) physician's (b) physicians examined him.   2._____

3. The fluid that came out of the drains (a) is (b) are recorded.   3._____

4. Each doctor wrote (a) their (b) his or her orders.   4._____

5. The nursing home violated (a) its (b) their standards.   5._____

6. The patient was diagnosed with (a) Hypertension (b) hypertension.   6._____

7. The Trent Home Care Agency staff is larger than Wilson Home Care
(a) Agency (b) Agency's.   7._____

8. (a) He said he couldn't pass his board certification exam.
(b) He said he could not pass his board certification exam.   8._____

9. The nausea (a) effected (b) affected the resident.   9._____

10. The (a) LNCs (b) LNC's were aware of the task.   10. _____

11. (a) The patient said, "I need medication."
(b) The patient said, "I need medication."   11. _____

12. (a) She liked oranges, apples, and pears.
(b) She liked oranges, apples and pears.   12. _____

13. (a) The doctor examined the lab results but he did not comment on them.
(b) The doctor examined the lab results, but he did not comment on them. 13._____

14. (a) She was responsible for stocking the operating room, writing
the purchase orders, and greeting the salesman.
(b) She was responsible for stocking the operating room, purchase orders,
and salesmen.   14. _____

15. (a) They are planning to go over there to collect their documents.
(b) Their planning to go over they're to collect there documents.   15. _____

16. (a) Various different nurses all told the same story.
(b) Various nurses told the same story.   16. _____

D. Letter

Instructions: This letter needs to be typed, formatted, edited, proofed, and printed. Please prepare this letter for Ms. Taylor's signature.

March 2 1 2005 This is a letter to Marjorie Wall who is the director of medical records at Gutter memorial hospital, 233 Main street, Califon, New York 10221 Dear Mrs. Wall, I am contacting you once again to request hospital records for the admission of Peter Quic whom we represent in a personal injury action Mr. Quic was amitted to your hospital on January 3 2003 and discharged on Janary 7 2003 we reqested his records three months ago and as of yet we have not recieved them once again I am enclosing a copy of the patients hippa complaint authorization from which enables you to release them to our firm I would request that you direct your attention to fulfilling this request so that a supena of the records does not become necessary please contact me if you have any questions. Respectively yours, Ann Taylor esquire copy to Dennis Olaughlin esq.

E. Proofreading

Directions: Please correct the typos and other errors.

To: GW
From: LL

At the time of her final admission to Redwood City medical center Mrs. Mary Hockel was a 69-year-old woman who weighed 81 pounds (as of the preoperative checklist). (Her weight is also listed as 90 pounds on the nursing admission assessment. Her blood pressure was recorded as 132/76 on the preoperative checklist. She was admitted to the hospital for a total knee replacement. She was taken to the operating room on 9/16/04. She was estimated to have a blood loss of 200 cc in the operating room. The surgeon, Dr.Pullis, placed two hemovac drains in Mrs. Hockel's knee at the completion of the operation. One was connected to a cell saver unit to permit autotransfusion. In the recovery room, she lost 350 ccs, but received 125 ccs of her own blood, for a net loss of 225 ccs. Her blood pressure ran about 120/80 while in the recovery room. The physician wrote postoperative orders which included:

Routine postop vital signs
Morphine 6 mg IM every 4-? h (second number unreadable) and Vistaril 25 mg IM every 3-5 h prn
CBC, SMA 6 at 6 P.M., call with results
Accurate I and O (intake and output): reconstitute hemovac drain q2h and prn
Straight cath q 6-8 h prn bladder distension/retention.

Mrs. Hockel was transferred to the nursing unit at 2:15 P.M. according to the notes of the recovery room nurse. There is one recorded set of vital signs on the graphic record for this shift. The patient's vital sign's were blood pressure of 101/84 and a pulse of 72 at 3:00 P.M. The patient received Morphine 6 mg and Vistaril 25 mg at 3:15 P.M., according to the notes of Nurse Loomis. A hemovac output of 500 ccs is recorded on the graphic chart under the column marked "Day" (shift). There are no incremental amounts recorded on the graphic sheet or the intake and output sheet for this shift. The nurses notes by Nurse Loomis state that the patient had frequent voidings for small amounts of urine. Two voidings are recorded (150 cc and 25 cc). 800 ccs of urine was obtained when Sara Hockel RN straight catheterized her mother in law at 8:00 P.M.

A sample of blood was drawn at 6:00 P.M. for testing the hemoglobin and hematocrit. The results were hemoglobin: 11.0 (down from 13.7 on 9/12/94) and hematocrit 32.1 (down from 39.3 on 9/12/94.)

At about 8:00 P.M., the care of Mrs. Hockel fell to Maura Reilly. There are two recorded vital signs before midnight. Mrs. Hockel's blood pressure was 102/84 with a pulse of 114 at 8:00 P.M. Her hemovac output was recorded on the fluid intake and output form as 100 ccs at 9:00 P.M. At 9:25 P.M., the patient was given Morphine and Vistaril. At 11:30 P.M. Mrs. Hockel's blood pressure was 98/62 with a pulse of 104. Dr. Feinstein made rounds at 11:30 P.M., and entered a progress note labeled as Post Op Day #1. He removed the hemovac.

According to the nursing progress notes, Melanie Reilly gave the patient an injection of Morphine at 3:15 A.M. The next recording of blood pressure was timed for 4:00 A.M. and was recorded as 89/56 with a pulse of 93. Maura Reilly's notes stated that these vital signs were 'stable'. Her notes claim that she went into the patient's room at 5:00 A.M. and the patient was asleep with adequate color. The patient was found unresponsive (no pulse or respirations) at 5:50 A.M. A cardiac arrest effort was initiated. The patient was transferred to ICU. No nursing notes for the 8 P.M. to 8 A.M. shift were found at that time. The page in the medical record was written after the fact by Maura Reilly. The note did not include documentation that the hemovac drain was removed, the time of the addendum was not noted on the record. The patient expired three days later.

Appendix 20.8
Answer Key for Tests

A. Spelling Test 1

Bold signifies correct spelling.

accidently	**accidentally**
arguement	**argument**
competent	compitent
defendant	diffendant
irresistible	irresistable
referance	**reference**
seperate	**separate**
harrass	**harass**
indispensable	indispensible
liaison	liason
pursue	persue
privilege	priviledge
refferance	**reference**
subpoena	subpena
truely	**truly**
warrant	warrent
yeild	**yield**

B. Spelling Test 2

Key: Correctly spelled word is in right column.

Accommodate		Maintenance	
Administator	Administrator	Mangement	Management
A lot		Medial Malpractice	Medical Malpractice
Appenddix	Appendix	Murmur	
Attendance		Nusing	Nursing
Bussiness	Business	Occurred	
Calendar		Oxgen	Oxygen

Clincial	Clinical	Paient	Patient
Correspondence		Pennyslvania	Pennsylvania
Definately	Definitely	Philadephia	Philadelphia
Desperate		Postoperaive	Postoperative
Developement	Development	Priviledge	Privilege
Disabilites	Disabilities	Pscyology	Psychology
Eligible		Questionnaire	
Embarssment	Embarrassment	Receipt	
Equiptment	Equipment	Recieve	Receive
Existence		Rhythm	
Foreign		Seizere	Seizure
Forty		Sceinces	Sciences
Gauge		Strenuous	
Hemorrhage		Succes	Success
Hosptial	Hospital	Tendency	
Insitute	Institute	Theraputic	Therapeutic
Irregardless	Regardless	Trail attorneys	Trial attorneys
Leisure		Untied States	United States

Your name
(Please print clearly)
Date:

HR use only   /50 Score for this page_____

C. Word Usage

For each of the following sentences, decide which of the words in parentheses represents correct usage. Write the letter or letters in the answer column.

1. She believed she had nothing to (a) loose (b) lose.   1. __b__
Loose refers to something that is lax. Lose is the act of giving up something.

2. The (a) physician's (b) physicians examined him.   2. __b__
Physician's is possessive. Physicians is plural.

3. The fluid that comes out of the drains (a) is (b) are recorded.   3. __a__
Fluid is the subject of the sentence, and is singular, so (a) is correct.

4. Each doctor wrote their (a) his or her (b) orders.   4. __b__
Pronouns must agree in number. "Their" is plural and cannot refer to a singular noun.

5. The nursing home violated its (a) their (b) standards.   5. __a__
The nursing home is singular and not a person, so "its" is correct. "Its" is the possessive pronoun. "It's" means it is.

6. The patient was diagnosed with Hypertension (a) hypertension (b).   6. __b__
Medical diagnoses are not capitalized in the middle of a sentence.

7. The Trent Home Care Agency staff is larger than Wilson Home Care   7. __b__
Agency (a) Agency's (b).

Avoid inexact comparisons. The correct option uses the possessive.

8. (a) He said he couldn't pass his board certification exam.
(b) He said he could not pass his board certification exam.   8. __b__
Do not use contractions in a formal report.

9. The nausea (a) effected (b) affected the resident.   9. __b__
Affect is usually a verb. Effect is usually a noun. Remember: affect = action.

10. The (a) LNCs (b) LNC's were aware of the task.   10. __a__
Use an apostrophe to indicate the possessive.

11. (a) The patient said, "I need medication." (b) The patient said,
"I need medication."   11. __a__
Place commas and periods inside quotation marks.

12. (a) She liked oranges, apples, and pears. (b) She liked oranges,
apples and pears.   12. __a__
Use commas to separate items in a series. Always place a comma before the concluding "and" in a series of three or more items.

13. (a) The doctor examined the lab results but he did not comment on them.
(b) The doctor examined the lab results, but he did not comment on them.   13. __b__
Use commas to separate two complete sentences joined by a coordinating conjunction (e.g., and, or, but)

14. (a) She was responsible for stocking the operating room,
writing the purchase orders, and greeting the salesman.
(b) She was responsible for stocking the operating room,
purchase orders, and salesmen.   14. __a__
Items in a series should be presented in the same grammatical structure.

15. (a) They are planning to go over there to collect their documents.
(b)Their planning to go over they're to collect there documents.   15. __a__
"They're" is a contraction for they are. "Their" is possessive. "There" is a location.

16. (a) Various different nurses all told the same story.
(b) Various nurses told the same story.   16. __b__
The second choice eliminates the redundancy of repeating "different" and "all" in the same sentence.

HR use only   /16 Score for this page_____

D. Letter

March 21, 2005

Marjorie Wall
Director of Medical Records
Gutter Memorial Hospital

233 Main Street
Califon, NY 10221

Re: Peter Quic

Dear Mrs. Wall,

I am contacting you once again to request hospital records for the admission of Peter Quic whom we represent in a personal injury action. Mr. Quic was admitted to your hospital on January 3, 2003 and discharged on January 7, 2003. We requested his records three months ago, and as of yet we have not received them once again. I am enclosing a copy of the patient's HIPAA-compliant authorization form, which enables you to release them to our firm. I would request that you direct your attention to fulfilling this request so that a subpoena of the records does not become necessary. Please contact me if you have any questions.

　　　　Respectfully yours,

　　　　Ann Taylor Esq.

　　　　AT/(initials of person typing the letter)

　　　　Enclosure

　　　　Copy to Dennis O'Laughlin Esq.

E. Proofreading

To: GW
From: LL

　　　　At the time of her final admission to Redwood City **medical center [should be capitals]** Mrs. Mary Hockel was a 69-year-old woman who weighed 81 pounds (as of the preoperative checklist). (Her weight is also listed as 90 pounds on the nursing admission assessment). Her blood pressure was recorded as 132/76 on the preoperative checklist. She was admitted to the hospital for a total knee replacement. She was taken to the operating room on 9/16/94. She was estimated to have a blood loss of 200 cc in the operating room. The surgeon, Dr. Pullis, placed two hemovac drains in Mrs. Hockel's knee at the completion of the operation. One was connected to a cell saver unit to permit autotransfusion. In the recovery room, she lost 350 ccs, but received 125 ccs of her own blood, for a net loss of 225 ccs. Her blood pressure ran about 120/80 while in the recovery room. The physician **wro**te **[close up space after physician]** postoperative orders which included:

1.　"Routine postop vital signs"
2.　Morphine 6 mg IM every 4-? h **[second number unreadable]** and Vistaril 25 mg IM every 3-5 h prn
3.　CBC, SMA 6 at 6 P.M., call with results
4.　Accurate I and O (intake and output): reconstitute hemovac drain q2h and prn
5.　Straight cath q 6-8 h prn bladder distension/retention.

　　　　Mrs. Hockel was transferred to the nursing unit at 2:15 P.M. according to the notes of the recovery room nurse. There is one recorded set of vital signs on the graphic record for this shift. The patient's vital **sign's [sign's should be plural]** were blood pressure of 101/84 and a pulse of 72 at 3:00 P.M. The patient received Morphine 6 mg and Vistaril 25 mg at 3:15 P.M., according to the notes of Nurse Loomis. A hemovac output of 500 ccs is recorded on the graphic chart under the column marked "Day" (shift). There are no incremental amounts recorded on the graphic sheet or the intake and output sheet for this shift. The nurses notes by Nurse Loomis state that the patient had frequent voidings for small amounts of urine. Two voidings are recorded (150 cc and 25 cc).

800 ccs of urine was obtained when Sara Hockel straight catheterized her **mother-in-law [add hyphens]** at 8:00 P.M. **[Do not start a sentence with a number. It should be spelled out.]**

A sample of blood was drawn at 6:00 P.M. for testing the hemoglobin and hematocrit. The results were hemoglobin: 11.0 (down from 13.7 on 9/12/94) and hematocrit 32.1 (down from 39.3 on 9/12/94.)

At about 8:00 P.M., the care of Mrs. Hockel fell to Maura Reilly. There are two recorded vital signs before midnight. Mrs. Hockel's blood pressure was 102/84 with a pulse of 114 at 8:00 P.M. Her hemovac output was recorded on the fluid intake and output form as 100 ccs at 9:00 P.M. At 9:25 P.M., the patient was given Morphine and Vistaril. At 11:30 P.M. Mrs. Hockel's blood pressure was 98/62 with a pulse of 104. Dr. Feinstein made rounds at around midnight, and entered a progress note labeled as Post Op Day #1. He removed the hemovac.

According to the nursing progress notes, **Melanie [should be Maura]** Reilly gave the patient an injection of Morphine at 3:15 A.M. The next recording of blood pressure was timed for 4:00 A.M. and was recorded as 89/56 with a pulse of 93. Maura Reilly's notes stated that these vital signs were 'stable'. Her notes claim that she went into the patient's room at 5:00 A.M. and the patient was asleep with adequate color. The patient was found unresponsive (no pulse or respirations) at 5:50 A.M. A cardiac arrest effort was initiated. The patient was transferred to ICU. No nursing notes for the 8 P.M. to 8 A.M. shift were found at that time. The page in the medical record was written after the fact by Maura Reilly. The note did not include documentation that the hemovac drain was removed, the time of the addendum was not noted on the record. The patient **expried [word spelled wrong]** three days later.

Chapter 21

Working with Nursing Expert Witnesses

Patricia W. Iyer, MSN, RN, LNCC, and Raymond Fleming, Esq.[1]

21.1 Introduction

Location of expert witnesses may be the responsibility of the attorney, paralegal, legal nurse consultant employed by a law firm, or independent legal nurse consultant. This chapter shares some ideas on how to locate and work with nursing expert witnesses. The perspectives of nursing expert witnesses are included in this material. The challenging role of the nurse in testifying as a liability expert is discussed along with best practices for deposing nursing expert witnesses.

21.2 Preparation for the Search for the Liability Expert Witness

Identify and hire experts as soon as possible, and keep them abreast of all developments in the case. These two steps are essential to a successful attorney-expert relationship. Early retention, while the case is still being formulated, will help you frame the case and set the limits of the expert's involvement. Delaying the decision can lead to the wrong choice of expert and diminish the value of her opinion.[2] Before beginning the search for an expert, the attorney or legal nurse consultant should make sure he has all the relevant material. The plaintiff's attorney should closely question clients about any visits to emergency departments or hospitalizations relevant to the case. Attorneys need a complete, certified copy of all necessary medical records from relevant prior healthcare providers, including hospitalizations, incident reports (if discoverable in the jurisdiction), outpatient office visits, emergency department visits, or any other relevant documentation. Explanation of benefit forms and similar records from the plaintiff's medical insurance carrier may provide evidence of other medical treatment not identified by the plaintiff. These records should be carefully reviewed by the attorney and the legal nurse consultant helping with the case.

The plaintiff's attorney who feels the client is withholding information should follow up on this intuition to avoid unpleasant surprises after investing time and money in the case. The client should be told there is a need for complete candor. The goal is to avoid at trial a surprise disclosure of a prior injury, unrelated medical condition, or a history of criminal conviction which might have a bearing on the case.

TIP: Certain people, because of personal habits, contributory negligence, or criminal behavior, will not garner sympathy from a jury, no matter how good a liability case they may appear to have.

Before looking for a nursing expert, the plaintiff's attorney should ask herself one more time if this case is worth pursuing. Considering how difficult it is to win malpractice cases, many plaintiff's attorneys are increasingly reluctant to take cases without clear-cut violation of the standard of care and compensatory damages worth at least $100,000. It is not unusual to spend tens of thousands of dollars on the preparation of a malpractice case before it ever gets to trial. The attorney who does not specialize in malpractice or has not pursued many such cases should consider obtaining advice from a legal nurse consultant or other attorneys with malpractice experience. A legal nurse consultant is the most

qualified consultant to review nursing malpractice cases for merit. Defense attorneys have a higher probability of specialization in medical and nursing malpractice cases and will be able to form some conclusions about the validity of the case at an early stage.

In a nursing malpractice case, the most important decision counsel on either side has to make is which nurse to select as an expert. Some have extensive credentials and clinical experience, but little or no experience in testifying in court. For some nurses, this can be a benefit, since they have no "track record" for other counsel to research. On the other hand testifying in court is a unique experience and it is difficult for anyone to adapt to the vagaries of the court system and give their best presentation the first time they sit in the witness box. There are some nurses who have testified numerous times, but do not necessarily have the background or clinical experience that fits a particular case. On the defense side, counsel usually has the advantage of seeing which expert witness plaintiff's counsel has chosen. A defense attorney will always try to find a defense expert who has more clinical experience in the specific field at issue in the case than the plaintiff's expert. Some nurse experts who otherwise are very knowledgeable have not worked in a clinical setting in many years. Most attorneys feel that this exposes them to a significant attack on their credibility in court. Jurors are looking closely at what actions the defendant nurse took or failed to take, and want guidance from nurses who face the same challenges and responsibilities on a regular basis. Sometimes a lack of experience can be overcome when the expert's academic background is impressive enough, and especially if they teach other nurses.

The specific specialty of nursing involved in a particular case is important to consider. In some cases, for example, a plaintiff's attorney will retain a labor and delivery nurse to be critical of a nurse for an incident that occurred on the postpartum unit. If it turns out that the labor and delivery nurse has not worked on a postpartum unit for 10 or 12 years, it will certainly affect her credibility with regard to opinions against the postpartum nurse. Similarly, one would not want to retain a medical-surgical nurse to criticize an ICU nurse, or a same-day surgery nurse to criticize an operating room nurse.

In some states that require affidavits or certificates of merit in order to maintain a suit, the professional signing the affidavit of merit must work in the same specialty as the defendant. There are numerous rules and exceptions in this regard. In the New Jersey affidavit of merit statute, for example (*N.J.S.A.* 2A:53A-26), a plaintiff must serve an affidavit of merit against any "licensed person" which includes attorneys, dentists, physicians, and "a registered professional nurse." In our experience, any registered nurse can file an affidavit of merit against any other registered nurse and meet the threshold requirements of the statute. Being careful about choosing a nurse with the appropriate specialty. Experience is usually more of an issue for trial presentation and credibility before the jury.

New Jersey also has a statute (*N.J.S.A.* 2A:53A-41) specifically setting forth the requirements of an expert in a "medical malpractice case." It is unclear from the language of the statute whether it applies to nurses, but it does refer to giving testimony on the appropriate standard of care only if that expert "is licensed as a physician or other healthcare professional in the United States." Under that statute, if the defendant has a medical specialty, the expert testifying against the defendant must either be board-certified in the same specialty or credentialed at a hospital to treat patients for the medical condition that forms the basis of the case. There have been cases about whether or not a general surgeon can testify against a gastroenterologist who performed a colonoscopy, and whether a psychiatrist can testify against a family physician who prescribed psychiatric medications. There are no cases yet specifically applying this statute to nursing malpractice as opposed to "medical malpractice," but the argument could be made, and the issue will eventually reach the courts.

At the present time, it would not seem to be an issue for a registered nurse to testify against an LPN, although if one could find an LPN adequately qualified to act as an expert, that would be the best fit. Any time a nurse of a different subspecialty testifies there will be attacks on his experience and knowledge as compared to the defendant. While this might not disqualify him, it can affect his credibility in the eyes of the jury and ultimately affect the outcome of the case.

21.3 Limitations and Expansions of the Nursing Expert Witness Role

Many states require an affidavit of merit from an expert witness before a malpractice case can be pursued. Conservative and prudent plaintiff's attorneys are often more comfortable proceeding with a case after receiving validation from a nursing expert witness that the case has merit. The attorney must be attuned to the requirements in the state in which the case is filed as to the word and timing of supply of affidavits of merit. Refer to Chapter 14, *Screening the Nursing Malpractice Case*, for additional content on this topic.

An expert witness has "special knowledge, skill, experience, training and/or education that goes beyond the experience of ordinary members of the public."[3] An expert witness's testimony is allowed after two major requirements are met:

1. The subject of the testimony must be so related to some profession, science, or business as to be beyond the ken of the average layperson.
2. The expert witness must possess special skill, knowledge, or experience in a certain field so the expert's testimony will benefit the trier of fact.[4]

Also note the Federal Rules of Evidence [Rule 702], which states that, "If scientific, technical, or other specialized knowledge will assist the trier of fact to understand the evidence to determine a fact in issue, a witness qualified as an expert by knowledge, skill, experience, training, or education may testify thereto in the form of an opinion or otherwise." Nursing is a profession with associated educational qualifications, organizations, licensing requirements, and code of ethics. One of the distinctions of the profession is that it establishes its own standards of care. Most but not all nursing malpractice cases require testimony by a nursing expert witness to establish the standard of care.

TIP: State court rules regarding when expert testimony is required to establish a departure from the accepted standards of care can vary, so it is important for the attorney to verify this aspect of law in the venue where the case will be filed.

A. Physicians as Experts on Nursing Care

It is a generally held practice to have nursing expert witnesses testify about the standard of nursing care. Along with the trend toward naming nurses as defendants in malpractice cases grew the recognition that nurses rather than doctors as most qualified to act as expert witnesses on the standard of care. The expert witness in a nursing malpractice action must possess the requisite skill, training, knowledge, and experience to provide a reliable opinion.[5] While it seems self-evident that nursing is its own profession with a unique body of knowledge, standard of practice, ethical code, and requirement for licensure, the judicial system has permitted confusion to exist when physicians are allowed to testify about nursing standards of care. The American Association of Nurse Attorneys (TAANA) argues that a physician, who is not a nurse, is no more qualified to offer expert opinion testimony as to the standard of care for nurses than a nurse would be to offer an opinion as to the physician standard of care.[6] Although physicians have asserted that they are familiar with nursing standards based on observing nurses in a work environment, nurses have the same familiarity with physicians' standards, and yet are not permitted to testify about physician standards of care. Nursing has moved beyond its former dependence on the physician, and into a realm where it must and can legally account for its own professional practices.[7]

In a landmark Illinois case, *Sullivan v. Edward Hospital*,[8] a physician was retained by the plaintiff's attorney to testify that the nurse was negligent in permitting a patient to fall during an agitated state. The physician testified that the nurse was negligent in failing to more forcibly convey to the physician the condition of the patient, and that the "nurse missed the diagnosis of delirium completely." TAANA submitted an Amicus brief to the Illinois Supreme Court in this case, arguing that only nurses have the authority and responsibility to define the scope and practice of nursing. Therefore, only a nurse is qualified to offer expert opinion evidence as to the nursing standard of care. The Illinois Trial Lawyers also submitted an Amicus brief arguing that physicians can do anything a nurse can do, and therefore a physician can always testify as to the standard of care for nurses. The Illinois Trial Lawyers argued that physicians were familiar with nursing practice from observation, and that the question should not be whether the expert is a nurse or a physician, but rather whether the expert is familiar with the procedure in question. Under this rule, where both nurses and physicians are familiar with and perform a specific procedure, such as starting an intravenous, the physician should be allowed to testify as to the standard of care for a nurse. Under this logic, the nurse should likewise be permitted to offer expert opinion against a physician. However, no court permits this. The Illinois Supreme Court issued a decision, citing extensively to the TAANA brief, and ruled that only a nurse is qualified to offer opinion evidence as to the nursing standard of care.[9] Citing the *Sullivan v. Edward* case, the American Association of Legal Nurse Consultants issued a position paper in 2006 emphasizing that only nurses should testify about nursing standards of care (Figure 21.1). When deposing or cross-examining an opposing physician expert witness who prepared a report about the nursing standard of care, the attorney can probe the physician's qualifications by asking the questions in Figure 21.2. The answers to these questions are effective in demonstrating the separation of medicine and nursing as professions.

B. Proximate Cause

A nurse should ordinarily not be used to establish causation, although, in some cases, a nursing expert is able to testify to proximate cause. If a pediatric nurse leaves a crib rail down and the child falls to the floor, fracturing her skull, a nursing expert witness would be able to testify that the negligent act

of leaving the crib rail down caused the child's fall, although the testimony of a physician would still probably be needed to relate the fractured skull injury to the fall. In *Flanagan v. Labe* (690 A.2d 183 (PA 1997), the plaintiff sued the hospital for medical malpractice, alleging he received substandard nursing care after insertion of a tube into his chest wall led to progressively worsening subcutaneous emphysema. The plaintiff's only expert was a nurse, who testified that the subcutaneous emphysema resulted from the nursing staff's negligence. After ruling that the testimony was inadmissible, the Court of Common Pleas, Philadelphia County granted the hospital's motion for summary judgment. The plaintiff appealed. The Superior Court affirmed. The plaintiff appealed by allowance. The Supreme Court held that the nurse's testimony would have consisted of medical diagnosis of the patient's condition, thus precluding admission of that testimony. The nurse is permitted to diagnose human responses to health problems, but is prohibited from providing medical diagnoses. The acceptance of the testimony of the nursing expert would have consisted of medical diagnosis, as well as an opinion as to why that condition existed or worsened.

TIP: In almost all medical malpractice cases, the testimony of a physician is still needed to establish that the negligent act in question proximately caused the patient's injury or death.

In *Freed v. Geisinger Med. Ctr.*, the Supreme Court of Pennsylvania affirmed an appellate court decision allowing a nurse to give her opinion as to the cause of a plaintiff's pressure ulcers. At the trial level, the defense objected to such testimony since it arguably constituted "a medical diagnosis" which nurses are not permitted to give under the professional practice of nursing act in Pennsylvania. The court held that the act regulated nursing practice "in real life" but did not affect the rules of evidence or the testimony a nurse could or could not give in a civil action. The court remanded the case to the trial level to permit the nurse to give her opinion as to the cause of the patient's pressure ulcers. It should be noted, however, that Pennsylvania had just recently passed a statute more clearly defining who could give causation testimony in malpractice cases which would have barred the nurse's testimony. Accordingly, this is not a far-reaching decision. In addition, one would expect most judges to continue to prohibit a nurse from giving opinions as to medical diagnoses.

Position Statement
Providing Expert Nursing Testimony

Summary:

The purpose of this position statement is to establish that registered nurses are the only health care providers that should provide expert testimony related to nursing standards of care.

Introduction:

This position statement is the outcome of extensive review of literature and case law related to physicians testifying on nursing standards. Nurses are uniquely prepared to perform a critical review and analysis of clinical nursing care and administrative nursing practice which provide the foundation for testifying in nursing negligence issues.

Background and Discussion:

Medical malpractice is the failure of a professional health care practitioner to provide reasonable care. The required elements of proof in a medical malpractice case are a duty between the patient and health care practitioner, a breach of duty or departure from accepted practice and the departure being the proximate cause of the alleged injury. Expert opinion is typically required to establish the applicable standard of care and the actual departure from standard practice. The expert witness is required to possess the necessary skill, knowledge, training and experience to ensure that the opinion rendered is reliable. It appears elementary that the only expert qualified to render expert opinion testimony would be a member of the same profession who practices in a substantially similar manner to the potential defendant in the case. For many years, physicians have routinely been admitted into evidence to offer testimony to establish the standard of care for the nursing profession. On the other hand, many courts have found that physicians are best qualified to render testimony as to standards of care for physicians and that in many other health care professions, only a member of that health profession is qualified to testify to standards of care for that discipline. Recently, the courts have begun to acknowledge that nurses possess specialized knowledge that physicians do not have unless they have been trained and practice as a nurse. The Supreme Court of Illinois recently held that a board-certified internal medicine physician was not competent to testify as to the standard of care of a nurse. Citing the Amicus Brief submitted by The American Association of Nurse Attorneys, *the court noted:*

> "A physician who is not a nurse is no more qualified to offer expert opinion testimony as to the standard of care for nurses than a nurse would be to offer an opinion as to the physician standard of care. Certainly, nurses are not permitted to offer expert testimony against a physician based on their observances of physicians or their familiarity with the procedures involved. An operating room nurse, who stands shoulder to shoulder with surgeons every day, would not be permitted to testify as to the standard of care of a surgeon. An endoscopy nurse would not be permitted to testify as to the standard of care of a gastroenterologist performing a colonoscopy. A labor and delivery nurse would not be permitted to offer expert testimony as to the standard of care for an obstetrician or even a midwife. Such testimony would be, essentially, expert testimony as to the standard of medical care." (*Sullivan v. Edward Hospital.*, 806 N.E. 2d 645 (Ill. 2004).

Scholars and litigators have long held that "Physicians often have no first-hand knowledge of nursing practice except for observations made in patient care settings. The physician rarely, if ever, teaches in a nursing program nor is a physician responsible for content in nursing texts. In many situations, a physician would not be familiar with the standard of care or with nursing policies and procedures which govern the standard of care. Therefore, a physician's opinions would not be admissible in jurisdictions which hold the expert must be familiar with the standard of care in order to testify as an expert." (Elizabeth W. Beyer and Pamela W. Popp, Nursing Standard of Care in Medical Malpractice Litigation: *The Role of the Nurse Expert Witness*, 23A J.A. HEALTH & HOSP. L. 363-365 (1990) Nursing has evolved into a profession with a distinct body of knowledge, university based education, specialized practice,

Figure 21.1 *Position Statement: Providing Expert Nursing Testimony, American Association of Legal Nurse Consultants, reprinted with permission*

standards of practice, a societal contract and an ethical code. The practice of nursing requires decision making and skill based upon principles of the biological, physical, behavioral and social sciences as well as evidence-based research related to functions such as identifying risk factors and providing specific interventions. Each state has a Board of Nursing that is the authorized state entity with the legal authority to regulate nursing practice. State legislature has set forth licensing and regulations for the nursing profession in their respective Nurse Practice Acts and Advanced Practice Nursing Acts. It is evident that under the nursing act, only a nurse would meet the qualifications for sitting for nursing licensure examination, and as such be eligible for licensure as a registered nurse.

The American Association of Legal Nurse Consultants:
AALNC is the organization that:
- Provides the foundation for best practices within the multitude of legal nurse consultant roles.
- Incorporates cutting edge clinical and consultative education to promote the practice of legal nurse consulting.
- Supports "Legal Nurse Consulting: Scope and Standards of Practice."

Conclusion:
The profession of nursing is autonomous from the profession of medicine and other allied health disciplines. The profession of nursing has its own educational and licensing requirements which serve to identify registered nurses and, among registered nurses, further identify those with advanced training and certification in their nursing specialty. Nursing has the responsibility and knowledge to define its standards of practice and indeed has published these standards of care. Therefore, licensed registered nurses are competent to address these standards of nursing practice in the litigation arena.

It is the position of the American Association of Legal Nurse Consultants that when applicable nursing standards need to be established through expert testimony, that the expert shall be a licensed, registered nurse. Further, the only expert competent to testify on clinical and administrative nursing issues is a licensed, registered nurse.

Additional References:
American Association of Legal Nurse Consultants (AALNC). (Iyer, P., Ed.) (2003). *Legal Nurse Consulting: Principles and Practice.* (2nd ed.). Boca Raton, FL: CRC Press.
American Nurses Association, *Code of Ethics for Nurses with Interpretive Statements,* 2001, Washington, D.C.
American Nurses Association. (2004). *Nursing: Scope and Standards of Practice,* Washington, D.C.
American Nurses Association, *Nursing's Social Policy Statement, Second Edition,* 2003, Washington, D.C.
C. Kehoe, *Contemporary Nursing Roles and Legal Accountability: The Challenge of Nursing Malpractice for the Law Librarian,* 79 LAW LIBR. J. 419, 428-29 (1987)
Dolan v. Jaeger, 285 A.D. 2d 844, 846, 727 N.Y.S. 2d 784, 786-87 (N.Y. App. Div. 2001)
F. Cavico and N. Cavico, *The Nursing Profession in the 1990's: Negligence and Malpractice Liability,* 43 CLEV. ST. L. REV. 557, 558 (1995)
E. Beyer and P. Popp, *Nursing Standard of Care in Medical Malpractice Litigation: The Role of the Nurse Expert Witness,* 23 J. Health & Hosp. L. 363, 365 (1990)
National Council of State Boards of Nursing (1994). *Model Nursing Practice Act.* Chicago: Author
P. Sweeney, *Proving Nursing Negligence,* 27 Trial 34, 36 (May 1991)
State Nurse Practice Acts
State Statutes regulating Expert Witness Testimony
Sullivan v. Edward Hosp., No. 95409, 2004 WL 228956 (Ill. Feb 5, 2004)
Amicus brief submitted to Illinois Supreme Court – Karen Butler, Esq American Association of Nurse Attorneys
Vassey v. Burch, 45 N.C. App. 222, 226, 262 S.E. 2d 865, 867

Approved by the American Association of Legal Nurse Consultants Board of Directors, January 2006.

Figure 21.1 Position Statement: Providing Expert Nursing Testimony, American Association of Legal Nurse Consultants, reprinted with permission (continued)

- Did the physician go to nursing school?
- Does the physician know who accredits nursing schools?
- Is the physician eligible to sit for nursing licensure?
- In what nursing organizations does the physician hold membership?
- What offices has the physician held in nursing organizations?
- What nursing textbooks or professional nursing journals has the physician read?
- What policies and procedures has the physician written for nurses?
- When was the last time the physician read the standards of practice for the applicable specialty in nursing?
- What articles has the physician written for nursing journals?
- What chapters has the physician contributed to nursing texts?
- What does the physician know about the state's Nurse Practice Act?
- Has the physician ever read the American Nurses Association Nursing Scope and Standards of Practice?
- What does the physician know about Nursing's Social Policy Statement?
- Can the physician cite the points in the Code of Ethics for Nurses?
- Has the physician ever been previously qualified in any court to testify regarding the standards of care applicable to a nurse?
- What research of the medical/nursing literature has the physician conducted regarding the standard of care applicable to nurses for the particular case?
- In how many other cases has the expert written reports or testified regarding the standard of care applicable to a nurse?
- Would the physician defer to a qualified nursing expert regarding the standard of care applicable to a nurse?

Figure 21.2 *Cross-examination of the Physician Expert Testifying about Nursing Standards of Care*

The court in *Freed* may have also been influenced by the fact that pressure ulcer cases are particularly nursing oriented. Nurses are required to prevent, document and care for pressure ulcers; and if they fail to take appropriate steps to prevent pressure ulcers (such as following hospital procedures requiring them to turn certain patients every two hours), then their actions have likely been a cause of the development of the pressure ulcers. One could certainly make the argument that an experienced nurse, particularly a wound care specialist, could testify regarding the formation of pressure ulcers, how they are prevented and treated, and what caused a particular patient to develop a pressure ulcer. On the other hand, one might argue that other intrinsic medical conditions of the patient might be a significant factor in the development of a pressure ulcer and that only medical expert testimony should be permitted.

The unreported New Jersey decision of *Palmer v. Fiume* does not directly deal with the issue of nurses giving testimony on causation. In that case, a prisoner was bringing a dental malpractice action against several dentists and oral surgeons. One of his claims was a lack of informed consent. Plaintiff retained a registered nurse as an expert witness to

testify that the consent form utilized in the case in question "did not properly or completely advise plaintiff of the risks and complications of a molar extraction." The court held that the nurse expert did not have the proper qualifications to testify on plaintiff's lack of informed consent claim. Historically, the obligation to give informed consent falls on the physician (or dentist), and not a nurse. The court held that, "as a registered nurse [the expert] was not qualified to opine on dental treatment and the risks of such treatment," and noted that the expert and defendant "were not engaged in a common area of practice."

21.4 Qualifications of the Nurse Expert Witness

The desired qualifications of the expert witness are a function of the facts of the case, applicable statutes, and attorney preferences. The constants in the equation are thorough knowledge of the subject matter and related standards of care, pertinent clinical experience, honesty, objectivity, firmness of conviction, strong communication skills, and a pleasant personality. This section expounds on each of these qualifications.

A. Facts, Statutes, and Preferences

The facts of the case direct the qualifications of the appropriate nursing expert. Some allegations are directed to basic nursing care. Not every issue is on the cutting edge of new technology or methods. Many cases involve simple issues of ordinary good practice. The provision of nursing care to prevent an immobile patient from developing a pressure ulcer is important in many settings where nursing care is delivered, such as critical care or medical surgical units, home care, and nursing homes. A nurse with critical care experience may be qualified to opine about the care given to a medical surgical patient who developed a pressure ulcer. In other types of cases, the technical aspects of the care are best addressed by a nurse with hands-on experience in that setting at the time of the incident. For example, a labor and delivery nurse with expertise in interpreting fetal monitoring strips is the most qualified person to comment on whether the fetal monitoring strip changes warranted intervention by the nurse.

Applicable statutes define the qualifications of the nursing expert. Attorneys should be aware of any state regulations that define the qualifications of an expert witness. Active clinical practice within a specific period of time may be required. Some states limit the amount of medical legal work an expert may provide by stating that this role should not occupy a certain percentage of the expert's working hours. Other states may place geographical limitations on the location of the expert, such as coming from the same state or one that touches the state.

Attorney preferences direct the selection of nursing experts. Concepts about the desirable qualifications of experts are based in part on past experience working with nursing expert witnesses and observing how juries and opposing counsel react to the expert. An expert witness is expected to be thoroughly knowledgeable in the subject area in question, and to have a high level of clinical and academic preparation. Some attorneys feel that the most credible experts are ones with current, hands-on experience, who work or have worked in the same clinical area as the defendant nurse in the subject lawsuit. Other attorneys favor using educators or instructors in schools of nursing as expert witnesses, as they are responsible for teaching the standards of care. Rose comments that the length of the expert's résumé is not the most important factor for a jury: "Experts who win the war of credentials with the opposing side's expert usually win on the basis of how much hands-on experience they have with the topic in question."[10]

Some attorneys also prefer experts who are clinical specialists and staff or head nurses with advanced degrees. Extensive clinical experience is an asset. Aspects of the nurse's background that are considered include participation in professional organizations and public speaking, or presentation skills. Most attorneys agree the expert should have an advanced degree with a minimum of a bachelor's degree. The expert's experience reviewing cases and testifying is also important. The expert should be intelligent, knowledgeable in the area, and able to communicate with a jury.

B. Objectivity and Knowledge of the Standards of Care

The ability to be objective is another important quality for an expert. Some experts never take a case for defense attorneys while others never work for plaintiff's attorneys. There is general agreement that the most credible expert has established a reputation for objectivity for both defendants and plaintiffs in different cases. The expert should also be able to state that he has turned down cases because of an inability to support the side who contacted the expert. An expert who accepts every case that comes in is less credible and may be viewed as a hired gun. Some plaintiff's attorneys prefer experts who primarily testify for the defense. These experts may be perceived as more knowledgeable and credible.

Occasionally attorneys consider using a treating nurse as an expert witness. This is often not a desirable position in which to place the nurse. The treating nurses' knowledge of the standard of care in existence at the time of treatment may be discoverable. This is often explored during depositions of the defendant nurses and raises questions about how willing the nurses would be in this situation to be critical of their employer. This is the major reason why it is desirable to locate an expert witness who is not affiliated with the hospital who can provide an objective opinion.[11]

TIP: Factors that could disqualify the expert from taking a case may include a personal relationship with the plaintiff or the defendant healthcare professional, feelings of animosity toward the opposing side, employment status at the defendant hospital, or healthcare system.

Nursing expert witnesses should understand the legal aspects of nursing and malpractice. A basic knowledge of the legal process is helpful, but until recently there has been little emphasis in nursing educational programs on malpractice issues. The expert witness should be familiar with the standards of care that apply to the specialty area. According to Cady, the most important qualification is clinical experience.[12] The amount of time spent caring for patients with similar conditions or spent teaching or supervising others is paramount. Additionally, neophyte experts must understand the legal definition of standard of care, and that the nurse defendant is not to be judged according to the most skilled clinician. Nursing experts may be even more critical of their peers than are physicians of each other.

Many nurses have a very basic understanding of how the legal system functions. They rely on the retaining attorney to explain their role if they are neophyte experts. Several publications provide the expert with knowledge about the responsibilities of the expert witness.[13-19]

C. Publications and Communication Skills

Ideally, but not of paramount importance, the nurse should have published an article or book related to the field of nursing. The nursing journal should be a peer-reviewed publication as opposed to a journal sent at no cost to nurses within a specific geographical area. If the expert has published on the subject of the lawsuit, the opinions expressed in the publication must be consistent with the expert's testimony. At the very least, the expert should be well versed in the nursing literature pertaining to the nursing issues in the case.

Good written and oral communication skills are essential to success as an expert witness. The expert must be able to prepare written or oral reports that help others understand the standards of care to illustrate what should have been done in a particular case. The expert's oral communication skills will be tested at a deposition, hearing, or trial. The jury, judge, arbitrator, and attorneys rely on the expert to explain complex medical or nursing concepts in terms that everyone can understand. The ability of the expert to communicate and establish rapport is often evident during initial contact. The expert should be someone the jury and judge will respect and trust. Evaluate the expert's responsiveness. Does the person return phone calls promptly? Is she easy to reach? Can the expert explain complex concepts? If so, this person is likely to be able to effectively teach the jury.

D. Honesty

Expect the expert witness to tell the retaining counsel the strengths and to emphasize the weaknesses of the case. There is often a lot riding on a malpractice case, including the costs associated with litigating and defending a case. Although written by a physician to other physicians who act as expert witnesses, the following advice applies to the nurse expert witness as well: "He [the expert witness] must remember that his improper testimony may prevent injured parties from receiving compensation, may ruin the lives of innocent defendants and their families, may destroy the reputations of individuals or companies, or may financially destroy an individual or company. The expert witness should never forget this burdensome responsibility."[20]

E. Firmness of Convictions and Personality

The expert must be able to define and hold an opinion on the standards of care without being swayed by the attorney's position. At times an attorney may be tempted to talk the expert into taking a position contrary to the standards of care. The expert must avoid being manipulated by the attorney into becoming a partisan and must be able to withstand this type of pressure and hold firm to convictions. Avoid experts who seem to tailor their opinions to fit the attorney's needs. On the other hand, the expert should also be flexible and willing to change an opinion based on new evidence. The expert needs to understand that honest answers are needed.

As Rose[21] points out, if experts are hired on the basis of expertise, personality should not matter. But personality does count. If the attorney finds the expert to be annoying, egotistical, or long-winded, so will the jury. They are likely to not listen to the expert's testimony. Personable experts who are open, have an appropriate sense of humor, and convey their enthusiasm and expertise are most likely to gain favor with the jurors. Most nurses, by virtue of the skills needed to succeed in nursing, are able to get along well with others. They are accustomed to interacting with stressed, irritable, and pressured people. Occasionally the attorney encounters a nurse whose personality interferes with communication skills and the effectiveness as an expert. Some direct coaching may be effective in neutralizing these issues.

F. Cost

It is common for attorneys to ask about hourly rates, flat rates, and retainer requirements when contacting experts about a case. The prepared expert will have a fee agreement to provide to the attorney. A psychiatric expert witness advise attorneys not to pick an expert because she charges less than others: "Too often lawyers collect the CVs and fee schedules of experts. They pick the expert whose fees are lowest without stopping to think about why the expert is less expensive. You should not expect experts to discount their fees. This is not a flea market. A good expert is not supposed to be a 'bargain.' Find someone whose skills you feel comfortable paying for, hire her on retainer and let her do her job."[22]

21.5 Finding the Nurse Expert Witness

Experts can be located by reviewing summaries of jury verdicts, reading the nursing literature, contacting nursing schools, using expert witness referral services, speaking with other attorneys, consulting information about speakers on nursing topics, and using computer searches. In addition, experts who have reviewed cases for the law firm or a legal nurse consulting expert witness location service may recommend someone they respect. Many state nurses associations maintain an expert witness referral list or can put the attorney in touch with clinical subgroups within their organization. For example, psychiatric nurse practitioners may have formed a subgroup within the state nurses association. The headquarters of a national nursing organization often provides information about local chapters and officers. From there, local expert clinicians can be located.

Set up a filing system for the résumés of well-qualified experts. In addition to having the résumé for future use, on occasion discrepancies will be spotted in an expert's résumé. One of the authors (PI) knows of one attorney who was able to launch an effective cross-examination of an opposing expert witness who had concealed information that had appeared on an earlier version of his résumé. Contradictory information on the subject of the testimony may be found in the author's publications.

Testimony databanks for experts such as IDEX are relatively limited. Some insurance carriers automatically run IDEX searches on plaintiff's experts in each case and send them to the defense attorney. Often the information is either incomplete or repetitive. Except for certain physicians who have testified for decades, most IDEX searches reveal very little information. When the IDEX search does list the name of a case where a particular nurse expert has given previous testimony, it then becomes the lawyer's job to communicate with the attorneys in that case (if the attorneys' names are listed) in an effort to obtain the deposition transcripts and trial transcripts, if any, from that earlier case. Often it is difficult to obtain the cooperation of other counsel, particularly if they are out of state. Many attorneys do not maintain copies of deposition transcripts or are hesitant to copy them and send them to a lawyer they do not know. On the other hand, on of the authors (RF) has received several depositions of an expert's prior testimony; and after poring through hundreds of pages, there is often little useful information since the facts of the cases themselves were so disparate. It is worth making this effort in significant cases, since sometimes the information an expert gives about his background and training can differ from one deposition to another.

Generally, the best way to find expert witnesses, including nurses, is word of mouth among counsel doing similar work, or using one of the legal nurse consultant services. Lawyers who have done a considerable amount of nursing malpractice work either on behalf of plaintiffs or defendants, will build up their own library of résumés and reports on the various nurse experts. If a nurse expert places her name with a service and a lawyer hires her by contacting a service which provides names and résumés of experts, this is fair ground for cross-examination. Some attorneys try to show that the nurse who is aggressively seeking cases to review has an economic motive and may not be the most caring nurse. Nurses also have to be careful about what they write in articles and on the Internet or on blogs. One of the authors (RF) works in a firm that, through a service, hired a nurse expert who had published an article which was readily available on the Internet about how she was burned out from nursing and how much easier it was to make money writing reports than doing clinical work. Plaintiff's counsel tried to show that her mind was not really on nursing care and that she would likely write any opinion to earn a fee. This was an unfair attack on the very nice and well-qualified nurse involved, but this is part of advocacy. On the other hand, absent such problems, the mere fact that experts list their names with a referral service does not seem to have a significant impact on jurors, in the authors' experience.

Critically evaluate the skills and credentials of the experts retained by the other side. They may be interested in reviewing a case for the firm at some point after the current case is resolved. In general, nurses are less reluctant than most physicians to become involved as expert witnesses, as they are less likely to know a nurse from another facility.

Another factor that influences a nurse's willingness to review a case is that nurses have not been affected by malpractice suits or increasing malpractice insurance rates to the same degree as physicians. Nursing malpractice insurance rates are usually under $100 a year unless the nurse practices in an advanced role such as a midwife or nurse anesthetist, or in a high-risk specialty such as obstetrics. See Chapter 17, *View of the Actuary*, for more information.

Some nurses are reluctant to review a case as an expert witness on behalf of the plaintiff. While nurses see themselves as patient advocates by protecting the rights of patients, they often do not appreciate the role of the plaintiff's attorney as a protector of the patient's rights. There is a certain amount of paranoia and distrust among nurses about the role of plaintiff's attorneys. While most nurses questioned will admit to having seen malpractice committed by another healthcare professional, few would speak up for the patient who was affected. Refer to Chapter 5, *Medical Errors: Roots of Litigation*, for more on this topic.

21.6 Screening an Expert

Once a likely candidate has been located, insist on speaking with him directly. To effectively screen the expert, obtain the information listed in Figure 21.3 from the expert. Ask the expert for a copy of a curriculum vitae (CV) or résumé. Impressions are often formed by the appearance of the résumé. The neatness, spelling, and type of printer used may provide a prediction of the type of report the expert will

The following information would be helpful to obtain directly from the expert:

- How many cases has the expert reviewed?
- What percentage of the cases reviewed were for the plaintiff, and how many for the defendant?
- Who are some of the attorneys with whom the expert has worked?
- Has the expert been published in the field of nursing or on the issues associated with the case?
- Does the expert teach in the field of nursing, or about the issues associated with the case?
- What are the expert's fees for reviewing the case?
- Does the expert charge different rates for different services, such as reviewing records, meeting with clients, or testifying at depositions or trial?
- Does the expert require a retainer?
- Does the expert have the specialty nursing experience that relates to the nursing aspects of the case; is the expert familiar with the standard of care (in labor and delivery, critical care, and so on)?
- What percentage of the time does the expert devote to expert witness work?
- What percentage of the time does the expert devote to clinical practice?
- In what area does the expert perform clinical services?
- Does the expert know the defendant or plaintiff, and is there any conflict of interest?
- Can the expert complete the review within the allotted time?
- Has the expert ever been found to be unqualified to testify in a court?
- Has the expert been sued for malpractice; if so, how many times, and with what outcome?
- Has the expert ever been disciplined by a licensing board?
- If you wish to meet the expert in person, is there a charge for this meeting?

Figure 21.3 *How to Screen the Expert Witness*

prepare. Look for the expert's level of education, applicable clinical experience, publications, and professional association memberships, offices, and honors. Examine the résumé for formatting, typos, and whether the expert actually states that he is an expert witness, a practice most attorneys discourage.

Opinion is divided on whether the expert should list everything or just the basics in the CV. Some experts maintain a short version of their CV which lists the highlights including education, certifications, experience, and publications. A longer version might list membership in professional associations and seminars at which the expert has presented or attended. Many nurses have been drilled in the concept that a résumé should not exceed two pages and do not make the transition to the more extensive CV. This may result in omitting some qualifications as their experience expands. Consider these points when evaluating the CV:

- Does the expert's CV demonstrate expertise in the area of nursing in question?
- Does the expert's educational background include advanced degrees?
- Has the expert published on the subject of nursing or the issues involved in this case?

21.7 Explaining the Case

The first opportunity to size up the expert and establish rapport occurs during the initial phone call. Listen to how the expert answers questions. Is the expert approachable and professional, or reluctant to become involved? If the expert has a bias towards one side of the bar, question whether the person can give the case an objective reading.

TIP: Be very clear about what is expected of the expert. Is a screening opinion needed or a testifying role essential?

Explain the case, providing a brief overview of the facts. This allows the expert to determine if she has the necessary expertise to review the case, and to request any additional material that would be helpful in forming an opinion. The attorney or legal nurse consultant should avoid offering opinions at this stage. The expert should be advised that the attorney wants absolute candor. If the case is flawed, the attorney wants to be told so as to avoid the expenditure of substantial resources.

Most nursing and medical experts shy away from an explanation that includes the implied message of, "this is what I want you to say...." Being pressured can turn off a potentially good expert. An infectious disease doctor told one of the authors after his first and last experience as an expert witness that, "I felt like I was being manipulated to say what the lawyer wanted me to say, not to tell the truth." By emphasizing that the expert's role is to assist in the search for the truth, the expert will understand the role.

Although it is tempting to obtain an opinion over the phone from an expert without sending the records, such an approach is flawed. A careful, thorough expert cannot form an opinion without seeing the records. Both the seasoned attorney and expert witness recognize this to be true in all but the most blatant cases. Even in the most obvious cases, the expert must review the records to proceed with the case.

The expert should be approached by a person who knows the case well and can give specific details. The preparation for this phone call will result in a feeling of confidence, and reassure the expert that the person is familiar with the case. If practical, it is also helpful to review the medical literature before speaking to the expert so an informed discussion of the medical issues can occur. This is especially facilitated when the attorney appoints a legal nurse consultant (either as in-house employee or independent consultant) to conduct this discussion.

Recognize that everything said or given to the expert is usually considered discoverable. Everything the expert produces or says may be subject to discovery. One of the advantages of involving a non-testifying legal nurse consultant in a nursing malpractice case is the opportunity it affords the attorney to frankly discuss the case without fear of disclosure.[23] The legal nurse consultant supplements the skills of the expert witness and may be asked to help prepare questions for depositions, and perform literature searches and other activities that may be more costly and discoverable if performed by the expert.

21.8 Orienting the New Expert

On occasion, the nurse most qualified to review the case has never acted as an expert witness. With proper explanations and orientation, this person can be developed into an effective and invaluable expert. Many inexperienced experts are unaware of the nuances of this role but are happy to accommodate the attorney's needs once they understand what is expected.

TIP: Novice expert witnesses may be reluctant to ask questions for fear of appearing uninformed or stupid.

Assuming the role of expert witness involves entering a new world with its own language and rules. Terms that are commonplace to attorneys can be bewildering to the expert.

The neophyte expert is lost when attorneys use terms like "motion for summary judgment," "requests for production," "dismissed with prejudice," "affidavit of merit," "standard of care," and "reasonable degree of nursing probability." The vocabulary needs to be explained to the new expert with explicit reassurances that the expert should ask questions. The cooperation that is gained will more than justify the extra minutes spent in explanation.

Provide instructions to the novice about the importance of not writing on or highlighting portions of the medical record, the implications of note taking, the confidentiality of the case, and the importance of not discussing it with others. Inform the expert that putting preliminary opinions or thoughts in writing makes them discoverable in some, but not all, jurisdictions.

Be sure the expert understands the importance of evaluating the nursing care using the reasonably prudent nurse, not the super clinician, as a standard. The expert must understand the need to avoid criticizing physician care.

21.9 Preparing the Documents

Proper organization of the case materials and medical records can turn a paper nightmare into a dream for an expert witness. (Chapter 7, *Nursing Documentation*, explains how to organize medical records.) Nothing is more frustrating to an expert than opening an envelope containing medical records that look like they have been thrown together without any organization. Double-sided copies of documents that have not been appropriately organized into sections of the chart are particularly difficult to review. A legal nurse consultant or a paralegal can organize the file before it is sent to the expert at far less cost than the expert's hourly rate. The retention letter that accompanies the records is discoverable and is usually brief. A recommended format is shown in Figure 21.4.

TIP: A full, certified copy of the medical record related to the incident or care in question is needed. A chart missing nursing documentation is virtually worthless for analyzing nursing liability.

21.10 Ethical Aspects of Preparing the Case

It is assumed the expert will prepare a report for the attorney if required by the jurisdiction and if the expert can support the attorney's side. One of the authors (PI) is still troubled by the ethics of a situation involving a plaintiff's attorney who wrote a report for a nurse expert witness. Although the nurse was in the process of preparing the report, the attorney created a letterhead for the expert, wrote the report, and

RE: *JONES v. SMITH*, file #94-006425
Dear Expert,
Enclosed is the following material:

- Complaint
- Certificate of Merit
- Medical records of Lewis Lister's hospitalization at Cape Hope Medical Center from 3/14/05-3/19/05
- Autopsy report 3/20/05
- Incident report 3/19/05
- Investigation report of the State Department of Health 4/1/05
- Plaintiff's answers to interrogatories
- Defendants' answers to interrogatories
- Cape Hope Medical Center's answers to notice to produce
- Report of Nurse Crittle, plaintiff expert witness
- Report of Doctor Almente, defense expert witness
- Deposition transcripts of Nurse Godden, Nurse Newhart, and Nurse Kingerly
- Deposition transcript of Doctor Mulhaney

This will confirm that you have agreed to review the materials enclosed and to provide me with your thoughts on them. I understand that your fees are as follows:

Record analysis	$_____
Deposition testimony	$_____
Trial appearance	$_____

A $_____ retainer is enclosed.
If for any reason you determine you are familiar with any of the parties or treating healthcare providers, please contact me immediately.

If you determine you will need additional material to review, please let me know. I look forward to hearing from you by the week of _____.

Very truly,

Attorney, Esq

Figure 21.4 *Sample Retention Letter*

faxed it to the nurse's place of employment for her signature. What the attorney saw as a helpful act created ill will. The expert was annoyed the attorney had written a report for her, and embarrassed the attorney sent it to her hospital without her permission. The attorney was puzzled that the expert objected. He defended his actions by saying he wrote reports for experts all the time. Clearly, the expert and the attorney had very different perspectives on the ethics of this incident. The report the attorney prepared may have been discoverable and would have been devastating if the defense had obtained a copy of the draft. Withholding such a report also poses ethical problems.

Another issue with ethical implications is withholding information or material from an expert witness. Files can become voluminous, and certainly the expert does not need to read material that is not germane to the expert's role in the case. The experienced expert soon learns which parts of the file are most important to review and which can be skimmed or skipped, depending on the nature of the case. On the other hand, a few attorneys have tried to withhold important evidence in the case, such as the depositions, because they "didn't say anything." Provide the expert with all of the information available and do not make excuses if all relevant materials are not available. Let the expert know it may affect the analysis of the expert. One of the worst things the attorney can do is hide information from the expert if the missing information will not support the attorney's case. It is far worse for the expert to be confronted with this information on the witness stand in cross-examination that goes like the following:[24]

> Attorney: Nurse Jones, at the time you formed your opinions, you wanted all of the available information, correct?
>
> Expert: Yes.
>
> Attorney: Did you have the deposition of the patient's son at the time you formed your opinions?
>
> Expert: No.
>
> Attorney: Have you ever seen the deposition of the patient's son?
>
> Expert: No.
>
> Attorney: Didn't you think that knowing the son's version of the events would be important in your review?
>
> Expert: I was unaware that the deposition of the patient's son was taken.
>
> Attorney: Did you ask the attorney for the deposition transcript?
>
> Expert: No.

No matter how the expert reacts, she looks less than thorough in the eyes of the jury for forming an opinion without this information.

- The attorney was not clear about when the report was needed.
- The expert was overwhelmed by the size of the file, and put it aside for review at a better time.
- The expert's schedule was crowded, and the expert has difficulty saying no to demands on her time.
- The expert was ambivalent about taking on this case, and therefore procrastinated in reviewing the file.
- The case was difficult and required extensive review of material, including the medical literature.
- Unanticipated demands on the expert's time prevented the timely review of the case.
- Pertinent documents were missing, such as the appropriate institution's records.

Figure 21.5 Reasons for Delays in Hearing from the Expert Witness

Occasionally an unethical attorney will identify a person as an expert when there has been no contact with that expert. This strategy prevents the opposing attorney from retaining the services of that expert. The authors are aware of this practice occurring with certain hard-to-find experts. The expert who learns that his name has been used without permission is likely to demand a retainer and case materials.

21.11 Review and Report Preparation

Ideally, the attorney contacts the expert and provides a reasonable time frame for review of the material. The deadline for the submission of the opinion should be clearly defined. After packing up all of the material, the attorney sits back and waits for the expert's opinion. Delays in receiving the expert's reading on the case could happen for the reasons listed in Figure 21.5. The attorney may be watching the clock tick closer to the date when the expert's report must be supplied, if required in the jurisdiction, while the expert is oblivious to the pressures on the attorney. To avoid last minute panic, be very clear about the time frame when the expert witness is first contacted.

One of the pet peeves of experts is being sent a case at the last minute with an unreasonable deadline. "Waiting too long to hire an expert, whether it's because you did not realize the deadline was nearing or because you were hoping the case would settle before you had to pay the expert's retainer fee, is asking for trouble."[25] With a comfortable deadline, the expert may be able to suggest additional documents that would be helpful for review, suggest other defendants who should be named, or offer ideas for strategic handling of the claim. Sometimes through no fault of the attorney, the expert's opinion is needed with very little time for the expert to review the file. Explaining to the expert the valid reasons for this rush will make it more acceptable when the expert has to shift priorities to review the case and meet the deadline. When there is a particularly tight deadline, keep in touch with the expert to see how the review is going, and to keep the case in the forefront of the expert's mind. Explain what will happen to the case if the opinion is not received in time. The consequences may be obvious to the attorney, but the novice expert witness is often unaware of the legal implications of deadlines. Pay the expert's invoice in a timely manner according to the terms of the fee agreement, to express appreciation for the rush job, and to maintain the good will of the expert.

A. When the Expert Cannot Support the Attorney's Side

When the expert can provide a careful, coherent rationale for not going further with a case, this advice may save needless time, energy, and expense. Unless the attorney is convinced the expert is dead wrong, it is futile to argue with the expert. Beware of trying to convince the expert that the attorney is right and the expert is wrong. Even if the expert agrees to view the case through the attorney's eyes, this may come back to haunt the attorney later. An expert who does not truly believe the case has merit can be effectively cross-examined in a deposition or at trial. Use the expert to play devil's advocate and identify the flaws of the case. Expert witnesses are called that because they are experts. They have education, training, or experience that makes them more knowledgeable in their field than the attorney. The attorney should respect that. The attorney may not like hearing what the expert says about the issues in the case, but should recognize that the expert is fulfilling an ethical obligation to tell the truth and exhibit integrity. Expert witnesses can get reputations for ethical or unethical behavior. Avoid the hired gun who will skirt the edges of junk science to please the attorney and support the theory of the case.[26]

TIP: Rarely does an attorney win when trying to convince the expert he is wrong when a case is turned down. Typically both the attorney and expert become impatient and defensive, leaving each feeling frustrated.

B. Obtaining the Written Report

Many attorneys request a phone call after the initial review of the material before preparation of a written report, if required by the venue. At this time, the attorney commonly asks for the nursing expert's conclusions regarding liability. The expert should identify any missing records or materials needed for rendering a more complete opinion or for developing the case. The analytical expert should be able to help anticipate the position of the opposing counsel's expert. The expert may suggest the need for medical literature to strengthen an opinion or impeach an opposing expert.

When the expert has completed the review and is ready to render a written opinion that favors the attorney's side, ensure the expert understands the format for the report. To avoid receiving an unacceptable product from a new expert, explain in detail the format preferred and required in the jurisdiction. Expert witness reports commonly include three components:

- A list of documents reviewed.
- A summary of the medical facts.
- Description of the standards of care with an explanation on how the nurse adhered to the standard of care (if the report was written for the defense) or deviated from the standard of care (if the expert

was retained by the plaintiff's attorney), and a description of how the deviations proximately caused any event or events, if applicable.

A more detailed report can consist of this additional information, as applicable:

- An outline of key events by date, time, and personnel involved
- Identification of contradictions within the medical record
- Identification of contradictions between the medical record and testimony of defendants, fact witnesses, and experts
- Critique of the opposing expert's position

In some cases, the information outlined above may be elicited at the time of deposition or trial rather than included in a written report. If the expert is unfamiliar with the format of a typewritten report, send the expert an old report from a resolved case, with the names redacted, so the expert can see the type of information and format that is expected. Let the expert know if quotes from the medical literature supporting the expert's position are needed. Many nursing experts who write for publication are accustomed to footnoting their comments. They may not realize that the attorney on the other side is likely to read and review the sources to search for statements that contradict the expert's opinion. Case law regarding use of published sources varies from state to state.

Explain the expected length, and what not to include in the report, such as sweeping statements that cannot be justified by the facts of the case or criticisms of the medical rather than nursing care. Be specific about whether the report should be read to the attorney over the phone, faxed in advance, or sent in final form. Go over the requirements of Rule 26 so the expert knows what should be included in the report and what records may be kept separately (Figure 21.6). A major revision of Rule 26 proposed to take effect in December 2010 would allow communications between the expert and attorney to fall under the protection of the work-product doctrine. The amendments would prohibit discovery of draft expert reports and limit discovery of attorney-expert communications. Still allowed would be full discovery of the expert's opinions and the facts or data used to support them.[27]

When evaluating the report, consider:

- Has the expert defined the basis of his opinions or simply provided a net opinion?
- Does the report read well?

Rule 26(b)(2): Disclosure of Expert Testimony

(2)   Disclosure of Expert Testimony

(A)   In addition to the disclosures required by paragraph (1), a party shall disclose to other parties the identity of any person who may be used at trial to present evidence under Rules 702, 703, or 705 of the Federal Rules of Evidence.

(B)   Except as otherwise stipulated or directed by the court, this disclosure shall, with respect to a witness who is retained or specially employed to provide expert testimony in the case or whose duties as an employee of the party regularly involve giving expert testimony, be accompanied by a written report prepared and signed by the witness. The report shall contain a complete statement of all opinions to be expressed and the basis and reasons therefore; the data or other information considered by the witness in forming the opinions; any exhibits to be used as a summary of or support for the opinions; the qualifications of the witness, including a list of all publications authored by the witness within the preceding ten years; the compensation to be paid for the study and testimony; and a listing of any other cases in which the witness has testified as an expert at trial or by deposition within the preceding four years.

(C)   These disclosures shall be made at the times and in the sequence directed by the court. In the absence of other directions from the court or stipulation by the parties, the disclosures shall be made at least 90 days before the trial date or the date the case is to be ready for trial or, if the evidence is intended solely to contradict or rebut evidence on the same subject matter identified by another party under paragraph (2)(B), within 30 days after the disclosure made by the other party. The parties shall supplement these disclosures when required under subdivision (e)(1).

Figure 21.6 *Rule 26(b)(2): Disclosure of Expert Testimony*

- Does the report contain typographical errors?
- Is the report logical and consistent with the facts?
- Has the expert altered facts?
- Has the expert omitted significant information?

TIP: Most importantly, give the expert a phone call after the written report is received. Congratulate the expert if the job was well done. If the report could have been improved, explain the problem so the expert will learn from the experience. Feedback like this enhances the expert's skills and is a wise investment in the creation of a strong expert.

C. *Daubert, Joiner,* and *Kumho Tire*

The Supreme Court provided federal trial attorneys with guidelines on the qualifications and methodologies of expert witnesses in an effort to refine the admissibility of expert witness testimony. Palmer[28] notes that in *Daubert v. Merrell Dow Pharmaceuticals, Inc.,* 509 U.S. 579 (1993), the Supreme Court held that federal trial judges must perform a gatekeeping function to decide whether proposed expert testimony is reliable and relevant and therefore admissible under Federal Rule of Evidence 702.

The four *Daubert* criteria for evaluating the admissibility of expert testimony are:

1. whether the methods upon which the testimony is based are centered upon a testable hypothesis;
2. the known or potential rate of error associated with the method;
3. whether the method has been subject to peer review; and
4. whether the method is generally accepted in the relevant scientific community.[29]

After *Daubert,* the Eleventh Circuit held that appellate courts should apply a particularly stringent standard of review when trial courts exclude expert testimony, but not when they admit such testimony[30] In *General Electric Co. v. Joiner,* 541 U.S. 136 (1997), the Supreme Court rejected this proposition, holding that an abuse of discretion standard applies regardless of whether evidence is admitted or excluded. In *Kumho Tire Co. v. Carmichael,* 526 U.S. 137 (1999), the Supreme Court reversed the Eleventh Circuit's decision that the Supreme Court had explicitly limited its holding in *Daubert* to the "scientific context." The Supreme Court clarified its position in *Kumho Tire* by holding that the *Daubert* gatekeeping factors apply to all experts testifying, including economists, psychiatrists, physiologists, and so on. This area of law affects all nursing experts, but is particularly troublesome for life care planners.

Palmer[31] recommends that attorneys consider how these guidelines apply to the location and preparation of expert witnesses. The following suggestions are offered for application of these guidelines to nursing malpractice cases:

- The expert should be able to clearly identify the methodology used and be able to establish that it is generally accepted in the field as the method used to analyze or resolve a particular issue. For example, the life care planner should rationalize including certain items in the life care plan, or how prices were established for services or equipment.
- Experts should be encouraged to publish in peer-reviewed journals. The expert without publications should be able to cite peer-reviewed articles and books showing that the opinions and methodology have solid support in the discipline.
- The experts must test their alternative design to establish that it would have prevented the injury. (This may apply when a piece of equipment, coupled with nursing error, is associated with an injury to a patient.)

While we seldom see *Daubert* motions in nursing malpractice cases, the "net opinion" rule comes up quite frequently. *Daubert* is designed to make certain that the witness is giving her expert opinion based on some accepted scientific knowledge, and not just personal opinion. By the same token, a nurse or physician who gives a personal opinion without any scientific basis can be barred in state court pursuant to the net opinion rule. We have seen this in some nurse expert reports. Some nurse experts painstakingly summarize the medical chart at issue and comment upon the actions taken by the defendant nurse. They then conclude in a sentence or two that the nurse did or did not deviate from accepted standards of care. This is a net opinion. A nurse expert must not only review the facts of the case, but must specifically base her opinion on those facts. To be safe, a nurse should spell out the standard of care at issue, and then explain in detail how that standard of care was met with or deviated from by the defendant nurse. She should refer specifically to certain notes or entries in the chart and explain how those facts support her opinion that the defendant nurse met with or deviated from the standards described. The nurse expert can then go on to give her opinion as to whether or not that caused the harm or injury in question, which is usually permitted, as long as the nurse does not get into a medical discussion. Suffice it to say that a nurse can certainly testify that the failure to strap a patient onto a stretcher was the cause of the patient falling, but would not be able to testify as to the type of fracture that resulted, or the medical treatment needed.

21.12 Communicating with Nurse Expert Witnesses

The attorney and the nurse have different perspectives. Many nurses have been taught to be indirect in their communication, as in, "Doctor, the usual dosage of Morphine is 5 to 10 milligrams. Are you sure you want to order 100 milligrams?" Indirect communication allows the nurse to function within the healthcare hierarchy by preserving the egos of physicians. Attorneys, in contrast, are taught to be direct and powerful in the adversarial legal system. It is advisable to explicitly tell the nurse, "I want to hear the downside of this case so there are no surprises later on and I can make appropriate legal decisions." Attorneys are often taught to function autonomously. Nurses are taught to be team players. They are quite comfortable working with others and can be valuable assets as the case develops. Nursing school emphasizes the need to be helpful.[32] Nurses are taught in school to evaluate a set of medical facts and to draw conclusions from them. Attorneys are often taught to use their theories of the case and frame the facts accordingly. This difference in perspectives can result in communication problems between nurses and attorneys.

It can be awkward at times for the nurse expert witness to receive phone calls at work. Some employers frown upon expert witness work, particularly on behalf of a plaintiff. Depending on the role of the nurse, it may be difficult to receive or make calls in privacy. Therefore, the attorney should schedule the call at the nurse's convenience. A degree of sensitivity to this issue is helpful when establishing a relationship with the expert witness.

21.13 Paying the Expert's Bill

To avoid the unpleasantness of an unexpectedly large bill, explain the limitations of the budget before sending the case to the expert. Emphasize the need to communicate if the time spent on the case is going to exceed the amount available for the review.

The attorney, not the client, is responsible for paying the expert's bills. Attempting to pass on financial responsibility may create animosity with some expert witnesses. Experts expect to be paid in a timely manner for the services rendered. Some experts require large or replenishing retainers, or structure the retainer so it is applied to the final bill and not the first bill.

The attorney may experience one of the following remedies available to experts for recovering payment for services rendered:

1. Receiving a series of letters demanding payment
2. Being the subject of a complaint with the ethics committee of the local bar association
3. Receiving a claim in small claims or other branches of the court system
4. Being contacted by a collection agency
5. Being advised that all work on the file is being stopped and that the expert will not appear for a deposition or trial without payment

---

TIP: Prompt payment of expert witness bills is a positive way to build a firm relationship with the expert.

21.14 Additional Services of the Expert Witness

In addition to preparing the written or oral report or affidavit, the nursing expert can assist in a number of other ways as the case progresses. The expert can assist in the discovery phase by:

*   suggesting policies, procedures, and other documents that should be obtained from the defendant facility,
*   identifying additional potential defendants,
*   developing questions for deposition or cross-examination of the opposing expert witness, fact witnesses, or defendants,
*   attending the depositions of these individuals to detect the nuances that cannot be captured on the transcript,
*   obtaining information about the opposing expert's reputation,
*   helping the attorney develop a theme for the case,[33]
*   assisting in case development,
*   obtaining other expert witnesses, and
*   assisting with the preparation of demonstrative evidence.

The nursing expert may be able to help the attorney critique the curriculum vitae of the opposing expert to identify weaknesses in publications or experience. It is not true that "a nurse is a nurse is a nurse." The expert should have experience in the particular specialty area of nursing involved in the case. The authors have seen attorneys hire obstetrical nurses to review medical surgical cases, for example, whereas the same attorney would not hire an obstetrician to opine about the standard of care for an internist.

One of the most important areas of investigation is examination of the publications of the opposing expert for in-

consistencies with the expert's opinion. The nursing expert witness may be invaluable in helping obtain the published work of the opposing expert. Figure 21.7 summarizes the major responsibilities of the nursing expert.

---

*   Offering opinions based on the standards of care, not on the morals, motivations, reputation, or scruples of any party.
*   Rendering an opinion based on knowledge, abilities, training, and the information reviewed.
*   Basing an opinion on "a reasonable degree of nursing certainty" for each alleged act of negligence demonstrating a deviation (major or minor) from the acceptable standard of care.
*   Avoiding offering opinions on causation, since physicians must testify to the question of causation, "if not for (the negligent act) the injuries would not have occurred."
*   Avoiding commenting on the standard of care for physicians involved in the case.

Figure 21.7 Nursing Expert Witness Responsibilities

21.15 Assisting the Expert with Depositions

Some experts find testifying at depositions to be stressful. The attorney should prepare the expert with some explicit instructions and information.

A. Preparation

Remember the first time you rode a roller coaster? You probably had little forewarning and approached it with considerable anticipation. Most roller coasters begin with a slow climb to the top of a hill that quickly crests and cascades downward through unknown valleys and turns, thrusting you hither and yon, and leaving you short on oxygen and physically exhausted. The roller coaster experience is not unlike a first deposition at the hands of a skilled lawyer. Unlike a roller coaster ride, the expert can be prepared for a deposition. If the retaining counsel neglects to properly prepare the expert, the expert is back on the roller coaster.[34]

One of the biggest complaints experts have is not having adequate time to prepare for a deposition with retaining counsel before the event.[35] The neophyte expert needs to understand the importance of reviewing the case again before the deposition so that the facts are very clear, and that everything in the file is discoverable. The expert should be informed of what to bring to the deposition, particularly if this individual is new to the process.

B. What to Bring

The expert should bring an accurate, updated CV. Providing an inaccurate CV can result in needless damage to credibility. The expert should bring his file. Surprises may be found within files. An attorney found a note in an opposing expert witness's file that marked one page of the medical record. The note said, "The attorney wants me to say this, but I believe the opposite." During deposition, the expert first testified consistent with the attorney's opinion on the point. Then he was confronted with the note. This experience caused this expert to stop expert witness work. In another case, the opposing counsel found two reports written by the expert. They were both sent by the retaining law firm, stapled to each other. One was a confidential memo written to the insurance company. It had one set of opinions; the official report had another.[36] The expert should bring all of the records and a copy of the report, even if this requires a luggage cart.

C. Pre-Deposition Session

A meeting before a deposition is advisable for preparing the expert. This serves several purposes: meeting the expert, discussing issues and developments, reviewing strategies, and describing opposing counsel. This session is often the attorney's first opportunity to meet the expert. The attorney has a chance to determine:

- Does the expert have jury appeal? (In the terms of one attorney, "Does the expert have a good 'court face'?")
- Is the expert able to speak in layperson's terms?
- Can the expert speak with spirit and conviction?
- Can the expert think quickly and extemporize?
- Can the expert follow a hypothetical question and respond in a meaningful manner?

Part of the preparation of the expert witness, especially the neophyte, is defining who is likely to be present at the deposition, especially the identities of the other attorneys. The expert should be advised that one of the purposes of the deposition is to size up the expert, and that opposing counsel is taking the expert's deposition to learn every opinion he has and the factual basis for each opinion. The information is used to attempt to discredit the opinion by discovering

bias or prejudice. The expert is expected to commit to statements under oath that can be used later as sound bites at trial.[37]

The pre-deposition session is an opportunity to review the issues and late-breaking developments. The retaining counsel should make the expert fully aware of the key premises in the opposition's case. This may damage the viability of his own opinion and the overall success of the case, to the extent that the expert is forced to agree to such a key premise. Where possible, the expert should be thoroughly prepared to avoid admitting any key premise of the opposition's case or of the opposition's expert testimony.[38] It is helpful to understand what has occurred in recent depositions of defendants or opposing experts so as to understand the information that has been revealed so far.

Experts may ask about the style of opposing counsel. Understanding the personality and level of experience of the opposing counsel is useful to the expert. Some styles likely to be used include:

- Broken record: Repeats questions multiple times to induce the expert to provide inconsistent answers to the same question, or to get the expert to answer a question favorably to the questioning attorney, when the expert's first answer is not favorable;
- Bully: Attempts to browbeat or intimidate the expert into answering questions favorably to the attorney's interests;
- Simple country boy: Tries to charm the expert into favorable answers by appearing simple, humble, and down to earth, projecting a desire to obtain only "honest" answers;
- Hurt puppy: Acts disappointed by the expert's answers, hoping the expert will want to please the attorney by providing different (and more favorable) answers;
- Good ole boy: Insincerely attempts to charm the expert by coming across as a "buddy," believing that "you can catch more flies with honey than vinegar";[39]
- Jumper: Quickly and frequently changes the pace and subject matter to keep the expert from anticipating the next series of questions or to obtain inconsistent answers to the same questions asked more than once at different points throughout the course of the deposition.

Sometimes opposing counsel has unusual habits. If the retaining attorney is aware of these, it is useful to forewarn the expert so as to be better prepared to ignore facial tics,

---

Prepare the expert for these deposition strategies:

- Detailed probing into the expert's background, fee structure, experience as an expert—the expert should calmly and non-defensively provide the answers to these questions.
- Asking questions in no obvious order—this is designed to prevent the expert from seeing a pattern in the questions. The expert should answer each question as clearly as possible.
- Deliberate mispronunciation of words—the attorney is trying to present an uneducated air so that the expert's guard will be let down. The expert should ignore the mispronunciations.
- Flattery—the opposing attorney acts impressed with the expert's credentials in order to lower the expert's guard. The expert should politely acknowledge the compliment and wait for the next question.
- Goading the expert—the attorney is hoping the expert will lose her temper or respond in a flippant way. The expert should remain calm.
- Using body language to intimidate—pointing fingers, shouting, leaning into the expert's space are often tactics that the attorney who retained the expert can bring to a halt by objecting.
- Asking questions rapidly—the attorney may be hoping the expert will mimic the pace of questioning and give a careless answer in haste. The expert should think through the answer to each question and establish a pace that is comfortable for the expert, remembering that a pause does not show up on a transcript.
- Asking repetitive questions—the expert should provide consistent answers to the same question asked several times.
- Asking complex convoluted questions—whether done on purpose or because of difficulty framing questions, the attorney should be asked to rephrase the question so that it is clear.
- Questioning the expert about details in the medical record to test the expert's memory—the expert is allowed to refer to the materials that were reviewed and does not have to answer questions based on memory alone.
- Use of silence—the attorney may pause after the expert's answer hoping the expert will elaborate on the answer.
- Asking about nursing literature to identify "reasonably reliable and authoritative texts"—the attorney should prepare the expert to answer these questions based on the jurisdiction's case law.
- Hypothetical questions—the expert needs to be sure the details included in the hypothetical question match the case issues, and does not include facts unsupported by the evidence.

Figure 21.8 Deposition Strategies

cleaning fingernails with hunting knives, chewing tobacco and spitting in a cup, clicking pens, and other distracting behavior.

The expert may need assistance in anticipating the strategies that may be used. See Figure 21.8. Other information to impart includes the following:

- How to stay focused during the deposition.
- How hypothetical questions are used in depositions.
- How to answer questions about reasonably reliable or standard texts.
- How to respond to questions regarding the total amount of annual income from expert witness work.

- The need to answer questions about fees for this case and other cases.
- What not to do at a deposition, including losing one's temper, making rash statements, guessing, allowing the attorney to interrupt the expert's answer, volunteering information, giving flippant answers, looking at the attorney for the answer to a question, talking to the opposing attorney during break under the illusion that it is "off the record," relaxing before the deposition is over, and so on.
- The importance of requesting the opposing attorney to clarify ambiguous questions.
- How to avoid letting the expert's ego get in the way of testimony.
- The importance of addressing the adverse facts.

- The need to concede the obvious.
- The need to listen to the entire question before formulating an answer.
- How to appear in front of the camera if the deposition will be videotaped.
- Not permitting the opposing attorney to inaccurately summarize or characterize the expert's testimony.
- The importance of being comfortable with silence.
- Thinking before answering questions.
- That it is okay to answer "I don't know." The expert may be pushed into making an on-the-spot analysis of information without adequate time to think it through.
- The importance of not overstating the client's position, which can devastate the expert's credibility.
- The need to attend to questions and to ask an incomprehensible question to be repeated or rephrased. The expert cannot ask the attorney client for help in answering a question.
- The fact that the expert cannot ask questions of the opposing counsel, unless the question is not clear.
- That the attorneys may request to speak to a judge to get clarification on controversial questions.
- The fact that the expert was not hired to impress people, but to be persuasive. It may be possible to do both, but if the expert has to choose between looking impressive and being likable, it is better to be liked. The expert should think of herself as a personable teacher, not as the ultimate arbiter of fact.
- The explanation for the term "reasonable nursing probability or certainty." The expert may think of this term in a very different way than the attorney.
- The importance of making testimony understandable by avoiding technical jargon.[40]
- The need for the expert to not follow opposing counsel's lead, if she is leading the expert astray. The expert should listen for red flag questions. If the opposing counsel asks a question that sounds like legalese, it may be an effort to trick the expert into making a damaging concession.
- Why it is important to be definite, when possible. The expert should avoid, "I think," "as far as I can tell," "to the best of my knowledge," and "I believe." These terms sound imprecise.[41]
- How to deal with "possible" versus "probable"—the expert may not understand that the law makes a legal distinction between possibilities and probabilities. Opinions based upon possibility are not

necessarily admissible. If the nursing expert uses any of the following phrases in connection with her opinion, such testimony may be stricken:
- It might be true.
- It might be possible.
- It might have that effect.
- It could have that effect.[42]

TIP: Leshner[43] notes: "A big red flag is raised when the opposing attorney attempts to summarize considerable deposition questioning in a one or two sentence summary statement. I simply answer 'that's not what I said,' or 'That's not the way I would say it.' This answer is not too clumsy and usually gives me an opportunity to summarize in my own words." Fruehan[44] adds that, "Since these questions typically start with 'So your testimony is…,' I simply answer (in a very flat tone) 'No,' which usually forces the attorney to break it down. This may have an additional value for the shock of the simplicity, and for placing the burden totally on him/her to clarify." Many inexperienced experts take some deposition questions personally and feel defensive after undergoing a difficult deposition, and need the attorney's help to keep the experience in proper perspective.

Mester advises following a step-by-step process for preparing the attorney and the expert for a deposition. The key tenants of his model are as follows:

1. Plan two expert preparation sessions; the first a week before the deposition and the second the day before or the day of the deposition. Prior to the first session, review the medical records and previous depositions so the attorney can identify the most important documents and be prepared to review them with the expert.
2. Assemble a binder for the expert with key medical records, articles on the issue, including the expert's own publications, and important deposition transcripts.
3. Write down every document you send to the expert and ask the expert to check the list to be sure nothing is missing.
4. At the preparation session, explain the basics of a deposition and the specifics of the case.
5. Make sure the expert knows the facts of the case, and the temperament or style of questioning of opposing counsel.
6. Discuss the theories of the opposing side and the goals of the deposition—to learn the facts and

opinions that the expert plans to present, to memorialize the expert's testimony in anticipation of impeachment at trial, and to evaluate the expert as a witness.

7. Look at every document in the expert's file, including notes, highlighting of testimony, indexing of records or research performed.

8. Review the expert's report and curriculum vitae and ask the expert to bring a copy to the deposition.

9. Find out if the expert needs anything else before forming a final opinion for deposition. Get those materials for the expert.

10. Consider having the expert write a summary list of opinions to use at deposition, to ensure that all areas are covered.

11. Explain legal terminology. Go over the meaning of "more likely than not" and "to a reasonable degree of medical probability/certainty."

12. Review any articles the expert has written and make sure the testimony is consistent with what's in those articles.

13. Tell the expert to always refer to the article or records before answering a question that is posed.

14. Ask whether the expert performed any literature searches; if yes, run the same search yourself to see if you see something the other side may seize upon.

15. Go over the definition of the standard of care applicable in your jurisdiction.

16. Complete a mock question and answer session.[45]

21.16 Best Practices When Deposing Medical Experts: Retaining Counsel

It is instructive to consider the perspectives of expert witnesses who possess a wealth of information about effective and ineffective practices of attorneys during depositions. The next section of the chapter reflects these perspectives. The following information was gathered by requesting expert witnesses to share their perspectives and experiences in deposition.

A. Use the Expert to Learn About Nursing

An attorney who wants to learn everything about the case and requests time with the expert for "education" is smart.[46] The expert should be used to help develop the case. The attorney who knows as much or more than the expert is wasting money. Only hire experts who know more than the attorney, and use their knowledge to help build the case. For example, experts can often help draft interrogatories or

prepare questions to ask at the depositions of the opponent's expert. Although the expert must be paid for this time, the time the attorney saves is worth far more. Also, a good expert suggests questions and theories the attorney is unlikely to discover on his own without investing a vast amount of time and energy.[47]

B. Request Optimal Time and Date Choices for Deposition

Do not assume the expert will be available when it is convenient for the attorney. Plenty of advance notice is always appreciated.

C. Help the Expert Anticipate Questions

The retaining counsel should spend sufficient time with an expert before she testifies, and ask questions in rehearsal. This gives the expert an opportunity to think through the questions.[48] Do a rehearsal of the questions counsel expects the opponent to use during deposition—and allow the expert to answer "on the spot" in that rehearsal, so that both the attorney and the expert are prepared. The expert (if new at this) will get a clue as to what types of questions might be asked. The attorney will get a very clear picture of the expert's opinion, if it has not been made clear already.[49]

It is often helpful to make a checklist of important issues likely to come up during the deposition. Also, when assisting a more novice expert, it is important to review definitions, such as "standard of care" (as it applies to the given jurisdiction) and "reasonable degree of probability" (when explaining proximate cause opinions).

D. Carefully Plan the Environment for a Videotaped Deposition

Consider the location of the deposition: will it be in the expert's office? If so, counsel should see the expert's office before the day of the deposition. Is the size of the room adequate? Should a plant be moved so it does not look like it is engulfing the expert? Is there a distracting picture in the background? Should the videographer bring a backdrop to conceal the background? Have the expert and videographer get together for 15 minutes before the deposition if exhibits are going to be used. The expert and videographer can work out a system so that the camera follows the expert who is pointing to exhibits. Check the noise level in the office. Is the air conditioner sounding like a jet plane taking off? If so, it will come through on the videotape.[50] Discuss wearing conservative, dark clothes. The expert should look directly in the camera when testifying and avoid long pauses. Avoid eating, drinking, or chewing gum, hair, or pencils. Turn off cell phones, pagers, and beepers.[51]

E. Inquire About Out-of-Town Travel Arrangements for Expert

Recognize that some experts prefer to make their own travel arrangements, so the best practice is probably to inquire of the expert first. Have a staff person meet the expert at the airport and escort the individual to the hotel or courthouse. Also, with the advent of videoconferencing technology, it may be a good idea to offer to conduct the deposition of an out-of-town expert by videoconference. Many experts are more appreciative of the convenience of not having to leave their home state to testify. This also seems to be less costly than paying for the travel expenses.

F. Provide Accurate Directions to Site of Deposition to All Involved Parties

Attach directions to the deposition site to the letter to the expert that confirms the date. Do not rely on Internet directions. Do not expect the expert's staff to provide directions to multiple attorneys in anticipation of a deposition being held at the expert's office. Many experts do not have the resources to provide this type of service.

G. Provide Encouragement and Support

During the preparation phase, counsel should set a positive tone for the expert by providing support, projecting confidence, and being enthusiastic about the case. During breaks, smile at the expert. Use that time to determine how the witness is feeling instead of checking voicemail or sorting through the mail. Often a calm face in the middle of a potentially stressful experience helps the expert maintain focus.

H. Curb Opposing Counsel's Abusive or Difficult Behavior

Abusive types of questions include repetitive, lengthy questioning, vulgarity, hostility, personal attacks, and demeaning and sarcastic remarks by counsel. How far is too far is ultimately decided by a judge. "I had a deposition where the deposing attorney kept asking the same question over and over—changing maybe one word in it each time. I kept saying the same answer each time. He finally told my attorney, 'She's not answering it right.' My attorney stated, 'She's been answering it—you just want it your way and it's not going to happen—get over it and go on with another question.'"[52] Advise the expert that he is being paid for his time, and if the opposing counsel wants to ask the same question over and over, the expert should be tirelessly patient.

The retaining counsel should intervene if the conduct of the opposing attorney becomes harassing or abusive. If the opposing attorney begins behaving in that manner, the retaining counsel should state, "If this type of conduct continues, the deposition is going to be terminated."

Lawyers have an ethical obligation to be respectful to all involved in the litigation process. In New Jersey, for example, there is a specific ethics rule which states that, "in representing a client, a lawyer shall not use means that have no substantial purpose other than to embarrass, delay or burden a third person [such as a nurse expert...]." In New Jersey, the ethic rules specifically require lawyers to "treat with courtesy and consideration all persons involved in the legal process." Unfortunately, in practice, many attorneys become overzealous in their attempt to advocate for their client. However, if an attorney's questioning of a witness at a deposition becomes nasty and abusive, the opposing counsel who hired that witness as an expert has an obligation to protect that witness and make certain that the proceeding maintains a certain decorum. There is a significant difference between asking probing questions which make a poorly prepared witness feel uncomfortable, and meaningless questions designed to embarrass or harass. The lawyer objecting has to be careful that an instruction to a witness to stop answering such questions (or to end the deposition altogether) has a sound basis, or she could end up paying the costs of a re-deposition. Again, the attorney should not interfere with the proceeding just to protect a witness who is not properly prepared or may be about to give up an important point in the case; but the lawyer should not hesitate to protect that person from abusive behavior.

In one author's practice (RF), a couple of warnings to the other attorney to lower his voice or to redirect the other attorney to asking more relevant questions has usually been found to prevent the problem. The better alternative to walking out of the deposition is to suggest a phone call to the court where the matter can be discussed, and hopefully the deposition can then proceed to a conclusion to save everyone time and expense. The threat of a phone call to the judge usually calms down the attorney who has unintentionally become somewhat overzealous.

I. Give Feedback When It Is Over

A brief session with the expert following the deposition is invaluable. Use this opportunity to offer feedback on the performance during the deposition. Most experts find this information essential in improving their skills, and have been grateful for both praise and suggestions for being more effective the next time.

J. Express Thanks After Deposition

A best practice is to send a letter, e-mail, or call the expert after the deposition to thank the individual for her assistance.[53]

21.17 Worst Practices When Deposing Medical Experts: Retaining Counsel

The practices listed below address each of the issues that increase the discomfort of the expert, interfere with the deposition process, or engender ill will, and thus should be avoided.

A. Failing to Listen to the Expertise of the Expert

Feedback from some experts reveals that, at times, attorneys do not listen to their own experts. Inexperienced attorneys may create traps for themselves instead of tapping the expertise of the experienced expert.

B. Dumping Several Last-Minute Requests

Supplying the expert with several depositions or a new set of medical records to read at the last minute is particularly stressful for an expert. The need to read and assimilate the new information interferes with the ability to prepare for the deposition.[54]

C. Arranging Telephone Depositions

Telephone depositions, while convenient for out-of-town counsel, can be challenging if there is a delay of a few seconds with the phone.[55] From the standpoint of opposing counsel, there is a missed opportunity to evaluate the appearance and file of the expert.

D. Misleading the Expert About the Scope of Testimony

Do not tell the nurse expert it is acceptable to testify about physician practice standards in a deposition, but then contradict this position in the courtroom.[56] The nurse is expected to focus on nursing standards, not physician standards.

E. Attacking the Expert

Experts sometimes share stories of being attacked by the attorney who retained their services. For example, one expert was subjected to profanities, screaming, and berating because the deposition was not going as expected. This is not the optimal way to instill confidence in the expert, and calm the expert in the midst of a long, nasty deposition. No matter how poorly the expert is doing, the attorney should give a "pep talk" to get the expert through—ultimately helping the attorney's own case outcome.[57]

F. Exhibiting Distracting Body Language

"One of the most disconcerting deposition experiences for me involved the attorney's non-verbal communication, es-

pecially bodily noises. Every time a question was asked, answer given or objection raised, she grunted, groaned, scowled, squirmed in her chair, threw down her pen, etc. The worst part is she was the attorney for whom I was testifying."[58] Other experts advise:

- Do not throw your pen across the table or on the floor when your expert gives an answer you do not like.
- Do not slouch in your chair.
- Do not drop your head to the table.
- Do not emit huge sighs/groans.
- Do not berate your own expert in deposition—in front of opposing counsel, i.e., very disdainfully stating, "You're not answering the question they asked you!"
- Do not dress sloppily just because the deposition is in your office.
- Do not ask the expert to refund the law firm for an unused plane ticket.
- Do not distract the expert by reviewing mail or other material, signing mail, checking e-mails or text messages, or doing other work during the course of the deposition.

21.18 Best Practices for Deposing the Opposing Expert

Figure 21.9 provides some suggestions for taking the deposition of the opposing expert. The goals of deposing an expert witness may include:

- Laying the foundation for cross-examination at trial,
- Showing the expert's bias or otherwise undermining the expert's credibility,
- Gaining concessions from the expert to help prove the attorney's points,
- Obtaining as much information as possible regarding the expert's opinions and the basis for them,
- Attempting to get the expert to support even a small part of the attorney's case,
- Discovering the weaknesses in the attorneys' own client's case, and
- Judging the demeanor of the expert.[59]

A. Organize One's Own Materials and Be Prepared

The attorney who is in command of the file has a sense of confidence, organization, and precision. The expert witness will recognize and respect this individual as a professional.

1. Personal information—address

2. Professional background
   a. Education not listed on the curriculum vitae (CV)
   b. Special training in the subject matter of the suit
   c. Areas of expertise
   d. Teaching positions
   e. Certifications including eligibility requirements
   f. Number of attempts to pass certification exam
   g. Is CV current
   h. Information left off of CV
   i. Termination, suspension, disciplinary action taken against expert
   j. Suits filed against expert and their outcomes
   k. How expert keeps up with advances in the field

3. Employment experience
   a. Practical experience in the subject matter of the suit
   b. Past and current job descriptions
   c. Consulting experience

4. Professional societies, honors, and activities
   a. Criteria for membership in associations
   b. Honors and grants, research interests
   c. Proudest accomplishments
   d. Presentations of the subject of nursing negligence to any groups

5. Publications
   a. Articles in peer-reviewed journals
   b. Texts
   c. Thesis, or dissertation, or both
   d. Publications by expert on topic of suit
   e. Any publications by expert not listed on curriculum vitae
   f. Nursing books in expert's library on this subject
   g. Subscriptions to nursing journals with articles on this subject

6. Media presentations (radio and television shows)

7. Continuing education programs taught or attended

8. Licenses
   a. States in which licensed
   b. Status of license—active or inactive
   c. Reason sought each license
   d. Number of times took licensing exam
   e. Any suspension or termination of license or employment at a hospital or other facility

9. Experience as an expert
   a. Understanding of role of an expert.
   b. How learned what is needed to become an expert
   c. Number of cases reviewed over what period of time

   d. Prior court appearances
   e. Instances of being found not qualified to testify
   f. Subject areas in which testimony was given
   g. Percentages of defense versus plaintiff work
   h. Prior cases reviewed for this firm
   i. Social or personal relationships with attorneys of this firm or any of the parties, or employment relationships with defendant hospitals, if applicable
   j. Names of attorneys for whom expert has worked
   k. Identification of other cases expert has reviewed that relate to subject matter of this case[1]
   l. Percentage of cases expert reviews that result in a conclusion that the expert cannot support position of attorney
   m. Advertising as an expert witness[2]
   n. Expert's definition of nursing negligence
   o. Motivation for acting as an expert

10. Compensation
    a. How derived fee structure
    b. Are there different rates for plaintiffs and defendants[3]
    c. Usual rate of pay when not doing expert work
    d. Record review and report preparation
    e. Deposition testimony
    f. Trial testimony
    g. Number of cases reviewed annually
    h. Percentage of reviews for plaintiffs and defendants
    i. Cancellation fees
    j. Percentage of income from expert witness work
    k. Insurance carrier of expert

12. Initial contact on this case
    a. Source of referral
    b. When contact first occurred
    c. Phone versus letter contact
    d. Explanation of case given at the time of the initial contact
    e. Expert's understanding of the role in this case
    f. Materials provided on the case-review of transmittal letter
    g. Missing materials, if any, requested

13. Contact with attorney's office after review of material
    a. Phone call made?
    b. E-mail contact?

14. Basis of opinions
    a. Where expert learned information used to form opinions
    b. Reasonably reliable literature supporting opinion
    c. Publications used for this case
    d. Publications contrary to the expert's position
    e. Sources of standards of care used in this case
    f. Texts used in nursing school on the subject matter of this case

Figure 21.9 Outline for Deposing the Opposing Expert

g. Professional organization materials; technical bulletins, position statements, etc.
h. People recognized as qualified in the field or to whom expert would go for advice in field
i. Knowledge of details of the case[4]
j. Identification of all of the facts upon which the expert based opinion
k. Expert's understanding of why defendant did each thing
l. Other acceptable ways to accomplish the care provided
m. Identification of facts that would change opinions
n. Degree of certainty of opinions
o. Defendant's responsibility toward plaintiff
p. Anything that could have been done by anyone else to prevent or correct the unfortunate event
q. Expert's opinion about what he would have done had the patient been his
r. Any credibility judgments made by expert as part of analysis

15. Preparation of report
a. Identity of person who prepared report
b. Consultations with other professionals before writing report
c. List of all materials reviewed in preparation of the report[5]
d. Did expert rely on the material sent in rendering opinions[6]
e. Was a draft report prepared
f. Changes made in draft report
g. Amount of time spent on preparing report
h. Missing materials requested and not supplied and their influence on opinions
i. Anything the expert felt important that was left out of the report [7]
j. All issues about which the expert will testify
k. What expert did to prepare for deposition and length of time of preparation
l. Materials supplied to expert after report preparation and before deposition
m. Materials supplied to expert the day of the deposition
n. Is entire file present with expert
o. Materials removed from file before deposition[8]
p. Plans to prepare supplemental report based on new material

16. Other services provided for attorney
a. Literature search

b. Preparation of deposition questions
c. Selection of demonstrative evidence
d. Recommendation of other experts
e. Other services

17. Information related to deposing attorney's expert
a. Knowledge of your own expert's reputation
b. Critique of your own expert's opinion

18. For defense expert
a. Circumstances under which plaintiff's condition could have been caused by negligence of a healthcare provider
b. Current condition of plaintiff preventable, and how
c. Belief that no one deviated from standards of care
d. Opinion about whether it is right for a patient to sue a nurse for negligence
e. Expert's trust of the system to adjudicate malpractice cases

Endnotes

1. Details of other cases would include name of case, name of attorney, docket number, court, and so on.
2. Question about advertising in telephone books, billboards, newspapers, legal journals, mailings, and so on.
3. Anything the attorney can gather in this area such as different rates for different cases or sides may impeach the credibility of the expert.
4. Ask specific questions on what is in the records. The expert probably has not read all of them. You may be able to get him to agree about things being in the records that are not there.
5. It is very possible that the opposing counsel did not give the expert material that is important to the case.
6. By pinning the expert down, the intent is to make certain the expert will not be able to testify beyond the limits of the report at the time of trial. Do not give the expert the opportunity to expand upon the report in the deposition.
7. Get the expert to admit he relied on all material sent in rendering an opinion. It could be that some of the material is helpful to your case, such as your expert's reports, and that the reports can be read by the attorney at trial in cross-examining the expert.
8. What materials were removed; who removed them, and why?

Figure 21.9 *Outline for Deposing the Opposing Expert (continued)*

Preparation enables the deposition to proceed smoothly and be conducted faster; it also identifies exhibits needed at trial, eliminates the expert's resentment over a waste of time, encourages the expert to be more forthcoming, and establishes the attorney as a person with whom opposing counsel must reckon.[60] Research the expert by reading publications of the expert and deposition transcripts.

B. Have the Person Who Knows the Case Best Take the Deposition

Experts comment that having the attorney most familiar with the file conduct the deposition promotes a productive experience. The attorney who takes the time to learn as much as possible before the deposition will have a solid foundation for learning what the witness can teach during the deposition.[61]

C. Be Courteous

Being pleasant to one's adversary, respecting the needs of the expert, and not being abrasive make the deposition a professional experience. As Horowitz notes, relaxing the witness is a good thing; engaging the witness in a conversation, on the record, is even better. Almost everyone is more giving and forthcoming when relaxed.[62]

D. Make the Expert Feel Comfortable

Sherri Hill notes, "I think the best thing I've seen attorneys do is make the person feel comfortable and treat him with respect even if the attorney and expert disagree."[63] A nurse attorney comments, "The deposing attorney should make the deponent feel comfortable with coffee, smiles, and conversation prior to getting started, etc. This communicates to the inexperienced expert that this is an informal friendly talk and the expert may let his/her guard down and say 'too much'" (to the opposing side's benefit).[64] By allowing a discernable pause after the witness has given an answer, the attorney nonverbally encourages the witness to add more to the answer. Answers that otherwise may not have come from direct questioning may be offered.[65] Be sensitive to the impact of the phrase "I get only one bite at the apple" when referring to the opportunity to depose the expert. The expert, who is the apple, may not appreciate the reference.

E. Make It Possible to Take a Break or Meal

Experts are entitled to ask for a break. Do not make it difficult for that to happen by saying, "But I just have a few questions." Recognize the needs of the participants to eat at a meal time. Do not attempt to continue through meal time without letting the expert eat. Expect to be charged for the expert's time spent eating. Consider that when scheduling the start time.

F. Spend Time on Case Issues, Not on Trivia

Focus on the issues and the expert's experience related to the issues. One expert shared this story: "One attorney spent 30 minutes asking me questions about my duties as a nurse's aide in the mid 1970s. I'll answer questions like that all day long if he wants to pay."[66] Once a valuable answer has been given to a question, immediately move on rather than allowing the expert to recant the answer.[67]

G. Do Not Attempt to Decimate the Expert

Recognize the risks associated with attempting to systematically destroy an expert's credibility, self-esteem, and confidence. A vicious attack may result in an expert being totally unable to safely drive home. One expert subjected to such an attack had to pull over on the highway because she was crying so hard she could not see. There are legal risks to prematurely destroying the other side's expert. In one notable case, a bright yet inexperienced attorney did a remarkable job of demolishing the credibility and conclusions of the expert at deposition. At the end of the deposition, he gloated, "If you're going to take this case to trial, you had better get a better expert." The opponent did just that, and won at trial. Had the attorney saved his devastating impeachment for trial, he probably would have won the case.[68]

It is probably best for the attorney to save the most useful cross-examination material for the time of trial. Certainly, the attorney wants to elicit as many favorable answers as possible from the opposing side's expert. This may cause opposing counsel to question whether she would want to have the expert testify at trial. If the attorney does too good a job of cross-examining the expert, the other team will likely get a new expert, and the attorney may have already exposed the adversary's most significant weaknesses. This ensures the new expert is better prepared to deal with them at the time of deposition. The caveat here is that in many jurisdictions, the time to serve expert reports are strictly governed by court order, so an adversary may not have time to retain a new expert if the expert is decimated at a deposition.

H. Ask What Facts the Expert Assumes to Be Correct

When facts are in dispute, ask what facts the expert assumes to be true to form opinions. If the opinions are based on facts in dispute, ask why the expert presumed those facts were true, rather than the facts obtained through discovery. Hypothetical questions may be asked when there are contradictory facts. The expert may have a different opinion if the facts more favorable to the attorney's case are presumed to be true. The jury who believes the attorney's set of facts may negate the opinion of the expert.[69]

I. Ask for All Opinions

Some attorneys end a deposition by asking for any additional opinions. Wendy Jones shares this story: "I recently heard a fantastic OB expert say that if the attorney asks 'Have you shared with us all of the opinions that you intend to express at trial?' he often adds more information. If they do not ask the question, he most certainly will not offer the added information. He said only the best attorneys ask this question at the end of the depositions and the least experienced usually do not."[70]

On the other hand, there are risks with this strategy. For example, if the expert does not comment on a particular area in the report (if in a state where the expert has written a report), such as causation, why open the door and ask if there are other opinions? It may be better to limit the scope of the expert's opinions by asking, "Are all of the opinions you have in this matter set forth in your report?" The expert may say "no" and begin to offer completely new opinions. Some attorneys might then tell the expert, "Since these opinions are not set forth in your report, I'm not going to ask you about them today. If you write a new report with these opinions in them, and a court lets you testify about these opinions offered out of time, then I will ask to come back and re-depose you about your new opinions, since I have not had enough time to evaluate your new opinions and properly prepare to ask you about them."

J. Confront the Non-Responsive Answer

The attorney can establish authority in the deposition by acknowledging an unresponsive answer and ask the witness to listen carefully as the attorney repeats the question. The court reporter can read the question back so that the witness can give a responsive answer. The judge should never be called unless it is absolutely essential, and the judge should always be called when it is necessary.[71]

K. Do Your Homework About the Expert

Due diligence about the expert may reveal surprising information. In one case, a plaintiff's nursing expert testified she had a chronic illness. The attorney contacted the Board of Nursing to find out if the expert had an active license. The board revealed her license had been suspended for writing prescriptions for herself using her husband's physician prescription pad. The attorney confronted the expert with the Board of Nursing documentation after the expert denied being disciplined. At trial, the judge permitted the jury to hear about the expert's disciplinary action. Trial was won by the defense.

Although researching experts requires consulting many different sources, valuable information can be uncovered.

Consider looking for trial documents, court and judge reports, challenge information, and deposition transcripts.[72]

L. Consider the Objectives of Questioning

Depositions are the only time you should ask experts open-ended questions. Ask a series of specific, leading questions that require the expert to concede facts and opinions that help your case. Use the literature to spin out the logical extremes of the expert's opinions until they sound absurd. Finally, try to get the expert to agree with the specific opinions that your expert has rendered. If he refuses, ask why. This may help you bolster weaknesses in your own expert's testimony.[73]

21.19 Worst Practices for Deposing the Opposing Expert
A. Not Arranging for the Court Reporter to Be at Deposition

It is not the job of the expert to arrange for a court reporter. Do not expect the out-of-state expert to contact local court reporters or arrange for a video deposition. If the expert is required to do this, be prepared to be billed at the expert's hourly rate to make the arrangements. When the court reporter does not show up, the expert will need to be paid by opposing counsel for the waiting time. An alternative to canceling the deposition is the use of a tape recorder in lieu of a court reporter.

B. Asking the Expert to Review or Comment on a Document the Expert Has Not Seen

The expert should be given the opportunity to fully review any document about which she is going to be asked questions. The expert should not assume that she is already sufficiently familiar with the document without having to look at the paper.[74]

C. Not Acting Like a Guest in the Office of the Expert

Always remember you are a guest on the expert's premises. Guests do not steal books from the expert's library. Guests do not pop into other worker's offices without permission or rifle through the expert's desk. Guests ask to use the phone. Guests do not park illegally. A defense attorney from another state thought she could pull up and park in front of the court reporter's office in midtown Manhattan in a no parking zone. Her rental car with all of her luggage was towed within ten minutes.[75] If the deposition extends beyond the allotted time, do not go overtime and assume the expert is able to stay.

D. Being a Bull Dog

Aggressive cross-examination at deposition may be designed to eliminate surprises at trial, to look for openings, and to test the reactions of the expert. Aggressive behavior may work to the disadvantage of the attorney. This approach gives the expert more preparation and makes him less vulnerable at trial.[76] The retaining counsel should prepare the expert to deal with this behavior. The expert should not lose his temper no matter how hard pressed. Losing the temper can mean losing credibility and the case. A break should be requested at any point the expert feels an explosion is imminent. An emotional response to a question can come back to haunt the expert.

The expert may be exposed to an interrupter—the opposing counsel. In this situation, the expert should let the attorney finish speaking, and then politely say, "I'm sorry, but you interrupted my last answer before I was finished. I would like to complete that answer before I move on to your next question. As I was saying...."[77] The expert, not the attorney, should control the pace of the deposition. If opposing counsel asks questions in a rapid fire manner, the expert should not feel rushed.[78] Giving the expert negative feedback or being harsh, angry, or aggressive will encourage the expert to say less and to become guarded. Giving no feedback to the expert (flipping through notes, avoiding eye contact, and treating the expert like an inanimate object) discourages open, candid responses.[79]

E. Making Erroneous Assumptions in a Hypothetical or Mischaracterizing Testimony

Retaining counsel should prepare the expert for hypothetical questions. Unfairly worded questions may contain untrue facts. The attorney may be trying to confuse the expert or make the expert doubt the findings. The expert should be careful about accepting the opponent's facts. Before the deposition, the retaining counsel and expert should discuss the key facts, and understand which facts are in dispute. This prevents the expert from accidentally conceding a point that is in dispute.[80] The expert should keep a sharp lookout for questions that have a double meaning and questions that assume the expert has testified to a fact when she has not done so.[81]

F. Trying to Win At All Costs

Although the following quote is written by a physician, it applies equally to nursing expert witnesses:

> I note that some attorneys openly detest experts, surprisingly especially their own. Amazingly, I see little insight into the dual truths that doctors in no way created the process by which experts are used. And more importantly, doctors do not want it to be that way. Somehow, an expert is expected to both

perform in the narrow constraints of a system made, and entirely controlled by others, yet hated for doing so. Doctors far prefer to be seen as champions of truth, honor, and humanitarianism, especially in the legal arena. Physicians are typically dismayed to find that the majority of time spent in testimony revolved more around casting aspersions upon the honor of witnesses instead of on issues of medical substance. Doctors by their very natures and training are nurturers, not adversaries.[82]

G. Not Bringing a Check to the Deposition or Quibbling About Fees

Most experienced experts recommend that experts be paid prior to giving a deposition. The expert who does not require payment in advance runs the risk of late payment, no payment, and collection problems with counsel. The attorney should not quibble about fees. For example, the attorney should not use the time displayed in Internet map programs to calculate how long it should have taken the expert to get to the deposition site, and then shortchange the expert accordingly.

H. Asking Obvious Questions About Expert's Résumé

Why ask the expert where he went to nursing school when it is on the curriculum vitae? Use the time to ask about experience or details not listed on the résumé.

I. Avoid Using Deposition to Settle a Score with Retaining Counsel

Regardless of how adversaries feel about each other, the expert should not be caught in the middle. Professionalism mandates setting aside personal animosities and gracefully getting through the procedure.

21.20 Preparing the Expert for Trial

If the case is settled or dropped before trial, be sure to tell the expert witness. It is gratifying to get the feedback, particularly if the expert was on the winning side, as well as to know that it is finally all right to shred the case materials.

If the case goes to trial, the expert will need some very specific preparation. Clearly, if the expert has never testified before, the type of preparation required is going to be very different from the information the experienced expert will want to know. A careful, thorough preparation for the neophyte can yield rich rewards in terms of increasing the expert's confidence, and can result in a smooth performance.

Although it seems basic, do not forget to explain the probabilities of the trial actually taking place on the scheduled day. Inexperienced experts may take the first day of the trial off from work and sit by the phone waiting to be called to testify, having spent preparation time for which the attorney will be billed. If the courts are backed up, and it is the norm for a trial to be rescheduled several times before it begins, explain this to the experts. Have the law firm staff keep them informed of postponements. Many experts prefer a phone call rather than waiting for a letter to appear in the mail several days after the date the trial was supposed to have begun. Lack of communication with the expert at this stage contributes to the expert's frustration. Expect cancellation fees to be required. Nurses employed by a healthcare agency may have difficulty scheduling a day off without adequate notice.

It is becoming increasingly common for experts to ask to be paid in advance of testifying in the trial. Payment of the fee before the witness gets on the stand is a safeguard for the attorney. If the opposing attorney elicits testimony that the expert has not been paid for coming to court, the jury is able to infer that the payment is contingent upon the expert's performance in court. Receiving a check before getting on the stand promotes peace of mind for the expert.

Keeping in touch with the expert before the court date is an essential practice to avoid the surprise of finding that the expert is unavailable for trial. Ask the expert for a home, work and cellular phone number and e-mail address. A discussion the night before the expert will appear in court is useful for covering any last-minute changes in the shape of the case. This is also a good opportunity to thoroughly review the expert's curriculum vitae. The attorney should ask the expert to go over any experience particularly related to the nursing issues in the case so that it may be brought out in voir dire.

When the trial actually begins the expert's anxiety level may also increase. Although the expert's period of stress is shorter than the attorney's, it can be just as intense in the time interval before and during the day in court. Note one attorney's description of how the nursing expert witness may feel:

> If you are like most everyone else, you lose your comfortable coolness when you take your seat on the witness stand, with the eyes and ears of one judge, two lawyers, 12 jurors, and a room full of spectators trained on YOU. Because, suddenly, you are not in control. You are not directing the scene. You are on somebody else's turf. This is the realm of lawyers, and now they are going to put YOU through some kind of interrogation like you are used to seeing on TV. Sure, somebody else is

on trial, the one whose guilt or innocence, whose money or career or property or liberty or conceivably whose life is in the balance. But you are on trial too—your credibility, your professionalism, your knowledge, your competence, your judgment, your adherence to policies and procedures, your respect for the rights of others—they are all on trial. Suddenly, you would like to trade the safe, calm, clean courtroom for the most chaotic nursing situation.[83]

Ideally, the expert will have reviewed several cases and testified at many depositions before the first day in court. However, that does not always happen. It is also helpful to experts to provide them with at least a verbal outline of how their direct examination will proceed. There is nothing worse during a trial than to ask experts a question on direct examination and have them give you a blank stare. You should remind them that it is necessary to review their background and to qualify them as an expert in front of the jury. At that point, they should be reminded that the other lawyer will be able to ask them questions on their qualifications before the direct examination proceeds to the merits of the case. At that point, they will be asked if they are familiar with the standard of care and what it is and whether or not the nurse in question met the standard of care. Then the nurse will be asked on direct examination to explain the basis for her opinion. This is the most important question in the case. This is where the nurse's opinion can be ruled a net opinion and stricken from the case unless the nurse can tie her opinion to the facts of the case. Let the nurse know that her explanation of the basis of her opinions is her opportunity to expound on the facts of the case and how they support her opinion and how they prove that the nurse was or was not negligent.

The attorney should also go over any demonstrative evidence with the nurse and make her comfortable with the portions of the chart that might be enlarged for presentation to the jury and ask her in advance if she is comfortable standing up in the courtroom and going to the easel to testify about the document in question. Likewise, the nurse should be prepared for cross-examination. It is the lawyer's job to point out the weaknesses in the case and anticipated questions on cross-examination so that the nurse expert is not startled or surprised by anything that happens in the courtroom. The nurse wants to maintain a calm objective demeanor so that the jury has confidence in her opinions and accepts her explanations of proper nursing care.

In preparing one's own nurse expert for trial, there has to be a careful balance between proper preparation and "coaching the witness." In preparing for trial, it is acceptable for a lawyer to indicate what answers he expects to certain questions based on the nurse's report, her deposition testimony and their conversations throughout the pendency of the case. It is wholly improper to insist that a nurse expert, or any expert, give a particular answer. In preparing a witness, the lawyer must re-educate the witness on the importance of certain concepts such as deviations, standards of care and reasonable probability. There have been cases where experts have been asked to define these concepts; and if the definition is not in accord with the law of the state, the expert's testimony has been stricken.

The attorney preparing the expert for testifying at trial should cover these points:

- What to wear to court
- To avoid any insignias or jewelry that identifies the expert as a member of a group to avoid antagonizing anyone who dislikes that group[84]
- The need to thoroughly review the file before testifying and to know the report inside and out
- The security at the entrance to the courthouse may include searching belongings
- What to bring to court, including a résumé, medical records, and the report
- The exhibits that will be used
- The qualifications the expert should stress during voir dire
- The importance of emphasizing the expert's experience and credentials related to the issue at hand
- The questions planned for direct examination, and whether the attorney prefers brief answers or wishes the expert to give narrative answers
- The need to refer to the medical records, exhibits, and other documents to strengthen the expert's position
- The importance of looking at the jury while answering questions posed by the attorney
- Not to memorize any testimony
- To never lie in court
- To focus on explaining the standard of care to the jury rather than being an advocate
- The need to avoid sounding hesitant by using words such as "I think" or "I believe"
- The importance of avoiding medical jargon
- The need to be an effective teacher
- The importance of not answering a question that has raised an objection until the judge has made a ruling
- The importance of using good analogies and demonstrative evidence to make points

- To treat everyone as if they could be jurors on the case, and to stay away from people if possible
- How to bring out all of the points favorable to the theory or theme
- The importance of not trying to read the mind of a defendant or another person involved in the care of the patient
- The need to avoid referring to the fact that the defendant nurse is likely covered by an insurance policy
- To avoid testimony on any areas that the judge has ruled as off limits

21.21 Cross-Examination

As attorneys and experts approach trial, we carefully study the discovery deposition. The nurse expert knows that he will be questioned about statements made in depositions, and the slightest inconsistency will likely be pointed out. Sometimes both sides forget to go back and look at the nurse's original report which may have been written one to three years earlier. It is usually easy to find an issue in the case that has developed that is not mentioned at all in the nurse's expert report. A nurse expert should be prepared for cross-examination on whether or not he carefully reviewed the record in the first instance and why the report does not include reference to that particular issue. Did he take his job seriously, did he read the record carefully to be as accurate as possible; would he come to court and criticize a nurse without being certain of all of the facts, etc. A nurse who did not address a particular issue in the report, and who wrote no supplemented report, must be prepared for questions along these lines. The nurse will be asked if an opinion which was important enough to mention at deposition or trial, and is not in the report, reflects a certain amount of inattention or sloppiness. This is very effective cross-examination in a case where the nurse is criticizing the defendant nurse's record-keeping or lack of documentation.

Some nurse experts are critical of a defendant nurse for failing to "go up the chain of command" or call a supervisor about a particular problem. It is important to explore that issue with the expert at depositions to find out how often that nurse has gone up the chain of command in his own practice. In our experience, this is a relatively uncommon situation, and, if the nurse acknowledges that at deposition, this can be brought out during cross-examination at trial.

The attorney should prepare the expert for the realities of cross-examination, including:

- How to reiterate points that undermine the opponent's position

- Avoidance of sarcasm, defensiveness, displays of flippancy or anger, or being a crusader
- The importance of being uniformly polite, calm, and respectful to the cross-examining attorney
- The importance of avoiding being cocky, overly helpful, fawning, overly emotional, or biased
- How to emphasize that the expert is being paid for time, not for testimony
- The importance of being truthful and admitting it if the expert does not know an answer
- How to respond to the directive to "Just answer yes or no" (If unable to answer yes or no, the expert should say so or qualify the response.)
- How to handle indirect questions
- The need to remember that the expert is there to advise the jury, not to win a case, beat a cross-examining lawyer, or play strategic games[85]
- To be brief in answering questions, to know when to stop
- The importance of remembering that the difficult questions in cross-examination are not personal attacks on the expert, just the attorney being an advocate for the client
- That the retaining attorney has the opportunity to use redirect to cover points that need to be clarified

TIP: Zafren notes, "Everyone has their own style, but I find that addressing attorneys as Sir and Ma'am works for me and sounds respectful. If someone is badgering you and you keep answering their questions and calling them Sir or Ma'am, they will look like a bully. Most attorneys realize this, so it tends to keep the questions on a professional level."[86]

Fruehan[87] comments, "One technique I learned (from opposing counsel) is the art of indirection such as to ask a leading question of a witness that supposes the opposite of the answer that is expected. This has the effect of disarming most people, and in their attempt to 'help' they answer too much....I wondered why this attorney, who seemed to understand the issues, was 'so stupid.' Of course that is a clue to 'watch out' and I did. I figured out his game and started using it myself."

Perhaps the most stressful aspect of the trial from the expert's perspective is the cross-examination. If possible, the attorney should have another member of the firm act as the opponent to put the witness through a cross-examination before the day of the trial. The experience, especially for the novice expert, should take some of the sting out of the actual cross-examination.

TIP: It is essential to know what to expect and how to respond to the tactics used during this portion of the trial.

Review these common mistakes made by expert witnesses and suggest ways to avoid them:

- Failing to read and consider all information
- Failing to listen to the question; failing to stay focused
- Failing to be responsive, especially giving more explanation or more information than is asked for
- Failing to speak to all of the issues or cover all the points
- Failing to stand behind the expert report
- Going too far out on a limb—not being flexible and sticking to their guns too much
- Testifying to issues outside their expertise
- Failing to know the topic
- Using terms such as "always" and "never"
- Trying to be a lawyer
- Being an advocate
- Being argumentative, aggressive, or too clever
- Being arrogant
- Appearing to be biased
- Underestimating the opposing attorney
- Letting their guard down on cross-examination
- Being too wrapped up in themselves and losing track of why they are in the courtroom
- Charging fees that are difficult to justify to the jury
- Failing to think like a juror
- Talking over the heads of the jury or talking down to them
- Failing to use demonstrative evidence properly, for example blocking an exhibit from the jury's view while making a point about it[88]
- Making statements that defy the common sense of jurors
- Speaking too softly
- Nodding the head instead of answering orally

TIP: Contact the expert after the trial is over to discuss the verdict. This is an opportunity to further strengthen the relationship with the expert by expressing gratitude.

21.22 Cross-Examination of the Opposing Expert

Kiesel[89] recommends questioning the opposing expert about these issues:

- The number of forensic cases the witness is involved in each year
- The number of times the expert has testified as an expert in the prior year
- The percentage of work for plaintiffs and defendants
- The charges on the particular matter at issue and the breakdown of those charges
- The average charge in a litigation case (using broad estimates, if necessary)
- The total number of litigation cases worked on per year
- The number of cases reviewed for this particular firm

Investigation of the expert's prior testimony can be accomplished using depositions available from colleagues or the banks of depositions accessible to attorneys (Idex/Defense Research Institute for defense attorneys or Trialsmith for plaintiff's attorneys). Additional information about expert witness testimony can be found in Chapter 25, *Trial Techniques*.

The chapter already discusses some of the background questioning that an attorney cross-examining an expert may want to do. In one of the author's (RF) experience, it can sometimes backfire to try to show that the expert has testified on numerous occasions, especially if the expert continues to maintain an active clinical practice. Some jurors believe that the more an expert has been qualified as such and has testified in court, the more important she is. Good lawyers try to focus their cross-examination more on the individual facts of the case and not those general issues that jurors may not find very convincing. A lawyer always wants the jury to trust his credibility and does not want the jury to think he is "nitpicking." It does not seem significant to show that the plaintiff's nurse expert charges $350 per hour and the defense nurse expert charges $250 per hour. Will the jury be convinced that the nurse expert who charges less money is more credible; or possibly just the opposite?

Points made on cross-examination are the most important points made during a trial. Points that fail on cross-examination make the loudest thud. The lawyer must be very thoroughly prepared before cross-examining any expert and must make certain to know the facts and documents of the case even better than the expert, if at all possible. Sometimes even the best experts who do not "live and breathe the case" like the lawyer does will overlook something in the chart or record.

In cross-examining a nurse expert, the lawyer wants to get that nurse to agree with as many propositions as possible. It is usually not very difficult to get the nurse expert to agree that the defendant nurse was an experienced nurse; that the defendant nurse had an adequate and appropriate education and training for the job undertaken; that the nurse's motives were pure and she was trying to do her best to care for the patient in question. One can then move to the record and get the expert to agree that—even though there are certain criticisms of the defendant—it must be recognized that the defendant did properly record, for example, the patient's input and output; did accurately record the patient's respirations at the appropriate intervals, etc. It is usually helpful on behalf of a nurse to get a plaintiff's nurse expert to agree that there is an element of judgment involved in nursing. If the issue is what time a doctor should have been called, most nurses will agree that it is a matter of judgment even if the plaintiff's expert asserts that the doctor should have been called "sooner." The nurse expert will usually acknowledge that some nurses might have called a few minutes earlier or a few minutes later and still been within the standards of care depending upon the clinical situation at the time.

The more important background questions are the questions regarding the expert's experience. If he is being critical of the manner in which the defendant nurse performed a certain procedure, when is the last time the expert performed that procedure? The attorney better be certain that the nurse will not answer "last night" which the authors have seen in one case. But usually, based upon the information gleaned from the nurse's curriculum vitae and deposition, it can be established that the expert had not performed the procedure in question or attended to precisely the same type of patient for many years. This is important to bring out since the expert has not had to exercise the judgment that has been admitted as relevant in caring for a patient like the defendant nurse had to do in this case.

21.23 Summary

The nurse expert witness plays an important role in reviewing the liability of the potential or actual nursing defendants, and in testifying to the standards of care. Careful preparation and establishment of good communication with the expert will substantially improve the outcome of the case. The attorney should consider asking the expert witnesses to provide feedback about the attorney's performance. Some helpful information may be learned to assist with the attorney's continuing development, and to gain a new perspective.

Endnotes

1. The authors appreciate the contributions of Michael Zerres, Esq. and Cindy Banes, RN to earlier versions of this chapter.

2. Tomaras, P. and Smith, A. "Closing the attorney-expert gap," *Trial*, October 2008, 22-27.

3. "How attorneys use experts," 1998 www.expertpages.com.

4. Scholin, M., "The use of nurses as expert witnesses," *Houston Law Review* 19 (1982): 555.

5. The American Association of Nurse Attorneys, "TAANA Position Paper on Expert Testimony in Nursing Malpractice Actions," *Journal of Nursing Law* 9, no. 4 (Winter 2004): 18-25.

6. *Id.*

7. *Id.*

8. *Sullivan v. Edward Hospital* (No. 95409, 2004 WL 228956 (Ill. Feb 5, 2004).

9. Butler, K., "Experts on Nursing: TAANA Takes a Stand," *Journal of Nursing Law* 9, no. 4 (Winter 2004): 15-17.

10. Rose, J., "How jurors perceive expert witnesses," *Trial* (June 2000): 51.

11. A New Jersey case, Hutchinson, allows an attorney to ask a defendant nurse (or other defendant) what the standard of care was under the circumstances. *Hutchinson v. Atlantic City Medical Center*, 314 N.J. super. 468 (App. Div. 1998). *Carey v. Lovett*, 132 N.J. 44 (1993) states that a defendant may testify regarding the applicable standard of care pertaining to his or her specialty. Similar cases may exist in other states.

12. Cady, R., "Focus on the law: so you want to be an expert witness? Things you need to know," *Maternal Child Nursing* 25, no. 1 (2000): 49.

13. Babitsky, S. and J. Mangraviti, *How to Become a Dangerous Expert Witness*, Falmouth, Massachusetts: SEAK, 2005.

14. Babitsky, S. and J. Mangraviti, *How to Excel during Depositions*, Falmouth, Massachusetts: SEAK, 1999.

15. Babitsky, S. and J. Mangaviti, *Cross-examination: The Comprehensive Guide for Experts*, Falmouth, Massachusetts: SEAK, 2003.

16. Babitsky, S. and J. Mangraviti, *Writing and Defending Your Expert Report: The Step by Step Guide with Models,* Falmouth, Massachusetts: SEAK, 2004.

17. *Guidelines for Practice as a Nurse Expert Witness,* Chicago: AALNC, 2003.

18. Matson, J., *Effective Expert Witnessing,* Boca Raton, Florida: CRC Press, 2004.

19. Lubet, S., *Expert Testimony,* Notre Dame, Indiana: NITA, 1998.

20. Brent, R., "The irresponsible expert witness: a failure of biomedical graduate education and professional accountability," *Pediatrics* 70, no. 5 (November 1982): 754.

21. See note 10.

22. Bonne, G., "Working with expert witnesses. The seven deadline sins," www.law.com, accessed 4/12/06.

23. Suplee, D. and M. Woodruff, "Talking with experts," *Litigation* 19, no. 1 (Fall 1992): 8.

24. See note 22.

25. *Id.*

26. *Id.*

27. Ambrogi, R. Rule 26: "Major changes for attorneys and experts," *Bullseye* February 2010.

28. Palmer, R., "Opening the gates," *Trial* (June 2000): 86.

29. *Id.*

30. www.daubertexpert.com/basics_daubert-v-merrell-dow.html, accessed 02/25/11.

31. See note 28 at 90.

32. Miles, R., "Communicating successfully with attorneys," *National Medical-Legal Journal* 1, Fourth Quarter (1991).

33. "Success as a consulting or testifying expert involves principles of TQM," *The Testifying Expert* 2, no. 10 (October 1994): 7.

34. Moscato, F., "Malpractice: How to prepare for deposition," www.dynamicchiropractic.com/mpacms/dc/article.php?id=41423, accessed 02/25/11.

35. Personal communication, Howard Weiss, October 2004.

36. Personal communication, Howard Richman Esq., October 2004.

37. Spohrer, R. and D. Maciejewski, "Modus operandi for the expert witness," *Chemical Health and Safety*, 3(1):8–12, (January-February) 1996.

38. "How to attack and defend expert witnesses," www.dicarlolaw.com/ExpertWitnesses.htm, accessed 02/25/11.

39. Godec and Middletown, "Wolves at the Door," www.sccs-law.com.

40. Larson, A., "Expert Witnesses," www.expertlaw.com/library/expert_witness, accessed 02/25/11.

41. "Preparing the Plaintiff's Medical Expert," www.lectlaw.com.

42. *Id.*

43. Personal communication, M. Leshner, March 2000.

44. Personal communication, G. Fruehan, March 2000.

45. Meister, C. Expert preparation, *Trial*, May 2010, 16-20.

46. Personal communication, Barbara Levin RN, October 2004.

47. See note 40.

48. Herschberg, S. and J. Gentile, "What attorneys should avoid when handling medical malpractice cases," www.lectlaw.com/filesh/tabartmm.htm.

49. Personal communication, Barbara Boschert RN, October 2004.

50. Personal communication, Steve Appelbaum, October 2004.

51. See note 15.

52. Personal communication, Martie Hawkins RN, October 2004.

53. See note 50.

54. *Id.*

55. *Id.*

56. See note 49.

57. *Id.*

58. Personal communication, Karon Goldsmith RN, October 2004.

59. Feldman, M., "Winning strategies for deposing the adverse expert," *Trial* (January 2000): 83.

60. Horowitz, D., "Deposition tips your parents taught you," *Trial* (July 2005): 40.

61. *Id.*

62. *Id.*

63. Personal communication, Sherri Hill RN, October 2004.

64. Personal communication, Arlene Klepatsky Esq. RN, October 2004.

65. See note 60.

66. Personal communication Vicki Turner, October 2004.

67. See note 60.

68. See note 34.

69. See note 40.

70. Personal communication, Wendy Jones RN, October 2004.

71. See note 60.

72. Lazarus, S. "Wielding a double-edged sword: overcoming risk in engaging experts in litigation," Annual Law Practice Management Review, 2008, 36-43.

73. Gander, D., "Prescription for powerful expert testimony," *Trial,* May 2007, 40-44.

74. See note 38.

75. Personal communication, Jeffrey Levine MD, October 2004.

76. "Making the best use of expert witnesses," www.expert4law.org/ewc/bestuse.html.

77. See note 37.

78. See note 38.

79. Morris, C., "Effective communication with deposition witnesses," *Trial* (July 2000): 75.

80. See note 40.

81. Harney, D., "Preparing the plaintiff's medical expert witness for trial," www.lectlaw.com/files/med35.htm, accessed 02/25/11.

82. Davies, A., "First, kill all the experts," www.lectlaw.com/filesh/medscn1.htm, accessed 02/25/11.

83. Salovesh, C., *Presentation of Evidence,* Cypress, California: Professional Development Systems, 2001.

84. *Id.* at 15.

85. Personal communication, H. Kilpatrick, March 2000.

86. Personal communication, K. Zafren, March 2000.

87. See note 44.

88. "Mistakes consultants and experts make," National Medical-Legal Journal 3, no. 1 (First Quarter, 1992): 3.

89. Kiesel, P., Kiesel, and Larson, "For lawyers only: cross examining the defense expert," www.kiesellaw.com.

Additional Reading

Clifford, R., Wagner, K, and Hunter-Adkins, D, "Effective preparation of the expert witness for deposition," *Journal of Legal Nurse Consulting,* Fall 2008, vol. 19, No. 4, 26-29.

DiCecco, K., "The battle of the experts: The aftermath and peer review of expert testimony," *Journal of Legal Nurse Consulting*, Winter 2008, Vol. 19, No. 1, 7-17.

"Expertly done," *Trial,* October 2008, 28-37.

Henry, B, and Keplinger, B. "Defining the standard of care," *For the Defense*, November 2006, 34-66.

Miller, P., "Taking exceptional depositions," *Trial,* June 2008, 40-45.

Morkan, L. "No room for elephants," *For the Defense*, 64-68.

Olson, L. "Ten things I wish I'd known before my first deposition," *For the Defense*, April 2008, 6-8.

Pillersdorf, G. "Put the medical experts in the best light," *Trial,* October 2008, 38-41.

Sullivan, R. and Langdon, B., "Developing memorable expert testimony," *Trial,* October 2008, 44-46.

Zimmerman, P. "Providing expert witness testimony: lessons learned," *Journal of Legal Nurse Consulting*, Spring 2008, vol. 19, No. 2, 15-17.

Chapter 22

Demonstrative Evidence

Stephen Appelbaum, CEP, EPIC, Patricia W. Iyer, MSN, RN, LNCC, and John M. Parisi, Esq.[1]

22.1 Introduction

Trial lawyers face the question of how to dramatize their cases and emphasize their positions in a manner that is both permissible under the rules of evidence and, at the same time, compelling. One of the best ways to accomplish this is through demonstrative evidence. Demonstrative evidence is not limited as much by the rules of evidence or procedure as by the imagination and creativity of the lawyer handling the case. During long nursing malpractice cases, demonstrative evidence simplifies complex issues, removes boredom from the courtroom tedium, and educates the jurors on both the liability and damages aspects of the case.

Presenting the case with pictures, computer animations, illustrations, anatomical models, storyboards, timelines, graphics, and video will help tie together key pieces of evidence and facts. Using the power of television and computers in the courtroom reinforces the way most jurors receive information (through the screen), and is a persuasive way to make points at trial.[2]

Planning the use of demonstrative effort takes a team approach. A behind-the-scenes legal nurse consultant (LNC) should be brought into the case as early as possible. The LNC's role is to sort through the accumulating mass of hospital records and nursing notes, as well as to establish the basis for the presence or absence of negligence on the part of the potential defendants. The skills of the attorney and expert witness are needed to define the key issues to be illustrated. The LNC is a vital part of the team in helping to prepare witnesses and formulate the demonstrative evidence that will communicate the information as efficiently as possible. Nurses are trained to be effective patient educators. The LNC's ability to communicate the medical issues combined with the attorney's grasp of the liability themes and the perspective of the expert witness create a powerful team. Refer to Chapter 20, *Working with Legal Nurse Consultants*, for additional perspectives on this role.

Without first teaching the lay jurors the technical background in, for example, a failure to recognize fetal distress case, the jurors may never understand the opinions regarding the alleged errors in fetal monitoring and assessing cervical dilation. The force on a baby's shoulder during a stressful vaginal delivery performed by a nurse midwife may never be perceived as a mechanism of injury until the anatomy and physiology of the labor process is explained with the use of clearly marked models or an animation of the birth process. The safeguards built into an infant warming unit cannot be explained effectively without a photograph, the actual machine in the courtroom, or a clear graphic or video.

Demonstrative evidence is defined in *Black's Law Dictionary* as "that evidence addressed directly to the senses without intervention of testimony." It may consist of photographs, enlargements of hospital records, charts, anatomical models, diagrams, or computer animations. This form of evidence is clearly more powerful than oral testimony alone because it empowers jurors to recall details with greater accuracy and for a longer period of time.

TIP: Some attorneys might define demonstrative evidence as the "charts and photographs that get blown up for trial." Sometimes demonstrative evidence is seen as the "necessary evil expense one must incur on a Friday

when you have not settled your case and trial is the following Monday." It is this narrow thinking that is the stimulus for this chapter.

Picture memory is stronger than word memory in all age groups. When pictures are used in combination with spoken words to tell a story, people remember 65 percent of the information after 72 hours. With just pictures alone, they remember 20 percent. With words alone, they remember 10 percent. Recall is even greater if the pictures are presented before the words.[3]

In trial, "show and tell" is vital to successful communication. Think back to when you came into class to discover that the teacher was showing a film that day. Jurors have the same reaction. Because they must retain testimony for a week or more before using it in deliberations, retention time is a critical consideration. Some jurisdictions now permit jurors to take notes and ask questions; consequently, demonstrative evidence takes on a more important role in helping jurors formulate their ideas in a more organized manner.

Demonstrative evidence actually goes back to biblical times. Remember that Moses did not come off the mountain and tell the children of Israel the words spoken to him by God…he brought charts. Six-hundred and thirteen commandments in the Bible, digested down to two boards, with five key items on each chart, numerically indexed. This may have been the first use of Federal Rule 1006, which allows for the use of summary charts of otherwise voluminous material.

As the courts are becoming more liberal with the use of visuals during opening statements, the trial attorney has an increasing obligation to use that portion of the trial to organize the case for the jury. The process of jurors' hearing testimony is similar to that of being given pieces of a jigsaw puzzle, one at a time, with the objective to assemble the final picture. Imagine how difficult this could be if one is not first shown the picture on the cover of the box. Using visuals during the opening statement is like showing the jury the cover of the box. Now they know what they are supposed to do with the pieces (testimony), and like the pieces of a puzzle, there is only one way they will fit together to make the picture that the attorney has proposed. During the opening statement each attorney has a chance to show the picture on the cover of the box as it illustrates the theme and focus of the case. This technique is not always effectively used. Ralph Waldo Emerson once said, "Thunder is good, thunder is impressive, but it's lightning that does the work." Demonstrative aids should be like lightning: sporadic and intense, powerful and simple.

TIP: A structured image of the facts and theories that parallel the theme and strategy can be burned into the jurors' minds by using effective visuals during opening statements. This can be done with pre-made charts, magnetic charts that can build the theme while being presented, or with more formal presentations using software programs such as PowerPoint.

The laws of recency and primacy dictate the innovative use of visuals during opening statements and closing arguments and should be considered when planning for these points in the trial presentation. Visual evidence should be incorporated into the presentation of every key point in both the plaintiff's and the defendant's case. It helps to focus potentially cynical jurors on the strength and logic of the attorney's case and the weaknesses of the adversary's.

Jurors now expect to have engaging presentations of the facts. They have come to believe that big cases, both civil and criminal, will have substantial visual components incorporated into them. Demonstrative evidence has come to play an increasingly larger role in trials for several reasons. The pioneering efforts of Melvin Belli in the last half of the twentieth century toward the effective use of visual aids set the stage for the attorney to "think outside of the box" in terms of courtroom persuasion. Law, by tradition, has been a profession of words and oratory in the courtroom, but we are living in a visual society. The baby boomers and Generation X'ers have been brought up in front of television sets. They are more accustomed to seeing and hearing news than reading it from a printed page. The success of the newspaper *USA Today* is an example of color visual support (in the form of maps, charts, and graphics) to supplement the printed story. Even the television medium has maximized the use of visual support for the spoken word, by going to the video of the actual event as opposed to the reporter's summary and retelling of the events. When introducing a story for a news segment, there will usually be a graphic icon or symbol of some kind on the screen next to the reporter to visually anchor the general theme of the story. Anchoring is an important technique to be considered throughout the trial and should be considered for each key witness or expert. Visual anchors are set up in a nursing malpractice trial when a blowup is positioned in a certain place while a witness testifies. It would be set in the same place during summation.[4]

As little as ten years ago, demonstrative evidence in a typical malpractice case would consist of enlarged photographs of the plaintiff, the site of the incident, radiographic studies, portions of the medical chart, and bar graphs used by the economist. The defense bar frequently abstained from the presentation of any visual support except for chart en-largements. Over the last decade, however, there has been an explosion in the frequency, quality, and array of demonstrative evidence techniques being used by both sides. Insurance companies are seeing the value in paying for visual support for their trial attorneys because the techniques work. Newer tools such as computer animations and videos intended for medical teaching purposes allow jurors to fully understand the complex issues they need to evaluate. When used properly, the more sophisticated trial presentation software programs can add new levels of flexibility to trial presentations. Care should be taken, however, to assure that the operator in court is familiar with both the program and computers in general to assure a smooth and error-free presentation. Figure 22.1 summarizes key reasons when demonstrative evidence should be used.

1. Demonstrative evidence should be used when jurors are unfamiliar with anatomy, procedures, or techniques the expert witness will explain.
2. Concepts are difficult to visualize when described verbally.
3. Jurors must choose between divergent opinions or theories on an issue.
4. Relationship of details to the whole must be shown.
5. Statistical or numerical data show trends.
6. The effects of the injury cannot be appreciated through testimony alone.
7. Images or photographs are needed to acquaint jurors with a scene they cannot visit.
8. In a long trial, jurors must be stimulated to maintain their interest.

Figure 22.1 *When to Use Demonstrative Evidence*

22.2 The Courtroom as a Classroom

The courtroom can be compared to a classroom. The presentation of the facts of a case becomes an exercise in teaching and learning for the participants. In litigation today, it is usually necessary to teach the jurors the science and mechanics of a particular subject before they can judge the conduct of the defendant accused of violating a nursing standard of care. Whether it is a piece of medical equipment or a professional responsibility, the jury has to first learn enough information to be able to judge the merits of the case.

The attorney (through the testifying expert) becomes the teacher and the jurors become the students. Who does not remember the excitement felt in the room when, as students in a particularly boring class, we learned that we were going on a field trip, or going to the auditorium for the period instead of sitting there for another day listening to the teacher's lecture? The same thing happens in the courtroom.

TIP: Demonstrative evidence breaks up the otherwise monotonous stream of questions and answers, many of which are only intended to lay foundations for the important trial issues. By the time the case gets interesting, the jury has tuned out.

Teachers consider the learning styles of their students. So should attorneys consider the learning styles of mediators, arbitrators, judges and jurors. Learning styles are simply different approaches or ways of learning. There are three primary groups of learning style.

- **Watchers or visual learners** need to see something. They will learn from reading the exhibits. Some jurisdictions permit jurors to take notes, which helps the visual learners make sense of what they hear.
- **Listeners or auditory learners** need to hear. Some auditory learners can listen to lectures and almost memorize what has been said from just one time heard. There is a lot of listening that occurs during a trial, which is ideal for the auditory learner. Because auditory learners understand information when it has been spoken to them, often they will have a hard time staring another person in the eye when they are being spoken to. They do not need to see where the voice is coming from; they comprehend the information while staring at an object. It might seem that they are ignoring others by "staring into blank space" when actually their brain is carefully comprehending and storing the information given in a much more efficient manner than non-auditory learners. This "storing" of information challenges their brain, so the person often disregards the use of vision to help the brain work easier.
- **Doers or kinesthetic learners** learn by doing. They learn through moving, doing and touching, through a hands-on approach, actively exploring the physical world around them. They may find it hard to sit still for long periods, as occurs in a trial, and may become distracted by their need for activity and exploration. Tactile learners are hands-on learners. They will want to manipulate the equipment being shown to the jury during a trial.

Address all three types of learners as you prepare your report. Paint word pictures, use bullet points, and hand out demonstrative evidence to the jury.[5]

22.3 Right-Brain/Left-Brain Learning

People can be considered either right-brain or left-brain dominant, which translates to many aspects of life including hand dominance as well as learning styles. When you ask for directions to a destination, do you prefer a diagram or turn-by-turn instructions? Right-brain learners tend to be artistic, intuitive, and creative people. Left-brain learners, on the other hand, are more symbolic in their thought processing and are rational thinkers. They will tend to process more easily what they hear while right-brain learners will more easily process what they see. Right-brain learners, therefore, need to see information in visual, spatial relationships, whereas left-brain learners can easily assimilate information that is heard.

TIP: Some persons claim to be able to tell if people are right- or left-brain learners by merely observing them (which wrist their watch is on, the way they cross their arms and legs, and so on). Trial attorneys need to prepare for both learning styles. The outcome of a case is too important to chance a missed opportunity to effectively convey all aspects of the presentation.

A nursing malpractice trial is an exercise in two complementary processes: education and persuasion. The jurors are presented with information that forms the basis for their verdict. Rarely is a doctor, a nurse, or another healthcare provider allowed to become part of a jury in a malpractice case. Therefore, as a rule jurors are laypeople who must be quickly familiarized with the general area of medicine. They must then be educated on the complexities of the case. Imagine taking a college course taught by ten or twenty different professors, in which one is not allowed to take notes, ask questions, or talk to fellow students about the subject matter, and no one knows what will be on the final so that studying for the exam is impossible. Yet, this is what we expect of jurors. Fortunately, organizations such as the National Jury Project are working diligently for change. It is starting to make some headway in several jurisdictions.[6]

22.4 Preservation of Evidence

Demonstrative evidence should be considered during the initial investigative phase of the case. This aspect is called the "preservation" phase, as opposed to the "presentation" phase, which is the use of the material in pre-trial presentations or trial. As in any type of case, much evidence can be considered transient. This evidence must be recorded and documented as soon as possible to prevent loss. In hospital or other care environments, furniture, fixtures, and equipment are easily moved or replaced. Lighting is changed, and partitions and walls are added and removed. Nursing stations are relocated, and windows are added or blocked. Doors are removed, and locks and security devices are added or moved. Storage cabinets and rooms for drugs and other supplies are often moved to different locations, or locks and signage are often added after an incident. These changes prevent reconstruction of the environment as it existed at the time of the incident. All these elements and more can be relevant to the case and should be documented through photographs, video, and diagrams as soon as possible.

Suppose a nursing home resident fell on a highly polished, freshly waxed floor. Plaintiff's attorneys should preserve the evidence as soon as possible after the fall. Use large, labeled zip-close bags for the shoes so that wax build-up or other injury-producing substances can be viewed and tested later.[7]

Some demonstrative evidence may be lost if prompt efforts to find and save it are not made. In an emergency, the recorded dispatches of radio transmission between a mobile ICU and the hospital emergency room may contain useful data not found in the hospital chart. If available, these recorded dispatches serve as a powerful tool to capture the urgency of the plaintiff's pre-hospital care. These recordings may be kept by a hospital rescue squad for only a very short period of time before they are reused or replaced, so requests for copies should be made as soon as possible. This advice also applies to x-ray films, MRI, CT, and other types of diagnostic studies. Hospitals will not keep this material on file forever. Transfer to microfilm makes retrieval difficult and impairs image quality, although today most facilities have gone to electronic recordkeeping including digital preservation of x-ray and other radiological studies. Medical equipment implicated in a medical error might be sent to the biomedical department for analysis rather than preserved.

Another important area of evidence that counsel should attempt to preserve early in the investigation of a case is any electronically stored information on diagnostic testing equipment and medical devices. Requests should be made for downloads of the electronic data contained in diagnostic equipment and medical devices. For example, Patient Controlled Analgesic (PCA) pumps are programmed to dispense medication. In the case of a suspected overdose of pain medication, the PCA pump should be secured immediately and the information downloaded before the pump is cleared by the healthcare facility for use by another patient, which would result in the data being lost. Requests should also be

made early in the case for the "raw data" for CT images. Once obtained in a digital format, the raw data of the CT image can be used to create 3D images that make very powerful demonstrative exhibits at trial.

Many facilities today use surveillance video recording equipment for both security and monitoring purposes in key areas. Every attempt should be made to review all video made at or near the time of the subject incident. Even if the camera does not record the actual event, a camera in another location within the facility might show an employee was in a certain location when she testified to the contrary. Cameras monitoring elevators, exits, and public areas can support or counter the statements of key parties to the case. Many of these systems record multiple areas onto one device. This is called multiplexing, and there is equipment available that can "de-multiplex" these videos as well as slow them down and enhance them (to certain limits) for study and analysis.

TIP: Do not be fooled by some of the advanced technology seen on television or in the movies. There are limits to what the best technician can do with video enhancement; but depending on the quality of the original, video images can be processed to assist in analyzing them for the particular needs of the case. Always try to get the original videotape. Digital images can be downloaded for further analysis and processing without any loss in quality.

22.5 Evidentiary Considerations

The attorney must understand how to use it in the courtroom before investing time and money into demonstrative evidence. This section addresses the legal considerations that should be examined when planning visual support for the trial.

A. Relevance

It is axiomatic that evidence must be relevant in order to be admissible. The Federal Rules of Evidence define "relevant evidence" as evidence that has "any tendency to make the existence of any fact that is of consequence to the determination of the action more probable or less probable than it would be without the evidence."[8] Relevant evidence can be excluded from a trial when the probative value of the proffered evidence is substantially outweighed by the danger of being unfairly prejudicial to the other parties, confusing the issues, or misleading the jury. It can also be excluded if admission would result in undue delay, a waste of the court's time, or needless presentation of cumulative evidence.[9] Relevant evidence may be either direct or circumstantial. Direct evidence is given by witnesses on the stand who testify based on their personal experience. Witnesses testify to what they saw or heard. Direct evidence can also consist of physical evidence relevant to the case. The actual sponge removed from a patient's body a year after the initial surgery, the IV pump involved in a medication error, or the patient's MRI showing a hemorrhage are examples of direct evidence.

In contrast to direct evidence, circumstantial evidence is derived from inferences reasonably made from other admissible facts. The classic examples of circumstantial evidence are footprints in the snow. Even without testimony of an eyewitness who saw someone walking, the prints themselves are circumstantial evidence of a person's presence at the scene. Photographs or time charts documenting a large number of unexplained bruises or falls suffered by a patient could be used as to infer that the patient was unsupervised, abused, or both.

TIP: Relevance depends in part on the particular type of evidence sought to be admitted and the issues of each case. When offering an exhibit into evidence, counsel must explain why the exhibit is relevant to an issue in the case. Counsel must also be ready to explain how the proffered exhibit will help the jury better understand that issue or assist the witness in providing testimony.

B. Materiality

Materiality was an important consideration for the admissibility of evidence under common law. Now the concept of materiality has been codified in Federal Rules of Evidence 401 and 402. Materiality is based on the concept that admissible evidence must be of "consequence" to the case. What is of consequence to the case depends upon the scope of the pleadings and the theories of the case, as well as the substantive law. In jurisdictions that use a pre-trial order to supersede the pleadings, care must be given to ensure that the evidence is material to a theory of liability contained in the pre-trial order. Thus, it is important to develop demonstrative evidence throughout the pendency of the case. Preparing exhibits to support legal theories or evidence that will not be part of the case at trial should be avoided.

C. Unfair Prejudice

Relevant evidence is not always admissible. Relevant evidence can be ruled inadmissible if it is unfairly prejudicial. Obviously, all evidence is prejudicial in the sense that it hurts one party and helps the other. Only when the probative value of the evidence is "substantially outweighed by the danger of unfair prejudice" can the evidence be excluded.[10] An objection that a particular exhibit is unfairly prejudicial

is usually directed to exhibits that display injuries or an accident scene in overly graphic or gruesome detail.

The trial judge determines whether the proposed evidence or exhibit is unfairly prejudicial. A judge's decision is discretionary and will be reviewed under a narrow abuse-of-discretion standard. The judge's decision will be given great deference on appeal. Thus, if counsel is concerned that an opponent will attempt to introduce a particularly graphic or unfairly prejudicial exhibit, a motion to bar or limit admissibility should be considered.

Pre-trial motions, or motions in limine, give the trial judge the opportunity to consider objections to an exhibit, outside of the pressures of an ongoing trial. It also provides for a ruling before the jury has already seen or heard the evidence sought to be excluded. On the other hand, the proponent of a gruesome exhibit, such as photographs of pressure

---

Opponents may object to the admission of otherwise relevant demonstrative evidence. The force and effectiveness of the objections to the introduction of demonstrative evidence will vary with the skill of the opposing attorney, the nature of the particular item being offered, and the purpose and value in the particular case. The trial judge has broad discretion to rule upon the admissibility of many types of demonstrative evidence. Common objections to the admission of evidence include:

1. Relevance
2. Improper authentication
3. The evidence is not as it was on the date of the incident.
4. Best evidence rule violations (Fed. R. Evid. 1002)
5. The probative value of the exhibit may be substantially outweighed by one or more of the following:
    a. Danger of unfair prejudice or of inflaming the jury
    b. Danger of misleading the jury
    c. Danger of confusing the jury
    d. Undue delay or waste of time
    e. Needless presentation of cumulative evidence

Figure 22.2 *Objections to the Admissibility of Demonstrative Evidence Pregeant v. Pan-American World Airways, 762 F.2d 1245 (5th Cir. 1985).*

ulcers, may seek an evidentiary hearing with the court before trial to get rulings on admissibility of the photographs. By getting the court's ruling in advance, counsel for the proponent of the evidence can prepare for trial knowing whether the photographs will be able to be introduced over objection. The court's ruling may also direct counsel to modify a proposed exhibit to make it admissible. Waiting until midtrial to get a ruling should be avoided if counsel has any concern about the admissibility of the exhibit. Figure 22.2 summarizes objections to the admissibility of evidence.

Opponents may object to the admission of otherwise relevant demonstrative evidence. The force and effectiveness of the objections to the introduction of demonstrative evidence will vary with the skill of the opposing attorney, the nature of the particular item being offered, and the purpose and value in the particular case. The trial judge has broad discretion to rule upon the admissibility of many types of demonstrative evidence.

D. Hearsay

Counsel must also consider whether the proposed exhibit contains inadmissible hearsay that will prevent its use at trial.[11] While an in-depth discussion of the hearsay rule is well beyond the scope of this chapter, be mindful of the potential that inadmissible hearsay evidence contained in an exhibit will prevent its admission into evidence if an opponent properly objects to the admission of the exhibit.

1. Definition

Oral testimony, written documents, and even photographs can constitute hearsay. If an exhibit contains a "statement" that is oral, written, or consists of nonverbal conduct offered as an assertion that occurred out of court and is offered to prove the truth of the fact asserted, it contains hearsay and will be excluded on proper objection unless it falls under one of the exceptions to the hearsay rule contained in Fed. R. Evid. 803.

Greatly oversimplified, there are three essential elements in a hearsay statement. If any one element is absent, that statement is not hearsay:

a. the statement must be an oral or written assertion (or nonverbal conduct intended to be an assertion);

b. the statement must be "out of court"; and

c. the "out of court statement" must be offered to "prove the truth" of what the statement says.[12]

Not all out-of-court statements are hearsay. Pursuant to Fed. R. Evid. 801(d)(1) and (2), prior statements by witnesses who testify at trial, party admissions (or any statement attributed to a party by another witness), and statements of prior identification are not hearsay if the person making the statement testifies at trial and is subject to cross-examination. Thus, blowups of admissions made by a party and depositions of parties and witnesses testifying at trial are not subject to the hearsay rule. If you can reasonably anticipate an objection to the use of the blowup of testimony or an exhibit at trial, as discussed in the previous section, getting an advance ruling from the court can alleviate this problem.

2. Exceptions to hearsay

Even if a statement is hearsay, it may nonetheless be admissible into evidence because of one of the exceptions to hearsay found in Fed. R. Evid. 803-804, 807. These federal rules have codified 29 separate exceptions, and state law may recognize even more. Several of these exceptions to the hearsay rule are often important in determining whether an exhibit is admissible at trial notwithstanding that it contains hearsay. For example, statements of existing mental, emotional, or physical condition are excluded from being hearsay.[13] Thus, statements describing a patient's medical history or condition, made to a medical professional for purposes of medical diagnosis, are not hearsay. The majority of entries in a medical record may fall under this exception to the hearsay rule.

Business records are another important exception to the hearsay rule.[14] Records kept in the ordinary, regular course of business or other organizations are admissible under this exception. In order to be admissible, counsel must show that:

1. The entries were made at or near the time of the event or act;

2. A person with knowledge recorded the information or transmitted the information to someone who recorded it;

3. The records were kept in the ordinary course of a business activity which is a regular practice of the business;

4. The custodian or other qualified witness testifies to the above facts; and

5. The records are otherwise reliable and trustworthy.

In a nursing malpractice case involving a for-profit nursing home chain, many of the financial and other internal records of the operation of the facility may be admissible under the business record exception. In most jurisdictions, the proper foundation for business records is laid by taking the deposition of the records custodian. However, Fed. R. Evid. 803(b) (6) provides that a proper foundation of a business record can also be laid by certification of a qualified witness in compliance with Fed. R. Evid. 902(11), 902(12), or a statute permitting certification. This provision makes it unnecessary to call the records custodian as a live witness to lay the foundation at trial.

Another important exception to the hearsay rule in a nursing malpractice case relates to public records. Pursuant to Fed. R. Evid. 803(8), public records are deemed a reliable hearsay exception because government officials record the information pursuant to a public duty or specific statute and not to benefit either party. Department of Health inspection reports may be very persuasive and admissible exhibits, depending on their content. However, only those parts of the investigation report that are factual findings, factual conclusions, and historical facts are admissible. Conclusions or opinions such as expert witness testimony are not admissible without establishing additional foundation for the basis of the testimony.

Other exceptions to the hearsay rule that may be important in a nursing malpractice case are market reports and commercial data that are admissible pursuant to Fed. R. Evid. 803(17). Thus, commercial or financial data showing the profitability of a particular for-profit hospital at the time the patient was neglected because of inadequate staff, may be admitted if relevant.

Excerpts from learned treatises are often important exhibits for expert testimony. Pursuant to Fed. R. Evid. 803(10), learned treatises are also admissible as direct evidence. To admit a learned treatise into evidence in most jurisdictions, an expert must testify that the book, periodical, article, pamphlet, or other writing is a reliable authority. In some cases, the expert for the opposing party will admit or establish that a particular text or book or periodical is a reliable authority on the subject matter. With this foundation, the learned treatise may be used to provide substantive testimony or to cross-examine an opposing expert. Even if the opposing expert does not concede that the text is reliable, if the first expert establishes the text is reliable, most judges will allow its use in cross-examination.

E. Blunting the Effect of Sustained Objections

When evidence is excluded, the trial court must advise counsel of the specific ground for exclusion so that counsel can, if possible, cure the problem. See *United States v. Dwyer,* 539 F.2d 924-928 (2d Cir. 1976). Some objections may be easily anticipated. For example, if counsel objects to a color photograph of the decedent's autopsy, a black-and-white photo should be prepared for use if the color enlargement is kept out.

TIP: Requesting a limiting instruction is effective for weakening objections to demonstrative evidence.

Given the court's broad discretion to admit evidence, suggesting an appropriate limiting instruction might encourage the court to admit a critical piece of demonstrative evidence. For example, in the case of a patient who became a quadriplegic when a cervical collar was removed from his fractured neck, an animation may be effective. It would depict the mechanism of injury to the cervical spine and subsequent cord damage and draw from the foundation laid by the treating neurosurgeon. Opposing counsel may object to the speculative nature of the animation because the exact biomechanics of the injury are unknown. With the appropriate limiting instruction, the court may be persuaded to admit the evidence. A conditioned instruction to the jury might be, "You are free to accept this animation, but only as to the general type of injury and not as to how this specific injury occurred."

22.6 Types of Trial Exhibits

There are three primary types of trial exhibits: real evidence, demonstrative evidence, and visual aids. Although different terminology is used to describe these various types of exhibits, all three are generally well recognized.

A. Real Evidence

Examples of real evidence in a case may include actual physical objects, such as a syringe used by a patient to inject herself with insulin in an overdose attempt, the original medical record, an incident report, or a prosthetic device. These tangible items of real evidence are probative in and of themselves and are admitted into evidence as part of the trial record. Once admitted, real evidence is generally made available for the jury to view and is usually taken to the jury room during deliberations.

TIP: Real evidence consists of exhibits—which are actual objects—or writings that constitute facts in the case.

B. Demonstrative Evidence

Demonstrative exhibits are not derived from the actual event that is the subject of the litigation. They are usually created after the fact by counsel for the purpose of illustrating, describing, or teaching the jury about the events or issues in the case. Demonstrative exhibits commonly include diagrams, charts, graphs, models, movable figures, computer graphics, video, and any other exhibit that makes oral testimony more easily understood by the jury.

TIP: Demonstrative evidence refers to exhibits that are created or obtained for the trial of the case.

To admit a demonstrative exhibit, its proponent must establish (1) that the exhibit will assist a witness in testifying or (2) that the demonstrative exhibit will help the judge or jury better understand the evidence. Before using demonstrative evidence, counsel should request the court's permission to do so, out of the jury's presence. Demonstrative exhibits are often admitted into evidence and become part of the permanent trial record. Some judges may not permit demonstrative exhibits to be used by the jury during deliberations because they are not part of the "real" evidence of the case.

Because demonstrative evidence can be a powerful influence in determining the outcome of a case, use of exhibits is vital to courtroom persuasion. Demonstrative exhibits need not be complicated or expensive to be effective. A simple line drawing of an accident scene can provide great assistance to a witness describing the event. A photograph of the scene, even if taken long after the event in question, can provide details of the scene that would otherwise be difficult to describe by oral testimony alone. In a case of a patient who committed suicide in a hospital psychiatric unit, a videotape of the unit can literally bring it into the courtroom. This will greatly enhance the jurors' understanding of the physical surroundings of the patient. By gaining an understanding of the surroundings, the jury is in a much better position to be able to see how the staff could not have observed the patient at the time of the incident.

TIP: Use of demonstrative evidence during examination of a witness will usually enhance the jury's attention to the testimony being provided, especially if the witness uses the exhibit to orient the jury to the scene.

C. Visual Aids

Visual aids are generally not considered to be real or demonstrative exhibits and are not considered or admitted into evidence. Visual aids may be used during final argument, opening statement, direct examinations, and cross-examinations. Visual aids include charts summarizing evidence, overhead transparencies summarizing expert testimony, part of an opening statement prepared for an overhead projector, or an enlargement of the verdict form to be used during final argument. Other examples are a white marker board, flip chart, easel, or other blank surface on which counsel lists terms, dates, names of witnesses, or other summaries of testimony of a witness during direct examination or cross-examination.

TIP: Visual aids are primarily created and used by attorneys to communicate information and ideas to the jury and to help the jury understand the client's case. In New Jersey, for instance, a 1960 case says that if it can be said in the courtroom, it can be put on a chart. This case ruling that originally dealt with an objection to an economist writing numbers on a blackboard cleared the way for the use of many types of visual support for both attorneys and witnesses. (See *Cross v. Lamb,* NJ Super, 1960.)

The line between a demonstrative exhibit and a visual aid is not very distinct, and some judges treat them in the same fashion. However, visual aids are not usually marked as exhibits and are not received into evidence as part of the court record. It is advisable to alert the court to the intended use of the visual aids before their use, especially during opening statement or the presentation of testimony. The judge has discretion to permit or deny the use of visual aids in the courtroom. Since they are not admitted into evidence, visual aids are generally not given to the jury during deliberation.

22.7 Basic Considerations for Use of Exhibits at Trial

As noted above, during discovery and trial preparation, counsel must select the exhibits to use as real and demonstrative evidence. In many jurisdictions, preliminary witness and exhibit lists are exchanged between the parties. Even if preliminary exhibit lists are not exchanged, final exhibit lists are often required as part of a pre-trial order. To comply with such a rule, attorneys must select the exhibits they intend to use, well in advance of trial.

Look at the trial as if it were a scripted stage play. Use the transcripts of pre-trial discovery as the script, then add the "set design." Many attorneys attempt to create exhibits without thinking about who will use them and how they will be used. The attorney should determine the identity of the witnesses and what the jury should understand from testimony, and then design a supporting visual or anchor exhibit that reinforces that information.

Before deciding to use an exhibit, counsel must decide if the exhibit will enhance the effectiveness of a witness's testimony. Unless an exhibit assists a witness in describing or explaining testimony, it should not be used. Obviously, if the exhibit detracts from the testimony or serves to confuse a juror, it should not be used. Perdue[15] cautions that demonstrative evidence can unintentionally distance the attorney, the plaintiff, and the plaintiff's story from jurors. When demonstrative evidence is presented before the testimony it illustrates, the jurors may focus on the visuals and tune out the words. Demonstrative evidence should be presented at the right time.

Any significant case (with a value of $400,000 and up), certainly warrants the use of some kind of research. Consider previewing exhibits using focus groups or mock trial sessions. This will require advance preparation and coordination, but can be time and money well spent. A "trial run" to determine how the exhibit "plays" before a live audience can pay big dividends at trial. The information provided by a focus group can be used to decide if an exhibit should be modified or used at all. It is also useful to determine how the exhibit may be perceived and understood by the "real" jury. Fox stresses that "We sometimes fall in love with our exhibits after spending substantial amounts of time and money on them. Test drive your evidence in front of focus groups or disinterested parties to ensure that it illustrates the point you are trying to make. If your exhibits do not help to prove or clarify a point, don't use them, no matter how much time and money you've spent on them."[16]

Ideally, exhibits have been well planned, designed and thought out. A focus group enables the attorney to find out what people from that particular venue by county feel about the issues in the case: what is important, what is not important, what are some of the speed bumps. This gives the attorney a tremendous opportunity to test out the exhibits. Appelbaum advises:

> Very often what we will do when an attorney comes to us if we have enough lead time and he wants exhibits we will recommend doing the focus group first. Let the jury tell us what's important, what's not important and what they would like to see. The way we do the focus groups and there is a very distinct difference between focus groups and mock trials, but we always say that focus groups are like taking the x-ray before you do the surgery. We ask the panelists, 'Would a timeline have helped you? Would an illustration of the anatomy have helped you?' Or if we started to prepare one we ask if the timeline was helpful and if they say 'yes', we ask 'Is there any way we can improve it?' Or they may say 'No, it wasn't helpful because it didn't show this or it didn't show that.' We know what we have to add to it.
>
> Same thing with the medical illustrations—did you understand them? Were they helpful? They will tell you what they liked about it, what they didn't like about it. We may show them a surgical storyboard and they may say it was too confusing or we really need to see the steps individually or it needs

to be explained differently. We also ask them which photographs may have been helpful. The attorney will bring in a lot of photographs of the plaintiff. We know we cannot use them all. So we will show some to the jury and ask them what they thought of the pictures and they will say whether they were impressed or they weren't impressed. We will show them, sometimes, all of the photographs and have them tell us which ones they are impressed with, which ones are meaningful, which helped them understand the extent of the injury, the nature of it and the pain and suffering that the plaintiff went through.

> Focus group participants have also told us that they don't like to see pictures taken in the hospital unless the probative value is extremely high from a pain and suffering stand point. Once we had a focus group where a young fellow had cut his some of his fingers off in a high school wood shop accident and there were photographs of him in the hospital. He is sitting on the edge of his bed holding his arm up and the arm is bandaged and you see a bandaged arm and the hand is covered. The jury said 'Who took the photographs?' The attorney said 'We had a photographer come in.' They asked how long after the accident was this and he said 'Two days.' They said, 'You mean two days after the accident they had already gotten a lawyer and were thinking of suing?' So we have been finding that unless the probative value is considerable that it outweighs that prejudice against the client, usually prejudice is towards a client when they talk about that, but here it goes the other way. We generally suggest not using those photographs and that's why we like the focus participants to pick out the photos because it is hard to be objective.
>
> I look at a photograph that shows all of the healed pin sites from external fixation and I can look at those holes and I know what was there. The jury looks at it and they are not impressed by it. The holes look like four pimples, so unless they understand that they were rods and nuts and bolts and you have corresponding pictures of the hardware, chances are those photographs are not going to be valuable and we probably should not use them. An exhibit that backfires, or is more helpful to the other side's case, should be identified before offering it into evidence at trial.[17]

See Chapter 23, *Keeping the Jurors in Mind*, for more information.

Some exhibits, especially in nursing malpractice cases, can be too graphic. Counsel must determine whether the exhibit, although probative, is too provocative to survive objection. Usually, vivid photographs will draw objection. Photographs of lacerations, pressure ulcers, or autopsies are vulnerable to objection. It is useful to preview these exhibits with the judge to determine how far admissibility extends before the judges rules the prejudicial effect of the evidence outweighs its probative value.

TIP: Graphic photographs should be used sparingly. If overused, they lose their effect and draw an objection that they are cumulative. Decide which photographs need to be shown to the jury during testimony and which ones can be identified and marked, to be viewed later during deliberations.

Consider as well that gruesome photographs or exhibits can backfire with the jury. If the jury feels it is being manipulated by counsel, the effect of an otherwise persuasive exhibit can be lost. Also, an attorney should be mindful of the number and kinds of exhibits the other side may use. Some jurors may regard the presentation of many expensive exhibits as a sign of weakness. This may be particularly important if the opponent tells a simple story with few or no exhibits. Sophisticated persuasion is different from slick salesmanship.

22.8 Authentication of Exhibits

An exhibit must have factual foundation to show that it is authentic before it will be admitted into evidence. This is ordinarily done by testimony of a witness with sufficient knowledge to lay the proper foundation.[18] The attorney must be prepared to meet any objection to an exhibit's authenticity. Ordinarily, this task is fairly easy to meet and is ordinarily done through a witness who is knowledgeable about the exhibit.[19] The minimum evidentiary foundation needed to establish admissibility for an item of real evidence is met when a witness identifies the exhibit by its distinctive characteristics and states that it is in substantially the same condition as it was at the relevant time. Pursuant to Fed. R. Evid. 901(b)(4), identification can be made by the witness based on "distinctive characteristics" such as "appearance, contents, substance, internal patterns or other distinctive characteristics...." For real evidence consisting of physical objects, products, appliances, and so forth, counsel must establish the prerequisite elements to get the exhibit admitted into evidence. For example, to show a back brace needed after a fractured vertebra, the attorney must:

1. Demonstrate that the exhibit is relevant to the case;
2. Elicit testimony that the witness recognizes and identifies the exhibit;
3. Determine that the witness can recall the exhibit's appearance at the relevant time, and must say that the exhibit is in the same or substantially the same condition as when the witness previously saw it.

This is a summary of the necessary evidentiary foundation.

1. Relevance. To be admissible, all evidence, including visual exhibits, must be relevant.[1] To be relevant, evidence must tend to "make the existence of any fact that is of consequence to the determination of the action more probable or less probable than it would be without the evidence."

2. Authentication. The Rules of Evidence universally require that demonstrative evidence be, as a precondition for admission, identified and properly authenticated.[2] Simply put, authentication requires the proponent of an exhibit to demonstrate that the item offered is what it is claimed to be. The testimony of a qualified witness is required unless the evidence is stipulated to or is self-authenticated.[3]

3. Sponsorship by a competent witness. "A witness may not testify to a matter unless evidence is introduced sufficient to support a finding that the witness has personal knowledge of the matter."[4] A witness who seeks to introduce an exhibit must display knowledge or training in the subject matter pertaining to this exhibit. The extent of the witness's knowledge goes to the weight of the evidence rather than its admissibility.

Endnotes

1. Fed. R. Evid. 401 and 402.
2. Fed. R. Evid. 901.
3. Fed. R. Evid. 901 and 902.
4. Fed. R. Evid. 602

Figure 22.3 Summary of necessary evidentiary foundation

Sample foundation for admissibility of a medical illustration

1. Nurse, I show what has been marked as plaintiff's exhibit 1 for identification. Do you recognize it?
2. Who prepared this exhibit?
3. Is this medical illustration a fair and accurate depiction of the plaintiff's pressure ulcers as you saw them on December 8, 2009?
4. Your Honor, I offer plaintiff's exhibit 1 into evidence and ask permission to show this illustration to the jury.

Sample foundation for admissibility of photographs and videotapes

1. I show you what has been marked as P2 for identification. Nurse, do you recognize what is shown in this photograph?
2. Does the image shown in P2 fairly and accurately represent the condition of Mr. Kenney's body as you saw it on December 8, 2009?
3. Your Honor, I offer plaintiff's exhibit 2 into evidence and request that it be shown to the jury.

Sample foundation for admissibility of subpoenaed hospital charts, medical records, x-rays/MRIs by custodian of records

1. Are you employed by Little Sisters of Mercy Hospital in the records department?
2. What is the position you hold?
3. Are the hospital records of Little Sisters of Mercy Hospital maintained under your care, custody and control?
4. Did you receive a subpoena duces tecum for certain hospital records pertaining to Mai Wong?
5. Did you bring these records?
6. Can you identify the hospital records which have been marked as P3 for identification as the complete and unaltered record of Mai Wong's hospitalization from January 9, 2010 until the date of her death on January 12, 2010?
7. Did you retrieve the hospital records yourself?
8. Was this hospital record made in the regular course of business?
9. Is this hospital record regularly kept or maintained as required by law? (Certified copies of hospital charts are admissible into evidence under Federal Rule 803 as an exception to the hearsay rule. However, if the accuracy, authenticity, or completeness of the chart is questioned or if it is alleged that medical records have been altered, sponsorship by the custodian of records is advisable. Note that other rules governing included hearsay may also apply.)

Figure 22.4 *Sample Foundation Questions*

During the discovery process, counsel may obtain information that will build the foundation for the admission of demonstrative evidence. Requests for admission can sometimes avoid more complicated methods of authenticating demonstrative evidence. For example, a well-crafted request for admissions can authenticate an enlargement of a nurse's critical chart entry or establish that a device or instrument is identical to one that played a role in the patient's injury. While such actions may not ensure the demonstrative evidence will be admitted, several steps in the authentication

process are eliminated, saving the jury the delay and distraction of evidentiary arguments. Federal Rule of Civil Procedure 36 provides for requests for admissions. Any matter admitted under this rule is conclusively established unless the court permits withdrawal or amendment.

A pre-trial conference to negotiate the use and admissibility of demonstrative evidence avoids delay and disruption at trial. When negotiation fails, hearings on the admissibility of certain evidence may be required.[20] Counsel opposing demonstrative evidence that may be improper or unduly

1. Show the exhibit to the judge and your adversary.
2. If not already marked, request permission to mark the exhibit for identification.
3. Lay the foundation for having the exhibit admitted into evidence.
4. Request that the exhibit be admitted into evidence. If admitted, the marking on the exhibit will be changed to reflect "P" or "D in evidence" and the date admitted.
5. Show the evidence to the jury at the appropriate point of the case and avoid interrupting the flow of the testimony. Often, the expert who is using the exhibit as part of testimony should control the presentation of the exhibit to the jury.
6. If the court sustains an objection to the introduction of the exhibit, a record must be made of how the witness would have used the exhibit had it been allowed. This "offer of proof" can be argued at sidebar, or preferably by the witness after the jury is excused. The record should emphasize the inability of the witness to clarify an opinion or to avoid confusion without the exhibit.

Figure 22.5 Procedure for Introducing Demonstrative Evidence

prejudicial should object and move to bar its use before it is shown to the jury, thereby avoiding the potential for a mistrial. Pre-trial conferences under Fed. R. Civ. P. 16 can resolve actual or anticipated objections to the admissibility of demonstrative evidence. Figure 22.3 summarizes evidentiary foundation.

See Figure 22.4 for a sample dialogue to establish the admissibility of evidence. Figure 22.5 outlines a procedure to introduce demonstrative evidence. Exhibits can be used to summarize evidence, such as a chart detailing the financial data of a corporation, the testimony of multiple witnesses, or the medical records. These exhibits are allowed pursuant to Fed. R. Evid. 1006. The foundation to admit a summary is the same as that already discussed. The exhibit must be relevant, the witness must have knowledge of the information that is summarized, and the witness must review the exhibit and verify its accuracy. For example, a life care plan used in a birth injury case can be reduced to a single exhibit outlining the cost of the various items of future care. This type of exhibit effectively streamlines closing argument. It should

be considered instead of a page-by-page presentation of the entire plan.

TIP: Demonstrative exhibits marked for identification but not admitted into evidence may not be allowed as a visual aid in summation, nor will they become a part of the factual record during the jury's deliberations. Get them admitted into evidence before resting your case. Be creative and think visually. Use simple, powerful demonstrative evidence in as many media as the case and the budget permits.

22.9 Commonly Used Types of Demonstrative Evidence in Nursing Malpractice Cases

This section describes various types of demonstrative aids that can be used in the courtroom. This is not meant to be an exhaustive list. The aids to be discussed include:

1. Photographs
2. Scene diagrams
3. Radiology and diagnostics
4. Anatomical models
5. Medical illustrations
6. Nursing notes and treatment records
7. Liability exhibits
8. Timelines or chronologies
9. Organizational chart
10. Damages and medical expense chart
11. Lost earnings chart
12. Videotape
13. Computer animations
14. Medical equipment
15. Standup cardboard figures
16. Plaintiff in the courtroom

A. Photographs

Photography has been used in the courts of this country for as long as the technology has existed. Two recent landmarks for the use of photographs as evidence have been the routine acceptance of color images (1960's into the '70's) and the increasing acceptance of digital images. Many photographs should be taken in nursing malpractice cases for several reasons. First, they can document the presence and location of important features of the facility or hospital that will be referred to during the course of the lawsuit. Beds, bed tables, furniture in the patient's room, or the location of medication carts, appliances, signs, or larger equipment should be recorded. Photographs also document lines of sight available to nursing staff, for example, as part of their responsibility

Figure 22.6 Hallway with blind spots

Figure 22.9 Woman pushing cart to solarium entrance

Figure 22.7 Hallways with safety mirrors

Figure 22.8 Woman pushing cart taller than she

to observe the movements of visitors near the newborn nursery. A question may arise about the ability of a staff member to observe a visitor in an infant abduction case. The same issue may come up in a hospital or nursing home regarding the ability to see past equipment. Figure 22.6 involves a case of a patient who was struck by a cart while he exited from the solarium. The photo shows the layout of the hallway, the blind spot created by the walls and the location of the reflectors and mirrors that allow for observation around the blind spots in the hallway. Figure 22.7 shows the opening at the right leading to and from the solarium and the safety mirrors mounted on the ceiling. Figure 22.8 shows a model who is the same height as the hospital employee involved in the accident. She pushed the cart, as documented in the testimony. Figure 22.9 shows her inability to see over or around the cart. Hospital policy stated the carts were to be pulled, not pushed.

Photos should be taken as soon as possible to document any injuries. Photographs should be taken of the equipment or appliances used in the care of the injured patient. Overall photos of the patient's room should be taken. If the patient has been moved to another facility following an incident, be aware that hospitals may have specific procedures for permitting photography of patients for legal purposes. This contrasts with photography for treatment purposes, an area which is probably covered in the admission forms signed by the patient or family member. In some facilities, the permission for photography is handled by the nursing, administration, public relations, risk management, or security department. The attorney should request and review the procedure before sending a photographer to the hospital. When a treating doctor's permission is needed, get the written authority before dispatching the photographer. Usually, the preferred time for this type of photography is the afternoon because the patient usually receives some type of treatment or tests in the morning. Advising the nursing floor supervisor of the attorney's intention can also avoid scheduling problems. It may be helpful to keep a file or database on all hospitals or facilities within the immediate area. This file should include the correct address and phone number of the hospital (many hospitals have similar sounding names), and the name of the contact person from whom permission is needed before sending a photographer. The file should indicate the kinds of permission needed, as well as copies of release forms, if any. Facility-specific files will save time and possibly the need for repeat trips by the photographer. The Health Insurance Portability and Accountability Act (HIPAA) of 1999 has made it more difficult to make arrangements with facilities, and a photographer should be provided with an appropriate HIPAA release when requesting information or permission to photograph a patient.

Consider the impact of using a series of photographs. One of the authors (PI) created an exhibit of photographs of a man who lost 70-80 pounds after a medical malpractice event. She arranged them so the oldest, most healthy photo was at the top left corner of the exhibit, and the photo taken days before he died was in the lower right corner. The pictures were laid out on a diagonal to show that change of a man who became almost unrecognizable by the time that he died.

Surveillance photographs and videography can be effectively used to dispute assertions of damages. Alternatively, photographs of the injury site, the client's scars, the durable medical equipment in the patient's home, the home modifications such as ramps, railings, lifts, bars, and special toilets, after a patient lived independently for many years, can send a message to jurors.[21]

1. Lighting and film choice

It is important to consider lighting when photographing the interiors of rooms, hallways, and nursing stations. In these types of cases it is preferable to take the photographs by natural or ambient lighting.

The exposure should use the smallest lens aperture possible. This will ensure the entire image is in focus from the nearest to the farthest point in the scene. Getting the greatest "depth of field" usually requires long exposure time under such conditions. As a result, a tripod or other such equipment must be used to steady the camera during the exposure. Generally, traditional "flash" photography will light the foreground but leave the background poorly lit, creating an unfair and unrealistic representation of the scene. Multiple flash units or the technique of "painting with light" may also misrepresent an interior scene. Hence, professional consultation should be considered in advance.

The decision to use color or black-and-white film depends on the subject matter. Sometimes the environment being photographed is illuminated by a mix of light sources such as incandescent, fluorescent, and natural daylight. Color films react differently to each type of light source, which will affect the quality of the final image. Color accents detail; black-and-white photography records only shape and spatial relationships. Color photographs are better for depicting conspicuous signs warning of dangerous conditions, improper exits, or some other hazard. Black-and-white photographs are reliable for depicting the distance between a bed and wheelchair involved in a patient's fall and may be the better choice if the inability to record color renders the photograph misleading. With digital printing, however, black-and-white prints are easily made by a simple change in the software application, such as Photoshop, which is a standard in the industry.

TIP: When the accuracy of color reproduction is important, such as with bruises or pressure ulcers, a color chart should be part of the exhibit. Color print laboratories can then match the known colors in the chart, which will ensure the proper representation of all the other colors in the scene. A photo should be taken with and without the chart in the frame. The image with the chart is there only for evidentiary reasons in case opposing counsel challenges the photo.

All photographs involving injuries and bruises should contain at least one frame with a color reference chart. This is especially important because of the relationship between skin tones and scars or bruises. Supplemental flash units should be considered to overcome any ambient light that might affect color reproduction. For example, fluorescent room lighting might look too green if the flash unit is not powerful enough to overcome the intensity of the room lights. Again, professional consultation can mean the difference between an admissible and inadmissible exhibit. In a pressure ulcer case, consider having the photographer take a wide view of the scene or of the patient (Figure 22.10, taken of a patient in a morgue), and a close up of the pressure ulcer with a ruler to provide dimensions (Figure 22.11).

Close-up photographs should provide clear images of any printing on an object. Figures 22.12 and 22.13 are photographs of a vial of insulin that was stolen from an unlocked medication cart. The patient used the needle shown in Figure 22.14 to inject the contents of the vial. Figure 22.15 shows a ruler next to the syringe to show the size of the needle. (At trial in this case, the jury found no liability on the part of the nurses responsible for this medication incident.)

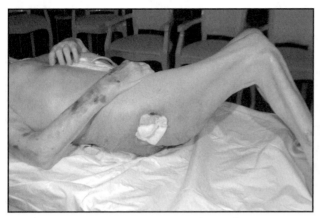

Figure 22.10 *Patient on a Morgue Table with Packing in a Pressure Ulcer*

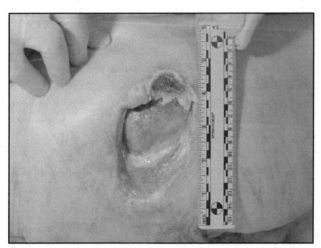

Figure 22.11 *Packing Removed to Show the Depth of the Pressure Ulcer. A Ruler Provides Important Information about Dimensions of the Pressure Ulcer.*

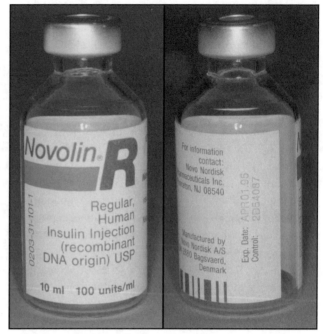

Figures 22.12 *and* **22.13** *Insulin Stolen by a Patient*

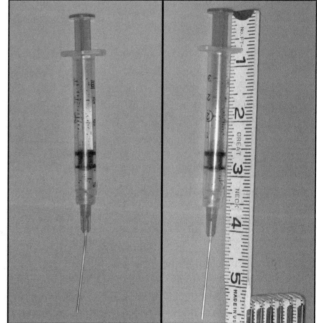

Figures 22.14 *and* **22.15** *Syringe Used by Patient to Inject Herself with Insulin*

The location of the artificial or natural light source must also be considered. Flash units built into the camera tend to flatten the appearance of the subject, hiding the appearance of raised marks or swelling. Photos should be made with equipment that allows movement of the light source away from the camera, the subject, or both. The flash can be placed above, and to either side of, the subject to record the depth and texture of injuries more accurately. Human vision is three-dimensional because we see through two eyes. Unfortunately, the camera sees only through one lens, creating two-dimensional images. It is therefore extremely important to remember this when attempting to capture injuries with a camera, and one should not expect them to look the same as the subject in person. If you are using film, take advantage of one-hour "mini-labs" to process important photographs as soon as possible if there is any doubt about the success of the photo mission, or monitor results as you shoot with your digital camera. Today, there is a drugstore on almost every corner that has the ability to print your photos while you wait. Do not trust the image on the camera screen. It is usually not large enough to assure that your picture is sufficiently in focus, even though the exposure may look suitable. If your camera has the feature, magnify the image on the screen to make sure your image is sharp.

2. Lenses and print size

Proper lens selection is critical in this type of medical-legal photography. There is a popular conception that the use of wide-angle or telephoto lenses "distorts" the reality of a scene. Actually, the distortion results from the improper relationship of lens choice, viewing distance, and print size. To determine the proper print size and viewing distance for photographs, forensic photographers use a formula based on the focal length of the lens. For practical purposes, this formula allows the photographer to create fair and accurate representations of scenes using wide-angle (short focal length) lenses. These permit the recording of larger areas of space when making interior photos in patients' rooms or crowded hospital corridors.

If a wide-angle lens is used to capture a scene, the print may be enlarged so that the intended viewing distance retains its true appearance. Assume, for example, that a nurse leaves a wheelchair outside a bathroom stall, and a patient trips over it after opening the door. A wide-angle lens will capture the essence of what the patient could see while sitting on the toilet including the door to the stall, the width of the stall, the space under the door, and so on. A print size of approximately 11×14 inches will create a more accurate representation of the scene than would a smaller image. Think of it this way: objects seem farther away (smaller)

when viewed through a wide-angle lens so the print should be larger to compensate. Extra care must be taken when applying this formula using digital cameras, as the relationship of the lens to the camera's sensor differs from that with a film camera. (Newer digital cameras have larger sensors that eliminate this discrepancy.)

Nevertheless, these techniques and theories may be lost in a courtroom. Distance from the exhibit stand to the jury box may interfere. Also the visual abilities of jurors may diminish a photo's effect. It is nonetheless important for the attorney to at least be aware of these issues in advance of trial to allow for the effective presentation of such photos. Counsel should prepare and anticipate objections to photos that do not meet the proper criteria. The formula also comes into play when enlarging photographs for use on an easel in front of the entire jury.

TIP: An 8 x 10-inch print traditionally circulated among jurors should be about 30 x 40 inches when placed in a fixed mount six feet away from jurors. Doubling the viewing distance of a photo or document requires doubling of exhibit size to maintain legibility and proper perspective.

B. Scene Diagrams

Exhibits that show a jury the nature and geometry of the incident's location may help explain the occurrence. While photographs show the appearance of a person or object from a particular viewpoint, diagrams, plan views, or aerial photos show the relative positions of important features. Diagrams can show the layout of a patient's rooms, the relationship of the patient's bed to the bathroom or exit, or the relationship of the patient's room to nursing stations or closets where drugs or chemicals are kept.

Preparing site diagrams need not be a major task, as most facilities usually have plans on file that are used for fire or general safety purposes. This information may be right next to the elevator, with the "YOU ARE HERE" arrow affixed. Ask for a photocopy from the files, or photograph the diagram, and have it enlarged and traced at a later date. Figure 22.16 was made from the field measurements of the hospital hallway involved in the cart striking the patient. It shows the specific accident area, and a scale is included for reference. Figure 22.17 shows the same diagram, with the addition of a scale version of the cart, and a circle representing the employee. Lines are drawn to demonstrate the limited view of the food cart when it is pushed in this manner. The blind spot can be colored yellow in the final exhibit to more effectively show that most of the hallway is out of view from this position.

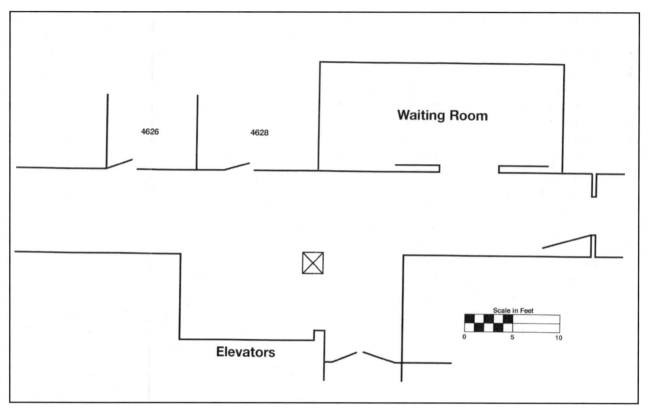

Figure 22.16 *Diagram of hallway involved in cart incident*

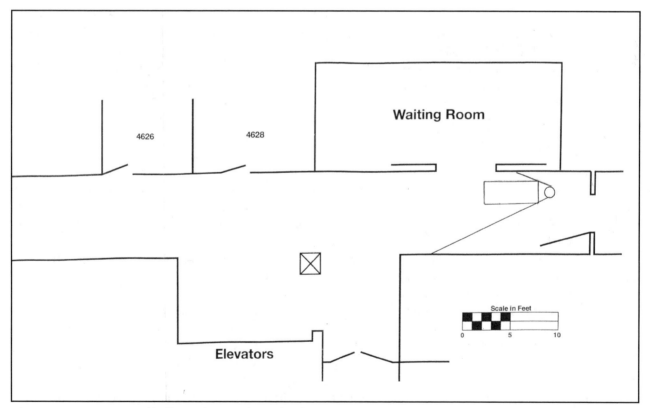

Figure 22.17 *Diagram of hallway showing line of sight*

An experienced forensic photographer will be able to assist with the preparation of such a diagram at the time the photos of the area are being made. Measurements of hallways and rooms, the location of stairways and exits, and linear distances from point to point can all be recorded and drawn to scale to meet the needs of the case. Site inspections are typically done with a group of attorneys, hospital personnel, and claims people. Generally the photography should be done in a separate session. The photographer can then work his way up and down the halls taking time to measure accurately to avoid the need for a return trip. Some agreement should be made, however, to allow for a return visit to verify any measurements before preparing the final exhibit. All parties may agree, for instance, that the photographer can schedule a return visit only to check measurements in a previously inspected and photographed location. The return can be done in the presence of one hospital employee, avoiding the need to coordinate the schedules of multiple law firms and hospital departments.

Diagrams can be equipped with overlays or magnetic pieces so that key elements of the testimony can be noted in different ways at trial. It may make sense to create two diagrams for the trial. One diagram would show the overall general layout of a specific area, such as an entire floor or wing of the facility, with a second, scaled diagram concentrating on the immediate location of the key events. This would result in an exhibit large enough for all jurors to view easily. Properly scaled exhibits are readable but too cumbersome for transportation and handling.

C. Radiology and Diagnostics

Paper prints from x-ray or other diagnostic films can be made and distributed easily to insurance adjusters or attorneys. Not only do they reinforce the facts of the condition or injury, they also enhance the perception of a well-prepared, creative advocate. Prints and exhibits based on the films themselves can be included in settlement brochures, arbitrations, or settlement conferences as precursors to more elaborate trial presentations.

TIP: Some of the most critical forms of visual evidence preservation are radiology films and other diagnostic imaging studies. Diagnostic tests such as x-rays, MRI or CT scans, and EKGs yield visual proof of injury or deviation that can support the otherwise written or verbal descriptions of a patient's care and treatment.

The nomenclature of "positive" and "negative" images is an important consideration when working with x-ray films or MRI and CT scan films. It is important to understand that the films themselves are not really "negatives" in the traditional photographic sense. X-ray films are what the doctor uses to assess injury. They are not intermediate images that are later transformed. This is critical, especially in cases in which a dark spot that was missed on an x-ray must be a dark spot on the exhibit, not reversed into a "positive."

Some attorneys believe that fractures look more impressive when the image is reversed on paper, but the human eye is drawn to the lightest part of any visual image. Therefore the most important part of the x-ray image, the bone, should remain light, not dark. A "positive" x-ray image forces the fracture line to compete with what now is a massive white background image. This is even more crucial when the films show some form of internal fixation or other hardware of treatment. On the original x-ray film, metal or plastic objects show up white on the print and are generally more identifiable for the same reason.

Most forms of diagnostic films can be used as the foundation for enhanced exhibits such as colorizations or illustrative interpretations. These are addressed below in Section 22.9.E. No matter what format is used to present the films, it is important to have the doctor who will describe the exhibits at trial choose which images should be presented. Very often there are many more films than need be marked as exhibits. Counsel must have the treating doctor or expert take an active role in exhibit selection. Because of busy schedules, this selection process should occur in one or more pre-trial meetings or perhaps for a few minutes in the doctor's office following the taking of her deposition. If the deposition is being videotaped, have the prints made ahead of time, so that any marking made at the deposition can be preserved for the trial. As with all exhibits, advance selection and preparation will avoid delays and confusion during trial.

Many hospitals have gone to digital imaging for their x-rays and are delivering the results on disk rather than film. In some instances it is still possible to request film print-outs of selected images, which will require the use of a traditional x-ray light box for viewing and use at depositions and trial. The advantages of the images being on disk are many. Firstly, they take up much less room and store more easily in the files. Second, they are much less expensive to duplicate when sending them to your adversary or experts. Be aware, though, that some hospitals are using proprietary software that might not allow for printing or export to a graphics program, making it difficult to make enlarged exhibits or display in court, other than from the original disk. The disk should be tested before making assumptions, especially on the eve of trial.

Diagnostic test results such as EKG strips also make effective trial exhibits. Copies of the strips can be enlarged and mounted on rigid backing, with overlays or laminate material added to give the witness a way to mark the exhibit during trial. Color markers can highlight areas of irregularity and contrast them with normal readings. Lines can be added across the strips to mark the "high-low" range of normal results. Such material can also be presented effectively using one of the various computer presentation programs, allowing for the images to be enlarged on a screen for better juror comprehension. In the digital world, fetal strips can be annotated and programmed to "scroll" through the critical time periods. Hot links can be inserted leading to relevant documents or records that relate to the portion of the treatment timeline. Consult with your demonstrative evidence vendor to discuss the best way to present this material.

Laboratory test results are also included in the diagnostic category. Enlargements of these printed sheets from a hospital chart can show deviations in blood work or other chemistries that point to the issue of improper care and treatment. Rather than simply enlarging several sheets for use at trial, the critical entries can be summarized and combined onto one exhibit for ease of comparison and tracking. This material can also be included in timeline exhibits, which are discussed below in Section 22.9.H. When showing printed material such as EKGs or other medical printouts, it is helpful to have a baseline exhibit to first use as a reference. There are stock illustrations that show a normal EKG. Only after showing one of these orientation illustrations can a juror best appreciate any deviations from normal results. The same is true with blood pressure readings, for example, in which a chart can be created showing the normal ranges in one color and the actual readings in another for contrast. This is when working with a graphics professional can really pay off.

D. Anatomical Models

Each juror's rudimentary knowledge of human anatomy can be quickly and effectively enhanced by models and charts. Just as with the preparation of x-ray exhibits, any meeting with a medical witness should include a review of a model or chart that can be used at trial. Medical witnesses, particularly specialists, can be a valuable source for such material. Practitioners sometimes have functional anatomical models in the office that can be brought to court. It is important, however, for the attorney to see these models or charts ahead of time. Often the models in the doctor's possession are small "freebies" that the drug companies give out, and may not be suitable for courtroom use because of their lack of detail or size. The most accurate anatomical models are cast from natural specimens and are better for trial use. They are also unlikely to draw objections. Some models, such as those of the eye, ear, and heart, come in larger sizes for use

as teaching tools in classrooms and make better trial aids for the courtroom.

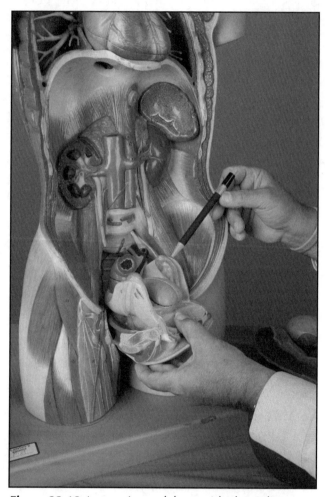

Figure 22.18 *Anatomic models provide three dimensional views of the body*

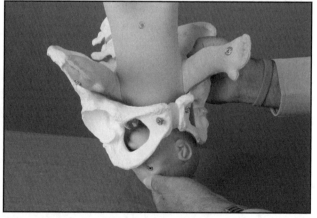

Figure 22.19 *A pelvis fetal model is flexible enough to be realistic*

TIP: For trial, try to get the largest accurate model available for each part of the anatomy. Accuracy counts. An improperly designed or constructed model is inadmissible evidence.

Anatomical models still serve an important purpose in the courtroom. Figure 22.18. They allow for the presentation of anatomy in a 3-dimensional manner, giving the jury an opportunity to become oriented to the relative position of important parts. The downside is that the testimony or demonstration is not preserved for jury deliberations. Also, some models are life size, which means that they are small. That makes them difficult to be seen by the jury. Models, such as skeletal models, can be held next to x-ray prints to show the jury how the film related to the specific part of the body. A baby model (Figure 22.19) is scaled to the proper size for a shoulder dystocia case. The expert can easily explain the mechanism of injury. This baby is flexible enough to be passed through the pelvis to show rotation and proper techniques for this condition.

Anatomical models are available from Lawyers & Judges Publishing Company. They can also be found on the Internet. Catalogues of anatomical models geared to paramedics and first aid squads and medical or nursing schools are also rich resources. Order them early and ask about the return policy in case the model does not completely suit the case. Ask about rental for more expensive models that may only be needed once. Some businesses, and some of the manufacturers, may rent models that they have on display or normally use for trade show or promotional purposes. They may also have some models in stock that are slightly "shop-worn" but would be completely suitable for trial needs at reduced cost.

Manufacturers who cater to orthopaedic surgeons provide models useful in teaching surgery. Special models can also be created on demand using the patient's x-rays. For example, an osteoporotic (soft) bone or a fracture can be replicated in material that has the look and feel of bone. The substance can be drilled in the courtroom with standard orthopaedic instruments. Hardware can be attached to illustrate fixation of fractures or correction of vertebral fractures. Other body parts may be made into models using a process called stereolithography. A plastic-based model is created using two-dimensional data. For example, a skull containing a hemorrhage can be created from the patient's diagnostic studies.

One advantage of models is that they give the jury a three-dimensional sense of the body or organ. Models can also be compared with radiology films of the injury to better show the nature and extent of an injury. If an x-ray print or illustration shows an AP or lateral view, for instance, hold the model up to the exhibit in the proper position so the jury can make the association between the anatomy and the image being displayed. Models, however, require a witness to identify and describe them effectively. On the other hand, a model admitted into evidence and left on counsel table can be a powerful reminder of important testimony as trial progresses. The attorney should be careful about renting a model that would have to be marked by an expert during testimony. Most models are made of a porous plastic and it is almost impossible to remove ink markings without damaging the rest of the model. Some models have numbers on them that correspond to a key guide supplied by the manufacturer. Using a solvent for the witness' marks could also remove the numbers in the surrounding areas of the model, making them less valuable for future use. Check with the supplier first.

E. Medical Illustrations

Anatomical charts and illustrations may be a less expensive alternative to cumbersome models. Illustrations may also have the advantage of captions and labels that teach without the need for testimony. They can also be brought into the jury room for further analysis.

1. Case law

Medical illustrations that are substantially correct reproductions of the injured part of the body are admissible within the trial court's discretion.[22] If a medical illustration or animation is "reasonably accurate" yet not drawn precisely to scale or contains some abstractions, it should still be admissible.[23] Courts look to whether demonstrative evidence will "aid the jury in understanding testimony" as the primary litmus test for admissibility. Because medical and nursing testimony is often complex and confusing to a lay jury, most trial courts have acknowledged that jurors can absorb and comprehend "better what is seen than what is heard."[24]

2. Sources of illustrations

One source for anatomical charts is the doctor who will be testifying about the patient's injuries. The doctor may have examples in the office or may have them as part of a lecture package. Counsel should ask the doctor for any textbooks that might illustrate the condition or injury. The illustrations can be copied from these books, with permission, and made into demonstrative evidence. The expert may have an extensive library from which to select potential exhibits, especially concerning unique surgical procedures. For copyrighted materials, counsel should get written permission to reproduce illustrations for courtroom use. Some authors and publishers will require a fee for one-time use; others might only require that the exhibit cite the source text and the publisher. Images are readily available on the Internet by performing a Google image search. The suitability of the images will vary depending on the size of the image. High resolution images are suitable for printing and enlarging. Low resolution images may be useful for incorporation into media presentations.

TIP: The attorney should adhere to all copyright laws when using images.

Many companies sell laminated and foldout anatomical posters that may be suitable for trial use. Generally, however, they are made for the classroom and are too detailed. They may contain too many images or too much text for effective use. Medical books or illustrations intended for consumers may contain clearer descriptions, particularly those directed at children and young adults. These simple illustrations may be adaptable for trial use, assuming again that permission is obtained from the publisher. They can be electronically scanned into the computer and altered to remove unnecessary information.

There are many books on human anatomy directed to a wide range of readers. Some contain color photographs of cadavers, and are too graphic for the courtroom. Books such as *Grant's Atlas of Anatomy* are good sources for material. *The Atlas of Human Anatomy* by Frank H. Netter, currently published by Saunders, is probably the most widely recognized collection of anatomical illustrations. Originally published as the Ciba Collection, Dr. Netter's life work has been placed in one volume, carefully organized by region of the body, with a complete index for easy reference. While also copyrighted, the Netter material is now available through a network of licensed vendors who are authorized to make enlargements from computerized data files. In addition, these images are also available for purchase online at www.netterimages.com. When purchasing through vendors, attorneys can reference the plates in the atlas and order trial exhibits that can be customized for each case. While not allowed to change the art itself, Netter agents can add or delete any or all of the captions as they appear on the page, making the exhibits more "jury-friendly" and case-specific. Titles can be changed to better address the topic of the exhibit, and the background can even be changed to black so that the opposing counsel cannot write on the exhibit. Look for Netter agents on the web at www.netterimages.com.

3. Custom illustrations

Colorizations of x-rays, CT scans, or MRI films can highlight various anatomical structures so that they can be identified easily. Color adds a focal point to conditions such as hematomas, tumors, and clots. Herniated discs can be colorized to identify the disc components, the spinal cord,

and the surrounding anatomy. Ligaments in the knee can be colored to isolate the relevant structures. Tears in a meniscus can be colored to correspond with the diagnosis and subsequent surgical treatment. A photograph of the surgical scar placed next to the x-ray adds to the effect.

Consider making custom, "case-specific" illustrations to show surgical procedures or unique injuries. These should be based on the diagnostic films and can help the jury understand the nature of the injury or condition. An effective way to personalize the illustration is to superimpose the anatomical images over the patient's actual face or body. Consideration should be given, however, to any embarrassment such an illustration might cause the client, and the use of such a display should be approved beforehand.

Surgical storyboards assist the medical witness in explaining the procedures used to treat a particular problem or injury. It is important to select a medical illustrator with proper training and experience in medical-legal work to interpret the medical reports. Medical illustrators work closely with the doctor in creating exhibits that accurately recreate the surgery performed. When working with an illustrator for the first time, ask to see samples of previous work. Examine the presentation of the anatomy and the procedure from a juror's point of view:

- Is the exhibit well organized?
- Are the captions legible?
- Does the art allow the attorney or expert to explain the procedure to someone?

It is critical to give the medical illustrator sufficient lead-time to prepare exhibits. An effective image requires a number of drafts before it is finished. Medical illustrators will need the operative reports, pertinent films, and radiology reports to create a case-specific medical exhibit. Whenever possible, good quality copies of these items should be provided, along with the name and phone number of the attorney's expert.

TIP: Experts should be notified that a particular medical illustrator will be working on the attorney's case. Ask the expert to cooperate if the illustrator asks for assistance. Of course, counsel should expect to be billed for time spent by the expert.

If possible, the attorney should submit a sketch, no matter how rough or crude, of what the final board should look like. Even this small input can save time and money in delivering a finished product that satisfies everyone and is within budget. Allow the illustrator, whenever possible, to have direct contact with the medical witness, and allow plenty of time to permit changes and revisions based on the expert's suggestions. Files can be e-mailed for review or placed on an extranet (a secure part of a website) if all parties have the proper access, which can save time when necessary. However, try not to rely on fax and e-mail to shorten the lead-time; the time required to create such exhibits is not affected by these modern delivery mechanisms.

The illustrator should use labels for anatomical parts in a large bold font (60-72 point). The exhibits should include orientation drawings so that a jury can identify the location of the close-up. Presentation of the normal anatomy next to an image of the injury permits the jury to make the needed comparison. To avoid confusing the trier of fact, the normal image should be in the same anatomical position as the image of the client's injury.[25] The images should be simple. Medical illustrations should be carefully checked by the expert witness to ensure they are accurate.

Since most medical-legal illustrators now work in computer format, the attorney can request 8.5 × 11 inch printouts for preliminary use, settlement brochures, and expert approval, ordering the final enlargements for trial only when they are needed. This also allows the finished work to be delivered in digital format for direct importing into trial presentation software. The attorney should also test the images before trial to make sure the resolution is sufficient when enlarged on the screen. Some trial presentation programs allow for smaller portions of the image to be enlarged; however, if the resolution is not high enough, the jury will be looking at a checkerboard image of the drawing. If you are using traditional easel presentations in your trial, consider breaking up your multi-image surgical storyboard into individual frames and creating a "flip-chart" of each step. The image will be proportionally larger and you will have more room for an appropriate caption in a font size that will be more legible.

F. Medical Records and Deposition Transcripts

The medical record is an important source for demonstrative evidence. The presence or absence of information, comments, key events, and entries regarding times, medications, and dosages can be used effectively to reinforce the theories and strategies of the case. The admission of these documents into evidence is often routine, but the dynamics of their publication to the jury have changed considerably in recent years.

The traditional method of publishing exhibits at trial is to circulate it among the jurors after its admission. Not only does this take time but it dampens the jury's psychological reaction to the exhibit. The practice of enlarging documents is not new, but it is generally done in an unfocused manner.

Enlarging a document does not always make it more effective unless counsel tells the jury the point of an exhibit. It may be the absence of an entry in the chart, or an unusual entry that appears to be squeezed in between lines in a questionable manner. The point might also be the inconsistency of time entries or a difference in handwriting within a specific nursing shift.

If an exhibit focuses on specific wording, it may be preferable to create "call-out" or "isolation" exhibits, enlarging only the key words or phrases the jury needs to understand. This can be done in many ways. Figure 22.20 is an example of a call out exhibit using the original document in an enlarged version when the handwriting is legible. A call out exhibit sometimes includes the entire page in the corner of the exhibit in its original size with arrows leading to enlarged versions of the key text. If the original document is handwritten, it is often helpful to have a typeset transcription made of the otherwise illegible script, and enlarge that rather than the original. Enlarging an otherwise illegible entry may improve its readability. This is especially helpful when the document is written with abbreviations and symbols unknown to lay jurors. The transcription can be made using the actual words represented by the symbols, but care must be taken to obtain an accurate reading of the entry from its creator, or the witness who will interpret it. Translation of abbreviations or symbols is an important goal of pre-trial depositions. In cases when handwriting is not legible, an overlay can be brought down with a typeset transcription falling over the original version.

Figure 22.21 shows a deposition isolation exhibit which is effective for focusing the jury on a specific question and answer when there is no evidentiary need to show the original context of the exchange. It might be more suitable for use in closing arguments, but may be useful during cross-examination at the discretion of the court. Figure 22.22 is a call-out exhibit that incorporates the original page for context and uses the actual image from that page. Some jurisdictions are more comfortable with this format. Some attorneys prefer it also because it anchors the quote to a document which may have a more powerful psychological effect on the jury as to the official nature of the statement. Note the actual document would have yellow highlight to help the image stand out on the page. Figure 22.23 is an isolation exhibit that contains portions of the original document, concentrating on only key parts needed for emphasis. Ellipses are used to indicate there are missing parts. This type of exhibit can be done as a fully prepared board, a magnetic board where the individual entries are added on as the attorney addresses them, or digitally so the attorney can click on each line one at a time to build the exhibit.

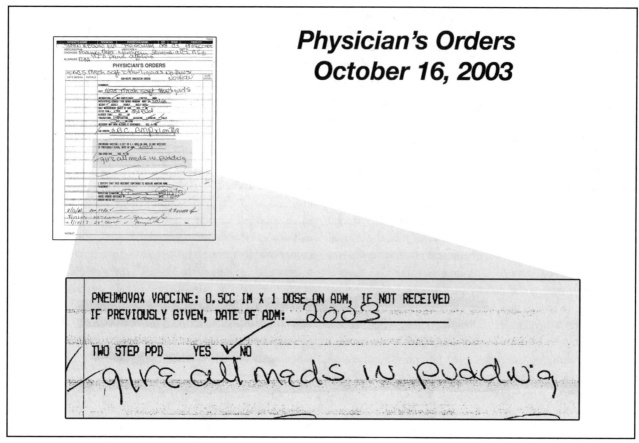

Figure 22.20 *A call-out exhibit using the original document*

Deposition of Jane Doe
October 27, 2006

Cross Examination By Mr. Brown

Q: And it's your understanding that, even back in November of
     2003, up until today, that the policies and procedures that
     control the conduct within ABC Home are consistent with
     any implementation of OBRA regulations?

A: Correct.

Page 91, lines 15-20

Figure 22.21 *A deposition isolation exhibit*

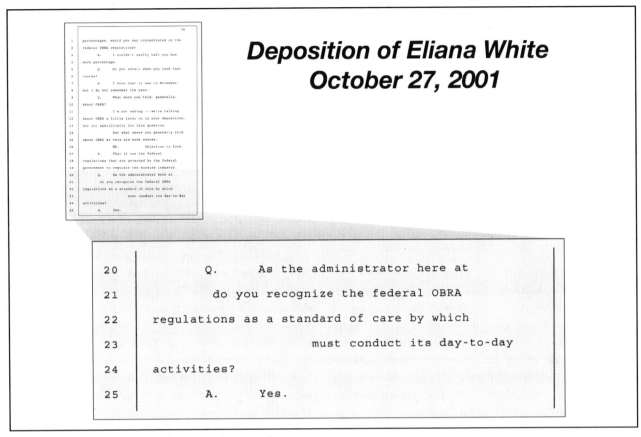

Figure 22.22 A call out exhibit using the actual page

Letter from Assistant Director of Nursing to Department of Health and Senior Services

*   *   *

On 11/02/03 at 3:50 PM, resident John Doe was found sitting outside on the concrete patio.

*   *   *

He was assessed and denied pain. He was lifted into the wheel chair and shortly thereafter grabbed his right thigh. When questioned about pain again he stated that it hurt. A call was placed to 911.

*   *   *

He has been admitted with a fractured right hip.

*   *   *

Figure 22.23 An isolation exhibit that concentrates on key parts for emphasis

If the intention is to review a document quickly with a witness, and the importance is more in its volume than its content, a flip chart can be prepared. It may consist of a series of enlargements of the pages, bound at the top with only the bottom page mounted for use on an easel. This gives the trial attorney the dynamic tool needed to work both quickly and economically through a document when it is not the primary exhibit but warrants more than mere identification.

Highlighting portions of documents for jury focus depends on the court and the jurisdiction. Some judges do not allow highlighting in yellow or other colors before the exhibit is used. Others prefer that the exhibits be shown with highlighting. A transparent overlay containing yellow film material that emphasizes key words or entries accomplishes the same goal. Of course these techniques, such as highlighting and "call-outs" are effective tools to consider when using trial presentation software. Complete familiarity with the programs will help the user make the best choice of which tool to use but care should be taken not to overuse these techniques which could easily detract from the message intended.

TIP: Generally, if the attorney asks a witness a question that begins with "I would now like to draw your attention to...," this is the time to consider some form of highlighted exhibit so the jury can properly follow along. One technique is to offer the original document to be marked and identified, and then put up the highlighted enlarged document to emphasize a key point. If you are planning on using a video document camera at trial (also known as an "ELMO") you should consider pre-highlighting a copy of the page you will be showing so that the jury can focus in on only those lines that are at issue. Unlike trial presentation programs, the zoom feature of the document camera does not allow for exclusion of words and content adjacent to the subject material.

G. Liability Exhibits

In addition to photographs and diagrams that address the key issues of injury, one component of nursing cases involves malpractice that caused the illness or injury. A deviation from accepted standards of care can be medically oriented or based on agency policies and procedure. Isolation exhibits are visually effective ways to address the content of these documents. Portions of the policies or procedures can be enlarged and highlighted, and if the context of the information is important, the entire page can be enlarged with highlighting of important text.

All standards that were violated can be extracted from the original source and converted into exhibits listing the failures and negligence of the defendants. One effective way to do this is with magnetic exhibits. Magnetics are an effective way to "build" an exhibit as the attorney or witness presents information. These types of exhibits were done with Velcro for many years, but modern materials available on the market allow the construction of lightweight and inexpensive magnetic exhibits. You can accomplish the same effect with a well-designed series of PowerPoint images; but as with any digital exhibit, if you do not have multiple uses, it may not make sense to set up the projector and screen for just a few minutes of presentation. Many trial attorneys today, however, use a document camera, laptop and projector for every trial, just to be prepared for last minute changes or for the presentation of material not previously prepared.

In cases in which comparative negligence is an issue, a magnetic exhibit can be created that uses the image of a scale, wherein the lone mistake made by the plaintiff can be contrasted with the many acts of negligence of the defendant. Each instance is typeset onto its own magnetic piece, and each piece can be "piled on" during closing argument for emphasis. If well crafted, the exhibit can be used in different cases, changing only the movable pieces to fit the needs of the case.

Mounted enlargements of the hospital chart or incident report are persuasive exhibits and can be used by both sides in a nursing malpractice case. The exhibit allows the jury to see what happened on the record in its actual form, in the subject's actual writing, just the way it existed on the day of the incident. Such exhibits can be made more effective as testimony aids by using overlays with markers and highlighting. Overlays marked in advance can be affixed to avoid impromptu editing. Separate excerpt boards or isolation exhibits can "zoom in" on the critical parts of the document or chart. In an electronic courtroom documents can be scanned into the computer, called up within seconds using a variety of techniques, and annotated by attorney or witness while being projected on a screen for the jury to view.

A less expensive approach to the presentation of documents is preparation of overhead transparencies and use of a projector to display the images. This is less costly, yields a bright image, and needs less lead-time than digital methods. When producing overheads for courtroom use, be careful to copy them at about 60-80 percent of the original size. The glass plate on the projector is somewhat smaller than the 11 inches of most documents, and by reducing the copy slightly it will not be necessary to move the sheet around to get it all in at one time. In addition, depending on the placement of the projector and screen, you may find the image too large for the screen if it is not reduced. As with all types of courtroom presentations, practice with the materials and the equipment and test your overheads on the first day in court. When using any type of audio-visual equipment the attorney may have an assistant run the show so it does not distract from the main job of formulating questions, listening to the answers, and keeping an eye on the judge, jury and the adversary.

H. Timelines

Timelines, or chronologies, are invaluable whenever the jury is expected to understand a sequence of events. Noted trial lawyer Gerry Spence preaches the importance of "telling a story" to the jury. A timeline suggests by its very nature that a sequence of events led up to the event, followed by another sequence of events as a result of it. Timelines help put the incident and its aftermath into perspective. This demonstrative tool can give the jury a better understanding of the time span in which the events took place and assist in the analysis of the relationship of events in time.

TIP: There is almost no case that cannot benefit from the preparation of a timeline exhibit. It can be used during opening statement, as an anchor during testimony, or during closing argument.

1. Examples of timelines

In a nursing context, a timeline can illustrate the time between the last observation of the patient and the discovery of the patient lying on the floor; the stages of skin breakdown as pressure ulcers worsened over time; or the evolving signs of fetal distress that went unreported. Timelines can illustrate the last notations in a patient's chart, such as last known activity and location. In an elopement or escape case, these notes can be security camera tapes that document the patient walking out of the facility unobserved. In another example, a patient may have fallen down a stairwell and not have been noticed because of a faulty alarm. A timeline might assist in explaining the installation and maintenance history of the alarm system, helping to point the liability in the proper direction. Timelines can also be used for collateral attack on a nurse's testimony. When evidence exists that a nurse cared for many patients, a timeline can demonstrate that, based upon the nurse's charted entries, all of the tasks indicated could not have been performed as claimed. A timeline can highlight discrepancies by showing conflicting documentation or testimony. While there are some commercially available timeline design software packages on the market, timelines need to be designed to tell a story.

Whether by layout, flow of information or color, the jury should be able to tell what the important elements are before there is any verbal explanation. When designing a timeline, determine what is the most important element or fact, and make sure it stands out. In some cases, such as a delay in treatment, the empty space on the exhibit will be the most important element. Timelines can serve multiple purposes. They can be used as anchor exhibits: something that stays up for the duration of the trial as a continual reference point. They can be used as a "cue-card" for the attorney as a reminder of the events needed to be covered in the testimony. They can be designed for an expert or they can be designed for a lay witness to assist during direct examination. A foundation must be laid that the witness "assisted in the preparation" of a diagram that would help the jury and is a fair and accurate representation of what it purports to depict.

Some jurisdictions will allow the use of timelines at any point in the trial with proper foundation. Some may allow them to be used as "assistive" demonstrative exhibits only and some courts will allow them to go into evidence under the prevailing rule allowing for "summaries" such as in Federal Rule 1006, which relates to the admission of summaries of voluminous books, records, or documents.

Alternatively, the defense may use a timeline to support its position on the case and to bolster the nurse's testimony.

In one case, a plaintiff alleged that no one came in his hospital room for hours. A timeline can illustrate the multiple visits to a patient's hospital room to make assessments and perform treatments. An effective method of presenting a timeline involves placing the time in a bar across the top of the chart or along the middle of the page. Arrows are used to point to key events. Timelines can be presented in traditional board format or electronically using presentation software that allows for them to become interactive. One technique is to create the timeline with hot links that will take the viewer to key medical records, radiology images related to that date, photographs of the injuries as they appeared at that time, or video of physical therapy being administered during that portion of the hospital stay. Such a technique is very helpful when preparing digital settlement presentations. Interactive disks can be created that allow the viewer (opposing attorney, claims representative, mediator) total flexibility in choosing what portions of the presentation to watch, and in what order. A recent presentation contained the total story involving three plaintiffs in one family, with the option of choosing which plaintiff to review and what portion of the treatment chronology to address. Summaries of the life care, vocational and economical damages reports were included as well as pre- and post-injury videos and statements by each person as to how his life had been affected by the injury.

2. The pain and suffering chart

Timelines are often used as part of the damages presentation, documenting the course of treatment of the patient. Refer to Figure 22.24. A timeline should include length of hospitalizations, duration of critical care, surgeries, and follow-up therapies. A pain and suffering chart depicts in hourly, daily, or monthly units, the patient's hospitalization, treatment, and medication over time. A timeline can highlight in red all of the subsequent surgeries that were needed to treat the injuries sustained by the plaintiff. It may show peaks in pain levels (Figure 22.25). These charts are essential to support a time unit argument regarding damages based, for example, on the value of each day spent on IV pain medication. These types of exhibits can be prepared as either linear timelines or calendar chronologies. The litigation support specialist can assist in deciding which type of exhibit might work best for the attorney's case. (Please see Chapter 10, *Pain and Suffering*, for more information on these charts and for examples.)

The client, as well as family members, should help prepare such exhibits. It is more likely to survive objection with its substance based on the personal knowledge of client and witnesses. Under Federal Rule 1006 a summary chart of otherwise voluminous evidence is permissible.

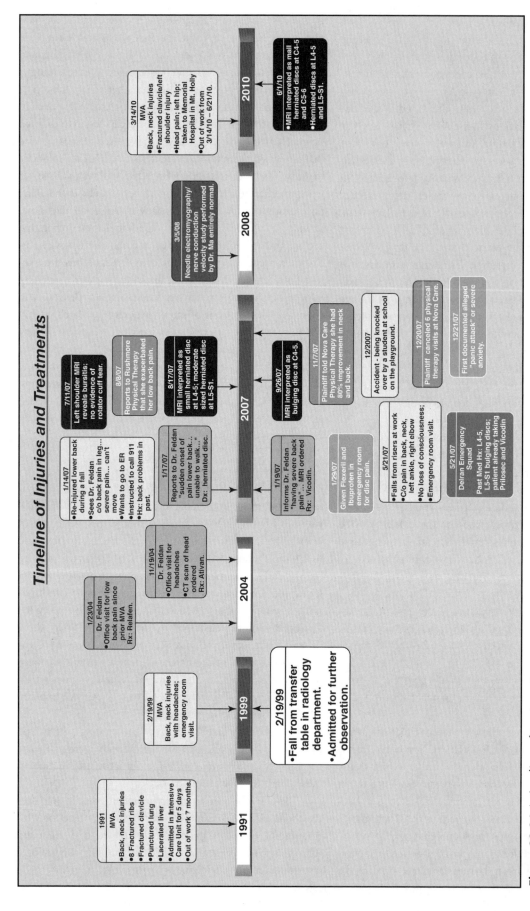

Figure 22.24 *A timeline of treatment*

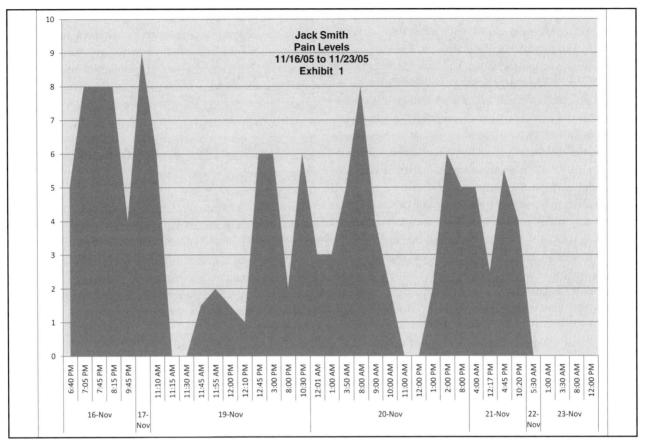

Figure 22.25 A display of pain levels

TIP: It is not necessary to put every detail on a timeline. This type of exhibit merely summarizes facts for the jury and illustrates key points on liability or damages.

---

3. Design principles for timelines

Color is an important element in the design of timelines. Color should enhance rather than distract from the facts presented. Color can convey important messages by creating emotional responses with complementary and contrasting hues. Using red for intensive care periods, orange for acute hospital stays, yellow for surgeries, and green for physical therapy periods can effectively carry themes throughout the exhibit portfolio. Yellow (with black lettering) is used to highlight surgery as the most critical time of treatment. Multiple surgeries will jump off the chart by using this color combination. The color combination of black on yellow or yellow on black is the one that most stimulates the eye for attention. It is important that counsel understand the psychology of color and use it as part of a presentation strategy.

A number of exhibit formats can be created. A traditional display for this type of information uses a horizontal line with boxes containing key data above and below the

dateline. A "who did what?" timeline uses space to identify the actions of each party. Combined with appropriate colors, the location of each entry as well as the lack of entries for certain parties clearly illustrates the critical facts of the case. If a doctor or supervisor issued orders and they were not followed, this deviation will clearly show on a properly designed timeline exhibit. If the goal of the timeline is to focus on precise times, clock faces with the applicable time can be included. Each event can be placed next to or under each clock to illustrate the elapsed time.

Timeline exhibits should generally be prepared to scale; that is, each time period represented should be similarly sized to avoid distorting the relationship of events. Chronologies, on the other hand, can be prepared by listing events in sequence no matter how much time passed between each one. In timelines that span a long period of time, it may be better to prepare two exhibits: one showing the "big picture" and the other a larger scale exhibit highlighting the time or date of the specific event.

One inherent problem with timeline exhibits is that they tend to be larger than most charts. This in turn leads to crowding too much information onto one page. All options regarding sizing, mounting, supporting, and transporting the exhibit should be explored. Attorneys who drive small sports cars will be more concerned with this than those who have the family van available to take to court. Exhibits can be hinged for ease of transportation, and carry cases are made that can accommodate large folding exhibits.

It is essential to check and double-check all the information that goes on any timeline, especially one that plots medical treatment. One flaw in an important entry may render the entire exhibit objectionable. A legal nurse consultant may help digest all the records into categories and dates of care for this purpose. Such a consultant should be used in all major cases to assist with the extraction and organization of the medical entries, especially when there are handwritten progress notes that contain abbreviations and language not familiar to a non-medical person such as a paralegal. Very often it is possible to confuse insurance payment dates on doctors' bills for dates of treatment, which can cause enough errors in an exhibit to warrant its exclusion from use.

4. Use of the timeline in settlement negotiations and the courtroom

Displaying trial exhibits during settlement conferences can be a valuable strategy. Not only does it help the defendant see the merits of the plaintiff's case, it shows counsel's preparedness and commitment to the case. It also demonstrates that the attorney is prepared to fund demonstrative evidence and suggests that other exhibits may be in the works. This is a win-win situation for the attorney. Even if the case settles before trial, early preparation of demonstrative evidence can be viewed as an investment rather than an expense. They may help increase any offer that is on the table at the time.

A timeline offers the trial attorney a visual and verbal focus throughout the presentation. As with the case itself, each exhibit needs an introduction, an explanation, and reinforcement to be most effective. The purpose of the timeline might be to illustrate multiple events leading up to the date of injury. Alternatively, an exhibit with no prior history might illustrate the sudden and unexpected nature of an incident or injury. This could be very powerful in a nursing case if evidence shows that there was no training in a hospital or facility before an event, or if nothing was done after an incident.

TIP: The process of creating a timeline or chronology forces counsel to organize case information in advance of trial. As a result, counsel is better prepared for trial or early settlement conferences.

I. Organizational Chart

Many nurses work in large hospitals. As hospitals and other healthcare institutions continue to merge and grow, tiers of overlapping authority must be explained to show each medical professional's responsibilities. The jurors must be given a clear picture of who makes important decisions, and how they are made. Charts and storyboards effectively present the chain of command in the modern medical center. Plaintiff's counsel will want to demonstrate the nurse's area of responsibility, while defense counsel will want to show how far removed she was in the policy or decision-making process. A job description chart can also be used to show the responsibilities of nurses and can be a useful adjunct to the organizational chart. Adherence to the job requirements or deviations from the responsibilities in a job description can then be highlighted. See Chapter 8, *Inside the Healthcare Environment*, for a description of a typical organizational structure in a nursing hierarchy.

TIP: Magnetic exhibits are helpful because they can be "constructed" as the testimony unfolds and the pieces can be moved around to correspond to testimony as it develops.

J. Damage and Medical Expense Charts

The medical expense chart summarizes medical bills and, indirectly, the severity of treatments the plaintiff has endured. This is a component of a life care plan, as described in Chapter 12, *Life Care Planning*. Damages and medical expense charts cover lost income, present and future medical expense, and lost enjoyment of life. It is important to document past costs and project future medical costs. A final chart can show all categories of damages and also allow addition or deletion of items during the trial as evidence is presented. The final product should be dramatic, persuasive, and easy to read. It must be a guide to the obvious and hidden costs of the injury over the plaintiff's lifetime. A magnetic chart would be useful to summarize costs. There are generic exhibits available from many vendors that allow the attorney to reuse the components as needed for each case, writing the numbers and dollar amounts in blank spaces provided. Different jurisdictions have varying rules as to what can be included on such a chart; but whether the amount is filled in or not, the jury can see each element that needs to be considered during deliberations.

TIP: Counsel should pattern a proposed jury verdict form on the categories of damages found in the damages chart.

In less significant cases, damages can be expressed in monetary terms using fill-in-the-blank charts. As the "costs" of malpractice are determined, they are placed on the chart. Elements may include special damages, such as medical expenses, nursing care, physical therapy, medication, and special housing requirements. In catastrophic cases, life care planners prepare such charts based on expected medical testimony, mortality tables, and the planner's expertise.

K. Lost Earnings Chart and Life Activity Calendars

If earning capacity is lost or impaired, a vocational expert assesses the plaintiff's earnings capacity and the net economic loss caused by the malpractice. This expert can also detail current and future income losses from a forced career change. This chart, completed by the economist, should be supported by the testimony of the plaintiff, the spouse, family, friends, and employer. Data from the Bureau of Labor Statistics can quantify, for example, the value of loss of household services.

Jurisdictions vary in what testimony they permit from an expert economist. Some jurisdictions allow an economist to make assumptions and provide a total dollar amount based on those assumptions. Others may limit an economic expert to presentation of a methodology and facts only. Regardless, counsel should keep an economist's testimony short, simple, and to the point. Lengthy technical discussions of present or future value will confuse the jury. See Chapter 13, *The Role of the Forensic Economist in Nursing Malpractice Actions*, for more information on how this expert contributes to trial testimony. In any presentation of dollar amount, whether it is for life care or past/future lost income, the final total amount should be in a larger type size, and preferably in color, to stand out from all the other numbers on the exhibit. This is the figure the jury will carry into their deliberations and use as a springboard for other aspects of the case value.

TIP: While explanations may include discount rates, inflation, and other economic factors, an economic chart should be limited to a series of simple items that the jury can easily add. The expert witness should present more technical explanations of discount rates and other factors.

A life activity calendar is typically constructed by collecting data about the activities of the plaintiff before versus after an injury. Landau advises plaintiff's attorneys to consider using a life activity calendar or other demonstrative aid to show how the client filled his days before the fall and how a fractured hip or other injury has replaced many of those activities with doctor's visits, therapy, dependence on others, boredom and pain.[26]

L. Videotape

The widespread use of video technology has changed the way many lawyers prepare and try their cases. It has also created its share of problems. Counsel should avoid the tendency to overuse or misuse video because of its relative simplicity. Videotaped evidence, without thorough planning, can be confusing and unduly prejudicial. This section will review how videotape can assist counsel in the specific areas of nursing malpractice litigation.

Note that when using the term "videotape" we are referring to a form of "motion picture" presentation that can be both recorded and presented using either older analog equipment or more common digital equipment. At the time of this writing, most professionals in this field are recording digitally and delivering a finished product on DVD. It is critical to communicate with the video vendors to assure the compatibility of their product with the equipment that will be used. Not all DVDs play on all computers or in all DVD players. While this format is becoming a standard, the standardization process has not yet reached its maturity.

1. Videotape of the facility

Like photography, video may be used to document the scene of any incident. While still photographs best address specific issues to be presented later on in the case, videotape can thoroughly survey a scene, room, or hallway, often capturing images missed by still photography. Video presentations can better illustrate the path a confused patient may have taken from a room to an unprotected exit door.

If the issue is an automatic door, video can document the speed at which the door closes, possibly creating a hazardous condition that may have precipitated a fall. The movement of elevator doors is often similarly documented on videotape, especially when patients and nurses cannot move quickly through doorways with wheelchairs or other medical equipment.

2. Videotape of the patient

Videotape can also be used to document the condition and demeanor of the patient in ways not possible with still photos. When appropriate, videotape should be used as soon as possible to record any abnormalities in speech, body movement, or any dynamic trait that may have been changed as a result of the accident or event. Interaction between the patient and family members, the ability to respond to questions, or changes in a patient's mobility are all important areas that may be documented. In cases involving nerve or brain injury, recording reactions or lack of response may document conscious pain and suffering. Again, when appropriate, an informal question and answer session by a family member can preserve testimony at, or immediately after, an event. The patient may be able to recall conversations that took place with and among caregivers during treatment and care, especially when it is thought that the elderly or unconscious patient may not be able to hear conversations spoken in normal volume.

TIP: Compact, lightweight video equipment can be an effective substitute for a snapshot camera, but remember that impromptu recordings may be discoverable in litigation.

There is generally no need for additional lighting with most video cameras. Their small size and unobtrusive nature, particularly when held at hip level, will not likely intimidate or upset a patient. Footage from these tapes can later be converted to other formats and included in video settlement brochures or trial presentations. Digital formats now allow for maximum flexibility for most postproduction needs.

Videotape material should also be considered for use in the settlement process. A video montage of the subject's life before the injury can be an effective negotiating tool. If photos or video footage exist from family gatherings, they can be made into an effective presentation that contrasts with the patient's current condition.

Settlement or mediation presentations using video technology are extremely effective because they combine the emotional effect of the injury with the persuasive facts of the case. Defense attorneys as well as insurance adjusters can preview the effect of the plaintiff's case and better evaluate the risks of taking the case to a jury. It is to the attorney's advantage to be creative with the use of video in these types of cases. Preservation is more crucial within shorter time frames.

Presentation of demonstrative evidence by videotape may include depositions of witnesses and the plaintiff, day-in-the-life films (described below), statements of fact witnesses, surgical procedures necessitated by the alleged negligence, or home movies of family events or dying loved ones. After showing a two-hour videotape of the testimony of the nursing expert witness, for example, the attorney may use a brief segment to reinforce a point during summation. Because of its conciseness and clarity, the tape segment reinforces the full length deposition.[27]

3. Day-in-the-life films

Video depositions and day-in-the-life films may be considered if the injury and the resulting change in lifestyle

warrant, or the plaintiff's condition prevent an appearance at trial. A day-in-the-life videotape is particularly effective in cases involving catastrophic injury. In such cases, a 15- to 30-minute day-in-the-life film can illustrate the claimed damages better than verbal testimony.

TIP: Check into the case law in the particular jurisdiction as an objection to such a presentation as being cumulative of oral testimony has been brought up on many occasions. One way to approach this is to have the witness introduce the video as to its authenticity, play a small portion of it, and follow up with additional explanation of what was just shown. There is no rule that mandates such a video needs to be shown in its entirety at one time. The portion of the video showing the home care can be shown at a different time than the video of the hospital rehab therapy. Foundation can be made by differing witness at different times during the trial. In addition, the issue of the right of adverse counsel to attend and the need for notification of the intent to film such a presentation should be addressed. For example, some New Jersey attorneys refer to *Balian v. General Motors* (121 N.J. Super 118, app.div 1972) when citing the need to be notified of such a filming session. However *Velazquez v. Jimenez*, (336 N.J. Super. 10 (app Div 2000) distinguishes day-in-the-life videos from reconstructed events, holding that defense counsel are not entitled to be present during the taping of a day in the life video.

A film showing the plaintiff's condition immediately after the accident and during the recovery period, will visually express the scope and nature of the plaintiff's injuries, pain, and suffering. Day-in-the-life films, introduced by Melvin Belli's law office in the mid '50s, are necessary to "show the jury just what the life of the plaintiff is like, and what it will continue to be like for the rest of his days. Shortened versions of these films taken at the peak of plaintiff's discomfort convey to the jury a message the spoken word alone could not even begin to approach."[28] Each juror sees that the plaintiff can no longer care for even the simplest needs and how the condition demands constant attention. In short, "The jurors watch as the plaintiff suffers through a typical day, which will be repeated over and over again until death."[29] Care must be taken not to exceed 30 minutes for this demonstrative evidence. Longer tapes will lose the jury's interest or dampen the visual effect. Haviland notes: "You want to capture the care from the time they wake up to the time they go to bed—what it takes to care for someone. Jurors can get a clear picture rather than just hearing someone talk about the fact that he has a feeding tube; he needs to be fed every night; he has IVs and sites that need to be cleaned and so on. Showing a day in a life is much more effective."[30]

Day-in-the-life films do not have to show an entire day in the plaintiff's life, contrary to what its name suggests. A short video showing how a plaintiff needs to change a colostomy bag on a daily basis or take out and clean a prosthetic eye is an example of such a use for video in demonstrating damages. It is important to know that the video must be, like a photograph, a fair and accurate representation of what it purports to depict. Scenes should not be directed by the videographer in terms of lengthening their duration or in any way showing them in an unauthentic manner. Morning activities of daily washing and dressing should not be re-staged in the afternoon to make it more convenient for attorneys or videographers. A plaintiff may be more rested in the morning whereas re-staging the process in the afternoon, after what may be a tiring day of treatment or therapy, could yield a totally different appearance for the camera.

4. Videotape of experts

Videotapes can substitute for experts or witnesses who cannot testify in person at trial. Digital video images allow counsel to edit a specific segment and play selected portions during closing argument. Combining video images with deposition text may be particularly effective when cross-examining an expert witness with a videotaped deposition transcript.

Many attorneys are reluctant to present key liability testimony by videotape. Often taken a few weeks before trial, the testimony may not be congruent with changes in legal theories or facts as they emerge during trial. Advance taping also permits the adversary to have a longer opportunity to prepare a rebuttal of the witness' position. In addition, with the spontaneity of interaction lost, jury boredom with a lengthy videotape becomes a factor.

TIP: Video teleconferencing provides new options to get around logistical issues. It can permit an out-of-state physician to testify "in person," thus saving travel expenses and time. After being brought up to speed on the trial, the expert can be prepared to address the case as it is unfolding in the settlement discussions or at trial. The trial attorney should confer with the video conference facility in advance regarding the technique to be used to record the deposition. If exhibits are being used, a provision should be made to have the camera operated in such a way that the chart or model will appear clearly on camera if the intention is to use the video as trial testimony.

---

5. Teaching videotapes

When appropriate, instructional videotapes can replace expensive medical experts. Such videotapes, produced or endorsed by accrediting boards, cover most areas and standards involved in nursing malpractice. Teaching films can be helpful in conveying the details of a procedure that could not be well demonstrated in the courtroom. For example, the jury can watch the surgical correction of a fractured hip or how skin is removed from healthy tissue for grafting onto burned areas. Groups such as the American Academy of Orthopaedic Surgeons maintain a vast library of educational audiovisual material and videotapes showing surgical procedures. Instructional tapes usually feature well-credentialed specialists who present an overview of the anatomy and then an actual surgery. Portions of the tape can be played with the soundtrack to explain the intricacies of the procedure. The tape can also be played without soundtrack and narrated by the physician expert witness at trial. This allows the expert to verify accuracy and describe the similarities or differences between the textbook procedure and that performed on the plaintiff. These films are, however, classic hearsay and will not likely be admissible without the agreement of opposing counsel.

Tapes can illustrate the injury the patient has suffered as the result of a nurse's negligence. For example, the case may involve a pregnant woman who sustains a knee injury from falling over a wheelchair left in her path by a nurse. The attorney might use a tape to demonstrate the arthroscopic knee surgery used to repair this injury. In a case involving a head injury after a fall of an unattended patient, a tape of the evacuation of a subdural hematoma (blood pooling inside the skull) is used. A tape of a lumbar discectomy performed on a man who has sustained a herniated lumbar disc in a fall from a hospital window would be another example. In each of these cases, the instructional tape gives a jury of laypeople insight into the nature and seriousness of the procedures required to repair the injury. They may also be more likely to be stipulated into evidence because they relate to an uncontested fact of treatment.

Instructional videos can also be used to teach basic nursing techniques in some cases. These tapes demonstrate the standard of care applicable to fundamental nursing procedures. Excellent instructional tapes are available from Springhouse Corporation, the American Journal of Nursing, and Mosby Year Book. Much good resource material is available from various commercial sources and organizations that can be helpful in educating others about a particular procedure or medical issue. The Learning Channel and Discovery Channel have video material of surgeries that can also be purchased for courtroom use to educate juries. Nursing and medical publishers and professional associations are good sources of information. Internet searches of books and software sellers geared to healthcare professionals may yield other resources.

TIP: When using such an educational or institutional video at trial, consider reviewing it carefully with the witness and having it professionally edited to its shortest length possible to avoid objections in court or having to fast-forward the tape to get to key parts of the presentation.

For those attorneys who are more computer literate (and have the time and patience to learn the software), editing programs such as Final Cut and others provide the capability to do this in-house when needed.

M. Computer Animations
Animations used to recreate an event in normal or slow motion can be powerful and persuasive. Animation can explain and reinforce the disparate elements of complex testimony. Critical elements of the case are brought into focus.

TIP: Computer technology offers many possibilities in nursing malpractice litigation. Sophisticated medical testimony can be reduced to a series of computer-generated animations that illustrate key facts without unnecessary detail.

Animations can illustrate the structure, function, and processes that may be pertinent to a case. They may include three-dimensional models of a hospital to show the relationship of rooms, hallways, and other parts of the facility when presenting security-type cases. The outside of the building can be shown and the walls and floors can be programmed to dissolve away, revealing different parts of the building in a way that two-dimensional illustrations or conventional models cannot. A virtual walk-through can be created to take the jury through the simulated building. This tour can highlight the areas important to the litigation without showing unnecessary visual detail.

Computer graphics can also be used to demonstrate issues such as the malfunction of a hospital bed or another device that may have failed, such as when a patient fell head-first off of a lifting device because of a defective sling and an inattentive nurse. These types of events can be graphically shown along with the corresponding remedies as opined by the expert engineer in her report. Such aggressive preparation on the part of plaintiff's counsel can often move a case to settlement because of the persuasive nature of such exhibits.

Computer technology can also demonstrate the mechanism of injury, showing how a patient was strangled by a restraint. This can be combined with footage showing the effects of the injury by stripping away the body's anatomy in layers showing the injury to the muscular, vascular, nervous, and skeletal systems. Head injuries can be illustrated by showing how a damaged ceiling tile could have fallen causing injury. Information supplied by the expert about trips, slips, and falls of all kinds can be demonstrated to show how an injury could have occurred one way and not the other. The death of muscle caused by the failure of a nurse to detect compartment syndrome can be effectively illustrated by showing how swelling, over time, reduces blood flow and destroys tissue. Such visual support can go a long way in refuting adverse theories of liability or proximate cause.

Computer animations that merely illustrate the subject at issue are generally accepted as graphic depictions in the same way as diagrams that are hand-drawn on a blackboard. Computer animations generated solely by the software such as those that calculate motor vehicle crash data in accident reconstructions are subject to more stringent evidentiary requirements. One of the advantages of such a presentation is that, when combined with an audio track, animations can serve as "absentee advocates" in the settlement process, effectively making the case every time and anywhere the videotape is played. When included in a video settlement package, it gives the viewer a taste of how the jury may react to the presentation during trial.

Computer-generated animation or reenactment can provide a very persuasive visual presentation to the jury. Such animations are very time consuming and can be expensive to produce. Moreover, because of their expense, care must be taken to ensure that a proper foundation is laid to ensure admissibility at trial. Horst and Rosenberg[31] stress that these legal principles are essential:

1. In order to be admissible, the evidence must be supported by the testimony of an expert witness. If the animation is used to accurately illustrate expert testimony concerning general scientific principles, it is likely to be admitted.

2. If the animation is used to illustrate the expert witness's theories concerning an event in the case by presenting a reconstruction of the event, the evidence must accurately reflect the conditions of the event consistent with the evidence. The animation must reflect the testimony of the expert.

3. The probative value of the evidence should not substantially outweigh the danger of unfair prejudice, confusion of the issues, or misleading of the jury.

4. Attorneys seeking to present animations at trial should ensure that they comply with the particular evidentiary requirements specified by the courts for animations.

5. If attorneys are attentive to the purpose for which the animation is to be used, and tailor the evidence accordingly, the use of animations can be a powerful tool that will enhance the impact of expert witness testimony on juries. Refer to Horst and Rosenberg[32] for additional information on the topic.

TIP: Contact the vendor for computer animation as early in the process as possible so there will be clear and complete communication as to what is to be portrayed, the expert will have time to review it, and there will be ample time for revisions. Haste makes waste, especially in this type of work; and many hours of rush fees are often run up producing this type of work at the last minute. The animation vendor should first prepare a storyboard of what you want to demonstrate. This will include sketches of the content of each "scene" in the video to assure the correct placement, perspective and sequence of events. Changes in any of these elements are easy to do at the early stage and will avoid unnecessary fees for revisions at the digital stage of preparing the art.

N. Medical Equipment

Medical equipment in the courtroom powerfully conveys the realities of health care. Many jurors have some familiarity with medical equipment through life experiences or by watching popular television shows based on the events of hospitals. However, their knowledge is incomplete. Small pieces of medical equipment may be supplied by the treating physician, expert witness, or manufacturer of a product. The catalogues of many manufacturers are available on the Internet. Whenever possible, the equipment should be seen and touched by the judge and jury. Consider the effect of handling a capped syringe, a scalpel, or a vest restraint. Medical equipment helps convey the totality of the patient's experiences or to explain how an injury occurred.

While it is impractical or impossible to bring into the courtroom large or expensive pieces of equipment, such as ventilators, CT scanners, hospital beds, or operating room tables, it is possible to show them to a jury through photographs or videotape. Textbooks, articles, medical supply catalogs, and product brochures are all sources of photographs of medical equipment. Examples of images of medical equipment which can profoundly influence jurors include intracranial pressure bolts, tracheostomy tubes, halo traction devices, rotating beds, ventilators, suction equip-

ment, external fixators and splints used for fractures, plates, screws, rods, artificial hip joints, and dermatomes used for skin grafting. Procedures involving the injection of medications can provide graphic videotape footage. As already discussed, videotape of treatment procedures using complex equipment can portray a patient's ordeal more powerfully than can testimony alone. For example, few jurors could fail to react to a video showing debridement of a pressure ulcer or burn care.

O. Standup Cardboard Figures

Heninger[33] suggests using life-size cutouts of doctors, nurses, or other key witnesses or defendants in a case. Silhouettes of figures are useful for creating these demonstrative aids. The attorney can use a felt-tip marker to write identifying information on each figure. This may include the person's name, responsibilities, and short quotes of key testimony. The figures are helpful reminders for jurors once the witnesses leave the courtroom.

P. The Plaintiff in the Courtroom

In many cases, the client is the most important demonstrative evidence. Counsel should carefully time the exposure of the client to the jury. In some cases, the plaintiff and available family members will become fixtures in the courtroom. In other cases, the plaintiff may appear only briefly or not at all. In all cases, counsel must remember that the jury will observe and evaluate the plaintiff and defendant, if present throughout the course of the trial.

TIP: Plaintiff's attorney should explain the rules of behavior to the plaintiff and family and not assume the client knows how to act or dress. The plaintiff should avoid the jurors during breaks and remember that jurors and others will be observing him.

Counsel should consider limiting the jury's exposure to the severely incapacitated client in cases involving quadriplegia or infant brain-damage, with attendant risk of jury desensitization. For example, prolonged jury exposure to a toddler with spastic quadriplegia with ventilator assistance may be less effective than a shorter well-timed presentation. Reference to the infant's condition during the earlier segments of the trial creates anticipation. The jury should only be exposed to the severely injured plaintiff once or twice during trial for a few minutes each time. The presentation should be done in a low-keyed and dignified manner. The jurors should be cautioned about the plaintiff's incapacity. Presenting such a plaintiff in a dignified way undermines any attempt by defense counsel to argue that counsel is manipulating the jury's sympathy for the purpose of obtaining or increasing the award. Plaintiff's counsel should apologize for causing the jurors' discomfort by showing them the plaintiff's condition.

Closed circuit video may be used to display a plaintiff's injuries without having the victim in the courtroom. This technique may create some psychic distance between the witness and the jurors,[34] which may work to the advantage of either side.

Q. The Remote Plaintiff in the Courtroom

The absence from court of a badly injured or infirm plaintiff may suggest disinterest in the case. In the past, lawyers accepted such a circumstance as unavoidable and struggled to minimize its effect on the jury. Today, lawyers can present "virtual" plaintiffs and witnesses in court using videoconferencing.

Jurors pay rapt attention when informed that such presentations are unusual and allowed only under compelling circumstances. The drama inherent in these moments, when used judiciously, adds poignancy to testimony. A brief videoconference introduction of a catastrophically injured client may be included in the opening statement. The jury sees the extent of the injuries and is made aware that the plaintiff is present. The client reappears as the last witness. Now less shocked by the plaintiff's condition, the jury can focus its attention on what is likely to be the most dramatic testimony of the trial. Finally, if the trial has been lengthy, the plaintiff's appearance during summation can be a graphic reminder of her plight.

Effective videoconference testimony requires preparation, practice, and money. Have an experienced professional assemble the technical elements (hardware, software, and communication lines) in a careful and timely manner. Multiple videoconference practice sessions can create a strong witness and hone the attorney's presentation. Practice is particularly important to test the influence of videoconferencing on trial dynamics. The attorney may need to develop new techniques to cue a remote witness or quickly stop unresponsive or damaging testimony.[35]

22.10 Considerations in Selecting an Approach to Presenting Demonstrative Evidence

The chapter concludes with information about factors that influence the selection of a demonstrative evidence approach. Four types of presentation systems are defined with advantages and disadvantages of each. Suggestions for designing effective computer-generated slides for use with presentation software are included.

A. Planning

Careful planning is essential for the successful use of any demonstrative evidence. Planning starts with identifying the purpose of the demonstrative evidence. Is the exhibit designed to introduce a framework for understanding the liability issues, to illustrate or refute damages, to point out inconsistencies in the facts of the case, or to present key opinions of experts? The purpose of the exhibit will drive its preparation and its use. The trial attorney must allow sufficient time for the production of the exhibit. Joye comments, "The night before trial is too late to think about how to incorporate accident scene photographs or diagrams into witnesses' testimony. Preparing demonstrative evidence early in the case forces the attorney to think about the progress of the case, the value of the evidence, and the order of the witnesses. It forces the attorney to choose and use the pieces of evidence that will best illustrate the important points in the case."[36]

TIP: Consider the visual presentation of demonstrative evidence months before trial. Last-minute planning will likely be less persuasive and successful.

A good rule of thumb is to estimate total production time for each exhibit and then double it. This is essential for incorporating the perspective of the witness who may be using the exhibit; this also avoids costly mistakes. Consider using a variety of exhibits to appeal to different senses. Select items that can be viewed (posters, slide shows), touched (medical equipment, anatomical models), and heard (the voice of the decedent on a home video) to draw on all of the learning styles of the jurors.

Consider the use of an anchor exhibit. This could be one exhibit that pulls together the theories of liability, for example, or an exhibit that ties the jury down at some place that the attorney returns to. Again, it depends on the case. But an anchor exhibit in a medical malpractice case would be a timeline that explains the chronology of the case, something that the attorney will repeatedly refer to. It would be something that the attorney can use on opening statement to tell the story, something that the fact witnesses can use to place their participation in the events along the chronology of time and, of course, something the experts could use.

For example, the plaintiff may argue that a pressure-relieving bed should have been used earlier in the hospital admission. The bed is not mentioned in the records until just before the patient was sent to a nursing home. It does not appear in any of the hospital records until the last day. The timeline will be used as an anchor exhibit to show that this patient went into the hospital with a rather lengthy history of medical problems. She was a high-risk patient, and not until the very last day did the hospital do certain things that should have been done from the beginning. It turned out to be too late and the patient was discharged. In that type of a case the timeline would be considered an anchor exhibit—something that is there all the time, that is used repeatedly and, hopefully, is not put up and taken down. A lot of defense attorneys request the judges to instruct the plaintiff's attorneys to please remove the exhibit when they are done because they find it prejudicial and inflammatory. It hurts their case and they want it out of there as soon as possible. If the plaintiff's attorney can successfully argue, "Your Honor, I am going to be referring to it many times during the trial, and it does not make sense to put it up, take it down, put it up, take it down," then the judge may overrule that objection. That would be a win on the part of the plaintiff's attorney in a very big battle to have that exhibit there throughout the duration of the trial.[37]

It is essential to be familiar with the room where the hearing, arbitration, mediation or trial will take place. Go to wherever you are planning to present the exhibits, for example, at a deposition. The important part is to find out where the deposition is going to be and to see the size of the room, working out what will be most comfortable for those sitting around the table versus the courtroom. This will help the attorney determine how much equipment to bring and what can be most effective and comfortable for everybody.

Look at the evidence from the viewpoint of the person who is going to be looking at it. It may look beautiful from the attorney's vantage point, but always view it from where the jury or the witness will sit, ensuring it has the same aesthetic and desired impact from there as well. If access to the room is not possible, call someone familiar with the room and say, "Look, I am going to be lugging a lot of equipment. I just need to know the room size so everyone is comfortable. Can you give me a little bit of an idea? Is there lighting in the room; is it a room with windows, versus a conference room with no windows? Are there enough plugs, enough outlets?" The attorney needs to be knowledgeable about these details before getting there. Avoid getting there and finding out there are not enough outlets and you did not bring enough extension cords or power outlets. Then you are scrambling at the last minute, and everyone is standing around waiting for you. The more prepared you can be, the better.[38]

Planning is also essential at the beginning of the trial. To avoid delays and disruptions with the flow of testimony, meet with opposing counsel before trial and review exhibits so that objections can be handled before the jury is seated. The judge and jurors resent time-wasting tasks that could have been handled earlier. Rogers[39] gave the attorney he was working with a CD of photos that were critical to the case, and uploaded them onto an FTP server so he and the defense attorneys could download the photos. He asked the attorney to send the photos to the defense counsel. At trial, the defense attorneys alleged they never received their copies and so could not tell whether the images had been enhanced. The judged barred the use of the photos because they had not been tendered to the other side. Be sure to prepare early and confirm the other side received the exhibits.

Plan the presentation of exhibits in the specific order of negligence, causation, and damages.[40] While liability in a nursing malpractice case may be self-evident to the attorney, it can be dangerous to assume the jury will view the case the same way.

The attorney should expect the unexpected during trial. A visual aid may be ineffective, not allowed, or become nonfunctional at the most inopportune time. The fall-back position might entail making the points verbally. Do not unravel before the audience when the unexpected occurs.[41]

B. Simplicity

The exhibits should use simple pictures or symbols with as few words as necessary. The use of consistent labels or titles provides context. Each slide or visual aid should present a single thought. Avoid excessive or bright colors, changes in font, more than six words per line and six lines per slide, or small font size.[42]

C. Budget

After developing a budget for the production or purchase of demonstrative evidence, consider a less expensive alternative. Some exhibits can be prepared in such a way as to make them reusable. Does the potential value of the case justify the amount of money needed to produce the demonstrative evidence? Other exhibits may be borrowed from another attorney, physician, or medical school. Other attorneys in the area may be willing to share the costs of a key piece of evidence for certain types of cases. Litigation is expensive. Exhibit preparation can be one of the largest expenditures for trial. The cost of exhibits can become prohibitive, in terms of both the time to make them and the cost to produce them. Obviously, the expense of the exhibit, in terms of the amount of time and money it takes to produce it, should not exceed the exhibit's overall usefulness at trial. The value of a case will in large measure dictate the sophistication and expense of the exhibits used.

D. Effect

Medical evidence can have a dramatic effect on the jury. In an effort to gauge the success of an exhibit, show the demonstrative evidence to laypeople well before the settlement meeting or trial. The staff of a law firm, although conveniently accessible, may not be the best audience. Focus groups or independent persons brought in for mock trials may provide useful reactions to the exhibits. At trial, introduction of a particularly vivid photograph should be timed to have the maximum effect on the jury. The exhibits should be covered and out of sight until it is time to present them to the jury.

When color, pictures, symbols, printed words, and spoken words are combined effectively, their impact as a whole is greater than the sum of the parts. The message is understood more easily and retained longer.[43]

Consider using large flat panel LCD or plasma monitors or LCD projectors with a good presentation screen so that the exhibits will be as large as possible. These can be rented from your exhibit consultant or local audio-visual vendor. Place demonstrative aides in a position to help the expert teach the jury. They should be situated so that opposing counsel is forced to move to see them and ideally is isolated from the jury.[44]

TIP: Show the strongest piece of evidence to the jury as early as possible.

E. Comfort Level

The attorney should be comfortable with handling the exhibits. Preparation with showing a computer animation, picking up and handling medical equipment, or presenting photographs will improve the confidence of the attorney. When using some of the new computer-based technologies, to be discussed in further detail below, consider the operator's skill and comfort level. If trial counsel finds that operation of the equipment is too distracting, an experienced assistant must be available to handle the exhibits and troubleshoot any technical problems. The exhibits are needed to assist the trier of fact, but should never be so elaborate that the trial attorney is distracted from the primary responsibilities in presenting the case. Also, consider the receptivity of the judge to this technology. Some judges may be tolerant, if not sympathetic; others may reject the offered evidence outright.

Ensure that equipment is working before turning to it during trial. Investing in purchased or rented equipment, being thoroughly familiar with how to use it, and having backup equipment available and an alternative way to present evidence will increase the attorney's comfort. One of the challenges of using digital presentation systems is that there really should be somebody in the courtroom operating it who is not fulfilling another role. If the attorney does not have somebody in the office who is fluent with the software,

then the attorney should not be running it himself. Very few attorneys can stand on their feet, look for documents, listen to the answers to the questions, watch the body language of the judge, watch the body language of the jury, think of the next question, and work the computer at the same time. That is a lot to ask of even the best attorneys. So you need somebody in the courtroom.

If there is somebody in the office who can master it, it should probably be a younger associate because it gives that associate time in the courtroom to watch and learn a superior. Many attorneys do not have that luxury, which means they hire a company to operate in the courtroom in addition to renting the equipment, which can get costly. These are some of the aspects to consider in planning.[45]

TIP: Effective demonstrative evidence should be objection-proof, time-saving, easy to understand, memorable, interesting and useful to the jury, and free of adverse inferences.[46]

22.11 Overview of Presentation Systems

Counsel can select from a variety of methods of presenting evidence. The four basic approaches include:

1. Paper system
2. Optical projector with screen
3. Electronic projector
4. Digital system

A. Paper System

The paper system uses flip charts, mounted exhibits, and enlargements of medical records as described above. This has historically been the most commonly used method of presenting demonstrative evidence. It has the highest comfort level for many attorneys and requires the lowest skill level.

Be sure the juror can easily see and read the exhibits. Sit in the jury box before the trial starts or during a break to ensure the chart is legible from all seats. A chart that looks sufficiently large in the confines of the attorney's office may appear very small once brought into a courtroom. Also, if using overlays or laminated exhibits, check if there is any glare or reflection on the plastic from nearby windows or light fixtures. Be careful also when using matte laminates on trial exhibits, as they may tend to mute colors and take away from the overall look of the chart. Ask the graphics vendor for samples of exhibits with different surfaces or laminates if concerned about this potential problem. After testing the exhibit in the courtroom, put a small tape mark on the floor as a reminder about where to set up the easel.

1. Advantages

Trial-size exhibits are familiar to most if not all trial attorneys and judges. The trial attorney is unlikely to encounter any resistance from the judge regarding enlarged documents. The use of posters or enlargements of medical illustrations or key documents does not rely on technology in the courtroom. There is no need to be concerned about electrical outlets or equipment failure. Successful use of this presentation system relies on adequate lighting and adequately sized exhibits. A minimum amount of equipment is needed. A clear, no-glare overlay can be added to the front of the exhibit to allow for annotations.

At trial, counsel is responsible for selecting the appropriate exhibits and mounting them without assistance. Little can go wrong with the use of enlarged documents, with the exception of forgetting to bring them to court, getting them hopelessly out of order if a large number of enlargements are to be used, or selecting documents for enlargement that have inadequate font size. It is relatively easy to create and use exhibit notebooks for the jury containing paper exhibits if permitted in the locale. Eight-and-one-half-inch by 11-inch reproductions of key documents can be placed in indexed binders so the jury can follow along and refer to the exhibit during deliberations.

2. Disadvantages

The printing and mounting of each exhibit can be costly, running from $50 for black and white material to $200 or more for each color board. The disadvantages of using enlarged pages include the need for advance preparation, and their unwieldy size. Companies that enlarge exhibits usually require some lead-time. The ability to add a finished, mounted exhibit after the beginning of trial may be severely hampered by the availability of the outside vendor. Some law firms with high-volume trial work have created their own in-house graphics departments. This staff can provide last-minute support, but it is available only to a select few. Most trial attorneys must plan exhibits ahead of time to avoid last-minute changes.

A final disadvantage is that when a full page of a record is enlarged and placed on an easel in front of the jury, the jurors may become distracted by reading the entire page instead of the section that is the subject of the witness's testimony.

B. Optical Projector-and-Screen Systems

The next step up from enlargements of documents is transparencies shown on overhead projectors. The image may appear on a screen or a light-colored wall. The transparency projector is versatile and a favorite tool of lecturers. With properly created transparencies, the projector can show key medical documents, major points in opening and closing arguments, medical illustrations, site maps, and so on.

TIP: Use masking tape to create a window or border on either side of the transparency to prevent light from leaking around the edges. This also makes it easier to align the transparency on the plate.

Another variation of the transparency projector is the erasable white board with a small printer. The attorney or witness draws on the board during key points of the trial. Hitting a print button coverts the image into a piece of paper, which can be admitted into evidence to preserve the drawings.

1. Advantages

Transparencies are easily made. Most office copiers or laser printers can be used to create transparencies using film specific to that machine. A box of transparency film is inexpensive. Film with colored borders, which add visual interest, is also available. It takes more time to plan and properly design a transparency than it does to print it on the copier. The actual production of the transparency takes seconds. Revision can be done easily and quickly. Key portions of the document can be highlighted with yellow or colored transparency film laid on top of the original film.

Expert witnesses with a teaching background are comfortable with the use of transparency projectors. They may already have appropriate transparencies prepared to teach some of the medical issues in the case. For example, an orthopaedic consultant may have transparencies of the hip joint or of the plates and screws commonly used to repair a fall-related fracture.

Another advantage of this equipment is that little can go wrong with the operation of the equipment. Bulbs in projectors rarely burn out, although it is important to have a spare bulb and know how to change it. Lightweight and portable projectors make transportation of the projector much easier than in the past when the units were bulkier.

Find a machine that allows changing the bulb by simply moving a lever from one side to the other. This can be done in seconds and avoids having to take the machine apart to remove an old bulb and install a new one. Also, look for a projector that will accommodate a full size sheet. Many machines have 9x9 inch openings, making it necessary to move the document around during the presentation.

2. Disadvantages

Courtroom wall surfaces and ambient light in the room may make it difficult to see the projected image unless the lights are dimmed. Dark panels on the walls may require the use of a screen, or tall windows may flood the room with too much light.

Familiarity with the courtroom is most important. The ability to place the machine in a position so that the jury and judge can see the screen may be impossible in certain courtrooms. If possible, experiment with different positions before trial begins. At the least, inspect the courtroom to locate electrical sockets and identify the need for extension cords. The ideal position for the jury is to have the screen parallel to the jury box. If the jury box is at a 90-degree angle from the judge, this may place the screen in such a way that the judge cannot see the image. The judge has more flexibility than the jury in terms of changing position but is sometimes reluctant to get off the bench in order to view an image, particularly when the projector is heavily used.

A small table for the projector is an important piece of equipment. Do not assume other courtroom furniture will be suitable. One of the authors (PI) once observed a judge become angry because the projector was balanced on the edge of the witness box in order to project an image onto the wall. The placement of equipment needs to be thought out ahead of time, well before the appearance of the projector in the courtroom.

TIP: Devise a system to keep transparencies in order and easily accessible. Consider the use of an associate, a paralegal, or a legal nurse consultant to handle the transparencies while counsel focuses on the witness or the jury.

Most policies and procedure manuals or medical records are formatted in portrait mode (i.e., with the short dimension running across the top of the document). This layout is ideally suited for the transparency projector. However, it is common for some records to have different page formats. Nursing home medication administration records and treatment records are commonly in landscape format. The layout of the projector makes it difficult to show a landscape document without repeatedly sliding it across the glass in order to show the portions of the document.

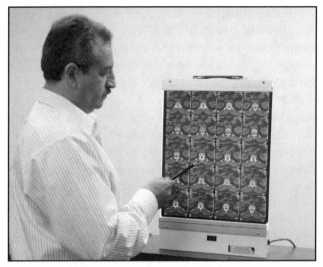

Figure 22.26 *A light box is an ineffective way to show radiological studies in court*

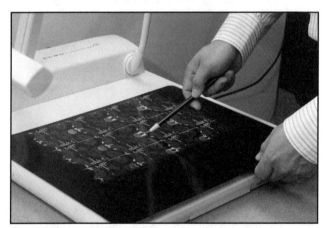

Figure 22.27 *A video document camera effectively projects images*

TIP: If using an overhead projector in court, make sure the glass opening is a full 11 x 11 inches. Most machines are only 9 x 9 inches, which means reducing the image in the copy machine to fully fit on the glass stage. Also, test the transparencies in the courtroom on the first day. Overhead projectors do not have zoom lenses, and it may be necessary to decrease the size of the image depending on the distance from the screen.

Transparencies have, for the most part, been replaced with PowerPoint presentations as more attorneys become comfortable with this presentation method. However, they are inexpensive and reliable for smaller cases.

C. Electronic Projectors

America is a visually oriented culture. Americans spend an increasing amount of time obtaining information from television and computer screens both at home and at work. Movies, network television, cable television, videos, MTV, computer games, digital video discs, and the Internet, among others, provide information visually and audibly. To effectively convey information to potential jurors in the courtroom, trial lawyers need to consider employing electronic technology.

Using an x-ray illuminator in court (Figure 22.26) is probably the worst way to testify from x-rays, MRI, CT scan or other radiological images. Especially with MRIs, the details that make up the important part of the testimony are small to begin with and the jury will be more than 10 feet away from the film image. Enlarged prints can be made from the selected frames and displayed on an easel, proving for marking and labeling by the witness.

A more common way to display images now is to use the video document camera (ELMO). See Figure 22.27. This avoids the need to pre-make exhibits, saving money by not preparing exhibits in the event the case settles, and allows more flexibility in showing only those portions of the film that are relevant. It is crucial that the trial attorney practice with the device before using it in court. She should be familiar with the controls and adjustments so that there can be a seamless presentation with the witness.

A number of companies sell video presenters, also called document cameras, which can be used to display a wide variety of objects. The camera on the presenter can zoom in on small objects, making it easy for the jury to see the object without the distraction of passing it around the jury box. The electronic presenter may be combined with a printer, video player, or laser disk. X-rays may be viewed with the use of the visual presenter with an artist's rendition of the x-rays to make the images more understandable to the jury.

A visual presenter combines projection equipment with either a camera or a computer. Visual presenters, including those originally marketed by DOAR and manufacturers such as Samsung and ELMO, are widely available commercially. They allow hard copies of documents to be placed on a machine and projected onto a screen for the jury to view. The set up is essentially a vertically mounted video camera that can zoom in on any document or object and send the signal to a projector or video monitor. They function as updated versions of overhead projectors, but do not require transparencies. The advantage of the visual presenter is that it allows a jury to see the exhibit at the same time the witness sees it. It also avoids having to hold up enlargements of pictures or other documents or placing them on easels, and it avoids the expense of enlarging documents for presentation on foam core boards. In addition to presenting documents, they are very effective in presenting x-rays and photographs.

1. Advantages

The visual presenter is a versatile machine that can be used for a wide variety of purposes. It has an unparalleled ability to display small objects or focus in on minute details of a medical record. If used with a projector of sufficient light output, it may not be necessary to dim the room lights. Be wary: if projecting photos where color and small details are critical, the images will look significantly better with the room lights off. Check the exhibits before the trial or during a break to see if it makes a significant difference to the viewer.

Alternatively, the output of the presenter may be hooked up to a television monitor or series of monitors that will permit the jury, counsel, witness, and judge to simultaneously see the images. The presenter may be attached to a DVD-R so that a record can be made of the presentation as it was made during the trial. With the decreasing cost of computers and graphics software, attorneys now have the means to create effective charts, graphs, and diagrams for courtroom presentation with minimal expense. Once generated, these graphics can be enlarged for traditional exhibits or they can be projected from a laptop computer through a digital projector. The primary benefits of using computer-generated graphics are their ease of modification and relative low cost. Key portions of the medical record can be transcribed and placed in boxes next to the actual page. In most cases, the typed text in the boxes will be much easier to read than the original.

A digital writing tablet is a useful tool that can be used with digital presentations. This is a device that allows the witness to annotate or mark an image being shown on the screen so that it can be preserved and marked into evidence, if needed. The device is similar to what one would see being used by commentators at football games during instant replays to show how the players move about the field. The imaging tablet is often used in conjunction with a light pen, which permits drawing on the image. With the touch of a button the highlighting can be erased, or the image printed for use by the jury during deliberations.

2. Disadvantages

Most documents are vertical (portrait) in format, and most video monitors are oriented horizontally (landscape). The image resolution of text in a video is not as good as transparency projection. The visual presenter is appropriate when the volume of work justifies its expense. Rental of projectors may be possible for law firms who have only an occasional use. The attorney planning to use this during a trial should allow plenty of time for setting up the equipment. It may be necessary to have another person available to run the equipment. There is a higher risk of equipment failure with this system. While problems can be quickly fixed, this is not the job of the trial attorney. An assistant should be on hand to handle unexpected emergencies. There was a time when jurors may have been suspicious of such a presentation, characterizing it as a slick show that may not be completely accurate. Nowadays, however, most people are accustomed to seeing these types of presentations and almost expect it of a competent attorney.

D. Digital System

Plaintiffs' personal injury attorneys have been on the forefront in terms of using technology to present their cases. "The second chair at the plaintiff's table these days is less likely to be an associate attorney than a $1,500-a-day technical director hired to spike the presentation with computer-generated graphics."[47] In a digital system, all documents including radiology films, video clips, and photos are converted to digital form and stored on a CD-ROM or hard drive of a computer. All applicable medical records are scanned, saved, and projected onto a large screen for the jury. Individual flat panel monitors are sometimes placed on counsel table, on the judge's bench, and near the witness box. Once stored, these documents can be indexed or bar-coded to allow immediate retrieval during direct or cross-examination. When using a visual presenter, the attorney can efficiently and effectively take a witness through a document, medical illustration, x-ray, photograph, or virtually any other record in the case. Depositions can be saved on the computer in digital or video form, and instantly used to cross-examine a witness. Presentation software can show images of medical equipment or key points in a summation.

Software programs used to create slide shows (Power-Point®, Sanction®, Trial Director®, and other packages) are valuable tools for creating effective presentations. Timelines, bulleted or numbered lists of key points, text quotes, and summaries of testimony can be easily created. Slides may be combined with scanned photographs of the client, medical equipment, the scene of the incident, or pages from the medical record. Ball[48] suggests the attorney accumulate visual evidence such as photographs of the witnesses and the scene of the injury, covers of standards, video footage of depositions, graphs, maps, scans of key documents, jury issues, bullet points, and so on as the case progresses.

1. Advantages

One consideration with regard to using newer technology in the courtroom is the cost-benefit ratio, taking into consideration the amount of material that will be presented and the cost to rent, transport, set up, and run the equip-

ment. This is not as much of a concern in firms that own their equipment and have an appropriate litigation support staff. In other firms that do not do as much trial work, the cost of setting up equipment, wiring, monitors, screens, and so forth, in courtrooms that are not so equipped can exceed the benefits of their use. If the attorney is showing a day-in-the-life videotape or a deposition in the courtroom, it is not complex to add a video document camera or laptop.

Many pages of exhibits or medical records can be economically stored and used in this type of system. The ability to project specific pages of the medical record, and to zoom in on or isolate key portions eliminates the need to enlarge and mount specific pages or documents. The attorney can switch from one exhibit or page to another with ease. The cost per exhibit is low. Generation X jurors, who have spent much of their time watching TV, or those who are computer literate may be most comfortable with this presentation style.

A presentation prepared with PowerPoint software can be very effective. In little time, slides can be prepared and modified, and can accentuate key points in a presentation, affording the fact finder the ability to see as well as hear what the attorney believes are the major facts and themes for the jury to remember. PowerPoint allows for a slide-by-slide presentation in a prepared sequence. It can be used easily with little practice by simply clicking on a wireless mouse to change the images and does not require much concentration taking away from the verbal presentation. Other programs, however, may require a more active role for an attorney or assistant in terms of calling up pages. An iPad (or other tablet) permits a more flexible presentation. A series of slides may be grouped into a category. Depending on the testimony, a specific category may be presented. This technology offers the trial attorney more flexibility. Care must be exercised in selecting the right tool for the job. Not everything that comes out of a projector and computer is "PowerPoint." Be wary of the desire to make a generic name out of a licensed trademark.

2. Disadvantages

Cost is a consideration in the use of technology. Many smaller firms are reluctant or unable to spend large amounts of money on outside consultants. Insurance carriers may be reluctant to fund the costs of this type of equipment and support service. These barriers may be overcome by the attorney who is willing to invest the time to become more technologically skilled.

The selection, scanning, and organization of key pieces of medical evidence takes time. This is not a presentation style that can be left until the last minute. The use of monitors and computers in the courtroom may meet resistance from the judge and jurors. Environmental barriers may be encountered, such as an inadequate electrical supply or glare. A technician may be needed to run the equipment, decreasing the attorney's control over the presentation of the material. There are risks of technical problems and equipment failures, such as the computer freezing or crashing. Unlike mounted exhibits, once the computer monitor is turned off, the image disappears and cannot be referred to later by the jury.

The size and layout of the courtroom is an important consideration. Smaller courtrooms create problems for placing monitors and screens. Some judges also have their own likes and dislikes regarding equipment choice and location. Counsel should take great care in deciding what material should be presented electronically and what material would be most effective in more tangible, board-on-easel presentations.

Even with these disadvantages, it is becoming clearer that more attorneys are exploring this type of technology. Younger attorneys in particular are usually more comfortable with computers than the previous generation. Courtrooms are being designed or renovated to permit use of computers and monitors. Some insurance carriers recognize that they need to invest resources to obtain advantages when it comes to presenting the evidence.

22.12 Design Principles of Presentation Software

Reinforcing the main points of the attorney's case through use of a variety of media helps jurors understand the details of a nursing malpractice case. Presenting the data in small chunks makes comprehension easier than showing jurors complex slides or exhibits. This is the same reason why telephone numbers are separated into three pieces and paragraphs are used in books.[49] The ability to create slides for a presentation has never been easier with the use of presentation software. The ease of use may mislead an attorney into believing that it is simple to create presentations. On the contrary, understanding the framework for building slides helps to create easy-to-view slides and memorable exhibits. Adherence to the design principles described below will enhance the jury's ability to understand the material presented on computer monitors and thus help the attorney achieve the objectives of the presentation. These design principles are also useful when preparing paper enlargements or charts.

A. Readability

The maximum number of letters per line on a slide should not exceed 30 to 35. The slide should be readable from the back row of a jury box or a distance of about 20 feet. A consistent format should be used. The font should not switch from italics to bold to underline without a logical reason. When a series of related slides are presented, the consistency of the format will help enhance comprehension of the material. An adequate amount of white space will increase readability. (White space refers to allowing sufficient borders and space within the slide to avoid crowding of information.)

Color combinations that are most effective include, in order of readability:

1. Black on yellow
2. Black on white, pale blue, or gray
3. Dark blue or green on white
4. White or yellow on dark blue

Look at the TV news and see what color combinations they are using for their graphics. Warm colors such as red, orange, yellow, and green draw attention to a key point. Cool colors, such as blue, green, or violet are useful for backgrounds. Make sure the colors contrast, however, in the event that there may be a juror who is color blind and will experience different colors as one shade of gray.

To increase readability, avoid having the exhibit printed on glossy paper or reflective surfaces. The sometimes uncontrollable glare in a courtroom due to nearby windows or light fixtures may render the board or screen difficult to read.

Consider also the associations jurors have with certain colors. Green is associated with safety and red suggests danger. To show that a defendant nurse "ran a medical stop sign" or ignored a warning signal, a plaintiff's attorney might use a graphic depicting a stoplight. Green might represent a safe condition, and red would depict the patient's clinical presentation. Red flags instead of bullet points might be used to highlight risk factors, such as those associated with developing pressure ulcers.[50]

B. Comprehension

Several techniques are useful for increasing the jury's comprehension. Allow the screen to be displayed for at least 30 seconds to enable the jury to read the material. Keep in mind that the material needs to be at the appropriate reading level for the jury.

TIP: The average reading level of adults is between the eighth and ninth grade level, with one in five adults reading at or below the fifth grade level. Studies have shown that adults read at levels four to five grades below the highest completed grade.[51]

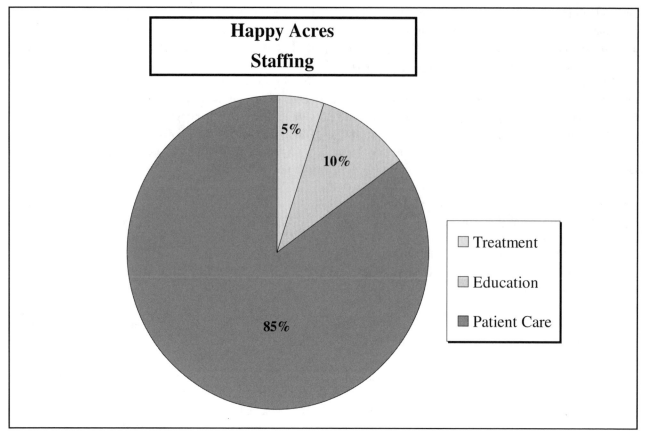

Figure 22.28 *Pie Chart Showing Dramatic Differences in Size of Wedges*

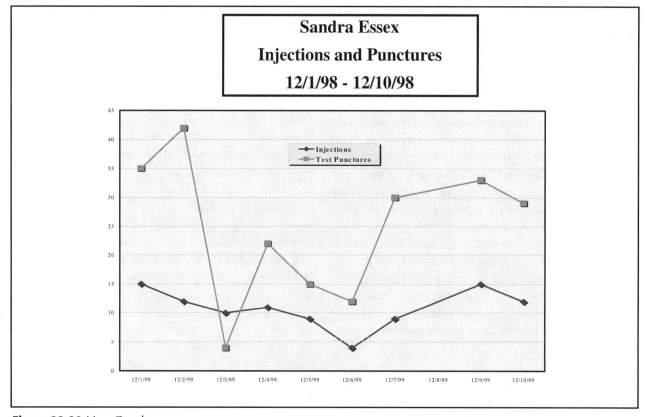

Figure 22.29 *Line Graph*

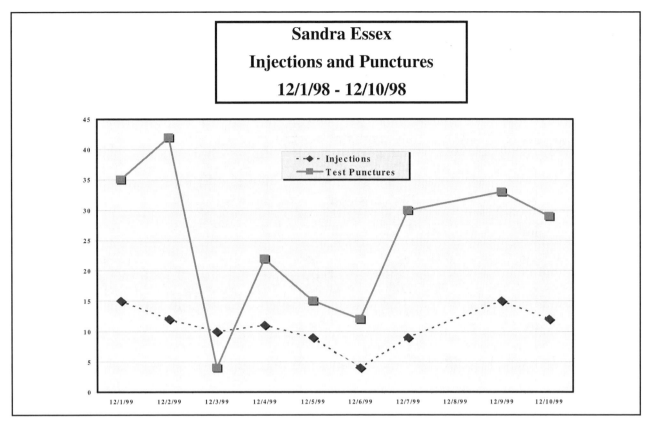

Figure 22.30 Variation in Style of Line

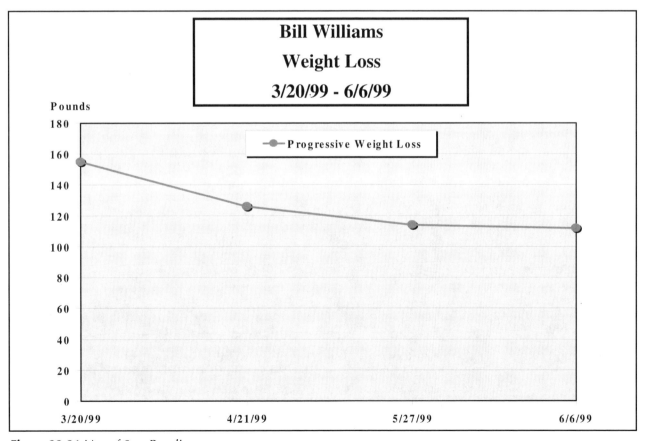

Figure 22.31 Use of 0 as Baseline

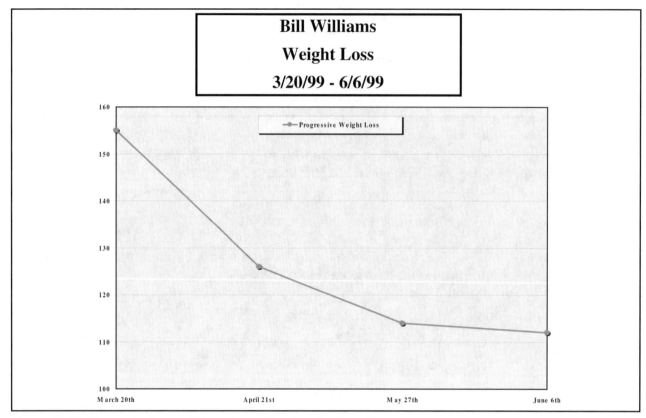

Figure 22.32 Change in Slope of Line when 100 is Used as Baseline

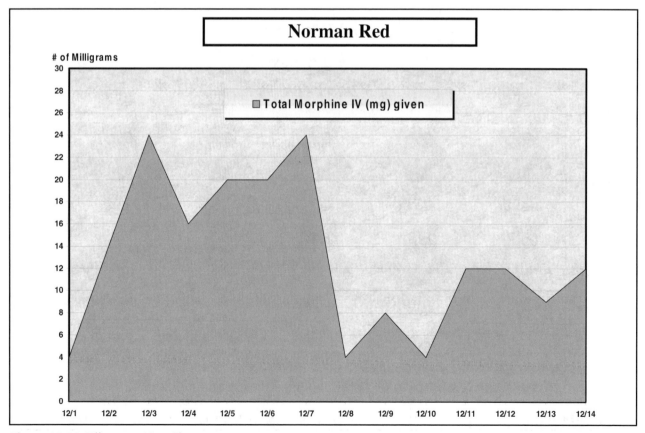

Figure 22.33 Silhouette Line Chart

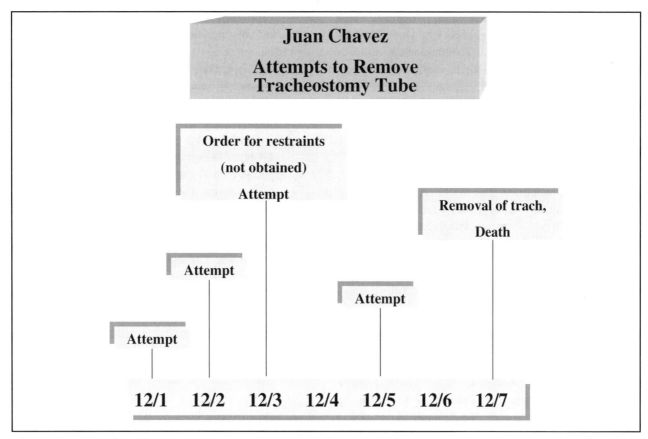

Figure 22.34 Timeline Showing Attempts to Remove Tracheostomy Tube

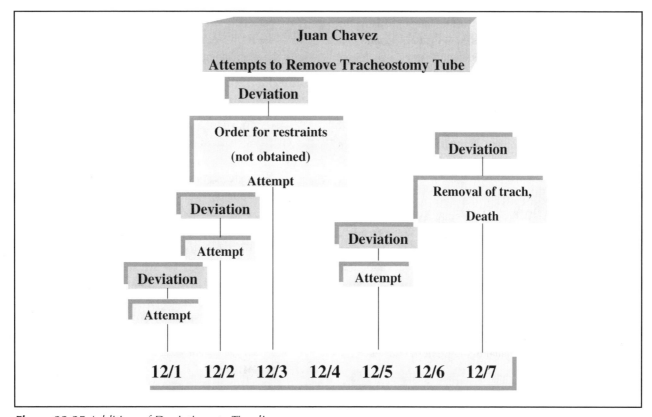

Figure 22.35 Addition of Deviations to Timeline

A safe assumption is that the average juror has a seventh grade education, and 10 percent of all jurors may be illiterate, although few will admit this. The attorney can indirectly address this by reading key points from an enlargement of a medical record or reading the screen as it is being presented. Comprehension of material will be enhanced by keeping it big, simple, and clear.

C. Chart Design

Several types of charts can enhance the presentation of key concepts. These include bar, pie, or line charts or timelines. Selecting sharply contrasting colors overcomes problems created when the colors are too close to each other in tone. Pie charts are most effective when there are significant differences in the size of the wedges (see Figure 22.28). It is easier to see the contrast in categories of information than if the pieces of the pie are about the same.

Line charts should incorporate labels that instantly identify the type of information being presented. The title should be in a large font with a brief name. If labels are used and the type of data is not obvious, the name of the vertical axis should be at the top of the axis and the name of the horizontal axis should be centered below the axis. A key can be included in the white space within the chart (see Figure 22.29). Varying the type of line that is used (Figure 22.30) makes it easier to differentiate between the two sets of data. To present data accurately and fairly, a baseline of zero should be used, as shown in Figure 22.31. Note what happens to the shape of the line when the baseline starts at 100 pounds instead of 0 (Figure 22.32). Silhouette line charts are useful for demonstrating fluctuations in data (see Figure 22.33).

Simple timelines can be created in a sequential manner. For example, consider a case of a patient who was ventilator-dependent and made multiple attempts to remove the tracheostomy tube. A timeline can show the sequence of events (Figure 22.34) step by step, coupled with the deviations for failure to obtain restraints (Figure 22.35).

22.13 Preparation

Consider the importance of being prepared. Rogers[52] offers some guidance to trial attorneys. The attorney who makes an opening statement that incorporates a slide presentation that is not rehearsed will look stilted, confused, or ineffective. His key points include:

1. The earlier you start preparing, the better. Start to think about the visual evidence at the outset of the case.

2. Digitize discovery information with an eye towards displaying it in the courtroom. Answers to interrogatories, statements, logs, and other important information should be displayed for the jury if they help the case.

3. Assemble the electronic documents in a workable chronology. Use a program, such as CaseMap, to create chronologies and timelines.

4. Take video depositions whenever possible. This enables a videographer or court reporter to synchronize the video deposition with the transcript, and permits the attorney to create video clips for use in mediations, opening statements, and cross-examination.

5. Keep adding to your case story board as you develop information. Integrate key documents, photos, and illustrations into a visual narrative.

6. Think about ways to illustrate the story. For example, Rogers worked on a nursing malpractice case and used photos from the surgery in the opening statement to underscore the gravity of the plaintiff's blood clot and to set the stage for damages considerations.

7. Think about how the jury will see the little things in your case, and use technology to emphasize them.

8. Be sure to turn all your exhibits over to the defense. Confirm they received them.

9. Use whatever you need to get your point across. Use a combination of media presentations to communicate with your jurors or mediators. Provide multisensory explanations of the case through boards, handouts, models, and computer presentations.

10. Practice with your technology before making any presentations. Do not be like the attorney who:
    - Talked ahead of his slides because he forgot to advance them
    - Switched off his remote during his opening statement instead of advancing the slides
    - Did not review his exhibits with the technician to coordinate how to get specific exhibits onto the screen
    - Called for a document the technician had never heard of
    - Called for exhibits that had not been given to the technician

11. Have a back up computer and other equipment available in the courtroom.

22.14 Summary

The attorney who walks into a courtroom should be an advocate on behalf of clients and possess certain communication skills that allow her to be effective in this position. The law, by tradition being oratory, does not prepare the practitioner during the school years for this additional role. It is one that must either come naturally or be honed through additional training and practice, often under the tutelage of seasoned colleagues and superiors. Many courses are available, some run by professional actors and drama specialists, that can help the trial attorney with the skills needed to present cases more effectively before a jury. It is necessary, however, to gain additional understanding of the dynamics of using demonstrative evidence as part of the courtroom presentation, and the more tools that are used, the more difficult it can be to orchestrate all the components of today's courtroom technology. The goal of making a seamless presentation of the evidence can be attained with some practice so that the jury is never aware of the medium being used, only the message.

Trial lawyers are using an increasing array of visual exhibits to assist the jury in understanding their cases. Simple, uncluttered formats assist in comprehension. Always keeping the juror in mind, the exhibits should be designed to persuade, aid in understanding, and inform the juror. As technology advances, means by which attorneys are able to present information to the jury will continue to expand. Computer-based presentation systems will undoubtedly play a larger role in the courtroom. Attorneys will need to familiarize themselves with these systems in order to take advantage of this technology and to meet jurors' expectations in terms of the way that they receive information. Regardless of the means by which exhibits are presented to the jury, attorneys still need to plan for the exhibits they will use, and to prepare them well in advance of trial.

Endnotes

1. The authors thank these co-authors for contributions to previous editions: Samuel L. Davis, Helen Griff Chalier (formerly Weisgal) Esq., and Wendy Neggers Esq.

2. Panish, B. and C. Spagnoli, "Take technology to trial," *Trial* (July 2002): 39-46.

3. Vesper, T., "Add dynamics to direct examination," *Trial* (September 2003): 46-50.

4. Perdue, Sr., J. M. and J. M. Perdue, Jr., "Putting the pieces together," *Trial* (May 2003): 39-47.

5. Iyer, P., *Writing Handbook for LNCs*, Flemington, NJ, Med League Support Services, Inc. 2010.

6. *Order in the Classroom Videotape. National Jury Trial Innovations' Project,* Chicago: International Association of Defense Counsel Foundation, 1998.

7. Landau, D. "After the fall," *TRIAL,* April 2009, 34-40.

8. Fed. R. Evid. 401.

9. See Fed. R. Evid. 403.

10. *Id.*

11. See Fed. R. Evid. 801 and 802.

12. Fed. R. Evid. 801.

13. Fed. R. Evid. 803(3).

14. Fed. R. Evid. 803(6).

15. Perdue, Jr. J. M., "The art of demonstrative evidence," *Trial* (May 2005): 46-51.

16. Fox, G., "Animate your medical negligence case," *Trial* (July 2002): 41.

17. Appelbaum, S. and Iyer. P. *Show, Not Tell Teleseminar,* Med League Support Services, 2009, www.medleague.com.

18. See Fed. R. Evid. 901(a).

19. Fed. R. Evid. 901(b) (1).

20. Fed. R. Evid. 104.

21. See note 7.

22. *Vergott v. Deseret Pharmco,* 463 F.2d 12 (5th Cir. 1972).

23. Vergott, supra.; *Wagner v. York Hospital,* 415 Pa. Super. 1, 608 A.2d 496 (1992).

24. See, e.g. *Carson v. Polley,* 689 F.2d 562 (5th Cir. 1982).

25. Personal communication Delilah Cohn, 1998.

26. See note 7.

27. See note 16.

28. Belli, M., "Demonstrative evidence: seeing is believing," *Best of Trial*. Washington, D.C.: ATLA Press, 1990.

29. *Id.*

30. Haviland, K. and Iyer, P. *Visual Evidence Teleseminar*, Med League Support Services, 2009 www.medleague.com.

31. Horst, R. and M. Rosenberg, "Animation Evidence in the New Millennium Courtroom," *For the Defense* (March 2002): 34-56.

32. *Id.*

33. Heninger, S., "Persuasive proof," *Trial* (April 2000): 55.

34. See note 15.

35. Davis, S., "A practical guide to videoconferencing," *Trial* (March 2000): 48-53.

36. Joye, M., "Avoiding 10 pitfalls of demonstrative evidence," *Trial* (November 2000): 94-101.

37. See note 17.

38. See note 30.

39. Rogers, M. "Practice makes perfect visual presentations," *TRIAL*, June 2009, 44-48.

40. See note 36.

41. Dempsey, D., "Create effective graphics in the courtroom," *New Jersey Law Journal* (June 9, 2003): 30.

42. See note 15.

43. See note 3.

44. See note 15.

45. See note 17.

46. See note 3.

47. Gottlieb, H., "Holding the high tech edge," *New Jersey Law Journal* (February 27, 2006).

48. Ball, C., "Winning with PowerPoint," *Trial* (January 2005): 34-40.

49. Maher, T., *Demonstrative evidence for complex litigation: A practical guide*, Tucson, Arizona: Lawyers and Judges Publishing Co., 2005.

50. See note 15.

51. Brownson, K., "Education handouts: are we wasting our time?" *Journal for Nurses in Staff Development* (July-August 1998): 176.

52. See note 39.

Additional Reading

Atkinson, C., *Beyond Bullet Points: Using Microsoft Powerpoint to Create Presentations that Inform, Motivate, and Inspire*, Redmond, Washington: Microsoft, 2005.

Paradi, D. *The Visual Slide Revolution*, www.visualslider-evolution.com, 2008.

Chapter 23

Keeping the Jurors in Mind: Jury Research, Jury Selection, Themes, and Comprehension

Diane Wiley

23.1 Introduction

In the early 1970s, social scientists began taking a serious look at the dynamics involving juror decision making, how to determine bias and prejudice in jury selection, and how attorneys' styles of communication and word choice affect juror comprehension. In the beginning, this work centered on cases involving political issues and potential racial bias, such as the *Attica* and *Wounded Knee* trials. However, it was not long before social scientists began advising attorneys on all kinds of cases, and this led to the development of the field of trial consulting. A large body of work involving research into juror decision-making, courtroom communication, jury selection, and other related aspects of jury trials now exists.[1]

Trial consultants come from a variety of disciplines, including sociology, psychology, communications, marketing, and acting. Trial consultants provide services including:

- consultation on case presentation,
- witness preparation,
- voir dire,
- jury selection assistance,
- focus groups and mock trials,
- venue evaluation surveys, and
- composition challenges.

Trial consultants contribute to many aspects of the jury trial process, including the use of open-ended questioning of jurors and an understanding of the problems of courtroom communication. Nursing malpractice cases involve many issues that many jurors will have experience with and/or opinions about. The chapter defines the basics about some of the services trial consultants offer and how those services can help the trial team in preparing for trial and jury selection in nursing negligence cases.

23.2 Understanding Jurors: Pre-Trial Jury Research

Pre-trial jury research refers to the use of focus groups and mock trials in preparation for trial. Many variations of focus groups and mock trials exist, but usually they consist of one or more groups of juror-eligible participants who listen to presentations by attorneys and then either discuss the case with a moderator or deliberate to a verdict. The participants are recruited from the jurisdiction in which the case will be tried.

A. Why Do Pre-Trial Research?

It is easy for attorneys immersed in their cases for years to forget that jurors do not approach the case the same way as attorneys do. Jurors do not know what the law and jury instructions are until the end of the case, after their impressions about the evidence and what it means are already formed. Of course, all jurors do not look at any given case the same way, so their life experiences and attitudes will play a formative role in how they view the issues. Understanding how different experiences, assumptions and attitudes will affect jurors' perceptions can inform attorneys' strategies for jury selection and case presentation.

The increasingly complicated and technological nature of health care creates a number of problems for plaintiffs and defendants in trial. There is now more medical jargon used in the field. Attorneys and medical witnesses often do not realize they are speaking a language not understandable to many of the jurors. It is difficult, if not impossible, to persuade jurors to assume a perspective if they cannot comprehend the attorney's position. Jurors often report in post-trial interviews that they did not understand key concepts at the beginning of the trial, or the mechanism of injury the plaintiff or defendant was asserting. Any lag in comprehension means a loss of valuable persuasion time.

Some jurors believe the standard of care is whatever care they received for the same or similar condition. Each year, jurors have a greater awareness of various medical conditions and treatments. Jurors' expectations about the kind of nursing care a person should receive are based on their own experiences or the experiences of people they know. They are bombarded with television shows and news articles about medical advances, medical treatment horror stories, medical malpractice insurance problems, tort reform, medical sitcoms, and dramas. The Internet reports news of medical errors announced by major hospitals. What used to be local stories are now available to people throughout the country. All this media information combines with jurors' ideologies and personal experiences to produce a "juror burden of proof," which may or may not have anything to do with the legal burden of proof. This also leads jurors to draw conclusions about what responsibilities a patient has for his own health and health care.

Many jurors think they know how the courts work and what the rules are, and see themselves as somewhat expert in relation to court issues. Increasing numbers of cases are being tried, so some jurors come to court having previously served as jurors.[2]

Attorneys often talk to people they know about their cases, getting feedback and insight into how those not connected to the legal field might look at the case. Pre-trial research is a systematic way of finding out what experiences, assumptions, attitudes, and ideologies jurors might bring to the case and how that will interact with the specific case facts.

Many ways to do pre-trial research exist, but the primary methodologies are focus groups and mock trials, sometimes called trial simulations.[3] These involve discussion groups of juror-eligible participants from the jurisdiction in which the trial is to be held and can be conducted by a trial consultant or the attorneys themselves.

1. Identify strengths and weaknesses of the case

Mock trials and focus groups help the trial team understand how potential jurors view the events that gave rise to the case, both as to liability and damages. By presenting the story of what happened and having the mock jurors discuss it, the trial team understands where more information is necessary for the jurors to understand the client's perspective. Most jurors do not understand a nurse's duties and responsibilities. They do not understand nursing standards, nursing charting responsibilities, or the chain of command used by nurses if they disagree with a doctor's decision. Consequently, jurors might make assumptions harmful to either side of a case. By hearing what mock jurors have to say, the trial team is better able to structure the voir dire, opening, and witness testimony to better address issues, misinformation, and questions the trial jurors might have.

2. Assess comprehension

One of the primary purposes of pre-trial research is to evaluate the ability of jurors to comprehend the material being presented. An evaluation can be made about comprehension by using questionnaires asking jurors about their opinions on the presentations they have heard and by listening to the discussions among the jurors and between the jurors and moderator. The technical complexity of medical conditions and their treatment modalities may or may not need to be broken down into more understandable pieces of information than the trial team originally thought. The trial team learns by careful listening and analysis of how much information (and misinformation) most jurors possess about a given subject and how much the presentation of technical medical data must be simplified. The trial team also evaluates how the attribution of liability is affected by jurors' comprehension of the medical aspects of the case as opposed to the behavior of the participants.

TIP: Mock jurors often make analogies to their own life experiences when discussing what occurred at the hospital or nursing home, and these can provide insight into how they simplify the issues to make them understandable and relevant to their own life experiences.

---

3. Develop themes

Attorneys are increasingly aware of the importance of using themes in case presentation for purposes of persuasion and comprehension. The use of themes in nursing negligence cases is particularly important due to the complex facts and medical terminology involved.

Themes and repetitive phrases can be tested in focus groups and mock trials to see if the mock jurors pick up on them and use them in their discussions. Often the mock jurors will identify themes that the attorneys missed or that are more powerful.

4. Identify juror traits

Focus groups and mock trials identify how mock jurors' experiences, assumptions, attitudes, and ideologies interact with the case-specific facts and issues. This information is invaluable in preparing for jury selection and case presentation. It is essential to learn what is likely to most affect potential jurors in their analysis of the case, because attorneys are allowed very few peremptory challenges.

The information gained is very useful in constructing voir dire questions and strategy for jury selection, but remember that due to the number of mock jurors involved in the discussion groups, it is rare that this information can be used to predict juror verdicts. The sample size is not large enough. Jury research can, however, help to identify experiences and attitudes to be explored during jury selection.

5. Test graphics and demonstrative evidence

Graphics and demonstrative evidence are essential tools in nursing negligence cases. However, not all graphics are of equal quality. Many trial consultants are dismayed by the complexity of the graphics used in court. Overly complex graphics confuse jurors and fail to convey what the attorney wants to communicate. By showing demonstrative evidence to mock jurors, the trial team can learn what conclusions the mock jurors draw from what they see. There are a number of excellent references available for preparing graphics, including *Demonstrative Evidence for Complex Litigation* and *Modern Visual Evidence*.[4]

6. Settlement evaluation

Focus groups or mock trials help evaluate settlement possibilities. The trial team can use this information when making recommendations to the client and guiding the client to more realistic expectations. As stated previously, the results of the focus group or mock trial cannot be relied upon to be predictive of the outcome of the actual trial; however, an analysis of the discussion and conclusions of the mock jurors provides the trial team with valuable information about the range of likely trial outcomes.

B. Confidentiality

Confidentiality agreements are essential. Examples of these agreements are in many of the references provided below. Mock jurors' signatures on confidentiality agreements do not guarantee they will not talk to anyone about their participation in jury research. For this reason, mock jurors must be carefully screened to assure they have no connections to the opposing parties or their attorneys.

C. Mock Trials

Mock trials involve two or more attorneys making presentations from the perspectives of the various parties to the case. They can last anywhere from four hours to two or three days. Most often mock trials on medical negligence cases are held on a Saturday for four to eight hours, which allows time for the mock jurors to hear enough about the case to fully understand the issues. At the National Jury Project, these presentations are called "clopenings," a phrase coined by one of the author's clients meaning a combination of opening and closing. Presentations are structured like an opening with a small amount of argument allowed. Depending on the time frame, there may also be testimony, preferably presented on videotape, and sometimes there is time for a short closing by each side. Many variations of mock trials, also called "trial simulations," exist. The biggest challenge is getting sufficient information to the mock jurors while still leaving time for deliberation amongst themselves. The various approaches share some characteristics, covered below.

1. Recognizing the importance of balance

The trial team must put as much energy into developing a compelling case for the opposition as it does in developing its own case. For example, if the plaintiff's attorney wants to show the mock jurors parts of the "Day in the Life" video of the client, there should be a video made for the defense expert who talks about the damages issue. If the defense attorney wants to present a video of the defendant nurse practitioner, then a video should be made of someone playing a plaintiff expert talking about the liability issues.

TIP: The results of any mock trial or focus group will only be as useful as the balance between the presentations of the plaintiff and defense cases.

---

2. Doing it yourself or hiring someone

Many attorneys conduct mock trials and focus groups on their own, without the assistance of trial consultants.[5] Trial consultants handle the logistical problems of finding a place, recruiting mock jurors, putting together questionnaires, helping with preparation of the presentations and exhibits to be shown to the mock jurors, and evaluating the data. Trial consultants keep a close eye on balance issues. They also possess an objectivity that may be lacking in the trial team due to their being immersed in the case.

3. Choosing the participants

The mock trial should occur in the jurisdiction in which the case will be tried. However, if the jurisdiction is very small, it might be wise to pick another county very similar in terms of population, size, and demographics. The mock jurors should be as representative as possible of the trial jurisdiction and of the types of jurors who might be able to sit on the actual jury. For example, if the trial will be long, the participants should not include people who would likely be excused by the judge for hardship.

Persons who have obvious bias or pose a security concern should not be allowed on the mock jury. For example, someone whose family member works for the defendant hospital should not be allowed to participate, nor should someone who knows the plaintiffs or their family members. Those who have had a medical negligence claim or have a family member who has made a claim should be excluded. Most trial consultants exclude people who work in the news media since there is a risk they will violate the confidentiality agreement and write a news story about the experience.

4. Scripting the presentations

Presentations made for the opposing side in both mock trials and focus groups should be written out in at least annotated outline form, considering the time constraints and need for balance. Most trial consultants suggest the presentations be scripted out in advance so they can be compared and evaluated for balance, comprehension, completeness, and accuracy. As with any good opening statement, the attorney should not give mock jurors the wrong impression of what the testimony will be.

The experience of writing out and critiquing the opposing presentations provides new insight to the trial team as to what the case involves. Mock jurors need to hear the story of what happened and what the conflicting testimony entails, not just a list of accusations and legal points.

Trial consultants can help the attorneys construct presentations that are understandable and persuasive for both sides.

TIP: Timelines given to the mock jurors for deliberations help them keep the facts straight and not waste time trying to reconstruct what happened instead of talking about their reactions to the presentation.

---

5. Using questionnaires

Most consultants use questionnaires at various points during mock trials and focus groups. Questionnaires can be used before mock jurors hear the presentations to evaluate their attitudes and life experiences, after each presentation to evaluate comprehension and opinions, and at the end of the mock deliberations. Again, balance is a key issue. If the questionnaires appear skewed towards one side or the other, the results will be skewed. Figure 23.1 provides examples of questions that could be asked after the plaintiff's attorney has presented the case in a mock trial.

1. The **strongest** or **most** convincing points in the case for Charles Patient are:
_____
_____
_____

2. The **weakest** or **least** convincing points in the case for Charles Patient are:
_____
_____
_____

3. At this point, what do you think caused Charles Patient to have a brain bleed?
_____
_____
_____

4. At this point, do you feel Nurse Cary did anything which violated the standard of care?
____ Yes ____ No
Why do you say that?
_____
_____
_____

5. At this point, do you feel Chuck Patient did anything which caused his injury?
____ Yes ____ No
Why do you say that?
_____
_____
_____

Figure 23.1 Examples of questions for mock trial participants

6. Evaluating the results

The most important point to remember about the results of any mock trial is that it *may or may not* predict the outcome of the actual trial. Mock trials identify what is most important to the mock jurors: what experiences, assumptions, attitudes and ideologies they bring to the case and how that affects their perceptions of the story and evidence. They identify motivations jurors ascribe to the various medical personnel and plaintiff. Mock trials identify how jurors analyze the case in relation to the jury instructions as well as the "juror burden."

Most consultants look for verdict shifts when analyzing data from the mock trial. A verdict shift occurs when a participant shifts from one position on an issue to the other, and provides information about what is most important to that mock juror in making that shift. Themes are tested to see if they assist jurors in coming to the conclusions the trial team wishes. They also help in evaluating damages perceived and what range of money award makes sense to the mock jurors.

Mock trials and other jury research help the trial team see how lay people respond to the issues and evidence. The trial team can learn what evidence is most important to the mock jurors and how to frame it by listening to how they approach the issues and argue their respective positions.

D. Focus Groups

Focus groups also involve a discussion with a small group of participants who are juror-eligible in the jurisdiction where the trial will occur. Focus groups are conducted several ways, but generally a moderator discusses aspects of the case with the mock jurors.

1. Opening statement groups

Attorneys have been practicing their opening statements before office staff, relatives, and friends for years. The opening statement focus group is a more formal way of getting feedback.

Remember that any feedback received based on hearing one side of a case will not tell the trial team how potential jurors will react after they hear both sides. Information learned includes:

- the level of comprehension the mock jurors have of the issues,
- whether they respond to the themes put forward,
- what questions they have that were not addressed, and
- what they anticipate the other side is saying.

TIP: The opening statement group allows attorneys to practice before a group of people similar to the jurors at trial who have no qualms about being brutally honest in their assessments.

---

2. Issues groups

Focus groups explore what experiences, assumptions, attitudes, and ideologies jurors bring to the case and how they interact with the case facts. These groups are particularly useful in the early stages of a case when attorneys are trying to identify the real issues. By conducting an issues group halfway through discovery, the trial team can learn what other questions it should try to answer through depositions or document requests.

The format for an issues group involves a moderator presenting short pieces of information and asking the mock jurors for their thoughts about those issues. The moderator must be neutral in the presentation of the facts if the information gained is to be useful.

3. Graphics groups

A focus group can be convened to evaluate the graphics to be used at trial. Good quality graphics are essential in communicating complicated information about nursing cases. Recent trends toward the overuse of graphics and the use of overly complicated graphics can obfuscate the issues they are supposed to illuminate, or in some cases leave jurors with an impression that is the opposite of what the trial team intended.

Exhibits intended to prove or disprove an argument can be shown to mock jurors for their reactions solicited if there is an accusation, for example, that the nursing chart was tampered with or not kept in real time. Medical illustrations can be shown to a focus group along with the testimony that will explain them, to determine if the mock jurors understand them.

4. Before taking the case

Some plaintiff's attorneys use focus groups to help them to decide whether or not to take a case. This can be particularly important if there is a question involving neg-

ligence of the patient or an issue with which the attorney is unfamiliar. In some instances, focus groups or mock trials completed before filing encouraged attorneys to request pre-filing settlements before a large investment has been made in a case in which the return is likely to be small.

Defense attorneys use focus groups before a case has been filed when they think there may be a reason to resolve the issue before litigation begins. Groups can be particularly helpful to defendants when negligence is clear and the only issue will be damages.

5. Evaluating witnesses

Controversy exists within the trial consultant community about whether or not witnesses should testify live before focus groups or mock trials. While useful feedback can be obtained from using live witnesses, this author feels the drawbacks outweigh the benefits. Opposing counsel might later ask the witness on the stand whether she has practiced testimony in front of a group of mock jurors, and how she changed the testimony as a result. Legal precedent on this subject cannot assure that this will not be viewed as breaching the attorney-client privilege. The risk is small, but the damage to the witness could be enormous at trial. Taping the witnesses and showing the tape to the mock jurors is a safer approach. The attorney and trial consultant can then use what they learned in preparing the witnesses without possibly compromising their trial testimony.

TIP: When taping witnesses, edit the tapes as little as possible. Some mock jurors become suspicious and obsess on the fact that a tape was edited, interfering with their evaluation of the witness.

E. Community Attitude Surveys

Community attitude surveys of the jurisdiction where the trial will take place are large-scale endeavors. Nursing and other medical negligence case issues are too complex to provide benefit from such surveys. They can, however, be useful if the case has received considerable news coverage.

The trial team can learn what effect the news coverage has had on the juror-eligible population. Such a survey can also be used to evaluate what attitudes potential jurors will have towards the hospital or clinic involved. They can determine how widespread knowledge is about the specific medical procedures or conditions involved, and what the expectations are about the type of nursing care a patient should receive. These surveys can be costly and are generally reserved for use in venue evaluation.

Figure 23.2 provides questions used to assess potential jurors' attitudes in medical malpractice cases. These same types of questions can be used in venue evaluation surveys:

1.   Have you or has anyone close to you ever been hospitalized overnight at General Hospital in West Egg?
      1.   Yes   (ASK Q1A)   3.   Refused   (SKIP TO Q2)
      2.   No   (SKIP TO Q2)   4.   Don't Know   (SKIP TO Q2)

      1A.   Is this: ____Yourself ____Spouse ____Child ____Other family member ____Friend

2.   Have you or has anyone close to you ever used the emergency room or any outpatient services at General Hospital in West Egg?
      1.   Yes   (ASK Q2A)   3.   Refused   (SKIP TO Q3)
      2.   No   (SKIP TO Q3)   4.   Don't Know   (SKIP TO Q3)

      2A.   Is this: ____Yourself ____Spouse ____Child ____Other family member ____Friend

3.   What is your opinion about the kind of care provided by General Hospital in West Egg?
      1.   Excellent   4.   Poor
      2.   Good   5.   Refused
      3.   Fair   6.   Don't Know

4.   Have you or has anyone close to you ever received any medical care from a nurse practitioner?
      1.   Yes   (ASK Q4A)   3.   Refused
      2.   No   4.   Don't Know

      4A.   Is this: ____Yourself ____Spouse ____Child ____Other family member ____Friend
      Please explain: _____
      _____

5.   How would you rate the kind of care you or someone close to you had from a nurse practitioner?
      1.   Excellent   4.   Poor
      2.   Good   5.   Refused
      3.   Fair   6.   Don't Know
      Why do you say that? _____
      _____

6.   Do you think medical care in Great County has been affected by lawsuits against hospitals and medical professionals in any way?

      1.   Yes   3.   Refused
      2.   No   4.   Don't Know
      Why do you say that? _____
      _____

7.   There have been claims made in the media that the high cost of medical malpractice insurance and large verdicts in court cases are driving doctors out of Great County. How do you think all of this discussion has affected your feelings about medical malpractice lawsuits?
      _____
      _____

Figure 23.2 Examples of questions used in a community survey

23.3 Venue Evaluation

Venue evaluation might consist of:

- a content analysis study of newspaper articles and other media stories which apply to a case or party,
- a review of census or hospital data relating to the percentage of patients in a jurisdiction, and
- an attitudinal survey done for purposes of evaluating potential jurors' attitudes towards a case or a party.

In most instances, the plaintiffs want to conduct a venue evaluation for purposes of making a motion for change of venue. It is very difficult to get a case moved to another venue. Changes of venue have been granted when the defendant hospital or doctor is the only or main source of medical care available in a county, and/or when there has been extensive news coverage of a case, but changes are rare.

Attorneys also file change of venue motions, knowing they are unlikely to prevail, with the hope of educating the judge as to issues in the case that warrant more extensive voir dire, individual voir dire, and the use of a voir dire questionnaire. If the attorney does not have the funds for a survey, or if there is extensive news coverage, affidavits from community members attesting to problems of bias and prejudice can be submitted in lieu of conducting a survey. An attorney who feels a change of venue is warranted should contact a trial consultant with experience in conducting, analyzing, and presenting testimony about such surveys, as they are both expensive and difficult to prepare and win. Trial consultants can also analyze news coverage and submit an affidavit in support of a change of venue.

Venue evaluation research can also be used when an option exists as to the county in which a case can be filed. This involves comparison of the counties as to the following:

- types of occupations and other demographic characteristics of the counties,
- usage of the defendant hospital or clinic and alternatives,
- news coverage of previous medical negligence cases,
- problems involving medical insurance and medical care, and
- tort reform issues.

23.4 Selecting and Working with Trial Consultants

Working with a trial consultant leads to a very close relationship, more so than other experts, because the trial consultant becomes a part of the trial team. In evaluating which trial consultant to hire, attorneys should contact other attorneys who do the same kind of work and ask about consultants with whom they have worked. Ask about the consultant's background and other attorneys with whom the consultant has worked. Call the attorneys for references. Obtain either a contract for the work or a letter of agreement. Most trial consultants expect to be paid by the hour or by the project. They will not agree to work on a contingency fee basis.

TIP: Most trial consultants provide a range of services from a small number of hours of consulting to full-scale mock trial projects. The attorney should discuss the specifics of the case and formulate a plan with the trial consultant, being clear about the dates by which the work should be completed.

It is the attorney's responsibility to provide the trial consultant with information relevant to the case. In general, the attorney should include:

- any motion papers which lay out both sides of the case and the issues involved, including mediation statements if available,
- a summary, either oral or written, laying out the opposing arguments and evidence,
- depositions of the plaintiff, defendants, and other relevant witnesses,
- expert reports and depositions, and
- jury instructions and verdict form from the case or a similar case in the same court or jurisdiction.

The more the trial consultant knows about the case, the more he will be able to identify the issues and the kind of help, which can be provided.

Many trial consultants perform much of the work over the phone without visiting the attorney's office except for witness preparation, research, and jury selection, so a consultant from anywhere in the country can be hired. Trial consultants should be hired by the law firm and not the law firm's client, so the trial consultant's work falls under the attorney-client privilege. (See Section 23.9 below for further discussion of the issue of privilege and discoverability of the trial consultant's work product.)

Most trial consultants keep a copy of the work product, whether it is a voir dire, opening statement, or research tapes. Since attorneys benefit from the previous work trial consultants did with other attorneys, it is mutually beneficial for the consultant to retain a copy of the material produced.

The consultant may use the tapes in giving presentations to attorneys or other trial consultants after the case has been resolved, depending on the confidentiality agreements with the mock jurors and the attorney. Trial consultants should ask for permission from the attorney before using excerpts from the research tapes in seminars or other presentations.

23.5 Jury Selection

Nursing negligence cases require thoughtful preparation of voir dire questions and jury selection strategy.

A. Preparation

1. Case analysis for jury selection purposes

The trial team should analyze the case from the perspective of the potential jurors when preparing for jury selection. The trial team should consider the following questions:

- What kinds of life experiences could a juror have had that will affect how she looks at the parties and the medical issues?
- What kinds of assumptions could jurors make about the parties in the case and about the medical issues that will help or hurt the case?
- What kinds of attitudes might a juror have about the parties and the medical issues?
- How might a juror's ideology impact how she evaluates the case?
- What does the juror have to believe in order for us to win?

2. Identify juror types

Every jurisdiction is different in terms of the range of occupations and circumstances of potential jurors. The trial team should think about the various types of jobs jurors have and how jurors' experiences at work might affect their perceptions of the case. Race and age are two other areas in which it is important to look at the impact on jurors' perceptions of the case. This will assist in preparing questions for jury selection. For example, jurors who have jobs which are highly structured and regimented might not understand the issues involved with a nurse making the independent decision to take a complaint up the chain of command.

Demographic characteristics of the jurors in a jurisdiction in which the attorney has not previously tried a case, or in a jurisdiction where there have been changes since the attorney last tried a case must be evaluated. Remember that attitudes are the most important, and attitudes can and do cross demographic lines.

3. Think through possible cause challenges

One of the biggest challenges to attorneys is convincing the judge to grant cause challenges. Attorneys who think ahead about the areas of questioning most likely to produce cause challenges are more likely to get them. Preparing voir dire questions to address these areas results in the attorney being better prepared to handle the issues more effectively when they arise.

Asking for a cause challenge too soon is a common mistake attorneys make in voir dire. If a juror says that she has been treated by one of the nurse practitioners involved in the case as a defendant, treating practitioner, or expert witness, the tendency of the plaintiff's attorney is to stop and ask for a cause challenge. The most likely outcome in that instance is that the judge will rehabilitate the juror by asking, "Can you be fair?" and most jurors will say, "Yes." A better approach is help the juror see for herself that she cannot be objective by asking the juror a series of questions, such as:

- How long have you seen the nurse practitioner?
- Do you think you would continue treatment with the nurse practitioner?
- Have you, or would you, recommend this nurse practitioner to a friend or family member?
- How would you describe the relationship you had with the nurse practitioner?
- Was your experience with the nurse practitioner pleasant and positive?
- Are there other people you know who have been to this nurse practitioner?
- Who recommended this nurse practitioner to you?
- Is the nurse practitioner connected to another doctor who you see regularly?
- Would you tend to believe this nurse practitioner if she testified about something related to the field of __?
- How do you think you will be able to be objective in this case when this nurse practitioner is going to testify for the [plaintiff or defense]?
- If this nurse practitioner testified to one thing, and another nurse practitioner you did not know testified to something else, do you think you would tend to believe the nurse practitioner you know?
- How would you put your positive or negative experience and feelings about this nurse practitioner out of your mind and be objective and impartial to both sides in this case?

TIP: Avoid asking jurors if they can be "fair." Everyone wants to believe they are a fair person. Use words such as "objective" and "impartial." Ask if the other side has an advantage, or if the connection or attitude would cause the juror to lean in one direction or another. Ask, "Are we starting out even with [the other side] with you?"

---

4. Research the judge's practice

If an attorney has never selected a jury in front of the judge handling the case, he should talk to other attorneys who have done so. Attorneys should ask the court clerk how the judge typically handles voir dire. Knowing the judge's practice well in advance of preparing voir dire questions is important. At the pre-trial hearing, attorneys should clarify how the judge expects to conduct voir dire. Attorneys should not assume anything. It is essential that attorneys in a new jurisdiction read the local rules of unfamiliar jurisdictions.

TIP: It is helpful for the attorney and trial team to observe the judge conduct a jury selection before trial.

---

5. Prepare the judge

A case might involve sensitive or controversial issues, which could result in a jury selection that is longer than usual. Attorneys should mention the possible need for sequestered questioning of some or all jurors, or the possible need for a case-specific voir dire questionnaire. The judge can then get used to the idea that the voir dire may take longer than expected.

6. Court questionnaires

The availability of the questionnaires filled out by jurors prior to coming to court varies from jurisdiction to jurisdiction, as does the amount of information they contain. Their usefulness is questionable in that they usually only ask very basic demographic questions, such as occupation, spouse, and children.

7. Ask for a case specific voir dire questionnaire

Over the last 30 years,[6] more courts have begun to allow case-specific questionnaires to be submitted to jurors before voir dire. Often called *voir dire questionnaires* or *supplemental juror questionnaires*, these are filled out by the jurors called specifically for the case before oral voir dire begins, and include questions relating specifically to the case.[7] A case-specific voir dire questionnaire is an efficient way to obtain information from the jurors and allows the attorneys to focus their voir dire questions on issues concerning each juror. They also provide jurors with privacy if there are experiences, attitudes, issues, or concerns they are reluctant to talk about in front of the other jurors in open court.

Many judges are impatient about allowing attorneys sufficient time to question jurors due to increasing caseloads and longer trials. Voir dire questionnaires can expedite voir dire, and help provide attorneys with the information they need for cause challenges and to intelligently exercise their peremptory challenges.

Voir dire questionnaires have three basic advantages over oral voir dire alone:

- Efficiency: Voir dire questionnaires can expedite the jury selection process and reduce wasted time.
- Privacy: Voir dire questionnaires offer potential jurors the opportunity to convey sensitive information to the court and the attorneys without revealing it to the rest of the jury panel.
- Honesty: The written format encourages more honesty and candor than oral questioning alone.

a. Motion and memorandum for questionnaire

Judges who have not utilized a voir dire questionnaire are often concerned about the practicalities involved. It is most effective to submit a written motion for a voir dire questionnaire, suggesting a process to be used and offering to make arrangements for copying the questionnaires and distributing them to the judge and opposing counsel. The memorandum should include any legal justification for the use of questionnaires in general, and a recitation of why the case issues included would best be handled by questionnaire. Attach a copy of a requested questionnaire to the motion. Sometimes judges who have not previously considered the use of a questionnaire will be more open once they see that the questionnaire is not lengthy and is a neutral document designed to gather relevant information.

b. Voir dire questionnaires are not a substitute for voir dire

Voir dire questionnaires do not replace oral voir dire. Attorneys and judges must still see the juror's demeanor in order to assess credibility. However, the questionnaire can efficiently collect demographic and attitudinal information about jurors, which may or may not require follow-up, and can identify jurors who should be examined out of the presence of the other jurors. The questionnaire allows the attorneys to focus their questions on relevant issues.

TIP: Voir dire questionnaires can be invaluable in courts where attorney-conducted voir dire is not allowed. In some instances, the use of a questionnaire will lead to the opportunity for more follow-up questioning than would have occurred without it.

---

c. The questions should be neutral

The voir dire questionnaire should be a neutral fact-gathering instrument. The attorney is less likely to face opposition from opposing counsel if the questions are designed to cover areas of concern to both sides, or pose a legitimate concern for one side. The judge might require that the parties agree on the questions to be used. Questions that advocate the attorney's position rather than simply gather information will undercut arguments that the questionnaire is being proposed in the interests of efficiency, respecting the jurors' privacy and benefiting all parties.

d. Length

Voir dire questionnaires might run from two pages to the 75-page questionnaire used in the O.J. Simpson case, depending on the jurisdiction. The length of the questionnaire submitted to the judge will likely influence whether or not it is permitted. Unless the case is a high profile case, most judges will not be inclined to grant a long questionnaire.

TIP: If the jurisdiction is one in which questionnaires have never been used, it is best to start out by submitting a four- to six-page questionnaire.

---

e. Sensitive Issues

Jurors may find many issues too sensitive to talk about in open court in front of the other jurors. These should be covered by the questionnaire and include such issues as:

* experiences in the hospital
* medical injuries or conditions they or family members have
* experiences with or feelings about the parties
* the jurors' religious affiliations if the hospital has a religious affiliation
* experiences with lawsuits
* attitudes about lawsuits

Many jurors are reluctant to discuss certain kinds of medical problems or conditions in public, such as prostate, bowel and bladder, and "female" problems, among the most common. The attorneys have a good argument for the use of a voir dire questionnaire if the case involves a potentially sensitive medical condition. Some jurors faced with a topic that is sensitive for them will not request a private interview with the judge during voir dire, but will instead simply not answer or minimize their answers.[8] A questionnaire allows jurors to answer these sensitive questions in private and without embarrassment. See Figure 23.3.

TIP: Put a question at the end of the voir dire questionnaire, which reads, "Are there any issues or questions on this questionnaire that you would prefer to talk to the judge and attorneys about in private?"

---

f. List of parties, witnesses, and attorneys

Nursing negligence cases often involve large numbers of witnesses or potential witnesses. The voir dire questionnaire allows the jurors to see the names of the witnesses at a slower pace and determine whether or not they know the witnesses. This process is much more efficient than reading a long list of names to the jurors. Jurors are reticent to say, "Could you read that again, Your Honor?" if they briefly hear a name that sounds familiar. Their most likely response is to sit quietly so as not to bring attention to themselves or look stupid. While they are trying to remember if they know someone with the same name, they are missing the next names being read. Having the names in writing also eliminates improper pronunciation. A questionnaire allows the jurors sufficient time to remember if the medical professional or other witness listed is one they know.

g. Oath

The jurors should be sworn in before they complete the voir dire questionnaire. The questionnaire should contain a statement at the beginning that the juror is under oath and must answer truthfully and completely. A statement such as the following, signed and dated by the juror, should be at the end of the questionnaire: "I affirm, under penalty of perjury, that I have given complete and honest answers to all of the questions above." Refer to Figure 23.3 for an example of questions used in case-specific voir dire questionnaires.

B. Voir Dire Questions

Most nursing negligence cases are tried in state courts, most of which allow some attorney-conducted voir dire. The end of this chapter contains suggestions for voir dire questions in cases involving medical negligence. The following are sample questions that can be used in cases involving various issues.

1. Using open-ended questions

The goal of voir dire is to encourage the jurors to talk. How much jurors talk is directly related to the skill of the attorney in using open-ended questions. Questions that can be answered "yes" or "no" are not open-ended questions. Another way to get jurors to talk is to say, "Tell me about...." Examples of open-ended questions are listed below.

* What are your feelings about the kind of medical care you and your family have received over the years?
* How did you feel about the care you received from the nurses when you were having your baby?
* What do you think are the most important skills a nurse can have?
* Do you think there should be changes made in the way our court system handles medical negligence cases? Why?

JUROR QUESTIONNAIRE

Please answer **all** of the following questions as **completely** and **honestly** as you can. Remember that you are **under oath**. As you answer the questions, please keep in mind that there are no "right" or "wrong" answers. Just read each question carefully and give an honest answer. You **must not** discuss your answers with any of the other jurors. If you need help, ask one of the clerks for assistance. Thank you for your cooperation.

1.   Name _____Age _____

2.   Please check all categories which apply to your current occupational status:

☐ Employed full-time   ☐ Employed part-time   ☐ Retired
☐ Temporarily laid off   ☐ Full-time homemaker   ☐ Student
☐ Unemployed   ☐ Disabled

3.   **If you are currently employed**, list your current occupation and employer and briefly describe your duties:
_____
_____
_____
_____

Length of employment: _____

If you are not currently employed, what type of work did you do most recently and when was that?
_____
_____

4.   List your last three jobs and briefly describe your duties:

Dates	Employer	Position	Duties

5.   City or town you live in or closest to:_____

Do you live in: ☐ the city or ☐ a rural area? How many years in county?

Where did you grow up?_____

Where else have you lived? _____

6.   Have you ever served in the military?   _____Yes _____No

IF YES, please list branch, rank at discharge, place and date of service:
_____
_____

Figure 23.3 Examples of questions for case specific voir dire questionnaires

7.   What is the highest grade or degree you completed in school? _____

IF SCHOOLING AFTER HIGH SCHOOL:

Name(s) of College or Vocational School	Major or Type of Training	Years Attended and Degrees or Certificates

8.   What is your marital status?

☐ Single (never married)   ☐ Separated for ___ years
☐ Married for ____ years   ☐ Widowed for ___ years
☐ Living with a partner for ____ years   ☐ Divorced for ___ years

If **married or separated**, list spouse's/partner's employer and occupation.
If **widowed** list spouse's/partner's last occupation.

His/Her occupation: _____

His/Her employer: _____

His/Her last grade level completed in school: _____   _____

If more than high school, list his/her major areas of study or special training:
_____

9.   If you have children, please list their age, sex, and if applicable their occupation and employer:
_____
_____
_____

10.   List the occupations and educational background of any other adults in your household and their relationship to you:
_____
_____
_____

11.   Please describe the occupation and education of your mother and father [if **retired**, **unemployed**, or **deceased**, please indicate and list their employment]:

Your Mother: _____

Your Father: _____

Figure 23.3 Examples of questions for case specific voir dire questionnaires (continued)

12. Please list any organizations you have belonged to or in which you participate. This could include veterans groups, service clubs, social clubs, unions, professional, volunteer, church, neighborhood, educational or political groups:

_____

_____

_____

13. Have you or anyone you know ever had any kind of brain injury? ____ Yes ____ No

IF YES, is this: ☐ Yourself   ☐ Spouse   ☐ Child   ☐ Family   ☐ Friend

Please describe: _____

_____

_____

14. Do you now have, or have you ever had, a mentally or physically impaired relative living at home? ____ Yes ____ No

IF YES, please explain: _____

_____

_____

15. How often do you go to the doctor or get medical care? _____ times per year.

16. Do you or anyone close to you have a medical condition or problem that requires ongoing, regular medical care? ____ Yes ____ No

IF YES, is this: ☐ Yourself   ☐ Spouse   ☐ Child   ☐ Family   ☐ Friend

Please explain, including how often medical appointments are necessary: _____

_____

_____

17. Have you, any family members or close friends ever been involved in any kind of medical situation where you or they were dissatisfied with the medical care that was received? ____ Yes ____ No

IF YES, is this: ☐ Yourself   ☐ Spouse   ☐ Child   ☐ Family   ☐ Friend

Briefly describe what happened: _____

_____

Was there a lawsuit or claim made about this situation? ____ Yes ____ No
IF YES, how was it resolved and how did you feel about the resolution?

Figure 23.3 *Examples of questions for case specific voir dire questionnaires (continued)*

18.   Have you or has someone close to you ever had a very positive experience with a doctor, nurse, or other medical professional in which you felt they saved your life or did an extremely good job of taking care of you or someone close to you? _____ Yes _____ No

IF YES, please explain, including when this was: _____

19.   Have you or has anyone close to you ever been paralyzed or had a physical disability—whether due to an injury or a medical condition?   _____ Yes _____ No

IF YES, is this: ☐ Yourself   ☐ Spouse   ☐ Child   ☐ Family   ☐ Friend

Please describe the person's disability and the cause (if known):

_____

_____

20.   Have you, a family member or close friend ever had a difficult labor or birth or had complications from a birth?   _____ Yes _____ No

Briefly describe what happened: _____

_____

_____

21.   Have you or any of your family ever been a patient at General Hospital? _____ Yes _____ No

IF YES, is this: ☐ Yourself   ☐ Spouse   ☐ Child   ☐ Family   ☐ Friend
IF YES, please explain: _____

_____

_____

22.   Have you or has anyone you know ever worked at, volunteered for or provided services to General Hospital? _____ Yes _____ No

IF YES, is this: ☐ Yourself   ☐ Spouse   ☐ Child   ☐ Family   ☐ Friend
IF YES, please explain: _____

_____

_____

23.   Do you or anyone you know have **any association** with the following people, law firms or hospitals? "Association" means that you or someone you know has any personal, family, business, or professional connection of any kind.

Name	I recognize the name	I have some association	Someone I know has an association	Please Explain
Nurse Nancy	_____	_____	_____	_____
Dr. Janet	_____	_____	_____	_____
General Hospital	_____	_____	_____	_____
Joe Attorney	_____	_____	_____	_____

Figure 23.3 *Examples of questions for case specific voir dire questionnaires (continued)*

24. This case involves a lawsuit being brought on behalf of Chuck Patient against Nurse Nancy, Dr. Janet and General Hospital. Chuck Patient claims that he was paralyzed when the medical professionals involved in his care negligently failed to diagnose the condition that led to his paralysis. Nurse Nancy, Dr. Janet and General Hospital deny that they were medically negligent.

Have you heard anything about this situation, do you know any of the people involved or is there anything else the judge and attorneys should know about you that may impact your ability to be an impartial juror in this case? ____ Yes ____ No

IF YES, please explain: _____

_____

_____

25. Do you feel that juries should provide money in compensation to an injured person for the loss of such things as physical pain, emotional distress and loss of enjoyment of life? ____ Yes ____ No

Please explain your answer: _____

_____

_____

26. Are any of your answers to the questions in this questionnaire so personal that you would not want them to be discussed in front of other jurors? ____ Yes ____ No

27. Do you have any physical, family or other problems which would make it difficult for you to sit as a juror for the next __ days/weeks? ____ Yes ____ No

IF YES, briefly explain: _____

_____

_____

_____

_____

28. There is a list of potential witnesses to this case attached to this questionnaire. Please put a checkmark by the names of any of the people that you **know of** or who you or anyone you know has ever had **any association** with. "Association" means that you or someone you know has any personal, family, business, or professional connection of any kind.

29. I affirm, under penalty of perjury, that I have given complete and honest answers to all of the questions above.

_____   _____
Signature   Date

Figure 23.3 Examples of questions for case specific voir dire questionnaires (continued)

In some jurisdictions, the judge will not permit attorneys to ask jurors questions unless the jurors have raised their hands in response to a closed-ended question directed at the entire group. In that situation, it can be helpful for the attorney to use the phrase, "How many of you…" rather than, "Do any of you…."

TIP: Attorneys must remember that open-ended questions generally begin with: "What, Where, Why, How, Who, or Tell me…." Any closed-ended question can be turned into an open-ended question by asking, "Why do you feel that way?" or "Tell me more about that."

---

2. Follow-up questions

Jurors are often reluctant to talk during voir dire. Many reasons exist, from the general fear of public speaking and the fear of divulging private information, to the desire to get on a jury for specific reasons involving bias for a particular party or side of the dispute. Some jurors are so cynical about the entire court process that they are unwilling to participate fully.

Attorneys intimidated by the reticence of jurors to open up find themselves without the information they need to exercise their peremptory challenges at the end of voir dire. One way to get jurors to talk more is to utilize a variety of different phrases as follow-up questions. The following are probes, which entice the jurors to expand on their answers:

- Tell me more about what you're thinking about that.
- Tell me more about what happened.
- Why do you think that?
- What else can you tell me about that?
- Can you tell me more about why you feel that way?
- I'm not sure I understand where you're coming from; can you explain a little more about what you're thinking?
- How do you feel about that?
- What do you think about that?
- It sounds like you care a lot about this issue.
- It sounds like that was a very difficult experience for you; how do you think that affected you?
- How did that affect you?
- How did that experience affect how you feel about the medical profession in general?
- That's very interesting, what else were you thinking about that?

TIP: Attorneys who look directly at the juror and remain quiet after asking a question will get fuller responses from jurors.

---

3. Importance of preparing written questions ahead of time

Many attorneys simply jot down notes about what they want to ask the jurors and do not prepare written questions. Most trial consultants highly recommend that a written voir dire be prepared and gone over in detail with the trial team, anticipating what the answers will be and what follow-up questions should be asked.

Utilizing themes and key phrases in voir dire is one way to begin the process of educating the jurors. The primary purpose of voir dire should be to better understand who the jurors are and what their experiences and values are. Themes and key phrases used in questions are likely to elicit information. Attorneys are unlikely to incorporate their themes unless they prepare questions ahead of the voir dire.

TIP: Attorneys who feel their ability to conduct voir dire is weak can convene a focus group and practice with the focus group, with or without a trial consultant to critique them.

---

4. Anticipate opposing counsel's questions

Whether the attorney is going to be questioning the jurors first, second, or in some cases third, preparation should include thinking through what types of questions, themes, and key words opposing counsel will be using. This planning allows the attorney to anticipate questions that come up after he finishes questioning, or to prepare to deal with issues brought up before he has an opportunity to question the jurors.

There are pros and cons in being the first or last attorney to question the jurors. Post-trial interviews of jurors found that they are irritated by attorneys asking questions they have already been asked. Attorneys should not repeat questions but should ask follow-up questions instead.

5. Stereotyping

Everyone stereotypes. There is no way for humans to get through the day without making assumptions about people based on stereotypes. And generally, there is some basis for the stereotype having developed. Attorneys can be heard to make many generalizations about jurors, such as, "If I'm representing a female plaintiff, I do not want women because they are more judgmental of other women than men are." Similarly, defense attorneys often say, "I want men because they do not take care of their family's healthcare needs so they have to rely more on the nurses and doctors." The attorney must be aware of her own stereotypes and be willing to challenge those stereotypes when a juror does not fit them.

Attorneys must also be prepared to confront the stereotypes their client might fit. A plaintiff's attorney with a client who is an African-American, single mom on welfare must consider how to question jurors about the kinds of stereotypes they may have and how those stereotypes might affect their ability to be objective in the case. Defense attorneys may have to confront the stereotype of the arrogant doctor who does not listen, and prepare questions to deal with that issue.

6. Identify and prepare questions on relevant subject matter

Medical negligence cases stir up strong emotions for many jurors. Considerable news coverage of lawsuits against medical providers and strong opinions have been expressed, both pro and con. On one hand, jurors are likely to believe that medical negligence lawsuits are driving up the cost of medical care, inhibiting providers in the delivery of health care and driving various professionals out of the field. On the other hand, jurors are also likely to believe that lawsuits are holding medical providers accountable and making medical care safer. Some jurors hold both sets of opinions at the same time. It is the trial team's responsibility to develop a voir dire strategy that identifies the juror's relevant experiences, the attitudes jurors hold, and the strength of their convictions.

Individual jurors have varying levels of understanding and appreciation of nurses' and nurse practitioners' roles in patient care. Some feel nurses should not make some of the decisions they have the authority to make, while others may feel protective of nurses and feel doctors do not listen to them.

a. Experience with a similar medical injury or condition

Almost every nursing negligence case involves a medical condition known to one or more of the jurors. Some jurors are likely to have experiences in everything from fetal monitoring strips to the correct order of testing a patient with chest pains. They will make assumptions about what role the nurses should play, versus the doctor, in treatment. Attorneys must understand jurors' life experiences that relate to the conditions involved in the case, what amount of familiarity they have with the subject matter, and how expert they see themselves in the subject matter.

Trial consultants are always asked: "Will a juror with a similar life experience be good for the plaintiff or defense?" Unfortunately, no simple answer to this question exists: the person could be good for the plaintiff or defense. It depends on the nature of her experience, the claims being made in the case, and the personality of the juror. As previously stated, for many jurors, what happened to them becomes synonymous with the standard of care. Some jurors feel, "Since I had an internal fetal monitor, then all women should have an internal fetal monitor," or, "Since I did not have an in-

ternal fetal monitor and my baby turned out alright, no one else needs one." Some jurors believe a nurse should spend a certain amount of time with the patient, because that was their experience in the hospital. These types of attitudes are generally a function of personality and limited life experience. It is the attorney's responsibility to talk to the jurors long enough to understand what their experiences were in the area and what they thought about it.

Jurors should be asked if they, or anyone close to them, have ever been treated in a nursing home, specific hospital department, or emergency room, depending on where the injury in the current case occurred. This relates back to the juror feeling that he understands what the standard of care is or should be.

If the issues in the case include the liability of both the hospital and doctor, the following questions should also be asked:

- How much of the treatment you received in the hospital actually came from the doctor as compared to the hospital staff?
- What responsibilities do you think nurses have for the care of patients, which might be different from or in addition to those of the doctor?

TIP: Remember it is not the experience, but the juror's reaction to the experience that counts.

---

b. Connections to medical personnel and institutions

Jurors' connections to medical personnel and institutions can be familial, social, or professional. Potential jurors' connections with and attitudes towards nurses, doctors, hospitals, medical technologists, and others involved in health care must be probed carefully and fully by both plaintiff and defendant, as these types of connections can produce bias and prejudice. Jurors who have relatives or friends who work in the medical profession might be protective of the medical profession. They have often been exposed to talk about the difficulties of being a nurse or other provider in today's healthcare system. They often have negative attitudes about malpractice lawsuits. These attitudes can affect different parties in different ways, depending on the position the attorney is taking. Other factors that can affect people with connections to the medical professions are rivalries between institutions.

For the most part, jurors with medical connections have biases in favor of the defense. Attorneys must delve into jurors' attitudes about the medical profession and lawsuits in general, based on their experiences. A nurse's aide and her family members might have negative attitudes about nurses and doctors. The son of a nurse might have negative prejudices and stereotypes about doctors. A former nurse might have negative feelings about doctors or a competing hospital. A doctor's family members might have bad attitudes about nurses.

Examples of questions attorneys should ask jurors with medical connections follow:

- How long have you known this person?
- In what area of medicine does this person work?
- What kinds of things does this person discuss about his work?
- How do you think it would affect you to be a juror on a case against the hospital where your sister works?
- How will you be completely objective?
- We're asking this jury to find that nurses at the hospital your sister works at were negligent and to provide a substantial amount of money compensation to (the plaintiff). How do you think your relationship with her might affect you in awarding damages against the hospital?
- My concern here is that you, as a juror, might be affected by your connection to General Hospital in a way that will make it difficult for you to be impartial. Sometimes people feel protective of their local medical people, and that's a perfectly legitimate feeling. Do you have any feelings like that when you hear that someone has sued a local hospital or clinic?

Jurors might have medical training or skills as volunteer first responders, CPR training, or experiences in the military. They might have a background in biology or other science. These experiences and skills can give certain jurors the feeling that they understand what the standard of care is or should be, and can also give them status with the other jurors, wherein they become "experts" in the jury room. It is difficult to predict whether these jurors will be more dangerous to the plaintiff or the defendants.

TIP: If the hospital has a religious affiliation, attorneys should inquire whether the jurors have a similar affiliation with or negative feelings about the denomination. This is a good question to include in the juror questionnaire as well.

---

c. Attitudes affecting the plaintiff

The defense might make a legal claim that the plaintiff's actions were negligent in a particular case. The strategy of the defense might involve undermining the plaintiff

and suggesting that the plaintiff is undeserving of compensation because of actions she took, or did not take. Many jurors are susceptible to these claims, whether based on a legal theory or not. In preparing for voir dire, the plaintiff's attorney must be prepared to confront these issues, and the defense to exploit them.

The theme of personal responsibility has been very successful for the defense in medical negligence cases. The defense should ask a question such as, "How important do you think it is for patients to take personal responsibility for their own health? Why do you say that?"

If the plaintiff is a smoker, the implication might be that since the plaintiff smoked, he did not care about his health and was unlikely to have done what the nurse practitioner advised. Plaintiff's attorneys must ask the jurors questions such as:

- How many of you believe that anyone who smokes doesn't care about his health?

The next step is to follow up with the jurors, asking them why they think that, and if they think that someone who smokes would automatically not do what the nurse practitioner advised.

Missed appointments is an issue that frequently arises for plaintiffs. The attorney must ask the jurors if they have ever missed or rescheduled an appointment:

- Have you ever missed or rescheduled an appointment with a healthcare professional? Why was that?
- Did you miss that appointment because you didn't care about your health?
- Do you think that if someone misses an appointment it means that they aren't taking responsibility for their health? Why do you say that?
- Do you think that there are times when nurses aren't clear about what they want a patient to do or under what circumstances a patient should reschedule an appointment?
- Have any of you personally or has someone in your family ever had a misunderstanding with a nurse or doctor?

Another problem plaintiffs frequently have in nursing malpractice cases is that many jurors think that the nurses do not have the power to challenge a doctor if they know that there is a problem with the medical care a patient is receiving. In that instance, plaintiffs should ask any healthcare providers on the jury:

- Do nurses have a responsibility to the patient if they see that medical care is not being delivered properly?
- Have you ever seen a situation where a doctor isn't doing what they should for a patient? What did you do about it?
- What is the policy at your hospital when a nurse feels that a patient isn't getting the proper care from a doctor?
- Does your nursing home have a chain of command where you are able to bring concerns you have about a doctor's treatment of a patient to someone else? Have you ever done that?

d. Attitudes affecting defendants

The media freely discusses problems at hospitals involving system breakdowns and injuries and deaths caused by provider negligence. Widespread resentment of the cost of care exists. Some jurors perceive that medical care is not what it should be. Others feel that managed care and health maintenance organizations unfairly restrict their access to necessary medical treatment. Some jurors or their family members have had negative experiences with healthcare providers. Staff shortages at hospitals can cause jurors to believe patient care needs are not being met.

Jurors with family members in nursing homes may have strong negative feelings about the quality of care their family members have received. These negative feelings may arise from a perception that the food is bad in nursing homes, the nurses do not care, or that the nurses are mean to the residents. Defense attorneys should explore the extent of these attitudes to determine how deep-rooted they are. Much is written about how medical professionals' bedside manner influences patients' perceptions of competence. The problem occurs when a juror generalizes this bad feeling to all medical professionals. Jurors in small towns sometimes have personal issues with local nurses or doctors that affect their ability to be fair to that defendant or to objectively listen to her testimony.

The same types of questions suggested in Section 23.5 and 23.6 about connections to medical personnel and institutions should be asked of these jurors and tailored to their experience:

- Tell us what happened.
- How did that affect how you feel about nurses and doctors?
- It sounds like you were pretty upset about that situation. How do you think this will affect you in being objective in this case in which…?

- Some people think that if a patient has a bad outcome, it must be the fault of the medical professionals. What do you think?
- How has that experience affected what you think when you hear that a nurse or doctor was sued?

e. Experiences with and attitudes towards lawsuits

Jurors come to court with a panoply of attitudes about lawsuits. Some jurors are incapable of finding against a medical defendant because of their opposition to lawsuits. Plaintiffs should be wary of jurors' attitudes about lawsuits. Most jurors in some jurisdictions believe there are too many lawsuits and are opposed to frivolous lawsuits. However, this does not mean every juror with this attitude is a bad juror for plaintiffs. Strong attitudes generally come from either an experiential or ideological base. To determine whether or not a juror's opposition to lawsuits is a strongly held view, attorneys must ask a series of questions. The following types of questions can be proposed to jurors to understand their attitudes toward lawsuits in general:

- How many of you think there are too many lawsuits? Why do you say that?
- Are there any particular lawsuits you think should not have been allowed? What was it about that lawsuit that bothered you?
- How many of you think that simply because a lawsuit was filed, the defendant must have done something wrong?
- What do you think are the negative effects that lawsuits have had on the practice of medicine?
- What do you think are the positive effects that lawsuits have had on the practice of medicine?
- What is it that makes a lawsuit frivolous in your opinion?
- Based on what you know about this lawsuit so far, do you think it is frivolous?
- How do you think the negative attitude you have towards lawsuits might affect you in being a juror in this kind of case? Are we starting out even with you?

Attorneys often ask trial consultants if someone who has been involved in a lawsuit will side with the same side as they were on. This is obviously a concern, but is not always determinative. A juror who has been a plaintiff in a worker's compensation case may or may not have an affinity for the plaintiff in a medical negligence case. A juror sued in relation to a car wreck or even a business contract may or may not identify with the defense. Attorneys should examine jurors thoroughly about their experiences with lawsuits and the impact on them, as opposed to making assumptions. In particular, attorneys should ask questions about how the lawsuit affected the juror:

- How did you feel about the way that case was handled?
- How did that experience affect how you feel about how the courts handle lawsuits?
- That must have been a difficult experience. How did you feel about the people and the attorney who (you sued)/(sued you)?
- How do you think that experience might affect you here in being a juror in this type of lawsuit?
- You were a (plaintiff or defendant). Do you feel you might be leaning towards the (plaintiff or defendant) because you were in the same situation in a lawsuit?

TIP: Jurors may have been involved in lawsuits involving companies they worked for. This could include being interviewed, having a deposition taken, working for someone or with someone who was involved, or worrying about the impact of the lawsuit on the business. Be sure to ask if an employer was ever involved in a lawsuit.

---

f. Attitudes towards damages

Many jurors believe money should not be provided in compensation for intangible damages such as pain and suffering, mental anguish, emotional distress, or psychological damages. This attitude affects plaintiffs more than defendants. Jurors should be asked questions such as:

- What do you think the psychological impact is on a person who has lost the use of his legs?
- How did being in the hospital for a long time affect you emotionally?
- How many of you have a problem of any kind with providing money to compensate a patient for physical pain or emotional distress that an injury has caused?
- How many of you feel that the courts should not allow people to sue for money compensation for pain and suffering? Why do you feel that way?
- How many of you feel that the emotional distress from having a serious injury can be as difficult as dealing with the injury itself?
- Do you think that psychological injuries are real injuries? Why do you say that?

g. Organizations

Many jurors belong, or have belonged, to organizations. The nature of the organization and jurors' levels of participa-

tion can provide valuable insight into their lives. People active in organizations are often accustomed to working with others or running meetings. These people might play a more active role in the jury deliberations because of their experiences. Organizational involvement can also provide insight into a juror's ideological beliefs and values. Most judges do not allow direct questions to jurors about their religious or political affiliations unless there is a direct link to the case facts. Religious affiliation might become an issue if abortion or disconnecting life-sustaining care is involved or, as mentioned earlier, if the hospital or clinic is a religious-based institution.

- What organizations do you belong to or have you belonged to in the past—such as civic groups, children's groups, political or religious or volunteer organizations?
- Do you do any volunteer work or have you done any in the past?
- Have you ever served in any offices or on committees?
- How active are you in this organization?
- What kinds of activities are you involved in?
- What is it you like best about that organization?

h. Hardship

The issue of hardships can come up in any case. Some judges are reluctant to excuse any jurors, while others are fairly liberal. The impact on jurors forced to sit on a jury when they really do not want to be there has not been adequately studied. Accepted wisdom is that jurors who do not want to sit will not want to find for the plaintiff, or will punish the party they think is lengthening the trial. Interviews with reluctant jurors in long cases have also found that some jurors become frustrated with the defense simply because they want the case to end. Most trial consultants advise both plaintiffs and defendants to ask the judge to excuse people who do not want to be there because of the inability to predict how their service will affect their opinion.

C. When the Judge Does the Voir Dire

Practicing in a court which does not allow attorney-conducted voir dire is difficult. Judges do not generally do as in-depth a voir dire as an attorney would like. In addition, they do not know the case issues as intimately as the attorney and often do not cover all the issues necessary to identify the biases and prejudices that might affect the jurors. Attorneys in such jurisdictions should routinely submit motions requesting that they be allowed to conduct the voir dire and include material from the social sciences which demonstrates that attorney-conducted voir dire is more thorough and likely to identify juror prejudice. While the chances of such a motion succeeding are small, some motions are granted. A judge might allow the attorney a short period of time to question the jurors or to follow-up. In addition, such a motion should include a recitation of the types of case issues which could produce bias or prejudice in the jurors.

When preparing questions for the judge to ask, note that the format of the questions can be the determining factor in whether or not the judge asks the questions. An endless stream of numbered questions is less likely to be used than one broken up into subject areas and labeled as such. Figure 23.4 is an example of how to structure a set of questions in a judge's voir dire on specific subjects, using labeling for the subject matter, bolding for the primary question, and indentation without bolding for the follow-up questions.

TIP: Voir dire questionnaires are very useful in jurisdictions where the voir dire is limited or conducted solely by the judge. Trial consultants have observed that even when judges reject the use of the questionnaire, they tend to ask more questions of the jurors.

D. In-Court Observations

The more preparation put into thinking about rating the jurors before the trial begins, the more efficient and successful the trial team will be. Once voir dire is over most judges want the attorneys to exercise their peremptory strikes quickly. In courts where the decision to strike or not must be made after questioning a certain number of jurors and then following each replacement juror, attorneys must prioritize ahead of time which issues are most important. Trial consultants can assist with this process both in and out of the courtroom, helping the trial team to plan the voir dire strategy and observing the jurors as they answer the questions.

When a trial consultant is involved in jury selection, the attorney should not introduce the trial consultant as a member or employee of the law firm. If the attorney does not want to divulge that the trial consultant is a trial consultant, she should simply use the trial consultant's name and say the person is helping with jury selection. In most instances, the opposing side will assume the consultant is a part of the firm, but it is important not to misrepresent the trial consultant.

1. Rating the jurors

A variety of systems can be used to rate jurors. A sense of what the key issues are in the case and assuring that the rating system takes all of those issues into consideration is important. Experiences, attitudes, assumptions, and ideology should be evaluated to get a sense of which jurors will be most biased against the attorney's side of the case.

2. Remember the jury is a group

Juries function as a group. Some jurors are more opinionated and more forceful than the others, or have expertise or experience in an area involved in the case. The potential leaders of the jury must be looked at more closely than followers.

Jurors who appear quiet may also be powerful. Attorneys must not underestimate a juror who seems uncomfortable or of insufficient social status to be a force in the deliberations. The quiet juror may be hiding behind his or her silence despite having strong opinions. The quiet juror may be a leader in his church or union or other social situations. If a juror is not answering any questions addressed to the group, it is imperative that the attorney address that juror individually. For example, "Mr. Smith, I notice that you haven't said much. What are your feelings about these issues involving medical care and suing nurses that we have been talking about?" If the juror still does not say much, the attorney should be prepared to ask specific questions. Assume a juror who is quiet during jury selection will be quiet with the other jurors at your own peril.

3. Exercising challenges

The trial team should assure they fully understand the method the judge uses for exercising peremptory challenges when trying a case before a new judge. When will strikes be exercised? How much time will there be for consultation with the trial team? Which jurors will be alternates and will they be allowed to deliberate at the end of the case? Will attorneys lose a strike if they pass a turn?

The chances of an alternate serving on the trial jury increases when the trial is expected to take more than a week. Thus, a "bad" juror who is an alternate becomes more of a concern when deciding which jurors against whom to exercise peremptory challenges.

E. Jurors and the Internet

The ubiquity of cell phones with Internet connections in recent years and the proliferation of blogging and tweeting present numerous issues for jury trials today. Besides the problems with jurors texting their friends or blogging about the trial, jurors doing their own research has become a huge problem. Blogging and texting jurors (and judges, attorneys and witnesses) have lead to mistrials and cases being overturned on appeal.[9]

Attorneys should talk to their judge before a trial begins to find out whether the judge will be giving the jurors a specific instruction about not using their phones or the Internet and what that instruction will be. Trial consultants are advising that the instruction not only tell the jurors what they cannot do, but give them the reasons for the instruction. Many jurors are used to simply going to Google for information they do not understand and will not think there is anything wrong with doing so during a trial unless they are told why they should not.

1.   **MEDICAL TRAINING:**

   - Have any of you ever had any kind of volunteer medical training—CPR or something else?
   - Tell us about that.
   - How often have you used this training?

2.   **SUPERVISION**:

   - Have any of you ever been involved with supervising or training anyone else?
   - Tell us about that.
   - How did you feel about having that responsibility?
   - Do/did your supervisory responsibilities involve hiring, firing, disciplining or training of people who you supervised?
   - Please tell us about what that involved.
   - Do/did you have any responsibility for staffing—for deciding which employees were qualified to provide a certain service?
   - Do you have any positions where a person has to have certain qualifications or it isn't safe to let them do a job?
   - Tell us about that.

3.   **STANDARDS**:

- **How many of you have standards or policies that you have to follow in your job?**
   - Where do those standards come from?
   - What happens if you do not follow them?
   - Do you think that's right?

   - In this case the Patient's contend that Nurse Nancy and Dr. Janet at General Hospital were negligent and that they violated certain medical standards of care during Baby Patient's birth which resulted in his permanent brain damage. Nurse Nancy, Dr. Janet and General Hospital deny that they violated any medical standards and that their care resulted in Baby Patient's injuries.

   - Do any of you have any feelings that the law should not permit nurses, doctors or hospitals to be sued even if they have acted carelessly or negligently?
   - Does anyone have any problem with doctors or hospitals being sued for being negligent?

4.   **GENERAL HOSPITAL**:

   - Have any of you, your family, or friends ever worked at General Hospital?
   - What did you do there? When?
   - What do you think about General Hospital?
   - Do you generally have positive or negative feelings about General Hospital?
   - How do you think it would affect you to be a juror on a case where General Hospital is being sued?
   - How will you be completely objective?
   - Have any of you or someone close to you ever gone to General Hospital for any kind of medical service, including tests, having a baby, or surgery?

Figure 23.4 *Examples of questions that can be submitted to a judge for voir dire.*

- How do you feel about the kinds of services you got there?

  - **IF GOOD**: How do you think the fact that you received good care from General Hospital will affect you?
  - Would the fact that you had a good experience make it hard for you to believe that someone else received such poor care that they were severely injured?
  - Do you think that someone else could have received such improper care from General Hospital that they would become severely disabled or injured?

  - **IF BAD**: How do you think the fact that you received good care from General Hospital will affect you?
  - Would the fact that you had a bad experience make you predisposed to believe that the hospital was in the wrong in this situation?

This case is about what happened 3½ years ago, when Baby Patient was born at General Hospital. Baby's family is suing the doctor, nurse and hospital for negligence because Baby was born with serious brain damage, which the family contends was caused by the fact that his mother was not given a C-section in time.

- Is there anything about your connection to General Hospital that would make it hard for you to believe that the Hospital and it's nurses were at fault?
- Is there anything about your feelings about suing General Hospital that would make you think that the family should not be suing the hospital and its nurses?
- Is there anything about your connection to General Hospital that would make you think, before you have heard any evidence, that the Hospital and it's nurses were at fault?

5. **DR. JANET:**

- Have any of you ever heard of Dr. Janet, who is an obstetrician who currently practices at General Hospital?
- How do you know Dr. Janet?
- How do you feel about the kind of care you or your family member or friend received from Dr. Janet?
- Would the fact that you had a good experience with Dr. Janet make it hard for you to believe that someone else received such poor care that they were severely injured?
- What is your opinion of Dr. Janet?
- Do you generally have good feelings about Dr. Janet?
- How do you think it would affect you to be a juror on a case where Dr. Janet is being sued?
- How will you be completely objective?

This case is about what happened 3½ years ago, when Ethan Krochmalny was born at General Hospital. Ethan's family is suing Dr. Janet and the hospital and its nurses for negligence because Ethan was born with serious brain damage, which the family contends was caused by the fact that his mother was not given a C-section in time.

- Is there anything about your connection to Dr. Janet that would make it hard for you to believe that she was at fault?
- Is there anything about your feelings about suing Dr. Janet that would make you think that the family should not be suing the hospital?

Figure 23.4 Examples of questions that can be submitted to a judge for voir dire (continued).

6.   **ATTITUDES TOWARDS NURSES**:

- Are your feelings about nurses generally positive or negative?
  - Why do you say that?

- Have you ever had a negative experience with a nurse?
  - What happened?
  - How does that affect how you feel about nurses in general?

- Have you ever had a particularly positive experience with a nurse?
  - Tell us about that.
  - How does that affect how you feel about nurses in general?

In this case, Baby Patient's parents are claiming that Nurse Nancy was medically negligent. Nurse Nancy denies that she was negligent. How do you think your feelings about nurses in general might affect how you look at this case?

- Do you feel that you are leaning one way or the other, either in favor of or against Nurse Nancy before the case starts?

7.   **CHILDREN'S HOSPITALIZATIONS**:

- How many of you have children who have had to stay in the hospital overnight for any reason?
- What happened?
- When was this?
- How long was he or she in the hospital?
- Is the child healthy now?
- How satisfied were you with the nurses who took care of your child in the hospital?
- Were there any problems with the care your child received?
  - IF YES: Please tell us about that.
  - How do you think that experience will affect you in being a juror in this case where....

Figure 23.4 *Examples of questions that can be submitted to a judge for voir dire (continued).*

Jurors doing research on the Internet is particularly problematic for medical malpractice cases. In addition to the standard problems of accurate or inaccurate information about parties, attorneys, expert witnesses and possible news coverage of the case or similar cases, there is a plethora of information on the Internet about medical conditions, standard of care issues and hospital and professional regulations. Much of this information is simplistic and some of it is simply wrong. No attorney wants their jury to be evaluating their case based on Internet "experts'" testimony.

Dealing with this problem should include two steps: questioning the jurors during jury selection and instructing them on every break and before they go home at night.

1. Voir dire on Internet usage

During jury selection, the following questions should be asked:

- How many of you blog or text or use the Internet for information gathering? Tell us about that.
- Have you ever looked up anything about your health on the Internet? Tell us about that. What did you think about that information?
- Do you think that everything you read on the Internet is true and accurate?
- Would you have any problem not blogging or texting about the trial?
- Trials are structured so that everyone has the same information—the judge, the attorneys and the jurors.

Do you think it would be fair if one of the jurors brought information into the jury room that the attorneys did not know about and could not question?

- The judge has made rulings on what testimony and documents will be allowed in this case. The attorneys have to follow the judge's rulings and jurors are not allowed to do their own research about the facts of the case. What do you think about this? Do you have any problem with this? Will you have a problem not looking things up on the Internet?

- Will you be able to follow the judge's instruction that you are not to do any independent research on the Internet or anywhere else?

2. Instructions to the jurors

Typical jury instructions, if they are given at all, are similar to these instructions from Illinois:

> The use of cell phones, text messaging, Internet postings and Internet access devices in connection with your duties violates the rules of evidence and you are prohibited from using them.
>
> You should not do any independent investigation or research on any subject relating to the case. What you may have seen or heard outside the courtroom is not evidence. This includes any press, radio, or television programs and it also includes any information available on the Internet. Such programs, reports and information are not evidence and your verdict must not be influenced in any way by such material.

We are recommending that the instructions be expanded to provide the jurors with an explanation of why they should not do their own research. Compliance with instructions that provide a rationale for following them is higher than when jurors are simply ordered to not do something:

> You should not do any independent investigation or research on any subject relating to the case. What you may have seen or heard outside the courtroom is not evidence. This includes any press, radio, or television programs and it also includes any information available on the Internet. Such programs, reports and information are not evidence and your verdict must not be influenced in any way by such material.
>
> The use of cell phones, text messaging, Internet postings and Internet access devices while you are a juror violates the rules of evidence and you are prohibited from using them. You are not allowed to look up definitions of words or descriptions of medical treatments. You are not allowed to do ANY research of any kind that relates to the case.
>
> It is not legal and also would not be fair to the parties in this lawsuit if someone were to bring in information they got from outside the courtroom. Many of you are probably used to using Google or some other program to look up the meanings of words or other information. As I am sure you know, not everything you read on the Internet is true. If you were to bring in outside information from research you did, that information might be wrong and the parties would have no way to respond to it.
>
> Also, if you are posting or receiving information from outside the courtroom, that could be seen as influencing you and the fairness of the trial would be questioned and the case may have to tried again, thus having wasted all of our time and resources. It is important to the integrity of our system that cases be decided only on the basis of the evidence you hear from the witness stand. That's why you are not allowed to use text messaging or to blog about the trial or to do your own research about the case, either on the Internet or anywhere else while you are a juror.

Given that many jurors are used to being able to find information about any question at any time, it may make sense for attorneys to lobby for the right of jurors to ask questions. This could alleviate jurors feeling that they need to find out the answers to questions they have that are not being answered during the course of trial.

23.6 Witness Preparation

Trial consultants can help attorneys plan the order of witnesses, prepare for direct and cross, and prepare both expert and lay witnesses for testimony. The order of witnesses and the testimony from each can have a huge impact on the ability of jurors to understand the material being presented. Having their trial consultant discuss how to integrate themes into their preparation of direct and cross is extremely helpful. Trial consultants look at the material more objectively and assist the attorney in using language accessible to the jurors.

Most lay witnesses are extremely nervous about testifying and some are downright terrified. Others have ineffective communication styles. Trial consultants work with the lay witnesses to help them be calm and present their testimony in a clear, concise manner.

Nursing cases almost always involve complicated medical testimony. The ability of expert witnesses to communicate in clear and understandable language cannot be overemphasized. Expert witnesses can sometimes be blind to the language they use and make assumptions that jurors will have more knowledge about the subject than is likely. Trial consultants work with the experts to break down their testimony into segments more easily understood. It can be helpful to have the trial consultant work with the witness before their deposition as well.

In order to assist in witness preparation, the trial consultant must understand the issues in the case and the rules of testimony in the jurisdiction. Most consultants prefer to read some of the case materials and have a meeting with the attorney before meeting with the witness if they are not already familiar with the case.

Many attorneys feel that the consultant's work with witnesses falls under the work product doctrine and is not discoverable by opposing counsel, but this issue is by no means settled. (See Section 23.10 below for a discussion about discoverability.) The safest way for trial consultants to work with witnesses is with the attorney in the room to preserve client privilege.

23.7 Developing Themes

The importance of having case themes cannot be overstated. Every case is a war of opposing stories. Did the nurses convey the information properly to the physician over the phone? Did they convey their perception that the physician needed to come in? Did the nurse really take the vital signs during the crisis and not have time to write them down, or did she simply not take them? Should the nurse have gone up the chain of command, or not? Often there are questions of whether or not the injury was going to occur despite all the care given. Often there are questions of whether it was the doctor's or the nurse's negligence which resulted in the injury. Jurors are bombarded with unfamiliar information about the standard of care, negligence, causation, and damages. They will be thinking about why the events unfolded the way they did and whether it was right or wrong. They will be looking at the motivation of the parties. Most importantly, they want to know if any rules were broken.

The prudent and creative use of themes assists the jurors in understanding the attorney's position on the pertinent issues. The attorney should have a theme, a phrase or sentence, which will summarize his position on the threshold issues.

A. What is a Theme?

Every case has themes. If the attorney does not give the jurors themes, they will use the opposing sides' themes or come up with their own. In order to process and remember information, people must use shorthand. Is this a case about a nurse who did not pay enough attention to the patient's blood pressure, or is this a case about a woman who had a rare condition that the reasonable nurse would not have recognized?

A theme is simply a set of words summing up some aspect of the case, or a phrase which counters a central problem in a case. The key to these words being a theme, and not just words, is that they stand for something larger than just the words. They create an image, remind the jurors of a part of the story the attorney does not want them to forget, and are repeated throughout the case. Repetition of the theme is essential, a theme means the same phrases or sentences are used throughout the case, preferably beginning in jury selection and stated at least three times during the opening, used with witnesses, and reinforced in the closing.

In every case, the trial team has a legal burden: what they must prove legally to win. However, there is also a juror burden, which often is not the same as the legal burden. The themes should address both the legal and the juror burden. What must be proven to the jurors in order to win? What must the jurors believe happened? Themes should provide the link between what the jurors must believe happened and structure of the law.

B. Where Do Themes Come From?

Themes work best if they grow out of the case. Themes come from the plaintiff, defendants, expert witnesses, hospital records, standards, or policies. The only requirement is that they be in English, not legalese or medicalese. They can be as simple as, "The hospital was cutting corners by not having enough nurses on duty," or "The plaintiff cared so little for his health that he continued to smoke after the nurse practitioner told him to stop." The plaintiff's liability themes should focus the jurors' attention on the hospital, nurses, doctors, and standards of care. The defense's liability themes should focus the jurors' attention on their strongest answer to the plaintiff's strongest argument. The plaintiff's damages themes should be directed at the strongest argument the defense has, and vice versa.

TIP: A theme is a simple symbol, and must be repeated throughout the case.

C. Incorporating Case Themes into Voir Dire

Some examples of how to integrate themes into voir dire questions follow. The theme phrases are in italics. Refer to Chapter 24, *Crafting Effective Themes*, for more on this topic.

- How many of you know of any situations where *the nurses and doctors tried their hardest, but there was nothing that could be done?*
- How many of you know of any situations where the *nurse's quick thinking* saved someone from dying?

- How many of you are troubleshooters or have to do a lot of problem solving in your jobs?
- Is *time of the essence* in terms of your ability to fix a problem?
  - Does it matter how soon you *identify and start to* work on a problem in terms of fixing it?
  - Are there some problems that you can't fix if they *go on too long*?
  - Are there some decisions more critical to your job than others — are there crisis situations — or *problems that can become a crisis if not handled quickly*?

23.8 Post-Trial Interviews

Post-trial interviews, if permitted in the venue, provide a gold mine of information to the trial team. It is best to have someone other than the attorney who tried the case interview the jurors because of biasing effects. A paralegal or trial consultant should conduct the post-trial interviews. Some jurors might feel embarrassed about telling an attorney what she did that was wrong or ineffective. Others may temper their answers due to not wanting to cause the attorney discomfort. And frequently, an attorney who has just lost a case is too emotionally invested to be objective. Some attorneys are unable to listen to what the jurors have to say, instead trying to reargue their case.

A. Why Interview the Jurors?

There is much to be gained from interviewing jurors. Often the trial team tells a consultant that this particular juror was on its side from the beginning and this one was not, only to find out after the interviews that neither assessment was true. Sometimes the trial team thinks a particular piece of evidence was important, only to find out it was not. The jurors often comment on the attorneys' or judge's communication style.

It is particularly important to interview jurors when an attorney has a number of similar cases going to trial. If a case similar to an upcoming case has been tried recently in the same jurisdiction, interviews with the jurors provide insight into what worked and what did not, how they perceived the expert testimony, what themes they responded to, and the level of comprehension of the medical issues. Finding out what the jurors thought and why they found as they did provides invaluable help in planning for the next case, whether it has similar issues or not.

B. Check Local Law and Custom Before Interviewing Jurors

Many jurisdictions do not allow any juror interviews. Others allow interviews only with the permission of the judge, or only with representatives of both parties present. The juror must be informed if the interviewer is taping the answers. If jurors are at all reluctant to be interviewed, they will be even more reluctant to be recorded. The interviewer should inform the jurors who has hired him to do the interviewing and who will see the interviews. If a reason exists to not tell the jurors who is sponsoring the interviews, the interviewer should tell the jurors that they do not want to reveal that information. Interviewers should not lie to the jurors. In some jurisdictions, the interviewer must stop the interview if he believes that something the juror has said indicates that there was juror misconduct during the trial. No interviews should ever be conducted without a complete understanding of the rules in the jurisdiction.

Due to the increased use of cell phones and caller ID, contacting jurors has become more difficult. Some consultants have had success with sending letters to jurors with a phone number to call at their convenience.

C. Plan the Interview Questions

The questions should be planned out carefully even if someone who worked on the case interviews the jurors. The person doing the interviewing must understand the testimony, witnesses, and jury instructions.

Most trial consultants start out the interview process by asking a number of open-ended questions of the juror. For example:

- "In your own words, what do you think this case was about?"
- "What was the most important evidence in the case as far as you were concerned?"
- "What were the biggest differences among the jurors?"

Open-ended questions encourage the juror to start talking about what she thought was most important and avoids skewing the interview.

Jurors generally do not want to identify which jurors said what during deliberations, although they are willing to discuss what was said. By prefacing questions with phrases such as, "I don't want to know which jurors felt (a certain way), but I'm wondering what things you disagreed about and what arguments were made."

D. Group Interviews

A group of jurors from the case can be interviewed together. This interaction amongst the jurors can result in jurors remembering their reactions to parts of the case they might not have remembered on their own. The downside is that there is not as much opportunity to get an in-depth analysis of the case from each juror.

23.9 Discoverability of Trial Consultants' Work

The U.S. Court of Appeals ruled *In re: Cendant Corp. Securities Litigation*,[10] that discussions during witness preparation attended by the non-lawyer trial consultant, witness, and attorney were protected under the federal work product doctrine. The court did not reach the attorney-client privilege issue. The court held that exchanges between the trial consultant and the witness have the same protection as communication with other non-attorneys who are covered by the work product doctrine. The concurring opinion held that it is impossible to dissect the information that the consultant has about the case into that which is privileged and that which is not, due to discussions between the attorney, client, and trial consultant.

The question of whether mock trial or other research is covered under the work product doctrine is less settled than the issue of witness preparation. The author is aware of a number of cases in which one of the parties attempted to obtain the work of the trial consultant.[11]

In order to protect the trial consultant's work under either the attorney-client privilege or the work product doctrine the following procedures are necessary:

- The trial consultant should be hired and paid by the attorney and not the client.
- The case material should come from the attorney and not the client.
- The trial consultant should report to the attorney and not the client.
- Any reports from the trial consultant to the attorney should be labeled "confidential work product" and make reference to the relationship between the material in the report and the theories and thought processes of the attorney.
- Reports should be labeled as being prepared for the specific attorney in relation to the specific case.
- Memos from the attorney to the trial consultant should be labeled "work product."

TIP: The contract with the trial consultant should include the specific case name and a clause similar to the following: "It is further agreed that all information learned by the trial consultant in consultation with (lawyer client) and others in preparation for and in relation to her work on the case is confidential and privileged information. All materials, research, including mock trial research, and reports produced for the (client) law firm are work product and subject to the appropriate legal protection."

23.10 Summary

Jurors approach nursing negligence cases with their own life experiences, assumptions, attitudes, and ideology. No trial team should proceed without thoroughly analyzing the possible interpretations jurors could make of the case facts. Pretrial research provides insights into what will be important at trial, and what both the juror burden and the legal burden will be.

Trial consultant use at any point in trial preparation can be helpful in gaining insight into how jurors evaluate case issues. By carefully analyzing the evidence with the jurors' perspectives in mind, the trial team can develop themes and prepare depositions, voir dire questions, opening, witness examinations, and closing to be as effective and persuasive as possible.

Endnotes

1. See Additional Reading section for a listing of relevant books on this subject.

2. According to a survey conducted by Sherry Diamond for the Brookings Institute in 1995, 17 percent of the population has served through an entire trial and 45 percent has been called.

3. See Joseph, G. *Modern Visual Evidence*. New York, NY: Law Journal Press 2005 and Maher, T., *Demonstrative Evidence for Complex Litigation*. Tucson, Lawyers and Judges Publishing Company, 2005.

4. For a more in-depth discussion of focus groups and mock trials, see Krauss and Rountree, National Jury Project, *JURYWORK: Systematic Techniques* Clark Boardman Callaghan, New York, NY (1983, updated yearly).

5. See Ball, D., *Do Your Own Focus Groups*. (2008) Videotape Series available from the National Institute for Trial Advocacy (NITA), Louisville, CO.

6. It is unclear when case specific voir dire questionnaires were first used. The first such questionnaire that the National Jury Project is aware of was used in 1975 in the nationally covered case of *North Carolina v. Joan Little*. See Krauss, E. and Rountree, W., National Jury Project (1983, updated yearly) *Jurywork: Systematic Techniques*, second edition. St. Paul, MN: Thomson/West, page 2-62.14.

7. A number of the books referenced in the chapter's Additional Reading have sections on juror questionnaires, with motions and suggested questions and formatting. The chapter in *Jurywork* is particularly comprehensive and was written by the author. It also has a list of states and jurisdictions which have allowed questionnaires over the years, which can be appended to the motion submitted to the judge.

8. Schwartz, John, *As Jurors Turn to Web, Mistrials Are Popping Up*, New York Times, March 17, 2009.

9. "Post-trial interviews with jurors often reveal that they are extremely reluctant to request a private interview for fear that others would think that those jurors have something to hide." Starr, V. Hale, *Jury Selection: An Attorney's Guide to Jury Law and Methods*, Little, Brown and Company, Boston, MA (1985, updated yearly), 1991 Supplement, page 92.

10. *In re: Cendant Corp. Securities Litigation*, [9] 3d Cir, No. 02-4386, 0/16/03.

11. See Davis, S.D., Beisecker, T. D. "Discovering Trial Consultant Work Product: A New Way to Borrow an Adversary's Wits?" *American Journal of Trial Advocacy*, Vol. 17: 581.

Additional Reading

Ball, D., David Ball on Damages: The Essential Update, Second Edition. National Institute for Trial Advocacy (NITA), Louisville, CO, 2005.

Bennett, C. and Hirschhorn R. Bennett's Guide to Jury Selection and Trial Dynamics. St. Paul, MN: West Publishing Co, 1993.

Blumenfeld, A. and James, K., Act of Communication – Consultants in the Art of Advocacy, What Can Lawyers Learn From Actors? Act of Communication, 2001.

Crawford, R.J. and Morris, C.A. The Persuasive Edge. Tucson, AZ: Lawyers & Judges, 2005.

Donner, T.A., and Gabriel, R.K., Jury Selection Strategy and Science. St. Paul, MN: Thomson/West, 1999.

Gertner, N., and Mizner, J. The Law of Juries. Little Falls, NJ: Glasser LegalWorks, 1977.

Goodman, J., Green, E. and Loftus, E. What Confuses Jurors in Complex Cases; Judges and jurors outline the problems. Trial Magazine, 21, November 1985.

Greene, E. "On Juries and Damage Awards: The Process of Decisionmaking," Law and Contemporary Problems 52, 1989

Hamlin, S. What Makes Juries Listen. New York, NY: Harcourt Brace Jovanovich., 1985.

Lilley, L.S. "Techniques for targeting juror bias." Trial Magazine, 74, November 1994.

Linz, D. and Penrod, S. "Increasing attorney persuasiveness in the courtroom." 8 Law and Psychology Rev. 1, 8 -11, 1984.

Matlon, R. Communication in the Legal Process. New York, NY: Holt, Rinehart and Winston, 1988.

Munsterman,, G.T., Hannaford, P. and Whitehead, G.M. Jury Trial Innovations. National Center For State Courts, 1997.

Oliver, Eric Facts Can't Speak for Themselves: Reveal the Stories that Give Facts their Meaning, NITA (National Institute of Trial Advocacy), 2008.

Pennington, N. and Hastie, R. "Explanation-based decision making: effects of memory structure on judgment." Journal of Experimental Psychology: Learning, memory and cognition, 521, 1988.

Pennington, N. and Hastie, R. "A cognitive theory of juror decision making: the story model." 13 Cardozo L. Rev., 519, 1991.

Pennington, N. andHastie, R. "Evidence evaluation in complex decision making." Journal of Personality and Social Psychology, 242, 1986.

Rifman A., et al. (1992). "Real jurors: understanding of the law in real cases" 16 Law & Human Behavior, 539.

Smith, L.J. and Malandro, L.A. Courtroom Communication Strategies. New York, NY: Kluwer Law Book, 1985.

Chapter 24

Crafting Effective Themes for a Nursing Malpractice Case

Sean J. Doolan, Esq., Monica M. Kenny, Esq., Nursine S. Jackson, MSN, RN, Samuel L. Davis, Esq., Douglas S. Grossbart, MD, JD, and Wendy Neggers, Esq.

24.1 Introduction

The first objective of trial advocacy is to focus the jurors on the essence of the case, from the start of the trial until its conclusion. In meeting this goal, the trial lawyer should develop a theme or motif that binds the case together. A case theme, both understandable and motivational, should be chosen well before trial and followed throughout. The theme is "a life preserver that jurors can hold onto throughout the trial's tempests and tumult. It helps jurors rationalize away all the case conflicts and justify the preferred viewpoint concerning the case facts."[1]

TIP: The value of a trial theme is that it (1) personalizes case issues and (2) helps jurors form impressions that win lawsuits.

Scientific jury research over three decades shows that:

1. Jurors deliberate in themes.
2. The case theme is the primary mental organizer that helps jurors remember facts.
3. A good theme enables jurors to recognize evidence that fits or does not fit the story.
4. Themes facilitate comprehension of the evidence and enable juries to reach predeliberation verdict decisions.[2]

24.2 How to Develop a Theme

There are no hard and fast rules on building a theme, because no two lawsuits are ever alike. Thinking in a legalistic manner is of no help in developing a compelling trial theme. Doing this usually results in a case focused on complex or arcane legal issues which jurors neither understand nor care about. Colorful descriptions make great theme summaries, because they use a few easily remembered words. Vivid words should be used in the theme. Themes based on one word are even better than themes of a few words. An example of a negligence case theme of a few words might be "paying for someone else's mistake." (See Figure 24.1 for additional examples of themes built on a few words.) One-word themes for a nursing malpractice case may include "indifference," "greed," "trust," or "caring." A good theme is consistent with the evidence and the jurors' beliefs. The theme should reflect a sense of values shared by the attorney, the client, and the jurors alike and should tap into that value system.

TIP: It is critical to present the central theme to the jury early on in the case; if possible, do so during voir dire.

In developing the theme, attorneys should not hesitate to adopt good themes about which they may have read or heard. Current and local events can be translated into themes by use of analogy or comparison. Literary references, such as the *Oxford Book of Humorous Prose, Roget's Thesaurus, The International Dictionary of Thoughts, The Little Brown Book of Anecdotes,* and *Bartlett's Familiar Quotations* are good sources of themes. The use of fairy tales, children's rhymes, song titles, and the Bible often create warm responses.

Developing a persuasive theme starts with selecting the right case. Lawyers probably learn the most from the cases that they regret taking. For example, if attorneys accept cases involving dysfunctional families, they will have difficulty defending against the defendant's theme that this is a greedy family that did not care about the deceased. Contrarily, if the family frequently visited their loved one in the nursing home or assisted living facility and had a close relationship, a jury will identify with the family and want to ensure this does not happen to anyone else.

In selecting the case, the plaintiff's attorney should be careful and thorough in determining whether the attorney is dealing with a caring or uncaring nurse. Ask the family members what they thought of the nurses. If they visited regularly, they should have an opinion. What is the reputation in town of the nurse? Is he a traveling nurse just passing through? Did he go to school with the jurors? Is his family intertwined with the community? How well trained was the nurse? What training, testing, or performance reviews did he receive? If the nurse received her degree in 1965 and did not actively pursue continuing education courses, your theme may be that the staff was not properly trained or current in training. How competent can this nurse be, especially if he was overworked?

Defendant

A doubtful remedy is better than none.
—*Bacon, Essays: Of Innovations*

A desperate disease must have a desperate cure.
—*Shadwell, The Humorist Act iv*

Doctors are authorized by the states to practice medicine, which is to diagnose, treat, prescribe, and operate on diseases, not people. Everything else is nursing.
—*Donna Diers, R.N.*

To preserve a man alive in the midst of so many chances and hostilities, is as great a miracle as to create him.
—*Jeremy Taylor, Holy Dying*

Plaintiff

You yourself do wrong when you do not punish it.
—*Publilius Syrus, Sententia*

In overlooking the offenses of a good man you impair the law.
—*Publilius Syrus, Sententia*

Pardon one offense and you encourage many.
—*Publilius Syrus, Sententia*

There are some remedies worse than the disease.
—*Publilius Syrus, Sententia*

Caring is the essence of nursing. This does not understate the science of nursing. Rather, nursing has identified the science of caring.
—*Nancy Sharts Engel, R.N.*

Modern nursing in a sentence?—Florence doesn't live here anymore.
—*Echo Heron, R.N.*

***Figure 24.1** Sample Themes for a Nursing Malpractice Case*

A. Discovering the Theme Through Psychodrama

Erich Fromm, a psychoanalyst, once said, "Man's task in life is to give birth to himself, to become who he potentially is." As the famed author and attorney Gerry Spence once said, "We are the psychic archeologists engaged in an archeological dig for the self."[3] The basic premise is that you cannot effectively convey the themes of your case unless you can relate to them in your own life. For example, you will be a far more effective advocate for your client if you can relate your client's case to something in your own life.

Lawyers are trained to view the facts and cases in a dispassionate way without emotion. We are trained to let logic and reason prevail over emotion. When interviewing our clients, we tend to hurry them along so we can get the facts that we need. You cannot uncover the themes of your case unless you listen patiently and carefully. It is often helpful to reveal something in your own personal life that demonstrates that you understand how the client and/or witness feels. We do not always have to be the all-knowing and powerful lawyers. For example, a personal story about who or how the lawyer became interested in handling these types of cases may put prospective clients at ease by making them realize the lawyer can relate to their experience and understand their position.

As lawyers interviewing witnesses and clients we are trained to get the facts and only the facts. Often when the witnesses or clients get emotional we view that as getting in the way of fact-finding. As a result of this approach, we often miss the true story. John Nolte, a well-known psychodramaticist, believes that there is no such thing as information, but rather only emotions and feelings. He further argues that facts are nothing more than attempts to explain our emotions and feelings. The famed trial attorney Gerry Spence would use a unique method through the use of psychodrama to discover the true story of the case. He would have the lawyers actually take the place of the clients, defendant, witnesses, etc. to act out each of the roles. For example, in a nursing malpractice case, two lawyers may use this method to discover the story by having one lawyer act out the part of the nurse and the other to act the part of the patient. By acting out the part of the client, a lawyer will get in touch with her own feelings and, more importantly, those of the client.

Development of the facts of the case through the discovery process creates the theme. The theme will not be credible if the facts do not support it. It is much better to have a specific theme than a generic one. Jurors want to believe they are doing something worthwhile and important. Below is an example of how to take the generic theme of "trust" and tailor it to the case specifically:

This case is about broken promises. In their advertisements, the defendant-assisted living facility promised that its residents would receive "skilled" care and "personal attention" in "clean surroundings." They broke each of these three promises. The staff providing care to the resident was not skilled. They lacked the basic understanding of her medical needs. The care was not personalized. She was treated like a number on a page. The surroundings were far from being clean. In fact, they were unfit for decent living. Skilled care, personal attention, clean surroundings—all a string of broken promises.

B. Discovering the Theme Through Jury Focus Groups

Jury focus groups are small groups of jury-qualified residents from the trial community. These individuals listen to arguments and information about the case and are then asked for their reaction and their "verdict." Jury focus groups are an excellent way to develop both sides' themes of the case. After having two lawyers present each side to the jury, you can have them deliberate or you can simply have them ask questions and talk about the case. Through either method, there is no question that you will uncover certain themes in your case.

TIP: You can hire a jury consultant firm to make the arrangements for a jury focus group. However, you can save money by hiring a local employment agency to gather six to eight people of different ages and backgrounds who are willing to participate. There are also trial guides that will assist you in conducting a jury focus group.

24.3 Factors that Influence Themes
A. Public Image of the Nurse

The public image of all healthcare providers has changed, and so have the perceived roles of nurses and health care. Nursing is no longer considered for women only and is widely regarded as a high-status profession. While gaining in prestige and acceptance, nursing continues to maintain its foundation of compassion and concern and its strong reputation for caring. A poll of students and adults concluded that the sample was most likely to agree that nursing provides the following:

- A sense of making a difference
- A sense of feeling that what you do is important
- Working with a group of people you enjoy

- Challenging responsibilities
- Needing a solid understanding of medical technology
- Needing to react quickly to situations in a fast-paced environment[4]

Seventy-five percent of the persons surveyed about nurses frequently chose the adjectives "caring" and "knowledgeable" to describe the typical nurse, and the vast majority rated "caring" as the most important quality a nurse can possess.[5]

Nurses are taking on more responsibility and exercising more independence in our society. Nurses are recognized as professionals responsible for independent nursing care. While many nurses may find such independence satisfying, it can expose them to greater liability. Nurses are also being looked to as providing a safety net for physicians. Because nurses are held to specific standards such as the American Nurses Association Standards of Practice,[6] individual liability can be imposed for their negligence. The distinction between nurses and doctors is not as clear as it used to be. Because nurses are so highly skilled today, jurors are more likely to agree that if a nurse is negligent then the nurse should be held responsible.

TIP: The public's image of the prototypical physician— someone who is kind, caring, reassuring, and proficient, like Dr. Marcus Welby of television fame—is more often than not embodied by a nurse.

The quality of care provided by hospitals will continue to be a front-runner in the public's expectations of a nurse. However, the public perception today is that the quality of health care is declining. More hospitalized individuals are complaining that they could not figure out who the nurse that cared for them was because nurses were too hurried or rushed to introduce themselves; they went days without linen changes and their call bell was not answered.[7] More experienced nurses are leaving the profession, stating that they are "burned out." Nursing groups have been concerned about this perception. On the flip side, with increased emphasis on preventative care, illness prevention and self-care, and the role of the nurse within that framework, the public's view of an independent nurse may emerge.[8] See Chapter 2, *Where Have All the Nurses Gone?*, for more information on the nursing shortage.

The attorney's ability to portray or detract from the defendant nurse's caring quality may be the single most important theme in a nursing malpractice case. The images of nurturer and handmaiden remain closely linked in the public's

eye. According to a recent survey, more than 80 percent of the public believe nurses are doing a "good job" of serving healthcare consumers. This contrasts with roughly 65 percent holding the same view for physicians, pharmaceutical companies, and hospitals, and only 34 percent for HMOs and managed care companies.[9] The ability to emphasize a nurse's lack of compassion for those who have placed their trust in these professionals is a strong point for a plaintiff.

Based on the public's feelings toward nurses, a jury may very well start the case with sympathy for the defendant nurse, unless it is somehow lost or dispelled by the evidence and testimony. The defense should take advantage of this by making all attempts to personalize the nurse defendant. The defense should suggest that this case will affect the nurse's professional and financial position. The defense can emphasize the ways in which an adverse judgment may affect the defendant nurse's family and stress the nurse's vulnerability because of this lawsuit. Since information about the defendant nurse's insurance coverage is not presented to the jury in most jurisdictions, the jurors never know whether the nurse is personally liable for an award. Jury research does suggest, however, that jurors are aware of insurance coverage and do discuss in deliberations who is responsible for paying the money.

Defense attorneys should humanize the nurse defendant, reminding the jury that their client, unlike the physician, does not drive a luxury automobile or enjoy the physician's wealth, power, or prestige. Most jurors can easily identify with the nurse who works all night, has kids at home, and is struggling to support a family. A plaintiff's attorney learned this the hard way when he began vigorously questioning a nurse in front of the jury about her work experience. She testified that she worked at a donut shop. When pressed, she answered that it was the only way she could get the money to go to nursing school. The attorney quickly dropped his sarcastic tone, but the jury picked up his ridicule and reacted negatively to it.

Defense attorneys can personalize the nurse through the use of historical themes that portray the profession as honorable and charitable. For example, Clara Barton was a nurse who selflessly assisted the victims of the Johnstown, Pennsylvania, flood of 1890. Descriptions of Florence Nightingale, the profession's best known figure, should focus on her acts of courage and selflessness. This may portray a positive association that may benefit the defendant. Many meritorious claims against nurses can be successfully defeated by the portrayal of the nurse in the historical role of an "angel of mercy." The nurse defendant can subtly exploit the public's perception of the nursing profession as comprising caring, compassionate professionals. The defense attorney should carefully prepare the nurse for trial by emphasizing the jury's natural inclination to admire the nurse. The nurse should avoid any expressions of dislike, distaste, or outrage over the plaintiff's conduct. Any derogatory comments made by the defendant about the plaintiff can convey the message that the nurse did not provide appropriate care because of antagonism toward the plaintiff.

TIP: It is important for the plaintiff's attorney to depersonalize the nurse defendant because juries are reluctant to hurt people whom they like or with whom they identify.

The flip side of this is that the plaintiff's attorney, while agreeing with the general caring image of the nurse, may be able to demonstrate that this nurse on trial does not conform to the image of a typical "good" nurse. Plaintiff's attorneys want to personalize their clients and simultaneously depersonalize the nurse. It is not easy for a jury to look a nurse in the eye and say, "You were careless in this case, and therefore you must pay." Plaintiff's counsel should point out that while nurses are "people too," they nevertheless have a job to do just like the rest of us. The job must be done correctly.

For example, a jury had no problem finding liability in a case in which a 38-year-old quadriplegic resident at a long-term care facility was being bathed by a LPN wearing rubber gloves. The patient requested hotter water for his bath and the nurse responded by using hot water from a coffee urn and pouring scalding hot water into the tub in which he was seated. Because the patient did not have any feeling below his shoulders, he was not aware that he was being scalded until he saw his skin floating to the surface of the tub. The patient sustained second and third degree burns over 40 percent of his body as a result of this. The patient underwent a bilateral amputation of his lower extremities below the knee because of circulatory deficiencies and severe pressure ulcers. The patient later succumbed to a bloodborne infection that spread from the infected pressure ulcer. Clearly, the nurse had a job to safeguard the patient, but did not follow the standard of care.

The groundbreaking book *Rules of the Road: A Plaintiff Lawyer's Guide to Proving Liability* is a trial advocacy book that provides useful insights in the handling of nursing malpractice cases.[10] The authors explain how all jurors who drive understand that if a driver breaks a "rule of the road," she should be held accountable. In other words, if the driver goes through a red light, the driver has violated the rules of the road and, therefore, must be held responsible for any resulting injury to another.

Nursing malpractice cases are often much more complex than a motor vehicle case but nursing malpractice cases can be simplified for the jury by demonstrating that the nurse failed to follow the "rules of the road" much like a driver in a motor vehicle case. The average juror has difficulty understanding the ill-defined liability standards that apply to nursing malpractice cases. Jurors are asked to measure the defendant's conduct based on what a reasonably prudent or reasonably competent nurse would have done in the same circumstances. Most jurors do not want to second guess a nurse's judgment. On the other hand, jurors are more willing to hold a nurse accountable if that nurse has failed to follow the basic rules—rules that the juror can understand and relate to. Most importantly, it is a basic fundamental rule of nursing that nurses are supposed to be advocates for their patients.

B. Deep Pockets and Big Business

Physicians and hospitals, not nurses, are perceived by the public to be the deep pockets in malpractice claims. This is still true, despite the worsening financial condition or charitable status of most hospitals. A nurse, as an employee of the hospital, can provide access into these deep pockets if liability can be proven.

> In *Ripnick v Heller*, a 29 year old man was left in a persistent vegetative state after he was injected with the wrong drug during surgery for a ruptured eardrum. He received $6 million under a structured settlement. The $6 million is to be paid in a lump sum, with $3 million being paid by the insurance company on behalf of three nurses and the ambulatory center, and the remaining $3 million to be paid by the doctor's insurance company (unpublished verdict).

Often, one law firm is assigned to represent a nurse and hospital insured under the same malpractice insurance policy. For strategic reasons, it may be highly prejudicial to the defendant nurse to reinforce the image of any unity of interest with other named defendants. By sharing the same defense firm, the nurse is deprived of the chance to create distance from the corporate image and other problems occurring in the hospital. With both the hospital and nurse represented by the same attorney, the defendant nurse is precluded from presenting evidence of staffing violations or inadequate training. Serious conflicts of interest may exist for an attorney providing joint representation of a nurse and hospital. The nurse defendant in any nursing malpractice case should seriously consider retaining his own counsel, especially in catastrophic cases in which a verdict for the plaintiff could exceed the coverage limits of any malpractice insurance. This issue is also mentioned in Chapter 16, *Defense Attorney's Perspective.*

C. Risk Apportionment

Plaintiff's counsel may also wish to approach the case from a perspective of who is better able to shoulder the risk. Patients seek medical treatment for a condition that is affecting them. They trust the medical personnel responsible for their care. Patients are not in a position to guard against the injuries that occur to them because of a trusted person's negligence. Patients lack the knowledge to effectively balance the risks and benefits of proposed treatment. The more serious the suffering or disability, the less likely they are to engage in rational choices or self-protective behavior.

TIP: The apportionment of loss creates an issue of fairness, with the ultimate question being, who should compensate the innocent party for the losses?

Jurors must be taught that patients should not suffer because of the inappropriate actions of relied upon professionals. Every patient has the right to a full explanation before beginning any type of treatment. The patient can make a reasonable response based on the facts presented. Often, it is the nurse's responsibility to secure the patient's signature on an informed consent form before a procedure is begun. The nurse must be knowledgeable about the procedure because the patient or family may ask questions before signing. The nurse who discovers that a patient has not been informed must proceed cautiously. The nurse should notify the physician to determine whether the information was deliberately withheld. If the nurse has divulged information to the patient that caused her to refuse treatment in a life-threatening situation, and the physician had intentionally withheld information, the nurse could be held liable for his actions. By framing the issues in this manner, the jury is not being asked to place blame or decide who was at fault, but rather who was in a better position to prevent this injury. The nurse, with whom the jury may sympathize, is no longer being judged on a moral basis.

D. Patient Advocacy

In many ways, nurses are the patient's advocates. The nurse spends more time with the patient than any other medical provider. The nurse is also the eyes and ears of the doctors. This is especially true in institutional settings. Nurses in a nursing home are full-time and usually are on-site 24 hours a day, seven days a week. On the other hand, a doctor may visit a nursing home only one time per week for less than a full day. The doctor must rely on the observations and notes of the nurse to effectively treat the residents. In a home care environment, the physician is heavily dependent on the nurses and home health aides to report changes of concern.

Controlling the flow of information is a function of the nurse in institutional settings. The nurse decides what information deserves noting in the patient's chart. The nurse will likely conduct the initial assessments of the patient and the doctor will briefly review it before signing. Care plans are then based on these assessments. Therefore, a nurse's job is more hands on and decisive than that of a physician.

While the status of nursing has changed, jurors may still feel that nurses are not supposed to be experts in diagnostic techniques or the mechanics of treatment. The defense may want to bring out this point during trial in an attempt to place the blame on someone else. It was not the nurse's job, for example, to diagnose the patient's medical problem, and thus the injury was caused by someone else's negligence. The plaintiff's attorney can counter this defense with a list of the responsibilities the nurse has on a daily basis, such as those stated above.

A theme for a case involving a failure of a nurse to inform the attending physician or other hospital staff of a change in the patient's condition might be, "The nurses acted like three monkeys—see no evil, hear no evil, speak no evil," or, "No one was listening. No one was putting together the pieces to the puzzle." This theme could have been used in a case such as the one involving a 26-year-old Croatian musician who was struck by a car and sustained open fractures of both lower extremities and probable internal and closed head injuries. He was taken by ambulance to a community hospital where his head and thoracic spine were CT-scanned. The scout film demonstrated prevertebral swelling, but the CT scan of C1-C7 was not ordered. The patient was brought to the operating room, where he was intubated in preparation for orthopedic surgery and an exploratory laparotomy. At some point, a nurse removed the hard cervical collar. Over the next four hours, the patient became quadriplegic. A subsequent CT scan revealed a burst fracture at C1. This fracture was not discovered by two trauma surgeons, a vascular surgeon, an orthopedic surgeon, two radiologists, and three anesthesiologists until 24 hours later. This case was settled (unpublished verdict).

With nurses' greater professional stature and independence, they are expected and required to meet the standards of care. The Nurse Practice Act adopted by each state makes this an absolute duty. Nurses who challenge a doctor's orders cannot be dismissed on those grounds.[11] A nurse is expected to speak up for what she believes without having to worry about professional ramifications. Many states have laws that require nurses to "blow the whistle" on incompetent medical acts. Courts in those states have upheld such laws and held that nurses unable to work out the problem with the doctor must inform their supervisors if they believe a patient is not receiving proper care.[12] In theory, a nurse may speak out on diagnosis and treatment-related matters without fear of retaliation and, consequently, jurors may be less forgiving if the nurse does not. Regardless of what the law and the code of ethics say, fear and intimidation are potent forces that inhibit the free reporting of incompetent behavior.

Generation X jurors (those born between 1966 and 1981) are likely to respond well to themes involving ethical and moral behavior. Foley and LeFevre[13] note that themes relating to ethics, rules, and morality tend to be persuasive for some members of Generation X. A theme likely to appeal to this age group is, "The nurse's job was to protect the patient from the doctor's mistake," or "The nurse was the last link in the chain of events that separated the patient from health and injury."

TIP: The ANA Code of Ethics for Nurses[14] states that it is a nurse's duty to promote, advocate for, and strive to protect the health, safety, and rights of the patient. Additionally, the Code sets forth the nurse's primary commitment: to the patient.

E. Personal Responsibility

In a recent survey, Americans were asked to rank 15 values in order of importance. More than 95 percent of those surveyed called personal responsibility "very important." This was consistent across sex, race, class, and political preference.[15] The theme of personal responsibility is useful for both plaintiff and defense attorneys. Jurors want both plaintiffs and defendants to take responsibility for their conduct. As a result of efforts to change the tort system, attacks on the plaintiffs' bar and plaintiffs have focused attention on the need to accept personal responsibility. A nursing malpractice suit involves responsibilities of the nurse and the patient. The plaintiff's attorney's goal is to draw attention to the responsibility of the nurse to provide care in accordance with standards of care. The plaintiff's attorney is asking the jury to hold the nurse responsible for the negligent care delivered by the nurse.

The defense attorney often focuses on the patient's responsibilities to adhere to instructions provided by the nurse. The tort reform efforts have been successful in drawing attention to the personal responsibilities of the plaintiff. Wenner and Cusimano[16] comment that, "[r]ight or wrong, the public is fed up with what appears to be the refusal of people to take responsibility for their own actions." Take for example the now infamous McDonald's case. How many times have attorneys had to defend our judicial system to those who think that a woman driving a car was awarded millions of dollars because she chose to put a hot cup of coffee in her lap as she drove away? But do those who question this verdict have all the facts? Likely, no. The facts in that case were different than the usual story: the woman was not driving, she was a passenger; McDonald's had been repeatedly warned that the temperature of its coffee was more than 20 degrees hotter than recommended and 50 degrees hotter than home-brewed coffee; McDonald's had received over 700 complaints about the temperature of its coffee; and the woman had simply asked McDonald's to pay her medical bills (approximately $20,000). McDonald's instead offered her only $800. Because of her severe injuries and the medical bills, she sued. It should also be noted that the verdict was later reduced by 80 percent by the judge and the parties later settled for an undisclosed amount.[17]

This anti-plaintiff bias places an obligation on the plaintiff to prove she was both a responsible citizen before entering the healthcare system and was in no way responsible for her injuries.

TIP: The plaintiff's attorney must dispel the myth that all lawsuits are frivolous. To do so, distinguish the plaintiff as severely injured and deserving of just compensation.

The theme of personal responsibility can be used by the defense in the empty chair theory. The nurse and physician may have been involved in an incident that led to a patient's injury. If the plaintiff's attorney failed to name the physician as a defendant, yet that individual was responsible for the injury, the defense attorney may exploit this situation. The defense attorney can persuasively argue that the client nurse should not have to accept personal responsibility for someone else's error.

F. Language Barriers

1. Foreign nurses

A high percentage of nurses today are either foreign-born or use English only as a second language. This clearly affects juror perceptions. A patient's reaction to encountering a foreign nurse may lead to doubts about training, qualifications, experience, and other competency issues not necessarily related to the actual ability of the nurse. Communication and cultural barriers may keep a nurse from understanding a co-worker or patient and, conversely, prevent someone from understanding the nurse, which can create hostility and put a patient's safety at risk.

This enhanced danger of alienating the patient and the increased safety risk caused by poor English skills have been recognized by the courts. An assistant head nurse in California filed a Title VII action against her hospital, which had prohibited the nurse and those she supervised from speaking their native Filipino dialect of Tagalog in the maternity unit where they worked. Hospital administrators asserted that the rule was necessary, because conversations in Tagalog had resulted in preferential treatment for those nurses who spoke it and adversely affected worker morale and supervision. The court found that the language restriction did not violate the nurse's civil rights, because it was motivated by a desire to eliminate dissension that could have compromised patient safety.[18]

Some foreign nurses come from male-oriented cultures that condition them to fit into a male-dominated hospital environment. These nurses may have great difficulty questioning a physician's orders. Some facilities have dealt with this problem by teaching a foreign nurse how to be assertive. Other nurses may come from cultures that discourage displays of any type of public intimacy, making it more difficult for them to discuss diseases with patients, to look them in the eye, or to touch them. These cultural predispositions may hamper a nurse's case by creating negative juror feelings. The defense may be able to counter these reactions by presenting a "cultural defense" that increases juror understanding and sympathy for the things that the nurse did or did not do. When preparing a foreign nurse for a trial, the defense counsel may want to emphasize the crucial importance of looking at the jury when answering questions. Lack of eye contact may be interpreted as the nurse being evasive or having something to hide.

Patient safety is at issue if communication is hampered by the nurse's accent. The ability to communicate with the public is an essential requirement of the nurse's job. The defense must take these communication problems into account when preparing the nurse client for trial. If a jury is unable to understand the defendant, it may be hostile. There may be a strong prejudice against the defendant. These biases must be explored during voir dire.

2. Language barriers and patients

The inability of the patient to understand English is another variable that affects liability. This may lead to themes such as, "No one took the time to get an interpreter" or "The patient received second class care when he deserved first class." These themes might be applied to a situation in which a patient who spoke broken English arrived at the nurse defendant's outpatient facility shortly after fainting. The nurse asked him if he was on any medication, and the patient misunderstood and shook his head "No." The doctor wrote a prescription and the patient later experienced side effects caused by a drug interaction. It turned out the patient had been taking antibiotics, but did not understand the nurse's question about medication.

Joint Commission standards require that the healthcare facility provide information in a language the patient can understand. The use of interpreters and translation services assist the nurse in meeting the applicable standard of care. Today's multicultural population requires intense efforts to maintain effective communication. If the nurse does not make these efforts, the nurse is jeopardizing the patient's safety and is being negligent.

24.4 Nurses in Advanced Practice
A. Expanding Roles

Potential jurors do not have a good idea of what a nurse's job entails or does not entail. There are misconceptions regarding a nurse's duty to diagnose illnesses and plan patient care. While a majority of jurors realize that the nursing profession has specialties, many are hard-pressed to identify exactly what those specialties are. As a group, non-physician clinicians are becoming increasingly prominent in providing health care. These clinicians include nurse practitioners, physician's assistants, nurse anesthetists, midwives, clinical nurse specialists, and others, including naturopaths, acupuncturists, and chiropractors.

Some of the responsibilities of these clinicians include:

1. Observing symptoms and reactions of patients and taking prompt, correct action when indicated.
2. Properly using all equipment. A nurse can be sued for inadvertent misuse of equipment which results in an injury to the patient.
3. Accurately documenting all patient care matters: dosages, times, readings, etc. "Human error" is no defense.
4. Supervising others under the nurse's level who are engaged in nursing care. Nurses can be sued for mistakes of unlicensed assistive personnel.
5. Carrying out "proper nursing procedure." But what is proper procedure? Following standing orders? Using best judgment?
6. Carrying out the orders of doctors, and for understanding the reason for, and the effect of, such orders. A nurse could be held liable along with the physician.
7. Providing adequate patient instruction.

As the nursing profession matures, nurses are moving into increasingly responsible and accountable positions, which in turn increases professional liability concerns. Liability risks associated with the role of the nurse midwife are discussed in Chapter 21, *Midwifery Malpractice and Litigation,* in Volume II. The special perioperative risks of the nurse anesthetist are presented in Chapter 20, *Nurse Anesthesia Malpractice Issues,* in Volume II. Clinical specialists function within a supervisory or educational role in hospitals, and act as a resource for the staff. They are accountable for their actions, just as with any nurse rendering patient care.

Nurse Practitioners (NPs) fit into the grey zone as professionals capable of practicing independently. The amount of physician supervision of the NP is loosely defined in many areas. As patients increasingly view NPs or nurse midwives as primary caregivers, patients will expect them to bear responsibility for their actions.

The role of NPs has expanded largely because of their cost-effective manner of providing care. As courts come to view them as professionals capable of independent practice, these NPs increasingly are held independently liable for their actions. With the addition of prescriptive privileges, NPs have in some instances replaced physicians in the primary delivery of health care. While the elements of a NP malpractice action are the same as a medical malpractice action, the standard of care for a NP is that of the reasonable NP.

A juror who has had any experience with a NP may hold registered nurses (RNs) to a higher standard of care; this could be dangerous to the defense. This could also be very advantageous to the plaintiff's attorney. The defense should stress that the standard of care required by a registered nurse is established by those nurses with the same level of educational preparation.

TIP: The defense must ensure the jurors do not subconsciously compare the RN on trial with their prior experiences with a NP, who is a specially trained practitioner providing all the services necessary for health promotion, prevention of disease, and, in some cases, rehabilitation.

Because NPs are moving into territory once controlled by physicians, some doctors feel threatened and may be very critical of or hostile towards the nurse. The basis of the doctor's argument is that nurses acting independently could be a threat to patients' health.[19] A similarly trained advanced practice nurse is the most appropriate expert witness to act for the plaintiff and for the defense. Using a physician to testify in a case that involves a NP confuses the issue and may result in the misapplication of the standard of care.

See Chapter 21, *Working with Nursing Expert Witnesses,* for information on The American Association of Nurse Attorneys (TAANA) and the American Association of Legal Nurse Consultants' (AALNC) position statements on use of nursing experts to review nursing cases. With a recent study showing that NP care is comparable to physician care for primary care follow-up and ongoing care, the line between NPs and physicians could blur.[20] If NPs claim increased abilities, they may be setting themselves up to higher standards in a court of law. This point is further emphasized as the autonomy of both NPs and certified registered nurse anesthetists increases.

Hostility relates more to the economic threat of the doctor's practice. NPs and nurse midwives are educated to deliver primary health care at a cost less than that delivered by doctors, with no sacrifice in quality. Many studies have found that advanced NPs spend more time with patients, patients have higher levels of satisfaction with the care provided by NPs, and patients are more knowledgeable about their conditions.

The plaintiff's attorney needs to deal with the affection and fondness many people have developed toward NPs and nurse midwives. Many women prefer a nurse midwife rather than a physician for normal pregnancy care. Some patients describe their relationships with NPs as more personal than their relationships with doctors. The NP actively listens to the patient as a person, rather than avoiding personal involvement as some physicians do.[21] Jury perceptions of NPs should be explored during voir dire.

The physician may be legally in charge of the patient, but the nurse is indispensable in the healing process, an art belonging to the nursing profession. The profession will not get the support it needs if the public remains ignorant of the complex care nursing can provide. Defense attorneys may wish to distinguish between the duties of a doctor and those of a nurse, stressing that, even though a registered nurse may have additional training, the nurse is nevertheless not a doctor, and that the nurse's primary expertise lies in prevention and care, not diagnosis and treatment. The primary reason why patients are admitted to hospitals and long-term care facilities is to receive nursing care, not physician care.

Many believe that as long as nurses receive adequate additional training requirements, they should have additional duties delegated to them. The plaintiff's attorney, in an attempt to overcome the public's aversion to questioning the professional judgment of a nurse, should concentrate on framing the issue as one in which the defendant stepped over the boundaries of what she was qualified and trained to do.

B. Changing Public Perception Toward Nurse Practitioners

Though nurse practitioners have long been viewed as trusted and effective caregivers, as they step into acute care and get pushed into the more frantic pace of care in managed care settings, they are increasingly restricted in their ability to provide the personalized care and individualized education that has endeared them to their patients. Available measures of trends in litigation have not yet reflected a noteworthy increase in malpractice occurrences; however, attorneys are hearing an increasing number of health consumer complaints targeting NPs' care. Case reports suggest that NPs are at an increased risk of being involved in a lawsuit.

The National Practitioner Data Bank for 2004 shows that nurses represent only one out of every 100 malpractice payments paid. Of all nurse payments, NPs were responsible for 7.3 percent (of the advance practice nurses, nurse anesthetists were responsible for 62.7 percent, nurse midwives for 9.2 percent, and clinical nurse specialists for the lowest percentage at 0.2). In 2004, there were 368 malpractice payments for NPs, up from 290 in 2003 and 242 in 2002. Of the problems that led to malpractice payments for NPs in 2004, diagnosis-related payments comprised 44.8 percent and treatment-related problems were responsible for another 23.9 percent of the 368 payments.[22]

In managed care settings, NPs, who are generally reimbursed for services at a significantly lower rate than physicians, are pushed to provide assembly line care, seeing an increasing number of patients in shorter periods of time. Time constraints predispose the NP to overlooking noteworthy symptoms and physical findings; overlooking the need to schedule routine health maintenance diagnostics; and, in general, performing in a manner by which they are predisposed to misdiagnoses. Taking a patient's history and performing examinations have become perfunctory to meet the demands of many practice settings, in contrast with the past when NPs proffered patient education and personalized care. Acute care NPs face similar issues as they provide a wide range of treatments, while dealing with increasingly complex equipment; all the while, inpatient acuity is increasing and staffing of their nurses and ancillary staff has become tighter.

Meanwhile, in this evolving role of the NP as "physician extenders," NPs no longer have the opportunity to develop relationships with patients and provide the special attention that has thus far immunized them from legal issues. NPs are increasingly at risk for making mistakes, and at risk for being named in a lawsuit resulting from injury from nursing negligence.

The defense attorney for the NP will likely characterize the client as the nurturer, as the public has historically viewed nurses, and emphasize the "core values" described by the American College of Nurse Practitioners.[23] The NP is a skilled, effective, and well-educated individual with master's and doctoral preparations plus specialty certifications. The public and many patient populations are indebted to NPs, since they are often practicing in lesser desirable communities, serving populations underserved by physicians. They are vital team members in acute and critical care settings, where they provide high quality, cost-effective care around the clock, and cover patients with complex needs in a very technically challenging environment.[24]

The plaintiff's attorney, on the other hand, is likely to paint the NP in the less appealing persona of "little doctor," where the importance of the bottom line and status supersedes patient needs. The attorney will use the case example to illustrate how this NP failed the client, because the NP was too busy or distracted to provide proper care. Finally, the attorney will show the injuries that flowed from the negligence of this hassled and harried NP, who has lost focus of the core values of NPs.

C. Themes in Nurse Practitioner Cases

1. Improper training and certification

While nurse practitioners obtain their educational preparation in a specific practice area, such as acute care, pediatrics, oncology, or psychiatry, most Nurse Practice Acts permit NPs to gain additional experience in the field and to acquire additional skills through training and/or certification in the field. NPs are too often released into employment before training and certifications are completed, even though nurses and their employers begin the NP's growth process with good intentions for providing safe opportunities to acquire new skills.

For example, a hospital built a state-of-the-art neonatal unit, only to find that they were unable to find enough certified neonatal nurse practitioners (NNP) to staff the unit around the clock. The state in which this facility was built had a nursing code mandating that NPs must be educated and certified as NPs before being permitted to work autonomously in this role. As a result, this new facility hired pediatric nurse practitioners (PNPs) with the plan to have them mentored at all times by a certified NNP, until they qualified for and passed the NNP certification examination.

Only a few weeks into her on-the-job training, a new graduate PNP found herself alone on the neonatal intensive care unit, because her mentor was ill, and a replacement NNP could not be found at short notice. She was then confronted by an ethical dilemma, for which there was no right choice. One of the babies in the unit, a healthy newborn who was an inpatient because he had contracted a serious viral respiratory infection from his older siblings, developed sudden respiratory distress. He had a pneumothorax (collapsed lung) and needed immediate treatment—a needle aspiration to re-expand the collapsed lung.

The covering neonatologist, who was required by law and by hospital policy to be constantly accessible to the NP and physically within 30 minutes of the hospital, was tied up with another emergency and could not come, so this new NP was left to insert a needle into this newborn's tiny chest. There was no one else to perform this procedure and no time to waste, so she proceeded after reviewing a procedure manual and having the procedure described over the phone. Unfortunately, her needle placement was poor and she nicked the infant's left ventricle, which led to his death from cardiac tamponade.

The superficial observer (such as the plaintiff's attorney reviewing the records) of these events saw a NNP performing a procedure that she had to perform due to circumstances, but misplaced the needle in the baby's tiny chest, where there is no room for error. However, a jury could perceive this as a forgivable error in which there is no negligence.

The attorney discovered a rich web of bad behaviors and cost-cutting measures by the hospital, overreaching by an untrained nurse, and serious lack of planning for a foreseeable emergency—all at the expense of their consumers. Because of this, an otherwise healthy newborn died.

Plaintiff's attorneys should look during discovery for the information in Figure 24.2.

2. Substandard collaboration with supervising physician

Whether in the heart transplant unit where the NP's role is to medically manage the fresh transplants, or the family practice office of the rural NP in an old farmhouse, the problems are the same. Busy lives, illnesses and vacations, lack of organization, and personalities interrupt communications and effective collaboration. NPs are independent practitioners with their own patients; often their own insurance policy; and in many states, independence in prescription writ-

ing. However, behind this "independence," many NPs are mandated by statute to have a supervising physician, whose role and responsibilities are defined in state laws. Generally, the supervising physician must be "immediately available through direct communications, or by radio, telephone or telecommunications." A predetermined plan for emergency services should be in place in the event the supervising physician is unavailable.[25]

While NPs can be functioning independently in performing negligent acts, the supervising physician may also be named in a suit if the physician fails to fulfill the state-mandated or institution-directed responsibilities to properly collaborate with the nurse practitioner. In case development, the plaintiff's attorney should determine whether the supervising physician was negligent in his role and responsibilities.

- Evidence on file at the institution of RN education and current licensure;
- Nurse practitioner education;
- Nurses' and NPs' license numbers;
- Additional coursework, continuing education, and/or training of nurses and NPs;
- Evidence of certification, certifying board, date of certification, date of renewal;
- Evidence of continuing education and training in the proper performance of the routine procedures necessary to fulfill the role and responsibilities of the position in which they are working;
- Any prior disciplinary actions, restrictions to practice, and criminal charges;
- Name of physician with whom NP is in collaborative practice;
- Medicare billing number of NP;
- State Code for Professional and Vocational Standard that defines NP preparation;
- Policies and procedures and privileging as defined by the institution governing NP preparation and practice;
- Policy statement regarding nurse practitioner role in the associated physician specialty organization.

Figure 24.2 Information that Plaintiff's attorneys Should Look for During Discovery

- She was supervising too many NPs to provide safe and effective support. See e.g., PA§21.287 wherein an MD is limited to supervising no more than four CRNPs who prescribe and dispense drugs.
- She was unavailable to accept or to plan for the appropriate referral of a patient whose needs exceeded the scope and training of the NP.
- She was unable to produce the state-mandated collaborative agreement between the prescribing NP and supervising MD. See e.g., PA§21.285.
- Her error failed to provide routine consultations and chart reviews, which were evidenced in her failure to co-sign the NP's patient's charts.
- She failed to establish and update standing orders, drugs, and other medical protocols within the practice setting.
- She failed to afford the NP the opportunity to attend the mandatory ongoing continuing education or additional training and certifications necessary to function within her current role.
- She failed to establish protocols and was willing to accept overloaded patient schedules for financial gains.

Figure 24.3 *Themes to Consider in Contributory Negligence by the NP's Supervising Physician*

Plaintiff's and defendant's attorneys should consider the themes in Figure 24.3 surrounding contributory negligence by the NP's supervising physician.

A case example involves a 50-year-old male, who was added into an office schedule on a busy Friday afternoon. He had been experiencing intermittent chest discomfort for the past week, which he attributed to muscular pains from picking up an air conditioner. On Friday while he was at work, his pains worsened and he felt generally bad, finally motivating him to call his family physician's office. The NP who saw him was new to the practice and somewhat overwhelmed by the demands of the overscheduled day.

Appropriately, the NP took his history and immediately took an EKG. Also appropriately, the NP identified that the ST changes represented an ischemic heart. The NP then asked the office staff what the protocol was to get an acutely ill patient to the hospital, and found that none had been devised. Feeling badly that he had complicated an already heavy day for this new NP, the patient said he could drive himself to the nearby hospital. There is no evidence as to how much the NP resisted this idea. The next information available is from the paramedic report describing how this patient had caused a head-on collision; and when his car came to rest on the roadside, he was found slumped over the wheel in complete cardiopulmonary arrest. He was dead on arrival to the emergency department.

3. Ego and personality issues

Only a small subset of registered nurses go on to fulfill additional education and training to become NPs. Personality, more than intelligence, financial motivations, or other, inspires this move. Registered nurses (RNs) in general, like to be in charge, and those with additional drive tend to seek out this advanced role for the autonomy, challenges, and status it affords.

NPs are also risktakers, a valuable trait as they face daily challenges in caring for patients with complex needs. Whether in rural or big city medical center settings, NPs are faced daily with performing new, technically challenging procedures and making diagnoses using sophisticated diagnostic testing, both of which are at the cusp of the scope of their education and training. Just as they chose this career path based on personalities, their styles of managing daily challenges are shaped by their personalities and ego needs.

Legal cases often involve the NP overstepping the bounds of training and education. Sometimes the NP, who characteristically takes on more than can be managed well, is just moving too fast and not making good judgments about what should be done when problems require extra time for consultations or when patients need to be referred out. Other times, most often in a medical center setting, the NP falls into the spirit of a resident physician and forgets the constraints of his training.

An ideal collaborative relationship between a NP and the supervising physician bolsters the autonomy and safe practicing of the NP. Establishing the guidelines of the collaborative relationship and defining the hierarchy to access in case of emergencies assists in maintaining this balance. Too often, personality issues intercede to yield bad outcomes.

An example of insufficient planning to overcome personality issues arose in a labor and delivery setting. A healthy 30-year-old mother of one healthy child at term with her second pregnancy was admitted to a medical center on her due date for an elective induction. Her family physician, who had provided her antepartum care and planned to perform her delivery, made intermittent visits to the hospital during the course of the labor. As per their established mode of operation, a team of NPs and residents responded to calls from the labor nurse between the obstetrician's visits.

During the course of this induction and augmentation with medications to induce labor, the mother started reporting increasing pain, and the monitor showed a pattern consistent with uterine hyperstimulation. Fifty-five minutes prior to delivery, the mother felt a serious tearing pain in her left upper abdomen, then the fetal tracing started showing serious signs of distress. When the family physician was notified, he had become tied up with a concurrent issue, so he instructed the nurses to call an OB who often covered for him.

The NPs and residents were clearly concerned with the ongoing evidence of fetal distress, but they failed to seek the assistance of the covering OB for an inexplicably extended period of time. Ultimately, they relented and called him. The OB came immediately when called and performed an emergency cesarean section. Upon entering the abdomen, the surgeon found the fetus lying in the mother's peritoneum, having been completely expelled from the uterus through a massive uterine tear. The baby suffered profound ischemic brain injury but survived.

Plaintiff's attorneys should seek the following in discovery in such cases:

- The hospital protocols for induction of labor
- The hospital protocols for use of the specific agent (in this case, Cytotec) used in the induction
- The American College of Obstetricians and Gynecologists (ACOG) standards for induction, and specifically, for induction with this agent[26] because the NP's practice is governed by the standards set by the corresponding MD organization
- The collaborative relationship established for the NPs covering the OB service
- The hierarchy of supervisory support, both physicians and nursing supervisors, to whom the labor nurses and NP seek assistance

- The NP's testimony explaining why she failed to implement the chain of command to seek assistance for the fetus in distress
- The dearth of NP's continuing education, in regard to interpretation of fetal monitoring and regarding the adverse effects of Cytotec when it is employed off-label and against the warnings of its manufacturer and FDA, as an induction agent

In the case example above, discovery revealed that the hospital had developed and maintained appropriate policies and procedures, defined a clear chain of command, and had documents reflecting good emergency planning in general. What they did not account for was the personalities involved. The OB on call proved to be intimidating and mean-spirited. The OB team knew that in the past, calls to him for guidance had resulted in such derision that they chose to wait out the fetal distress, hoping it would go away, rather than having to endure his wrath.

As a result, not only were the NPs named as defendants, but so was the covering OB, who in this case came immediately when called and performed a timely and appropriate cesarean section. Because of circumstances caused by his personality, overwhelming the personalities and judgments of the OB team, he was called far too late to prevent serious injury to the baby. That personality came through loudly in deposition, but might have been toned down for trial, and was memorialized for use in trial via the videotaping of the deposition.

The resulting trial theme came to be about failure of the OB team, including the NP, to advocate for a laboring mother and fetus in distress. This theme was intertwined with substandard continuing education of the NP and the OB team, in that they failed to appreciate the significance of the electronic fetal monitoring evidence of uterine hyperstimulation, and particularly did not appreciate the serious potential for uterine hyperstimulation during the use of this specific induction agent—Cytotec—known to cause such severe hyperstimulation that its package insert warns of its potential to cause uterine rupture. Knowledge deficit superimposed on personality issues yielded a catastrophic outcome for this baby and his mother.

4. Documentation, or lack thereof

What exactly should the NP be documenting? The attorneys involved in medical malpractice litigation have the burden of learning the standard of care from the medical literature, practitioners, and educators to establish what the NP had the duty to document for each particular problem or issue at hand.

For example, a NP charted that a 46-year-old male presented to a rural urgent care with complaints of "midsternal chest pain and vomiting." In this setting, the NP had the duty to follow the diagnostic tree that an emergency department physician would employ. Clinical policies developed by the American College of Emergency Physicians (ACEP) would have been a helpful tool to the attorney to get a sense of the issues in working up a patient presenting with chest pain.[27] In this case the attorney learned that the NP had failed in her duty to explore and document the characteristics of the pain:

- What precipitated the pain? (His wife later reported that he was sitting on a commode straining with constipation.)
- Had he had this pain before? (Never—it was of sudden and dramatic onset.)
- Were there associated symptoms like diaphoresis or shortness of breath? (He suffered near-syncope when the pain came on.)
- Was there radiation of the pain? (It radiated to his back.)

The NP also had the duty to assess the patient's risk factors for a cardiovascular etiology of the pain. When the NP considered the possible etiology of the presenting complaint, she needed first to consider and rule out the life-threatening causes of chest pain (e.g., myocardial infarction, pulmonary embolism, aortic dissection, and so on) before accepting a working diagnosis of a non-life-threatening etiology. The NP's selection of diagnostic studies indicated that she gave some consideration to the possibility of acute coronary syndrome, but failed to obtain serial cardiac markers after the first set of studies and EKG were essentially within normal limits.

She concluded he was at low risk for cardiovascular or pulmonary disease without taking a good history of his cardiovascular risk factors or symptomatology, so she did not obtain a chest x-ray or any additional studies. Had she given due consideration to his risk factors, she would have

appreciated he was at a significant risk for cardiovascular disease: being male, over 40, slightly overweight, sedentary, stressed, and suffering the effects of unmanaged hypertension.

By failing to take a standard history, perform a standard battery of diagnostics, and continue to observe him, as per the standard of care (established by both the expert retained and the gold standard literature), she missed his diagnosis of aortic dissection.

This emergency department NP failed to obtain a chest x-ray, which according to experts later enlisted by the plaintiff would have showed a widened mediastinum "to a reasonable degree of medical certainty." Because he was discharged prematurely, the patient was no longer in the hospital when he started suffering pain radiating to his back. Following a couple of hours of monitoring, she discharged this patient with continuing chest pain to home with a diagnosis of viral gastroenteritis (his white blood count was somewhat elevated), and within a couple of hours, his aorta ruptured and he died.

The theme of this case lies in the research and literature that supports that:

1. Good history-taking was the key to making this diagnosis.[28] The decedent presented with a textbook presentation of aortic dissection, which the NP failed to appreciate due to substandard history-taking and a cursory physical examination.[29-30]
2. Her shortcut in history-taking, as demonstrated by her dearth of documentation, predisposed her to missing this life-threatening diagnosis.
3. Her patient had lived long enough to have definitive intervention, i.e., he had time to be taken to the operating room, had the diagnosis been made in a timely manner.

Documentation issues also encompass billing by NPs, who must also learn to bill for services rendered. While billing and coding may be unpleasant tasks in their professional lives, they quickly become habituated to performing this "documentation" because they are at risk for nonpayment for services by third-party payers and charges of Medicare abuse and fraud. Coding and billing alone are not sufficient, because if NPs do not justify the coding through appropriate documentation of physical findings, a plan of care, and justification for diagnostics and procedures for which they have charged, they can suffer serious repercussions, even loss of license if their billing practices are deemed fraudulent.

Despite this constant threat of serious ramifications from substandard documentation, harried and sometimes disorganized, or ill-disciplined NPs take shortcuts in documentation, leaving subsequent caregivers and attorneys developing a case in the dark. More consistently than charting, NPs habitually code itemized statements for reimbursement, using diagnostic codes and procedure codes to describe the care provided. By decoding these billing statements as part of case development, the attorney can uncover missing pieces to the puzzle that should have been noted in the medical records. In more than one case, evidence of whitewashing of the medical records has been discovered through decoding items on billing statements. Within the codes the decoder may discover that telling diagnoses and procedures may have been charged, but were not documented as having been performed in medical records (or at least in the records provided).

Evidence contained within itemized statements may take some of the weaknesses out of "he said, she said" situations. For example, in a case where a patient suffered from respiratory depression and died from what the family claimed was Morphine overdose, the itemized statements supported the family's claim that a significant overdose of Morphine had been administered in the emergency department, though none was charted. This discovery explained the toxicologist finding a high level of opiates in the blood stream at the time of autopsy, and allowed a causal connection to apparent negligent dosing and administration.

5. Little doctors

Instructors in many NP educational programs encourage their students to have their names and credentials embroidered into their lab coats' pockets. This built-in name tag assures that the NPs' credentials are always apparent to the patients. NP students are taught to correct a patient if mistakenly called "Doctor," and immediately clarify that they are nurse practitioners, not doctors. They function according to the standards of care for nurse practitioners, and are taught that they should hold themselves out to the world as nurse practitioners. When their practice is the focus of a lawsuit, it is appropriate to have a nurse practitioner, not a physician, testify to the standards of the NP's care.

Unfortunately, there are times when a NP forgets the scope of her practice, forgoes reminding patients that she is not a physician, and does not consult with a supervising physician or refer a patient to a specialist when the patient's needs exceed the NP's abilities or training. Particularly in remote vicinities, whether low income urban settings or rural communities underserved by physicians, NPs tend to be placed on a pedestal by patients and become isolated from colleagues, who might reorient them to the scope of their practice.

In a very rural pediatric clinic, a ten-year-old girl presented to her NP with complaints of increasingly bothersome headaches. Initially, the headaches were thought to be related to allergies and actually seemed to respond to allergy treatment. Over several years they worsened, lasting days then weeks at a time and got labeled as "migraines." The associated symptoms with the "migraines" evolved, and when one would occur, the young girl reported blurred vision and episodes of vomiting. Once the headaches were deemed unresponsive to allergy medication, the NP tried Paxil, then tried other psychotropic drugs, analgesics, and antiemetics.

The slender child started losing weight, so the NP obtained food histories and counseled the child about food choices, and he told her to make certain she did not skip breakfast. He never sent her for a diagnostic study or consultation.

Approximately four years after the onset of her "migraines," the child had a syncopal event on a weekend when the clinic was closed, so her parents took her to an emergency department. During this visit she had a radiologic study of her brain, which showed a 4 x 5 cm mass compressing her optic nerve and hypothalamus, and causing a significant hydrocephalus. Surgical pathology of this mass, obtained when she underwent a debulking operation, showed this mass to be an astrocytoma, an incurable cancer. The surgery left her with severely diminished vision and with intractable nausea, after which she needed to receive nourishment through a feeding tube. These problems will probably continue for the remainder of her short life. The family wondered why their "doctor" had not sent them for diagnostic studies earlier.

The theme of the mediation focused on the importance of the quality of each remaining day, when only a finite number remain; and on the inexplicable overreaching of the NP, who had dozens of indications and opportunities to send this child for timely testing and timely interventions that would not have left her in such misery.

See Chapter 19, *Nurse Practitioner Liability Issues*, in Volume II, for more information.

24.5 Who are the Defendants in Long-Term Care Settings?

The plaintiff's attorney cannot properly develop the theme without first deciding who are the defendants. Because of vicarious liability, the facility is responsible for the negligence of its staff, including nurses. Accordingly, the attorney will almost always name the facility as a defendant but not necessarily the nursing staff. Typically in the long-term care setting, the attorney is faced with the decision of whether to name a nurse as a defendant. The nurse practicing in a long-term care facility often makes clinical judgments without a physician readily available.

The nurse should not be a "tag along" defendant but rather a significant focus of the lawsuit. Naming the nurse as a defendant must fit nicely with the theme. Themes must be consistent. Naming a nurse as a defendant along with the facility may not always be consistent. If the complaint alleges a facility was understaffed but a nurse is a defendant, the nurse may assert the defense that he was not provided with the necessary staff to perform his job. This can cause inconsistency that may confuse the jury and lead to an unfavorable verdict.

Jurors realize the patient may not be the only victim in a malpractice case. They also realize a lawsuit could have devastating emotional and professional impacts on a nurse. Accordingly, it is the authors' view that the plaintiff's attorney should not name nurse defendants unless their conduct significantly deviated from the standard of care so that a reasonable person would be angered by their behavior. Of note, in some states, a nurse must be named in order to exceed the charitable immunity cap.

If there is a sweet nurse native to the area who made a simple mistake, the plaintiff's attorney may not be wise to name her as a defendant. Nor should she be vilified. Rather, the attorney should show that she is the victim because, although she did her best, someone in a corporate position made the decision to intentionally understaff the facility. The further logical extension of this theme is that this corporate decision to understaff the facility led to simple mistakes. On the other hand, the attorney may want to name as a defendant a temporary nurse or an agency not native to the area and whose conduct would anger the jury. Consider if the nursing process was followed in determining whether to name the nurse as a defendant. If not followed, consider naming the nurse as a defendant. The steps of the nursing process are as follows:

- Assessment
- Nursing diagnosis
- Planning

- Implementation
- Evaluation

While the failure to follow the nursing process is a good start, there must be something additional to anger the jury.

TIP: Another consideration is whether the family likes the nurse. Interview the family and find out what they thought of the nurse. Patients tend to remember nursing care more than anything else. If the family thought the nurse was rude and uncaring, chances are the jury will as well.

The following case is an example of conduct that angers a jury:

> Two nurses in Colorado stepped over the line dividing nursing and practicing medicine. A resident was in a long-term care facility when one morning he was making it difficult for a housekeeper to clean his room. At that point, a nurse and a nurse's aide strapped him down and gave him a shot of Thorazine (a major tranquilizer). The resident died later that day. The resident's physician testified he never prescribed Thorazine for him while at the facility. The doctor further testified the resident was incapable of consenting to the drug's administration. The nurses were found guilty of practicing medicine without a license.

24.6 Common Plaintiff Themes
A. Profits Over People

A common generic plaintiff's theme is that the facility put profits over people. Typically, two types of cases fit this theme: understaffed facilities, or improper admission and retention. Both are discussed in more detail later. If the plaintiff's attorney can show intentional understaffing that prevents nurses and aides from performing their jobs, the focus will shift from a single act of nursing negligence to the profit-motivated corporate decision that made the delivery of health care less than standard. Negligence related to corporate greed is likely to happen to someone else. This is no longer an isolated incident.

Defendant attorneys should counter this theme by arguing the facility is entitled to make a profit and there is no crime in doing so. In fact, that is why it is in business. A defense attorney may be able to show that the federal government does not reimburse enough money for them to provide perfect care and still make a profit.

When appropriate, the defense should also counter this theme by stating that the plaintiff is greedy. The defendant may show that the plaintiff never or rarely visited the patient, but now wants to hit the legal lottery and collect money based on the patient's suffering. For more information on this, see Section 24.8 below.

Another common defense counter to this theme is that the facility is not-for-profit. The argument is that its focus was on quality care since it was not motivated by profit. Many not-for-profit facilities award owners handsomely. Plaintiff's counsel must mine the facts to determine whether the owners and managers are overly compensated. The plaintiff should also point out that, regardless of the not-for-profit status, the facility must still provide the same level of care for patients. There should not be a different standard of care for not-for-profit facilities.

B. Trust

Trust is really a variation of the personal responsibility theme. It goes as follows: "We (the patient and family) trusted the nursing home, hospital or home care agency to provide the care we contracted for and provide the care we could not perform at home. The facility knew about all of her medical conditions and was getting paid to care for her. They accepted the job and implicitly promised they could care for her. The purpose of a nursing facility or agency is to provide compassionate nursing care. The facility and its staff are the professionals and know the required care."

In developing this theme, the plaintiff's attorney has to answer the question of who broke that promise—was it the corporation or was it an individual nurse or was it both? The facility did if it made a business decision to be intentionally understaffed.

A common counter defense to this theme is, "If the family members did not trust the facility, why did they continue to keep their loved one there after the accident? Or if there was a pattern of neglect, why did the family keep its loved one there?" This ties into the underinvolvement of the family and thus they are undeserving of any award from the jury. The defense will further argue that nurses are only expected to follow the standard of care for an ordinary nurse, not the much higher standard of care the plaintiff suggests. The standard of care does not require that exceptional care be provided. If a plaintiff's attorney has selected the case carefully, he will be able to respond that the case concerns basic nursing 101—something that would have been learned in school. This is textbook nursing and nothing exceptional.

Another common defense theme to counter the trust argument is that they are just nurses, not the doctors responsible for ordering the necessary care. The defense will argue, "We should not be held responsible for the mistakes of doctors."

The plaintiff's counter to that theme is that nurses are the eyes and ears of the doctors. While in many instances carrying out a physician's orders insulates a nurse from liability, blindly carrying out questionable orders does not protect the nurse. A nurse has an obligation to advocate on behalf of the patient. While nurses cannot change an order simply because they disagree with it, they do have options. They can consult with a nurse supervisor or another physician in the facility. Nurses are an important part of the healthcare team. In any setting, nurses are available much more than the doctors. Nursing assistants report back directly to the nurses, provide most of the care in long-term care, and have more contact with patients than do doctors. The nurses and aides care for this patient 24 hours a day, seven days a week. As stated earlier, nurses' roles are changing in the direction of them acting more independently with a higher skill level. Commensurate with that is more responsibility and thus greater liability.

TIP: Remember that a failure of a nurse's aide is a failure of the nurse. Aides are supervised and answerable to the nurse. It is the nurse's responsibility to make sure the aides are doing their jobs properly.

C. Insufficient Staff

In some hospital cases and most long-term care cases, the plaintiff's attorney's theme is that the facility's understaffing was a contributing factor in the bad result. In some cases, the understaffing theme supports the broader theme of profits over people—that there was a corporate decision to intentionally understaff the facility.

A defense response to the understaffing theme is, "The nursing shortage is not our fault. We try to get qualified people but cannot find them." There is ample evidence that the United States is in the midst of a nursing shortage expected to increase as the baby boomer generation enters long-term care facilities. By 2012, more than one million new and replacement nurses will be needed.[31] This shortage is expected to intensify over the next two decades with 44 states expected to have RN shortages by the year 2020.[32] In May 2005, the National Commission of Nursing Workforce for Long-Term Care released a report, *Act Now for Tomorrow*, which indicated that there are nearly 100,000 vacant nursing positions in long-term care facilities on any given day and the nurse turnover rate is 50 percent. Americans are aware of this healthcare crisis: 40 percent think the quality of health care has worsened in the last five years. Americans feel the most important issues causing medical errors are workload, stress, and fatigue among healthcare professionals. Sixty-nine percent of Americans in the study felt there were too few nurses.[33] Furthermore, 65 percent of the general public cited the shortage of nurses as the leading cause of medical errors.[34]

To counter this theme, defense counsel cannot simply offer statistics, but rather must show that the facility has made reasonable efforts to increase staffing. Did the facility make recruitment efforts and offer financial incentives to attract new recruits?

D. Failure to Follow Regulations or Facility Policies and Procedures

Often when a facility demonstrates a pattern of failing to comply with regulations or to follow its own policies and procedures, it ties in nicely with other plaintiff's themes of profits over people, understaffing, breaching trust, and so on. An understaffed facility that has put profits over people may have an increased incidence of pressure ulcers. Evidence may show that their staff members failed to comply with their own policy to turn and reposition patients every two hours.

This theme can be further developed by showing that policies and procedures are required to be followed by OBRA and/or The Joint Commission, if applicable. Facilities can be disciplined when the policies and procedures are not followed. This argument will defeat the defense counter that defendant's policies and procedures were not followed because those policies and procedures are only guidelines and not requirements. A facility's policies and procedures are published in a book or available on a computer for all staff and nurses to review. The plaintiff's attorney must assert during the trial that those policies and procedures are important and must be followed. It is generally believed that policies and procedures create a standard of care.

TIP: The plaintiff's attorney should carefully review any survey reports, deficiency reports, and the facility's policies and procedures. This review will likely show if there is a pattern of failing to follow the policies and procedures.

If the plaintiff's attorney can show a systemic habit of the nurses failing to follow regulations or the facility's own policies and procedures, it may further develop the theme of understaffing and properly trained staff being unaware of the policies and procedures. This theme, properly developed, will anger a jury.

TIP: The plaintiff's nursing expert witnesses should select rules that are easy to understand, hard to disagree with, and can show that violations would lead to the patient's injury.

Nurses in our society are viewed favorably and as having the best interests of the patient in mind. A plaintiff's attorney does not have to demonize a nurse for a jury to hold the nurse accountable. Rather, demonstrating that the nurse failed to follow a regulation or policy and procedure and that such failure resulted in the patient's injury will suffice.

For example, there was a case where the nurse failed to verify the placement of a feeding tube prior to commencing tube feeding. As a result, the patient suffered a severe abdominal infection that eventually resulted in her death. The plaintiff's nursing expert witness assisted in finding that a basic nursing principle had been violated.

In another case, the patient fell and fractured her hip because of poor supervision by an aide. The aide had seen that the patient was up and moving around, but did not stop putting away dishes to supervise the patient. The basic rule broken was that patient safety should always be the first priority.

TIP: The attorney can look for "rules of the road" in statutes, regulations, case law, textbooks and articles from professional literature, ethical standards, and common sense. Review the Nursing Practice Act that has been adopted by each state and explore if there are any violations in your particular case.

The importance of good documentation cannot be overstated. For example, in a pressure ulcer case, it will often be found that the nurse did not fully assess the wound for stage, size, depth and color. The aides often do not document that the resident was turned and repositioned or toileted regularly. The plaintiff's attorney must establish the importance of documentation for the jurors. It is a good practice to have the defendant nurse testify as to all of the reasons documentation is done; for example, communication between staff, quality assurance, and consistency among the staff. The nurse could also be asked if he knows the old adage, "If it's not documented, it wasn't done."

24.7 Common Themes in Assisted Living Facilities

Many of the themes set forth herein are suitable to assisted living facilities (ALFs). However, unlike nursing homes, ALFs are not directly regulated by the federal government, but rather by the individual states. Thus, definitions, terms, and rules governing ALFs vary throughout the country. ALFs have become another option in long-term care and are no longer part of an industry in its infancy. According to one study, there were 36,451 licensed care facilities/ALFs with 937,601 units/beds in 2004, about 168 more facilities nationwide than in 2002.[35]

Also unlike nursing homes, training and licensing varies considerably from state to state. Only 11 percent of ALF staff members had to complete a minimum of 75 hours of training and pass an exam before they could work in a unit providing direct care.[36] Further training time ranged from one to sixteen hours. According to the Hawes study, most staff in ALFs lacked the necessary knowledge about the normal aging process, resulting in a failure to alert nurses or other licensed professionals to a resident's decline. For example, almost 90 percent of the study thought that confusion was a normal part of the aging process.

In the last several years there has been an explosion in the growth of the assisted living industry. In the mid to late 1990s, ALFs grew at a rate of nearly 30 percent.[37] As a result of this growth, one-third of ALFs have been in business for no more than five years.[38] Sixty percent of ALFs have opened in the last ten years.

As a result of this rapid growth, two issues have developed: oversupply and consolidation. In 2003, the ten best performing chains achieved a median growth rate of 53 percent, while in 2004 their median growth rate slipped to 26 percent, resulting in a drop of nearly 50 percent.[39] In 2004, Benchmark Assisted Living, a New England Company, purchased Village Retirement facilities, resulting in Benchmark becoming the largest provider of assisted living in its region.

Of the states that do regulate ALFs, the trend is to permit more services so residents can age in place.[40] Accordingly, many ALFs are providing services for those that suffer from Alzheimer's disease. In 1997, about 30 percent of ALFs had units dedicated to Alzheimer's residents; by 2000, that figure was 51 percent.[41]

The typical ALF resident is likely to be a woman, 85 years of age, who requires assistance with several activities of daily living (ADLs). In 2000, 76 percent of ALF residents were women.[42]

Because of the growth of this unregulated industry, most ALF cases involve the improper admission or retention of residents. Some of the same themes used in nursing homes are present in ALF cases, such as profits over people, understaffing, or breach of trust. One new theme in ALF cases is that this rogue industry must be reigned in. Plaintiff's attorneys will give the jurors the sense they are part of something much bigger than this case—that they are doing something important in sending a message to this rogue industry; that the industry will pay a price for putting profits over people.

The obvious defense retort is that, because this is a new industry, it should not be held to the same standards as federally regulated nursing homes. This is an experiment society is conducting and there will be a period of trial and error. An extensive discussion of ALFs and residential healthcare facilities can be found in Chapter 11, *Assisted Living Liability*, in Volume II.

24.8 Common Defense Themes

There are several defense themes seen regularly in nursing malpractice cases. This section discusses some of the more prevalent ones. Defense themes are very subtle. Defense lawyers rarely openly argue them but simply imply the theme. For example, the defense will imply a theme of nursing shortages by trying to show that the nurse made a simple mistake because she is overworked and the facility is understaffed.

A. Nursing Shortages

The nurse is not part of the power structure of a facility and is virtually powerless to affect the decisions of the corporation concerning staffing and cost-cutting in health care. The defense, by framing the issues in this manner, allows the nurse to become a victim of the circumstances of corporate indifference in the managed health care system or a part of an overworked, undertrained, and underpaid staff. This allows the defense to distance the nurse from the corporate image of health care. The nurse is not a decision maker but merely an employee whose job may be jeopardized as a result of this trial.

A theme that can be used by both defendant's and plaintiff's attorneys is the effect of cutbacks on staffing. An understaffed facility increases liability for nurses, but it also gives jurors the opportunity to place "blame" on a doctor or corporate entity rather than on the "good" nurse with a strong moral commitment to the care of patients. The number of nurses does make a difference. See Chapter 2, *Where Have All the Nurses Gone?*, for information on how nursing care affects outcomes.

It is essential that the plaintiff's lawyer continually remind the jury that a malpractice suit does not imply criminal or unethical conduct by the defendant or jeopardize the professional's license, membership in professional societies, or status in the eyes of colleagues. Even though a nurse may be competent and have high professional standards, the nurse can do nothing about the fact that the hospital is understaffed or poorly managed. This theme allows a jury to render a pro-plaintiff verdict without a moral condemnation of the nurse.

There is a perception among the public that nurses are overworked and that the cost-cutting trends have increased the use of nurse's aides and other unlicensed assistive personnel as substitutes for RNs. A plaintiff's attorney can portray the nursing shortage as an intentional profit-making endeavor undertaken by the facility. Of significant note, California was the first state to pass legislation that requires all patient care units in hospitals to meet minimum nurse-to-patient ratios. California's Department of Health Services must establish these minimal ratios. This legislation also prohibits hospital use of unlicensed, minimally trained personnel to perform procedures normally done by nurses. It additionally prohibits nurses from being assigned to areas in which they lack proper clinical training. The hospital industry and business groups lobbied hard against the bill.[43]

That a majority of people believe nurses are overworked is a point defense attorneys can use to their advantage in selecting jurors sympathetic to a nurse's workload, such as working mothers who work the night shift and run a household as well. The quality of bedside care can be expected to decline in facilities that shrink their nursing staff. Higher workloads for nurses occur when they are required to take on the responsibility of non-nursing tasks, such as housekeeping chores and clerical work. As nurses increasingly absorb non-nursing assignments, they have less time to spend with patients and more errors necessarily occur. Additionally, to fill scheduling gaps, nurses are given assignments for which they may not be qualified. As discussed in Chapter 1, *The Roots of Patient Injury*, and Chapter 8, *Inside the Healthcare Environment*, the reduced number of licensed nurses within a facility can have serious consequences. This is also discussed in Volume II, in Chapter 7, *Medical Surgical Malpractice Issues*. These include inadequate staffing, delays in providing basic care, inexperienced staff ill-prepared to report or recognize significant symptoms, and the discharge of patients without adequate instructions. State licensing boards do not regulate the education of nurse substitutes. There are no requirements on the amount of training for unlicensed personnel being assigned nursing work. The danger is that care is being compromised to cut expenditures, as facilities are forced to comply with the dictates of the managed healthcare companies. These shortcuts inevitably lead to increased numbers of readmissions, medication errors, and patient accidents. Not only do registered nurses have to care for a greater number of patients in less time, but they must supervise untrained technicians for whose mistakes they also are responsible.

TIP: Hospitals and other facilities are clearly walking a tightrope between profitability and the quality of care provided.

A patient could face injury or death if a NP is the most skilled person present. In this situation, what should the NP do? He has an ethical duty to attempt to treat the problem at hand even though it is beyond the scope of the NP's training. This situation can arise much more than expected. For example, a responsible physician may be responding to an emergency at another facility and be unavailable. Therefore, if a NP is faced with an emergency situation and the physician cannot respond, the NP must overstep his training and treat the patient.

TIP: An attorney should know if the specific emergency was one the NP should have anticipated and prepared for, to deal safely with the population or environment in which he was working.

Both plaintiff's and defendant's attorneys must determine several things when dealing with a case involving a NP caught in this situation. Was the NP required to obtain certification or continuing education to function in each role or setting? Also, the attorney must determine whether there was a chain of command protocol in place—for example, an emergency department physician in house that the NP should have consulted before assuming responsibility. In discovery, the attorneys should inquire if the NP is on or has a representative on the Ethics Board of the institution to assist in planning actions to be taken if placed in such a situation.

Jurors become aware of serious patient injuries through personal experiences and the media. They do not live in a vacuum. The theme that profits are compromising the quality of care given in medical facilities may very well lead to a higher percentage of pro-plaintiff verdicts. One nurse observed that, while there are fewer nurses, "nursing care standards don't change. I'm still expected to give the same level of care."[44]

Particular attention should be paid to a careful review of all original documentation of nurses' notes, shift assignments, time cards, and other nursing records that reflect professional nursing services rendered on weekends, holidays, and other times when nurses are generally short-staffed. During these periods negligence is most likely to occur or when problems arising from incomplete or inaccurate medical records are noted. Using the term "skeleton crew" may be particularly effective in describing the minimal staffing available during these times.

As medical facility staffs shrink, nurses are being forced to function outside their areas of expertise and become, in essence, nurse generalists. This has caused a fair amount of anxiety within the nursing community. A group of nurses who work at the nation's smallest hospitals have already gone this route. Many nurses at less-than-50-bed facilities located mostly in rural areas have been generalists for years.

These nurses are called upon to care for almost any type of patient. A generalist must be able to change focus at a moment's notice. The nurse might be caring for an adult surgical patient when a child with a respiratory problem needs assistance. Dealing with this wide range of patients presents many difficulties. These generalists must be competent in a range of technical skills that includes cardiac and fetal monitoring, pulse oximetry, drawing blood specimens, adult and neonatal resuscitation, and traction setup. The trend in medical facility administration is to add more responsibilities to nurses. The cross-training has spread to larger hospitals as well.

Since many hospitals rarely have the resources to provide the support services needed, acquiring and maintaining diverse nursing skills can be difficult. In an effort to reduce costs, education positions are being cut from the nursing budget. In many instances, these nurses are on their own and must provide for their own continuing education. The defense may wish to stress that nurses are expected to do everything without any support services to fall back on. Plaintiff's attorneys may wish to stress the difficulty these nurses have in keeping up-to-date with current techniques, which may result in more deviations from the accepted standard of care.

Hospital patients are now sicker than before because of changes in reimbursement. Today's outpatients would have been treated in hospitals in the past. Patients cared for on medical surgical units might have been in critical care units in the past. More complex technology together with a sicker population and higher patient-to-nurse ratio, may pave the way for increased adverse outcomes in the future. This has implications for nursing malpractice as well as the public perception of the nursing profession.

B. Victims of Obedience

Nursing, perhaps more than any other profession, has been influenced by social conceptions regarding women. Nursing originated at a time when Victorian ideas dictated that the role of women was to serve men's needs and conveniences. Nursing's development was greatly influenced by the attitude that women were less independent, less capable of initiative, and less creative than men and needed their guidance. This background continues to influence the trial of a nursing malpractice case. Note that jurors may have different perspectives on this issue. Older jurors may still adhere to traditional male and female roles and behavior. Baby boomers who saw and participated in the battles for equality for women may have strong feelings about a female nurse subservient to a male doctor. Generation-X women, according to Foley and LeFevre, "think feminist battles are over.

Women of the Baby Boomer generation, some of whom spent a life time opening new opportunities for women, are understandably puzzled when Generation-X women preface a statement with 'I'm not a feminist but....'"[45] This may be due in part to the media portraying feminists as "femi-nazis," suggesting it is not fashionable to be a feminist.

The duty to obey physicians' orders is one of many issues that arise in a nursing malpractice case. The jury debates whether the nurse acted responsibly and followed the doctor's orders. This debate surfaced in a case involving an unstable six-month-old preemie born at 30 weeks, weighing eight pounds, who was accidentally given an overdose of potassium chloride (KCl) administered intravenously by an overworked Filipino nurse. Minutes later, a cardiopulmonary arrest occurred. The nurse subsequently failed to advise the team of physicians who attempted resuscitation that an overdose had occurred. As a result, the resuscitation took almost 45 minutes, leaving the child brain damaged and quadriplegic. If the nurse did in fact follow the doctor's orders and tragedy resulted, she could be perceived as the victim of an act of obedience. If no such order was written, she could be perceived as an "angel of death." Jurors become less punitive in their judgment when the defendant is perceived as engaging in such an act of obedience.

NPs frequently blame delays in getting referrals to specialists or diagnostic studies on the limitations imposed by the patient's health insurance. Paperwork, calling insurance companies for approval, limited providers available in-network, difficult communications within the bureaucracy—all complicate getting the patient the care she needs.

TIP: Plaintiff's attorneys should use available documentation to demonstrate that the NP failed to recommend the procedure or consultation in a timely manner or that the NP failed to document any efforts to expedite the process.

In *Cline v. Lund,* a nurse and her employer hospital were found negligent in failing to check a patient's vital signs every 30 minutes as the attending physician had ordered.[46] The physician had instructed the nurse to notify him immediately if the patient's condition deteriorated. The nurse failed to check the patient's vital signs and the patient subsequently died. The nurse obviously failed to follow the doctor's orders.

The plaintiff's attorney faced with this scenario must stress that nurses no longer function as handmaidens following physicians' orders without independent thought.

For example, in a Louisiana case, the attending physician left orders for an infant patient to receive a certain drug. The nurse felt the order was unclear as to the proper administration, so she approached two physicians in the nursing unit for clarification. The physicians felt there was no need for concern. The nurse did not contact the attending physician and administered the drug by injection in the amount of the order. The dosage was lethal and the patient subsequently died. The testimony at trial was that a nurse who encounters a confusing or ambiguous order should seek clarification from the attending physician who wrote it. The failure to seek clarification was, in fact, a deviation from the standard of care required of a professional nurse. The nurse was found negligent by the court, which concluded: "While apparently strict adherence to physicians' orders may in some cases protect the nurse from a finding of negligence, the nurse cannot rely on faithful and strict adherence to the physicians' orders when the nurse knows that the orders are incorrect."[47]

TIP: If the plaintiff can show that a nurse should have called a treating physician or that a doctor gave orders that were subsequently not followed, he may very well be able to counter the jurors' sympathy for the defendant.

C. The Nurse is in Over Her Head

There is no excuse for malpractice if a medical problem can be easily remedied by the right person, technique, or tool. With the constant emphasis in the managed care era of economy and limited services, nurses and NPs are now often confronted with this dilemma. Just as there have been predictions that pharmacists under greater pressure to fill more prescriptions in a shorter period of time will make more significant errors, nurses and NPs will also face a similar dilemma. The public is well aware of this problem and will likely not tolerate this type of defense.

Another potential problem for especially NPs is a patient that presents with symptoms consistent with two concurrent diagnoses. In this case, the patient's symptoms lead to one diagnosis, which obscures a separate and distinct diagnosis. Additionally, if the presenting signs and symptoms are atypical, the NP may have no reason to entertain a particular diagnosis, even though it may be the correct one.

TIP: Attorneys should scour the records to make sure the NP ruled out life-threatening diagnoses before ac-

---

cepting a less serious diagnostic possibility. Review of records should verify that the patient had adequate clinical indications of diagnosis A to end the NP's diagnostic investigation, even though the patient may have had risk factors for diagnosis B. It must also be noted that sometimes one diagnosis completely obscures another, and this cannot be avoided.

The plaintiff's attorney should remind the jury that a nurse or NP in over her head should seek assistance: you cannot simply bury your head in the sand if you are unsure about what to do. That is not a valid excuse for negligence—in fact, it is a classic example of negligence.

D. The Perfect Hindsight Defense

Address the question of, what is known now that was not known before the alleged deviation? Resentment towards the "Monday morning quarterback" is a common theme that plays into the tort-reform arguments. The hindsight rationale is best countered by using timelines that demonstrate to jurors how the events unfolded.

In the case of NPs, defense could argue it was appropriate the NP did not consider the actual diagnosis within his differential diagnoses, because the patient did not have the risk factors for that diagnosis. Plaintiff's attorneys should use the medical records to demonstrate that the NP did not take a proper history to adequately assess the patient's risk factors; the physical examination missed significant findings that should have raised red flags; the patient had or probably had physical findings and symptoms overlooked by the NP; and the patient had risk factors. As discussed above, the plaintiff's attorney can use documentation to claim the patient was given improper care. Defense could argue that just because there is poor documentation does not mean there was necessarily poor care. The staff can sometimes just forget to document the care that was provided.

Defendant attorneys should remind jurors that hindsight is 20/20 and it is easy to judge the correct action after the fact. However, it is not easy when faced with an emergency situation that demands immediate attention.

E. The "Patient's Body Failed" Defense

This is a common theme in long-term care cases and in cases involving critically ill patients. Some injuries are not caused by any negligence. Simply stated, "Stuff happens. It was nothing the nursing staff did." The patient was already very sick. You cannot prevent all medical conditions or the inevitable. Once again, the broader themes of trust and personal responsibility are triggered. The plaintiff's attorney's response should be that everyone dies, but it did not have to end this way and the defendant had no right to give substandard care because the patient was sick. The attorney can counter that the plaintiff is not here because the patient died, but rather because of the manner in which death occurred. Also, the patient had a quality of life and deserved to be cared for. The facility had no right to take away what little quality of life the resident had.

The following quote by Jeff Rusk, Esq. sums up the plaintiff's response to this defense theme: "Remember that it is not the damages to the family which drives a nursing home case. It is the conduct of the defendant. Someone has to take a stand."

TIP: Plaintiff's attorneys should respond to this theme with care plans indicating what future goals the resident had. If the patient was in the facility for rehabilitation and was expected to be released in the near future, then why say the resident was going to die anyway?

Advocates must attempt to anticipate the questions that will arise in the jurors' minds as they decide a case. These issues are frequently overlooked because they are not, strictly speaking, the mandatory legal components of the case: that is, the standard of care, deviations from that standard, proximate cause, and damages. The most common overriding question in nursing malpractice cases is whether the body failed or the nurse failed.

Jurors rationalize. They try to "make right what was done wrong." On any given jury, some members will seek out alternative explanations for bad outcomes. They will search for if the patient's body failed or the family failed. These jurors will come to the conclusion that the healthcare provider was responsible only after ruling out other causes, such as patient conduct, genetic predisposition, or "fate." In the case of the baby who received an overdose of potassium chloride, the jurors must be freed from lingering doubts on the cause of the brain damage. Failure to do this results in the jurors' wondering whether the infant had significant brain damage before the overdose occurred. In the case of the undiagnosed cervical fracture that rendered the patient quadriplegic, it may be difficult to believe that eight physicians dropped the ball and failed to make a proper diagnosis. Both cases settled out of court. Plaintiffs must teach jurors to distinguish fate from human error.

TIP: Plaintiff's attorneys should show the jury that the patient deserved and would have had a better quality of life for the time she had left, were it not for the malpractice. Also, show the jury the patient would at least had time for closure had it not been for the malpractice.

F. Aggravation of a Preexisting Condition

In the usual medical or nursing negligence case, the doctor will have been called upon to treat some preexisting injury or illness. In the case of the baby given an overdose of potassium chloride, the premature baby was unquestionably neurologically impaired before getting the overdose from the defendant nurse. The defendants attempted to emphasize the fact that the outcome, especially in regard to higher functioning and employability, would not have been dramatically different even without the overdose. Damages in these cases may well be increased by the argument that the defendant created further anguish and mental pain for someone who already suffered greatly.

TIP: The plaintiff could stress the following theme: when you have limited capacities to begin with, any additional problems are even more devastating. The nurse's actions deprived the plaintiff of the little he had.

The fact that the plaintiff had a mental or physical problem before the alleged deviation is no defense. If counsel for the plaintiff proves that such a preexisting condition was aggravated, it is as much a basis for just and adequate compensation as a new injury or condition. However, some apportionment may exist depending on the facts.

G. No Guarantee of Positive Outcome

A defendant's attorney must look to the care the nurse gave the patient. If the nurse used professional judgment properly and there was a bad outcome, the nurse should not be the guarantor of a positive outcome for the plaintiff. A negative outcome does not necessarily imply malpractice or negligence on the part of the nurse.

H. Bad Family

In many cases, the defense can use the bad family theme. There are many different variations of this theme—the family did not visit and therefore are not deserving of money; the family was uncooperative and made it difficult for the nurses and staff; if the facility was so bad why did the family not move the patient; the health care proxy signed a DNR so they must not have loved the patient, and so on.

Plaintiff's attorneys can avoid this problem by accepting cases only where there is family involvement. The attorney must also distinguish between family being difficult and a family being an advocate for the patient. The plaintiff's attorney should also explore with family members why they did not remove the patient from the facility if they believed the care was poor. Some family members may explain that the facility had become the patient's home and moving would have been disruptive. They may say there were no other facilities nearby. Additionally, the facility may have made promises that the care would improve and that the problems would be corrected.

TIP: Review the social services progress notes to see what was said about the family. Also review any sign-in sheets that family members would have to sign when visiting.

24.9 Case Examples
A. Nursing Home

A nursing home resident sued for damages sustained as a result of personal injuries she suffered in a fall while at a nursing home in New York. The resident was admitted to the nursing home in October 2000. She had suffered over ten falls in less than one year following admission. The last fall resulted in a fractured hip requiring surgery. The resident never regained her ability to self-ambulate after the fall, rendering her bedridden. The plaintiff alleged the nursing home was negligent in the care and treatment of the resident and was also liable for violations of state statutes.

The theme, with respect to the nurses, would have included personal responsibility and patient advocacy. The medical records in the case included physician progress notes, completed by the treating physician on a monthly basis. A review of those progress notes revealed that the physician indicated there were no falls suffered during the pertinent time period. However, other medical records, as well as state-required incident reports, indicated falls occured during those time periods. Based on these discrepancies, it was the plaintiff's theory that the nursing staff and the nursing home failed to notify the treating physician of the falls, in violation of the nursing home's own policies and procedures. The theme was that the nurses should take responsibility for their failure to follow their own policies and procedures and their failure to advocate for the patients.

B. Assisted Living Facility

Consider the case of an 87-year-old woman who moved into an unlicensed assisted living facility. She exhibited some confusion at the time she moved in. As time went on, however, her confusion increased and the resident's neurologist notified the assisted living facility that a higher level of care was needed for the resident. The neurologist suggested the resident be moved to the facility's dementia unit. (The facility also had an unlicensed unit for Alzheimer's and dementia residents.) However, the resident was not moved due to the unavailability of rooms in the unit.

Several months later, the resident, who had a history of wandering through the facility, eloped from the facility in frigid northeastern winter temperatures. It was not until some four hours later that the facility noticed the resident was unaccounted for. A search was performed in the facility and the police were notified. The resident was found the following day, when her body was discovered a short distance from the facility. Due to the weather conditions, she suffered hypothermia resulting in death.

The facility employed a RN who held the title of Wellness Director. The RN acted as a liaison among the resident, the resident's family, and the facility. On several occasions prior to the resident eloping, the RN had contacted the resident's family and reported unusual behaviors in the resident. However, the RN did not suggest the family move the resident from the assisted living facility to a facility that could provide additional care and supervision. Even after being directed by the resident's neurologist that the resident be moved to the dementia unit, the RN did nothing other than tell the family she would be moved when a room became available.

The main theme in this case was greed with an undercurrent of this being a rogue facility. The facility was relatively new, was unlicensed, and had many vacancies to fill in the non-dementia units. It was the plaintiff's position that the RN should have recommended to the family that the resident be moved out of the facility and placed in a nursing home or other facility that could provide the necessary care and supervision. However, the RN was also involved in the process of filling vacancies. If the resident had been moved out of the facility, there would have been another vacancy to fill and a loss of monthly fees. Assisted living facilities are usually more expensive and the residents are likely private-pay clients. Therefore, it makes a large difference each time a vacancy occurs in these facilities. The theme was that this nurse failed to exercise her independent judgment and advocate for the residents.

C. Hospital

An 87-year-old patient was admitted to the hospital for flu-like symptoms and dehydration. The cause of these symptoms was determined to be a hernia requiring surgery. Upon admission, the patient was assessed as a fall risk. After her surgery, she suffered a fall from her bed that resulted in a fractured hip requiring surgery. The patient had apparently tried to climb over the bedrails and fell. Although there was an order for a bed alarm, the alarm was not on the bed at the time of the fall. Furthermore, the call bell was not within reach of the patient so she could not call the nurses for assistance.

The theme used in this case could be profits over people. It could be argued that, had the hospital had the correct amount of staff or properly trained staff, the bed alarm would have been on the bed, the call bell would have been within reach of the patient, and the fall would never have occurred. If the bed alarm had sounded and the hospital had the correct nursing staff, the fall could have been prevented by a prompt response.

The plaintiff could have also used the theme of personal responsibility against an individual nurse. There were orders that this patient have a bed alarm in place at all times. Additionally, the patient was assessed as a fall risk upon admission to the hospital. Therefore, it was the nurse's responsibility to ensure the orders were carried out.

24.10 Tort Reform Movement and the Role of the Media

Plaintiffs almost certainly feel the effects of anti-plaintiff information spread by the healthcare and insurance industries. The median jury award for medical malpractice claims rose to $1,045,000 in 2004,[48] and is higher now. This image of money-hungry, exaggerating plaintiffs has reached a national level—even being included in the following quote from President Bush's State of the Union Address on January 31, 2006, in which the affordability of health care in America was being discussed: "…because lawsuits are driving many good doctors out of practice—leaving women in nearly 1,500 American counties without a single OB/GYN—I ask the Congress to pass medical liability reform this year."[49]

A study conducted by the Henry J. Kaiser Family Foundation and the Harvard School of Public Health found that, while Americans favor malpractice reform, they rank it low on the list of priorities for Congress and the President. In fact, malpractice jury awards were ranked 11 out of 12 healthcare priorities, while federal funding for stem cell research ranked twelfth. When discussing damages caps for pain and suffering, 63 percent of those surveyed supported caps and 69 percent thought a law limiting pain and suffering awards would help a lot or some in reducing the overall costs of health care.[50] However, real-world experience has shown that caps do not work in reducing malpractice insurance premiums. Take for example Texas. Voters in 2003 capped medical liability to $250,000. Yet, not more than a year later, one of the nation's largest medical malpractice insurance companies applied for a 19 percent increase in its rates. It should also be noted that the top ten medical liability insurers in the United States had combined profits in 2003 of $25 billion.[51] Refer to Chapter 17, *View of the Actuary*, for more information.

The numerous lawyer advertisements on television can create a false impression that the alleged victims of medical malpractice or any personal injury case are cash-hungry lottery players. However, when done tastefully, they may inform the public that when something goes wrong during medical treatment, not only is someone to blame, but there may be an industry-wide effort to conceal the details of the alleged malpractice.

Some jurors have been negatively influenced by the media's hostility against the plaintiff's attorney. The plaintiff's attorney therefore must distinguish himself and the clients from the negative, unsympathetic images jurors have been exposed to; the plaintiff's attorney should stress that, were it not for the jury, the wrongs of the medical profession and the injuries to a deserving plaintiff would go unaddressed. If the plaintiff's injuries are severe enough, this should not be a hard obstacle to overcome. The plaintiff's attorney should weave notions of fairness, morality, and righteousness into this concept. The plaintiff's attorney should stress that the jury is to come to a decision based upon presentation of the facts and its own practical views of what is right and wrong.

24.11 Summary

Nursing malpractice is one of the most difficult and complex types of litigation for the trial attorney and the juror. Overcoming the generally sympathetic sentiments for the nurse and a badly damaged plaintiff requires the artful crafting of a plaintiff's trial theme. Trial themes are an essential tool of persuasion designed to develop a common thread and keep jurors focused. The theme should be formulated well before trial and presented to the jury as early as possible during the voir dire or opening statement. This theme should be repeated and alluded to often and left with the jury during summation.

Endnotes

1. Singer, A., "Jury-validated trial themes," American Trial Lawyers Association handouts, October 2004.

2. *Id.*

3. Spence, G., *Win Your Case: How to Present, Persuade, and Prevail—Every Place, Every Time*, St. Martin's Press, 2005.

4. Erickson, J., L. Holm, L. Chelminiak, and M. Ditomassi, "Why not nursing?" *Nursing* 35, no. 7 (July 2005): 46-49.

5. Begany, T., "Your image is brighter than ever," *RN* (October 2004): 28-34.

6. *American Nurses Association Standards of Professional Practice and Performance,* Washington, D.C., 2004.

7. Meier, E., "The Image of a Nurse—Myth vs. Reality," *Nursing Economics* 17, no. 5 (September-October 1999): 273-275.

8. Flood, C. M., "Conflict Between Professional Interests, the Public Interest and Patients' Interests in an Era of Reform: Nova Scotia Registered Nurses," *Health Law Journal* 5 (1997): 27.

9. "Trouble in the Nurse Labor Market? Recent Trends and Future Outlook; As managed care has spread across the country, registered nurses have felt the pinch in earnings and employment. Are changes on the horizon?" *Health Affairs* (January-February 1999).

10. Friedman, Rick and Malone, Patrick, Trial Guides, LLC, 2006.

11. *Kirk v. Mercey Hosp. Tri-County,* 851 S.W.2d 617 (1993).

12. Trudeau, S., "Legally speaking: the law adds force to your voice," *RN* (January 1994): 65-66.

13. Foley, E. and A. LeFevre, "Understanding Generation X," *Trial* (June 2000): 58.

14. American Nurses Association, *Code for Nurses,* 2001.

15. Cherlin, A., "I'm OK, You're Selfish," *New York Times* (October 17, 1999): 44.

16. Wenner, D. and G. Cusimano, "Combating juror bias," *Trial* (June 2000): 30.

17. Duffy, T., "The Enduring Legend of McDonald's Coffee," *Lawyers Weekly USA* (November 22, 2004).

18. *Dimaranan v. Pomona Valley Medical Center,* 775 F.Supp. 338 (C.D. Cal. 1991).

19. Herbert, B., "In America, nurses on the advance," *New York Times,* Sec A, (December 15, 1993): 27.

20. "Study Shows NP Care Is Comparable to Physician Care," *American Journal of Nursing* 100, no. 3 (March 2000) citing *JAMA* 283, no. 1 (2000): 59-68, 106-8.

21. Lewin, T., "Advanced nursing practices are invading doctors' turf," *New York Times* Sec. A (November 22, 1993): 1.

22. www.npdb-hipdb.com/resources/reports/2004NPDBAnnualReport.pdf, accessed 02/25/11.

23. www.acnpweb.org/i4a/pages/index.cfm?pageid=3282, accessed 02/25/11.

24. Hravnak, M., et al., Scope of practice, credentialing, and privileging. *Practice issues for the acute care nurse practitioner. (1998):* 41-63.

25. PA Code§21.251 adopted July 22, 1977, effective July 23, 1977, 7 Pa.B. 2063.

26. American College of Obstetricians and gynecologists (ACOG) Committee Opinion, Number 228, November 1999; and Number 283, May 2003.

27. www.acep.org/practres.aspx?id=30060, accessed 02/25/11.

28. Klompas, M., "Does this patient have an acute thoracic aortic dissection?" *JAMA* 287, no. 17 (May 1, 2002): 2264.

29. Hagan, P. G., et al., "The international registry of acute aortic dissection," *JAMA* 283, no. 7 (February 16, 2000): 897.

30. *Id.*

31. U.S. Bureau of Labor Statistics, "Monthly Labor Review," February 2004.

32. www.kaiseredu.org/topics_im.asp?imID=1&parentID=61&id=138, accessed 02/25/11.

33. *National Survey on Consumers' Experiences with Patient Safety and Quality Information,* sponsored by the Kaiser Family Foundation Agency for HealthCare Research and Quality and Harvard School of Public Health.

34. Sandroni, S. and L. G. Sandy, "Homeostasis without reserve-the risk of health system collapse," *New England Journal of Medicine* 347, no. 24 (December 12, 2002): 1971-1975.

35. The Senior Care Source, 2006, Vol. 3, citing Johnson-Lamarche, Mollica R., *Residential Care and Assisted Living Compendium,* 2004.

36. *The Senior Care Source,* 2006, Vol. 3, citing Hawes C, Philips CD, High-Service or High-Privacy Assisted Living Facilities, Their Residents and Staff: Results from a National Survey, 2000.

37. *The Senior Care Source,* 2006, Vol. 3, citing National Center for Assisted Living, Facts and Trends: The Assisted Living Sourcebook, 2001.

38. *Id.*

39. "Largest Assisted Living Providers," *Assisted Living Today* (June 2004).

40. The Senior Care Source, 2006, Vol. 3.

41. *The Senior Care Source,* 2006, Vol. 3, Assisted Living Federation of America, 2001 Overview of the Assisted Living Industry.

42. *Id.*

43. "California Nurses Win Landmark Victory," *American Journal of Nursing* 100, no. 1 (January 2000): 20.

44. Henneberger, M., "For nurses, new uncertainties; managed care means specialized needs and less hiring," *New York Times* Sec. 1 (August 21, 1994): 45.

45. See note 13.

46. *Cline v. Lund,* 107 Cal. Rptr. 629 (1973).

47. Leatherwood, J., "Special problems of the hospital defendant," *C342 American Law Institute—American Bar Institute* 133, 139, 1988.

48. *Current Award Trends in Personal Injury,* LRP Publications, 2006.

49. www.washingtonpost.com/wp-dyn/content/article/2006/01/31/AR2006013101468.html, accessed 02/25/11.

50. "Americans Favor Malpractice Reform and Drug Importation, but Rank Them Low on Health Priority List for the Congress and President," The Henry J. Kaiser Family Foundation, January 11, 2005.

51. "Tort Reform Group Names 'Judicial Hellholes'," *CNN, December 15, 2004.*

Chapter 25

Trial Techniques

Kenneth F. Fulginiti, Esq., Samuel L. Davis, Esq., Helen Griff Chalier (formerly Weisgal), Esq., and Wendy Neggers, Esq.

25.1 Introduction

This chapter addresses varying styles of trial techniques, from juror selection through verdict. A great deal of thought must be given to the trial to formulate the theory of the case. It is important with all cases, but especially the more complex cases, that they be distilled to their necessary elements and kept focused on the theory. The attorney must be aware of the adversary's theory, but should not get lured into trying the case. Stay focused!

25.2 Voir Dire
A. Introduction

There are those who say they win the case in voir dire. There are others who say the process, while important, is virtually impossible to control. Since it is an attorney's first opportunity to interact with the potential jury, it is certain that a case can be lost during jury selection. However, let us not minimize the importance of the trial itself.

Jury selection is important; it is the first opportunity to address the jurors directly. It is the jurors' first opportunity to see the plaintiff. The jurors will see the attorneys interact with the court as well. It is important to be respectful, deferential to the court and mindful of the eyes upon the attorneys. Behavior during jury selection is jurisdiction- and judge-depedent. Some judges and jurisdictions get the process completed in 30 minutes with no interaction with counsel. Other judges and jurisdictions permit the attorneys to conduct and complete voir dire without the judge being present in the courthouse, allowing questions not only intended to elicit potential bias, but also to begin the persuasion process. And there are all those situations that fall somewhere between those two. If unclear about what is permitted, contact people such as the president of the local Trial Lawyers Association or Defense Research Institute. The tipstaff and court attendants may answer procedural questions or the judge's procedures may be detailed online. One of the authors (KF) has seen attorneys chastised during the voir dire process for overstepping their permitted role. Know the boundaries. They might be soft. There might be few rules; there might be many. It is up to the attorney as to whether and how much the rules will be tested. Clearly there is risk in doing so.

B. Court-Restricted Voir Dire

Some judges limit voir dire exclusively to the items on the court-approved voir dire questionnaire. In Pennsylvania the same questionnaire is used for both criminal and civil cases. Far more questions on the questionnaire focus on criminal rather than civil cases. If a prospective juror responds negatively to all of the questions (i.e., no prior lawsuits, will not disregard the court's instructions, not biased, and so on), then no questioning is permitted of that juror. If there are affirmative responses, questioning is permitted but limited to those affirmative responses. Little can be done in jurisdictions that restrict voir dire in this fashion.

Even with such restrictions, the court must inform the jurors of what kind of case is at issue. Some judges restrict that description to "slip and fall," "medical malpractice," "auto accident," and so on. No further detail or description may be provided. The court must also identify the witnesses who will testify. Typically the judge will simply read their names. Sometimes the judge, even in these restricted jurisdictions, will allow the attorneys to identify their own witnesses and wait to see if any jurors know them. This may provide a brief opportunity to introduce the attorney and client, and provide some relevant information (i.e., "I represent Joe Smith, he lives in South Philadelphia and is a member of the Benevolent Mothers of our Great Lord Parish. Does any-

one know Joe Smith from his neighborhood or church?") It may be possible for the attorney to provide an introduction to himself, and offer some personal information (i.e., "My name is John Esquire. I am supposed to ask if anyone knows who I am. I wouldn't expect you to know me...I don't advertise on TV or have a billboard on Route I-95, but maybe I represented your aunt or son or daughter...so, does anyone know who I am—John Esquire?").

One of the jurors could possibly be familiar with a party, particularly in smaller towns. One of the authors (KF) tried a case that occurred in Delaware which involved one business owner against another. Of the 45 individuals in the jury venire, approximately 90 percent knew one or both of the parties. These potential jurors advised it would not affect their decision. After jury selection, the judge recused himself as he was personally familiar with both parties. If proper voir dire had not occurred, this trial could have very well been a mistrial once the names of parties and witnesses were ultimately disclosed. If the court does limit the attorney's involvement, or what can be asked, it is still important to provide a set of proposed voir dire to the jury. If for no other reason, it may be necessary to preserve an issue for appeal. In a climate of intense media focus on lawsuits, some jurisdictions are considering it to be reversible error not to allow some limited questioning on this issue.[1] Media attention to a particular subject before jury selection can be a perceived benefit to one side of the claim, For example, a story that the attorney general is investigating abuse and neglect in a nursing home could impact a panel of jurors selected to hear a case involving a nursing home resident who wandered out of a facility before being hit by a car. A story that orthopaedic surgeons are leaving the state because of rising insurance premiums, whether or not this has any bearing on lawsuits, could affect the jurors being considered to sit for a case involving an orthopaedic nurse and physician. Since flushing out juror bias is the intended goal of jury selection, it would seem consistent with this goal to allow the court or counsel to delve into the issue of jurors' attitudes toward certain types of cases (i.e., medical malpractice, nursing home). It would seem inconsistent with this goal to bar this limited line of inquiry.

TIP: As part of its submissions to the court, counsel should provide the court with a narrow list of defined questions. If the attorney's concern is medical malpractice bias, it would be a good idea to have questions backed up with some statistics (for the court's review, not the jurors'). Such biases may very well be the most important factor in deciding how to use peremptory challenges. Again, be specific and focused. It is easier for a judge to refuse a list of 73 "absolutely necessary" voir dire questions than to refuse the three that are focused on the pivotal issues in the case.

C. Challenges for "Cause" and Peremptory Challenges

1. Challenges for cause

Challenges for cause are quite judge-depedent. The issue is often based upon the number of jurors needed not only for the attorney's case, but also within the system in general. For example, "cause" may be found more liberally when there is only one case requiring a jury panel compared to a day when there are 15 trials requiring jury selection. Also, some judges are simply more strict on what is perceived to be "cause" than others. While one judge may allow a juror to be excused due to "financial hardship," another judge may not honor such a generic request as it might be difficult to draw the line as to more or less legitimate "financial hardship" claims. Personal "cause" is often determined uniquely by each juror in issue. There are issues personal to the jurors that might affect their ability to sit as jurors. A juror may be required to provide care to an elderly parent or a young child. While some attorneys argue against "cause" in those personal situations when they feel a particular juror might be helpful to their cause, this is a difficult position to take. Consider what might happen when the juror learns which attorney kept her on the jury. Tipstaffs do talk to jurors.

Challenges for bias are based on a concern that some juror has some preconceived notion of how the type of case should turn out before hearing any evidence. Some jurors use this as a means of getting off jury duty, and there is little that can be done about that. No matter how many times the judge asks if they will follow the court's instructions, they will always say "no." They know it is a free ride off the jury. There is an old line by judges trying to get a case settled before the start of trial—"Do you really want your case decided by 12 people who can't figure out how to get out of jury duty?" Nevertheless, there are certainly jurors who do have preconceived notions about certain types of cases. These notions may be either in favor or against the attorney's position. "All nursing homes deliver bad care" or "All nurses are hardworking saints facing difficult situations every day" are biases. Some jurors have been, or know someone, involved in a similar matter. Juror 1 may say, "My husband was the victim of nursing malpractice." The defense attorney may respond, "Don't you think that will influence your thought process in this case?" Jurors may be sympathetic to the defense. Juror 2 may say: "My sister is a physician and she is always complaining about frivolous lawsuits." In those situations the defense attorney may ask, "But if the judge explains the law to you, you will follow the court's instructions, won't you?" As stressed in Chapter 23, *Keeping the Jurors in Mind,* avoid asking jurors if they can be fair. Everyone wants to believe they are fair. Use words such as "objective" and "impartial." Ask if the other side has an advantage or if the connection or attitude would cause the juror to lean in one direction or another. Ask, "Are we starting out even with [the other side] with you?"

In the example above, both jurors have a bias. Both might ultimately agree they will follow the court's instructions. Each judge handles these situations differently. Sometimes the most the attorney can do is make a record, argue the point, and be prepared to use a peremptory challenge. There is no limit to challenges for cause. The judge has the final decision on whether such a challenge will be granted.

2. Peremptory challenges

The number of peremptory challenges is jurisdictional, as is the manner in which the jurors are seated following challenges. In federal court, each side is entitled to six peremptory challenges.[2] State courts may widely vary on their rules. The attorney must know the rules in the state to avoid unpleasant surprises. In New Jersey State Court, the number is six.[3] In Pennsylvania, four.[4] In Delaware, three.[5] This number is typically "per side," meaning the plaintiff is entitled to four challenges and the defendants, cumulatively, are entitled to four. If the defendants are not aligned and have cross-claims and very different issues, courts may allow each defendant to have four challenges. However, other jurisdictions provide each party with the same number of peremptory challenges, thereby creating inequities in cases with one plaintiff but multiple defendants. The court evaluates whether the defendants are aligned. The New Jersey Rules specifically provide for such an issue. When there is similarity of interest among defendants, the court, upon motion, may grant the plaintiff additional peremptory challenges. In that circumstance, the New Jersey rules provide that the court "in its discretion may, on application of counsel prior to the selection of the jury, accord the adverse party such additional number of peremptory challenges as it deems appropriate in order to avoid unfairness to the adverse party."[6]

In some jurisdictions, it is possible to know exactly who is being seated as the next juror when the attorney exercises a peremptory. The entire panel is already numbered and present. If a case is being tried with 12 jurors and two alternates, and each side gets four challenges, the attorneys need only look to Juror 22 despite the fact that 40 jurors may be seated for jury selection. Therefore, there is no need to start looking at Juror 23, 24, 25, and so on. Focus on the first 14 jurors. If Juror 6 is struck, it is apparent Juror 15 is ready for consideration. It might very well be that the first 14 are the best 14. Therefore, start striking jurors after number 14, if at all. Be mindful of the fact that it may not be necessary to strike any jurors. Attorneys are not required to strike any jurors. One of the authors (KF) has tried cases where peremptory challenges were not used, feeling that the jurors "in the box" were the best of the venire.

In some jurisdictions, the attorney does not know who will be replacing the dismissed juror. Only accepted jurors are seated in the box; there is only an opportunity to strike the next juror called. If the attorney strikes that juror, the next juror is randomly chosen from the venire. Therefore, it is not possible to make the decision that the juror being struck is going to be worse than the one taking his place.

TIP: It is important to question the conventional wisdom that an attorney must use all peremptory strikes. It is not necessary to use all or even any of them. If the panel in the box is acceptable, consider waiving challenges. Naturally, if there were challenges for "cause" that the court did not strike, the attorney will want to exercise those with peremptory challenge or likely lose any appellate issue on that for failing to exercise peremptory challenge.

The use of peremptory challenges in general is liberal. The attorney may not like the way the juror looked at the attorney upon entering the room; the attorney may be concerned about the job the juror holds; and the attorney may not like the juror's responses to certain questions. However, peremptory challenges cannot be based on race.[7] A *Batson* challenge must be raised if it is perceived the adversary is simply striking jurors based on race. The basis of each strike must be supportable in the event challenged. Depending on the response a mistrial may be requested. A *Batson* challenge may be made after the adversary's second or third strike, causing the adversary to rethink how she will exercise the remainder of the strikes.

D. Sample Voir Dire

Figure 25.1 is a sampling of some proposed voir dire in medical negligence cases. Whether or not the judge allows these particular questions, or whichever questions are proposed, is judge-dependent and may be jurisdiction-dependent. Providing just a few pointed questions on this issue, which are not drafted in a misleading or inappropriate manner, may be acceptable to the court. For example, a court might permit the plaintiff's attorney to ask if any jurors "have a preconceived notion that would prevent them from providing a substantial

award if the evidence warranted such an award." The same judge would likely prevent the plaintiff's attorney from asking if any jurors "have a preconceived notion that would prevent them from providing a massive financial award after the plaintiff proves to you that the defendant committed egregious malpractice causing all kinds of serious harm to Mr. Jones." Obviously the second question is more of an argument than an unbiased question intended to solicit juror bias.

E. How Do You Know Who to Strike?

Prior to selecting the jury, the attorney must give some thought as to the nature of the desirable juror. A small percentage of cases have the value that would justify hiring a jury consultant or performing mock trials. Consider the principal witnesses, the target defendants, and who might be likely to align themselves with or against those individuals. Naturally, in a nursing malpractice case, it is undesirable to have a nurse on the panel. However, consider these individuals:

- Engineers
- Elderly men
- Middle-age women
- Business owners
- Secretaries

Each of these individuals has family. Each of these individuals has life experiences, and likely each knows a nurse, has a family member who is a nurse, or has met a nurse in a healthcare environment. While the attorney might be thinking that the person who indicated he was a plaintiff in a prior lawsuit might be favorable, it might not be apparent that the potential juror is married to a nurse anesthetist and is bombarded with information about frivolous medical malpractice cases. Perhaps he was not reluctant to file an auto accident case, but feels very strongly against nursing malpractice cases. Therefore, the attorney must learn more about the prospective jurors as well as their family (and possibly close friends).

Once past the issue of "alignment," consider the general issues of who will be best or worst for the issues in the case. Will a business owner be preoccupied with the rising cost of insurance and the constant "frivolous" claims contended with every time one of her truck drivers opens a car door into another in a parking lot? She might come to the trial with a skeptical attitude about litigation in general, possibly holding the plaintiff to a higher burden of proof than the law requires. If an important witness in the case is a young male nurse, consider how an older audience might react to him. If you intend to aggressively attack a particular witness who is a union member, consider how that might sit with certain members on the jury.

1. Are any members of the juror's family in the nursing or medical profession?

2. Does the juror consider any members of the nursing profession to be among her close friends?

3. Has the juror had any experience as a nurse's aide, hospital volunteer, Red Cross worker, or the like?

4. What experiences, if any, has the juror had with nurses?

5. What are the juror's general attitudes toward the nursing profession? Is the juror unduly sympathetic or hostile?

6. Can the juror accept the fact that nurses are held to a professional standard of care in treating patients?

7. Can the juror accept the principle that a departure from the applicable standard of care can result in medical injury to a patient?

8. How important do you believe it to be that victims should be compensated when they have been injured as a result of someone's negligence?

9. How would you feel about returning a large monetary award to the plaintiff if the nurse's negligence and substantial damages are proven?

10. How do you feel about providing monetary compensation to victims of malpractice?

11. Do you believe that every effort should be made to compensate people who are negligently injured by a healthcare professional?

12. Do you believe that just because a plaintiff files a lawsuit that she is entitled to money?

13. Do you believe that all injured people deserve to be compensated, even if that means a defendant who is not negligent pays the award?

14. How do you think you would feel if the defendant was not negligent and, therefore, the plaintiff was not entitled to any compensation whatsoever from the defendant?

15. Do you feel that justice would be done if you found the defendant not negligent, and hence, that the plaintiff is not entitled money?

16. Have you seen or heard, or read anything about what has been called the "lawsuit crisis" or "malpractice crisis"? What do you think about this?

17. What are your feelings about lawsuits brought by patients against nurses?

18. Do you believe that patients have a right to expect quality professional care from a nurse?

19. Have any of you participated in discussions with family, friends, or co-workers about lawyers, lawsuits, people who bring suits or are being sued, or the jury system? Based on your discussions, have any of you developed strong feelings either for or against the American justice system or the people involved in the system such that it would be difficult for you to be a fair and impartial juror to both parties?

The attorney should continue with any follow-up questions necessitated by the answers provided to the above questions.

Figure 25.1 *Sample of Potential Voir Dire Questions*

Much of this is a guessing game, but it requires thought before sitting in the courtroom with people staring at the attorney waiting for a decision. Come up with a plan and stick with it. While it is impossible to know how the panel will be comprised ahead of time, at least some thought has been given to the type of juror the attorney believes might be most helpful (or least destructive) to the issues in the case.

F. The Need to Uncover Attitudes and Beliefs

Once voir dire is over, only in a rare case can a juror be removed without risking a mistrial. Voir dire is the only real chance to uncover a juror's potential attitudes and beliefs. A juror's underlying attitudes and beliefs may drive a heated debate during deliberations.

One's attitudes and beliefs are formed from life experiences. Those experiences may be direct (i.e., the juror's father died in a nursing home) or indirect (i.e., the juror read a newspaper article regarding claims against nursing homes). One would expect a juror's direct experiences to be more influential than indirect experiences. Nevertheless, both may play a role in the juror's evaluation of the case. By delving into such experiences, both direct and indirect, counsel begins to understand how potential jurors may respond to the case. After uncovering core values and beliefs during an effective voir dire, jury verdict behavior becomes more predictable.

Counsel must evaluate how direct a potential juror's exposure has been to relevant situations. Jurors with direct experience possess the potential for greater empathy, identification, understanding, and emotional reaction (either positive or negative) than do jurors with only indirect experience. The latter's knowledge is based on exposure to the media or to third parties who have been in similar situations. Some jurors have no related experiences. The more direct and relevant the experience, the greater role it may play in the jurors' decision making during deliberations.

Jurors may relate their own experiences as patients to their evaluation of the actions of the plaintiff. Thus, jurors may focus on the conduct of a postoperative patient who falls after getting out of bed without asking for help. The jury may penalize the patient for perceived comparative negligence even in the absence of testimony of specific nursing warnings not to get out of bed. This phenomenon, in which jurors tend to blame the patient, is called defensive attribution.

It must also be remembered that, as a plaintiff, at some point you will be asking for compensation for your client under your state's law. There has been a recent trend towards aggressively flushing out juror beliefs on compensation during voir dire. Rather than merely ask if a juror can "provide compensation in the event plaintiff meet's his burden," attorneys are using "buzz words" that normally trigger adverse

sentiment towards lawsuits, to see if a juror is triggered into a particular position. For example, an attorney representing an accident victim, might ask if any jurors would have a problem providing "an award" for "pain and suffering" in a particular matter. Normally words such as "award" or "pain and suffering" are linked with trial lawyers, cervical collars and the lottery. Historically, attorneys representing accident victims shied away from such parlance. However, recent trends suggest to pepper voir dire with such language in an effort to locate and strike those jurors who might be biased against personal injury claims.

G. The Educational Component of Voir Dire

Voir dire is an appropriate time to familiarize jurors with legal concepts, case issues, and the juror's responsibilities. A well-conducted voir dire integrates gathering information with educating the jury. Counsel should encourage jurors to reflect upon the issues of the case. Toward this end, use open-ended questions requiring multiword responses. In contrast, a question that begins with "Do you understand" allows a "yes or no" answer. It will not be very helpful in uncovering a prospective juror's attitudes.

TIP: Frame questions based on experiences that potential jurors have had relevant to the case at hand.

Figure 25.2 provides an example of dialogue between an attorney and prospective juror, intended to determine the juror's perspective of issues involving negligent supervision.

H. Questioning Techniques

Questioning may be in the open group setting or with individual voir dire. Consider the setting before applying the questioning technique. If the jurors are being questioned while still seated in the jury venire, be mindful of polluting the jury. A stray comment that resonates with the jury may affect the remainder of the trial.

Attorney: "Juror 1, do you have an opinion concerning nursing home medical care that might affect your ability to decide this case fairly?"

Juror 1: "Yes."

Attorney: "Why is that?"

Juror 1: "My father was a physician who helped the sick and elderly at nursing homes when their family would just dump them off and forget about them, and he would get sued every time some 93-year-old person died of natural causes—the attorneys would find some way to blame my father."

> Q. What does your job as a receiving inspector entail?
>
> A. Okay. I have the responsibility, I think to myself at least, to tell the foremen or the area supervisors what I think shouldn't be used even though it may be close to the specifications and they haven't got anything else to use, and so forth. I may go up and say, "I wouldn't use this." I have some background, engineering, and I have a little more understanding about what is going to happen when you put it together. And I say, "I wouldn't use this because you are going to have to scrap it later." I tell them the consequences they can expect. It's ultimately up to them whether or not to use it.
>
> Q. So, the people you are supervising still reserve the right to make an independent decision?
>
> A. They have a right to do what they want. I can't really tell them what to do because I am hourly and not salaried. I am not managerial, but because I know more than they do about certain things, I can voice my opinion by saying "don't use this" but I do not really have the authority. But they hear me, 99 percent of the time they listen to me because they know I am right.
>
> Q. If I understand what you are saying, you feel that in the course of your employment, you can go over to somebody and say, "Don't use that piece of equipment." Is that an order?
>
> A. No, not exactly. I don't exactly say "Don't use it." I give a reason why not to: "I wouldn't use that because it is going to be too short and when you put it together with the other piece you are going to have an unsatisfactory piece of machinery and you can't sell a dump truck with a gap in the floor.
>
> Q. But still the person could use it?
>
> A. Yes.
>
> Q. And a person has independent judgment and choice?
>
> A. Right.
>
> Q. This person is not accountable to you?
>
> A. Correct.
>
> Q. So regardless of whether it sounds like an order, it is not an order?
>
> A. That's right.
>
> Q. So would you agree that there are things that can be said, one person to another, that sound like orders, but are not orders?

Figure 25.2 *Dialogue Between an Attorney and a Prospective Juror*

In the individual setting, avoid closed-ended voir dire questioning. Narrow responses are produced by closed-ended questions. Questions should promote expansive answers from jurors. A one-word response may not be as informative as a response from a juror that explains the answer. "Ms. Smith, do you believe that a patient receives adequate care in the emergency room?" This is a typical closed-ended question in the voir dire phase of a nursing malpractice case. This answer tells the attorney little. Attorneys should frame questions that require jurors to answer "I think," "I believe," or "I feel." "Ms. Smith, how do you feel, in general, regarding patient care received in emergency rooms?" Any response, if not detailed, can be further probed with "tell me more about that" or questioning along those lines.

Open-ended questions begin with such phrases as "What are your feelings about…" or "Please share your thoughts about…" or "Please tell us your feelings about…." Questions usually end with actual case issues: "jury verdicts," "medical malpractice," and so on. The goal of an open-ended question is to promote an honest exchange about primary case issues and how jurors feel about these issues. Whatever the response may be, do not get argumentative with a juror. Let the juror expose bias and attempt to have the juror stricken for cause. If the bias is "cured," the attorney will likely need to use a peremptory. Attorneys need to be sociable during voir dire. Some attorneys may share personal information about themselves in order to encourage the jury to do the same. For example, the attorney might say, "I am a 42-year-old father of two daughters and grew up in South Philadelphia. My ten-year-old plays soccer for the neighborhood youth organization and my seven-year-old is on the swim team. My wife volunteers at St. Barnebies on 5th and Porter Streets." The attorney's brief introduction of himself on a personal level is designed to encourage the jurors to do the same. Explain to the jurors that there are no "wrong answers," except for inaccurate or incomplete ones.

TIP: Counsel might consider beginning voir dire by explaining to the jury that he is not there to pry and that, while everyone is qualified to sit on a jury, this does not mean they should be sitting on this jury. Because of the specific facts, evidence, and witnesses in this case, certain prospective jurors may have some level of knowledge or information, or some life experience that might simply make this jury panel an inappropriate one.

The defendant, on the other hand, wants to establish that jurors are not simply compensation-oriented. She needs to determine if the jurors will consider fairness to all parties. Figure 25.3 includes appropriate questions for defense.

I. Dealing with the Term "Malpractice"

Attorneys for the plaintiff recognize that the jury may have sympathy for the defendants. In many states, the number one employer in the vast majority of the counties is a healthcare institution. Efforts should be made to determine if prospective jurors have a bias in favor of the nurse. It might be that the jurors simply misunderstand the concept of malpractice. The term "malpractice" connotes general incompetence and almost intentional misconduct, if not an evil motive. Use of the term blurs the setting of a negligence claim and increases the plaintiff's burden of proof. Jurors must be reminded that a finding for the plaintiff in no way infers that the defendant is a criminal, a bad person, or even a bad nurse.

TIP: The plaintiff's attorney should avoid using the term "malpractice" at trial. Focus instead on the defendant's failure to act as required.

One tactic is for plaintiff's counsel, during voir dire, to repeatedly remind the jury that the word "malpractice" is simply another word for negligence. This makes the position of the defendant similar to that of any other defendant being sued in a negligence case, such as an automobile accident. Plaintiff's counsel should remind the jury that the subject matter of these cases is nothing more or less than negligence by a professional who happens to be a healthcare provider. The defense attorney, on the other hand, should stress the gravity of a suit against a professional and persuade the jury to avoid likening it to a simple negligence action.

J. Dealing with Negative Responses

What should be done when a contaminating response in the courtroom setting happens? An unexpected answer may provide an opportunity to uncover the key attitudes of other jurors. It might be advisable to inquire as to how many other jurors share the expressed viewpoint. Negative attitudes and beliefs expressed during voir dire may be shared during jury deliberations, but it is unlikely that a stray comment during voir dire will somehow control the outcome of the case. It is, nevertheless, important to solicit negative beliefs in a controlled manner during the voir dire process. At that time, something can be done about it. Some potential jurors believe large damage awards, no matter how justified or deserved, raise their insurance rates and lessen the availability of medical services for themselves and their families. A plaintiff's attorney must be able to impanel jurors who can approach damage awards with an open mind. Some potential jurors believe all nursing homes, including non-profit ones, cut every possible corner and provide totally substandard care while their executives get large paychecks. A defense attorney must select jurors who will approach liability issues in this situation with an open mind.

"Do you believe that just because a plaintiff files a lawsuit that he is entitled to money?"

"Do you believe that all injured people deserve to be compensated, even if that means a defendant who is not negligent pays the award?"

"How do you think you would feel if the defendant was not negligent and, therefore, the plaintiff was not entitled to any compensation whatsoever from the defendant?"

"Do you feel that justice would be done if you found the defendant not negligent, and hence, that the plaintiff is not entitled money?"

Figure 25.3 *Potential Questions for the Jury on Fairness—Defense's Perspective*

Jury selection is a capricious process. Counsel is well served by making a good first impression and sensitizing the jurors to the issues to be addressed at trial. "Never forget, you are not picking your jury; you don't have that many challenges. You are trying to find individuals you must eliminate from the panel while trying to educate those whom you will allow to serve."[8]

Refer to Chapter 23, *Keeping the Jurors in Mind*, for additional information about voir dire.

25.3 Opening Statement
A. Introduction

The opening statement is the attorney's first opportunity to develop rapport with the jurors. This is especially true in light of the limited involvement judges are providing to attorneys in the voir dire process. The opening statement is the attorney's first chance to persuasively inform the jury of the evidence, the applicable law, and the central theme. All this can be done while the jury is fresh, uncommitted, and ready to be persuaded.

A widely quoted study conducted by the University of Chicago in the early 1970s reported that 65 to 80 percent of all jurors decided the case consistent with their first impressions immediately following the opening statements. This means the remainder of the trial is devoted to maintaining those who agree with you and persuading those who do not. As is true in life, the psychological phenomenon of primacy applies. Initial impressions become lasting impressions. That is not to say that primacy rules, and recency also has an impact, but first impressions are important. The opening is the attorney's first opportunity to tell the jury what the case is really about. There are many experienced trial lawyers who believe cases are won or lost at the opening statement. Attorneys can make great openings, or serious mistakes in their opening, but it is important to maintain credibility and control from the beginning.

B. The Opening Statement as a Story

The opening statement, like the final argument, is a form of storytelling. The most effective attorneys can convey the theme of their case in a distilled narrative, easy-to-understand story, whether by use of analogy or simply recounting what occurred. Their openings are provided in simple terms, no legalese, and flow like a well-written story. They talk about "nurses," not "healthcare professionals"; they talk about "testimony," not "submissions"; they talk about "March 3, 2005," not "the date in question." Attorneys must remember that they have been living their cases for the previous two to three years. Jurors are hearing details for the first time. They need to hear the story in an understandable

manner. It is distancing to use big words and legalese. The attorney should just tell the jury what happened, like he would to a friend.

An effective trial attorney brings to life the facts of something that happened in another place, at another time, and to other people. This is done so that a jury of strangers can decide what result will be just. Attorneys must both educate and persuade. For that to happen, jurors must "see" what counsel is saying. They must be able to understand and follow the story being told to them. Counsel must make them visualize the scene as if something were happening before their eyes. Appendix 25.1 is an opening statement from a product liability case handled by one of the authors' firms (KF) (the names have been changed). Appendix 25.2 is an opening statement from a nursing and medical malpractice case handled by one of the authors' firms (KF) (the names have been changed). These opening statements were approximately 15 minutes. They included background and details of the case sufficient for the jurors to have a sense of where this journey will take them. The opening is factual but more than a mere recitation of the facts.

TIP: Keep the jury's attention during the opening by keeping the story active and relatively short. Even in jurisdictions where note taking is permitted, note taking is not permitted during the opening or closing. There is no need to get hypertechnical or hyperdetailed in the opening. In general jurors will not remember a bunch of names, or measurements, or dates, etc. Keep it simple.

The opening statement should be no more than 30 minutes or thereabouts. Avoid repetition; repetition of facts will come during testimony. Avoid what might be considered argument to avoid having the opening interrupted with objections; what is or is not considered argument may fall upon the tone of the attorney's voice. The same thing said softly, as opposed to loudly, might be overlooked as fact, rather than argument. The attorney may say softly as part of the opening "You will hear from Nurse No. She will take the stand, take an oath, and then explain how the defendant's conduct was totally proper; how the defendant followed the physician's orders when she...." However, yelling that "The evidence will prove to you that these defendants did not commit malpractice; that these defendants did everything they were supposed to do" will likely draw an objection during the opening. Explain the case, but do not act in a manner that might provoke an objection.

The opening statement is a preview of the case that will follow. Certain things are purposefully omitted to create suspense or perhaps because the jury simply may not be prepared to view the evidence that early in the litigation. For instance, plaintiff's counsel, in a case with catastrophic injuries, may give the jury only the briefest glimpse of the appearance of the injuries during the opening statement and will not have the plaintiff present until her testimony. This instills in jurors feelings of both anticipation and dread. Also, the plaintiff's attorney does not want the jury to become desensitized to the gravity of the injury. If a jury sees the same person for nine consecutive trial days with the injury, they may become desensitized. If the jury sees the injury once during the trial and then again in the closing, they are less likely to become desensitized to it. However, it must be clear for a plaintiff that your case is about damages. You do not want to ignore damages or back-burner them. The jury must know the case is about damages. Even if liability is the more heavily contested issue, do not minimize your damages issues. Simply because the defense wants to focus on liability does not mean you need to do this.

Defense counsel's opening may consist of a story of a dedicated, hard-working nurse. The themes of the defense may be presented during the opening. Defendants have other important tasks in their opening. In response to a strong plaintiff's opening, defense counsel will often remind the jury that no evidence has been presented, that the jury should be cautioned not to "rush to judgment," and that there are two sides to the story. While acknowledging the serious nature of the plaintiff's injuries, the defense attorney will underscore that the defendant is not responsible for them. Sensitized by tort reform, jurors identify with the notion that defendants should not be held responsible for the carelessness of others or when an honest judgment call caused injuries. At this point in the trial, the defense counsel will explain the factual basis for their client's defense. Storytelling that uses analogies and imagery is a very effective way to get, and keep, the juror's attention. Consider the following excerpt from the book, *What Makes Juries Listen*:

> There is much in any trial that is easily identifiable, images that can be brought to everyone's mind. Yet unfortunately, lawyers so often lose sight of the fact that a case is a narrative. Stories have appealed to all people from the beginning of time. In wanting to get out the facts and listing of the issues, you can forget that people don't like listening to dry data to which they don't relate and which reminds them of those abstract math problems at school.[9]

Begin with a tease, a glimpse into where you are going and a little excitement about what is going to happen next. Use the story in your trial to begin the narrative. Do not say, "Ladies and gentlemen, this case deals with certain issues of compensation which the law provides...." Instead, begin with "It was a Saturday morning, three years ago, when Nurse No was caring for her patients at the Better Care Nursing Home...."

TIP: Stories do not have to be told chronologically, and can be presented in first or third person. The plaintiff's attorney can combine the patient's perspective with the spouse's point of view to create a very effective opening statement. The defense attorney might start with describing the nurse defendant, how she worked through nursing school to achieve her dream job as a nurse anesthetist, and how she always got glowing evaluations. Use active verbs in the present tense, bringing the juror into the story by moving further toward persuading rather than merely educating.

Jurors tend to believe the story they hear first. Good or bad, that impression will be retained. If the attorney misleads the jury about the facts in the case, or omits important information, that attorney has lost credibility with the jury. Maintaining credibility at all times is an important part of being successful in the courtroom.

The attorney must also be aware of how biases affect the juror's perception of evidence. According to Wenner and Cusimano,[10] three biases affect the way the juror views evidence presented in the trial following the opening statement:

1. Confirmation bias—the juror will search for evidence that confirms his beliefs, will critically scrutinize inconsistent evidence and interpret ambiguous evidence as consistent with his belief. "Attorneys should never underestimate the extent to which jurors' prior experiences influence their perception of the evidence."[11]

2. Belief perseverance bias—the juror will have a tendency, once she has adopted a trial story, to cling to it even in the face of conflicting or discrediting evidence. Information that is presented early has an inordinate influence in how the evidence is constructed. Presenting strong evidence early is imperative.

3. Availability bias—whatever most occupies the juror's attention during the trial will most influence what the juror focuses on during deliberations. This evidence will be disproportionately used in

rendering a verdict. A simple rule of thumb is that the focus of the trial (the defendant's conduct, the plaintiff's conduct, or causation issues) will be foremost during deliberations.

C. Anticipation of Your Adversary's Opening Statement: Jury Inoculation

As indicated above, plaintiff's counsel's strong, fact-based opening can have a lasting effect on the jury. However, the plaintiff's attorney should not underestimate the adversary's ability to deliver an equally strong opening. A plaintiff's attorney must be mindful of the defense position and address it to the extent necessary to undermine it. Advance refutation of anticipated defenses is inoculation.[12] However, the plaintiff's attorney should also be mindful not to simply buy into and begin trying the defendant's case. It is very easy to get caught up with the defendant's defense, and then the plaintiff's attorney begins defending her own case. By being mindful of the defense position, the plaintiff's attorney may refute it appropriately. The plaintiff's attorney will mention in the opening if the defense's position is based upon nonexistent evidence or is unsupported in literature. Plaintiff's counsel should be prepared to inoculate the jury, but be mindful not to dwell on the defense position.

The term "inoculation" comes from medicine. In medical inoculation, the patient is exposed to a small amount of a disease, causing a mild illness. As a result of this exposure, the patient develops antibodies that ward off a strong attack of the disease. In similar fashion the jury, having been exposed to anticipated opposing arguments and then persuaded that the arguments are either irrelevant or incorrect, becomes resistant to the actual opposing argument. The major difference between medical inoculation and jury inoculation is that the body develops antibodies on its own while the jury develops "antibodies" only if the lawyer supplies convincing counterarguments.

Effectively inoculating a jury involves a three-step process. The first step is prediction of the defense's arguments, such as, "Mr. Barkas will probably make such and such an argument." The plaintiff's counsel should present the defense's predicted arguments in an objective manner and refer to opposing counsel in a professional manner. Second, the plaintiff's attorney explains why the counterarguments may at first appear true, and some people might believe them. This must be done sincerely and without sarcasm. To do otherwise risks alienating a juror who feels the counterargument is legitimate. Finally, the attorney explains why the reasoning of the counterargument is fallacious by showing that it is incorrect or irrelevant, or outweighed by better and stronger arguments on the plaintiff's side.

What follows is an example of how an inoculation works:

> Ladies and gentlemen, in a few moments, Ms. Esquire will have the opportunity to address you as well. She will explain to you that her client, Nurse Practitioner Alwater, is not responsible for this incident because she acted properly and timely. As I have explained the facts that I intend to prove, those same facts are what the defense experts have had to ignore to make their theory work. For example, I explained that Nurse Alwater actually received six telephone calls regarding Mrs. Tory's condition and complaints over a two-day period. You will hear that these telephone calls did occur and we will show you the telephone records to confirm what we are saying. The defendants, in order to maintain their position, deny this fact occurred. So, I would ask you to pay attention to Ms. Esquire's explanation of the existence of the telephone records and how she intends to disprove the accuracy of the Verizon records in that regard.

Again, do not dwell on the topic. Provide a couple of sentences of explanation and move on. Remember, when inoculating the jury, counsel should not give a complete version of the expected arguments of opposing counsel. Only give enough to "inoculate" them, without giving them the actual "disease." Of course, defense counsel has an opportunity to respond to plaintiff's attorney's efforts to inoculate the jury. The points made by the opposing counsel may be addressed directly or ignored based on the most strategic defense position. If plaintiff's counsel mischaracterizes the defense position or omits important factual information, defense counsel may seize upon that mischaracterization or omission to create credibility issues at the outset.

D. The Use of Visuals in Opening Statement

Jurors expect a lot. High-tech television shows create competition. Matlock is out, Crime Scene Investigation is in. With the court's permission, the attorney should provide a visual presentation in every aspect of the case, including the opening statement. The use of models or demonstrative evidence is an excellent way to bring a jury to the scene. In complex litigation, the trial attorney can show the facts to the jury with the aid of a model, videotape, photograph, computer simulations, graphs, charts, slides, exhibits, and diagrams.

The general flow of information in trial drags in contrast to what jurors experience through electronic media. There is a crucial distinction: courtroom time is measured in hours, media time in seconds. The average TV news program takes only one minute and 30 seconds to cover a story: 30 seconds to set the stage, 30 seconds to tell the details, and 30 seconds to wrap up. For much of this time, a picture, diagram, or cut-away to a location shot on a screen provides visual interest. Yet to express points no more complex, a trial lawyer often consumes an hour or more in the courtroom with very few visuals. The net effect is juror boredom.

Demonstrative evidence in the opening is not only appropriate, but perhaps necessary, if the adversary has been informed and it has been cleared by the judge. The type and format of demonstrative visual evidence varies with the proof problems unique to each case. Computer animation might be the key to success in one case and a waste of money in another. A simple storyboard may be more effective in one and a filmed surgery in another. This technology can describe a very complex situation in a short period of time. Typically, if the demonstrative evidence is authentic and is not too lengthy or graphic, the opening statement is an entirely appropriate time for the evidence. Refer to Chapter 22, *Demonstrative Evidence*, for more details of the types and uses of demonstrative evidence.

E. Build Rapport with the Jury

As touched upon previously, effective trial attorneys abandon complex legalese when addressing the jury. They do not treat the language appropriate to the trial the same way as an appellate argument. Simple, conversational language builds rapport with the jury and helps it easily understand the case. For example, "prior" and "subsequent" should be abandoned in favor of "before" and "after." An attorney, especially in a nursing malpractice case, must remember that he is not addressing a panel of lawyers. Jurors are irritated by unexplained technical terms. By not using unnecessary technical jargon, there is no need to waste time explaining that jargon.

The attorney should speak to the jury as if she were relating an experience to a group of friends sitting in her living room. Describing an aunt who went into a nursing home, was basically ignored for three weeks, developed horrible infections, and had a leg amputated would likely garner a warm, sympathetic response. Convey the same message with the same tone in the courtroom, using simple language explaining uncomplicated theories. The attorney should tell the jury, straight out, what is going to be proven and why the jury will be asked to find in the attorney's favor at the end of the case.

Rapport can be built with the jury by striking a common thread between the jurors and the aspects of the case.

The average juror is middle-aged, works, and is a creature of habit: going to Dunkin' Donuts in the morning, counting down the years until retirement, or bragging about kids. The attorney should tap into the common thread with the jurors and the case. The attorney should talk to them as she would outside the legal environment. The author (KF) was advised of a case involving a woman who was addicted to heroin and managed to overdose herself with insulin obtained from an unlocked hospital medication cart. It took two days to find 12 jurors who could answer yes to the question, "Do you believe people with substance abuse are entitled to the same quality of care as those who do not abuse drugs?" The trial took place in an inner city where the jurors were well aware of problems associated with substance abuse. Liability was strong, since the cart was supposed to be locked whenever it was unattended. The plaintiff's brain damage from her low blood sugar was clearly linked to injecting herself with insulin. But a common thread of being concerned about how addicts affected the city was effectively used by the defense. The jury did not award the plaintiff a penny.

To build rapport with the jury, the attorney should look professional (jurors expect that), but not gaudy. Act in a deferential manner to the judge (as it is her house, and she is the host). Missteps in this area can cause serious disruption to the flow of the case and earn the judge's disapproval. Be aware of the need to assist other people to behave in such a way as to maintain their rapport with the jury. Instruct expert witnesses and the client (whether the nurse defendant or the plaintiff) about the general and specific rules of courtroom demeanor so they do not unsuspectingly make errors. Multiple and usually invisible rules affecting demeanor become apparent only after they are broken. Defendants or plaintiffs who cheer, moan, or clap after a particularly strong point is made are likely to be swiftly silenced. Discuss with your client how to dress, not to chew gum, and not bring her 32 oz. refillable Wawa mug to court. While you might think these are things that need not be discussed with a client or witness, you would be surprised.

TIP: In a nursing home malpractice case, the plaintiff's counsel can explain to the jury that it is being asked not to condemn the profession of nursing, but to recognize that this particular nurse defendant simply did not do what was supposed to be done. The defendant is not going to jail as a result, but is merely being held accountable for actions or inactions.

The plaintiff's attorney must prove the nurse was negligent by failing to adhere to the prescribed standard of care and failing to exercise that level of professionalism required of the average nurse under the circumstances. Depending upon the case and the individual defendant, plaintiff's counsel can advise the jury that the case in question deals only with one incident and does not attempt to damage the defendant nurse's reputation and assign a label of good or bad. Additionally, even when negligence has occurred, the nurse's actions may have had no impact on the damages. This position is effectively used in disputing causation in birth injury cases in which it is established that cerebral palsy resulting from prenatal causes had nothing to do with the events occurring in the labor and delivery suite. Refer to Chapter 1, *Obstetrical Nursing Malpractice Issues*, in Volume II, for additional information on this topic.

The attorney must maintain credibility with the jury by not exaggerating, overstating, or misstating what will be proved. One author (KF) usually keeps a "red herring" tablet on his table. Throughout the trial, the only entries on that tablet are mistated points, irrelevant topics or pure wastes of time that the jury would likely remember. During closings, he even refers to it as his "red herring" tablet and advises the jury what he wrote down on it to remind the jury how the other side wasted hours of the jury's time talking about a 15-year-old prior soft-tissue neck injury lawsuit (in a case involving an amputated leg), or a person's mediocre high school grades (in a case where the plaintiff went on to achieve sufficient educational success that high school was immaterial), or discussing the person's "beach house" (which really turned out to be a camp site that had been abandoned at some point following the accident).

Weaknesses in the case should be disclosed before the opposing counsel has the opportunity to disclose them. By doing this, not only is the effect on the jury minimized, but the attorney's credibility is also enhanced. The attorney should stay calm. While it is useful to change one's tone while speaking, purely as a matter of effective public speaking, save dramatic confrontations or arguments for the appropriate time. The defense attorney who yells at the plaintiff and opposing experts, and yells throughout closing, is likely to offend the jurors and provoke unwanted attention from the judge.

F. Personalize the Client

Throughout the trial, counsel should attempt to humanize its client so the jury can relate to that client. From the plaintiff's attorney's perspective, the plaintiff is a victim, not a litigant. The plaintiff wanted answers as to what happened, not to be in a courtroom four years after the incident, tied up in some lengthy legal battle. The plaintiff did not ask to be put in this position and is unable to get out of it. The plaintiff lived his entire life, going to school, getting a job, getting married,

having children, and looking forward to vacations, family time and retirement, without ever hoping he would someday get to be a litigant in a lawsuit that would drag out for four years. He never expected to watch his wife die in the same-day surgery recovery room because the nurses did not monitor her blood pressure after the surgeon punctured her vena cava during surgery.

Counsel should refer to his client by name rather than as the "plaintiff," "claimant," or "defendant." Some courts will not allow the attorney to refer to the client by first name only. Older jurors expect the attorney to refer to older clients as Mr., Mrs., or Ms.

TIP: In 2004, the most recent year for which data is available, statistics show that the average length of time from incident to trial was 54 months.[13]

The defense should describe the hospital as a collection of people who, in the eyes of the law, are entitled to the same treatment as an individual. The defense should always have a "face" of the institution. That may be someone who has no real connection to the case, but it should have someone sitting at counsel table the entire trial. Otherwise, the jury may believe that the defense institution does not care about the case. In some trials, the claims adjuster attends much if not all of the trial in order to report back to the insurance carrier and be prepared to enter into settlement negotiations. Refer to Chapter 19, *Working with Claims Adjuster*s, for more on this role. While it is important to personalize the institution, do not attempt to suggest the case is necessarily about that person. In a recent case with one of the authors (KF), the plaintiff was suing a very large institution. The defense attorney had seated with him a designee, who he not only identified, but claimed he represented. The designee was not even a party to the litigation, and had no knowledge of the events. In fact, there was no individual defendant, just the institution. Nevertheless, counsel opened with the claim that he represented Joe Smith, a hard-working employee, who cares deeply about his job. That went on the red herring list.

The defense attorney should personalize the nurse. For example, "Nurse Williams has worked in this hospital's labor and delivery unit for 25 years. She has helped to deliver many of the babies in this town. In a few cases, she has helped to deliver the next generation of those children. Nurse Williams is a familiar figure about town."

G. Choice of Language

The opening is a critical part of the trial. Depending on how voir dire is handled by the trial judge, the opening is likely to be the first interaction with the jury. It is essential to give the jury the accurate impression that the attorney cares about the case, is intimately familiar with the facts, is credible and should be believed, and that the client's claims are meritorious. More than one trial has been lost because the jury disliked the attorney. Do not be flat or monotone. Counsel should be passionate, but not argumentative. Use sensory-awakening nouns and adjectives.

The plaintiff's attorney is seeking compensation for pain, suffering, wage loss, and other damages suffered by the plaintiff. At a later point, the attorney will ask the jury to return an award for a large sum of money. The attorney should use descriptive language to present the facts of the case. The attorney must tell the client's story. Do not state that "The plaintiff fell out of bed and was injured because the nurse had left the room." Rather, "Mary, deeply sedated, was in the same-day surgery recovery room after the operation on her foot. In spite of knowing that Mary had previously tried to climb out of the bed, the nurse primarily responsible for Mary's care left the room. It was during that absence when Mary, unattended and in her sedated state, tumbled from the bed, cracking her skull as her head hit the tile floor."

The current philosophy for plaintiff's counsel is to explain to the jurors early and often that you are seeking financial compensation. There is not to be any confusion down the road as to what this trial is about. It is about money. There is no "eye for an eye, tooth for a tooth" anymore. You do not want the jury simply focusing on liability, as if that is all the case is about. It is about money.

H. An Appeal to Emotion

At the onset of the trial, the jury does not know the attorneys, their clients, or their claims. Rather than standing up and starting to go into the intricate details of the case, recognize the need to win over the jury with a brief explanation of what the case is about and a credible explanation of the theory of the case. The plaintiff's attorney must discuss the losses suffered by the client, including wage loss (if applicable). The jury may hear about significant wage loss without needing to hear dollar amounts. They will also hear about other losses, such as loss of companionship, self-esteem, or body image. They may be told that the plaintiff's life has been torn apart because somebody was not paying attention to what she was doing, or for whatever reasons. The jury should be thinking from the beginning that it is a big case. To throw out numbers or show pictures of a gaping wound might be premature in the opening. Early presentation of startling information might be seen as grandstanding.

The defense attorney may appeal to emotion by expressing remorse or sorrow over what has happened to the plaintiff, but swiftly pointing out that the actions of the defendant had nothing to do with the outcome. The defense attorney might point out that the plaintiff was seriously injured in a car accident and not expected to survive. The inconsequential medication error had no impact on the outcome. Another defense argument might be directed to pointing out that the seriously ill patient, who beat his cancer with the excellent help of the hospital staff, developed an unavoidable extravasation of chemotherapy into his arm, causing a small burn. What is a burn in comparison to being able to live? It might be that the serious injury suffered by the plaintiff may have very well resulted in amputation in the normal course of events, and the infection that developed can occur in the absence of negligence; so merely because the plaintiff has suffered an amputation, in and of itself, does not equate to malpractice.

Be mindful of the composition of the jury when deciding how far to go in the opening. Foley and LeFevre[14] observed that Generation X jurors are cautious and practical. "These values are not compatible with hyperbole and drama. Xers are on the lookout for over-statement and flash. They resist emotional appeals." The authors suggest that rather than editorializing about what happened to the plaintiff, tell descriptive stories in the active voice from the plaintiff's perspective. Legal discussions serve a specific purpose but do not belong in the opening statement. Intellectualizing drains a case of the emotional appeal needed for a just and adequate decision. When liability is weak and potential damages enormous, the plaintiff's lawyer may focus on the damages, hoping that discussion will sway the jury. This tactic is dangerous. Defense counsel may emphasize that the plaintiff's counsel is trying to get a verdict on sympathy alone. Similarly, when injuries are minor, exaggeration can be fatal.

The jury must see the attorney's emotion as sincere and heartfelt. Be honest without being overly dramatic. The attorney should act naturally as she projects a belief in the correctness and the righteousness of her cause. Be impassioned but not out of control. Maintain a professional demeanor and etiquette. Bellicose ranting will only gain the jury's and judge's reproach. The lawyer becomes more credible when the jury believes the lawyer honestly feels the emotions being expressed. This credibility leads to trust. Trust allows the jury to accept the attorney's positions. The converse is also true. Jurors can recognize rehearsed displays and feigned emotions. Such efforts lead to distrust of the attorney and his motives.

For plaintiff's counsel

1. Ensure that the opening paragraphs capture the jurors' attention and evoke feelings that something horrible has happened to the plaintiff that was caused by something the defendant did wrong.

2. The jurors need a basis for identifying with the client and a basis for believing that this type of event could have happened to them or someone they love.

3. Direct the jurors down the path of knowing what is right and wrong. An issue of morality can be injected into the opening to emphasize that the defendant's knowledge of the danger, means to avoid it, and failure to do so has led to this tragedy.

4. Start leading toward the consideration of major damages, painting a vivid picture of the contrasts in the life of the plaintiff before and after the tragedy. Give the jury a strong sense of what the plaintiff's future offers.

5. Take full advantage of the first opportunity to exploit the weaknesses of the defendant's case or witnesses before the defendant has had a chance to mitigate the effect. At the same time take steps to bring out and soften the weaknesses of the plaintiff's case, so that the jurors hear about them from the plaintiff's attorney rather than from opposing counsel.

For defense counsel

1. Emphasize the role of healthcare professionals or the nurses in providing compassionate care by personalizing the defendant.

2. Introduce the primary defenses in the case.

3. Listen to the plaintiff's attorney's opening statement and revise your opening statement to counter the arguments.

4. Counter the appeal to emotion by presenting a strong, calm demeanor.

5. Emphasize your client's position in the community.

6. Highlight the weaknesses of the plaintiff's case, particularly any ignored by the plaintiff in opening.

For both plaintiff and defense counsel

1. The major themes should be woven in several times. Frame the issues of the trial in the manner in which you want them to be perceived.

2. Humanize the client's story by creating images that bring these jurors close to the action, rather than leaving them with detached reports about it. The use of carefully chosen words and phrases helps to convey the effects of what has happened.

3. Use the words and language of the jury, leaving the big words, medical terminology, and legalisms at the office. Explain any relevant medical terms in layperson's language. Weave in key phrases that will appear in the judge's instructions. The jury will understand these terms when they hear them used by the court.

4. Impress upon the jury that this is an important case, one in which these jurors play a major role.

5. Make the opening statements credible and avoid overstatement.

6. Make effective use of exhibits and various other demonstrative evidence to emphasize major case themes and points.

Figure 25.4 *Opening Statement Checklists and Tips*

The plaintiff is advantaged by getting the first speech; the defense attorney is advantaged by hearing the plaintiff's opening statement before speaking. The defense counsel can stress moderation, reason, withholding judgment, and calm deliberation. Fairness to the healthcare facility is stressed in the defense's opening statement. The defense attorney will counter the plaintiff's passion with her own calm voice of reason. Refer to Figure 25.4 for an opening statement checklist and opening statement tips.

Both plaintiff and defense attorneys should be aware of the length of the opening statement. Jurors are likely to grow impatient with long-winded opening statements. Although Generation Xers are particularly focused on the bottom line and do not want to wait an hour for the attorney to get to the point,[15] jurors of all ages are likely to appreciate a well-organized and concise opening statement. Keep in mind that the opening statement provides the key points and the overview of how the data supports the attorney's essential arguments. Many jurors come to trial with some suspicion. A clear and simple opening statement will impress them. A soft, conventional manner of speech may be effective in gaining the trust and sympathy of the jurors.

TIP: The jurors must be able to trust the attorney. The attorney must convey sincerity, directness, and honesty in everything that is said or done.

Excessive bickering over minutia, negative personalization of opposing counsel and witnesses, and innumerable sidebars combine to confirm the general opinion that lawyers are untrustworthy. Many jurors view objections and sidebars as "lawyer games" designed to win cases by preventing the truth from coming out. They hate the lawyers and judge whispering "little secrets." They usually view unfavorably any "sabotage" by an attorney who is "afraid" to present certain evidence or testimony. In essence, jurors become irritated and view the continuously objecting attorney as a spoiled kid saying "no fair."[16] It is imperative the trial attorney display a high level of professionalism as she leads the jury to the truth. The attorney must not be perceived as preventing the jury from discovering the truth. To truly understand how sidebars, bickering, and trial delay affects jurors, try and sit on a jury. While it is difficult to get selected as no attorney wants an attorney on the jury, you can try to sit on a mock trial, or any similar set up. Go watch a trial that you are not familiar with, and sit there, as jurors do, for three days, with the same breaks they take, and without stepping out and checking e-mails, voicemails, and so on. It can be very challenging.

25.4 Witnesses
A. Plaintiff Preparation

The attorney should carefully prepare his or her client for the courtroom. The plaintiff needs explicit information on appropriate clothing, demeanor, and behavior. Outbursts or angry reactions to the testimony of witnesses or judicial decisions will not win any favor with the judge or the jury. The attorney must not assume the plaintiff will understand these issues without adequate preparation.

Some attorneys have plaintiffs review all of the medical records so they can discuss any issues therein. Other attorneys shield their clients from the medical records except to possibly address an issue or two, so the witnesses can plausibly testify they have not seen the records, but will answer what she can from personal knowledge.

Consider what is most effective for the attorney. Clients should meet with the attorney as many times as needed to ensure their comfort level with the process.

It is always a good idea for the plaintiff's attorney to meet clients at their home, especially seriously injured clients to see what type of accommodations they have made at their home, and discuss those accommodations. Those accommodations might become important evidence that support the plaintiff's damages claims. Additionally, the defense attorney meeting the nurse defendant at home will gain a more complete picture of the nurse defendant. Refer to Chapter 16, *Defense Attorney's Perspective*, for more on preparing the nurse defendant for trial.

B. The Nurse as an Expert Witness

1. Introduction

The presentation of expert testimony is a crucial element of any malpractice trial. The proper presentation of a nursing expert witness involves thought and preparation. At one time, controversy existed over the need for experts in nursing malpractice actions. Traditionally, nurses performed routine, "non-technical" tasks. Today, some states go so far as to require an affidavit of merit by an expert in nursing to bring an action for negligence.[16] Refer to Chapter 21, *Working with Nursing Expert Witnesses*, to learn why it may be imperative to not use a physician expert witness to testify about nursing standard of care, based on the position statements of the American Association of Legal Nurse Consultants and The Association of Nurse Attorneys. Expert testimony is required to support a finding of negligence and to prove causation.

2. Negligence versus malpractice

There is a distinction between acts constituting negligence and acts constituting malpractice. This distinction may determine the need for an expert witness if a special malpractice statute is applicable. Negligence must include a failure to meet a standard of care, and the failure must be the proximate cause of damage to a person to whom a duty is owed. Malpractice is limited to the omission, lack, or misuse of a professional skill. Malpractice is a specialized form of negligence, applicable only to professionals. As one writer has pointed out, "A nurse, notwithstanding the stage of her training, may be liable for certain acts. It does not require a technical education to know that hot objects burn persons."[18]

It becomes important to select a competent expert witness once the decision has been made that the act complained of constitutes malpractice and not negligence. This topic is addressed in Chapter 21, *Working with Nursing Expert Witnesses*, Chapter 15, *Plaintiff's Attorney's Perspective*, and Chapter 16, *Defense Attorney's Perspective*.

3. Preparation of the expert

The attorney must ensure that his nursing expert is thoroughly familiar with the facts of the case. The adversary will attack the expert based upon his factual predicate if the retaining attorney fails to provide relevant materials or important information to the expert. The expert must be completely conversant with all the relevant facts of the claimed malpractice. The expert should be informed about any general or specific details of courtroom demeanor associated with a particular courthouse or judge. Camera-containing cell phones are not allowed in certain courthouses. Some judges have their own rules, which may be undefined until broken. The author is aware of an expert witness who was chastised for talking quietly on a cell phone during a break when the jury was out of the room, and who was screamed at for walking in front of the judge's bench instead of taking a circuitous route around the courtroom. An expert heard whispering in the courtroom too close to the jury bench may provide a reaction from the bailiff. In some courthouses, attorneys and expert witnesses share the bathroom or elevator with jurors. An overheard discussion may impact the case. Experts should be advised that they are to have no conversation at all about the case in or near the courthouse. They should not be seen joking around, conducting other business, or fraternizing with the opposing side or expert. Anything a jury sees may be misinterpreted. It is better they see nothing at all.

TIP: Pre-trial preparation is the key to ensuring the expert is able to deal with anything presented in the courtroom. The attorney must have the expert completely review the file before coming to court. Sit down with the expert on multiple occasions and ensure that all relevant facts are covered. If your expert is available, have her sit through as much of the trial as possible. It is not uncommon for a witness to testify to something differently at trial than during the deposition. That testimony might impact the opinion of the expert. Your expert will be better prepared to process the information if she hears it hours or days before her testimony, than if during cross-examination. Example: the expert is confronted with "Nurse Jones, did you know that Ms. Smith has now indicated that she pressed the call button 11 times in 2 hours without a response? Wasn't your opinion premised upon your understanding that she never pressed the call button?"

a. Legal terms

Experts need to understand the requisite legal terms of art. The expert must be comfortable using terms such as "reasonable nursing probability," "proximate cause," and "deviation from accepted nursing standards." A good expert uses these terms appropriately both in pre-trial reports and at trial. The attorney must explain the significance of these essential terms if the witness has not previously testified in court. Good preparation by the attorney can keep the expert from falling into the adversary's traps.

b. Authoritative texts

Experts and the attorney must familiarize themselves with every detail in the authorities to be used. Advance preparation can save the attorney and the expert the embarrassment of having the expert's testimony conflict with other authorities. The attorney must anticipate the texts the opposing counsel will use on cross-examination. At best, the expert will quickly refer to another section of the same text that modifies or more specifically refers to any section that the adversary contends impeaches the expert.

It is also important to review the expert's curriculum vitae (CV) carefully. If there are any articles or books the expert has written on the relevant topic, make sure this material is reviewed to ensure the expert has never taken a position contrary to the current one. That should occur prior to selecting the expert.

c. Anticipation of cross-examination

The plaintiff's attorney should help the expert anticipate the medical defenses so that any argument that the standard of care was followed may be quickly countered. The expert witness should be thoroughly familiar with the report or position of the opposing experts. The expert should be prepared to explain to the jury why his position has greater credibility, and to point out the flaws in the other expert's assertions. The defense nursing expert may use one of several arguments consistent with opinions expressed prior to trial: "the standard of care was followed," "the injury was not foreseeable," "the nurse used appropriate judgment," and "the outcome, while unfortunate, was not under the control of the nurse." A physician expert is most qualified to comment that the injuries did not have any bearing on the plaintiff's outcome, such as death.

Counsel should present examples of attacks on opinions that can be expected from opposing counsel when preparing the expert. Counsel must watch for any inconsistencies, contradictions, and evasive answers given by the expert. Instruct the witness to answer the question asked, not to be evasive, and not to go off on tangents. The expert will look as though she is hiding something if unable to answer a question directly; the expert should not feel as though it is necessary to fight every question on cross-examination. Giving up incidental points will not make a significant difference so long as the expert maintains her beliefs and position.

d. Avoiding arguments

The expert chosen by counsel need not be a total advocate for the case, but should be an advocate for his opinions. The expert does not need to fight the opposing counsel on everything. One of the authors (KF) has seen experts get caught up fighting issues ranging from their company logo to the definition of a "critter." The questioning was completely irrelevant, but pointed out that the expert was not providing an impartial opinion, but was merely an extension of the party's law firm. The expert was an advocate. This costs the expert credibility, and may often cost the client the case.

Similarly, the attorney must prepare the expert witness for attacks on the expert serving as a "professional witness." Such cross-examination is primarily concerned with diminishing the credibility of the testimony, the witness, or both. Honest and direct answers are the way to go with these questions. Squirming around an uncomfortable question will damage an expert's credibility with the jury.

25.5 Direct Examination During Presentation of the Expert (Voir Dire)

The expert must be qualified by reason of "knowledge, skill, experience, training, or education."[19] Counsel should begin the direct examination of the expert witness with questions directed toward the expert's qualifications to testify. Her educational background, training, work experience, certifications, publications, presentations, awards, and so on, should be explained to the jury. In addition to the "standard" background information, anything unusual and interesting is often impressive to the jury. One of the authors (KF) has presented experts who have been professional team physicians, Olympic athletes, and identified as "The Best of" by local magazines. While, in and of itself, this is not as impressive as a degree from MIT, Harvard, or Yale, jurors find this information fascinating and impressive. Provide the jury with enough information so that the court will accept the witness as an expert and the jury will accept the expert's testimony as authoritative.

TIP: The expert should show genuine interest in explaining the material to the jury. Counsel should avoid treating this portion of the examination in a mechanical manner. The jury must believe the expert is the best possible person for this type of case.

Counsel should highlight the "super spots" in the expert's CV and focus on those elements that enable this witness to assist in this particular case. Counsel may ask the expert the significance of the nurse midwife expert having written an article about obstetrical trauma, when the case at hand deals with improper treatment during a miscarriage. The connection must be clear to the jury. Counsel should also focus on those special qualifications that your expert may possess but the opposing expert may not. Examples include: if the expert has board certification, patents on devices, or testifying before Congress (in a good way). These qualifications may allow the jury, torn between two experts, to say, "Yes, but that one woman was Board Certified and the other was not."

TIP: Opposing counsel may offer to waive the requirement of qualification of a witness who will certainly be deemed an expert by the court. Counsel presenting this witness should not accept this stipulation. Presentation of qualifications is an opportunity to impress the jury with the witness' education, training, research, and other accomplishments. Also, the adversary will fully explain the expert's qualifications. Therefore, in order for the jury to be able to compare the two opposing experts, the jury must hear both experts' qualifications.

When an adversary advises he will stipulate to the expert's qualifications, it is appropriate to tell the court that, "While I appreciate that Mr. Esquire recognizes our witness to be an expert in the field of pediatric nursing, I would like the jury to hear why this nurse is particularly qualified to serve as an expert in this case." When qualifying the expert through accomplishments, counsel need not go overboard and discuss every publication, accomplishment, and so on. Juries will lose interest if every item on an extensive CV is highlighted and explained. It is appropriate to indicate, "Ms. Nurse, I see that you have written 73 articles on issues related to your fields of expertise, and 12 of them specifically on wound care of geriatric patients; is that accurate?" This question is followed by, "Were they all published articles?" and "What is entailed in having an article, or 73 for that matter, published?"

Direct examination of a witness is "bricklaying." The lawyer builds evidence "brick by brick," preparing for a closing argument that persuades the jury of the justice of the case.[20] The expert witness explains the complex issues to the jury, but does so in a simplified manner. Ideally, the expert is perceived as truthful, unbiased, qualified, and properly prepared. The expert must convey his position in terms or images clearly understandable to laypeople. Jurors are often unfamiliar with specialized medical terms. The expert must clearly explain his opinion and the basis of that opinion. If factual contentions support the expert's opinion but contradict the adversary expert's opinion, the expert must clearly explain why those facts are so important to the outcome of the case.

25.6 Videotaped Depositions in Lieu of Live Testimony

Medical experts often testify by videotape deposition. This is less common in medical malpractice cases. Physician and nursing experts must be advised at the inception of their retention that they will be expected to testify live at the time of trial. Live testimony is more effective than taped testimony. Additionally, videotape testimony will often occur as much as one month before trial. If there are new developments prior to trial, or even from the testifying witnesses, there is no ability to correct the videotape.

If presenting an expert by videotape is unavoidable, the tape should be handled the same way as live testimony. Use demonstrative evidence when appropriate and keep the pace lively. Consider going off camera for transition scenes. Rather than having the videographer pan from the witness's face to a piece of evidence and take a moment or two to focus, go off the record when the witness is done with her answer. Allow the videographer to pan over and focus, and then go back on record. It will provide for a more seamless transition. Also consider the use of two cameras: one on the witness and the other on the evidence. Both can roll and the tapes can be edited. Content is not being deleted or altered; rather, a more entertaining but accurate production is made.

TIP: There is always concern that jurors are drowsy after lunch and at the end of the day. Use of any evidence during this time period should be kept lively. Videotapes are a bit dangerous during these time periods as the lights are often dimmed and a juror may not feel rude closing his eyes when the person testifying cannot actually see him. Be mindful of when the videotape will be played.

Keep the direct exam on videotape short and simple, perhaps shorter than would occur if the witness was in the courtroom. Videotape presentations are not as interesting as live presentations, and watching an hour long show without commercials is difficult even if the jury wanted to see it.

After completing the videotape, it may be helpful to watch it again before the trial. Sometimes when you are caught up in the moment you might miss points, or answers that have significance. Also, in some jurisdictions, portions of the videotape can be withdrawn.[21] An attorney from one of the author's (KF) firms was involved in a case, defending the claims. A videotape of the defense doctor was taken. Plaintiff counsel's expert did not testify on direct examination with the requisite certainty. However, on cross-examination, the doctor did provide such testimony. During trial, defense counsel "withdrew" all of his videotape questions (i.e., presented no cross-examination of the doctor). Plaintiff's counsel argued that the questioning already occurred, and the entire video should be played. The trial court disagreed and allowed all of the questions to be withdrawn on cross-examination (which was affirmed on appeal). The plaintiff failed to meet his burden. In a similar manner, during a trial that was proceeding well for the defense, one of the authors (KF) videotaped his defense doctor. The examination, cross-examination, redirect examination, re-cross-examination, re-redirect-examination, etc., was contentious and unnecessarily lengthy. But, in the heat of the moment, it seemed like the way to go. Nevertheless, during the trial, as it seemed things were going well for the defense, counsel withdrew his redirect examination, which automatically eliminated everything that flowed thereafter, saving about 1.5 hours of video time.

25.7 The Timing of the Expert's Testimony

When to use the expert is a case-by-case decision. If the liability is particularly egregious, consider putting on the liability expert first. Some jurors might very well "make up their mind" at the conclusion of such testimony, and then it is a matter of running out the clock. A strong expert in a strong liability case can also bolster the credibility of the remainder of the case. If the first witness corroborates everything said by the attorney in the opening, this brings an air of credibility.

Depending upon the length of the case, the plaintiff's attorney may be concerned that the jury will be deliberating seven to eight days after the plaintiff's attorney's strong expert has testified. If the plaintiff's expert can be available for the purpose of potential rebuttal, then the attorney has the best of both worlds—calling the strong expert first and last. However, there must be some legitimate reason to call a rebuttal witness. It might be helpful to have the expert issue a supplemental report after she has reviewed the defense reports. During the expert's testimony, ask that she comment upon the defense experts. Some defendants will object on the grounds that they do not know if they are definitely calling that expert. This opens the door to allow the plaintiff's attorney to call his expert in rebuttal. The defense has essentially invited the court to rule that the plaintiff's expert cannot criticize other experts until after they have testified. In that situation, the plaintiff's expert should be able to testify in rebuttal.

From the defense's perspective, presenting the second half of the case immediately before the jury's deliberation has the advantage of recency. In jurisdictions in which the jurors are not allowed to take notes or ask questions, the defense may have an advantage in being the last side to present to the jury. The plaintiff's part of the case has been rebutted if the defense has been effective, and plaintiff's arguments were neutralized or made to look unreasonable or incorrect. Any significantly damaging evidence is softened by the passage of time. While the damages evidence will have not been forgotten, the jury will have heard days of evidence focusing on the defendant, the "medicine," and the defense experts prior to deliberations.

25.8 Educating the Jury

An expert who has the ability to teach makes it easy for the jury to understand. Many nursing expert witnesses are effective in the teaching role, as it is a skill developed to teach patients in the clinical setting. Armed with a greater knowledge of standards of care and of medical and nursing practice, the jurors can support their arguments during deliberations. A jury who does not understand the attorney's position cannot advocate that view during deliberations. Jurors want experts to explain concepts so they can make their own decisions. But the jurors need to understand the decision each attorney wants them to make.

Ask open-ended, non-leading questions when questioning your expert on direct-examination. Allow the jury to hear the words from the expert, and allow the expert to explain the standard of care and the facts that support the opinion. On redirect examination, it is more likely that the attorney may ask leading questions, as the questions need to be pointed to the topics addressed on cross-examination. Remind the expert witness that redirect is the expert's opportunity to clarify and strengthen the opinions offered.

25.9 Basis of Expert's Opinion

An expert's opinion cannot simply be a conclusory claim of negligence. This would violate what is known as the "net opinion" rule. To avoid violating the net opinion rule, the expert must always give reasons for her opinions. An expert may base opinions on personal knowledge or on facts and data made known to her before and during the trial.[22] An opinion may also be based on facts or data that are not themselves admissible into evidence, if they are "of a type reasonably relied upon by experts in the particular field in forming opinions or inferences upon the subject."[23] Opinions without factual support are not admissible; however, the factual support itself need not be independently admissible during the trial. For example, an expert may rely upon information contained in a police report of a suicide at a hospital as support for his testimony, even if the police report is not authenticated or otherwise admissible, so long as the expert testifies that police reports are the type of information customarily relied upon by experts in his field.

25.10 Demonstrative Evidence During the Expert's Direct Examination

Demonstrative evidence can assist the jury in understanding the topic and make the presentation more animated. Medical illustrations, timelines, photographs, models, or other materials must be authenticated.[24] Authentication is not a difficult process. The burden has been met as long as someone can testify that the evidence is what it purports to be.[25] Some evidence is self-authenticating. Refer to Chapter 22, *Demonstrative Evidence,* for additional information on the legal aspects of presenting demonstrative evidence.

No matter what evidence is being used—photographs, day-in-the-life video, and so on—be sure the expert has had an opportunity to see it before trial, so it can be assured the expert will be able to authenticate the exhibit. The ideal time to review the evidence with the expert before trial, is when there is time to revise the material in a timely and professional manner. Waiting until a few days before trial to create exhibits is a recipe for errors and stress.

Consider the best way for the jury to view the material, based upon the evidence in issue. Medical illustrations can be enlarged for the jury, presented on a rear view screen, or duplicated for individual viewing by the jurors. If it is authentic, the exhibit should aid in the presentation of complex matters to the jury.

25.11 Cross-Examination of the Expert

Experts are often cross-examined on the materials they viewed or did not view, facts they knew or did not know, or other information they may not have considered. Make sure the expert has everything. Do not allow the adversary to spend a half-hour cross-examining the expert on materials the expert never saw (which the attorney did not send because they were completely irrelevant to her opinion). It damages the credibility of the expert (and retaining attorney) to be repeatedly asked, "Mr. Esquire never sent you that deposition either, did he?" Send the expert everything and let her testify that a particular deposition had no bearing on the opinion rendered.

Make sure the expert reviews the opponent's expert reports, especially any criticisms of the expert's own opinions. Request that the expert provide a supplemental report addressing the adversary's experts. This will allow him to discuss those reports during direct exam (unless the court restricts that to rebuttal testimony). It will also give the expert a feel for where the attorney's adversary believes the expert's weaknesses lie. Once the expert sees how he is being attacked on paper, he can prepare for a similar attack in the courtroom.

Prepare the expert to be questioned about fees. This is fair game. On direct exam, the retaining attorney may wish to ask the expert:

- Are you testifying upon my request?
- Have you taken the time to review all of the file materials?
- Was there anything you needed that was not sent to you?
- Have you given some thought and consideration to the issues in the case?
- Are you ready to discuss your opinions about this matter?
- Have you sent bills to my office for payment?
- Have they been paid?
- Are you being paid for the time you are spending here today?

Most jurors expect an expert or consultant to be compensated for time. When the bill gets out of hand, jurors become concerned that an expert's opinion may be swayed by what has been compensated. If one expert has charged $8,000 to date for the case and the opposing expert of the same field has charged $32,000 for the same job, the jurors (and attorneys) will likely be taken aback by that. Although this is less of an issue when nursing experts are used as opposed to physician experts, a discrepancy may still arise. Sometimes the attorneys can reach an agreement on this issue ahead of time that neither counsel will ask each other's expert about compensation or what is being paid.

25.12 Effective Cross-Examination of the Opposing Nursing Expert

Cases often come down to what is referred to as "the battle of the experts." Will the jury believe the plaintiff's or defendant's expert? While other witnesses and issues in the case can determine the outcome of the case, certainly the expert's opinion is pivotal.

Depending upon the jurisdiction, the adversary will have a certain level of knowledge about the expert. Depositions of the expert are permitted in courts that follow the federal rules, such as Delaware and New Jersey. That is not permitted in Pennsylvania. Federal rules require the expert to identify the previous four years' worth of case information in cases in which the expert testified at deposition or trial. Transcripts may be tracked down through this method or by using one of the deposition databanks reserved for the use of plaintiff or defense attorneys. Invaluable information can be obtained from prior transcripts the expert provided in other litigation. Track down articles, books, and so on. Perform Internet research and download pages from the expert's website. One of the author's firms (KF) has obtained more information devastating to an expert's testimony from the Internet, websites, and other cases in which the expert took an adverse position, than any other source. It is often much easier to confront an expert with this type of information than trying to tangle with the expert "on the medicine." Give consideration to whether it is necessary to depose an expert if permitted to do so. An expert may see the flaws in her opinion through the deposition and provide supplemental analysis to try to correct those flaws, and the retaining counsel may substitute in a different expert if permitted to do so.

It is helpful to meet with the attorney's expert or a legal nurse consultant on the relevant issues prior to cross-examining the opposing expert. Retain a consultant, who need not be identified as a witness, to assist with preparation of the case and plan of attack. Such consultants will often provide the literature and relevant standards of care, and pick out significant issues in medical records that might appear to merely be semantics to a layperson (i.e., "no complaints of pain" is different than "denies complaints of pain": the latter suggests the patient was specifically asked if he had any pain, while the former might be written even if there was no conversation at all between the nurse and the patient). Refer to Chapter 20, *Working with Legal Nurse Consultants*, for expanded information concerning this role.

Professor Irving Younger has published his *Ten Commandments of Cross-Examination*:

1. Be brief.
2. Use short questions and plain words.
3. Always ask leading questions.
4. Do not ask a question to which you do not already know the answer.

5. Listen to the witness's answers.

6. Do not quarrel with the witness.

7. Do not allow the witness to repeat direct testimony.

8. Do not permit the witness to explain the answer.

9. Do not ask one question too many.

10. Save the ultimate point of the cross-examination for summation.

A. The Purpose of Cross-Examination

Cross-examination is the opportunity to punch holes in the adversary's case as well as bolster the attorney's position. If the adversary's expert has omitted relevant information from her analysis, assumed a fact to be true that is not true, or otherwise made an error, the cross-examining attorney must note the issue so the jury can consider that when assigning weight to the witness's testimony. It may not be enough for the jury to completely discredit the witness's testimony, but it may be enough to cause them to question the testimony, especially when considered alongside other factors (i.e., other errors in the testimony, the witness's relative qualifications, bias issues, and so on). Jury instructions provided by the judge at the end of the trial will address this point.

Additionally, the cross-examining attorney should make an effort to get the expert to agree with as much of his own expert's opinion as possible. It may very well be that the experts agree on 75 percent of what they are saying, but only disagree regarding one small issue, which can be addressed some other way. In closing argument, the attorney may reiterate how the experts are in agreement on "A," "B," and "C," and their disagreement on "D" is merely because the opposing side's expert misunderstood a relevant fact.

TIP: Attempt to "box in" the adversary's expert as much as possible. Take as much out of the case as possible; get the expert to agree on as much as possible and then focus on why there is a disagreement on the remaining issues.

B. Methods of Impeaching an Expert

An expert can be impeached like any other witness on grounds of bias, interest, or motive if she failed to consider important facts or if key evidence was misunderstood. Some typical "hot spots" to examine for potential cross-examination include:

1. Lack of qualifications or lack of hands-on nursing experience

2. Lack of nursing knowledge

3. Status as a professional witness

4. Fee expected for testifying

5. Number of times witness has testified or reviewed cases for each side

6. Total income for each appearance as an expert versus income as a nurse

7. Contradictory statements made in other reports, testimony, articles, and so on

The attorney may find a prior relationship between the opposing side's expert and a party to the litigation when reviewing the expert's CV In such a situation, the expert's self-proclaimed unbiasedness will likely be lost when the jury hears the connection. In the closing highlight the connection, and question why—with all of the potential experts that could have been retained by the adversary—someone was hired who formerly or presently worked with the other party.

C. Discrediting a Witness's Knowledge of the Facts

Proving a faulty observation or recollection is discrediting because it demonstrates that the witness did not accurately present the facts. Review the expert's report carefully. See if he or she omitted an important record, or did cite it but omitted an important piece of information in the record. Once confronted with the important information, the expert will either have to abandon the opinion or stick with the opinion no matter what. Note on cross-examination those important facts overlooked by the expert (i.e., "Can we agree there is no mention in your report of reviewing Dr. Smith's file?"). You may not need to ask the expert what impact such things would have on his opinion, as the point you want to make is that the facts are irrelevant to this expert. You can generally ask the expert, "Certainly you would want a complete set of records before rendering an opinion?" Of course, even with that, a seasoned expert who realizes he is missing records will likely respond, "Counsel, I have a very clear understanding of what happened here, so do I need every piece of paper? No. Would I like to have it so we could avoid this dialogue and get to what is important? Yes." Point out what is missing, and that might be enough for the jury to see that the expert is missing information. This will allow the cross-examining attorney to argue that the facts are totally irrelevant to this expert; the expert was going to provide the same opinion no matter what the facts were because when the expert was confronted with relevant contradictory facts, he still did not change his opinion. This will show some flaws in the expert's alleged objectivity.

Sometimes it is not the expert who failed to review records, but the attorney who failed to provide all relevant records. In that case, the expert might become noticeably upset that she has been "set up" by the hiring attorney. The expert might turn against her own side because she feels like a fool in front of the jury since not all of the facts were provided. Experts have reputations to protect and are aware that attorneys talk about their effectiveness. They do not want stories getting around that they "lost the case" for a particular side. They will let it be known that they did not receive certain records if that is the case. In contrast to the above comments, an expert will typically admit that they should have a complete file. Consider this line of questioning:

Attorney: Expert, you would agree that it is important to have all of the relevant medical records to render an opinion?

Expert: Yes.

Attorney: Expert, you would agree that it is a good thing to have a complete file?

Expert: Yes.

Can there be any other answer? Questions such as these must be admitted. The only possible avenue for the expert is to assert that everything that was relevant was sent to and considered by the expert. This argument works only if all of the key material was made available to the expert, and falls apart when something that was key was omitted.

These questions are often posed to the expert who seeks to deny that a relatively significant injury is not all that significant:

- "Expert, you would agree that breaking your leg is not a good thing?"
- "Expert, you would agree that falling from a bed in a nursing home is bad, right?"

What is the expert going to say? Some experts have written so much or testified so often that it is relatively easy, though time consuming, to gather information about them. The attorney who has sought out this information should let the expert know early on in the cross-examination. If the attorney has other depositions, articles, writings, texts, and so on, they can be piled on the table. Just the sight of a text flagged with multiple post-it notes may convince the expert during cross-examination that the attorney is cross-examining the expert with her own words. Sometimes the attorney will get the expert to agree with everything asked, out of the expert's fear that she has stated something differently some time in the past. Enlargement of pages of a text or prior reports that appear to contradict the expert's position on this case may be damaging to credibility, even if the facts of the

other case were entirely different. The expert is put on the defensive, attempting to convince the jury not to consider words that are in front of the jury in black and white. While the attorney might spend hundreds, if not thousands, of dollars accumulating this information, it only takes one prior comment or contradiction to destroy an expert's credibility.

D. Dealing with an Aggressive Lawyer on Cross-Examination

Many experts dread cross-examination; others enjoy the battle of wits. An expert witness almost always welcomes a discussion about how to deal with an aggressive attorney. Many experts appreciate knowing that if the attorney has difficulty attacking the expert's opinions about a case, the attorney will instead attack the expert's credibility, reputation, and so on. The intensity of this attack may catch an inexperienced expert off guard. Advance preparation for a personal attack is essential, because if not done properly it can severely backfire. Also, no matter how skilled opposing counsel appears, unless that attorney has a healthcare background, the expert invariably knows more about the clinical issues than the attorney. That is why it is imperative to meet with the attorney's own expert to fully understand the medical issues in the case.

Whether the cross-examining attorney is loud, soft, or demonstrative, the witness controls the pace of the examination. No matter how fast the attorney asks questions, the witness can take time to think about his answer, and provide a well-reasoned answer. If the attorney appears to be inappropriately losing her temper, the calm witness will amplify the attorney's demeanor. The attorney will look even more unreasonable in contrast to the calm witness. If the attorney does appear to be high strung and "losing it," a quiet, well-placed objection that the attorney is being argumentative and unnecessarily hostile might alert the judge to the attorney's antics. Unlike depositions, the expert can rarely ask for a break when this type of behavior is exhibited by opposing counsel. Breaks in trial are often rigidly scheduled. An expert who asks for a break during intense cross-examination may be perceived as having a difficult time with the questioning. It is also unlikely to be granted.

Should the expert react to the annoying behavior of the opposing attorney by responding in an angry or sarcastic way, he may appear more as an advocate than an independent evaluator of the circumstances. The retaining attorney familiar with the style of the adversary should advise the retained experts that they are not to argue with counsel. They can certainly disagree with counsel and explain the basis of their disagreement, but loud, confrontational argument is never appropriate. The retaining attorney is responsible for objecting when the aggressive cross-examining attorney interrupts the witness or repeatedly asks the same question. When the opposing counsel is asking questions, the retaining attorney must listen closely and be prepared to make a timely, concise, and appropriate objection. A finite list of objections should be committed to memory or paper, but easily recalled when needed. This list includes:

- the question is argumentative,
- the question assumes facts not in evidence,
- the question calls for hearsay testimony,
- relevance,
- leading,
- the question is compound,
- the question seeks privileged information,
- the question calls for speculation, and
- asked and answered."[26]

25.13 The Nurse as a Defendant
A. Direct Examination of a Nurse Defendant

Direct examination of a nurse defendant is an attempt to establish a link between the jury and defendant. Defense counsel humanizes the client with discussion of nursing background, hobbies, family, and work ethics and values. A jury may be less inclined to find for a cold, uncaring nurse defendant who seemingly followed the appropriate standard of care than a pleasant, likeable defendant who may have deviated from the appropriate standard of care. Defense attorneys should school their clients to act with restraint and politeness even if the nurse defendant wholeheartedly disagrees with the allegations.

TIP: Jurors are instructed by the court to think with their heads and not with their hearts. Nevertheless, jurors are human and tend to lean in the direction most tasteful to them. All else being equal, it is reasonable to assume the jurors would be more likely to relate to the person they feel they could be friendly with outside the courtroom than the one they could not stand.

The nurse defendant needs advance preparation for trial to understand the proceedings, pace, and rules of trial. Explain to her the importance of using lay terms. There is a scene in the movie *The Verdict* when the defense team is preparing the defense doctor on how to testify, and the doctor explains that the patient "aspirated vomit" into her mask. The defense attorney told the doctor to testify that the patient "threw up" in her mask. This humanizes the witness and allows the jury to better relate to the witness.

The defense attorney should ask the defendant nurse to read his deposition before testifying. While this is not necessarily done to help remember the "story," it is effective in allowing the witness on cross-examination, if confronted with

the deposition, to recall a particular answer he provided. Refer to Figure 25.5 for a sample dialogue.

If the nurse defendant is familiar with the transcript, it is not fatal that some recollection of the facts has changed. That happens over time. Memories fade, or perhaps after reflection and speaking with other people present, people simply have a different recollection. If the nurse defendant's recollection has changed, she should advise the defense attorney of such, so it can be handled on direct examination as well as cross-examination. The defense attorney may not advise the client to "stick with" what was said before, because the witness no longer believes it. The witness will testify as to what the witness believes, even if her memory has changed. The witness will need to be able to explain that memories have changed.

Consider the use of demonstrative evidence. Whether it is medical summaries, timelines, illustrations, or anatomical models, such tools are useful and assist the jury in understanding the issues. For example, in a case involving allegations of injection injury from improper landmarking, have the nurse defendant use an anatomical model to show where he gave the injection, using correct technique.

Some attorneys believe it is useful to perform mock direct and cross-examinations to help the nurse client prepare. While these may be helpful, the defense attorney also wants to avoid the potential of having the client's testimony appear rehearsed. There should be some liveliness and spontaneity in the questions and answers which adds to the credibility of the testimony. The witness should be advised to directly answer the question posed and look at the jury when answering. The witness should avoid fidgeting and should act properly the entire trial. Even when not testifying, the nurse witness must remember to be mindful of demeanor:

- Do not roll eyes at answers.
- Do not sigh.
- Do not chew gum.
- Do not leave on a cell phone.
- Dress appropriately.

Advise people to dress appropriately, but comfortably. One of the authors (KF) recalls a witness (not his) who appeared at trial in clothing that appeared to be a prom dress from decades ago. When asked why she was wearing the dress (after being complimented on her appearance ten separate times), she responded that she "was told to dress nice and this was the nicest thing" she had. Some people need very concrete instructions. The attorney should ask what they plan on wearing. If they say jeans and a nice sweatshirt, then discuss more appropriate clothing. If a woman says she plans to wear a skirt and a sweater, then no alteration in plans may be needed.

Q.   Nurse Jones, you testified on direct examination that you were in the patient's room within five minutes of being called; do you remember saying that?

A.   Yes, I do.

Q.   Do you remember me asking you that same question during your deposition?

A.   Yes, I saw in my deposition that I stated "Ten or maybe fifteen minutes," and I guess that is what I said, but that just is not how I remember it at this time.

Q.   But you did say that in your deposition, under oath?

A.   Yes, apparently, as I have seen the deposition and it says that, and I have given some thought to it, and I just remember it being more like five minutes, but this is just an estimate; everything seemed so fast.

The nurse has an opportunity to take some of the sting out of an inconsistent statement if she knows where the questioning is going. Consider this line of questioning.

Q.   Nurse Jones, you testified on direct examination that you were in the patient's room within five minutes of being called, do you remember saying that?

A.   Yes, I do.

Q.   Do you remember me asking you that same question during your deposition?

A.   No, I do not.

Q.   Well then, let me back up—you remember being in my conference room seated directly next to your attorney?

A.   Yes, I do.

Q.   I told you I needed you to tell me the absolute truth about whatever it is that I ask you, see on page five where I was giving you the instructions?

A.   Yes, I do.

Q.   I told you on page seven to let me know if anything I asked was vague or confusing. Do you see that?

A.   Yes, I do.

Q.   I asked you questions generally about what occurred the day of the incident that brings us to this courtroom.

A.   Yes.

Q.   And I asked you how long it took you to get to the room after being called?

A.   I don't remember that specifically.

Q.   Well, take a look at page 42, line eight; I asked you, "how long did it take you to get to the room after being called?" Do you see that?

A.   I do now.

Q.   And please read your answer to the jury.

A.   "Ten or maybe fifteen minutes."

Q.   Do you see that now?

A.   I do now.

Q.   So that is what you said eight months ago when asked the same question under oath in my office, while seated next to your counsel?

A.   Yes, I guess.

Q.   And neither you nor your counsel interjected and said "maybe it was closer to five minutes"?

Figure 25.5 Impeaching a Nurse Defendant

B. Medical Records and the Nurse Defendant

The accuracy and thoroughness of a medical record can be a critical factor in a nursing malpractice trial. Jurors can be swayed, regarding nurse credibility, by the manner in which medical records were kept. Sloppy or erratic recordkeeping can create the inference that patient care was rendered in a similar fashion. Plaintiff's attorneys stress that the documentation process is completely under the control of the healthcare providers. Evidence of altered or missing charts is a devastating blow to a defendant's credibility. Required by law, documentation is a vital part of communication between doctors and nurses. Evidence of tampering destroys the credibility of the author and any defendant who, in the eyes of the jury, knew or should have known of attempted deception. Jurors abhor attempts to deceive them. A record with damaging facts hurts less than a record that has been altered. Once available as a plaintiff's theme, an alteration can expand a defendant nurse's exposure. Jurors may add a punishment factor to the compensation.

The defense attorney should have the original medical file available in the courtroom, divided using the section index tabs familiar to the nurse defendant. This advance preparation of the chart will increase the nurse's ability to locate key pieces of information in the medical record, and thus improve confidence in what is an extremely intimidating procedure.

C. Plaintiff's Attorney's Goal in Cross-Examining the Nurse

Ideally, the plaintiff's attorney wants the nurse to concede a deviation from the standard of care. Sometimes that occurs if the nurse's defense is on disputing causation. Depending on what was obtained in discovery, the plaintiff's attorney must decide if it is important to read portions of the deposition in the case-in-chief, if a witness should be called on cross, or if she simply wishes to cross the witness when called in the case-in-chief. As with cross-examining the expert, the attorney must gauge what can be obtained from the nurse defendant by way of admission. If the plaintiff's attorney does not believe it will be possible to make many points using the medical issues, the focus shifts to what the attorney and nurse agree on, and what separates the attorney and nurse from agreeing on liability. It might just be a single fact. Or, the attorney may want to at least have the nurse agree that if he deviated from the standard of care, there should be liability. This allows the attorney to argue the nurse's words during the closing, as shown in Figure 25.6. This now allows the plaintiff's attorney to argue in the closing that even the nurse defendant agrees he should be held responsible civilly if the jury believes he did not act as professionally as possible. The attorney has essentially obtained the nurse defendant's permission for liability.

Q.   Nurse, you would agree that you are a professional?

Q.   And you understand that people depend upon you for proper medical care?

Q.   People who are sick and in need of proper medical attention rely upon you to help them?

Q.   And you would agree that you have an obligation to those people?

Q.   You would agree that it is important for you to do the best job you can do to help these people in their time of need?

Q.   Your patients deserve that don't they?

Q.   And if a particular medical issue is over your head, you should go get someone to help you?

Q.   Because that is what a professional does, right?

Q.   So, you would agree that if the jury believes you didn't act in the professional manner that you should have, and that harmed your patient, Mr. Jones, then you should be held responsible?

Q.   That would be fair, would it not?

Figure 25.6 Questioning to Get the Nurse Defendant to Admit to Liability

Be mindful of the theme of the case when cross-examining the nurse. Do not feel compelled to try to crush the nurse with a devastating knockout if the facts do not support it. The trial is centered around a theme, and each witness, including the nurse, should help develop that theme. Be focused with the nurse. Ask short, simple questions. Have the nurse agree with those points not in dispute. Highlight the clear failures to act on the nurses' parts—even if the defense concedes the conduct but challenges causation—as, during deliberations, each element of the case will spill over into the next. Be respectful. Do not be misleading with evidence or information. Many jurors have negative attitudes about lawsuits and claims. Do not give them a reason to feel as though the presentation has bolstered their beliefs.[27]

D. Multicultural Issues

As nurses from other cultures have found employment in the United States, some have also found themselves named as defendants in nursing negligence claims. A common misperception among some nurses from other cultures is that they will be deported or lose their licenses as a result of losing a nursing malpractice case. Naturally such concerns may interfere with the ability to testify effectively both on direct examination and cross-examination. Awareness of cultural differences helps the defense attorney assist the nurse prepare for cross-examination. Cross-examination by male attorneys may be particularly difficult for some nurses to withstand. Female nurses from cultures that emphasize deference to male authority will often need more assistance from the defense attorney to recognize the importance of adhering to their testimony and position that they were not negligent.

Nurses with significant language barriers may not present well in a courtroom, triggering jury prejudices about the nurse's background and capabilities. Attorneys from both sides need to be aware of cultural issues affecting the nurse's understanding of the proceedings and the jurors' reactions to the defendant. A nurse with longevity in the United States may be much better prepared to deal with courtroom dynamics than the nurse who was a recent immigrant at the time of care in question. Additionally, the multicultural nature of the jury may result in a juror sitting in judgment on a nurse from her own country. How this will affect jury deliberations must be considered at the time of jury selection and throughout the trial.

25.14 Closing Argument
A. Focus

The closing statement gives the attorney the "opportunity to wrap a ribbon around the trial package that has been craft-

ed."[28] The closing argument ties the evidence into the theme of the case. Remind the jury of the favorable evidence from the favorable witnesses who supported the case. Remind the jury of the witnesses who contradicted the adversary's case. Remind the jurors of the "red herrings." Ask the jury, "Why would someone raise all of these issues if she knew she would never prove them at the time of trial?" The answer is obvious: "To muddy the water, and distract you from the real issues in the case." Ask the jury why the opposing attorneys would waste time going over irrelevant topics. "Why not just focus on what is relevant? The trial should be focused on relevant issues, and we would be done sooner. If the facts and evidence support someone's position, they focus on that. If the facts and evidence do not support someone's position, they blow smoke and try to shift the jury's focus." There was a saying in law school: "If the facts are in your favor, pound the facts; if the law is in your favor, pound the law; if neither are in your favor, pound the table." This saying is particularly applicable against the attorney who is a lot of argument, but not a lot of substance.

Consistent with the "red herring" argument is the general rule that many attorneys thank the jurors for their time. Some attorneys elaborate on thanking the jury. Rather than just stating "thank you for your time, you have been most attentive and we appreciate your civic duty" (which perhaps some jurors expect, but others see as nothing more than hollow words), the attorney who has not thrown "red herrings" into the case might state, "Thank you for your time. It is easy for anybody to stand here and simply say the words 'thank you.' However, I hope you have seen my appreciation of your time by not wasting it. Appreciation goes beyond words. I believe I have shown you my thanks by coming to court every day, filling the days with relevant testimony, and being to the point in our proofs—not wasting your time with 'red herrings.' Nevertheless, beyond my actions, I do want to also say the words—'thank you.'"

Continue the theme of the case and explain the evidence that supports that theme. Reuse key exhibits presented throughout trial. Tell the jury what evidence is not in dispute and what finite issues might be in dispute. Review not only the burden of proof issues, but also the law. Explain how the facts, applied to the law, warrant a finding in the attorney's favor.

B. The Applicable Law

Initially, the attorney provides the judge with requested and proposed jury charges. The judge will have a charging conference with both sides' attorneys and explain with what he will charge the jury. When possible (and when it is the law), it may be preferable to stick to the standard points as much as possible. Attorneys want to both win the case for their client and avoid having the case retried. It does little good to obtain a verdict based upon an incorrect charge that the attorney argued was proper, only to have the case later reversed at the appellate level. There are, however, standard charges which have either not been accepted as the law by appellate courts, or do not completely and accurately reflect the state of appellate law. Be mindful of these issues and be sure to provide the court with the current law. At the conclusion of the charging conference, but before the closing arguments, the judge will tell the attorneys what he is going to state to the jury during the jury charge.

During closing, each side's attorneys can then explain the relevant sections of the law. If it is anticipated that there is one particular charge the case is going to turn on, then highlight it with the jury. State the law to the jury as the judge will phrase it, but then explain what it means in layperson's terms. It can be effective to have a trial exhibit of the charge so the jurors can see it. Break it down as to what it means and the evidence that supports the client's position.

C. Defense Summation Techniques

In closing, defense counsel should remind the jury that the plaintiff has two important advantages: the right to speak twice and the opportunity to have the last word. Therefore, the fact that defense counsel does not stand up and provide a rebuttal closing does not mean it agrees with the plaintiff's rebuttal closing, it merely means that it is simply not allowed to argue further. The defense should also remind the jury that to prevail, the law requires the plaintiff to prove her case by a preponderance of the evidence. The defense does not have a burden and need not prove that the defendant was not negligent. Rather, the plaintiff must prove negligence by a fair preponderance of the evidence.

The defense will often emphasize that it is easy to file a lawsuit for any amount of damages upon any claimed facts. The filing fee is $130, and a lawsuit is filed. This can be effectively used against the defense in rebuttal (i.e., "it is unlikely there is anyone in this room that thinks it took only $130 to get this case to this point—it is three years old, there have been 20 depositions, expert testimony and five days of trial").

The defense must point out what evidence supports its position and theory of its case, and how the plaintiff has failed to meet its burden of proof. The defense should remind the jury that if it believes the evidence is equally balanced for the plaintiff and the defense, then its verdict must be for the defense.

Because the defense has no burden of proof (except on its affirmative defenses), it often focuses on credibility. The

defense attorney will often attempt to diminish the credibility of the plaintiff's witnesses and proofs, as that might be enough for the jury to decide the plaintiff has not met his proof. Did the plaintiff's testimony change on a material point from deposition to trial? Did the plaintiff's expert testify inconsistent with a proposition previously stated in a different case or publication? Did the plaintiff ignore a significant piece of evidence? Did the plaintiff change her theory from that which was pled to that which was proven? While any of these issues may not be fatal to the plaintiff's case, many defense attorneys have been successful in merely piling up the "inconsistencies" so as to later argue the evidence does not deserve the weight that would allow the plaintiff to meet the burden of proof. The verdict should be for the defense because the plaintiff's case is based upon misstatements and changed stories. If the plaintiff's case was righteous, then why would he need to misrepresent a key point? Why change his theory? Why hire an expert who does not even know his own opinion from day to day?

Attacking credibility may not be an option for the defense. The case might simply be a battle of the experts on the standard of care or causation. In such a situation, the defense should remind the jury that there is not a great deal in dispute. The parties do not dispute that the plaintiff was a patient seeking medical care and that he received the care consistent with the medical records, but unfortunately did not make a complete recovery. That happens sometimes and nurses live with the pain of knowing they cannot help every person they encounter. These nurses are not in their profession to harm people; they are in their profession to help people. They are not in their profession to ignore or neglect people; they are in their profession to heal the sick and injured. That does not mean that even if they do everything they are supposed to do, as they did in this matter, that cancer will be cured, heart attacks will not occur, and people will not suffer. What a great world we would live in if nurses could cure everything.

D. Plaintiff's Summation Techniques

1. Key points

There are considerations in closing a nursing malpractice case that may not exist in other types of litigation. In a nursing malpractice case, the plaintiff's lawyer can address a topic that affects every juror: concern about good nursing care. Every juror is at risk of medical error.

The tone the plaintiff's attorney takes in the closing is sensitive to the case: the venue in which the case is being tried, as well as the personality of the judge all play a role. If the healthcare facility is in a large metropolitan city and there were a number of egregious errors, the attorney can afford to be more righteous. If, however, the attorney is dealing with a small community medical facility, she should be mindful of the criticisms of the facility in general rather than just the conduct in issue.

Similarly, if the nurse is a nice, likable person, the plaintiff's attorney can explain that even good people make errors. If the plaintiff's attorney has solicited agreement from the nurse defendant that if the jury finds that he erred, then the nurse should be held liable, the attorney can also tie in that when good people, such as the nurse defendant, make mistakes even they acknowledge they must be held accountable. That is our system. Remind the jury that the nurse defendant is not going to jail, not losing his job, and not going to be condemned in the community because of what occurred. The plaintiff is merely looking for the jury to apply the law to the facts and determine if the nurse's conduct, on the particular date(s), met the proper standard of care. If it did not then the jury must so decide. The case merely involves the care given by one hospital and one nurse (or a nursing home over a period of time, a same-day surgery facility on the day in question, and so on). If the patient was harmed as a result of that care, the healthcare professionals must be held accountable. That is our system.

Remind the jury that the plaintiff's burden of proof is a preponderance of the evidence. Remind them about the balanced scale. Remind them that if the scales tip ever so slightly to the plaintiff's side, then the plaintiff prevails. There is no higher burden of proof than that.

Avoid legal jargon like "pain and suffering" and "award." Those expressions are often synonymous with what jurors think are frivolous lawsuits. Tell the jurors that because of the defendant's medical error, Mrs. Jones lost her leg, lost her freedom, and lost her ability to care for and provide for her family. Our only system in America to evaluate the life that has become Mrs. Jones is through a civil jury system, so that a group of citizens, such as the jurors, can evaluate the value of the level of harm with which Mrs. Jones now lives.

An effective closing will cause the jurors to think how they relate to the facts of the litigation. Everyone, at one time or another, has required health care or knows someone who required health care. Explain to the jury that health care plays an important role in our society, and the individuals who work at healthcare facilities are responsible for their patients, who are depending upon them when they need it the most. When medical care is good, all is fine, but when it is not, there can be very serious consequences. Jurors should understand that a verdict for the defendant is a signal that bad nursing care is acceptable in the community. To take the case out of the confusing realm of medical malpractice, remind the jurors that when auto operators make mistakes, they are held accountable; when construction companies make mistakes, they are held accountable; when large petroleum companies make mistakes, they are held accountable; and when nurses make mistakes, they must be held accountable.

If the facts of the case lend themselves to a righteous tone at select moments of the closing, then the attorney may properly remind the jury of that particular evidence. Listen carefully to the defense's closing for misstating evidence, taking a position that discounts the seriousness of the claim, or incorrectly attempting to inoculate the jury to the arguments expected from the plaintiff's attorney.

Use rebuttal as the last speech. Let the jury know that although it is called closing "argument," the plaintiff's attorney did not want to argue during the closing, but wanted merely to remind them of the evidence. However, after hearing the adversary say "X," "Y," and "Z," it was important to correct that misinformation. And then go on to explain how the adversary's argument is disingenuous or misleading. If the defense attorney suggests that sympathy should not play a role in the jurors' deliberations, tell the jurors you are not now, nor were you ever looking for sympathy. You do not want the defense lawyers' sympathy, or the jurors'. Let the jurors know all the things you did not do, but could have done, if you wanted sympathy (i.e., brought in the plaintiff's four children to sit in the front row during closings, brought in pictures of the plaintiff's house that is falling apart since the incident, etc.).

The plaintiff's attorney stresses that the jury is being asked to do the right thing. They are to apply the facts of this case to the law as explained by the judge, and if the evidence tips ever so slightly on the issues of liability, then they are to move on to damages. The plaintiff's attorney asks the jury to remember the opening argument and the promises made to the jury. Emphasize that the promises have been kept; the points to establish liability have been proven; and the adversary did not prove what she claimed was going to be proved to establish how her client was not culpable.

2. Jury verdict sheet

Next, review the verdict sheet with the jury. Some attorneys prefer to make the sheet into an enlargement or display it in some other way to illustrate how it is to be completed. Review that the question of whether the defendant was negligent should be answered "yes," and the issue of causation should also be answered "yes." Review with the jury that if they do not answer those questions "yes," the plaintiff is forever barred from recovery, and can never return to the courthouse and the case is over. This finality can be conveyed to the jury so they understand the importance of answering "yes" to the questions regarding the defendant's fault. Then begin review of the verdict sheet on damages. Explain to the jury how to answer those questions; review the factual information and law regarding damages.

E. Damages

Various elements of damages must be discussed. The plaintiff's attorney reviews the elements being pursued and recalls the evidence developed on those issues. Do not minimize the significance of some of the larger damages with discussion of every conceivable element of damages if some of those elements are weak or minimal. If the client's injury resulted in an amputation, but little past medical bills or treatment (i.e., $15,000), consider not putting that number "on the board." Emphasizing a $15,000 figure when a seven-figure recovery is being requested could hurt the plaintiff's cause. It might be more effective not to show the jury any numbers at all, rather than a relatively small number. If the evidence was presented in the case, then the jury charge is appropriate and the jury can render the verdict, but it need not be discussed in closing. Prior consideration of this issue will determine whether the bills should be put into evidence at all. Conversely, if the plaintiff has only $15,000 in bills, defense counsel may wish to ensure that he establishes plaintiff's medical bills so the amount can be discussed during closings. The small number might have the jury thinking smaller, despite the serious injury. One author (KF) was involved in a trial where the injury in issue was a broken wrist where there was no surgery, but the break never healed properly. As such, post-traumatic arthritis set in, and a fusion of the wrist was to be performed at some point in the future. The total medical bills were $6,500. Plaintiff did not put the medical bills into evidence. At the end of plaintiff's case, the defense moved for a non-suit on past medicals. Plaintiff did not oppose the non-suit. As the court was about to grant the non-suit, defense counsel withdrew his motion as he realized that he wanted to argue the meds. However, he never put them into evidence either and plaintiff's counsel urged that the non-suit was proper, which the judge granted. The jury returned a seven figure verdict.

1. Economic damages

Economic damages include medical bills, lost household services, wage loss, and lost benefits. The plaintiff may have lost economic damages up to the time of trial and anticipate future lost damages. Experts will work up these numbers pre-trial. However, consider which numbers are most reliable, and be conservative. For example, the economist

might run calculations of lost future wages with retirement ages of 60, 65, and 70. Present all of this information to the jury. The plaintiff's attorney should consider suggesting to the jury in the closing that they can accept any of these numbers, but that 65 is one everybody might be able to agree upon; it is right down the middle. Remind the jury that this is the last time the case will be in a courtroom. If Mr. Plaintiff runs out of money at the age of 60 because of the surgeries, rehabilitation, and living expenses, another jury will not be reconvened to deliberate further. They need to make sure the money awarded is satisfactory to last the plaintiff's lifetime.

Both defense and plaintiff's attorneys may have retained experts pre-trial to calculate numbers of past and future damages. Reevaluate the numbers after impaneling the jury. Some or none of these experts may be called to testify. Credibility is key. An otherwise strong case may result in losing credibility if the plaintiff's attorney begins overreaching with damages. That is not to say that such experts should routinely be jettisoned. It is merely a suggestion to reevaluate how things look at every step of the way. Do not feel locked into presenting damages experts simply because they have been retained.

TIP: Avoid making a commitment during opening statements that the witness will testify, if uncertain whether a certain witness will be called.

---

2. Non-economic damages

Non-economic damages include pain and suffering, disfigurement, loss of life's pleasures, loss of consortium, and similar elements. It is difficult for a jury to place a number on these damages and for the attorney to communicate these issues to the jury; however, the attorney must devise effective ways to explain how the client's life has been affected. For example, using a summary of the medical records and an expert fact witness has helped juries to understand what the plaintiff went through as a result of the medical negligence. (Refer to Chapter 10, *Pain and Suffering*.) It is helpful to get the jury to relate to the plaintiff's injury. In this regard, analogies of pain might be helpful. Why do people hate to go to the dentist? Because they might be in some discomfort for 20 minutes. Yet, Mr. Plaintiff is in pain every minute of every day and will continue to experience that pain for the rest of his life. What do people do when they feel a small pebble in their shoe? They do not walk around like that for a second more than they must. They immediately take all weight off that foot, remove their shoe, and remove the pebble. Mr. Plaintiff cannot do that; he cannot remove the pebble. Every step he takes is the pebble in the shoe.

If the client endured surgical procedures, the plaintiff's attorney should clarify with the expert the risks associated with those procedures. Make sure the jury knows that each time Mr. Plaintiff had this procedure, he ran the risk of death, paralysis, and so on. Yet he was in so much pain that he elected the procedure with those risks rather than living with the pain. How much pain must someone be in that he would willingly run the risk of never waking from a procedure, or being confined to a wheelchair? That is the pain Mr. Plaintiff is in every day.

Whether someone has little pain or a great deal of pain is purely subjective. Attorneys representing plaintiffs must convey to the jury a foundation to establish why the particular plaintiff's complaints of pain are legitimate. Whether the plaintiff has arthritis, a soft-tissue injury, a herniated disc, or some other injury, the jury should hear and see what it is about a particular plaintiff that is causing the pain. This task becomes easier with the use of demonstrative evidence. Demonstrative evidence, properly qualified and authenticated, can be used to assist the jury to understand the damages. Depending on the nature of the injury, demonstrative evidence may be useful in a variety of contexts, including proving the nature or severity of pain and suffering, the ultimate effects of an injury, or the financial consequences to an injured person.

Pain and suffering are two distinct entities and should be treated as such. Pain is typically considered the actual sensation one feels due to an injury. Pain is a "localized sensation of discomfort, distress, or agony."[29] Pain is attendant to posttraumatic arthritis, nerve compression from a herniated disc, or CRPS (complex regional pain syndrome). Suffering, on the other hand, is the manner in which one's life has been affected by pain or an injury. One who is suffering is "subject to disability or handicap."[30] Suffering is not being able to dance at your daughter's wedding because you are in a wheelchair. Suffering is sitting home on prom night because you are self-conscious of a facial scar. Suffering is not being able to play in the yard with your child because of back pain. The proper use of demonstrative evidence can convey an accurate picture of both pain and suffering to the jury. While those words should not be used much by plaintiff's counsel, as they have connotations of what is "wrong" with our system, they are the terms the jury charges may encompass, and should, therefore, be explained.

Demonstrative evidence must be properly authenticated, as indicated above, and should be professionally prepared or created. The requirements for authentication have been codified with the adoption of rules 901 of the Federal, New Jersey and Pennsylvania Rules of Evidence, or other states' rules as applicable. The requirement is not significant, but it is necessary.

Additionally, demonstrative evidence should not distort the evidence or exaggerate a condition. Inaccurate or incomplete demonstrative evidence can successfully be used against the offering party, thereby nullifying its effect. It is important that any demonstrative evidence be prepared in conjunction with the witness or expert who is needed to properly authenticate the evidence during the trial. Properly prepared demonstrative evidence may be critical in assisting the jury to fully understand how a particular incident has affected one's life, depending upon the nature or severity of the injury. The case might involve a patient whose physical injury is not readily apparent. Demonstrative evidence is necessary in conveying the full pain and suffering picture to the jury (i.e., a case involving arthritis, a herniated disc, or other internal injury which is not perceptible to the jury during a trial). There may be a readily apparent physical injury but the actual impact that the injury has had on one's life cannot be fully and accurately conveyed to a jury without demonstrative evidence (i.e., a case involving an amputation). The patient's injuries and their consequences might be readily apparent to a jury. Understanding the difficult jobs jurors have, and that they are required to evaluate a great deal of frequently technical testimony in a short period of time, demonstrative evidence may be vital to ensure the injuries are fully communicated in an appropriate fashion that maintains the jurors' attention.

Keep in mind that a jury is being asked to fully digest the case in what is often a three to five day trial, with conflicting testimony of witnesses whom they have never met, after being provided only a 45 minute primer on the law of the case. This is certainly in marked contrast to the attorney's three years of law school, two to three year evaluation of the case, and position as advocate for the client. So, what may appear obvious to the attorney can often be more easily and accurately conveyed to the jury with professionally prepared and properly authenticated demonstrative evidence.

Consider the following types of evidence to assist in proofs:

- medical records, diaries, and calendars;
- photographs;
- day-in-the-life films; and
- charts and illustrations.

However, be creative and find ways unique to the case to convey the plaintiff's message. Home movies, a collection of prescription pill bottles, tennis trophies, and the like can be effective ways of communicating to the jury the effect post-injury limitations have played on one's life.

F. Motivating the Jury

Generally, juries want to know they are making a difference with their verdict: whether it is sending a signal to a plaintiff they believe filed a case that should not have been filed, or letting the defense know their conduct was negligent and they are going to see to it that the plaintiff is adequately compensated. The jury wants to side with the side that is "just." Let the jury know why your side is the "just" side. Explain how the facts and law squarely support a verdict for the client, and how a finding for the adversary would be because of the adversary's ability to cloud and confuse the issues (assuming that to be the case).

A plaintiff's attorney can let the jury know that a sympathy-driven verdict is not being sought. The jury is being asked to provide a verdict based upon the law and the facts as applied to that law. That verdict needs to compensate the plaintiff for the rest of her life. Explain how that can work.

While asking for compensation may be distasteful to the plaintiff, it is all that is left. The plaintiff cannot be granted the restoration of a limb or life as it formerly existed (whatever the case may be). This is not Biblical times when we would take the defendant out and inflict "an eye for an eye and a tooth for a tooth." This is the American system. It has worked for over 200 years and it is the system that holds Mr. Plaintiff's fate and future. Consider the influence of frequently used terms. Foley and LeFevre[31] suggest that Generation X jurors respond better to the term "human losses" rather than "pain and suffering" or (the rather oblique term) "non-economic damages." They advise the plaintiff's attorney to avoid persuading Generation X jurors to award money to compensate the victim. Instead, describe how the money will make a difference in the patient's life. The components of a life care plan are particularly important in achieving this goal. The plaintiff's attorney will help the jury identify with the plaintiff by describing the plaintiff as a fighter rather than a whiner.

25.15 The Jury Verdict Form

As indicated above, the verdict form should be reviewed with the jury. (Refer to Figure 25.7.) Both sides' attorneys must explain to the jury exactly how it is being requested to complete the form—which boxes must be checked "yes" and which checked "no." Some jurisdictions require the damages in medical malpractice actions to be specifically itemized; some jurisdictions do not. Different people have different philosophies as to whether they prefer the damages itemized or in a lump sum. The rationale for putting them in a lump sum is that it is less susceptible to serious scrutiny. If the jurors intend to award $1 million, but their itemized damages total something different, they need to go back and redeliberate. If they then change an itemized number, as opposed to the total, there will be objections that the jurors are manipulating the outcome. If the number is all one lump sum, it is difficult to attack the number on anything other than it being excessive in general. However, proponents of itemizing the damages believe that if the verdict is reviewed on appeal, the appellate division, using this information, is better able to determine if the jury's conclusion mirrored the evidence presented on damages, and then affirm or perhaps reverse on only an item of damages.

25.16 Jury Instructions
A. Introduction

Typically, both sides will provide their proposed jury instructions to the trial court for review. The adversary's proposed points are usually available at least a day or two before the charging conference. The judge will hold a charging conference to review what law he intends to read. Any objections must be clearly stated on the record or the issue might very well be considered waived at the appellate level. File and submit every point. Do not mischaracterize the law. Even if the attorney gets the point read to the jury, the verdict could, and should, be reversed at the appellate level once the mischaracterization of the law is revealed. The standard of review on a legal issue before the appellate courts is typically *de novo* (basically, their own independent review), while the standard of review on evidentiary issues is abuse of discretion (meaning the appellate court defers to the trial judge). Keep points short and simple. If one of the points is two pages long and single-spaced, the court will not read it. Provide each point on a separate page, double-spaced, with the citation to the standard point or case that supports the point. If the point is from a case, try to make it an exact quote so the court knows the attorney is not merely paraphrasing, and possibly "massaging" the law.

Some courts request that the parties provide agreed-upon points to the extent possible, and then provide the disputed points separately. This reduces the likelihood of error and focuses the court more on the real charges in dispute. Often there is no real dispute on the standard charges regarding burden of proof, preponderance of the evidence, evaluation of witnesses and evidence, proximate cause, injuries, and damages. The instructions concerning the exact liability or malpractice in issue might create more conflict. It is the court's discretion as to whether it will introduce facts into its charge. Some judges explain what evidence supports certain charges; some judges refrain from commenting upon that completely. Because of the impact of the charge, it is extremely important to clearly state objections on the record.

Itemized damages

1. Was the defendant Nurse Johnson negligent? YES_____ NO_____

If "Yes," proceed to question 2.
If "No," cease your deliberations and return your verdict.

2. Was defendant Nurse Johnson's negligence a proximate cause of plaintiff, Mr. Plaintiff's, injuries and resulting losses? YES_____ NO_____

If "Yes," proceed to question 3.
If "No," cease your deliberations and return your verdict.

3. State what amount of money would fairly and adequately compensate plaintiff, Mr. Plaintiff, for his injuries and losses:

ECONOMIC:
    Past Medical Bills $_____
    Future Medical Bills $_____
    Past Lost Wages $_____
    Future Lost Wages $_____
NON-ECONOMIC:
    Past Pain and Suffering and Disability and Impairment $_____
    Future Pain and Suffering and Disability and Impairment $_____

4. Is plaintiff, Mrs. Plaintiff, entitled to recover for the loss of her husband's services? YES_____ NO_____

5. If "yes," total amount of Mrs. Plaintiff's compensatory damages: $_____

Lump sum

1.   Was the defendant Nurse Johnson negligent? YES_____ NO_____

If "Yes," proceed to question 2.
If "No," cease your deliberations and return your verdict.

2. Was defendant Nurse Johnson's negligence a proximate cause of plaintiff, Mr. Plaintiff's, injuries and resulting losses? YES_____ NO_____

If "Yes," proceed to question 3.
If "No," cease your deliberations and return your verdict.

3. State what amount of money would fairly and adequately compensate plaintiffs, Mr. and Mrs. Plaintiff, for his injuries and losses: $_____

Figure 25.7 Jury Verdict Form

B. The Burden of Proof in a Civil Case

Most of the public is familiar with the "beyond a reasonable doubt" burden of proof in criminal actions. Plaintiff's counsel may wish to distinguish that burden from the civil plaintiff's burden of proving his case by "a preponderance of the evidence." Counsel should clarify that a verdict must be rendered against the defendant if the scales tip just slightly in favor of the plaintiff. The jury need only find that the proof offered has left the jury with the notion that the existence of the contested fact is more probable than not. Sometimes introduction of the criminal burden, even to contrast it, might be confusing. Therefore, consider if it is appropriate to contrast the two different burdens, or if it more desirable to simply address this case's burden.

C. Standard of Care: Definition of Malpractice

The instruction defining nursing malpractice should clearly state that in order for the nurse defendant to be found negligent, she must have violated standards of ordinary nursing skill and care expected of nurses. By undertaking professional services to the patient, a nurse represents that she possesses, as a duty, the degree of learning and skill ordinarily possessed by nurses of good standing practicing in the same community under similar circumstances. It is the nurse's further duty to use the care ordinarily exercised in like cases by reputable members of the profession practicing in the same or a similar locality and under similar circumstances. The nurse is to use reasonable diligence and best judgment in the exercise and application of skills and learning in an effort to accomplish the purpose of employment. A defendant nurse must violate one of these duties before being found to have committed malpractice.

Furthermore, an instruction should emphasize that the defendant nurse is only required to possess and exercise the skill and care possessed and exercised by the average nurse in the field. The law does not require perfection, prophetic insight, or infallible judgment of a nurse. It only requires that the nurse possess a reasonable ability to carry out professional work, and that the nurse exercise reasonable care, skill, and judgment in doing this.

The defense attorney will want an instruction dealing with mistake of judgment as distinguished from malpractice. A defendant nurse is usually not liable for a simple mistake in judgment. An instruction for this might be included by the defense:

A mistake in judgment on the part of the nurse is not evidence of negligence. If a nurse possesses reasonable and ordinary skill and uses care ordinarily used in like or similar situations by nurses of reasonable and average skill, practicing in the community at the time in question, he is not guilty of negligence even though his judgment may be subsequently proven incorrect.

Some courts do not allow an "error in judgment" charge. An example of this is found in *Pringle v. Rapaport*, 2009 PA Super 171, P1 (Pa. Super. Ct. 2009)). Pennsylvania, along with many other states find the charge misleading, and adds nothing to the standard of care instruction. So long as the court's instruction is a fair recitation of the law, it need not provide any of the one or two sentence passages often provided by way of case citation. The court need only advise the jury as to the definition of negligence. Plaintiffs should argue against the inclusion of multiple additional charges exculpating the defense. These tend to highlight the reasons for finding for the defense, as opposed to the law of negligence.

In a case of clear negligence, the defense will often focus on "causation." In that regard, the plaintiff's attorney's evidence must also focus on the strong causal connection, the proper instruction on causation, and the burden on causation (i.e., preponderance of the evidence). Naturally, if the evidence also supports a conclusion that the plaintiff's injuries were the result of some cause other than the nurse's conduct, the defense will focus on that evidence. Review all of the evidence with the jury; do not ignore the "adverse" evidence; explain the weaknesses in it.

25.17 Final Thoughts

After having finished the closing, and the judge has charged the jury, it is common to second-guess your efforts. Attorneys often wonder if all of the important points were covered, if one too many or one too few witnesses were called, and whether the case was oversold or undersold. Following the theme for the case and staying on track may not yield a perfect case, but will yield a well-thought out, well-strategized trial. You tried a case that did your client justice. You have conveyed the message you intended to convey, presented the evidence you needed to present and convinced the jury that your client's cause is a just cause. The case is now out of your hands and you can drive yourself crazy with retrying the case in your head. Since you developed your theme before trial and stuck with your theme through trial, rest assured that you have represented your client effectively.

Endnotes

1. *Capoferri v. Children's Hospital of Philadelphia*, 893 A.2d 133 (Pa. Super. 2006).

2. Fed. R. Civ. P. 47.

3. N.J. Court Rules, R. 1:8.

4. Pa.R.C.P. 221. A party need not show prejudice in the event a trial judge limits peremptory challenges to an amount less than four. See *Bednar v. Dana Corp.*, 2008 PA Super 283, 962 A.2d 1232 (Pa. Super. Ct. 2008).

5. De.R.P. 47.

6. N.J. Court Rules, R. 1:8.

7. *Batson v. Kentucky*, 476 U.S. 79, 90 L.Ed. 2nd 69, 106 S.Ct. 1712 (1986).

8. Weaver, D. 1992. "Selecting a Jury," In *A Celebration of Justice: ATLA 1992 Annual Convention Reference Materials*. Washington, DC: ATLA Press.

9. Hamlin, S. 1985. *What Makes Juries Listen*. New York: Harcourt Brace Jovanovich.

10. Wenner, D. and G. Cusimano. 2000. "Combating Juror Bias," *Trial* (June 2000): 35.

11. *Id.*

12. Hanagan, M., "How to inoculate a jury against counter persuasion," Washington, D.C.: ATLA Annual Convention Materials, 1995. Audiocassette.

13. *Current Award Trends in Personal Injury,* 45th edition, Jury Verdict Research, Horsham, Pennsylvania: LRP Publications, 2006.

14. Foley, E. and A. LeFevre, "Understanding Generation X," *Trial* (June 2000): 62.

15. *Id.*

16. Boyll, J., "Winning over the jury: tips from the mouths of jurors," *INLIT* 6, no. 10 (October 1992): 23.

17. See Pennsylvania Rule of Civil Procedure 1.023.

18. Creighton, H., *Law Every Nurse Should Know*, Third edition, 122. Philadelphia: W.B. Saunders, 1975.

19. Fed. R. Evid. 702.

20. Warsaw, J., *Build a Theme for the Jury, Effective Utilization of Expert Witnesses*. Sherman Oaks, California: Medi Legal Institute, 1986.

21. *Smith v. Barker*, 368 Pa. Super. 472, 475 (Pa. Super. Ct. 1987).

22. Fed. R. Evid. 703.

23. *Id.*

24. N.J. R. E. 901.

25. *Id.*

26. Lipson, A., "Know your testimonial objections," *Trial* (July 2005): 70.

27. Mandell, M., "Cross-examining the defendant doctor," *Trial* (May 2006): 28.

28. Givens, B., "Closing argument: consolidating your theme," *Trial* (January 1990).

29. *Dorland's Medical Dictionary,* 28th Edition.

30. *Webster's Ninth New Collegiate Dictionary.*

31. See note 13.

Appendix 25.1
Sample Opening Statement

Counsel: May it please the Court, Mr. Defense Counsel 1, Mr. Defense Counsel 2, Mr. Plaintiff, Your Honor. Ladies and gentlemen of the jury, when you make a product and you sell that product and you make money off of manufacturing and selling that product you have to make sure that that product has every element that can make it safe. We are here today because the Defendants made and sold a product that did not have every element necessary to make it safe. We are here today because that product caused serious injury to Mr. Plaintiff.

I have just painted with a very broad brush what this case is about. I would like to spend a few moments explaining to you the evidence that I will present about the product, about Mr. and Mrs. Plaintiff, and about the liability that should rest with the Defendants.

In order to know about the plaintiffs you're going to have to turn back the clock to Woodbury High School in the early 80s. Mr. Plaintiff graduated from Woodbury High School on June the 14th, 1984. He had known Mrs. Plaintiff at that time. They were what you would call high school sweethearts, childhood sweethearts. A few years after high school they got married.

While attending high school, Mr. Plaintiff worked in the Acme. He was not academically oriented. He was in the Votech (vocational and technical) program and in Votech he took design and drafting courses. When he graduated high school he started to work almost immediately in heavy construction. He was a member of the Laborer's Union Local 172. His father had been a laborer before him. He performed heavy labor. He went out to construction sites where they were usually putting down roads, sewer systems, building foundations. Mr. Plaintiff loved that kind of work. You'll hear that he never missed a day's work—with two exceptions—one was when his wife was giving birth, and then he usually went to the hospital the day the baby was born and then was usually there when Mrs. Plaintiff came home. And the other time he missed work was in the winter, when like many construction workers when work would get slow, he would get laid off. He never missed work otherwise; never took a vacation. In lieu of a vacation he would wait until he was laid off in the winter.

After Mr. and Mrs. Plaintiff were married, they lived in a little house in Williamstown and eventually moved to Elmer, New Jersey, down in the heartland of South Jersey. They have a farm. They don't grow crops, but they have sheep and animals like that they raise with their children. They went on and had five children. Mr. Plaintiff was

healthy. He was active. He was doing what he wanted to do, and he and his family had a good life together.

You'll hear about how Mr. Plaintiff was energetic. When he wanted to build a sandbox for his children, he wasn't happy getting a little five-by-five box from the hardware store. Instead, Mr. Plaintiff built a 40-by-40 sand box; a sand box that required two tractor trailer sized dump trucks to dump sand on his property so his kids could play there.

In addition to working full-time in construction during the day, Mr. Plaintiff did knock down jobs. If a lady in the neighborhood needed a Bilco door, he would put it in and pay for it. If someone needed concrete steps fixed, he would do it. That's the way their life was going.

You'll hear that Mr. Plaintiff was very active in his church, the Living Hope Worship Center in New Jersey. You're going to hear from his pastor. The reason you're going to hear from him is about how things with Mr. and Mrs. Plaintiff were going before and how things have been since Mr. Plaintiff's injury. The last thing they wanted in their life was me, Mr. and Mrs. Plaintiff's counsel.

On April the 29th, 1998, Mr. Plaintiff was working for a company called Plaintiff's Employer Construction Company. He had worked for them for a number of years. He had been working in the City of Wilson in Wilson County on new sewer systems they were putting in. Part of his work was digging down putting sewer pipes into the ground. These were 36 inch sewer pipes. The way they put in the 36 inch sewer pipes—and I believe you're going see these exhibits—is the sewer pipe would be put in and then in order to stop water from rushing out of the sewer pipe, they had to put a plug or some type of device to stop the water. The device that was used by Mr. Plaintiff on the day of the accident was called a Muni-Ball. You're going to hear a lot of testimony about Muni-Balls. I believe Muni stands for municipal ball, meaning they use it on municipal sources.

This was the first time that Mr. Plaintiff had actually worked with this Muni-Ball. The Muni-Ball—and we have it here—is about seven feet by four feet and it looks like a pillow. It gets filled with air and when it's filled with air it blocks the sewer pipe so that water that's in the sewer pipe won't run down into the work that the men are doing further down stream. Mr. Plaintiff is going tell you he worked there on the crew with a fellow named Junior. And when he worked on Junior's crew he was the top man. He stayed up out of the ditch while other men worked down in the ditch. And he would go and fetch equipment; he would turn on the pumps when they wanted them.

When he worked with Junior's crew as the top man he would take the hose, the air hose that would fill up the ball, and he would drop it down into the hole. The way they showed him to use it is they would then fill up the ball down in the hole. Then they would take the air hose from the compressor and take it up out of the hole, and you'll see illustrations about this. When he worked on Junior's crew Mr. Plaintiff was never responsible for filling up the ball himself.

On April the 28th, which was a Tuesday, Mr. Plaintiff's crew had been assigned to work on a section of pipe that Junior and his crew had been working on a couple weeks before. Junior and his crew had taken one of these Muni-Balls and filled it up and put it in a pipe and left it there to keep water from flowing down the line. On Tuesday the 28th, Mr. Plaintiff was made a foreman of a crew. You'll hear how sometimes he was foreman, sometimes he was a laborer. But on this crew, because it involved digging out heavy rock he worked with an operator, a fellow that works the pick, the shovel, to dig out the rock. They asked him to dig out the rock.

On Tuesday Mr. Plaintiff dug out the rock to put in a new section of pipe, and he put in a new section of pipe that was about 13 feet in length. Around that section of pipe they put what's called a trench box, which is a metal case to keep the trench from falling in. The trench box was two layers high; about 20 feet high.

Mr. Plaintiff had gotten to work that day about 6:00 or 6:30 because he had always gone to work early, and when he got there he had set up for the day. He went down in the ground to make sure the pipe was level. He came out of the pipe while the men were taking a coffee break and Mr. Plaintiff had them place the new section of pipe down in the hole. Mr. Plaintiff then went and got the Muni-Ball that was put there by Junior's crew, which is the Defendant's product. You'll see it has ropes attached to it. He crawled down in the 36-inch pipe and he pulled the Muni-Ball from one section of pipe to the next section of pipe. In order to do that, he had to let a little air out of the ball because the ball was filling the inside of the pipe. He pulled it to the new section of pipe. He went to fill it up, and you're going hear a lot of testimony about what he did and how he did it. You'll hear and you'll see there's a 30-foot line with two 30-foot hoses onto the pipe, and he went and picked up the gauge that goes with the pipe, that goes with the pillow, and he saw that the gauge was cloudy. You're going to hear testimony that these gauges that are supplied by the Defendant break all the time. They don't work all the time. Mr. Plaintiff's going to tell you this is the first time he worked with this particular ball. He picked up the gauge, and the gauge wasn't working and he knew that he had a crew that was finishing up their coffee break that would need to start working again. So what Mr. Plaintiff did is what any reasonable workman would do,

he said "I'll try to fill this up even though the gauge isn't working." He looked at the ball and he saw that it was letting water underneath, and he assumed that if it was still letting water underneath it would be okay to put air in. Mr. Plaintiff is going to tell you what he did is he cracked the handle—you'll see the handle—he cracked the handle to let air in and he looked, and even before the water stopped running beneath the ball it exploded.

The explosion let out a tremendous force. The force hit him in the face. It broke the orbit under his eye. You'll hear testimony about how there are metal plates in his face. It shattered his arm, both bones in his arm; you'll see pictures of that. It struck him backwards and caused injury to his knees.

You'll hear from Dr. Orthopaedic, who is a board certified orthopaedic surgeon at the Hospital of University of Wilson, about these injuries. Mr. Plaintiff's employer, of course, brought over a bucket truck. They lifted him out of the hole. They took him down to CC Medical Center where they started repairs. They did some surgery where they put plates in his arm. You'll see illustrations of that.

Eventually he was having trouble seeing and his wife took him to see a doctor who fixed the orbit in his face. The main injury he had, or one of the main injuries he had, is to his frontal lobe. You're going to hear from Dr. Neurologist, he's a board certified neurologist. He will tell you that when Mr. Plaintiff got hit in the face he had an injury to his front lobe. He'll explain, and you may see x-rays or illustrations to show that right behind the cheek where his eye was broken is the front orbit. The lobe behind the orbit is the front lobe, and Mr. Plaintiff, because of his shock, had injury to his front lobe. This frontal lobe injury has caused neuropsychological problems to Mr. Plaintiff. You'll hear from Dr. Neuropsychologist how he was tested and how he was shown to have problems. You'll hear from his wife. She'll talk about the confusion he has, about how he gets lost easily, and how he has to sleep all the time.

You'll hear how Mr. Plaintiff, in August of 1998, tried to go back to work. At the jobsite he was confused and his wife worried about him getting hurt by a piece of equipment. You'll hear expert testimony about how he can't go back to this type of work. You'll hear from his pastor about how he works part-time at the church. You'll hear him tell how instead of now being a construction worker he's a custodian of the church a couple days of week where he cleans the lady's and men's rooms, sets up for services, and so on. You'll hear him talk about how his life has changed with his wife and his children.

All of that happened because the product sold by their client was defective. It didn't have every element to make it safe. We're going to show you what it lacked. A product like this should have what's known as a relief valve. A relief valve is a very simple device used on any type of product that has pressure. If it gets too much pressure the valve opens it and lets the pressure out and the product keeps from blowing up. You'll see or hear testimony that these relief valves have been around for decades. They're on most every device that has any kind of pressure, hot water heaters for example. You'll hear testimony about how if it gets too hot, even the ones on your hot water heater down in your basement will open up and let the hot water out and not explode. That's the first defect, that it didn't have a relief valve.

The second example our expert will show as an alternative to a relief valve is that it could have had some type of patch. You're going to hear that's the second way this product was defective. It didn't have any type of patch or relief valve; they sort of overlap. The third thing that it should have had, and you'll see illustrations about this, is what we'll call an internal tether. Inside it should have had a nylon strap or rope, so if it did get over pressurized and explode, the pressure wouldn't be released all the once and the pieces wouldn't go flying and hit somebody.

The fourth problem that you're going to hear about is the Defendant's safety information, or lack thereof. I want you to pay attention to it because I'm going ask the Defendants it. You're going to hear that the Defendants do not have any safety information about the development of this product except for one thing that states they did a couple of tests where they took five of these balls and they blew them up. They filled them full of pressure until they popped. And that's how they set their safety standard. They figured the amount of pressure when they broke—and you're going to hear they all broke around 27, 28, 31 pounds of pressure—so they decided "we'll tell people to put in half of that pressure."

We have tried to get records from the Defendant. I will challenge them to bring an engineer in or to bring anyone from the product development part of their company in here to take the stand, put his hand on the Bible and show us one document that shows that they did anything about safety other than these few burst tests. They are negligent. You're going to hear that the concept of a relief valve is not crazy. You're going to see that the Defendants themselves have two patents for relief valves. One of those patent applications says it is to be used with pneumatic tubes, pneu-

matic balls such as this. So we're going to show you that our idea of a relief valve is not only feasible but the Defendants themselves were thinking about it before this, although for some reason they didn't put it on the ball. And they will not bring in an engineer from the company to address you and tell you why they didn't. And they don't have any records to show they are tested to do what they did with the relief valves.

The other thing we'll show is that the warnings on this bag and the instruction manual is not even the correct instruction manual. If you try to look at the instruction manual to find this ball in the manual, it's not even listed in there. This is an instruction manual that was printed in 1992 before this device was even made or invented. And you'll see in our claim that they are defective and negligent for failing to provide the right instruction.

These are the things I am going to establish and prove. I want you to keep your eye on the ball. Certainly there's going to be a lot of evidence saying that Mr. Plaintiff should have known better, that he shouldn't have been filling the ball up. You're going to hear him explain that the way they always did it at that job was down in the hole. And I'm going to show you literature from the Defendants where they show men filling up the balls down in the hole. And Mr. Plaintiff is going to say, "yeah, the gauge was cloudy and I knew that if I said let's stop the job, let's go look for a new gauge, maybe there's one in the shop, maybe there isn't," that isn't what they want to hear on construction sites. "And if I did that all the time the next time there was a layoff I would be the guy who wouldn't be called back."

This accident should not have happened. It happened because in Minnesota in 1986, 1987, 1988, 1989, 1990 they didn't spend one nickel on looking into making this product safe. Other than these, you'll hear about what I'll call flimsy burst tests. It happened because they didn't give adequate instructions and because they didn't contain every safety element. And the Judge will instruct you at the end of the case what the law is on that.

I hope that we can move along. I didn't think we were going to eat up this morning. I will get an opportunity to stand up and talk to you in a few days, possibly as early as Friday, maybe early next week. I will try to move the case along. And when I stand up here and I've proved the case, I'm going to ask you at that time to enter a verdict for my client, my clients Mr. and Mrs. Plaintiff.

Thank you.

Appendix 25.2
Sample Opening Statement

Mr. Plaintiff's counsel: Thank you, your honor—may it please the court, your honor, Nurse T, Nurse N, Nurse P, Nurse C, Mrs. Plaintiff, William, Donald, David, and Constance, ladies and gentlemen of the jury:

This is a case about a man who went to the hospital on a weekend, whose care was neglected.

This is about a man who, for 18 hours and 33 minutes, was a patient at Community Hospital—and during those 18 hours and 33 minutes, this man was ignored by the nurses and by the doctors. Standard medical tests were not done; standard medical consults were not done; and standard medical care was not rendered. As a result of that, this man died. He was 39 years old. He was a brother; he was a son; he was a father.

This case is going to be presented in three parts: one part is going to be about who he was prior to his admission to Community Hospital; one part is going to be about the effect that this loss has had on his son, his mother, and his family; and the other part, which will probably be longest in time for presentation of evidence, is about those 18 hours and 33 minutes that he was at Community Hospital.

I have just painted, with a very broad brush, what this case is about. I will try to get into some of the specifics of what I will prove on behalf of the plaintiffs and Constance.

David Plaintiff grew up in West Hudson, went to Lincoln High School and all through high school he worked. Like his brothers, he worked in supermarkets. He graduated from high school and he got a job as a butcher. You will see a picture of him with his brothers. And this picture will be relevant not only to show what kind of person that he was and the relationship he had with his family, but to show his size. He was a big fellow. His nickname was "Iron Hand." He had his own set of butcher knives. He and his brother were twins. His brother taught him how to be a butcher; he got in the union for butchers and became a union butcher.

He liked to do two things. He liked to work, and he liked to take care of his family. You will hear how he met Constance and they were engaged to be married. Constance delivered their son David and, for whatever reason, like many people they didn't stay together, and they were not married. But you will hear how David stayed active in his son's life, how he supported his son and how he supported his mother and took care of his family. That will be one part, ladies and gentlemen.

Let me now talk about the 18 hours and 33 minutes, which is the crux of this case. On the night of January 3rd, 1997, David, who lived with his mother, started to feel ill. It was unusual for him to be ill or sick. He spent New Year's Eve with his mother at the house. His mother asked David to come from his room to her room, and he told her "Mom, I am not feeling well." And his mother will tell you—this may be in dispute—he said he had pain somewhere over here (indicating) right below his breast. And this was unusual for David. You will see a picture of him, he's a man, a strong man and for him to be crying about any kind of pain and to be in pain, was unusual, he told his mother that he was really in a lot of pain. He and his mother finally realized he was not getting better and they called 911 and Medic 3 took him to Community Hospital. The medical records will show that he was seen by the triage nurse at five minutes after 2:00 A.M. That begins the 18 hours and 33 minutes.

When he was in the ER—and he remained in the ER until about 6:00 A.M.—a standard chest x-ray was not done. When he was in the ER, neither a CAT scan of his stomach nor his chest was ever done. Neither was a consult by a specialist—either a surgeon or gastroenterologist (that's a GI specialist)—called. They did not do a CBC, a complete blood count, even though he had complaints of pain and, again, the medical records said they were epigastric, which means they were right here (indicating). Everybody will agree that this is not too far from the heart. An EKG was never done. David was ignored most of the time he was in the ER He was not attended to.

At around 6:00 in the morning a call was made to a doctor. The doctor was an attending doctor with privileges at Community Hospital. This doctor, Dr. T, agreed that this patient would be admitted under his service.

Stacked up in that corner (indicating) are most of, or a lot of the medical records. I will be showing them to you over the next couple of days. Today I will call Dr. T as a witness. When David was admitted, the intern or the resident who admitted him (you will see records) says—"admit to general medicine floor," he was to have a GI consult.

It is now 8:00 A.M. David is alone. He is not being seen by a nurse or a doctor. No diagnosis has yet been made.

Even though he had been admitted to the hospital with pain in his epigastric area, they still had not taken a simple x-ray of him. He was admitted to the floor and the records will show that no nurse saw David for quite some time. And no doctor saw him up on the floor until Dr. T came in to see him around 11:00 A.M. Dr. T said he saw him for about 20 minutes or a half an hour, ladies and gentlemen.

A resident did take a history when they admitted David. That history is important because one of the things in the history and in the records is that David had hypertension. You will hear how David had a little bit of a speech impediment, how he stuttered, but even with the stutter David told the doctors that he had hypertension. It's in the records that he told the doctors that his family had a history of hypertension. Even with the doctors knowing that, a cardiologist was never called in to see him; an EKG was never done; and a simple x-ray was never taken at that time.

One blood sample was taken and it showed he had increased amylase, and increased lipase. Those two things—and I am sure you will hear the defendants talk about this—do indicate someone could have pancreatitis, which is an inflammation of the pancreas. And you will hear about the pancreas and how it makes enzymes for the digestion of food. But you are also going to hear that increased lipase or an increased amylase can be an indication of some other problem. You are also going to hear, from our experts—a doctor from Harvard, a doctor from Columbia, and other doctors, too—that it was very unlikely that it was pancreatitis. Most pancreatitis cases involve people who have a history of alcoholism or have an acute alcohol poisoning—that's a fraternity brother who drinks down a quart of vodka all at once, and that will inflame the pancreas. The ducts to the pancreas could be blocked by gallstones.

David did not have any of those conditions. You will hear about the medical texts. You will see Harrison's on Medicine. Harrison's on Medicine says if you are diagnosing pancreatitis and you are not sure, you have to look for what is called a differential diagnosis—what else could be the problem? I have an enlargement of a page from Harrison's and one of the things you have to be aware of is whether or not the patient may be having what's known as a dissecting aorta. Now, in a medical malpractice case you have to look at it as if you are taking a little lesson at medical school. You are going to hear—aside from information about the pancreas—about the aorta. The aorta is one of the main blood vessels in the body, it goes from the heart, it loops up and it goes all the way down, almost to your iliac crest, which is your hip, and different branches come off it (indicating). What a dissecting aorta is is this: your aorta is like a hose—for want of a better way to put it—that has different layers. Actually it has three layers, but we are only concerned with two. What happens in a dissection is this bottom layer, the one where the blood is going through—if I can use my hose analogy—breaks. And now instead of going through the hose, the blood is going between the two linings and it slowly, slowly, slowly pushes the linings apart. That's what David had going on in his body during those 18 hours and 33 minutes on January 4, 1997.

Who is Nurse N? One of the things that you will see clearly from the records is that the nurses should be monitoring David and if there is something happening or you do not know what you are doing, you call a doctor. You will

hear and you will see from the records that the nurses should have called a doctor. They did not.

Dr. A, who now teaches at University of Hudson, was supposed to be called if there was any issue whatsoever. The nurses claim they did call him at some point. You will hear from Dr. A. He was never contacted. Dr. A testified in his deposition that he never saw this patient; and he never heard of this patient until a lawsuit was filed. You are going to hear that this now switches from being a straight medical malpractice to a little bit of a mystery, trying to figure out what actually went on and whose story is right. Instead of Dr. A coming in—you will see the form which requests Dr. Junior Resident, who will testify, if he testifies consistent with deposition—he was not even sure, what specialty he wanted to go in to, and since this incident I think he is now in dermatology; and, a junior resident are all who saw David. You will see the records about what that junior resident saw.

Then we get to about noon. David has been at Community Hospital for about ten hours. He is still being ignored. There is still no diagnosis. They have not done an x-ray; they have not done a CAT scan.

Finally, another doctor arrived around noon. He immediately indicated that David should be brought to radiology for an x-ray. He wrote "stat." What "stat" means is right away—we need it now; it is important. The nurses brought David to radiology at 1:53 P.M. Here is a picture of the x-ray (indicating); you will hear testimony about it. Essentially, what this x-ray shows, and you will hear doctors explain it to you, that this part over here (indicating)—this knob sticking up means it is an aorta that is swollen, it is an aorta that has a problem.

Even though the x-ray was supposed to be read stat, there is no record in the hospital that this x-ray was ever read, until the following morning; at that time, David was already dead.

After the x-ray at 1:53 P.M., David is taken to a room. For the remainder of that afternoon, no nurse checks on David and no doctor comes to see him.

Now, around five o'clock that night, 5:40, David began to have even more pain. You will hear how his brother, William, came in to see him, to visit him and he says: "Brother, I'm hurting." And David asked for more pain medication around 5:40 P.M., and even though he asked for more pain medication, no doctor came to see him.

William saw David fall asleep, kissed him on the forehead and said, "I will be by to see you tomorrow." Around eight o'clock David had more pain. No doctor came to see him.

Over the phone, a doctor told a nurse—"give him more Demerol." You will hear and see from the records that the nurse finally got the okay to give him more Demerol for pain, but when the nurse went into the room, David's heart had stopped beating. She called a code 9.

You will see the records from the code 9, that around 8:22 P.M. the hospital staff arrived, and at that time they tried to resuscitate him, and they pronounced David dead at 8:38 P.M.

The family was notified maybe 15 or 20 minutes later. An autopsy was eventually done on David, and they found that he died from a condition known as a cardiac tamponade. What that means is that when this dissecting aorta broke, the cavity around his chest filled with blood, and eventually that blood just stopped, squeezed his heart until his heart stopped beating.

On January 4, 1997, David died 39 years young; he died in pain; he died alone. Ladies and gentlemen—that's why we are here.

In a couple days, I am going to get an opportunity to stand up and talk to you again and I'm going to ask you to award a verdict to his son and his mother and his family for their loss. And I will prove to you over the next couple of days that that loss didn't have to occur and that the nurses and doctors at Community Hospital are responsible for that loss.

Thank you.

About the Editors

Patricia W. Iyer, MSN, RN, LNCC is one of the editors of this text and wrote or coauthored 12 chapters: *Roots of Patient Injury, Where Have all the Nurses Gone? Medical Errors: Roots of Litigation, Foundations of Nursing Practice, Pain and Suffering, Nursing Documentation, Patient Safety Initiatives, Subacute and Long-term Care Nursing Malpractice, Demonstrative Evidence, Working with Legal Nurse Consultants, Working with Nursing Expert Witnesses,* and *Medication Error*s. Ms. Iyer's experience as an author and editor began in 1980. She has written, coauthored, or edited over 125 articles, chapters, textbooks, case studies, and online courses. Prior to this text, her most recent editorial involvement was serving as the co-editor, with Barbara Levin, of *Medical Legal Aspects of Medical Records.* She is the chief editor of *Principles and Practices of Legal Nurse Consulting, Second Edition* (2003) the core curriculum of legal nurse consulting and *Business Principles for Legal Nurse Consultants* (2005). Most recently, she completed an online course for Sigma Theta Tau directed to legal issues for the new nurse.

Ms. Iyer is a frequent lecturer to attorneys, paralegals, nurses, and legal nurse consultants. She has appeared several times on Law Journal TV and on American Airlines inflight entertainment radio programming as part of a program on the nursing shortage. After entering the field of legal nurse consulting as a medical surgical expert witness in 1987, in 1989, she established Med League Support Services, Inc., an independent legal nurse consulting firm. Ms. Iyer has served on the national board of the American Association of Legal Nurse Consultants in the role of secretary, director at large, president elect, president, and past president. She served two years as the chair of the AALNC Education Committee, during which time she was the chief editor of the AALNC online legal nurse consulting course. AALNC awarded Ms. Iyer with the Lifetime Achievement Award in 2005 and the Volunteer of the Year Award in 2006. Certified by the American Association of Legal Nurse Consulting as a Legal Nurse Consultant Certified (LNCC), Ms. Iyer began her nursing career by earning a diploma in nursing from Muhlenberg Hospital School of Nursing in Plainfield, New Jersey. She earned her bachelor of science degree in nursing and a master of science degree in nursing from the University of Pennsylvania in Philadelphia. She can be reached at Med League Support Services, Inc., Flemington, New Jersey, or through patmedleague@gmail.com or www.medleague.com or www.patiyer.com.

Barbara J. Levin, BSN, RN, ONC, LNCC co-authored and updated the *Orthopaedic Malpractice* chapter and co-authored a new chapter: *Falls and Their Consequences.* Ms. Levin was a co-editor of *Medical Legal Aspects of Medical Records, Second Edition* (2010) and co-authored the chapter *Orthopaedic Records.* In addition, she was an associate editor of *Principles and Practices of Legal Nurse Consulting, Second Edition.* Ms. Levin is a certified orthopaedic nurse and has received recognition as a Clinical Scholar at Massachusetts General Hospital where she works in the orthopedic trauma unit. Her dedication to orthopaedics has inspired her to co-author the chapter *Orthopaedic Complications* for the National Association of Orthopaedic Nurses Core Curriculum.

Ms. Levin is an accomplished NAON instructor who teaches review classes to nurses in preparation for the ONC (orthopaedic nurses' certification) exam. She earned the distinction of Legal Nurse Consultant Certified and served as president of the American Association of Legal Nurse Consultants (2004-2005). She participated with the American Nurses Association to define and publish *Legal Nurse Consulting: Scope and Standards of Practice.* During Ms. Levin's term on the AALNC Board of Directors, she assisted in the development of the position statement *The Specialty Practice of Legal Nurse Consulting.* She also received the prestigious 2006 Partners in Excellence award for exemplary performance in "Outstanding Community Contributions." In 2007, Ms. Levin received the AALNC Member of the Year award. Ms. Levin draws on a wealth of nursing experience in a myriad of clinical settings. She has published and lectured to nurses nationwide about patient safety, orthopaedics, and documentation practices. Assisting facilities in redesigning key policies and procedures, Ms. Levin has improved patient safety and reporting of such incidents. Ms. Levin serves as a valued member of the Massachusetts Tribunal, working together with a judge and an attorney to determine the direction of medical malpractice claims. In her role as a legal nurse consultant, she educates at court mediations and has been an appreciated asset during these appearances. Ms. Levin and Ms. Iyer have collaborated on many projects which include teaching two programs to the International Council of Nurses, 2007 conference, in Yokohama, Japan. Additionally they have given presentations to nurses, physicians, medical students, nursing students and attorneys nationally. Ms. Levin earned her bachelor of science degree in nursing from Boston University. She can be reached at bjllnc@aol.com.

Kathleen C. Ashton, PhD, APRN, BC is a Professor of Nursing in the Jefferson School of Nursing at Thomas Jefferson University in Philadelphia, Pennsylvania, and a Professor Emerita at Rutgers University in Camden, New Jersey, where she taught for 16 years. She has conducted numerous funded research studies on women and heart disease and has published her work in leading medical and nursing journals. She coauthored the *Critical Care Nursing Liability Issues* chapter.

She obtained her basic nursing education at Mercer Medical Center in Trenton, New Jersey, her BSN from Coe College in Iowa, her MS in nursing from the University of Maryland, and her Ph.D. from Temple University in Philadelphia. As a legal nurse consultant for over 15 years, she reviews cases for plaintiff and defense firms and serves as an expert witness at depositions and trials. She also serves on various boards for community and professional organizations and volunteers for medical missions to Lima, Peru where she practices as an Advanced Practice Nurse. She has received numerous awards for research, service and teaching, including the New Jersey Governor's Merit Award for

Advanced Practice Nursing. Dr. Ashton may be reached at ashton834@comcast.net.

Victoria Powell, RN, CCM, LNCC, CNLCP, CLCP, MSCC, CEAS is an editor of this text and co-author of the *Life Care Planning* chapter. Ms. Powell is the author of *Business Plan* and *Marketing* chapters for the core curriculum of nurse life care planning. She sits on the editorial board for the American Association of Nurse Life Care Planners and has written several articles on amputation for the publication. Ms. Powell is also an avid blogger. She is the owner and current president of VP Medical Consulting, a professional nurse consulting firm in central Arkansas. She provides case management services to the catastrophically injured and life care plans for both clinical use and litigation with a special interest in amputation. She holds certifications in case management, nurse life care planning, Medicare Set Aside, legal nurse consulting and ergonomic assessment. She has a worldwide client base.

Ms. Powell is a nationally recognized speaker, having made numerous presentations on a variety of business and health-related topics to healthcare providers, attorneys, public and civic groups. She currently serves as the state's chapter president for the AALNC and is the marketing chair for the AANLCP as well as a conference committee member. She is a current member of the American Association of Legal Nurse Consultants, American Association of Nurse Life Care Planners, National Association of Medicare Set-Aside Professionals, National Nurses in Business, Case Management Society of America, Academy of Certified Case Managers, and the Amputee Coalition of America. Ms. Powell is also one of the adjunct faculty for University of Florida's Forensic Science for Nurses. Ms. Powell began her nursing career in 1994 after having graduated from Baptist School of Nursing in Little Rock, Arkansas. She can be reached at VP Medical Consulting in Benton, Arkansas or by e-mailing victoria@vp-medical.com. For more information on Ms. Powell, visit www.vp-medical.com.

About the Contributors

Tonia D. Aiken, JD, BSN, RN, is President and co-owner of Nurse Attorney Institute, LLC, along with Diane T. Warlick, RN, JD. Their company provides education and consultation services to healthcare providers.

They have created a Legal Nurse Consulting Program with Louisiana State University Health Sciences Center School of Nursing and have provided legal and ethical seminars and educational materials for over 23 years. Ms. Aiken has extensive experience in medical malpractice litigation and healthcare issues. She is a past president of The American Association of Nurse Attorneys (TAANA) and the Foundation. Ms. Aiken is a nationally recognized author, speaker, educator, facilitator, mediator, adjunct professor, and consultant. She serves on the Board of Directors for the National League for Nursing Foundation. She is president of the New Orleans District Nurses Association and on the Board of Directors for the Louisiana State Nurses Association. Ms. Aiken is also the editor and a contributing author of *Legal, Ethical, and Political Issues in Nursing, Second Edition* and *Legal and Ethical Issues in Health Occupations*, which are textbooks and resources for health professionals. She is a contributor to Nursing Ethics and the Law, a video from the National League for Nursing. She served as a medical-legal consultant to Mosby Publishing Company for a videotape series on legal and ethical issues in nursing. She is a contributor to Taber's Cyclopedic Medical Dictionary. Ms. Aiken is also a presenter in two national videotapes for patients and nurses entitled: 1) *Advance Directives: What You Need to Know*, and 2) *Advance Directives: What the Healthcare Provider Needs to Know*, produced by Long Term Care Network. Honors received by Ms. Aiken include Who's Who in American Nursing, Who's Who in Practicing Attorneys, Who's Who in American Woman, Who's Who in the South and Southwest and Who's Who Worldwide.

Stephen Appelbaum, CEP, EPIC is a graduate of Rochester Institute of Technology with a degree in photographic illustration. He began his legal career doing fire photography for insurance companies and expanded to include all forms of forensic work including liability claims assignments and work for plaintiff's attorneys as well. In 1988, he started The Evidence Store, which is a walk-in retail store in Union, New Jersey, for trial attorneys. When Mr. Appelbaum moved into his new facility in 1998, he added a full size courtroom for the purpose of conducting mock trials and for teaching demonstrative evidence techniques. The Evidence Store provides all forms of legal photography, video and litigation graph-

ics. Mr. Appelbaum has lectured nationally to photography organizations, local and state bar associations, and numerous Inns of Court, and has been featured on national and local radio and television programs. He is a former editor of the *Journal of Evidence Photography* and is a member of the Board of Directors of the Evidence Photographers International Council. He is also a member of the American Society of Trial Consultants and the Professional Photographers of America. Mr. Appelbaum is a recent recipient of the R.C. Hakanson Award from the Evidence Photographers International Council, presented for service to the organization and accomplishment in the field of evidence photography. Currently Mr. Appelbaum specializes in night visibility photography and video for the reconstruction of accidents as well as the adjudication of criminal cases involving low light conditions.

Peter I. Bergé, JD, RPA contributed a chapter to *Medical Legal Aspects of Medical Records, Second Edition* (2010): "Attorney Use of Medical Records in a Medical Malpractice Case," and has authored articles, abstracts and a textbook chapter in the medical literature. He has been an attorney with the litigation law firm of Bendit Weinstock since 2004. His concentration is medical malpractice. He is a member of the New Jersey State Bar Association, the Essex County Bar Association, the New Jersey Association for Justice, the American College of Legal Medicine and the American Academy of Physician Assistants in Legal Medicine. Mr. Bergé is a licensed physician assistant (PA) in New York State, and has over 30 years of experience in health care. Prior to attending law school Mr. Bergé was a member of the full-time faculty of the St. Vincent Medical Centers—St. John's University Physician Assistant Education Program. He continues to lecture on medicine, law and medicolegal topics at the Pace University-Lenox Hill Hospital Physician Assistant Studies Program, and to local and national groups. He received a BS from Hahnemann Medical College and Hospital, an MPA from Baruch College, City University of New York and a JD from Seton Hall University School of Law. He is proficient in Spanish.

Robert B. Buckalew, Esq. is a sole practitioner where he has practiced in the area of personal injury since 1979. He has dealt with such issues as automobile accidents, products liability, the Jones Act, industrial accidents, nursing home cases and workers' compensation. Mr. Buckalew earned his undergraduate degree from Hendrix College and his law degree from the University of Arkansas at Little Rock School of Law. He is licensed to practice in

Arkansas and Missouri as well as Federal Courts and United States Supreme Court.

Stephanie B. Camarda, Esq. is an associate and member of Stark & Stark's Employment Litigation Group. Ms. Camarda concentrates her practice in corporate litigation matters, with an emphasis on employment trial litigation, arbitration, mediation and employment counseling.

Helen Griff Chalier (formerly Weisgal), Esq., of Mahwah, New Jersey, is a member of both the New Jersey and New York bars where she practices tort litigation. Currently she is working at Lesniak, LLP in Parsippany, New Jersey, where she divides her litigation time between medical malpractice and mass tort/asbestos defense. Following her association with Sokol, Behot & Fiorenzo in Hackensack, New Jersey, she became Senior Associate with the law firm of Winne, Banta, Hetherington, Basralian & Kahn, P.C., in Hackensack, New Jersey. She earned a BS degree and Physical Therapy certificate from New York University. After several years practicing as a physical therapist, she became Editor-in-Chief of Surgical Communications, Inc., which produced medical educational materials in video and print media. Ms. Chalier earned her JD degree, with a Health Law concentration, from Seton Hall University School of Law in 1998. She became of member of the New Jersey bar in December 1998 and the New York Bar in January 1999. She continues preparing cases for trial and on occasion had the opportunity to take a verdict.

Barbara Cohen, RN, M.S., M.Ed., JD, is currently a professor at Berkeley College in New York City and is pursuing a doctorate of nursing science at The Graduate Center. She has been admitted to practice law in New York and New Jersey since 1983. Ms. Cohen's legal experience includes over 20 years in the fields of medical malpractice, claims and litigation services and professional licensure issues. She was a team supervisor for a claims and litigation service corporation for a number of years and, in that capacity, had ongoing experience in working with defense counsel to the successful resolution of cases across the full range of verdict values.

David Cohen, Esq. is a shareholder in the Personal Injury Group of Stark and Stark, Princeton, New Jersey. He concentrates his practice in nursing home negligence and abuse claims, elder abuse and assisted living facility litigation. He is certified by the Supreme Court of New Jersey as a Certified Civil Trial Attorney. Mr. Cohen is a past Chair of the American Association for Justice's Nursing Home Litigation Group and a frequent lecturer and writer throughout the country on litigating nursing home abuse cases. He is a former member of the Minority Concerns Committee of Mercer County Vicinage. Mr. Cohen has served as faculty for the New Jersey Institute for Continuing Legal Education (ICLE) on Nursing Home Malpractice in New Jersey every year from 2001 through 2010. Mr. Cohen has also lectured extensively on attorney review of medical records for NBI, American Association for Justice, New Jersey Association for Justice and the Institute for Continuing Legal Education. He has guest lectured at Rutgers University, The College of New Jersey,

Rider University and has served as advisor for the Hunter Advanced Moot Court Team. Mr. Cohen has authored numerous faculty papers for national and local seminars, and was co-host and moderator of the weekly radio/television show "In the Public Interest" for 13 years. In 2007, 2008, 2009, and 2010, Mr. Cohen was named as a New Jersey Super Lawyer by New Jersey Monthly Magazine.

Deborah D. D'Andrea, BSN, BA, RN received her BSN from Lewis University in Illinois and is the founder and president of D'Andrea Consulting, Ltd., in Chicago. Ms. D'Andrea has been providing litigation support to attorneys who have cases focusing on healthcare issues, since 1986. She has been employed as an in-house legal nurse consultant for one of Chicago's leading plaintiff's attorneys and has testified as an expert witness. Ms. D'Andrea has lectured on nursing standards of care and on various nursing liability issues. Her honors include Who's Who in American Nursing. She is the past president of the Greater Chicago Chapter of the American Association of Legal Nurse Consultants and is a member of the Association of Trial Lawyers of America and the American College of Legal Medicine. Ms. D'Andrea also coauthored a chapter in *Nursing Home Litigation: Investigation & Case Preparation* edited by Patricia Iyer, and published by Lawyers & Judges Publishing Company. She is a contributing author of *Business Principles for Legal Nurse Consultants* edited by Patricia Iyer, and published by Taylor & Francis Publishing Company.

Samuel L. Davis, Esq. is the founding partner of Davis, Saperstein & Salomon, P.C., a firm with offices in Teaneck and Edison, New Jersey and Manhattan. He graduated from Tufts University in 1973 and Rutgers School of Law in 1977. Mr. Davis is a sustaining member of ATLA and concentrates his practice in the areas of personal injury, medical and nursing malpractice, medical and pharmaceutical product liability, and class actions. Mr. Davis has written and lectured extensively about trial techniques and the evolving use of videoconferencing in the trial of significant cases. His article "A Practical Guide to Videoconferencing" appeared in the March 2000 issue of *Trial Magazine*. In 1998, he was the first attorney in the United States to utilize videoconferencing and the Internet to present evidence in a civil action. In this medical negligence case, the plaintiff, a ventilator-depedent quadriplegic testified in a New Jersey courtroom from his bed in Chicago. Mr. Davis lectures to medical and legal professionals regarding liability. He runs the nonprofit Burn Advocates Network, dedicated to assisting burn victims.

Alisa Mintzer Dayanim, RN, BSN, MSN, CRRN received a bachelor of science degree in nursing (BSN) from the University of Maryland in 1985 and a master of science degree in nursing (MSN) from Thomas Jefferson University in Philadelphia in 1997. She has achieved certification in Rehabilitation Nursing (CRRN) and Life Care Planning (CLCP). Ms. Dayanim has 25 years of rehabilitation nursing experience and has taken numerous continuing education courses. She is a member of the Association of Rehabilitation Nurses, the American Association of Nurse Life Care Planners, and the International Academy of Life Care Planners. Ms. Dayanim has been preparing life care plans since 2006.

Sean J. Doolan, Esq. graduated from Law School in 1994. He started his legal career as an Assistant District Attorney in Bronx County prosecuting white-collar crimes, and as the DWI Prosecutor in Greene County, NY. He currently resides in Greene County, New York, with his wife and son. Mr. Doolan has recently been honored to coauthor (along with Monica Kenny, Esq.) a chapter on litigation strategies in two books, both published by Lawyers & Judges Publishing Company: *Nursing Home Litigation: Investigation and Case Preparation, Second Edition*, and *Nursing Malpractice, Fourth Edition*. Mr. Doolan is also a guest lecturer at numerous Nursing Home/Assisted Living Litigation and Negligence seminars. Some of the organizations that he lectures for include: American Association of Legal Nurse Consultants (AALNC), Lorman Education Services, Professional Education Systems Institute, LLC (PESI), Greene County Department of Aging, New York Bar Association, Rockland County Bar Association, and the Albany County Bar Association. Mr. Doolan is a member of the Greene County, Albany County, Rockland County, and New York State Bar Associations, the New York State Trial Lawyers Association, and the American Association for Justice. He is also a member of the Nursing Home Group of the American Association for Justice.

Susan Egger, MSN, RN is a full-time faculty member at Thomas Jefferson University School of Nursing in Philadelphia, Pennsylvania. Ms. Egger received a bachelor of science degree in nursing from Neumann University, Aston, Pennsylvania, a master of science degree in nursing specializing in Adult Health and Nursing Education from Widener University, Chester, Pennsylvania, and is currently a PhD candidate at Widener University. Her clinical career has included adult health and critical care nursing. She has functioned as an Administrative Nursing Supervisor and Staff Development Educator in adult health and critical care. In addition to her role as faculty for prelicensure students, Ms. Egger is a member of Jefferson's Interprofessional Education faculty team, advisor for the Jefferson chapter of the Student Nursing Association of Pennsylvania and currently the Vice President of the Congress on Policy and Procedure for the New Jersey State Nurses Association, Region 5.

Raymond Fleming, Esq. has degrees from Seton Hall University and Rutgers Law School. He is admitted to practice before the New Jersey Courts and the United States District Court for the District of New Jersey, the Third Circuit Court of Appeals, and the Supreme Court of the United States. He is a member of the American Bar Association, the New Jersey State Bar Association and the Essex County Bar Association. He has served on the Essex County Ethics committee. Mr. Fleming has represented hospitals and medical professionals for more than 25 years, and has presented numerous educational programs for hospital staffs on medical legal issues, including mock trials. He has also lectured on medical malpractice at the Institute for Continuing Legal Education. He is regularly involved in the trial of serious and complex matters on behalf of defendants in medical malpractice cases. He has tried more than 100 jury trials to a conclusion. Mr. Fleming has argued several cases before the State Supreme Court and numerous cases in the Appel-

late Division. He was elected by his peers as a New Jersey "Super Lawyer" in 2006 and 2007.

Kenneth F. Fulginiti, Esq. is a partner in the Philadelphia firm of Duffy + Partners, where he practices in the area of catastrophic injury litigation, with specific focus on product defect, industrial and work-related accidents, premises liability, motor vehicle and trucking accidents, as well as professional negligence. He received a BS from the University of Delaware and his JD from Villanova University School of Law. Mr. Fulginiti is a graduate of the Temple University Academy of Trial Advocacy and is a member of the Million Dollar Advocates Forum. Mr. Fulginiti has been designated a Pennsylvania Super Lawyer, a title bestowed upon the top 5 percent of attorneys in the Commonwealth, as determined by his peers. He is a member of the American and Pennsylvania Associations for Justice. Mr. Fulginiti is "AV" rated by Martindale Hubbell, the highest rating awarded by Martindale Hubbell. He is a frequent lecturer on topics within his fields of practice.

G. Ann Geyer, Esq. is licensed to practice law in California where she splits her time as managing director of Tunitas Group, a health IT consulting firm, and as a private practice attorney at CRMLaw where she specializes in healthcare compliance and risk management issues. She is a member of the E-Discovery and Digital Evidence Committee of the American Bar Association, the California Privacy and Security Advisory Board, and the American Society of Health Risk Management. She borrows heavily from governance principles to advocate stronger alignment between risk, IT, and legal departments. Ms. Geyer received a BA in literature from McGill University, BA in psychology and a MA in statistics from the University of California Berkeley, an MBA from Claremont Graduate School, and a JD from Concord Law School.

Peter A. Greene, Esq. is a graduate of Rutgers Law School. Mr. Greene is a partner in Sachs Maitlin Fleming & Greene in West Orange, New Jersey where his areas of expertise include professional malpractice defense of nurses and doctors. As a certified civil trial attorney, Mr. Greene has tried over 160 jury cases. He has been counsel to the State Board of Medical Examiners.

Douglas S. Grossbart, MD, JD is a physician/attorney specializing in medical negligence and other significant personal injury matters, including brain injury. A summa cum laude graduate of Seton Hall University, Dr. Grossbart attended UMDNJ before completing a medical internship and subsequently attending Seton Hall Law School. He has been involved in the review and pursuit of numerous medical negligence matters and has both lectured and written material for the Association for Justice—New Jersey. At the time of preparation of the chapter, Dr. Grossbart had a private practice in personal injury litigation in New Jersey.

Louise H. Hayes, Esq. recently retired as founder and senior partner of the law firm Hayes, Finger & Wenick in New York City. The firm was affiliated with FOJP Service Corporation, an insurance advisory group that provided coverage for many of the area's major medical centers, nursing homes, physicians, nurses, and other healthcare providers. Ms. Hayes and her firm handled medical malpractice and personal injury cases for the above entities. Prior to forming the above firm, Ms. Hayes was a trial attorney and partner in the New York firm Jones Hirsch Connors & Bull, where she handled medical malpractice cases for such carriers as Medical Liability Mutual Insurance Company, AIG, Cigna, and Royal. Early in her career Ms. Hayes was with the Office of Corporation Counsel, Law Department of the City of New York where she defended in court the hospitals and medical staffs of New York City Health and Hospitals Corporation. She organized a special medical malpractice unit that took over handling and trying of medical cases for 14 city hospitals.

Nursine S. Jackson, MSN, RN is a master's degree prepared Cardiovascular Clinical Nurse Specialist with more than 25 years of clinical experience who has provided support to plaintiff's attorneys since the mid-1980s. She graduated from the University of Pittsburgh with her BSN in 1977 and her MSN in 1983, then returned to the Adult Nurse Practitioner program for additional coursework. She currently has a full-time role as a legal nurse consultant, supporting the Law Offices of Mark R. Bower, PC in Manhattan, in addition to having an independent practice in which she provides support to plaintiff's attorneys across the nation. She teaches in the Graduate and Undergraduate Nursing programs of the University of Pittsburgh, in which she addresses "Liability of the Nurse Practitioner" and provides practical information regarding the LNC role and case development for the Forensic Nursing/ Legal Nurse Consultant course. Ms. Jackson has published and lectured extensively on challenges in caring for cardiovascular patients, on safe nursing and preventing medical errors, and on the medical-legal analysis of cases, among other topics. Ms. Jackson has been active in many nursing organizations, most recently with board positions in the Pittsburgh Chapter of the American Association of Legal Nurse Consultants and in Sigma Theta Tau International. She has been the editor of the LiNC, the newsletter of the Pittsburgh Chapter of AALNC for six years and is on the Editorial Advisory Board of the Forensic Examiner.

Monica M. Kenny, Esq. is a sole practitioner with an office in Catskill, New York. She is a graduate of Albany Law School, where she was named the Arthur F. Mathew's Scholar, receiving a full scholarship. Ms. Kenny began her legal career earning a paralegal certificate from Marist College in 1999, and continued with her education at the State University at Albany, graduating *summa cum laude* with a bachelor's degree in Criminal Justice in 2002. Upon graduation from the State University at Albany, she was the recipient of the Donald J. Newman Award for Academic Achievement. Ms. Kenny previously worked for her coauthor, Sean J. Doolan, Esq., for over eight years. Mr. Doolan's practice includes personal injury litigation with a concentration on Nursing Home/Assisted Living Facility Abuse and Neglect. Ms. Kenny has been in private practice as a sole practitioner for approximately two years and practices primarily in the areas of family law, criminal defense, and civil practice.

Sharon L. Koob, RN, BSBA, CPHRM, ARM is currently a Healthcare Risk Consultant at Princeton Insurance in Princeton, New Jersey. Ms. Koob began her career as an acute care nurse in Michigan, leaving after almost ten years to work as a Risk Consultant in Chicago. Risk Management turned out to be her niche and after ten years in Chicago she has continued that work for over a decade more in Pennsylvania, Delaware, and New Jersey. Ms. Koob received her bachelor's degree in business from St. Joseph's College of Maine; her masters work is in spirituality and healthcare through Chestnut Hill College, Chestnut Hill, Pennsylvania. Having spent so many years in healthcare risk management, working in different roles and with a variety of institutions, Ms. Koob has a multifaceted view of healthcare and its issues. From an early point in her career she identified problems that negatively impacted patients, staff and practitioners. Her work in risk management has given her an opportunity to make positive changes in some of these situations and it continues to guide her in identifying future needs for improvement in the industry.

Mark F. Kowal, Esq. is an associate and member of Stark & Stark's Employment Litigation Group. Mr. Kowal concentrates his practice in employment litigation, arbitration, mediation and employment counseling.

Thomas B. Lewis, Esq. is a Shareholder and Chair of Stark & Stark's Employment Litigation Group. Mr. Lewis practices in the area of corporate litigation, with an emphasis on employment trial litigation, arbitration, mediation and employment counseling. Mr. Lewis represents companies and their executives in employment disputes and litigation including restrictive covenant issues, noncompete agreements, claims of sexual harassment, workplace discrimination, wrongful discharge, employment agreements, and severance agreements. He has litigated and arbitrated cases in numerous states and jurisdictions and regularly appears before state courts, federal courts, the EEOC and various state civil rights agencies. Mr. Lewis also litigates restrictive covenant issues on behalf of individuals, medical practitioners, small to mid-sized companies and Fortune 500 companies.

Bryan A. Liang, MD, PhD, JD is Executive Director and E. Donald Shapiro Distinguished Professor, Institute of Health Law Studies, California Western School of Law; Co-Director and Associate Professor of Anesthesiology, San Diego Center for Patient Safety, University of California San Diego School of Medicine; and Adjunct Associate Professor of Public Health, College of Health and Human Services, San Diego State University, all in San Diego, California. Dr. Liang's patient safety activities include serving on the Patient Safety Health Literacy Advisory Panel of the American Medical Association, the Medication Reconciliation Work Group of the American Medical Association, the Patient Safety Workgroup of the Federation of State Medical Boards, the Research Program Committee of the National Patient Safety Foundation, the board of directors of the Partnership for Safe Medicines, and the editorial boards of the *Journal of Patient Safety* as well as *Quality and Safety in Health Care*. He received his BS from MIT; PhD in Health Policy from the

Harris School of Public Policy Studies, University of Chicago; MD from Columbia University College of Physicians & Surgeons; and JD from Harvard Law School. Dr. Liang is also a licensed private pilot, and is instrument rated with high performance aircraft, complex aircraft endorsements. He flies N2MH, a Piper Turbo Lance.

Mark Lukas, Ed.D., CRC has been a vocational rehabilitation consultant in private practice for 20 years. He offers rehabilitation services to individuals and forensic vocational evaluation services to the legal community encompassing primarily Pennsylvania, Delaware, New Jersey, and Maryland. His educational background includes both a master's degree in rehabilitation counseling and a doctorate in education. He holds certifications including Certified Rehabilitation Counselor and Licensed Professional Counselor in addition to board certification by the American Board of Vocational Experts. Dr. Lukas's professional work history in the rehabilitation field encompasses a period of 35 years devoted to the evaluation and rehabilitation of injured persons.

Timothy Mackey, MAS is employed with the Institute of Health Law Studies as a Senior Research Associate. He completed a master's in applied studies (MAS) from California Western School of Law and UCSD, San Diego, California; a MAS from the Joint Program in Health Law, California Western School of Law-University of California San Diego; and a BA from the University of California, San Diego.

Irmo Marini, PhD, CRC, CLCP is currently a Professor and the Ph.D. Coordinator of the Rehabilitation Counseling Program at the University of Texas Pan-American. Dr. Marini has numerous teaching and research awards, has chaired several national rehabilitation organizations, and is on the editorial boards of three rehabilitation journals. Dr. Marini has published one book, ten book chapters and 65 refereed journal articles. Dr. Marini is CEO of Marini & Associates (forensic rehabilitation consultants), providing life care plans and vocational damage assessments in litigated cases.

Susan Mellott, RN, CPHQ, FNAHQ, PhD is currently the CEO of Mellott & Associates, a healthcare consulting and legal nurse consulting firm located in Houston, Texas. Dr. Mellott has been working in the healthcare field for over 30 years, specializing in healthcare quality and patient safety for the last 15 years. She holds a bachelor's degree in nursing from Indiana University of Pennsylvania, a master's degree in pediatric nursing from University of Pennsylvania, and a doctorate in health education and wellness from Texas A&M University. She is a certified professional in healthcare quality (CPHQ), and is a Fellow of the National Association for Healthcare Quality. Dr. Mellott is also an adjunct faculty member of Texas Women's University in Houston, Texas Masters Administration in Nursing program, and a faculty member of the University of Phoenix Online program's baccalaureate healthcare administration program. At Mellott & Associates, she is the owner and primary consultant assisting healthcare facilities to prepare for Joint Commission accreditation, and to improve patient safety and improve healthcare processes and outcomes. Dr. Mellott is also a legal nurse consultant, assisting attorneys with their cases involving aspects of health care.

Wendy Neggers, Esq. graduated from Rutgers School of Law. At the time the chapter was written she was an associate of Davis, Saperstein and Salomon in Teaneck, New Jersey. Ms. Neggers concentrated in personal injury, medical malpractice, and environmental law. She was a member of the American Bar Association, the American Trial Lawyers Association, the New Jersey State Bar Association, and the New Jersey District Court.

John M. Parisi, Esq. is a graduate of the University of Missouri, with a B.A. in Anthropology in 1978 and is a graduate of the University of Kansas, with an M.A. in Anthropology in 1983. He obtained his law degree from the University of Missouri at Kansas City in May of 1989 where he graduated with distinction. Prior to obtaining his law degree in 1989, Mr. Parisi was a professional archaeologist for ten years and conducted numerous archaeological excavations and surveys, including sites in the Republic of Egypt in the Western Sahara Desert. Mr. Parisi has practiced law with the firm Shamberg, Johnson & Bergman, Chtd. since 1989, and became partner in 1994. He has successfully handled personal injury, medical malpractice, products liability, false claims act (*qui tam*), nursing home abuse, class action and environmental law cases. Mr. Parisi is active in a number of bar associations, including the Kansas Trial Lawyers Association as a Past-President, and the Association of Trial Lawyers of America as the current Chair of the Small Firm and Solo Practitioner Section. Mr. Parisi is also a member of the American Bar Association, the Association of Trial Lawyers of America, the Kansas Bar Association, the Kansas City Metropolitan Bar Association, and the Missouri Bar Association, among others. He currently serves as a Commissioner for the Kansas Client Protection Fund and as an Investigator for the Johnson County Bar Ethics & Grievance Committee. Mr. Parisi is a two-time recipient of ATLA's distinguished Wiedeman & Wysocki award, for 2001 and 2002; and was named as a Missouri and Kansas Super Lawyer in both 2005 and 2006.

Judith D. Rottkamp, MA, RN, CNA serves as the Vice President of Clinical & Professional Service at St. Francis Medical Center in Trenton, New Jersey. A registered nurse with over 30 years' experience, Ms. Rottkamp is a graduate of the St. Francis School of Nursing. Ms. Rottkamp furthered her education by obtaining her BSN from Stockton State College and her master's degree in health administration from Rider University. Ms. Rottkamp also holds a post-master's Certification in Nursing Administration from Villanova University as well as certifications from the ANCC in Washington, D.C. and an Ethics Associate from Catholic Health Initiatives in Denver, Colorado. A leader and advocate of Nursing Standards, she is an active member of the New Jersey State Nurses Association. Additionally she chairs, co-chairs and holds memberships on several committees at St. Francis Medical Center. These committees include but are not limited to Nursing Leadership, Infection Control, Quality Council, Corporate Compliance, Pharmacy and Therapeutics, Patient Safety Council and Medication Safety. Ms. Rottkamp also maintains active memberships within the community such as the Mercer County LPN Advisory Board, the Mercer County Child Placement Review Board and the Children's Home Society.

Mindy M. Steichen, FCAS, MAAA is currently a consulting actuary with the Milwaukee office of Milliman. She holds a BA in mathematics from Drew University and a MA in actuarial science from the University of Wisconsin, Madison. She has over ten years experience in the actuarial science field. Ms. Steichen's particular area of focus has been in professional liability coverage. She provides annual reserve and prospective funding analyses for a number of self-insured healthcare organizations as well as reserve support to several professional liability insurers.

Frank D. Tinari, PhD is Professor Emeritus of Economics at Seton Hall University, and Principal Economist of the Tinari Economics Group, a litigation consulting practice. He has taught at Fordham, Pace, Purdue, William Paterson and Drew Universities, and was a repeat invited lecturer at the University of International Business and Economics in Beijing. Dr. Tinari is a member of the American Academy of Economic and Financial Experts, the National Association of Forensic Economics (NAFE), and the American, Eastern and Western Economic Associations. He has served as the elected President of NAFE and chaired its ethics committee. In April 2010 he was appointed to the New Jersey State Advisory Committee to the U.S. Commission on Civil Rights, Dr. Tinari lectures widely at economics conferences and bar association programs including the New Jersey Institute for Continuing Legal Education, Inns of Court, National Employment Lawyers Association, New York State Trial Lawyers Institute, Columbian Lawyers Association, and many others. From 2002 through 2004, he worked closely with Trial Lawyers Care to assist claimants of the 9-11 Victims Compensation Fund and testified at dozens of hearings before Special Master Ken Feinberg. Dr. Tinari has extensive experience in litigation consulting and has testified hundreds of times in federal and state courts. The author of a college text, *Economics: The Options for Dealing with Scarcity*, Dr. Tinari is widely published in the *Journal of Economic Education, Review of Social Economy, Journal of Forensic Economics, Journal of Legal Economics, New Jersey Law Journal The Legal Intelligencer* and other publications. He serves as editorial reviewer for several journals. Dr. Tinari earned a BS from Fordham College and his MA and PhD degrees in economics from Fordham University's Graduate School of Arts and Sciences.

Diane Warlick, JD, BSN, RN is a nurse attorney with more than 25 years experience in nursing law, medical malpractice litigation and appellate law practice. A conflict with a physician over an order which violated hospital regulations drove her to law school to make some sense over the legal and ethical boundaries of nursing practice. Since graduating from Boston University School of Law, Ms. Warlick has represented both plaintiffs and defendants in malpractice litigation, healthcare providers in regulatory and disciplinary actions and a Board of Nurse Licensure as a consultant for development of disciplinary standards and procedures. She was

a founder and the second president of The American Association of Nurse Attorneys (TAANA) and represented TAANA and the American Nurses Association as amicus curiae before the United States Supreme Court in the landmark case, *Cruzan v. State of Missouri*, which addressed the difficult issues of patient self-determination. In partnership with Tonia Dandry Aiken, RN, JD, a noted nurse attorney, Ms. Warlick founded the Nurse Attorney Institute, LLC. The Institute is dedicated to bringing knowledge of the law to the nursing profession, fostering healthy working relationships between professional groups in health care facilities, and teaching facilitative leadership skills. She also practices law part-time in Dallas, Texas.

Peter G. Wick, FCAS, MAAA is currently a principal and consulting actuary with the Milwaukee office of Milliman. He holds a BA in business administration from the University of Wisconsin, Madison. He has more than 30 years experience in the actuarial science field. Mr. Wick's area of expertise is property and casualty insurance, particularly ratemaking, loss reserve analysis and financial planning. Mr. Wick has extensive experience in commercial lines, including professional liability, workers' compensation, reinsurance and other long-tailed lines of business.

Diane Wiley is the President of the National Jury Project Midwest® in Minneapolis, Minnesota. Ms. Wiley is a pioneer in the field of trial consulting and a founder of the National Jury Project®, the nation's first trial consulting firm. She began her work in trial consulting in 1973, and since then she has consulted in thousands of civil and criminal cases, in both state and federal jurisdictions throughout the United States. Her work includes conducting mock trials, focus groups, and attitudinal surveys for venue evaluation; consulting with attorneys on themes, case presentation, witness preparation, and voir dire; and assisting with jury selection. Medical negligence cases and nursing home negligence are two of her specialties.

Mona Goldman Yudkoff, RN, BSN, MPH, CRRN, CCM, CLCP received a bachelor's degree in nursing (BSN) from the University of Pennsylvania in 1971 and a master's degree in public health (MPH) from Hebrew University in Jerusalem in 1978. She has taken numerous continuing education courses and has achieved certification in Rehabilitation Nursing (CRRN), Case Management (CCM) and Life Care Planning (CLCP). Ms. Yudkoff has more than 35 years of pediatric and rehabilitation nursing experience, including three years as the Assistant Director of Nursing at Children's Seashore House in Philadelphia, Pennsylvania. Ms. Yudkoff is a nationally recognized leader in the field of Life Care Planning. She has authored chapters on life care planning in three textbooks and has been invited to speak about life care planning to healthcare providers, parent groups and attorneys. Ms. Yudkoff is a member of the Association of Rehabilitation Nurses, a charter member of the Academy of Certified Case Managers, a member of the American Association of Nurse Life Care Planners and a member of the International Academy of Life Care Planners.

Index